Contents

1 Introduction and hints   7
Introduction; routes; special interest holidays

2 Horizons   29
The Land; Religion; Culture; History; Modern Indonesia

3 Indonesia

Java   79
Jakarta; West Java; Central Java and Yogyakarta; East Java

Bali   310
Horizons; Island information; Denpasar; South Bali; Bukit Peninsula and Nusa
Dua; North from Denpasar to Ubud; North of Ubud; North of Denpasar; Pura
Besakih and Mount Agung; The East; From Padangbai to Candi Dasa; North
from Denpasar to Lake Bratan; The North Coast; The West

Sumatra   424
Horizons; Island information; Northern Sumatra: Medan; The Route North:
Medan to Bukit Lawang and Banda Aceh; The West Coast: Banda Aceh to
Sidikalang; The Route South from Banda Aceh to Sidikalang; The Route
South to Lake Toba; The Route North; Lake Toba South to Padangsidempuan;
Southern Sumatra: The Minang Homeland; The Riau Archipelago; The Riau
Islands to Pekanbaru and Bukittinggi; The West Coast; The Mentawi Islands;
Padang South to Sungai Penuh; Padang to Jambi and Palembang; Palembang
to Bengkulu; Muaraenim to Bandar Lampung, Bakauheni and Java.

Kalimantan   542
Horizons; Banjarmasin and South Kalimantan; Tanjung Puting National Park
and Central Kalimantan; Balikpapan and East Kalimantan; Pontianak and
West Kalimantan

4

Sulawesi   609
Horizons; Island information; Ujung Pandang; Ujung Pandang to Toraja;
Toraja; Southeast Sulawesi; Pendolo to Palu; Palu to Mandado

Lombok and Sumbawa   686
Lombok; Horizons; Island information; Ampenan-Mataram-Cakranegara;
Lombok's West Coast; The Gilis; The Northwest Coast and Mount Rinjani;
Central Lombok and the West; South Lombok and the South Coast. Sumbawa;
Horizons; Sumbawa Besar to Bima-Raba

East Nusa Tenggara and East Timor   727
Horizons; Komodo. Flores; Horizons; Island information; Ende to Larantuka;
Lembata; Alor. Sumba; Horizons. Timor; Horizons; West Timor; Roti; Savu;
East Timor; East from Dili to Los Palos; South from Dili to Maubesi

Maluku   795
Horizons; Ambon; The Lease Islands; Seram; Banda Islands; Ternate and
Tidore; Halmahera; Morotai; South East Maluku

Irian Jaya   835
Horizons; Island information; Jayapura; The Baliem Valley

4 Information for travellers   859
Before travelling, Getting there, On arrival, Where to stay, Food and drink,
Getting around, Communications, Holidays and festivals

5 Rounding up   881
Acknowledgements; Further reading; Internet and radio; Words and phrases;
Eating out; Health; Travelling with children; Fares and timetables; Glossaries;
Index; Maps

Indonesia
Handbook

Joshua Eliot, Jane Bickersteth
and Liz Capaldi

Footprint Handbooks

We have left you,
the calm lagoon without a ripple,
sheltered by a leafy mountain
from wind and storm.
For once we have woken up from a pleasant dream.

Soetan Takdir Alisjahbana, 'To sea, the new generation'

Footprint Handbooks

6 Riverside Court, Lower Bristol Road
Bath BA2 3DZ England
T 01225 469141 F 01225 469461
E mail handbooks@footprint.compulink.co.uk

ISBN 0 900751 78 9   ISSN 1363-7355
CIP DATA: A catalogue record for this book is
available from the British Library

In North America, published by

PASSPORT BOOKS
a division of *NTC Publishing Group*

4255 West Touhy Avenue, Lincolnwood
(Chicago), Illinois 60646-1975, USA
T 847 679 5500 F 847 679 24941
E mail NTCPUB2@AOL.COM

ISBN 0-8442-4910-6
Library of Congress Catalog Card
Number 96-69591
Passport Books and colophon are registered
trademarks of NTC Publishing group

©Footprint Handbooks Limited
September 1996

First published in 1992 as part of *Indonesia,
Malaysia & Singapore Handbook* by Trade &
Travel Publications Ltd

**Every effort has been made to ensure that
the facts in this Handbook are accurate.
However travellers should still obtain
advice from consulates, airlines etc about
current travel and visa requirements and
conditions before travelling. The editors
and publishers cannot accept responsibilty
for any loss, injury or inconvenience,
however caused.**

**Maps - neither the coloured nor the black
and white text maps are intended to have
any political significance.**

Cover design by Newell and Sorrell;
photography by Tony Stone Images and TRIP

Production: Design by Mytton Williams;
Typesetting by Jo Morgan, Ann Griffiths and
Melanie Mason-Fayon; Maps by Sebastian
Ballard, Alasdair Dawson and Kevin Feeney;
Proofread by Rod Gray and Tim Heybourne.

Printed and bound in Great Britain by
Clays Ltd., Bungay, Suffolk

The Editors

Joshua Eliot

Joshua has had a long-standing interest in Asia. He was born in Calcutta, grew up in Hong Kong, has a PhD on rural development in Thailand from the University of London, and lectures on Southeast Asia. He is the author of a book on the geography of the region and has also written well over 30 papers and articles on Southeast Asia. He has lived and conducted research in Thailand, Sumatra and Laos and has travelled extensively in the region over a period of nearly 15 years. He speaks Thai, and some Lao and Indonesian.

Jane Bickersteth

Jane has worked on the guidebooks since the first edition in 1992. She has been visiting the region for over 10 years, spending a year there whilst she researched the first edition. Jane is an artist by training and is particularly inspired by the Khmer ruins of Thailand and the candis of Java and Bali.

Liz Capaldi

Liz Capaldi is a freelance writer with a long-standing interest in the East having grown up in Japan. She began as a researcher and writer in the art world and her articles have appeared in such publications as *The International Herald Tribune*, *The Chicago Tribune*, *Collector's Guide* and *Arts Review*. More recently she was editor and joint organizer of a festival of Japanese culture and art in Britain. She has travelled extensively in Indonesia and speaks some Indonesian.

Acknowledgements

Much help has been received from friends, colleagues, researchers and fellow travellers during the preparation of this edition. All contributions have been tremendously helpful and are acknowledged on page 881. However, we would particularly like to thank John Moxey of Garuda in London and Captain Harry Hilliard of Pelni in Jakarta for their assistance.

Introduction and hints

INDONESIA is the unlikeliest of countries. Geographically it encompasses 13,677 islands spread over 5,000 kilometres of tropical seas, linking Asia with Australasia. It is a human mosaic of vivid complexity with around 300 ethnic groups speaking close to 600 languages and dialects. Seemingly every guidebook is tempted to attach the epithet 'diverse' to the place it describes, whether that is New York, Singapore, Hawai'i or the United States. But in the case of Indonesia this is not mere journalistic hyperbole. One of the country's defining characteristics is its sheer diversity, from its complex and in places unique flora and fauna, to its stupendous geography and multitude cultures.

Indonesia – or the East Indies as it was then – was haphazardly pieced together by the Dutch over a period of three centuries. From 1610 when they gained their first toehold in the Spice Islands of Maluku, an area of magical wealth in the eyes of contemporary Europeans, through to the early decades of the twentieth century when West Irian (Irian Jaya) was finally incorporated, Indonesia was created more by historical accident than by design. The result, by the outbreak of the Second World War, was a vast, sprawling territory of diverse people cemented by little more than the colonial glue of the Dutch. That this artificial creation should have survived intact is one of the greatest achievements of Indonesian independence – and, to some, one of its greatest surprises.

Will you help us?

Our authors explore and research tirelessly to bring you the most complete and up-to-date package of information possible. Yet the contributions we receive from our readers are also **vital** to the success of our Handbooks. There are many thousands of you out there making delightful (and sometimes alarming!) discoveries every day.

So important is this resource that we make a special offer to every reader who contacts us with information on places, experiences, people, hotels, restaurants, well-informed warnings or any other features which could enhance the enjoyment of our travellers everywhere. When writing to us, please give the edition and page number of the Handbook you are using.

So please take a few minutes to get in touch with us - we can benefit, you can benefit and all our other readers can benefit too!

Please write to us at:

Footprint Handbooks,
6 Riverside Court, Lower Bristol Road, Bath BA2 3DZ England
Fax: +44 (0)1225 469461 E Mail handbooks@footprint.compulink.co.uk

Where to go

For most people seeing 'Indonesia' – *in toto* – is an impossibility. The country is simply too large. In addition, overland travel in some areas of the country is slow and exhausting and travelling from Aceh in the north of Sumatra to Jayapura, the capital of Irian Jaya as the crow flies (and it is rarely possible to fly like a crow in Indonesia!) involves a journey of around 5,000 km – the equivalent of travelling from Athens to Delhi or Vancouver to Mexico City. Many people are happy to explore Bali alone – an island, albeit a special one, which accounts for less than half a percent of Indonesia's total land area.

The sheer size of Indonesia, coupled with poor roads in some areas, and the special problems of skipping through an archipelago of over 13,000 islands, means that an itinerary has to be carefully planned. Those with two months to spare (the length of a standard visa) can work their way from Sumatra to Timor, or vice versa, but even with the luxury of 8 weeks they will be forced not just to miss the odd town but entire regions – Sulawesi, Kalimantan or Maluku, for example.

TRANSPORT AND TRAVELLING

Compared with roads in the W, those in Indonesia are poor. Even in Java, Indonesia's heartland and the centre of economic activity, there are just a handful of stretches of road that could even remotely be labelled 'highways'. Over much of the rest of the country all-weather roads only link the most important centres. In the wet season even these may be periodically impassable due to flooding, subsidence and land slips. Large areas of Sumatra, Kalimantan and Irian Jaya are, to all intents and purposes, inaccessible to even the most determined traveller.

That, so to speak, is the bad news (or the good news, depending on one's viewpoint). The good news is that many of the horror stories of the past, when bus passengers were regularly stranded for days in towns that they would now wish to forget are, to a large extent, history. It is possible – though perhaps not enjoyable – to catch a bus through the entire length of Sumatra or Sulawesi, for example.

A second factor to bear in mind is the challenge of travelling between the smaller islands. This is particularly pertinent in Nusa Tenggara and Maluku where there may be just one ferry a day between some islands, sometimes just one a week. Flying, though in theory a much faster alternative has its own problems. It is often impossible to book flights between the more out of the way spots, and even a booked seat may magically disappear if a VIP (and there are an awful lot of VIPs in Indonesia) should suddenly decide to make the journey.

JAVA AND BALI

Java and Bali have slow but abundant year round public transport including train on Java as well as bus. The comparatively short distances involved means that even travelling from one end of Java to the other is possible in a day. The concentration of people and economic enterprise means that there are many bus services from luxury a/c 'Vip' buses to slow and cramped 'Ekonomi' vehicles. There are also tour buses geared to foreigners on many routes. Jakarta and Denpasar, Bali's capital, are also serviced by more international airlines than any other cities in the country. Note that Jakarta suffers from serious road congestion.

SUMATRA

Sumatra's size – it is the fourth largest island in the world – makes travelling an ordeal. Most visitors take a well-defined route from Medan (where there are sea links with Malaysia) through to Brastagi, Toba, Bukittinggi and Padang. Transport between these towns is fairly well provided for with tour and a/c buses. Beyond these towns, though, bus transport is less well developed, although provincial centres will always have some a/c and Vip services. There is a limited rail service in the south of the island and domestic airlines serve the main provincial centres. There are also international air links with Medan from Singapore, Penang and Kuala Lumpur; and with Padang via Pekanbaru from Singapore. Regular ferries link the southern tip of Sumatra with Java.

KALIMANTAN

Kalimantan's size and geography – it has vast swamps – makes overland travel difficult. The major towns have coastal locations and there are reasonable road links between Bajarmasin, Balikpapan and Samarinda, and from Pontianak to Sarawak. However it is not possible to travel overland across Kalimantan, even following the coast. To travel inland – or 'upriver' – it is often necessary to fly or go by boat. There are international connections with Singapore from Banjarmasin, Pontianak, Tarakan and Palangkaraya, and it is also possible to enter Kalimantan overland from Sarawak.

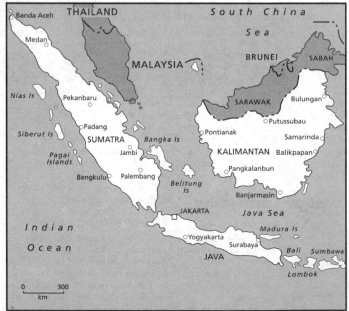

SULAWESI

Sulawesi's strange spidery shape means that nowhere is far from the sea and coastal ships work their way up, down and around the coasts. With the completion of the (almost) all-weather trans-Sulawesi highway it is also possible to bus it all the way from Ujung Pandang in the south to Manado in the north. But beyond this main 'highway' roads are poor and bus services may be limited. Ujung Pandang has good air and sea links with others parts of the country and Manado in the north is also well-served. There are international air connections between Manado and Singapore, and domestic airlines serve the main provincial towns.

LOMBOK, EAST NUSA TENGGARA AND EAST TIMOR

Transport on Lombok is comparatively good and roads are reasonable. Travelling east from here road conditions tend to

deteriorate, although the main highway rarely – except after torrential storms or an earthquake! – descends into impassability. Ferries link the main islands, usually daily, although smaller islands off the main east-west route may be served less frequently. There are air services to most islands but these are often over-booked, un-booked and multi-booked without apparently any consideration to the number of seats on the aircraft. There are international air connections between Kupang and Darwin. East Timor, because of the on-going strife there, presents particular problems when it comes to overland travel and in the past the province has been closed to visitors.

MALUKU

Maluku consists of a multitude of islands spread over a vast area of sea. There are air links between many of the larger and more important islands but as in Nusa Tenggara there is a tendency for booked seats to

disappear. Passenger ships serve many ports in Maluku but they may call infrequently. On the larger, but often sparsely populated and thickly jungled islands like Seram, Buru and Halmahera bus services are usually slow and intermittent, and in some cases non-existent.

IRIAN JAYA

Indonesian New Guinea remains one the great unknown corners of the world. Large areas are inaccessible except to those with months on their hands, a pocket full of anti-malarials, and very stout walking boots. The main towns are linked by air and sometimes by sea with other parts of the country and there are also international air connections between Biak and the US. A road between Jayapura and Wamena is under construction although some people believe (and hope) that it will be washed away just as soon as the tarmac is dry. The government requires visitors to obtain a *surat jalan*, or travel letter, before venturing beyond the main towns.

TIMETABLING A VISIT

Indonesia is so vast that even two months – the length of a visitor's visa – is not nearly enough time to see the country. Two months is sufficiently long to whizz through the archipelago, see the key sights and lie on the main beaches, but little more. This is why many people consider that visitors should restrict themselves to exploring one or two areas rather than just scratching the surface of many places. Two weeks is a good length of time to discover Bali, a month to experience Java or Sulawesi. Those intending to go to the more out of the way spots in Maluku or Nusa Tenggara might find they need a full two months for those regions alone.

HIGHLIGHTS

Wildlife

Java: Ujung Kulon at the far west of Java for the very slim chance of seeing one of the rarest large mammals in the world; and Sukamade at the far east of the island for turtle egg-laying.

Sumatra: Bukit Lwang to visit the Orang Utan Rehabilitation Centre; Gunung Leuser National Park for possibly the richest fauna on the island.

Kalimantan: the Tanjung Puting National Park and Orang Utan Rehabilitation Centre is the most visited park in Kalimantan.

Sulawesi: Bantimurung Falls with its diminishing butterflies that astounded Alfred Russel Wallace when he visited in 1856; the Tangkoko Batu Angus National Park for its unique fauna.

East Nusa Tenggara and East Timor: Komodo's dragons.

Irian Jaya: a unique flora and fauna, vast uncharted areas, great potential but poorly developed except in the Wasur National Park.

Hill stations

Java: Bogor, Indonesia's most venerable hill station within easy reach of Jakarta; Cisarua, Cibodas and Cipanas, three hill resorts in a stunning position but marred by ugly architecture; Tawangmangu, Sarangan, Tretes, Batu and Selekta, five more hill resorts in Central and East Java.

Bali: Ubud for the most sophisticated and foreigner-centric hill resort in Indonesia.

Sumatra: Brastagi is Sumatra's original colonial hill retreat, a good location for trekking in the surrounding hills; Bukittinggi in the Minang area of West Sumatra is now more popular and more attractive.

Sulawesi: Malino, 70km outside Ujung Pandang at over 1,000m and Kakas Kasen close to Manado and near the active Mount Lokon.

National Parks and Botanical Gardens

Java: Ujung Kulon, possibly Java's best-run national park and the last home of the Javan rhino in Indonesia; the Botanical Gardens at Bogor, established in 1817; the upland Cibodas Botanical Gardens created in 1899 for high altitude and temperate plants and the adjoining Gede-Pangrango National Park; Bromo-Tengger-Semeru National Park encompassing a series of imposing volcanoes.

Sumatra: the well-run Gunung Leuser National Park and the important but less developed Kerinci-Seblat National Park; the Way Kambas National Park with its herd of elephant.

Kalimantan: the Tanjung Puting and Kutai National Parks both have a reasonable level of amenties for visitors.

Sulawesi: the Morowali National Park is possibly the finest on Sulawesi but with a low level of facilities; the Lore Lindu National Park has good trekking and interesting megaliths; Tangkoko Batu Angus National Park with good facilities and a unique fauna.

East Nusa Tenggara and East Timor: Komodo National Park for its dragons and good amenities.

Maluku: Manusela National Park on Seram – rarely visited and lacking in facilities but a natural wonderland.

Irian Jaya: the Wasur National Park outside Merauke is the most accessible park in Irian Jaya with the best facilities.

Trekking

Java: the Gede-Pangrango National Park east of Bogor and Mount Merapi and Kaliurang near Yogyakarta for moutain treks; the Bromo-Tengger-Semeru National Park for trekking from volcanic cone to cone; Mount Ijen in the far east of Java for more adventurous trekking.

Sumatra: Bukit Lawang and the Gunung Leuser Reserve for good trails and a convenient base; Brastagi and Mount Sibayak for upland walks; Lake Toba for walks in an incomparable location within the world's largest volcanic crater; challenging treks on Nias and Mentawi islands; walks in the hills around Bukittinggi including stiff mountain climbs.

Kalimantan: trekking in the Meratus Dayak area around Loksado and in the Kutai and Tanjung Puting National Parks; exploring the Dayak areas of the Mahakam and Kapuas Rivers and the Apo Kayan.

Sulawesi: excellent trekking in the uplands of Toraja; good hikes in the Lore Lindu National Park with its megaliths; walks in the volcanic hills to the south of Manado.

Lombok and Sumbawa: climbing Mount Rinjani is one of the most rewarding and spectacular climbs in the country; Mount Tambora on Sumbawa is less commonly climbed – and very hot!

East Nusa Tenggara and East Timor: climbing Mount Kelimutu for the sunrise is popular.

Irian Jaya: excellent trekking around Wamena in the Baliem Valley.

Natural features

Java: Krakatau offers a fascinating glimpse of the makings of the world; the Puncak Pass, perhaps Java's most spectacular stretch of road; the Tangkuban Prahu Crater outside Bandung provides an easily reached view into a steaming volcanic crater; Dieng is a mystical volcanic upland plateau, cold and often shrouded in cloying mists; Mount Bromo is Indonesia's most famous volcano; Mount Ijen a less visited alternative.

Bali: the volcanoes of Mount Batur and Mount Agung, upland Lake Bratan, and the irridescent terraced paddy fields of the south and east – all well trodden by countless tourists.

Sumatra: Takengon for its upland lake in the Gayo Highlands; Lake Toba and the stupendous crater which it occupies; Lake Maninjau and Lake Singkarak not far from Bukittingi for their peaceful and remarkable locations.

Sulawesi: the caves at Taman Purbakala Leang Leang outside Ujung Pandang; Lake Tempe with Sengkang nearby; Lake Poso, an upland lake with a rich and unique fauna; active Mount Lokon south of Manado; Lake Tondano and its hot water springs.

Lombok and Sumbawa: Mount Rinjani for its views (when clear), crater and crater lake; Mount Tambora for a hot but rewarding climb to the summit of a volcano that changed the world's climate.

East Nusa Tenggara and East Timor: Mount Kelimutu on Flores and its three-coloured crater lakes.

Beaches and coastal idylls

Java: Pulau Seribu for island resorts within easy reach of Jakarta; Labuan and Carita beaches are popular weekend getaways for frazzled Jakartans but scarcely remarkable save for their proximity to Krakatau; Pelabuhanratu, Pangandaran and Parangtritis are three south coast beach resorts that all offer poor water, a stiff pronounciation challenge and at times dangerous currents; Pacitan is probably the most attractive of the south coasts resorts; Pasir Putih on the north coast is a distinctively Indonesian-style beach resort with family planning posters and demure swimming gear.

Bali: the island has a succession of beach resorts: frenetic Kuta, ersatz Nusa Dua, more refined Sanur, emerging Candi Dasa and Lovina Beach, plus other quieter places.

Sumatra: Sabang and Weh Island off Sumatra's northern tip for an alternative place to catch a tan; Lagundi Bay on Nias Island, best known for its surfing; the Riau Islands (Batam and Bintan) for sophisticated but rather generic resorts geared to Singapore's beach starved population.

Sulawesi: the Tongian Islands for a place close to paradise; Donggala outside Palu for somewhere closer at hand; the Bunaken National Marine Park, best known as a dive site.

Lombok and Sumbawa: Senggigi, Lombok's most developed beach resort; the Gilis (islands) for a more traveller-oriented destination; while Kuta is Lombok's emerging beach area.

East Nusa Tenggara and East Timor: modest beaches and islands near Kupang in West Timor.

Maluku: poorish beaches near Ambon, excellent on Saparua, suprisingly poor on Banda, superb on lesser visited islands but expect almost no amenities.

Irian Jaya: good beaches near Biak; modest beaches around Jayapura.

Diving

Java: Pulau Seribu and Carita and Labuan beaches for accessible but only modest diving.

Bali: lots of dive outfits and some reasonable dive sites but better for beginners than for the cognoscente.

Sumatra: Sabang and Weh Island off Sumatra's northern tip for good diving.

Sulawesi: the Tongian Islands for excellent snorkelling; the Bunaken National Marine Park for superb diving with good dive companies and a wide range of amenities.

Lombok and Sumbawa: reasonable diving and dive companies at Senggigi and on the Gilis in Lombok; good snorkelling on Moyo Island off Sumbawa.

East Nusa Tenggara and East Timor: diving near Maumere in Flores, now much recovered from the earthquake of Dec 1992.

Maluku: modest diving at Ambon, excellent on Banda

Irian Jaya: good snorkelling off the islands around Biak.

Surfing and rafting

Java: Grajagan Bay on the south coast of East Java for a fine left break.

Bali: the most popular surfing in Indonesia with some good breaks but a tendency to become over-crowded at peak times of year (see page 343); rafting on the Ayung River.

Sumatra: rafting on the Alas River through the Gunung Leuser National Park; surfing at Lagundi Bay on Nias Island.

Kalimantan: rafting on the Amandit.

Sulwesi: white water rafting on the Sadang River.

Lombok and Sumbawa: modest surfing at Taliwang and Maluk on Sumbawa, better at Hu'u also on Sumbawa.

Historical sites: temples and palaces

Java: Cirebon, Yogyakarta and Suakarta (Solo) have the finest kratons (palaces) in the country; Imogiri, outside Yogyakarta, is the site of the tombs of the Mataram rulers, Borobudur and the candis of the Prambanan Plain are the two most spectacular collections of historical monuments in the country; enigmatic Candi Ceto and Candi Sukuh are beautifully positioned at 1,000m; the candis of the Dieng Plateau and Bandungan though plain and small also enjoy wonderful upland locations; Sangiran is the site where 'Java Man' was unearthed; the mausoleum of Indonesia's first President Sukarno is situated in Blitar while 14th century Candi Panataran lies outside the town; the elegant east Javanese candis all lie within easy reach of Malang; Trowulan, the formerly grand capital of the Majapahit Empire is also accessible from Malang as well as Surabaya.

Bali: Bali's most notable temples are Besakih, Uluwatu and Tanah Lot; other historical sites include the caves of Goa Gajah and ancient stone carvings of Yeh Pulu, the burial chambers of Gunung Kawi; and the royal bathing pools of Tirtagangga.

Sumatra: the Batak tombs, houses and megaliths of Lake Toba; Padang Lawas, a rarely visited collection of around 25 temples spread over a large area; the megaliths near Pagaralam.

Sulawesi: Old Gowa outside Sulawesi was the heart of the Sultanate of Gowa; the Megaliths of the Bada and Banua valleys in the Lore Lindu National Park; the megalithic sarcophagi at Sawangan near Manado.

Lombok and Sumbawa: though not comparable with similar places on Bali, the Mayura Water Palace and Gardens and Pura Mayura in Mataram-Cakranegara on Lombok are worthwhile and so too is the Taman Narmada and the Waktu Telu Temple; the modest Sultan's Palace on Sumbawa.

East Nusa Tenggara and East Timor: megaliths, tombs, traditional houses, festivals and weaving villages of Sumba.

Maluku: remnants of the Portuguese and Dutch presence in the Spice Islands, evident on Ambon, Saparua, Tidore and Ternate, but particularly Banda.

Historical sites: towns

Java: Kota or Old Batavia in Jakarta offers a glimpse of the old Dutch East Indies while Banten, a day's outing from Jakarta, has the ruins of a once great pre-colonial trading sultanate; Bandung is one of Indonesia's architectural gems with possibly the finest collection of 'tropical' Art Deco architecture in the world; Tegal, Kudus and Tuban were formerly important sultanates on Java's north coast with three of Java's oldest and most revered mosques; Surabaya's Kalimas Harbour for its *penisi* schooners.

Bali: Tenganan, the village home of Bali's 'original' inhabitants.

Sumatra: the traditional houses and villages of the Batak and Minangkabau of West and North Sumatra, and of Nias Island; Bengkulu is arguably the most charming modern town in Sumatra.

Kalimantan: Banjarmasin's floating market.

Sulawesi: Ujung Pandang's Paotere Harbour usually has a number of elegant penisi schooners docked; the villages around Rantepao for traditional soaring-roofed houses; Gorontalo retains more of its colonial architectural heritage than most Indonesian towns.

Culture

Java: Madura island, cut off from the Java 'mainland', has a distinctive culture most evident in the enthusiastic annual bull races.

Bali: for the greatest concentration of things 'cultural' in Indonesia from dances to funeral ceremonies and traditional villages.

Sumatra: Banda Aceh is one of Indonesia's most staunchly Muslim areas; the Batak area encompassing Lake Toba and Brastagi is worth exploring; equally distinctive are their culture are the Minankabau of West Sumatra (Bukittinggi) with their distinctive high-roofed houses; the cultures of the Nias and Mentawi islands is often paraded as 'stone age', with Nias offering particularly fine traditional villages.

Kalimantan: the Dayak culture of Kalimantan is less well preserved than that of the neighbouring East Malaysian states but the Mahakam and Kapuas rivers and the Apo Kayan are all worth exploring.

Sulawesi: the incomparable culture of the Toraja.

East Nusa Tenggara and East Timor: central and west Flores for its traditional villages; Larantuka in east Flores for its unique Christian cultural tradition; whaling in Lamalera.

Irian Jaya: much of Irian Jaya offers interesting cultural possibilities but they are best developed and most accessible in the Baliem Valley where the Dani live.

Museums

Java: the National Museum in Jakarta is Indonesia's best and largest collection; the Museum Prabu Geusan Ulun in Sumedang and the Ambarawa Railway Museum are both charming with slightly wacky collections; the kraton (palace) museums in Cirebon, Yogyakarta and Solo are worthwhile; while Kudus has a wonderfully politically incorrect kretek (cigarette) museum.

Bali: the Museum Bali in Denpasar for one of the best – and best presented – provincial collections.

Sumatra: Medan's North Sumatra Museum contains a motley collection; the Ethnological Museum of Simanindo on Lake Toba's Samosir Island recreates Batak culture in a traditional village;

Palembang's South Sumatra Museum contains some fine pieces.

Kalimantan: Musium Negeri in Pontianak for provincial exhibits.

Sulawesi: the Ujung Pandang State Museum, and for a reasonable provincial collection the Museum of Central Sulawesi in Palu.

East Nusa Tenggara and East Timor: the Blikan Blewut Museum outside Maumere; Kupang's good Museum of East Nusa Tenggara.

Fairs and Entertainment Parks

Java: Taman Mini for Indonesia in miniature and Taman Impian Jaya Ancol for Indonesia's stab at Disneyland, both in Jakarta.

Shopping and Handicrafts

Java: Jakarta for most things; Yogyakarta for handicrafts and especially batik and silver jewellery; Solo for batik and 'antiques'; Pekalongan for its distinctive batiks; Jepara for its woodworking and furniture.

Bali: for an array of products including paintings, jewellery, woodcarving, batik and garments often skilfully designed for Western tastes.

Sumatra: traditional woodcarvings from Nias Island.

Kalimantan: for 'tribal' handicrafts and some textiles.

Sulawesi: Rantepao for Torajan handicrafts, textiles and 'antiques'.

Lombok and Sumbawa: Lombok for pottery and textiles.

East Nusa Tenggara and East Timor: Flores, Sumba and Timor for their varied traditional textiles.

Irian Jaya: tribal handicrafts, the best coming from the Asmat people of the south-east, but more commonly made in the Wamena area of the Baliem Valley.

NB The above is only a selection of places of interest and is not exhaustive. It is designed to assist in planning a trip to the region. Any 'highlight' list is inevitably subjective.

How to go

BEST TIME TO VISIT

Indonesia is a vast country and although the whole area is 'tropical' – in others words it is hot (at sea level) – it encompasses several rainfall zones. This means that there is no particular 'best time to visit' – it just depends where you are going. The map on see page 34 and the chart on page 36 give a broad idea of the seasons across the archipelago and the levels of rainfall in different parts of the country at different times of year. Bear in mind that some areas have annual rainfall of just 500 mm, while others receive a drenching 6,000 mm. There are monthly climate graphs on pages 105 (Jakarta, Java), 433 (Medan, Sumatra), 512 (Padang, Sumatra), 581 (Balikpapan, Kalimantan) and 801 (Ambon, Maluku).

Travelling overland in the wet season in some areas can present problems, especially if intending to venture off the main highways. Parts of Sumatra, Sulawesi, Kalimantan, Nusa Tenggara and Irian Jaya can all be cut off after severe storms. However the main highways that the government has now largely built through the major islands – like the Trans-Sumatran highway – are usually open year-round. Travelling during the wet season can also have advantages. Hotel prices are generally negotiable and resorts that may be excessively crowded at peak times of year can be wonderfully quiet.

HEALTH

Medical care in Indonesia is not up to the standards of neighbouring Malaysia and Singapore. Many foreigners living in Indonesia fly to Singapore for more serious operations. In 1996 even President Suharto caught a plane to Hanover for a medical check-up rather than trust his life to the administrations of local doctors and technology. However for most minor ailments and injuries, the level of medical care is fine. Every provincial capital and most district towns have hospitals. Nonetheless, it is advisable that visitors take out health insurance with an emergency evacuation clause should they be struck down in some out-of-the-way spot.

For a comprehensive roundup of health related issues, see page 899.

WHAT TO TAKE

Travellers usually tend to take too much. Almost everything is available in Indonesia's main towns and cities – and often at a lower price than in the West. Remoter areas, inevitably, are less well supplied.

Suitcases are not appropriate if you are intending to travel overland by bus. A backpack, or even better a travelpack (where the straps can be zipped out of sight), is recommended. Travelpacks have the advantage of being hybrid backpacks-suitcases; they can be carried on the back for easy porterage, but they can also be taken into hotels without the owner being labelled a 'hippy'. **NB** For serious hikers, a backpack with an internal frame is still by far the better option for longer treks.

In terms of clothing, dress in Indonesia is relatively casual – even at formal functions. Suits are not necessary except in a few of the most expensive restaurants. However, though formal attire may be the exception, dressing tidily is the norm. Women particularly should note that in many areas of Indonesia, they should avoid offending Muslim sensibilities and dress 'demurely' (ie keep shoulders covered and wear below-knee skirts or trousers). This is particularly true in Aceh in North Sumatra and West Sumatra, in parts of Java, and in Sumbawa. Note that this does not generally apply in beach resorts.

There is a tendency, rather than to take inappropriate articles of clothing, to take too many of the same article. Laundry services are cheap, and the turn-around rapid.

Checklist

Bumbag
Earplugs
First aid kit
Insect repellent and/or electric mosquito mats, coils
International driving licence
Passports (valid for at least 6 months)
Photocopies of essential documents
Short wave radio
Spare passport photographs
Sun protection
Sunglasses
Swiss Army knife
Torch
Umbrella
Wet wipes
Zip-lock bags

Those intending to stay in budget accommodation might also include:
Cotton sheet sleeping bag
Money belt
Padlock (for hotel room and pack)
Soap
Student card
Toilet paper
Towel
Travel wash

MONEY

Travellers cheques denominated in most major currencies can be exchanged in provincial centres. However off the beaten track it may be difficult and US$ TCs are recommended. A small amount of cash (in US$) can also be useful in an emergency. Keep it separate from your TCs.

● ISIC

Anyone in full-time education is entitled to an International Student Identity Card (ISIC). These are issued by student travel offices and travel agencies across the world and offer special rates on all forms of transport and other concessions and services. The ISIC head office is: ISIC Association, Box 9048, 1000 Copenhagen, Denmark, T (45) 33 93 93 03.

GETTING THERE

AIR

There are direct flights to Jakarta from Europe, the US, Australia, and many Asian cities. However some people find that it is more convenient to catch a flight to Singapore and then a connection to Jakarta. There are also direct flights to Bali from Europe and Australia; flights to Kupang (Timor) from Darwin (Australia); to Biak (Irian Jaya) from the US; to Medan from Kuala Lumpur (Malaysia); and connections with Singapore from Medan and Padang on Sumatra, Manado on Sulawesi, and Banjarmasin and Potianak on Kalimantan.

Exchange rates (August 1996)

	US$	£	DM
Brunei (dollar)	1.41	2.18	0.94
Indonesia (rupiah)	2,343	3,628	1,569
Malaysia (ringgit)	2.49	3.86	1.67
Singapore (dollar)	1.41	2.18	0.94

Discounts

It is possible to obtain significant discounts, especially outside European holiday times, most notably in London. Shop around and book early. It is also possible to get discounts from Australasia, South Asia and Japan. Note that 'peak season' varies from airline to airline – many using 8-10 bands. This means one airline's high season may not be another's.

Air passes

The national airline Garuda in conjunction with its sister domestic carrier Merpati offers a Visit Indonesia Decade Pass which must be booked outside the country and offers internal flights at roughly US$100 each up to a maximum of 8 legs (see page 871 for more details. As air passes on offer change frequently, check with a good travel agent before booking flights. Be particularly careful to check any restrictions on either international or internal flights.

SEA

The two most popular routes into Indonesia by sea are from Singapore to Batam and Bintan in the Riau Archipelago (Sumatra), and from Georgetown, Penang's (Malaysia) capital, to Medan's port of Belawan. No regular oceanic passenger ships call in Indonesia.

For those interested in booking a passage on a cargo ship travelling to Indonesia, contact the Strand Cruise Centre, Charing Cross Shopping Concourse, The Strand, London WC2N 4HZ, T 0171-836-6363, F 0171-497-0078. Another company booking berths on freighters is Wagner Frachtschiffreissen, Stadlerstrasse 48, CH-8404 Winterthur, Switzerland, T (052) 242-1442, F (052) 242 1487.

OVERLAND

The only overland road links into Indonesia are between Kalimantan and the East Malaysian states of Sarawak and Sabah. The most popular crossing is at Entikong, linking Kuching in Sarawak with Pontianak in West Kalimantan. The border between Irian Jaya and Papua New Guinea is closed.

SAFETY

Confidence tricksters

Most common of all are confidence tricksters: people selling fake gems and antiques, informal currency exchange services offering surprisingly good rates, and card sharps. Confidence tricksters are, by definition, extremely convincing and persuasive. Time, as they say, is cheap in Southeast Asia, and people are willing to invest long hours lulling tourists into a false sense of security. Be suspicious of any offer that seems too good to be true. That is probably what it is.

Theft

Thieves favour public transport; confidence tricksters frequent popular tourist destinations. Personal valuables – money, TCs, passports, jewellery – should be kept safe. Do not leave valuables in hotel rooms; place them in a safe deposit box if possible, or keep them with you.

Drugs

Penalties are harsh for trafficking in even modest quantities.

Police

Report any incident that involves you or your possessions. In general, police will act promptly and properly.

PRISONERS ABROAD

Prisoners Abroad is a charity dedicated to supporting UK nationals in prison abroad. As the charity writes: "Arrest, trial and imprisonment are devastating in a familiar environment, supported by family and friends. Abroad it is much worse." Young men and women caught with drugs may find themselves facing sentences of 10 years or more, often in appalling conditions. Volunteers can help Prisoners Abroad, and similar organizations, by becoming a pen pal, donating a magazine subscription, or sending books, for example. If you or a friend find yourself in the unfortunate position of being in jail, or facing a jail term, then contact the charity at: Prisoners Abroad, Freepost 82, Roseberry Avenue, London EC1B 1XB, UK, T 0171 833-3467, F 0171 833-3460 (if telephoning or faxing from abroad then the code is +44171). Further information on the charity and its work can also be obtained from the above address.

WOMEN TRAVELLING ALONE

Women travelling alone face greater difficulties than men or couples. Young Southeast Asian women rarely travel without a partner, so it is believed to be strange for a western woman to do so. Western women are often believed to be of easy virtue – a view perpetuated by Hollywood and in local films, for example. To minimize the pestering that will occur, dress modestly – particularly in staunchly Muslim areas such as Aceh and West Sumatra and in more out-of-the-way spots where locals may be unfamiliar with tourists. Comments, sometimes derogatory, will be made however carefully you dress and act; simply ignore them. Toiletries such as tampons are widely available in Indonesia's main towns.

WHERE TO STAY

Indonesia's major tourist destinations, particularly Bali and the capital Jakarta, offer a wide range of accommodation with some hotels that are among the very best in the world. These are also comparatively moderately priced by western standards. Major provincial centres will also offer a reasonable range of accommodation although there may not be many – or any – hotels geared to the vicarious demands of the tourist. Budget accommodation is well provided for on the main travellers' routes. However, outside the main towns and tourist areas, accommodation can be surprisingly limited – restricted to one or two 'Chinese' hotels with neither budget places for backpackers, nor more expensive establishments. In the very remotest areas, homestays are sometimes the only option. The Indonesian government has identified a lack of adequate accommodation as one of the major factors restricting the growth and geographical spread of tourism beyond the handful of places like Bali that have an established reputation.

Camping

Camping is not common in Indonesia and even in national parks camping facilities are poor and limited. Indonesians find it strange that anyone should want to camp out when it is possible to stay in a hotel.

FOOD AND DRINK

Food

Food in Indonesia is generally good, and excellent value for money. Levels of hygiene are reasonable. All towns have local restaurants and stalls serving cheap, tasty and nourishing dishes.

In tourist areas and more expensive hotels, western food is also widely available. In areas popular with backpackers, so-called travellers' food is available: dishes such as chocolate fudge cake, pancakes, fruit shakes (or 'smoothies'), and garlic toast. Across the region, fruit can be a life-saver. It is varied, cheap, exotic, safe to eat (if peeled oneself) and delicious.

Water

Bottled water is easily obtainable in Indonesia. It is not advisable to drink water straight from the tap.

GETTING AROUND

AIR

Domestic air services are generally efficient and safe, although in Maluku and Nusa Tenggara overbooking is common. Fares are cheap by western standards but considerably more expensive than the overland alternatives. See page 871 for details on the Visit Indonesia Air Pass.

TRAIN

There is a reasonable railway network on Java and a limited one in southern Sumatra. **NB** Theft can be a problem on long-distance train journeys.

ROAD

Road is the main mode of transport in Indonesia. **Buses** link nearly all major and secondary towns, while minibuses and bemos link smaller settlements. Air-conditioned VIP buses are available on routes between provincial capitals. The more popular tourist destinations are also often linked by tour buses. Bus travel is cheap although journeys can be very long and uncomfortable, and occasionally dangerous (accidents are not infrequent). **NB** Security can be a problem on long-distance bus journeys.

CAR HIRE

Cars for self-drive hire are available from reputable firms in the largest cities and the more popular tourist destinations. Some people recommend hiring a driver as well if travelling long distances beyond tourist areas like Bali. Road 'courtesy' is not a feature of Indonesian drivers, and larger vehicles expect smaller ones to give way, even where the latter may have right of way.

HITCHHIKING AND CYCLING

Hitchhiking is not common in Indonesia. However there are small but increasing numbers of visitors who tour Indonesia by **bicycle**. It is strongly recommended that cyclists arrange their route on minor roads; drivers use the hard shoulder. See page 873 for further information on cycling in Indonesia.

BOAT

Ships, boats and ferries are important forms of transport and communication in a country of over 13,000 islands. Ferries link the various islands, the state-run shipping company Pelni operate a fleet of ships that run fortnightly circuits around the archipelago, and in Kalimantan river transport to the interior is also important.

LANGUAGE

English is not widely spoken beyond the main tourist centres and a smattering of Bahasa Indonesia always comes in handy. Indonesian is an easy language to pick up.

Tourism: counting the costs

"Tourism is like fire. It can either cook your food or burn your house down". This sums up the ambivalent attitude that many people have regarding the effects of tourism. It is one of Indonesia's largest foreign exchange earners, and the world's largest single industry; yet many people in receiving countries would rather tourists go home. Tourism is seen to be the cause of polluted beaches, rising prices, loose morals, consumerism, and much else besides.

The word 'tourist' is derived from 'travail', meaning work or torment. Travail, in turn, has its roots in the Latin word *tripalium*, which was a three-pronged instrument of torture. For many people struggling through interior Borneo this etymology should strike a chord. And yet, as *The Economist* pointed out in a survey of the industry in 1991:

"The curse of the tourist industry is that it peddles dreams: dreams of holidays where the sun always shines, the children are always occupied, and where every evening ends in the best sex you have ever had. For most of its modern life, this has been matched by a concomitant dreaminess on the part of its customers. When asked, most tourists tell whopping lies about what they want on holiday..." (Economist, 1991).

Most international tourists come from a handful of wealthy countries. Half from just five countries (the USA, Germany, the UK, Japan and France) and 80% from 20 countries. This is why many see tourism as the new 'imperialism', imposing alien cultures and ideals on sensitive and unmodernized peoples. The problem, however, is that discussions of the effects of tourism tend to degenerate into simplifications – culminating in the drawing up of a checklist of 'positive' and 'negative' effects, much like the one on page 25. Although such tables may be useful in highlighting problem areas, they also do a disservice by reducing a complex issue to a simple set of rather one dimensional 'costs' and 'benefits'. Different destinations will be affected in different ways; these effects are likely to vary over time; and different groups living in a particular destination will feel the effects of tourism in different ways and to varying degrees. At no time or place can tourism (or any other influence) be categorized as uniformly 'good' or 'bad'. Tourism can take a young Australian backpacker on US$5 a day to a losmen on one of the islands off Lombok, an American tourist to a luxury hotel on Bali where a room can cost over US$200 a night, or an elderly couple on a cruise through the islands of Nusa Tenggara.

SEARCHING FOR CULTURE

Indonesia is one of the richest cultural areas in the world, and many tourists are attracted to the country because of its exotic peoples from the Dayaks of Borneo to the Dani of Irian Jaya and the Minangkabau and Bataks of Sumatra. When cultural erosion is identified, the tendency is to blame this on tourists and tourism. Turner and Ash have written that tourists are the "suntanned destroyers of culture", while Bugnicourt argues that tourism:

"...encourages the imitation of foreigners and the downgrading of local inhabitants in relation to foreign tourists; it incites the pillage of art work and other historical artefacts; it leads to the degeneration of classical and popular dancing, the profanation and vulgarization of places of worship, and the perversion of religious ceremonies; it creates a sense of inferiority and a cultural demoralization which 'fans the flames of anti-development' through the acquisition of undesirable cultural traits" (1977).

The problem with views like this is that they assume that change is bad, and that indigenous cultures are unchanging. It makes local peoples victims of change, rather than masters of their own destinies. It also assumes that tourism is an external influence, when in fact it quickly becomes part of the local landscape. Cultural change is inevitable and on-going, and 'new' and 'traditional' are only judgements, not absolutes. Thus new cultural forms can quickly become key markers of tradition. Tourists searching for an 'authentic' experience are assuming that tradition is tangible, easily identifiable and unchanging. It is none of these.

'Tribal' people wearing American baseball caps are assumed to have succumbed to western culture. But such changes really say next to nothing about an individual's strength of identity. There are also problems with identifying cultural erosion, let alone linking it specifically with tourism, rather than with the wider processes of 'modernization'. This is exemplified in the case of Bali where tourism is paraded by some as the saviour of Balinese culture, and by others as its destroyer. Michel Picard in his paper "'Cultural tourism' in Bali" (1992) writes: "No sooner had culture become the

Tourism development guidelines

● Tourism should capitalize on local features (cultural and natural) so as to promote the use of local resources.

● Attention should be given to the type of tourist attracted. A mix of mass and individual will lead to greater local participation and better balance.

● Tourist development should be integrated with other sectors. Co-ordination between agencies is crucial.

● Facilities created should be made available to locals, at subsidised rates if necessary.

● Resources such as beaches and parks must remain in the public domain.

● Different tourists and tourist markets should be exploited so as to minimize seasonal variations in arrivals and employment.

● A tourist threshold should be identified and adhered to.

● Environmental impact assessments and other surveys must be carried out.

● Provision of services to tourists must be allied with improvements in facilities for locals.

● Development should be focused in areas where land use conflicts will be kept to a minimum.

● Supplies, where possible, should be sourced locally.

● Assistance and support should be given to small-scale, local entrepreneurs.

emblematic image of Bali [in the 1920s] than foreign visitors and residents started fearing for its oncoming disappearance. ...the mere evocation of Bali suggested the imminent and dramatic fall from the 'Garden of Eden': sooner of later, the 'Last Paradise' was doomed to become a 'Paradise Lost'" (Picard, 1992:77).

Yet the authorities on Bali are clearly at a loss as to how to balance their conflicting views:

"...the view of tourism held by the Balinese authorities is blatantly ambivalent, the driving force of a modernisation process which they welcome as ardently as they fear. Tourism in their eyes appears at once the most promising source of economic development and as the most subversive agent for the spread of foreign cultural influences in Bali" (Picard, 1992:85).

TOURIST ART: FINE ART, DEGRADED ART

Tourist art, both material (for instance, sculpture) and non-material (like dances) is another issue where views sharply diverge. The mass of inferior 'airport' art on sale to tourists demonstrates, to some, the corrosive effects of tourism. It leads craftsmen and women to mass-produce second rate pieces for a market that appreciates neither their cultural or symbolic worth, nor their aesthetic value. Yet tourism can also give value to craft industries that would otherwise be undermined by cheap industrial goods. Some people argue that the craft traditions of Indonesia should be allied with tourism to create vibrant new rural industries. The corrosive effects of tourism on arts and crafts also assumes that artists and craftsmen are unable to distinguish between fine pieces and pot-boilers. Many produce inferior pieces for the tourist market while continuing to produce for local demand, the former effectively subsidising the latter.

Some researchers have also shown how there is a tendency for culture to be 'invented' for tourists, and for this to then become part of 'tradition'. Michel Picard has shown in the case of Bali how dances developed for tourists are now paraded as paragons of national cultural heritage. The same is true of art, where the anthropologist Lewis Hill of the Centre for South-East Asian Studies at the University of Hull has demonstrated how objects made for the tourist market in one period are later enthusiastically embraced by the host community.

ENVIRONMENT AND TOURISM

The environmental deterioration that is linked to tourism is due to a destination area exceeding its 'carrying capacity' as a result of overcrowding. But carrying capacity, though an attractive concept, is notoriously difficult to pin down in any exact manner. A second dilemma facing those trying to encourage greater environmental consciousness is the so-called 'tragedy of the commons', better described in terms of Chinese restaurants. When a group of people go to a Chinese restaurant with the intention of sharing the bill, each customer will tend to order a more expensive dish than he or she would normally do – on the logic that everyone will be doing the same, and the bill will be split. In tourism terms, it means that hotel owners will always build those few more bungalows or that extra wing, to maximize their profits, reassured in the knowledge that the environmental costs will be shared among all hotel owners. So, despite most operators appreciating that over-development may 'kill the goose that lays the golden eggs', they do so anyway. In short, tourism contains the seeds of its own destruction.

But many developing countries have few other development opportunities. Those in Southeast Asia are blessed with beautiful landscapes and exotic cultures, and tourism is a cheap development option. Other possibilities cost more to develop and take longer to take-off. It is also true that 'development', however it is achieved, has cultural and environmental implications. For many, tourism is the least environmentally corrosive of the various options open to poor countries struggling to achieve rapid economic growth.

THE 'POST-TOURIST' AND THE TRAVELLER

In the last few years a new tourist has appeared; or at least a new type of tourist has been identified – the 'post-tourist'. The post-tourist is part of the post-modern world. He or she is aware that nothing is authentic; that every tourist experience is new and different; that tourism begins at home, in front of the television. The whole globe is a stage on and in which the post-tourist can revel; the crass and crude is just as interesting and delightful as the traditional and authentic to the post-tourist. He – or she – is abundantly aware that he is a tourist, not a brave and inquisitive searcher for culture and truth; just another

A tourism checklist	
Costs	**Benefits**
Vulnerable to external developments – eg oil price rises, 1991 Gulf War.	Diversifies an economy and is usually immune to protectionism.
	Requires few technical and human resources and is a 'cheap' development option.
	Requires little infrastructure.
Erodes culture by debasing it; strong cultures overwhelm sensitive ones (often tribal).	Gives value to cultures and helps in their preservation.
Leads to moral pollution with rising crime and prostitution.	Changing social norms are not due solely, or even mostly to tourism.
Often concentrated in culturally and environmentally sensitive areas, so effects are accentuated.	Helps to develop marginal areas that would otherwise 'miss out' on development.
Lack of planning and management causes environmental problems.	Poor planning and management is not peculiar to tourism and can be rectified.
Foreigners tend to dominate; costs of involvement are high so local people fail to become involved and benefit.	Costs of involvement can be very low; tourism is not so scale-dependent as other industries.
Tourism increases local inequalities. Jobs are usually seasonal and low-skilled. Economic leakages mean revenue generated tends to accrue to foreign multi-nationals.	Leakage is less than with many other industries; local involvement generally greater and value added is significant.
Tourism is not sustainable; tourism ultimately destroys tourism because it destroys those attributes that attracted tourists in the first place.	Tourism is not monolithic; destination areas evolve and do not have to suffer decay.

sunburnt, probably over-weight, almost certainly ignorant foreigner spending money to have a holiday (not a travel 'experience') in a foreign country. Paradoxically this lack of apparent discernment is what is seen to identify the post-tourist as truly discerning. Feifer, in 1985, stated that the post-tourist is well aware he is "not a time-traveller when he goes somewhere historic; not an instant noble savage when he stays on a tropical beach; not an invisible observer when he visits a native compound. Resolutely 're-alistic', he cannot evade his condition of outsider". Of course, all this could be discounted as the meaningless meanderings of a group of academics with little better to do than play with words and ideas. But, there is something akin to the post-tourist of the academic world beginning to inhabit the real world of tourism. These people might have once been described as just cynics, marvelling in the shear ironies of life. They are tourists for whom tourism is a game to be taken lightly; people who recognize that they are just another 'guest', another consumer of the tourist experience. No-one, and nothing, special.

The 'traveller' in contrast to the post-tourist finds it hard even to think of him or herself as a tourist at all. This, of course, is hubris built upon the notion that the traveller is an 'independent' explorer somehow beyond the bounds of the industry. Anna Borzello in an article entitled 'The myth of the traveller' in the journal *Tourism in Focus* (no. 19, 1994) writes that "Independent travellers cannot acknowledge – without shattering their self-image – that to many local people they are simply a good source of income. ...[not] inheritors of Livingstone, [but] bearers of urgently needed money". Although she does, in writing this, grossly underestimate the ability of travellers to see beyond their thongs and friendship bracelets, she does have a more pertinent point when she argues that it is important for travellers realistically to appraise their role as tourists, because: "Not only

are independent travellers often frustrated by the gap between the way they see themselves and the way they are treated, but unless they acknowledge that they are part of the tourist industry they will not take responsibility for the damaging effects of their tourism."

GUIDE BOOKS AND TOURISM

Guide books themselves have been identified by some analysts as being part of the problem. They are selective in two senses. First, they tend to selectively pick destination areas, towns and regions. This is understandable: one book cannot cover all the possibilities in a country. Then, and second, they selectively pick sights, hotels and restaurants within those places. Given that many travellers use guide books to map out their journey, this creates a situation where books determine the spatial pattern of tourist flows. As John McCarthy writes in *Are sweet dreams made of this? Tourism in Bali and Eastern Indonesia* (1994, IRIP: Victoria, Australia):

"Such is the power of guide books that, unless they are carefully written, one writer's point of view can determine the commercial success or failure of a hotel or restaurant for years after. Even when the enterprise changes, the loathing or love of a travel writer who passed through a village 3 years ago remains too potent a testimony" (page 93).

There are no easy answers to this. If guide books were more diverse; if travellers really were more independent; and if guide books were not so opinionated and subjective, then this would all help in spreading the tourism phenomenon. But none of these is likely: guide books exist to 'guide'; humans are by nature subjective; and the notion of the free spirit 'traveller' has always, in the most part, been a mirage brought on by a romantic collective sense of what tourism *should* be. One answer is for books to become more specialist, and certainly one identifiable trend is towards guide books covering sub-national regions – Jakarta, Bali and

Sumatra, for example. It seems that people are now more willing to spend an extended period of time exploring one area, rather than notching up a large number of 'must do's'. Although even such specialist books also tend to suffer from the dangers of selectivity noted above, those people who do spend a longer period of time in an area are in a position to be more selective themselves, and to rely more on their own experiences rather than those of a guide book writer who may have visited a town in a bad mood 3 years previously.

In the opening page to his *Illustrated Guide to the Federated Malay States*, Cuthbert Woodville Harrison wrote:

"It has become nowadays so easy and so common a venture to cross the world that the simple circum-navigation of the globe 'merely for wantonness' is very rapidly ceasing to be in fashion. But as the rough places of the earth become smooth to the travellers, and they no longer fear 'that the gulfs will wash us down', there is growing amongst them a disposition to dwell awhile in those lands whose climate and inhabitants most differ from ours. The more completely such places are strange to us the more do they attract us, and the more isolated they have lived hitherto, the more do we feel called upon to visit them now."

Cuthbert Woodville Harrison's book was published in 1923.

SUGGESTED READING AND TOURISM PRESSURE GROUPS

In the UK, **Tourism Concern** aims to "promote greater understanding of the impacts of tourism on host communities and environments", "to raise awareness of the forms of tourism that respect the rights and interests of [local] people", and to "work for change in current tourism practice". Annual membership is £15.00 which includes subscription to their magazine *In Focus*. Tourism Concern, Froebel College, Roehampton Lane, London SW15 5PU, T (0181) 878-9053.

The most up-to-date book examining tourism in Southeast Asia is: Hitchcock, Mike *et al.* (edits) (1993) *Tourism in South-East Asia*, Routledge: London.

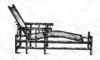

Horizons

INDONESIA is the world's largest archipelago with 13,677 islands, stretching along the equator for 5,120 km (twice the distance from London to Moscow) – or, as Indonesians say, from 'Sebang to Merauke'. It has a population of nearly 190 million – making it the fourth most populous country in the world – comprising 300 ethnic groups who speak an estimated 583 languages and dialects. Indonesia also has the world's largest Muslim population. Its geography is just as varied. There are glaciers in the central highlands of Irian Jaya, and vast expanses of tropical swamps in Kalimantan and Sumatra. Across the archipelago there are over 300 volcanoes, more than 200 of which have been active in historical times. From the floor of the Weber Deep in the Banda Sea, to the summit of Mt Jaya, Indonesia's highest mountain in Irian Jaya, it is 12,470m.

No wonder Indonesia's motto is *Bhinneka Tunggal Ika*, officially – and rather loosely – translated as 'Unity in Diversity'. Indonesia's coat of arms is the Garuda, the eagle of ancient Indonesian mythology, symbolizing creative energy. With such a bewildering mosaic of cultures, landscapes and histories, it often makes more sense to break the country down into its constituent parts. With this in mind, each of the major regions of the country has been given a separate introduction: Java, Bali, Sumatra, Kalimantan, Sulawesi, Nusa Tenggara, Timor, Maluku and Irian Jaya. This general introduction is intended to provide an overview of Indonesia's geography, history, politics and economy.

THE LAND

Who first coined the term 'Indonesia' is disputed. Traditionally the glory has gone to the German ethnographer Adolf Bastian who is said to have latched onto the word at the end of the 19th century. But some scholars credit the English lawyer George Windsor Earl with coining the name in an article he wrote in 1850. Another English lawyer, JR Logan, practising in Singapore is said to have read Earl's articles and as a result took to using the term in his own papers. It was only then that Bastian, after reading Logon's publications, began to refer to 'Indonesia' in his own work. The Teutons and the Anglos will probable be fighting over this rich prize for some years yet!

THE REGIONS OF INDONESIA

With a country of such enormous size, how it is divided takes on great importance. Many people – although rarely Indonesians themselves – simply talk of the 'Inner' or 'Metropolitan' islands of Java, Bali and Madura, and the Outer Islands – the rest. This division is one of core and periphery, in a political, economic, cultural and historic sense. Jakarta and Java are the main centres of political and economic power, and Javanese culture has an overriding effect upon the rest of the nation. As the anthropologist Clifford Geertz wrote in 1966: "If ever there was a tail which wagged a dog, Java is the tail, Indonesia the dog."

The country can also be broken down into the Greater and Lesser Sunda Islands. The Greater Sundas comprise Sumatra, Java, Kalimantan and Sulawesi; the Lesser Sundas, Bali, Timor and the myriad islands of Maluku and Nusa Tenggara. This division has a certain zoological and geological logic: plants and animals of the two broadly reflect their contrasting Asian and Australasian origins.

Officially however, the country is divided into 27 provinces (which includes three special administrative areas – see below) or *propinsi* (including the disputed territory of E Timor), each administered by a governor (*gubernur*). The administrative unit beneath the province is the district or *kabupaten*, of which there are between three and 29 in each province (242 in total); each of these is headed by a *bupati*, known as a regent during the colonial period. Urban municipalities – 56 in total – which have the same administrative status as districts, are known as *kotamadya*. Kabupaten are in turn divided into sub-districts or *kecamatan* of which there are 3,639, and they into villages or *desa*. Each village – and in 1991 there were 62,061 – is headed by a *kepala desa*, literally 'village head'.

In addition to this division, there are three special administrative units: the Special Territories or *Daerah Istimewa* of Aceh and Yogyakarta, and the Special Capital District or *Daerah Khusus Ibukota* (DKI) of Jakarta.

The regions of Indonesia

	Population (millions 1990 census)	Land area (sq km)
Java	107.6	132,186
Bali	2.8	5,561
Sumatra	36.6	473,481
Kalimantan	9.1	539,460
Nusa Tenggara*	7.5	82,927
Sulawesi	12.5	189,216
Maluku	1.9	74,505
Irian Jaya	1.6	421,981
INDONESIA	179.3†	1,919,317

* Nusa Tenggara = the islands of West and East Nusa Tenggara and East Timor.
† There is a rounding error in this figure.

GEOGRAPHY

In total, Indonesia covers a land area of 1,919,317 sq km – or eight times the land area of Britain. The country also claims sovereignty over 3,272,160 sq km of sea, stretching from Asia to Australasia. The political, historic and economic heart of the country are the islands of Java and Bali, which support 60% of the population but account for only 7% of the land area. On Java's N coast is the capital or 'mother city' (*ibu kota*) of Jakarta, formerly Batavia. Ranged around these so-called Inner Islands, are the Outer Islands: Sumatra, Kalimantan, Sulawesi, Timor and Irian Jaya, and the assorted islands of Maluku and Nusa Tenggara.

An active volcanic arc runs through Sumatra, Java and the islands of Nusa Tenggara, and then N through Maluku to Sulawesi. It marks the point where two tectonic plates plunge, one beneath the other. This is an area of intense volcanic activity – a 'ring of fire' – most dramatically illustrated when Krakatau erupted and then exploded in 1883 (see page 144). Off the coast of these islands is a deep sea trench, in places more than 7,000m deep. Within the arc is the more stable Sunda Shelf with shallow seas and a less dramatic landscape.

Another division that has attracted

Volcanoes

Indonesia has more active volcanoes than any other country – 13% of the world's total. It has also experienced more eruptions known to have affected people and their activities (156) than any other country. Over the last 200 years an estimated 175,000 people have died from volcanic activity in Indonesia and between 1985 and 1995 alone the country experienced no fewer than 38 eruptions. Indonesia, in short, is a vulcanologist's dream. The volcanoes are concentrated in an arc that marks the boundary between the Pacific, Australian and Philippine tectonic plates, running through W Sumatra, Java, Bali, the islands of Nusa Tenggara, and which then sweeps N to include N Sulawesi and Halmahera in Maluku. Not suprisingly, Indonesia also suffers numerous earthquakes. From a human perspective, it is Java where volcanoes pose the greatest threat. Around 2.5 million people on Java live in designated 'high risk' areas and if Mount Guntur between Bandung and Garut showed signs of activity around 750,000 people would have to be evacuated.

The best known eruption was the one which vaporized a large part of the island of Krakatau off the W coast (not the E coast as the film *Krakatau east of Java* tried to maintain in a futile attempt – presumably – to sound more romantic and Oriental) of Java in 1883 (see page 144). But far larger was the eruption of Mt Tambora on Sumbawa in 1815 which catastrophically altered the global climate in the following year (see page 720). More stupendous still, though, was the truly massive eruption that created Lake Toba in N Sumatra about 75,000 years ago – probably the largest explosion anywhere in the last million years (see page 461).

With Indonesia's wealth of volcanoes there is also a correspondingly impressive infrastructure for coping with eruptions. Some of this is traditional, but the modern Vulcanological Division of the Geological Survey, building on previous Dutch work, is highly professional and effective – belieing Indonesia's comparative poverty in other respects. When Colo volcano on the island of Una Una in Central Sulawesi erupted in 1983, the 7,000 inhabitants had already been evacuated, following the advice of the Survey which had been carefully monitoring seismic activity in the area. The eruption of Mount Merapi on Java, at the end of Nov 1994, led to more than 5,000 villagers being evacuated from the mountainside; there were also a considerable number of deaths.

considerable attention is a biological divide: between Indonesia's Asian and Australasian faunal realms. This 'line' runs between Bali and Lombok, and N to divide Kalimantan and Sulawesi. It is known as Wallace's Line after the great Victorian naturalist Alfred Russel Wallace who first observed the distinction in the 19th century (see page 690). To the SE of the line, animals tend to be Australasian in origin – for example, marsupials are found in the Kai Islands and in Sulawesi. By contrast, to the NW of Wallace's Line, no marsupials are found but there are many of the large Asian mammals, including tigers, elephants, orang utans and rhinoceros.

The two Indonesian landscapes that are most striking are the **terraced rice field** and the **tropical forest**. The terraced rice field, exemplified by those on Java and Bali are cut from the land, bunded by small embankments, irrigated, and can support well over 1,000 people/sq km. They are managed, artificial ecosystems in which nature is reworked and harnessed in the interests of humans. In contrast, the tropical forest is a natural ecosystem. Hunter, gatherers and shifting cultivators (see page 33) do not so much replace the forest, as work with and within it. Population densities rarely exceed 10 people/sq km, and their livelihoods are dependent on maintaining the forest resource. But although the tropical lowland rainforests contain a greater variety of species than any other terrestrial ecosystem, they are also one of the most sensitive. If the forest is cleared over large areas, then the land and soil suffer from erosion and degradation.

The cycle of wet rice cultivation

There are an estimated 120,000 rice varieties. Rice seed – either selected from the previous harvest or, more commonly, purchased from a dealer or agricultural extension office – is soaked overnight before being sown into a carefully prepared nursery bed. Today farmers are likely to plant one of the Modern Varieties or MVs bred for their high yields.

The nursery bed into which the seeds are broadcast (scattered) is often a farmer's best land, with the most stable water supply. After a month the seedlings are uprooted and taken out to the paddy fields. These will also have been ploughed, puddled and harrowed, turning the heavy clay soil into a saturated slime. Traditionally buffalo and cattle would have performed the task; today rotavators, and even tractors are becoming more common. The seedlings are transplanted into the mud in clumps. Before transplanting the tops of the seedlings are twisted off (this helps to increase yield) and then they are pushed in to the soil in neat rows. The work is back-breaking and it is not unusual to find labourers – both men and women – receiving a premium – either a bonus on top of the usual daily wage or a free meal at midday, to which marijuana is sometimes added to ease the pain.

After transplanting, it is essential that the water supply is carefully controlled. The key to high yields is a constant flow of water, regulated to take account of the growth of the rice plant. In 'rain-fed' systems where the farmer relies on rainfall to water the crop, he has to hope that it will be neither too much nor too little. Elaborate ceremonies are performed to appease the rice goddess and to ensure bountiful rainfall.

In areas where rice is grown in irrigated conditions, farmers need not concern themselves with the day-to-day pattern of rainfall, and in such areas two or even three crops can be grown each year. But such systems need to be carefully managed, and it is usual for one man to be in charge of irrigation. In Bali he is known as the *kliang subak*. He decides when water should be released, organizes labour to repair dykes and dams and to clear channels, and decides which fields should receive the water first.

Traditionally, while waiting for the rice to mature, a farmer would do little except weed the crop from time to time. He and his family might move out of the village and live in a field hut to keep a close eye on the maturing rice. Today, farmers also apply chemical fertilisers and pesticides to protect the crop and ensure maximum yield. After 90-130 days, the crop should be ready for harvesting.

Harvesting also demands intensive labour. Traditionally, farmers in a village would secure their harvesters through systems of reciprocal labour exchange; now it is more likely for a harvester to be paid in cash. After harvesting, the rice is threshed, sometimes out in the field, and then brought back to the village to be stored in a rice barn or sold. It is only at the end of the harvest, with the rice safely stored in the barn, that the festivals begin.

Fields in the forest

Shifting cultivation, also known as slash-and-burn agriculture or swiddening, as well as by a variety of local terms, is one of the characteristic farming systems of Southeast Asia. It is a low-intensity form of agriculture, in which land is cleared from the forest through burning, cultivated for a few years, and then left to regenerate over 10-30 years. It takes many forms, but an important distinction can be made between shifting field systems where fields are rotated but the settlement remains permanently sited, and migratory systems where the shifting cultivators shift both field (swidden) and settlement. The land is usually only rudimentarily cleared, tree stumps being left in the ground, and seeds sown in holes made by punching the soil with a dibble stick.

For many years, shifting cultivators were regarded as 'primitives' who followed an essentially primitive form of agriculture and their methods were contrasted unfavourably with 'advanced' settled rice farmers. There are still many government officials in Southeast Asia who continue to adhere to this mistaken belief, arguing that shifting cultivators are the principal cause of forest loss and soil erosion. They are, therefore, painted as the villains in the region's environmental crisis, neatly sidestepping the considerably more detrimental impact that commercial logging has had on Southeast Asia's forest resources.

Shifting cultivators have an intimate knowledge of the land, plants and animals on which they depend. One study of a Dayak tribe, the Kantu' of Kalimantan (Borneo), discovered that households were cultivating an average of 17 rice varieties and 21 other food crops each year in a highly complex system. Even more remarkably, Harold Conklin's classic 1957 study of the Hanunóo of the Philippines – a study which is a benchmark for such work even today – found that the Hanunóo identified 40 types and subtypes of rocks and minerals when classifying different soils. The shifting agricultural systems are usually also highly productive in labour terms, allowing far more leisure time than farmers using permanent field systems.

But shifting cultivation contains the seeds of its own extinction. Extensive, and geared to low population densities and abundant land, it is coming under pressure in a region where land is becoming an increasingly scarce resource, where patterns of life are dictated by an urban-based élite, and where populations are pressing on the means of subsistence.

CLIMATE

Straddling the equator, and stretching over 5,000 km from E to W and almost 2,000 km from N to S, Indonesia encompasses several climatic zones. It is possible to fly from one region's wet season to another area's dry, and from towns with annual rainfall of nearly 5,000 mm, to places where it is less than 500 mm. The only constant – at least at sea-level – is the temperature, which averages about 26°C.

Much of Indonesia has what climatologists term an **'equatorial monsoon'**

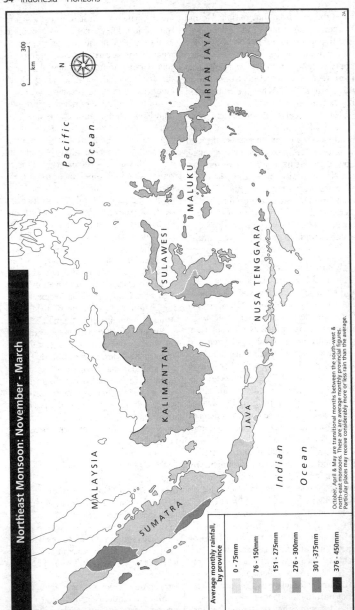

Northeast Monsoon: November - March

300
0 __ km

N

Pacific Ocean

IRIAN JAYA

MALUKU

SULAWESI

NUSA TENGGARA

KALIMANTAN

MALAYSIA

JAVA

Indian Ocean

SUMATRA

Average monthly rainfall, by province

- 0 - 75mm
- 76 - 150mm
- 151 - 275mm
- 276 - 300mm
- 301 - 375mm
- 376 - 450mm

October, April & May are transitional months between the south-west & north-east monsoons. These are average monthly provincial figures. Particular places may receive considerably more or less rain than the average.

Southwest Monsoon: June – October

Pacific Ocean

Indian Ocean

MALAYSIA

SUMATRA

KALIMANTAN

JAVA

SULAWESI

MALUKU

NUSA TENGGARA

IRIAN JAYA

N

0   300
km

Average monthly rainfall, by province

- 0 - 75mm
- 76 - 150mm
- 151 - 275mm
- 276 - 300mm
- 301 - 375mm
- 376 - 450mm

October, April & May transitional months between the south-west &
north-east monsoons. These are average monthly provincial figures.
Particular places may receive considerably more or less rain than the average.

climate. This broad classification covers a multitude of climate types. Annual rainfall usually exceeds 2,000 mm, but can be more than twice that, or less than a quarter of it. Close to the equator rainfall is distributed evenly through the year, and there is no marked dry season. However, moving N and S from the equator, the dry season becomes more pronounced, and rainfall becomes concentrated in one or two seasonal peaks. Indonesia's worst storm on record resulted in 802 mm (31") of rain falling in just 1 day. Over a period of 13 days, 3,220 mm (127") of rain fell, with 80 mm (3") falling in the space of just 30 mins.

This pattern of rainfall is determined by two monsoons: the NE monsoon and the SW monsoon. The NE monsoon prevails from Nov/Dec to Feb/Mar and forms the wet season. The SW monsoon extends from Jun to Aug/Sep and brings dry conditions to the area. But, there are a large number of exceptions to disturb this general pattern. The effect of local wind systems and climates, and the shadowing effect of mountainous areas means rainfall can either be significantly higher than the 'norm', or lower. Palu in Sulawesi, for example, is on exactly the same latitude as Padang on the W coast of Sumatra, yet the former has an annual rainfall of only 530 mm, while the latter receives a drenching 4,500 mm.

Eastern Indonesia has a rather different climate from the rest of the country. It too is affected by two monsoons: the W monsoon from Dec to Mar, and the E

Indonesia's climate

REGION	SEASON		RAINFALL
	Dry	Wet	
Java	Jun-Aug	Dec-Feb	West 2,360 mm
			Central 2,400 mm
			East 1,660 mm
Bali	May-Oct	Nov-Apr	Average 2,150 mm
Sumatra	Jun-Jul	Oct-Apr	West coast 4-6,000 mm
			Other areas 3,000 mm
Kalimantan	Jul-Sep	–	Average 3,810 mm
Sulawesi	Aug-Sep	Dec-Feb	Manado 3,352 mm
			Ujung Pandang 3,188 mm
			Palu 533 mm
Nusa Tenggara	Apr-Oct	–	E Flores & Sumba 8-900 mm
North Maluku	–	May-Oct	Ambon 3,450 mm
SE Maluku	Dec-Mar	–	Ceram 1,400 mm
Irian Jaya	–	–	North coast 2,500 mm
			Interior 5-8,000 mm
			Merauke 1,500 mm

NB The distinction between the wet and dry seasons is least pronounced in Sumatra, Sulawesi, North Maluku and Irian Jaya; and most pronounced in Nusa Tenggara and Southeast Maluku.

monsoon from May to Sep. The W monsoon is a continuation of the Asian NE monsoon after it has changed direction on crossing the equator. However, by the time it has arrived, the monsoon has picked up moisture over the warm seas of the Indonesian archipelago. It therefore brings large quantities of rainfall to the area between the months of Dec and Mar. By May the NE monsoon has retreated and E Indonesia comes under the influence of the hot and dry South Pacific Trade-winds. This E monsoon generally extends from May to Sep, although the dry season (which is very dry) can be as much as 7 months long.

The climate of each of the regions of Indonesia is discussed in the relevant introductory section. The characteristics of each is summarized in the climate box above. For monthly rainfall and temperature figures for some of Indonesia's cities see the following pages: 105 (Jakarta, Java), 432 (Medan, Sumatra), 511 (Padang, Sumatra), 581 (Balikpapan, Kalimantan), and page 105 (Ambon, Maluku).

FLORA AND FAUNA

The greatest naturalist to have travelled through the islands of Indonesia was the Victorian, Alfred Russel Wallace (1823-1913). His book *The Malay Archipelago: the land of the Orang-utan and the Bird of Paradise* (1869), is a *tour de force*, dedicated, significantly, to the other great Victorian naturalist Charles Darwin "not only as a token of personal esteem and friendship but also to express my deep admiration for his genius and his works". Darwin first appeared to take notice of Wallace's work in 1855 or 1856 when Charles Lyell, the great geologist, recommended that he read Wallace's paper 'on the law which has regulated the introduction of new species' in the *Annals and Magazine of Natural History* (vol. 16, 1855). Wallace was clearly on the same evolutionary path as Darwin – or at least an allied one – and it was probably the fear that Wallace might pre-empt Darwin which led the latter to fully develop his evolutionary ideas which had been gestating for so many years.

Wallace was enchanted by the animals and people that he encountered during his 8 years away from England. He travelled 14,000 miles through the archipelago, made 60 or 70 separate journeys, and collected 125,600 specimens – which he shipped back to London and donated to the British Museum.

Straddling the equator and marking the interface between the Asian and Australasian worlds, Indonesia has the richest flora and fauna of any country in Southeast Asia. Although it accounts for only 1.3% of the earth's land area, Indonesia supports 10% of the world's flowering plants (25,000 species), 12% of mammal species (500), 16% of the world's amphibian and reptile species, 17% of bird species (1,600) and 25% of the world's species of fish (8,500). In total there are 816 endemic species of fauna – animals found no where else in the world except Indonesia – including 210 mammal species, 356 bird, and 150 reptile. Along with Australia, there are more endemic vertebrates in Indonesia than in any other country. Many of the large Asian mammals are represented: tigers, elephants, two species of rhinoceros, tapirs, buffalos, gibbons and orang-utans

Durian: king of fruits

In Southeast Asia, the durian is widely regarded as the most delicious of fruits – to the horror of many foreign visitors). In his book *The Malay Archipelago* (1869), Alfred Russel Wallace describes it in almost orgiastic terms:

"The consistence and flavour are indescribable. A rich butter-like custard highly flavoured with almonds gives the best general idea of it, but intermingled with it come wafts of flavour that call to mind cream-cheese, onion sauce, brown sherry and other incongruities. Then there is a rich glutinous smoothness in the pulp which nothing else possesses, but which adds to its delicacy. It is neither acid, or sweet, nor juicy, yet one feels the want of none of these qualities, for it is perfect as it is. It produces no nausea or other bad effect, and the more you eat of it the less you feel inclined to stop. In fact to eat Durian is a new sensation, worth a voyage to the East to experience."

(see Borneo, page 548). There are also oddities such as the bird of paradise (page 837), the maleo bird (page 684), the Komodo dragon (page 731) and the Rafflesia flower (page 490). The characteristic flora and fauna of each region are discussed in the relevant introductory section.

Sadly, not only has Indonesia got one of the richest flora and faunas in the world, it also suffers from rapid loss of habitat as forests are cleared for timber and human settlement. The Javan wattled lapwing (*Vanellus macropterus*) and the caerulean paradise flycatcher (*Eutrichomyias rowleyi*) of the Sangihe Islands off N Sulawesi are both extinct, as are the small Balinese and Javan (probably) tigers, both subspecies of tiger. Other ani-

National Parks & Protected Areas

Rubiah Sea Garden
Gunung Leuser National Park
SUMATRA
Siberut National Park
Kerinci Seblat National Park
Bukit Barisan Selatan National Park
Ujung Kulon National Park
Gunung Gede-Pangrango National Park
Way Kambas National Park
Pulau Seribu Marine Park
Bromo-Tengger-Semeru National Park
Meru Betiri National Park
Gunung Palung National Park
Tanjung Puting National Park
Gunung Kawi-Kelud
JAVA
Alas Purwo National Park
KALIMANTAN
Kutai National Park
Bali Barat National Park
Moyo Island
BALI
Gunung Rinjani National Park

mals are represented by such small populations that they are probably unsustainable – the Javan gibbon, for example. As Tony and Jane Whitten remark in their book *Wild Indonesia*, the "term 'living dead' has been applied to such species". In Feb 1994 the Environment Minister Sarwono Kusumaatmadja announced that all companies which explore for and exploit natural resources would be required to undertake an annual environmental audit. At the time this statement was widely discounted as environmental PR. However, in an apparent further hardening of the government's position on the environment, at the end of 1994 President Suharto refused to extend the licences of 75 logging companies on the grounds that they had not met the necessary minimum forest management requirements – stipulating such things as selective logging, sustainable yield tech-

niques, and reafforestation. He proposed to nationalize 33 other companies for the same reason. For more detail on Indonesia's regional flora and fauna see the relevant regional introduction.

NATIONAL PARKS

As of early 1991, 24 **national parks** had been gazetted by the Indonesian government covering 6.9 million ha. Three of these have been adopted by the IUCN as World Heritage Sites: Ujung Kulon in W Java, Komodo in Nusa Tenggara, and Lore Lindu in Sulawesi. In general, Indonesian parks have limited tourist facilities when compared with parks in Malaysia and Thailand, although those in Java (eg Ujung Kulon) and Bali represent exceptions to this rule. The Indonesian government also recognizes separate categories of Recreational Forests, Grand Forest Parks and Hunting Parks. These areas are

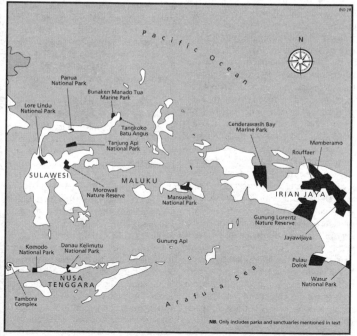

NB: Only includes parks and sanctuaries mentioned in text

less rigorously protected. The fact that 1993 was heralded as Visit Indonesia Environment and Heritage Year possibly indicates that some people are beginning to accept that the environment is worth preserving on sound, pecuniary grounds.

In Oct 1994 a new 800,000 ha forest reserve and wildlife sanctuary was created spanning the borders of Sarawak and Kalimantan, not far from the infamous Malaysian dam at Batang Ai. This is the first example of environmental cooperation between Malaysia and Indonesia, and officials state that the two reserves – the Lanjak Entimau in Sarawak and the Bentuang-Karimun in Kalimantan – together constitute the largest protected area of wet tropical forest in the world. The two reserves support important populations of such rare mammals as the Sumatran rhinoceros, clouded leopard, wild orang utan (as opposed to 'rehabilitated' animals) and bearcat; recently six entirely new species of animal have been discovered in the Sarawak side of the park, including a terrestrial crab and a snake.

But the task facing the Indonesian government is how to protect the country's plants, animals and wild areas when the population is growing at nearly 2% a year, and when economic pressures on resources are escalating at an even faster rate. About 10% of the country's land area is now protected. An environmental movement has also emerged in Indonesia, spurring the government to take greater notice of infractions of environmental laws. But in the Outer Islands it is difficult for farmers and settlers to appreciate that any environmental crisis exists. In Sumatra, Kalimantan, Sulawesi and Irian Jaya it is all too easy to believe that the forest is a limitless resource. When families have to be fed and clothed, and children sent to school, cutting-down trees to sell the timber and clear the land for agriculture, seems not just a reasonable response but often also the only response.

HISTORY

PREHISTORY

After Thailand and East Malaysia, Indonesia – and particularly Java – has probably revealed more of Southeast Asia's prehistory than any other country in the region. Most significant was the discovery of **hominid fossils** in Central Java in 1890, when Eugene Dubois uncovered the bones of so-called 'Java Man' near the village of Trinil. He named his ape-man *Pithecanthropus erectus*, since changed to *Homo erectus erectus*. These, and other discoveries – particularly at Sangiran, also in Central Java and Mojokerto – indicate that Indonesia was inhabited by hominids as long as 1.8 million years ago (see page 229). Excavations in Central Java have also revealed other fossils of early Man – *Pithecanthropus soloensis* and *P modjokertensis*. Among the skulls of *P soloensis* a number has been found to have had their cranial bases removed, leading scientists to postulate that the species practised anthropophagy – less politely known as cannibalism – which involved gouging the brains out through the base. Alternatively, the surgery might have been part of a post mortem ritual.

Following the end of the last Ice Age 15,000 years ago, there began a movement of Mongoloid peoples from the Asian mainland, S and E, and into the Southeast Asian archipelago. As this occurred, the immigrants displaced the existing Austromelanesian inhabitants, pushing them further E or into remote mountain areas.

The practice of **settled agriculture** seems to have filtered into the islands of Indonesia from mainland Southeast Asia about 2,500 BC, along with these Mongoloid migrants. Settled life is associated with the production of primitive earthenware pottery, examples of which have been found in Java, Sulawesi and Flores. Later, **ancestor cults** evolved, echoes of which are to be seen in the megaliths of Sumatra, Java, Sulawesi, Bali, Sumbawa and Sumba. These cultures reached their height about 500 BC. Among the various discoveries has been evidence of the mutilation of corpses – presumably to prevent the deceased from returning to the world of the living. In some cases, ritual elements of these megalithic cultures still exist – for example on the island of Sumba in Nusa Tenggara, among the inhabitants of Nias Island off W Sumatra, and among the Batak of N Sumatra.

The technology of **bronze casting** was also known to prehistoric Indonesians. Socketed axes have been discovered in Java, several islands of Nusa Tenggara (eg Roti) and in Sulawesi. But the finest bronze artefacts are the magnificent kettledrums of E Indonesia (see page 377). It is thought these were made in Vietnam, not in Indonesia, and arrived in the archipelago when traders used them as barter goods. Later, locally made equivalents such as the *moko* of Alor (see page 753) were produced, but they never achieved the refinement of the originals.

PRE-COLONIAL HISTORY

Unlike the states of mainland Southeast Asia which did enjoy a certain geographical legitimacy prior to the colonial period, Indonesia was a fragmented assemblage of kingdoms, sultanates, principalities and villages. It is true that there was a far greater degree of communication and intercourse than many assume, so that no part of the archipelago can be treated in isolation but nonetheless, it is still difficult to talk of 'Indonesian' history prior to the 19th century.

The great empires of the pre-colonial period did range beyond their centres of power, but none came close to controlling all the area now encompassed by the modern Indonesian state. Among these empires, the most powerful were the Srivijayan Kingdom based at Palembang in S Sumatra; and the great Javanese Dynasties of Sailendra, Majapahit and Mataram. There was also a string of less powerful, but nonetheless influential, kingdoms: for example, the Sultanate of Aceh in N Sumatra, the Gowa Kingdom of S Sulawesi, the trading sultanates of the Spice Islands of Maluku, and the Hindu kingdoms of Bali. The history of each of these powers is dealt with in the appropriate regional introduction.

Major pre-colonial powers		
Empire, kingdom or sultanate	**Date (century)**	**Centre of power**
Srivijaya	7th-14th	Palembang
Sailendra	8th-10th	Central Java
Sanjaya	8th-11th	Central & East Java
Kediri	11th-13th	Kediri, East Java
Banten	12th-17th	Banten, West Java
Singasari	13th	East Java
Majapahit	13th-15th	East Java
Gowa	16th-17th	Makassar, South Sulawesi
Mataram	16th-18th	Central Java
Aceh	16th-19th	Aceh, North Sumatra
Karangkasem	18th-19th	Bali & Lombok

Sir Francis Drake in Indonesia

🐾 During his epic circumnavigation of the world, Sir Francis Drake sailed through a large part of the Indonesian archipelago between late 1579 and early 1580 in his ship the *Golden Hind*. From the Philippines, his last port of call before entering Indonesian waters, Drake set a south-westerly course, towards the fabled Moluccas (Maluku) or Spice Islands – one of the key objectives of his voyage. The log records:

"October 25 we passed by the Iland named Talao, in 3 deg. 40 min. We saw to the North-ward of it three or foure other Ilands, Teda, Selan, Saran (three Ilands so named to vs by an Indian), the middle whereof stands in 3 deg."

These are the most northerly islands in Indonesia. He embarked two fishermen en route who agreed to pilot him to the Moluccas. On the 3 Nov the log notes:

"...we fell with the islands of MOLUCCA, which day at night (hauing directed our course to runne with TYDORE) in coasting along the island of MUTYR, belonging to the King of TERNATE..."

Reaching the Spice Islands and loading a cargo of cloves was a key objective of the whole voyage. Although concerned about the Portuguese – reflected in the fact that the *Golden Hind* was intentionally 20 miles W of her destination on arrival in the area – Drake loaded 6 tons of cloves and verbally agreed a trading treaty with the king. The evidence seems to indicate that he either anchored between Ternate and Tidore and was then towed to the fort, or anchored off the fort and was towed to the palace on Ternate. Sultan Baab (Babullah) was invited on board Drake's vessel and after he returned to shore sent a meal of sago, rice, hens and sugar to the captain and his men. The following day, the Sultan sent his brother to the ship to act as a hostage while Drake was invited to visit the Sultan at his court. The captain's advisors were suspicious of the Sultan's intentions and recommended that a delegation of 'gentlemen' be sent instead. They reported that the palace was poorly defended with "two lonely cannons". The gentlemen were, according to contemporary accounts, accorded great honour during their visit. The location of the palace was almost certainly the same as that of the current palace, on a hill to the N of town. However, the original building has been demolished and today's building is a 19th century construction.

Some of the exhibits in the palace museum correspond with the artefacts and costumes described in the account of the visit:

"The king at last came in garded with 12. launces the points turned downward: [the Sultan was] couered ouer with a rich canopie [and at his feet] were a paire of shoes, made of CORDOUAN skinne ... [the people were attired] all in red, downe to the ground, and...on their heades [were turbans] like the Turkes..."

From Ternate, and with a cargo of valuable spices, Drake sailed W "...till November 14, at what time we arriued at a little Iland, standing in 1 deg. 40 min.". This island was the smaller of the two **Potil Islands**, not far from **Luwuk** on Sulawesi's eastern limb and 3 miles E of the much larger island of Peleng. Here Drake and his crew re-watered and careened their ship. It seems that the locals thought the ship wrecked, and that repairs were underway. During the stay on the island, Drake records the sight of fireflies:

"Among the trees, night by night, did shew themseulues an infinite swarme of fierie-seeming-wormes flying the aire, whose bodies (no bigger than an ordinary flie) did make a shew, and giue such light as if euery twigge on eury tree had beene a lighted candle, or as if that place had beene the starry sphaere..."

Drake named the island Francisca Island, after one of the two negroes he had taken aboard in the Americas.

Drake sailed westwards through the Kaloembangan Strait and entered an area of treacherous reefs and shoals. His ship ran over the **Vesuvius Reef**, not far from **Kendari** on Sulawesi and the vessel was struck hard aground. This event occurred at 2000 hours on 9 January 1580. It is recorded that although the ship suffered no damage, the crew prostrated themselves on the deck and offered their souls to the Lord. To float the ship off the reef, Drake ordered the jettisoning of two tons of valuable cloves, eight cannon and some food. It was at this dark time that Frances Fletcher gave a sermon effectively blaming Drake for the predicament the ship and its crew found themselves in. Shortly after refloating the *Golden Hind*, Drake excommunicated Fletcher from the Church. Drake chained one of the man's legs to the forecastle deck hatch and had the legend "Frances fletcher, ye falsest knave that liveth" enscribed and attached to his arm.

From Vesuvius Reef, Drake sailed southwards through foul weather, past the islands of **Buton** and **Muna**. A westerly gale then blew off course and towards the islands of **Nusa Tenggara**. He probably sighted the island of **Wetar** on 1 Feb, and then **Damar Island** which lies 300 miles east of Alor. Here he "cast anchor, and the next day [7 Feb] watred and wooded". He then sailed and anchored for 2 days at "Barativa", which is probably the present-day town of **Bebar**, also on Damar. He recorded that "The people are Gentiles, of handsome body and comely stature..." and was immensely impressed with their "civill demeanour very iust in dealing, and courteous to strangers...". Bebar was the most welcoming anchorage for Drake since Ternate and he and his crew took comfort and refreshment while there. He was amazed at the wealth of fruit and noted the use of sago.

From Damar Island, with a favourable easterly wind, Drake began his journey home passing and recording the islands of Moa, Leti and Kisar, and skirting the southern coast of Wetar. He sailed through the Alor Strait and anchored at **Rusa Island** on the 18 Feb.

From Alor, Drake continued westwards towards **Java**, following the S coast of the island "when in the morning [of 9 March] wee espied land, some part thereof very high... This Iland we found to be the Iland of Jaua...". This was probably Mt Slamet, some 26 miles inland. That night Drake anchored at **Cilacap** as this is one of the few safe havens on the ocean-lashed S coast. A boat was sent ashore the next morning where they had "...traffique with the people of the country...". At this stage in the voyage, Drake's mind was focussed on getting back to England. He needed to re-provision and careen his ship. By all accounts he found the people of the area very hospitable – so much so that his departure was delayed. As the record of the voyage puts it, they were "...louing, a very true and just dealing people". In late Mar, Drake set sail for England, leaving the islands of the Indonesian archipelago astern.

NB The above is condensed from the manuscript of Michael Turner of Somerset, England who is researching and writing a book recounting Drake's voyages, entitled *In Drake's wake*. We are grateful to him for allowing us to use his work.

Even after the European powers arrived in the archipelago, their influence was often superficial. They were concerned only with controlling the valuable spice trade, and were not inclined to feats of territorial expansion. To get around this lack of a common history, historians tend to talk instead in terms of common processes of change. The main ones affecting the archipelago were the 'Indianization' of the region from the 1st century AD and the introduction of Hinduism and Buddhism; the arrival of Islam in N Sumatra in the 13th century and then its spread E and S during the 15th century; and the contrast between inwardly-focused agricultural kingdoms and outwardly-orientated trading states.

COLONIAL HISTORY

During the course of the 15th century, the two great European maritime powers of the time, Spain and Portugal, were exploring sea routes to the E. Two forces were driving this search: the desire for profits, and the drive to evangelize. At the time, even the wealthy in Europe had to exist on pickled and salted fish and meat during the winter months (fodder crops for winter feed were not grown until the 18th century). Spices to flavour what would otherwise be a very monotonous diet were greatly sought after and commanded a high price. This was not just a passing European fad. An Indian Hindu wrote that: "When the palate revolts against the insipidness of rice boiled with no other ingredients, we dream of fat, salt and spices".

Of the spices, cloves and nutmeg originated from just one location, the Moluccas (Maluku) – the Spice Islands of eastern Indonesia. Perhaps because of their value, spices and their places of origin were accorded mythical status in Europe. The 14th century French friar Catalani Jordanus claimed for example that the clove flowers of Java produced an odour so strong it killed "every man who cometh among them, unless he shut his mouth and nostrils".

It was in order to break the monopoly on the spice trade held by Venetian and Muslim Arab traders that the Portuguese began to extend their possessions eastwards. This finally culminated in the capture of the port of Melaka by the Portuguese seafarer Alfonso de Albu-

Locals bringing nutmeg to sell to Dutch factors in Banda, the Moluccas, 1599.

querque in Jun 1511. The additional desire to spread the Word of God is clear in the speech that Albuquerque made before the battle with the Muslim sultan of Melaka, when he exorted his men, stressing:

"...the great service which we shall perform to our Lord in casting the Moors out of this country and of quenching the fire of the sect of Mohammet so that it may never burst out again hereafter".

From their base in Melaka, the Portuguese established trading relations with the Moluccas, and built a series of forts across the region: at Bantam (Banten), Flores, Ternate, Tidore, Timor and Ambon (Amboyna).

Many accounts of Indonesian history treat the arrival of the Portuguese Admiral Alfonso de Albuquerque off Malacca (Melaka) in 1511, and the dispatch of a small fleet to the Spice Islands, as a watershed in Indonesian history. As the historian MC Ricklefs argues, this view is untenable, writing that "...in the early years of the Europeans' presence, their influence was sharply limited in both area and depth".

The Portuguese only made a significant impact in the Spice Islands, leaving their mark in a number of Indonesian words of Portuguese origin – for example, *sabun* (soap), *meja* (table) and *Minggu* (Sun). They also introduced Christianity to E Indonesia and disrupted the islands' prime export – spices. But it was the Dutch, in the guise of the *Vereenigde Oost-Indische Compagnie* or VOC (the Dutch East India Company), who began the process of western intrusion. They established a toehold in Java – which the Portuguese had never done – a precursor to later territorial expansion. But this was a slow process and it was not until the early 20th century – barely a generation before the Japanese occupation – that the Dutch could legitimately claim they held administrative authority over the whole country.

The idea of Indonesia, 1900-1942

The beginning of the 20th century marks a turning point in Indonesian history. As Raden Kartini, a young educated Javanese woman, wrote in a letter dated 12 January 1900: "Oh, it is splendid just to live in this age; the transition of the old into the new!". It was in 1899 that the Dutch lawyer C Th van Deventer published a ground-breaking paper entitled *Een eereschuld* or 'A debt of honour'. This article argued that having exploited the East Indies for so long, and having extracted so much wealth from the colony, it was time for the Dutch government to restructure their policies and focus instead on improving conditions for Indonesians. In 1901, the Ethical Policy – as it became known – was officially embraced. Van Deventer was commissioned to propose ways to further such a policy and suggested a formulation of "education, irrigation and emigration". The Ethical Policy represented a remarkable change in perspective, but scholars point out that it was very much a creation of the European mind and made little sense in Indonesian terms.

The Indonesian economy was also changing in character. The diffusion of the cash economy through the islands and the growing importance of export crops like rubber and coffee, and minerals such as tin and oil, were transforming the country. Christianity, too, became a pow-

The expansion of Dutch influence and control	
	Date of Establishment of Control*
Maluku	1610
Java	1811
Kalimantan	1863
Lombok	1894
Sumatra	1903
Sulawesi	1905
Nusa Tenggara	1907
Bali	1908
Irian Jaya	1928

* Marking the date when effective Dutch control over the bulk of the area had been established.

erful force for change, particularly in the islands beyond Muslim Java. There was large-scale conversion in central and N Sulawesi, Flores, among the Batak of Sumatra, in Kalimantan, and Timor. In response to the inroads that Christianity was making in the Outer Islands, Islam in Java became more orthodox and reformist. The 'corrupt' *abangan* who adhered to what has become known as the 'Javanese religion' – a mixture of Muslim, Hindu, Buddhist and animist beliefs – were gradually displaced by the stricter *santris*.

At about the same time, there was an influx of *trekkers*, or Dutch expatriates, who came to the East Indies with their wives and Dutch cultural perspectives, with the intention of going 'home' after completing their contracts. They overwhelmed the older group of *blijvers* or 'stayers', and there emerged a more racist European culture, one that denigrated *Indische* culture and extolled the life-style of the Dutch. The Chinese community, like the Dutch, was also divided into two groups: the older immigrants or *peranakan* who had assimilated into Indies culture, and the more recent *totok* arrivals who zealously maintained their culture, clinging to their Chinese roots (see box, page 67).

So, the opening years of the 20th century presented a series of paradoxes. On the one hand, Dutch policy was more sensitive to the needs of the 'natives'; yet many Dutch were becoming less understanding of Indonesian culture and more bigoted. At the same time, while the Chinese and Dutch communities were drawing apart from the native Indonesians and into distinct communities based upon Chinese and European cultural norms; so the economy was becoming increasingly integrated and international. Perhaps inevitably, tensions arose and these began to mould the social and political landscape of confrontation between the colonialists and the natives.

A number of political parties and pressure groups emerged from this maelstrom of forces. In 1912, a Eurasian – one of those who found himself ostracized from European-colonial culture – EFE Douwes Dekker founded the Indies Party. This was a revolutionary grouping with the slogan 'the Indies for those who make their home there'. In the same year, a batik merchant from Surakarta established the Sarekat Islam or 'Islamic Union', which quickly became a mass organization under the leadership of the charismatic orator HOS Cokroaminoto. 7 years later it had over 2 million members. In 1914, a small group of *totok* Dutch immigrants founded the Indies Social-Democratic Association in Semarang. Finally, in 1920 the Perserikatan Komunis di India (PKI) or the Indies Communist Party was established.

In 1919, the Dutch colonial authorities decided to clamp down on all dissent. The flexibility that had characterized Dutch policy until then was abandoned in favour of an increasingly tough approach. But despite the rounding-up of large numbers of subversives, and the demise of the PKI and emasculation of the Sarekat Islam, it was at this time that the notion of 'Indonesia' first emerged. In Jul 1927, Sukarno founded the Partai Nasional Indonesia or PNI. In Oct 1928 a Congress of Indonesian Youth coined the phrase "one nation – Indonesia, one people – Indonesian, one language – Indonesian". At the same congress the Indonesian flag was designed and the Indonesian national anthem sung for the first time – *Indonesia Raya*. As John Smail writes in the book *In Search of Southeast Asia*:

"The idea of Indonesia spread so easily, once launched, that it seemed to later historians as if it had always existed, if not actually explicitly then inchoate in the hearts of the people. But it was, in fact, a new creation, the product of a great and difficult leap of the imagination. The idea of Indonesia required the denial of the political meaning of the societies into which the first Indonesians had been born".

In spite of Dutch attempts to stifle the nationalist spirit, it spread through Indonesian, and particularly Javanese, society. By 1942 when the Japanese occupied the country, the idea of Indonesia as an independent nation was firmly rooted.

The Japanese occupation, 1942-1945

Although the Japanese occupation lasted less than 4 years, it fundamentally altered the forces driving the country towards independence. Prior to 1942, the Dutch faced no real challenge to their authority; after 1945 it was only a question of time before independence. The stunning victory of the Japanese in the Dutch East Indies destroyed the image of colonial invincibility, undermined the prestige of the Dutch among many Indonesians, and – when the Dutch returned to power after 1945 – created an entirely new psychological relationship between rulers and ruled.

But the Japanese were not liberators. Their intention of creating a Greater East Asia Co-Prosperity Sphere did not include offering Indonesians independence. They wished to control Indonesia for their own interests. The Japanese did give a certain latitude to nationalist politicians in Java, but only as a means of mobilizing Indonesian support for their war effort. Sukarno and Muhammad Hatta were flown to Tokyo in Nov 1943 and decorated by Emperor Hirohito. For the Dutch and their allies, the war meant incarceration. There were 170,000 internees, including 60,000 women and children. About a quarter died in captivity.

One particularly sordid side of the occupation which has come to light in recent years is the role of 'comfort women'. This euphemism should be more accurately translated as 'sex slaves' – women who were forced to satisfy the needs of Japanese soldiers to aid the war effort. For years the Japanese government denied such comfort stations existed, but documents unearthed in Japan have indicated beyond doubt that they were very much part of the war infrastructure. Much of the attention has focused upon comfort women from Korea, China and the Philippines, but there were also stations in Indonesia. These women, so long cowed and humiliated into silence, are now talking about their experiences to force the Japanese government to accept responsibility. Dutch-Australian Jan Ruff is one of these brave women. A young girl living in Java before the war, she was interned in Camp Ambarawa with her mother and two sisters. In Feb 1944 she was taken, along with nine other girls, to a brothel in Semarang for the sexual pleasure of Japanese officers. In her testimony at a public meeting in Tokyo in Dec 1992 she recounted: "During that time [at the brothel] the Japanese had abused me and humiliated me. They had ruined my young life. They had stripped me of everything, my self-esteem, my dignity, my freedom, my possessions, my family." Belatedly, the Japanese government offered its "sincere apologies and remorse" in Aug 1993, 48 years afterwards. The fact that the apology came on the last day of the Liberal Democratic Party's government detracted from the honesty of the remarks. Many still feel that Japanese leaders find it difficult to be sincere about events almost half a century old.

As the Japanese military lost ground in the Pacific to the advancing Americans, so their rule over Indonesia became increasingly harsh. Peasants were forcibly recruited as 'economic soldiers' to help the war effort – about 75,000 died – and the Japanese were even firmer in their suppression of dissent than the Dutch had been before them. But as the military situation deteriorated, the Japanese gradually came to realize the necessity of allowing nationalist sentiments greater rein. On 7 September 1944, Prime Minister Koiso promised independence, and in Mar 1945 the creation of an Investigating Committee for Preparatory Work for Indonesian Independence was announced. Among its members were Sukarno, Hatta and Muhammad Yamin. On 1 June Sukarno mapped out his philosophy of Pancasila or Five Principles which were to become central tenets of independent Indonesia. On 15 Aug, after the second atomic bomb was dropped on Nagasaki, the Japanese unconditionally surrendered. Sukarno, Hatta, and the other independence leaders now had to act quickly before the Allies helped the Dutch re-establish control. On 17 August 1945 Sukarno read out the Declaration of Independence, Indonesia's red and white flag was raised and a small group of onlookers sang the national anthem, Indonesia Raya.

The revolutionary struggle, 1945-1950

In Sep 1945, the first units of the British Army landed at Jakarta to re-impose Dutch rule. They arrived to find an Indonesian administration already in operation. Confrontation was inevitable. Young Indonesians responded by joining the revolutionary struggle, which became known as the Pemuda Movement (*pemuda* means youth). This reached its height between 1945 and mid-1946, and brought together young men and women of all classes, binding them together in a com-mon cause. The older nationalists found themselves marginalized in this increasingly violent and fanatical response. Men like Sukarno and Hatta adopted a policy of *diplomasi* – negotiating with the Dutch. The supporters of the Pemuda Movement embraced *perjuangan* – the armed struggle. Not only the Dutch, were also minorities like the Chinese, Eurasians and Ambonese suffered from atrocities at the hands of the Pemuda supporters. The climax of the Pemuda Movement came in Nov 1945 with the battle for Surabaya (see page 280).

In 1947, the Dutch were militarily strong enough to regain control of Java, and E and S Sumatra. At the end of 1948, a second thrust of this 'Police Action', re-established control over much of the rest of the country. Ironically, these military successes played an important role in the final 'defeat' of the Dutch in Indonesia. They turned the United Nations against Holland, forcing the Dutch government to give way over negotiations. On 2 Nov the Hague Agreement was signed paving the way for full political independence of all former territories of the Dutch East Indies (with the exception of W Irian), on 27 December 1949.

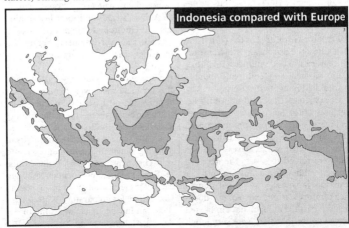

Indonesia compared with Europe

A stroll along Jalan history

✒ Many important figures in Indonesia's independence movement, as well as heroes from history, have lent their names to thoroughfares throughout the archipelago.

Abdul Muis – Sumatran independence writer.

Jend A Yani, *Brig Jend Sutoyo*, *Lets Jend Haryono*, *Panjaitan*, S Parman, and *Suprapto* – were the six generals (along with one captain) killed on 30 September 1965 in the attempted PKI coup (see page 50).

Cik di Tiro (1836-1891) – most famous of the *ulamas* or religious leaders who led the resistance against the Dutch in Aceh.

Cokroaminoto (1882-1934) – a leader of the Sareket Islam (Islamic Union), the first mass organization to be established in Indonesia in 1912. He was a forceful orator and highlighted numerous grievances against the Dutch.

Diponegoro, Prince (1785-1855) – led the Java War of 1825-1830 against the Dutch (see page 192), was captured in 1830 and then exiled to Manado and Ujung Pandang in Sulawesi where he died (page 617).

Gajah Mada – famous Prime Minister of the Majapahit Kingdom who served from 1331-1364 during the first 14 years of Hayam Wuruk's reign. Gajah Mada University in Yogya is one of the country's premier universities.

Haji Agus Salim – leader of the political Reform Islam movement, and right-hand man to Cokroaminoto.

Hang Tuah – naval hero who's exploits are immortalized and glorified in the *Sejarah Malayu* (Malay History), the literary masterpiece of the Malay world. Hang is an honorific equivalent to Sir.

Hasanuddin (r.1653-1669) – Sultan of Gowa in S Sulawesi who resisted the Dutch (see page 615).

Hayam Wuruk (r.1350-1389) – less well known as King Rajasanagara, he presided over Majapahit's golden age.

Imam Bonjol (1772-1864) – the most influential leader of the religious Padri movement in W Sumatra (see page 486). He was captured by the Dutch in 1837 and exiled to Priangan, then to Ambon and finally to Manado where he died in 1864 (page 674).

Jendral Sudirman (1915-1950) – Islamic teacher who became an officer in the Japanese volunteer army Peta (Pembela Tanah Air, Protectors of the Fatherland) and later a leading force in the revolution.

Kartini, Raden Ajeng (1879-1904) – the daughter of a noble bupati, educated at a European lower school in Jepara, Kartini is seen as an early Indonesian suffragette (see page 257). She tragically died in childbirth at the age of 25. Her moving letters have been published in Dutch (*Door duisternis tot licht* – 'Through darkness into light') and in English (*Letters of a Javanese princess*).

Majapahit – the Java-based empire (see page 84).

Pattimura (1783-1817) – a Christian Ambonese soldier who's proper name was Thomas Matulesia and who led a rebellion against the Dutch from Saparua, near Ambon in Maluku (see page 803).

Srivijaya – the Palembang-based empire (see page 426).

Teuku Umar – Acehnese leader who helped lead the *ulama* movement against the Dutch in the late 19th century (see page 444).

From independence to Guided Democracy to coup 1950-1965

In 1950, Indonesia was an economic shambles and in political chaos. Initially, there was an attempt to create a political system based on the western European model of parliamentary democracy. By 1952 the futility of expecting a relatively painless progression to this democratic ideal were becoming obvious, despite the holding of a parliamentary general election in 1955 with a voter turnout of over 90%. Conflicts between Communists, radical Muslims, traditional Muslims, regional groups and minorities led to a series of coups, rebel governments and violent confrontations. Indonesia was unravelling and in the middle of 1959, President Sukarno cancelled the provisional constitution and introduced his period of Guided Democracy.

This period of relative political stability rested on an alliance between the army, the Communist PKI, and Sukarno himself. It was characterized by extreme economic nationalism with assets controlled by Dutch, British and Indian companies and individuals being expropriated. The *Konfrontasi* with the Dutch over the 'recovery' of W Irian from 1960-1962, and with Malaysia over Borneo beginning in 1963 (see page 554), forced Sukarno to rely on Soviet arms shipments and Indonesia moved increasingly into the Soviet sphere of influence. Cracks between the odd alliance of PKI and the army widened and even Sukarno's popular support and force of character could not stop the dam from bursting. On 1 October 1965, six senior generals were assassinated by a group of middle-ranking officers, thus ending the period of Guided Democracy. MC Ricklefs writes:

"...on that night the balance of hostile forces which underlay guided democracy came to an end. Many observers have seen tragedy in the period, especially in the tragedy of Sukarno, the man who outlived his time and used his popular support to maintain a regime of extravagant corruption and hypocrisy."

The coup was defeated by the quick-thinking of General Suharto whose forces overcame those of the coup's leaders. However, it undermined both Sukarno and the PKI as both were linked with the plot – the former by allowing the PKI to gain such influence, and the latter by allegedly master-minding the coup. Most Indonesians, although not all western academics, see the coup as a Communist plot hatched by the PKI with the support of Mao Zedong and the People's Republic of China. It led to massacres on a huge scale as bands of youths set about exterminating those who were thought to be PKI supporters. This was supported, implicitly, by the army and there were news reports of 'streams choked with bodies'. The reaction was most extreme in Java and Bali, but there were murders across the archipelago. The number killed is not certain; estimates vary from 100,000 to one million and the true figure probably lies somewhere between the two (500,000 is widely quoted). The difficulty is that the body count kept by the military is widely regarded as a gross under-estimate. Oei Tjoe Tat, a cabinet minister under Sukarno, was sent on a fact-finding mission to discover the scale of the massacres. He calculated that by January 1966 half a million people had died. The military's figure at that time was 80,000. As it was an anti-Communist purge, and as China had been blamed for fermenting the coup, many of those killed were Chinese who were felt, by their mere ethnicity, to have leftist-inclinations and Communist sympathies. Few doubt that the majority were innocent traders and middlemen, whose economic success and ethnic origin made them scapegoats. While these uncontrolled massacres were occurring, power was transferred to General Suharto (although he was not elected president until 1968). This marked the shift from what has become known as the Old Order, to the New Order.

That the events of 1965 remain contentious is reflected in the government's attempts to re-write, and in places to erase, this small slice of history. In 1995, three decades after the events of 1965-1966, the authorities banned Oei Tjoe Tat's autobiography *Oei Tjoe Tat: assistant to President Sukarno*. It seems that the account of the anti-communist purge diverged too much from the official history. The fact that banned novelist and former political prisoner Pramoedya Ananta Toer had a hand in the book also can not have endeared it to the authorities. By the time it was banned, however, around 15,000 copies had already been sold. The government wants them all returned, although thoughts of stable doors and bolting horses come to mind. Documents relating to the 1965-1996 upheaval are restricted, and instead the government produces its own sanitised version of events. This has it that the Communists were behind the attempted coup, that President Sukarno was misguided in allowing the Communists to gain so much power, and that only the quick-thinking and courageous military, with Suharto at the fore, thwarted the attempt and saved Indonesia from turmoil.

Political and economic developments under the New Order, 1965-present

When Suharto took power in 1965 he had to deal with an economy in disarray. There was hyper-inflation, virtually no inward investment and declining productivity. To put the economy back on the rails he turned to a group of US-trained economists who have become known as the Berkeley Mafia. They recommended economic reform, the return of expropriated assets, and a more welcoming political and economic climate for foreign investment. In terms of international relations, Suharto abandoned the policy of support for China and the Soviet Union and moved towards the western fold. Diplomatic relations with China were severed (and only renewed in 1990), and the policy of confrontation against Malaysia brought to an end.

Pancasila: Sukarno's five principles

- Belief in the One Supreme God
- Just and Civilized Humanity
- Unity of Indonesia
- Democracy guided by the inner wisdom of unanimity
- Social Justice for all the people of Indonesia

Indonesia's national symbol is the mythical bird, the Garuda. On its chest is emblazened the pacasila while its claws clasp the legend *Bhinneka tungal ika* - 'unity in diversity'.

The period since 1965 has been one of political stability. Suharto has now been president for more than a quarter of a century, and he has presided over a political system which in a number of respects has more in common with the Dutch era than with that of former President Sukarno. Suharto has eschewed ideology as a motivating force, kept a tight control of administration and attempted to justify his leadership by offering his people economic well-being. He is known as the 'Father of Development'.

ART AND ARCHITECTURE

Indonesia has one of the richest artistic inheritances in the world, embracing the sublime Buddhist and Hindu monuments of Central Java, including Borobudur and Prambanan; the elegant vernacular architecture of the Toraja of Sulawesi and the Batak of Sumatra; the skilled woodcarvings of the Asmat of Irian Jaya; the ikat cloth of Sumba and batiks of Java; the soaring-roofed palaces of the Minangkabau in W Sumatra; and the mountainside *puras* (temples) of Bali.

The problem is that given this enormously diverse heritage, it is not possible to talk of 'Indonesian' art and architectural style. The country's material culture is a diffuse collection of different regional inspirations, that occasionally overlap with one another but which scarcely comprise a unified 'national' output. For this reason, the distinctive regional arts and architectures of Indonesia are discussed in the relevant regional introductions of this book.

CULTURE

RELIGION – ISLAM IN INDONESIA

Indonesia has the largest population of Muslims in the world – about 80% of the country's 180 million inhabitants call themselves Muslims. Despite pressure from Javanese Muslim leaders during the formative years of the independence movement, Sukarno resisted attempts to make the country an explicitly Islamic state. Indeed, a feature of both President Sukarno and President Suharto's rule has been their common dislike and fear of Islamic zealotry. When it has threatened stability, such movements have been vig-

The practice of Islam: living by the Prophet

Islam is an Arabic word meaning 'submission to God'. As Muslims often point out, it is not just a religion but a total way of life. The main Islamic scripture is the Koran or Quran, the name being taken from the Arabic *al-qur'an* or 'the recitation'. The Koran is divided into 114 *sura*, or 'units'. Most scholars are agreed that the Koran was partially written by the Prophet Mohammad. In addition to the Koran there are the hadiths, from the Arabic word *hadith* meaning 'story', which tell of the Prophet's life and works. These represent the second most important body of scriptures.

The practice of Islam is based upon five central tenets, known as the Pillars of Islam: Shahada (profession of faith), Salat (worship), Zakat (charity), *saum* (fasting) and Haj (pilgrimage). The mosque is the centre of religious activity. The two most important mosque officials are the *imam* – or leader – and the *khatib* or preacher – who delivers the Friday sermon.

The **Shahada** is the confession, and lies at the core of any Muslim's faith. It involves reciting, sincerely, two statements: 'There is no god, but God', and 'Mohammad is the Messenger [Prophet] of God'. A Muslim will do this at every **Salat**. This is the daily prayer ritual which is performed five times a day, at sunrise, midday, mid-afternoon, sunset and at night. There is also the important Friday noon worship. The Salat is performed by a Muslim bowing and then prostrating himself in the direction of Mecca (in Malaysian *kiblat*, in Arabic *qibla*). In hotel rooms throughout there is nearly always a little arrow, painted on the ceiling – or sometimes inside a wardrobe – indicating the direction of Mecca and labelled kiblat. The faithful are called to worship by a mosque official. Beforehand, a worshipper must wash to ensure ritual purity. The Friday midday service is performed in the mosque and

orously suppressed. Significantly, Pancasila stipulates a belief in One Supreme God – this god being seen to be the same whether Muslim, Christian, Hindu or Buddhist – and despite the difficulty of nominating a single supreme Buddhist or Hindu god.

Over the centuries, the people of Indonesia have been influenced by a succession of religions. Each has left its imprint on aspects of Indonesian culture. Buddhism and Hinduism were introduced from India in about the 5th century, and made an impact in Sumatra and Java where they fused to become a composite Hindu-Buddhist religion. The Islamization of the Indonesian archipelago began in Sumatra, filtering SE to the N coast of Java, and from there to the Javanese interior during the 15th century (see page 94 and also page 52 for a summary of the practice of Islam). Christianity meanwhile, did not begin to make significant inroads in eastern Indonesia until the 19th century.

Despite the overwhelming numerical dominance of Muslims today, many of them feel threatened by the advance of other religions, particularly Christianity. In 1933, 2.8% of the population was Christian; in 1971 this figure had risen to 7.4%; and by 1995 it was estimated to be 9% (comprising 6% Protestant and 3% Roman Catholic. Other religions are represented as follows: Hindu, 2%; Buddhist, 1%; other, 1%.) Meanwhile, some Muslims feel that their position is being eroded: over the period of the last generation, the proportion of the Indonesian population who are Muslim has fallen by over 6 percentage points – from 93% to 87%. The spread of Christianity, allied

---

includes a sermon given by the *khatib*.

A third essential element of Islam is **Zakat** – charity or alms-giving. A Muslim is supposed to give up his 'surplus' (according to the Koran); through time this took on the form of a tax levied according to the wealth of the family. In Malaysia there is no official Zakat as there is in Saudi Arabia, but good Muslims are expected to contribute a tithe to the Muslim community.

The fourth pillar of Islam is **saum** or fasting. The daytime month-long fast of Ramadan is a time of contemplation, worship and piety – the Islamic equivalent of lent. Muslims are expected to read one-thirtieth of the Koran each night. Muslims who are ill or on a journey have dispensation from fasting, but otherwise they are only permitted to eat during the night until "so much of the dawn appears that a white thread can be distinguished from a black one".

The **Haj** or Pilgrimmage to the holy city of Mecca in Saudi Arabia is required of all Muslims once in their lifetime if they can afford to make the journey and are physically able to. It is restricted to a certain time of the year, beginning on the 8th day of the Muslim month of Dhu-I-Hijja. Men who have been on the Haj are given the title *Haji*, and women *hajjah*.

The Koran also advises on a number of other practices and customs, in particular the prohibitions on usury, the eating of pork, the taking of alcohol, and gambling. In Indonesia, these are not strictly interpreted. Islamic banking laws have not been introduced, and drinking is fairly widespread – although not in all areas. There is quite a powerful Islamic revival in Malaysia and Brunei and some scholars and commentators identify the beginnings of a similar trend in Indonesia. But while the use of the veil is becoming *de rigeur* in Brunei and increasingly in Malaysia it is still only rarely encountered in Indonesia. The Koran says nothing about the need for women to veil, although it does stress the necessity of women dressing modestly.

with an Islamic revival has led to greater religious tensions in a country where they have been expressly played-down in an effort to promote unity.

Muslim-Christian tensions came to a head at the end of 1992 when there were a series of attacks on churches in Java. Abdurrahman Wahid, the moderate Muslim leader of the Nahdlatul Ulama (NU), an Islamic group with 35 million members (making it the world's largest Muslim organization), wrote a letter to Suharto warning the president that Indonesia risked a religious conflagration if he did not act to prevent "war-mongering against the Christians". Suharto pointedly ignored the missive while earlier supporting the establishment of the Organization of Indonesian Muslim Intellectuals (ICMI) in Dec 1990, headed by the president's great friend BJ Habibie. There are worries that ICMI will mobilize, or at least focus, discontent as Muslims try to regain – as they see it – the initiative. There is a feeling that Christians have economic and political power that far outweighs their number. Christian, in Muslim eyes, is often equated with rich. They also point out that both of Indonesia's leading newspapers, *Kompas* and *Suara Pembaruan* are controlled by Christians while, at least until the recent reshuffle, the cabinet also had a surfeit of Christians. While Muslims continue to count Christian and Muslim heads it is likely that the issue of religion will remain prominent. At the beginning of 1995 Abdurrahman Wahid, himself increasingly embattled as his moderate position was attacked, said "If there's only one or two *santri* [devout Muslim] generals, then what's the danger. But as soon as they are given domination in the context of Islamizing or promoting a new type of politics, for example promoting ICMI candidates at the expense of other factions in Golkar, then that would be dangerous."

LANGUAGE AND LITERATURE

The Indonesian language – Bahasa Indonesia

There are more than 500 languages and dialects spoken across the archipelago, but it was Malay that was embraced as the national language – the language of unity – at the All Indonesia Youth Congress in 1928. Republicans had recognized for some time the important role that a common language might play in binding together the different religions and ethnic groups that comprised the East Indies. Malay had long been the *lingua franca* of traders in the archipelago, and, importantly, it was not identified with any particular group. Most importantly of all though, it was not a Javanese language. This muted any criticism that Java was imposing its culture on the rest of the country. Before long, Malay was being referred to as *Bahasa Indonesia* – the Indonesian language.

As visitors to Indonesia will quickly notice, the written language uses the Roman script. Through history, three scripts have been used in the country: 'Indian', Arabic and Roman. Indian-derived scripts include Old Javanese or Kawi, and Balinese. Arabic was associated with the spread of Islam and has tended to be confined to religious works. It proved to be particularly unsuited to use with Javanese. At the beginning of the 20th century, the Dutch assigned Ch A van Ophuysen to devise a system for Romanizing the Malay language. The Roman script gained popularity during the 1920s when the Indonesian nationalist movement associated its use with political change and modernity. In 1947 a number of spelling reforms were introduced of which the most important was the change from using 'oe' to 'u', so that 'Soekarno' and 'Soeharto' became, respectively, 'Sukarno' and 'Suharto'. Another series of spelling changes were introduced in 1972 to bring Bahasa Indonesia in line with Bahasa Melayu (Bahasa Malay). Nonetheless, as Bahasa Indonesia gained acceptance as a 'national' language, so it

Much ado about *adat*

Commentators on things Indonesian probably use the Indonesian word *adat* more than almost any other. The word is taken from the arabic word *'ada*, meaning custom, and it refers to any locally accepted code of norms, behaviour, laws, customs or regulations. Often a society's *adat* is the totality of all these, and there is therefore not just one *adat*, but many *adats*, both within and between societies. It has enormous breadth of coverage including, for example, the accepted duties of husband and wife, customary practices in village wood lot use, the correct procedure in rituals, the accepted allocation of duties between different ranks, and rules on inheritance.

Adat is often viewed as the glue which helps Indonesian people to function and interact without conflict – or at least with a minimum of conflict. Any local leader was expected to be conversant with the accepted *adat*, and this was traditionally passed down the generations through verse, proverb, adage and aphorism. An intimate awareness of *adat* was akin to wisdom. The Dutch quickly grasped the importance of *adat*, and they codified it and used the resultant laws to help govern and administer at the local level.

Today, *adat* is in decline. Success and wisdom is less likely to be measured in terms of an intimate awareness of *adat* than in terms of academic achievement and economic power. Increasingly, the core of modern *adat* is the state 'ideology' of *pancasila* (see page 51), not the inherited layers of customary behaviour enshrined in the traditional meaning of the word, *adat*.

began to diverge from the Malay spoken in Malaysia. Today, although the two are mutually intelligible, there are noticeable differences between them in terms of both vocabulary and structure. The two countries' respective colonial legacy can be seen reflected in such loan words as *nomor*, from the Dutch for number in Indonesia, and *nombor* from the English in Malaysia.

The government has avidly promoted Bahasa Indonesia as the language of unity and it is now spoken in all but the most remote areas of the archipelago. Children are schooled in the national language, and television, radio and newspapers and magazines all help to propagate its use. But although most Indonesians are able to speak 'Bahasa', as it is known, they are likely to converse in their own language or dialect. Of the 500 other languages and dialects spoken in the country, the dominant ones are Sundanese, Javanese and Madurese (all three spoken on Java or Madura), Minang and Batak (on Sumatra), and Balinese.

Literature

Many of Indonesia's hundreds of languages have produced no written literature – although oral traditions do exist. However, the distinction between oral folk traditions and written literature is often blurred, as is the distinction between local traditions and imported literatures. For example, the series of popular stories which tell of the exploits of the *kancil* or mousedeer, who through guile and cleverness is able to overcome far stronger beasts, are Indian in influence, as are some of the Batak and Dayak tales.

But Indian influence is clearest in Old Javanese literature (900-1500 AD) when the Ramayana and Mahabharata were translated from Sanskrit (see box). However, this was not merely a case of absorbing outside influences wholesale. Most notably, *Kakawin* literature – though derived from an Indian genre – is clearly a Javanese art form. *Kakawin* poetry was commissioned by noblemen and performed at court. They were regarded not merely as stories, but as spiritual works of worship – almost as a form of written yoga. Perhaps the finest of the *kakawin* is the 14th century *Nagarakertagama*, discovered in 1894.

With the fall of the Hindu Majapahit Empire and the rise of Islam, so 'modern' Javanese literature evolved, from around the beginning of the 18th century. This combined Indian and Muslim traditions and produced such works as the *Babad Tanah Jawi*, a historical text, and the *Hikayat Aceh*, a record of Sultan Iskander Muda of Aceh's reign (1607-1636). The greatest source of dispute among scholars is how far such texts can be regarded as historically accurate – some scholars use them as a template to recreate Javanese life of the time, while others maintain that they are fundamentally inaccurate. Among religious texts of this period, the most highly regarded – for example the 3,000 page *Serat Centhini* – were produced at the court in Aceh, where they took on an almost mystical tone.

With the arrival of the Dutch and the gradual extension of their control over the archipelago, so a modern literature emerged. Many of the finest novelists of the early years of the 20th century were from Sumatra – and particularly from Minangkabau (W Sumatra) – men such as Adbul Muis, Marah Rusli (who wrote the highly regarded *Sitti Nurbaya*) and Nur St Iskander. The Japanese occupation of the country stifled publication, but following the 1945 revolution a group of idealists formed the *Angkatan 45* – the generation of 1945 – to support and develop Indonesian literature. Foremost among its members was Chairil Anwar. *Angkatan 45* became caught up in the political maelstrom of the 1960s, and following the attempted coup of 1965 many of its members were imprisoned. The years since have seen an emasculation of Indonesian literature, and the radicalism and invention of the 1950s and 1960s has still yet to be equalled.

DANCE, DRAMA AND MUSIC

Like Indonesian art and architecture, the dance, drama and music of the archipelago also spans a large number of regional styles and forms. Many of these are discussed in the relevant regional sections. Nonetheless, the influence of Javanese drama and music has spread beyond Java to the Outer Islands – in a process of artistic imperialism. In so doing these art forms have begun to take on a 'national' character, and have become repre-

---

The Ramayana and Mahabharata

Across much of Southeast Asia, the Indian epics of the Ramayana and Mahabharata have been translated and adapted for local consumption. The stories of the **Mahabharata** are the more popular. These centre on a long-standing feud between two family clans: the Pandawas and the Korawas. The feud culminates in an epic battle during which the five Pandawa brothers come face to face with their 100 first cousins from the Korawa clan. After 18 days of fighting, the Pandawas emerge victorious and the eldest brother becomes king. The plays usually focus on one or other of the five Pandawa brothers, each of whom is a hero.

The **Ramayana** was written by the poet Valmiki about 2,000 years ago. The 48,000 line story tells of the abduction of the beautiful Sita by the evil king, Ravana. Sita's husband Rama, King of Ayodhia, sets out on an odyssey to retrieve his wife from Ravana's clutches, finally succeeding with the help of Hanuman the monkey god and his army of monkeys. Today it is rare to see the Ramayana performed; the orchestra needs to be large (and is therefore expensive), and in the case of *wayang* (see page 96) few puppet masters have a sufficiently large collection of puppets to cover all the characters.

Art form	Centre of performance	Further information
Dance and drama		
Barong or kris	Bali	page 329
Kecak	Bali	page 329
Legong	Bali	page 332
Pencak silat	West Sumatra	page 483
Wayang kulit	Java	page 96
Wayang topeng	Java	page 97
Wayang wong	Java	page 100
Ramayana ballet	Java	page 100
Court dances	Java	page 100
Bambu gila	Maluku	page 807
Cakalele	Maluku	page 807
Music		
Angklung	Sundanese, Java	page 162
Gamelan	Java	page 101

sentative of the country as a whole. This applies, for example, to the gamelan orchestra and the wayang shadow puppet theatre.

Indonesian music available on CD and tape Most Indonesian towns have shops selling traditional Indonesian music – although the quality is often poor. Outside the country it is rather harder to obtain recordings. However, the US Library of Congress, as part of its Endangered Music Project, released *Music for the Gods* (Catalogue nos. RCD 10315 [CD] and RAC 10315 [cassette]) in 1994, a selection of 13 pieces from The Fahnestock South Sea Expedition to Indonesia in 1941. The pieces on this CD were recorded largely in Bali. The two Fahnestock brothers, Bruce and Sheridan, along with the latter's wife Margaret, sailed for Indonesia in the 137-ft schooner *Director II* with two state of the art Presto disc-cutters and 3 km of microphone cable so that they could record from shore to ship. After making recordings in Bali and the South Seas, the boat sank off Australia in 1941, but not before the precious discs had been taken back to New York. The Fahnestock's then proceeded to spy for President Roosevelt, noting the

sea defences of Java, all the while continuing to record performances in E Java and Madura, as well as Bali. Bruce was killed in New Guinea during the war, while Sheridan later became a publisher. The original recordings were donated to the Library of Congress in 1986 by Margaret Fahnestock.

In total the Smithsonian are planning 20 'volumes' of Indonesian music. Others currently available are:
- *Songs before dawn* (Smithsonian/Folkways SF40055)
- *Indonesian popular music* (Smithsonian/Folkways SF40056)
- *Music from the outskirts of Jakarta* (Smithsonian/Folkways SF40057)
- *Music of Nias and North Sumatra* (Smithsonian/Folkways SF40420)
- *Betawi and Sundanese music of the north coast of Java* (Smithsonian/Folkways SF40421)
- *Night music of West Sumatra* (Smithsonian/Folkways SF40422)
- *Music from the forests of Riau and Mentawai* (Smithsonian/Folkways)
- *Vocal and instrumental music from east and central Flores* (Smithsonian/Folkways)
- *Vocal music from central and west Flores* (Smithsonian/Folkways)

Further information from: Smithsonian/Folkways, Center for Folklife Programs and Cultural Studies, 955

L'Enfant Plaza, Suite 2600, Smithsonian Institution, Washington DC 20560, USA.

SPORT

Badminton

Only in one sport is Indonesia unrivalled: badminton. In 1994, the world grand prix rankings placed seven Indonesians in the top ten male badminton players, and three in the top ten women. In both the men (Ardy Wiranata) and women's (Susi Susanti) games, Indonesians were top of the rankings. Badminton made its debut as a full Olympic sport only at the 1992 games in Barcelona, and in Europe and North America there is still a tendency to look down on the sport as a child's game. Nothing could be further from the truth. The shuttlecock, made of white goose feathers, cork and goat leather, can be smashed at over 200 km/hr, while there is a subtlety of play, touch and finesse that is absent from most championship tennis matches. Like so many sports it was devised in England. It is said that the daughters of the Duke of Beaufort began playing 'battledore and shuttlecock' in Badminton House around 1860. Officers of the British Army then took the game to the East where, like cricket, it evidently appealed to the minds of the British Empire's Eastern subjects. The problem that badminton faces in trying to become a global sport is that it is not much played professionally in Europe and North America. As a result sponsorship, television coverage and advertising are all lacking.

MODERN INDONESIA

POLITICS

Since 1965, albeit with a few hiccups – most recently in July 1996 – Indonesia's political landscape has remained unchanged. President Suharto still holds power, and influence still lies with a loose grouping of businessmen, civilian politicians and the army. This military-bureaucratic élite has exercised popular power through Sekber Golkar, a political party based upon the armed forces or Abri.

Golkar is, in effect, the state's own party. All state employees are automatically members of Golkar, and during election campaigns the state controls the activities of other parties. The two opposition parties, for example, are not permitted to campaign in rural areas. Not surprisingly therefore, Golkar has been able consistently to win over 60% of the votes cast in parliamentary elections, and controls the Parliament (DPR) and the People's Consultative Assembly. The most recent elections were held in June 1992 and Golkar once again achieved a convincing majority, winning 68% of the vote.

That said, at each election, 'opposition' parties have claimed that they are well set to eat into the Golkar majority. The Indonesian Democratic Party (PDI) and the United Development Party (PPP) (which represents a coalition of Muslim groups), were hoping for more success in 1992. Both recorded modest increases in their share of the popular vote: the PDI from 11% to 15%, and the PPP from 16% to 17%. But Golkar had reason to be satisfied with the result, even though its share of the vote declined from 73% in the previous election to 68% in 1992. The main area of concern was the loss of support in Java, the country's heartland. As the people of Java are the most politically aware, this may give an indication of things to come.

In the Indonesian context, **'opposition'** is a relative term: there is really little to choose in matters of substance between the policies and perspectives of Golkar, and the PPP, although the PDI in recent months has been more overtly critical of the government in an attempt, apparently, to put clear blue water between it and Golkar in the run up to the next elections. This culminated in the demonstrations and riots of late July. Given the current electoral system, even should an opposition party win a majority, there is no chance that it might wield power. In the People's Consultative Assembly, only slightly over 400 out of 1,000 seats are up for election. Of the remaining 600, 500 are appointed directly by the President, and 100 are reserved for army members.

Notwithstanding the above, with economic growth so the demand for more political freedom does seem to be growing – although Asianists point out that assuming that a 'free' market economy necessarily means a free political 'economy' is naive. Towards the end of 1993 two university students were tried for "spreading of hatred", an odd colonial-era article in the criminal code which in this instance was a euphemism for political opposition. The two students from Java's Diponegoro University had led the Golput movement. Golput stands for *golongan putih*, or white group, and they were encouraging voters to cast blank ballots in protest at the lack of democracy in the country. The attorney-general's office put it another way when it stated that "We don't call this a Golput case. This is a general crime". Interestingly, the accused garnered considerable support in the media, which appeared to be able to report the case with relative freedom (but see below). Individuals siding with the defendents were also willing to speak out. Ariel Heryanto who teaches as the Satya Wacana Christian University was reported in the *Far Eastern Economic Review* as complaining: "This is a case of political terrorism. ... It [does not] teach people to obey the law, but to fear power."

Another development in opposition politics was the election of former president Sukarno's daughter, **Megawati Sukarnoputrii**, to the leadership of the PDI in 1994. The government tried – in a rather cack-handed way – to have her nomination quashed and pro-government nominees placed on the 29-person executive board. They forced many of the 1,500 PDI delegates to sign pledges that they would not vote for her at the convention held in the East Java city of Surabaya

at the beginning of 1994. In this they failed, although at the beginning of 1995 accusations of Communist sympathies – the Great Evil that is invoked whenever anyone or any organization needs to be cut down to size – were also levelled at the party and its key members. A few months later, in mid-1996, the military and government again appeared to try and orchestrate the marginalisation of Megawati within her party by trying to arrange an 'alternative' congress in Medan. This time they were successful and Suryadi, a former Golkar member, was 'elected' the new leader of the PDI. It was his election, and the fury of Megawati stalwarts, which directly led to the riots of July (see below).

The **PDI**, though a small party, is important because it is the only party which comes anywhere close to representing an 'opposition'. It has also consistently increased its vote over the last two elections – to 56 seats in parliament, as compared with Golkar's 282 and the PPP's 62. When in Feb 1995 it appeared that Abdurrahman Wahid, leader of the mass Muslim organization Nahdlatul Ulama (see page 52, lent his support to Megawati, Golkar appeared distinctly uneasy about a possible alliance of the country's largest Muslim organization and the charismatic Megawati, flying the Sukarno name. Megawati appears to dislike what she regards as an increasing Islamicization of Indonesian politics, and would wish to put the business of government firmly back on the secular road – one that her father avowedly set out to promote. She has also become more outspoken about the role of the military in Indonesian politics – a dangerous course for her to take given the power and influence of the army. Those who like to examine the tea leaves of Indonesian politics saw a powerful axis developing between Megawati and Mr. Wahid, and Megawati possibly standing for the presidency in 2003 – perhaps even in 1998. Megawati's political future, though, has been even

Rising hopes

In 1991, the Central Bureau of Statistics asked a sample of Indonesian families what they thought about the change in the welfare of themselves and their neighbours by comparing conditions at the time of the survey with those 3 years earlier. Although most respondents thought that their situation had improved, there were some areas where a significant proportion – between a fifth and a half – felt that their welfare had deteriorated (see table).

The negative responses are just as likely to reflect a rising level of expectation, than a decline in provision or access. Nonetheless, the areas of concern are enlightening. There is a clear disatisfaction with the level of access to secondary schooling. This highlights parents' concern not so much for their own well-being and prospects, but for their children's. Primary level education may now be virtually universal in Indonesia, but this has created a heightened demand and expectation for secondary level schooling. There also seems to be a significant demand for better housing and utilities and – surprisingly perhaps – for access to reading material. This latter point hints at a difficult and nebulous area – that of political freedoms. The Indonesian government now accepts, in broad terms, that economic development also creates demands for greater press freedom and freedom of expression. But most striking is the dissatisfaction among two-thirds of those surveyed with the level of access to formal jobs. This shows that despite rapid economic growth, security of employment in formal sector jobs was perceived to be a major shortcoming.

further muddied by the events of July 1996.

The crass ejection of Megawati from the leadership of the PDI by government stooges transformed Sukarno's daughter from a rather lack-lustre opposition politician into – in some people's eyes – Indonesia's very own Aung San Suu Kyi. In manipulating the PDI's electoral process the government made a gross miscalculation: it turned up the heat on a simmering pressure cooker of discontent, poverty, and repressed democratic forces. Megawati loyalists barricaded themselves inside the PDI's headquarters in Jakarta, preventing the new leader of the party, Suryadi, from entering the building. The stand-off continued for over a month. PDI supporters demonstrated their dislike of Suharto and Golkar ever more openly until the government, it seems, decided that enough was enough. Waiting until visiting foreign ministers attending the Asean Regional Forum in Jakarta had quit town, the army ordered riot police backed by army units to storm

the PDI HQ and remove the malcontents. What might have been seen in the briefing room as a surgical military operation turned into the worse **street fighting** Jakarta has seen for over a decade. Banks, government offices and cars were set alight, shops were looted, streets were cut off, and government forces were stoned and petrol bombed. After a weekend of skirmishes, 3 people were dead, 100 injured and over 250 arrested. The government had regained control of the situation by the beginning of the week but commentators were asking themselves why Suharto was willing to pay such a high price for so minor a political prize. As one person with links to the army complained, "They [the army] think the old man has lost his touch. The government is using an atomic bomb to kill a fly."

The most important question beyond the demonstrations themselves is what implications they hold for Indonesia's political and economic future. Is Indonesia going the way of South Korea, the

	Great improvement			Much worse			% in response cat's
	1	**2**	**3**	**4**	**5**	**6**	**4-6**
Household income	0.7	31.9	53.5	10.4	3.4	0.1	*13.9*
Food expenditure	0.3	22.3	66.7	9.5	1.2	0.0	*10.7*
Housing quality	0.7	22.4	61.1	14.5	1.3	0.0	*15.8*
Utilities	0.5	21.6	58.6	18.1	1.1	0.1	*19.3*
Clothing	0.5	27.4	64.1	7.4	0.7	0.0	*8.1*
Health	0.8	29.0	64.3	3.8	2.1	0.1	*6.0*
Health services	1.4	38.1	52.8	6.8	0.8	0.2	*7.8*
Family planning service	2.1	42.6	50.9	3.6	0.6	0.2	*4.4*
Access to drugs	1.4	33.6	51.4	12.0	1.1	0.4	*13.5*
Access to primary school	2.8	36.9	57.8	1.8	0.6	0.1	*2.5*
Access to junior high school	1.4	25.5	59.5	11.2	2.0	0.4	*13.6*
Access to senior high school	1.5	22.9	51.2	18.9	4.6	0.9	*24.4*
Access to transport	5.1	49.6	32.4	11.2	1.2	0.5	*12.9*
Religious services	3.0	39.3	57.0	0.6	0.1	0.0	*0.7*
Religious holidays	1.8	29.1	66.4	2.2	0.6	0.0	*2.8*
Security from crime	2.1	30.9	57.0	7.7	2.1	0.2	*10.0*
Access to radio	2.5	35.3	52.6	8.3	1.0	0.3	*9.6*
Access to television	2.9	38.7	41.0	14.8	1.7	0.8	*17.3*
Access to reading material	1.4	21.2	44.0	29.4	3.0	1.1	*33.5*
Formal jobs	0.1	4.4	26.6	46.7	18.4	3.7	*68.8*
Sports	0.5	15.8	63.2	18.2	1.9	0.4	*20.5*

Philippines or Thailand where autocratic governments were removed by popular uprisings? Or will it more closely mirror the experiences of China and Myanmar (Burma) where popular uprisings were brutally put down? Neither scenario is particularly convincing. The army in Indonesia seems to be firmly behind the government and is not likely to switch sides – as it did in the Philippines. In addition, support for confrontational and violent opposition politics seems to be very limited – particularly when it becomes a front for looting and thuggery which appeared to be sporadically the case in the capital. Economically, the effect of the violence was to cause the stock-market to slide and the rupiah to weaken. No doubt, had the demonstrations escalated – or should they re-occur – then foreign investors will shy away from the country with grievous medium-term economic consequences. How Suharto handles the situation over the next few months will be critical in determining Indonesia's longer term future. The initial response was to blame events on a left wing political party, the Democratic People's Party or PRD. The government alluded to the PRD's 'communist' leanings hoping, as usual, to scare the public into associating it with the bloody events of the mid-1960s. Only the government, though, appeared convinced by this attempt to drum up the ghosts of the past. Activists were arrested across the capital and also in Surabaya, Solo and Yogyakarta in an apparent attempt to strangle the nascent democracy movement at birth. Megawati first action was to challenge the government in the courts – in an effort to convince ordinary Indonesians that she would play the game by the book. Few people believed, as this book went to press, that the demonstrations would have changed Indonesia's political landscape to any significant extent.

The next **parliamentary elections** are due in May 1997. Although few doubt that Golkar will win a substantial majority, there are those within the government who are worried that Golkar's dominance will be further eroded – and that their share of the vote might dip below that symbolic two-thirds figure. The fact that Indonesia's population is a very 'young' one means that something like 20 million people will be voting for the first time in 1997 (amounting to around a fifth of the electorate) and it is clear that it is among the youth that dissatisfaction with Golkar is greatest. As in the case of the opposition PDI (see above), the response by the government has been to conjure up bogeymen and warn of the dangers of *organisasi tanpa bentuk* or 'formless organizations'. This is code for those with Communist sympathies. Most local commentators, however, find little evidence that these 'OTBs' – as they are popularly known – amount to a significant threat. Nonetheless, there can be no doubt that Communism remains a source of concern. In 1995 an issue of the London weekly magazine *The Economist* was banned because there was a hammer and sickle on the cover, while in the city of Solo (Surakarta) the ever-watchful police seized 100 pairs of children's jeans that flaunted the Communist symbol on their labels. The key question is whether these warnings will cut much ice with an electorate that, increasingly, was born after 1965 and sees little evidence of Communism, let alone a threat from a political ideology which much of the world views as virtually moribund.

Perhaps the most vexed question of all, though, is that of **President Suharto's succession**. Understandably, this arouses considerable consternation. President Suharto has brought great stability to Indonesia, but he has now been in power for almost 3 decades since he was inaugurated as President in 1967, and in Jun 1996 turned 75. Only such paragons of democracy as General Ne Win of Myanmar (Burma) have held power for so long. In Mar 1993 Suharto began his sixth consecutive 5-year term as president. Despite this remarkable political longevity – or perhaps because of it – there is the looming issue of who will replace him at the head of a potentially fractious and divided nation. Mrs Suharto slyly commented before her husband's 71st birthday on 8 June 1992 that "a coconut has more juice the older it gets", but even President Suharto is not thought to have found the elixir of everlasting youth. In July 1996 the President flew to Germany for medical 'tests'. Presidential aides tried to convince reporters that these were routine, but the fact that he cancelled a scheduled meeting with the Prime Minister of Malaysia led most to question this version of events. The stock market and rupiah fell in sympathy.

In Mar 1993 some indication of a **possible successor** was provided by the election of Try Sutrisno, the retired armed forces commander, to the post of vice-president. Significantly, Sutrisno was the army's choice, and after their nomination Suharto had little choice but to follow Golkar's lead. There lingers the impression that the army is manoeuvring skilfully to be in a strong position to influence events when Suharto is expected to retire in 1998. It seems that Suharto's favourite candidate – although this is only conjecture – is Science and Technology Minister BJ Habibie. However Habibie is dis-

In the nick of time

👣 Money can buy you most things, but people tend to assume that being in prison means being in prison. The case of Eddy Tansil, a wealthy businessman jailed in 1994 for 20 years for defrauding Bapindo, a state bank, of US$448mn (see page 74), shows even this does not always hold true in Indonesia. His prison cell was more like a hotel suite. He had a television, video and fan, and allegedly even a mobile phone and pager. There were rumours that he was permitted to visit his office regularly, and, incredibly, to play golf. So when, in May 1996 the media got wind that Eddy had 'escaped', thoughts of him tunneling out with nothing more than a toothpick seemed unlikely. It seems that it took the prison authorities 2 days to report his disappearance – they had apparently been hoping that it was just a rather extended session on the 19th hole.

trusted by influential army leaders, who see him using his leadership of the Association of Muslim Intellectuals (ICMI) for political purposes (see below). The army is steadfastly against any political grouping with a religious or ethnic *raison d'être*. Another wild card in the pack is Sukarno's eldest daughter Megawati, leader of the Indonesian Democratic Party (see above) while a new entrant in the game has been the President's son-in-law Prabowo Subianto who masterminded the release of the hostages held by Irianian rebels in early 1996. Megawati has alienated many of the élite by her association with the demonstrations and riots of July 1996, while General Prabowo's rapid rise is said to be resented by key members of the military. The next presidential election in due in 1998. The conduct of that election is likely to be very interesting, and although Suharto looks almost certain to win – if he stands – his succession is still not clearly mapped out.

That even the most powerful of men and women are mortal was brought home with the death of Siti Hartinah, better known as **Ibu Tien – Suharto's wife** and right-hand woman – on April 28th 1996. Married during the independence struggle and descended from nobility, Suharto, himself of lowlier stock, was widely felt to have made a good match. Ibu Tien became the president's most trusted advisor, and although it does not seem that she became closely involved in government affairs, she did lie at the heart of the Suharto family and as such was a stabilizing influence. In particular she may have brought a moderating influence on the actions of her children. Her body was flown from Jakarta on an airforce plane to Surakarta (Solo), where the family mausoleum is located. Suharto, flanked by his children and close relatives and friends, looked drained. How the death of his cherished wife will influence his decisions – such as whether to stand for another term as president – was not yet clear as this book went to press.

Although Suharto's 30 years in power has brought unparalleled political stability to Indonesia, there is increasing criticism of his family's economic power. Nepotism may be a way of life in Southeast Asia, but there are limits to what is deemed acceptable. **Suharto's six children** (three sons and three daughters) have built up considerable business empires on the basis of their family connections. The two biggest non-Chinese conglomerates – Bimantara and Humpuss – are both run by sons of the president, Bambang Trihatmodjo and Hutomo 'Tommy' Mandala Putra. They have managed to do this by drawing on their ties with the President to secure lucrative contracts and licences – even enjoying preferential rates of interest on loans from the central Bank of Indonesia.

'Tommy' is the youngest and the most flamboyant of the children and he has been closely involved in two of the country's most contentious economic stitch-ups: the creation of a clove monopoly (see page 256, and the recent deal on the production of an Indonesian 'national' car. Tommy has always had a penchant for cars – especially fast ones. He was a key player in the purchase by an Indonesian company of the luxury Italian sports car maker Lamborghini from Chrysler. He has built a Formula 1 racing track in Java and heads the country's motor-racing association. In 1996 his Humpuss group announced a US$1 billion joint venture with the South Korean car manufacturer Kia Motors to manufacture the 'Timor' (an oddly insensitive choice of name), a re-badged Kia sedan, in Indonesia. The deal awards Kia-Timor Motors 'pioneer status', effectively giving it a 30% to 50% cost advantage over rival car makers in the country, and Humpuss an inside track into dominating the country's car market. Analysts were said to be 'astonished' by the scale and audacity of the coup and Sir Leon Brittan, the European Commission's Vice President, suggested during a visit to Indonesia that the national car might contravene the World Trade Organization's rules. Even more put out, by all accounts, were the Japanese car firms who for so long have been assembling vehicles in Indonesia. It seems almost certain, if the project gets off the ground, that their market share will evaporate in a puff of gasolene, and some analysts wondered whether the Japanese might challenge the decision under the WTO's articles. Ironically, it was President Suharto who pushed for free trade at the Asia-Pacific Economic Cooperation meeting that he hosted at Bogor towards the end of 1994. Since the initial announcement it has transpired that for the first year at least, Timors will not even be made in Indonesia, but by a small army of transplanted Indonesian workers in Korea. (As the *Far Eastern Economic Review* put it in an editorial, "Thus we have the absurdity of an Indonesian national

car which has to be manufactured in South Korea.") Only in March 1997 – if all goes well – will the proposed assembly line outside Surabaya begin producing cars in Indonesia – and even they will have a local content of only 20%, rising to 40% by the end of the third year, and 60% by the end of the century. Suharto's middle son Bambang is said to have been seething with frustration at the announcement too. His company Bimantara which already produces cars with another Korean firm, Hyundai, was far better placed than his brother's – at least they had an assembly line producing vehicles and a 100,000 car-a-year factory on the drawing board.

One Asian ambassador in Jakarta was quoted in the *Far Eastern Economic Review* in Apr 1992 as saying: "The central question is whether the avarice of the children will ultimately undermine 25 years of pretty good leadership". An *Economist* survey of the country in 1993 reflected similar sentiments, when – likening him to former Javanese kings – it described Suharto as having: "A paternal style, a professed lack of interest in power, a circle of deferential courtiers and the ability to dispense seemingly unlimited patronage ...". Despite the obvious sensitivity of the subject, opposition leaders and academics are becoming less reticent in voicing their thoughts, believing that the system of nepotism could begin to undermine the country's economic progress.

A key institution in any transfer of power to a more representative system of government is the **army**. The army lies at the very centre of political life and is the only group in the country (beyond Suharto and Golkar) with the necessary cohesion and unity of purpose to influence political events at a broad level. This wider role is enshrined in the constitutional principle of *dwifungsi*, or dual function, which gives the army the right to engage in politics and administration as well as defend the nation from external aggressors and internal insurrection.

Around two-thirds of army personnel, according to political scientist Harold Crouch, are assigned to territorial rather than combat duties. As such they are engaged in such things as "overseeing the activities of political parties and non-governmental organizations, intervening in land disputes, [and] dealing with striking workers or demonstrating students...". While the emerging urban middle classes may wish to see the further development of civil society and a diminished role for the military in these areas that would seem to lie outside the bounds of national security, in the countryside the army is seen as a stabilizing force and the guarantor of ethnic and religious peace. The army, rather like the military in Thailand, regards itself as the protector of the nation, and more particularly the protector of ordinary Indonesians against potentially venal civilian politicians and their business associates. The key role that the military played in Indonesia's independence movement – after the civilian revolutionary government had capitulated to the returning Dutch after the end of World War II – gives it further credibility to speak not just for itself, but also for the country as a whole.

There can be no doubt that the major stumbling block to Indonesia's full acceptance into the fold of international nations is **East Timor**. The most recent sequence of public relations disasters began when the army killed at least 50 **East Timorese** in Nov 1991 (see page 783) – and it has continued ever since. The government's sensitivity over the issue was demonstrated at the end of May 1994 when President Ramos of the Philippines was rather crudely pressurized by the Indonesians to cancel a conference being held on East Timor in Manila. When Ramos pointed out that the Philippines was a democracy and he had little control over such events, the Indonesians called-off bilateral talks and arrested Philippine fishermen operating in Indonesian waters. In the end, the fracas only raised the profile of the rather obscure conference and reflected badly on the Indonesian government. As one of the conference organizers explained: "without the Indonesians' help, this conference would not have been such a huge success."

The legacy of East Timor was in evidence still more recently at the **Asia-Pacific Economic Cooperation** (APEC) summit held in the W Java hill town of Bogor in Nov 1994. The least of the organizers' worries were the logistics of looking after 15 presidents or prime ministers, a sultan, and an economic minister. Some 9,000 soldiers, a mini-hospital, and a fleet of Mercedes S600s (and Bill Clinton's armoured Cadillac) were on call to deal with that. What the Indonesian government could not control was embarrassing and unscripted questions from nosey foreign journalists and the possibility of some sort of demonstration. A week before the summit, 29 East Timorese climbed into the grounds of the US Embassy, while during the meeting there were demonstrations in East Timor itself. With Jakarta and Bogor, even East Timor, seething with international journalists and film crews, the military could do little to curb the protests and audiences abroad were treated to images of the summit set against those from the US Embassy compound. Since then, activists have managed to keep East Timor in the news. During 1995 and into 1996 demonstrators occupied, at various times, the Dutch, Japanese, Swedish, French and Russian diplomatic missions in Jakarta.

Despite some evidence of a loosening of political control, the government treats all pressure groups – whether radical Muslim or secular human rights-orientated – with suspicion. Continuing difficulties in Aceh (see page 444) and Irian Jaya (see page 839) as well as in East Timor, ensures that the government will keep a tight rein on what it perceives to be critical areas of dissent. Nonetheless, as living standards grow and the economy is reformed, it is difficult not to see how pressure for greater political reform and openness will also continue to grow. Perhaps this is already occurring: at the end of 1992, the number of people on the government's immigration blacklist was reduced from 17,000 to 9,000.

The process of political change in Indonesia today is highly confused and confusing. In some fora and on some occasions, the leadership appears to be willing to allow 'democratic' principles to run their course (for example in the recent rash of labour disputes – see below); in other instances, it has cracked down with surprising vigour (for example in the trial of the students noted above and the 4-year jail sentence handed out to Nuku Sulaiman for distributing stickers allegedly insulting the President). In the same vein, while some developments seem to indicate that Suharto has a firm grip on power, other events – such as the election of former President Sukarno's daughter to the leadership of the opposition PDI (see above) – indicate the opposite.

This confusion of signals over Indonesia's political 'progress' is exemplified in the recent treatment of **the press** by the authorities. As recently as 1994, informed commentators were noting the increased freedom of the press to print stories mildly critical of government leaders. At the time, it appeared that Suharto and his advisors accepted that Indonesia's rapidly expanding middle classes were becoming more informed, more critical, and therefore less willing to be fobbed off with state propaganda. This freeing-up of the press became known as *keperbukaan*, or openness, and was widely welcomed by Java's élite. The question, as John McBeth wrote in the middle of 1994, was whether that "now the genie [of press freedom] is half out of the bottle ... [it will be possible] to force it back in again if things don't go quite the way [Suharto] wants them to".

Just a few months later, at the end of Jun 1994, and against the tide of events, the government closed three weekly publications – the respected news magazine *Tempo* with a circulation of 200,000, and *DeTik* and *Editor* – apparently over articles which were too critical of certain government ministers. The closures came as a great shock, and were widely viewed as a gross over-reaction to articles (especially in *Tempo*) that were only slightly daring. After the closure of the magazines, the Information Department called in the editors of the *Jakarta Post*, *Sinar Pagi*, *Media Indonesia* and *Forum Keadilan* for a spot of finger wagging. Journalists and human rights activists demonstrated outside the Department's offices, only to have the military break up the protests. There was widespread disapproval of the closures, and even members of the military were heard to murmur discrete criticism. Information Minister Harmoko – widely disliked – found himself booed in July at a Parliamentary meeting when he disingenuously explained that he had not banned the publications (which would have contravened the amended 1982 Press Act) but merely revoked their licences. As in Malaysia and Singapore, there is a line – perhaps none too clear – between acceptable and unacceptable criticism. Harmoko asked that Indonesians not lower themselves to "deceitful acts incompatible with the moral values of the nation". As the *Far Eastern Economic Review* put it, that is just the problem, for it brands anyone "Expressing divergent views on such popular issues of the day as press freedom, land distribution, labour unions and the nation's credit structure ... as enemies of the state."

Ordinarily, this sequence of events would simply have come stuttering to an end, and the dissatisfied, digruntled and disenchanted would have have faded from view. But in this case the story, as they say, ran and ran. In Aug 1994 the Alliance of Independent Journalists (AIJ) was formed to fight against "all kinds of interference, intimidation, censorship and media bans". In Sep, the founder of *Tempo*, Goenawan Mohamad brought a suit against the closure order. The closure

The politics of envy: the Chinese in Indonesia

The Chinese make up about 5% of Indonesia's population and are still treated with suspicion. There are still 300,000 Chinese living in Indonesia who have yet to choose whether they are Indonesians by nationality, or Chinese. The community adopts a low profile – in Glodok (Jakarta's Chinatown), for example, there are few Chinese signs on the shopfronts. Indeed, until recently there was a ban on displaying Chinese characters. The so-called *masalah Cina* – or 'Chinese problem' – continues to be hotly discussed, much of the debate centering on whether the Chinese should be assimilated or integrated into Indonesian culture.

The animosity between the 'Indonesian' and Chinese communities is based upon the latter's economic success, and their role as middlemen, shopkeepers and moneylenders. Most of the country's largest firms are Chinese-owned – known as *cukong* – and the richest families are also Chinese. Such evident success has given rise to envy. Even President Suharto has publicly stated that the Chinese should be prepared to redistribute their wealth to prevent a 'social disturbance'. Some indigenous businessmen, known as *pribumi*, have called for the implementation of an explicit economic policy of positive discrimination in favour of native Indonesians modelled on the New Economic Policy in Malaysia.

So far at least, President Suharto has scorned such an idea. Perhaps part of the reason is because influential indigenous politicians make considerable fortunes through their links with the *cukongs*. The politicians provide political protection, and they in turn are rewarded financially by the *cukong*. The Chinese still have codes on their ID cards which identify them as Chinese – although this may soon change – and there are numerous other ways in which they face discrimination. In 1990, President Suharto invited 30 of the country's top Chinese businessmen to his palace and was seen, on television, explaining to them that if inequalities were not reduced – implying the gap between the Chinese rich and the Indonesian poor – "social gap, social envy and even social disturbance will happen". This barely concealed warning of a possible repeat of the events of 1965 was not lost on the Chinese community. The volatility of the *masalah Cina* was demonstrated in Mar 1994 when labour unrest in the Sumatran city of Medan became an anti-Chinese riot. Chinese-owned shops were burned down and one Chinese factory owner killed in the violence.

of the magazines also brought a number of illegal political newsletters onto the streets – publications like the satirical *Independen* with far more barbed and personal comment that licensed publications like *Tempo*. At the beginning of 1995 the state-recognized Association of Indonesian Journalists expelled 13 of its members for suggesting that it was not the sole representative of Indonesian journalists. Then, in May 1995, Goenawan Mohamad's case against the closure of *Tempo* was heard by a court in Jakarta. To great surprise, the three judges found that In-

formation Minister Harmoko had acted unlawfully and in an 'authoritarian' manner. The judges ordered that Harmoko reissue the licence and pay costs. The judgement was something of a milestone as it went against the wishes of the establishment. The Minister's appeal was heard by the State Apellate Court at the end of 1995 and to yet greater surprise the court upheld the verdict of the lower court. Fukri Jufri one of *Tempo's* founders said that he "couldn't believe [the verdict]...All I could say was 'Praise God'". Following the State Apellate court's decision, Harmoko appealed to the Supreme Court which, as many observers predicted, overturned the two lower courts' decisions and rule in favour of Harmoko in a judgement in June 1996. But although the verdict – ultimately – went against Gunawan, the whole affair seemed to show that the heavy hand of the government is not quite as heavy as it once was. Harmoko himself has been in hot water recently when it was alleged that he had intentionally manipulated the words of the Koran's most holy prayer, the *Al-Fatihah*, to make a political point at a wayang kulit performance. Islamic scholars felt this was insulting to Islam and although Harmoko subsequently issued an apology and claimed it was simple human error the whole rumpus has further tarnished his already muddied reputations

All in all, it would be a brave person who would predict the path of change over the next 5 years. The Western obsession with the superiority and 'natural' evolution towards greater political pluralism and a market economy makes it hard to imagine that things might go 'backwards'; the experience of China following the Tiananmen Square massacre illustrates the dangers of such blithe assumptions. Nor does the pressure from the West for progress on human rights take into account Indonesia's unique set of conditions. The country's middle classes were estimated in 1995 to number just 14 million people – about 7% of the total population – and the evolution of civil society is still in its infancy. (By comparison, there are around 1.3 million people who have 'ET', standing for *Eks-Tahanan-politik* or former political prisoner, stamped on their ID cards. It labels and stigmatises them and the effect is to confine most to the margins of society. Indonesia's National Commission on Human Rights lobbied to have the system scrapped and in August 1995, in the lead-up to the 50th anniversary celebrations of Indonesia's proclamation of inde-

pendence, the government promised to do so.) It is highly unlikely that the army will give up its influence and the sheer geographical, social and cultural complexity would make the country extremely hard to hold together in the event of free-for-all democracy. With Suharto coming to the end of his term, there are many who accept that the tensions of transition will stretch Indonesia's unitary status to the limit, with or without the helping hand of democracy. Foreign Minister Ali Alatas, interviewed for London's *Financial Times* in 1995, summed up the difficulties of predicting the future when he said:

"We are far from our democratic ideals. That I admit readily. We must more and more democratise. But after 10 years, after 30 years, I guarantee you we will still not be the US or Australia... In 10 years' time, I am sure we will be more democratised. But we will still be different. That's the problem."

ECONOMY

Since 1965, the Indonesian economy has gradually recovered from the extreme mismanagement that characterized the period from independence in 1950. With the advice of the so-called Berkeley Mafia – a group of reform-minded, US-trained economists – there has been an attempt to increase efficiency, reduce corruption and entice foreign investment. Like the other countries of the region, export-orientated development has become the name of the game. President Suharto is known as the 'Father of Development' – and sometimes as the '5% President' (because his legitimacy is based on maintaining at least a 5% economic growth rate). So far things have gone well on the economic front at least. Annual per capita economic growth averaged 4.2% between 1980 and 1993, and in 1994 and 1995 the economy grew by 7.5% and 8.1% respectively. The forecast for 1996 and 1997 is for growth to continue at between 7% and 8%. In 1996 Dennis de Tray, the World Bank's country managed heaped praise on Indonesia's economic performance. "We give Indonesians a very good report card", he said, adding that in 1995 "few countries [in the world] have had better economic performance".

On 17th August 1995, at the celebrations marking the 50th anniversary of Indonesia's proclamation of Independence, President Suharto squinted into the skies as the N-250, a home-built and home-designed 70-seat commuter aircraft, made its maiden flight. The plane, named *Gatot Kaca* after one of the characters in a Hindu epic, is the brainchild of Minister for Research and Technology BJ Habibie, and illustrates more than anything else Indonesia's technological 'coming of age'. Critics of the project regard the investment of so much money in a single project as wasteful. Although Habibie claims that 192 aircraft have already been ordered, and the company (IPTN in Bandung, see page 000 [cross ref to Bandung intro page 693]) only needs to sell 259 to break even, most of these aircraft are destined for domestic airlines which are said to have little choice in the matter. The concentration of funds, skilled workers, and technological excellence in one machine of dubious commercial value is seen to be crazy in the context of Indonesia, a country with immense potentially but, currently, a very narrow technological base. Nonetheless, the pride and self-confidence that Indonesians have gained in producing the N-250 is immense, and as the plane left the tarmac Suharto gave the go-ahead for Habibie to produce a jet airliner – codenamed the N-2130 – by 2003.

Development has been based upon a series of 5-year plans known as *Repelitas* (standing for *Rencana Pembangunan Lima Tahun*), the first beginning in 1969. Indonesia's GDP/person was about US$800 in 1994; in 1967 it was only US$70. At that time, the average Indonesian – statistically – was twice as poor (or half as rich) as the average Indian or Bangladeshi. At the beginning of 1995 Indonesia made the transition from being a 'low income' to becoming a 'middle income' country according to World Bank criteria. For those with a love of acronyms, it is now classified as a MIMIC – or Moderately Indebted Middle Income Country. As if to cement Indonesia's economic coming-of-age, the World Bank now includes the country as one of its eight High Performing Asian Economies or HPAEs. These countries, the subject of considerable academic study (see page 72), are regarded as role models for the rest of the developing world.

Indonesia has benefited from its **oil wealth** (see page 70). This has enabled the government to pursue ambitious programmes of social, agricultural and regional development. After the first oil price rise in 1973 following in the wake of the Arab-Israeli Yom Kippur War, when the cost of a barrel of oil quadrupled in less than a year, the government was awash with funds. These were used to build 6,000 primary schools a year, expand roads into the less accessible parts of the Outer Islands, and subsidize rice cultivation so that the country attained self-sufficiency by the 1980s. But the oil boom also promoted **corruption** on a scale that was remarkable even by Southeast Asian standards. It was said, for example, that importers were having to pay US$200mn a year in bribes to the notoriously corrupt Customs Department, and that even the lowliest coffee boy had to pass US$1,000 under the table to buy himself a job. This investment would, of course, be repaid in a few months, as the coffee boy's share of the bribes trickled down through the system. Such was the degree of corruption that in 1985 Suharto was forced to take the unprecedented step of calling in a Swiss firm, Société Générale de Surveillance, to oversee import procedures. They did much to clean up the Customs Department, but their contract was only temporary and in 1992 SGS began to hand back control to the Indonesian customs – a process which should be completed by the end of 1995.

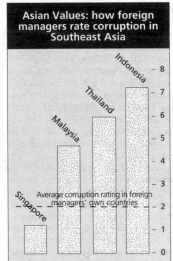

In 1995, the Hong Kong-based firm *Political and Economic Risk Consultancy* asked managers working in the Asian region – mainly of European and North American nationality – how they rated levels of corruption in Asian countries compared with their own, on a scale from 0-10. Indonesia 'topped' the poll.

Regrettably, the department does not seem to have been reformed. Corruption is on the increase again, and the *Economist* reported that "sadly, an unruly child seems to have matured into a delinquent adolescent". In 1996 customs official at Tanjung Priok, Jakarta's port, were accused of rampant bribery by the Indonesian Importers Association.

The decline in oil prices since the early 1980s has forced the government to become rather more hard-headed in its approach to economic management. Growth in recent years has been rapid, and the value of **non-oil exports** has expanded particularly impressively – today, over 20% of Indonesia's GDP is produced by the manufacturing sector and oil and

gas account for less than a quarter of total exports. Foreign investors have been attracted by Indonesia's low wage rates when compared with Malaysia and Thailand, its political stability when compared with China, and its comparatively investor-friendly environment when compared with Vietnam. In 1994, approved foreign direct investment totalled nearly US$24bn, and in 1995 it jumped to almost US$40bn. (In prior years, of 'approved' investment, 54% was 'realized'.)

Other than oil and gas which contributed US$9.7bn out of total exports of just over US$40bn, Indonesia's major exports in 1994 were wood products (US$5.1bn), garments and textiles (US$5.0bn), electronic goods (US$1.3bn), coffee (US$720mn) and jewellery (US$670mn). This illustrates the continued importance of **agriculture** and other primary products in the economy. Much of the glitz may be attached to prestige projects such as the aircraft manufacturer IPTN (see page 157), but agriculture remains highly important employing nearly half the country's workforce and producing a fair slice of exports.

Many economists emphasize the need for further **deregulation** of the economy if past growth rates are to be maintained. The problem for the government is that standing still is not enough. Indonesia has one of the world's largest **foreign debts** – about US$100bn. Although this translates into a manageable debt service ratio of 30% (the cost of servicing this debt as a % of export earnings), it does not leave any room for complacency. On top of the need to service this massive debt (so far Indonesia has had a spotless reputation for meeting its obligations), the government also has to expand its development expenditure. All in all, it means that the economy has got to continue growing at 6%+ per year, and foreign companies have got to continue investing in the country – which many people translate as continuing deregulation.

Nor is Indonesia's rapid economic growth without **human costs**. People are being displaced from the countryside to swell the ranks of the urban labour force, causing social tensions to escalate. Many of the jobs in industry are non-formal, and non-contractual, so few workers feel that they have much security. American labour activists have highlighted this when they argue that many factories contravene the International Labour Organization's standards on the treatment of workers. Although the Indonesian constitution in theory allows workers to freely organize themselves into unions, two recent attempts have been quashed by the government in favour of the tame, institutionalized, All-Indonesia Workers Union. The problem is that the internal security agency Bakorstanas is able to intevene in strikes and other activities when they threaten political and social stability. This can be, and is, interpreted in a very loose fashion to include almost any workers' action.

It was only with the creation of the Indonesian Prosperous Labour Union (SBSI) in early 1994 that a truly independent union appeared. And the arrest of the union's chairman in Feb 1994 demonstrated that the authorities were not going to make it easy for the union. This action was preceded in Jul 1993 by the murder of an E Java labour activist, Marsinah. As John McBeth in the *Far Eastern Economic Review* records: "Marsinah was tortured for 3 days and then sexually violated with a sharp instrument before being dumped on a roadside and left to bleed to death". Nine people, including a local military commander and the owner of the factory where Marsinah worked, 40km S of Surabaya, were charged in connection with the murder. Even at the time, the charges were widely regarded as unsound. In 1995, Indonesia's Supreme Court surprised many commentators by exonerating six of the nine – who had argued that their 'confessions' had been obtained under torture. The case has therefore been re-opened,

and the police are investigating a crime which has become a cause célèbre among labour activists. The defending council believes that Marsinah died in detention, which implies that the crime was covered-up, and then nine people framed for the murder. Whether the new investigation turns up any new evidence is seen as a test case in Indonesia where the courts seem to be becoming more willing to confront entrenched power interests.

There are also many examples of **child labour** and of poor workplace safety. Officially there are 2.4 million child workers in the country, although some NGOs believe the real figure is four times as large. The difficulty of determining whether child work is exploitative is reflected in the term that the government prefers to describe underage labourers: *anak yang terpaksa bekerja* or 'children who are compelled to work'. If children work below a certain minimum number of hours a day and if their labour is crucial to household survival then it is, officially, permitted. Strikes in favour of better working conditions and wages are becoming more common – and more successful. In Apr 1994 there was violent labour unrest in the Sumatran city of Medan which rapidly turned into an anti-Chinese riot involving 20,000 people. Since then there have been further strikes and demonstrations in this Sumatran city.

Despite this unprecedented bout of labour unrest, it is still true that few unskilled workers are in a position to complain. The minimum wage in theory is about US$2 a day in Jakarta, but there is ample evidence that people will work for less than this. At the time, some commentators argued that the strikes and demonstrations were only allowed to occur because the Indonesian government was trying not to antagonize the Americans before the country's Most Favoured Nation status came up for review in late 1994 – a review which was successfully negotiated. There seems little doubt that some leaders, especially in the army, would simply like to imprison the trouble-makers. Nonetheless, the labour unrest does seem to have had some positive effects on conditions and wages, and it seems to be more difficult now for employers to pay less than the minimum wage. In Medan, for example, it was estimated at the end of 1994 that as a direct result of workers' actions, nine out of ten factories in the city pay at least the local minimum wage of 3,750Rp (US$1.70) a day.

Much press comment in the West paints Indonesia as ruled by an authoritarian government which brooks no dissent and ignores – or suppresses – protest. This is far too simplistic. The president, his closest aides, and the army are not only divided among themselves but find that they must also take into account the views of a wide range of other interest groups. As civil society and the middle classes strengthen and grow, this inability to dictate terms will become more pronounced (see above, Modern Indonesia: politics). The success of the campaign against the national lottery, the increase in the minimum wage, the success of the environmenalists' campaign to halt the building of golf courses, and Suharto's attempts to establish an Asian commission on human rights, all show the extent to which the government does bow to public pressure.

Tourism is Indonesia's third largest foreign exchange earner: it generated US$5.2 billion in 1995, up from US$4.8bn in 1994 and US$3.6bn in 1993. President Suharto has tipped the sector to become

The Asian miracle: why it happened: the story according to the World Bank

In 1993, the World Bank published a study which tried to make sense of the Asian economic success story, with the title *The East Asian miracle: economic growth and public policy*. The unprecedented rate of economic growth in Asia, including in a number of Southeast Asian countries, demanded an explanation so that other, less fortunate regions of the world might also embark on this road to fortune. Of course, not everyone is so sanguine about Asia's success, past or future. These critics point to, for example, human rights violations, poor working conditions, widening rural-urban disparities, environmental degradation on a monumental scale, the exploitation of child labour, and corrupt and corrosive government.

Although the World Bank study begins by pointing out that there is no 'recipe' for success, it does highlight a number of critical elements which countries and governments need, in their view, to get right. As the World Bank puts it, the so-called High Performing Asian Economies or HPAEs (including Singapore, Malaysia, Thailand and Indonesia) "achieved high growth by getting the basics right". Not all the below can be applied to all the countries in question all of the time; nonetheless, they represent a checklist of 'right' policies and government.

● **The principle of shared growth**: although the countries of Asia are not, in most cases, democracies, their governments have tried to ensure that the fruits of development have been relatively widely shared. This is particularly true in the case of the 'dragons' (including Singapore) where rapid growth has been achieved with relative equity. This has helped to establish the legitimacy of their governments and usually won the support of the populations at large – despite the fact that those governments may still be authoritarian in complexion.

● **Investment in physical capital**: the countries of Asia have, in general, been saving and investing a greater proportion of their total wealth than countries in any other region of the world. This includes both private and public investment, but is most

the country's largest foreign exchange earner by the end of the century. In 1995 4.3 million foreigners visited the country, as against just over 4 million in 1994 and 3.4 million in 1993. This latter figure is well over double that for 1988. The tourist authorities in Indonesia are predicting that 6-6.5 million tourists will be visiting the country by 1998, 8 million by 2000, and 11 million by 2005. Some analysts doubt that these targets will be met, and point to the slow down in tourist arrivals since the spurt of the late 1980s and early 1990s. In comparison to fellow Asean members Singapore, Malaysia and Thailand, the Indonesian Tourist Promotion Board is wonderfully amateur. The rotund rhino that became the symbol of the 1991 Visit Indonesia Year is still propped up outside hotels, indicating

that while neighbouring countries fine tune their PR campaigns month-by-month, Indonesia stumbles along with Stalinist-style Five Year Plans. Nor is it just a question of marketing; there is a real shortage of facilities and tourist infrastructure beyond a few key destinations like Bali. Lombok, for example, has been waiting to explode now for close to a decade and the upgrading of the island's Selaparang Airport to international status – which has been imminent for years – will still probably not be complete until the 21st century. Tourist arrival figures are low compared with Thailand, Singapore or Malaysia. In terms of tourists per sq km, Thailand receives around 10 tourists/year, Indonesia about a tenth of this figure.

To more fully exploit the country's

dramatic in terms of private investment (the World Bank, as one might expect, views private investment as more efficient and effective in promoting growth).

● **Investment in human capital**: although the proportion of spending allotted to education is not very much higher in Asia than elsewhere in the developing world, this money has been primarily allocated to primary and secondary schooling, not to higher education. Among developing countries, the families of most of those entering higher education can pay for it anyway, and need little government support; the best way to improve general levels of education is by targetting primary and secondary schooling. Asian governments have also tended to educate girls nearly as well as boys.

● **Allowing the market to determine prices**: as one might expect from the World Bank, the report also highlights the importance of allowing the market to determine the price of labour, capital and goods. The Bank skipped around the tendency for Asian governments to intervene in economic decision-making (with the exception of Hong Kong) by arguing that this was judicious intervention which reinforced, rather than tried to buck, the market.

● **That vital intangible**: Lee Kuan Yew, former prime minister of Singapore, visited Vietnam – one of the poorest countries in the world with a per capita income of US$220 – and pronounced that the country's prospects were bright because it had that 'vital intangible'. Economists talk rather less poetically in terms of Total Factor Productivity (TFP). In effect, this is what cannot be explained in a country's growth by looking at such variables as investment in physical and human capital. The former Soviet Union, on paper, should have grown as fast as Singapore and S Korea. As is now abundantly clear, it did not. The problem is identifying this ghostly missing catalyst.

● **Creating a business-friendly environment**: the countries have usually welcomed foreign investment and have sought to create the conditions in which foreign companies can thrive. They have also created a cadre of efficient technocrats to manage the economy.

tourism potential, 1991 was declared Visit Indonesia Year by the government with the slogan 'Let's Go Archipelago'. Unfortunately, this promotion blitz happened to coincide with the Gulf War and recession in the West, so numbers were rather disappointing – about 2.5 million. It is also true that many areas have limited facilities. About one third of all tourists visit Bali, and beyond one or two other destinations like the Riau Islands, Jakarta and Yogya, travel is only for the more adventurous. This is unlikely to change without considerable investment in facilities and infrastructure: 'starred' hotels are limited beyond the main tourist and commercial centres (there are only 29 5-star hotels and 51 4-star), only the airports at Jakarta, Bali, Medan and Biak (in Irian Jaya, an important refuelling stop) can accommodate Boeing 747s, and transport facilties (roads, frequency of flights etc) are poorly developed across vast swathes of the archipelago. Nonetheless, the government has big plans for tourism, seeing it as one of the country's leading growth sectors. To illustrate its enthusiasm, the government, not satisfied with just one or two Visit Indonesia Years – and in a fine example of over-egging the pudding – declared 1991 to 2000 Visit Indonesia Decade.

Though at one level it is possible to marvel at Indonesia's economic progress and to extol the wonders of its 'miracle' economy, businessmen complain of the *pungli* or hidden taxes that make doing business so difficult. John McBeth has written of the "army of 4 million underpaid bureaucrats [who] lurk in ambush in thickets of red tape" waiting to pounce on unsuspecting businessmen. Indonesia comes close to the top in the World Corruption Stakes: in 1996 it was thought to be running close behind China and Vietnam, while Transparency International put Indonesia at the top of a field of 41 countries. But it is not just corruption which worries businessmen. The way in which the politically well-connected gain

access to lucrative contracts and licenses, the burgeoning business empires of the various Suharto children (see above), and the lack of transparency in the system are all also sources of concern.

In addition to corruption, foreign investors and local businessmen still highlight poor infrastructure, lack of skilled workers, a cumbersome bureaucracy and high interest rates as major **constraints to growth**. The liberalization programme also has its own risks, as exemplified in the collapse of Bank Summa, one of the country's largest private banks, in late 1992. The fundamental weakness of many private and publically-owned banks was highlighted again in 1994 when Bapindo, a state-owned development bank, was shown to have lost around US$450m in a shady deal which implicated aides of President Suharto. Eddy Tansil, the businessman at the centre of the scandal was later jailed for 20 years (see box page 63). Many other banks are thought to have similar skeletons in their loan cupboards, reflecting the importance of political connections over financial probity in securing loans. At the end of Apr 1994, Standard and Poor's, an American credit rating agency, classified Indonesia as a "high risk environment" for foreign investors.

The largely hidden difficulties of the banking sector highlights the deep-seated problem of political patronage. This means it is often more useful for a businessman to cultivate close connections with influential politicians, and thereby secure lucrative government contracts, than it is to produce the best product at the lowest price. This is particularly true of Chinese businessmen who often feel politically exposed in a country where there is ingrained mistrust of the Chinese community, founded partly on their economic success and partly on the perception that they do not show total allegiance to their adopted country. The two best examples of this approach to business are Liem Sioe Liong, who was

Suharto's quartermaster in the 1960s, and Bob Hasan, who helped to finance the president's Central Java Command, also in the 1960s. They are both Chinese; they both have impeccable links with Suharto; and they are both highly successful and very rich. As the saying goes, this success has been based more on know-who, rather than know-how.

In Mar 1993 Suharto reshuffled his cabinet. Many western commentators identified a shift in influence away from the Berkeley Mafia – the technocrats who have been instrumental in Indonesia's economic liberalization – towards the economic nationalists led by BJ Habibie. A number of Habibie's acolytes gained cabinet portfolios in the reshuffle and some observers at the time argued that Indonesia was on the verge of a highly significant change in economic policy – towards what is known as 'Habibienomics'. Events since then have shown that such predictions placed too much emphasis on 'people-watching'. To an extent the changes are generational, and there is little doubt that, for the time being at least, Suharto remains firmly in control.

Uneven development

One major cause for concern in the country is the uneven nature of development. This has both a spatial and a human component. To begin with, the great bulk of investment is concentrated in Java – some 64% of total foreign investment. Over vast swathes of the archipelago, the export-driven boom is just hot air.

'Social justice for all Indonesians' is one of the principles enshrined in *pancasila*, the state ideology, and Suharto clearly does feel under pressure to ensure that at least some of the fruits of development accrue to those at the bottom of the economic pile and at the geographical edges of the country. It seems that with the economy growing strongly and the powerful also now wealthy, the glaring inequalities between the rich and the poor, and between different regions of the country, has become an issue of driving concern.

This was reflected in the initiation of a new **poverty alleviation** programme at the beginning of Apr 1994, *Inpres Desa Tertinggal* or the Presidential Instruction Programme for Less Developed Villages. This aims to reduce poverty from roughly 15% today to 6% by 1998 by specifically targetting those for who wealth has not 'trickled down'. In preparing for the programme, the National Development Planning board drew up a map of 20,633 villages where poverty was endemic and by 1996 some 2.3 million families had been accepted on to the scheme. The intention is to involve local people and

Total and percentage of the population defined as poor, 1976-1990 using the BPS* poverty line

Year	Poor in millions			Percentage of the population		
	Urban	Rural	Total	Urban	Rural	Total
1976	10.00	44.2	54.2	38.8	40.4	40.1
1980	9.5	32.8	42.3	29.0	28.4	28.6
1984	9.3	25.7	35.0	23.1	21.2	21.6
1987	9.7	20.3	30.0	20.1	16.4	17.4
1990	9.4	17.8	27.2	16.8	14.3	15.1

Sources: Based on Booth (1992), Firdausy (1993) and Biro Pusat Statistik (1992). * BPS = Biro Pusat Statistik (Central Bureau of Statistics).

NGOs to a far greater degree than has hitherto been the case. The problem is that although the numbers of Indonesians living below the poverty line has fallen dramatically over the last 2 decades (see table on page 75), there are still perhaps a third or more of the population who live very close to what is, ultimately, an arbitrarily designated poverty 'line'. These 'close to poor' – the 'striving poor' as they are sometimes called – were rather unfortunately termed 'pre-prosperous' in a 1994 Population Ministry Survey. In 1996 the poverty line for people living in urban areas was just 930 rupiah per person per day (less than 50 US cents), and for people in rural areas a measley 608 rupiah (close of 25 US cents). These people are also living hard lives, without many of the basics of life, and often feel frustrated and dissatisfied. They represent as much a political worry as an economic concern. Significantly, many household who applied for inclusion in the Inpres Desa Tertinggal programme were told they were ineligible because they were too wealthy.

In mid 1996 President Suharto tried another tack to narrow the glaring **inequalities** within the country. He made a personal plea for rich individuals and companies to hand over 250 billion rupiah to finance a poverty alleviation programme. 11,000 people and firms, selected on the basis that each had an income after tax of over 100 million rupiah – were sent a booklet asking them to share their wealth with the needy. This caused quite a stir and executives found themselves looking at each other seeing who would jump first and how much they would donate. If they didn't contribute to the fund, would they find themselves out in the cold? If they did, how little could they get away with? The booklet asked these favoured few to "carry out the noble task of poverty alleviation together with the government". One Western business advisor was quoted in the *Far Eastern Economic Review* as saying that most American companies weren't signing any cheques – yet. He suggested that they would "batten down the hatches and wait for skilful intimidation". Another local businessman exclaimed "It's extortion". One of the difficulties is how the whole programme is going to be administered. The beneficiary, initially, will be the cozily named Prosperous Self-reliant Fund. But the chairman of the fund is the President himself and the treasurer is Suharto's son Bambang Trihatmodjo. This rather heavy-handed approach to redistributing wealth is one of a series of proposals in the air. Companies have been floating the idea of making a small percentage (1-2%) of their profits available for development and charitable purposes, or for financing credit schemes for the poor. Many, if they are going to donate funds to the poor, would prefer that these funds go to organizations without political associations and which maintain as much transparency in their dealings as possible in a country as opaque as Indonesia.

Although Indonesia's population of poor and near-poor are the most evident source of concern, there is also growing discontent among those groups who, so far, have gained most from the country's rapid economic growth. High school leavers and even university graduates are finding that jobs in private business or the public sector, previously virtually guaranteed by dint of their having a degree or secondary school certificate, are increasingly hard to find. With expectations growing as the consumer culture bites, so these individuals are finding their aspirations thwarted. A disgruntled, educated, largely urban-based mass of young men and women is the last thing the government wants as it tries to stem the desire for greater political pluralism. The next parliamentary elections in 1997 should show whether the government has cause for concern in this regard.

Indonesia: fact file

Geographic

Land area	1,919,443 sq km
Arable land as % of total	8.7%
Average annual rate of deforestation	0.8%
Highest mountain, Mount Jaya	5,030m
Average rainfall in Jakarta	1,766 mm
Average temperature in Jakarta	26°C

Economic

GNP/person (1994)	US$880
GDP/person (PPP*, 1994)	US$3,600
GNP growth (/capita, 1980-1994)	6.0%
GDP growth 1994	7.0%
GDP growth 1995	7.2%
GDP growth 1996	7.0% (est)
% labour force in agriculture	55%
Total debt (% GNP)	57.4%
Debt service ratio (% exports)	32.4%
Military expenditure (% GDP)	1.4%

Social

Population	191 million
Population growth rate (1980-93)	1.7%
Adult literacy rate	84%
Mean years of schooling	4.1 years
% of age group enrolled in tertiary education	10
Population in absolute poverty	25%
Rural population as % of total	67%
Growth of urban population (1980-93)	4.8%/year
Urban population in largest city	17%
Televisions per 1,000 people	60

Health

Life expectancy at birth	63 years
Population with access to clean water	42%
Calorie intake as % of requirements	122%
Malnourished children less than 5 years old	8.6 million
Contraceptive prevalence rate†	55%

*PPP = Purchasing Power Parity (based on what it costs to buy a similar basket of goods and services in different countries).

† % of women of childbearing age using a form of modern contraception.

Source: World Bank (1996) *Human Development Report 1995*, OUP: New York; World Bank (1996), *World development report 1996*, OUP: New York; and other sources.

Java

Horizons	79	Central Java and Yogyakarta	180
Jakarta	105	South Central Java and Yogyakarta	182
West Java	134	Yogyakarta	184
The Far West	136	Central Java's North Coast	244
West Central Highlands and		East Java	261
South Coast	146	The Rump of East Java	263
The North Coast Plain	174	Madura Island	290
		The Far East	295

JAVA is the cultural and economic heart of Indonesia. Although the island covers only 6% of the country's land area, well over 100 million people live here – more than 60% of Indonesia's total population. This makes it one of the most densely populated islands on earth. Historically, Java has been home to Indonesia's most glorious kingdoms (an exception being Sumatra's Srivijayan Empire), and has produced the archipelago's finest art and architecture. Today, it is the centre of political and economic power, generating more than half of the country's GDP and dominating Indonesia to the extent that inhabitants in the Outer Islands decry the so-called 'Javanization' of their cultures.

HORIZONS

The immense population of Java has not just been a concern of recent years. From the beginning of the 19th century, Dutch administrators and commentators had been talking of the island's 'overpopulation'. Nederburgh in 1802 wrote of Java as overcrowded and its population unemployed. In 1827, LPJ du Bus de Gisignies painted a picture of an island that before too long would be populated by millions of tenants living at the very margins of existence; even Stamford Raffles in his *History of Java*, published in 1817, believed there would have to be an emigration of surplus population from Java to other, less densely populated, islands. Yet, the predictions of the prophets of doom – who had forecast famines on a scale hitherto unimagined – have not been fulfilled. This is all the more remarkable when it is considered that in 1845, Java's population was just one tenth of today's figure. This astonishing feat has been achieved by continually increasing the output of wet rice or *sawah* (see box, page 80). A lesser, though still significant role has been played by the programme of 'transmigration' – the resettlement of Javanese in sites

Sawah: wet rice cultivation in Java

Every visitor to Java is struck by the immense patchwork of verdant rice paddys, often terraced down precipitous hillsides. Rice (*Oryza sativa* L) cultivation seems to have been introduced into Java some time during the first millennium BC. But at that time the crop was grown in dry fields in the same way as other grains such as millet, wheat and corn. The cultivation of 'wet' rice – rice grown in flooded conditions – probably did not begin until the early centuries of the first millennium. By the 8th century rice was being grown in irrigated fields in E Java, while the Chinese adventurer Ma Huan reported at the beginning of the 15th century that in N-E Java "the rice ripens twice in one year", indicating that double cropping was practiced. By the time European mariners began to arrive in Southeast Asia during the 16th century, Java had become the greatest rice exporter in the region. Central Java was sending 50-60 rice junks each year to Melaka on the Malay Peninsula, while the Dutch reported in 1615 that they could purchase 2,000 tonnes a year at the N coast town of Jepara.

The logic of cultivating rice in flooded conditions is that higher yields can be achieved. In Java today, there are areas where three crops are harvested every year, each crop producing up to five tonnes per hectare. Hectare for hectare, the wet rice system of cultivation in Java probably produces more calories than almost any other agricultural system. The lack of land and an exploding population – which has grown 10-fold over the space of less than 150 years – has forced rice farmers to search for new ways to increase yields. In response, terraces have been built up ever-steeper slopes, irrigation systems have been perfected to ensure year-round supplies of water, and the land has been cultivated ever-more assiduously and minutely.

By squeezing a few extra kilograms of grain from each minutely cultivated field, the Javanese farmer has managed to feed each extra mouth. But only just: in the mid-1980s, the government estimated that over three quarters of the rural population were living below the poverty line. Some scholars believe that the system of cultivation has perpetuated poverty, by preventing the accumulation of any surplus.

Historically, rules of harvesting guaranteed that everyone in a village had the right to harvest any piece of land – all they had to do was to turn up on the day. This *bawon* ('share') system of harvesting guaranteed that even people with no land could secure enough rice to feed themselves and their families. For land owners today this is not always a desirable tradition – there have been reports of up to 600 people harvesting a single hectare, leading to trampling of the crop and the loss of production. To get round this, land owners have taken to harvesting their land at night or very early in the morning, and not announcing the date of the harvest. Even so, the *bawon* system has now been replaced in many villages with the *tebasan* system, where the standing crop is sold to a middleman before it is harvested, thereby getting around such community obligations.

cleared from the forest in the Outer Islands (see box, page 427).

(see box, page 427)

THE LAND

GEOGRAPHY

Java stretches more than 1,000 km from E to W, but is only 81 km broad at its widest point, and covers an area of 132,187 sq km. The island lies over a volcanic arc that marks the boundary between two tectonic (continental) plates, making it one of the most volcanically active places on earth. There are 121 volcanoes on Java – more than any other country – of which between 27 and 35 are classified as active. This degree of vulcanicity has periodically led to catastrophe. Most famously, in 1883, the island of Krakatau just off Java's W coast exploded killing 36,000 people (see page 144). Further back in history, in 928 or 929AD, it is thought that Mt Merapi erupted leading to the mass migration of the court and people of Central Java eastwards (see page 89). More recently, in 1982, Mt Galunggung in E Java erupted causing 60,000 people to lose their homes and livelihoods.

But Java's volcanoes have not just been a source of misery and disruption; they are the reason why the island has some of the richest soils in the world. Fertile ash coats the land and volcanic rocks are slowly eroded to release more nutrients. Admittedly, not all the discharge is fertile – a distinction needs to be made between the good, neutral-basic volcanic soils, and the poor acidic volcanic soils of parts of E and W Java. Nonetheless, Java's fertility explains how agricultural populations, crowded at densities of up to 2,000 per sq km, can produce enough food to support themselves. It also explains why farmers continue to cultivate the land around volcanoes that are at constant risk of eruption. Thomas Stamford Raffles in 1830 wrote that "whoever has viewed the fertile plains of Java or beheld with astonishment the surprising efforts of human industry, which have carried cultivation to the summits of the most stupendous mountains, will be inclined to consider that nothing short of a permanent interest in the soil could have effected such a change in the face of the country...". In Raffles' view, it was Java's extraordinary natural fertility which allowed great civilizations to arise on the island.

CLIMATE

The 'E monsoon' from Jun to Aug brings dry weather to Java while the 'W monsoon' from Dec to Feb corresponds with the wet season. During the transitional months between these two seasons, rainfall can be even heavier than during the wet season. In general it becomes drier from W to E, and while the western two thirds of the island receives rain throughout the year, the eastern third of Java has a pronounced dry season. Average annual rainfall in W Java is 2,360 mm, in Central Java, 2,400 mm, and in E Java, only 1,660 mm. Temperatures vary little through the year, averaging 26°C-27°C at sea-level.

THE HISTORY OF JAVA

Java's epic and convoluted history encompasses an array of kingdoms, empires, sultanates and dynasties. Although the history portrayed below might give the impression that one kingdom neatly followed another in dominating the island, there were always a number of powers vying for influence at any one time. It was only a case of which dominated, when.

Sailendra (Central Java, mid-8th-10th century)

The Sailendra Dynasty of Central Java, which lasted for only two centuries, was the greatest of all the Javanese kingdoms and produced architectural monuments of such grandeur and artistic brilliance that they are among the finest not just in Indonesia, but in the world.

In the middle of the 8th century a descendant of Funanese immigrants from S Vietnam established a kingdom called Sailendra, meaning 'King of the Mountain' – a name that associates it with the temple mountain-builders of Cambodia. At the height of its power, Sailendra's sphere of influence stretched as far as Champa on the Vietnamese coast and Angkor in Cambodia.

The kings of the Sailendra Dynasty derived their wealth and power from agriculture, rather than trade which was the backbone of Sumatra's Srivijayan Empire. Exploiting the year-round rains, tropical warmth, and fertile volcanic soils of Java, the farmers of Sailendra produced a substantial rice surplus. This allowed a large court, with its holy men, artisans and soldiers to be maintained, and a series of impressive monuments to be constructed. The Sailendras were Buddhists, and they attracted Buddhist scholars from all over Asia to their court. It also seems that the kings were linked through marriage with the rulers of Srivijaya.

Of all the monuments erected by the Sailendras, none is more imposing than **Borobudur** – possibly the single most magnificent temple in Southeast Asia. This enormous edifice, built between 778 and 824, represented the cosmological and spiritual centre of the kingdom. Along its terraces, row upon row of superbly executed reliefs, depict the Sailendra world order: the nine previous lives of the Gautama Buddha, princes and carpenters, dancers and fishermen. Borobudur offered a religious justification for Sailendra rule, and at the same time gave the kings religious authority over Srivijaya. Johann Scheltema, a German traveller, on seeing Java's monuments wrote – rather pompously – at the beginning of this century that they were "...eloquent evidence of that innate consciousness which moves men to propitiate the principle of life by sacrifice in temples as gloriously divine as mortal hand can raise".

Sanjaya (Central and East Java, 8th-11th century)

At about the same time as the Sailendra kings were building Borobudur, another Central Javanese Kingdom was also engaged in an extensive monument-building programme: Sanjaya (sometimes known as Mataram). In this instance, Hinduism, rather than Buddhism, was the dominant religion, but no less energy was expended. Foremost among this kingdom's temples was **Prambanan**, the finest Hindu shrine on Java. The Sanjaya Kingdom derived its wealth from controlling the spice trade between Maluku (the Moluccas), China and the sultanates of the Arab world. The control of port facilities focused on the strategic Strait of Melaka (Malacca). This led Sanjaya into open conflict with the more powerful kingdom of Srivijaya based at Palembang, Sumatra. In 1006, Srivijaya defeated Sanjaya and sacked its capital, slaughtering many of its inhabitants. It was not until 1026 that Srivijaya's hold over the Strait of Melaka was relinquished following an expedition headed by a prince from S India.

Before the conflict between Sanjaya and Srivijaya, at the beginning of the 10th century, the kingdoms of Central Java mysteriously moved E to the area of the Brantas River. This move was associated with the reign of King Sindok, whose power is reflected in a multitude of inscriptions recording his successes and decrees. Various explanations have been proposed to explain the shift in focus from Central to E Java, including war, pestilence and the eruption of Mt Merapi. A century later, in 1020, a new figurehead emerged in the Sanjaya Kingdom – Airlangga – the son of a Balinese prince and a Sanjaya princess. His reign was peaceful and he restored relations with Srivijaya by marrying a Srivijayan princess. Religious syncretism was at its height during Airlangga's reign and he pragmatically recognized both Buddhism and Hinduism, hoping to appeal to supporters of both faiths. He also eroded the strength of the Brahmin priests by appropriating their land. Towards the end of his life, Airlangga became a Buddhist monk, while at the same time styling himself as a reincarnation of Vishnu (Hindu). His biggest mistake was to divide his kingdom just before his death in 1049. He had no direct heir and feared a dispute between two of his children, born of concubines. His fears were realized when – following his death – the empire was divided into two kingdoms – Kediri and Janggala.

Kediri and Janggala (1050-1222)

Kediri was centred in the Brantas River valley nr the site of the modern day city of the same name; while it is thought that Janggala was focused S of Surabaya, nr Malang. Inscriptions indicate that Kediri became a locally powerful maritime kingdom, operating on the N coast of Java. It traded extensively in spices from Maluku with India, and was preferred as a port over Srivijaya because of its proximity to the source of those spices. Of Janggala, historians know almost nothing. However, in 1222, Ken Angrok of Kediri captured the lesser kingdom of Janggala and then went on to kill the ruler of Kediri and establish his new kingdom at Singasari.

Between 1486 and 1512, the capital was moved from Majapahit, SW to Kediri, perhaps to escape from the powerful Islamic incursion from the N coast. The move did nothing to prevent Demak from overpowering Kediri in 1527.

Singasari (1222-1292)

The short-lived Singasari Kingdom was founded in E Java by Ken Angrok in 1222 after the defeat of Kediri and Janggala. The kingdom's greatest king was its last, Kertanagara (1268-1292). His aggressively expansionist policies took Singasari's influence beyond the confines of E Java and in 1290 he defeated the once powerful empire of Srivijaya.

Although Singasari lasted just 70 years, a considerable temple-building programme was undertaken, which included the construction of Candi Kidal and Candi Jago, to house the funerary remains of the kings. In 1289 the Chinese Emperor Kublai Khan sent a diplomatic mission to Singasari, ordering Kertanagara to accept the suzerainty of the Middle Kingdom and pay tribute. Kertanagara ignored his demands and after torturing the members of the Chinese mission, sent a message back to Peking carved into the forehead of the Emperor's delegate. The enraged Kublai Khan responded to this diplomatic slap-in-the-face by dispatching a large army to attack Singasari. A rival prince from the old kingdom of Kediri took advantage of the disarray caused by the imminent arrival of the Chinese force and seized the kingdom of Singasari, killing Kertanagara in the process. Kertanagara's heir, Vijaya, promptly fled to Majapahit. The Chinese arrived to find a country in

The curse of the kris-maker

The Singasari king Ken Angrok fell in love with a Queen of Tumapel, called Ken Dedes. However, to marry her he first needed to murder her husband. This required the forging of a *kris*, or sword (see page 118), endowed with supernatural powers. Unfortunately, the swordsmith engaged to make the weapon took so long to forge the *kris* that, in his impatience, Angrok stabbed the poor man to death. As he lay dying, he cursed the king and his descendants, claiming they would all die by the kris Angrok held in his hand. The curse did not take long to take effect; Angrok was murdered by his stepson Anusapati, having been betrayed by his new wife Ken Dedes. Anusapati, in his turn, and despite taking precautions such as building a moat around his bed, was also murdered by the same sword after ruling Singasari for 20 years (his memorial shrine is at Candi Kidal).

turmoil. Vijaya, sensing Chinese reluctance to return home without some recognition of suzerainty, promised to become a vassal of China if the Chinese fleet would assist him in overthrowing the rebel from Kediri. In such inauspicious circumstances, the great Majapahit Dynasty was founded.

Majapahit (1292-1478)

The Majapahit – or 'Bitter Gourd' – empire was the last and most powerful of the Javanese kingdoms and at the height of its influence claimed suzerainty over parts of Sumatra, Malaya and Borneo. The capital of this far-flung empire was Trowulan, which at the time was one of the largest cities in Asia.

The flowering of the Majapahit Kingdom spanned the middle years of the 14th century and is associated with two brilliant men: **Gajah Mada** and **Hayam Wuruk**. Gajah Mada was a skilled general and consummate politician – and filled the post of Prime Minister from 1331 to 1364. Hayam Wuruk, the grandson of Majapahit's founder Vijaya, acceded to the throne after the death of Vijaya's widow in 1350 and reigned until 1389. His formal title was Rajasanagara and he was the greatest king of the Majapahit Period. During Hayam Wuruk's reign, and under the guidance of Gajah Mada, Java experienced what many regard as the island's golden years, during which there was a flowering of the arts. The kingdom of Majapahit had contacts as far afield as Burma, Thailand, Cambodia and Vietnam. Though ostensibly Buddhist, the king and his subjects also worshipped the Hindu gods Siva and Vishnu. All three were incarnate in the king, who was known as Siva-Buddha or Niruna.

By 1402, Melaka (Malacca), on the Malay Peninsula, had been established as a trading-post and the importance of Java waned. At the same time as Majapahit was losing its economic *raison d'être*, the infiltration of Islam began to undermine the religious legitimacy of the kingdom.

Majapahit finally fell to Demak, the Islamic state on Java's N coast, in 1478.

Java in disarray: 1400-1600

Following the decline and subsequent fall of Majapahit at the beginning of the 15th century, Java entered a 200-year period of in-fighting between numerous small kingdoms and sultanates. Along the N coast, trading sultanates (so-called *pasisir* states) drew their religious inspiration from Islam and their wealth from controlling the spice trade between Maluku and Melaka. Foremost among these trading states was **Demak** which reached the height of its power under Sultan Trenggono in the 16th century. At that time its influence, if not its power, spread through Central and E Java. Meanwhile, a group of weak agriculturally-oriented kingdoms dominated the interior. These maintained their links – religious and cultural – with the preceding Hindu-Buddhist empires. Hardly worthy successors to Sailendra and Majapahit, they maintained a tradition that was on the wane. It was not until the early part of the 17th century that Java was once again to come under the influence of a single dominant power: Mataram.

Mataram (16th century-1757)

The last of the great Javanese kingdoms was Mataram, focused on Central Java nr Yogyakarta and Surakarta. Mataram's greatest king was Sultan Agung (r.1613-1645), a devout Muslim. With the help of the Dutch, he vanquished the coastal trading states and promoted Islam in Java's interior. At its peak, his kingdom encompassed Surabaya in the E and Cirebon in the N. He had every intention of uniting the whole of Java, but was prevented from achieving this aim by the presence of the Dutch in Batavia (Jakarta). His two attempts to dislodge the Dutch in 1628 and 1629 failed, with great loss of life.

Although Mataram's kings were not the god-kings of earlier empires they were still regarded as divine. Their names indicate as much: Hamengkubuwono means 'He who holds the World on his

Lap', while Pakubuwono can be translated as 'Axis of the World'. The king and his capital – or *negara*, from the Sanskrit – lay at the centre, not just of the kingdom, but of the cosmos. To live close to a King was to bask in his reflected glory and power – a notion which links the rulers of Mataram with their Hindu-Buddhist predecessors. The kings of Mataram ruled through an assortment of hereditary lords and appointed officials. The officials were servants of the king and

A summary of Javanese history 400-1870

400	First Hindu Kingdom of Tarumanegara is established

Central Javanese Period 600-929

Sailendra Dynasty (mid-8th-10th century)
Sanjaya Dynasty (8th-11th century)

East Javanese Period 929-1527

	King Sindok of Sanjaya (928-950)
1006	Srivijaya defeats Sanjaya Kingdom
	King Airlangga of Sanjaya (1020-1049)
1045	Partition of Sanjaya into Kediri and Janggala
	Kediri Dynasty (929-1222)
	Singasari Dynasty (1222-1292)
	King Ken Angrok (1222-1227)
1222	King Ken Angrok conquers Janggala
	King Kertanagara (1268-1292)
	Majapahit Dynasty (1292-1527)
	Chief Minister Gajah Mada (1331-1364)
1343	Javanese colony established on Bali
	King Hayam Wuruk (1350-1389)
1400	Decline of Majapahit

Islamic Period 1527-1757

1500	Sultanate of Demak
1527	Demak overpowers Kediri
	Wali Dynasty in W Java
	Foundation of Jakarta
1575	Islamic Kingdom of Mataram
	King Senopati (1575-1601)

Colonial Period 1513-1870

1513	Portuguese land at Sunda Kelapa; first European contact with Java
1522	Portuguese establish a godown at Sunda Kelapa
1602	VOC established
	Sultan Agung of Mataram (1613-1645)
1619	Batavia established by Jan Pieterszoon Coen
1628-29	Sultan Agung attacks Batavia, but fails to dislodge Dutch
1757	Dutch conquer Mataram and divide kingdom into 3 vassal sultanates
	Governor-General Daendels (1808-1810)
	British administration under Raffles (1811-1816)
	Java War (1825-1830)
	Culture System (1830-1870)

were called *bupati* or regents, a word which is still in use today. Through this network, the king was able to draw taxes in food and labour. There was no Majapahit money in circulation – although the Spanish silver dollar and Chinese copper coins were in use.

In a number of respects the Mataram Kingdom was weak. It generated 'income' by extracting the small agricultural surplus that a peasant family produced each year. By doing this many thousands of times, the king accumulated considerable wealth. But the basis of this wealth was wholly different from the coastal or *pasisir* kingdoms, whose economic power was founded on trade. Historians argue that Mataram managed to unite Java as a political whole because there existed a common language and culture, and as John Smail says "a political myth that was universally accepted because it rested on common religious beliefs". Such an explanation is only partially convincing, and the Mataram Empire was beginning to degenerate even as it reached the greatest extent of its power. Sultan Agung's son, Amangkurat I (r.1645-1677), faced a rebellion in 1672 after Mt Merapi erupted, and it was only with Dutch assistance and the crowning of a new king, Amangkurat II, that the kingdom was pieced-back together. Ironically, the assistance afforded by the Dutch gave them a foothold and presaged their domination of Java by 1757.

Colonial expansion and control (1513-1870)

Colonial contact with Java dates back to 1513, when a Portuguese expedition arrived off Sunda Kelapa (Jakarta). But the Portuguese were in no position to make their presence felt. Instead, it was the Dutch who were to extend their control over the archipelago. This was a gradual affair (see box, page 45), and for the first 150 years, Dutch influence was restricted to the town of Batavia (Jakarta) and its environs. The history of this period is recounted in the introduction to Jakarta (see page 107).

The Dutch, in the guise of the **Vereenigte Ooste-Indische Compagnie (VOC)** or Dutch East India Company, only began to expand their influence inland as the Mataram Kingdom went into decline. They did this with little enthusiasm, merely filling a political vacuum that otherwise might have been occupied by another colonial power. On conquering Mataram in 1757, the VOC divided the kingdom into three: the senior sultanates of Surakarta and Yogyakarta, and a junior sultanate also at Surakarta. Over the rest of the island, the VOC appointed *bupati* to rule in their name, effectively duplicating the traditional system and structure of control. An important difference however was that the focus of power was reversed. Under the VOC, it was the coast and particularly Batavia that was the centre; the *negara* of the former Mataram Kingdom had become unimportant backwaters.

Under the rule of the VOC there was a modicum of expansion in commercial activity in Java. Looking for a means to justify the expense of managing what was fast becoming a colonial empire, the Dutch forced the Priangan regents of W Java to deliver a fixed quota of coffee beans each year. The arabica coffee bush had been found to grow well in the highlands of Priangan in the early 18th century and it quickly became one of Java's most valuable exports. To produce the coffee to pay the Dutch, the Priangan regents in turn imposed a quota on their peasants. Road and river tolls, the 'leasing' of villages and other forms of taxation all generated wealth for local lords, Dutch officials, Chinese businessmen and for the Company. The cost, invariably, rested on the bony shoulders of the Javanese peasant who was, more often than not, mired in poverty.

In 1795 the French occupied the Netherlands and the Dutch King William V fled to Britain where he asked the British to take control of his colonies. But before the English were to make their mark on the island a new, reformist, governor-general was to arrive in Batavia: **Herman Daendels**, a Dutchman, but also a supporter of Napoleon. Daendel's period as governor-general spanned only 2 years, from 1808 to 1810. But it led to a revolutionary change in the way in which Java was administered. In place of the existing system of regencies, he introduced a far more structured, centralized and bureaucratic system of colonial rule. Like the Englishman Thomas Stamford Raffles who would follow him as governor-general, Daendels recognized the inequities of the existing system. He introduced courts based on *adat* or traditional law, rather than on Dutch law, and he successfully reduced corruption. But by doing this he alienated the Javanese aristocracy, whose powers had been diminished, and angered the Dutch administrators, for whom the possibilities of graft had been substantially reduced. Such was the discontent that he was recalled in 1810 – leaving with the title that had been informally bestowed on him, Tuwan Desar Guntur or Great Thundering Lord, ringing in his ears.

Although it took a few years, the English acted upon King William's request and the **English East India Company** occupied the Dutch East Indies between 1811 and 1816. Just as the VOC had expanded into Java with some trepidation, so the English were equally reluctant to commit men and resources to an enterprise which appeared to offer little financial return.

Thomas Stamford Raffles was to follow in Daendels' footsteps when he became governor-general at the age of 30 in 1811, after forces of the English East India Company landed on Java unopposed. There is some dispute over the extent of the reforms that Raffles wrought in Java. In the past both he and his actions have been, respectively, excessively idolized and idealized. But the recent tendency to denigrate his efforts are similarly unconvincing. There is little reason to doubt his

libertarian outlook, and particularly his liberal economics. He introduced economic, political and social reforms and improved the lives of the local population. The great colonial economist JS Furnivall noted that the reforms removed most of the more iniquitous laws and ensured that the peasant retained some of the rewards of his labour. However, Raffles did not end the quota system of coffee cultivation in the Priangan Highlands, and some view the commercialisation of peasant life that the more liberal economic policies introduced as heralding a shift from village self-sufficiency to dependence. Raffles was also a keen botanist and helped to establish the **gardens at Bogor** (see page 146). His keen interest in the history and culture of Java led him to write the two-volume *History of Java* in 1817, and to commission the first archaeological survey of Borobudur. With the defeat of France, the British – to Raffles' chagrin – returned Java and the Indies to Dutch rule.

Less than 10 years after Java was returned to Dutch rule, the **Java War** erupted in 1825. Several factors combined to spark the rebellion. First, the revolt's leader, **Prince Diponegoro** (see page 192), had been given short shrift by the Dutch who had overlooked his rights of succession to the Sultanate of Yogyakarta. He was able to gather support due to disaffection over the Dutch decision to allow Chinese to exact tolls at border crossings, and the ruling that forced landowners to repay rent to their tenants. To add insult to injury, the Dutch were building a road that passed through the site of a sacred Muslim tomb. Diponegoro called for a *jihad* – or holy war – against the Dutch, and this clarion call received widespread support. The war, focused on Central Java, lasted until 1830 when Diponegoro, his support dwindling, was forced to negotiate. His arrest and subsequent exile to the Celebes (Sulawesi) marked the end of the movement and resulted in a considerable loss of power in the Javanese court. During the war, 8,000 Europeans are thought to have died, along with 200,000 Javanese – mostly victims of the famine that accompanied the conflict.

The end of the Java War saw the introduction of possibly the most infamous of all Holland's economic policies in the Indies: the **Cultuurstelsel** or **Culture System**. Reverting to the pre-colonial system of taxation, the colonial government, under a new governor-general **Van den Bosch**, required that each peasant family deliver a certain quantity of produce for export – or the equivalent labour and land for its production. The latter was estimated at one-fifth of a farm's land area or 66 working days each year.

Export crops such as **sugar cane, indigo** and **coffee** were often cultivated on land that was previously reserved for subsistence crops, like rice. For some cultivators, the Culture System became an intolerable burden and some historians have directly blamed it for a series of famines. For the Dutch government, it brought great wealth, enabling Holland to pay off its public debt. In 1861, the English writer JB Money published a book extolling the virtues of the system, entitled *Java, or How to Manage a Colony*. Not everyone was so impressed, and from the 1850s liberals in Holland began to campaign for the Culture System's abolition. It was finally rescinded in 1870, although many elements of it continued to operate until the early years of the 20th century. The English merchant William d'Almeida in his visit to Java in the 1860s wrote:

"Nature has blessed Java with a healthy climate, genial temperature, and fertile soil, and the Dutch – notwithstanding their former arbitrary measures, modified of late years by a more liberal system of government – have made it what it is, a happy contented land, yielding a splendid revenue".

From the final decades of the 19th century, the history of Java becomes intertwined with the history of Indonesia (see page 45).

ART AND ARCHITECTURE

Of all the islands of Indonesia, none is more richly endowed with architectural monuments than Java. It is here that the former great empires of the country were centred, and their artistic achievements are still reflected in the temples and palaces that lie scattered across the mountains and plains of the central and E regions. Joseph Jukes, the British naturalist aboard the ship *HMS Fly*, who travelled through the Indonesian archipelago in the 1840s, wrote after seeing the temples of Java:

"The latest date that can be assigned to these ruins is in the time of our (King) Edwards; – making allowance for the difference of climate and race, was the civilization of England at that time more advanced than that of Java?"

There are two major periods of Javanese art and architecture, usually referred to as the **Central** and **East Javanese** periods. But this does not necessarily mean that all the monuments linked to these two periods are to be found in those two regions – it only indicates their respective centres of influence. Nonetheless, W Java has far fewer remains, possibly because Buddhism never spread to the W.

The art and architecture of both the Central and East Javanese periods is known as '**Classical**', because it was influenced by the art and architecture of India. The question which still preoccupies scholars is whether the Indian or the Indonesian element should be stressed. During the 5th to 7th centuries, Indian culture arrived in Southeast Asia along with Indian merchants (*vaisyas*) and religious men (*brahmanas*) – a period which is sometimes termed the 'Indianization' of Southeast Asia. In fact, before the term Southeast Asia was used to describe the region, it was called Further India or Greater India. The candi of Java appeared just at the time when

The building sequence in Java (late 6th-late 15th century)

The Central Javanese Period
The Early Javanese Style
(late 7th-9th century)

Dieng Plateau	c end 7th century
Candi Gunung Wukir	732
Candi Badut (East Java)	760
Gedung Songo	c early 8th century

The Early Classical Style
(late 8th-9th century)

Candi Borobudur	778-824
Candi Mendut	800
Candi Pawon	800
Candi Ngawen	?
Candi Kalasan	778-810
Candi Sewu	782-792
Candi Sari	835
Candi Plaosan	835
Candi Loro Jonggrang	835-856

The East Javanese Period
(11th-15th century)
The Early Classical Style
(11th-12th century)

Gua Gajah (Bali)	1000
Gunung Kawi (Bali)	late 11th century

The Later Classical Style
(1197-1470)

Candi Panataran	1197
Candi Kidal	1247
Candi Jago	1268
Candi Jawi	1292
Candi Singasari	early 13th century
Candi Tikus	1350
Candi Jedong	1385
Candi Plumbangan	1390
Candi Sukuh	1430
Candi Ceto	1470

NB These dates are approximate; inscriptions do give exact dates, but they only refer to one period of construction. Many monuments were built, redesigned and then rebuilt on a number of occasions spanning a long period.

Indian influence was strongest and there are stylistic links between the earliest candi of the Dieng Plateau and Gedung Songo and some N and S Indian structures. But, in the late 19th century, scholars began to question how far these buildings should be seen in terms of Indian influences, and how far in terms of local art and culture. In recent years, the tendancy has been to stress the 'local genius' rather than the imported Indian traditions.

The search for specifically Indonesian artistic styles was emphasized when Indonesia was searching for a wider national unity in the run up to independence. It is now argued that by the 8th and 9th centuries, Javanese artists had effectively created their own Javanese style of architecture and ornamentation. The Indonesian art historian Soekmono, for instance, writes that the candi is "an unquestionably Indonesian art form, based upon the Indian world of thought, nevertheless created and developed by Indonesians themselves in accordance with their own native potential and tradition".

CENTRAL JAVANESE PERIOD (730 AD-929 AD)

The **Central Javanese Period** embraces one of the most extraordinary periods of monument-building anywhere in the world. This was associated with the advent of the Sailendra Dynasty and the arrival of Buddhism. The building boom spanned two centuries from 730, during which Candi Kalasan, Candi Prambanan and Candi Borobudur were all built, along with numerous smaller temples. The temples were built of andesite, a porous volcanic stone found in abundance across Central Java. The period came to a spectacular end in 928 or 929 when Mt Merapi is thought to have erupted. Not only would such an eruption have affected agricultural production by coating the land in a deep layer of ash and lava, but it would doubtless

Balinese door guardian or *karang sae*, closely related to the *kalamakara* or *banaspati* of Java (adapted from Ramseyer, Urs (1986) *The art and* culture of Bali, OUP: Singapore).

have been taken as a sign that the gods were displeased, thus necessitating a move on religious grounds as well. From 928 until the 15th century there are no epigraphic – or carved – records from Central Java. This gives some indication of the scale of the disaster.

From the 10th century, the magnificent monuments of Central Java were left to be ravaged by earthquakes and storms, and consumed by the forest. When the Dutchman, Ijzerman discovered Borobudur's base in 1885 he found only "pityful ruins, dismantled by

The Javanese Candi

The *candis* of Java – the word has been variously translated as 'sepulchral monument' and 'ancient shrine' – are the equivalent of the cathedrals of Europe. They were places of worship or homage, and dedicated either to deified kings or to gods and spirits. An important difference though is that while cathedrals are designed to accommodate large numbers of the faithful, candis were exclusively the abodes of the gods. The gods descended to inhabit the monuments during special ceremonies attended by only a handful of priests. Drawing heavily upon Indian cosmology, candis were representations of the universe in microcosm, with Mt Meru, the cosmic mountain and abode of the gods, at the centre and surrounded by concentric circles of mountains, separated by oceans. The frequent presence of the lotus flower is linked to the belief that gods were born out of these flowers and then sat upon them.

A candi has three distinct elements: a square base, on which rests a single-celled, usually cuboid, shrine, and a stepped roof. This three-fold division mirrors the symbolic three-fold division of the universe into a lower Sphere of the Mortals (*bhurloka*) and an upper Sphere of the Gods (*swarloka*), between which is the Sphere of the Purified, where the objects of worship are placed (*bhuwarloka*). The base is larger than the shrine, so leaving room for the movement of people around the building. Under the shrine, a hole in the base contained the ashes of a dead king – perhaps explaining why they were called candis (= sepulchral monument).

The summit of the stepped roof is often surmounted with a stupa or *linga* shape. On the E side of the shrine, steps lead up to a portico which houses an icon. Numerous embellishments were added to this basic design: external niches, porticoes built out on all four walls, and steps added to the base to provide more wall space for decoration. Sculptural decoration also varied, but again there were common elements: for example the *kalamakara* and *kalanaga* motifs above doorways (known as *banaspati* in E Java), which acted as door guardians, warding-off evil spirits.

The names given to most candis in Java – a notable exception being Borobudur – are not original. They date from the late 19th or early 20th century and rarely indicate the king or deity to which a particular shrine is dedicated. The names are often linked to nearby towns or villages, and other geographical features.

bastardized descendants incapable of appreciation for the greatness of their ancestors". Central Javanese temples were coated with *vajiralepa*, literally 'plaster as indestructable as diamond'. This white plaster helped to prevent moisture from entering the porous building stone. The question that still has to be satisfactorily answered is whether the monuments were left bleached white like those in Burma, or whether they were subsequently painted.

EAST JAVANESE PERIOD (929 AD-1527 AD)

The **East Javanese Period** is associated with the dramatic move of the palace of King Sindok, along with his subjects, E in 929 to the fertile lands of E Java and the Brantas River. It seems that this massive migration followed the catastrophic eruption of Mt Merapi. The East Javanese Period spans just over six centuries and is dominated by the dynasties of Kediri (929-1222), Singasari (1222-1292) and Majapahit (1293-1527).

Javanese Candi

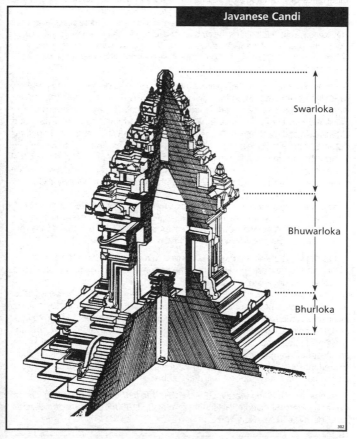

Swarloka

Bhuwarloka

Bhurloka

302

During the East Javanese Period, the plan of the temple complex gradually changed, so that the primary shrine no longer sat in the middle of the complex but was to be found towards the rear of the enclosure. Panataran is the greatest achievement of this age (see page 267). The movement away from symmetry led to the inclusion of different kinds of building within the compound, for instance, assembly halls. The deeply carved reliefs of Central Javanese monuments also made way for a much flatter style of decoration, more akin to the form of the *wayang* puppet. In general, ornamentation moved away from the sculptural

The Javanese Kraton

While the candi is the characteristic building of the ancient kingdoms of Java, the kraton is of more recent times. The links between the two are clear in the importance of cosmology, or orientation. Aart van Beek in his book *Life in the Javanese Kraton* writes of the kraton of Yogya and Solo that:

"Both Kraton face N in the direction of the life-giving volcanoes...these peaks represent the Kraton's sentinels. South is the ambivalent direction for the Javanese, for Ratu Loro Kidul, the Goddess of the Southern Ocean, lives there. It is an unsafe place, in a way a place of death... The N and S sections of the palaces are in some ways mirror images of each other".

The word *kraton*, sometimes spelt *keraton* or *karaton*, is derived from *ke-ratuan*, which literally means the abode of the monarch. This, in turn, links with the Sanskrit word *negara* which means both kingdom and capital. The word kraton is usually translated into English as 'palace'. The king and his family, court officials, court entertainers and royal servants – the *abdi dalem* – lived within its walls. Traditional clothing of the *abdi dalem* include a sarong, a kris and *iket* (cloth head-covering).

But the kraton was more than just a 'palace' in both a physical and a spiritual sense. It included squares, mosques, streets and houses, and also served as the spiritual centre of the kingdom. Every part of the complex is symbolically important. Again, van Beek writes:

"As clouds are heavy with the promise of rain towards the rainy season, so is the Kraton pregnant with meaning. It is a magical world to the Javanese, full of rules and codes of proper conduct. A sacredness and cosmic energy is attributed not only to the Sultan or Susuhunan but also the buildings and the weapons within them".

Just as the kings of Mataram were conceived to radiate power, so too is a kraton's sultan. And to be close to the walls of the kraton is to be close to the protective, life-enhancing powers of the sultan.

The most distinctive building within the kraton is the open-sided pavilion or *pendopo*. The name is probably derived from the Sanskrit word *mandapa* which means a pillared hall. The links between the pendopo and earlier candis are clear in the temples of the late East Javanese Period with their raised platforms and columns, such as those at Panataran. The pendopo is not just a feature of kraton architecture though; its essential elements can be seen repeated in the square pillared mosques of Indonesia, in the mosque pavilions or *surambi* of Sumatra and Kalimantan, and in the *bale* of Bali and Lombok.

Recommended reading: Aart van Beek (1990) *Life in the Javanese Kraton*, Oxford University Press: Singapore. Helen Ibbitson Jessup (1990) *Court arts of Indonesia*, Asia Society Galleries: New York.

order of Central Java, into extravagant fantasy. Many monuments were built at this time, but none on the scale or artistic magnificence of Borobudur or Prambanan. The most significant are Candi Kidal and Candi Singasari – more slender and steeper-roofed than their predecessors in Central Java. Candi Jago displays wayang-style reliefs while Candi Jawi shows the blend of Buddhism and Hinduism in having both Siva and Buddha displayed on the one shrine. It is often observed that although plastic arts suffered a decline during the East Javanese period, it represented the golden period of Javanese literature.

The last structures to be built during this period were the mountain-top candis of Sukuh and Ceto (see page 225), and a handful of lesser monuments on Mt Penanggungan, where the last inscription dates from 1512. These later candis resemble Balinese temples as they are designed as a series of stepped courtyards, with the holiest shrine at the highest level (so that the god could descend into the temple from his home on the mountain).

THE ISLAMIC PERIOD (1527-PRESENT)

The end of the Indianized period of monument building in Java during the 15th and 16th centuries coincided with the arrival of **Islam** from W India via Sumatra. Temple-building stopped, and mosque construction began. But this did not mean the rejection of local styles for imported ones. The early mosques had square floor plans like Javanese candis, and tiered roofs like the *pura* of Bali. They also had courtyards and split gates. The brick-built minaret at Kudus for example, mirrors the *kulkul* tower of Bali and even displays the Hindu-Buddhist *kalamakara* motif.

CULTURE

PEOPLE OF JAVA

Although it is common to hear people talk of the 'Javanese', Java supports a number of different cultural and linguistic groups of which the Javanese are only one, albeit the most numerous. The **Javanese** occupy the island's geographical and cultural heart, encompassing such royal cities as Surakarta and Yogyakarta, along with the important trading ports of the N coast. A broad distinction can be drawn between the courtly, refined and reserved *Kejawen* of the interior, and the more extrovert, 'coarse' and religiously orthodox inhabitants of the coastal *pasisir* areas. The Javanese are wet rice farmers *par excellence*, although population growth has meant that land holdings are growing smaller by the year – today they average 400 sq m per family (0.035 ha) – and many farmers have become landless agricultural labourers. The Javanese often have only one name, the upper classes choosing their own family name. This invariably ends in an 'o'.

The **Sundanese** are concentrated in the Priangan Highlands of W Java and share many of the same traditions as the Javanese. However, the great court culture of Central Java never made a great impact here. The land is less fertile, and villages tended to be more isolated and self-sufficient. The Sundanese are therefore less encumbered with complex rules of etiquette and behaviour. Like the Javanese of the N coast, they are orthodox Muslims. Sundanese family names commonly end in an 'a'.

Among Java's patchwork of peoples are the **Madurese**, inhabitants of the island of Madura. During the Dutch period the Madurese made up a disproportionate share of the colonial army and have a reputation as fierce warriors. Also in E Java, the Hindu **Tenggerese** are thought to be descended from the Majapahit refugees who fled Central Java in the 10th century, following the eruption of Mt Merapi. Finally, the enigmatic **Badui** of W Java live in 35 isolated villages nr Rangkasbitung. Outsiders are expressly excluded from the remote 'inner' Badui villages, although the 'outer' communities permit some limited contact.

ISLAM IN JAVA

Java is a Muslim society: 90% of its population of over 100 million are nominal Muslims. However, as Clifford Geertz pointed out in his brilliant book *The religion of Java* (1960), less than half of this 90% can be viewed as Muslim in the sense that Islam is central and paramount to their beliefs. These people Geertz termed *santri*. The remainder he called the *abangan*: people for whom Islam is intertwined with pre-Islamic religions and beliefs. Peacock writes of the Javanese world that it is "composed of spiritual energies contained in forms and images, such as magically potent swords, sacred shrines, spirits, deities, teachers and rulers; the Javanese syncretistic world is what Weber termed a 'garden of magic' – indeed, animist jungle". The roots of this mixture can be traced back to the reign of the great Majapahit King Agung (1613-1645), a devout Muslim. He had the Islamic title of sultan, but at the same time bore the Hindu-Javanese title of *susuhunan*. The calendar Agung introduced in 1633 numbered its years according to the Hindu Shaka Era (1 Shaka = 78 AD), but borrowed from the Islamic system adopting a lunar year, in place of the Hindu solar one.

Most Javanese Muslims maintain that the mysticism and spirituality so evident in Java – though a departure from the Prophet Mohammad's original teachings – are nonetheless derived from Islamic traditions. Orthodox Islam is based upon the *shariah* – Islamic law – together with the Koran and the Hadith (the sayings, practices and rites not contained in the Koran) (see page 52). A **Sufi** is a Muslim who follows the mystical path, or secret doctrine. Sufism aims to free the soul from earthly concerns, but the doctrine – which is believed to be the key to salvation – is kept secret from the masses because it is often in conflict with orthodox Islam and therefore should only be revealed to those able to appreciate its subtleties. Through history, the Sufis have been in periodic conflict with the scholars of orthodox Islam or *Ulama*. The former taught the path of mysticism, the latter the path of orthodoxy.

The introduction of Islam to Java and the nine Walis

One of the most significant processes in Indonesian history was the spread of Islam. When and how it occurred are not clear. Muslim traders had, presumably, been visiting Java and other islands in the archipelago from early in the second millennium and some had probably married local women and settled. When Marco Polo's expedition stopped in Sumatra in 1292 on its return from China, he recorded that the town of Perlak was Muslim. But it was not until the 14th century that Islam appears to have spread from Trengganu on the Malay Peninsula, to Sumatra and from there to Java. It is assumed that Islam first made an impact on the N coast, and then diffused to the interior, which was Hindu. The discovery of Muslim graves at Trowulan, dated 1368-1369, indicates that there were Muslims of considerable prestige living there, even when the Hindu Majapahit Empire was at its height. But Indonesians have their own accounts of the spread of Islam. They say Islam arrived by magic, not diffusion. In his history of Indonesia, Riklefs relates one such tale:

"In this story, the Caliph of Mecca hears of the existence of Samudra and decides to send a ship there in fulfilment of a prophesy of the Prophet Muhammed that there would one day be a great city in the East called Samudra, which would produce many saints. The ship's captain, Shaikh Ismail, stops en route in India to pick up a Sultan who has stepped down from his throne to become a holy man. The ruler of Samudra, Merah Silau, has a dream in which the Prophet appears to him, magically transfers knowledge of Islam to him by spitting in his mouth, and gives him the title Sultan Malik as-Salih.

The nine walis of Java

🐾 The title *wali* is an Arabic word meaning saint, while *Sunan* is a Javanese title, probably derived from the word *suhun* meaning 'honoured'. The nine walis were of mixed origin. Some were clearly non-Javanese, while at least three (Sunan Giri, Sunan Bonang and Sunan Walilanang) are thought to have studied Islam in Melaka before arriving in Java. The *Babad Tanah Jawi* recounts numerous stories about the lives of the nine walis and how they came to embrace Islam and arrive in Java. Many involve miraculous conversions. For example, Sunan Kalijaga – at that time named Said (an Arabic name) – is said to have lost at gambling while working for the Majapahit court and became a highway robber. One day he accosted another future wali named Sunan Bonang who convinced Said not to rob him but to wait for the next traveller who would appear wearing blue with a red hibiscus flower behind his ear. Three days later, a man dressed as Sunan Bonang described came along the path and Said duly pounced on him. The man in blue was, of course, really Sunan Bonang in disguise, who quickly turned himself into four people. Understandably, Said was taken aback by this turn of events, renounced his evil ways, embraced Islam and the life of an ascetic, became a wali, and married one of Sunan Gunung Jati's daughters.

Historians find it difficult to hold much store by these legends. There is disagreement over who should be counted a wali, how many there actually were (nine is a significant number to the Javanese and it may have been for this reason that it has become accepted that there were nine walis), or what their origins were as different legends tell of different origins – Chinese, Indonesian, Indian and Arabian. However, whatever their disagreements, all the legends appear to agree that the walis were travelling preacher-teachers. This links them with the trading network which first brought Islam to Java.

Upon awakening, the new Sultan discovers that he can read the Qur'an although he has never been instructed and that he has been magically circumcized."

The influential manuscripts that comprise the *Babad Tanah Jawi* or 'History of the Land of Java' ascribe the conversion of Java to Islam to the work of nine saints – or *wali sanga*. Unfortunately, the manuscripts are not agreed on who the nine wali were, and whether there might not have been more. Usually, the nine are listed as: Sunan Ngampel-Denta, Sunan Kudus, Sunan Murya, Sunan Bonang, Sunan Giri, Sunan Kalijaga, Sunan Siti-jenar, Sunan Gunung Jati, and Sunan Walilanang. Sometimes a tenth wali, Sunan Bayat, is also listed. Today the graves of the nine walis, to be found in towns along the N coast of Java, are important pilgrimage centres for Indonesians.

But these stories of the nine wali do not explain why Islam suddenly took hold in Indonesia in the 14th century. The accepted view used to be that Islam, as an egalitarian and populist faith, was simply more attractive than the corrupt Hindu-Buddhist religion that existed at the time. But some historians maintain that Islam seems to have been imposed from above, and not embraced from below. Others believe Sufism was instrumental, as it, like Hindu-Buddhism, was a mystical faith and could compete on equal terms. That said, there is little evidence to support the notion that large numbers of Sufis were actively proselytising across the country at the time. Another possibility is that Muslim traders were responsible for introducing Islam, and spreading it through the island.

DANCE, DRAMA AND MUSIC

The wayang: shadow puppet theatre

Wayang means 'shadow', and the art form is best translated as 'shadow theatre' or 'shadow play'. Some people believe that the wayang is Indian in origin, pointing to the fact that most of the characters are from Indian epic tales such as the Ramayana and Mahabharata. Others maintain that wayang was established before the Indianisation of Java and Sumatra and that the art form stems from ancient Malayo-Polynesian culture. They say the puppets represented ancestral spirits, who were summoned to solve the problems of the living. It was only later that the medium was used to teach Indian spiritual values through such Hindu epic stories as the Ramayana and Mahabharata (see page 56).

Wayang is possibly first hinted at in two royal charters dated 840 and 907 which mention officials who supervised musicians and performers, and talk of a play called *mawayang*. But historians are dubious whether the inscriptions refer to wayang at all. The first certain reference – by which time it was already a well established art form in Java – is in an 11th century poem, *The Meditation of Ardjuna*, composed by the court poet of King Airlangga (1020-1049):

"There are people who weep, are sad and aroused watching the puppets, though they know they are merely carved pieces of leather manipulated and made to speak. These people are like men, thirsting for sensual pleasures, who live in a world of illusion; they do not realize the magic hallucinations they see are not real".

An important development in wayang, was the introduction of articulated arms in 1630 at the court of Mataram, which in turn led to further changes in the plays themselves. Most of the classic repertoire, which puppet masters – or *dalang* – are expected to absorb dates from this period.

There are various forms of wayang, and not all are 'shadow' theatre in the true sense. *Wayang purwa* or *wayang kulit* is the original shadow play and is performed using flat puppets, chiselled out of leather, and is associated with the Javanese and Balinese. *Wayang golek* uses three dimensional cloth and wood puppets and is a Sundanese adaptation of wayang

---

Making a wayang kulit puppet

Wayang kulit puppets are made of buffalo hide, preferably taken from a female animal of about 4 years of age. The skin is dried and scraped, and then left to mature for as long as 10 years to achieve the stiffness required for carving. After carving, the puppet is painted in traditional pigments. In carving the puppet, the artist is constrained by convention. The excellence of the puppet is judged according to the fineness of chisel-work and the subtlety of painting. If the puppet is well made it may have *guna* – a magical quality which is supposed to make the audience suspend its disbelief during the performance. Puppets accumulate *guna* with age; this is why old puppets are preferred to new ones.

Each major character has a particular iconography, and even the angle of the head and the slant of the eyes and mouth are important in determining the character. Some puppets may be called on to perform a number of minor parts, but in the main a knowledgeable wayang-goer will be able to recognise each character immediately.

The *cempurit* or rods used to manipulate the puppet are made of buffalo horn while the studs used to attach the limbs are made of metal, bone or bamboo. Court puppets might even be made of gold, studded with precious stones.

kulit. *Wayang berber* is enacted using painted paper or cloth scrolls which are unrolled while the narrator chants the story. *Wayang topeng* is performed by masked, live actors, while *wayang wong* or *wayang orang* uses maskless live actors.

The commonest and oldest form of wayang is the *purwa* or *kulit*. These are finely carved and painted leather, 2-dimensional puppets, jointed at the elbows and shoulders and manipulated using horn rods. In order to enact the entire repertoire of 179 plays, 200 puppets are

Semar: the most sacred of all the puppets.

Kresna: a King and spiritual guide of Ajuna (a warrior and hero in the Pandawa cycle of plays).

needed. A single performance can last as long as 9 hrs. The plays have various origins. Some are animistic, featuring, for example, the Rice Goddess, Dewi Sri. Others are adapted from the epic litera- ture; these are known as *pondok* or 'trunk' tales and include the Ramayana. Others have been developed over the years by

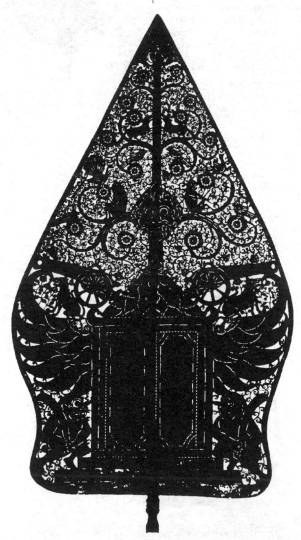

Gunungan: the tree of life.

influential puppet masters. They feature heroic deeds, romantic encounters, court intrigues, bloody battles, and mystical observations, and are known as *carangan* or 'branch' tales.

The *gunungan* or 'Tree of Life', is an important element of wayang theatre. It represents all aspects of life, and is always the same in design: shaped like a stupa, the tree has painted red flames on one side and a complex design on the other (this is the side which faces the audience). At the base of the tree are a pair of closed doors, flanked by two fierce demons or *yaksas*. Above the demons are two garudas and within the branches of the tree there are monkeys, snakes and two animals – usually an ox and a tiger. The gunungan is placed in the middle of the screen at the beginning and end of the performance – and sometimes between major scene changes. During the performance it stands at one side, and flutters across the screen to indicate minor scene changes.

Traditionally, performances were requested by individuals to celebrate particular occasions – for example the seventh month of pregnancy (*tingkep*) – or to accompany village festivities. Admission was free, as the individual commissioning the performance would meet the costs. Of course, this has changed now and tourists invariably have to pay an entrance charge.

Javanese puppets are characteristically highly stylized, with long necks, very long arms and extended shoulders. To the wayang cognoscenti, every nuance of the puppet is significant. It tells, so to speak, a tale. There are 15 eye shapes, 11 mouths and 13 nose shapes for example. Heroes are required to conform to the Javanese physical ideal. They must be slender, with long, elegant noses, down cast eyes (denoting humility and restraint) and balanced proportions. Major characters like Arjuna in the Mahabharata have numerous – more than 10 – puppet shapes, deployed according to the scene being enacted.

Traditionally, the shadows of the puppets were reflected onto a white cotton cloth stretched across a wooden frame using the light from a bronze coconut oil lamp. Today, electric light is more common – a change which, in many people's minds, has meant the unfortunate substitution of the flickering, mysterious shadows of the oil lamp, with the constant harsh light of the electric bulb. There are both day and night wayang performances. The latter, for obvious reasons, are the most dramatic, although the former are regarded as artistically superior.

The audience sits on both sides of the screen. Those sitting with the puppet master see a puppet play; those on the far side, out of view of the puppet master and the accompanying gamelan orchestra, see a shadow play. It is possible that in the past, the audience was segregated according to sex: men on the dalang's side of the screen, women on the shadow side.

The puppet master or *dalang*, is a consecrated priest. The word is said to be derived from *galang*, meaning bright or clear, the implication being that the dalang makes the sacred texts understandable. He sits on a plinth, an arm's length away from the cloth screen. From this position he manipulates the puppets, while also narrating the story. Although any male can become a dalang, it is usual for sons to follow their fathers into the profession. The dalang is the key to a successful performance: he must be multi-skilled, have strength and stamina, be able to manipulate numerous puppets simultaneously, narrate the story, and give the lead to the accompanying gamelan orchestra. No wonder that an adept dalang is a man with considerable status.

Wayang topeng: masked dance

The masked dance either evolved from initiation rites in which a masked man indicated the ideal human state, or from the story of the Hindu god, Vishnu. In this story, Vishnu on seeing the world to be an evil place descended from the heavens to dance and try to change it by a release of spiritual energy. To preserve his anonymity, Vishnu danced disguised by a mask. We know from Tomé Pires' account of his visit to Java in the early 16th century, that wayang topeng dances were already being performed on the N coast. This seems to indicate that far from being a court innovation of the interior – as previously believed – it was a popular coastal form of entertainment.

Nonetheless, the carving of topeng has always been regarded as a suitable way for royalty to occupy their time. Princes have become skilled artists as well as dancers. The kraton in Surakarta has a particularly fine collection of topeng masks (see page 225). Most wayang topeng performances are based on the *Ramayana* and *Mahabharata*. However, of the repertoire of dances, perhaps the most ritually important is the Panji dance based on *The Adventures of Prince Panji*, a tale which dates from the Majapahit period and which has produced – in the character of Prince Panji – the archetypal Javanese hero along with Arjuna in the *Mahabharata* and Rama in the *Ramayana*. The Panji dance consists of four parts, personifying the spirituality and worldliness of men. A well-performed Panji is regarded as being among the most graceful of dances. Unfortunately, full-length topeng performances are rare today, a fact which may well be linked to the spread of Islam.

Wayang wong and the Ramayana ballet

Wayang wong is the grandest form of dance drama performed on Java. It is thought to post-date wayang kulit, although it shares many of the shadow puppet theatre's characteristics. It draws its repertoire of stories primarily from the Indian epics, the play is accompanied by the music of the gamelan orchestra, and the aesthetic is essentially the same as that of wayang kulit. The principal difference

is that actors, often masked, play the characters, not puppets – although the movements of the actors often imitate puppets.

Like many performing arts in Java, wayang wong was intimately linked to the kratons of Yogyakarta and Surakarta and reached its apogee during the 18th century. The costs of staging a performance were so great that only a sultan could raise the necessary funds, making it a strictly élite affair. In Yogya only men performed wayang wong; in Surakarta, though, women played the female roles. The movements are highly stylized; females dance slowly, in a restrained manner, rarely allowing their feet to leave the floor; men – especially those playing powerful figures – adopt an open-legged position and raise their legs high off the floor to indicate their strength and masculinity.

At the end of the 19th century, a variant of wayang wong known as **wayang orang**, emerged. This was an attempt to popularize the dance-drama and bring it to a wider audience. But perhaps the dance most likely to be seen by tourists is the **sendratari**, better known today as the **Ramayana ballet**. This dance was first performed in 1961 and is now staged most notably at Prambanan, outside Yogyakarta (see page 221). The open-air 'ballet' is held once a year and is mounted on an epic scale, with large numbers of actors playing four episodes of the Ramayana over 4 days: namely, the abduction of Sita, Hanuman's mission to Lanka, the conquest of Lanka, and the fall of Ravana.

Court dances

Various court dances evolved in the kratons of Java of which the most important are *bedhaya* and *serimpi*. Both are subdued dances performed by groups of women to the accompaniment of gamelan music and singing. Jukka Miettinen in her book *Classical dance and theatre in South-East Asia* describes the bedhaya as "extremely slow and solemn", writing that the "face is kept strictly expressionless, and the eyes look down, while the dancers undulate to the *gamelan* music in a continuous flow of movement like underwater plants". The serimpi dance is similarly slow and languid, but is performed by only four dancers who are presumed to represent both the four cardinal points and the four elements (fire, water, earth and air). Although some private dance academies teach these court dances, the best place to see them performed is at the kratons in Yogyakarta and Surakarta (Solo).

Music

The **angklung** is a traditional and ancient Javanese instrument used to accompany story-telling and marching. It probably originated in W Java, although it is used throughout Java and Bali (see box, page 162).

The **gamelan orchestra** is the most important assemblage of musical instruments in Indonesia. It is essential to the performance of wayang plays, accompanies celebrations at the royal kratons, and is inextricably bound-up in ceremonies at Balinese temples. The gamelan is a Javanese and Balinese musical form, although there are important differences between the music of the two islands.

Gamelan orchestras vary according to the context in which they are being played. However, it is usual to have large hanging gongs or *gong*, medium-sized hanging gongs or *kempul*, inverted bronze bowls – either single (*ketuk*) or grouped in fives (*kenong*) – bronze xylophones constructed of heavy bars (*saron*) or lighter hanging bars (*gender*), a wooden xylophone or *gambang*, finger drums or *kendang*, a zither or *celempung*, and a 2-stringed fiddle or *rebab*. Many of the instruments are made of bronze, and most are struck like percussion instruments. The only remaining workshops making these instruments are to be found in Bogor and Yogyakarta.

If there is more than one example of a particular instrument, then these are usually tuned to connecting or overlapping octaves, giving the orchestra a range of six or seven octaves. Each octave is divided into either five (*slendro*) or seven (*pelog*) notes. This means that instruments are usually designed for one or other scale. The most important members of a gamelan are the kendang drummer, who sets the tempo, and the lead gender player. The latter plays the *gender barung* and cues the other members of the orchestra.

TEXTILES

Batik

Batik is the characteristic textile patterning technique of Java and Madura, and to a lesser degree, Bali, Lombok and Central Sulawesi. It is also prominent on the Malay Peninsula. Like *ikat* (see page 408), it is a method of **resist-dyeing**. But in this instance, the resist – beeswax – is applied to the woven cloth rather than to the yarn. The word batik may be derived from the Malay word *tik*, meaning to 'drip'. It is believed that batik may have replaced

A cockerel motif printed with a *cap* metal stamp, Central Java.
Adapted from: Gillow, John (1992) Traditional Indonesian textiles, Thames & Hudson: London.

A batik primer

There are two principal batik-producing areas in Java, each with its own distinctive designs: N coast and Central Java. However, within this crude division there are countless variations:

Central Java The batik of Central Java is characterized by the use of **repeated geometric motifs**, today invariably produced using a *cap* or stamp. Rouffaer counted 3,000 named motifs in the early 20th century. The introduction and spread of Islam from the 12th-16th centuries led to a change from portraying living creatures realistically, to their abstraction into geometric designs. By creating people and animals realistically, the artist was seen to be trying to compete with God. Brown, black and blue are the traditional colours and patterns are very dense with an absence of straight lines and empty areas. There are three principle designs: *ceplokkan* (inter-linking squares, diamonds and other shapes), *garis miring* (geometric shapes which run diagonally across the cloth) and *semen* (more flowing, with tendrils linking the design).

In Central Java, the art of batik is linked with the *priyayi* gentry class who have traditionally viewed it as one of the 'high' arts. Certain motifs were reserved for the sole use of sultans, and people of high rank. The garuda motif for example, was reserved for the crown prince and his consort. Today, no such restrictions exist.

North coast Because of the trading tradition of the N coast, this part of Java has tended to assimilate foreign cultural influences. From the 17th century, Chinese from Fukien province began to settle along the N coast, and by the late 19th century they had cornered the trade in cambric cloth and dominated the batik industry. As a result, batik produced along the N coast shows **Chinese influences**. It is also notable that whereas most batik designs in Central Java were court-inspired, those from the N coast – with the exception of Cirebon – were commercial in origin. In general, designs are less geometric and fussier than those of Central Java; colours are brighter and realistic designs more common. Centres include:

Indramayu: where the *luk cuan* bird – an adaptation of the Chinese phoenix – is a common motif, colours are dull, and the use of linking tendrils is widespread.

Cirebon: the **most distinctive designs** in Java originate from Cirebon, and many are Chinese in inspiration. Palaces, gardens, mountains and fantastic animals are drawn as if on a landscape, making the cloth suitable for wall hanging. The renowned cloud designs (*megamendung* and *wadasan*), produced for the court, died out some time ago but have now been resuscitated. Again, they are Chinese in inspiration (see page 175).

Pekalongan: more batik is produced here than anywhere else in Java. Chinese influence is clear in the use of the *luk cuan* and other motifs. Pekalongan batik also – and unusually – shows Dutch influence, for example in the floral bouquets. Fortunately, just at the time that imported printed cloth and stamped batik was pushing hand-drawn Pekalongan batik into extinction, a group of Dutch women began to promote and support this traditional industry. At this time batik artists also began to sign their works – again a European influence. **Very fine designs, minutely detailed**, often with a profusion of dots (known as *citcik*) are characteristic of Pekalongan cloth.

Batik from other parts of Indonesia

Toraja, Sulawesi: the Torajans produce simple batik known as *sarita*, using large motifs similar to those carved on Torajan houses and rice barns. Rarely produced today, sarita was worn as a headdress by Torajan warriors. The sarita is viewed as magical and can bring good fortune to its owner.

tattooing as a mark of status. In Eastern Indonesia, the common word for tattoo and batik is the same.

Traditionally, the **wax was painted onto the woven cloth** using a *canting* (pronounced 'janting'), a small copper cup with a spout, mounted on a bamboo handle. The cup is filled with melted wax, which flows from the spout like ink from a fountain pen – although the canting never touches the surface of the cloth. In areas such as the town of Pekalongan where batik is finely detailed, waxers are sometimes taught meditation and deep-breathing exercises to help soothe the mind. Batik artists have a number of canting with various widths of spout, some even with several spouts, to give varied thicknesses of line and differences of effect.

The canting was probably invented in Java in the 12th century, whereupon it replaced the crude painting stick, enabling far more complex designs to be produced. Inscriptions from this period refer to *tulis warna*, literally 'drawing in colour', which was probably some sort of resist dyeing technique similar, but ancestral, to batik. Cloth produced using a canting should be labelled *tulis* (literally, to write) and one sarong length can take from 1 to 6 months to complete. Reflecting the skill and artistry required to produce such batik, waxers used to be called *lukis* or painters. Drawing the design with a canting is a laborious process and has largely been replaced by stamping.

In the mid-19th century, **the 'modern' batik industry** was born with the invention of the *cap* (pronounced 'jap') – a copper, sometimes a wooden, stamp. This is dipped in wax, and then pressed onto the cloth. The cap revolutionized batik production. As Wanda Warming and Michael Gaworski say in their book *The world of Indonesian textiles* "...it took a small cottage industry, a fine art, an expression of Javanese sensibilities, and a hobby for aristocratic women, and turned it into a real commercial enterprise". With the invention of the cap, so there

evolved a parallel cap-making industry. Old copper stamps have become collectors' pieces, and now are only produced in large numbers in the towns of Solo, Pekalongan and, to a lesser extent, in Yogyakarta. Not only did the cap speed-up production, it also took the artistry out of waxing: waxers merely stamp the design onto the cloth. Some designs are produced using both the canting and the cap – such cloth is called *combinasi*.

Two types of wax are often used in the batik process. *Klowong* is a light and brittle wax that is used for the first stamping only, on both sides of the cloth. *Tembok* is darker and more durable, and needs to survive numerous washings, rewaxings and dyeings. If it cracks, then dye will reach the cloth. The marbled effect that is often viewed by visitors as characteristic of batik is due to this cracking of the tembok – Javanese regard such work as inferior.

Unlike ikat where women perform all the stages of cloth production, in the case of batik they usually only draw the design, while men dye the waxed cloth. In recent years, male batik artists, many of whom are based around Yogya, have taken to both waxing and dyeing. At the same time, there has been a decline in home-produced batik and an expansion in the number of small workshops and factories. Like weaving in many societies, the ability to produce finely-worked batik was expected of well-bred Javanese girls. Far fewer women make their own batik today, but they still appreciate and recognize well-made and well-designed cloth, and batiks worn at weddings and other functions are carefully, though surreptitiously, scrutinized by the guests.

Distinguishing hand-drawn from stamped batik It can be hard differentiating drawn (*tulis*) and stamped (*cap*) batik, particularly in the case of the repetitious geometric designs of Central Java. Look for irregular lines and examine repetitive motifs like flowers carefully – stamped batik will show no variation.

On poorly-executed stamped cloth, there may be a line at the point where two stamps have been imperfectly aligned. **NB** There is also machine printed cloth with traditional batik designs: this can be identified by the clear design and colour on one side only; batik, whether drawn or printed, will have the design clearly revealed on both sides of the fabric.

Books on Textiles Hitchcock, Michael (1985) *Indonesian textile techniques*, Shire Ethnography: Aylesbury, UK. Hitchcock, Michael (1991) *Indonesian textiles*, British Museum Press: London. Warming, Wanda and Gaworski, Michael (1981) *The world of Indonesian textiles*, Serindia: London.

Jakarta

JAKARTA is officially named the Special Capital Region of Jakarta or in Indonesian, *Dearah Khusus Ibukota*. Hence the prefix, DKI Jakarta. With a population of over 9 million, it is the centre of commerce and communications, of manufacturing activity and consumption, of research and publishing. It has the highest per capita income and the greatest concentration of rupiah billionaires. Just as "cream rises to the top of the milk" economist Lance Castles writes, so "surpluses from whatever industries are currently flourishing [in Indonesia] tend to gravitate to the metropolis".

DKI Jakarta is administered as a province, yet covers a meagre 656 sq km (about the same area as Singapore) – making it the smallest in the country. During the last half century its population has grown spectacularly. In 1942 the city had 563,000 inhabitants; in the next 10 years this more than doubled and by the census of 1971 had reached 4,579,000. In the most recent census in 1990, a figure of 8,254,000 was recorded. In other words, over the space of just 48 years, the population of Jakarta has increased 15-fold – a far higher rate than the country as a whole. Its economic attractions have effectively sucked people in from other parts of Java and the Outer Islands. It is also true that census figures considerably understate the actual numbers of people living and working in the city, as they do not account for so-called 'circular migrants' – those people who still 'live' in the countryside, but who spend most of the year sojourning in the capital.

Over the years, Jakarta has grown from its original position at the mouth of the Ciliwung River, on the Java Sea, and sprawled inland. Jakarta has, in effect, outgrown its borders. The town of Bogor, for example, 1-hr drive to the S, acts as a

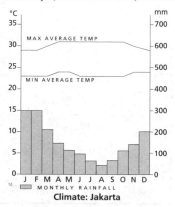

Climate: Jakarta

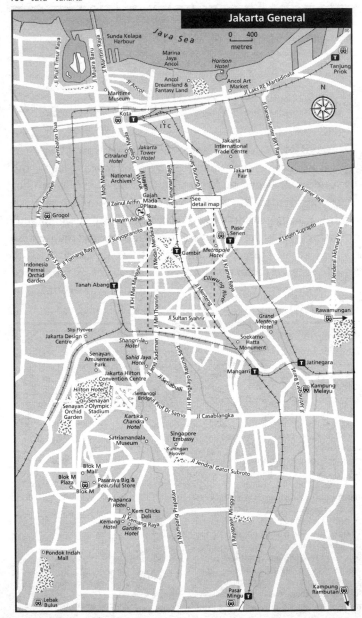

Jakarta General

0   400
metres

Jakarta highlights

Museums and galleries: the *National Museum* (see page 116) is one of the most impressive museums in Southeast Asia. Other museums include the *Fatahillah Museum* (see page 112), the *Wayang Museum* (see page 112), the *Textile Museum* (see page 119) and the private *Adam Malik Museum* (see page 120).

Religious sights: the *Istiqlal Mosque* (see page 117) is the largest mosque in Southeast Asia.

Areas of historical interest: *Kota*, the core of old Batavia (see page 110), and the mosque and ruined fortress at *Banten*, 100 km W of Jakarta (see page 138).

Sights of natural interest: day excursions to the beaches, swimming and snorkelling at *Pulau Seribu* (see page 136) and to the renowned *Bogor Botanical Gardens* (see page 146).

Shopping areas: *Jalan Surabaya flea market* for 'antiques' (see page 129) and *Blok M* for anything else (see page 130).

Culture and performance: the *Taman Mini-Indonesia* (see page 120) and the *Taman Ismail Marzuki* (see page 128).

dormitory town for Jakarta. For this reason, planning agencies and economists now talk of Jabotabek – an area which encompasses Jakarta, along with the three W Java *kabupaten* (or regencies) of Bogor, Tangerang and Bekasi, and the municipality of Bogor.

A HISTORY OF JAKARTA

FROM TRADING POST TO QUEEN OF THE EAST, 16TH-18TH CENTURY

Evidence suggests that there was a Hindu settlement on the site of modern-day Jakarta as early as the 5th century. By the 12th century, Sunda Kelapa, the name of the old harbour of Jakarta, was already flourishing as a port serving the Sundanese Kingdom of Pajajaran, S of Bogor. In 1513, the first Portuguese mariners arrived from Melaka (in Malaysia) in search of spices. No trading-post was established during this first visit, but a few years later they returned bearing gifts for the King of Sunda. In 1522 a Treaty of Friendship was concluded, and the Portuguese were given permission to erect a godown.

The proud and independent Hindu Sundanese probably agreed to such a treaty because they felt threatened by the encroaching Muslims from the powerful N coast sultanate of Demak. However this alliance failed to deter the aggressive instincts of the Muslim leader, Fatahillah. He attacked and took Sunda Kelapa in 1527, making it a vassal state of Demak, and renamed the town **Jayakarta**, meaning 'Complete Victory'. The date of the victory – 22 Jun – is still celebrated annually as the anniversary of Jakarta's founding.

By the end of the 16th century, the Dutch had superseded the Portuguese in their race to dominate the lucrative trade in spices centred on the E Indonesian islands of the Moluccas or Maluku (see page 795). Appreciating the commercial attractions of the large harbour at Sunda Kelapa, the Dutch began to shift their operations from Banten (see page 138), and in 1610 they were given permission by Prince Fatahillah to build a godown on the E bank of the Ciliwung River. By 1618 they had abused their agreement by converting the godown into a fort. At the same time, the English were also busy jostling for position and Prince Fatahillah gave them permission to build a lodge, in the hope of keeping the increasingly powerful Dutch at bay. In spite of limited English support, it was all to no avail. In

The Chinese of Java and Jakarta

🐾 From as early as the 17th century, the Chinese formed an indispensable element of Jakarta's population. But it was not until the middle of the 18th century that large numbers of Chinese began to arrive in the city, driven out of S China by famine and economic hardship, and attracted by the lure of employment.

Unfortunately, many of the immigrants failed to secure work and were seen as a nuisance by the VOC. The Dutch attempted to control the situation by deporting unemployed Chinese to Ceylon, but rumours spread that deportees were being dumped in the Java Sea. The Chinese formed gangs and attacked Dutch outposts, resulting in a government search for arms in all Chinese homes in 1740. When the search began, shots were heard, a fire broke out and bedlam ensued. Chinese were attacked, robbed and killed by Dutch citizens, soldiers and sailors. Five hundred who were being held prisoner in the City Hall were slaughtered after the bailiff gave the order for them all to be killed. It is estimated that in all between 5,000 and 10,000 Chinese were massacred. During the riot, much of the old city was destroyed. Batavia never really recovered from this incident, not so much because the fabric of the city had been destroyed, but because the economic heart – the Chinese – had been decimated.

This incident did not prevent the Chinese population of Jakarta achieving great economic power – although it did presage an even more horrific massacre of Chinese in 1965 (see box, page 67). By the 19th century, there were already the beginnings of a deep-seated antipathy towards the Chinese on the part of the indigenous Javanese population. But even then, the numbers of Chinese were hardly large: in 1870, Chinese in the Indies numbered only 250,000. These were known as *peranakan* – literally 'half-caste' – Chinese men intermarried and, to a large degree, assimilated into Javanese society. Many lost their ability to read, write, or even speak Chinese. Their position in society was often as middlemen, marketing rice, selling fertilizers, and providing credit to farmers. However, this gradual process of assimilation was not to last. The increasing nationalism of mainland China broke upon the shores of the Indonesian archipelago, making the *peranakan* conscious of their roots.

Peranakan families began to enrol their children into Chinese language schools, and to verse them in the culture and ideals of their homeland. But far more important than this change of heart, was the influx of large numbers of Chinese *totok* attracted to the Indies by the economic opportunities to be found there. Importantly, the men were also accompanied by large numbers of *totok* women, so that pure Chinese families could be formed. Peranakan Chinese found themselves alienated from Dutch, Javanese and Chinese society. As was said of one Peranakan, Kapitein Cina Tan Jin Sing of Yogya in 1813: *Cina wurung, Londa durung, Jawa Tanggung* – "No longer a Chinese, not yet a Dutchman, a half-baked Javanese." In the 1930s the Partai Tionghoa Indonesia (Chinese Indonesian Party) was formed to represent the interests of the Chinese in the country, who by that time numbered about 1,250,000, or 2% of the total population of Indonesia.

Since independence, the Chinese have found themselves facing government-sanctioned discrimination – at least until very recently. The Chinese language was outlawed in the 1960s, the use of Chinese characters in public made illegal at the same time (the ban was only lifted in Aug 1994), and the position of Chinese businessmen sometimes made very difficult.

1619, a Dutch fleet arrived led by Jan Pieterszoon Coen who led an attack on the town, and razed it to the ground. A new town, renamed **Batavia**, was built and became the property of the Dutch East India Company (or VOC), with Coen as its first governor-general. Under Dutch rule, Batavia became a thriving centre for trade and the most powerful city in the archipelago.

The Javanese kingdoms of Banten and Mataram (based near Yogyakarta and Surakarta) did try to dislodge the Dutch – unsuccessfully. Sultan Agung attacked the town in 1628, and again in 1629; each time the forces of the VOC prevailed. But it would be wrong to think of the Dutch 'ruling' Java during these early decades. The VOC was only interested in Batavia as a port and base from which to manage the spice trade. The city was a bustling centre of enterprise, but there was no attempt at territorial expansion. It was not until the end of the 17th century, as Mataram and the other sultanates went into terminal decline, that the VOC began to expand and annex these former kingdoms. By 1757, Banten, and the sultans of Mataram were vassals of the VOC based at Batavia, a city which had become known by then in Europe as the 'Queen of the East'.

FROM HEALTH HAZARD TO CAPITAL CITY, 18TH-20TH CENTURY

During the 18th century, Batavia developed a reputation as the unhealthiest town in the East – a White Man's graveyard. When designing the city, the Dutch had made the mistake of attempting to recreate Holland, digging canals and ditches in an already swampy area surrounded by marshland and jungle. The effect, though, was to create – to use a word popular at the time – a noxious 'miasma'. The canals were often stagnant and quickly became open sewers – there was scarcely a toilet in the city – choked with rotting carcasses, human 'ordure', slime and filth: perfect conditions for the spread of disease, notably cholera and malaria.

The mortality rate was stunningly high; in 1806 the English traveller Sir John Barrows concluded, from studying a register of deaths, that *every* soldier sent out to Batavia had 'perished there'; a posting to the city was, in effect, a death sentence. The geographer Victor Savage in his book *Western impressions of nature and landscape in Southeast Asia* writes that Batavia was "in the western sphere, the most notoriously insalubrious place in Southeast Asia, and possibly the world".

At the beginning of the 19th century, under the leadership of Governor-General Daendels (1808-1810), a clean-up operation was undertaken. Canals were filled in, rivers were cleared and became free-flowing, and swamps were drained and brought under cultivation. Paddy fields close to the city were abandoned, and a new Batavia was built on a higher elevation, 4 km from the old city. These efforts did much to control disease and improve the health of the population.

When the Napoleonic Wars in Europe resulted in the annexation of Holland by the French, the British, led by Thomas Stamford Raffles, invaded Java in 1811 and took control of the island (see page 87). Raffles' administration only lasted until 1816, when he was forced to hand control back to the Dutch. He left Java to establish Singapore, which eventually eclipsed Batavia as the most important regional trading centre. From 1820 through to the early part of the 20th century, Batavia flourished and once again earned itself another glowing title – this time the 'Pearl of the Orient'.

Certainly, improved sanitation and the construction of wide boulevards and leafy parks leant it a more sophisticated air and by the early 20th century the city had a population of 300,000. However, the improvements to the physical infrastructure of Jakarta only served to disguise the dissatisfaction felt by the Indonesians, who continued to live in appalling conditions. The Dutch were also too slow to share any power with the indigenous population, and nationalist groups began to gain support and influence (see page 46). This was aided by the concomitant rise of a more orthodox Islam.

At the end of 1941, the Japanese began their whirlwind invasion of Southeast Asia, taking Batavia on 5 March 1942. They renamed the city **Jakarta**, a shortened version of Jayakarta. During the relatively short period of Japanese wartime occupation, Jakarta lost many of its colonial buildings – destroyed in civil disturbances or demolished to make way for new structures. With the imminent defeat of the Japanese, Indonesia proclaimed its independence on the 17 August 1945, under the leadership of Sukarno and Mohammad Hatta. However, the Dutch were not prepared to give up sovereignty so easily and in 1946, Jakarta again became the capital of a decidedly shaky colony. Over the next 3 years, nationalist groups throughout the country gained in influence and the Dutch came to realize that their colonial ambitions had reached the end of the road. In 1949, Sukarno returned to the capital in a blaze of glory to become the first President of the new Republic of Indonesia (see page 48).

MODERN JAKARTA

Today, Jakarta is a sprawling, cosmopolitan city, the centre of government, commerce and industry, with a population approaching 10 million – making it much the largest city in Indonesia. Growth has been extremely rapid. During the 1965 attempted coup for example, journalists holed-up in the *Hotel Indonesia* were at the S extremities of the city; today the hotel sits in the heart of a sprawling conurbation. Like Bangkok, Jakarta is perceived by the poorer rural Indonesians as a city paved with gold and they have flocked to the capital in their thousands. A survey in 1985 revealed that 40% of Jakarta's population had been born outside the city.

The central area is dominated by large office blocks, international hotels and wide, tree-lined roads. Off the main thoroughfares, the streets become smaller and more intimate, almost village-like. These are the densely inhabited *kampungs* where immigrants have tended to live – one-storey, tile-roofed houses crammed together and linked by a maze of narrow paths. Initially, kampungs developed their own identity, with people from particular language and ethnic groups, even from particular towns, congregating in the same place and maintaining their individual identities. Today those distinctions are less obvious but the names of the kampungs are a reminder of their origins: Kampung Bali, Kampung Aceh (N Sumatra), and Kampung Makassar (Ujung Pandang) for example. The diverse mix of cultures is something Jakartans are particularly proud of; visitors to the capital are frequently reminded that the city is a 'melting pot' of the country's many ethnic groups (an example of Indonesia's motto 'Unity in Diversity').

It seems that Jakarta may be attempting to become another Singapore; first-class hotels have sprouted-up and there are any number of sophisticated shopping-malls, restaurants and nightclubs. Jakarta is not often rated very highly as a tourist attraction but if visitors can tolerate the traffic, then it is possible to spend an enjoyable few days visiting the excellent museums, admiring the architectural heritage of the Dutch era, strolling through the old harbour or discovering some of the many antique or arts and crafts shops.

PLACES OF INTEREST

KOTA OR OLD BATAVIA

The city of Jakarta developed from the small area known as **Kota**, which stretches from the Pasar Ikan, or Fish Market, to Jl Jembatan Batu, just S of Kota train station. The area is about 8 km N of both Monas

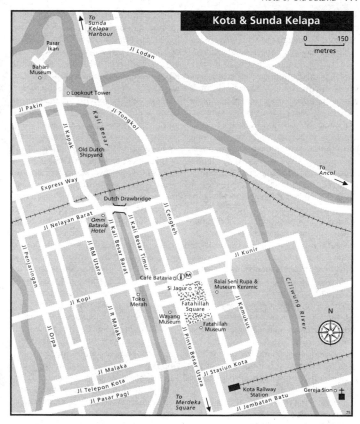

Kota & Sunda Kelapa

0 _____ 150
metres

To
Sunda
Kelapa
Harbour

Pasar
Ikan

Bahari
Museum

Lookout Tower

Jl Lodan

Jl Pakin

Kali Besar

Jl Tongkol

Jl Kapak

Old Dutch
Shipyard

Express Way

To
Ancol

Dutch Drawbridge

Jl Nelayan Barat

Omni
Batavia
Hotel

Jl Kali Besar Barat

Jl Kali Besar Timur

Jl Cengkeh

Jl Penjaringan

Jl RM Utara

Jl Kunir

Café Batavia

Si Jagur

Balai Seni Rupa &
Museum Keramic

Jl Kopi

Toko
Merah

Fatahillah
Square

Jl Kemukus

Ciliwung River

Jl R Malaka

Wayang
Museum

Fatahillah
Museum

N

Jl Orpa

Jl Pintu Besar Utara

Jl Malaka

Jl Stasiun Kota

Jl Telepon Kota

Kota Railway
Station

Gereja Sion

Jl Pasar Pagi

To
Merdeka
Square

Jl Jembatan Batu

and many of the city's hotels and guesthouses, so a bus or taxi ride is needed to
get here (see the end of this section for
details on transport). North of Pasar Ikan
was the old harbour town of **Sunda Kelapa**
which thrived from the 12th century to
1527. *Sunda* refers to the region of W Java
and *Kelapa* means coconut, and the port is
still worth a visit today. Impressive Bugis
or Makassar schooners dock here on their
inter-island voyages and can be seen
moored along the wharf (see page 620).
Gradually, they are being supplanted by
modern freighters, but for the time being
at least it is possible to se e these graceful

ships being loaded and unloaded by wiry
barefooted men, who cross precariously
between the wharf and the boats along
narrow planks. It is also sometimes possible to arrange a passage on one of the boats
to Kalimantan and elsewhere in the archipelago – ask around. Admission to harbour area 200Rp (800Rp for a car). Open
0800-1800 Mon-Sun.

Much of the original town of Sunda
Kelapa was demolished after the area was
declared unhealthy in the 18th century.
On its S edge and close to the Lookout
Tower (see below) is the original, and still
functioning, **Pasar Ikan** (Fish Market).

The market is an odd mixture of ship chandlers, tourist stalls and food outlets. Amongst the merchandise on sale are sea shells, toy kijangs, carvings and unfortunate stuffed animals. Close by at Jl Pasar Ikan 1 is the **Bahari** (or Maritime) **Museum** which was one of the original Dutch warehouses used for storing spices, coffee and tea. It was built in stages between 1718 and 1774. Today, it is home to a generally rather unimpressive maritime collection. However, upstairs is an interesting display of photographs dating from the late 19th and earlier 20th centuries recording life on board the steamships that linked Batavia with Holland. This new permanent exhibition was opened to commemorate the 50th anniversary of independence in 1995. The museum is worth a visit for the building rather than its contents. Admission 150Rp (extra for cameras). Open 0900-1500 Tues-Thur, 0900-1500 Fri and Sun 0900-1230 Sat. Other warehouses behind this museum were built between 1663 and 1669. The area around the Pasar Ikan is due to be developed further as a tourist attraction (this has been on the cards for some years now and has yet to manifest itself), recreating the atmosphere of the Dutch period by renovating and reconstructing the original buildings.

Overlooking the fetid **Kali Besar** (Big Canal) is the **Lookout Tower** (or *Uitkijk*) built in 1839 on the walls of the Dutch fortress Bastion Culemborg (itself constructed in 1645). The tower was initially used to spy on (and signal to) incoming ships, and later as a meteorological post – a role it continued to fill until this century. From the top of the tower there are views N over the port of Sunda Kelapa and S to the city, over an area of poor housing and urban desolation.

Less than 1 km from the Bahari Museum and Sunda Kelapa, S along either Jl Cangkeh or Jl Kapak, is one of the last **Dutch-era drawbridges** across the Kali Besar. It was built over two centuries ago and is known as the Chicken Market Bridge. The canal here is choked with rubbish and biologically dead. Continuing S for another 200m or so, walking past old Dutch warehouses, godowns and other commercial buildings, is **Fatahillah Square**, or **Taman Fatahillah**. This was the heart of the old Dutch city and the site of public executions and punishments – hangings, death by impalement and public floggings. It was also a bustling market place. In the middle of the square is a small, domed building (rebuilt in 1972), the site of the old drinking fountain. The Dutch were unaware that the water from this fountain was infested, and it contributed to the city's high incidence of cholera and consequently high death-rate (see page 109). On the S side of the square is the **Fatahillah Museum**, on the site of the first City Hall built in 1620. A second hall was constructed in 1627 and today's building was completed in 1710. A fine example of Dutch architecture (reminiscent of the old city hall of Amsterdam), it became a military headquarters after independence and finally the **Museum of the History of Jakarta** in 1974. It is a lovely building but, like so many Indonesian museums, the collection is poorly laid out. It contains Dutch furniture and VOC memorabilia. In the courtyard behind the museum, two *ondel-ondel* figures stand outside another room of rather down-at-heel exhibits. Below the main building are the prison cells. Admission 150Rp. Open 0900-1600 Tues, Fri and Sun 0900-1300 Sat.

The **Wayang Museum**, previously called the Museum of Old Batavia, is on the W side of the square at Jl Pintu Besar Utara 27. All that remains of the original 1912 building is its façade. Until 1974 it housed the collection now in the Fatahillah Museum and today contains a good collection of wayang kulit and wayang golek puppets (see page 96). Well made examples are sold here for 50,000-100,000Rp. Admission 250Rp. Open 0900-1500 Tues-Thur and Sun, 0900-1100 Fri, 0900-1300 Sat. Performances of wayang kulit or wayang golek are held here on Sun from 1000 (see entertainment). West from the Wayang Museum and over the Kali Besar (canal) is the **Toko Merah** or Red House. This was once the home of Governor-General Gustaaf van Imhoff. There are some other interesting 18th century Dutch buildings in the vicinity.

On the N side of Fatahillah Square is an old Portuguese bronze cannon called **Si Jagur**, brought to Batavia by the Dutch after the fall of Melaka in 1641. The design of a clenched fist is supposed to be a symbol of cohabitation and it is visited by childless women in the hope that they will be rendered fertile. On the E side of the square is the **Balai Seni Rupa**(the Fine Arts Museum), formerly the Palace of Justice at Jl Pos Kota 2. Built in the 1860's, it houses a poor exhibition of paintings by Indonesian artists. The building is shared with the **Museum Keramik**, a collection of badly displayed ceramics. Admission 150Rp. Open 0900-1600 Tues-Thur, 0900-1100 Fri, 0900-1300 Sat, 0900-1400 Sun. The most stylish place to eat and drink on the square is at the *Café Batavia* – itself something of an architectural gem in Indonesian terms. It was built in stages between 1805 and 1850 and is the second oldest building on the square (after the City Hall). Particularly fine is the renovated Grand Salon upstairs, made of Java teak. The café was opened at the end of 1993 and is frequented by foreigners and the Indonesian wealthy (see bars and restaurants). There is a *Tourist information office* next to the café and, next to this, a **clothes market** which functions every day except Sun.

East of Kota railway station on the corner of Jl Jembatan Batu and Jl Pangeran is the oldest church in Jakarta, **Gereja Sion**, also known as the 'old Portuguese Church' or 'Gereja Portugis'. It was built for the so-called 'Black Portuguese', Eurasian slaves brought to Batavia by the Dutch from Portuguese settlements in India and Ceylon. These slaves were promised freedom, provided that they converted to the Dutch Reformed Church. The freed men and women became a social group known as *Mardijkers* or 'Liberated Ones'. The church was built in 1693 and is a fine example of the Baroque style, with a handsome carved wooden pulpit, black ebony pews and an elaborately carved organ. The four chandeliers are of yellow copper.

● **Transport** To get to Kota or the Old City from the centre of town, take bus P16 or P17 to Terminal Bis Kota or microlet M08 or M12 (among others), or a taxi.

CENTRAL JAKARTA

South of Fatahillah Square is **Glodok**, or **Chinatown**. This lay outside the original city walls and was the area where the Chinese settled after the massacre of 1740 (see page 108). Despite a national ban on the public display of Chinese characters which was only rescinded in Aug 1994, Glodok's warren of back streets still feels like a Chinatown: shophouses, enterprise and activity, and temples tucked behind shop fronts. Midway between Fatahillah Square and Merdeka Square is the **National Archives** or **Arsip Nasional**. This building (which no longer holds the National Archives) was erected in 1760 as a country house for Reiner de Klerk, a wealthy resident who subsequently became governor-general. After de Klerk's death, the house was bought by John Siberg, who likewise was later to become governor-general. But its most interesting owner was a Polish Jew named Leendert Miero. It is said that Leendert, a mere guard at the house, was given 50 strokes for falling asleep whilst on duty. From that day, he swore that he would one day own the building. He duly made his fortune as a goldsmith and purchased the house in 1818. Since 1925, it has been owned by the state and now houses an interesting collection of Dutch furniture.

The enormous **Medan Merdeka** or Liberty Square dominates the centre of Jakarta. It measures 1 sq km and is one of

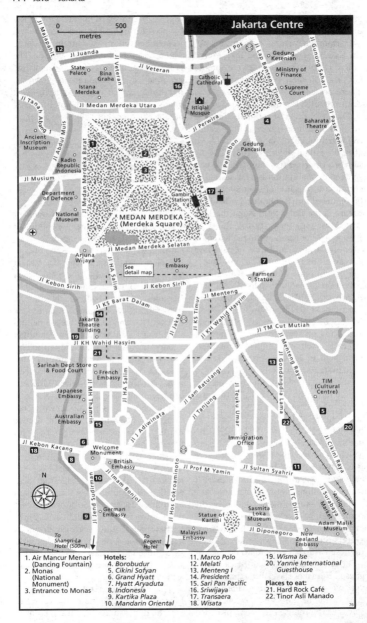

Jakarta Centre

1. Air Mancur Menari (Dancing Fountain)
2. Monas (National Monument)
3. Entrance to Monas

Hotels:
4. *Borobudur*
5. *Cikini Sofyan*
6. *Grand Hyatt*
7. *Hyatt Aryaduta*
8. *Indonesia*
9. *Kartika Plaza*
10. *Mandarin Oriental*
11. *Marco Polo*
12. *Melati*
13. *Menteng I*
14. *President*
15. *Sari Pan Pacific*
16. *Sriwijaya*
17. *Transaera*
18. *Wisata*
19. *Wisma Ise*
20. *Yannie International Guesthouse*

Places to eat:
21. *Hard Rock Café*
22. *Tinor Asli Manado*

Jakarta's heroic monuments

A particular feature of the city is the monumental heroic sculpture which dominates many busy intersections. Commissioned by Sukarno, these sculptures were conceived as one element in his remodelling of Jakarta as a great modern city. In the same vein as Communist heroic art, they also romanticise Indonesia's struggle for independence. Examples include the two waving figures of the **Welcome Monument** on the traffic circle between the *Hotel Indonesia* and the *Mandarin Hotel*. The so-called **Farmers' Monument** or Patung Tani depicts a couple bidding farewell, as the husband leaves to join the revolution. Sculpted by two Russians and with Communist overtones, it has not been the favourite monument of Jakartans in recent years; a group even lobbied for its removal. Other monuments include the muscular **Irian Jaya Freedom Monument** (also known as the Incredible Hulk) in the centre of Lapangan Banteng which shows a man symbolically breaking free from his chains; and the distinctly uninspired **Youth Monument**, to the S on Jl. Jend Sudirman, known as Hot Plate Harry or The Pizza Man. Indonesians call this last monument *Adu, Panas* ('Ow, Hot') or Pertamina – a reference to the national oil company and the volatility of its product. Finally there is the **Dirgantara Monument** (or Pancoran), which can be seen from the highway to Bogor. It has various names: the Dutch in Jakarta call it *Ard Schenk* because the figure's arms are like those of a skater in motion; some Indonesians call it Truper (a corruption of Trooper), because the ragged clothes look like the remains of a parachute; while many English-speaking residents refer to it as the 7-Up Man because of the statue's pedestal. The latest addition to Jakarta's monuments is the figure of **Arjuna Wijaya** (Arjuna driving a chariot of galloping horses) near the National Museum on the corner of Jl. Thamrin, which looks as though it has been sculpted out of white chocolate.

the largest city squares in the world. In 1818, it was renamed King's Square or Koningsplein and since independence, following its enlargement by Sukarno, it has been known as Merdeka Square. President Sukarno imagined Merdeka Square lying at the centre of a new city – one fitting of a new country. Sukarno, before becoming a full-time independence leader, was a student of Architecture and Civil Engineering and was steeped in the ideas of Le Corbusier and the modernists. In the centre of Medan Merdeka is the **National Monument** (**Monas**), a 137m-high pinnacle meant to represent a *lingga* and thus symbolize fertility and national independence. This massive obelisk was commissioned by President Sukarno in 1961 to celebrate Indonesia's independence from the Dutch. Construction entailed the bulldozing of a large squatter community to make way for the former President's monumental ambitions. It is known among residents of the city, rather irreverently, as Sukarno's Last Erection. Covered in Italian marble, it is topped by a bronze flame (representing the spirit of the revolutionaries), coated in 35 kg of gold leaf. Take the lift to the observation platform for magnificent views over the city. In the basement below the monument is a *museum* housing dioramas depicting the history of Indonesia's independence. The entrance to the museum is N of the road immediately in front of the monument (access is through an underground tunnel), where there is a **statue of Diponegoro** (a Javanese hero, see page 192) on horseback. He was held prisoner by the Dutch at the Batavia town hall, before being exiled to Manado in N Sulawesi.

Admission 500Rp for museum, 2,000Rp to take the lift to the top, 300Rp for camera, 500Rp for video, 2,500Rp for booklet with English description of the dioramas. Open 0800-1700 Mon-Sun.

On the W side of the square is the neo-classical **National Museum**. Established in 1860 by the Batavian Fine Arts Society, it is an excellent museum and well worth a visit. Set around a courtyard, the collection consists of some fine stone sculpture (mostly of Hindu gods), a textile collection (recently skilfully reorganized), and a collection of mainly Chinese ceramics found in Indonesia and bequeathed to the museum by a Dutchman, Orsoy de Flines, in the 1930s. Next to the ceramics is a display of bronzeware including some magnificent Dongson drums (see page 377) and krisses (see box). The pre-history room is well laid out. Its collection includes the skull cap and thigh bone of Java Man, a rare example of *Homo erectus*, discovered by Eugene Dubois in 1890 (see page 228). The ethnographic collection has been reorganized recently and includes an excellent range of masks, puppets, household articles, musical instruments and some models of traditional buildings representing cultures from several of the main islands in the archipelago. Upstairs there is a display of archaeological finds including recently discovered gold treasures found in Klaten, Central Java. Outside the museum entrance is the bronze statue of an elephant presented by King Chulalongkorn of Thailand, in 1871. Admission 300Rp (plus camera charge). Open 0830-1430 Tues-Thur and Sun, 0830-1130 Fri, 0830-1330 Sat. Good volunteer guides available: English (Tues, Wed, Thur), German (Thur), French (Wed), Dutch and Japanese (Tues) language tours are available, usually between 0900 and 1000. See the *Jakarta Post* for details as times and days vary. There is a handicraft shop and a telecommunications centre here (visitors can make faxes, telexes and long distance phone calls), set up by a museum co-operative.

To the W of the National Museum, down Jl Tanah Abang 1, is the rarely visited **Museum Taman Prasasti** or the **Ancient Inscription Museum**. This open-air museum occupies part of a former Christian cemetery, the Kebon Jahe Kober, where high-ranking Dutch officials were buried from the late 18th century onwards. The gravestones of important Dutchmen such as JHR Kohler who was killed in battle in Aceh (see page 444), and Dr MF Stutterheim are to be found here along with Soe Hok Gie and Mrs Olivia Marianne Raffles (Stamford Raffles' first wife) among others. The curators have also felt the site appropriate for the display of traditional gravestones from Indonesia's 27 provinces. Admission 150Rp. Open (in theory – do not be surprised to find it closed): 0900-1500 Tues-Thur, 0900-1430 Fri, 0900-1230 Sat, 0900-1500 Sun.

On the N side of the square, is the neo-classical Presidential Palace or **Istana Merdeka**, built in 1861 and set in immaculate gardens. Originally named **Koningsplein Paleis**, it was renamed after the independence ceremony was held in front of the building on 27 December 1949. The large crowd that assembled for the ceremony is reputed to have shouted 'merdeka, merdeka' ('freedom, freedom') as the new red and white flag of the Republic of Indonesia was raised; this ceremony and episode is re-enacted each year on Independence Day. President Sukarno resided at the Istana Merdeka, but President Suharto moved to a more modest residence and the building is now only used for state occasions. Behind the palace is the older **State Palace** (Istana Negara), next to the Bina Graha (the presidential office building). This palace was built for a Dutchman at the end of the 18th century and was the official residence of Dutch Governors-General, before the Koningsplein Palace was built. To get to the State Palace, walk down Jl Veteran 3 and turn W on Jl Veteran.

In the NE corner of Medan Merdeka is the impressive **Istiqlal Mosque**, finished in 1978 after more than 10 years work. The interior is very simple and is almost entirely constructed of marble. It is the principal place of worship for Jakarta's Muslims and reputedly the largest mosque in Southeast Asia with room for more than 10,000 worshippers. Non-muslims can visit the mosque when prayers are not in progress (women should take a scarf to cover their heads, and dress modestly). Facing the mosque, in the NW corner of Lapangan Banteng (see below), is the strange neo-gothic **Catholic Cathedral**; its date of construction is unknown, but it was restored in 1901.

Due E of the mosque is **Lapangan Banteng**, or 'Buffalo Field', used by the Dutch military during the late 18th century. Daendels built a huge palace on this square in 1809; it is now the Department of Finance. Next door is the Supreme Court. In 1828, the Waterloo Memorial was erected in the centre of the Lapangan Banteng. Demolished by the Japanese during their wartime occupation, it has since been replaced by the **Irian Jaya Liberation Monument**. Positioned as it is in front of the Treasury, residents wryly joked that the figure's stance with raised, open hands was not one of freedom but represented the exclamation 'kosong', or 'empty' (referring to the Treasury).

From the S corner of Lapangan Banteng, Jl Pejambon runs S past **Gedung Pancasila**, the building where Sukarno gave his famous *proklamasi*, outlining the five principles of Pancasila (see page 51). At the S end of Jl Pejambon, backing onto Merdeka Square, is the **Gereja Immanuel**, an attractive circular domed church, built by Dutch Protestants in the classical style in 1835.

OTHER PLACES OF INTEREST

Jakarta's kampungs, usually translated as 'village' but really untranslatable into English, are home to the bulk of the city's population and one of the most memorable excursions is simply to wander through these effervescent, vivacious communities with their labyrinthine streets. (They are clearly seen on the approach to Jakarta airport – look out for the patchworks of ochre rooftiles.) The kampungs still tend to be inhabited by migrants from particular parts of the archipelago, and are named accordingly: Aceh (N Sumatra), Bali and Ujung Pandang Makassar (Sulawesi) for example. They often have stalls and *warungs* (restaurants) which serve regional specialities and offer an insight into the lifestyle of ordinary Jakartans. Population densities can reach 100,000 per km^2 as migrants squeeze into small *pondoks*, or traditional boarding houses. Some kampungs have been improved and upgraded, but in many sanitation is poor, flooding during heavy rains is common, and disease remains a serious problem. Drinking water has to be bought from vendors in some places such is the shortage of standpipes. Yet residents remain because of attractions or benefits which out weigh the costs: their central location, low rents, access to employment, and community spirit among them. In a sense, urban kampungs are parts of rural Indonesia transplanted into a city environment. Although crime is a minor problem, visitors are far more likely to suffer the indignity of getting lost.

The older urban kampungs of Jakarta are in the northwestern and eastern portions of the city. Newer kampungs are situated more peripherally, for example, around Tanjung Priok. Generally, the newer settlements have less of a sense of 'community'; they are inhabited by large numbers of transient migrants who have less of an affinity with their temporary places of residence. Although many kampung dwellers, with insecure tenure, have found themselves evicted to make way for modern development (they often occupy prime inner city locations), other sites have been improved through the Kampung Improvement Programme or KIP.

The kris: martial and mystic masterpiece of the Malay world

The kris occupies an important place in Malay warfare, art and philosophy. It is a short sword – the Malay word *keris* means dagger – and the blade may be either straight or sinuous (there are over 100 blade shapes), sharpened on both edges. Such was the high reputation of these weapons that they were exported as far afield as India. Krisses are often attributed with peculiar powers – one was reputed to have rattled violently before a family feud. Another, kept at the museum in Taiping, has a particularly bloodthirsty reputation. It would sneak away after dark, kill someone, and then wipe itself clean before miraculously returning to its display cabinet. Because each kris has a power and spirit of its own, they must be compatible with their owners. Nor should they be purchased – a kris should be given or inherited.

The fact that so few kris blades have been unearthed has led some people to assume that the various Malay kingdoms were peaceful and adverse to war. The more likely explanation is that pre-Muslim Malays attributed such magical power to sword blades that they were only very rarely buried. The art historian Jan Fontein writes that "the process of forging the sword from clumps of iron ore and meteorite into a sharp blade of patterned steel is often seen as a parallel to the process of purification to which the soul is subjected after death by the gods".

The earliest confirmed date for a kris is the 14th century – they are depicted in the reliefs of Candi Panataran and possibly also at Candi Sukuh, both on Java. However, in all likelihood they were introduced considerably earlier – possibly during the 10th century. A European visitor to Java in 1515 commented "Every man in Java, rich or poor, must have a kris in his house ... no man between the ages of 12 or 80 may go out of doors without a kris in his belt". Even women sometimes wore krisses.

The *Kampung Improvement Programme* dates from 1969, and is still on-going – making the KIP one of the longest-running development projects in the country. In 1969 the government finally accepted that the capital's burgeoning and densely settled urban *kampungs* were woefully lacking in basic services, represented concentrations of poverty, and the people living in them had a life expectancy considerably below the average. The KIP aimed to bring the inhabitants an improved physical infrastructure by building roads and walkways and providing piped water, and a better social infrastructure by constructing local schools and health clinics. This was to be achieved while retaining most of the existing housing stock. Although the *kampungs* of Jakarta represent high concentrations of poverty, the KIP has undoubtedly helped to improve conditions for many thousands of Jakarta's poor. It has also created an environment in which people are likely to invest in the maintenance and improvement of their houses and their neighbourhoods.

The poorest inhabitants of these urban kampungs, for whom even the KIP has passed them by, are the room renters with a monthly income of barely 100,000Rps (US$50). *Gubuk* are one-roomed rental units; *petak* have two or three rooms. The temporary rural migrants who live in these crowded units share facilities. One of the best books on Jakarta's kampungs is Alison Murray's *No Money, no honey: a study of street traders and prostitutes in Jakarta* (1992, OUP: Jakarta). She lived for many months within a kampung and recounts the lives of the inhabitants first hand and with great sensitivity. She writes, for example:

Krisses are forged by beating nickel or nickeliferous meteoritic material into iron in a complex series of laminations (iron from meteors is particularly prized because of its celestial origin). After forging, ceremonies are performed and offerings made before the blade is tempered. The *empu*, or swordsmith, was a respected member of society, who was felt to be imbued with mystical powers. After forging the blade, it is then patinated using a mixture of lime juice and arsenicum. Each part of the sword, even each curve of the blade, has a name and the best krisses are elaborately decorated. Inlaid with gold, the cross-pieces carved into floral patterns and animal motifs, grips made of ivory and studded with jewels, they are works of art.

But they were also tools of combat. In the Malay world, a central element of any battle was the amok. Taken from the Malay verb *mengamok*, the amok was a furious charge by men armed with krisses, designed to spread confusion within the enemy ranks. Amok warriors would be committed to dying in the charge and often dressed in white to indicate self-sacrifice. They were often drugged with opium or cannabis. It was also a honourable way for a man to commit suicide. Alfred Russel Wallace in *The Malay Archipelago* (1869) writes: "He grasps his kris-handle, and the next moment draws out the weapon and stabs a man to the heart. He runs on, with the bloody kris in his hand, stabbing at everyone he meets. 'Amok! Amok!' then resounds through the streets. Spears, krisses, knives and guns are brought out against him. He rushes madly forward, kills all he can – men, women and children – and dies overwhelmed by numbers...". The English expression 'to run amok' is taken from this Malay word.

Recommended reading: Frey, Edward (1986) *The Kris: mystic weapon of the Malay world*, OUP: Singapore.

On one occasion, for example, I watched one of the RW 'B' women dying of tuberculosis in a hospital in Jatinegara. Even though her husband was a civil servant and she received some health insurance benefits, conditions were appalling. There were cockroaches everywhere, cats were scavenging in the garbage under the bed, and she had to walk herself to the toilet and bathroom at the end of the corridor even though she was barely strong enough to stand. Friends and relatives raised hundreds of thousands of rupiah for a course of injections for her, but she had lost the will to live and asked to be taken home to die. She was 43.

Death in the *kampung* is a common occurrence and is treated fatalistically. On another occasion I came home to the water tower house and found it adorned with the yellow flag that signifies a death. Franki, one of the youths who hung around the

chicken porridge stall there, had died after a late night (helmetless) motorbike smash into a telegraph pole. The other members of the gang had gathered and enlisted my motorbike for the funeral cortège. Three to a bike and waving yellow flags to warn other traffic, we roared off with the truck carrying the body careering at breakneck speed behind. Arriving at the cemetery, the hole in the ground turned out to be too small for the body, which was placed aside while more earth was dug out so the burial could continue. The youths were deferential towards Franki's parents, and were briefly solemn before returning to the porridge stall to drink cheap wine late into the night as usual.

WEST OF THE CITY CENTRE

The **Textile Museum**, nr the Tanah Abang Market (and railway station), Jl Satsuit Tuban 4, is housed in an airy Dutch colonial house set back from the road W of the centre of town. It contains a good range of Indonesian textiles, both batik and ikat. Admission 150Rp. Open 0900-1500 Tues-Thur and Sun, 0900-1130 Fri, 0900-1230 Sat. Get there on Bus S6 or S4.

SOUTH OF THE CITY CENTRE

The **Adam Malik Museum** is on the N side of Jl Diponegoro at number 29, W from the junction with Jl Surabaya. This unique private collection was only opened to the public in 1985, 1 year after the death of Adam Malik who was Foreign Minister and Vice President of Indonesia. His widow still lives in the house. The quirky collection includes cameras, radios, walking sticks, watches, as well as Chinese ceramics, wood carving from Irian Jaya, stone carvings from Java, rather ostentatious furniture, guns, krisses and some interesting Russian icons. Upstairs is a scene carved on a grain of rice, and in a separate gallery outside a small collection of paintings by local artists. The problem with this museum is its lack of discrimination. The interesting and the commonplace, the skilled and the inept, are massed together in a generally poorly displayed and labelled collection. Admission 1,000Rp. Open 0930-1500 Tues-Sat, 0930-1600 Sun. Get there by bus or taxi.

The **Satriamandala Museum**, or Armed Forces Museum lies to the S of the city on Jl Gatot Subroto, opp the *Kastika Chandra Hotel*. It was formerly the home of Dewi Sukarno, wife of the late President. Today it houses a display of armaments and a series of dioramas, showing steps towards Indonesia's independence. Open 0900-1530 Tues-Sun.

A night-time drive, or perhaps even a walk, down **Jl Latuharhary**, in Menteng reveals a seedier – or at least an alternative – side of life in Jakarta. Transvestites, dressed up to the nines, and known as *banci* (meaning hermaphrodite or homosexual) or *waria*, hawk their wares. Foreign visitors may be astonished not only by the beauty of these 'imitation ladies', but also by the fact that this is countenanced in an otherwise relatively strict Muslim society. Transvestites have, in fact, a long and honourable tradition not just in Indonesia but throughout Southeast Asia.

The large, wholesale, **Pasar Cikini**, in the district of Menteng, is worth a visit to see the range of fruits, vegetables, fish and other fresh products trucked in from the surrounding countryside and the coast for sale in Jakarta. The second floor houses a gold market.

EXCURSIONS

Taman Mini-Indonesia is a 120-ha 'cultural park', 10 km SE of Jakarta (but closer to 20 km from the centre). Completed in 1975, there are 27 houses, each representing one of Indonesia's provinces and built in the traditional style of that region. All the houses are set around a lake with boats for hire. It is possible to drive around the park on weekdays or alternatively, walk, take the mini train, cable car or horse and cart (small charges for these). The cable car takes passengers over the lake, upon which there is a replica of the whole archipelago. The **Keong Mas Theatre** (so-called because its shape resembles a golden snail) presents a superb not-to-be-missed film on Indonesia, projected on to world's largest imax screen (check in *Jakarta Post* for viewing times). Admission 1,000Rp. The **Museum Indonesia**, a Balinese-style building, houses a good collection of arts and crafts and costumes from across the archipelago. Open 0900-1500. The **Museum Komodo** is, as the name suggests, built in the form of the *Varanus komodiensis*, better known as the Komodo dragon (see page 731). It houses dioramas of Indonesian fauna and flora. Open 0800-1500. Visit Taman Mini at the weekends for cultural performances but on weekdays to avoid the crowds. Admission to the park 2,000Rp. Open 0800-1700 Mon-Sun. **Accommodation D** *Desa Wisata*, close to Museum Komodo, popular with families and student groups. *Getting there*: take a bus to Kampung Rambutan terminal and from there a T55 to the park (1-1½ hrs).

Taman Impian Jaya Ancol lies 10 km N of Merdeka Square, on the waterfront E of Sunda Kelapa. Built on reclaimed land, it is Southeast Asia's largest recreation park, with Disneyland-type rides, a 'fantasyland' – really just a glorified funfair – drive-in cinema, sporting facilities (including a golf course) and the *Pasar Seni* art market. There is also an *oceanarium* (6,000Rp) and a *swimming pool complex/waterworld* (2,500Rp). Accommodation, restaurants and foodstalls are all available. The park can become very crowded at weekends. Admission at main gate 1,000Rp; additional 5,000Rp for *Fantasyland* (a Disneyland copy, with plenty of rides and very popular with children), 13,000Rp gives free use of all the rides, 15,000Rp includes water world. **NB** All prices increase over the weekend and on holidays. Open 1500-2200 Mon-Fri, 1000-2200 weekends and holidays. *Getting there*: by bus number 64 or 65 from the Kota station, or by minibus M15. **NB** Taxis are hard to find at the end of the day; avoid venturing onto the main road after dark – both locals and foreigners have been robbed.

Lubang Buaya (or 'Crocodile Hole') **Heroes Monument** is a memorial park that lies 15 km SE of town. It is dedicated to the six army generals and one officer slain in the abortive Communist-inspired coup d'état in 1965 (see page 50). The centrepiece is the *Pancasila Monument*, with statues of the seven heroes standing nr the well in which their bodies were thrown, after having been tortured and then executed by Communist militia squads. *Getting there*: by bus from the Kampung Rambutan terminal, S of the city.

Ragunan Zoo is in Ragunan, 15 km S of the city centre; see the famous Komodo dragon (see page 731) and other regional animals. Admission 1,000Rp, 500Rp for children. Open 0800-1800 Mon-Sun.

Getting there: take a P19 bus from the centre of town.

Pulau Seribu or the 'Thousand Islands' are situated just off the coast, NW of Jakarta (see page 136). The closest thing to a tropical island paradise within easy reach of the capital. *Getting there*: by ferry, hydrofoil, helicopter or speedboat from Ancol Marina.

Banten is a historic town 100 km W of Jakarta on Java's N coast (see page 138). *Getting there*: Banten can be visited in a day from the capital, provided you hire a car or taxi.

Bogor is a hill resort 60 km S of Jakarta and famous for its *Botanical Gardens* (see page 146). Nearby is the *Safari Park* at Cisarua (see page 148) and the *Puncak Pass* (see page 152). *Getting there*: by bus from the Kampung Rambutan terminal (1,000Rp, 1½ hrs); by train from Gambir station 1-1½hrs (500-1,500Rp).

Bandung is one of Indonesia's largest cities, almost 200 km from Jakarta (see page 155). *Getting there*: by bus from the Kampung Rambutan terminal 5 hrs (8,000Rp); by train from the Gambir station 3 hrs (9,000-18,000Rp) or by minibus with Media, Jl Johar 15 T 343643 (10,000Rp).

TOURS

The tours outlined below can be organized by any of the travel agents or tour operators found in the major hotel complexes. City tours can include a visit to the National Museum, Old Batavia, Pasar Ikan and Sunda Kelapa, Taman Mini and a batik factory or the flea market on Jl Surabaya. Evening tours can be arranged to Ancol Amusement Park and the Pasar Seni (an arts and crafts market within Ancol), with dinner included. Out-of-town tours can be arranged to Bogor and the Puncak Pass, the Safari Park at Cisarua, Bandung and the Tangkuban Perahu crater. 1-day tours by hovercraft to Pulau Seribu are organized on Sun and holidays, 0700-1700, 1 hr 20 mins ride, T 325608 for more information. There are also day tours to the W, to visit the historic site of Banten and the beach at Anyer, on the W coast.

Cruise holidays starting from Tanjung Priok, Jakarta's port, are available with the *Island Explorer*, a luxury 18 cabin ship. From Dec to Mar it travels from Jakarta to Krakatau, the Ujung Kulon National Park and to Sumatra to see an elephant training centre. The rest of the year it cruises between Bali and Kupang (Timor) (see page 339), Jl Let Jen S Parman 78, Slipi, Jakarta Barat, T 593401, F 593403.

FESTIVALS

Apr: *Anniversary of Taman Mini* (20th), performances of traditional music and dance.

May: *Jakarta International Cultural Performance*, a festival of music and dance from around Indonesia and also from other areas of Southeast Asia.

Jun: *Anniversary of Jakarta* (22nd), commemorates the founding of Jakarta. Followed by the *Jakarta Fair* which lasts 1 month.

Aug: *Jl Jaksa Street Fair*, 7 days of entertainment, incl dance and music.

LOCAL INFORMATION

● **Accommodation**

Around Merdeka Square: **L** *Borobudur*, Jl Lapangan Banteng Selatan, T 3805555, F 3809595, a/c, several restaurants, large pool, large hotel block set amidst extensive gardens, on the S side of the square; shopping arcade and airline offices all found here; **A+** *Hyatt Aryaduta*, Jl Prapatan 44-46, T 3861234, F 380990, a/c, restaurant, pool, recently renovated; **A+** *Sari Pan Pacific*, Jl MH Thamrin 6, T 323707, F 323650, a/c, several restaurants, pool, large tower block (over 500 rm) in central position, with good facilities incl a health centre; **B** *Sriwijaya*, Jl Veteran 1, T 370409, good location; **B** *Transaera*, Jl Merdeka Timur 16, T 357059, old colonial hotel.

Menteng and Cikini: **L** *Grand Hyatt*, 4th Flr, *Plaza Indonesia*, Jl Jend MH Thamrin, PO Box 4546, T 3901234, F 334321, a/c, restaurant, pool, very smart new block in central location next to *Plaza Indonesia* – an extensive new shopping mall, 5th flr facilities incl landscaped garden with pool, tennis and squash courts and fitness centre, the 450 rm are plush and very sophisticated, an excellent hotel with prices to match; **L** *Shangri La*, Jl Jend Sudirman, T 5707440, F 5703531, a/c, restaurant, bars, pool, fitness centre, very plush, very sophisticated, newest and glitziest of the luxury hotels; **A+** *Indonesia*, Jl MH Thamrin, T 3140008, F 3141508, a/c, restaurant, pool, Jakarta's original premier hotel, built in 1962 for the Asian Games, reputedly with war reparations from the Japanese, recently refurbished and still popular, although there is no way of getting rid of its ugly exterior, the 586 rm are only average at this price and the whole hotel still feels rather dated; **A+** *Mandarin Oriental*, Jl MH Thamrin, PO Box 3392, T 3141307, F 3148680, a/c, several restaurants, pool, sandwiched in between Jl Thamrin and Jl Imam Bonjol, this hotel is immaculately maintained, with superb service and large rooms; **A+** *President*, Jl MH Thamrin 59, T 2301122, F 3143631, Japanese owned and frequented almost entirely by Japanese businessmen and tourists, 315 Japanese minamalist rooms, not much of Indonesia evident here; **A+** *Sahid Jaya*, Jl Jend Sudirman 86, T 5704444, F 5733168, a/c, restaurant, pool, recently renovated, popular with tour groups and Indonesian businessmen but still rather lacking in ambience; **A** *Cikini Sofyan*, Jl Cikini Raya 79, T 3140695, F 3100432, a/c, restaurant, 115 well-appointed rooms, health centre, a small(ish) hotel which makes a good alternative to the larger mid-range places; **A** *Grand Menteng*, Jl Matraman Raya 21, T 882153, F 882398, a/c, restaurant, pool, fitness centre, central; **A** *Kartika Plaza*, Jl MH Thamrin 10, T 3141008, F 3225470, a/c, restaurants, good pool, recently renovated, with central position in city and popular with businessmen, gym; **A** *Menteng 1*, Jl Gondangdia Lama 28, T 3106468, F 3144151, a/c, restaurant, pool, snooker parlour, rather a tacky hotel with no style whatsoever; **A** *Wisata*, Jl MH Thamrin, T 2300406, F 324597, a/c, restaurant; **A-B** *Marco Polo*, Jl Cik Ditiro 19, T 325409, F 3107138, a/c, restaurant (with cheap, excellent buffet dinners and breakfasts), pool, a rather unprepossessing hotel with 181 featureless rooms and lobby, but recently renovated, clean and good facilities incl satellite TV and fridge in each room, just like rooms in any other city on the planet; **B** *Yannie International Guesthouse*, Jl Raden Saleh Raya 35, T 3140012, a/c, hot water, price incl breakfast, good value, very clean rooms, popular.

Jalan Jaksa

Hotels:
1. Arcadia
2. Bloem Steen
3. Cemara
4. Cipta
5. Djody
6. Indra International
7. Karya
8. Kresna
9. Nick's Corner
10. Pondok Wisata Jaya
11. Rita
12. Sabang Metropolitan
13. Wisma Delima
14. Bintang Kejora Hostel
15. Borneo Hostel
16. Hostel 36
17. Jusran Hostel
18. Norbek Hostel
19. Tator Hostel

Places to eat:
20. Angie's Café
21. Asmat Bar & Café
22. Memories Café
23. Merry's Café
24. Sizzlers Restaurant

Other parts of the city: **A+** *Ambhara*, Jl Iskandarsyah Raya I, T 7396759, F 7220582, a/c, pool, new 250-room hotel located nr Blok M in the southern part of town and therefore away from many of the sights, comfortable enough but rather clinical; **A+** *Citraland*, Jl S Parman, T 5660640, F 5681616, a/c, restaurant, pool, new hotel set above a shopping plaza and run by the Swiss Belhotel group; **A+** *Hilton*, Jl Jend Gatot Subroto, T 587981, F 583091, a/c, several restaurants, large pool, considered by many to be the best hotel in town, it incl a penthouse with its own swimming pool, set in lovely gardens, with good sports and business facilities; **A+** *Horison*, Jl Pantai Indah, Jaya Ancol, T 680008, F 689322, a/c, restaurant, pool, fitness centre, tennis courts, health spa, rather out of town, within the entertainment park on the beach, good for children and for sport; **A+** *Omni Batavia*, Jl Kali Besar Barat 44-46,

Kota, T 6904118, F 6904092, a/c, restaurants, pool, out of the centre in the Kota area. 400-odd rooms in this grand new hotel; **A** *Jayakarta Tower*, Jl Hayam Wuruk 126, T 6294408, F 6295000, a/c, restaurant, pool, not a very convenient location; **A** *Kartika Chandra*, Jl Jend Gatot Subroto, T 5251008, F 5204238, a/c, restaurant, pool, uninspired, plain decor but good sized rooms; **A** *Kemang*, Jl Kemang Raya, T 7993208, a/c, restaurant, pool, inconvenient location S of the city; **A** *Setiabudi Palace Hotel*, Jl Setiabudi Raya 24, T 5254640, F 5254651, a/c, restaurant, pool, a first rate hotel with very competitive rooms rates, large rooms and friendly, professional management, good pool, rec; **B** *Chitra*, Jl Otoko Tiga Seberang 23, T 6291125, a/c, friendly, good service, big breakfast incl, clean hotel, seems to be frequented mainly by Chinese, long way to city centre, area around hotel is dirty but very interesting (markets etc); **B** *Fabiola*, Jl Gajah Mada 27, T 6394008; **B** *Garden*, Jl Kemang Raya, T 7995808, F 7980763, a/c, restaurant, pool, quiet position S of the city, rec; **B** *Melati*, Jl Hayam Waruk 1, T 377208, F 360526; **B** *Paripurna*, Jl Hayam Wuruk 25-26, T 376311; **B** *Prapanca*, Jl Prapanca Raya 30, T 712630, F 7395030, S of the city, good value; **B-C** *Wisata Jaya*, Jl Hayam Wuruk 123, T 6008437, a/c, hot water.

Jalan Jaksa and nearby streets: the area around Jl Jaksa has quite a number of budget hotels as well as some new tourist hotels. There are also a number of travel agents on this road as well as a post office, laundry services and several travellers' eating houses and second-hand bookshops. To get to Jl Jaksa from Pulo Gadung bus terminal, take Bus no. 507. To get to Tanjung Priok (for PELNI boats), catch Bus no. P14 on Jl Kebon Sirih Raya.

A *Cemara*, Jl Cemara 1, T 3908215, F 324668, a/c, restaurant, excellent mid-range hotel, small, central position, enthusiastic service, rec; **A** *Cipta*, Jl KH Wahid Hasyim 53, T 3904701, 48 plain rooms with TV and fridge, it claims to have the personal touch other, larger hotels cannot provide, from the street it looks somewhat like a Tuscan pagoda, good central location; **A** *Sabang Metropolitan*, Jl Agus Salim 11, T 3857621, F 372642, a/c, restaurant, pool, jazz club, good central location but rooms and hotel give off an aura of the mid-1970s; **A-B** *Arcadia*, Jl KH Wahid Hasyim 114, T 2300050, F 2300995, modern Art-Deco in style, the 96 rm are small but decorated with more panache than usual, lots of chrome and deep colours, excellent showers, huge pillows and green or blue light-infused aquarium-esque lifts, opened in 1994, small with personal service, rec; **B** *Le Margot*, Jl Jaksa 15C, T 3913830, a/c, restaurant, ensuite bathroom, brand new upmarket (for Jl Jaksa) hotel, 'business centre', car rental, restaurant in basement, same style as *George and Dragon Pub*, live music; **B-C** *Karya*, Jl Jaksa 32-34, T 320484, a/c, attached shower rooms, rooms are run down but the hotel is expanding and under renovation so maybe things have improved, even so it is clean and quiet with friendly staff, the rooftop restaurant has views over the local neighbourhood to Monas, but the food is poor and over priced; **B-C** *Indra International*, Jl Wahid Hasyim 63, T 337432, some a/c, unattractive, rooms with hot water showers and cable TV, rather expensive even with these perks; **B-D** *Djody*, Jl Jaksa 27-35, T 332368,

some a/c, attractive quiet courtyard set back off the road, reasonable rooms but some rather small (we have also had complaints of some rooms being rather grubby), more expensive with a/c and attached mandi, but no hot water, good, fast laundry service, dorm beds (**F**), rec; **C** *Norbek*, Jl Jaksa 14, T 330392, a/c, restaurant (limited menu, but good value), popular, clean but small rooms, some with attached mandi, organize taxis to the airport; **C-E** *Nick's Corner*, Jl Jaksa 16-18, T 336754, F 3107814, a/c, new place, dormitory rooms as well as hospital-clean rooms with attached bathroom, suffers from unfriendly management; **B-E** *Tator*, Jl Jaksa 37, T 323940, F 325124, some a/c, plain rooms, clean bathrooms, more expensive rooms with a/c and attached shower rooms, no hot water, friendly management, tea and coffee incl in the price; **D-E** *Borneo*, Jl Kebon Sirih Barat Dalam 35, T 3140095, café, small rooms, some with attached mandi, popular but recent visitors report rather surly management (**F** for dorm beds); **D-E** *Wisma Delima*, Jl Jaksa 5, T 337026, some a/c, restaurant, popular (it was one of the original budget places on Jl Jaksa), but rooms are cramped and rather worn, some with attached mandi, however the house has an attractive garden; **D-F** *Jusran*, Jl Kebon Sirih Barat 616 (off Jl Jaksa), T 3140373, simple rooms with shared mandi, quiet and friendly, down a narrow alley.

E *Bintang Kejora Hostel*, Jl Kebon Sirih Barat Dalam 52 (off Jl Jaksa, S end), T 323878, rooms are large (relatively) with fans, shared showers and toilets, popular, a cut above the average but also slightly more expensive – not that downstairs rooms are noisy and rather scruffy at this price; **E** *Bloem Steen*, Jl Kebon Sirih Timur 1, small, popular, rooms upstairs are better, with small balconies; **E** *Kresna*, Jl Kebon Sirih Timur 1 175, T 325403, clean, some rooms with attached bathroom, rooms can be rather dark, but friendly and set back off the road down a quiet alley, rec; **E** *Hostel 36*, Jl Jaksa 36B, tatty losmen with cockrels, small oriental garden, shared mandi, down a quiet alley off Jl Jaksa (S end), larger rooms than most around Jaksa, relatively peaceful, rec; **E** *Wisma Ise*, Jl KHW Hasyim 168, just W of Jl MH Thamrin, T 333463, some a/c, some private bathrooms, friendly owners, central location, good value; **E-F** *Hotel Rita*, Jl Kebon Sirih Barat Dalam 36A (off Jl Jaksa, S end), small rooms, rather hot and cramped, grubby; **E-F** *Pondok Wisata Jaya*, Jl Kebon Sirih Barat Dalam 10 (off Jl Jaksa, S end), T 3104126, quiet, larger and more airy than most, with small garden and clean rooms, rec.

● **Places to eat**

Jakarta is a good place to eat out, with a wide choice of Indonesian, other Asian and international cuisines.

Indonesian: ♦♦♦♦+*Oasis*, Jl Raden Saleh 47, T 326397, also serves International food, Dutch governor's house built in 1928 the walls are adorned with Indonesian arts and crafts, rijstaffel served here, one of the best restaurants in town, local music performances, reservations necessary; ♦♦♦*Bengawan Solo*, Sahid Jaya Hotel, Jl Jend Sudirman 86, central Javanese cuisine; ♦♦*Handayani*, chain of restaurants – Jl Abdul Muis 36 and Jl Kebon Sirih 31, rec; ♦♦*Tinoor Asli Manado*, Jl Gondangolama 33A, simple but tasty Sulawesi (N) dishes served in dusty canteen-esque restaurant catering almost entirely to locals; ♦*Bami Gajah Mada*, Jl Gajah Mada 92, and Studio 21 cinema, Jl MH Thamrin, cheap noodlehouse, rec; ♦*Sari Kuring*, Jl Silang Monas Timur, popular with locals, cheap and good; ♦*Sari Nusantara*, Jl Silang Monas Tenggara (all regions of Indonesia); ♦*Sate House Senayan*, Jl Kebon Sirih 31A, sate and gado gado, rec.

Several cheap restaurants in the Jl Jaksa area for both Indonesian and international dishes. For Padang food (from W Sumatra), there is a concentration of excellent restaurants along Jl Tanah Abang 1 (running off Jl Abdul Muis, not far from the National Museum). All are in our ♦–♦♦ categories; try the *Sepakat* or the *Surya*. The ♦♦*Natrabu*, Jl Salim (between Jl Hasyim and Jl Sirih), is also an excellent Padang restaurant, clean and cosy.

Other Asian cuisine: ♦♦♦♦+*Nippon-Kan*, Hilton Hotel, Jl Gatot Subroto, expensive but good value Japanese; ♦♦♦♦*Arirang*, Jl Makaham 1/28, Korean barbecue, rec; ♦♦♦♦*Chikuyo-Tei*, Summit Mas Tower, Jl Jend Sudirman, Japanese, rec; ♦♦♦♦*Keyaki*, Sari Pacific Hotel, Jl MH Thamrin 6, Japanese, rec; ♦♦♦♦*Korea Tower*, Bank Bumi Daya Bldg, 30th Flr, Jl Imam Bonjol 61, Korean, rec; ♦♦♦♦*Shima*, Hyatt Aryaduta Hotel, Jl Prapatan 44, reputedly serves the best Japanese food in town; ♦♦♦♦*Spice Garden*, Mandarin Oriental Hotel, Jl MH Thamrin, Sezchuan, rec; ♦♦♦♦*Tokyo Garden*, Jl Rasuna Said 10, tapanyaki, rec; ♦♦♦*Hazara*, Jl KH Wahid Hasyim 11 (next to the *Arcadia Hotel*), good N Indian food incl fine tandoori dishes, succulent goat curry and oddities like curried crab; ♦♦♦*Yakiniku*, Jl Mahakam 1/166, set price for all you can eat, buffet stylep; ♦♦♦*Summer Palace*, Tedja Buana Bldg, 8th Flr, Jl Menteng Raya 29, Sezchuan,

large but reliable restaurant, rec; ♦♦*Kikugawa*, Jl Cikini IV 13, Japanese, central location, good value; *Gang Gang Sulai*, Jl Cideng Timur 65 and Jl Kemang Raya 10; *Phinisi floating restaurant*, Ancol, also serves seafood.

International: ♦♦♦♦++*Club Room*, Mandarin Oriental, Jl MH Thamrin, exclusive French; ♦♦♦♦+*Jayakarta Grill*, Sari Pacific Hotel, Jl MH Thamrin; ♦♦♦♦*Maxis*, Plaza Indonesia, Jl MH Thamrin, small Italian café, classic Italian dishes, average quality; ♦♦♦♦++*Taman Sari*, Hilton Hotel, Jl Gatot Subroto, rec; ♦♦♦♦*Ambiente*, Hyatt Aryaduta Hotel, Jl Prapatan, best Northern Italian in town, but nonetheless overpriced for Jakarta; ♦♦♦♦*Le Bistro*, Jl Wahid Hasyim 75, Jakarta's first French restaurant, established 15 years ago, classic French favourites such as bouillabaisse and Lamb Provençale; ♦♦♦♦*Toba Rotisserie*, Borobudur Intercontinental Hotel, Jl Lapangan Banteng, French, expensive but excellent; ♦♦♦♦–♦♦♦*Café Batavia*, Fatahillah Square, T 6926546, open 24 hrs, stylish and sophisticated bar and restaurant serving Indonesian and international dishes in superbly renovated early 19th century building, good food in great surroundings but very expensive for Indonesia, rec; ♦♦♦*A La Bastille*, Jl Yusuf Adiwinata 30, traditional French, BYOB; ♦♦♦*Green Pub*, Jakarta Theatre Bldg, Jl MH Thamrin 9, best Mexican available in the city, or so the cognoscente tell us; ♦♦♦*Hard Rock Café*, Jl Thamrin (1st flr of Sarinah block), burgers and fries, lively atmosphere and live music after 2300, relatively expensive but a taste of the West for those who need it – a good place to check out Jakarta's growing numbers of trendies, open 1100 until 0200; ♦♦♦*La Rose*, Landmark Centre, Jl Jend Sudirman 1, intimate and romantic; ♦♦♦*Memories*, Wisma Indocement Bldg, Jl Jend Sudirman, interior decorated with Dutch memorabilia, Dutch cuisine, rec; ♦♦♦*Pinocchio*, Top Flr, Wisma Metropolitan I, Jl Jend Sudirman, Italian, good place for families – birds and monkeys in cages nr the dining area, fixed price Sun lunch and dinner; ♦♦♦*Pizzaria*, Hilton Hotel, Jl Gatot Subroto, outdoor, set in Balinese garden, overloud live music; ♦♦♦*Planet Hollywood*, Jl Gatot Subroto (beside *Kartika Chandra*), recently opened, overpriced, limited menu but still the place to be seen by the young and trendy; ♦♦♦*Ponderosa*, Lippo Bldg, Jl Gatot Subroto 35 and Jl Jend Sudirman 57, chain of standard steakhouses – carvery and salad; ♦♦♦*Prambors Café*, 2nd basement, Blok M Mall, a new café, with live radio broadcasting from a booth in the centre of the café, lively, offering a variety of entertainment and a selection of western and Asian food; ♦♦♦*Rugantino's*, Jl Melawai Raya 28, indifferent Italian; ♦♦♦*Sizzlers*, Jl HA Salim, good steaks, buffet salad bar; ♦♦♦*The Stage*, Ratu Plaza, Jl Jend Sudirman, Greek food, with unusual decor and live music; ♦♦*Amigos*, Arthaloka Bldg, Jl Jend Sudirman, Mexican food to accompaniment of live country and western music after 1800; ♦♦*Family*, Jl HA Salim, on corner with Jl Wahid Hasyim, modern decor, clinically clean, friendly 'American' style service, Indonesian and European food, on expensive side, but good; *Casablanca*, Jl RH Rasuna Said; *Jaya Pub*, Jl MH Thamrin, pub food; *Kon Tiki*, 16th Flr, Wisma Metropolitan II, Jl Jend Sudirman, Waikiki salad, seafood chowder, baked crab Honolulu, good views of the city.

Seafood: ♦♦♦*Kuningan*, Jl HOS Cokroaminoto 122; ♦♦♦*Ratu Bahari*, Jl Melawai V11/4 Blok M, Chinese style; ♦♦♦*Seafood Senayan*, Jl Pakubuwono V1/6 and Jl HOS Cokroaminoto 78, fresh, Chinese style; ♦♦♦*Yun Nyan*, Jl Batuceper 69 (off Jl Hayam Wuruk) and Jl Panglima Polim Raya 77 (in S Jakarta), closed Mon, rec; ♦♦*Nelayan*, Manggala Wanabakti Building, Jl Gatot Subroto, T 5700248, also serves Chinese, large, very popular, reservations necessary, rec.

Travellers' food: Jl Jaksa has the greatest concentration and of these the most popular are *Memories* at Jl Jaksa 17 which serves waffles, shakes, steaks, fries and some Indonesian dishes, and *Angie's* at No 15, serving much the same; *Merry's Café*, Jk Jaksa.

Fast food: ♦♦*Pizza Hut*, Jakarta Theatre Bldg, Jl MH Thamrin, all-you-can-pile-on-your-plate salads and pizzas. There are now *McDonald's*, Jl Thamrin, Sarinah Bldg, beside *Hard Rock Café*, open 24 hrs – popular with Indonesian middle class and those who can't quite afford *Hard Rock Café*; *Wendy's* and other fast food outlets in many shopping centres.

Foodstalls: *Hotel Indonesia*, Jl MH Thamrin, buffet of different Indonesian cuisines, a good place to survey the variety; *Jl HA Salim* has a great number of cheap regional restaurants, western, Padang, Sundanese etc; *Jl Mangga Besar* has night-time warungs; *Jl Pecenongan* (also known as Jl Used Cars) – warungs at night, used car workshops by day, particularly good seafood, rec (BYOB); *Sarinah's Department Store* on Jl MH Thamrin (at the intersection with Jl KH Wahid Hasyim) has a *Foodcourt* in the basement, good range of cheapish Indonesian dishes (♦♦) served in pristine a/c restaurant with English language menu explaining what each

dish consists of, rec; the basement of *Pasar Raya*, Blok M, has a variety of reliably good 'stalls' (not just Indonesian); the top flr of *Sogo*, in the Plaza Indonesia, has similar stalls.

Bakeries: popular (and good) in Jakarta. There are a number down Jl Hayam Wuruk and in some hotels, eg *Hilton*, *Sari Pacific*, *Hyatt* and *Mandarin*. *Sakura Anpan* on Jl HA Salim has been rec.

● **Bars**

Café Batavia, Fatahillah Square, very stylish bar and restaurant in renovated 19th century building, great atmosphere, skyhigh prices for Indonesia, every cocktail from Sex on the Beach to an Orgasm; *Captain's Bar*, Mandarin Oriental Hotel, Jl MH Thamrin, good for lunch, largescreen sports news, live bands; *Chequers*, Mandarin Oriental Hotel, 5th Flr, Jl Thamrin, newly opened upmarket bar competing with O'Reilly's, live music, expensive drinks, huge screen for watching satellite sport; *George and Dragon*, Jl Teluk Betung 32; *Green Pub*, Jakarta Theatre Bldg, Jl MH Thamrin 9, Country and Western band; *Hard Rock Café*, Jl MH Thamrin (1st flr Sarinah block), expensive drinks in one of Indonesia's trendier places, occasional live music; *Jaya Pub*, Jaya Bldg, Jl MH Thamrin 12, an expat hangout, can get lively, live music; *Kudus Bar*, Jakarta Hilton, Jl Gatot Subroto; *Morgans*, Dai Ichi Hotel, Senen, decor based around this make of British convertible sports car; *O'Reilly's*, Grand Hyatt, Plaza Indonesia, upmarket Irish pub with style, live music and bar food, expensive; *Pendopo Bar*, Borobudur Hotel, Jl Lap Banteng Selatan, open 1100-0100, Mon-Fri; *Sportsmans Bar*, Jl Pelatehan I, No 6-8 (Blok M), Kebayoran Baru, very popular expat haunt for sports fanatics, TV shows live sport and pre-recorded from around the world, bar meals; *Sundance*, Jl Pelatehan Blok K, Kebayoran, darts and pool; *Tavern*, Hyatt Aryaduta, Jl Prapatan 44/48.

Karaoke: bars abound.

● **Airline offices**

International airline offices: Air India, Wisma Dharma Niaga, Jl Abdul Muis 6-8-10, T 3858845; British Airways, World Trade Centre, 10th Flr, Jl Jend Sudirman Kav 29-31, T 5211500; Cathay Pacific, Borobudur Hotel, Jl Lap Banteng, T 3806660; China Airlines, Jl Jend Sudirman 32, T 2510788; Emirates, Sahid Jaya Hotel, 2nd Flr, Jl Jend Sudirman, T 5742440; Japan Airlines, Mid Plaza, Grd Flr, Jl Jend Sudirman Kav 10-11, T 5703119; KLM,

New Summitmas 17th Flr, Jl Jend Sudirman Kav 61-62, T 2526730; **Korean Air**, Wisma Bank Dharmala, 1st Flr, Jl Jend Sudirman, T 5212175; **Lufthansa**, Panin Centre Bldg, 2nd Flr, Jl Jend Sudirman 1, T 5702005; **Malaysian Airlines System**, World Trade Centre, Grd Flr, Jl Jend Sudirman Kav 29-31, T 5229682, F 5229790; **Myanmar Airways**, Lippo Life Bldg, 7th Flr, Jl HR Rasuna Said Kav 10, T 5200202; **Philippine Airlines**, 11th Flr, Suite 1105 Mashill Tower, Jl Jend Sudirman Kav 25, T 5267780, F 5267789; **Qantas**, BDN Bldg, Jl MH Thamrin 5, T 2300655; **Royal Brunei Airlines**, World Trade Centre, 11th Flr, Jl Jend Sudirman Kav 29-31, T 5211843; **Royal Jordanian**, 3rd Flr *Borobudur Intercontinental Hotel*, Jl Lapangan Banteng Selatan, T 3441915; **Scandinavian Airlines System**, S Wijoyo Bldg, Jl Jend Sudirman 71, T 2524081; **Saudi Arabian Airlines**, Bumiputera Bldg, 7th Flr, Jl Jend Sudirman Kav 75, T 5710615; **Silk Air**, *Chase Plaza*, 4th Flr, Jl Jend Sudirman Kav 21, T 5208023; **Singapore Airlines**, Chase Bldg, Jl Jend Sudirman Kav 21, T 5704422; **Swissair**, *Borobudur Hotel*, Jl Lap Banteng, T 373608; **Thai International**, BDN Bldg, Jl MH Thamrin 5, T 3140607.

Domestic airlines offices: Bouraq, Jl Angkasa 1-3, T 6295150; **Garuda**, BDN Bldg, Jl Thamrin 5, T 2300925, also ticket sales offices at *Hotel Indonesia*, T 3100568, *Borobudur Hotel*, T 360048 and in the Jakarta International Trade Centre, T 2600244; **Mandala**, Jl Veteran I no. 34, T 368107; **Merpati**, Jl Angkasa 2, T 4247404; **Sempati**, *Hotel Borobudur*, Jl Lapangan Banteng Selatan, T 3805555, also ticket sales offices in *Hotel Indonesia*, T 320008, *Sari Pan Pacific*, T 323707 and *Le Meridien*, T 5711414.

● **Banks & money changers**

Most of the larger hotels will have money changing facilities, and banks and money changers can be found throughout the city centre, particularly, for example, in shopping centres. Note that on Sun it can be difficult to change TCs. Below is a list of the head offices of the main local banks, and international banks only.

Local banks: Bali, Jl Sudirman, cashpoint (Mastercard, Access); **Bumi Daya**, Jl Imam Bonjol 61; **Central Asia**, Jl Asemka 27-30; **Dagang Negara**, Jl MH Thamrin 5; **Duta**, Jl Kebon Sirih 12; **Ekspor Impor**, Jl Lapangan Stasiun; **Indonesia**, Jl MH Thamrin 2; **Negara Indonesia**, Jl Jend Sudirman 1; **Niaga**, Jl Gajah Mada 18; **Rakyat Indonesia**, Jl Jend Sudirman 44-46.

Foreign banks: American Express, Jl Jend

Sudirman; **Bank of America**, Wisma Antara, Jl Merdeka Selatan 17; **Bangkok Bank**, Jl MH Thamrin 3; **Banque Nationale de Paris**, Skyline Bldg, Jl MH Thamrin 9; **Barclays Bank**, Wisma Metropolitan 1, Jl Jend Sudirman Kav-29; **Standard Chartered Bank**, Atria Sq Bldg, Jl Sudirman 33; **Chase Manhattan**, Jl Merdeka Barat 6; **Citibank**, Jl MH Thamrin 55; **City Bank**, Jl Sudirman, cashpoint (Visa, Mastercard, Access); **Deutsche Bank**, Gedung Eurasbank, Jl Imam Bonjol 80; **Hongkong and Shanghai Bank**, Jl Hayam Wuruk 8 and 1st Flr, World Trade Centre, Jl Sudirman 29-31, cashpoint (Visa, Global); **Westpac**, Summitmas Tower Bldg, Jl Jend Sudirman.

● **Embassies & consulates**

Australia, Jl HR Rasuna Said Kav C 15-16, T 5227111, F 5227101; **Austria**, Jl Diponegoro 44, T 338090, F 3904927; **Belgium**, Jl Wisma BCA, 5th Flr, Jl Jend Sudirman Kav 22-23, T 5710510, F 5700676; **Brunei**, Wisma BCA, 8th Flr, Jl Jend Sudirman, T 5712180; **Burma** (Myanmar), Jl H Agus Salim 109, T 3140440, F 327204; **Canada**, Wisma Metropolitan I, 5th Flr, Jl Jend Sudirman Kav 29, T 5250790, F 5712251; **Czechoslovakia**, Jl Gereja Theresia 20, T 3904075, F 336282; **Denmark**, Bina Mulia Bldg, 4th Flr, Jl HR Rasuna Said Kav 10, T 5204350, F 5209162; **Finland**, Bina Mulia Bldg I, 10th Flr, Jl HR Rasuna Said Kav 10, T 516980, F 512033; **France**, Jl MH Thamrin 20, T 3142807; **Germany**, Jl Raden Saleh 54-56, T 3849547, F 3144984; **Greece**, Jl Kebon Sirih 16, T 347016; **Hungary**, Jl HR Rasuna Said Kav 10, T 5203459, F 5203461; **Italy**, Jl Diponegoro 45, T 337440, F 3107860; **Laos**, Jl Kintamani Raya C-15 33, T 5202673, F 5229601; **Malaysia**, Jl HR Rasuna Said Kav 10, 6, T 5224947; **Netherlands**, Jl HR Rasuna Said Kav S-3, T 511515; **New Zealand**, Jl Diponegoro 41, T 330680, F 3153686; **Norway**, Bina Mulia Bldg, 4th Flr, Jl HR Rasuna Said Kav 10, T 5251990, F 5207365; **Philippines**, Jl Imam Bonjol 6-8, T 3100334; **Singapore**, Jl HR Rasuna Said Block X, Kav 2, T 5201489; **Spain**, Jl H Agus Salim 61, T 335937, F 325996; **Sweden**, Bina Mulia Bldg I, 7th Flr, Jl HR Rasuna Said Kav 10, T 5201551, F 5252652; **Switzerland**, Jl HR Rasuna Said Block X, 3/2, T 516061, F 5202289; **Thailand**, Jl Imam Bonjol 74, T 3904225; **UK**, Jl MH Thamrin 75, T 330904, F 3141824; **USA**, Jl Medan Merdeka Selatan 5, T 360360; **Vietnam**, Jl Teuku Umar 25, T 3100358, F 3149615.

● **Entertainment**

For a schedule of events, look in the 'Where to Go' section of the *Jakarta Post*, or buy Jakarta Program's *'What's On and Where'*, obtainable from most bookstores for up-to-date information on the city's entertainment.

Cinemas: Jakarta is a city for cinema-goers; there are many complexes in the shopping malls, showing the latest American films. Little censorship of violence but no sex or anti-religious action allowed. The Indonesian way is to provide subtitles rather than to dub, so soundtracks are in English.

Cultural shows: *Ganesha*, a volunteer group interested in Indonesian culture, organize a Tues evening lecture series at the Erasmus Huis, Jl HR Rasuna Said (T 360551), check the *Jakarta Post* and hotels for details; *Gedung Kesenian*, Jl Gedung Kesenian 1, organizes wayang orang performances, piano recitals, theatre and other cultural events, a modern art gallery is attached to the theatre, hotels should provide information on their programme or phone, T 3808283; *Manari Theatre Restaurant*, Jl Jend Gatot Subroto 14, T 5204036; *Pasar Raya Theatre*, 2000-2100 Fri; *Pondok Garminah*, Jl Taman Kebon Sirih 11/6, T 335716, combine an evening meal with entertainment, Indonesian traditional dance and music, 1900-2100 Sun and Wed; *Taman Ismail Marzuki* (or TIM) just off Jl Cikini Raya is the focal point of cultural activities in the city with performances almost every night, the centre contains exhibition halls, 2 art galleries, theatres, cinema complex and a planetarium (admission 1,000Rp, tours on Tues-Thur, 0930, 1100 and 1330, Fri 1000, 1330, Sat 0930), their monthly calendar of events is usually available at hotel-counters or from Jakarta Tourist Office, or call T 322606 for information; *The Indonesian/American Cultural Centre* on Jl Pramuka Kav 30, T 8583241, has exhibits, films and lectures on Indonesia.

Discos: *Big Fire*, Plaza Indonesia, teens and twenties congregate here for excellent sound and light effects; *M Club*, Blok M Plaza – similar to *Big Fire*; *Ebony*, Kuningan Plaza, Jl Rasuna Said; *Hollywood East*, Harmoni Plaza, Blok B; *Music Room*, Borobudur Hotel, popular with locals, good dance floor; *Pitstop*, Sari Pacific Hotel, Jl MH Thamrin, good live bands but quite small; *Tanamur*, Jl Tanah Abang Timur 14, one of the oldest discos, popular with expats, tourists and every variety of Jakarta night life – definitely an experience, packed at weekends.

Gamelan: *Miss Tjitjih's Theatre*, Jl Kabel Pendek, Sundanese folk drama, 1900 and 2100 Mon-Sun; *National Museum*, 0930-1030 Sun; *Taman Mini*, Sun.

Jakarta Fair: annual event from 15 Jun-13 Jul, now at a new site, the old Kemayoran Airport NE of the city centre, entertainment, art market etc. Admission 1,000Rp. Open 1700-2300.

Music: *The Blue Note*, Atria Sq Bldg, Jl Sudirman 33, Standard Chartered Bank Bldg, new jazz club and restaurant, top night spot, with international artists. Country and Western music at the *Green Pub*, Jakarta Theatre Bldg, Jl MH Thamrin. Jazz at *Jamz*, Blok M, Jl Panglima Polim II – the city's leading jazz venue, with bench seating and big crowds, and at *Borobudur Kintamani Garden*, Borobudur Hotel and *Captain's Bar*, Mandarin Hotel; *BATS*, Shangri La Hotel, Jl Jend Sudirman, new place with live music and a New York basement feel, in 1996 was one of the hippest places for the wealthy Jakarta youth, food is American-Mediterranean, cappuccino culture comes to Jakarta!

Traditional dance: *Bharata Theatre*, Jl Pasar Senen 15, has nightly performances of wayang orang and Ketoprak from 2015-2400 (except Sat); *Taman Mini*, Sun and hols 1000-1400.

Wayang: *Wayang Museum* has alternate wayang kulit and wayang golek performances 1000-1400 Sun (200Rp). Alternate wayang kulit and wayang golek shows at the *National Museum*, 2000 Sun (entrance incl in museum entry ticket); *Bharata Theatre*, Jl Kalilio 15, Pasar Senen puts on Wayang Orang performances, T 4214937 for more information; as do *Teater Populer*, Jl Kebun Pala I (in Tanah Abang), T 3143041 for details.

● **Hospitals & medical services**

24 hrs emergency ambulance service: T 334030.

Hospitals: *Cipto Mangunkusumo*, Jl Diponegoro 71, T 332029; *Metropolitan Medical Centre*, Jl HR Rasuna Said Kav C21, Kuningan, T 5203435, F 5203417, rec by Swiss Embassy, reasonable facilities, doctors speak English, service is good; *Pondok Indah*, Jl Metro Duta 1, T 767525; *St Carolus*, Jl Salemba Raya 41, T 8580091.

Pharmacy: *Guardian Pharmacy*, Plaza Indonesia on Pondok Indah Mall or Blok M Plaza, only place supplying a strong mosquito repellent – *Mijex*.

Private clinics with English speaking doctors: *Medical Scheme*, Setia Budi Bldg, Kuningan; *SOS Medika*, Jl Puri Sakti 10/10, T 7393014.

Red Cross: Jl Kramat Raya 47.

● **Libraries**
British Council Library, T 5223311, Wijoyo Centre, Jl Jend Sudirman 56, open 0900-1300 (visitors must join to use the library); *Australian Cultural Centre*, Jl Rasuna Said (at the Embassy), library open Mon-Fri 1030-1530.

● **Places of worship**
Anglican: *All Saints*, Jl Prapatan, opp *Hyatt Aryaduta Hotel*; *St Patrick's Cathedral* (see *Jakarta Post* for times of services).

Catholic: *St Canisiut*, Jl Menteng Raya.

Methodist: *Jemaat Anugerah*, Jl Daan Mogot 100, every Sun, 0800.

● **Post & telecommunications**
Area code: 021.
General Post Office: Jl Pos Utara 2, Pasar Baru (or access from Jl Lapangan Banteng). Poste Restante open Mon-Fri 0800-1600, Sat 0800-1300.
Post Offices: on Jl Gajah Mada, Jl Fatahillah 3 (Kota); Jl Sumenep 9 (Menteng); Jl Cikini Raya.
Telegraph office: Jl Merdeka Selatan 12.
Telephone office: Telkom, Jakarta Theatre Bldg, Jl M H Thamrin 81 (open every day, 24 hrs; IDD and fax service available). There are numerous Warpostel and other telephone offices dotted around the city.

● **Sports**
Ancol Waterworld: 7,000Rp.

Bowling: at Ancol, Monas and Kebayoran Bowling Centres.

Fitness centres: many of the big hotels have these.

Golf: there are several courses around town. *Jakarta Golf Club*, Jl Rawamungun Muka Raya, T 4891208; *Kebayoran Golf Course*, Jl Asia Afrika Senayan, T 582508; *Padang Golf Jaya Ancol*, Jl Lodan Timur Ancol, T 682122.

Spectator sports: *jai alai* (similar to pelota) – said to be the fastest ball game in the world – can be seen at Ancol, 2100 Mon-Sun.

Swimming: all the major hotels have pools, some will allow non-residents to use their pools for a small charge, eg *Kartika Plaza*, Jl MH Thamrin (5,000Rp) – pleasant and not overcrowded, with poolside service; *Hotel Indonesia*, Jl MH Thamrin (10,000Rp). Other pools are at *Ancol Waterworld* and *Taman Mini*.

Waterskiing: at Ancol.

● **Shopping**
Fixed priced stores are becoming more common in Jakarta but bargaining is still the norm. When buying antiques and handicrafts, bargain down to 30%-40% of the original asking price, especially on Jl Surabaya.

Antiques: *Jl Kebon Sirih Timur Dalam* supports a row of antique shops said to be among the best in town – the goods on sale here are more likely to be genuine than anywhere else. The street is only 200m or so long and it is worth wandering along it to check out the shops. Among the best (from N to S) are: *Guci* at No 39; *Mitra Budaya* at No 21; and *Djody* at 20/22. Jl Palatehan 1 (nr *Blok M*), S of town in Kebayoran has several shops selling antiques and Indonesian handicrafts. The mass of stalls which line the famous *Jl Surabaya* is a great place to browse for smaller objects – anything from Golek puppets, wood carvings to brass ship's chandlery. There is little genuine for sale here – men sit by the side of the road openly 'distressing' newly-made objects. The quality of the 'antiquing' is quite high and it's easy to be fooled into believing they are antiques. Bargain hard (offer third or quarter of price). *Jl Majapahit*, NW of Merdeka Square, houses a number of shops with genuine antiques. *Jl Ciputat Raya* is quite a distance S of town, with better quality antiques and good furniture.

Bangka tin: locally mined pewter from *Pigura*, Palatehan 1/41; also at *Pasar Raya*, *Sarinah* and hotel boutiques.

Batik: *Ardiyanto*, Pasar Raya (3rd Flr), Jl Iskandarsyah 11/2; *Batik Keris*, Danar Hadi, Jl Raden Saleh 1A; *Batik Semar*, Jl Tomang Raya 54; *Government Batik Cooperative (GKBI)*, Jl Jend Sudirman 28; *Iwan Tirta*, Jl Panarukan 25 or *Hotel Borobudur*; one flr of *Pasar Raya, Blok M*, is devoted to batik; *Pasar Tanar Abang*, a market W of Merdeka Square, has good modern textiles, batik and ikat by the metre; *Srikandi*, Jl Melawai VI/6A. A batik factory at Jl Bendungan Hilir 2, in Senayan, is open to visitors.

Bookshops: *Gunung Agung Bookstore* on Jl Kwitang 6 (E of Jl Jaksa) for English books; *Gramedia*, Jl Gajah Mada 109 and Jl Melawai IV/13 Blok M; the new Plaza Indonesia has a couple of bookshops incl a *Times Books Store*; as do many of the major hotels. Jl Jaksa is a good place to buy second-hand books – both novels and travel guides – in most European languages; **Book Exchange**: there are also 2 book exchanges on Jl Jaksa.

Blok M & Pasar Raya

Sketch map: not to scale

Jl Trunojoyo

Jl Wolter Monginsidi

N

Jl Panglima Polim

Jl Sultan Haamudin

Blok M Plaza

Blok M Mall

Hotel Ambhara

Pasar Raya

Jl Iskandardjah

Melawal Plaza

Clothes: children's clothes are good value at *Pasar Raya* (*Blok M*). Adult fashions are improving and are also good value. *Sarinah Department Store* for international designs at reasonable prices and rack upon rack of ethnic clothing (such as batik shirts, dresses and jackets). Some of the large chain batik shops now supply ready-made batik, hand-painted silk and ikat in modern designs.

Electronic goods: for the best bargains, try the narrow crowded walkways of Kota in the northern part of the city.

Furniture: Jakarta is a good place to buy Indonesian specialities such as Palembang chests, painted Madura chests, Javanese chairs, planters' chairs, cupboards and boxes. Jl Kemang Raya and Jl Ciputat Raya (the latter is rather out of town, SW) both contain a number of furniture shops and are good places to start.

Gold: gold market on the second flr of *Pasar Cikini*, off Jl Pegangsaan Timur (an extension of Jl Cikini Raya), Menteng. Other suppliers can be found in *Blok M*.

Handicrafts: found at *Pasar Raya* and the *Sarinah Department Store*, in *Blok M* and Jl Palatehan 1 (Pigura at 41, Djenta at 37); *Indonesian Bazaar*, *Hilton Hotel*; *Pasar Seni* in Ancol. Jl Pasar Baru for Balinese woodcarving, silver workshops etc. Another *Sarinah Department Store* with 2 flrs of handicrafts and batik from across Indonesia is on Jl MH Thamrin (at the intersection with Jl KH Wahid Hasyim).

Jewellery: *Pasar Raya*, *Blok M*; *Sogo*, *Plaza Indonesia*, Jl Kemang Raya. For precious stones, try the *Indonesian Bazaar*, *Hilton Hotel* or *Pasar Uler*, NE of town in Tanjung Priok. For 'cheap' jewellery the prices are higher than in Yogya or Bali.

Maps: the *Discover Jakarta City Map* is adequate (and free from the Jakarta Tourist office). *Nelles* produces a good street map and for the most detail the *Jakarta Street Atlas* (published by Falk) is invaluable.

Markets: for more information on the markets of Jakarta, buy *A Jakarta market* by Kaarin Wall, published by the American Women's Association (5,000Rp).

Newspapers: *Jakarta Post* is an English language paper with information on events around town.

Paintings: *Duta Fine Arts Foundation*, Jl Bangka 1/55A; *Hadiprana Galleries*, Jl Palatehan 1/38; *Harris Art Gallery*, Jl Cipete 41; *Oet's Gallery*, Jl Palatehan 1/33; *Pasar Seni* (art market) at Ancol.

Pharmacies: *Guardian Pharmacy*, Plaza Indonesia or Pondok Indah Mall or Blok M Plaza

Shopping centres: there is now a glut of these ultra modern, ultra expensive malls in town; full of imported goods beyond the pocket of the average resident. The showcase is *Plaza Indonesia*, *Grand Hyatt Hotel*, Jl MH Thamrin. Avoid malls at the weekend, especially Sun, when Jakartans take their families to also 'cuci mata' (window shopping). *Blok M*, S of town in Kebayoran Baru is still the largest, it incl *Matahari*, *Melawai Plaza* and *Pasar Raya*, *Blok M* is well served by buses and is easily accessible; *Glodok Plaza* is N of town on Jl Hayam Wuruk and is another large shopping complex; *Pasar Baru* is N of Merdeka Sq.

Supermarket: for all westerners' deli cravings, visit *Kemchicks*, Jl Kemang Raya 3, S of town. *Hero's* and *Galael's* supermarkets are two chains which have stores across the city. *Sogo Department Store* (basement), part of Plaza Indonesia, Jl MH Thamrin, good selection of imported food, expensive. *Sarinah* (basement), Jl Thamrin, expensive.

Watches: copy watches in Blok M.

● **Tour companies & travel agents**

Most of the larger hotels have travel agents. The list of tour firms below is not comprehensive but incl many of the larger outfits. Most will arrange city tours, out-of-town day tours and also longer tours throughout the Indonesian archipelago. For agents and companies geared to the needs of those on a lower budget, Jl Jaksa is probably the best bet. Bus and train tickets are booked for destinations across the archipelago and other services provided. Of the larger companies are: *Atlantictour*, B-15, Harmoni Plaza Bldg, Jl Suryopranoto 2, T 2310011, F 376760; *Colors of Asia Travel*, Niaga Tower, 16th Flr, Jl Jend Sudirman, T 2505370, F 2505371, run tours to all parts of the archipelago, professional and well-run; *Continental*, Komplek Duta Merlin Blok A/22, Jl Gajah Mada 3-5, T 3803442; *Kalpataru Adventure*, Jl Galur Sari II/54, T 882150, organize wildlife tours to Krakatau and Ujung Kulon as well as further afield to Komodo, Kalimantan and Flores; *Kaltim Adventure Tour*, Jl Tanah Abang 11/23, T 361950, F 3802678, specializes in trekking tours to E Kalimantan; *Musi Holiday Travel Agency*, Jl Wahid Hasyim 12C, T 3800727; *Natrabu*, Jl Agus Salim 29A, T 331728; *Pacto*, Jl Taman Kemeng II Blok D2, T 7975874, F 7975881; *Pantravel*, Kartika Plaza, Jl MH Thamrin 10, T 320908; *Puri Tour*, Duta Merlin Complex Blok C 56-57, Jl Gajah Mada 3-5, T 3844646; *Rakata Adventure*, Jl Matraman 102, T 8582436, specialists in adventure destinations around Indonesia, reliable; *Robertur Kencana*, Jl Jaksa 20B, T 332926, can organize visa extension (50,000Rp for 2 weeks) or cheap trips to Singapore to renew visa; *RTQ*, Jl Jaksa 25C, T 3904501, efficient service, Mr Baginda speaks good English and is used to dealing with foreign visitors, rec for cheap flights and bus travel around Indonesia, photocopying, telephone calls, maps; *Satriavi*, Jl Prapatan 32, T 3803944, F 3806556; *Seabreeze*, Jl Jaksa 38, T 3902996; *Setia Tour*, Glodok Plaza, Jl Pinangsia Raya, T 336183; *Sona Topas*, Panin Bank Bldg, Jl Jend Sudirman 1, T 710636, *Borobudur Hotel*, 3rd Flr, T 361738 and *Hotel Indonesia*, T 3107567; *Tomaco*, Jakarta Theatre Building, Jl MH Thamrin 9, T 317435; *Universal Tour*, Jl Pintu Besar Selatan 82C, T 6901669; *Vayatour*, *President Hotel*, Jl Thamrin, T 3100720.

● **Tourist offices**

Directorate General of Tourism, Jl Kramat Raya 81, T 3103117, F 3101146, handouts on all regions of the country but many of limited use for those travelling independently. The **Jakarta Tourist Office** is in the Jakarta Theatre Bldg, Jl MH Thamrin 81, T 332067. They supply maps and information on sights in the city, open: Mon-Sat 0900-1630. There is a tourist information desk run by the Jakarta Tourist Office at the airport and another office at Fatahillah Square, in Kota, next to the *Café Batavia*.

● **Useful addresses**

American Express: T 5703310.

British Council: Wijoyo Centre, Jl Jend Sudirman 71, T 587411, F 586181 (visitors must join to use the facilities).

Immigration: Jl Warung Buncit Raya 207, T 7996340 or Jl Tengku Umar 1, T 3909744 or Jl Batutulis Raya 1, T 3845459 or at the airport T 5501764.

Police: Jl Jend Sudirman 45, T 587771.

The PHPA office: provides permits for Java's National Parks, Jl Gatot Subroto (Forestry Department Bldg [Departemen Kehutanan]).

● **Transport**

Local Bajaj: (orange motorized 3-wheelers, Indian made, pronounced *bajai*), sometimes known as 'panzer' bajaj because of their tank-like behaviour. There have been rumours that the government would like to do away with bajajs, as they have been deemed 'anti-humane'. They are already barred from Jakarta's main thoroughfares. Nonetheless, they remain the cheapest way to get around other than by bus or on foot. Negotiate price furiously before boarding and expect to pay a minimum of 1,000-1,500Rp for a short journey.

Bus: most fares 300Rp, up to 550Rp around town. Crowded, beware of pickpockets. Express buses (marked 'P' for Patas) are smaller and less crowded, 600Rp. Patas a/c express buses, 1,300Rp.

Car hire: most international companies strongly rec a driver and local expats believe it is pure madness to attempt tackling the streets of Jakarta oneself, visitors do, though, and survive. Cars with driver can be hired by the day for about US$50. **Avis**, Jl Diponegoro 25, T 3142900, also desks at Soekarno-Hatta Airport and the *Borobudur Intercontinental Hotel*, T 380555; **Bluebird**, Jl Hos, Cokroaminoto 107, T 332064, F 332175; **Hertz**, Plaza Podium, 7th Flr, Jl Jend Sudirman, T 5703683; **National**, Kartika Plaza Hotel, Jl MH Thamrin 10, T 333423; **Toyota Rentacar**, Jl KH Hasyim Ashari 31, T 362672.

Helicak: strange looking motorized bubbles, now rather rare.

Microlets: similar to colts; blue vans with set routes, 300-500Rp.

Taxi: the most comfortable and convenient way to get around the city. There are numerous companies in Jakarta, some more reliable than others. The company with the most cars is *President Taxis* (red and yellow cabs). But with the exception of the newest vehicles, they tend to be driven by migrants who have recently arrived in Jakarta and have little knowledge of the city. Meter fiddling is common. Among the most reliable are *Blue Bird* (T 7941234) and *Dian Taksi* (T 5807070). Avoid taxi drivers who refuse to use their meters (*Argos*) and make a point of locking the doors (especially after dark). Theft while stuck in traffic is becoming more common – most thieves are after just watches and money. Tipping is not usual, but round up the fare on the meter to the nearest 500Rp or 1,000Rp. Remember to have sufficient small bills to pay the fare, 900Rp flagfall and 450Rp for each additional kilometre.

Air Jakarta's **Soekarno-Hatta Airport** lies 25 km NW of the city, and connects Jakarta with all other major cities and towns in the country, as well as regional and global destinations (see pages 912-913 for route map). State-owned Garuda and Merpati Airlines operate out of Terminal A, all other international airlines from Terminal B (for airport facilities, see page 862). Terminal C is used by domestic airlines other than Garuda and Merpati – namely, Bouraq, Sempati and Mandala. Shuttle buses link the international and domestic terminals, but they stop early evening. **Transport to town**: there is a city 'air terminal' on the street flr level of the *Plaza Indonesia* (taxi drivers know it better as *Sogo*), Jl MH Thamrin 28-30. For US$20 they will organize reconfirmation of flights, airport transfer and baggage check-in – although this fee is pretty extortionate considering the buses only leave twice a day! Limousine service, 80,000Rp, metered taxis, 25,000-30,000Rp (plus a toll fee of 6,000Rp and surcharge of 2,300Rp). The unofficial taxi drivers who solicit for fares from unsuspecting tourists are usually a more expensive option than metered taxis. The airport authorities now hand out complaints cards for visitors to complete, setting out the toll charges and surcharges applicable. Allow at least an hour to reach the airport for the centre of town. Damri a/c bus connections with the Gambir railway station every hour from 0500-2400 (60 mins, 4,000Rp), a problem with this way of getting into town is that few taxi drivers at Gambir want to take fares down-town – consequently they overcharge. But it is convenient for Jl Jaksa (the centre for budget accommodation) which is just a 10-min walk away. A/c Damri buses also run to *Blok M*, Jl Bulungan; and Kemayoran (former domestic airport). Many of the first class hotels lay on transport. In addition, if travelling on Merpati, it is possible to check in at Gambir and then take advantage of their free airport shuttle.

Train Jakarta has 4 railway stations. The main station is **Gambir**, on the E side of Merdeka Square (Jl Merdeka Timur). Regular connections with Bogor 1 hr 20 mins (800Rp) on 3rd class, or non-stop, 50 mins (1,500Rp) on business class and Bandung 3 hrs, and connections with Yogya 10 hrs, Solo and Surabaya 14½ hrs. Left luggage locker facility here in upstairs restaurant, **Kota** station, in the old town also services Bandung and Yogya, and Surabaya (via Semarang and Cirebon). Night trains tend to depart from Kota. **Tanah Abang** station connects towns in W Java with Jakarta, incl the port of Merak 4 hrs – the ferry departure point to Sumatra. **Pasar Senen** connects the N coast towns of Cirebon, Semarang and Surabaya (see timetable on page 917).

Road Bus: there are 3 city bus terminals, all some distance from the city centre. **Kalideres Terminal**, T 592274, on the W edge of the city, 15 km from the centre, serves the W coast, incl Merak with a handful of connections on to Sumatra. Bus Nos 20, 26, 46A, 204, 913, 208, P02, P03, P6A, P7A and P18 all serve Kalideres terminal. **Kampung Rambutan**, about 15 km S of the city is a relatively new terminal primarily serving Bogor, Bandung and other towns and cities in West Java, 20 mins (1,000Rp) to Bogor. Buses to Sumatra and some other major long haul destinations incl Surabaya and Yogya also leave from Kampung Rambutan. Bus no. 502 from Jl Kebon Sirih, at the N end of Jl Jaksa, goes to Kampung Rambutan. **Pulo Gadung Terminal**, T 881763, 12 km E of the centre at the junction of Jl Bekasi Timur Raya and Jl Perintis Kemerdekaan, serves Central and E Java incl the towns of Cirebon 5 hrs, Yogya 12, Surabaya 15 hrs and Malang 18 hrs. Pulo Gadung is also the main bus terminal for Sumatra, with buses going to all the major towns – even as far as Banda Aceh, some 3,000 km N. Bali is served from Pulo Gadung, often via cities in East Java, and this terminal is by far the busiest of the three. Bus Nos 42, 44, 50, 51, 52, 55, 56, 57, 58, 59, 77, 501, 502, 504, 507, 508, 509, 907, P4, P5, P7, P7A, P9 and P13A all serve Pulo Gadung terminal. **Booking bus tickets**: private bus companies have their offices at these terminals. Alternatively, purchase tickets from a travel agent. The largest concentration of agents who book bus tickets is to be found on Jl Jaksa.

Sea Boat: Jakarta's port is Tanjung Priok, 15 km from the city centre. The state-owned shipping company PELNI has its head office at Jl Gajah Mada 14, T 343307. Its ticket office is at Jl Angkasa 20, T 4217406. A counter on the 2nd flr of the bldg is much less crowded for ticket purchase (entrance on right of building). Two photocopies of passport are required (photocopying shop on left of building, as you face it). There are also many more Pelni agents in town, which though they levy a small surcharge are often far more convenient. The

Jakarta Tourist Board, Jakarta Theatre Bldg, has information on sailing schedules (see page 921). **Getting to Tanjung Priok**: Bus no 60 from Jl Pos or bus no P14 from Jl Kebon Sirih, off Jl Jaksa. Or take a taxi. Allow at least an hour. It is less than 1 km from the bus station at Tanjung Priok to the Pelni dock.

West Java

The province of West Java accounts for much of the west third of the island of Java, bar the Special Territory of Greater Jakarta which is a province in its own right. Long regarded as the most prosperous of the provinces of Java (excepting Jakarta), West Java supports the greatest concentration of people and the most prestigious universities in Indonesia, as well as two of the country's most important industrial enterprises: the Krakatau Steelworks and the aircraft manufacturer, IPTN. The province covers 46,300 sq km and has a population of 35 million – giving it a population density of over 750 people per sq km. The capital of West Java is the hill city of Bandung with a population of over 2 million.

West Java consists of three distinct geographical regions: the S and W coasts, the central highlands, and the northern coastal plain.

A lack of good agricultural land, poor natural harbours, and the difficulties of overland communication, makes the **S and W coast region** the poorest area in W Java. For the visitor, the S coast offers the beach resorts of Pangandaran and Pelabuhanratu, while the W coast has Carita and Anyer, as well as the famous Ujung Kulon National Park.

The **Central Highlands** is an area of spectacular scenery, dominated by a series of impressive volcanoes. During the colonial era, the highlands were developed as an area of plantation agriculture, with stands of coffee, tea, cinchona (the bark of which was used to produce quinine) and other crops. The two hill towns of Bogor and Bandung expanded on the back of the plantation economy. With the gradual decline of the plantation sector Bogor lost out to more dynamic Javanese cities, although Bandung has managed to make the transition and is now a centre of manufacturing and higher education. In place of plantation crops, farmers now grow so-called *palawija* (non-rice food) crops – cassava, maize, groundnuts, sweet potatoes and various beans. It is this region which holds the greatest attractions for the visitor: the cool, hill resorts of Bogor and those in the vicinity of the Puncak Pass; the university city of Bandung, and hiking in the highlands around towns such as Garut.

The third region is the **Northern Coastal Plain**, an area of intensive rice production. At the very NW corner of this

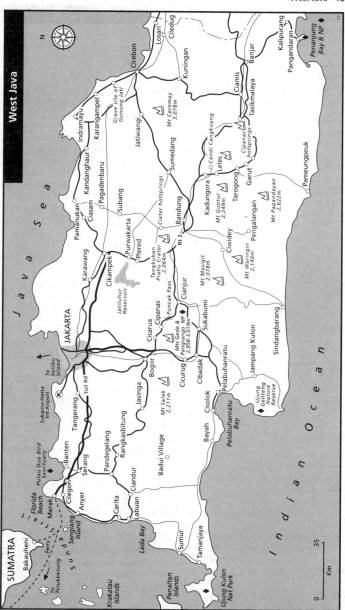

region, an industrial centre has developed around the town of Cilegon, exploiting the improved communications which link Jakarta with Sumatra via the port of Merak. Other than Jakarta, the largest town on the N coast is Cirebon, at the E edge of the province and famous for its distinctive style of batik.

THE FAR WEST

PULAU SERIBU

Pulau Seribu, or 'Thousand Islands' was clearly named by someone who was either intent on deception, or had no idea how many islands there are here, or was mathematically challenged: just 112 small islands make up this mini-archipelago in the Java Sea. They are situated off Java's N coast, just to the W of Jakarta, and are becoming increasingly popular as a tourist destination. The Dutch VOC had a presence on the islands from the 17th century, building forts, churches and shipyards.

Pulau Onrust is one of the closest islands to the mainland. It was used by the Dutch from the early 17th century and became an important ship repair centre; by 1775 as many as 2,000 people were living on the island. But in the 1800's the British sacked and burnt the small settlement, so that today only ruins remain. **Pulau Bidadari** also has ruins of a fort and leper hospital built by the VOC. It lies 15 km from Ancol (45 mins by speedboat). **Pulau Laki** is one of the inner islands situated 3 km offshore from Tanjung Kait W of Jakarta.

Venturing further N into the Java Sea, there are a succession of privately-owned resorts including **Pulau Ayer**, **Pulau Putri**, **Pulau Pelangi**, **Pulau Kotok** and **Pulau Panjang**, in that order. They have beautiful beaches and offer snorkeling, scuba diving, jet skiing, and windsurfing.

● **Accommodation Pulau Bidadari: A-B** Cottage accommodation and restaurant, managed by *Marina Ancol*, Taman Impian Jaya Ancol, T 680048. **Pulau Ayer: A** *Pulau Ayer Resort Hotel*, cottages available, some built over the sea, pool, tennis, jetski, fishing, snorkeling facilities, contact *Sarotama Prima Perkasa*, Jl Ir H Juanda 111/6, T 342031, F 358142. **Pulau Putri, Pulau Pelangi, Pulau Perak, Pulau Melintang and Pulau Petonden: A+-A** Cottage-style accommodation managed by *Pulau Seribu Paradise*, Jl Wahid Hasyim 69, T 348533, F 344039, a/c, restaurants, diving, fishing and sailing facilities. **Pulau**

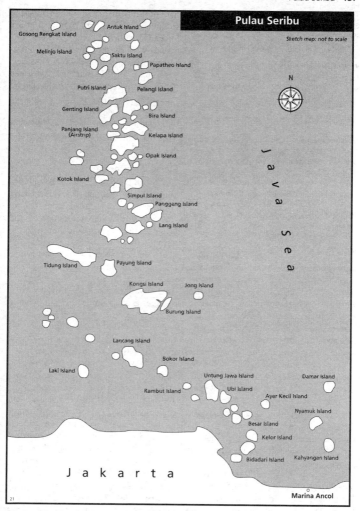

Pulau Seribu

Sketch map: not to scale

Gosong Rengkat Island
Antuk Island
Melinjo Island
Saktu Island
Papatheo Island
Putri Island
Pelangi Island
Genting Island
Bira Island
Panjang Island (Airstrip)
Kelapa Island
Opak Island
Kotok Island
Simpul Island
Panggang Island
Lang Island
Tidung Island
Payung Island
Kongsi Island
Jong Island
Burung Island
Lancang Island
Bokor Island
Laki Island
Untung Jawa Island
Damar Island
Rambut Island
Ubi Island
Ayer Kecil Island
Nyamuk Island
Besar Island
Kelor Island
Bidadari Island
Kahyangan Island

Java Sea

N

J a k a r t a

Marina Ancol

Kotok: **A** Simple wooden bungalow accommodation (a/c and non a/c) and restaurant, together with a full range of watersports facilities incl diving, contact *Kotok Island Resort*, Duta Merlin Shopping Arcade, 3rd Flr, Jl Gajah Mada, T 362948, F 362499. **Pulau Laki**: **A** Cottages with pool, tennis, jetski, windsurfing, scuba, fishing, etc, contact *Fadent Gema Scorpio*, Jl HOS Cokroaminoto 116, T 44353. **Pulau Macan Besar**: **L-A+** *Matahari Island Resort*, cottage accommodation on 6 ha island with bathrooms and TV, swimming pool, price incl all meals and transfer from Ancol Marina, contact *Matahari Impian Indah*, Jl Pangeran, T 6281234, F 6296652. **Pulau Barat** and **Pulau Timur** are amongst the most northern islands: **Barat** has 34 cottages, Japanese restaurant, swimming pool and dive shop.

Timur has 56 cottages, restaurant, tennis courts and marine sports rental shop. Contact *Pantara Wisata Jaya*, Mid Plaza 19th Flr, Jl Jend Sudirman Kav 10-11 Jakarta, T 5706200, F 5706286.

● **Transport Air** There is an airstrip on Pulau Panjang. The trip takes 25 mins from Jakarta. Boat transfers to other islands. **Helicopter**: transfer available on request from Fadent Gema Scorpio (see above), who have cottages on Pulau Laki. **Sea Boat**: a regular ferry service leaves from the Marina Jaya at Ancol at 0700, returning from the islands at 1430. The trip takes 2-4 hrs to the outer islands, 30 mins-1 hr to Onrust and Bidadari. **Hydrofoil**: Hover Maritime Semandera (HMS) operate a service taking 90 mins to the islands, departing 0700 from Ancol, returning 1500, T 325608 for more information.

Pulau Seribu Paradise (see above) organize transport to their islands by speedboat, or small airplane to Panjang Island and speedboat on.

BANTEN

West of Jakarta and 10 km N of Serang lies a rather scruffy little port; all that remains of the once powerful Banten (or Bantam). This town was the centre of an Islamic Empire from the 12th-15th century which managed to retain its independence from neighbouring Mataram. It derived its wealth from controlling the lucrative trade in pepper and other spices. Situated on the strategic Sunda Strait, the kingdom conquered Lampung in S Sumatra and Pajajaran in W Java.

Banten reached the height of its power during the reign of Sultan Agung (1651-1683), ironically just at the time that the Dutch and English were intensifying their presence in the area around Batavia (Jakarta). It is likely that Banten was the largest city in Java (possibly Indonesia) until as late as the 19th century; Raffles in his *History of Java* thought the sultanate had a total population of 232,000. Even so, contemporary accounts record that people living on the outskirts of the city still had to contend with the threat of tigers.

Sultan Agung, suspicious of Dutch and, to a lesser extent, English intentions, made frequent attacks on Batavia, finally declaring war in 1680. But the Sultanate had nothing to match Dutch military technology and by 1684 Agung, after his forces had suffered great losses, was defeated. With Agung vanquished, Banten became a vassal state of Batavia. However, it was not until 1832 that the last vestiges of the Sultans' power were eliminated by the Dutch when they finally formally annexed the territory and abolished the sultanate. By that time, the harbour had silted-up and the focus of Javanese trade had shifted to other locations.

Places of interest

The site of the historic city of Banten lies outside 'New' Banten, at **Banten Lama** (Old Banten). The road from Serang crosses a bridge and the minaret of the mosque can be seen in the distance. To the right of the path to the mosque is the **Museum Situs Kerpurbakalaan**, with a modest display of archaeological artefacts unearthed in the surrounding area. Open 0900-1600 Tues-Sun. Close by is the **Mesjid Agung**, an example of Hindu-Islamic architecture, built in 1556 by Sultan Maulana Jusuf, son of Hasanuddin, and still very much in use. There are good views from the top of the adjacent minaret, designed by a Dutch Muslim (some sources maintain it was built by a Chinese Muslim) at about the same time as the mosque. Near and just to the S of the mosque are some ruined walls and excavated foundations – all that remains of the **Surosowan Palace**, built by Sultan Hasanuddin, destroyed during the reign of Sultan Agung, rebuilt, and then finally levelled by the Dutch Governor-General Daendels in 1832.

Northwest of the mosque are the ruins of **Spellwijck Fortress**, built by the Dutch in 1682 (and subsequently extended), in an attempt to keep Sultan Agung at bay. Near the fort are tombs of the Dutch soldiers who died in the battle for Banten. West of the fort is a large 200-year-old renovated Chinese temple, **Klenteng**, which is still in use today. Just outside the town, back on the road to Serang and just before the bridge over the

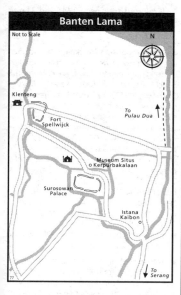

Banten Lama

Not to Scale

N

Klenteng

To
Pulau Dua

Fort
Spellwijck

Museum Situs
o Kerpurbakalaan

Surosowan
Palace

Istana
Kaibon

To
Serang

77

river, are the ruins of the **Istana Kaibon**, the palace of Queen Aisyah, mother of Banten's last sultan. It was destroyed by the Dutch in 1832, at the same time that Banten lost its final struggle with Batavia for even a small morsel of independence. The Dutch, symbolically, used the bricks to construct their own buildings.

Excursions

Pulau Dua is a low-lying island off the coast from Banten and an ornithologist's dream, being Indonesia's (and one of the world's) major **bird sanctuaries**. The island is best visited between Mar and Jul when migratory birds arrive on the island to breed. There are good, though sometimes poorly maintained, observation towers for viewing nesting sites. The island has no accommodation, but guides are available to point out birdlife. *Getting there*: from Karanghantu Harbour, 1 km from Banten. The boat ride takes 30 mins and a 2-hr tour costs about 50,000Rp. The island can also be reached by land, along a recently made causeway.

● **Accommodation** None available in Banten. The nearest town with accommodation is Serang, 10 km S of Banten where there are **E** *Abadi*, Jl Jend Sudirman 36, T 81641; and **E** *Serang*, Jl Jend A Yani 38.

● **Places to eat** Foodstalls surround the carpark by the mesjid.

● **Transport** 10 km from Serang, 100 km from Jakarta. **Road Bus**: from Jakarta's Kalideres station to Serang, 2 hrs. From Serang, catch an angkutan to Banten from the minibus station at Pasar Lama. They drop off by the mosque. **Taxi**: from Jakarta, 2½-3hrs (100,000Rp). **Train** Slow local trains run from Tanah Abang Station in Jakarta to Serang.

MERAK

Merak is the point of departure and arrival for **Sumatra** and is one of the dirtiest and noisiest towns in Java.

Excursions The massive **Krakatau Steelworks** are 14 km outside Merak on the road to Jakarta, nr the town of Cilegon. PT Krakatau Steel is one of the two largest state enterprises in the country (the other being PT Nusantara at Bandung). Built by the state oil company Pertamina during the period of booming oil prices between 1973 and 1982, it received investments totalling nearly US\$4bn. It is an impressive monument to the wealth and excesses of the oil boom. It is said that the construction of the plant involved corruption on a scale unheard of even in Indonesia. Many people believe the money could have been more productively spent in some other way and, in Indonesian terms, it is hard not to see it as a monumental white elephant. In short, it was a prestige project which gained a momentum of its own. Tours can be taken around the steelworks.

Florida Beach is a few kilometres N of Merak and has good sand, but is too close to Merak to be attractive to most visitors.

● **Accommodation** in Merak is over-priced and poor; only people waiting for a ferry stay here. **B** *Merak Beach*, Jl Raya Merak, T 3106440, a/c, most comfortable hotel in town, but only rec as a stopover while waiting for the ferry; 2 km from the ferry sandwiched between the road and the sea; **D-E** *Hotel Anda*, Jl Florida 4, T 71041, some a/c, close to the ferry, rooms are serviceable; **E** *Hotel Robinson*, Jl Florida 7, close to the ferry, just about OK to stay the night, but hardly out of choice; **E** *Nirmala*, Jl Pelabuhan Merak 30; **E** *Sulawesi I*, Jl Pelabuhan 8; **E** *Sulawesi II*, Jl Pelabuhan 8.

● **Transport** 140 km from Jakarta. The fast Jl Toll road is complete all the way from Jakarta to Merak. The old road, used by many lorries and buses, is slow and busy. **Road Bus**: the station is close to the ferry dock. Regular connections with Jakarta's Kalideres station, 2½ hrs. Buses are also available from Merak to major regional centres in Java including Bandung, Yogya, Bogor, Solo and Cirebon, but these leave less frequently. For Anyer Carita and Labuan buses leave from the Cilegon terminal. **Train** The station is close to the ferry. Connections with Jakarta's Tanah Abang station early morning and early afternoon 3½-4 hrs (1,500Rp). **Sea Boat**: regular car ferries link Merak with Bakauheni on the S tip of Sumatra. Times of departure vary through the year, but normally there are about 15 crossings/day, 1½ hrs (24,200Rp/car, 1,300-2,400Rp pp, depending on class).

ANYER

South of Cilegon and Merak is the small town of Anyer, once an important Dutch port. Much of the town was destroyed by the tidal wave which followed the eruption of Krakatau in 1883. The most notable feature of the town is the elegant white **lighthouse**, built by Queen Wilhelmina of the Netherlands in 1886, following the Krakatau disaster.

Anyer is more popular with Jakarta residents than with foreign visitors, and there are innumerable holiday bungalows along the coast S from Merak.

Excursions Pulau Sangiang is a jungle-clothed island in the Sunda Strait. The waters around the island offer good diving and snorkelling (both coral and WW2 wrecks). There is no accommodation on the island. *Getting there*: chartered traditional wooden boats take about 1½ hrs from Anyer Kidul, a speedboat takes about half the time.

Krakatau (see page 144) and **Ujung Kulon** (see page 141) can both be reached from Anyer.

● **Accommodation** Weekday rates are often less than those at weekends. Accommodation is strung out along the coast. **A+-A** *Mambruk Beach Resort*, Jl Raya Karang Bolong, T 601602, F 81723, J 716318, a/c, restaurant, pool, tennis courts, diving and fishing, expensive, but professionally run and highly rec by those who stay here; **A** *Ancott*, Jl Raya Anyer Km 21, T 601556, J 7994809, a/c, pool, some bungalows self-catering, located on a quiet strip of beach, popular; **A** *Anyer Beach Hometel & Resort*, Jl Raya Karang Bolong Km 17/153, T 629224, F 6295000, a/c, pool, large, clean bungalows; **A** *Anyer Seaside Cottages*, Jl Raya Karang Bolong Km 35; **A** *Patra Jasa (Anyer Beach Hotel)*, Jl Raya Karang Bolong, T 81376, F 81872, J 510503, a/c, built in 1973 by Pertamina, comfortable enough; **A** *Villa Ryugu*, T 91894, a/c, 2 bedroom 'units'.

● **Transport** 119 km from Jakarta, 12 km from Cilegon, 26 km from Merak, 41 km from Labuan. **Road Bus**: regular connections with Jakarta's Kalideres station, Merak and Cilegon. **Note** that it may be necessary to change buses in Cilegon.

LABUAN/CARITA BEACH

Labuan is the main point of departure for the Ujung Kulon National Park (see page 141) and for Krakatau (page 144). There are holiday bungalows all along the coast, as well as some hotels. Like Anyer, Carita is a resort for tired Jakartans rather than foreign visitors. There is an attractive 3 km-long sandy beach here with reasonable surf (best in the afternoon).

● **Accommodation** A selection of hotels and losmen along these 2 beaches incl: **Carita Beach**: **A** *Carita Beach Resort*, T 202222, J 5720361, F 5720360, next door to *Mutiara Carita Cottages* and owned by the same group, a/c, restaurant, pool, rooms in main block and some cottages, tennis court, good for families; **A** *Mutiara Carita Cottages*, J 5720361, F 5720360, pool, wooden cottages with attached kitchens, beach is only average here; **A-C** *Desiana*, T 201010, J 593316, a/c, restaurant, boat trips, the beach here is poor and rather dirty, although the hotel is homely and friendly; **B-D** *Carita Krakatau Beach*, T 81206,

J 320252, most popular base from which to visit Krakatau and Ujung Kulon, good information with excellent beach front position, a one-time favourite among budget travellers – now rather too expensive, although also offers cheaper hostel accommodation, showing its age (**B-C** at weekends); **E** *Rakata Hostel*, linked to *Carita Krakatau Beach Hotel*, popular base for those on lower budget; **E-F** *Black Rhino*, T 81072, best of the cheap places, simple clean rooms with shared mandi, good source of information, organize tours. **Labuan Town and Carita Village**: **E** *Caringin*, Jl Caringin 20 (Carita side of Labuan town); **E** *Losman Sunset*, Carita Village, simple but well kept rooms, friendly, away from beach, good budget accommodation.

● **Useful addresses PHPA office**: Jl Perintis Kemerdekaan 43 (Labuan-Carita road, 2 km from Labuan towards Carita), T 81217.

● **Transport** 158 km from Jakarta, 41 km from Anyer, 67 km from Merak. **Road Bus**: regular connections with Jakarta's Kalideres station and with Merak and Cilegon. To reach Carita Beach, take one of the frequent colts from Labuan.

UJUNG KULON NATIONAL PARK

This peaceful wilderness occupies 162,000 ha of land and sea on the SW tip of Java, and contains some of the last stands of tropical lowland rainforest on densely populated Java. It is a little-visited haven for people wishing to escape the crowds and enjoy some walking on the cool trails through the forest. The park comprises a chunk of the 'mainland' along with several islands (including Panaitan, Peucang and Handeuleum), and the surrounding sea. The eruption of Krakatau in 1883, and the subsequent tidal wave, destroyed some of the lowland tropical rainforest here; trees fossilized by volcanic dust bear witness to the event. The area was first declared a protected area in 1921, was designated a Nature Reserve in 1958, and was upgraded to National Park status in 1980. It has recently been given World Heritage status – one of only two natural World Heritage sites in Indonesia (the other being Komodo Island). *Best time to visit*: Apr-Nov.

The Park's main claim to fame is its small population of Javan Rhinoceros (see box) – although these are very rarely seen by visitors to the park. Other, more accessible, wildlife include wild pig, barking deer (*muntjak*), wild buffalo (*banteng*), leopard, the rare leaf-eating monkey, crab-eating macaques and civets. Nine of the mammals to be found at Ujung Kulon are on the Red List of threatened mammals, and there are over 50 species of rare plants. The park also supports a diverse community of birdlife – about half of the known species of bird to be found on Java are present in the park, including hornbills. There are a number of established trails through the park's forests, the most popular being the 3-day hike from Tamanjaya to Peucang Island. Marine life is abundant around Peucang Island and off the northern coast. In contrast to the calm waters of the N coast, the S is rugged and wave-swept and in consequence is becoming increasingly popular with surfers.

Handeuleum Island's attractions include an area where banteng (wild buffalo) can be seen grazing, canoe trips up the Cigenter River, a 2-hr walk to the Curung Waterfall through an area frequented by rhino, and motorboat trips up the Cikabeumbeum River through mangrove forest.

Best time to visit: during the dry season, Apr-Oct.

Park information
● **Permits & guides**

The PHPA office (park office) recommends that visitors hiking through the park employ a guide (7,500-10,000Rp/day); porters and cooks are also available. Enquire at the PHPA office in Labuan. Admission: a permit must be obtained, available from the PHPA office in Labuan at Jl Perintis Kemerdekaan 43, T 81217. 2,000Rp pp, plus 1,500Rp pp insurance (for search and rescue), for a period of 7 days. Office hours 0730-1400 Mon-Thur and Sat, 0730-1100 Fri.

● **Accommodation**

Guesthouses are managed by *Wanawisata Alam Hayati*, Gedung Manggala Wanabakti, Blok 4, Jl Jend Gatot Subroto, Senayan, Jakarta T 5700238. Bookings can be made through them or at the Labuan PHPA office (see address above). Advance booking is rec.

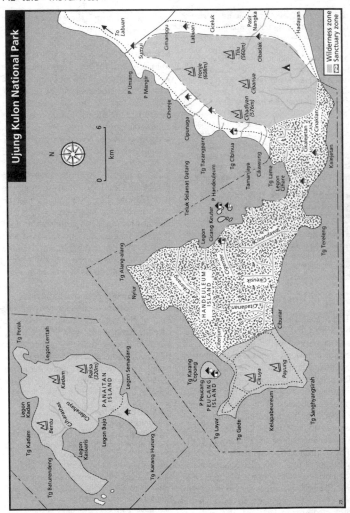

Ujung Kulon National Park

Wilderness zone
Sanctuary zone

Peucang Island: **A** *Peucang Lodges* (opened 1991) has 16 bedrooms and holds a max of 32 people, a/c, restaurant, hot water, tv, all meals provided; **B** *Peucang Guesthouse* (the original guesthouse in the park) holds a max of 12 people in 5 double/triple rooms, with attached bathrooms for 3 rm, price inclues breakfast.

Handeuleum Island: **C** Attractive Swiss-style cottages, with 4 bedrooms, sleeping a max of 10 people, shared bathroom.

Tamanjaya (mainland village): **C** *Wanawisata Lodges*, 2 lodges recently renovated, each with 3 bedrooms and shared bathroom.

● **Camping**
Camping sites are available throughout the park, but no facilities are provided.

The Javan Rhinoceros (*Rhinoceros Sondaicus*): the rarest mammal on Earth?

The Javan (also known as the lesser, or Javan one-horned) rhinoceros was once distributed from Upper Burma S to Java but is now thought to be restricted to a small population in the Ujung Kulon National Park, W Java and a second, even smaller group, in Vietnam. When Europeans first arrived in Southeast Asia, the Javan rhinoceros was still to be found in Sumatra, Malaya, Thailand, Burma and Vietnam. Their disappearance was due to over-hunting. A Hoogerwerf notes that the Belgian big game hunter, Baron Robert de Charcourt, killed 300 rhinoceros in his lifetime (mostly in Africa). He met his end in Sumatra when, appropriately, he was killed by one of the wounded beasts that he had been terrorizing for so many years. A British newspaper, recording his fate, reported: "Shortly before he died, de Charcourt opened his eyes once more and said with a loud, clear voice to his head boy: 'Mark him down, Latiki. He is number 300...'". As A Hoogerwerf notes "it is only to be regretted that such 'heroes' lived so long".

In 1930, various estimates of the numbers of *sondaicus* left ranged from five to 100. By 1970 there was thought to be only a single herd of 28 animals, giving it the dubious honour of being the rarest large mammal in the world. However, with the protection against poaching now given by the guards of the Ujung Kulon National Park, the numbers have increased to approximately 60 animals. In 1990 Vietnamese naturalists discovered to their – and the world's – amazement, another small herd in Vietnam.

The Javan rhinoceros' distinctive 'armour plated' appearance is due to the folds of skin which delineate the neck and legs from the body. With an average shoulder height of 1.6m, they carry a single horn, and inhabit dense lowland forest. They particularly enjoy wallowing in mud and are rarely found far from water. Their small stature (for a rhino) and tendency to inhabit thick forest, rather than the open savannas and grasslands like their African cousins, makes them difficult to spot.

As with other rhinos, the value of the powdered horn as a universal medicine to the Chinese led to widespread hunting and its extermination throughout Southeast Asia bar these two small, relict populations. The female only gives birth once every 3-4 years so rebuilding the population will be a long, perhaps a fruitless, process. The supposed effectiveness of rhino horn as a cure-all was noted by George Rumphius in his *Amboinese rariteitenkamer* written during his long stay in the East Indies from 1654-1702 as a VOC official. He claimed it cured snakebite, could indicate the presence of poison in drink (the drink was said to foam if drunk from a horn cup) and, of course, was an aphrodisiac. But it is not just the horn (*say kak*) that is prized. Hooves (*sie kok sze*), 'salt' from the hide (*say goe phwee*), 'two blunt teeth lying between the canine teeth', and even the undigested contents of the stomach, are believed to have medicinal powers. Gee (1964) notes that the horn placed under the bed of pregnant mothers would alleviate the pain of birth, writing: "Persons owning a horn would rent it out to expectant mothers for the equivalent of 30 pounds each time!". He goes on: "Yet another absurd belief was that a rhino horn left to soak in a filled bucket turned the water into a sort of elixir of life, of which members of a family would sip a spoonful every day!". The outcome of these unfounded beliefs was not a happy one for the Javan, as well as other, rhinoceros.

● **Places to eat**

Visitors should take their own food and water. Restaurants are available at the accommodation site on Peucang Island. For campers, take all your food and drink with you.

● **Tour companies & travel agents**

Wanawisata Tours and Travel, Jl Jend Gatot Subroto, T 5700238, F 5701141, organize 2-4 day tours to the park and Krakatau.

● **Transport**

Road Bus: regular connections with Jakarta's Kalideres station to Labuan. From there, take a bus to Sumur, and then an *ojek* to Tamanjaya. 4WD vehicles can also negotiate the road to Tamanjaya. Alternatively, go by boat from Labuan (see below).

Sea Boat: available from Labuan. The *Wanawisata Alamhayati* company provides a boat every Mon and Fri at 0800 for trips to Peucang Island, via Tamanjaya and Handeuleum Island. The boat returns to Labuan every Thur and Sun; for further information contact the PHPA office or *PT Wanawisata*, the company that operates the vessel, in Jakarta (T 5700238)

(see **Accommodation** for address). Boats also run from Tamanjaya to the islands. Approximate cost is 60,000Rp from Labuan or Tamanjaya to Peucang Island. Faster launches can be chartered to the park from Anyer, Merak and Carita.

KRAKATAU

Krakatau is the site of the largest volcanic eruption ever recorded. The explosion occurred on the morning of the 27 August 1883, had a force equivalent to 2,000 Hiroshima bombs, and resulted in the death of 36,000 people. Tidal waves (*tsunami*) 40m high, radiating outwards at speeds, reportedly, of over 500 km per hour destroyed coastal towns and villages. The explosion was heard from Sri Lanka to Perth (Australia) and the resulting waves led to a noticeable surge in the English Channel. The explosion was such that the 400m-high cone was replaced by a marine trench 300m deep.

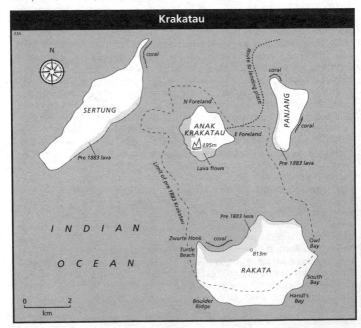

Krakatau

Rupert Furneau writes in his book *Krakatoa* (1965):-

"At ten o'clock plus 2 mins, three-quarters of Krakatoa Island, eleven square miles of its surface, an area not much less than Manhattan, a mass of rock and earth one and one-eighth cubic miles in extent, collapsed into a chasm beneath. Nineteen hours of continuous eruption had drained the magma from the chamber faster than it could be replenished from below. Their support removed, thousands of tons of roof rock crashed into the void below. Krakatoa's three cones caved in. The sea bed reared and opened in upheaval. The sea rushed into the gaping hole. From the raging cauldron of seething rocks, frothing magma and hissing sea, spewed an immense quantity of water......From the volcano roared a mighty blast, Krakatoa's death cry, the greatest volume of sound recorded in human history".

In 1927, further volcanic activity caused a new island to rise above the sea – Anak Krakatau (child of Krakatau). Today this island stands 200m above sea-level and visitors may walk from the E side of the island upon the warm, devastated landscape through deep ash, to the main crater. It remains desolate and uninhabited, though the other surrounding islands have been extensively recolonized (a process carefully recorded by naturalists; the first visitor after the 1883 explosion noted a spider vainly spinning a web). Check that the volcano is safe to visit and take thick-soled walking shoes (Krakatau is still avowedly active: between 1927 and 1992 it erupted no less than 73 times). There is good snorkeling and diving in the water around the cliffs; the undersea thermal springs cause abundant marine plant growth and this in turn attracts a wealth of sea creatures, big and small. *Best time to visit*: the sea crossing is calmest and the weather best Apr-Jun and Sep-Oct. Between Nov and Mar there are strong currents and often rough seas.

NB Check either at the PHPA office in Labuan or at one of the hotels or tour agents regarding Krakatau's state of activity. In 1993 travellers died approaching too close to the active cone.

● **Tours** Although it is possible to charter your own boat (see **Transport**, below), the cheapest and safest way to visit the island is on a tour where the cost can be shared. Many of the hotels in Carita – incl *Black Rhino*, and *Carita Beach Resort* – run tours. Expect to pay about 50,000Rp pp.

● **Transport Sea Boat**: boats can be chartered from Anyer, Carita and Labuan. Locals have gained a reputation for overcharging and then providing un-seaworthy boats. (It is said that two Californian women spent 3 weeks drifting in the Sunda Strait, living on sea-water and toothpaste, before being washed ashore nr Bengkulu, W Sumatra.) The *Mambruk Beach Resort* at Anyer has a fast launch for hire to Krakatau (2 hrs) while the *Carita Krakatau Beach Hotel* has two boats, one costing 300,000Rp to charter, taking 4 hrs each way, the other costing 750,000Rp and taking 2 hrs (they also have a waiting list for single travellers). If chartering a local boat from Carita, Labuan or Anyer, make certain that there is sufficient petrol for the two way journey and that it is understood at what time you wish to return to the mainland – visitors have been stranded on Krakatau, no doubt with visions of a repeat of the 1883 event. Prices vary according to the size and condition of the vessel, but expect to pay 250-300,000Rp. The PHPA office in Labuan (see page 141) can help in chartering a vessel.

THE WEST CENTRAL HIGHLANDS AND SOUTH COAST

BOGOR

Bogor is best known as the site of one of the finest Botanical Gardens in Southeast Asia. But the town's history pre-dates the Gardens. It seems that during the 5th century the Hindu Kingdom of Tarumanegara had its capital in the vicinity of Bogor. Rather later, a second Hindu Kingdom, Pajajaran, was focused here from the 12th-16th century. Little remains of this period save for the Batutulis monolith which records the reign of King Surawisesa who ascended to the throne of Pajajaran in 1533 (see below).

The town lies 290m above sea-level in an upland valley, surrounded by mounts Salak, Pangrango and Gede. Average temperatures are a pleasant 26°C, significantly cooler than Jakarta, but rainfall is the highest in Java at 3,000-4,000 mm per year. The Dutch, quite literally sick to death of the heat, humidity and the swampy conditions of Jakarta, developed Bogor as a hill retreat.

In 1745, Governor-General Imhoff built a palace here which he named 'Buitenzorg' ('Without a Care'), modelling it on Blenheim Palace in Oxfordshire, England. The palace later burnt down, but was rebuilt and became the official residence of successive governor-generals from 1870-1942. Stamford Raffles, governor-general of Java during the Napoleonic Wars, stayed here, so it was not just the Dutch who found the town enticing. A memorial to Raffles' first wife who died while he was governor-general of the Dutch East Indies stands in the Botanical Gardens.

Bogor is centred on the lush botanical gardens, with views over red-tiled roofs, stacked one on top of the other, and toppling down to the Ciliwung River which runs through the middle of the town and gardens. The Ciliwung, which has cut a deep gorge, has also become a convenient place to discard rubbish, marring some of the views in the process. The town has a large community of Christians, and a surprising number of Western fastfood outlets and department stores. These serve the population of wealthy Indonesians who live here and commute into Jakarta. A scattering of old colonial buildings is still to be found around town – for instance, set back from the road on Jl Suryakencana.

Places of interest

The superb **Botanical Gardens (Kebun Raya)** dominate the centre of the city, covering an immense 87 ha. The gardens are usually thought to have been established under the instructions of Sir Stamford Raffles. Certainly, Raffles was a keen botanist – borne out in his numerous publications. However, it was the Dutch Governor-General Van de Capellan who commissioned the transformation of the gardens into arguably the finest in Asia. The botanist Professor Reinhardt from Kew Gardens in England, assisted by James Hooper and William Rent, also from Kew, undertook the major portion of the work in 1817. As early as 1822 the Gardens contained 912 recorded plant species, and today there are said to be 2,735. The gardens became world renowned for their research into the cash crops of the region (tea, rubber, coffee, tobacco and chinchona – from the bark of which quinine is derived). The giant water lily, as well as a huge variety of orchids, palms and bamboos can be seen here. It used to be possible to see the giant Rafflesia flower as well (see page 490), although it is reported that the specimen has now died. Admission 2,100Rp, Mon-Sat, 1,100Rp Sun and holidays. Open 0800-1600 Mon-Sun.

Deer graze in front of the imposing **Presidential Palace** or **Istana Bogor**, which lies within the Gardens, directly N of the main gates (there is also an entrance on Jl Ir H Juanda). The building is not the original 'Buitenzorg' of Governor-General Imhoff. That building was

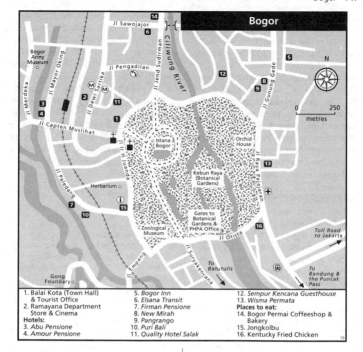

Bogor

N

0   250
metres

1. Balai Kota (Town Hall) & Tourist Office	5. Bogor Inn	12. Sempur Kencana Guesthouse
2. Ramayana Department Store & Cinema	6. Elsana Transit	13. Wisma Permata
Hotels:	7. Firman Pensione	**Places to eat:**
3. Abu Pensione	8. New Mirah	14. Bogor Permai Coffeeshop & Bakery
4. Amour Pensione	9. Pangrango	15. Jongkolbu
	10. Puri Bali	16. Kentucky Fried Chicken
	11. Quality Hotel Salak	

destroyed by fire, rebuilt by Governor-Generals Daendels and Raffles and again destroyed in 1834 after an earthquake, triggered by the eruption of Mt Salak. It was not until 1850 that reconstruction commenced, and the present one-storey building was designed to be able to withstand violent earth tremors. The Palace was a particular favourite of President Sukarno and contains a large collection of his paintings, sculpture and ceramics (he had a passion for the female nude). Sukarno lived here under 'house arrest' from 1967 until his death in 1970. Today, it is used as a guesthouse for important visitors (for instance, the King of Thailand and former President Sadat of Egypt both stayed here) and for high-level meetings (the Cambodian talks of 1990 were held at the palace and so was the APEC meeting at the end of 1994). Those planning to visit the Istana Bogor must think ahead. Only groups of 10 or more are admitted after permission has been secured through the Istana or the tourist office (see below), at least a week ahead of the planned visit. Guests must be formally dressed and children under 10 are not admitted because of the value and fragility of the objects. If visitors can meet all these requirements they deserve a prize.

The **Zoological Museum** is on the left of the entrance to the Botanical Gardens and was founded in 1894. It contains an extensive collection of stuffed, dried and otherwise preserved fauna (over 15,000 species) of which only a small proportion is on show at any one time. The museum also has a library. Admission 500Rp. Open 0800-1600 Mon-Sun, except Fri when it is closed between 1100 and 1300.

There is also a **Herbarium** associated with the Botanical Gardens, on Jl Ir H Juanda, across the road from the W gate to the Gardens. It is said to have a collection of 2 million specimens, which seems suspiciously inflated. Admission 300Rp. Open 0800-1330, Mon-Thur, 0800-1000, Fri. A second museum, probably even less interesting to the average visitor, is the **Bogor Army Museum** on Jl Merdeka which mainly charts Indonesia's struggle for independence. Admission 300Rp. Open Mon-Thur 0900-1400.

Jalan Otista (also known as Otto Iskandardinata) is a road running along the S edge of the Botanical Gardens. The street is lined with stalls selling fruit, rabbits (not to eat), some batik, children's clothes and unnecessary plastic objects. The main **market area** is along Jl Dewi Sartika where stalls, hawkers, shoppers, colts and becaks struggle for space. A fascinating area to walk and watch, absorbing the atmosphere.

The **gong foundry** at Jl Pancasan 17, nr the river and SE of the Gardens, is one of the few foundries left in Indonesia – on one side of the street is the foundry, and on the other the gong stands are carved from wood. Visitors can watch metalsmiths making gongs in the traditional manner – a process which takes between 1 and 3 days per gong. The factory is about a 35-min walk SE from the town centre. Walk S down Jl Empang and then turn right onto Jl Pahlawan (see map).

A **batutulis** (meaning 'inscribed stone') dating from the 16th century and erected by one of the sons of a Pajajaran king is housed in a building 3 km S of town on Jl Batutulis (which runs off Jl Bondongon). Admission by donation. Open 0800-1600 Mon-Sun. *Getting there*: take an Angkutan (Green Colt) No 02.

Excursions

Taman Safari 2½ km off the main road just before Cisarua is an open-air safari park. It also houses a mini zoo and offers amusement rides, elephant and horse riding, various animal shows throughout the day, a waterfall, swimming pool, restaurant and camping facilities. Admission: 5,000Rp. Open 0900-1700 Mon-Fri, 0800-1700 Sat, Sun and holidays. **Accommodation** The **B-C** *Safari Garden Hotel* is on the main road, Jl Raya Puncak 601, T (0251) 4747, F 4111, J 7695482, restaurant, pool and sports facilities, 170-odd rm, some bungalows. *Getting there*: take a bus heading for Cisarua and ask to be let off at the turning to the park. Motorbike taxis ply the route from the main road to the park gates.

Local information
● Accommodation

A-C *Hotel Salak*, Jl Ir H Juanda 8, T 322092, F 322093, some a/c, this old hotel (it was built in 1906 and was called *Hotel Binnenhof*), was being 'renovated' during our last visit, although it looked more as if it were being demolished, locals wonder whether it will ever open again – apparently there are doubts over the financial probity and solidity of those funding the redevelopment, however, assuming that the contractors have found a way to put it back together, and funds have been forthcoming, it should be the glitziest place in town – and probably in our A-A+ categories.

B-C *Bogor Inn*, Jl Kumbang 12A, T 328134, most a/c, hot water, Imelda Marcos could have been commissioned to do the interior decorating for this hotel, charming owner called Mary, with good English; **B** *Pakuan Palace*, Jl Pakuan 5, T 323062, F 311207, a/c, good range of business facilities for a hotel in this bracket, clean, comfortable; **B** *Wisma Mirah II*, Jl Mandalawangi 3, T 312385, some a/c, price incl breakfast, peaceful and welcoming.

B-C *New Mirah*, Jl Megamendung 2, T 328044, some a/c, a large villa set above the town centre in a quiet, leafy area of Bogor, the rooms are set around numerous courtyards, most with hot water, clean and professionally managed, popular with Indonesians but rarely frequented by overseas visitors; **B-C** *Pangrango*, Jl Pangrango 23, T 328670, F 314060, a/c, pool, price incl breakfast, a good hotel with large rooms set in a courtyard around the pool, very clean with numerous enthusiastic staff, rec.

C *KWIK (International Youth Hostel)*, Desa Tonjong Km 36, T 31523, pool, new, not really a hostel, with tennis and conference facilities, outside Bogor at Km 36; **C-D** *Puri Bali*, Jl Pledang 30, T 317498, big rooms and friendly, but running to seed, price incl breakfast, discount for longer stay.

C-D *Elsana Transit Hotel*, Jl Sawojajar 36, T 322522, rooms set around an attractive courtyard, but the courtyard is better than the rooms which are rather shabby, especially the bathrooms, no hot water, price incl breakfast; **C-D** *Permata*, Jl Raya Pajajaran 35, T 323402, F 311082, a/c, hot water, price incl breakfast, a couple of years ago this was an immaculate little hotel – it has gone downhill and is now rather shabby and lacklustre, an extension programme further disfigures a hotel which has all too rapidly gone to seed; **C-D** *Wisma Mirah I*, Jl RE Martadinata 17, T 323520, some a/c, price incl breakfast, out of town, more expensive rooms with a/c and hot water, cheapest with shared mandi and cold water, rooms are darkish, small garden and low rise, extension work underway in 1994, not very attractive.

D *Pakuan Homestay*, Jl Pakuan 12, T 319430, small new pensione on the outskirts of town on the road to Cisarua run by a Dutch woman, only 19 large and very clean rooms, small garden at the back, attached bathrooms, attractive views of tiled roofs, well-managed but rather inconvenient location for the sights of the centre of town, to get to the homestay, take Angkutan 06; **D** *Ramayana Rest-U*, Jl Ir H Juanda 54, T 320364, price incl basic breakfast, tea and coffee all day; **D** *Sempur Kencana*, Jl Sempur 4, T 328347, restaurant.

D-F *Abu Pensione*, Jl Mayor Oking 15, T 322893, probably the best place to stay in Bogor for most people on most budgets, the hotel/pensione has rapidly expanded and now has accommodation from dormitory beds to rooms with hot water and views over a deep (but sadly rather rubbish-filled) ravine, Mr Abu is a vigorous entrepreneur and the pensione is well-run and a good source of information, tours available, dorms hold 8 people – rather prison-like (don't forget the insecticide!); **D-E** *Firman Pensione*, Jl Paledang 48, T 323246, small rooms (some very small), but friendly and popular, the manageress and her daughter speak good English, views over fields and rooftops from its hilltop position, some bathrooms, price incl breakfast.

E *Amour Pensione*, Jl Mayor Oking 11A, T 326261, next to the *Abu Pensione*, a cheap alternative, but not as good.

● **Places to eat**
Indonesian: Bogor, like many towns, has a profusion of Padang restaurants, but in this case they are almost all owned by one man and the food is virtually the same so there is nothing to choose between them gastronomically. Two local specialities are *asinan Bogor*, sliced fruit in sweet water, and *tuge gorehg*, fried bean-sprouts served with a spicy chilli sauce. ✦*Dewi Sri*, Jl Raya Pajajaran, nr bus station, simple Indonesian food; ✦*Jongko Ibu*, Jl Ir H Juanda 44, simple Indonesian food, rec; ✦*Ponyo*, Jl Raya Pajajaran, specializes in Sundanese food; *Ramayana*, Jl Dewi Sartika 34, also serves Chinese and International; *Simpang Raya*, Jl Pajajaran 7, nr the bus station, Padang food; *Trio*, Jl Ir H Juanda 38, Jl Pajajaran, nr the bus station.

Western: *Kentucky Fried Chicken*, Jl Raya Pajajaran, nr the bus station; *Lautan*, Jl Jend Sudirman 15, also serves Chinese food; *Pizza Hut*, Internusa Bldg, Jl Raya Pajajaran.

Foodstalls: on Jl Dewi Sartika (during the evening) and Pasar Bogor (during the day and evening) and along Jl Suryakencana; *Taman Jajar* 'food court' on Jl Mayor Oking.

Bakeries: *Bogor Permai*, Jl Jend Sudirman 23A, good coffee in modern a/c restaurant attached to small supermarket, cakes are rather sickly but a good place for a break; *Jumbo Modern Bakery*, Jl Raya Pajajaran 3F; *Singapore*, Jl Suryakencana.

● **Banks & money changers**
A number on Jl Ir H Juanda and Jl Capten Muslihat, eg **BNI 46**, Jl Ir H Juanda 42 and **Central Asia**, Jl Ir H Juanda 24. **Pembangunan Daeran**, Jl Capten Muslihat 13. There is a money changer at Jl Siliwangi 62, but it does not accept TCs nor is it open on Sun or public holidays.

● **Entertainment**
Cinema: *Ramayana Cinema*, Jl Dewi Sartika.

Sundanese dance, gamelan and Wayang golek: Mekah Galuh Pakuan, Jl Layung Sari Rt 6/XIV, S of town, just off Jl Pahlawan, performances once a month on 4th Sat, (5,000Rp).

● **Hospitals & medical services**
Chemist: Jl Raya Pajajaran, nr bus station.
Doctor: Jl Ir H Juanda 40.
Hospital: Jl Pajajaran 80, T 24080.

● **Post & telecommunications**
Area code: 0251.
Post Office: Jl Ir H Juanda 3, almost opp Tourist Information Centre.
Telephone exchange: Jl Pengadilan 8 for

international calls, fax, telex; 50% discount between 2100 and 0600.

● **Shopping**

Batik: *Batik Semar*, Jl Capten Muslihat 7.

Books: *Gunung Agung*, Jl Raya Pajajaran (Internusa Shopping Centre); *Toko Buku Bookstore*, Jl Otto Iskandardinata 80 (nr intersection with Jl Raya Pajajaran).

Handicrafts: *Kenari Indah*, Jl Pahlawan; *Pasar Bogor* on Jl Suryakencana.

Market: *Kebon Kembang* on Jl Dewi Sartika.

Shopping centres: *Dewi Sartika Plaza*, Jl Dewi Sartika; *Internusa Bldg*, Jl Raya Pajajaran; *Ramayana Department Store*, Jl Dewi Sartika.

Wayang golek: Lebak Kantin Rt 2/Vl.

● **Sports**

Golf: Jl Dr Semeru, T 322891. Clubs are available for hire. To get to the course take angkutan No 03 from the bus station.

Swimming pool: *Villa Duta Real Estate*, Jl Pakuan (4,000Rp).

● **Tour companies & travel agents**

Arcana Safariyah Tours, Jl Jend Sudirman 23A, T 328629; *Budhy Persada*, Jl Siliwangi 37H, T 328788; *Finisa Jasa Lestari*, Jl Jend Sudirman 14A; *Mulia Rahayu*, Jl Mayor Oking 1-2 (opp *Pensione Abu*), T 324150, rec; *Panorama*, Jl Suryakencana 214, T 321847; *Tropical Wind*, Jl Sempur 30, T 320272;

● **Tourist offices**

The **tourist office** has moved from Jl Ir H Juanda to an office in the grounds of the distinctive Balai Kota or town hall, also on Jl Ir H Juanda but further N. Otong Soekander who runs the office, speaks good English and is very knowledgeable, maps and pamphlets available. Open 0700-1400 Mon-Thur, 0800-1100 Fri, 0700-1300 Sat.

● **Useful addresses**

Immigration: Jl Jend A Yani 65, T 22870.
Police: Jl Capten Muslihat 16.
PHPA: Jl Ir H Juanda 9 (for permits to visit National Parks).

● **Transport**

60 km S of Jakarta. A fast toll road makes the trip to Bogor rapid, though scenically unexciting.

Local There are **becaks**, **bajajs** and **taxis**. **Colts** (Angkutan): omnipresent green machines; seem to be more of them than there are passengers. Fixed fare of 300Rp around town, destinations marked on the front. **Delman**

(horse-drawn carts): from outside the bus station or the entrance to the Botanical Gardens, 500-1,000Rp. **Taxis**: *Omega Motor*, Jl Pajajaran 217, T 311242; *Tropical Wind*, Jl Sempur 30, T 320272. **Car hire**: car and driver are available for charter from *Abu Pensione*, Jl Mayor Oking 15.

Road Bus: the station is just off Jl Raya Pajajaran, S from the Botanical Gardens and opp the intersection with the toll road from Jakarta. Frequent connections with Jakarta's **Kampung Rambutan**, 20 mins (1,000Rp). Green bemos from here to the centre of town cost 300Rp. Regular connections with Bandung, via the Puncak Pass 3 hrs. For a/c buses to Yogya, Solo and Bali, it is best to go to one of the tour companies which run bus services. *Budhy Persada*, *Arcana*, *Safariyah*, *Panorama* and *Mulia Tahayu* all operate such services. See Tour companies & travel agents for addresses. Also connections with Merak, Labuan and Pelabuhanratu.

Train The station (a colonial building) is NW of the Botanical Gardens on Jl Rajapermas, also known as Jl Stasiun. Regular connections every 30 mins or so with Jakarta 50 mins-1 hr 20 mins (750-1,500Rp). Trains leave from Jakarta's Kota station but also stop at Gambir on their way through the capital, then stopping en route to Bogor. Note that there are no trains on to Bandung.

PELABUHANRATU

Pelabuhanratu is a small beach resort, more popular with Jakartans than with foreign visitors, with kilometre after kilometre of rather dirty-coloured sand beaches. The surf is generally moderate although Cimaja (see Excursions) has a reputation of sorts as a surfing beach. Local folklore has it that the waters off Pelabuhanratu are home to a mythical goddess, **Nyi Loro Kidul**, the Queen of the South Seas. In the large *Samudra Beach Hotel*, a room is kept permanently empty for her. The goddess is said to claim anyone who ventures into the sea wearing green, especially men, whisking them away to her watery lair. Why she has a penchant for green has never been adequately explained but visitors who worry about such things are advised to have more than lizard green swimming gear with them.

There is not much to Pelabuhanratu and the better hotels are all E of town on the road to Cisolok. At the end of Jl Siliwangi, right on the beach and next to the petrol station, is the **Pasar Ikan** or fish market, with a good array of denizens of the deep, and a smell which permeates the whole town. Fish auctions are held at 1000 and 1800. There are a number of good seafood restaurants in town. Close to the Pasar Ikan, fishing boats – among them large outriggers – are pulled up onto the beach, and boats are still being built here.

Excursions

Fishing expeditions can be arranged from Pelabuhanratu, but it's quite expensive at 200,000-300,000Rp for the day, incl tackle. Ask at the hotels or nr the fish market in town.

Pantai Citepus is the most popular beach, about 3 km from town on the road to Cisolok. The beach is lined with official stalls, restaurants and tank traps (presumably put there by the Japanese to thwart an American landing – there are very few places along Java's inhospitable S coast where it is possible to mount a landing). The beach is wide and sandy and paddy fields descend from the hills to within yards of the beach. It's an attractive spot. *Getting there*: take any colt heading for Cisolok.

Cimaja beach, popular with surfers, is about 9 km W from town and 100m walk off the road. **NB** Currents here can be vicious and swimming dangerous – possibly explaining the legend of Nyi Loro Kidul. **Accommodation** Two very basic losmen, both **E**, the *Andrias* and *Kamboja*. Rather better is the *Mustika Rata* (**D**). *Getting there*: take any colt heading for Cisolok.

Karanghawu 'cliff' beach is W of Cimaja and 12 km from town. The beach is popular, but the 'cliff' is really just a finger of rock jutting into the sea. *Getting there*: take any colt heading for Cisolok.

The Legend of Nyi Loro Kidul, The Queen of the South Seas

Nyi Loro Kidul, the Queen of the South Seas, is mentioned in the ancient history of Java the *Babad Tanah Jawi*, as well as a number of other manuscripts. She was born a princess in the ancient W Javanese kingdom of Pajajaran, but her thirst for power forced her father to place a curse upon her head. He said that she would, indeed, have greater power than he but that she would wield it only over the Southern Seas. Re-incarnated as the extraordinarily beautiful Nyi Loro Kidul – more powerful than all the spirits – the Goddess has been closely associated with kingship. Even during the coronation of Hamengkubuwono X of Yogyakarta in 1989, some of the participants said that she was present wearing a transparent green *kabaya*.

One of the nine walis (Muslim saints, see page 95), Sunan Senopati, is said to have found her sleeping – naked, fat, and snoring, with huge breasts. Nonetheless, in the *Babad Tanah Jawi*, Senopati is recorded as having asked, with about as much subtlety as a latterday Casanova: "Dear, I would like to see how your bedroom is arranged". He was whisked off to her watery palace where he became her lover. After 3 days of bliss he was allowed to return home. Sultan Hamengkubuwono IX of Yogyakarta also claimed he was visited by the temptress on many occasions, and that she gave him strength in times of difficulty.

Throughout Java there are places linked with the legend of Nyi Loro Kidul – Mt Merapi, Mt Lawu, Parangtritis, the Kraton in Yogya, Solo and Tawangmangu. Even today, male swimmers in the sea off Java's S coast are advised not to wear green. If they do, they too are at risk of being taken by the goddess to her abode beneath the sea.

Note that room rates can double during holiday periods.

Cisolok Hot Springs can be found 16 km from Pelabuhanratu and about a 20-30 min walk from Cisolok. The springs are set in a verdant valley. **Accommodation** C *Wisma Tenang*; **B-C** *Pantai Mutiara*, a/c, swimming pool. Both these places are near Cisolok, close to the beach. *Getting there*: take a bemo from Pelabuhanratu to Cisolok and walk.

Festivals

Apr: *Pesta Nelayan* (movable), a thanksgiving to Nyi Loro Kidul, the Goddess of the South Seas. Flowers are scattered on the sea from a decorated boat and a buffalo is sacrificed. Various events – competitions and cultural shows – are held on the previous evening.

Local information
● **Accommodation**

Cheap accommodation can be found in town, but most of the better hotels are on the road running W from Pelabuhanratu towards Cisolok. Note that room rates can double during holiday periods.

Pelabuhanratu town: **D** *Wisma Karang Naya*, Jl Siliwangi 82, T 88, best of a poor bunch, the opulence of the lobby is not reflected in the rooms, some bathrooms; **E** *Penginapan Laut Kidaul*, Jl Siliwangi 148, T 41041, rather run down but friendly management and the rooms are kept clean despite the decrepitude; **E** *Wisma Putra*, Jl Siliwangi 86, T 35, rooms are rather dark, some with mandi.

Hotels on the coast: **A** *Samudra Beach*, Jl Cisolok (6 km from town), T 41023, J 340601, a/c, good pool, large international-style hotel, tennis, right on the beach, special deals on weekdays; **B** *Pondok Dewata*, Jl Cisolok (1 km from town), T 41022, a/c, small pool, individual cottages on the beach, clean, fishing trips arranged; **B-D** *Karang Sari*, Jl Cisolok, T 41078, some a/c, above the beach, cheaper rooms are very average and rather dark, more expensive bungalows are good with views over the bay; **C** *Cleopatra*, Jl Raya Citepus 114, T 41185, some a/c, small pool, friendly and clean; **C-D** *Bayu Amrta*, Jl Cisolok, T 41031, has a rather unfinished feel, but rooms are fine, above beach with views back to the town, fishing trips arranged; **E** *Penginapan Simpang Raya*, Jl Cisolok (Km 3).

● **Places to eat**

Seafood: *Maya Sari*, Jl Siliwangi 19, also serves Chinese, Indonesian; *Nelayan*, Jl Raya Citepus (Km 3 – at E end of Citepus Beach), Sundanese, Chinese, western; *Sederhana*, Jl Kidang Kencana, also serves Indonesian; *Wantilan*, Cisolok road 1 km from town just past Pondok Dewata.

● **Banks & money changers**
Bank Central Asia, Jl Siliwangi 109.

● **Post & telecommunications**
Area code: 0266.

● **Transport**
90 km from Bogor.

Local Becaks, horse-drawn carts, colts. Regular colts run from nr the bus terminal in town to Cisolok passing all the hotels and beaches en route.

Road Bus: the station is nr the centre of town, just inland from the Fish Market. Regular connections with Bogor, 2½ hrs and Bandung via Sukabumi. There are no direct buses from Jakarta – catch a bus to Bogor and get a connection onward, or a bus to Sukabumi getting off at Cibadak (17 km before Sukabumi) where there are numerous colts to Pelabuhanratu.

Train From Bogor to Cibadak, and then take a colt.

ROUTE-WISE: BOGOR TO BANDUNG VIA THE PUNCAK PASS The journey from Bogor to Bandung via the Puncak Pass includes one of the most spectacular stretches of road in Indonesia. From Bogor, Route 2 climbs from 300m to the Puncak Pass at 2,900m, passing rice terraces and tea plantations, and with magnificent views (on a clear day) over the surrounding landscape. The invigorating climate led to the creation of a number of hill resorts in the vicinity of the pass including Cisarua and Cipanas. The Gede-Pangrango National Park offers fine hiking. From the Puncak Pass, the road descends to the town of Cianjur, and from there runs 68 km to the capital of W Java, the university city of Bandung.

PUNCAK PASS AND CISARUA

The road from Bogor to Bandung begins by passing through several kilometres of rather ugly ribbon development with numerous restaurants and hotels – the latter almost entirely frequented by Indonesians taking a break from Jakarta or Bandung life. It is only after Cisarua that the journey begins to become more attractive; the views open up, the developments disappear and the road begins to wind through immaculately kept tea plantations, rice terraces and bamboo forest, climbing steadily in the process to the **Puncak Pass** at 2,900m.

On the road up to the pass, **Cisarua** nestles in the foothills; a potentially attractive place to stop for walks but now disfigured by uncontrolled development. Just before Cisarua is the **Taman Safari**, an open air safari and amusement park with accommodation (see page 148 for details). While just after Cisarua, travelling up to the Puncak Pass is the **Gunung Mas Tea Factory and Estate**. The plantation is open to visitors who are shown the tea factory and can walk in the plantation watching pickers pluck off the young leaves. Admission 1,000Rp to see the factory, 500Rp to simply walk around. Open Tues-Sun. To get to the plantation, take one of the bemos that continually ply up and down the road. Ask for Pabrik Teh Gunung Mas.

After the Tea Plantation the road spirals its way up the last few kilometres to the Puncak Pass itself where daytime temperatures are 20°C or less, and the night distinctly cold. There is only one place to stay up here – the *Puncak Pass Hotel* which is also an excellent food/coffee stop. The hills are often shrouded in mist but on clear days it is said that it is possible to see all the way to Jakarta. There are a surprising number of places to stay (and eat) along this road, catering largely to Indonesian tourists attempting to escape from the heat of the plain.

● **Accommodation** Hotel rates escalate during weekends and holidays when rooms are in demand by domestic tourists. Even on weekdays the room rates are inflated when compared with most other areas of Java. **A-B** *Puncak Pass Hotel*, Jl Raya Puncak, T 512503, F 512180, restaurant, pool, tennis, just over the pass itself, in a spectacular position, dating from the colonial period, it is still the best hotel in the area,

bungalows have wonderful views (sometimes) and some, log fires at night; **B** *Cibulan Indah*, Jl Raya Puncak, Km 82, Cisarua, T 4055, positioned just outside Cisarua going up to the Puncak Pass, this small hotel appears shabby but the new rooms are large and clean with attached bathrooms and hot water; **B** *Parama*, Jl Raya Puncak, Km 32, Cisarua, T 4728, bungalows built in 'Balinese' style set in a fantasy grotto of concrete, despite the kitschness, the rooms are reasonable with attached bathrooms and hot water; **B-C** *Permai International Hotel*, Jl Raya Puncak, Km 82, Cisarua, T 4864, the restaurant has good views down the valley but the rooms are poor, no hot water and badly maintained with squat loos, often dirty; **C** *Kopo Hostels and Bungalows*, Jl Raya Puncak 557 (next to the petrol station in Cisarua), T 4296, private rooms and dormitory accommodation, the best of the cheaper places to stay in Cisarua.

● **Places to eat** *Rindu Alam*, almost at the Pass, surprisingly good food for such a large, ugly restaurant, and a wonderful position; *Puncak Pass Hotel*, Jl Raya Puncak, the food here is reasonable but the position makes a stop almost essential; on the terrace it is possible to sip fresh Javanese coffee and eat Hollandsche Poffertjes (deep fried batter balls dusted with sugar) and Puncak Pannekoek (pancakes) while looking down (sometimes) to the plain below. An alternative place for a meal is the *DC-6 Aero Restaurant* easily identified by the DC-6 which has seemingly crashed on the hillside. The plane is suspended 35 ft in the air and a spiral staircase leads up to the cabin door, the food is only average though.

● **Post & telecommuniccations Area code**: 0251.

● **Shopping** Cisarua specializes in the production and sale of brass and glass lamps which are sold from numerous shops along the main road. Basketry and rattan and bamboo work is also widely sold.

● **Sports Horse riding**: small ponies, scarcely strong enough – one would have thought – to take the weight of the average *orang putih* can be hired. 'Riders' are then led around in a rather desultory fashion.

● **Transport** 20 km from Cisarua to Bogor, 98 km from Cisarua to Bandung, 9 km from Cisarua to Puncak Pass. **Road Bus**: regular connections from Jakarta's Kampung Rambutan terminal to Cianjur or Bandung via the Puncak Pass; ask to be let off, the buses don't officially stop here. Also regular bus connections with Bogor. Bemos continually run up and down the pass linking Cisarua with Puncak and beyond.

CIBODAS AND CIPANAS

Cibodas and Cipanas are two hill resorts that, with recent rapid ribbon growth along the road, now effectively merge with one another. Like Cisarua, an apparent lack of any planning controls has almost ruined an area with a massive natural selling point: its position. The two towns are garish and noisy, the hotels almost without exception unsightly and only occasionally does the truly stupendous location shine through. Nonetheless these two resort towns are a place to stop before descending to Bandung – indeed there is nowhere else – and some of the hotels are decent enough.

10 km beyond Puncak Pass and 1.5 km before Cipanas town there is a turning to the right (easily missed – look out for a sign to the Cibodas Youth Hostel – Pondok Pemuda Cibodas) leading to the **Cibodas Botanical Gardens** which cover 60 ha. The 3½ km drive or walk up to the gardens from the turn-off is through a spectacular array of flowering shrubs and other plants; 'nurseries' line the route. The beautifully maintained Gardens were created in 1889 and are an extension of the Gardens in Bogor but for temperate and high altitude species. They remain an important research centre. Admission 1,500Rp.

The Gardens are also the starting point for climbs up Mt Gede (2,958m) and Mt Pangrango (3,019m), through the **Gede-Pangrango National Park**. The Park was established in 1862, covers 150 sq km and is the oldest in Indonesia. It is largely the sheer age and accessibility of the Park which explains why it has so many plant species found here but nowhere else: botanists have had well over a century to root them out. The most famous botanical sight is a field of Javanese Edelweiss (*Anaphalis javonica*) – the so-called *alun-alun* – found

to the N of Mt Gede. The climb to the summit of either of the two peaks takes a full day – 6-8 hrs. It is possible to camp on the slopes, but warm clothing and sleeping bags are essential. There are also other, shorter, hikes for the less ambitious. Permits must be obtained from the PHPA office (just before the entrance to the gardens); permission is not always granted. PHPA office open: 0700-1430 Mon-Thur, 0700-1100 Fri, 0700-1330 Sat. The best time of year for climbing is from May-Oct and guides are recommended for those who have not climbed the routes before. *Getting to the gardens*: catch a colt from Cipanas to Ranahan, or charter one.

1½ km on down the road towards Bandung from the turn-off for the Cibodas Gardens is the spa town of **Cipanas**. Here hot sulphur baths are fed by springs that issue from the slopes of Mt Guntur which last erupted in 1889. These public baths are crowded and rather unpleasant. The mountain resort is centred on the **Istana Cipanas** – looking rather like an elegant cream hunting lodge – where former President Sukarno would come, so it is said, to write his more inspired speeches. The palace even has its own private hot spring and spa. Like Cisarua, this is primarily an Indonesian resort town, although it makes a good stopping place on the road to Bandung.

● **Accommodation** There is a profusion of hotels and holiday homes in the area. Note that room rates increase at the weekends and holidays. **A+-A** *Indo Alam*, Jl Raya Cipanas, T 512071, F 512703, restaurant, pool, a sprawling series of bungalows, some designed for large families, a tennis court, but rather poorly designed and over-priced; **A** *Summit Panghegar*, Jl Sindanglaya Raya 180, Cipanas, T 511335, F 512785, a new and relatively well-designed hotel with an excellent position on a spur, geared mostly to the conference market, the rooms are very comfortable and prices competitive; **B-C** *New Puri Meru*, Jl Singdanglaya 184, Cipanas, T 512415, F 512259, the hotel was recently extended and the rooms in the new wing are the most luxurious, but even the older rooms are surprisingly well maintained compared with the stairwells and corridors, with clean bathrooms, hot water and satellite TV, although it is not clear what the advertised 'Ding Dong Game' entails; **C** *Hotel Sentosa*, Jl Raya Cipanas 87, Cipanas, T 512612, F 512369, an older hotel with some new rooms, consists of bungalows with sitting areas and bathrooms, all with hot water, plain and rather dark but well maintained, more expensive with TVs, one of the best places to stay in this category; **D** *Botanical Gardens Guesthouse*, T 512233, in the Gardens, restaurant, large rooms, rec for its position and atmosphere, bookings can be made at the Bogor Botanical Gardens; **E** *Pondok Pemuda Cibodas*, nr PHPA office, T 512807, attractive position and usually empty during the week.

● **Post & telecommunciations Area code**: 0255. **Post Office & telephone office**: nr the centre of Cipanas at Jl Raya, Cipanas 109 (after the main market and before the Istana Cipanas).

● **Transport** 32 km from Cipanas to Bogor, 86 km from Cipanas to Bandung, 12 km from Cipanas to Puncak Pass. **Road Bus**: regular connections from Jakarta's Kampung Rambutan terminal to Cianjur or Bandung via the Puncak Pass; ask to be let off, the buses don't officially stop here. Also regular bus connections with Bogor. **Bemos**: these constantly run up to the Puncak Pass and from there to Cisarua, as well as down to Cianjur. They can be hailed with no trouble.

ROUTE-WISE: PUNCAK PASS TO BANDUNG After descending from the **Puncak Pass** and reaching the large market town of Cianjur, the road passes through the comparatively rich and fertile agricultural lands of the **Bandung Plain**. The route crosses the **Tarum River**, which at this point in its course has cut a deep, spectacular gorge. The **Saguling Dam**, which helps to irrigate the rice lands of the area, is 15 km S. A speciality of the area is *tapai*; dried, peeled, white cassava which is sold from numerous stalls along the road. Also sold are painted pottery animals, and over-sized carved wooden fruit. About 20 km W of Bandung is the brick and tile making town of **Pandalarang**. The town is coated in a thin layer of dust. and kilns rise up between the houses, providing work and a livelihood – and probably pulmonary illnesses too – to many of the people living in the area.

BANDUNG

The first reference to Bandung dates from 1488, and in 1614 Juliaen de Silva wrote of "a city called Bandung comprising 25 to 30 houses". Known as Kota Kembang (the flower city), Bandung was developed by the Dutch in the late 19th century as a cool retreat from the sweltering plains of Jakarta and it became the country's first resort town. In 1811, Governor-General Daendels encouraged the regent, Dalem Wiranatajusumah II, to move his capital 10 km to the N, so that the town would link up with the new 1,000 km-long Great Post Rd which was under construction. In the 1880s a railway was completed linking the city with Batavia (Jakarta) and Bandung's future was assured. By the end of the century, the town had become the headquarters for the Dutch army and the centre of the plantation industry centred on the Priangan Highlands. There were even plans tabled to move the capital from Batavia to Bandung – plans that were interrupted by the Japanese invasion in 1942.

Set in a huge volcanic basin, at an altitude of 700m and surrounded by mountains, Bandung has one of the most pleasant climates in Java with temperatures averaging 22°C. It is also the third largest city in Indonesia and is the capital of the province of W Java. Bandung has a population of over 2 million, with a further 3 million living in the surrounding area, making this one of the most densely populated regions of Java. Such has been the growth of the city that in 1989 its administrative boundaries were extended, doubling the area of the city overnight. The farmland around the town, though hilly, is relatively fertile – though the volcanic soils are not as fertile as those of Central and E Java.

Bandung is regarded as the intellectual heart of Java, with over 50 universities and colleges situated in and around the city. It is no accident that the Minister for Science and Technology, Dr Habibie, decided to establish Indonesia's first

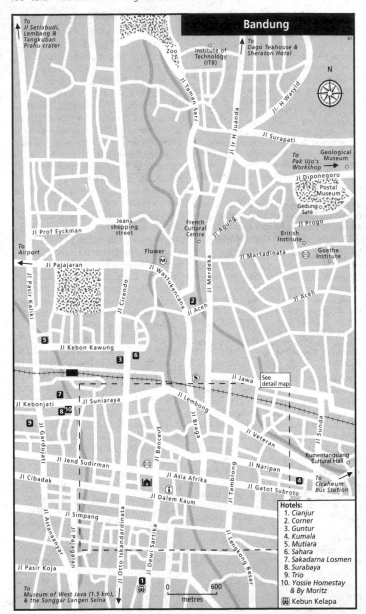

Bandung

To Jl Setiabudi, Lembang & Tangkuban Prahu crater

Zoo

Institute of Technology (ITB)

To Dago Teahouse & Sheraton Hotel

N

Jl· H Wasyid

Jl Taman Sari

Jl Ir H Juanda

Jl Surapati

To Pak Ujo's Workshop

Geological Museum

Jl Diponegoro

Postal Museum

Gedung Saté

French Cultural Centre

Jl Agung

British Institute

Jl Progo

Jl Prof Eyckman

Jeans shopping street

Jl Martadinata

Goethe Institute

To Airport

Flower (M)

Jl Wastukencana

Jl Pajajaran

Jl Cicendo

Jl Aceh

Jl Aceh

2

Jl Merdeka

Jl Pasir Kaliki

5

Jl Kebon Kawung

3 6

See detail map

(S) Jl Jawa

7

Jl Kebonjati

Jl Suniaraya

Jl Lembong

Jl Sunda

8 10

Jl Braga

Jl Veteran

9

Jl Gardujati

Jl Jend Sudirman

Jl Banceuy

Rumentangsiang Cultural Hall

Jl Cibadak

Jl Asia Afrika

Jl Naripan

Jl Tamblong

To Cicaheum Bus Station

(i)

Jl Gatot Subroto

4

Jl Dalem Kaum

Jl Simpang

Jl Astananyar

Jl Pajagan

Jl Otto Iskandardinata

Jl Dewi Sartika

Jl Lengkong Besar

Jl Pasir Koja

To Museum of West Java (1.5 km), & the Sanggar Langen Selna

0   600
metres

Hotels:
1. Cianjur
2. Corner
3. Guntur
4. Kumala
5. Mutiara
6. Sahara
7. Sakadarna Losmen
8. Surabaya
9. Trio
10. Yossie Homestay & By Moritz

🚇 Kebun Kelapa

aircraft industry – IPTN or Industri Pesawat Terbang Nusantara – just outside the city in 1976. The company is one of the largest state operations in Indonesia, and employs over 2,000 university graduates. The factory assembles helicopters and aeroplanes under licence from CASA of Spain, Messerschmitt of Germany, Bell of the USA and Aerospatiale of France; it also makes parts for Boeing. In 1995 an Indonesian-built commuter aircraft, the N-250 was wheeled out of a hangar here for its maiden flight – on the 50th anniversary of Indonesia's independence.

In the early part of the century, Bandung was a centre of the fledgling independence movement. It was here in 1928 that the historic 'Youth Pledge' committed students to serve only one Indonesia and speak one language – Bahasa Indonesia. A remarkable pledge considering that at the time the Dutch still had complete control over the country, and the islands were divided into sultanates and a heterogenous patchwork of ethnic, cultural, religious and linguistic groups.

Rather later, Bandung was the site of the inaugural meeting of the Non-Aligned Movement in 1955. 29 countries attended the conference, which showed Sukarno and Indonesia leading the developing world for the first time. Jalan Asia-Afrika, one of the city's main thoroughfares, is named after the event. In 1992, Indonesia hosted the NAM conference for a second time; on this occasion though, Indonesia was very much less revolutionary, its leaders radiating moderation and pragmatism.

The Institut Pasteur (now called the Bio Farma) became famous as a centre for research and production of the smallpox vaccine as well as a serum against rabies. Before the war, Bandung produced 90% of the world's quinine (from the bark of the cinchona tree). The Bandung Institute of Technology, arguably Indonesia's most prestigious university, was founded in 1920 by the Dutch. Sukarno, Indonesia's first president, studied here. In the realm of culture, Bandung is also the centre for *wayang golek* (see page 96) and the *angklung* orchestra (see box, page 162).

Bandung's Art Deco heritage

The Three Locomotives: three identical houses in streamline modern Art Deco style, Jl. Ir H Juanda 113, 115 and 117 (architect: AF Aalbers).

Twelve Houses: 1939, in Prairie style Art Deco, Jl. Pager Ceunung (architect: AF Aalbers).

Tiga Warna: 1938, Curvilinear Functionalism Art Deco, Jl. Dr Haji Juanda and Jalan Sultan Agung (architect: AF Aalbers).

Dinas Rendapatan Daerah: 1930-1935, Early Functionalism, Jl. Juanda 37 (architect: AF Aalbers).

Villa Merah: 1922, Jl. Tamansari 78 (architect: Wolff Schoemacher).

Boekkit Tinggi: 1925, Jl. Taman Sari (architect: Wolff Schoemacher).

Mesjid Cipaganti: 1933, the only mosque designed by Schoemacher, Jl. Cipaganti 85 (architect: Wolff Schoemacher).

St. Peter's Cathedral: 1932, Jl. Merdeka 10 (architect: Wolff Schoemacher).

Villa Ang Eng Kan: 1930, Geometric Art Deco building of great beauty (architect: FW Brinkman).

The Singer Building: 1930, functionalist Art Deco, this was the original Singer Sewing Machine Company Office in Indonesia, now part of an office complex (architect: FW Brinkman).

The Tourist Information Centre on the alun-alun or town square produces a good booklet giving more detail on Bandung's Art Deco heritage – the *Bandung city tours*.

Places of interest

The centre of town is modern, unattractive and overcrowded; some patience is needed in seeking out Bandung's main attraction: namely, its fine collection of Art Deco architecture, built between 1920 and 1940 when Bandung was *the* sophisticated European town of the Dutch East Indies.

Bandung is recognized as one of three cities in the world with **'tropical Art Deco' architecture** (the others being Miami, Florida and Napier, New Zealand). The Bandung Society for Heritage Conservation has a register of well-over 600 category I and II monuments in Bandung (see box). Of all the Art Deco architects the one most closely associated with Bandung was Wolff Schoemacher. He graduated with Ed Cuypers from the Delft Technical University in the Netherlands, and then moved to Bandung where he designed hundreds of buildings. As Frances Affandy of the Bandung Society for Heritage Conservation observed in 1995 when commenting on the city's architectural wealth, "Poverty is the friend of conservation". Now that money is flowing in from Jakarta in increasing amounts, Affandy and others fear the effects on Bandung's incomparable architectural treasures. In theory, any building over 50 years old is protected and the Mayor of Bandung is said to be appreciative of the need to preserve this heritage. But with the cowboy atmosphere that pervades many other towns and cities, the preservationists will need to be ever watchful.

The most impressive Art Deco building, lying in the centre of town, is the **Savoy Homann Hotel** on Jl Asia Afrika, built in 1938 by AF Aalbers and still retaining period furniture and fittings. It has been meticulously renovated at a cost of US$2mn so that visitors can savour a hotel that numbers Charlie Chaplin, Ho Chi Minh and Zhou En-lai among its guests. From the exterior it has been likened to a radio; the interior to an ocean liner. Aalbers is said to have wanted to remind Dutch guests of the ships that brought them to the country. Opposite is the **Preanger Hotel**, built in 1889 but substantially redesigned by Wolff Schoemacher in 1928. The remaining Art Deco wing faces Jl Asia Afrika. West on Jl Asia Afrika is the **Gedung Merdeka** (also known as the Asia Afrika building). Originally built in 1895, it was completely renovated in 1926 by Wolff Schoemacher, Aalbers and Van Gallen Last, and today houses an exhibition of photographs of the first Non-Aligned Movement conference held here in 1955 (hence the name of the street). **Jalan Braga** is often said to be Bandung's colonial heart – the Fifth Ave of Indonesia. Sadly though, most of the original façades have been disfigured or entirely replaced. North of the railway line also on Jl Braga is the **Bank of Indonesia** designed by Ed Cuypers in the 1920s. Either side are church buildings designed by Schoemacher. Additional notable Art Deco buildings in Bandung are listed in the box on page 157. For visitors interested in learning more about Bandung's architectural heritage, a visit to the Bandung Society for Heritage Conservation (Bandung Paguyuban Pelestarian Budaya), *Hotel Savoy Homann*, Jl Asia Afrika 112 is worthwhile. Their offices are open Mon-Sat 0900-1700, and they welcome interested travellers as well as professional researchers.

The N suburbs of Bandung are the most attractive part of the city, leafy and green – this is University Land. **Gedung Sate** on Jl Diponegoro was built in the 1920s and is one of Bandung's more imposing public buildings, with strong geometric lines and a formal garden. Within the building but rather hidden away, is the **Museum Post and Philately**, at Jl Cilaki 37. Almost opposite is the **Geological Museum** at No 57 (reputed to be the largest in Southeast Asia). It houses skeletons of prehistoric elephants, rhinos, fossilized trees and a meteor weighing 156 kg which fell on Java in 1884. But most notably, it is home to the skull of

'Java Man' (see page 40). Unfortunately, there's no information in English. Open 0900-1400 Mon-Thur, 0900-1100 Fri, 0900-1400 Sat. Also N of the city centre on Jl Taman Sari, the **Bandung Institute of Technology** or **ITB** was built by Maclaine Pont in 1918 and represents another good example of the architecture of the Art Deco era. Off Jl Taman Sari, just before the ITB travelling N is the **Kebun Binatang**, Bandung's **zoo** with Komodo dragon among other beasts. Very crowded on Sun and holidays. Admission 1,750Rp (2,000Rp on Sun and holidays).

Bandung – factory visits

The excellent and innovative Bandung City Council are encouraging visitors to see more of 'real' city life. One element of this is to encourage people to seek out the small factories that are the life blood of Bandung.

Lilian Candle Factory (Jl Aksan 18, T 612200): run by the Chinese Tan family, this factory is a home industry producing candles from paraffin that range in size from a few centimetres to over 2m in height. Most are produced for Chinese temples – of which the most complex take 2 years to complete – but Christmas candles and others can be made to order. Prices range from 400Rp to 20,000Rp. Open 0800-1800 Mon-Sat. *Getting there*: best by taxi.

Yun Sen Tofu Factory (Jl Jend Sudirman): tofu or tempe (see box page 870) is made from soybean paste coagulated with acetic acid or a fungal spore and then pressed to remove excess water. The Yun Sen factory welcomes visitors Mon-Fri 1300-1500.

Chinese Paper Houses (Jl Cibadak-Gang Ibu Aisah): Bandung's large Chinese population, despite attempts at assimilation, retain many of their Taoist and Confucianist rites and rituals. Paper houses with all the paraphernalia of a real home are made for the deceased to furnish them in their life after death. And not just beds and kitchens; modernity demands that bamboo and paper swimming pools, cars and satellite dishes are also painstakingly produced. Every element must be made of flammable material so that the dead receive the gifts in heaven. The best place to see paper houses and their accoutrements being made is on Jalan Cibadak, near the Vihara Leng An in Gang [Lane] Ibu Aisah. Vihara Leng An is open 1000-1600 Mon-Sat.

Kerupuk Factory (Jl Kopo-Gang Pak Sahdi 27): kerupuk or krupuk, deep-fried spiced tapioca (cassava) crackers, are produced in their zillions in Bandung. One survey (how it was done, goodness knows) estimated that 2.2 million were consumed every day; nearly a billion a year. Bandung's first krupuk factory was established in 1925 by Haji Sukarna and his descendants continue to run four enterprises in the same street – just off Jl Kopo. The crackers are moulded out of tapioca flour and then dried in the sun before being deep-fried just before selling. Dried (but un-fried) krupuk can be stored long-term. *Getting there*: Jl Kopo-Gang [Lane] Pak Sahdi is opposite the Immanuel Hospital. Open: working hours.

Wayang Golek Factory (Jl Pangarang Bawah IV No 78/17B): wayang golek puppets are produced by numerous workshops in Bandung (see page 96 for details on wayang theatre). Some of the finest are made by Pak Ruchiyat, in whose factory they are carved from light-weight albasia wood and then painted and decorated by his wife, Ibu Ruchiyat and her assistants. See Shopping, below, for details on buying puppets. Open 0800-1600 Mon-Sat.

Open 0900-1700 Mon-Sun. Not far S of the zoo is the rather bizarre **'Jean Street'** on Jl Cihampelas. Shopkeepers vie for the most elaborate shopfront in an attempt to lure trade. It is almost surreal with larger-than-life plaster Rambos, sausages, helicopters, James Bonds and other figures and images. Worth a visit even if not intending to shop. There are not just jeans for sale here: all types of clothes, tapes and merchandise for Bandung's large population of students and trendies. To get to the street, take an Angkutan kota running up Jl Pasir Kaliki and then walk through Jl Prof Eyckman (Jean St itself is one-way running S). **Jalan Pasar Selatan** is a more recent imitation of the original, lined with stores selling denim.

South of town, the **Museum of West Java** (Negeri Propinsi Jawa Barat) is on the corner of Jl Otto Iskandardinata and the ring road. It houses artefacts tracing the development and history of W Java. Admission 200Rp. Open 0900-1400 Mon-Thur, 0900-1100 Fri, 0900-1200 Sat-Sun.

Like many Indonesian cities, Bandung has a number of markets – useful for shopping as well as places to visit. **Pasar Kota Kembang** runs along a narrow lane linking Jl Asia-Afrika and Jl Dalem Kaum, and specializes in clothes, shoes and accessories. **Pasar Baru** is in Chinatown and is a good place to buy textiles, including batik; the basement houses a vegetable market. **Jalan Pasar Utara** is a food market selling snacks and many W Javanese culinary specialities. Not far from the Ciroyom Terminal is the **Pasar Jatayu** on Jl Arjuna which houses a few antique and junk shops among the second hand motorcycle outlets; there are also some places selling military memorabilia nearby. Bandung's largest **flower market**, supplied from the many upland nurseries around the city, is on Jl Wastukencana.

Further N still is the **Dago Teahouse**, to be found behind the Pajajaran University housing complex at the end of Jl Ir H Juanda. It was renovated in 1991, and provides a cultural hall and open-air theatre for evening Sundanese dance performances. Good views of the city from here. *Getting there*: catch a Dago colt up Jl Ir H Juanda (the colts terminate at Terminal Dago, not far from the Tea House).

Walks The Bandung tourist office has identified a number of walks in the city through the CBD, chinatown and elsewhere. For maps and further information contact the tourist office – good background information on buildings and the city's history is available.

Excursions

Most visitors who venture out of the city travel N into the volcanic Priangan Highlands that surround Bandung, to see neat tea plantations, colossal craters and natural hotsprings.

Villa Isola lies on the route N on Jl Setiabudi, 6 km from the city centre, and is yet another fine Art Deco building, set on a hill overlooking the city. *Getting there*: regular minibuses and colts ply this route out of Bandung. Either travel direct from the train station or via Terminal Ledeng at the northern edge of the city.

Lembang, 16 km N of Bandung, is a popular resort town on an upland plateau with restaurants, hotels and pony-drawn carts. The town can be used as a base to explore the uplands and visit such places as the Tangkuban Prahu crater and the Ciater Hot Springs (see Excursions, below). Garden nurseries line the road into Lembang and the town also supports the internationally respected **Bosscha Observatory** (visits must be prearranged). **Accommodation B** (for new wing), **C** (in old building) *Grand Hotel*, Jl Raya Lembang 272, T 286671, F 286829, is the best place to stay in Lembang, an old hotel with swimming pool and tennis courts renovated by Aalbers of Savoy Homann fame now with an additional new wing, large garden compound, hot water in all rooms, the older wing is cheaper and remains the more stylish; **C** *Sindang Reret II*, Jl Raya Cikole, Km 2,

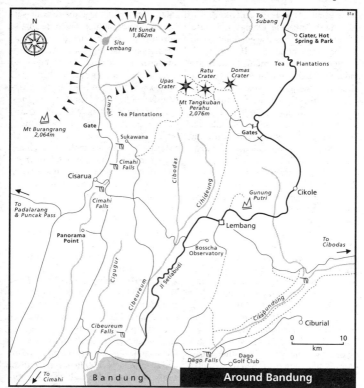

Around Bandung

T 286129, F 286119, a large resort above Lembang with a profusion of bamboo and concrete, a stagnant pool holds massive carp which children feed crisps and other nutritious snacks, but the rooms are OK and the water is hot. *Getting there*: regular minibuses connect Lembang with Bandung's Terminal Ledeng, on Jl Dr Setiabudi on the northern edge of the city. To get to Terminal Ledeng, take a colt going up Jl Pasir Kaliki. There are also colts running direct to Lembang from the train station in the centre of town.

Tangkuban Prahu Crater (the capsized boat crater) is one of the most popular tourist sights in the vicinity of Bandung and possibly the most accessible volcanic crater in Indonesia. The route up to the volcano from Lembang passes through rich agricultural land, with terraces of market garden crops clawing their way up the hillsides, chincona trees (the bark is used to produce quinine), teak and wild ginger. Nine km from Lembang is the entrance to the 'park'. The drive from the gate snakes through a forest of giant pines reminiscent of a set from *Jurassic Park*. 3 km from the gate is the lower car park (with restaurant and tourist stalls). From here the road continues upwards for another 1 km to the rim of the impressive Ratu Crater. Alternatively, there is a footpath from the lower carpark to the Ratu Crater (1.5 km), and another from there to the smaller Domas Crater (1 km). Another path links the Domas and Ratu Craters (1.2 km). It is also possible to walk all the way round the Ratu Crater. Though visited by numerous tour buses and inhabited by large numbers of souvenir sellers, the natural splendour of the volcano makes the trip worthwhile. Ratu rises to an altitude of 1,830m, and the crater drops precipitously from the rim. Bursts of steam and the smell of sulphur bear witness to the volcanic activity latent beneath the surface.

The curious shape of the summit of Tangkuban Prahu has given rise to the Sundanese *Legend of Prince Sangkuriang* who unknowingly fell in love with his mother, Dayang Sumbi. She tried to prevent their marriage, insisting that her betrothed create a lake and canoe before sun-rise on their wedding day. Sangkuriang seemed to be endowed with magical powers and he nearly achieved this impossible task when Dayang Sumbi called upon the gods to hasten the sun to rise, in order to prevent their forbidden union. Sangkuriang was so angry, that he kicked his nearly finished canoe, which landed upside down on the horizon, thus creating this silhouette. Admission 1,250Rp, 400Rp for car. Guides are available for off-path treks (inadvisable without a guide because of the emissions of sulphurous gases) and the wildlife in the surrounding forest includes a small population of native gibbons. At the summit hawkers sell anklungs to bemused tourists while tapping out *Auld Lang Syne*, or *Happy Birthday To You*. They also vigorously proffer assorted lurid clothes, synthetic fur hats, bags and rucksacks as well as wooden carvings, animals made of small seashells and herbal remedies, such as *kayu naga*. This resembles green, hairy twiglets and is reputedly good for rheumatism and backache. The twiglets are boiled in water and the resultant malodorous brew is drunk. *Getting there*: bus or colt heading for Subang – and ask to be dropped off at the entrance to the crater (about 25 km from the city). Hitch or walk (3.5 km) from here. At the weekend there are colts which go all the way up to the summit.

Ciater Hot Springs are 6.5 km on from Tangkuban Prahu, the road following the mountain side and winding through tea plantations. There are brilliantly clear hot water pools and waterfalls here situated on the side of a hill; unfortunately, the complex is rather seedy and run down. Admission 1,000Rp, car 1,250Rp, and another 1,500Rp to bathe. **Accommodation B** *Sari Ater Hotel*, on site,

The Angklung

🦶 The *angklung* is an ancient Sundanese instrument used to accompany story-telling and marching. It consists of a number of different length open bamboo tubes; in Bali these are sometimes assembled into an orchestra or *gamelan angklung* for certain ceremonies. The angklung is thought to have originated in W Java. It is still used by the Badui tribe in a number of their rituals, including the dance that precedes rice planting. In the past it probably accompanied the Badui into battle – hence its association with marching.

The antiquity of the angklung is indicated by the fact that its scale has only four notes (pentatonic). The name is thought to be onomatopoeic – the word imitates the sound of the instrument, *klung...klung...klung*. Along with the gamelan (see page 101), the angklung is peculiar to Indonesia – although there is a similar instrument in N Thailand – and in 1968 the Department of Education declared that it should be taught throughout the archipelago as a national instrument. To listen to the angklung: the best angklung workshop and orchestra is Pak Udjo's (see Entertainment below).

T 200319, F 200772; **D** *Pondok Gunung-sari*, Jl Raya Ciater, small, clean homestay. *Getting there*: take a colt or bus towards Subang, asking to be let off at Air Panas Ciater; the hotel and springs are 150m off the main road.

Mount Papandayan is 74 km from Bandung and a full day's trip (see page 170).

Ciwidey is a small town about 14 km S-W of Bandung. Continuing along the road, up the Ciwidey valley, the route climbs up past Cimanggu (at the 42 km marker) where there is a small park and hot pools fed from Mt Patuha (2,400m). The hill sides here are planted with tea bushes. Among the largest estates are the Rancabali and Malabar estates.

Candi Cangkuang is an 8th century Hindu monument and can be visited in a day from Bandung (see page 169). The temple is 48 km from the city on the road to Garut. *Getting there*: catch a bus from Bandung's Cicaheum terminal on Jl Jend A Yani travelling E towards Tasikmalaya and Banjar; get off 2 km after Kadungura, in the village of Leles.

Tours

The tourist office on Jl Asia Afrika will organize tours in and around town, as will many of the travel agents. Typical tours visit the Tangkuban Prahu crater and Ciater hotsprings (5 hrs, 64,000Rp per person), architecturally interesting buildings around town (3 hrs, 30,000Rp per person) and an angklung music performance, plus traditional Sundanese dancing (3 hrs, 24,000Rp per person). For those who want to hire a car and driver to visit the surrounding area, men hang around the Tourist Information office on the town square (alun-alun). Expect to pay about 100,000Rp for a day.

Local information
● **Accommodation**

A+ *Grand Preanger*, Jl Asia Afrika 81, T 431631, F 430034, a/c, restaurant, pool, original art deco wing (1928), refurbished to a high standard and offering the most interesting rooms, now 'complemented' by a 10-storey modern addition, central location, fitness centre, good facilities and well-run; **A+** *Chedi Hotel*, Jl Ranca Bentang 56-58, T 230333, F 230633, a/c, restaurant, pool, 51 rooms in this new, modernist and minimalist hotel, lots of style, situated several kilometres N of the city centre overlooking countryside to the N so not well placed for that spontaneous, spur-of-the-moment stroll around the sights; **A+-A** *Savoy Homann*, Jl Asia Afrika 112, T 432244, F 436187, a/c, restaurant (see places to eat), bars, pool, superb art deco building, renovated but retaining original furnishings, central mature garden with caged birds, good location – the most interesting place to stay in town – if you can afford it – rec; **A** *Abadi Gardens*, Jl Dr Setiabudi 287, T 210987, F 211999, a/c, restaurant, pool, good sports facilities (incl tennis courts) but 5 km N of town; **A** *Istana*, Jl Lembong 44, T 433025, F 432757, a/c, good restaurant, pool, 51 comfortable rooms, most facilities but rather lacklustre and colourless, a place to stay for those who are looking for function rather than style; **A** *Kumala*, Jl Asia Afrika 140, T 445141, F 438852, a/c, restaurant, pool, a rather featureless hotel, but comfortable enough, Sundanese dance and music every Wed and Sat evening; **A** *Panghegar*, Jl Merdeka 2, T 432286, F 431583, a/c, restaurant, pool, health club, 200 rooms and most facilities, but now rather dated compared with the competition and cannot even claim heritage status to make up for it; **A** *Papandayan*, Jl Jend Gatot Subroto 83, T 430788, F 430988, J 587303, a/c, pool, fitness and business centres, 245 rm and most facilities, a little way from the centre of town, E along Jl Gatot Subroto, good base if location is not an issue; **A** *Perdana Wisata*, Jl Jend Sudirman 66-68, T 438238, F 432818, a/c, Japanese restaurant, Irish bar, modern hotel, central courtyard with pool; **A** *Sheraton*, 3 km N at Jl Ir H Juanda 390, T 2500303, F 2500301, a/c, restaurant, pool, international standard hotel with good facilities (fitness centre); **A-B** *Trio*, Jl Gardujati 55-61, T 615756, F 431126, a/c, courtyard style hotel, rooms rather kitsch with velverette coverings, hot water bathrooms, rather out-of-the-way for the main sights, but clean and comfortable.

B *Mutiara*, Jl Kebon Kawung 60-62, T 4200333, F 4204961, a/c, close to the train station, clean 3-storey motel-style hotel, rooms are large and well-equipped; **B** *Selekta Permai*, Jl Pasir Kaliki 68-88, T 432279; **B** *Utari*, Jl Ir H Juanda 50, T 56810, some a/c, nice area,

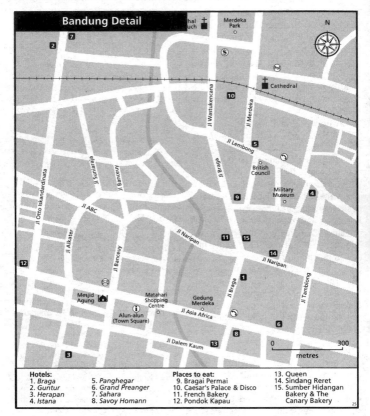

Bandung Detail

Hotels:
1. Braga
2. Guntur
3. Herapan
4. Istana
5. Panghegar
6. Grand Preanger
7. Sahara
8. Savoy Homann

Places to eat:
9. Bragai Permai
10. Caesar's Palace & Disco
11. French Bakery
12. Pondok Kapau

13. Queen
14. Sindang Reret
15. Sumber Hidangan Bakery & The Canary Bakery

professional, but slightly out of town; **B-C** *Braga*, Jl Braga 8, T 4204685, some a/c, faded old Dutch hotel, rooms with sitting areas, large clean shower rooms in new wing with hot water, antiquated telephone system and some character coupled with a central location, but some of the older rooms are a shambles, dark, dirty and mosquito-ridden, so see a range of rooms first and be ready to be shocked and pleasantly surprised in turn, price incl breakfast; **B-C** *Famili*, Jl Pasir Kaliki 96, T 50181.

C *Guntur*, Jl Otto Iskandardinata 20, T 4203763, 1960s hotel apparently stuck in a time warp, bathrooms with hot water, low rise, central courtyard "where you can get rid of your fatigue"; **C** *Herapan*, Jl Kepatihan 14-16, T 51212.

D *Melati 2 Kenangan*, Jl Kb Sirih 4, T 432239, friendly, but not very central.

● **Budget hotels**

Budget hotels can be found around the railway station on Jl Kebonjati and Jl Pasir Kaliki.

C-D *Corner Hotel*, Jl Wastukencana 8, T 436871, dark rooms with a surfeit of mosquitoes and a deficit of sheets, friendly enough but only worth staying here if pushed, rooms have attached showers with hot water, breakfast incl; **C-D** *Dewi Sartika*, Jl Dewi Sartika 18, T 431190, small hotel with central location, hot water, unprepossessing and crammed in along a row of shops but rates are competitive and rooms are clean and serviceable.

D *Sahara Hotel*, Jl Oltoiskandardinata 3,

T 4204684, villa in large garden, cheaper rooms with shared mandi, metal frame beds in bare rooms, 300m from the railway station; **D** *Surabaya*, Jl Kebonjati 71, T 436791, Victorian railway hotel, one of the few cheaper hotels with some style, a rambling place with wooden flrs and large rooms, currently undergoing renovation, the more expensive rooms with opium beds and Chinese object d'art and attached cold water shower rooms, cheaper, rooms are small and dark with shared facilities and the hotel is noisily positioned on a main road, rec.

E *Cianjur*, Jl Abdul Muis 169, T 56834, attractive guesthouse, rec; **E** *Mawar*, Jl Pangarang 14, T 51934, central with clean rooms, popular with Indonesian travelling salesmen; **E** *Sakadarna*, Jl Kebonjati 34, T 439897, restaurant (basic), much nicer than the other Sakadarna at No 50 and closer to the railway station, small rooms but clean; **E-F** *By Moritz*, Jl Kebonjati (Kompleks Luxor Permai 18), T 437264, new budget place run by a German, good reports – clean, well managed and a good source of information, dorm beds available, rec; **E-F** *Yossie Homestay*, Jl Kebonjati 53, T 4205453, F 441224, food made to order, communal mandi, tours to local sights, run by friendly young people, some German spoken, noisy (close to road), very cheap dormitory, rec.

● **Places to eat**

Local dishes incl *gorengan*, a form of vegetable-based tempura, *bandrek* and *bajigur*, both drinks made of ginger and sweetened coconut milk respectively, *pecel lele* (fried eels with a piquant sauce) and *comro* made from cassava and tempe. There are also a remarkable number of bakeries in Bandung, the best selection concentrated on Jl Braga.

Indonesian: ***Savoy Homann Hotel*, Jl Asia Afrika 112, traditional Rijstaffle dinner served nightly; **Handayani*, Jl Sukajadi 153, best Javanese restaurant in Bandung; *Sate Ponorogo*, Jl Jend Gatot Subroto 38, very good value open-air saté restaurant.

Chinese: **Queen*, Jl Dalem Laum 79, large menu, popular restaurant; **Tjoan Kie*, Jl Jend Sudirman 46, popular Cantonese restaurant.

Japanese: ****Dai Shogun*, Jl Cihampelas 125, serves probably the best, but also the most expensive Japanese food in town; ***Paregu*, Jl Martadinata 91, cheaper Japanese restaurant with good value buffet lunch.

Sundanese: **Babakan Siliwangi*, Jl Siliwangi 7, nr the zoo, open-air restaurant with large menu,

rec; **Pondok Kapau*, Jl Asia Afrika 43, excellent Padang food, with seafood specialities, try the whole spicy octopus; **Ponyo*, Jl Malabar 60, rec by locals for its Sudanese specialities, popular.

International: ****Savoy Homman Hotel*, Jl Asia Afrika 112, good T-bone steaks; **Sukarasa*, Jl Tamblong 52, T 438638, steaks and omelettes; *Eliza Garden*, Jl Kepatihan 21, attractive courtyard, simple food.

Foodstalls (*): probably the best are arrayed down a tiny alley off Jl Bungsu nr the Puri Nas Bakery (open 1730 on). Stalls are also to be found on Jl Merdeka, Jl Martadinata, Jl Diponegoro (nr the RRI building), Jl Cikapundung Barat, and Jl Dalem Kaum, W of the *alun alun*. Most are night stalls only. Of all the stalls, the one with the greatest local reputation is Pak Aceng's *Es compur* (mixed ice) cart which he sets up on Jl Kapatihan nr the Damai shop. He has been selling here for over 25 years. Another way of trying Bandung's range of food is by going to the *Food Centre* at the *Matahari Department store* on Jl Cikapundung Barat, good, cheap dishes and it is possible to see what you are getting.

Bakeries: *Braga Permai*, Jl Braga 58, large bakery-cum-restaurant with tables outside, very clean but the cakes are rather sickly; *French Bakery*, Jl Braga, the best bakery in town, authentic French cakes, pastries and bread for the westerner looking for a fix; *Sumber Hidangan*, Jl Braga; *The Canary Bakery* and restaurant (nr intersection with Jl Naripan), Jl Braga.

● **Bars**

Tempo Doe Loe Terrace, Grand Preanger, Jl Asia Afrika 81, large deco bar with terrace, some good cover bands play here, but drinks are pricey, 2 for 1 happy hour from 1730-2000.

● **Airline offices**

Bouraq, Jl Cihampelas 27, T 438795; **Garuda/Merpati**, Jl Asia Afrika 73-75, T 441226, F 4204497, opp *Hotel Savoy Homann*; **Sempati**, at *Hotel Panghegar*, Jl Merdeka 2, T 430477.

● **Banks & money changers**

Arta Mulia, Jl Jend Sudirman 51; **BPD**, Jl Braga; **Djasa Arta**, corner of Jl Suniaraja and Jl Otto Iskandardinata; **Dwipa Mulia**, Jl Asia Afrika 148; **Golden Money Changer**, Jl Otto Iskandardinata 127; **Interstate Investment**, Jl Naripan 28; **Metro Jasa**, Jl Jend Gatot Subroto 21; **Sejahtera Bagian Utama**, Jl Suniaraja 55.

● **Embassies & consulates**

Austria, Jl Prabu Dimuntur 2A, T 439505,

F 430505; **France**, Jl Purnawarman 32, T 445864; **Netherlands**, Jl Diponegoro 25, T 431419.

● **Entertainment**

Adu Domba (ram fights): every other Sun at **Ranca Buni**, nr Ledeng, N of town on Jl Setiabudi.

Angklung (hand-held bamboo chimes): performances at **Pak Udjo's workshop**, Jl Padasuka 118 (8 km NE of the town centre), when there are 20 or more people, T 71714. Admission 3,000Rp, beginning 1530. *Getting there*: take a Cicaheum colt getting off at the intersection with Jl Padasuka, nr the Cicaheum bus station. Pak Udjo's workshop is a 7-min walk, on the right hand side of the street. *ASTI, Institute of Fine Arts*, Jl Buah Batu 212, T 304532 for angkung and other performances; information on performance schedule from the tourist information office.

Art galleries: Bandung is a centre of modern art, possibly because of ITB's excellent fine art faculty. Galleries incl *Bandung*, Jl Siliwangi 16, N of town, predominantly Bandung artists are shown here, some ceramics and specialist art books, changing exhibitions by international artists; *Braga*, Jl Braga 68, displays well known Indonesian artists, both living and dead; *Hidayat*, Jl Sulanjana 36, paintings, graphics and ceramics. See Shopping, below, for telephone details.

Cinemas: opp *Hotel Braga* on Jl Braga. *Sartika 21* nr intersection of Jl Aceh and Jl Merdeka; *Vanda*, Jl Merdeka, nr Jl Jawa and the City Hall.

Cultural shows: martial arts, dances, etc every Sun morning at the zoo, 0900-1300. Admission is the entrance fee to zoo. *Museum of West Java* on Jl Otto stages a cultural performance every Sun.

Discos: *La Dream Palace*, Jl Asia Afrika, Plaza Lt 2 (2100-0200); *Lipstick Discoskate*, Gedung Palaguna Lt IV (1200-2100 for discoskating, 2130-0200 for standard standing disco); *Studio East*, 2nd Flr, Premier Bldg, Jl Cihampelas 129 (2100-0200).

Jaipongan dance: another traditional Sundanese dance form – which is now popular in parts of Kalimantan and Sumatra – performances at *Museum of West Java*, Jl Otto Iskandardinata, Wed 1400.

Ketuk Tilu dance: a traditional social dance accompanied by gamelan music at the *Sanggar Langen Selna*, Jl Otto Iskandardinata 541A. Professional dancers encourage you to join them in a dance (for which you pay). Nightly from 2100, show becomes more lively later on, cover charge 3,000Rp.

Nightclubs: there are a number on Jl Jend Sudirman, eg *Panama* at No 72, *Oriental* at No 134 and *Paramount* at No 291 (all 2000-0200). But the nightclub housed in the most beautiful building must be *Caesar's Palace and Disco* on Jl Braga, nr the intersection with Jl Lembang. Open 0800-late.

Sundanese dance & gamelan recitals: at *Hotel Panghegar* on Jl Merdeka on Wed and Sat at 1930, no charge but the audience is expected to eat or drink.

Wayang golek: performances at *Sindangreret restaurant*, Jl Nirapan 7-9 (nr Jl Braga) on Sat from 0700-2300 or an epic 8-hr performance every 2nd Sat of the month at the *Rumentangsiang Cultural Hall* (an Art Deco building), nr the Kosambi market on Jl Jend A Yani.

● **Hospitals & medical services**

Chemist: *Dewi Sartika*, Jl R Dewi Sartika 89 (24 hrs).

Hospital: *Adventist Hospital*, Jl Cihampelas 161, T 82091.

● **Post & telecommunications**

Area code: 022.

Post Office: Jl Asia Afrika 49, corner of Jl Asia Afrika and Jl Banceuy. Poste Restante available. Also Jl Pahlawan 87.

Telephone and fax: Wartel, Jl Asia Afrika (opp *Savoy Homann Hotel*) for international calls and fax.

● **Shopping**

Angklung instruments: Jl Madurasa.

Antiques: *Tasin Art*, Jl Braga 28.

Art galleries: Bandung is viewed as a centre for Indonesian arts and there are a number of galleries in town exhibiting work by promising young Indonesians. Centrally located are the *Braga Art Gallery*, Jl Braga 68, T 438058, open 0900-1930, Mon-Sat; and the *Elegance Art Gallery*, Jl Banceuy 8, T 437061, open 0930-1900 Mon-Sat. North of the town centre are two more galleries: *Bandung Gallery*, Jl Siliwangi 16, T 81199, open 0900-1700, Mon-Sat; and *Hidayat Gallery*, Jl Sulanjana 36, T 436038, open 1000-1700, Mon-Sat.

Bookshops: all over town, but especially N of the centre around the university.

Ceramics: there is a *Ceramics Research Institute* on Jl Jend A Yani nr the Pasar Cicadas; examples can be purchased from *Bandung*

Gallery, Jl Siliwangi 16, *Kundhika*, Jl Gunung Batu 178 and *Uun Kusnadi*, Jl Kenangan 9A.

Handicrafts: next to *Sarinah department store* on Jl Braga. Opp is the *Indonesian National Crafts Council* (No 15).

Jeans: Jl Pasar Celatan, off Jl Otto Iskandardinata, for whacky shop fronts and cheap jeans, also Jl Cihampelas for more weird shop fronts and bargain clothing.

Jewellery: *Runa*, a husband and wife team, produce perhaps the best modern jewellery in Bandung. It is on sale at many of the major hotels, eg *Preanger*, *Savoy Homann* and the *Sheraton*.

Leather: Jl Braga 113, Jl A Yani 618.

Rubber stamp production: an area of stalls and shops carving out stamps, Jl Cikapundung Barat and Jl Asia Afrika – have your name carved in rubber for 5,000Rp.

Shoes: good buy here, Jl Cibaduyut (S of town on Jl Kopo) for a wide variety.

Shopping centres: an abundance, eg *Plaza Bandung Indah*, Jl Merdeka 56; *Matahari Shopping Centre*, Town Square (Alun-alun); *Sarinah Dept Store*, Jl Braga 10.

Wayang Golek: *Pa Aming*, Jl M Ramdhan 4 and *Pa Ruchiyat*, Jl Pangarang Bawah IV No 78/17B (behind No 20 in the alleyway). Both are workshops where you can also buy and the latter is reputed to sell perhaps the finest worked examples. Pak Ruchiyat has over 35 year's experience; note that prices – which range from 20,000-60,000Rp for most puppets – are fixed. Shops along Jl Braga sell puppets.

● **Sports**
Golf: *Dago Golf Course*, top end of Jl Ir H Juanda.

● **Tour companies & travel agents**
There are about 25 travel agents in town; most are branches of Jakarta-based companies. *Interlink*, Jl Wastukencana 5; *Natrabu*, Braga Hotel, Jl Braga 8 (be careful – they overcharge for reconfirmation of flights); *Nitour*, Jl Tamblong 2; *Pacto Tours and Travel*, Jl Asia Afrika 112 (in the *Savoy Homann Hotel*); *Satriavi*, Grand Preanger Hotel, Jl Asia Afrika 81, T 50677 or at *Hotel Panghegar*, Jl Merdeka 2, T 440192.

● **Tourist offices**
In their office at the NE corner of the city square on Jl Asia Afrika, the staff of the **Bandung Visitor Information Centre** can tell you anything you want to know about Bandung and

the surrounding area, open 0900-1700 Mon-Sat (in theory). The office organizes 'designer' tours, custom made to suit each visitor's interests. For example, an architectural tour of the town, a pre-historic tour, a trip to the volcanoes, or a tour to Sundanese tribes and a Dragon village. There is also an office at the railway station. **West Javan Regional Tourist Office** is at Jl Cipaganti 153, T 81490, F 87976, on the N edge of the city, open 0700-1900 Mon-Sun.

● **Useful addresses**
American Express: T 51983.
British Council: Jl Lembong, nr *Hotel Panhegar*.
Immigration (local office): Jl Surapati 82, T 72081.
PHPA: Jl Jend A Yani 276.

● **Transport**
187 km SE of Jakarta, 400 km W of Yogya.

Local Most roads in the centre of town are one way. This, coupled with the dense traffic, makes it quite a struggle getting around town. Bandung must have more orange-suited traffic wardens than any other town on Java, ready to dangerously direct traffic (and collect their 300Rp *parkir*). **Bus**: city buses go N-S or E-W; W on Jl Asia Afrika, E on Jl Kebonjati, S on Jl Otto Iskandardinata, N on Jl Astanaanyar, 250Rp. **Becaks** (very colourfully painted). **Car rental**: Avis, *Grand Hotel Preanger*, Jl Asia Afrika 81, T 431631 and *Sheraton Inn Bandung*, Jl Ir H Juanda 390, T 2500303; **National Car Rental** at *Istana Hotel*, Jl Lembong 21. **Colts** (Angkutan kota): 300Rp around town, up to 500Rp for longer journeys. Station on Jl Kebonjati. **Delmans**. **Taxi**: 3 or 4 companies run metered taxi services. Taxis can also be chartered for 5,000Rp/hr, minimum 2 hrs.

Air Bandung's airport is 4 km from the city, T 614100. *Transport to town*: by taxi, 5,000Rp. Regular connections with Garuda/Merpati, Sempati and Bouraq with other destinations in Java, Sumatra, Kalimantan, Sulawesi, Bali, Lombok, Nusa Tenggara, Maluku and Irian Jaya (see page 912 for route map).

Train The station is in the centre of town behind the bemo station, on Jl Stasion Barat, T 50367. Regular connections with Jakarta's Kota and Gambir stations, although the best service is the hourly *Parahyangan* express from Gambir. Journey time 3-4 hrs (3,000Rp in Ekonomi, 12,000Rp in Bisnis, 25,000Rp in Exekutive). The journey between Jakarta and Bandung is spectacular, and highly rec. There are 2 trains daily to Surabaya 13 hrs and 3 to Yogya.

Road Bus: Bandung has 2 long-distance bus terminals: Kebon Kelapa on Jl Dewi Sartika for all traffic W incl Dago, Cicaheum, Sukajadi, Cicadas and Buah Batu, as well as destinations farther afield such as Jakarta, Bogor and Sumatra. A/c and non-a/c buses leave from here. Terminal Cicaheum on Jl Jend A Yani serves destinations to the E and N incl Yogya, Solo, Surabaya, Cirebon and Semarang. Tickets for a/c night buses can be bought on Jl Kebonjati, nr the *Hotel Surabaya*. Regular connections with Jakarta's Kampung Rambutan terminal $2^{1}/_{2}$-3 hrs (10,000Rp) on an a/c bus (with *P.T. Pakar Utama*, Jl Pramuka, East Jakarta), Bogor $3^{1}/_{2}$ hrs, Pelabuhanratu 4 hrs, Cirebon, $3^{1}/_{2}$ hrs, Yogya 12 hrs. **Minibus**: 2 companies from Jakarta – 4848, Jl Kramet Raya 23, T 357656, and Media, Jl Johar 15, T 343643 – run minibuses to Bandung 4 hrs. **Taxi**: share taxis for 6 cost about the same as the train.

ROUTE-WISE: THE GREAT POST ROAD
18 km E of Bandung, the road divides, turning NE along the Great Post Rd, constructed under the direction of Governor-General Daendels between 1808 and 1810 for the defence of the island against the English. An engineering feat which required unprecedented numbers of *corvée* labourers, stretches of the road are carved through steep gorges and along narrow river valleys, and cost many lives. The route ends at the coastal city of Cirebon, a total of 130 km from Bandung.

SUMEDANG

Sumedang is a medium-sized town rarely visited by tourists, but makes for a pleasant enough stopping off point between Bandung and Cirebon, especially if taking the back roads from Bandung via Tangkuban Prahu Crater and Ciater (see Excursions, below). The town's most notable point of interest is a good provincial museum (see below). Sumedang was once an important principality and the Acehnese heroine Tjoek Njak Thien, who helped to lead the fight against the Dutch in N Sumatra, was sent into internal exile here at the end of the 19th century.

The **Museum Prabu Geusan Ulun** (at Jl Prabu Geusan Ulun 40) is situated in the grounds of the District Office, on the SE side of the town square, about 2 km from Sumedang's commercial heart on the road to Bandung. The museum is housed in four colonial buildings and among the more interesting pieces on display are VOC cannon, a good selection of krisses, the uniforms of the Bupati's (Regent's) bodyguards, fine songket cloth woven with gold thread, a bed for the prince to recuperate following the circumcision ceremony, and old hand-written korans. The museum also houses a considerable library of historic books and manuscripts. But the museum's finest pieces are the crown and associated regalia (*pusaka*) of the princes of Sumedang which are locked away in a strong room. To be certain of seeing these 'crown jewels' it is necessary to arrange a viewing beforehand. The curator can sometimes open the strong room without prior notice, but do not count on it. In addition to the regalia, there is a good collection of gamelan orchestral instruments – the largest suspended on wooden frames made in Bangkok and dating from the late 19th century. The largest gong went missing in Europe while the orchestra was touring, only to be returned to Indonesia by the Dutch ambassador in 1989. There are gamelan performances held at the museum each Sun and Tues, 0800-1200 (with singing on Tues). Admission: 1,000Rp (with guided tour by the curator in English, Dutch or Indonesian). Open: 0800-1200 Mon-Thur, 0800-1100 Fri, 0800-1200 Sun.

Excursions

The trip between Sumedang and Bandung via Ciater and Tangkuban Prahu Crater is worthwhile in itself – a beautiful journey through terraced rice fields and small villages. Java at its bucolic finest. For details, see page 161.

Local information
● **Accommodation**
B-C *Hanjuang Hegar*, Jl Mayor Abdul Rachman 165, T 201820, F 201829, some a/c, new hotel looking rather like a wedding cake on the Cirebon side of town about 500m from the

centre, hot water, rooms are clean and comfortable but stylish in only the kitschest sense.

C-D Kencana Hotel, Jl Pangeran Kornel 216, T 201642, some a/c, a villa hotel on the Bandung side of town about 2 km from the centre, clean rooms with TVs and attached bathrooms but no hot water, the rooms at the back are quieter (the hotel is on the main road), an excellent and well-run place for such a small town.

D-E Wisma Gumer, Jl Grabu Geusan Ulun, simple room with shared basic facilities, on the Bandung side of town.

● **Places to eat**
Most restaurants and stalls in Sumedang specialize, unsurprisingly, in West Javanese cuisine incl hot, spicy potato with liver, deep fried slivers of spicy tahu or bean curd (tahu Sumedang), and assorted offal.

Rumah Makan Bandung, Jl Prabu Geusan Ulun 93 (1 km from town centre towards Bandung), limited choice of Sundanese dishes.

Foodstalls: there is a small night food market selling Sundanese snacks on Jl Palisari, which runs off the main Bandung-Cirebon road, 1 km from the town centre towards Bandung.

● **Entertainment**
Cinema: Diana Cinema in town centre, with a/c and showing English language films.

Gamelan performances: at the Museum Prabu Geusan Ulun, Jl Prabu Geusan Ulun 40, 0800-1200 Sun and Tues (with singing on Tues). See Places of interest, above, for further details.

● **Post & telecommunications**
Area code: 0261.
Post Office: Jl Prabu Geusan Ulun (1 km out of town on the road to Bandung).

● **Transport**
40 km from Bandung, 90 km from Cirebon.

Road Bus: the terminal is on the Cirebon side of town 2 km from the centre and colts constantly ply the route between the two. Regular connections with Bandung and Cirebon along the Great Post Rd. **Minibus**: there are also minibuses linking Sumedang with Bandung via Ciater and Tangkuban Prahu Crater (see Excursions, above).

GARUT

Garut lies 65 km SE of Bandung and was once a Dutch hill station, magnificently set at an altitude of over 700m amidst towering volcanoes. Gunung Guntur is a source of some concern and has been the object of interest by volcanologists since 1985 when local villagers noticed that spring water was rising in temperature. The volcano last erupted in 1847, but the long period of dormancy since then worries the experts who fear a cataclysmic event. The rocks in the surrounding area show evidence of pyroclastic lava flows – a superheated mixture of molten rock and gas – spreading 40 km outwards from the volcano. Such flows can travel at 100 km/hr, so if the worst occurs remember to check out quickly.

The area is also renowned for its orchards and tobacco, and in the 1920's was a popular hill resort for wealthy residents of Batavia. It is a good point from which to visit Candi Cangkuang, volcanoes (eg Mt Papandayan), hot springs and lakes (see below). Few foreign tourists stop here, although the town is large enough to provide most amenities. The surrounding area is also known for its batik. Running off Jl Jend A Yani is a colourful **fruit and general market**.

Excursions

Candi Cangkuang is a small 8th century temple set on an island in the middle of a peaceful, water lily-covered lake. The **Candi** was first listed in a report of the Dutch Archaeological Service in 1914. It was then 'rediscovered' in 1966, and restored in 1976. The temple is simple in design, square, only 8.5m high and built of andesite. It is one of the only Hindu temples to have been found in W Java and is thought, because of the absence of architectural ornamentation and the primitive building techniques, to predate Borobudur and the candis of the Dieng Plateau. It is believed to date from the 8th century, although some authorities consider it to be even older. Within the candi there is a statue of Siva riding upon his vehicle, the bull Nandi. Compared with other monuments in Java it is quite plain, although the position could hardly be more beautiful. At the foot of the temple, is the **Tomb of Arief Mohammad**, a 17th century warrior who is said to have been a very holy man who resisted the Dutch in Batavia. Surprisingly, when the tomb was excavated, no human remains were found. His descendants live in a **hamlet** 150m W of the temple, where one of the traditional houses has been restored. There are several taboos connected with this strange village: the houses cannot be altered, pilgrims are not permitted to pay homage at the tomb on Wed, four legged animals cannot be kept within the village compound, and musical instruments are forbidden during festivals. It is almost as if the inhabitants made up the prohibitions on an evening when there was nothing better to do. There is a small **museum** 50m NW of the candi. Admission to area 200Rp, 300Rp for a car; admission to candi 200Rp. *Getting there*: take a regular bus or colt travelling out of town on the Bandung road and ask to be let off at the turning for the lake and candi. This narrow road off to the right is easy to miss – there is only a small sign. The turning is 13 km N of Garut in the village of Leles (also known as Cangkuang). Travelling from Bandung, the turning is 2 km S of Kadungura (48 km from Bandung). Horse-drawn carts wait at the turning to transport visitors the 3 km from the main highway, through beautiful countryside, to Lake Cangkuang (about 6,000Rp). To reach the candi, take one of the (modified for tourists) bamboo rafts across the lake to the island (approx 2,000Rp per raft). It is also possible to walk the 2 km around the edge of the lake.

The turning for the **Cipanas hot springs** is at the Km 4 mark travelling N from Garut towards Bandung. The waters are supposed to have healing properties. The springs are 2 km above Cipanas town, an easy and attractive walk. Some female visitors found bathing here rather embarrassing, as a crowd of men gathered to ogle. **Accommodation A-D** *Sumber Alam*, T 21027, range of rooms, attractive and relaxing place, discounts available on

weekdays; **A-B** *Tirtagangga*, Jl Raya Cipanas 130, T/F (0262) 22549, restaurant, pool, bungalows with hot spring water, sports facilities. *Getting there*: regular bemos (No 04) from the bemo terminal in Cipanas town.

Mount Papandayan is an active volcano (2,622m) with remarkable bubbling sulphur pools, 36 km SW of town. Entrance: 1,000Rp. *Getting there*: catch a bus to Arjuna and hike, 2-3 hrs or take a minibus from Garut to Cisurupan, then an ojek (4,000Rp return) to the crater.

Local information
● Accommodation
C *Kota Indah*, Jl Otto Iskandardinata 236, T 61033, some rooms with hot water, clean, price incl breakfast; **C-E** *Paseban*, Jl Otto Iskandardinata 260, T 81127, restaurant, some rooms with hot water, average, bungalows set amongst gardens, older rooms a little shabby, newer ones better, with hot water, price incl breakfast.

E *Hotel Familie Ayu*, Jl Ranggalawe 66, T 81247, just off the main road and not far from the Alun-alun, rooms are rather dark but otherwise fine; **E** *Penginapan & Pemandian Cipta Rasa 2*, Jl Raya Cipanas 101, large private mandi with non-stop running hot water from the springs; **E-F** *Penginapan Kota*, Jl Ciledug 241, basic rooms.

● Banks & money changers
Bank Central Asia, Jl Ciledug 156; BNI 1946, Jl Jend A Yani 56.

● Entertainment
Cinemas: *Sumbersari*, Jl Jend A Yani 162, not very modern, but the best there is.

● Post & telecommunications
Area code: 0262.
Post Office: Jl Jend A Yani 40.

● Shopping
Department stores: *Asia Department Store*, Jl Jend A Yani 142.

● Tourist offices
Garut Tourist Office, Jl Pamuka 5, like other small tourist offices, enthusiastic but not much of substance to offer the independent – or dependent – tourist.

● Transport
65 km from Bandung.

Local The bemo station is nr the intersection of Jl Jend A Yani and Jl Cikuray; bemos from here to local towns.

Train The railway station is a Dutch-period building a few hundred metres from the town square, off Jl Jend A Yani – but no passenger trains stop here.

Road Bus: Garut's Guntur terminal is on the N edge of town. Regular connections with Bandung, Tasikmalaya, Yogya and Banjar.

TASIK MALAYA

Tasik, as it is known, is a thriving – but rarely visited – town. The main reason for this, frankly, is that there is not a great deal to do or see here. Mt Galunggung, an active volcano, lies 20 km NW of Tasik. It most recently erupted in 1982 after a 63-year-long period of dormancy. Around 35,000 people had to be evacuated from the surrounding area and a British Airways jumbo lost power in all its four engines as it flew through the 16 km-high plume of ash and smoke. Fortunately the pilot, descending faster than he might have liked in a controlled 'glide', managed to restart the engines. At the top end of Jl Pancasila is a good **bird market**. The **Alun-alun** has some attractive gardens in its centre while the **Mesjid Agung** facing onto the Alun-alun is unremarkable. One of Tasik's saving graces, though, is that it is a important **handicraft centre**. In particular, rattan products are made in the surrounding villages and a distinctive form of batik is also produced here. For details on buying handicrafts in town, see Shopping, below.

● **Accommodation A-C** *Crown Hotel*, Jl RE Martadinata 45, T 332282, F 333967, a/c, pool, slightly out of town on the road to Bandung, 60-odd modern rooms with good facilities, all rather plasticky – like an over-sized Pizza Hut, popular with tour groups; **B-C** *Yudanegara Hotel*, Jl Yudanegara 19, T 331922, a/c, new hotel in central location, rather Indonesian kitsch in style, rooms are fine though, and good value; **B-E** *Pencuk Widuri*, Jl RE Martadinata 51, T 334342, some a/c, out of town on the road to Bandung, converted villa with gardens, quiet rooms with sitting areas, a trifle dark; **C-D** *Wisma Galunggung*, Jl Yudanegara 32-34, T 333296,

some a/c, the best place to stay in Tasik, old Dutch villa in central location, spotless rooms and bathrooms, attractive verandah, good rates and friendly service, highly rec; **D-E** *Kencana Hotel*, Jl Yudanegara 17, range of rooms, very central, no a/c but more expensive rooms are graced with TVs; **E-F** *Hotel Timur*, Jl Gang Kaum (just off Jl Yudanegara, in the centre of town nr the Alun-alun) 5, T 30928, grubby, narrow, uncomfortable beds, basic.

● **Places to eat** ◆◆*RM Arum Sari*, Jl RE Martadinata 185, excellent grilled, spicy chicken and fish for which this restaurant has a reputation; *Ramona Bakery*, Jl Sutisana Sanjaya 51, for the best pastries in town.

● **Banks & money changers** Bank Bali, Jl Dr Sukarjo; **Bank Bumi Daya**, Alun-alun (town square).

● **Post & telecommunications Area code**: 0262. **Post Office**: Jl Otto Iskandardinata 6. **Telephone & fax**: Wartel, Simpang Lima (Jl Martadinata)

● **Shopping Handicrafts**: numerous art and handicraft shops in town selling rattan products and the area's distinctive batik cloth. Try the shops along Jl Dr Sukarjo, which runs off the Alun-alun.

● **Tourist offices** *Dinas Pariwisata*, Jl Otto Iskandardinata 2.

● **Transport** 57 km from Garut, 121 km from Bandung, 116 km from Cirebon, 101 km from Pangandaran. **Train** The station is on Jl Cinulu, nr the centre of town. **Road Bus**: the bus terminal is just off Jl Ir H Juanda (or Jl By-pass), which is to the SW of town, several kilometres from the centre. Regular connections with Bandung, Cirebon, Garut, Pangandaran and other centres.

PANGANDARAN

Pangandaran is situated on the neck of a narrow isthmus and offers the best beaches on the S coast of Java – which is not saying a great deal. Originally a fishing village, many of the local people now derive their livelihoods from tourism. At weekends during peak season the town is crowded with Indonesian tourists; out of season on weekdays it is like a ghost town and hotel and losmen prices can be bargained down accordingly. The high season runs between Jun and Sep, the low season from Oct to Mar. Admission to the isthmus: 1,000Rp.

The best beach is on the W side of the isthmus and is named **West Beach** (*Pantai Barat*). Swimming is best at its S end; to the N, currents are vicious and swimming should be avoided. Souvenir shops line the beach front and it is here that most accommodation is concentrated. The E side of the isthmus (**East Beach** or Pantai Timur) is less developed; the water is often rough and swimming is poor, sometimes dangerous. Fishermen cast their nets from this shore and land their catches along the beach.

The promontory of the isthmus is a park – the **Penanjung National Park**. On both the E and W sides of the promontory are white sand beaches. It is possible to walk the 10 km around the shoreline of the peninsula, or hike through the jungle which is said to support small populations of buffalo, deer, tapirs, civet cats, porcupines and hornbills, although how they tolerate the herds of tourists is a mystery. The Rafflesia flower can, it is claimed, be seen here in season (see page 490). The park also has some limestone caves. Admission to the park 1,000Rp.

Excursions

Parigi Bay is W of Pangandaran, and offers better and quieter beaches than the isthmus, namely Batu Hiu, Batu Karas and Parigi, and good water for surfing. *Getting there*: regular buses run from Pangandaran bus station on Jl Merdeka (360Rp).

Boat trip A worthwhile alternative to the bus trip back to Banjar is the much more enjoyable ferry journey from Kalipucang to Cilacap (see Transport below).

Tours

Tour agencies (see travel agents) organize jungle, boat (fishing, snorkeling), home industry, village and other tours. Prices range from 5,500-23,000Rp per person. Almost every hotel organizes trips to Yogya, Wonosobo and Bandung etc.

Local information

● **Accommodation**

Accommodation is concentrated on the W side of the isthmus; in total there are something like 100 hotels and losmen, so below is only a selection. Rates can be bargained down during the low season (Oct-Mar). At Christmas, prices rise steeply, when Indonesian tourists flock here. Many of the hotels and guesthouses rent out family rooms – usually consisting of 2 double rooms and a living area.

East Beach (*Pantai Timur*): **B** *Sunrise*, Jl Kidang Pananjung 175, T 379220, some a/c, restaurant, pool, good for this price-range; **B** *Bumi Pananjung*, a/c, rather dark; **B** *Pantai Indah Timur*, Jl Talanca 153, T 379327, F 39327, a/c, hot water, clean, rather bare but good room

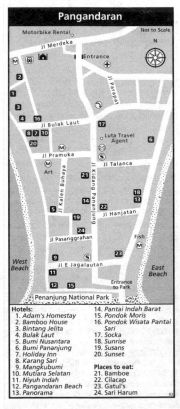

Pangandaran

Motorbike Rental
Jl Merdeka
Entrance
Jl Parapat
Jl Bulak Laut
Luta Travel Agent
Jl Pramuka
Art
Jl Talanca
Jl Kalen Buhaya
Jl Kidang Pananjung
Jl Hanjatan
Jl Pasanggrahan
Fish
West Beach
Jl E Jagalautan
East Beach
Entrance to Park
Penanjung National Park
Not to Scale

Hotels:
1. Adam's Homestay
2. Bamboo House
3. Bintang Jelita
4. Bulak Laut
5. Bumi Nusantara
6. Bumi Pananjung
7. Holiday Inn
8. Karang Sari
9. Mangkubumi
10. Mutiara Selatan
11. Niyuh Indah
12. Pangandaran Beach
13. Panorama
14. Pantai Indah Barat
15. Pondok Moris
16. Pondok Wisata Pantai Sari
17. Socka
18. Sunrise
19. Susans
20. Sunset

Places to eat:
21. Bamboe
22. Cilacap
23. Gatul's
24. Sari Harum

facilities, large pool and tennis courts, one of the plushest places in Pangandaran; **D** *Panorama*, T 379098, some rooms with verandahs face the sea, bathrooms attached, breakfast incl, good value for Pangandaran.

West Beach (*Pantai Barat*): **B** *Pangandaran Beach*, S end, T 62, some a/c, clean, large rooms; **B** *Pondok Putri Duyung*, N end, a/c, attractively built, 2 double rooms, living area, more luxurious than most, hot water, rec; **B** *Sunset*, N end, a/c, clean, bit dark, living room with 2 double bedrooms, bathrooms attached; **B** *Susan's*, inland from the beach, T 379290, some a/c, restaurant, pool, large bungalows with 4 rm, rec; **B-C** *Adam's Homestay*, T 379164, bungalows or large rooms, excellent and unusual spot; **B-C** *Pantai Indah Barat*, Kidang Pananjung 139-141 and 188, T 379006, F 379327, a/c, restaurant, pool, tennis courts, above average accommodation but not popular; **C** *Bintang Jelita*, N end, clean, with living area and 2 double bedrooms, well-run and popular, rec; **C** *Bumi Nusantara*, central section, some a/c, very clean, well designed and efficiently run, friendly, rec; **C** *Karang Sari*, N end, living room with 2 double rooms, bathrooms attached; **C** *Niyur Indah*, S end, a/c, clean, friendly, price variation for old and new rooms, rec; **C** *Pondok Wisata Pantai Sari*, Jl Bulak Laut, T 379175, inland from beach, N end, some a/c, restaurant, attached bathrooms, a/c, rooms are good value; **D** *Bulak Laut*, T 379171, N end, chalet style with sitting-room and unusual bathrooms, discounts available and room rate incl breakfast – good value; **D-E** *Christina's Delta Gecko Lodge*, 4 km W of Pangandaran, Bejak drive from bus station – too far to walk, attractive estate with little bungalows and gardens, youth hostel atmosphere, tours organized, bicycles for rent and games room. Run by a friendly Australian women, rec; **E** *Bamboo House*, N end and not on beach, T 379419, price incl breakfast, good, clean place, shared bathrooms; **E** *Mutiara Selatan*, T 379416, inland from beach at the N end, small rooms but well priced; **E** *Pondok Moris*, southern end of Peninsular, nr the park, T 379490, discreet little homestay, well-managed; **E-F** *Holiday Inn*, Jl Bulak Laut 50, T 327285, inland from beach at the N end, popular place with squat loos and bamboo rooms, excellent value.

● **Places to eat**

With something like 100 places to stay there are also innumerable places to eat. Many are geared to western tastes. Not surprisingly, the seafood is the best bet. *Bagus*, N of telephone exchange, very good value, healthy food and friendly owner; *Bamboe*, Jl Kidang Pananjung, just S of Luta Travel Agent; *Chez Mama Cilacap*, Jl Kidang Pananjung 187, a travellers' haven; *Gatul's*, East Beach, nr the fish market, excellent seafood; *Mumbo's*, West Beach, next to Mangkubumi, seafood, Chinese, Indonesian; *Pantai Timur*, Jl E Jaga Lautan, East Beach, seafood, Chinese, Indonesian and International; *Sari Harum*, Jl Pasanggrahan 2, Sundanese; *Scandinavian*, West Beach, just N of *Karang Sari Hotel*.

● **Banks & money changers**

Bank Rakyat Indonesia, Jl Kidang Pananjung 133 (nr the intersection with Jl Talanca). Rates here are poor.

● **Entertainment**

Cinemas: *Nanjung Cinema*, Jl Kidang Pananjung, N of post office.

Discos: the '*Cultural Centre*' on the West Beach Rd is no longer very cultural; it didn't make enough money and is now a disco.

● **Post & telecommunications**

Area code: 0262.

Post Office: Jl Kidang Pananjung 111 (Poste restante available here).

Telephone office: Jl Kidang Pananjung (N end).

● **Shopping**

Stalls on the beach and some shops on the central isthmus road, Jl Kidang Pananjung (for instance Luta at 107) – shell jewellery, shells, clothing, knick-knacks.

● **Sports**

Swimming: the *Socka Hotel* on Jl Kidang Pananjung, N of the cinema, opens its pool to non-residents.

● **Tour companies & travel agents**

Luta, Jl Kidang Pananjang 107, T 39294, organizes local tours and transport to and from Pangandaran; *Mumbo's*, West Beach (next to *Mangkubumi Hotel*), will organize buses to Jakarta, Yogya and Bandung. They also arrange the backwater boat trip from Kalipucang to Cilacap with connecting minibus to Yogya (13,500Rp).

● **Tourist offices**

PHPA Office on the borders of the park at the S end of the isthmus, nr the East Beach. Private tour companies and travel agents also often bill themselves as 'tourist information centres' to help attract business.

● **Transport**
400 km from Jakarta, 129 km from Bandung, 66 km from Banjar and 312 km from Yogya.

Local Becaks & bicycle hire: along the beach and from guesthouses, approximately 2,500Rp/day. **Motorbike hire**: Luta, Jl Kidang Pananjung 107, 9,000Rp/day. **Car hire**: Luta, Jl Kidang Pananjung 107.

Train There are no direct trains linking Pangandaran with Jakarta, Yogya, Bandung, or Solo. It is necessary to change in **Banjar**, a small town on the Bandung-Yogya road, and 66 km from Pangandaran. There are a number of cheap losmen over the railway bridge from the rail and bus stations in Banjar for those who arrive too late to make a connection. The train and bus stations are 500m apart; becaks wait to take travellers between the two. Regular connections with Jakarta 10 hrs, Bandung 5 hrs, Yogya 6-8 hrs and Surabaya to Banjar. Regular buses link Banjar with Pangandaran.

Road Bus: station is on Jl Merdeka, a 15-min walk N of most of the hotels and guesthouses (outside the main gates). Regular buses link Pangandaran with Banjar from where there are frequent buses onward to Jakarta 7-10 hrs, Bogor (via Ciawi), Bandung (7 hrs), Yogya and Solo, and less frequent buses to Wonogiri and Madiun. Jakarta-Banjar buses leave Jakarta's Cililitan station every hour. There are also some direct connections with Jakarta (8 hrs) and Bandung. More regular connections with Ciamis 2½ hrs and Tasik Malaya 3 hrs. Travel agents in town sell tickets on the more popular routes.

Sea Boat: an alternative to the bus or train is to take the boat between Kalipucang (Pangandaran's 'port') to Cilacap through the Anakan Lagoon, an 'inland' sea. A recommended 4-hr journey and a gentle form of transport, the boat sails down the mangrove-clothed Tanduy River, stopping-off in various fishing villages on the way, before crossing the Anakan Lagoon. The boat docks at Sleko, outside Cilacap (see page 184). Kalipucang is 15 km from Pangandaran; take a local bus there. **NB** To catch a bus connection in Cilacap get either the 0600, 0700 or 0800 from Kalipucang, 4 hrs (1,100Rp) (there are also 2 afternoon departures at 1200 and 1300). From Cilacap the boats leave from Sleko harbour, 4 departures a day (0700, 0800, 1100 and 1300).

THE NORTH COAST PLAIN

CIREBON

At the end of the 15th century, the kingdom of Cirebon reached its golden age under Sunan Gunung Jati, an ardent Muslim and one of the first *wali* – Muslim missionaries, now regarded as saints – to bring Islam to Java. He built the Pakungwati Kraton here in 1529. In 1677, the court was split into the Kasepuhan (elder) and Kanoman (younger) kratons. Unlike the kratons of Yogya and Solo, the kratons at Cirebon were not centres for the arts. Work was produced in nearby villages by guild-like organizations.

Today Cirebon is a busy port and one of the N coast's industrial centres, with a population of 250,000. The city itself is open and breezy and feels coastal despite the fact that the sea is usually out of sight. The city is famous for its distinctive batik, heavily influenced by Chinese designs (see box, page 175). The area around Cirebon is a centre of chilli, mung bean and sugar cultivation.

Places of interest

Cirebon's main attractions are its **kratons**, of which there are four, all still inhabited by their powerless sultans. The most interesting is the large **Kraton Kasepuhan**, which was built on the site of the earlier Hindu Pakungwati Kraton of 1529 (the home of Sunan Gunung Jati's queen, Pakungwati). It is the oldest palace, built in 1677 – although since much remodelled (the last extensive renovation was in 1928). It is set on the S side of a square, and is approached along Jl Kasepuhan through red brick split gates (*candi bentar*) – similar to Balinese temple gates (some of the newer hotels in Cirebon have imitated the same design element). In front of the kraton is the *Siti Inggil* – a very attractive brick enclosure, with split gates and small wooden, tiled pendopos. Plates, brought here by Chinese traders, are set into the brick – it is regarded as the finest Siti Inggil in Java.

In the first of the kraton's white washed walled courtyards is a rather down-at-heel museum, with a badly displayed collection of gamelan sets, rice harvesting knives (*ani ani*), European glass, Indian chests and Portuguese armour. Towards the back of the compound, through some weathered wooden doors, are the Palace's three main rooms. They are wonderfully cool and airy, painted in soft greens, with Delft tiles and Chinese plates set into the walls. The painted ceiling of the first room is original (although the rattan roof is new), as is the second pillared room. The beautiful pendopo *Langgar Alit*, with its unusual 4-branched central pillar, was part of the earlier Hindu Pakungwati Kraton and was used for private worship by the Sultan's family.

Back in the main courtyard, visitors should not leave the kraton without asking to see the main attraction: the *Singa Barong Carriage*. It is housed in a stable opposite the museum and is an extraordinary amalgam of Hindu, Buddhist and Islamic elements. Made in 1548 in the shape of a fantastic animal, the carriage would have been yoked to four white buffalo. It has the body and trunk of an elephant, the head of a naga, and the wings of a garuda, and when the carriage moved, the wings flapped. In its trunk the beast holds a 3-pronged spear (symbolizing the three religions). On the back of the carriage is the distinctive Cirebon cloud and rock design carved in wood. It was used by former sultans on ceremonial occasions, although it is said that the carriage has not left the stable since it was installed there in the 1940s. Behind the carriage are three palanquins, the central one, constructed in 1777, was used for circumcision ceremonies and has a garuda head and fish tail. The one on the left was for carrying the sultan's children, the one on the right for his wife. Admission 2,000Rp (with an extra charge for cameras and video). Open 0800-1700 Mon-Sun.

Next to the kraton, facing the square is the **Mesjid Agung** on Jl Jagasatru. Built in 1480 it is one of the oldest (and most revered) mosques in Indonesia, with the characteristic 2-tiered roof found along the N coast of Java. Like other mosques in Demak and Kudus, the design shows links with pre-Islamic Hindu-Buddhist structures (see page 52). The city's main mosque is the modern Mesjid Raya Al-Taque at the intersection of Jl Kartini and Jl Siliwangi, which imitates traditional Javanese style.

Kraton Kanoman is reached by walking from Jl Kanoman through the **Pasar Kanoman** and across a rough piece of ground grazed by sheep. The market sells meat, fish, vegetables and cooked foods along with dry goods of various kinds. Less attractive than Kasepuhan and less well cared for, the walls of the Kraton Kanoman at the entrance are of red plaster, again with Chinese plates set into them. It was probably built in the 17th century, but has been substantially remodelled since then. Ask to see the 'museum' on the left-hand side of the compound with an even more motley collection than the Kasepuhan Museum. Noteworthy are two more carriages, dat-

---

Cirebon rock : and cloud designs

The distinctive rock and cloud formations found not only on the batik of Cirebon but also in carvings on the carriages at the kratons, in the gates of the Kasepuhan kraton, and in decoration at the strange water garden Sunyaragi, are known as *megamendung* and *wadasan*. They are assumed to be derived from Chinese designs, probably adopted by local artisans after seeing ceramics and paintings brought by Chinese traders to the port. Each of the four courts developed their own particular styles, but all the designs featured clouds, rocks, gardens and heraldic animals.

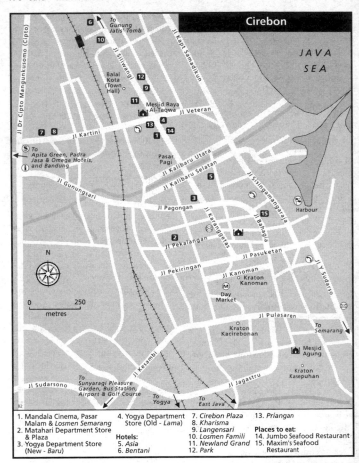

Cirebon

1. Mandala Cinema, Pasar Malam & *Losmen Semarang*
2. Matahari Department Store & Plaza
3. Yogya Department Store (New - *Baru*)
4. Yogya Department Store (Old - *Lama*)
5. *Asia*
6. *Bentani*
7. *Cirebon Plaza*
8. *Kharisma*
9. *Langensari*
10. *Losmen Famili*
11. *Newland Grand*
12. *Park*
13. *Priangan*

Hotels:

Places to eat:
14. Jumbo Seafood Restaurant
15. Maxim's Seafood Restaurant

ing from the period of the 16th century Pakungwati Kraton. The *Jempana Setia* may have been a litter used to carry the senior wife, or it may have been used to transport princes to the circumcision ceremony. It is of ornately carved wood in the Cirebon *megamendung-wadasan* style. The *Paksinagaliman* carriage is in the shape of a fantastic animal (an inferior version of the carriage at the Kraton Kasepuhan, see above) – a garuda, elephant and naga rolled into one ungainly

beast. Admission 500Rp. Open 0800-1700 Mon-Sun. Not too far from the Kraton Kanoman is the **Kraton Kacirebonan** – not really a palace at all but a house. It is an early 19th century off-shoot of the Kanoman and is the least interesting of the three. Admission 500Rp. Open 0800-1700 Mon-Sun.

Sunyaragi is a rather ugly 'grotto', built as a large pleasure garden (connected to the Kasepuhan Kraton) between 1720 and 1741. It was constructed on two levels, the upper area being an ornamental lake, with a small island only accessible by boat. Since then, it has been extensively altered, many would say ruined, and is now a maze of concrete caves built for the vertically or horizontally challenged and is remarkably unattractive. Locals promenade and picnic here on weekends and holidays. Admission 500Rp. Open 0700-1800, Mon-Sun. Sunyaragi is 3 km SW of town; take an angkutan 'G2' down Jl Kesambi (or 'G4', '0IB' and 'BX' which also pass the Cave) and get off at the intersection with Jl Bypass (also known as Jl Jend A Yani); the grotto is 500m N (right) on Jl Bypass. Ask for *Gua* (cave) *Sunyaragi*.

Exploring the town on foot can be rewarding as there are some attractive old buildings and a number of Chinese temples. The **Balai Kota** (town hall) was built in the 1920s and is a good example of Art Deco design. At the time, Cirebon was known as Kota Udang (City of Shrimps) and to celebrate this title the hall has moulds of shrimps climbing up the towers. Another notable building is the colonial offices of the **Bank Indonesia** at the

Chinese bird motif from a Cirebon batik
Adapted from: Gillow, John (1992)
Traditional Indonesian textiles, Thames &
Hudson: London

intersection of Jl Kartini and Jl Tuparev. Cirebon supports a number of markets: among the most accessible is the **Pasar Kanoman** on Jl Kanoman; the 'morning' market or **Pasar Pagi** on Jl Siliwangi is also worth a wander.

Excursions

The Tomb of Sunan Gunung Jati, one of Java's nine 'Walis', is 5 km N of town, 100m off the road to Karangampel and Indramayu (it is signposted *Makam* [grave] *Gunung Jati*). This 15th century mosque and cemetery is a popular pilgrimage site for devout Muslims (see page 95). The whitewashed walls, like those of Cirebon's kratons, are inlaid with Chinese and Dutch plates and tiles. Gunung Jati's tomb is through wooden doors and is not open to visitors (the doors are sometimes opened on special occasions); the tomb in the open pavilion is that of Sultan Sulaeman. Also buried here is the Wali's Chinese wife Ong Tien who fell in love with Sunan Jati while he was on a mission to China and implored her father to allow her to follow him to Java. She converted to Islam, but died 3 years after arriving in Cirebon. Admission free, officially, but donations include parking a car, entering the cemetery, leaving shoes, and entering the tomb site. *Getting there*: take an angkutan 'GG' or '06' which runs down Jl Siliwangi/Raya Klayan, and ask to be let off at *Makam Gunung Jati*.

Trusmi is a village 6 km W of town, and is the best known of the various *batik villages* in the vicinity of Cirebon. Linked to the courts of the Sultans for many years, the small workshops produce high quality batik tulis (hand drawn designs) as well as stamped cloth (see page 103). Prices start at 15,000Rp and go as high as 165,000Rp for the very best quality cloth. One of the largest and best known workshops is the *Masina Batik Factory*. *Getting there*: by blue angkutan 'GP' or '04', which runs from Jl Gunungsari, down Jl Tuparev to Plered (300Rp). In the village of Plered (really a suburb of Cirebon), turn right and walk down a becak-choked lane to Trusmi and its workshops (signposted).

Local information
● Accommodation
Most hotels are to be found along Jl Siliwangi.

A *Park Cirebon*, Jl Siliwangi 107, T 205411, F 205407, a/c restaurant, pool, karaoke bar, the flashiest place in town with some style and incorporating Islamic and Indonesian architectural elements, the rooms are the best available in Cirebon, good value, rec; **A-B** *Apita Green*, Jl Tuparev 323, T 200748, F 200728, a/c restaurant, pool, new high-tech hotel 2 km out of town on road to Bandung, large attractive 'river' pool, rooms are rather bland though, friendly and enthusiastic; **A-B** *Patra Jasa*, Jl Tuparev 11 (2 km out of town on the road to Bandung), T 29402, F 27696, a/c, pool, tennis, good facilities.

B *Bentani*, Jl Siliwangi 69, T 24269, F 27527, a/c, restaurant, pool, efficient new hotel with some style; **B** *Cirebon Plaza*, Jl RA Kartini 64, T 202062, F 204258, a/c, restaurant, 34 rm with satellite TV and minibar, modern hotel, the brochure maintains that: "The interior and furnishing manifest a fantastic conglomeration of Sundanese, Javanese, Islamic, Chinese and Dutch civilizations", this though, is scarcely evident, the *Plaza* is just another modern, albeit comfortable, Indonesian hotel; **B** *Kharisma*, Jl RA Kartini 60, T 200645, F 200646, a/c, restaurant, disco, karaoke, gym, tennis court, pool, recently expanded, 99 rm, built around pool and sunken bar, standard rooms, on edge of town centre, pretensions of provincial grandeur but it works well enough.

C *New Land Grand*, Siliwangi 98, T 208867, a/c, new disco, impressive colonial and colonnaded exterior, large suite rooms with the biggest doors in Cirebon, outside rooms are the best, TV, green baize carpets, hot water, large with mothballs liberally strewn; **C** *Omega Hotel*, Jl Tuparev 20, T 204291, a/c, modern Indonesian kitsch with surfeit of plastic and velvet, rather run down but expansion underway, OK for a night but not for much longer, inconvenient location nearly 2 km from centre of town on road to Bandung; **C** *Priangan*, Jl Siliwangi 106, T 200862, a/c, good mid-range hotel, hot water and a/c, central, clean and well-run with rooms on courtyard; **C-D** *Langensari*, Jl Siliwangi 127, T 204449, some a/c, some with own bathrooms, basic, plain rooms, convenient for railway station; **C-D** *Nooraini*, Jl Jend A Yani 55, T 201352, clean, next to the bus station.

D-E *Asia*, Jl Kalibaru 15-17, T 202183, old building, popular and clean with courtyard, on quiet street, the rooms are well maintained and the owner, Bontot Komar, is very switched-on, a good central place to stay, rec.

E *Famili*, Jl Siliwangi 66, T 207935, clean, plain rooms on a courtyard, shared mandi, excellent value, good location for railway station; rec; **E** *Islam*, Jl Siliwangi 116, T 203403; **E** *Losmen Semarang*, Jl Siliwangi 124, clean rooms, old building, good management, central, although rather noisy location in the middle of town.

● Places to eat
Local specialities incl *nasi jamblang* (rice served in dried teak leaves), *mie kocok*, *sate kalong* and *nasi tengko*. Cirebon has a reputation for producing some of the best seafood in Java. Try the spicy *udang mantegna* (prawns with tomato and cucumber) and the excellent squid (*cuci*).

Indonesian: ◆◆◆-◆◆*Jumbo Seafood Restaurant*, Jl Siliwangi 185 (opp the Mandala Cinema), locals rec as one of the best seafood restaurants in the city, fish and seafood are displayed and cooked to Sundanese and Chinese recipes, rec; ◆◆*Maxim's*, Jl Syarif Abdurachman 45-47, also serves Chinese and seafood, large, popular with locals, rec; ◆◆◆*Yogya Department Store*, Jl Karanggetas, food market on the ground flr selling good range of Indonesian dishes, excellent place to browse and try a range of dishes; *Baraya*, Jl Yos Sudarso 45.

Chinese: ◆◆*Canton*, Jl Syarif Abdurachman 72.

International: ◆◆*California Fried Chicken*, Jl Siliwangi 169.

Foodstalls: *Pasar Kasepuhan*, on the square nr Kraton Kasepuhan; *Pasar Malam*, a good place to try Cirebon's seafood is the night market by the Mandala Cinema on Jl Siliwangi.

Bakeries: *La Palma Bakery*, Jl Siliwangi (nr the Balai Kota); *Orchid German Bakery*, Jl Karanggetas 122.

● Banks & money changers
Bank Central Asia, Jl Siliwangi (nr Mandala Cinema); Bank International Indonesia, Jl Siliwangi 49; Bumi Daya, Jl Siliwangi 127; Djasa Valasmas Artha, Jl Yos Sudarso 56; Valuta Sejati, Jl Bahagia 53.

● Entertainment
Amusement parks: Ade Irma Suryana Nasution Taman Rekreasi. Admission 1,000Rp. Open 0900-2100 Mon-Sun.

Cinemas: there are a number in town, with a/c

showing English soundtrack films. *Mandala*, Jl Siliwangi; *Matahari Dept Store*, Jl Pekiringan.

Dance: *Topeng* (masked dance), at the Kraton Kasepuhan, 0800-1000 Sun.

Disco & karaoke: big in Cirebon; try the *Aquarius* at the *Park Hotel*; the *Blue Diamond* at Jl Yos Sudarso 1 is open 1900-0200/0300, or the *Grand Disco* at the *Grand Hotel*.

Theatre: open air theatre at Sunyaragi.

● **Post & telecommunications**
Area code: 0231.
General Post Office: Jl Yos Sudarso 7.
Telephone & fax: *Warpostel*, Jl Kartini 7 (opp the mosque).

● **Shopping**
Best buys here are batik, rattan, topeng masks, wayang kulit and wayang golek puppets.

Batik: the Cirebon area produces its own style of very distinctive batik (see box above). The town contains many batik shops; a good number can be found on the ground flr of the *Matahari Plaza*, on Jl Pekiringan; other good shops incl *Batik Keris*, Jl Pasuketan 81; *Batik Permana*, Jl Karanggetas 16; and *Batik Semar*, Jl Bahagia 36B.

Department stores: *Matahari*, Jl Pekiringan; *Yogya Department Store* (Baru), Jl Karanggetas; *Yogya Department Store* (Lama), Jl Siliwangi 173.

● **Sports**
Golf: *Ciperna Golf Course*, owned by the state oil company Pertamina, is 6 km SW of town and open to visitors. Angkutan 'GC' runs there.

● **Tour companies & travel agents**
Leo Star, Jl Karanggetas 227, T 28395; *Mitra Tour*, Jl Siliwangi 69, T 27726; *Nenggala Tour*, Jl Pasuketan 41, T 26421.

● **Tourist offices**
Cirebon Information Office (Dinas Pariwisata Daerah), Jl Cipto 1 (at intersection with Jl Kartini). Open 0800-1400 Mon-Thur, 0800-1100 Fri, 0800-1300 Sat. Not particularly helpful, indeed the office seems entirely empty. A brochure may be offered but the map is jealously guarded.

● **Useful addresses**
Immigration: Jl Sisinga Mangaraja 33, T 202955.

● **Transport**
248 km from Jakarta, 317 km from Yogya, 237 km from Semarang.

Local Blue angkutans (colts) criss-cross town in their hundreds (300Rp) and there are also multitudes of becaks. A few meter taxis make up Cirebon's public transport system.

Air Lapangan Airport is 5 km SW of the city, T 27085; angkutan 'GC' and 'GG05' go past the airport (300Rp). Daily connections by Garuda/Merpati with Jakarta, Bengkulu, Bandar Lampung, Balikpapan and Banjarmasin (see page 912 for route map).

Train The station, a rather attractive colonial-period structure, is at the N end of Jl Siliwangi, set back from the road on Jl Stasiun Kereta Api. Angkutans 'G6' and 'G5' run past the station. Cirebon connects with the southern line, which arrives at Gambir station in Jakarta and links up with Yogyakarta. There are also services on the northern coastal line, which departs from the Kota station in Jakarta and links up with Semerang and Surabaya. Regular connections with Jakarta 3¼-4 hrs, Yogyakarta 6¾ hrs, or along the coast to Semarang (see page 917 for timetable).

Road Bus: the station is 2 km S of town, on Jl Bypass, also known as Jl Jend A Yani. Numerous Angkutans (colts) ply the route into town almost continually. All long distance buses leave from here and express and a/c companies have their offices at the station. Regular connections with Jakarta 5 hrs, Semerang 5 hrs, Yogya 7 hrs, Bandung 3½ hrs and other major urban centres. **Minibus**: minibus connections with Bandung, Yogyakarta and Semarang. The minibus office is at Jl Karanggetas 7.

Sea Boat: few people reach Cirebon by sea, but the Pelni vessel *Sirimau* does call here on its fortnightly circuit between Java and Kalimantan. The Pelni office is at the harbour (see timetables on page 921).

Central Java and Yogyakarta

THE CENTRAL portion of Java comprises the province of Central Java and the Special Territory of Yogyakarta – the latter being one of only two such regions in Indonesia (the other is Aceh at the north tip of Sumatra). Although this part of Java contains some of the most magnificent monuments in the world, it is at the same time one of the poorest areas of Indonesia. Part of the explanation lies in the incredibly high population densities: combined, Central Java and Yogyakarta had a population of nearly 32 million in 1990, and in places farmers are crammed on to the land at a density of 2,000 per sq km.

In the 1960s, commentators were generally pessimistic about the ability of the region to escape the effects of what seemed to be such an intolerable burden of people. They highlighted the high incidence of malnutrition, the depths of poverty that existed, and could see little that might off-set a forthcoming 'Malthusian' catastrophe. Although conditions are still poor, the crisis has not materialized. Industrial growth – mostly small-scale, cottage industries – has been encouraging, while agriculture with the aid of the technology of the 'Green Revolution' – has managed, in the main, to keep production growing faster than population.

This central portion of Java lacks a city on the scale of Bandung in W Java or Surabaya in E Java. The largest towns are the historic towns of Yogyakarta and Surakarta (Solo). Central Java was the focus of the magnificent Buddhist Sailendra and Hindu Sanjaya dynasties which built, respectively, Borobudur and the temples on the Prambanan Plain. It was also the focus of the later Mataram Kingdom, and the sultanates of Yogyakarta and Surakarta. It is to visit these archaeological and historical sites, and to stay in what has become one of the most popular tourist towns in Indonesia – namely Yogyakarta – that visitors make their way here in droves. A general introduction to the art and history of Central Java can be found beginning on page 81.

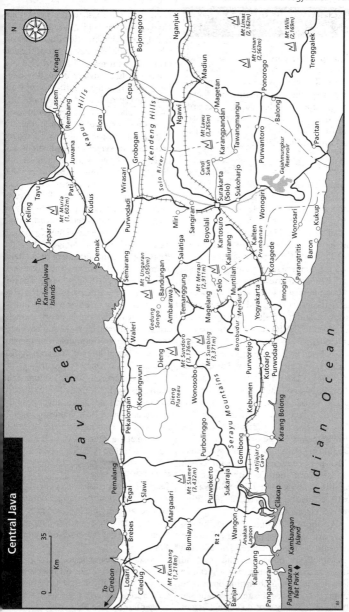

SOUTH CENTRAL JAVA AND YOGYAKARTA

Cilacap is the port for the ferry which runs four times daily to Pangandaran. The E-W route two skirts Cilacap, running across the coastal plain at the foot of the Serayu Mountains towards Yogyakarta. Yogyakarta is a total of 415 km from Bandung, 351 km from Garut and 216 km from Cilacap.

CILACAP

This coastal town has little to offer the tourist, but it is associated with the 'port' (really just a jetty) of Sleko where the daily ferry from the beach resort of Pangandaran (see page 171) docks. Because the bus journey to Pangandaran is a circuitous 163 km from Cilacap, it makes sense to take the far more relaxing ferry, a journey of 4 hrs. There are numerous hotels in Cilacap for visitors who arrive too late to catch the ferry to Pangandaran or a bus on to Yogya, and it can also be used as a base for visits to the Jatijajar Caves (see Excursions).

Sir Francis Drake, in his circumnavigation of the globe, anchored at Cilacap on 9 March 1580. The town offers one of the very few good anchorages on the wavelashed S coast. Drake was favourably impressed by the locals, writing that they were a "... loving, a very true and just dealing people". (See page 42 for a fuller account of Drake's stay at Cilacap.) Today Cilacap is a (comparatively) important industrial/trading area with a large Pertamina complex nearby. The whiff of fish in the air also hints that the town's fishing roots remain vibrant.

For those with time on their hands, there are one or two places of interest in Cilacap. At the southern end of town the Cilacap River flows into the sea, and along its course through the town can be seen brightly coloured fishing boats. The main port, in fact quite an important one as there are very few good anchorages along Java's S coast, is the **Pelabuhan Cilacap** at the end of Jl Martadinata. This is not the Sleko jetty (for Pangandaran) which is on the W side of town, at the end of Jl Jend Sudirman. Also marketed as a 'sight' is **Teluk Penyu** or **Turtle Bay**. This lies to the E of town, a 10-15 min walk from the centre. It vividly illustrates that in some places at least 'environmentalism' is no more than a slogan: numerous stuffed turtles, pangolins, civets, snakes and other animals along with shells and gruesome souvenirs are on sale at this dirty beach. The animals are not even well stuffed. Also here is the **Pasar Ikan** or fish market, where women sell fish, crabs and prawns on the beach. The beach may be interesting, but it is neither attractive nor pleasant. Walking S along the beach road, past the Pertamina oil storage tanks, is the **Benteng Pendem** or **Pendem Fort** (about 1 km or so, or 2 km from the centre of town, near the small lighthouse). The fort was built by the Dutch between 1861 and 1879 and is now an 'objek wisata' (tourist sight) – it is a warren of caves, tunnels, storage rooms and barracks and boys with torches offer to illuminate the fort for foreign visitors at exorbitant rates. Admission 500Rp. Open Mon-Sun.

A good market to browse around is the **morning market** (mostly fish and fruit) at the eastern end of Jl Sutoyo, near the intersection with Jl Dr Wahidin. There is also a **Chinese temple** in the centre of Cilacap at the intersection of Jl Martadinata and Jl Jend A Yani.

Excursions

Jatijajar caves consist of gardens, pools and concrete figures arranged within and around a cave complex (see page 194). *Getting there*: take a bus N to Route 2 and then another one E towards Kebumen and Yogya.

Nusa Kambangan is a narrow island and nature reserve just off the coast and is worth a visit if you have time to kill in Cilacap. *Getting there*: regular car and passenger ferries from Sleko pier.

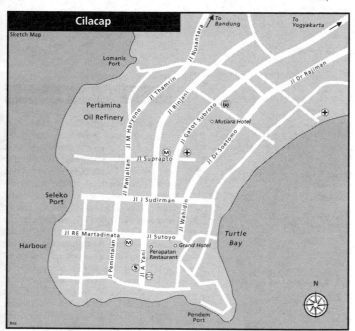

Cilacap

Sketch Map

To Bandung

To Yogyakarta

Lomanis Port

Jl Nusantara

Jl Thamrin

Jl Dr Rajiman

Pertamina Oil Refinery

Jl Rinjani

Jl Gatot Subroto

Mutiara Hotel

Jl M Haryono

Jl Panjaitan

Jl Suprapto

Jl Dr Soetomo

Seleko Port

Jl J Sudirman

Jl Wahidin

Harbour

Jl RE Martadinata

Jl Sutoyo

Turtle Bay

Jl Pemintalan

Jl A Yani

Grand Hotel

Perapatan Restaurant

N

Pendem Port

Local information
● Accommodation

A-B *Mutiara*, Jl Jend Gatot Subroto 136, T 31545, F 31547, a/c, restaurant, pool, part of a chain of hotels, good facilities with very comfortable and well kitted-out rooms, some way N of town before the bus station, prices seem rather steep for a small town; **A-B** *Wijaya Kusuma*, Jl Jend A Yani 12A, T 22871, F 31150, a/c, restaurant, pool, attractive hotel in large garden compound in centre of town.

B-D *Grand*, Jl Dr Wahidin 5-15, T 21381, F 22964, some a/c, pool, great sprawling hotel with 94 rm from cheap to expensive, check rooms as some are a mess, good pool and relatively central but could do with a management shake-up and a good clean – surface ostentation masks sloppy upkeep.

C *Cilacap Inn*, Jl Jend Sudirman 1, T 21543, some a/c, hot water in better rooms, 60s building washed in pink-red, rooms are fine and has a central location.

D-E *Delima*, Jl Jend Sudirman 3, T 21410, some a/c; **D-E** *Harnita Agung*, Jl Gatot Subroto 88,

T 21876, some a/c, more of a truckers stop than a place for travellers from abroad. As buses go straight from the Sleko Pier for most there will be no need to take advantage of this place's one plus point – its position close to the bus terminal; **D-E** *Teluk Penyu*, Jl Dr Wahidin 42-57, T 21488, some a/c, this hotel is split between two sides of the road and offers a range of rooms; fan rooms are clean with attached cold water mandis, the most expensive a/c rooms are large and well-decorated with hot water bathrooms and TVs (for some reason set into the wall between the beds), very good value compared with the established 'starred' hotels in town, the manager is keen and seems to be investing in improving his small hotel.

E *Losmen Sultana Adhi*, Jl Kol Sugiono 102, T 22750, large rooms and small mandis, walking distance from the centre of town, a little the worse for wear, quiet and reasonably friendly; **E-F** *Anggrek*, Jl Anggrek 16, T 21835, the best of the cheaper places, rooms are clean with bright, white sheets, airy, set down quiet street not far from centre of town and the Sleko Pier; **E-F** *Losmen Tiga*, Jl Mayor Sutoyo 61, good central locations, bare and basic rooms with shared bath but clean and welcoming, relaxing garden at rear.

● **Places to eat**
♦♦*Perapatan*, Jl Jend A Yani (nr intersection with Jl Martadinata), best Chinese food in town, moderate prices.

Bakeries: *Top Bakery*, Jl Jend A Yani (nr Rita Supermarket).

● **Banks & money changers**
Bank Central Asia, Jl Jend A Yani 118; **Bank Danamon**, Jl Jend Sudirman; **Lippo Bank**, Jl Jend A Yani.

● **Post & telecommunications**
Area code: 0282.

Post Office: Jl Jend A Yani 32.

● **Shopping**
Supermarket Rita, Jl Jend A Yani (in centre of town).

● **Sports**
Golf: there is an 18-hole course N of town, said to be one of the best on Java. Ask at your hotel for further information regarding green fees.

● **Tour companies & travel agents**
MIC Holidays, Jl DI Panjaitan 42 (at Sleko Jetty), T 2232.

● **Tourist offices**
Dinas Pariwisata, Jl Jend A Yani 8 (opp *Wijaya Kusuma Hotel*), T 22481, little English, handouts all (so far) in Indonesian, but pamphlet has a map which is marginally useful.

● **Transport**
216 km W of Yogya, 50 km S of Purwokerto.

Road Bus: minibuses leave for Yogya from the Sleko pier, and for Wonosobo (and Dieng), 5 hrs. The town's main bus terminal though is several kilometres N of the town centre at Jl Gatot Subroto 127. Buses to major regional centres from here. Private a/c minibus companies also run services to Yogya and Jakarta. *Rahayu*, Jl Martadinata operate buses to Yogya, and *Erny Travel*, Jl Sutoyo 54 to Bogor and Jakarta.

Sea Boat: the ferry to/from Kalipucang, Pangandaran's 'port', docks at Sleko Jetty on the western edge of town, at the end of Jl Jend Sudirman (where it becomes Jl DI Panjaitan). Departures at 0700, 0800, 1100 and 1300. It is possible to walk to the centre of town and hotels or losmen from here – about 15 mins, or take a bemo (see page 174 for details on the journey).

The ferry leaves for Pangandaran at 0700, 0800, 1200 and 1300 and takes 4 hrs (1,100Rp pp). To catch a bus onwards from Pangandaran, take a morning ferry from Cilacap, and then catch a becak and bemo to the bus station on the edge of town.

YOGYAKARTA

Yogyakarta – usually shortened to Yogya and pronounced 'Jogja' – is probably the most popular tourist destination in Java. It is a convenient base from which to visit the greatest Buddhist monument in the world – Borobudur – and the equally impressive Hindu temples on the Prambanan Plain. The town itself also has a number of worthwhile attractions: the large walled area of the kraton, with the Sultan's palace, the ruined water gardens or 'Taman Sari', and a colourful bird market. Yogya is arguably the cultural capital of Java and the ISI (Indonesian Art Institute) is based here, with faculties of Fine Art, Dance and Music. The town is the best place to see wayang performances and traditional dance (see page 200). In recent years it has become a popular town for Indonesian artists to base themselves. On the northern edge of the city is Indonesia's oldest, and one of its most prestigious, universities: Gadjah Mada University or UGM. It was 'founded' in Dec 1949 when Sultan Hamengkubuwono IX allowed students and their teachers to use the Siti Inggil within the precincts of the kraton. For the tourist, it is also one of the best centres for shopping and offers a good range of tourist services from excellent middle range accommodation to well-run tour companies.

Yogya is situated at the foot of the volcano Mt Merapi, which rises to a height of 2,911m, to the N of the city. This peak is viewed as life-giving, and is set in opposition to the sea which is life-taking and situated to the S. The importance of orientation vis à vis Mt Merapi and the ocean is seen most clearly in the structure of the kraton, or Sultan's palace (see below).

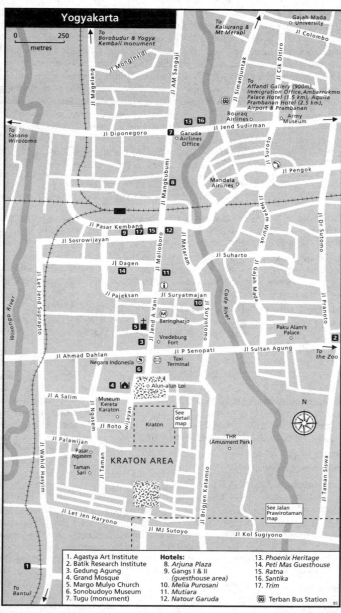

Yogyakarta

0 — 250
metres

To Borobudur & Yogya Kembali monument

To Kaliurang & Mt Merapi

Gajah Mada University

Jl Colombo

Jl Magelang

Jl Monginsidi

Jl AM Sangaji

Jl Simanjuntak

Jl Cik Ditiro

To Affandi Gallery (900m), Immigration Office, Ambarrukmo Palace Hotel (1.5 km), Aquila Prambanan Hotel (2.5 km), Airport & Prambanan

To Sasono Wirotomo

Jl Diponegoro

Bouraq Airlines

Jl Jend Sudirman

Army Museum

Garuda Airlines Office

Jl Mangkubumi

Mandala Airlines

Jl Suroto

Jl Pengok

Jl Dr Sutomo

Jl Pasar Kembang

Jl Sosrowijayan

Jl Matram

Jl Suharto

Jl Hayam Wuruk

Jl Gajah Mada

Jl Dagen

Jl Maliuboro

Jl Let Jend Suprapto

Winongo River

Code River

Jl Pajeksan

Jl Suryatmajan

Jl Jend A Yani

Beringharjo

Suryotomo

Paku Alam's Palace

Jl Pranoto

Jl Ahmad Dahlan

Vredeburg Fort

Jl P Senopati

Jl Sultan Agung

To the Zoo

Negara Indonesia

Taxi Terminal

Jl A Salim

Alun-alun Lor

Jl Ngasem

Museum Kereta Karaton

Jl Roto Wijayan

Kraton

See detail map

N

Jl Palawijan

Pasar Ngasem

Taman Sari

Jl Taman

KRATON AREA

THR (Amusement Park)

Jl Brigjen Katamso

Jl Taman Siswa

Jl Let Jen Haryono

See Jalan Prawirotaman map

Jl MJ Sutoyo

Jl Kol Sugiyono

To Bantul

1. Agastya Art Institute
2. Batik Research Institute
3. Gedung Agung
4. Grand Mosque
5. Margo Mulyo Church
6. Sonobudoyo Museum
7. Tugu (monument)

Hotels:
8. *Arjuna Plaza*
9. *Gangs I & II* (guesthouse area)
10. *Melia Purosani*
11. *Mutiara*
12. *Natour Garuda*

13. *Phoenix Heritage*
14. *Peti Mas Guesthouse*
15. *Ratna*
16. *Santika*
17. *Trim*

Terban Bus Station

85

History

The name Yogyakarta, or Yogya, is derived from the Sanskrit 'Ayodya' – the capital city of Rama in the Hindu epic, the Ramayana. The city was officially founded in 1755, although there were a succession of earlier settlements near the site, most notably the capital of the great Mataram Kingdom in the early 17th century (see page 84).

In the 1670s, the Mataram Kingdom based near Yogyakarta, under Amangkurat I, began to decline. At the same time, the Dutch East India Company (VOC) based at Batavia – present-day Jakarta – was growing in military might and commercial influence. By the mid-18th century, the VOC – whose leaders up until then had been loathe to expand territorially – were forced to make their move. Worried that the power vacuum left by the crumbling Mataram Kingdom might be filled by competing colonial powers, the VOC sent a force to Mataram. In 1755, the Treaty of Giyanti partitioned the kingdom into three sultanates: the two senior

---

The Hamengkubuwono Sultans of Yogyakarta (1749 to the present day)

Hamengkubuwono I or Mangkubumi (1749-92)
Established the Sultanate and the City of Yogyakarta after fighting the Dutch for almost a decade. Built the Kraton and the water gardens.

Hamengkubuwono II (1792-1810, 1811-12, 1826-28)
Not a man to match his father in stature, his undiplomatic behaviour made him unpopular with the Dutch. He was deposed three times by the Dutch and English, had two queens, 31 concubines and 80 children.

Hamengkubuwono III (1810-11, 1812-14)
Popular with the colonial powers and, as a result, unpopular with the Javanese aristocracy. It was during his reign, and that of his father, that the Sultanate lost all effective power.

Hamengkubuwono IV (1814-22)
Ascended to the throne at the age of thirteen and died under mysterious circumstances 8 years later.

Hamengkubuwono V (1822-26, 1828-55)
Ascended to the throne at the age of three, under the tutelage of a Dutch-appointed committee. It was at this time that Prince Diponegoro (Hamenkubuwono V's uncle) stirred up rebellion and led the Java War from 1825-1830.

Hamengkubuwono VI

Hamengkubuwono VII

Hamengkubuwono VIII (1921-39)
His great love was *wayang* theatre, and his reign saw a revival of this and other Javanese arts.

Hamengkubuwono IX (1940-1988)
Reigned through the difficult periods of the Japanese Occupation and then the formation of the Republic. He gave support to the fledgling independence movement, and allowed the kraton to become a focus of resistance. Died in 1989, highly respected and loved by his people.

Hamengkubuwono X (1989-)
Said to be both an astute politician and businessman.

houses of Pakubuwono (meaning 'Nail of the Universe') of Surakarta, and Hamengkubuwono (meaning, 'He who holds the World on his Lap') of Yogyakarta, and the junior house of Mangkunegara, also of Surakarta. These three sultanates retained considerable independence but ultimate power from that point rested with the Dutch. Pangeran Mangkubumi, the brother of Susuhunan Pakubuwono II of Surakarta (see page 227) became Sultan of Yogyakarta, and was known as Hamengkubuwono I. He reigned until his death in 1792 at the age of eighty, during which time he had built up a powerful and prosperous state, which his son and successor Hamengkubuwono II was unable to maintain. Hamengkubuwono II was contemptuous of the Dutch, who were creating ill-feeling with their oppressive policies. Tension between the new French-backed Governor-General Daendels and the Javanese resulted in a rebellion led by Raden Ronggo. Daendels sent a force to Yogya in 1810, which succeeded in killing Ronggo and forcing the Sultan to step down in favour of his son, Hamengkubuwono III.

During the Napoleonic Wars, Daendels's successor Janssens surrendered to the British in Batavia in 1811. Taking advantage of this colonial upheaval, Hamengkubuwono II regained the throne from his son. The British Lieutenant-General in Batavia, Thomas Stamford Raffles, subsequently became aware of an alliance between the Sultan of Yogya and the Susuhunan of Solo, and mounted a force to attack the city in 1812. Hamengkubuwono II, never a great success in military matters, was again defeated and deposed. He was sent into exile on the island of Penang (Malaysia), and his pro-British son returned to the throne once more. At the same time as the Hamengkubuwono family were at war with one another, a certain Prince Notokusomo took advantage of the confusion by establishing a second kraton in the city, naming himself Pangeran Pakualam I in 1813. For the next 16 years there were four princes in the two cities of Yogya and Solo.

Daendels and Raffles were both committed to ruling Java, not just controlling the island, and they introduced numerous administrative reforms that effectively emasculated the sultans of Yogyakarta. Yet this period saw a flowering of Javanese culture, and one of the centres was the city of Yogya. As the historian John Smail writes a "large new court literature grew up...the art of *batik* achieved its classical form and colours (indigo blue and rust brown), the repertoire of the *wayang kulit* was enlarged and its music refined and developed, and a new dance drama, *wayang orang*, grew out of the *wayang kulit* tradition". Smail goes on to note how "the Javanese language was polished into an instrument of superb social precision, so that Javanese came to speak what were almost different dialects, according to whether they were addressing social superiors, inferiors or equals". It is as if the sultans and *priyayi* or aristocracy of Yogyakarta and elsewhere, denied power, had redirected their energies into the arts and into the perfection of social custom.

The **Second World War** effectively ended the Dutch colonial period in Indonesia, and a focus of the conflict between the independence movement and the colonial authorities was Yogyakarta. Sukarno and Hatta, who had both publicly supported the Japanese, announced the independence of Indonesia on 17 August 1945 in Jakarta, just 2 days after the Japanese had surrendered to the Allies. The Dutch, with British support, managed to retake Jakarta, and Sukarno and Hatta were forced to flee into the Javanese interior. The kraton of Yogyakarta, the residence of the Sultan, became the centre of rebellion and the city itself the informal capital of the Republic of Indonesia. The first university of the new nation – Gajah Mada – was established within the kraton's walls.

In Dec 1948, the Dutch launched their **second Police Action** and Yogya was taken without a struggle. The leaders of the independence movement made the mistake of believing that world opinion would be on their side and prevent the Dutch from taking any precipitous action. Sukarno and Hatta were captured, and dispatched into exile. The rump of the independence army managed to flee into the countryside, from where they conducted a guerrilla war against the Dutch, capturing Yogya once again in 1949. 1 year later, Indonesia was to become truly independent and the focus of politics moved back to Jakarta.

Places of interest

Yogya's main street is Jl Malioboro which runs from N to S. At its S end, the street becomes Jl Jend A Yani and then Jl Trikora, which leads into the kraton and the grassed square known as the **Alun-alun Lor**. This square was the site of major events such as tiger and buffalo fights, which were staged here from 1769. A raised stand afforded the sultan and any visiting Dutch dignitaries a good view of the spectacle. The tiger was deemed to represent the foreigner and the buffalo, the Indonesian. Invariably, the buffalo would win the contest – often with some help – but the symbolism was lost on the Dutch. Nonetheless, the unperceptive Dutch still succeeded in dominating Yogya and Indonesia. There are two sacred *waringin* trees (*Ficus benjamina*) in the centre of the square. The *waringin* represents the sky and the square fence or *waringin kurung* surrounding the trees, the earth with its four quarters. At the same time, the tree is said to symbolize chaotic nature, and the fence human order.

At the NW edge of the Alun-alun Lor is the **Museum Sonobudoyo**. It was established in 1935 as a centre for Javanese culture, and the collection is housed, appropriately, within a traditional Javanese building. It contains a good selection of Indonesian art, largely Javanese, including a collection of wayang puppets, but also some Balinese woodcarvings. Admission 250Rp. Open 0800-1300 Tues-Thur, 0800-1100 Fri, 0800-1230 Sat and Sun (see Entertainment, page 200). On the SW side of the Alun-alun Lor is the **Grand Mosque**, built in Javanese style, with a wooden frame and a tiled roof.

The Kraton of Yogyakarta

The **Kraton** or *Keraton* (see page 92) of Yogyakarta was one of three such palaces that came into existence when the kingdom of Mataram was partitioned after the Treaty of Giyanti was signed with the VOC in 1755. It has been described as a city within a city; it not only houses the Sultan's Palace but also a maze of shops, markets and private homes supporting many thousands of people. This section only deals with the inner palace; the kraton actually extends far further, 'beginning' 1 km N at the far end of Jl Malioboro.

The kraton was started in 1756 by the first Sultan, Mangkubumi (who became Hamengkubuwono I in 1749) and finished almost 40 years later near the end of his reign. The teak wood used to construct the palace came from the sacred forest of Karangkasem on Mt Kidul. It is largely made up of *pendopo* or open pavilions, enclosed within interconnecting rectangular courtyards. The entire complex is surrounded by high white washed walls. John Crawfurd, who was an assistant to Raffles and later to make his mark in both Siam and Burma, wrote of the kraton in 1811:

"...The actual palace occupies the centre and is surrounded by the dwellings of the princes, and those of attendants and retainers...The principal approach..is from the N, and through a square..called the *alun-alun*..it is here that the prince shows himself to his subjects..."

Facing the Alun-alun Lor is the **Pageleran**, a large open *pendopo*, originally employed as a waiting place for government officials. Today, this pendopo is used for traditional dance and

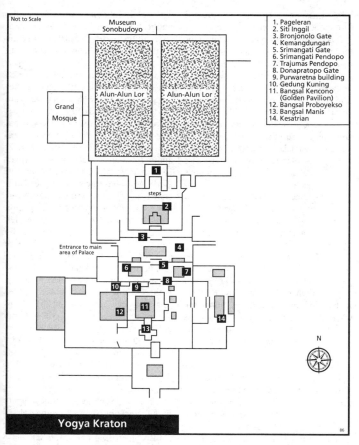

Not to Scale

Museum Sonobudoyo

Grand Mosque

Alun-Alun Lor | Alun-Alun Lor

steps

Entrance to main area of Palace

1. Pageleran
2. Siti Inggil
3. Bronjonolo Gate
4. Kemangdungan
5. Srimangati Gate
6. Srimangati Pendopo
7. Trajumas Pendopo
8. Donapratopo Gate
9. Purwaretna building
10. Gedung Kuning
11. Bangsal Kencono (Golden Pavilion)
12. Bangsal Proboyekso
13. Bangsal Manis
14. Kesatrian

N

Yogya Kraton

86

theatrical performances. There are a number of further *pendopo* surrounding this one, containing mediocre displays of regal clothing. The very first classes of the newly-created Gajah Mada University were held under these shaded pavilions. To the S of the Pageleran, up some steps, is the **Siti Inggil**, meaning 'high ground'. This is the spot where new sultans are crowned. Behind the Siti Inggil is the **Bronjonolo Gate**, which is kept closed. Admission to this area of the kraton is 300Rp. Open 0800-1300 Mon-Sun, 0800-1100 Fri.

The entrance to the main body of the Palace is further S, down Jl Rotowijayan – on the W side of the Pageleran complex. The first courtyard is the shaded **Kemangdungan** or **Keben**, with two small pendopo, where the *abdi dalem* or palace servants gather. The 'black' sand that covers most of the ground around the pendopo and other buildings in the kraton is from the beaches of the S coast. In this way, it is ensured that the Queen of the South Seas, Nyi Loro Kidul (see page 151), with whom the Sultan is believed to have intimate relations, is present throughout the palace.

The **Srimanganti** (meaning 'to wait for the king') **Gate** leads into a second, rather more impressive, courtyard with two *pendopos* facing each other; the *Srimanganti* to the right and the *Trajumas* to the left. The former was used to receive important guests while the latter probably served as a court of law. The Srimanganti now contains gongs and other instruments that make up a gamelan orchestra. The Trajumas houses palanquins, litters and chairs as well as a cage in which the Sultan's children played. It is said that the children were placed in here at 8 months of age and given a selection of objects – pens, money, books – to play with; whichever took their interest indicated their future careers.

The **Donapratopo Gate**, flanked by two *gupala* or *raksasa* statues to protect the palace from evil, leads into the heart of the palace where the Sultan and his family had their private quarters. Notice the way that gateways never give direct access to courtyards; they were designed in this way to confuse spirits attempting to make their way into the complex.

Inside this gate, immediately on the right, is the Sultan's office, the **Purwaretna**. Beyond it is the **Gedung Kuning**, an impressive yellow building which continues to be the Sultan's private residence. Both are roped-off from the public.

The central and most impressive pavilion in the complex is the **Bangsal Kencono** or Golden Pavilion. The four teak pillars in the centre represent the four elements. On each is symbolized the three religions of Java: Hinduism (a red motif on the top of the columns), Buddhism (a golden design based on the lotus leaf) and Islam (black and gold letters of the Koran). Unfortunately, because the pavilion is roped-off it is difficult to see the pillars clearly. Behind the Golden Pavilion to the W is the **Bangsal Proboyekso** (which contains the armoury) and the **Gedung Keputrian**, the residence of the Sultan's wives and children, both closed to the public. Immediately to the S of the Golden Pavilion is the **Bangsal Manis**, the dining room. **Kemakanan**, a pendopo to the S reached through a set of gates, is used for wayang performances at the end of Ramadan. To the E, through another gate (to the side of which is a large drum made from the wood of the jackfruit tree) there is another courtyard, the **Kesatrian**. The Sultan's sons lived here. In the central pendopo of this courtyard there is another gamelan orchestra on display. Performances are held every Mon and Wed, 1030-1200 (the performance is included in the price of the entrance). At the E side of this courtyard is a collection of paintings, the best being by Raden Saleh, a 19th century court painter who gained a reputation of sorts (and whose grave can be found in Bogor). The photographs of the sultans and their wives are more interesting. North of the Kesatrian is the **Gedung Kopo**, originally the hospital and now a museum housing gifts to the sultans. There are also a pair of rooms given over to memorabilia of Hamengkubuwono IX, who died in 1988. Admission to complex 1,500Rp. Open 0830-1300 Mon-Thur, 0830-1100 Fri, 0830-1200 Sat, 0830-1300 Sun. Guide obligatory.

Close to the Palace, on Jl Rotowijayan, is the **Museum Kereta Karaton**, which houses the royal carriages. Admission 500Rp. Open 0800-1300, Mon-Sat.

From the Palace it is a 5-10 min walk to the Taman Sari. Walk S along Jl Rotowijayan and turn left at the Dewi Srikandi Art Gallery. A number of batik painting galleries are down this road which leads into Jl Ngasem and then onto the **Pasar Ngasem** or bird market, an interesting place to wander. Song birds, and particularly turtle doves (Genus *Streptopelia*), are highly-prized by the Javanese. It is sometimes said that wives take second place to a man's song bird and that they can cost as much as US$15,000, although this seems hard to believe.

Popular are the spotted-necked dove (*Streptopelia chinensis*), the Javan turtle dove (*Streptopelia bitorquata*) and the zebra dove (*Geopelia striata*). Hand-made, split bamboo bird-cages are a good buy.

By picking your way through the Pasar Ngasem it is possible to reach the **Taman Sari**, which was known to the Dutch as the waterkasteel or 'Water Castle', as it is still called. This is a maze of underground passageways, ruins and pools built as a pleasure garden by the first Sultan, Mangkubumi, in 1765 at the same time as the Kraton. The *Babad Mangkubumi* gives a slightly later date – 1683 according to the Javanese calendar or AD 1757-8. Surrounded by high walls, it was the sultan's hideaway. He constructed three bathing pools – for his children, his *putri* (girls) and himself. A tower allowed the Sultan to watch his 'girls' bathing and to summon them to his company. In addition, there were a series of underwater corridors and even a partly underwater mosque. It is these labyrinths which have led some historians to speculate that it was also built as a retreat in times of war. By climbing the stairs over the entrance gate it is possible to look over the surrounding kampung: this was originally an artificial lake, with a large colonnaded pavilion in the middle. Unfortunately, the gardens were damaged during the British attack on Yogya in 1812 and restoration programmes have been rather unsympathetic. It is difficult to imagine the gardens as they were – as a place of contemplation. Most visitors enter the water gardens from Jl Taman, through the E gate, which leads into the bathing pool area or Umbul Binangun. This small section is the most complete area of the gardens, having been reconstructed in 1971. The gardens fell into disrepair following the death of Hamengkubuwono III, a process which was accelerated by a devastating earthquake in 1865. Admission 500Rp. Open 0700-1700 Mon-Sun.

To the SE of the kraton and Taman Sari on Jl Kol Sugiyono is the small **Museum**

Perjuangan or the struggle for Independence Museum. As the name suggests, this commemorates Indonesia's Declaration of Independence on 17 August 1945 and has a less than inspiring collection of historical artefacts relating to the episode. Admission 250Rp. Open 0800-1300 Tues-Thur, 0800-1100 Fri, 0800-1200 Fri and Sat.

The **Vredeburg Fort** lies to the N of the kraton on the E side of Jl Jend A Yani, near the intersection with Jl P Senopati. It was built in 1765 by the Dutch as a military barracks. Restored in the late 1980s, the fort has lost what character it may have had, and today looks rather like an American shopping arcade (piped music adds to the effect). Now a museum, the fortress houses a series of dioramas depicting the history of Yogyakarta. Admission 250Rp. Open 0900-1300 Tues-Thur, 0900-1100 Fri, 0830-1400 Sat and Sun. Close by is the **March 1st Monument** which commemorates the taking of Yogya from the Dutch in 1949 by a band of guerillas led by (then) Colonel Suharto. The **Beringharjo Market** is set back from Jl Jend A Yani on the same side of the street and just N of the Vredeburg Fort. A dimly-lit mixed market, it is an interesting and colourful place to wander with fruit, vegetables, fish and meat, batik and household goods – all jumbled together and seemingly fighting for air. Locals warn that numerous pickpockets operate here. On the other side of Jl Jend A Yani is **Margo Mulyo Church**, which dates from 1830.

Across the road from the fort is the **Gedung Agung** built initially in 1823 and then rebuilt in 1869 after the devastating earthquake of 1865. It was the former home of the Dutch Resident in Yogya and is now a state guesthouse. Queen Elizabeth II of Great Britain, former Prime Minister Nehru of India and Queen Sirikit of Thailand have all stayed here. Between 1946 and 1949 President Sukarno lived in the Gedung Agung, while Yogya was the capital of

Diponegoro: Prince and early freedom fighter

Prince Diponegoro (1785-1855) was the son of Sultan Hamengkubuwono III. He was both a learned and a devout man, dedicating much of his life to the study of the Islamic scriptures and to prayer. But he was also a man with a mission. He fervently hoped to return Java to its religious roots – by which he meant Islam, not Hinduism or Buddhism – and to cast off the infidel European yoke. Yet, even though he was a devout Muslim he also believed in the power of the Southern Ocean Goddess, Nyi Loro Kidul (see page 151) and he visited the ancient sites of the Mataram Kingdom, hoping that their past power might somehow invigorate him. Prince Diponegoro still remains a symbol of the nationalist movement in Indonesia, and virtually every town in the country has a road named after him.

In 1825, Prince Diponegoro led a rebellion against the colonial powers based in Batavia (Jakarta). This heralded 5 years of war – the Java Wars – during which time half the population of Yogya either fled the sultanate, were killed, or died of starvation. With the defeat of Diponegoro and his supporters in 1830, the Dutch were in a position to exercise yet firmer control. From that moment on, the Javanese courts never regained their authority in the country and became merely centres of the arts and of etiquette. Power in Yogya was from then on in the hands of the Dutch resident.

an emerging independent Indonesia. South of the fort, on Jl P Senopati, are three impressive **colonial buildings**, the General Post Office (1910), Bank Indonesia and the Bank Negara Indonesia (1923).

North from the Vredeburg Fort, Jl Jend A Yani becomes **Jl Malioboro**. The origin of the name is shrouded in mystery; there has been a tendency in recent years to associate it with the English Duke of Marlborough, even with a certain brand of cigarettes. Both explanations are highly unlikely. Whatever the origin of the name, this is the tourist heart of Yogya with shops, restaurants and a smattering of hotels. The town has the largest student population in Indonesia, and in the evenings they congregate along Jl Malioboro for intellectual discussions, eating and music, staying there till 1600 or 1700 in the morning; it has become known as the 'Malioboro culture'. At its N extension, Jl Malioboro becomes Jl Mangkubumi. To the W of Jl Mangkubumi in Tegalrejo is **Sasono Wirotomo**, or the **Diponegoro Museum**, a house built on the site of

Prince Diponegoro's residence, which was levelled by the Dutch in 1825. The museum contains the prince's memorabilia including a collection of weapons. Open 0800-1600 Mon-Sun. At the end of Jl Malioboro is an **obelisk** or *tugu* which marks the N limit of the kraton. The original tugu was erected in 1755, but collapsed; the present structure dates from 1889. Aart van Beek in his book *Life in the Javanese Kraton* explains that this was "the focal point for the Sultan who would sit at an elevated place near the entrance of the palace and meditate by aligning his eyes with the *tugu* and the 3,000m high Merapi volcano behind, in the distance".

To the E of the town centre on Jl Sultan Agung, is **Paku Alam's Palace**. A small part of the palace in the E Wing is a museum. Admission 500Rp. Open Mon and Thur. Further E still, on Jl Kusumanegara is the **Gembira Loka Zoo and Amusement Park**. It contains a reasonable range of Indonesian animals including the Komodo dragon, orang utan, tiger and rhinoceros. Admission 550Rp. Open 0700-1800 Mon-Sun.

Kota Gede, also known as Sar Gede, lies 5 km to the SE of Yogya and was the capital of the 16th century Mataram Kingdom. Nothing remains except for the **tombs** of the rulers of Mataram. In particular, Panembahan Senopati, the founder of the kingdom and his son Krapyak (the father of the famous Sultan Agung). Senopati's son-in-law, Ki Ageng Mangir is also buried here, his tomb protruding into common ground as he was Senopati's foe. About 100m from the cemetery is the Watu Gilang, a stone on which Senopati killed Ki Ageng Mangir by smashing his head against it. Walled gardens and ponds with fish and a yellow turtle with claimed magical powers ('several hundred years old') add to the atmosphere. Like the tombs of Imogiri (see Excursions, below) visitors must wear traditional Javanese dress which can be hired at the entrance (500Rp). Admission by voluntary contribution. Open 1300-1600 Fri for the actual cemetery but the other areas are open daily. Kota Gede is better known for its **silver workshops** which date back to the 17th century rule of Sultan Agung. Both traditional silver and black (oxydized) silverwork can be purchased. Get to the tombs and workshops by taxi or by town bus (bis kota) No 4 or 8 from Jl Jend Sudirman, No 11 from Umbunharjo terminal and No 14 from Jl Prawirotaman.

Taru Martani is a cigar factory on Jl Kompil B Suprapto, on the E side of town, which visitors can visit to watch the process of cigar manufacture. Open 0630-1500 Mon-Fri. There are English, Dutch and German speaking guides.

Excursions

Hindu and Buddhist monuments including the largest Buddhist monument in the world, **Borobudur** (see page 204), the magnificent Hindu temples at **Prambanan** (see page 215) and the small Hindu temples on the **Dieng Plateau** (see page 237) can all be visited on day trips from Yogya.

The **Yogya Kembali Monument** is situated to the N of the city, on Yogya's ring road, about 7 km from the centre. It is visited more by Indonesian than by foreign tourists, and commemorates the proclamation of Yogya as the capital of the newly-'independent' Indonesia on 6 July 1945. The monument is a 31m-high cone, symbolizing Mt Meru, and is positioned on an axis that runs N from the kraton, through the Tugu monument, then to the Kembali Monument, and finally to the sacred Mt Merapi. On the first floor of the building is a museum, on the second floor 10 dioramas depicting the fight against the Dutch for Yogya, while the third floor houses the Garbha Graha – a room for meditation containing little but the national flag. On the balustrade around the monument are 40 reliefs again recording the fight against the Dutch for independence. The monument was officially opened by President Suharto on 6 July 1989. *Getting there*: by bus from the Umbunharjo terminal on Jl Kemerdekaan, towards Borobudur (a visit here can be combined with a trip to Borobudur).

Mount Merapi lies 30 km N of Yogya and on its slopes is the hill resort of **Kaliurang**. Both are accessible on a day excursion, although staying overnight is recommended (see page 204). *Getting there*: see the transport details in the Mt Merapi and Kaliurang entry.

Imogiri 17 km to the S of Yogya, is the site of the **tombs of the Mataram sultans** as well as the rulers of the Surakarta Kingdom. Perhaps the greatest Mataram king, Sultan Agung (reigned 1613-1646), is buried here. He built the cemetery in 1645, preparing a suitably magnificent site for his grave, on a hillside to the S of his court at Kartasura. It is said that he chose this site so that he had a view of the Queen of the South (the sea goddess Nyi Loro Kidul). To reach his tomb (directly in front at the top of the stairway), and those of 23 other royal personages (Surakarta susuhunans to the left, Yogya sultans to the right) the visitor must stag-

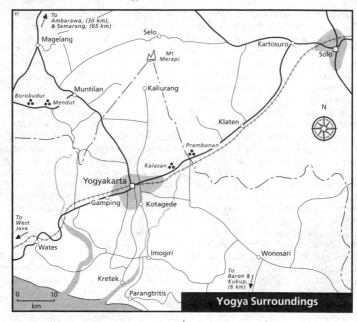

Yogya Surroundings

ger up 345 steps. Walk behind the tombs to the top of the hill for fine views of the surrounding countryside. Javanese dress, which can be hired at the site, is required to enter the mausoleums. The Yogyakartan equivalent of Chelsea Pensioners, with turbans and krisses, make sure correct behaviour is observed at all times. Admission by donation. Open: Agung's tomb is only open 1000-1300 Mon, 1330-1630 Fri and 1000-1330 Sun, although it is possible to climb up to the site at any time. A **traditional ceremony** to thank God for water involving the filling of four bronze water containers – known as *enceh* – is held in the Javanese month of Suro; the first month of the year (Jun). The containers are placed at the gates of the cemetery and are an expression of gratitude to God for the provision of water. *Getting there*: by bus or colt (buses continue on to Parangtritis from here – see below) (350Rp); it is a 1 km walk E to the foot of the stairs from Imogiri town (ask

for the *makam* or cemetery). The bus journey is lovely, along a peaceful country road past paddy fields.

Parangtritis is a small seaside resort 28 km S of Yogya (see page 203). It is accessible on a day excursion although there are a number of places to stay. *Getting there*: regular connections with Yogya's Umbunharjo bus terminal either via Kretek along the main road and over the Opak River, or via Imogiri and Celuk (see above). The longer, rougher, trip via Imogiri passes through beautiful rural scenery.

Jatijajar Caves are to be found in the side of a strange ridge of jagged hills, SW of the small town of Gombong and 157 km from Yogya. Outside the entrance is a large concrete dinosaur which acts as a spout for the underground spring (bathing pools here). Inside, there are stalactites and stalagmites, springs and theatrical statues of human beings and animals which apparently recount the history of the kingdom of Pahaharan. Admission 450Rp. *Getting there*: 7 km W of Gombong, turn left; the caves are 13 km off the main road. There are minibuses from Kebumen (50 km) and from Gombong. Gombong is accessible from Yogya, Cilacap, and Semarang, among other towns.

Karang Bolong Beach near to the Jatijajar Caves, is known as a site for collecting bird's nests for the soup of the same name.

Tours

For visitors without their own transport, one way to see the sights around Yogya is to join a tour. Although it is comparatively easy to get around by public transport it can mean waiting around for the appropriate bus or bemo. Yogya has more than its fair share of companies offering tours to the sights in and around the city. Listed below are a selection on offer; visit the tourist office for the latest information.

Tours include: *city tours* to the Kraton, Taman Sari, batik factories, wayang performances and Kota Gede silver workshops. *Out of town tours* to Prambanan, Borobudur, the Dieng Plateau, Kaliurang, Parangtritis, Solo and Candi Sukuh, Gedung Songo, Mt Bromo and Mt Merapi. The least expensive companies charge 15,000-20,000Rp/day, depending on the distance to be driven. Check various companies to select the vehicle and time of departure to suit your budget and needs (tours on non-a/c buses are considerably cheaper, for example).

Festivals

Being an ancient kingdom and a sultanate, Yogya is host to a number of colourful festivals.

Apr: *Grebeg Syawal* (movable – end of Ramadan). A celebration by Moslems, thanking Allah for the end of this month of fasting. The day before is *Lebaran Day*, when the festivities begin with children parading through the streets. The next day, the military do likewise around the town and then a tall tower of groceries is carried through the streets, the provisions being distributed to the waiting people.

Apr/May: *Labuhan* (movable – 26th day of fourth Javanese month Bakdomulud) (also held in Feb and Jul). Offerings made to the South Sea Goddess Nyi Loro Kidul. Especially colourful ceremony at Parangtritis, where offerings are floated on a bamboo palanquin and floated on the sea. Similar rituals are held on Mts Merapi and Lawu.

Jun: *Tamplak Wajik* (movable) ritual preparing of 'gunungan' or rice mounds in the Kraton, to the accompaniment of rhythmic gamelan and chanting to ward off evil spirits. *Grebeg Besar* (movable) a ceremony to celebrate the Muslim offering feast of Idul Adha. At 2000 the 'gunungan' mound of decorated rice is processed from the inner court of the Kraton to the Grand Mosque, where it is blessed and then distributed to the people.

Jul: *Siraman Pusaka* (movable – first month of the Javanese year) ritual cleansing ceremony, when the sultan's heirlooms are cleaned. The water used is said to have magical powers. *Anniversary of Bantul* (20th) celebrated with a procession of sacred heirlooms in Paseban Square, Bantul, S Yogyakarta.

Aug: *Kraton Festival* (movable), range of events including ancient ritual ceremonies, cultural shows, craft stalls. *Turtle dove singing contest* (second week) a national contest for the Hamengkubuwono X trophy, held in the S alun-alun from 0700. *Saparan Gamping* (movable), held in Ambarketawang Gamping village, 5 km W of Yogya. This ancient festival is held to ensure the safety of the village. Sacrifices are made of life-sized statues of a bride and groom, made of glutinous rice and filled with brown sugar syrup, symbolizing human blood.

Sep: *Rebo Wekasan* (2nd), held at the crossing of the Opak and the Gajah Wong rivers, where Sultan Agung is alleged to have met the Goddess Nyi Loro Kidul. *Sekaten* (movable – the 5th day of the Javanese month Mulud) a week long festival honouring the

Courtship Javanese-style – the *Lamaran*

Many elements of traditional Javanese life are disappearing in the wake of western-style commercialization. **Lamaran** – the formal request by the parents of the groom to the bride's parents – is one such traditional ceremony. Like the Javanese language, it is laden with hidden meanings and metaphors.

Initially, the groom's family visits the bride's to broach the subject of marriage. But this must be done according to elaborate rules, and there should be no direct reference to the purpose of the visit. The father of the prospective groom might explain, opaquely, that 'frost in the morning means rain in the evening', implying that he has come to discuss a 'cool' matter, which should not stir up strong emotions. The bride's father might reply by exclaiming that his daughter is a 'good for nothing', a spoilt girl and not yet an adult.

Two or three visits later, the matter is finally settled and a meeting is arranged at the prospective bride's house. This occasion is known as the *nontoni* (the 'looking over'). Again governed by tradition and formality, the girl serves her husband-to-be a cup of tea, avoiding any eye-contact. In the past, this would have been the young man's – or probably a boy's – first opportunity of stealing a sideways glance at his bride. The marriage itself is called the *panggihan* and is held at the bride's home.

Prophet Mohammad's birthday. The festival starts with a mid-night procession of the royal servants (abdi dalem), carrying two sets of gamelan instruments from the kraton to the Grand Mosque. Here they are placed in opposite ends of the building, and played simultaneously. A fair is held before and during Sekatan in the Alun-alun Lor. *Tamplak Wajik* (5th day of Sekaten). Ritual preparation of 'gunun-gan' or mounds of rice, decorated with vegetables, eggs and cakes at the palace, to the accompaniment of a gamelan orchestra and chanting to ward off evil spirits. *Grebeg Mulud*, religious festival celebrating the birthday of Mohammad, and the climax of Sekatan. It is held on the last day of the festival (12th day of Mulud) and features a parade of the palace guard in the early morning from the Kemandungan (in the kraton) to the Alun-alun Lor.

Local information
● Accommodation

Yogya's different categories of accommodation tend to be grouped in particular areas of town. Most of the more expensive, (our categories **A+-A**), international-style hotels are to be found either on Jl Malioboro, in the centre of town, or on the road E to the airport (Jl Adisucipto). The former are in a convenient position if visitors wish to explore the city on foot from their hotels. Many of the middle-priced guesthouses (our categories **B-D**) are concentrated on Jl Prawiro-taman, to the S of the Kraton, about 2 km from the city centre (a becak ride away). These are smallish private villas converted into hotels, some with just a handful of rooms. A number also have small swimming pools. On Jl Prawiro-taman a gaggle of restaurants, shops and tour companies have grown up to service the needs of those staying here. Finally, there is the budget accommodation (our categories **D-F**), which is concentrated on and around Jl Pasar Kembang and Jl Sosrowijayan, close to the train station. Again, there is a concentration of tour companies, travel agents, restaurants, car and motorcycle hire outfits, bus booking companies, and currency exchange offices here. Note, of course, that there are also hotels and losmen outside the above areas.

Jalan Malioboro, off Jalan Malioboro and Jalan Mangkubumi: A+ *Melia Purosani Yogyakarta*, Jl Suryotomo 31, T 589521, F 588070, a/c, restaurant, pool, opened in 1994, almost 300 rm in grand marble-filled hotel, facilities incl huge pool, gym, extensive garden, satellite TV and also benefits from a central location – unlike many others in this price category; A+-A *Natour Garuda*, Jl Malioboro 60, T 586353, F 563074, a/c, restaurant, pool, large hotel block, with new addition that rather swamps the original hotel, but good facilities, international standard rooms and a central location; **A-B** *Mutiara* (new wing), Jl Malioboro 18, T 514530, F 561201, a/c, overpriced restaurant, pool, rooms and food rather expensive, but central position; **B** *Arjuna Plaza*, Jl P Mangkubumi 48, T 561862, a/c, pool, rooms are small and rather dark.

Jalan Sosrowijayan and Jalan Pasar Kembang: **B** *Mendut*, Jl Pasar Kembang 49, T 563435, F 564753, a/c, restaurant, pool, hotel is squeezed on to a small area, rooms are good for the price, if very pedestrian in terms of style, central position; **B** *Royal Batik Palace*, Jl Pasar Kembang 29, T 587012, F 563824, a/c, small pool, price incl breakfast, attached mandi, attractive courtyard, rather over-elaborate in terms of decoration, reasonable mid-range value; **B-C** *Peti Mas*, Jl Dagen 39, some a/c, restaurant (slow service), nice pool, central cramped rooms and rather over-priced;

C-D *Hotel Asia Afrika*, Jl Pasar Kembang 21, T 566219, F 560139, some a/c, restaurant, pool, small rooms set around an attractive peaceful courtyard, price incl breakfast, set back from road so not too noisy, popular with tour groups; **C-D** *Hotel Trim*, Jl Pasar Kembang 2, T 4113, some a/c, cool marble tiled rooms with clean showers and hot water, a good mid-range place to stay; **C-D** *Kenchana*, Jl Pasar Kembang 15, some a/c, modern, clean and comfortable, attached shower, but most rooms look out onto a car park.

D *Asia Afrika Guesthouse*, Jl Pasar Kembang 9, T 587654, some a/c, central courtyard, attached showers; **D** *Bladok Losmen*, Jl Sosrowijayan 76, T 560452, 12 immaculately clean rooms, lovely gardens, good restaurant, enthusiastic and friendly staff, central location, rec; **D** *Karunia*, Jl Sosrowijayan 78, T 565057, F 565057, some a/c, clean and well managed small hotel with good information, attractive roof terrace and small restaurant; **D** *Nusantara*, Jl Pasar Kembang 59, T 588149, large rather grubby rooms but still remains popular – there are better places about; **D** *Oryza*, Jl Sosrowijayan 49, price incl breakfast; **D-E** *Ratna*, Jl Pasar Kembang 17A, T 561851, big rooms, with sitting area, fan and mandi, the rooms are better, and better maintained than one would imagine from the exterior.

E *Aziatic*, Jl Sosrowijayan 6, price incl breakfast, all rooms off a central hallway but no fans so tend to be hot as well as rather noisy, however the management are very friendly, it is immaculate, secure and good value, tours arranged, rec; **E** *Indonesia*, Jl Sosrowijayan 9, average rooms, some with attached mandi; **E** *Kartika*, Jl Sosrowijayan 10, T 562016, some with attached mandi; **E-F** *Ella Homestay*, Jl Sosrodipuran Gang I/487 (signposted off Jl Sosrowijayan), good food, quiet location away from the mass of losmen, rooms are a cut above the average, clean, good source of information, rec.

F *Gandhy*, Jl Sosrowijayan Wetan Gang II/75, although they, incredibly market themselves as "we're not the best, we're better" (who are they kidding?) this is, in fact, better than most with slightly lighter and cleaner rooms; **F** *Hotel Yogya*, Jl Sosrowijayan 1/30, basic rooms, some rather grubby but good value at the price; **F** *Rama*, Gang 1/32A, small dark rooms; **F** *Setia*, Jl Sosrowijayan Gang I/172, dark rooms with no window, cheap rates but conditions to match ... you pay the lowest rates and you get the equivalent.

Jl Prawirotaman: a good selection of middle range accommodation is to be found on Jl Prawirotaman, S of the Kraton. The hotels are the best of their kind in Yogya. The area's single obvious disadvantage is that it is not very central but the street provides numerous restaurants, shops, travel agents and cultural shows.

B *Airlangga*, Jl Prawirotaman 6-8, T 563344, F 571427, a/c, restaurant, pool, hot water, the largest hotel on Jl Prawirotaman, professional management, good pool, live music in the evenings, some rooms rather dark with narrow beds, the atmosphere is more that of a hotel than guesthouse, price incl breakfast, good value; **B** *Metro*, Jl Prawirotaman 71, T 572004, F 572004.

C *Kirana Guesthouse*, Jl Prawirotaman 30/38, T 513200, F 571175, characterful old house with wildlife packed central courtyard, rooms are spacious and clean, staff are helpful and knowledgeable, large and airy atmosphere, rec; **C** *Perwita Sari*, Jl Prawirotaman 31, T 577592, some a/c, good pool; **C** *Prambanan Guesthouse*, Jl Prawirotaman 14, T 513033, some a/c, small pool, some rooms with hot showers, opened in 1994, good rooms, enthusiastic staff and attractive surroundings, the fan rooms are particularly good value for money, rec; **C** *Rose*, Jl Prawirotaman 22, T 577991, a/c, big pool (for the area), hot water, set around a rather jaded courtyard, scruffy rooms, but remains popular nonetheless, a bit of a shake-up would help, price incl breakfast, free pick-up from airport, tours arranged; **C** *Sumaryo*, Jl Prawirotaman 22, T 377522, F 573507, pool, price incl breakfast and afternoon tea, large rooms in spacious

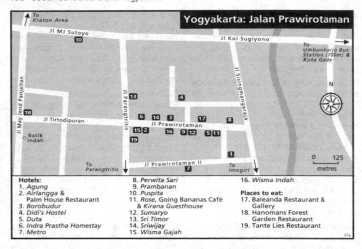

Yogyakarta: Jalan Prawirotaman

Hotels:
1. Agung
2. Airlangga & Palm House Restaurant
3. Borobudur
4. Didi's Hostel
5. Duta
6. Indra Prastha Homestay
7. Metro
8. Perwita Sari
9. Prambanan
10. Puspita
11. Rose, Going Bananas Café & Kirana Guesthouse
12. Sumaryo
13. Sri Timor
14. Sriwijay
15. Wisma Gajah
16. Wisma Indah

Places to eat:
17. Baleanda Restaurant & Gallery
18. Hanomans Forest Garden Restaurant
19. Tante Lies Restaurant

50s house with a fair amount of 50s furniture, clean and friendly, a peaceful and quiet place to stay, attached mandi, there is also a cheaper annex – guests staying here have access to the pool too, rec; **C** *Wisma Gajah Guesthouse*, Jl Prawirotaman 4, T 575659, F 572037, some a/c, small but attractive pool, well managed with spacious rooms, popular with tour groups, rec; **C-D** *Duta*, Jl Prawirotaman 20/26, T 72177, F 72064, some a/c, small pool with waterfall flowing into it, homely atmosphere, friendly girls on front desk, pleasant garden and sitting area, the indoor garden is Japanese in flavour and is filled with songbirds, price incl a good breakfast, having said all this, the owners have signed a contract with a tour company which has rather changed the atmosphere, still rec; **C-D** *Sri Timor*, Jl Parangtritis 51, some a/c, price incl breakfast; **C-D** *Sriwijay*, Jl Prawirotaman 7, T 571870, non a/c, breakfast incl, old house with attractive, small swimming pool, set around courtyard, fairly clean and ordered, rather curt staff, cold water showers and western toilets; **C-D** *Wisma Indah*, Jl Prawirotaman 4, T 576021, F 576021, some a/c, pool, rooms are rather small and dark, not up to the standards of other places along Jl Prawirotaman, price incl breakfast.

D *Borobudur*, Jl Prawirotaman 5, T 576891, F 573507, in an old house set around a central courtyard, small, friendly hostel, clean and well maintained, no a/c but with mandi, breakfast incl, Beethoven busts for sale at reception;

D-E *Indra Prastha Homestay*, Jl Prawirotaman, T 374087, non a/c, behind main street, a small quiet, new guesthouse set around a green brick road, young, enthusiastic staff, rooms are simple but spotless with cold shower, showers ensuite, peaceful garden, very good value in a medium priced area, rec.

E *Agung*, Jl Parangtritis 42/30, T 571811, own bathroom with hot water, restaurant, pool, good value; **E** *Didi's Hostel*, Jl Prawirotaman, down an alley off main street opp *Duta Guest House*, whose pool residents can use, small, clean, low budget for the area, mandi, all non a/c, pleasant, small rooms but clean, breakfast not incl; **E** *Puspita Guesthouse*, Jl Mayjend Sutoyo 64, T 571065, price incl good breakfast, helpful staff.

Jalan Jend Sudirman and Jalan Adisucipto: **A+** *Ambarrukmo Palace*, Jl Adisucipto, T 566488, F 563283, a/c, several restaurants, large pool, large, ugly block, one of the first international hotels to be built in Yogya in the 60s and it shows despite some attempt at modernization, inconvenient location out of town on the road to Borobudur; **A+-A** *Aquila Prambanan*, Jl Adisucipto 48, T 565005, F 565009, a/c, restaurant, pool, new hotel rather sacrilegiously modelled on Prambanan itself with inconvenient location nr the airport (beyond the *Ambarrukmo Palace*), 200 rm and atmosphere to match; **A+-A** *Sriwedari*, Jl Adisucipto, Km 6, T 588288, F 562162, a/c, restaurant, E of town; **A+-A** *Yogya Palace*, Jl

Adisucipto, Km 8, T 566244, F 566415, a/c, restaurant, pool, large new hotel someway out of town on road to Surakarta, free shuttle service into town, but still rather inconvenient, for quality of the rooms the rates are good.... if you can bear travelling for 20 mins to get just about anywhere; **A** *Phoenix Heritage*, Jl Jend Sudirman 9-11, T 566845, F 566856, a/c, restaurant, pool, new, central hotel, with friendly efficient staff; **A** *Santika*, Jl Jend Sudirman 19, T 563036, F 562047, a/c, restaurant, good pool, new and plush with reasonable rates; **A** *Yogya International*, Jl Adisucipto 38, T 561827, F 564171, a/c, restaurant, pool, E of town.

B *Sahid Garden*, Jl Babarsari, off Jl Adisucipto, T 513697, F 563183, a/c, restaurant, pool, E of town with range of accommodation.

● **Places to eat**

Central Javanese cooking uses a lot of sugar, tapped from the *aren* palm which produces 'red' sugar. Typical dishes incl *tape* (a sweet dish made from fermented cassava), and *ketan* (sticky rice). Yogya specialities incl *ayam goreng* (fried chicken) and *gudeg* (rice, jackfruit, chicken and an egg cooked in a spicy coconut sauce).

Indonesian: ♦♦♦*Griya Bujana*, Jl Prawirotaman, range of Indonesian, Chinese and International food, overpriced but remains popular; ♦♦*Hanoman's Forest Garden*, Jl Prawirotaman 9, incl entertainment (see below), a little run down; ♦*Shinta*, Jl Malioboro 5, also serves Chinese food; ♦*Tante Lies*, corner of Jl Prawirotaman and Jl Parangtritis, cheap Indonesian food and popular meeting place for travellers (mostly Dutch), cheap tours organized from here, however its reputation belies the quality and range of food; *Bu Citro*, Jl Adisucipto Km 9, opp the entrance to the airport, serves an excellent *gudeg*, the Yogya speciality; *Happy*, Jl Jend A Yani 95, speciality *ayam goreng*; ♦♦*Nusa Dua*, Jl Prawirotaman, happy hour 1700-1900, western, Indonesian, Chinese, 'Jappanesse' food, good, extensive menu worth investigating for itself alone – 'grilled fish served with aluminium foil'; *Simco*, Jl Prawirotaman 29, a medium sized, bamboo dominated restaurant with usual mix of travellers' and Indonesia/Chinese fare; *Sina Budi*, Jl Mangkubumi 41, popular for Padang food; *Suharti*, Jl Adisucipto 208, excellent *ayam goreng*.

Other Asian: *Sintawang*, Jl Magelang 9, excellent Chinese and seafood, rec; *Oshin Yakiniku*, Jl Malioboro 33, Japanese and some European; *Tempura Hana*, Jl Monumen Yogya Kembali 16, Japanese; *Yashinoki*, Jl Adisucipto 6, Japanese and some Indonesian.

International: ♦♦*Baleanda*, Jl Tirtodipuran 8, T 76114, garden, restaurant and art gallery serving good, well prepared Indonesian and western dishes in relaxing and beautiful surroundings, moderate prices and managed by Angelika, a European who has successfully blended Indonesian and European culinary tastes; ♦♦*Legian*, Jl Perwakilan 9, roof-top restaurant overlooking Jl Malioboro, slow service but worth waiting for, good-value food (plus cocktails); ♦♦*Palm House*, Jl Prawirotaman 12, range of Indonesian, Chinese and International food, excellent food at a good price, attractive ambience, popular, the chef worked on the French ship Mermoz, rec; ♦♦*Going Bananas*, Jl Prawirotaman 48 (E end of street), snacks and light meals in stylish restaurant with bar; ♦♦*Prambanan*, Jl Prawirotaman, Indonesian, Chinese, European – good.

Fast food: *McDonald's* has arrived in Yogya – a large branch at the S end of Jl Malioboro; *Pizza Hut*, Jl Jend Sudirman 3; *Kentucky Fried Chicken*, Jl Adisucipto 167 and Jl Malioboro 133.

Foodstalls: on the E side of Jl Mangkubumi, along Jl Malioboro (best after 0900) and outside Pasar Beringharjo (excellent *martabak*), also along NE corner of the alun-alun.

Travellers' food: ♦*Ana's*, Jl Sosrowijayan Gang 2, good pancakes, yoghurts etc, popular and usually a good source of information; ♦*Busis Garden*, Gang 1; ♦*Foodstall* at the N end of Gang 1, rec; ♦*Mamas*, Jl Pasar Kembang 71, long-established and still popular; ♦*Manna*, Jl Dagen 60; ♦*No Name Café* – southern end of Gang I, Jl Sosrowijayan, very good value, basic food in characterful atmosphere; ♦*Superman New and Old*, Jl Sosrowijayan, Gang 1, good breakfasts, rec; *Capuccino*, Jl Pasar Kembang 17, restaurant and bar; *Eko French Grill*, Jl Sosrowijayan Gang 1.

● **Airline offices**

Bouraq, Jl Mataram 60, T 562664; **Garuda**, Jl P Mangkubumi 56, T 561440; **Mandala**, Jl Yos Sudarso 1, T 54610; **Merpati**, *Java Palace Hotel*, Jl Jend Sudirman 63, T 54272; **Sempati**, *Natour Garuda Hotel*, Jl Malioboro 60, T 566315, F 566316.

● **Banks & money changers**

Artamas Buana Jati, Jl P Mangkubumi 4; **BNI**, nr General Post Office, on Jl Senopati; **Bumi Daya**, Jl Sudirman 42; **CV Intan Biru Laut**, Jl Malioboro 18; **Dagang Negara**, Jl Sudirman

67; **Intrabilex**, Adisucipto Airport; **Niaga**, Jl Jend Sudirman 13; **Summa**, Jl Laksda Adisucipto 63. Money changer next to the *Hotel Asia Afrika*, Jl Pasar Kembang 17. Two money changers on Jl Prawirotaman.

● **Embassies & consulates**
France, Jl Sagan 1, T 566520.

● **Entertainment**
Information on shows can be obtained from the tourist office, travel agents or from hotels. There is a wide choice of performances and venues, with something happening somewhere every night. Details given below may have changed since going to press.

Batik art galleries: 3 batik painters from Yogya have achieved an international reputation – Affandi, Amri Yahya and Sapto Hudoyo. The *Affandi Gallery* is at Jl Adisucipto 167 (town bus 8) on the banks of the Gajah Wong River. It lies next to the home of the Indonesian expressionist painter Affandi (1907-1990). The gallery displays work by Affandi and his daughter Kartika. Open 0900-1600 Mon-Sun. The *Amri Gallery* is at Jl Gampingan 67 and *Sapto Hudoyo* has a studio on Jl Adisucipto.

Batik lessons: at the *Batik Research Centre* on Jl Kusumanegara 2, plus a good exhibition; *Gapura Batik*, Jl Taman KP 3/177, 3 or 5 day courses (nr main entrance to Taman Sari); *Lucy Batik* on Jl Sosrowijayan Gang 1.

Cinemas: *Empire 21* and *Regent*, Jl Urip Sumoharjo (next to one another); *Indra*, Jl Jend A Yani 13A; *Ratih*, Jl P Mangkubumi 26.

Classical dance: *Rehearsals*, Kraton, 1030-1200, Sun.

Gamelan: performances at the Kraton 1030-1200 Mon and Wed; *Ambarrukmo Palace Hotel* lobby 1030-1230 and 1500-1700 Mon-Sun.

Indonesian language courses: *Sanata Dharma Research Centre*, Jl Gejayan Mrican Baru Tromolpos 29. The centre runs a 4 week (120 hrs) intensive course with lodging and meals for US$1,150. *Realia Language School* has been rec, 16,000-20,000Rp/hr, but if there are several people wishing to learn it is a reasonable price.

Ketoprak: traditional Javanese drama at the auditorium of RRI Studio Nusantara 2, Jl Gejayan 2030, twice a month (see Tourist Board for details).

Massage: *Anna Restaurant and Homestay*, Jl Sosrowijayan Gang II/127.

Modern art gallery: *Cemeti*, Jl Ngadisuryan 7A (nr the Taman Sari) has changing exhibits of good contemporary Indonesian and western artists. Open 0900-1330, Tues-Sun.

Modern Javanese dance: *Hanoman's Forest Garden*, Jl Prawirotaman, Sat.

Ramayana: at the Kraton on Sun (1,500Rp); *Ambarrukmo Palace Hotel*, Jl Adisucipto, Mon, Wed, Sat 2000 (either Pool Terrace or *Borobudur Restaurant*); *Arjuna Plaza Hotel*, Jl Mangkubumi, 1900-2100 Thur. Open-air performances at *Prambanan*, held on 'moonlight nights' between May and Oct, starting at 1900 and year-round at the *Trimurti Covered Theatre*, 1930-2130 Tues, Wed and Thur. There are also regular performances at *Dalem Pujokusuman*, Jl Katamso, 2000-2200, Mon, Wed and Fri (9,000Rp); and at the *Purawisata Open Theatre (THR)*, Jl Katamso, 2000-2200, Mon-Sun. Admission: 10,000Rp or 15,000Rp if paying through an agency (it's worth it). Good buffet dinner served before performance (though not cheap).

Samba music: *Slomoth*, Jl Parangtritis 109, 2000-2230 Wed and Sat.

Wayang kulit: performances held at the *Agastya Art Institute*, Jl Gedongkiwo, 1500-1700 Sun-Fri; *Ambarbudaya* (Yogya's Craft Centre), Jl Adisucipto, across from *Ambarrukmo Palace Hotel*, 2030-2230, Mon, Wed and Sat; *Ambarrukmo Palace Hotel*, Jl Adisucipto 2000-2100 Thur (*Gadri Bar*); *Auditorium Radio Republic Indonesia*, Jl Gejayan, every second Sat of the month, 2100-0530; *French Grill*, *Arjuna Plaza Hotel*, Jl Mangkubumi 48, 1900-2100 Tues; *Hanoman's Forest Garden*, Jl Prawirotaman, 2030-2130 Wed and Fri; *Museum Sonobudoyo*, Jl Trikora, 2000-2200 Mon-Sun; *Sasana Hinggil* (South Palace Square-Alun-alun Selatan), every second Sat of the month, 2100-0430; *Gubug Wayang-44*, Kadipaten Kulon, Kp 1/44, is a wayang kulit puppet workshop run by Olot Pardjono who makes puppets for the Museum Sonobudoyo. Ask at the museum for information on when his workshop is open and how to get there (see page 188).

Wayang gedhog (*Classical masked dance*): performances at the *Purawisata Open Theatre*, Jl Katamso, every Sun 1300-1400 hrs.

Wayang golek: performances held at the *Agastya Art Institute*, Jl Gedongkiwo, 1500-1700 Sat (Menak story), 1100-1300 Mon-Sat (Ramayana story); *French Grill*, *Arjuna Plaza*

Hotel, Jl Mangkubumi 48, 1900-2100 Sat; *Hanoman's Forest Garden*, Jl Prawirotoman, 1930-2130 Mon and Thur; *Nitour*, Jl Ahmad Dahlan 71, 1100-1300 Mon-Sat; and at the Kraton on Sat (1,500Rp).

Wayang orang: at the Kraton every Sun 1030-1200 (1,000Rp), nightly performances at the THR (the People's Amusement Park), Jl Brig Jen. Katamso (1,000Rp); *Ambarrukmo Palace Hotel*, Jl Adisucipto, 2000-2100 Tues, Fri and Sun (at the *Borobudur Restaurant*); *French Grill*, Arjuna Plaza Hotel, Jl Mangkubumi 48, 1900-2100 Thur; *Hanoman's Forest Garden*, Jl Prawirotaman, 98, 1930-2100 Tues and Sat.

● **Hospitals & medical services**
Hospitals: *Bethesda*, Jl Sudirman 81, T 81774; *Ludira Husada Tansa Hospital*, Jl Wiratama 4, T 3651.

● **Post & telecommunications**
Area code: 0274.

General Post Office: Jl Senopati 2.

Post Office: Jl Pasar Kembang 37 (for international phone calls and faxes).

Telephone office: Jl Yos Sudarso 9. Open Mon-Sun, 24 hrs. IDD international calls.

● **Shopping**
Yogya offers an enormous variety of Indonesian handicrafts, usually cheaper than can be found in Jakarta. Avoid using a guide or becak driver to take you to a shop as you will be charged more – their cut. The main shopping street, Jl Malioboro also attracts more than its fair share of 'tricksters' who maintain, for example, that their exhibition of batik paintings is from Jakarta and is in its last day, so prices are good...don't believe a word of it. The W side of Jl Malioboro is lined with stalls selling batik, wayang, topeng, woven bags. **NB** The quality of some of the merchandise can be very poor – for example the batik shirts – something that may be difficult to see at night.

Antiques: several shops along Jl Tirtodipuran and Jl Prawirotaman (S of the Kraton) and Jl Malioboro sell a range of curios.

Bamboo: split bamboo bird cages are a cheap and unusual buy; available from the Pasar Ngasem or bird market (see page 190).

Batik: Yogya is a centre for both batik *tulis* and batik *cap* (see page 103) and it is widely available in lengths (which can be made up into garments) or as ready-made clothes. There are a number of shops along Jl Malioboro. Contemporary 'European' fashions can be found in a couple of shops on Jl Sosrowijayan Gang 1. Batik factories are to be found on Jl Tirtodipuran S of the Kraton, where visitors can watch the cloth being produced. Batik paintings are on sale everywhere, with some of the cheapest available within the Kraton walls. There are some more shops down Jl Prawirotaman and off Jl Malioboro. But perhaps the best known outlet is the *Ardiyanto Studio*, Jl Magelang Km 5.8, T 562777, F 563280. The cloth may be expensive, but it is top quality. The Emperor of Japan and Hilary Clinton are reputed to be among the owner's clients. To get there take any bus running towards Borobudur/Dieng, which pass the shop some 6 km out of the city.

Bookshops: *Kakadu*, Jl Prawitotaman 41, for second hand volumes; *Prawirotaman International bookstore*, Jl Prawirotaman 30; *Sari Ilmu*, Jl Malioboro 117-119, for maps and guidebooks.

   Book exchange: two on Jl Sosrowijayan, one opp Gang 2. Another (*Kakadu*) on Jl Prawirotaman.

Handicrafts: Government crafts centre – *Desa Kerajinan* on Jl Adisucipto (Jl Solo) and some shops along Jl Prawirotaman, as well as the stalls lining Jl Malioboro.

Ikat: Jadin Workshop, Jl Modang 70B.

Leatherware: bags, suitcases, sandals and belts. All made from buffalo, cow or goat. Jl Malioboro has a selection of roadside stalls as well as several shops specializing in leather goods.

Pottery: earthenware is produced in a number of specialist villages around Yogya. Best known is Kasongan, 7 km S of the city, which produces pots, vases and assorted kitchen utensils. Get there by bus towards Bantul; the village is 700m off the main road.

Silverware: in Kota Gede, to the SE of the city (most shops are to be found along Jl Kemesan). Two major workshops – *MD Silver* and *Tom's Silver*. Two shops on Jl Prawirotaman.

Topeng masks: widely available from stalls along Jl Malioboro and nr the Taman Sari.

Wayang kulit & wayang golek: widely available from roadside stalls along Jl Malioboro. They come in varying qualities of craftsmanship, so ask to see the best and the cheapest. Hard bargaining should buy a puppet for about 75,000Rp.

● **Sports**
Golf: *Adisucipto Golf Course* (9 holes), T 3647, 9 km out of town on Prambanan road.

Panahan: traditional archery, performed to celebrate the birth of Sultan Hamengkubuwono X.

Swimming: hotels allow non-guests to use their pools, eg *Ambarrukmo Palace*, Jl Adisucipto (3,500Rp); *Colombo*, Jl Gejayan (700Rp); *New Batik Palace*, Jl Mangkubumi (750Rp); *Sri Wedari*, Jl Adisucipto (1,250Rp).

● **Tour companies & travel agents**
Colors of Asia Travel, Ambarrukmo Palace Hotel Arcade, Jl Laks Adisucipto, T 566488, F 563283; *Intan Pelangi*, Jl Malioboro 18, T 562895; *Jaya*, Jl Sosrowijayan 23; *Natrabu*, Ambarrukmo Palace Hotel, Jl Adisucipto, T 588488; *Nitour*, Jl KHA Dahlan 71, T 375165; *Pacto*, Ambarrukmo Palace, Jl Adisucipto, T 566488; *Sahid*, Hotel Sahid Garden, Jl Babarsari, T 587078; *Satriavi*, Ambarrukmo Palace Hotel, Jl Adisucipto, T 566488; *Setia*, Natour Garuda Hotel, Jl Malioboro 72, T 566353; *Tante Lies*, Jl Prawirotaman, 'Heri' in this restaurant organizes inexpensive tours around Java; *Vayatour*, Ambarrukmo Palace Hotel, Jl Adisucipto, T 566488; *Vista Express*, Natour Garuda Hotel, Jl Malioboro, T 563074. There are a number of companies around Jl Sosrowijayan and Jl Pasar Kembang as well as Jl Prawirotaman who will organize onward travel by *bis malam* and train. Many of the hotels offer similar services.

● **Tourist offices**
Tourist Information office, Jl Malioboro 14, T 562811 ext 218. Free maps of the town and environs, information on cultural events, bus routes etc. One of the most helpful tourist offices in Indonesia. Open 0800-2100 Mon-Sat. There is also a tourist office counter at the railway station and a second at the airport.

● **Useful addresses**
Immigration Office: Jl Adisucipto Km 10, T 4948 (out of town on the road to the airport, close to *Ambarrukmo Palace Hotel*).
Police: Jl Pisang l, T 88234.
Tourist police: Tourist Information, Jl Malioboro.

● **Transport**
565 km from Jakarta, 327 km from Surabaya.

Local Andong (horse-drawn carriage): traditional carriages with 4 wheels, the 2 in front being smaller, drawn by either 1 or 2 horses. They wait outside the railway station, the Kraton and next to the Bird Market. **Becak**: probably the best way to get around. Agree a price before boarding: approximately 500Rp/km – or charter one for the day, approximately 1,000Rp/hr. **Bemos & colts**: colts around town (300Rp). Beware of the drivers who seem to offer a very good price; they will almost certainly take you to batik or silverware shops. **Bicycle hire**: along Jl Pasar Kembang or Gang 1 or 2, approximately 2,000Rp/day. **Bus**: Yogya town buses (*bis kota*) travel 17 routes criss-crossing the town; the tourist office sometimes has bus maps available (300Rp). Minibuses leave from the Terban station on Jl C Simanjuntak, NE of the train station. **Car hire**: self-drive from *Avis*, at *Nitour*, Jl KH Ahmad Dahlan 71, T 75165; **Bali Car Rental**, by the airport, 70,000-90,000Rp/day, a driver will cost an extra 20,000Rp/day and it usually means the hire is for 12 hrs rather than a full 24 hrs; **Fortuna**, Jl Jlagran 20-21 and on Jl Pasar Kembang; **National Car Rental** from *Sahid Garden Hotel*. **Motorbike hire**: along Jl Pasar Kembang and at **Fortuna**, Jl Jlagran 20-21, approximately 10,000-15,000Rp/day depending on size and condition of the machine. Check brakes, lights and horn before agreeing; bikes are sometimes poorly maintained. **Taxi**: there are a few metered taxis, or taxis can be rented (from Jl Pasar Kembang 85, or from Jl Senopati, nr the Post Office) for trips around town (7,000Rp/hr) or for longer trips to Borobudur, Prambanan etc (30,000-50,000Rp/day).

Air Adisucipto Airport is 8 km E of town, along Jl Adisucipto (aka Jl Solo). *Transport to town*: minibuses from the Terban station on Jl Simanjuntak travelling to Prambanan pass the airport (400Rp), a taxi costs 8,500Rp. (Taxi desk in Arrivals Hall.) Regular connections on Garuda/Merpati, Sempati and Bouraq with other destinations in Java, Sumatra, Kalimantan, Sulawesi, Bali, Lombok, Nusa Tenggara, Maluku and Irian Jaya (see page 911 for route map).

Train The railway station is on Jl Pasar Kembang. Regular connections with Jakarta's Gambir station, 12 hrs (the night train leaves at 1930 and arrives at 0630), Bandung 9 hrs, Solo 1 hr, and with Surabaya 8 hrs (see page 917 for timetable). **WARNING** Thieves are notorious on the overnight train between Jakarta and Surabaya via Yogya. **NB** The night train (Utama Solo) is hot, smoky and slow, with hourly awakenings by hawkers. There is a hotel reservation desk at the railway station.

Road Bus: Yogya is a transport hub and bus services are available to most places. Because it is such a popular tourist destination, there are also a/c tourist buses and minibuses in profusion. Agents are concentrated in the hotel/losmen areas. The Umbunharjo bus station is 4 km SE of the city centre, at the intersection of Jl Veteran and Jl Kemerdekaan. Fastest services are at night (*bis malam*). Check times at the bus station or at the tourist office on Jl Malioboro. Regular connections with Jakarta, 9 hrs, and Bandung, 6 hrs, as well as many other cities and towns. To get to Solo, 1½-2 hrs, or N to Semarang, 3½ hrs, it is better to take a local bus, which can be hailed on the main roads. A/c buses from various agents along Jl Sosrowijayan (board bus here too) or from Jl Mangkubumi to, for example, Jakarta, Bandung, Surabaya, Malang, Mataram, Probolinggo, Pangandaran and Denpasar. **Colt**: private company colt offices are on Jl Diponegoro, to the W of the Tugu Monument. Seats are bookable and pick-up from hotels can be arranged. Regular connections with Solo and Semarang (5,000Rp).

PARANGTRITIS

Parangtritis is a small seaside resort 28 km S of Yogya and 20 km from Imogiri. It caters largely to Indonesian weekend daytrippers. Warungs line the black sand beach and the bay is enclosed at its E end by cliffs. Horse-drawn carts take tourists on trips along the beach, and the resort has a wonderfully dated and innocent air. An attractive avenue houses warungs and most of the losmen. The beach is a centre for the worship of the South Sea Goddess Nyi Loro Kidul; offerings to her from the Sultan (consisting of food, clothes, the Sultan's hair and cuttings from his nails) are made at the annual *Labuhan* ceremony (see page 195). **NB** The currents and undertow at the resort are vicious, and swimmers should exercise extreme caution.

Excursions Inland from Parangtritis are **fresh water swimming pools** fed by natural springs, and to the W are the **Parang Wedang hot springs** (*air panas*), said to cure skin infections (which might keep people from even considering swimming there). Caves can be found to the E of town, most notably **Langse Cave** which is at sea-level and can only be reached along rickety bamboo ladders. The cave is a meditation spot.

There are some less frequented **beaches** to the E of Parangtritis, not far

from the town of Kemadang – Baron, Kukup and Krakal. Snorkeling is reported to be reasonable at **Krakal**, a white sand beach stretching for 5 km (which developers have their eye on). Swimming is relatively safe at **Baron** – it is protected from the sea and currents by coral ridges. **Kukup** is a white sand beach with strong currents.

● **Accommodation**
(Rates on Fri and Sat tend to be higher) **A** *Queen of the South*, T (0274) 567196, F (0274) 567197, on a cliff above the beach, elegant thatched bungalows, cliff-edge pool and bar, great views; **D** *Rang Do*, 300m on from main avenue, popular; **E** *Agung Gardens*, mandi and fan, popular, reasonable source of information and average rooms, on main avenue; **E** *Budi*, small, with mandi, friendly, on main avenue; **E** *Yenny Homestay*, on main avenue; **F** *Widodo*, with mandi and fan, on main avenue. Both *Yennys* and *Agung Gardens* have restaurants selling travellers' food. The latter rents out motorbikes (8,000Rp/day). Entrance to resort area 300Rp, 1,500Rp for car.

● **Transport**
Regular connections with Yogya's Umbunharjo bus terminal either via Kretek along the main road and over the Opak River, or via Imogiri and Celuk (see page 193). The longer, rougher, trip via Imogiri passes through beautiful rural scenery.

Mount Merapi

Mount Merapi, whose name means 'giving fire', lies 30 km N of Yogya and is possibly the best known of all Java's many volcanoes. It rises to a height of nearly 3,000m and can be seen from the city. Because Merapi is still very active it is closely watched by Indonesia's Directorate of Volcanology who have an observatory here. Its first recorded eruption was in 1006 AD when it killed the Hindu king Darmawangsa. To climb Merapi most people start from the village of **Selo** (on the N slope) from where it is a 3-hr trek up and 2 hrs down. The trail is easy to follow. The spectacular views from the summit are best in the morning (0600-0800) which means an early start. To see dramatic fireholes, take the path off to the left, about 25m from the summit. The route passes a ravine before reaching the fireholes – a 10-min walk. Guides at Selo charge about 5,000Rp and will offer their houses for overnight stays. Tours are not recommended, as the guides urge the group to walk fast, and walking in a group in volcanic cinder can be dusty.

Kaliurang

The mountain resort of **Kaliurang** is 28 km N of Yogya, on the southern slopes of Merapi at just under 1,000m. It is an alternative setting-off point for a climb to the summit of Mt Merapi. There are facilities here for tennis and swimming, and a waterfall near the bus station (admission 300Rp). Good walks include a short 2.5 km trek to *Plawangan Seismological Station*, with views of the smoking giant (best in the morning, until about 0900-1000). **NB** As of mid-1995 the Seismological Station and the road leading to it were closed. If this route is closed, there is an alternative 2 km walk from the bus station to a belvedere which overlooks the lava flow resulting from Mt Merapi's 1994 eruption. There are good views of the volcano on clear days.

● **Accommodation**
C *Agung Merapi Hotel*; **C** *Kinasih*, Jl Boyong Kaliurang; **E** *Safari*, Jl Pramuka 55; **D-E** *Vogel's Homestay*, Jl Astomulyo 76, T 95208, the most popular place to stay here, excellent source of information, well run, range of rooms available; **F** *Astorenggo II*, Jl Pramuka 56.

● **Camping**
Pitch tents some distance from the trail, or you are liable to be woken by guided groups (from 0300), and theft is common.

● **Transport to and from Kaliurang**
A bus from Yogya to Kartosuro and then another bus to Boyolali, finally by minibus to Selo; leave Yogya in the morning, as afternoon buses are scarce. A more challenging climb can be made from Kinahrejo, on the S slope. The village, which has no accommodation, is a 1-hr walk from Kaliurang, and is 9 km from the summit (a 10-hr walk). *Getting to Kinahrejo via Kaliurang*: see below. Guides available. *Getting there*: take a Baker bus from the Umbulharjo terminal or a bus from in front of the Beringharjo market (1 hr) on Jl Jend A Yani.

BOROBUDUR

The travel business is only too ready to attach a superlative to the most mundane of sights. However, even travellers of a less jaundiced and world-weary age had little doubt after they set their eyes on this feast of stone that they were witnessing one of the wonders of the world. The German traveller Johan Scheltema in his 1912 book *Monumental Java* wrote, in truly monumental prose, that he felt the "fructifying touch of heaven; when tranquil love descends in waves of contentment, unspeakable satisfaction".

Borobudur was built when the Sailendra Dynasty of Central Java was at the height of its military and artistic powers. Construction of the monument is said to have taken about 75 years, spanning four or five periods from the end of the 8th century to the middle of the 9th century. Consisting of a 9-tiered 'mountain' rising to 34.5m, Borobudur is decorated with 5 km of superbly executed reliefs – some 1,500 in all – ornamented with 500 statues of the Buddha, and constructed of 1,600,000 andesite stones.

The choice of site on the densely populated and fertile valleys of the Progo and Elo rivers seems to have been partially dictated by the need for a massive labour force. Every farmer owed the kings of Sailendra a certain number of days labour each year – a labour tax – in return for the physical and spiritual protection of the ruler. Inscriptions from the 9th and 10th centuries indicate that there were several hundred villages in the vicinity of Borobudur. So, after the rice harvest, a massive labour force of farmers, slaves and others could be assembled to work on the monument. It is unlikely that they would have been resistant to working on the edifice – by so doing they would be accumulating merit and accelerating their progress towards nirvana.

Art historians have also made the point that the location of Borobudur at the confluence of the Elo and Progo rivers was probably meant to evoke, as Dumarçay says, "the most sacred confluence of all, that of the Ganga (Ganges) and the Yumna (Jumna)", in India. Finally, the monument is also close to a hill, just N of Magelang, called Tidar. Although hardly on the scale of the volcanoes that ring the Kedu Plain, this hill – known as the 'Nail of Java' – lies at the geographic centre of Java and has legendary significance. It is said that it was only after Java, which was floating on the sea, had been nailed to the centre of the earth that it became inhabitable.

The temple is made of grey andesite – a volcanic rock – which was not quarried but 'mined' from river beds. Huge boulders are washed down volcano slopes during flood surges and these were cut to size and transported to the building site. The blocks were linked by double dovetail clamps – no mortar was used in construction. It is thought that the sculpture was done *in situ*, after the building work had been completed. The stone was then covered in stucco and probably painted.

The large base platform was added at a later date and remains something of an enigma. It actually hides a panel of reliefs, known as the 'hidden foot'. Some authorities believe that this series of reliefs always meant to be hidden, because they depict earthly desires (this was true of a similar series of panels at Angkor Wat in Cambodia). Other art historians maintain that this is simply too elaborate an explanation and that the base was added as a buttress. Inherent design faults meant that even during initial construction, subsidence was probably already setting in. In 1885 these subterranean panels were uncovered by Yzerman to be photographed, only then to be covered up again to ensure the stability of the monument.

Aspects of Borobudur's design were brilliant: the removal of rain-water, for example, was achieved by the use of gargoyles placed on the diagonals of the monument, transferring water down each level to the base, where it was collected in a gutter before being soaked up by the earth. Despite annual rainfall of 1800 mm/year, this system would have coped admirably. Unfortunately, the latent instability of the overall structure led to subsidence, which in turn caused cracks to appear between the closely-laid stones, and this permitted water to seep into the heart of the man-made mountain, beginning a process of gradual deterioration.

The symbolism of Borobudur

Symbolically, Borobudur is an embodiment of three concepts. It is, at the same time, a *stupa*, a replica of the cosmic mountain *Mt Meru*, and a *mandala* (an instrument to assist meditation). Archaeologists, intent on interpreting the meaning of the monument, have had to contend with the

Borobudur: what's in a name?

The origin and meaning of the name Borobudur has been a source of dispute for many years. Some experts have maintained that it is derived from the Sanskrit words *Vihara Buddha Uhr*, meaning 'Buddhist Monastery on the Hill', and certainly it is situated on a slight rise above the surrounding plain. Other authorities reject this explanation, believing that *boro* is derived from the word *biara*, which means *vihara* or monastery, while *budur* is a place name, giving the monument the title 'Monastery of Budur'. De Casparis meanwhile, who uncovered a stone dated to the year 842 with the inscription *Bhumisambharabhudara* carved upon it, plumps for yet another explanation. The inscription means the 'Mountain of Virtues of the Ten Stages of the Bodhisattva', and he believes that the name is taken from the last part, *Bharabhudara*.

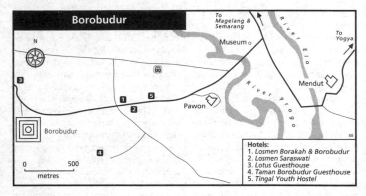

Hotels:
1. Losmen Borakah & Borobudur
2. Losmen Saraswati
3. Lotus Guesthouse
4. Taman Borobudur Guesthouse
5. Tingal Youth Hostel

fact that the structure was built over a number of periods spanning three-quarters of a century. As a result, new ideas were superimposed on older ones. In other words, it meant different things, to different people, at different periods.

Nonetheless, it is agreed that Borobudur represents the Buddhist transition from reality, through 10 psychological states, towards the ultimate condition of *nirvana* – spiritual enlightenment. Ascending the stupa, the pilgrim passes through these states by ascending through 10 levels. The lowest levels (including the hidden layer, of which a portion is visible at the SE corner) depict the Sphere of Desire (*Kamadhatu*), describing the cause and effect of good and evil. Above this, the five lower quadrangular galleries with their multitude of reliefs (put end to end they would measure 2.5 km), represent the Sphere of Form (*Rupadhatu*). These are in stark contrast to the bare upper circular terraces with their half-hidden Buddhas within perforated stupas, representing the Sphere of Formlessness (*Arupadhatu*) -- nothingness or nirvana.

The monument was planned so that the pilgrim would approach it from the E, along a path which started at Candi Mendut (see below). Architecturally, it is horizontal in conception, and in this sense contrasts with the strong verticality of Prambanan. However, architectural values were of less importance than the sculpture, and in a sense the monument was just an easel for the reliefs. Consideration had to be made for the movement of people, and the width of the galleries was dictated by the size of the panel, which had to be seen at a glance. It is evident that some of the reliefs were conceived as narrative 'padding', ensuring that continuity of story line was achieved. To 'read' the panels, start from the E stairway, keeping the monument on your right. This clockwise circumambulation is known as *pradaksina*. It means that while the balustrade or outer reliefs are read from left to right, those on the main, inner wall are viewed from right to left. The reliefs were carved in such a way that they are visually more effective when observed in this way.

The reliefs and the statues of the Buddha

The inner (or retaining) wall of the first gallery is 3½m high and contains two series of reliefs, one above the other, each of 120 panels. The upper panels relate events in the historic Buddha's life – the *Lalitavistara* – from his birth to the sermon at Benares, while the lower depict his former lives, as told in the *Jataka* tales. The upper and lower reliefs on the balustrades (or outer wall) also relate Jataka stories as

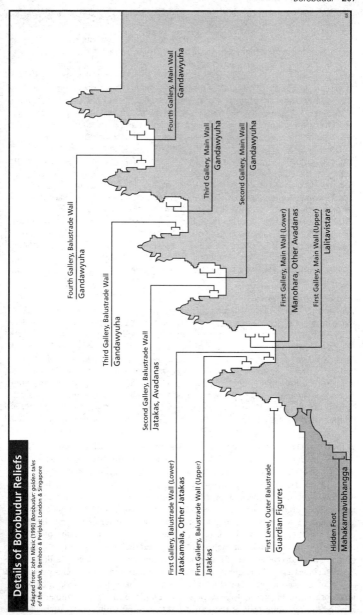

Details of Borobudur Reliefs

Adapted from: John Miksic (1990) *Borobudur: golden tales
of the Buddha*, Bemboo & Periplus: London & Singapore

Fourth Gallery, Balustrade Wall
Gandawyuha

Third Gallery, Balustrade Wall
Gandawyuha

Second Gallery, Balustrade Wall
Jatakas, Avadanas

First Gallery, Balustrade Wall (Lower)
Jatakamala, Other Jatakas

First Gallery, Balustrade Wall (Upper)
Jatakas

First Level, Outer Balustrade
Guardian Figures

Hidden Foot
Mahakarmavibhangga

Fourth Gallery, Main Wall
Gandawyuha

Third Gallery, Main Wall
Gandawyuha

Second Gallery, Main Wall
Gandawyuha

First Gallery, Main Wall (Lower)
Manohara, Other Avadanas

First Gallery, Main Wall (Upper)
Lalitavistara

Mudras and the Buddha image

An artist producing an image of the Buddha does not try to create an original piece of art; he is trying to be faithful to a tradition which can be traced back over centuries. The Buddha can be represented either sitting, lying (indicating *paranirvana*), or standing, and (in Thailand) occasionally walking. Each image will be represented in a particular *mudra* or 'attitude', of which there are 40. The most common are:

Abhayamudra – dispelling fear or giving protection; right hand (sometimes both hands) raised, palm outwards, usually with the Buddha in a standing position.

Varamudra – giving blessing or charity; the right hand pointing downwards, the palm facing outwards, with the Buddha either seated or standing.

Vitarkamudra – preaching mudra; the ends of the thumb and index finger of the right hand touch to form a circle, symbolizing the Wheel of Law. The Buddha can either be seated or standing.

Dharmacakramudra – 'spinning the Wheel of Law'; a preaching mudra symbolizing the teaching of the first sermon. The hands are held in front of the chest, thumbs and index fingers of both joined, one facing inwards and one outwards.

Bhumisparcamudra – 'calling the earth goddess to witness' or 'touching the earth'; the right hand rests on the right knee with the tips of the fingers 'touching ground', thus calling the earth goddess Dharani/Thoranee to witness his enlightenment and victory over Mara, the king of demons. The Buddha is always seated.

Dhyanamudra – meditation; both hands resting open, palms upwards, in the lap, right over left.

Other points of note:

Vajrasana – yogic posture of meditation; cross-legged, both soles of the feet visible.

Virasana – yogic posture of meditation; cross-legged, but with the right leg on top of the left (also known as *paryankasana*).

Buddha under Naga – a common image in Khmer art; the Buddha is shown seated in an attitude of meditation with a cobra rearing up over his head. This refers to an episode in the Buddha's life when he was meditating; a rain storm broke and Nagaraja, the king of the nagas (snakes), curled up under the Buddha (seven coils) and then used his 7-headed hood to protect the Holy One from the falling rain.

Buddha calling for rain – a common image in Laos; the Buddha is depicted standing, both arms held stiffly at the side of the body, fingers pointing downwards.

well as *Avadanas* – another Buddhist text, relating previous lives of the Bodhisattvas – in the NE corner. After viewing this first series of reliefs, climb the E stairway – which was only used for ascending – to the next level. The retaining wall of the second gallery holds 128 panels in a single row 3m high. This, along with the panels on the retaining walls and (some of the) balustrades of the third gallery, tells the story of Sudhana in search of the Highest Wisdom – one of the most important Buddhist texts, otherwise known as *Gandawyuha*. Finally, the retaining wall of the fourth

terrace has 72 panels depicting the *Bhadratjari* – a drawn out conclusion to the story of Sudhana, during which he vows to follow in the footsteps of Bodhisattva Samantabhadra. In total there are a bewildering 2,700 panels – a prodigious artistic feat, not only in terms of numbers, but also the consistently high quality of the carvings and their composition.

From these enclosed galleries, the monument suddenly opens out onto a series of bare, unadorned, circular terraces. On each are a number of small stupas, diminishing in size upwards from the first to third terrace, and pierced with lozenge-shaped openings. In total there are 72 such stupas, each containing a statue of the Buddha.

Including the Buddhas to be found in the niches opening outwards from the balustrades of the square terraces, there are a staggering 504 Buddha images. All are sculpted out of single blocks of stone. They are not representations of earthly beings who have reached nirvana, but transcendental saviours. The figures are strikingly simple, with a line delineating the edge of the robe, tightly-curled locks of hair, a top knot or *usnisa*, and an *urna* – the dot on the forehead. These last two features are distinctive bodily marks of the Buddha. On the square terraces, the symbolic gesture or mudra of the Buddha is different at each of the four compass points: the E-facing Buddhas are 'calling the earth to witness' or *bhumisparcamudra* (with right hand pointing down towards the earth), to the W, they are in an attitude of meditation or *dhyanamudra* (hands together in the lap, with palms facing upwards), to the S, they express charity or *varamudra*, (right hand resting on the knee) and to the N, the Buddhas express dispelling fear or *abhayamudra* (with the right hand raised). On the upper circular terraces, all the Buddhas are in the same mudra. Each Buddha is slightly different, yet all retain a remarkable serenity.

The main central stupa on the summit contains two chambers which are empty. There has been some dispute as to whether they ever contained representations of the Buddha. Those who believe that they did not, argue that because this uppermost level denotes nirvana – nothingness – it would have been symbolically correct to have left them empty. For the pilgrim, these spacious top levels were also designed to afford a chance to rest before beginning the descent to the world of men. Any of the stairways, except the E one, could be used to descend.

The decline, fall and restoration of Borobudur

With the shift in power from Central to E Java in the 10th century (see page 91), Borobudur was abandoned and its ruin hastened by earthquakes. In 1814, Thomas Stamford Raffles appointed HC Cornelis to undertake investigations into the condition of the monument. Minor restoration was undertaken intermittantly over the next 80 years, but it was not until 1907 that a major reconstruction programme commenced. This was placed under the leadership of Theo Van Erp and under his guidance much of the top of the monument was dismantled and then rebuilt. Unfortunately, within 15 years the monument was deteriorating once again, and the combined effects of the world depression in the 1930s, the Japanese occupation in WW2, and then the trauma of independence, meant that it was not until the early 1970s that a team of international archaeologists were able to investigate the state of Borobudur once more. To their horror, they discovered that the condition of the foundations had deteriorated so much that the entire monument was in danger of caving inwards. In response, UNESCO began a 10-year restoration programme. This comprised dismantling all the square terraces – involving the removal of approximately 1 million pieces of stone. These were then cleaned, while a new concrete foundation was built, incorporating new water channels. The work was finally completed in 1983 and the monument reopened by President Suharto.

There is a **museum** close to the monument which houses an exhibition showing the restoration process undertaken by UNESCO and some pieces found on site during the excavation and restoration process. Admission 300Rp (students, 150Rp with ISIC card; note that the 4,000Rp ticket to see the monument includes entrance to the museum). Open 0600-1800 Mon-Sun.

Best time to visit: early morning before the coaches arrive, although even by 0600,

Bhumisparcamudra – calling the earth goddess to witness. Sukhothai period, 13th-14th century.

Dhyanamudra – meditation. Sukhothai period, 13th-14th century.

Vitarkamudra – preaching, "spinning the Wheel of Law". Dvaravati Buddha, 7th-8th century, seated in the "European" manner.

Abhayamudra – dispelling fear or giving protection. Lopburi Buddha, Khmer style 12th century.

Abhayamudra – dispelling fear or giving protection; subduing Mara position. Lopburi Buddha, Khmer style 13th century.

there can be many people here. Some visitors suggest sunset is the best time to be there as the view is not affected by mist (as it commonly is in the morning). Consider staying the night in Borobudur, to see the sun rise over the monument. **Admission to complex** 5,000Rp (2,000Rp with ISIC card). Price includes a guide plus entrance to the museum and use of a camera/video camera. In theory, visitors

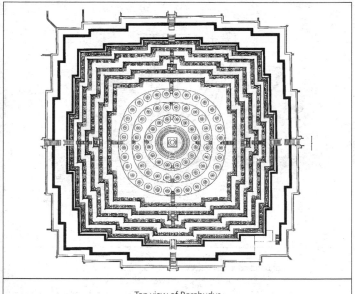

Top view of Borobudur

should wait for a group to accumulate and then be shown round by a guide. However many people simply explore the candi on their own. Guides vary, but visitors have reported them to be both useful and knowledgeable. It is also possible to hire a private guide (7,000Rp). Open 0600-1730 (ticket office closes at 1700) Mon-Sun.

Candis around Borobudur

Candi Pawon was probably built at the same time as Borobudur and is laid out with the same E-W orientation. It may have acted as an ante-room to Borobudur, catering to the worldly interests of pilgrims. Another theory is that it acted as a crematorium. *Candi Pawon* is also known as *Candi Dapur*, and both words mean kitchen. The unusually small windows may have been this size because they were designed as smoke outlets. The shrine was dedicated to Kuvera, the God of Fortune. The temple sits on a square base and contains an empty chamber. The exterior has some fine reliefs of female figures within pillared frames – reminiscent of Indian carvings – while the roof bears tiers of stupas. Among the reliefs are *kalpataru* or wish-granting trees, their branches dripping with jewels, and surrounded by pots of money. Bearded dwarfs over the entrance pour out jewels from sacks. Insensitive and poorly informed restoration of Candi Pawon at the beginning of the 20th century has made architectural interpretation rather difficult.

Candi Mendut lies further E still and 3 km from Borobudur. It was built by King Indra in 800. It is believed the candi was linked to Borobudur by a paved walkway; pilgrims may have congregated at Mendut, rested or meditated at Pawon, and then proceeded to Borobudur. The building was rediscovered in 1836, when the site was being cleared for a coffee plantation. The main body of the building was restored by Van Erp at the beginning of this century but the roof was left

Ship of the ninth century AD carved on the
temple of Borobodur, Central Java. The panel is on the eastern side of
the monument, first gallery, main wall (lower), see page 206.
Source: Horridge, Adrian (1981) *The prahu: traditional sailing boat of Indonesia*, OUP: Singapore.

incomplete (it was probably a large stupa). The temple is raised on a high rectangular plinth and consists of a square cella containing three statues. The shrine is approached up a staircase, its balustrade decorated with reliefs depicting scenes from the jataka stories. The exterior is elaborately carved with a series of large relief panels of Bodhisattvas. One wall shows the **4-armed Tara** or **Cunda**, flanked by devotees, while another depicts **Hariti**, once a child-eating demon but here shown after her conversion to Buddhism, with children all around her. **Atavaka**, a flesh-eating ogre is shown in this panel holding a child's hand and sitting on pots of gold. The standing male figure, may be the **Bodhisattva Avalokitesvara**, whose consort is Cunda. There are also illustrations of classical Indian morality tales – look out for the fable of the tortoise and the two ducks on the left-hand side – and scenes from Buddhist literature. The interior is very impressive. There were

originally seven huge stone icons in the niches; three remain. These three were carved from single blocks of stone which may explain why they have survived. The central Buddha is seated in the unusual European fashion and is flanked by his two reincarnations (Avalokitesvara and Vajrapani). Notice how the feet of both the attendant statues are black from constant touching by devotees. The images are seated on elaborate thrones backed against the walls but conceived in the round (similar in style to cave-paintings found in western Deccan, India). Admission 100Rp. Open 0615-1715 Sun-Mon.

There are no architectural remains of another, Sivaite, monument called **Candi Banon**, which was once situated near Candi Pawon. Five large sculptures, all fine examples of the Central Javanese Period, recovered from the site can be seen in the National Museum in Jakarta.

Festivals

May: *Waicak* (movable, usually during full moon), celebrates the birth and death of the historic Buddha. The procession starts at Candi Mendut and converges on Borobudur at about 0400, all the monks and nuns carry candles – an impressive sight.

Local information
● Accommodation

Most people visit Borobudur as a day trip from Yogya. The nearest up-market hotels are in Magelang, 17 km to the N (see page 213). Accommodation at the sight is expanding and incl:

B *Taman Borobudur Guesthouse*, Borobudur Complex, T 8131, a/c, peaceful location and good value but note that even by staying here – within the Borobudur complex – guests do not get access to Borobudur before the gates open at 0600.

C *Tingal Youth Hostel*, Jl Balaputradewa (about 2 km from the temple towards Yogya), T 8245, traditional-style wooden building set around courtyard, clean rooms with bathroom and character, incl breakfast.

D *Rositas*, Jl Syailendra Raya 8, some a/c, more expensive rooms with hot water and TV, although very plain, comparatively clean, but little obvious to rec this place, about 1.5 km from the entrance to Borobudur; **D** *Syailendra*, Jl Syailendra Raya 27, T 8163, some a/c, about 1.5 km from the main entrance, very plain rooms with little attempt to make this anything more than a place to sleep.

E *Losmen Borokah*, Jl Pramudawardani 2; **E** *Losmen Saraswati*, intersection of Jl Pramudawardani and Jl Balaputradewa, T 8283; **E-F** *Losmen Borobudur*, Jl Pramudawardani 1, clean, small rooms with mandi; **E-F** *Losmen Citra Rasa*, Jl Syailendra Raya (opp the bus stop and market) rooms are OK, mandis are tiny, the more expensive rooms have small balconies, although on the main road, the rooms are set back so not noisy, central position; **E-F** *Lotus Guesthouse*, Jl Medang Kamulan 2, T 8281, rather varying reports on this place, but generally favourable, looks onto Candi Borobudur itself, and is nr the entrance to the bus park about 1 km from the main entrance, set nr rice fields, rooms are clean and comparatively spacious, airy eating area, rec.

● Places to eat

There are two restaurants within the complex, and a number around the stall and carpark area, and in Borobudur Village. The *Saraswati* has a reasonable restaurant.

● Banks & money changers

Bank Rakyat Indonesia, nr the entrance gate to Borobudur temple, inside the complex.

● Post & telecommunications

Area code: 0293.

Post Office: Jl Pramudyawardani 10.

Wartel office (phone & telegram): Jl Pramudyawardani (opp market).

● Transport

42 km NW of Yogya, 90 km SW of Semarang, 17 km S of Magelang.

Local Bicycles: can be hired from some losmen/guesthouses (eg *Lotus Guesthouse*). An excellent way to visit candis Pawon and Mendut.

Road Bus: regular connections from Yogya's Umbunharjo terminal on Jl Kemerdekaan or from the street (ask at your hotel/guesthouse to find out where the bus stops. For those staying on Jl Prawirotaman, the best place is the corner of Jl Parangtritis and Jl May Jend Sutoyo). The buses run along Jl Sugiyono, Jl Sutoyo and Jl Haryono, 1½-2 hrs (1,000Rp). Note that the last bus back to Yogya leaves at 1800. Leave at 0500, to arrive early and avoid crowds. From the bus station in Borobudur it is a 500m-walk to the monument. *Bis malam* (night) and *bis cepat* (express) tickets can be booked from the office opp the market in the village. Buses to Yogya, Jakarta, Bogor and Merak. **Hire car or motorcycle:** travel N on the road to Magelang. After 32 km, turn left shortly after the town of Muntilan; 5.5 km down this road is Candi Mendut, and after another 3 km, Borobudur. It is well signposted. Borobudur itself is behind the market. **Taxi:** this may be the best option for 3-4 people travelling together – cheaper than a hotel tour and without time restrictions. **Tour bus:** most visitors reach Borobudur on a tour from Yogya; it is by far the easiest way to reach the monument and costs about 13,500Rp (see page 195 for list of tour companies).

MAGELANG

Magelang, although a sizeable town, is really only used by tourists as a base from which to visit **Borobudur**, which lies 17 km to the S. It is also within reach of the

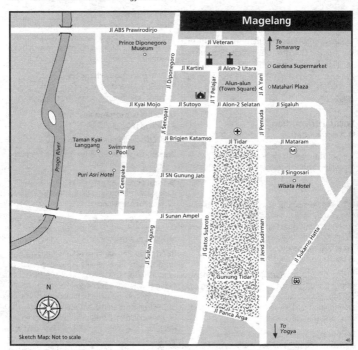

Magelang

- Jl ABS Prawirodirjo
- Prince Diponegoro Museum
- Jl Diponegoro
- Jl Veteran
- To Semarang
- Jl Kartini
- Jl Alon-2 Utara
- Gardena Supermarket
- Jl T Pelajar
- Jl A Yani
- Alun-alun (Town Square)
- Matahari Plaza
- Jl Kyai Mojo
- Jl Sutoyo
- Jl Alon-2 Selatan
- Jl Sigaluh
- Jl Senopati
- Jl Pemuda
- Taman Kyai Langgang
- Swimming Pool
- Jl Brigjen Katamso
- Jl Tidar
- Jl Mataram
- Puri Asri Hotel
- Jl Cempaka
- Jl SN Gunung Jati
- Jl Singosari
- Wisata Hotel
- Jl Sunan Ampel
- Jl Sultan Agung
- Jl Gatos Subroto
- Jl Jend Sudirman
- Jl Sukarno Hatta
- N
- Gunung Tidar
- Jl Panca Arga
- To Yogya
- Sketch Map: Not to scale
- 40

Dieng Plateau (see page 237) which lies 90 km to the NW. On the town square there are a number of colonial era buildings: for example the offices of the former Dutch resident, built in 1810. The **Prince Diponegoro Museum** dates from 1920 and lies just to the W of the Alun-alun (town square), on Jl Diponegoro. At the western edge of town is the **Taman Kyai Langgeng**, a zoo-cum-activity park-cum-fantasy land of concrete animals. There is also a rather more interesting **Chinese Temple** on the Alun-alun (town square) near the Post Office. The town also has rather more than its fair share of appalling heroic sculptures.

Local information
● Accommodation
Most of the town's hotels are to be found along Jl Jend A Yani.

A-C *Puri Asri*, Jl Cempaka 9, T 5114, F 4400, a/c, large pool, large hotel with 68 rm, garden position but relatively close to town centre, rooms are well maintained.

B *Borobudur Indah*, Jl Jend A Yani 246, T 4502; **B** *Magelang Plaza*, Jl Jend A Yani 4, T 4481; **B-D** *Trio Hotel*, Jl Jend Sudirman 68, T 5095, F 3727, some a/c, restaurant, good pool, tennis, good, well-run hotel with wide range of facilities, some distance from town centre, some rooms almost seem to be hewn from the living rock such is the degree of concrete rock encrustation, overall clean and comfortable.

C *City*, Jl Daha 23, T 2287; **C** *Sadewa Griya*, Jl Raya Mertoyudan, T 3990, some a/c, some hot water, little to rec this place, an all-round very average Indonesian motel some distance away from the town centre on the road to Yogya and Borobudur; **C-D** *Wisata*, Jl Jend Sudirman 367 (at the S of town), T 2593, some a/c, keenly priced rooms, clean but lacking any distinguishing features, large, mostly geared to local business-men, dark rooms, bare and empty corridors.

D-E *Bayeman*, Jl Tentara Pelajar 45, T 2050, some a/c, small garden and pleasant eating area, a private villa converted into a guesthouse, the cheaper fan rooms are the best value, the a/c rooms are generally a little tatty and don't warrant the doubling in price, friendly and enthusiastic manageress, fairly central location.

● **Places to eat**
Bakeries: *Probitas Bakery*, Jl Pajang.

● **Banks & money changers**
Bank Central Asia, Alun-alun (town square); Bank Rakyat Indonesia, Jl Jend Sudirman.

● **Entertainment**
Cinemas: *Magelang Tidar*, Alun-alun (town square), modern a/c cinema showing English soundtrack films.

● **Post & telecommunications**
Area code: 0293.
Post Office: Jl Jend A Yani 2 (town square).

● **Shopping**
Plazas/supermarkets: *Garden Pasar Raya*, Alun-alun (town square); *Matahari*, Jl Jend A Yani (town square).

● **Tourist offices**
Information centre at the entrance to the Taman Kyai Langgeng.

● **Transport**
43 km N of Yogya.

Local Bemos: run across town and out to the bus terminal. The bemo terminal is at the S of town on Jl Jend Sudirman.

Road Bus: the terminal is out of town to the E on Jl Sukarno-Hatta; bemos link the terminal with the town centre. Regular connections with Yogya and other regional centres.

PRAMBANAN

The Prambanan Plain was the centre of the powerful 10th century Mataram Kingdom which vanquished the Sailendra Dynasty – the builders of Borobudur. At the height of its influence, Mataram encompassed both Central and E Java together with Bali, Lombok, SW Borneo and S Sulawesi (see page 84 for more history). The magnificent temples that lie scattered over the Prambanan Plain – second only to Borobudur in size and artistic accomplishment – bear testament to the past glories of the kingdom. The village of Prambanan is little more than a way station with a handful of warungs, a market, and a bus stop. There are also a number of losmen and hotels here for those few people who might wish to stay overnight.

Places of interest

After Borobudur, Candi Prambanan is probably the best-known archaeological sight in Indonesia. But, in addition to Prambanan, there are another six major candis on the Prambanan Plain, each with its own artistic character, and all well worth visiting. The account below describes the temples from E to W, travelling from Prambanan village towards Yogya (see map). From Yogya, the monuments are approached in reverse order. The Prambanan temple group have recently been restored by the Indonesian Archaeological Service (1991-1994), and now stand in a neat, landscaped and well planned historical park.

Candi Prambanan or **Candi Lara Jonggrang** – Slender Maiden – as it is also known, stands on open ground and can be clearly seen from the road in Prambanan village. This is the principal temple on the Prambanan Plain, and the greatest Hindu monument in Java. In scale, it is similar to Borobudur, the central tower rising, almost vertically, over 45m. Built between 900 and 930AD, Prambanan was the last great monument of the Central Javanese Period and – again like Borobudur – the architects were attempting to symbolically recreate the cosmic Mt Meru.

Originally, there were 232 temples at this site. The plan was focused on a square court, with four gates and eight principal temples. The three largest candis are dedicated to Brahma (to the S), Vishnu (to the N) and, the central and tallest tower, to Siva. They are sometimes known as Candi Siva, Candi Brahma and Candi Vishnu. Facing each is a smaller shrine, dedicated to each of these gods' 'mounts'.

Candi Siva was restored by the Dutch, after an earthquake in the 16th century

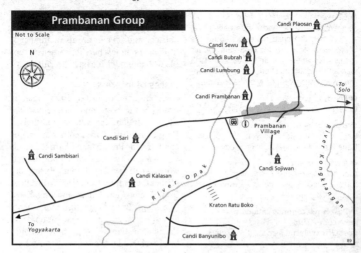

had left much of the temple in ruins. Like other Central Javanese candis, it was conceived as a square cell, with portico projections on each face, the porticos being an integral part of the structure. The tower was constructed as six diminishing storeys, each ringed with small stupas, and the whole surmounted by a larger stupa. The tower stands on a plinth with four approach stairways, the largest to the E, each with gate-towers imitating the main shrine and edged with similar shaped stupas. At the first level is an open gallery, with fine reliefs on the inside wall depicting the Javanese interpretation of the Hindu epic, the Ramayana (see plan page 56). The story begins to the left of the E stairway and is read by walking clockwise – known as *pradaksina*. Look out for the *kalpataru*, or wishing trees, with parrots above them and guardians in the shape of rabbits, monkeys and geese or *kinaras*. The story continues on the balustrade of Candi Brahma. Each stairway at Candi Siva leads up into four separate rooms. In the E room is a statue of Siva, to the S is the sage Agastya, behind him – to the W – is his son Ganesh and to the N is his wife Durga. Durga is

also sometimes known as Lara Jonggrang, or Slender Maiden, and hence the alternative name for the Prambanan complex – Candi Lara Jonggrang.

How the monument came to be given this name is linked to the legend of King Boko and his son Bandung Bondowoso. Bandung loved a princess, Lara Jonggrang, who rejected his advances until her father was defeated in battle by King Boko. To save her father's life, Princess Lara agreed to marry Prince Bandung, but only after he had built 1,000 temples in a single night. Summoning an army of subterranean genies, Bandung was well on the way to meeting the target when Lara Jonggrang ordered her maids to begin pounding the day's rice. Thinking it was morning, the cocks crowed and the genies retreated back to their underground lair leaving Bandung one short of his 1,000 temples. In an understandable fit of pique he turned her to stone – and became the statue of Durga. For those leaving Yogya by air, there is a mural depicting the legend at Adisucipto Airport.

The two neighbouring candis dedicated to Vishnu and Brahma are smaller. They have only one room each and one

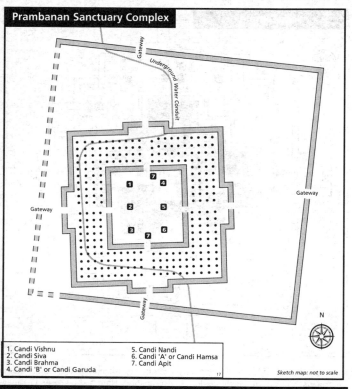

Prambanan Sanctuary Complex

1. Candi Vishnu
2. Candi Siva
3. Candi Brahma
4. Candi 'B' or Candi Garuda
5. Candi Nandi
6. Candi 'A' or Candi Hamsa
7. Candi Apit

Sketch map: not to scale

Prambanan as a holy water sanctuary

Water is a central element in the lives of many Southeast Asian societies. The Hindu myth of the Churning of the Oceans is reflected in the architecture of Angkor Wat in Cambodia and in the Khmer monuments of Thailand. The archaeologist Roy Jordaan believes that *amerta* – holy water – was also central to the symbolism and functioning of Prambanan. He writes: "On the basis of this myth [of the churning of the Oceans], the temple complex was built in such a way that the central temple area could be flooded with water on certain religious feast days, and function as a pool or a reservoir for the holy water that the priests made in a special temple ritual" (Jordaan, *IIAS Newsletter*, No 6, Autumn 1995). In searching out support for this theory of Prambanan as a swimming pool, Jordaan discovered reference to an underground water conduit in JW Ijzerman's *Beschrijving der Oudheden Nabij de Grens der Residenties Soerakarta en Djogdjakarta* published in 1891. He hypothesises that this was used to channel water into the temple precinct, transforming it into a holy water sanctuary. It also explains why Prambanan has drainage problems today: it was not because of some architectural slip, but because the temple was intended to be periodically flooded.

Siva Temple

N

1. Vishnu & Garuda (Panel 1)
2. Rama & Laksmana
   fighting demons (Panel 4)
3. Rama winning hand of Sita (Panel 5)
4. Rama, Laksmana & Sita flee
   to forest (Panel 7)
5. Rama fighting demons (Panel 10)
6. Laksmana rejects Curpankha;
   Rama chases deer (Panel 12)

7. Rawana abducts Sita (Panel 13)
8. Rama meets Hanuman (Panel 15)
9. Rama fights Valin with Surgriva (Panel 18)
10. Hanuman spots Sita in
    Rawana's Palace (Panel 20)
11. Hanuman imprisoned;
    then escapes (Panel 21)

staircase on the E side, but have equally fine reliefs running round the galleries. On **Candi Vishnu**, the reliefs tell the stories of Krishna, while those on the balustrade of **Candi Brahma** are a continuation of the Ramayana epic which begins on Candi Siva. On the exterior walls of all three shrines can be seen voluptuous *apsaris*. These heavenly nymphs try to seduce gods, ascetics and mortal men; they encourage ascetics to break their vows of chastity and are skilled in the arts – poetry, dancing and painting.

Opposite these three shrines are the ruins of **three smaller temples**, recently renovated. Each is dedicated to the mount of a Hindu god: facing Candi Siva is Nandi the bull – Siva's mount; facing Candi Vishnu is (probably) Garuda, the mythical bird; and facing Candi Brahma (probably), Hamsa the goose. The magnificent statue of Nandi is the only mount which still survives.

This inner court is contained within a gated outer court. Between the walls are 224 smaller shrines – all miniature and simplified versions of the large central shrine – and further enclosed by a courtyard. Admission to complex 5,000Rp (2,000Rp with an ISIC card). Open 0600-1800 Mon-Sun. Guidebook, with descriptions of reliefs available from tourist information, 8,000Rp. Guides will show you around the complex, pointing out the various stories on the reliefs for 7,500Rp.

Other candis near Candi Prambanan

From Candi Prambanan, it is possible to walk N to the ruined **Candi Lumbung**,

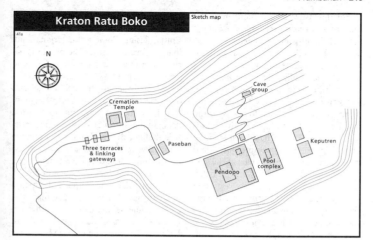

Kraton Ratu Boko
Sketch map

41a

N

Cave group

Cremation Temple

Three terraces & linking gateways

Paseban

Keputren

Pendopo

Pool complex

---

currently under restoration, as well as **Candi Bubrah**. Together with **Candi Sewu** (see below), they form a loose complex of three temples.

Candi Sewu – meaning 'a thousand temples' – lies 1 km to the N of Candi Prambanan and was constructed over three periods spanning the years 778-810. To begin with, the building was probably a simple square cella, surrounded by four smaller temples, unconnected to the main shrine. Later, they were incorporated into the current cruciform plan, and the surrounding four rows of 240 smaller shrines were also built. These smaller shrines are all square in plan, with a portico in front. The central temple probably contained a bronze statue of the Buddha. The candi has been recently renovated. The complex is guarded by *raksasa* guardians brandishing clubs, placed here to protect the temple from evil spirits.

2 km to the NE of Candi Prambanan is **Candi Plaosan** built, probably, about 835, to celebrate the marriage of a princess of the Buddhist Sailendra Dynasty to a member of the court of the Hindu Sanjaya Dynasty. Candi Plaosan consists of two central sanctuaries surrounded by 116 stupas and 58 smaller shrines – presently ruined. Like Candi Sari, the two central shrines were built on two levels with six cellas. Each of the lower cellas may have housed a central bronze Buddha image, flanked by two stone Bodhisattvas (similar to Candi Mendut, page 211). Again, the shrines are guarded by raksasa. The monument is currently undergoing restoration.

The ruins of the late 9th century **Kraton Ratu Boko** occupy a superb position on a plateau 200m above the Prambanan Plain and cover an area of over 15 ha. They are quite clearly signposted off the main road (S), 2 km. Because this was probably a palace (hence the use of the word kraton in its name), it is thought that the site was chosen for its strong natural defensive position. The hill may also have been spiritually important. Little is known of the 'palace'; it may have been a religious or a secular royal site – or perhaps both. Some authorities have even suggested it was merely a R&R centre for pilgrims visiting nearby Prambanan. Inscriptions found in the area celebrate the victory of a ruler and may be related to the supremacy of the (Hindu) Sanjaya Dynasty, over the Buddhist Sailendras.

For the visitor, it is difficult to make sense of the ruins – it is a large site, spread out over the hillside and needs some exploring. From the carpark area, walk up some steps and then for about 1 km through rice fields. The dominant restored triple ceremonial porch on two levels gives an idea of how impressive the palace must have been. To the N of the porch are the foundations of two buildings, one of which may have been a temple – possibly a cremation temple. Turn S and then E to reach the major part of the site. Many of the ruins here were probably Hindu shrines, and the stone bases held wooden pillars which supported large pendopo, or open-sided pavilions. Beyond the palace was a series of pools and above the whole complex a series of caves. To get to Kraton Ratu Boko: take the road S before crossing the Opak River, towards Piyungan, for about 5 km. On the road, just over a bridge on the left-hand side, are steep stone stairs which climb 100m to the summit of the plateau and to the kraton. Alternatively, it is possible to drive to the top; further on along the main road, a turning to the left leads to **Candi Banyunibo**, a small, attractive, restored Buddhist shrine dating from the 9th century. It is set in a well-kept garden and surrounded by cultivated land. Just before the candi, a narrow winding road, negotiable by car and motorbike, leads up to the plateau and Ratu Boko.

2 km to the S of Prambanan village is **Candi Sojiwan**, another Buddhist temple, undergoing restoration.

Candis on the road W to Yogya

About 3 km W of Candi Prambanan and Prambanan village, on the N side of the main road towards Yogya, is **Candi Sari**. This square temple, built around 825, is one of the most unusual in the area, consisting of two-storeys and with the appearance of a third. With three cellas on each of the two levels and porticos almost like 'windows', it strongly resembles a house. Interestingly, reliefs at both Borobudur and Prambanan depict buildings – probably built of wood rather than stone – of similar design. Some art historians think that the inspiration for the design is derived from engravings on bronze Dongson drums (see page 377). These were introduced into Indonesia from N Vietnam and date from between the 2nd and 5th century BC. There is an example of just such a drum in the National Museum in Jakarta. It is thought that both the lower and the upper level cellas of the candi were used for worship, the latter being reached by a wooden stairway. The exterior is decorated with particularly accomplished carvings of goddesses, Bodhisattvas playing musical instruments, the female Buddhist deity Tara, and male naga-kings. Like Candi Kalasan, the stupas on the roof bear some resemblance to those at Borobudur. Inside, there are three shrines, which would originally have housed Buddha images. Nothing remains of the outer buildings or surrounding walls, but it would have been of similar design to Candi Plaosan. The candi was restored by the Dutch in 1929 and like Candi Kalasan, is surrounded by trees and houses.

A short distance further W, and on the opposite side of the road from Candi Sari, is **Candi Kalasan** – situated just off the road in the midst of rice fields. The temple dates from 778, making it one of the oldest candis on Java. It is a Buddhist temple dedicated to the Goddess Tara and is thought to have been built either to honour the marriage of a princess of the Sailendra Dynasty, or as the sepulchre for a Sailendra prince's consort. The monument is strongly vertical and built in the form of a Greek cross – contrasting sharply with the squat and square Candi Sambisari. In fact, the plan of the temple was probably altered 12 years after construction. Of the elaborately carved kala-makaras on the porticos projecting from each face, only the S example remains intact. They would have originally been carved roughly in stone, and then coated with two layers of stucco, the second of which remained pliable just long enough for artists to carve the intricate designs. The four largest of the external niches are empty. The style of the reliefs is similar to SE Indian work of the same period. The roof was originally surmounted by a high circular stupa, mounted on an octagonal drum. Above the porticos are smaller stupas, rather similar in design to those at Borobudur. The only remaining Buddha images are to be found in niches towards the top of the structure. The building contains a mixture of Buddhist and Hindu cosmology – once again evidence of Java's religious syncretism. The main cella almost certainly contained a large bronze figure, as the pedestal has been found to have traces of metallic oxide. The side shrines would also have had statues in them, probably figures of the Buddha.

Another 5 km SW from Candi Kalasan towards Yogya is the turn-off for **Candi Sambisari** – the temple is 2 km N of the main road. If travelling from Yogya, turn left at the Km 12.5 marker – about 9.5 km out of town. Candi Sambisari, named after the village nearby, sits 6.5m below ground level, surrounded by a 2m-high volcanic tuff wall. It has only recently been excavated from under layers of volcanic ash, having being discovered by a farmer in the mid-1960s. It is believed to have been buried by an eruption of Mt Merapi during the 14th century and as a result, is well preserved. The candi was probably built in the early 9th century, and if this is so, then it was one of the last temples to be built during the Mataram period. A central, rather squat, square shrine still contains its original linga, indicating that this was a Hindu temple dedicated to Siva. There are also smaller boundary lingams surrounding the temple. On the raised gallery, in niches, there are fine carvings of Durga (N), Ganesh (E) and Agastya (S). Pillar-bases on the terrace indicate that the entire candi was once covered by a wooden pavilion. In front (and to the W) of the main temple are three smaller shrines in rather poorer condition.

Local information
● Accommodation
There are a number of losmen in Prambanan village. However few people stay here because the candis are so easily accessible from either Solo or Yogya.

A *Prambanan Village*, Klurak, Taman Martani, Kalasan, T 62674, a/c, restaurant, pool, overlooking Prambanan.

E *Losmen Muharti*, T 96103, opp entrance to Prambanan.

Other losmen/hotels incl the **C-D** *Kananga* (some a/c rooms) and the **E** *Mawar*, both on the road N past Candi Lumbung.

● Entertainment
Ramayana ballet (see page 100): at the open-air theatre at Candi Prambanan, 1900-2100, for 4 days every month over the full moon from May to Oct, 12,500-15,000Rp. Tickets available from tourist information at Candi Prambanan or from travel agents in Yogya. There are also performances year-round at the Trimurti Covered Theatre in Yogya (see page 200), 1930-2130.

● Tourist offices
There is a private tourist information office just E (towards Solo) of the bus stop.

● Transport
17 km E of Yogya, 46 km W of Solo.

Local In order to see the outlying candis, it is best to have some form of transport. If on a tour, enquire which candis are to be visited, or hire a taxi, minibus or motorbike from Yogya. Horse-drawn carts and minibuses wait at the bus station; they can be persuaded to drive visitors around. For the main temple group, a road 'train' now takes visitors around the candis, although it is also possible to walk – hot and tiring in the middle of the day. Alternatively, take a bus to Prambanan and work back, W or work E, ending at Prambanan.

Road Bus: regular connections with Yogya's Umbulharjo bus station, or by minibus from the main roads in Yogya, 30 mins. Connections with Solo, 1½ hrs.

SOLO (SURAKARTA)

Surakarta, better known simply as Solo, is Central Java's second royal city. It is situated between three of Java's highest volcanoes: Mt Merapi (2,911m) and Mt Merbabu (3,142m) to the W, and Mt Lawu

(3,265m) to the E. The kraton, or palace, of the great ancient kingdom of Mataram was moved to Surakarta in the 1670s. The town remained the *negara* or capital of the kingdom until 1755 when the VOC divided Mataram into three sultanates – two in Solo and one in Yogya. Although foreigners usually regard Yogya as Java's cultural heart, the Javanese usually attach the sobriquet to Surakarta. Solo's motto is 'Berseri', which is an acronym for Bersih, Sehat, Rapi, Indah (clean, healthy, neat, beautiful). It has won several awards for being the cleanest city in Indonesia.

Solo is quieter, smaller and more relaxed than Yogya – even though its population is more than half a million – and has pleasant wide, clean and tree-lined streets. It is also less touristy than Yogya. Solo is one of the few towns in Indonesia which has bicycle lanes (on the main E-W road – Jl Slamet Riyadi) and they are almost as busy as the main roads. Reflecting the bicycle-friendly character of Solo, many tour companies run cycling tours of the city's places of interest (see Tours, below). The city has gained a reputation as a good place to shop; not only is it a centre for the sale of batik – with a large market specializing in nothing else – but there is also an 'antiques' market which is worth visiting (see Places of interest).

As the courts of Solo were denied administrative powers during the two centuries of colonial rule from 1757, the sultans (or 'Sunans', as they are known) devoted much of their energy to the promotion of Javanese arts and culture. This is reflected today in the presence in Solo of a cultural centre (Pusat Kebudayaan), an academy of music (Konservatori Karawitan) and an academy of art (STSI).

Places of interest

The **Kraton Surakarta Hadiningrat**, better known as the **Kasunanan Palace** is the senior of the city's two kratons (see page 92) and the more impressive. It lies S of the main E-W road, Jl Slamet Riyadi. Like the kraton in Yogya, the Kasunanan Palace faces N onto a square – the Alun-Alun Lor – and follows the same basic design, consisting of a series of courtyards containing open-sided pavilions or pendopos. On the W side of the alun alun is the **Grand Mosque**, built by Pangkubuwono III in 1750, though substantially embellished since then.

The current Sunan is Pagkubuwono XII, a 70-year-old with six wives, 35 children and a playboy reputation. During 1992 and 1993 he was embroiled in a public relations war with the Sunan's 25th child, the princess Koes Moertiyah. The battle was over the Sunan's plans to turn a portion of the Kasunanan Kraton into a luxury hotel, a project which had the imprimatur of President Suharto and the support of Bimantara, a company controlled by Bambang, one of Suharto's sons. The logic of the scheme was clear: the Sunan has seen his kraton dissolve from glorious splendour into ramshackle decrepitude as funds for its upkeep have dwindled, and as the *abdi dalem* – the court servants – have declined from 3,000 to a mere 600 elderly retainers. But he had not counted on his daughter Koes Moertiyah who, alarmed at the prospect of uncouth tourists degrading the palace, arranged news conferences, encouraged demonstrations and confronted her father and his plans in a manner almost unheard of from a princess. Her actions led the governor of Central Java to impose a ban on building in the kraton and the hotel plans have now been shelved – for the time being.

Entering the Kasunanan Palace, the first pendopo – the **Pagelaran** – is original, dating from 1745 and is used for public ceremonies. This is where visiting government officials would wait for an audience with the Susuhunan. From here, stairs lead up to the **Siti Inggil** or High Place, the area traditionally used for enthronements. Like Borobudur and Prambanan, the Siti Inggil represents the cosmic mountain Meru, but on a micro-scale. On the Siti Inggil is a large pendopo. The fore section of this pavilion

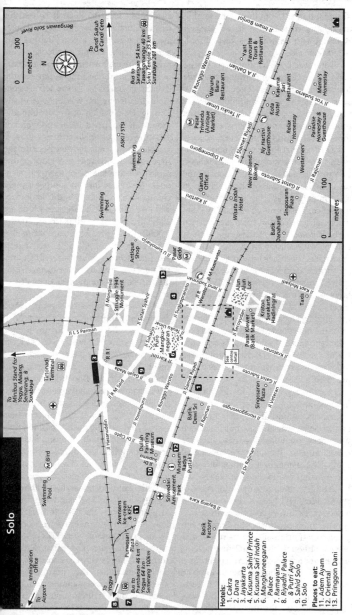

Solo

Hotels:
1. Cakra
2. Dana
3. Jayakarta
4. Kusuma Sahid Prince
5. Kusuma Sari Indah
6. Mangkuneegaran Palace
7. Ramayana
8. Riyadhi Palace & Putri Ayu
9. Sahid Solo
10. Solo

Places to eat:
11. Adem Ayam
12. Oriental
13. Pringgon Dani

was rebuilt in 1915 but the square section towards the rear (known as the **Bangsal Witana**), with its umbrella-shaped roof, is 250 years old.

Visitors are not permitted to enter the main palace compound through the large **Kemandungan Gates**. They must walk back out of the first compound, over a road, past the private entrance to the prince's quarters and an area used to store the royal carriages, through a second gate, to an entrance at the E of the main compound. Near the second gate is a school; this was originally a private school for the royal children but was opened to children of commoners at the time of independence. Walk through one courtyard to reach the large central courtyard, known as the *Plataran*. This shaded area, with its floor of black sand from the S coast, contains the main palace buildings. Much of the prince's private residence was destroyed in a disastrous fire in 1985, but has subsequently been restored. An electrical fault was the alleged cause of the fire, although local people believe that the Susuhunan neglected his duties and provoked the anger of the Goddess Nyi Loro Kidul (see page 151). Restoration was followed by extensive ceremonies to appease the goddess.

The three **pendopo** on the left are original, and are used for gamelan performances. Behind them, along the walls of the courtyard, are palanquins which were once used for transporting princesses around the city. An octagonal tower, the **Panggung Songgobuwono**, survived the fire and was supposedly used by the Susuhunan to communicate with the Goddess Nyi Loro Kidul. Songgobuwono means 'Support of the Universe'.

The main pendopo, the **Sasana Sewaka**, is not original – it was restored in 1987 – although the Dutch iron pillars which support it, are. Strictly speaking, if members of the public are to have an audience with the Sultan, they have to walk upon their knees across the pendopo; look out for the cleaners, who

crouch to sweep the floor. It is used for four ceremonies a year and sacred dances are held here once a year. Behind this pendopo is the private residence of the prince, with the **kasatrian** (the sons' quarters) to the right and the **keputren** (the daughters' quarters) to the left. A concrete area to the left was the site of the Dining Hall, which also burnt to the ground in the fire of 1985, and which is awaiting restoration, once funds allow.

The guide leads visitors back to the first courtyard, where two sides of the square are a museum, containing an interesting collection of enthronement chairs, small bronze Hindu sculptures and three fine Dutch carriages which are 200-350 years old. Admission 1,000Rp, 1,000Rp for camera. Open 0830-1400 Mon-Thur, 0830-1500 Sun. All visitors are asked to wear a *samir* – a gold and red ribbon – as a mark of respect. Guide obligatory (they are the *abdi dalem* or palace servants).

The less impressive kraton, **Pura Mangkunegaran** at the N end of Jl Diponegoro, is still lived in by the princely family who built it. In 1757, the rebel prince Mas Said established a new royal house here, crowning himself Mangkunegoro I. But his power was never as great as the Susuhunan, and Mangkunegoro's deference to him is evident in the design of his palace, which faces S, towards the Susuhunan's kraton. Much of the original structure has been restored. Built in traditional style, the layout is like other kratons, centred around a pendopo.

This central pendopo is the **Pendopo Agung**, built in 1810 and one of the largest and most majestic in Java. Note how the ceiling is painted with cosmic symbols. Mangkunegoro VII (1916-44), a scholar and patron of Indonesian performing and plastic arts, commissioned an addition to the kraton – the *pracimusono*. This octagonal pavilion was designed by a Dutch architect whose knowledge of Indonesian architectural traditions led to a sympathetic and innovative design. Behind the central pendopo is a large room – the **Paringgitan** – which houses, amongst other things, a good collection of antique jewellery and coins of the Majapahit and Mataram periods. In a corridor behind this room are a large number of topeng masks. Voyeurists can peer through the windows into the private rooms of the present prince. Beautiful cool gardens and verandahs give his quarters an air of a Victorian hunting lodge. Next to the ticket office are three fine carriages from London and Holland. Admission 1,500Rp. Open 0900-1400 Mon-Sat, 0900-1300 Sun. Guide obligatory (about 1 hr). Gamelan performances are held here (see Entertainment).

The small **Museum Radya Pustaka** housed in an attractive building on the main road, Jl Slamet Riyadi, next door to the Tourist Office. It contains a collection of wayang kulit, topeng, gamelan instruments, royal barge figureheads and some Hindu sculpture. Admission 500Rp. Open 0800-1200 Tues-Thur, Sat and Sun, 0800-1100 Fri.

Next door to the museum is **Sriwedari**, an amusement park. It is also the home of one of the most famous Javanese classical dancing troupes, specializing in wayang orang, who perform here from 2000-2300 Mon-Sat. Open 0800-2200 Mon-Sun.

There are several markets in Solo worth visiting. The antiques market **Pasar Triwindu**, is situated off Jl Diponegoro, on the right-hand side, walking towards the Pura Mangkunegaran. This is the only authentic flea market in Central Java and is a wonderful place to browse through the piles of goods. There are some antiques to be found but time is needed to search them out. Bargaining is essential. **Pasar Klewer**, situated just beyond the W gate of the Alun-alun Lor near the kraton, is a batik-lover's paradise. It is filled with cloth, mostly locally produced batik – a dazzling array of both *cap* and *tulis* (see page 103). Prices are

cheaper than the chainstores, but the market is very busy and first time visitors may be bemused into paying more than they should. It's best to go in the mornings, as it starts to wind down after lunch. Again, bargain hard. At the E side of the Alun-alun are a small number of shops and stalls selling fossils, carvings, krisses, puppets and masks. Don't expect to find anything of real quality, though. It is worth taking a becak to explore the streets of Solo to find some of the interesting colonial houses.

Excursions

Candi Prambanan is easily accessible on public transport from Solo (see page 215). *Getting there*: catch a bus from the Tirtonadi terminal, or a bus travelling W along Jl Slamet Riyadi. The other temples on the Yogya-Solo route are also just as easily accessible from Solo as Yogya (see page 218).

Kartasura is the abandoned site of a royal palace, the Kraton Kartasura, built in 1680 and abandoned 60 years later in 1742. Today all that remains are the beautiful moss-encrusted brick walls and, within the walls, a peaceful graveyard dotted with fragrant frangipani trees. Buried here are some minor members of the Solo royal family. Admission by donation. Open Mon-Sun, 0430-2300. *Getting there*: catch a bus from Solo towards Yogya and get off at the small town of Kartasura, by the Kartasura Market (Pasar Kartasura). From here walk due S for about 300m, and cross the main(ish) road; continue S for another 100m or so to reach the weathered walls. Ask for the *Kraton Kartasura* along the way.

Candi Sukuh and **Candi Ceto**, two of the most unusual and stunningly positioned temples in Indonesia, lie to the E of Solo, on the W slopes of Mt Lawu.

Candi Sukuh stands at 910m above sea-level and was probably built between 1434 and 1449 by the last king of the Majapahit Kingdom, Suhita. The enigmatic Candi Sukuh is situated in an area which had long been sacred and dedicated to ancestor-worship. The style is unlike any other temple in Java and has a close resemblance to South American Maya pyramid temples (which led archaeologists to believe, wrongly, that it was of an earlier date). It is built of laterite on three terraces, facing W. A path, between narrow stone gates, leads up from one terrace to the next, and steep stairs through the body of the main 'pyramid' to a flat summit. Good views over terraced fields down to the plain below.

The first terrace is approached through a gate from the W, which would have been guarded by dvarapalas (see page 272). The relief carvings on the gate are *candra sangkala* – the elements that make up the picture signify numbers which, in this instance, represent a date (1359 = 1437AD). On the path of the first terrace is a relief of a phallus and vulva: it is said that if a woman's clothes tear on passing this relief, it signifies excessive promiscuity and she must purify herself.

The gate to the second terrace is guarded by two more dvarapalas. On the terrace are a number of carved stones, including a depiction of two blacksmiths, one standing – probably Ganesh – the other squatting, in front of which is a selection of the weapons they have forged. The third, and most sacred, terrace is approached through a third gate. There are a number of relief carvings scattered over the terrace. The figures of many are carved in wayang form with long arms, and the principal relief depicts the Sudamala story. This story is performed in places where bodies are cremated, in order to ward off curses or to expel evil spirits. Also on the third terrace are standing winged figures (Garuda), giant turtles representing the underworld (strangely similar to the turtle stelae of pagodas in N Vietnam), and carvings of Bima and Kalantaka. It is thought Bima was the most important god worshipped here. A cult of Bima became popular among the Javanese élite in the 15th century: it was

Candi Sukuh

A short history of the Susuhunan of Surakarta

In 1745 Pakubuwono II (his name means 'Nail of the Universe'), inheritor of the older Mataram Kingdom, decided to move his capital from Kartasura to Solo – the former capital had been all but destroyed by E Javanese and VOC attacks. Three locations were carefully chosen as potential sites for a new kraton and after much prevarication and argument, Solo was selected. It seems that the architects were unhappy with the choice because of Solo's position on swampy ground, but they were over-ruled by the all-important seers or wise men who believed that by moving the capital here, the Javanese kingdom would again prosper and war would come to an end.

Despite the move, the royal family was still riven by dissent, with four princes in conflict with one another and with the Susuhunan, Pakubuwono II. Among the four, Prince Mangkubumi and Prince Mas Said were the most powerful. This dissent, coupled with the Susuhunan's agreement with the Dutch to lease the N coast of Central Java to the VOC for a nominal fee, led to the Third Javanese War of Succession (1746-57). Pakubuwono II did not live to see the end of this war and his heir was appointed the new Susuhunan, becoming Pakubuwono III. Prince Mangkubumi meanwhile, failing in his own attempt to become Susuhunan, established a second kraton, in Yogya, where he had developed a power base (see page 187). The only other person left to be placated was Prince Mas Said who became sultan of a third kraton (and the second in Solo) in 1757. From 1757-1795 he ruled his kraton as Mangkunegoro I and lived in harmony alongside Pakubuwono III.

believed that Bima could bring the dead back to life.

The 'topless' pyramid itself has little decoration on it. It is thought that originally it must have been topped-off with a wooden structure. A carved phallus was found at the summit; it is now in the National Museum, Jakarta. Although Candi Sukuh is often called Java's 'erotic' temple, the erotic elements are not very prominent; a couple of oversized penises, little else. Admission by donation (visitors are sometimes asked for a 100Rp fee at Ngolrok). Open 0615-1715 Mon-Sun. *Getting there*: take a bus from Solo's Tirtonadi station on Jl Jend A Yani to Karangpandan (41 km). Or pick up a bus on Jl Ir Sutami travelling E to Karangpandan. From Karangpandan take a minibus the 5.5 km to the village of Ngolrok; some minibuses continue right on up the steep road to the site of Candi Sukuh from the village – if not, it is an exhausting 1.6 km walk past women bringing wood down from the mountains. From Candi Sukuh there is a well-worn stone path to the mountain resort of **Tawangmangu** (see below), an easy 1½-2 hrs' hike.

Candi Ceto lies 7 km to the N of Sukuh, but is considerably higher at over 1,500m. It was built in 1470 and is the last temple to have been constructed during the Majapahit era. Candi Ceto shows close architectural affinities with the pura of Bali, where the Hindu traditions of Majapahit escaped the intrusion of Islam. Getting to the temple is an adventure in itself (although tours do run from Solo and Tawangmangu); the road passes tea estates, incredibly steeply terraced fields, and towards the end of the journey climbs seemingly almost vertically up the mountainside – the road ends at the temple.

Candi Ceto is one of the most stunningly positioned temples in Southeast Asia. It has recently been restored and is set on 12 levels. Nine would originally have had narrow open gateways (like those at Sukuh) but only seven of these remain. Pairs of reconstructed wooden pavilions on stone platforms lie to each side of the pathway on the final series of terraces. There is some sculpture (occasionally phallic) and strange stone decorations are set into the ground – again, very reminiscent of Mayan reliefs. Admission by donation. Open access. *Getting there*: from Karangpandan (see Getting there, above, for Candi Ceto for details on transport to Karangpandan) via Ngolrok there are minibuses to the village of Kadipekso; from Kadipekso it may be possible to hitch, or catch a motorcycle taxi, the final 2.6 km to the site. Alternatively walk, which is exhausting at this altitude. There are, however, now reportedly some direct bemos from Sukuh to Ceto, making this journey – until very recently an adventure in itself – much easier. The easiest way to reach Ceto, though, is to take a tour, see below.

Tawangmangu is a hill resort town set at 1,200m, 12 km on from Kawangpandan and a total of 53 km from Solo (see page 233). *Getting there*: buses leave regularly from Solo's Tirtonadi station, or pick up a bus on Jl Ir Sutami travelling E.

Sangiran, 18 km N from Solo, is one of Java's most important archaeological sites. In 1891, Eugene Dubois found the skullcap and upper jaw molar of what he took to be an ape. But 11 months later in Aug 1892 Dubois unearthed a femur which indicated that the 'ape' walked erect – he named this early hominid *Pithecantropus erectus* – popularly known as 'Java Man'. This 'ape-man' was far more advanced than Dubois presumed and is now classified as a subspecies of *Homo erectus* – namely *Homo erectus erectus*. Since then, excavations at Sangiran have revealed a wealth of fossil hominid remains, along with a hoard of other fossils. Until very recently it was assumed that Homo erectus evolved in Africa and migrated to Java, for while the African fossils were dated to 1.8 million BP, the examples from Java were thought to be only 700,000 years old (see box, page 193). The small

Trinil Museum (opened 1989) in the nearby village of Krikilan has a display including stegadon tusks, buffalo skulls, assorted fossils and, of course, examples of Java Man (craniums). Visitors are assaulted by locals selling fossils. Some (for example, the fish) are clearly of late 20th century origin and recent important discoveries in the area, have made the fossil sellers even more frantic and outrageous. Museum open 0900-1600, Mon-Sat. Admission: 500Rp. *Getting there*: take a tour or catch a bus from Solo's Tirtonadi station towards Purwodadi; just beyond the 14 km mark (in the village of Kalijambe) there is a road to the right signposted to Sangiran. The museum is 4 km along the road; take an ojek (1,500Rp), hitch or walk.

Miri is further N from Sangiran on the road to Purwodadi. This archaeological site and associated museum is less well known and not as well displayed as Sangiran. *Getting there*: turn left past the 21 km marker; the museum is some 2 km off the main road. Take a bus towards Purwodadi from Solo's Tirtonadi station and walk.

The hill village of **Selo** is accessible from Solo and from here **Mount Merapi** can be climbed (see page 203).

Pacitan is a small seaside resort 119 km S of Solo (see page 234). *Getting there*: there are a few direct buses from Solo's Tirtonadi station; alternatively get a bus to Wonogiri, from where there are regular connections to Pacitan.

Tours

Tour companies run cycling tours of Solo, trips to the Kraton, batik and gamelan factories, arak distillers, Prambanan, Sangiran, Candi Sukuh and Candi Ceto (see Travel agents). Many losmen and even some hotels, as well as independent guides, also run cycling or (horse) cart tours to surrounding villages to see rural life and crafts such as batik making, gamelan production, gold-smithing and leather-working. Prices vary considerably from 7,500Rp to 20,000Rp – those arranged

Out of Java: Homo Erectus

Most of the recent developments in human evolution have come from Africa, but at the beginning of 1994 Sangiran and Mojokerto in Java emerged as a star location to rival places like the Olduvai Gorge. The finds, or rather the re-interpretation of existing finds, even reached the dizzy hights of the cover of *Time* magazine.

Until these discoveries, it was assumed that *Homo erectus* evolved in Africa and from there dispersed to Asia, including Java. The remains of three humans from Sangiran and Mojokerto had been thought to be less than one million years old, making them the oldest hominids outside Africa, but not nearly as old as those unearthed in Africa. Now work by Garniss Curtis and Carl Swisher at the Institute of Human Origins in Berekely, California, using new radiometric dating techniques, has revealed that they are probably nearer 1.8 million years old. But doubts remain over the association of the dated crystals with the fossils: one of the problems are worries about the exact locations of the fossils (the Mojokerto fossil was found 60 years ago) and the complex geology of Java. Certainly, Curtis and Swisher have gone to great lengths to verify their early dates (for example by including fossil remains from two locations and including the discoverer of the Sangiran examples in the work), appreciating that because of their enormous implications there would also be intense scrutiny.

If the dates are verified, the work indicates that *H erectus* spread from Africa almost immediately, rather than hanging around for 800,000 years before venturing into Eurasia as previously believed. Anthropologists were always hard pressed to think of a reason why there was this 800,000 year delay. As Alan Walker at John Hopkins University remarks, they didn't "pack red-spotted handkerchiefs and set out for territories new" but gradually spread as the population grew, perhaps by 10 km per generation – reaching Java in a relatively speedy 25,000 years. The even more revolutionary notion that *H erectus* evolved in Asia and then spread to Africa is yet to gain many adherents, even though the dates for the Javanese and African fossils are almost the same. The reason is that there are no known antecedents to *H erectus* from Asia, while there are many from Africa. The belief that modern humans evolved in Africa has not been challenged by the new work, and in fact the multi-regional hypothesis (that humans evolved in numerous places and not just in Africa) has, it seems, been dealt a serious blow.

through homestays/losmen usually cheaper. Recommended are So'ud at the *Paradise Homestay* and Daniel K at *Westerners*. Most tours are 0900-1500.

Batik classes: some losmen and homestays will run batik classes (2 days for 8,000Rp), for example the *Relax Homestay*.

Festivals
Mar/Apr: 2 week-long fair held in the Sriwedari Amusement Park. On the first day a procession parades from the King's Palace to Sriwedari, with stalls selling handicrafts.

Jun/Jul: *Kirab Pusaka Kraton* (movable), a traditional ceremony held by the two kratons to celebrate the Javanese New Year. A procession of heirlooms led by a sacred albino buffalo (the Kyai Slamet) starts at the Pura Mangkunegaran at 1900 and ends at the Kasunanan Palace at 2400. The ceremony dates back 250 years, from the time of Sultan Agung.

Sep: *Sekaten* or *Gunungan* (movable), a 2 week long festival prior to Mohammad's birthday. The celebrations begin at midnight with the procession of two sets of ancient and sacred gamelan instruments from the kraton to the Grand Mosque. A performance is given on these instruments and at the end of the 2 weeks they are processed back to the kraton. A fair is held on the alun-alun in front of the mosque. The closing ceremony is known as *Grebeg Maulud* when a rice mountain (*gunungan*) is cut up and distributed to the crowds. The people believe that a small amount of 'gunungan' will bring prosperity and happiness.

Local information

● **Accommodation**

Solo has a good range of excellent places to stay at all levels, ranging from attractive, stylish colonial period hotels and villas, to clean, quiet and well-priced losmen and guesthouses. Newer hotels, for some unexplained reason, have a penchant for gross ostentation in terms of their interior decoration.

A+-A *Cakra*, Jl Brigjen Slamet Riyadi 201, T 45847, F 48334, a/c, restaurant, pool, garden, range of rooms available, but for many the Indonesian Louis XIV style of interior decoration may be simply too much to handle, gold, pillars and mirrors galore .... but as a place to stay OK if money is not an issue, price incl breakfast; **A+-B** *Kusuma Sahid Prince*, Jl Sugiyopranoto 20, T 46356, F 44788, a/c, restaurant, pool, rather run-down old colonial building but still the best hotel in Solo, some cottage-style accommodation, rec; **A** *Riyadhi Palace*, Jl Slamet Riyadi 335, T 33300, F 51552, a/c, overpriced and rather pretentious, a plush marble-filled lobby and cold rooms, price incl breakfast; **A** *Solo Inn*, Jl Slamet Riyadi 366, T 46075, F 46076, a/c, restaurant, varied rooms but rather overpriced, it looks as though Gracelands has come to Solo, with or without Elvis, Greek columns and neon signs vie uncomfortably with one another and although the rooms are comfortable and well provided, this is grandeur gone crazy.

B *Dana*, Jl Slamet Riyadi 286, T 33891, F 43880, some a/c, some private bathrooms, colonial building with charm and a lovely garden, rather bare, but it has a central location and feels stylish even if the service could be slicker; **B** *Sahid Solo*, Jl Gajah Mada 82, T 45889, F 44133, a/c, restaurant, pool, this was

a smallish hotel of just 40 comfortable rm, but at the end of 1994 a new block with 125 rm opened and the hotel underwent a revamping; no longer much of a 'home atmosphere', as they put it; **B-C** *Wisata Indah*, Jl Slamet Riyadi 173, T 43753, some a/c, dark rooms, not all very well maintained, central location.

C *Paradise Guesthouse*, Jl Gatot Subroto, Gang Kidul 1/3, T 52960, F 52960, a/c, the upmarket 'wing' of the *Paradise Homestay*, this place does seem somewhere close to paradise, just a handful of beautiful rooms in an old house down a quiet, central gang (alley), carvings and paintings adorn the walls, attached bathrooms, hard to beat at this price or, for that matter, any other, rec; **C-D** *Pondok Persada Bengawan*, Jl Kentingan, T 48616, a/c, tennis, on the banks of the Solo River, 4 km from town centre, large garden; **C-D** *Putri Ayu*, Jl Slamet Riyadi 293, T 46155, F 46155, some a/c, set around a green-painted garden courtyard (giving an aquarium feel), rooms can be rather small, cold water mandis but still good value, price incl breakfast; **C-D** *Ramayana*, Jl Dr Wahidin 22, T 32814, some a/c, attractive 1-storey private villa, rooms set around garden courtyard, large rooms with spacious cold water showers, works of art and sometimes elegant furniture (and less elegant cement murals), very quiet except when the caged birds begin to sing and squawk around 0500, friendly and popular, although some of the rooms are a trifle worn, price incl breakfast, rec; **C-D** *Sanashtri*, Jl Sutowijoyo 45, T 45807, some a/c, small, clean rooms, friendly management.

D *Ny Hartini Guesthouse*, Jl Gatot Subroto, Gang Empu Baradah 85, T 42152, some a/c, quiet private house down an alley in a central position, rooms are small and rather dark, but very clean, some of the cheapest a/c rooms available in Solo here.

E *Kota*, Jl Slamet Riyadi 113, T 32841, around courtyard, reasonable rooms, clean, TV, some with attached mandi, good location and price; **E** *Kusuma Sari Indah*, Kp Kestalan Rt4/III (just off Jl Monginsidi opp railway station), T 42574, clean, with attached mandi, rec; **E** *Mama's Homestay*, off Jl Yos Sudarso, T 52248, clean, friendly and good, shared bathrooms, prices incl breakfast; **E** *Paradise Homestay*, Jl Gatot Subroto, Gang Kidul 1/3, T 52960, F 52960, one of the most attractive and clean places to stay in Indonesia at this price, a beautifully converted old house down a quiet gang in the heart of Solo, works of art add character, rooms are not very large but spotless as are the shared showers and loos, rec; **E** *Relax Homestay*, Jl Gatot Subroto, Gang Empu Sedah 28 (off Jl Gatot Subroto), crumbling old house down quiet gang with large 'secret' garden, rooms are spacious, some with attached mandi, loos are clean and the place makes a wonderfully relaxed and peaceful place to stay in the heart of Solo, well managed by Manggus and his friendly assistant Amin; **E** *San Francisco*, down alley off Jl Monginsidi (nr train station), next to *Jayakarta Hotel*, basic; **E** *Sinar Dhady*, down alley off Jl Monginsidi (nr train station), next to *Jayakarta Hotel*; **E** *Tri Hadi*, Jl Monginsidi 181 (not far from train station), T 37557, mostly used by Indonesians, but rooms are spacious and airy, bathrooms are clean, and rates are very good – worth considering, although don't expect lots of traveller's information; **E-F** *Westerners* (*Pak Mawardi's Homestay*), Kampung Kemlayan Kidul 11 (right off Jl Yos Sudarso, from Jl Slamet Riyadi), T 33106 set in the old part of the city, this popular guesthouse is difficult to find but worth the effort, rooms are clean, relaxed, quiet homely atmosphere, good source of information, rec.

F *Moro Seneng*, Jl Ahmad Dahlan 49, average; **F** *Nirwana*, Jl Ronggo Warsito 59, T 2843; **F** *Timur*, Jl Keprabon Wetani I/5 (off Jl Ahmad Dahlan).

● **Places to eat**

Solo is renowned as a good place to eat, particularly local specialities; there is certainly no shortage of restaurants and warungs to choose from. Solo specialities incl *nasi gudeg* (egg, beans, rice, vegetables and coconut sauce), *nasi liwet* (rice cooked in coconut milk and served with a vegetable) and *timlo* (embellished chicken broth). The Yogyanese speciality *gudeg* is also popular here.

Indonesian: ♦♦*Adem Ayam*, Jl Slamet Riyadi 342, specializes in *ayam goreng* (fried chicken), which is done to perfection, large and relatively cheap; ♦♦*Pondok Bambu*, Jl Adisucipto 183 (out of town on way to airport), open restaurant with fish specialities; ♦♦*Pondok Segaran*, Sriwedari amusement park, good Javanese food; ♦♦*Pringgon Dani*, Jl Sutan Syahrir, good food and a pleasant atmosphere, rec; ♦♦*Sari*, Jl Slamet Riyadi 421, best Javanese restaurant in town; ♦♦*Timlo Sastro*, Jl Balong 28, locals maintain this serves the best *timlo* in town, open till after lunch; ♦♦*Tio Ciu*, N side of Jl Slamet Riyadi, nr the shopping plaza, fresh seafood; ♦*Bakso Triwindu*, Jl Diponegoro, good vegetarian

food; ♦*Bu Mari's*, Jl Jend Gatot Subroto, rec *gudeg*, open late; **E** *Mama's Homestay*, off Jl Yos Sudarso, T 52248, clean, friendly and good, shared bathrooms, prices includes breakfast; ♦*Malioboro*, N end of Jl Diponegoro, for excellent *ayam bakar* (barbecued chicken); ♦*Warung Baru*, Jl Ahmad Dahlan 8, travellers' food and more, popular, the charming manageress is an excellent source of information and the restaurant is also a rendezvous for Solo's community of foreigners, bicycle tours run from here, is highly praised, rec.

Other Asian cuisine: ♦♦♦♦*Nikkoo*, Jl Slamet Riyadi, best Japanese restaurant in town, but also, by Indonesian standards, very expensive; ♦♦*Centrum*, Jl RE Martinidata, a/c, best Chinese in town; ♦♦*Orient*, Jl Slamet Riyadi, a/c, good Chinese, good seafood, rec; ♦♦*Oriental*, Jl Slamet Riyadi (next to the Radya Pustaka Museum), open for lunch and dinner extensive menu incl pigeon, seafood, frog and pork, mostly Chinese dishes, watch two skilled cooks produce all the food on just 2 woks – Mossimann might even learn something here about economy of pans; ♦*Laris*, Jl Slamet Riyadi, Chinese noodles; ♦*Populer*, Jl KH Ahmad Dahlan, Chinese noodles.

International: there is little to offer the westerner who does not have the stomach for Indonesian or Javanese food. Listed under Indonesian are a couple of places serving travellers' food. The better hotels have a limited number of western dishes; *Kentucky Fried Chicken*, Jl Slamet Riyadi; *Kasuma Sari*, Jl Slamet Riyadi 111, icecreams; *La Tansa*, Jl Imam Bonjol 31, bakery with good range of well priced Indonesian sweet breads and western-style baked goodies; *New Holland*, Jl Slamet Riyadi, rec by many locals as the best bakery in the city; *Svensen's*, Jl Slamet Riyadi, icecreams.

Foodstalls: there are many *warungs* and food carts to be found around Solo, which vary enormously in quality; 3rd flr of *Matahari Dept Store* at *Singosaren Plaza* offers a variety of Indonesian food; those who are fans of *bakso* should try the excellent food stall *Mas Tris*, Jl Honggowongso (just S from the intersection with Jl Slamet Riyadi); night market at Pujasari (Sriwedari Park) next to the Radya Pustaka Museum on Jl Slamet Riyadi, most Indonesian favourites like *saté* and *nasi ranies* can be bought along with Chinese dishes and seafood like grilled fish and squid; carts set-up along the N side of Jl Slamet Riyadi in the afternoon and evening and sell delicious snacks (*jajan* in

Javanese). On the S side of town, nr Nonongan, saté stalls set-up in the evenings; stalls nr the train station on Jl Monginsidi.

● **Airline offices**
Bouraq, Jl Gajah Mada 86, T 34376; **Garuda Merpati**, Lippo Bank Bldg, Jl Slamet Riyadi 328, T 44955; **Sempati Air**, Solo Inn, Jl Slamet Riyadi 366, T 46240.

● **Banks & money changers**
Bank Rakyat Indonesia, Jl Slamet Riyadi; **Bumi Daya**, Jl Slamet Riyadi 16; **Central Asia**, Jl Slamet Riyadi 7; **Pan Indonesia**, Jl Major Kusmanto 7; **PT Grakarta** (money changer), Jl Slamet Riyadi 85.

● **Entertainment**
Solo has a cultural centre (Pusat Kebudayan), a Musical Academy and an Art Academy (STSI), with departments for dance, music, handicrafts and 'dalang' (the narrator of wayang kulit performances). The RRI (National Radio Station) Auditorium at Jl Marconi 51 (opp the railway station) organizes cultural performances.

Cinemas: multi-screen cinema, the **Solo 21**, in Sriwedari Park on Jl Slamet Riyadi.

Dance practices: Javanese classical dance at Pura Mangkunegaran every Wed 1000-1200. Also at the Kraton Surakarta Hadiningrat, Sun 0900-1100, 1500-1600.

Gamelan: at the Pura Mangkunegaran on Sat 1000-1200 and accompanied by dance on Wed at 0900. Admission – entrance fee to palace. Also at Kusuma Sahid Prince Hotel, 1800, Mon-Sun and Aski, 0900-1400, Mon-Thur, Sat.

Ketoprak: traditional folk drama performances at the RRI every fourth Tues of the month, 2000-2400.

Wayang Kulit: RRI, every third Tues and third Sat of the month from 0900-0500 the next morning.

Wayang Orang: at the Sriwedari Amusement Park on Jl Slamet Riyadi, 2000-2300 Mon-Sat, and at the RRI every second Tues of the month, 2000-2400.

● **Hospitals & medical services**
Hospital Kasih Ibu, Jl Slamet Riyadi 404, T 44422.

● **Post & telecommunications**
Area code: 0271.
General Post Office: Jl Jend Sudirman 7.
Telephone office: Jl Mayor Kusmanto 1 (24 hrs).
Wartel (telephone & fax): Jl Slamet Riyadi 275A (at intersection with Jl Prof Dr Sutomo).

● **Shopping**
Solo has much to offer the shopper, particularly batik and 'antique' curios.

Antique bric-à-brac: Pasar Triwindu, off Jl Diponegoro (see sights). Much of the merchandise is poor quality, 'antique' bric-à-brac, but the odd genuine bargain also turns up. Bargaining is essential. There is also a good jumble of an antique shop on Jl Urip Sumoharjo, S of Jl Pantisari – some good things to be had here for those with the time to search through the dust, incl batik stamps, old masks, bells, carvings, Buddhas, etc.

Batik: classical and modern designs, both tulis and cap, can be found at the Pasar Klewer, situated just beyond the W gate of the Alun-alun Lor, nr the kraton (see sights). Prices are cheaper than the chainstores, but the market is very busy and bargaining is essential. It is best to go in the mornings, as the market starts to wind down after lunch. Batik Danar Hadi, Jl Dr Rajiman 164; Ce Pe, Jl Ahmad Dahlan 4; Batik Keris, Jl Yos Sudarso 62; Batik Semar, Jl RM Said 148. It is also possible to see the batik-making process at Batik Semar.

Bookstore: Toko Sekawan, Jl Kartini, not much in English.

Ceramics: PKK Artshops, Jl Alun-alun.

Department store: Matahari, intersection of Jl Jend Gatot Subroto and Jl Dr Rajiman. New Matahari Store at eastern end of Jl Slamet Riyadi, NE of Alun-alun Utara.

Handicrafts (incl masks, wayang costumes, and leather puppets): Bedoyo Srimpi, Jl Dr Soepomo (opp Batik Srimpi); Pengrajin Wayang Kulit Saimono, Sogaten RT/02/RW XV, Pajang Laweyan Surakarta; Sriwedari Amusement Park, Jl Slamet Riyadi; Usaha Pelajar, Jl Majapahit 6-10.

Krisses: these traditional knives (see page 118) can be bought at Keris Fauzan, Kampung Yosoroto RT 28/RW 82, Badran (Bpk Fauzan specializes in Keris production and sale), and also from the stalls at the eastern side of the Alun-alun Utara. **NB** That a fine example will cost thousands of dollars.

Markets: Pasar Besar is on Jl Urip Sumoharjo and is the main market in Solo.

Music tapes: concentration of shops on Jl Gatot Subroto (at end nr Jl Slamet Riyadi).

Supermarkets: number in town, incl Galael's on Jl Slamet Riyadi (nr the Solo Inn).

● **Sports**

Golf: *Panasan Course*, NW of town, nr airport, T 42245, 80,000Rp.

Swimming: at *Kusuma Sahid Prince Hotel* (3,500Rp).

● **Tour companies & travel agents**

Mandira Tours, Jl Gadah Mada 77, T 54558; *Natratour*, Jl Gadah Mada 86; *Nusantara*, Jl Urip Sumoharjo 65; *Rosalia 121 Solo Indah Tour*, Jl Slamet Riyadi 380, T 41916; *Sahid Tours*, Jl Slamet Riyadi 318, T 41916, F 42012; *Sahid Tours and Travel*, Jl Slamet Riyadi 332, T 42105; *Warung Baru*, Jl Ahmad Dahlan 8, really a restaurant but this warung also run rec bicycle tours.

● **Tourist offices**

At Jl Slamet Riyadi 275 next to, and behind the Museum Radya Pustaka, T 41435, can supply town maps and some information on cultural events. Open 0800-1700 Mon-Sat. There are also tourist information centres at the bus station (very poor), the railway station and at the airport.

● **Useful addresses**

Immigration Office: Jl Adisucipto (out of town on way to airport), T 48479.

Police Station: Jl Adisucipto, T 34500.

● **Transport**

585 km from Jakarta, 63 km NE of Yogya, 262 km from Surabaya.

Local Angkutan: this is the local name for colts, which ply fixed routes around town, 350Rp. The station is close to the intercity bus terminal at Gilingan. **Becaks**: about 500Rp for a short trip in town, bargain hard. **Bicycles**: Solo is more bicycle-friendly than just about any other city on Java; bicycling is an excellent way to get around town. For hire from *Bamboo Homestay*, Jl Setyaki (behind Sriwedari); *Ramayana*, Jl Dr Wahidin 22; *Relax Homestay*, Jl Kemlayan; *Warung Baru*, Jl KH Ahmad Dahlan and *Westerners*, Gang Kidul 11. About 1,500Rp, 3,000Rp for a good mountain bike. **Bus**: double-decker town bus 200Rp. **Carts**: horse-drawn carts. **Taxis**: metered ones in town (800Rp flag fall).

Air Solo's Adisumarmo Airport is 10 km NW of the city. *Transport to town*: taxis are available for the trip into town (10,000Rp); there is no easy public transport. Regular connections with Garuda/Merpati and Sempati with other destinations in Java, Sumatra, Kalimantan, Sulawesi, Bali, Lombok, Nusa Tenggara, Muluku and Irian Jaya (see page 912 for route map).

International connections: *Silk Air* began operating direct flights from Singapore in early 1995.

Train Solo's Balapan station is on Jl Monginsidi (T 32228), a short distance N of the city centre. A/c connection with Jakarta 8-12 hrs, arrives Solo 0300, non-a/c arrives 0530 and on to Surabaya, 7 hrs. Crowded local train daily from Yogya 1 hr 20 mins (see page 917 timetable).

Road Bus: the Tirtonadi station (T 35097) is on Jl Jend A Yani, 2 km N of the city centre. Most bus companies have their offices on Jl Sutan Syahrir or Jl Urip Sumoharjo. Regular connections with most cities incl Jakarta, Bogor, Bandung 12 hrs, Malang 9 hrs, Surabaya 6 hrs, Semarang 2½ hrs, Denpasar. Local buses regularly leave Yogya for Solo 2 hrs. Night buses and express buses can be booked through most tour companies and many hotels and losmen. They run to most places in Java, and also to Lovina Beach, Lombok/Mataram and, in Sumatra, to Padang, Medan and Bukittinggi. Companies incl Java Baru, Jl Dr Setiabudi 20, T 52967. **Minibus**: regular a/c connections with Yogya, 2 hrs, Semarang, Surabaya and Malang. **Taxi**: connections with Yogya cost about 34,000Rp.

TAWANGMANGU

Tawangmangu is a hill resort at 1,200m set on the W slopes of Mt Sewu (which rises another 2,000m to 3,265m). Good walks, fresh air and pony 'trekking'. A short walk away is **Grojogan Sewu Waterfall** and up towards the top of town is the **Balekambang swimming pool** for cold dips. At the bottom of town, opposite the bus station, is a quaintly squalid **market**.

Excursions

Candi Sukuh (see page 225) can be reached on foot; it is a 1½-2 hr hike along the mountainside. Alternatively catch a bus down the mountain to Karangpandan. **Candi Ceto** can be reached from Sukuh or via Karangpandan (see page 227).

Sarangan is another hill resort 14 km to the E of Tawangmangu, and just into the neighbouring province of E Java. The town is centred around a lake (where there are facilities for fishing and rowing) and offers beautiful views of the surrounding countryside. Accommodation at Sarangan is more expensive than at Tawangmangu. Try the **C** *Hotel Mulia*, T 98059. *Getting there*: by colt from Tawangmangu.

Tours

Tours to Candi Sukuh and Ceto are arranged by *Komajaya Komaratih Hotel*.

Local information
● Accommodation

A good range of hotels and losmen; the better hotels are cheaper than Solo for the same standard of accommodation, making it a good 'alternative' hill resort. **NB** Over the weekend the resort is crowded with people from the plains, prices are therefore higher and the good places are often full.

A-C *Komajaya Komaratih*, Jl Lawu Kav 150-151, T 97125, F 97205, restaurant, pool, tennis, 'best' in town, good rooms, hot water, price incl breakfast, although it is a shame that more is not made of the views – the dining room, incredibly, has no windows bar those looking on to the parkway lot, **A** for a family room for 4.

C *Pondok Sari*, Jl Timur Balekambang (to left of main road going up), pool, clean, hot water, good value, price incl breakfast.

D *Muncul Sari*, Jl Lawu 87, T 97101, popular and the manager is friendly, rooms are darkish but clean with sitting areas to, in theory, admire the view, if there was one – which there isn't, attached cold water mandis, also rather dark and forbidding; **D** *Pondok Sari I*, Jl Utara Balekambang (100m from Pondok Sari), hot water and separate sitting-room.

E *Losmen Mekar Indah*, Jl Lawu Tawangmangu, T 97107, reasonable rooms with own mandi; **E** *Losmen Ngesti Sariro*, Jl Lawu Tawangmangu, reasonable; **E** *Losmen Tejo Moyo*, Jl Lawu, T 97149, attached cold water mandis, rather fusty, but cheaper than most places up here; **E** *Pak Amat*, Jl Lawu Kav (50m from bus station up hill), bungalows set around garden, rooms a little musty but clean.

● Places to eat

Pak Amat, Jl Lawu Kav, for cheap burgers, Wienerschnitzel and Indonesian dishes; *Sapto Argo*, Jl Lawu Tawangmangu.

● Post & telecommunications
Area code: 0271.
Wartel: Jl Raya Lawu 120A.

● **Transport**
40 km from Solo.

Local Horses: are available for rent for about 6,000Rp/hr.

Road Bus: regular connections with Solo's Tirtonadi station. Minibuses also run on, over the pass, and down to Magelang where there are buses to Kediri and on. The station is at the lower end of the village, opp the market. **Chartered minibus**: from the Balapan railway station in Solo. **Taxi**: from Solo, 1 hr (about 50,000Rp/day).

PACITAN

Pacitan is a small seaside resort 119 km S of Solo enclosed within a sweeping crescent-shaped bay. The beach is usually almost deserted and the swimming is generally good. The surrounding countryside and villages provide many lovely walks; a good place for a taste of 'real' Javanese life, with a beach to boot.

Local information
● Accommodation

Pacitan has only recently developed as a tourist destination and accommodation is generally simple.

C-E *Hotel Pacitan*, Jl Jend A Yani 37 (on the alun-alun), T 81244, some a/c, the Pacitan equivalent of the *Ritz*, large a/c rooms but the cheaper fan rooms are better value.

D-E *Happy Bay Beach Bungalows* (well signposted from the main road, get off the bus as it approaches Pacitan), T 81474, restaurant, at last count this place consisted of just 6 bungalows run by an Australian – Eric – and his Javanese wife, the bungalows, set in attractive gardens, have attached showers, deserted beach with good swimming, games room, motorbikes for hire, Eric visits Yogya once a week and will give guests free lifts, a favourite retreat for foreigners living in Yogya; **D-F** *Losmen Remaja*, Jl Jend A Yani 67, T 81088, some a/c, this place may be cheap but recent visitors have not said much else to rec it.

● **Banks & money changers**
Bank Rakyat Indonesia, will change US$ TCs.

● **Post & telecommunications**
Area code: 0357
Telephone: there is a **Wartel** office on Jl Jend A Yani.

● **Transport**
119 km from Solo.

Local: motorbikes for hire from the *Happy Bay Beach Bungalows*. **Bus**: the bus terminal is on the Solo side of town, a short walk from the centre. There are a handful of direct buses from Solo's Tirtonadi terminal; alternatively, catch a bus to Wonogiri where there are frequent connections to Pacitan.

SARANGAN

Sarangan is a hill resort on the E slopes of Mt Lawu (3,265m). It can be approached either from the E, from Madiun, or from the W, from Solo via Tawangmangu. The road up to the resort, from both directions, seems almost too steep for the public minibuses to negotiate. Sarangan itself is marketed as Indonesia's Switzerland, but do not expect a quaint alpine-esque mountain village. The resort is ugly and, if there is such a thing, Sarangan would be at risk of contravening the Trades Description Act.

Excursions
Cemora Sewu is the highest village hereabouts, almost at the pass. There are good walks amidst the mist and pines. **Accommodation** There is a camping ground at Cemora Sewu – only for those with warm sleeping bags. *Getting there*: minibuses travelling between Sarangan or Tawangmangu pass through Cemora Sewu.

Local information
● **Accommodation**
Hotels in Sarangan are over-priced. Even so it is often booked-out over the weekend, although considerable discounts can be negotiated during the week.

C *Hotel Mulia*, T 98059; **C** *Rahayu*, T 98019.

B-C *Hotel Sarangan*, T 98022; *Losmen Sri Maya*; *Wisma Dewi*.

● **Post & telecommunications**
Post Office: on the main road.

● **Tourist offices**
Dinas Pariwisata, on the main road in town.

● **Transport**
Road Minibus: Sarangan can be approached from either E or W. From the W, there are minibuses from Tawangmangu (another hill town), and from there regular connections with Solo. From the E, there are minibuses from Magetan, and regular bus connections between Magetan and Madiun.

WONOSOBO

A small mountain town with a cool climate, Wonosobo is the best base from which to visit the **Dieng Plateau** and its temples (see below). The town is built on a hillside and runs from the bus terminal (unfortunately) at the bottom, to the town square at the top, a total distance of about 2 km. There is a **market** running between Jl Jend A Yani (the main road) and Jl Resimen, at the N end of town.

Excursions
Dieng Plateau see below. *Getting there*: regular connections by bus from the minibus station nr the market in the centre of town (1 hr).

Tours
Angkutans can be chartered for tours to Dieng, from Jl Angkutan 45, T 21880 (30,000-35,000Rp).

Local information
● **Accommodation**
B-C *Sri Kencono*, Jl Jend A Yani 81, T 21522, some a/c, hot water, central position, rooms are far better than immediate impressions of the hotel might indicate, spotlessly clean, light and airy.

C *Nirwana*, Jl Resimen 18/36, T 21066, hot water, bath, clean and large rooms for the price, quiet, central for buses to Dieng, price incl breakfast, rec; **C-D** *Bhima*, Jl Jend A Yani 4, T 21233, hot water, bath, adequate accommodation, price incl breakfast.

D *Famili*, Jl Sumbing 6, T 396, nice building, average rooms, with outside mandi, a little overpriced; **D-E** *Perama*, Jl Jend A Yani 96, T 21789, hot water, bath, clean and airy rooms with some attempt at making a garden atmosphere, although the darkened glass makes the courtyard rooms rather dark, situated towards the bottom end of town, good value.

E *Citra Homestay*, Jl Angkutan 45, T 21880, clean and bright rooms, price incl basic breakfast, central location 5 mins' walk E from Dieng bus stop, rec; **E** *Sindoro*, Jl Sumbing 5, T 179,

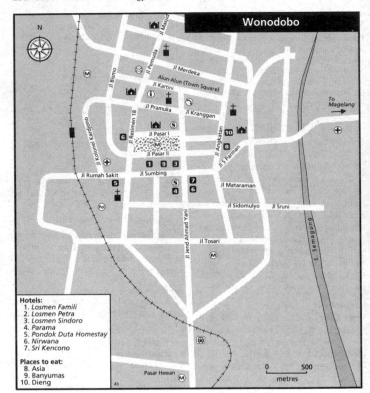

Hotels:
1. Losmen Famili
2. Losmen Petra
3. Losmen Sindoro
4. Parama
5. Pondok Duta Homestay
6. Nirwana
7. Sri Kencono

Places to eat:
8. Asia
9. Banyumas
10. Dieng

clean and central, nr the Plaza, a good, cheap place to stay, rec; **E-F** *Petra*, Jl Jend A Yani 97, T 21152, hot water in the more expensive rooms, overall impression is one of grubbyness; **E-F** *Pondok Duta*, Jl Rumah Sakit 3, T 21674, situated 500m W of the town centre, good travellers' information, clean rooms, popular.

F *Surya*, Jl Jend A Yani 4, T 272, central position in town, simple and basic rooms.

● **Places to eat**
✦✦*Asia*, Jl Kawedanan 35, good Indonesian/Chinese, rec; ✦*Banyumas*, Jl Sumbing (nr intersection with Jl Jend A Yani); ✦-✦✦*Dieng*, Jl Kawedanan 29, Indonesian as well as international food served here, good meeting place.

● **Banks & money changers**
Rakyat, Jl Jend A Yani, top end, on corner of Jl Kartini.

● **Post & telecommunications**
Area code: 0286.

Post Office: Jl Pemuda, top of town on main square.

Warpostel (fax & telephone): Jl Jend A Yani.

● **Shopping**
Batik: *Busaka Dewi*, Jl Jend A Yani, plus a number of shops around the market.

● **Tourist offices**
At Jl Kartini 3, T 21144. Open 0800-1400 Mon-Sat. Has a useful pamphlet on Wonosobo and Dieng to hand out, incl maps of both.

● **Transport**
107 km NW of Yogya, 134 km SE of Pekalongan, 119 km SW of Semarang.

Local Bus: local bus incl those for Dieng, leave from Jl Resimen nr the market, just up the road from the colt station, 800Rp. **Carts**: horse carts

or *dokar* are 5,000Rp for a tour of the town.
Colt: the station is in the market on Jl Resimen.

Road Bus: the long-distance bus terminal is at
the S end of Jl Jend A Yani, 1 km up hill from
the town centre. Regular connections with
Magelang 2 hrs and on to Yogya 40 mins,
Cilacap (via Purwokerto), and Semarang (via
Ambarawa) 4 hrs. A/c minibuses operated by
Rahayu Travel, Jl Jend A Yani 111 also run direct
to Yogya and Cilacap 6 hrs.

**ROUTE-WISE: REACHING THE DIENG
PLATEAU** From Wonosobo, the road
climbs steeply N through spectacular scenery. Every square inch of land is cultivated,
almost to the top of some of the mountains,
and often on precipitous slopes. On a clear
morning, there are stunning views back
down to the valley. Eventually, at 1,800m
and after 26 km the road reaches the Dieng
Plateau.

DIENG PLATEAU

The Dieng Plateau presents an extraordinary landscape; a rich volcanic basin of
sulphur springs, lakes and the oldest
Hindu temples on Java. Visitors sometimes report great disappointment on arriving at Dieng, having heard in advance
of the stunning journey up to the 2,000m-
high plateau. This is often because most
people do not get here until after midday

when it can be misty and grey. It is undoubtedly best to travel to Dieng and explore the plateau in the clear highland
mornings – this can only be achieved by
staying in Wonosobo (26 km S) or in Dieng
itself.

Places of interest

The Dieng Plateau (Dieng comes from the
Sanskrit word *Di-hyang*, meaning the
'Abode of the Gods') was occupied from
the end of the 7th century to the 13th
century. Eight temples remain, out of a
possible 200, all of which were on a small
scale and dedicated to Siva, the Hindu god
of destruction. Little is known of the history of these temples, but the volatile volcanic landscape probably had something
to do with the construction of so many
candis here – the area was almost certainly
considered an ideal place to communicate
with the ancestors. Beginning at the end
of the 7th century and ending in the late
8th or possibly early 9th centuries, these
candis are some of the oldest on Java. Their
construction was probably linked to the
Central Javanese Sanjaya Dynasty. The
names that the various candi have been
given are not original, and give no indication of their dedication. Built on swampy

Candis on the Dieng Plateau

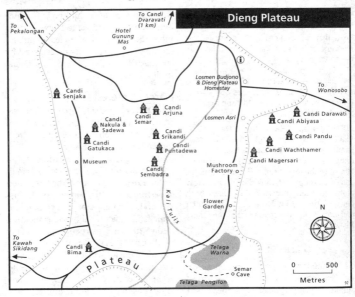

Dieng Plateau

ground, evidence remains of a vast, intricate underground drainage system, some of which still functions today.

At some point, and for some unknown reason, the Dieng Plateau was abandoned by the people who built the candis. Over the decades the natural swamp forest regenerated and when the first Europeans reached the plateau at the beginning of the 19th century, the temples were hidden from view. As the forest was cleared for firewood so the ruins were rediscovered, only to be slowly dismantled as the finely hewn stone blocks were transported away by stone robbers to be used for building. This explains why only a handful of candis remain. As Jacques Dumarçay and John Miksic point out, the climate on the plateau was too cold to grow any tropical crops and it is unlikely that there was ever any large resident population – bar "a few priests shivering in the cold air". The most recent inscription from Dieng is dated 1210, some time after which the plateau and its enigmatic temples were left to the swirling mists and bubbling sulphur pools.

Archaeologists believe that there were two building periods at Dieng. Candi Arjuna, Semar, Srikandi and Gatokaca all date from between the late 7th century to about 730, while Candi Puntadewa, Sembadra, Bima and Dvaravati were built between 730 and 780. The latter group were more elaborate. Nonetheless, the style of all the Dieng candis is box-like, with height and width of similar proportions, and little ornamentation. Outlined below is a circular route from Dieng village, which takes about 3 hrs to walk. It takes in most of the shrines, a couple of sulphur springs and a sulphur lake.

On arrival from Wonosobo, the major group of shrines can be seen, looking rather small, in the middle of the plateau. From the minibus/taxi stand next to the *Losmen Budjono*, walk along the main road (towards Pekalongan) for 300m. There is a small track on the right that leads up to **Candi Dvaravati** which dates from the middle of the 8th century. Returning to the main road, and walking

100m back towards the bus stop, is a road on the right leading to the main group of shrines.

Five small shrines remain amidst the foundations of a much larger group of buildings. They lack the ornamentation of candis on the lowlands, but their proportions are pleasing. The first temple to be reached by the footpath is **Candi Arjuna**. This and Candi Semar, which lies opposite, were probably the first temples to be built on Dieng. Arjuna originally housed a linga, which would have been ritually bathed each day. This necessitated the construction of a gutter through the N wall, which ends in an impressive gargoyle in the shape of a makara head. **Candi Semar**, is squat and rectangular in shape, and would originally have housed a statue of Nandi the bull – Siva's vehicle. It and Candi Arjuna were built as a unit, dedicated to the cult of Siva. The roofless **Candi Srikandi** is the squarest and possibly the most beautiful of the candis on Dieng. It retains some fine carving on its exterior walls with Vishnu on the N, Siva on the E and Brahma on the S wall – an unusual placement of these Hindu gods. Dumarçay postulates that at the early date that these shrines were built, the placement conventions evident in later temples were not yet established. **Candi Puntadewa** is the tallest and most elegant in this group, resting on a large plinth, with a stairway leading up to the shrine. It has the characteristic door frame ornamentation of the monster kala vomiting out foliage. **Candi Sembadra** is the smallest shrine here, with narrow niches, and a kala motif above the entrance. Open 0615-1715.

From this group of candis, walk over the grazing land to **Candi Gatukaca**, set apart from the main group. It is believed that the base of this candi was extended in the middle of the 9th century in order to house another shrine. In so doing, the foundations were weakened and its ruin hastened. Close by on the other side of the road is a rather unimpressive museum; more like a storehouse for sculptures of Hindu gods and lingam found on the plateau.

A 1 km walk S along this road leads to **Candi Bima**, built in a very different style, and unique in Java. The tower is a tall pyramid, with small heads in some of the niches on each layer. It shows strong stylistic links with the Orissan temples of E central India. It is thought that the architects must have had a plan of the Indian prototype, which they followed. The scale is very different however, presumably because the builders had no way of knowing the proportions of the original. It has been vandalized with graffiti, but remains one of the most impressive monuments on the plateau, being considerably more elaborate than the others.

From Candi Bima, turn W and after another 1½-2 km the path arrives at **Kawah Sikidang**, bubbling mud pools, sulphurous odours and a scarred landscape. The **thermal springs** here are used to produce power, the geothermal station being just a short distance on from the springs. From Kawah Sikidang, walk back past Candi Bima, and turn left at the 'T' junction, 50m on from the temple. Less than a kilometre along this road is **Telaga Warna**, an emerald green **sulphur lake**. From here there is a path skirting the lake and leading to further sulphur lakes and the **Semar Cave** (ask for *Gua Semar*), among others. Close to Telaga Warna is a terraced flower garden with such temperate plants as pansies, roses, marigolds and hydrangea. The garden is private. On past the mushroom factory, the road leads back to *Losmen Budjono*. Admission to area: 1,050Rp, 550Rp/car. Guide to temples 7,500Rp.

Excursions

Ask a guide to accompany you on a 2-hr walk to the highest village on Java, leaving at 0430, spectacular views. 4,000Rp for guide.

Local information

● Accommodation

If intending to stay overnight on the plateau, be sure to have some warm clothing as it gets very cold. One visitor reported the losmen here have the coldest mandi water in Indonesia.

D-E *Hotel Gunung Mas*, Jl Raya, opp road to main temples, more expensive rooms with attached mandis, there has even been talk of hot water – but otherwise much like the other places.

E *Dieng Plateau Homestay*, perhaps the best of the places here, good source of information, but popular, so rooms not always available; **E** *Losmen Asri*, left from T-junction into the village from Wonosobo; **E** *Losmen Budjono*, Jl Raya, basic facilities but friendly management.

● Places to eat

Losmen Budjono, Jl Raya, at intersection to Wonosobo road, simple Indonesian dishes, friendly atmosphere.

● Tourist offices

Dieng Tourist Information, Jl Raya (nr the bus stop).

● Transport

26 km from Wonosobo.

Road Bus: the bus stop is nr the *Losmen Budjono*. Regular connections with Wonosobo 1 hr, Yogya and Borobudur (3 buses a day). It is also possible to reach Pekalongan, with difficulty, from Dieng – a trip of 105 km and 3-4 hrs.

The Wonosobo-Dieng bus continues on to Batur. From there, there are minibuses to Kalibening, where it is possible to pick up another minibus to Pekalongan.

BANDUNGAN

Bandungan – yet another Javanese hill resort with a selection of wisma, losmen and one good hotel – is situated 1,000m above sea-level on the slopes of Mt Ungaran (which rises to 2,050m). It is the most convenient place to stay when visiting the temples at Gedung Songo (see below) and is a good alternative base.

Excursions

The Hindu temples of **Gedung Songo** are to be found 7 km W of Bandungan, close to the village of Duran. The road to the site passes through an area of highland agriculture, with a great diversity of crops being cultivated – including such strange tropical sights as roses intercropped with cabbages. Set on the S slopes of Mt Ungaran at 1,200 to 1,300m, the temples of Gedung Songo – meaning 'nine buildings' in Javanese – are all Hindu and were probably built between 730 and 780. Although the name of this site may mean 'Nine Buildings', there are in fact just six groups of candi. It seems that the Dutch thought

Gedung Songo

there were nine, and before they had properly surveyed the site had landed it with a name which leads many visitors to wonder what on earth happened to the other three. Stamford Raffles' *History of Java* mentions that locals called the site Candi Banyukuning or Yellow Water, probably a reference to the sulphur-coloured water from the hot springs.

The area has a number of volcanic vents which would have made it a revered site and probably explains the presence of these small candi, scattered over an area of several sq km. At weekends, the

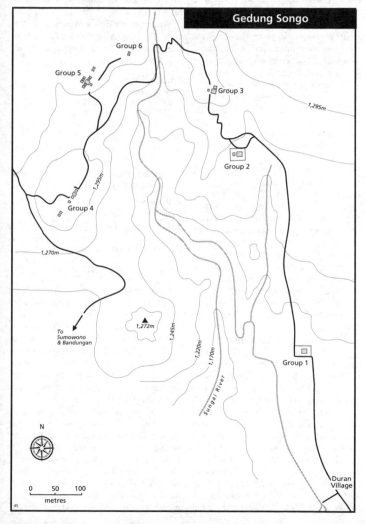

Gedung Songo

Group 6

Group 5

Group 3

1,295m

Group 2

1,295m

Group 4

1,270m

1,272m

1,245m

1,220m

1,170m

Sungai River

Group 1

N

0   50   100
metres

To
Sumowono
& Bandungan

Duran
Village

45

continuing magical and ritual importance of Gedung Songo becomes clear. Javanese come to the site to take the curative waters and to walk from complex to complex, carrying picnics to eat under the shady conifers. In the village of Duran, loudspeakers relay stories of the epics, drawing people under the spell of this magical place. The candis occupy one of the most spectacular positions of any group of temples in Java. The temperature is wonderfully cool after the plains, with mist characteristically hanging over the mountains behind.

The shrines are numbered one to six, starting from the bottom. Temples 1, 2 and 3 lie on the E side of the deep ravine through which runs a fast-flowing stream fed by a hot spring; 4, 5 and 6 lie on the western slopes. The main shrine in each group was dedicated to Siva. These temples became the prototype for subsequent Javanese Hindu temples. The sixth group is an excellent example; a square base is cut through by a stairway leading up to a portico on the W side of the building, which opens into a small square cella. The other three sides of the building are decorated by pilasters and a central niche which housed a statue. Three false storeys rise up above the central cella, decreasing in size and thus giving a deceptive impression of verticality. Group 3, though, is probably in the best state of preservation. The main Siva sanctuary shows the distinctive Javanese orientation of the Hindu gods: Durga, slaying the buffalo demon, on the northern face; elephant-headed Ganesh on the western wall (Ganesh is one of Siva's sons); and Agastya, a Saivite sage, on the southern wall. None of the shrines is particularly elaborate, although some display carvings of kala-makara heads and nagas. Admission 350Rp. Open 0700-1700, Mon-Sun. It is possible to walk around all the temples in 2-3 hrs, but it is exhausting at this altitude. An easier way of getting around is on horseback, 1½ hrs. Expect to pay about 2,500-3,000Rp for these old

animals. *Getting there*: catch a minibus towards Sumowono and get off after 3½ km at the junction where a minor road runs steeply up the mountainside (it is signposted). The entrance is 2½ km up this road and ojeks wait at the bottom. If coming from Ambarawa, catch a minibus to Bandungan or through Bandungan to Sumowono.

Ambarawa Railway Museum is 6 km from Bandungan (see page 249). *Getting there*: catch one of the regular buses or minibuses (200Rp).

Local information
● **Accommodation**

A-B *Rawa Pening I and II*, Jl Pandanaran 33, T (313) 91134, restaurant, good pool, tennis courts, wonderful views, attractive wooden chalets and extensive gardens, friendly, rec.

C *Kusuma Madya*, Jl Jend Sudirman 219, T 91136, a/c, hot water, tennis, average.

E *Wina Prawatya*, off Jl Pandanaran, mostly for families, good value, rec.

● **Transport**

6 km from Ambarawa, 35 km from Semarang.

Road Minibus: regular connections with Ambarawa; from Semarang or Yogya catch a bus or minibus to Ambarawa, then change.

SALATIGA

Salatiga is a relatively small town by Indonesian standards with a population of about 80,000. It is situated halfway between Semarang and Solo in the foothills of Mt Merabu, 600m above sea level. For a taste of unspoilt Java, this is an excellent place to visit. The locals are enormously friendly and welcoming and the numerous **churches** and **mosques** in town make wandering the streets a rewarding experience. A large **market** stretching along Jl Jend Sudirman sells goods from good quality T-shirts to foodstuffs – although recent visitors have warned to be wary of pickpockets. Salatiga supports a **university** – the Satya Wacana Christian University (SWCU) – with its campus situated on Jl Diponegoro. The SWCU runs a 1 month intensive Indonesian language and culture course which is very popular with Australians. Its hostel, or Asrama, on Jl Kartini is an excellent gathering place to meet people and make friends.

Best time to visit: the Jul-Aug dry season is the best time – climatically – to visit. However this is also the period when the Satya Wacana Christian University holds its 1 month intensive Indonesian language and culture course and 100-120 visitors (most from Australia) book up the town's hotels.

Local information
● **Accommodation**

B-C *Hotel Beringin*, Jl Jend Sudirman 160 (in the heart of town), T 81129/61082, a/c, restaurant, TV and shower, breakfast incl in rate, large and very clean rooms, staff are helpful and friendly and some English is spoken at the front desk.

C *Hotel Maya*, Jl Kartini 15A (10 mins from town centre), T 23179/23429, restaurant, price incl breakfast, no baths or mosquito nets, but clean and staff are very helpful, very little English spoken though.

● **Places to eat**

There are numerous Chinese and Indonesian rumah makan and warung in town.

◆-◆◆*Cafe Maya*, at the *Maya Hotel*, Jl Kartini 15A, a good selection of Salatigan food, particularly good bakmi and nasi goreng, fresh juices and Bintang available; ◆-◆◆*Pak Por*, Jl Kartini (nr *Cafe Maya*), specializes in chicken dishes from excellent ayam bakar (burnt chicken) to ayam goreng (fried chicken).

◆◆*Kentucky Fried Chicken*, Jl Diponegoro.

● **Banks & money changers**

Panin Bank, Jl Diponegoro (opp the Satya Wacana Christian University [SWCU] campus. The bank accepts Thomas Cook TCs in US and Australian dollars.

● **Post & telecommunications**

Area code: 0298.

Telephone: Wartel, Jl Diponegoro (next to the university campus) and *Hotel Beringin* both offer international calls.

● **Transport**

41 km N of Solo, 46 km S of Semarang.

Local: dokars charge about 2,000Rp for a 5-min ride. Angkutans, which run along fixed routes (destination displayed on the roof) can be flagged down. Taxis and minibuses can be booked at the front desks of the two hotels listed above.

Long distance: Bus – regular connection with Semarang and Solo. Taxi – 30,000Rp to/from Semarang.

CENTRAL JAVA'S NORTH COAST

TEGAL

Tegal is a N coast town with a history that belies its small size. Manageable, with good and reasonable accommodation and a breezy, coastal air, it is an attractive alternative stopping-off point on the N coast route.

Though Pekalongan may be best known for its distinctive batik, it is also remembered as the site of two days of riots in Nov 1995 after a mentally unstable Indonesian extraction tore pages from the Koran. He was savagely beaten for the offence against Islam – and later died – and the rioting crowd turned its attention to the homes and businesses of ethnic Chinese more widely.

'Sights', at least in the formalized sense of the word, are pretty thin on the ground in Tegal. The **Mesjid Agung Tegal** on Jl Jend A Yani exhibits classic

Tegal

Javanese lines. More interesting for many though is likely to be the **Pelabuhan Tegal** – Tegal Harbour at the end of Jl Veteran where traditional perahu moor to load and unload their cargoes of dry goods.

Local information

● **Accommodation**

A *Bahari Inn*, Jl Kolonel Soegiono 172, T 52222, F 58909, a/c, restaurant, pool, a new hotel 3 km W of the town centre with 80 modern and comfortable rooms, an excellent pool and geared mainly to the convention market, usually empty.

D-E *Hotel Semeru*, Jl Jend A Yani 168, T 61226, simple hotel in the centre of town, some attached bathrooms, no hot water, basic.

● **Banks & money changers**

Bank Bumi Daya, intersection of Jl Jend Sutoyo and Jl Diponegoro.

● **Post & telecommunications**
Area code: 0283.

Post Office: Jl Pemuda (nr the port).

● **Transport**
52 km from Cirebon, 57 km from Pekalongan.

Road Bus: regular connections with Cirebon and Bandung to the W, and with Surbaya via Pekalongan and Semarang to the E.

PEKALONGAN

Pekalongan is best known for the distinctive **batik** that is produced here and is known by the sobriquet 'Kota Batik'. Pastel shades, fine designs, and floral and animal motifs are all characteristic of the area's work (see page 102). There is a **Batik Museum** at Jl Majapahit 10 with a small display of characteristic designs from various areas of Java, along with a few tools. The museum is on the outskirts of town to the SW of the centre, tucked away along with government offices and not far from the Balai Kota. Get there by becak and ask for *museum batik* near the *Balai Kota*. If the building is closed, ask the caretaker to unlock it. Open (in theory) 0900-1400, Mon-Sat. Most of the best batik produced in Pekalongan and hereabouts is sold to outlets in Jakarta and elsewhere. There is surprisingly little good quality cloth

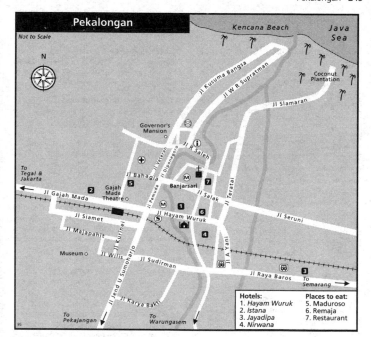

Pekalongan

Not to Scale

Kencana Beach

Java Sea

Hotels:
1. Hayam Wuruk
2. Istana
3. Jayadipa
4. Nirwana

Places to eat:
5. Maduroso
6. Remaja
7. Restaurant

available. The **Banjarsari market** on Jl Sultan Agung for example sells mostly low quality stuff, but is worth exploring. The smaller boutiques do have better cloth, and it can also be bought from the batik-making villages around town (see Excursions). Indeed, there is little reason to come to Pekalongan except to see, and perhaps to buy, batik – although the town does make a good stopping-off point on the N coast route.

The **town square** is off the main road, a short distance along Jl HM Wahid Hasim. The local mosque – a strange amalgam of lighthouse (the minaret), castle (the crenellated gateway) and Javanese (the tiered roof) – is situated on the W side of the square. There are also some **notable buildings** on the large roundabout to the N of town. The residence of the former Dutch resident of Pekalongan at Jl Diponegoro 1 is now the governor's

office. The Post Office also on Jl Diponegoro and close by is housed in another impressive colonial structure. Pekalongan is also said to have the biggest **fish auction** in Java. Few tourists venture here, but because it is on the main N route between Surabaya and Jakarta, it has a good selection of losmen and restaurants.

North of town is **Pekalongan Port** and **Pasir Kencana**. The latter is marketed as a coastal resort, but the water here is usually too dirty to swim without fear of infection.

Excursions

Kedungwuni, a town 9 km to the S of town, is a centre of *batik* production and sale where the production process can be observed. *Getting there*: regular colts from town. Another batik village, less well-known and rather harder to get to is **Pekajangan**, 7 km S of town and off the road to Kedungwuni. Again, all the processes of batik making can be observed and fine cloth purchased. *Getting there*: no bemos run to Pekajangan, but it can be reached by a long (and expensive) becak ride or by walking from the road.

Local information
● Accommodation
B-C *Istana*, Jl Gajah Mada 23-25, T 61581, F 21252, some a/c, popular with Indonesian business travellers but inconvenient location 2 km W of town centre, characterless modern hotel with hot water and attached bathrooms, little to rec it other than providing a clean room and bed; **B-C** *Nirwana*, Jl Dr Wahidin 11 (E side of town), T 41691, F 61841, some a/c, restaurant, large pool, most luxurious place in town looking rather like a 1970s-style hotel, rooms are a little worn but very good for a small place like Pekalongan, professionally run, price incl breakfast, rec; **B-D** *Jayadipa Hotel*, Jl Raya Boros 29, T/F 24938, some a/c, new hotel with inconvenient location out of town towards Semarang, clean rooms, Indonesian motel in style.

C-D *Hayam Wuruk*, Jl Hayam Wuruk 152-154, T 41823, some a/c, clean rooms with cool tiled floors and heavy furniture, the best rooms are outside rather than in the main block, central location, good value, no hot water but well-run, rec.

D *Losmen Sari Dewi*, Jl Hayam Wuruk 1, some a/c, friendly, rec.

E *Asia Losmen*, Jl KH Wahid Hasyim 49, T 41125; **E** *Gajah Mada*, Jl Gajah Mada 11A, T 41185, a small homestay on the W side of town some distance from the centre, basic, some rooms rather grubby; **E** *Losmen Cempaka*, Jl Cempaka 53 (20m off the main road, E of the bridge), T 21555, nothing special; **E** *Pekalongan*, Jl Hayam Wuruk 158, T 21021, old building with some character next to the *Hayam Wuruk Hotel*, reasonable rooms.

F *Losmen Kota Batik*, Jl Hayam Wuruk 1/4 (by the Danamon Bank), T 21521, dark and dirty, best to avoid unless there is absolutely no alternative.

● Places to eat
♦♦*Maduroso*, Jl Merdeka, Indonesian; *Purimas Bakery*, intersection of Jl Hayam Wuruk and Jl KH Wahid Hasim; *Remaja*, Jl Dr Cipto 17, serves Indonesian, International and Chinese (Chinese food rec).

● Banks & money changers
Bank Central Asia, Jl Diponegoro; Bank Danamon, Jl Hayam Wuruk; **Exspor Inspor Indonesia**, Jl Hayam Wuruk 5; **Lippo Bank**, Jl Hayam Wuruk.

● Entertainment
Cinemas: *Gajah Mada Theatre*, Jl Gajah Mada, a/c cinema showing films with English language soundtracks in centre of town.

● Post & telecommunications
Area code: 0285.

General Post Office: Jl Cendrawasih 1.

● Shopping
Batik: Pekalongan is famous as a centre of batik production and sale. The style is very different from that of Solo and Yogya; designs are fine, with intricate representations of flowers and birds. Colours tend to be softer, using pastel shades. There are many shops along the main road, Jl Hayam Wuruk such as *Batik Puspa*, *Queen Batik* and *Batik Aneka*. **BL Batik** at Jl KHM Mansyer 87 sells good quality made-up garments and lengths of cloth. *Jacky Batik*, Jl Surabaya 5A/1, is also a shop selling mostly high quality made up garments and is rather expensive. For cheap, low quality batik the best place to look around is the Pasar Banjarsari on Jl Sultan Agung in the centre of town. Salesmen also hawk batik direct to hotel residents: again, most of the batik is poor, low quality cloth. To see the various stages of the batik-making process, it is best to visit one of the batik villages outside town (see Excursions).

Shopping centres: Pasar Raya Sri Ratu, Jl Gajah Mada.

● Sports
Swimming: non-residents can swim at the *Nirwana Hotel*, Jl Dr Wahidin 11.

● Tour companies & travel agents
Amatama, Jl Mansyer 25, T 81121.

● Tourist offices
Dinas Pariwisata, Jl KH Wahid Hasyim 1. Open 0700-1330, Mon-Sat.

● Transport
384 km from Jakarta, 101 km from Semarang and 409 km from Surabaya.

Local Orange bemos (Angkutan kotas) are the main form of local transport (fixed fare 300Rp). Plethora of becaks.

Train The train station is just to the W of the centre of town at Jl Gajah Mada 10. Regular connections with Jakarta and Surabaya on slow daytime trains.

Road Bus: the intercity bus terminal is 2 km to the SE of the town centre, nr the intersection of Jl Dr Wahidin and Jl Dr Sutomo. Bemos constantly link the terminal with the town centre (300Rp). Connections with Semarang 2 hrs, Bandung, Cirebon 4 hrs, Solo, Dieng, Kudus, Demak, Sumedang, Tasik Malaya, Jakarta and other major centres.

SEMARANG

Semarang is one of the oldest cities in Indonesia, and was the seat of the Dutch Governor of the N-E Provinces. It is situated between the shore and a small ridge of mountains and consequently is very hot. The city was ceded to the Dutch VOC in 1677 by the Mataram king Amangkurat I, in lieu of debts. A base was established along the coast at Jepara (which was already a trading centre), with additional trading-posts at Semarang as well as at Surabaya, Rembang, Demak and Tegal. However, it was not until 1705 that the VOC finally brought Semarang firmly under its control. Only then did the Dutch move their headquarters here, and the town gradually grew in commercial influence.

Semarang's usefulness as a port waned with the gradual silting up of the harbour, and by the 19th century the city had been eclipsed as Java's premier port by Surabaya. Even so, Semarang remains the largest city in Central Java. It is an important commercial centre with a population of over a million, a third of whom are thought to be of Chinese extraction. In 1741, the Chinese of Semarang responded to the murder of their kinsmen in Batavia (see page 108) by, in their turn, attacking the Dutch of Semarang. This turned out to be a misjudgement. The VOC, with the help of Cakraningrat IV of Madura, defeated the Chinese and slaughtered all those they could lay their hands on.

Semarang is divided into two parts: the coastal lowland where most of businesses and industrial activities are to be found; and an inland, hilly, residential area.

Places of interest

Even though Semarang seems to be taking the shopping plaza route to urban development, Islamic, Chinese and European influences are still in evidence and there are numerous **beautiful buildings** dotted among the streets. Indeed, in parts at least, it is one of Java's most attractive cities. The best area to explore is N and E from the Post Office on Jl Pemuda (itself a notable building). Roads with interesting buildings include Jl Jend Suprapto, Jl Kepodang, Jl Garuda, Jl Suari and Jl Merak, and the maze of streets cutting across and between these roads. **Gereja Blenduk** (*gereja* meaning church, *blenduk* meaning dome) – the Immanuel Protestant Church – on Jl Jend Suprapto 32 is the oldest church in Central Java, and the second oldest on the whole island. Built in 1753, and rather Wren-like in appearance, it is in the shape of a Greek cross fronted by four pillars. It has a handsome classical portico, a faded copper dome and inside a Baroque organ and pulpit. Opposite is a fine 1920s-style commercial building, the offices of Jiwasraya Assurance. Unfortunately, many of the buildings in this area have been abandoned, and most are in a state of deterioration. Before long, they may disappear entirely. For architectural enthusiasts, other buildings of interest are to be found in the hills to the S, an area known as **Candi**, where there are some wonderful decaying villas.

Kelenteng Sam Poo Kong Temple (also known as **Gedung Batu**), dating from 1772, is one of the oldest Chinese temples in Java. It contains some good woodcarving and many ritual objects and brassware. *Getting there*: take a minibus to Banjir Kanal (300Rp) and then a becak to the temple (1,000Rp).

Simpang Lima (junction of five roads) is the huge main square in the centre of town. On the NW side of the square is the modern **Mesjid Baiturahan**. On most other corners seem to be the greatest concentration of shopping plazas in central Java (see Shopping, below).

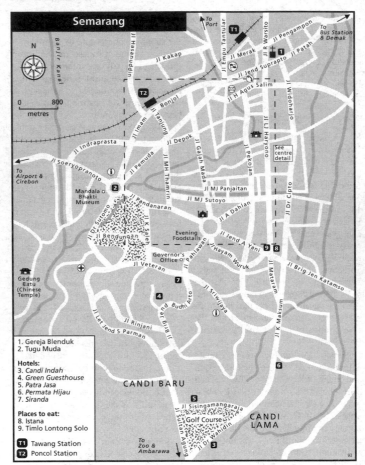

Semarang

To Port

To Bus Station & Demak

Jl Empu Tantular
Jl R Warsito
Jl Pengampon
Jl Patah

Jl Kakap
Jl Merak
Jl Jend Suprapto

Banjir Kanal

N

0   800
metres

Jl Hasanudin
Jl Imam Bonjol
Jl H Agus Salim
Jl Widoharjo

Jl Indraprasta

Jl Soeryopranoto

To Airport & Cirebon

Jl Tanjung
Jl Depok
Jl Gajah Mada
Jl Pekojan
Jl Harjono

Jl Pemuda
Jl MH Thamrin

Mandala Bhakti Museum

Jl Pandanaran

Jl Dr Cipto

Jl K Saleh
Jl MJ Panjaitan
Jl MJ Sutoyo
Jl A Dahlan

Jl Bendungan

Jl Dr Sutomo

Evening Foodstalls
Jl Jend A Yani
Jl Mataram

Governor's Office
Jl Ahlawan
Jl Hayam Wuruk

Gedung Batu (Chinese Temple)

Jl Veteran
Jl Sriwijaya
Jl Brig Jen Katamso

Jl Let Jend S Parman
Jl Rinjani
Jl Budhi Arto
Jl Brig Jend

Jl K Maktum

CANDI BARU

CANDI LAMA

Jl Sisingamangaraja
Golf Course

To Zoo & Ambarawa

Jl Sultan Agung
Jl Dr Wahidin

1. Gereja Blenduk
2. Tugu Muda

Hotels:
3. Candi Indah
4. Green Guesthouse
5. Patra Jasa
6. Permata Hijau
7. Siranda

Places to eat:
8. Istana
9. Timlo Lontong Solo

T1 Tawang Station
T2 Poncol Station

The **Tugu Muda** monument marks the centre of another square, about 1½ km NW from Simpang Lima. The monument commemorates the 5-day battle of Indonesian republican youth against Japanese troops at the end of the war. The square is surrounded by grand government buildings built by the Dutch (they planned more), the largest being the **Lawang Sewu** – the building of a thousand doors. Another Dutch era building contains the unremarkable **Mandala**

Bhakti Museum on Jl Sugiyopranoto. This used to be the Raad Van Yustitue but now recounts an episode in Indonesia's struggle for independence with a motley collection of photographs, weapons and other memorabilia. Open 0800-1400 Tues-Thur, 0800-1130 Fri, 0800-1230 Sat, 0800-1300 Sun.

Chinatown, S of Jl H Agus Salim, off Jl Pekojan, also contains some interesting buildings, notably those bordering the canal. There are a number of Chinese temples tucked away here, including the Confucian **Thay Kak Sie Pagoda**, along Gang Lombok. The main temple was built in 1772. Not far away and also on Jl H Agus Salim, opposite the *Metro Grand Park Hotel*, is the **Pasar Johar**, a good place to wander during the day and in the evening. The **zoo** (with botanical garden and recreation park) can be found S of town in Tinjomoyo, off Jl Teuku Umar. *Getting there*: charter a colt (3,000-5,000Rp) or take town bus (Bus Damri) No 04 (300Rp).

Excursions

Demak is an historic town on the road to Kudus and Surabaya, 25 km from Semarang. Raden Patah established the Sultanate of Demak in 1500, when it became the first Islamic Kingdom on Java. Islam was introduced via India by Muslim traders and Demak, as one of Java's most important ports, was rapidly converted to the new religion. The town gained a reputation for the community of scholars or *pesantren* who established themselves here, and pilgrims would travel from all over Java and beyond to be taught by these holy men. Demak remained powerful until the end of the 16th century when power shifted S to Mataram, near Yogyakarta. The oldest mosque in Central Java can be found in the town square, on the Semarang side of the centre. Founded by the nine *walis* (the first Muslim evangelists in Java, see page 95) in 1478, the **Agung Demak Mosque** has the characteristic 3-tiered roof of N Java. The *Babad Tanah Jawi*, a Javanese chronicle, records that the mosque was built by craftsmen from Majapahit, a Hindu Kingdom conquered by Demak in the 15th century. Certainly there appear to be some stylistic parallels between Majapahit and the mosque at Demak, but historians are loathe to hold too much store by the *Babad Tanah Jawi*. In the N part of the mosque is a graveyard of the family of Sultan Demak and the **tomb** of one of the nine walis is to be found here: Sunan Kalijaga. The minaret looks uncannily like a WW2 air raid tower, but does in fact echo earlier Hindu, Majapahit architectural styles. The mosque is an important pilgrimage spot and souvenir stalls line the outside walls, where posters of the nine walis can be bought. The main street leading from the square N towards Kudus, **Jalan Sultan Patah**, is lined by houses with graceful, sweeping tiled roofs. These are the distinctive, traditional houses of the Kudus area – *rumah adat Kudus*. The **market** is also on this street marked by the presence of an over-sized starfruit. *Getting there*: by bus from Semarang's Terboyo station on Jl Patah (get there by town bus – Bus Damri – or bemo); the Demak station is on the Semarang side of town, a walk of less than half a kilometre to the main square.

Kudus, 19 km on from Demak and 50 km in total from Semarang, is another historically interesting town – (see page 254). Another 30 km NW from Kudus is the **woodcarving port of Jepara** (see page 256) where it is possible to catch boats to the **Karimunjawa Islands** (see page 258).

Grobogan is an **active mud volcano** which lies about 85 km E of Semarang and 15 km E of Purwodadi. It makes rather a long detour from Semarang but is of interest to budding volcanologists and has a certain novelty value. Visitors can walk across spongy dried earth to within about 10m of the bubbling mud. Admission 150Rp. Open Mon-Sun. *Getting there*: catch a bus from the Terboyo terminal travelling E through Purwodadi towards Blora and Surabaya and get off at the crossroads in the village of Wirasari. From there catch a minibus going S (right), or take an ojek. The volcano lies 6 km along this road – ask for *berapi lumpur*.

Ambarawa town and its **Railway Museum** (*kereta api*) are 32 km from Semarang and 4 km off the main Semarang-Solo road. The Railway Museum is through the town, past the road to Bandungan, and about 1 km off Jl Pemuda. It is a charming, well kept museum set around the old railway

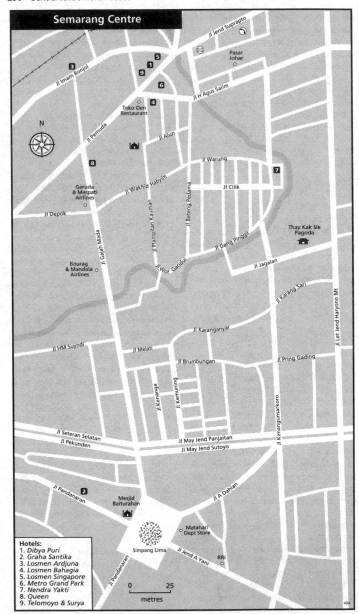

Semarang Centre

Hotels:
1. *Dibya Puri*
2. *Graha Santika*
3. *Losmen Ardjuna*
4. *Losmen Bahagia*
5. *Losmen Singapore*
6. *Metro Grand Park*
7. *Nendra Yakti*
8. *Queen*
9. *Telomoyo & Surya*

station and has a large collection of loco-motives, the oldest dating from 1891. It is possible to charter the single working cog locomotive and ride into the mountains to Bedono, 18 km away. The train seats 90 people and lunch is provided on the day-long outing. One day's notice required (write to: PJKA Wilayah Usaha Jawa, Jl MH Thamrin 3, Semarang, Jawa Tengah, Indonesia or contact one of the main railway stations). Admission 300Rp. Open 0700-1630 Mon-Sun. *Getting there*: 'medium' sized buses travel to the town, or catch a Semarang/Yogya bus, which pass through Ambarawa (45 mins from Semarang). Both leave from the Terboyo terminal. It is a 1½ km walk from the centre of town to the museum. The road from Semarang to Ambarawa is notable for a row of trees just outside Semarang which is home to thousands of white ibis.

The Hindu temples of **Gedung Songo** (see page 240) lie 13 km from Ambarawa, past the hill resort of **Bandungan**. *Getting there*: by bus from Semarang to Ambarawa, 45 mins (500Rp) and then one of the regular minibuses that climb up to Bandungan (200Rp).

Tours

Tour companies in Semarang run day tours around the sights of the city, as well as to Borobudur, the Dieng Plateau, Kudus and Demak, Gedung Songo, Solo, and cultural tours to, for example, Jepara (a woodcarving town). 'Teak plantation tours' to Cepu, 160 km E of Semarang: travelling in a steam locomotive, the tourist visits teak plantations in different stages of development. Contact Perum Perhutani, Jl Pehlawan 151, Semarang, T 311611.

Festivals

Feb: *Dugderan Festival*, marks the start of the month-long Muslim fast, held in front of Grand Mosque.

Jul: *Jarcn Sam Po*, Chinese ceremony, procession to Thay Kak Sie Pagoda.

Aug: *Semarang Fair*, month-long festivities every evening.

Oct: *Pertempuran Lima Hari* (14th), held around the Tugu Muda to commemorate the 5 day battle of Indonesian youth against the Japanese in 1945.

Local information
● Accommodation

A+ *Graha Santika*, Jl Pandanaran 116-120, T 413115, F 413113, a/c, restaurant, pool, new multi-storey hotel with central location overlooking Simpang Lima, facilities incl a fitness centre, the most convenient, efficient and well-run place to stay if money and character are no object; **A+** *Patrajasa*, Jl Sisingamangaraja, PO Box 8, T 314441, F 314448, a/c, restaurant, pool, good views, good facilities, sophisticated, if now rather dated, not very convenient for city centre, odd nagas flank the main entrance looking rather like Basil Brush.

A-B *Siranda*, Jl Diponegoro 1, T/F 313271, a/c, early 70s-style hotel built on the hill overlooking Semarang with 60 time-warp rm, but well maintained considering its age and the rooms have good views (as the blurb puts it 'the hotel with view') and are reasonable value, price incl breakfast; **A-C** *Metro Grand Park*, Jl H Agus Salim 2-4, T 547371, a/c, restaurant, a square, brown lump of a hotel with no redeeming architectural features, and now, to add insult to injury, rather down-at-heel.

B *Permata Hijau*, Jl Dr Wahidin 14-66, T 315671, a/c, new development in Candi Baru, rather like a housing estate, rooms are large and cool, geared mainly to people with own transport, offering discounts to entice custom, very comfortable; **B-C** *Dibya Puri*, Jl Pemuda 11, T 547821, F 544934, a/c, colonial hotel which has seen better days, rather scruffy, with odd mixture of modern and old, but central location and competitive rates, the best rooms are those at the back around a leafy courtyard with small sitting areas, price incl breakfast; **B-C** *Green Guesthouse*, Jl Kesambi 7, Candi Baru, T 312642, some a/c, attractive old-style hotel with large rooms (check the a/c though) and fine views looking S from Semarang, especially from the main terrace, efficiently run, out of town along quiet residential street in Candi Baru, price incl breakfast, rec; **B-D** *Candi Baru*, Jl Rinjani 21, T 315272, a/c, old hotel with character; **B-D** *Telomoyo*, Jl Gajah Mada 138, T 545436, F 547037, some a/c, modern, clean and comfortable, rooms are large and airy, tree-filled courtyard, friendly efficient service.

C *Bali Hotel*, Jl Imam Bonjol 146, T 511761,

some a/c, not a very convenient location, rooms are clean, no hot water, but acceptable for a night or two, Balinese split gates frame the entrance way and a leafy courtyard helps to add some character; **C** *Bukit Asri*, Jl Setiabudi 5, T 475743, a/c, 4 km from town on road to Ambarawa, clean rooms; **C** *Hotel Candi Indah*, Jl Dr Wahidin 112, T 312912, F 312515, some a/c, old house on a hill in Candi Baru, rooms are a little dark but the hotel is well run and maintained, located several kilometres from city centre; **C** *Nendra Yakti*, Jl Pekojan, Gang Pinggir 68, T 544202, F 550593, some a/c, central location in Chinatown, rooms are comparatively airy and also clean, good value although the block seems to have been designed by a prison architect; **C** *Surya Hotel*, Jl Imam Bonjol 28, T 544250, some a/c, small modern hotel, rooms have attached showers with no hot water or loo seats, a little dark but well maintained and the a/c rooms are a bargain; **C-D** *Queen*, Jl Gajah Mada 44-52, T 547063, a/c, large rooms, hot water, clean.

E *Losmen Ardjuna*, Jl Imam Bonjol 51, old style house, rooms are noisy at the front, clean enough and popular with locals, attached mandis, convenient location for train station, good value and atmospheric; **E** *Losmen Singapore*, Jl Imam Bonjol 12, T 543757, rooms set attractively around a courtyard, atmospheric, unfortunately the rooms themselves are rather grubby, shared bathroom; **E** *Losmen Tanjung*, Jl Tanjung 9-11, old Dutch era house, friendly management.

F *Losmen Bahagia*, Jl Pemuda 16-18, shared bathrooms, scruffy, small losmen in centre of town used largely by Indonesian travelling salesmen, cheap.

● **Places to eat**

Semarang has, seemingly, more restaurants per sq inch than any other town in Java. Jl Gajah Mada and Jl HM Thamrin, which run parallel to one another N-S, have restaurants serving virtually every variety of Asian food (particularly Chinese). In the evenings, the best place to eat is at one of the many **foodstalls** which set up along the S end of Jl Gajah Mada and the N end of Jl Pahlawan, both leading into the large square (Simpang Lima) dominated by the massive Matahari shopping complex. These roadside restaurants, protected by awnings, specialize in particular types of cuisine and food: seafood, Javanese food, Minang food, saté and so on. The awnings are clearly labelled with the specialities of the house and the food is usually cheap, fresh and excellent. Another possibility is to try the *Pasar Johor Yaik* opp the *Metro Hotel* at the NE end of Jl Pemuda, where excellent foodstall food is also available. The Semarang speciality is *bandeng* – a smoked fish.

Indonesian: ♦♦♦*Rumah Makan Gajah Mada*, Jl Gajah Mada (nr intersection with Jl Wahid Hasyim), excellent Chinese food in a/c splendour; ♦♦*Tan Goei*, Jl Tanjung 25, also serves Chinese food and icecreams, popular; ♦♦*Toko Oen*, Jl Pemuda 52 (N from intersection with Jl Gajah Mada), reasonable Indonesian food, good variety of ice-creams, some European food, all served in moth eaten colonial splendour with a menu which incl fried frogs, lamb chops, tournedos grillé and rather dry Dutch pastries (the best of the latter are those filled with nut paste); ♦*Nglaras Roso*, Jl Haryono 701, rec; ♦*Timlo Lontong Solo*, Jl Jend A Yani 182, Javanese.

Other Asian cuisine: ♦♦♦♦*Miyako*, Jl Semeru VI/16, T 475805, claimed by locals to be the best Japanese restaurant in Semarang, Sabu-Sab is especially rec; ♦♦♦*Istana*, Jl Haryono 836, Chinese and International food; ♦♦*Pringgading*, Jl Pringgading 54 off Jl LJ Haryono, excellent Chinese seafood; *Seoul Palace*, Jl Gajah Mada 99B, Korean.

International: ♦♦*Sukarasa*, Jl Ungaran, French food.

Fastfood: *McDonald's* in *Robinson's* on Simpang Raya.

Foodstalls: ♦♦*Simpang Raya*, Jl Imam Bonjol 40, reasonable Padang food; *Pasar Johar*, Jl HA Salim.

Bakeries: *Danish Bakery*, Jl Pandanaran; *Wijaya Bakery*, Jl Pemuda 38.

● **Bars**

Karaoke: Jl KH Wahid Hasyim 121.

● **Airline offices**

Bouraq, Jl Gajah Mada 16C, T 515921; **Garuda/Merpati**, Jl Gajah Mada 11, T 20178; **Mandala**, Jl Gajah Mada 16C, T 543021, F 543021; **Sempati**, *Graha Santika Hotel*, Jl Pandanaran, T 414086.

● **Banks & money changers**

Bank Central Asia, Jl Pemuda; **BNI** Jl LMT Haryono 16; **Bumi Daya**, Jl Kepodeng 34; **Ekspor Impor**, Jl M Tantular 19; **Supit Money Changer**, Jl Pemuda.

● **Entertainment**

Cinemas: *Gajah Mada*, Simpang Lima; *Manggala*, Jl Gajah Mada 119; *Studio 21*, *Citra Land Shopping Centre*, Simpang Lima.

Disco: *Xanadu*, *Metro Hotel*, Jl HA Salim.

Ketoprak & wayang orang: the Ngesti Pandowo, Jl Pemuda 116, Mon and Thur 2015.

Wayang kulit: the RRI (Radio station) on Jl Jend A Yani organize performances on the first Sat of every month.

● **Hospitals & medical services**
Hospitals: *William Booth*, Jl Letjen S Parman 5.

● **Post & telecommunications**
Area code: 024.

General Post Office: Jl Pemuda 4.

Telecommunication office: Jl Jend Suprapto 7 for fax and telephone services.

● **Shopping**
Batik: *Batik Keris*, *Gajah Mada Plaza*; *Batik Pekalongan*, Jl Pemuda 66; *GKBI*, Jl Pemuda 48; *Kerta Niaga*, Jl Stadion 1A and Jl Gajah Mada.

Handicrafts: *Toko Panjang*, Jl Widoharjo 31; *Wijaya*, Jl Gajah Mada 2.

Night market: *Pasar Johar*, Jl A Salim, good place to wander, vast range of goods on sale.

Shopping plazas: there are a number of shopping plazas and department stores around the Simpang Lima where Jl Gajah Mada, Jl H Dahlan, Jl Jend A Yani, Jl Pahlawan and Jl Pandanaran all meet: *Citra Land*, *Matahari*, *Robinson's* and *Simpang Lima*, for example. *Semarang Plaza*, Jl H Agus Salim (E of the market).

Woodcarving: *Kerta Niaga*, see above.

● **Sports**
Bowling: 10-pin bowling at the *Patrajasa Hotel*, Jl Sisingamangaraja.

Golf: *Semarang Golf Club*, Jl Sisingamangaraja 14, T 312582, close to the *Patrajasa Hotel*, 9-holes, green fees 8,500Rp Mon-Sat, 12,000Rp Sun.

Swimming: *Patrajasa Hotel* has a pool open to the public.

● **Tour companies & travel agents**
Chiara, Jl Seroja Selatan; *Electra Duta Wisata*, Jl Gajah Mada 1, T 288444; *Media Tour*, Jl Pandanaran 116-120 (*Hotel Graha Santika*), T 411729, F 415176; *Nitour*, Jl Indraprasta 97; *Nusantara*, Simpang Lima Shopping Centre, Blok C6; *Satura*, Simpang Lima Shopping Centre, Blok I, II, III; *Tedjo Express*, Jl Haryono 786.

● **Tourist offices**
Central Java Tourist Office (Dinas Pariwisata), Jl Imam Bonjol 209, T 510924. Contained in a grand old building on the square with Tugu Muda. Very

helpful staff. Open 0700-1400 Mon-Thur, 0700-1100 Fri, 0700-1230 Sat. **Semarang Municipal Tourist Office** (Dinas Pariwisata Kodia Semarang), Jl Srivijaya 29, T 311220 (at the old site of the zoo; colts drive down Jl Srivijaya).

● **Transport**
120 km N of Yogya, 485 km E of Jakarta, 308 km W of Surabaya.

Local Bus: fixed price city buses (300Rp). **Colts & becaks**: ply the streets, although becaks are outlawed on the main streets. **Taxi**: metered taxis, or rent them by the hour or the day.

Air Ahmad Yani airport is 5 km W of town off Jl Siliwangi. *Transport to town*: taxis charge 6,000Rp to town. No 2 town bus goes from Jl Pemuda as far as the roundabout (as too do bemos running along the Rejomulyo – Mangkang route), but it is a 1 km walk down Jl Kalibanteng to the airport itself. Take a becak from here or, easier still, a taxi from town. Regular connections on Garuda/Merpati, Sempati, Mandala and Bouraq with other destinations in Java, Sumatra, Kalimantan, Sulawesi, Bali, Lombok, Nusa Tenggara, Maluku and Irian Jaya (see page 912 for route map).

Train There are 2 train stations; Poncol is on Jl Imam Bonjol but is only for freight and some short trip passenger trains; passenger trains run from Tawang station on Jl Merak. Regular connections with Jakarta on the Mutiara Utara night express 7 hrs which continues on to Surabaya 8-10 hrs. The Senja Utama from Jakarta is non a/c night train 8-10 hrs, connections with Pekalongan 4 hrs (see page 917 for timetable).

Road Bus: Terminal Terboyo is on the E side of town, about 3½ km from the city centre, 200m N of the road towards Demak. Town buses travelling along Jl Pemuda travel out to the terminal as too do bemos. To buy tickets for onward journeys, plenty of bus companies have their offices here although a/c bis malam (night bus) and VIP bus companies are concentrated along Jl Haryono. There is a taxi rank for journeys into town. Regular connections with Kudus 1 hr, Yogya 3½ hrs, Solo 2½ hrs, Wonosobo 4 hrs, Surabaya 9 hrs, Cirebon 6 hrs, Pekalongan 3 hrs and Jakarta 9 hrs. **Minibus**: minibuses leave from the corner of Jl HA Salim and Jl MT Haryono with offices strung out S from this intersection. Regular connections with Solo, Yogya, Cirebon and Jakarta. **Sea Boat**: the Pelni ships *Kelimutu*, *Lawait*, *Leuser* and *Bukitraya* dock here, en route for Kalimantan, Sulawesi and Sumatra. See schedules on page 921.

KUDUS

Founded by the Muslim saint Sunan Kudus, Ja'far Shodik, Kudus developed as an important Islamic holy city and is still a pilgrimage centre today. Sunan Kudus is reputed to have been the fifth *imam* of the mosque at Demak – at that time the most powerful of the N coast *pasisir* states. The name Kudus is taken from the Arabic *al-Quds*, which means 'holy' or 'Jerusalem', and it is the only town in Java which has retained an Arabic name. Kudus and the surrounding countryside is still one of the most orthodox Muslim areas on Java. It is also relatively prosperous, enjoying the fruits of being a major kretek-producing town (see box).

Places of interest

Less than 1 km off the main road into town from Semarang is a **kretek museum** on Jl Jetas Pejaten – only Indonesia could have a museum in praise of the cigarette. Models, machinery, dioramas, photo portraits and a collection of kretek packets make up the display. In front of the museum, there is a statue of a family group with the man smoking an enormous kretek while remaining protective towards his wife and children. A traditional Kudus house (*rumah adat Kudus*) stands next to the museum (see below). Admission by donation. Open 0900-1400, Mon-Thur, 0900-1300 Sat, 0800-1400 Sun.

Down an alleyway off Jl Sunan Kudus, the main road to Jepara, is the **Al-Manar** or **Al-Aqsa Mosque** (on Jl Menara). Built in 1549 by Sunan Kudus (the year AH [Anno Hijrae, the Islamic era] 956, equivalent to AD 1549 is inscribed over the *mihrab* which indicates the direction of Mecca) on the site of a Hindu-Javanese temple, its name is the same as the mosque at Jerusalem. It is an important place of pilgrimage for Muslims and interesting for non-Muslims, with its attractive red brick **Kudus Menara** or **Clock Tower**. The tower was built in 1685, and shows clear architectural links with the Hindu Majapahit Kingdom and with similar towers in Bali, notably the Kulkul towers found in temple compounds. It is possible that it was built as a pre-Islamic temple. Today, the drum at the top of the tower is used to call the faithful to prayer and the porcelain plates set into the walls – similar to decoration found on other mosques and kratons – is thought to imitate Islamic tiles. It is possible to climb the steep stairs and then a wooden ladder to the top, where there are magnificent views of the town over a sea of tiled roofs. Behind the mosque, to the left of the main entrance, are a series of charming brick courtyards separated by weathered wooden doors. Each courtyard contains gravestones leading, eventually, to the revered **tomb of Sunan Kudus**. His mausoleum of finely carved stone is draped with a curtain of lace.

In town, on Jl Jend A Yani, is the large **Djarum kretek factory**, Kudus' major employer. Free tours of the factory are run on work days from 0800 (closed Fri). Not far S from the factory, and facing onto the large new *Kudus Plaza* shopping centre, is a **Chinese Pagoda**.

Kudus is also famous for its **traditional houses** or *rumah adat Kudus*. It was here, and at the nearby port of Jepara, that

The traditional Kudus house

A feature of the N coast, E of Semarang, is the traditional high-peaked wooden Kudus house. From the exterior they are immediately recognizable by their towering roofs; inside, they are known for their intricate and accomplished wood carving. Traditionally they were constructed of teak and consisted of three rooms: a guest room (*jogo satru*) used for receiving visitors, a large, main room (*gedongan*), and a family room (*pawon*) for cooking and eating. It is usually maintained that the art of carving wood was introduced in the 15th century by a Chinese immigrant, Ling Sing.

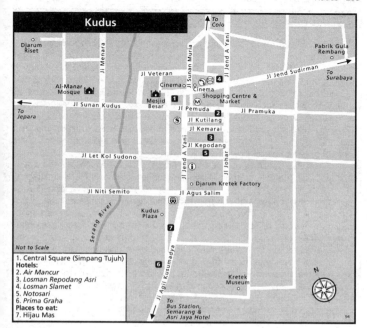

Kudus

Map labels:
- Djarum Riset
- Jl Menara
- To Colo
- Sunan Muria
- Jl Jend A Yani
- Pabrik Gula Rembang
- Jl Veteran
- Cinema
- Cinema — 4
- Al-Manar Mosque
- Jl Jend Sudirman
- To Surabaya
- Mesjid Besar — 1
- Shopping Centre & Market — M
- Jl Sunan Kudus
- Jl Pemuda — 2
- To Jepara
- Jl Pramuka
- S — Jl Kutilang
- Jl Kemarai
- Jl Jend A Yani
- Jl Kepodang — 3
- 5
- Jl Let Kol Sudono
- Jl Johar
- i
- Djarum Kretek Factory
- Jl Niti Semito
- Jl Agus Salim
- Kudus Plaza
- 7
- Serang River
- Not to Scale
- Jl Agil Kusumadya
- Kretek Museum
- 6
- N
- To Bus Station, Semarang & Asri Jaya Hotel

1. Central Square (Simpang Tujuh)
Hotels:
2. Air Mancur
3. Losman Repodang Asri
4. Losman Slamet
5. Notosari
6. Prima Graha
Places to eat:
7. Hijau Mas

woodcarving was developed to its highest degree of refinement and houses were decorated with elaborately carved internal and external screens. Abdul Syukur owns a traditional Kudus teak house on Jl Veteran, with just such intricately carved woodwork. To visit the house, contact the tourist office in Kudus and they will accompany you there.

Excursions

Rembang lies 60 km E of Kudus, on the N coast (see page 259). *Getting there:* regular connections with Kudus bus terminal.

The historic town of **Demak** is 19 km S of Kudus (see page 254). *Getting there:* regular connections by colt and bus.

Local information
● **Accommodation**

B-D *Asri Jaya*, Jl Agil Kusumadya, T 22449, F 21897, a/c, restaurant, pool, hot water, best accommodation here, 2.8 km from centre of town, rooms are a little grubby but good facili-

ties, 2nd flr rooms considerably cheaper but much the same as ground flr, corridors dark, dirty and grim, a lick of paint would do wonders.

C-D *Air Mancur*, Jl Pemuda 70, T 22514, some a/c, OK rooms with mandis; **C-D** *Notosari*, Jl Kepodang 12, T 21245, some a/c, restaurant, pool, central location but down quiet side street, VIP rooms have sitting area which makes the bedrooms rather dark, 'utama' are better and cheaper (especially those on the upper flr), some rooms with hot water, the best place from which to explore Kudus on foot; **C-D** *Prima Graha*, Jl R Agil Kusumadya 8, T 21820, some a/c, small hotel down quiet lane about 1 km from centre of Kudus, rooms are clean and well-maintained, some with attached mandis.

D-E *Losmen Kepodang Asri*, Jl Kepodang 15, down quiet side street nr centre of town, rooms are well kempt and the losmen is very popular, best of the cheaper places in town.

F *Losmen Slamet*, Jl Jend Sudirman 63, basic, but cheap.

● **Places to eat**

♦♦*Hijau Mas*, Jl Jend A Yani 1, good Indonesian

The life-blood of the Indonesian male: the clove or 'Kretek' cigarette

One of the most important upland crops in East Java is *cengkeh* or cloves. These are grown for a single purpose: to supply the massive *kretek* or clove cigarette industry. It is difficult to go anywhere in Indonesia where there is not the lingering scent of the spice. The centre of the industry is East Java where it employs about 100,000 workers. The giant Gudang Garam factory at Kediri alone has over 40,000 employees, while Bentoel in Malang employs another 20,000. In Central Java, the centre of kretek production is the Djarum factory in Kudus. Over the course of the 1980s and 90s the traditional hand-made kretek has been displaced by the machine-made variety. At the same time, the kretek has been eating into the market share of so-called 'white' cigarettes.

In late 1990, Suharto's youngest son, Hutomo 'Tommy' Mandala Putra, used his impeccable contacts to set up a clove monopoly, known as BPCC. He managed to convince his father that the best way to help 500,000 poor clove farmers was to create such a monopoly, enabling him to buy the spice from farmers at 7,000Rp/kg – double the prevailing market price – and then selling it on to the captive kretek manufacturers for 12,700-15,000Rp/kg. The powerful manufacturers resisted the move by paying less to tobacco farmers. Tommy, in turn, secured US$325 million in subsidized credits from the central Bank Indonesia and began to buy huge quantities of cloves, but mostly from powerful Chinese traders rather than from farmers. The monopoly seemed to be flying in the face of the government's attempts to de-regulate industry. By the beginning of 1992, BPCC was effectively bankrupt: it had no funds left to buy cloves, had built up a 2-year stock of the spice, and Tommy suggested – amidst much recrimination – that farmers burn half their crop to restore demand. BPCC became a semi-public monopoly with farmers receiving only 4,000Rp/kg for their crop, while kretek manufacturers were still required to buy their stocks from BPCC. In mid 1993, Tommy admitted that his company was no longer able to service its loan from Bank Indonesia, and suggested that he borrow money from a commercial - but state-owned - bank to repay the central bank.

food at good prices, closed Fri; *Pondok Gizi*, Jl Agil Kusumadya 59 (road into town from Semarang); *Sederhana*, Jl Agil Kusumadya 59B, excellent Indonesia, seafood specialities, rec; *Soto Ayam Pak Denuh*, Jl Agil Kusumadya. Night stalls at Pasar Bitingan nr the bus station.

● **Banks & money changers**
Bank Central Asia, Jl Jend A Yani 91; **Bank Rakyat Indonesia**, Jl Jend Sudirman (nr intersection with Jl Johar).

● **Post & telecommunications**
Area code: 0291.
Telephone office: Jl Jend Sudirman (about 1 km from town centre.

● **Sport**
Swimming: *The Asri Jaya Hotel* has a pool open to the public for 1,000Rp, 1,250Rp at weekends.

● **Tourist offices**
At Jl Jend A Yani 60, T 24000.

● **Transport**
51 km from Semarang.

Road Bus: the station is on the Semarang side of town, 4 km from the centre, on the main Kudus – Semarang road. Colts take passengers into town. Regular connections with Semarang 1 hr and Solo 2 hrs. **Colt**: the station is on Jl Jend A Yani, opp the *Kudus Plaza*, connections with Rembang and Jepara.

JEPARA

Jepara was once one of the N coast's, and therefore one of Java's, largest and most powerful cities whose wealth was based on trade. By the end of the 16th century it was surrounded by an impressive protective city wall and the kings and queens of

Jepara sent fleets to attack Portuguese Melaka, one of which was said to be 100 vessels strong. The city state reached the height of its powers under the rule of the renowned Queen Kali-nyamat. Even at that time, Jepara was already well-known for the quality of its wood carving, a reputation which it has maintained through to the present day. When the Dutch first arrived here they recorded that Jepara was supplying rice, palm sugar and cattle to other parts of Southeast Asia and Van Goens in 1656 estimated the population of Jepara at 100,000. That the tide of history has turned againt Jepara is clear: today it is a small provincial town with a flourishing furniture industry – an industry which owes much to the boat building skills of former years.

Once out of the suburbs of Kudus, the road to Jepara emerges onto a wide coastal agricultural plain where rice, sugar cane and beans are grown. About 20 km from Kudus the first wood carving and furniture making workshops appear. For the next 5 km, all the way into the centre of Jepara, the road is lined with enterprises ranging in size from one man on a stool with a hammer and chisel, to large warehouse-sized operations. Piles of rough-hewn logs are stored at lumber yards waiting to be transformed into furniture or carvings. Much is rather over-elaborate for western tastes, but there is also some elegant furniture of simpler design. Items such a garden benches, folding chairs and tables, are widely available. Many worshops also arrange packing and shipping, so getting the pieces home need not be a problem.

Jepara itself is an attractive, clean and well planned and airy town – testifying to the lucrative nature of the furniture business. It is a pleasant place to pass a few days away from the bustle of other, large cities. The **Kartini Museum** on Jl Alun-alun Jepara commemorates the local heroine RA Kartini who's statue can be seen waving as you reach the town. It contains an assortment of her possessions including photographs, paintings and furniture, as well as detailing her struggle

Raden Kartini

Raden Ajeng Kartini was born in 1880, daughter of the Regent or *bupati* of Jepara. She was fortunate in having a father who did not entirely disagree with the idea of female education, and he sent her to the European lower school in Jepara. Here, the distinctly revolutionary belief that women should be educated and emancipated, took hold. At the very end of the 19th century, the East Indies, like Europe, was caught up in the idea that with the dawn of the 20th century a new era would begin, one of enlightenment. Kartini was thrilled to be part of this change. She wrote to a friend on 12 January 1900 "Oh, it is splendid just to live in this age; the transition of the old into the new!".

Unfortunately, her dreams were not allowed time to unfold. She died at the tragically young age of 24 on 17 September 1904, while giving birth to her first child. Nonetheless, in her short life Kartini established a reputation for herself as a budding suffragette: she founded a school for the daughters of Javanese officials, and promoted the rights of Javanese women. For her rôle, Kartini is immortalised on a banknote. However, there are rumours of dissent emanating from some quarters. The fact that Kartini was so European in outlook, and apparently pro-Dutch in a number of respects, means that her nationalist credentials are slightly sullied. Her burial place, and that of her sons (at Desa Bulu, 20 km S of Rembang), has become a pilgrimage spot for Indonesian women nonetheless, and crowds travel here particularly on 21 Apr known as Kartini Day.

for greater female emancipation (see box page 257). Admission 200Rp. Open 0800-1700 Mon-Sat, 0900-1700 Sun. Also on the Alun-alun is the town's central mosque – the **Mesjid Baitul Ma'mur**.

On a small hill on the N side of town are the ruins of a **Portuguese fort**. The hill-top position affords a good view of the port and surrounding *tambak* fisheries (see box page 287). A worthwhile and pleasant late afternoon sortie.

Excursions

Bandengan Beach lies 5 km E of Jepara. It is pleasant enough and safe for swimming. There is a camping ground nearby.

Local information
● **Accommodation**

B-E *Kalingga Star Hotel*, Jl Dr Sutomo 16, T 91054, F 91443, good hotel with wide range of rooms, best with attached bathrooms, a/c, and hot water, surprisingly sophisticated for such a small place.

C-E *Ratu Shima Hotel*, Jl Dr Sutomo 13-15, T 91406, some a/c, wide range of rooms, best with attached mandi, hot water and TV.

D-E *Kencana Hotel*, Jl Pemuda 16, T 91217, some a/c; **D-E** *Menno Jaya Hotel*, Jl Diponegoro 40, T 91143, good central location, friendly management, the best of the lower range crop of hotels.

F *Losmen Asia*, Jl Kartini 32, dark, basic rooms in old, colonial villa, shared mandi, cheap.

● **Banks & money changers**
Bank Dagang Negara, Jl Pemuda; **Bank Negara Indonesia**, Jl Pemuda 46.

● **Entertainment**
Cinemas: *Mutiara*, Alun-alun Jepara.

● **Post & telecommunications**
Area code: 0291.
Telephone office: Jl Yos Sudarso 6.

● **Shopping**
Textiles: the area around Jepara town, and especially the village of Troso, is an important centre for the production of weft ikat, similar in design to that made at Gresik. The textiles are known as *tenunan lurik Troso* and their designs draw upon Gujarati (Indian) *patola* cloths.

● **Tourist offices**
Dinas Pariwisata, Jl Alun-alun Jepara 1.

● **Transport**
30 km from Kudus, 81 km from Semarang.

Road Bus: the terminal is off Jl Kol Sugiono on the NW side of town, but still a relatively easy walk from the centre. Regular connections with Kudus and Semarang.

KARIMUNJAWA ISLANDS

The 27 Karimunjawa Islands lie around 90 km off-shore from Jepara and have been gazetted as a Marine National Park. Among the endangered flora and fauna are red coral, eagles and an array of forest plants. The population of the islands – four of the 27 are inhabited – are staunchly Muslim and few tourists make it out here. Nonetheless there are a handful of losmen and homestays, and some good beaches and snorkelling (no diving facilities). The joy of Karimunjawa is the fact that this is a beach without the resort. Come with a stack of good books, expect simple food, and relax.

The biggest of the 27 islands in this small archipelago is Pulau Karimunjawa and most boats from the mainland dock on the island. Karimunjawa village has some homestay accommodation and the grave of Sunan Nyamplung – an hour's walk from the village. However, the only two chalet operations – at last count anyway – are on Pulau Tengah and Pulau Sambangan. This is because Karimunjawa Island is fringed with mangroves and has no good beaches, nor accessible coral for that matter. It is possible to base yourself at Karimunjawa village and then charter local boats to explore the other islands in the group.

Strictly speaking, to visit the national park it is necessary to obtain permission from the Office of Nature Conservation (KSDA), Jl Menteri Supeno 1/2, T 414750, Semarang or from the tourist office in Jepara at Jl Alun-alun Jepara 1 (on the main town square), T 118. Both can provide further information on the islands (although their English is limited).

Best time to visit: Apr-Nov.

Local information

● **Accommodation**

Karimunjawa Village (Pulau Karimunjawa): (**E**) homestay accommodation available in the village. Ask at the dock on arrival.

Sambangan Island: (**C**) beach chalets. These can be booked through *PT Pusakaraya Tours* in Kudus, or turn up and hope that they have rooms available.

Tengah Island: (**C**) beach chalets. These can be booked through *PT Satura Tours*, Jl Cendrawasih 4, Semarang, T 555555 or turn up and hope that rooms are available.

● **Transport**

90 km NW of Jepara.

Air There is a small airfield on Karimunjawa. It is possible to charter a plane from Deraya Air in Semarang but there are no scheduled flights.

Sea Boat twice weekly ferry connections on Mon and Fri mornings at 0900 from Jepara Port on Jl Patiunus on the NW side of Jepara town, 4½ hrs (15,000Rp). The ferry returns from Karimunjawa at 0800 on Tues and Sat. Chartering a boat to the islands is possible, as is simply pay your passage on one of the fishing boats that make the journey, but they seem flimsy affairs to be making this 90 km journey.

PATI

Pati is a small and rather neat market town in an area of rice and sugar production, with a good hotel for such a place. It can be used as a stopping-off point on the N coast route. The town authorities appear to have invested heavily in grandiose statuary and elaborate street lamps.

Local information

● **Accommodation**

C *Pati Hotel*, Jl Pangl Sudirman 60, T 81313, some a/c, pool, old villa in large compound nr the centre of town, range of rooms some with hot water, well-run, characterful and very acceptable for a small out-of-the-way place like Pati, rec; **C-E** *Merdeka Hotel*, Jl Diponegoro 69 (N side of town), T 81106, some a/c, 44 rm, quiet, set back from the road around a courtyard.

● **Post & telecommunications**

Area code: 0295.

Post Office: Jl Pangl Sudirman (opp the *Pati Hotel*).

Telephone & fax office: Jl Pangl Sudirman 61 (opp the *Pati Hotel*).

● **Tourist offices**

Dinas Pariwisata Tingkat II Pati, Jl Dr Wahidin 3, T 81422.

● **Transport**

24 km from Kudus, 35 km from Rembang.

Road Bus: the terminal is to the SE of town, off the road to Surabaya, not far from the centre. Regular connections with Kudus and on to Semarang, and E to Rembang, Tuban and Surabaya.

REMBANG

Rembang is another small, N coast town with a distinct coastal feel: bright light, white-washed walls and – usually – a brisk sea breeze. Also like some other towns on the N coast, it has languished into obscurity having once been a significant trading centre. Today it is best known for its associated with RA Kartini, the 'mother' of women's education and emancipation in Indonesia (see box page 257). A statue of Kartini clutching a book stands on the traffic island on the coast road, Jl Diponegoro, by the tourist office. Rembang also has a fair collection of traditional **Kudus houses** (see box page 254) and a large Christian community – evidenced in the number of churches.

The **railway station** has been closed for some years, but it is an attractive building with caged birds hanging from the rafters of the silent platform. **Rembang market** is on Jl Pemuda, the road to Blora.

Excursions

Lasem is a charming batik-making town 9 km E of Rembang. It was once one of the most important ship-building centres in Java, owing to the presence nearby of some of the finest stands of teak wood on the island. As ship-building fell into decline so, for a short time, Lasem became a thriving centre for *cap* and *tulis* batik-making, the business controlled by Chinese families. The houses here are Chinese-Portuguese colonial in style, and their weathered and rather ramshackle appearance makes Lasem an attractive place to spend a lazy few hours. Indeed, in its rather sub-provincial way, it is one of the most endearing towns on Java. The batik-making of old has withered and almost died, although there are still a handful of *tulis* batik factories in town. The cloth is distinctive for its deep red blood colour – not found anywhere else in Indonesia. There is a fine Chinese temple here and although its former wealth has now almost entirely trickled away, Lasem still exudes cultured sophistication rarely found elsewhere on Java. **Accommodation** Available in basic rooms at the run down **E-F** *Gadjah Losmen* on the main Tuban-Rembang road. *Getting there*: by regular bus from Rembang.

Bonang is a small fishing village 5 km N of Lasem and 14 km from Rembang. The village is well known for its dried fish which are sold from numerous stalls lining the road. Bonang is also famous, in Indonesian terms, as the home of one of Java's nine walis (see box page 95) – Sunan Bonang. A memorial to Sunan Bonang can be found at the top of a small hill just off the main road on the Tuban edge of the village. Sunan Bonang died here, but he is buried in Tuban (although this was not the intention – see the Tuban entry, below). Swimming at Bonang is not good; the shore is rocky, the water murky, and the currents can be strong. **Accommodation** is surprisingly good in Bonang at the **C-E** *Binangun Indah*, some a/c, set on a hill overlooking the sea on the Tuban edge of town, usually enjoying a cooling breeze, the rooms (some with attached bathrooms) here are clean and well maintained, a real alternative place to stay and take things extremely slowly, rec. *Getting there*: regular buses from Rembang (and Tuban), the town is on the main N coast route.

Local information
● Accommodation
C-E *Hotel Restu*, Jl P Sudirman 38, T 91408, some a/c, a small hotel on the coast road, better rooms with attached mandis, mostly frequented by travelling salesmen but this shouldn't put people off – the rooms are OK.

E-F *Losmen Perdana*, Jl P Sudirman 76, T 381, clean and very well priced basic rooms in a small villa, some with attached mandis.

● Banks & money changers
Bank Rakyat Indonesia, Jl Diponegoro (the coast road).

● Post & telecommunications
Area code: 0295.
Post Office: Jl Diponegoro.

● Tourist offices
Dinas Pariwisata (Rembang Regency office), Jl Diponegoro 77 (nr the centre of town), T 91403. They only have a short, rather uninformative pamphlet to hand out to the few visitors who venture here, but in mid-1994 were in the process of preparing a map which should now be ready for distribution to enthusiastic visitors.

● Transport
59 km from Kudus, 97 km from Tuban.

Road Bus: the terminal is not far from the centre of town, just off Jl Diponegoro, the seafront road. Regular connections with Semarang via Pati and Kudus, and E to Tuban and Surabaya. There are also buses to Bandung.

East Java

EAST JAVA covers an area of 47,922 sq km and includes not only the east portion of Java, but also the island of Madura. The province is drained by two principal rivers – the Brantas and Bengawan Solo. Two-thirds of East Java is mountainous, the highest peak – Mt Semeru – reaching 3,676m. The population of 32.5 million is made up largely of Javanese, Madurese and Tenggerese. The *ayam bekisar*, a cross-breed between a chicken and a green woodcock (and visible in most hotel lobbies), is one of East Java's symbols and so too is the *sedap malam*, a white flower.

For the visitor, the principal attractions of E Java are likely to lie in the magnificent volcanic scenery, the elegant candis and other architectural remains, and in the persistence – despite rapid economic change – of many facets of traditional life.

Like Central Java, E Java is rich in archaeological sites. The East Javanese Period of art and architecture began in 929 when King Sindok was forced to move his court to the rich Brantas River area following the eruption of Mt Merapi in 928 (see page 89). The East Javanese Period spanned six centuries and included the kingdoms of Kediri (929-1222), Singasari (1222-1292) and Majapahit (1292-1527). Among the various monuments, Candi Panataran is the greatest, although the elegant Candi Kidal and Candi Singasari, as well as Candi Jawi, are also significant.

In rural areas, traditional forms of dress are much in evidence, with women tending to carry loads on their heads, rather than tied with a sarong on their backs as in Central and W Java. Buffalo-drawn wagons, horse-pulled carts and carriages, and an abundance of bicycles show that the internal combustion engine is still facing a stiff challenge from less frenetic modes of transport.

Not only is E Java one of the country's most densely populated provinces, it is also one of the richest. An industrial 'golden triangle' (in fact a diamond) is centred on the port of Surabaya – the second largest city in Indonesia. Along with Surabaya, this golden triangle incorporates the towns of Malang, Jombang and Pasuruan. More people are engaged in industrial activities and live in urban areas in E Java than in any other province in the country, bar the capital Jakarta. These industries are dominated by *kretek* (clove cigarette) manufacturing – with the mammoth

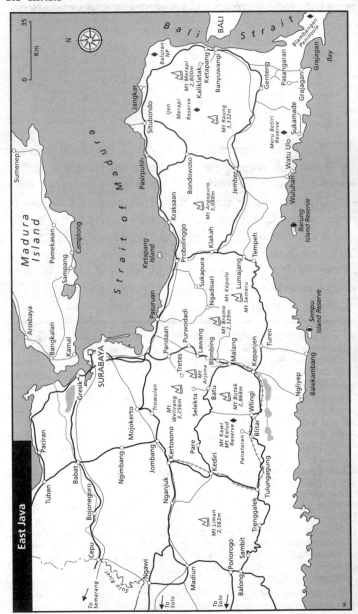

Gudang Garam factory at Kediri – sugar milling and weaving.

But this picture of E Java as a vibrant, modern province obscures great inequalities and continuing poverty in some of the more remote areas. In particular, Madura and the SW districts such as Pacitan have not benefited from E Java's recent economic growth. Although it has been the province's expanding industries which have generated much of the economic growth in recent years, E Java still has a larger area under plantations – sugar cane, coffee, cloves and tobacco – than any other province except N Sumatra. Other crops cultivated include rice, along with maize, cassava and fruit (particularly mango).

THE RUMP OF EAST JAVA

MADIUN

Madiun is the largest town in the western part of E Java (its population in 1990 was 166,000) and an important centre for the processing of sugar cane which is grown in the surrounding area – as it has been since colonial days. Entering or leaving by the NE (from Caruban), the road passes the **Rejo Agung sugar mill** built in 1894 and still in operation. There is also evidence of a vital past in the elegant villas that line roads such as Jl Yos Sudarso, and in the splendid governor's mansion on Jl Pahlawan. Madiun also remains an important centre for rolling stock production – again a role that it has inherited from the colonial period. The INKA works still occupy the same location they did under the Dutch.

Excursions

Sarangan, a hill resort, lies about 40km W of Madiun (see page 235). *Getting there*: take a bemo to Magetan via Maospati; from Magetan, catch a minibus up to Sarangan.

The Madiun affair

Historically, Madiun is best remembered for an abortive Communist revolt in 1948 which proved to be one of the key turning points in the Revolution. That year was one of turmoil in Indonesia. The Dutch were attempting to regain control through their police action, while the independence movement was split between the left – headed by the Communist PKI – and the fledgling Republican government. Ousted from government during a purge, the PKI attempt to regain control by encouraging a wave of strikes and demonstrations by peasants and workers. By the middle of 1948, effective warfare had broken out between pro-PKI and pro-government soldiers. Those supporting the PKI were driven out of Solo and retreated to Madiun. Here between 10,000 and 25,000 were out-numbered by government forces who backed Sukarno and his associates. When it became clear that ordinary soldiers had to choose between one side and the other, most sided with the Republican leaders. From that point, the insurrection was doomed. In all, it is thought, about 8,000 people were killed in and around Madiun. As Ricklefs writes in his *History of modern Indonesia*, the Madiun affair caused the left 'to be tainted forever with treachery against the revolution'.

Local information

● Accommodation

A-B *Merdeka Hotel*, Jl Pahlawan 42, T 2547, F 2572, pool, 120 a/c rm with hot water in a hotel that dates back, in parts at least, to 1904 when it was named *The Grand*; the Japanese renamed it the *Yamato* in 1942 during their occupation of the East Indies and it finally became the *Merdeka Hotel* in 1945; sadly there is little evidence of all this history, the rooms may be comfortable enough, but potential guests should not arrive with the impression that they will see a hotel dripping in colonial elegance.

B *Kartika Hotel*, Jl Pahlawan 54, T 51847, F 51847, a/c, restaurant, new hotel which scarcely seems to have been unwrapped (although these things have a habit of changing very fast), rather bare and clinical rooms and lobby, comfortable and good value, discounts available.

D-E *Hotel Madiun*, Jl Pahlawan 75, old villa, rather grubby but some character.

● Places to eat

Madiun is known locally for its *nasi pecel* – steamed rice with vegetables, peanut sauce and chicken. Another local delicacy is *brem*, a snack made from glutinous (sticky) rice.

● Banks & money changers

Bank Rakyat Indonesia, Jl Pahlawan.

● Entertainment

Cinemas: *Lawu Indah*, Jl Pahlawan (nr the *Merdeka Hotel*).

● Post & telecommunications

Area code: 0351.

Post Office: Jl Pahlawan 24.

● Transport

83 km from Kediri, 89 km from Solo.

Train Although very few people travel here by train, Madiun is on the main line between Jakarta, Yogya and Solo to the W, and Surabaya to the W. **NB** That not all the express trains stop here (the Bima express does).

Road Bus: regular connections E to Surabaya, Bali and Malang and W to Solo, Yogya and Jakarta.

KEDIRI

In theory, Kediri should be an attractive town. It has a glorious past when it was the centre of an important pre-Islamic Kingdom between the 11th and 13th centuries and its location, nestling between two volcanoes, Mt Liman (2,563m) to the W and Mt Kawi (2,551m) to the E, appears, cartographically, to also augur well. In reality though, Kediri is an ugly town of 235,000 people (1990), with little to show for past glories.

Today Kediri is not so much a one horse town as a one industry town: the massive **Gudang Garam** *kretek* cigarette factory employing over 40,000 people is based here, the largest single industrial concern (in terms of numbers employed) in all of Indonesia (see box). There are few sights either in town or roundabouts. At the end of Jl Pattimura there is the **Tri Dharma (or Tjoe Hwie Kiong) Buddhist monastery**.

Excursions

Surowono is a temple in the village of Canggu. It is currently undergoing renovation, but it exhibits some accomplished relief carving. *Getting there*: no public transport, and rather hard to find tucked away among the back roads. It is located about 5 km off the main Kediri-Pare road; turn right at a major intersection just outside Pare where a concrete policeman stands guard infront of the local police station. Ask for directions along the way (*dimana Candi Surowono?*) – and then get wonderfully lost.

Tegurwangi is a little visited candi about 8 km from the small town of Pare, NE of Kediri. **Gua Selomangleng** is a meditation 'cave', hewn out of the rock and reminiscent of a pill box. The rooms are decorated with episodes from the Jataka tales (the previous lives of the historic Buddha) and inscriptions indicate that the cave was created between the 12th and early 15th centuries. The cave is a few kilometres due S of the small town of Tulungagung, itself S of Kediri. *Getting there*: it is easiest to take an ojek (motorcycle); otherwise, a Microlet 'A', along Jl Mastrip runs in the right direction, although a change is necessary.

The magic saus of Gudang Garam

The 'Big Four' *kretek* cigarette manufacturers are all found in East Java: Gudang Garam, Bentoel, Djarum and Sampurna. However the Gudang Garam *kretek* cigarette factory in Kediri is by far the largest, and is in fact the largest single industrial enterprise in Indonesia, employing over 45,000 workers. Until the 1970s, *kretek* cigarette smoking was largely a lower class affair: the sophisticates of Jakarta spurned the *kretek* in favour of so-called 'white' (ie Virginia) cigarettes. Since then, though, a remarkable change in habits has occurred as *kretek* smoking has made in-roads into the middle classes and intelligentsia, to the extent that it has become *de rigour* – a mark of Indonesian-ness.

It seems that the practice of mixing cloves and tobacco originated in Java during the late 18th century. But it was not until the late 19th century that the industry really took off, and like most such activities, the industry was dominated by Chinese businessmen. Gudang Garam was founded in Kediri in the late 1950s by Surya Wonowijojo (or Tjoa Ing Hwie – his Chinese name), where production has always been concentrated. Ing Hwie was born in Fujian, southern China, in 1926. From modest beginnings (all such things have 'modest beginnings'), Gudang Garam grew to stupendous proportions: by the late 1980s, the firm was producing over 40 billion cigarettes a year – in the late 1960s it was scarcely one billion. The secret of the success of Ing Hwie's company lay in the clove *saus* (sauce) that he divined. When this was allied to the famous 'yellow pack' in 1962, the fortunes of his company began to change. It is said that the logo of the company – a salt warehouse or *gudang garam* – came to Ing Hwie in a dream, and for good luck since then he has had an image of a gudang garam emblazoned on every pack. His competitors, jealous at the success of Gudang Garam, put it about that his *saus* contained not only cloves, but also cannabis. Ing Hwie died in 1985 of heart disease, probably brought on by his smoking – doctors in New Zealand advised that he give up smoking; all he managed to was to 'cut down' to one pack a day.

Although Gudang Garam does not dominate the market as it did in its heyday during the early 1980s, it is still the largest single employer in Indonesia. Kediri is, to all effects, Gudang Garam, and the firm dominates the town.

NB This account is based on Kenneth Young's "Kediri and Gudang Garam: an industrial enclave in a rural setting", in: *Balanced development: East Java in the New Order* (edited by Howard Dick, James J Fox and Jamie Mackie), Oxford University Press: Singapore, 1993.

The famous logo of the Gudang Garam *Kretek* cigarette manufacturer. It depicts the salt warehouses, or gudang garam, after which the company is named.

Sri Aji Joyoboyo's tomb, a 13th-century king of Kediri, can be found in the village of Menang, near Pagu, 8 km from Kediri. The best time to visit the tomb is on Thur and Fri evenings, when there is a market and celebrations. *Getting there*: by bemo to Pagu.

Local information
● **Accommodation**

Kediri is not well-endowed with decent hotels, either at the top or at the bottom ends of the scale; there are no decent budget places to stay, and no classy joints.

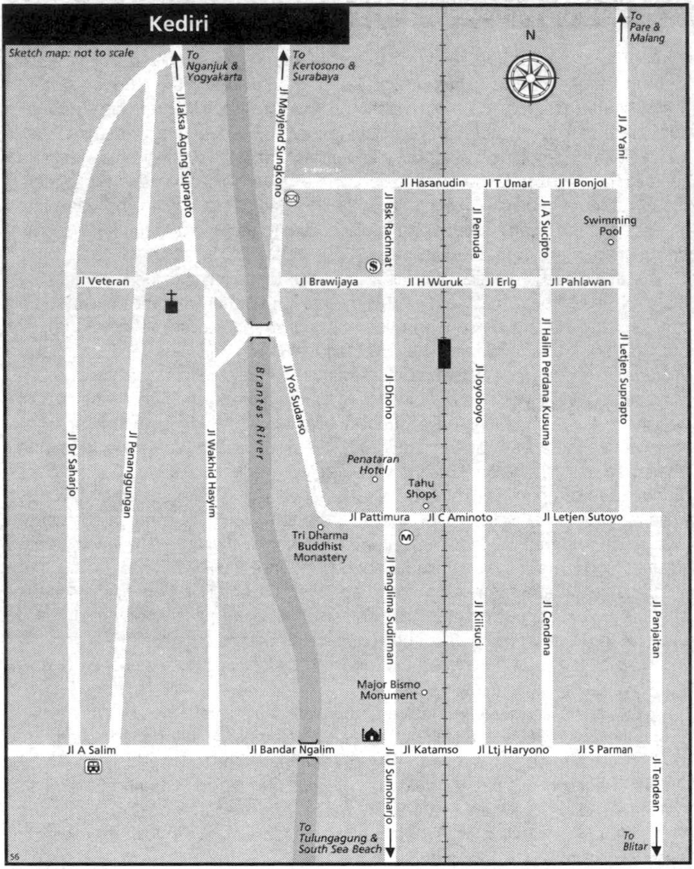

B-C *Hotel Penataran*, Jl Dhoho 190, T 84626, F 41799, a/c, best hotel in town, which is not saying a great deal, clean rooms and central location.

C-D *Safari Indah II*, Jl Panglima Sudirman 43, T 82466, some a/c, a rather scruffy, uninspired block of a hotel, although the rooms are just about OK, those at the front can be noisy, rather expensive for what you get.

D-E *Hotel Pelapa*, Jl Brawijaya (nr intersection with Jl Basuki Rachmat), old and rather attractive villa, but the rooms are poor.

E *Mustika*, Jl Panglima Sudirman 25, basic losmen in the centre of town.

● **Places to eat**

♦♦*Mirmar*, Jl Hayam Wuruk 12, Chinese restaurant serving tasty Chinese and Indonesian dishes in clean surroundings; *Zangrandl*, Jl Dhoho 10, ice creams in modern a/c comfort, hang out with the local high school drop outs.

● **Banks & money changers**

Bank Central Asia, Jl Brawijaya (nr the intersection with Jl Basuki Rachmat).

● **Entertainment**

Cinemas: *Golden*, Jl Hayam Wuruk, new and very comfortable.

● **Post & telecommunications**
Area code: 0354.
Post Office: Jl May Jend Sungkono.
Telephone & fax: Wartel, Jl Hayam Wuruk 30.

● **Shopping**
Two local food specialities are *getuk pisang* and *tahu* (bean curd) which are sold by numerous shops along Jl Pattimura.

● **Transport**
100 km from Malang, 83 km from Madiun.

Train The station is on Jl Stasiun, which runs off Jl Dhoho, in the centre of town. Kediri is on the main line between Jakarta, Yogya and Solo to the W, and Surabaya to the W. **NB** Not all the express trains stop here.

Road Bus: the terminal is on the outskirts of town on Jl Supratman. Regular connections with other major centres incl Madiun, Solo, Yogya, Surabaya, Bali, Malang and Jakarta.

BLITAR

Blitar, with a population in 1990 of 113,000, has two claims to fame: it is the site of former President Sukarno's mausoleum and is also the closest town to Candi Panataran. Blitar appears to have been founded after a Sailendra king built a Buddhist monastery here in about 860AD. Today, despite the presence of Sukarno's grave, the town is a quiet backwater in comparison with other E Javanese towns such as Malang or Solo.

Places of interest
The main road, Jl Merdeka, runs E-W. At its W end, close to the intersection with Jl Mawar, is a small **Chinese temple – Tri Dharma Poo An Kiong**. Just a short distance further W still, along the street that leads to the bus station, is an enjoyable **market** selling spices, dried fish and other local products. There is an **archaeological museum** on Jl Sodancho Supriyadi.

Sukarno's mausoleum is on the outskirts of Blitar, about 2 km NE of the town centre on Jl Slamet Riyadi, the road to Panataran. Following the attempted coup of 1965 and the consolidation of President Suharto's position, support for Sukarno among the army quickly dissipated. In Mar 1967 the Assembly held a meeting and relieved the former president of all power. He was forced to retire, an embittered man, to Bogor where he was held under effective house arrest until his death in Jun 1970. Following his death – and against his wishes – former President Sukarno was buried here in Blitar next to his mother. No doubt this backwater of Java was chosen to ensure that his grave did not become a focus of pilgrimage and dissent. In 1978 the grave was spruced-up; there is now an impressive open gateway, leading to a glass-enclosed pavilion which contains the engraved boulder marking the site of his burial. The number of stalls that line the road to the grave, and the abundance of becak drivers who wait hopefully around the entrance, demonstrate that Sukarno has not been entirely forgotten. Pilgrims prostrate themselves and flowers are scattered in front of the pavilion. Get to the grave by becak (ask for *makam Bung Karno*), or walk.

Excursions
Candi Panataran is 10 km N of Blitar and was built from 1345-1375 during the Majapahit Period, although work may have started during the Singasari era (1222-1292). It is the largest and most important candi of the East Javanese Period and anticipates the design of later Balinese temples. Asymmetrical in layout, it consists of three stepped courtyards surrounded by a wall. The visitor approaches the temple from the lowest level to the W, past a pair of *raksasa* or *dvarapala* (see page 272). The first courtyard originally contained two wooden buildings which would have been used as assembly rooms. All that remains is the base of a *terrace*, with fine bas-reliefs encircling it. These relate tales of the *kidungs*, with figures carved in the wayang-like stylization which is characteristic of E Javanese reliefs: flat, with no illusion of depth and with faces portrayed in profile. The N face of the terrace is the least weathered. Also in this courtyard is a small square building of vertical design, the so-called '*Date of the year temple*', built

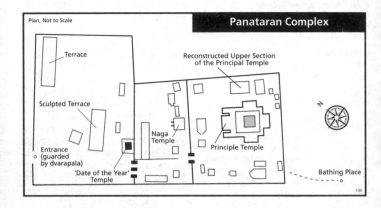

Plan, Not to Scale

Panataran Complex

Terrace

Reconstructed Upper Section of the Principal Temple

Sculpted Terrace

Naga Temple

Principle Temple

Entrance (guarded by dvarapala)

'Date of the Year' Temple

Bathing Place

N

100

in 1369 (since restored) and a good example of E Javanese candi architecture (it is similar in appearance to Candi Kidal, see page 273).

The second court contains the larger *Naga Temple*, which has lost its top section (originally of wood and similar to a Balinese *meru*, see page 412) but what remains is of very fine workmanship. It is identifiable by the four naga which wind around the top of the temple, supported by nine beautiful figures in royal attire. *Dvarapala* guard the entrance to the shrine, but the kala head above the door is now missing – although *tumpal* motifs can be seen at the front of each flight of steps. The building was used as a repository for sacred possessions.

The highest and most E court contains the *principal shrine*, which was originally surrounded by four smaller structures, remnants of which remain. The main shrine stands to the rear of the complex, nearest to the mountains, enabling the gods to descend into the temple. The base is decorated with relief carvings representing the Ramayana, interspersed with carved animal motif medallions. Four guardian figures patrol the steps upwards, rather disturbingly standing on bands of skulls (behind one of them the artist has carved a lizard, perhaps his signature). The steps lead up to a second level where there are carved winged creatures. To the left of the temple is its reconstructed upper section.

Down some stairs behind and to the right of the principal shrine is a clear pool, lined with stone and carved with animals. The pool, which would have been the king's 'mandi', is filled with fish. Admission: by donation. Open: 0700-1700 Mon-Sun. *Getting there*: take a colt direct to Panataran (500Rp) or go by ojek (about 3,000Rp).

Candi Sawentar lies a few kilometres SE of Blitar near the village of the same name. This temple was built at the beginning of the 13th century and is similar in style to Candi Kidal. For some reason, it was never completed and when the candi was discovered, it was almost completely covered in volcanic debris. *Getting there*: by colt to Sawentar.

Local information
● **Accommodation**

There are a number of hotels and losmen close to Sukarno's mausoleum catering mainly to Indonesian 'pilgrims'.

B-E *Sri Lestari*, Jl Merdeka 173, T 81766, some a/c, restaurant, good rooms, attractive main colonial building, well-run range of accommodation, in old and new wings, highly rec.

E *Losmen Damar Wulan*, Jl Anjasmoro 78, T 81884; **E-F** *Hotel Santosa*, Jl Manur 2, central position nr the bus terminal, simple rooms with attached mandi.

● **Places to eat**
♦♦*Sri Lestari*, Jl Merdeka, Indonesian incl Rijstaffel and European, rec.

● **Banks & money changers**
BNI, Jl Kananga 9.

● **Post & telecommunications**
Area code: 0342.
Post Office: Jl Wijaya Kusuma 1 (close to train station).

● **Transport**
225 km from Solo, 77 km from Malang.

Local Colts: the station is adjacent to the inter-city bus station on Jl Kerantil. **Dokars**: assemble nr the bus and rail stations. **Motorcycle taxis** (ojeks): available for trips out of town.

Train Station set back on Jl Wijaya Kusuma, to the S of Jl Merdeka. Connections with Surabaya via Malang 5 hrs (see timetable, page 917).

Road Bus: the station is on Jl Kerantil, the W continuation of Jl Merdeka. Connections with Solo 6 hrs, Malang 3 hrs, Surabaya 4 hrs and Jakarta.

MALANG

Surrounded by volcanoes – Mt Butak (2,868m) to the W, Mt Arjuna (3,339m) to the N, and Mts Kepolo (3,035m) and Bromo (2,329m) to the E – Malang is one of the most beautifully situated cities in Java. Lying at 450m, it is arguably Indonesia's largest hill resort with a population of 650,000 (Bandung residents might also, rather optimistically, call their city a hill resort too). During the colonial period, Malang was a small, quaint town where Dutch planters and civil servants could escape the heat of the lowlands. The elegant villas are still in evidence – for example along the wide, tree-lined Jl Besar Ijen – even if it has grown considerably in size since independence. Fortunately, the climate has not changed and it is still a good deal cooler than the plains. Malang is a friendly town, free from mass tourism and although it is not noted for its sights,

there are a number of places of interest within easy reach of the city, making it a good base or stopping-off point en route to or from Mt Bromo or Bali. The largest single industry in Malang is Bentoel's *kretek* factory which employs over 20,000 people (see box, page 256).

At the end of the Third Javanese War of Succession (1746-1757), Malang became a haven for the defeated rebels of the King, Surapati. They retreated here because of its inaccessibility. It was not until 1771 that the last of the Surapati line was finally captured. By then the area had been virtually de-populated such had been the turmoil caused by successive campaigns. Interestingly, because the VOC were worried about the Hindu Balinese coming to the rescue of Surapati's supporters, this was the only part of Java where the Company positively supported the spread of Islam.

Places of interest

The city is divided into two by the Brantas River which flows within a deep cutting. Tiled houses, some of colonial vintage, picturesquely – at least from a distance – tumble down the steep banks. In the E half of the city is Jl Tugu, with the uninspired **independence monument** as its centrepiece, facing which is the old Dutch town hall, renovated and renamed the **Balai Kota Malang**.

On the W bank of the Brantas, at the intersection of Jl Gatot Subroto/Laks Martadinata and Jl Zainal Zacse is the large **Eng An Kiong Chinese Pagoda**. Nearby is the **Pasar Besar**, on Jl Pasar Besar and Jl Gatot Subroto, a large and very colourful market selling everything from fruit, to live animals to batik. Other markets include the flower market, **Pasar Bunga**, and the nearby **Pasar Senggol**, a night market on Jl Brawijaya. The military **Museum Brawijaya** is at Jl Besar Ijen 25A, housed in a rather stylish 1940s or 50s building with military equipment arranged out the front.

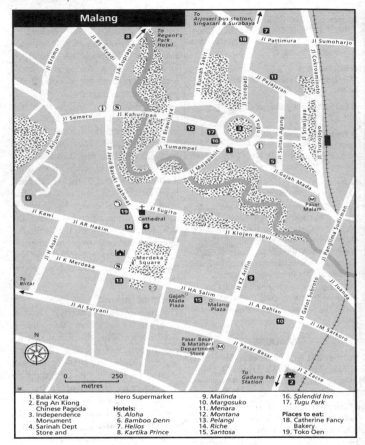

Malang

To Arjosari bus station, Singasari & Surabaya

To Regent's Park Hotel

Jl BS Riyadi · Jl A. Suprapto · Jl Bromo · Jl Rumah Sakit · Jl Pattimura · Jl Sumoharjo · Jl Cokroaminoto · Jl Pelajaran · Jl Arjuna · Jl Semeru · Jl Kahuripan · Jl Brawijaya · Jl Suropati · Jl Sultan Agung · Jl Srikelijaya · Jl Trunojoyo · Jl Tumampel · Jl Tugu · Jl Jend Basuki Rakhmat · Majapahit · Jl Gajah Mada · Jl Sugito · Cathedral · Jl Kawi · Jl AR Hakim · Jl Klojen Kidul · Pasar Malam · Jl H Agari · Jl K Merdeka · Merdeka Square · Jl KZ Arifin · Jl Panglima Sudirman · To Blitar · Jl Al Suryani · Jl HA Salim · Gajah Mada Plaza · Malang Plaza · Jl A Dahlan · Jl Gatot Subroto · Jl Juanda · Jl JM Sarkoro · Pasar Besar & Matahari Department Store · Jl Pasar Besar · Jl Z Zacse · To Gadang Bus Station

N

0 — 250
metres

1. Balai Kota	Hero Supermarket	9. *Malinda*	16. *Splendid Inn*
2. Eng An Kiong		10. *Margosuko*	17. *Tugu Park*
Chinese Pagoda	**Hotels:**	11. *Menara*	
3. Independence	5. *Aloha*	12. *Montana*	**Places to eat:**
Monument	6. *Bamboo Denn*	13. *Pelangi*	18. *Catherine Fancy*
4. Sarinah Dept	7. *Helios*	14. *Riche*	Bakery
Store and	8. *Kartika Prince*	15. *Santosa*	19. *Toko Oen*

Excursions

NB Candi Singasari, the Purwodadi Gardens and Candi Jawi are all on or just off the main road between Surabaya and Malang. It is easy to visit them en route between the two towns; simply hop-off one bus (there are many) and onto another.

Candi Badut this plain candi is thought to be the oldest surviving Hindu (Sivaite) temple in E Java, probably dating from 760 and built in honour of King Gajayana of the Kanjuruhan Kingdom (the earliest recorded kingdom in E Java).

The word *badut* is derived from a Sanskrit word meaning 'joker', or 'a man who is fond of making jokes'. The candi is similar in design to the temples of Gedung Songo, but on a larger scale. It seems that the building was altered in the 13th century, which caused it to become unstable and so hastened its ruin. The niches are framed by kalamakaras and some still contain Hindu gods. The central cella would originally have held a linga. The temple was discovered in 1923 and has subsequently been renovated up to the

Malang Surroundings

0   10
km

To Surabaya
To Pasuruan
Candi Jawi
Pacet
Pandaan
Prigen
Mt Welirang 3,156m
Tretes
Mt Arjuna 3,339
Selecta
Lawang
Purwodadi Botanical Gardens
Candi Singasari
Batu
To Kediri
Blimbing
Candi Jago
Malang
Tumpang
Mt Butak 2,868m
Candi Kidal
N
To Ngadas & Mt Bromo
Bulula-wang
Kepanjen
To Blitar
Turen
To Balekambang

lower section of the roof. It is located in an area of scrubland, on the outskirts of Malang, about 4 km to the NW of the city centre and past the university. The route here winds through narrow suburban lanes and quite suddenly passes into rice fields. *Getting there*: take one of the 'Jalur M-K' microlets, which travel between Madyupuro and Karang Besuki. The candi is 100m on from the end of the route.

Candi Singasari lies 9 km N of Malang just off the main road running towards Surabaya. The candi is E Javanese in style, with its heavy pyramidal roofs, and was built around 1300 as one of the funerary sanctuaries for Kertanagara, the last king of the Singasari Dynasty. Its design varies from other candis of the period in that the square base is much larger than normal. The cellas are – unusually – set within this base, rather than in the body of the candi. The body contains narrow niches, crowned by *banaspati* heads. Its shape implies that it was either a symbol of the *linga* or that it was meant as a replica of Mt Meru. A flight of stairs leads up to the first terrace where there are five chambers. About 150m on from the candi are two enclosures on either side of the street each containing an enormous, corpulent and demonic *dvarapala* statue with skull headbands and earrings, large staring eyes, sharp canine teeth and clasping a club. Traditionally these giant figures were placed at the gateway to ward off evil spirits (see box). Admission: 500Rp. Open 0700-1700 Mon-Sun. *Getting there*: take a bus or microlet (LA) towards Surabaya or Lawang from Malang's Arjosari station (500Rp). The candi is 600m to the left (W) off the main road in Singasari town.

The well kept and attractive **Kebun Raya Purwodadi** – the **Purwodadi Botanical Gardens** – lie 12 km N of Singasari (21 km from Malang), at the N edge of Purwodadi town. Admission 800Rp. Open 0730-1600 Mon-Sun. **Accommodation near Purwodadi D** *Niagara*, in Lawang, a few kilometres S of Purwodadi; on the main road, stylish but run-down. *Getting there*: take a bus or microlet (no LA) towards Surabaya or Lawang from Malang's Arjosari station.

Candi Jawi is a 13th century candi 49 km N of Malang, just off the road running to Surabaya. The monument was built as a commemorative shrine to the last king of the Singasari Dynasty, King Kertanagara (1268-1292). It is one of the most complete candis in E Java, and still shows the remains of the surrounding double enclosure as well as a brick-lined moat. Jawi is also perhaps the most graceful of all E Javanese shrines with its tall, tapering tower, rising to 17m. When the British naturalist Joseph Jukes saw Candi Jawi and the other temples around Malang in the 1840s, he wrote:

"The imagination became busy in restoring their former glories, in picturing

Dvarapala or temple guardians

Dvarapala are the terrifying temple guardians that flank and protect the entrances to candis. The demon is usually depicted kneeling on his right leg, with the left hand resting on his raised knee. In the right hand he holds a dagger, while his jewellery consists of ear pendants, a necklace, bracelets around the wrists and ankles, and armbands around the upper arms. Particularly fine dvarapala can be seen close to Singasari, in E Java.

Dvarapala from Candi Sewu

Source: Tissandier, M Albert (1986) *Cambridge et Java*, G Masson: Paris

large cities, adorned with temples and palaces, seated on the plain, and in recalling the departed power, wealth and state of the native kingdom that once flourished in a land so noble, so beautiful, and so well adapted for its growth and its security".

The architecture of the monument shows elements of both Sivaism, in its foundations, and Buddhism, in its stupa-like finial. It also originally housed both a statue of Siva and the Buddha Aksobhya, so revealing the King's belief in the unity of Sivaism and Buddhism. Weathered reliefs of stories as yet undeciphered decorate the base. The upper door frame holds kala heads and there are a pair of makaras at the end of the stairs. Up these stairs is a small chamber containing a stone block. The candi was redesigned in the 14th century and restored in 1938 and again in 1970. Close to Candi Jawi is the open air theatre Taman Chandra Wilwatika (see below). *Getting there*: the candi lies 49 km N of Malang, off the road to Surabaya. In the roadside town of **Pandaan** there is a turn-off for the hill resort of Tretes (see page 276), and 2 km up this road is Candi Jawi. Take a bus from Malang towards Surabaya and ask to be let off at Pandaan; walk the final 2 km or take a minibus heading for Tretes.

Taman Chandra Wilwatika this open air theatre, only 1 km from Candi Jawi and 48 km from Malang, stages performances of classical ballet on the second and fourth Sat nights of each month from Jun to Nov, 1930-2300. *Getting there*: the theatre lies 1 km downhill (and closer to the main road) from Candi Jawi (see above). Take a bus from Malang towards Surabaya and ask to be let off at Pandaan, walk the final kilometre or take a minibus heading for Tretes.

Candi Jago (also named Jajaghu) can be found down a side street (and before the minibus station) off the main road in the town of Tumpang, 22 km E of Malang. The candi feels rather enclosed, as it is squashed into a small space and surrounded by houses. This Buddhist shrine was probably built around 1270-1280 as a funerary monument to King Vishnuvardhana of the Singasari Dynasty. Today, the upper part of the cell and the tower are missing – it is thought that they were made of wood and palm, in the multitiered design characteristic of the Balinese meru. The candi is unusual in that the cella was placed at the back edge of a 3-tiered base and is approached up a steep stairway. The finely carved friezes on all three levels of the base are important as they appear to establish the existence of buildings with tiered roofs in the 13th century. The meaning of the friezes has not been firmly ascertained, although they seem to recount Hindu, Buddhist and local legends. However, on the basis of the reliefs, some commentators have argued that the temple dates from the later Majapahit Period. The four statues that were originally in the now ruined upper chamber are to be found in the National Museum, Jakarta (King Vishnuvardhana was portrayed in the form of a Buddhist god). *Getting there*: catch a minibus from Malang's Arjosari station to Tumpang (600Rp) and walk the short distance from the minibus station.

Candi Kidal is 7 km further on from Tumpang travelling SW, and was built in the mid-13th century as a memorial shrine to King Anusapati who died in 1248. Built of andesite, the shrine consists of a square cell with projecting porticos, set within low walls on a large plinth. The tower – now in ruins – would originally have been about 15m high and made up of three false storeys of diminishing height. However, its elegant proportions made it susceptible to earthquake damage and the structure has not survived the 750 years since it was built. Facing W, the stairway leads up to a chamber above which is a fearsome kala head. The icon within the inner chamber may have been the Siva statue which is in the collection of a museum in Amsterdam, or it may have been a post-mortem image of King Anusapati, or both – often shrines of this kind housed an image of a god whom the departed king was believed to have represented on earth. Around the base are some fine carvings of garuda, depicting the story of garuda liberating his mother Winata from the tyranny of the dragon Kadru. Admission by donation. *Getting there*: catch a minibus from Malang's Arjosari station to Tumpang (600Rp), and then a colt or ojek from Tumpang station (another 600Rp). The route to the site passes through Tumpang for 1 km before coming to a 'T' junction; turn right, the temple is on the left another 6 km along the road. It is set back from the street, so is easily missed.

Selekta and Batu are two hill resorts 4 km apart on the S face of Mt Arjuna and Mt Welirang, 23 km from Malang. Batu is marketed as Java's 'apple town' (apparently the first tree was planted in 1908 by a Meester Reyterdewitt) although the apples are second rate. **Candi Songgoriti** dated to 732 can be reached from either resort. The turn-off for the candi is just out of Batu on the road towards Pare. There are hot springs and pools, waterfalls and hiking trails around this beautiful scenery, sometimes referred to as Java's 'little Switzerland'. Batu and Selekta are popular with Malang residents and hotel rates rise considerably over the weekend, when hotels are often full. **Accommodation** In both towns, including the luxurious **A-B** *Kusuma Agro Wisata*, Jl Abdul Gani Atas, T 93333, F 93196 in Batu (with restaurant, swimming pool, tennis and various caged animals, set on hill above Batu, rather clinical, almost like a massive showhouse, but very comfortable nonetheless. Of the cheaper places – and most are pricey – the best are **E** *Losmen Kawi*, Jl Gajah Mada 19 (in Batu), T 91139, clean with attached mandi; **D** *Hotel Perdana*, Jl Gajah Mada 101, T 91104, hot water bathrooms, decent, clean and reasonably priced. *Getting there*: buses leave from Malang's new Lan-

dungsari station on Jl M Haryono, either direct to Selekta or via Batu.

Mount Bromo and Ngadas lie to the E of Malang. Most people visit Mt Bromo from Probolinggo (see page 296), although it is possible to climb the mountain from the village of Ngadas, on Bromo's S face. From Ngadas there are two trekking trails; one leads to the village of Ranupani, the highest community in Java, the other to Bromo's summit (12.5 km). The trekking here is more demanding than from Probolinggo, although the route is well worn and a guide is not required. It is possible to trek from Ngadas to Cemoro Lawang, from where minibuses run down to Probolinggo (see page 296). Villagers may offer their homes as guesthouses. **Getting to Ngadas** Catch a minibus from Malang's Arjosari station to Tumpang (22 km); from Tumpang catch a minibus to Gubuk Klakah and from there a 4WD vehicle (or hitch) up to Ngadas (another 22 km from Tumpang).

Ngliyep and Balekambang are two beach resorts, 67 km and 57 km S of Malang respectively. Both have accommodation. En route for the beach is the town of Kepanjen, where there is a hotel (**E** *Penginapan Panca Karya*, Jl Sawanggaling 18, next to the mosque, T 211, big clean rooms, no fans or mandis ensuite). *Getting there*: by bus from Malang's Gadang station. For Balekambang take a bus to Turen and then change. For Ngliyep take a bus to Kepanjen and change, or take a colt to Bantur and change.

Festivals

Nov: *Anniversary of Malang Regency* (28th), commemorated with traditional art performances and other shows.

Local information
● Accommodation
For a city which is not firmly on the tourist trail, Malang has a good selection of hotels adding to the city's already not inconsiderable attractions. However, there seems to be a dearth of rooms and hotels get booked up quickly; it is best to arrive early to secure a room in one of the better hotels.

A+-A *Regent's Park*, Jl Jaksa Agung Suprapto 12-16, T 63388, F 61408, a/c, poor restaurant, pool, western-style 'luxury' hotel with good rooms and general facilities, but a location on the edge of the city centre, there is little to distinguish it from a host of other such hotels.

A *Tugu Park*, Jl Tugu 3, T 63891, F 62747, a/c, restaurant, pool, stylish hotel (1990) by the independence monument, excellent, well-appointed rooms with a real attempt to create an attractive, atmospheric setting, good value by international standards and best in Malang in terms of style, location and price, rec; **A-B** *Kartika Prince*, Jl Jaksa Agung Suprapto 17, T 61900, F 61911, a/c, restaurant, pool, 'Chinese' style luxury hotel, on main road, the least obviously attractive of the high rise hotels although it works well enough; **A-B** *Montana*, Jl Kahuripan 9, T 62751, F 61633, adobe-style lobby not maintained throughout the hotel, average rooms but efficient service, good buffet breakfast incl, central.

B-C *Splendid Inn*, Jl Majapahit 4, PO Box 142, T 66860, F 63618, most a/c, pool, TV, characterful but slightly jaded hotel with 50s decor next to Balai Kota, huge TV, flanked by four large speakers dominates the lobby, quiet with large rooms but rather fusty, for those who prefer old Java to new western style, popular with foreign visitors and therefore often full, rec; **B-D** *Hotel Pelangi*, Jl Merdeka Selatan 3, T 65156, F 65466, some a/c, good central location, and attractive old high-ceilinged dining room (the hotel was built in 1915 when it was known as the *Palace Hotel*) decorated with old Dutch tiles, rooms are fine, but it has lost some of the jaded charm of hotels like the *Splendid Inn* during its rather over-enthusiastic renovation, the food here though is very good, reputedly because the cook at *Toko Oen* (see Places to eat) was enticed to come here.

C *Margosuko*, Jl Achmad Dahlan 40, T 25270, coffee shop, rooms with mandi and hot water, adequate; **C-D** *Malinda*, Jl KH Zainul Ariffin 39, T 64402, large rooms with 60s furniture, good central position, cold water showers, some style and good value, rec; **C-D** *Menara*, Jl Pejajaran 5 (walking distance from train station), T 62871, rather characterless, price incl breakfast; **C-D** *Santosa*, Jl KH Agus Salim 24, T 66889, F 67098, some a/c, good central position, rooms are immaculate, some with sitting areas outside, hot water showers, economy rooms are a little small and dark and the ones downstairs near the entrance lobby are very noisy, but still very clean,

a good and well-run little hotel; **C-D** *Willy's Indah* (nr the railway station), new hotel, rooms with a/c and hot water attached bathrooms, breakfast incl.

D *Aloha*, Jl Gajah Mada, wacky Hawaian-style hotel like a seedy fair ground show, rooms are less than average; **D** *Pejajaran*, Jl Pejajaran 17 (walking distance from train station), T 25306, set in quiet street but rooms are rather shabby; **D-E** *Helios*, Jl Pattimura 37 (walking distance from train station), T 62741, set around courtyard, the rooms in the new wing are immaculate and more expensive, the old rooms are quite serviceable, homely, rather ramshackle feel, rec; **D-E** *Hotel Riche*, Jl Basuki Rachmat 1, T 25460, excellent central location and friendly management but they are working with a poor product, bar has the quaint 50s feel, cinema style lobby, this is a warren of generally poor and rather grubby rooms, check carefully before booking in.

E-F *Bamboo Denn*, corner of Jl Arjuna and Jl Kawi, T 66256, very popular with cheapest dormitory rooms available, but still clean and well-managed, good source of information, a little out of town, hard to find (look out for the Bank Rakyat Indonesia; bus 'AT' runs there), rec.

● **Places to eat**

♦♦*New Hong Kong*, Jl AR Hakim, best Chinese in town; **♦♦***Minang Jaya*, Jl Jend Basuki Rakhmat 111, good Padang food; **♦♦***Toko Oen*, Jl Basuki Rakhmat 5, younger sister of Semerang branch, hangar-like fossilized restaurant serving an enormous array of Indonesian and European foods, also 26 varieties of ice cream, juices, sandwiches, Dutch breads and toast crackers 'flying saucers', mostly western clientele nowadays but good food and interesting surroundings, good for a western 'fix' in a cool setting, bakery and sweet shop serve large selection of rather dry cakes and biscuits; *Dirga Surya*, Jl Jend Gatot Subroto 81, good Chinese;

Fastfood: *Dunkin' Donuts*, Jl Semeru (next to East Java Information Office); *Kentucky Fried Chicken*, Jl Basuki Rachmat (nr the BNI Bank); *McDonald's*, Jl Basuki Rachmat (next to Sarinah's Dept Store and opp Toko Oen's).

Foodstalls: in the *Gajah Mada Plaza*, Jl H Agus Salimor or at the night market at the S end of Jl Majapahit.

Bakeries: *Catherine Fancy Bakery*, corner of Jl Pattimura and Jl Suropati (nr the *Helios Hotel*), good bakery, although some of the cakes look as though they might glow in the dark.

● **Airline offices**
Merpati (*Kartika Prince Hotel*), Jl Jaksa Agung Suprapto 17, T 27962; **Sempati**, *Regent's Park Hotel*, Jl Jacksa Agung Suprapto 12-16.

● **Banks & money changers**
A number in the town centre of which the most efficient are: **Bank Bumi Daya**, Jl Merdeka Barat; **Bank Central Asia**, corner Jl Basuki Rachmat and Jl Kahuripan; **BNI**, Jl Basuki Rachmat 75-77; **Lippobank**, Jl Merdeka Timur (on the main square).

● **Entertainment**
Cinemas: *Mandala*, Jl Agus Salim; Radio Republic Indonesia (RRI), first Sat of the month, 2100; Senaputra Amusement Park, last Wed of the month, 2000; *Studio Cinema*, Jl Merdeka Utara (central position on the main square).

● **Post & telecommunications**
Area code: 0341.
General Post Office: Jl Merdeka Selatan.

● **Shopping**
Antiques: *Art Shop Abu*, Jl May Jend Haryono 150 (on left hand side of road on way towards Batu), small antique shop with some good pieces.

Department stores & plazas: *Matahari*, Jl Pasar Besar; *Metro Dept Store*, Jl Merdeka Utara (on the main square); *Sarinah Dept Store* and *Hero Supermarket*, Jl Basuki Rachmat (next to *McDonald's*).

● **Tour companies & travel agents**
Tours can be arranged to most sights around Malang incl the Hindu-Buddhist temples of Jago, Kidal, Singasari and Badut, and the hill resorts of Batu and Selekta. Prices are much the same between companies, although *Toko Oen's Tour and Information Service*, Jl Basuki Rakhmat 5, T 64052, F 69497, offer the best and most imaginative deals. *Jack*, Jl A Yani 20i, T 471061, F 471062; *Mujur Surya*, 33A Jl Bromo, T 27955; *Penghela Swedesi*, Jl Basuki Rakhmat, T 62564; *Tanjung Permai*, Jl Basuki Rakhmat 41, T 66924.

● **Tourist offices**
Dinas Pariwisata Jawa Timur, Jl Kawi 41, T 68473, helpful and knowledgeable staff, and **East Java Information Office**, at Jl Semeru 2, T 61632, open Mon-Sun, 0830-1800, helpful staff with good knowledge and advice but not many handouts.

● **Useful addresses**
Immigration Office: Jl Raden Panji Suroso 4, T 4039.

PHPA office: Jl Raden Intan 6, T 65100.

● **Transport**
882 km from Jakarta, 89 km from Surabaya.

Local Becaks, colts & microlets: are the main form of public transport (there are no town buses). They run between the 3 bus stations, through the centre of town. Letters on the front indicate the route – A-D is Arjosari to Dinoyo, A-G is Arjosari to Gadang, and D-G, Dinoyo to Gadang. Rather confusingly, Gadang to Dinoyo is D, Gadang to Arjosari E, F or G, and Dinoyo to Arjosari, F (350Rp). **Metered taxis** (flag fall, 800Rp).

Train The central station, a building of perhaps 1930s vintage, is at the E end of Jl Kerta Negara. Trains leave here for Jakarta via Surabaya, the fastest service. There is another station to the S of the city, the Kota Lama Station. Trains leave here for Jakarta via Blitar. Trains coming in to Malang from the S continue on to the more convenient new central station. Regular connections with Surabaya 3 hrs and Jakarta 12½ hrs (see timetable page 917).

Road Bus: Malang has 3 bus stations. The largest is Arjosari on Jl R Intan to the N of town which serves Jakarta, Surabaya 2½ hrs, Probolinggo, Bandung, Denpasar (Bali), and Bogor. For Yogya and Solo, change in Surabaya. The Gadang station on Jl Kol Sugiono, to the S of the city centre and serves Blitar (from where there are connections by the S route for Solo and Yogya), Dampit and Lumajang. The new Landungsari station (formerly the Dinoyo station) on Jl M Haryono to the NW serves Kediri, Batu, Selekta and Jombang. Colts link the three terminals with each other through the centre of the city. For those wishing to book *bis malam* to Jakarta, Yogya, Mataram (Lombok), Bali and elsewhere, there are offices across town. The Tourist Information Service at *Toko Oen's*, Jl Basuki Rakhmat 5, has good information on the range of choice. Tickets can also be bought from most other tour companies and from the 'Post Office' on Jl Suropati (nr the *Helios Hotel*).

TRETES

Tretes is yet another Javanese hill resort, set at 700m above sea-level on the NE slopes of the twin peaks of Mt Arjuna (at 3,339m, one of the highest volcanoes on Java) and Mt Welirang (3,156m). The town is an attractive little place, cool at night, and with good views to the plain below and mountains above. Perhaps because it is a weekend retreat for wealthy Surabayans, accommodation is over-priced compared with Java's other hill resorts.

The **Kakek Bodo Waterfall** is a short walk S from town; walking uphill, take the road to the right before the river. The path begins before the *Dirga Hayu Hotel* and leads to the waterfall. There are numerous other **hiking trails** from Tretes; ask at hotels for information. The area around Tretes is said to produce some of the best fruit in Indonesia – particularly durians (see page 897). There is a **fruit market** towards the bottom of town near the intersection of Jl Ke Trawas and Jl Palembon.

Excursions

Candi Jawi is about 5 km down the mountain from Tretes (see page 271). *Getting there*: catch a minibus towards Pandaan.

The **Botanical Gardens at Purwodadi** are 22 km from Tretes (see page 271). *Getting there*: catch a minibus to Pandaan, and from there, one of the many S-bound buses which run between Surabaya and Malang. The gardens are about 15 km S of Pandaan.

Trowulan, the former capital of the Majapahit Kingdom, can be reached from Tretes. A beautiful mountain road winds for about an hour round the lower slopes of Mt Arjuna, past holiday homes for the Surabaya rich and famous, to the site of the city (see page 285). *Getting there*: no regular colts or buses take this route; hire a car and driver for the journey.

Local information
● **Accommodation**

NB There is additional accommodation a few kilometres down the mountain at Prigen. Like so many other mountain get-away resorts on Java, accommodation can seem expensive – especially at weekends when prices inflate.

A *Natour*, Jl Pesanggrahan 2, T 81776, F 81101, restaurant, pool, tennis, particularly good position on the edge of a gully, but rather spartan rooms and generally overpriced; **A** *Surya*, Jl Taman Wisata, T 81991, F 81058, pool, tennis, most luxurious hotel in town, lacking in hill resort character, recently extended;

B *Tanjung Plaza*, Jl Wilis 7, T 81102, rather scruffy.

C *Wisma Semeru Indah*, Jl Semeru 7, T 81701, good views and reasonable rooms.

D *Sri Katon*, Jl Taman Wisata.

Camping: there is a camping ground at the Kakek Bodo Waterfall.

● **Banks & money changers**
There are no banks in Tretes although hotels will change money.

● **Sports**
Horse riding: in the hills around. Men loiter outside hotels with their mangy looking animals, in the hope of luring some custom.

● **Transport**
55 km from Malang, 60 km from Surabaya.

Road Bus: buses between Surabaya and Malang will drop passengers off at Pandaan. From here minibuses travel up the mountain to Tretes.

SURABAYA

Surabaya is Indonesia's second largest city with a population of over 3 million – 10 times the figure for 1940. In 1900 it was the largest town in the Dutch East Indies, exceeding even Batavia in the size of its population. It was also the colony's most important port, and was only superceded by Jakarta's Tanjung Priok, in terms of tonnage handled, in the 1950s. Surabaya remains an important manufacturing centre, and the city lies at the heart of one of the fastest growing industrial regions in Indonesia.

Surabaya is not a popular tourist destination. It has no sights to compare with those around Yogyakarta, and lies to the N of the overland route between Bali, Yogya and Jakarta. However, it is an important port for vessels sailing to Sulawesi, Maluku, Kalimantan and Nusa Tenggara, and is frequently a port of call for local and foreign businessmen.

History

Surabaya emerged as an important port during the 16th century, although it was not until the 17th century that it became an influential power. By 1622, Surabaya exercised control over Gresik on the N coast, over parts of SW Kalimantan, and over the rich ricelands of the Brantas River valley. Ships from Surabaya were frequent visitors to Melaka, the ports of Ambon and Ternate in Maluku (the Moluccas), and other regional trading centres. However, as it expanded, the kingdom came into conflict with Mataram over control of E and Central Java.

The son of King Senopati of Mataram, Panembahan Sedaing Krapyak, began the war against Surabaya in 1610 and for the next 3 years he sent an army to devastate the surrounding ricelands on which the city's economy depended. Krapyak died in 1613, to be succeeded by his great warrior son, Agung. Like Krapyak, Sultan Agung harrassed the towns and villages of E Java that were loyal to Surabaya. It was not until 1620 that he turned his attention to the city itself. He besieged Surabaya with 80,000 troops – one of the largest armies ever assembled in pre-colonial Java – burning crops and killing livestock. Then he ordered the damming of the river Brantas and the poisoning of the city's water supply. By 1625, Surabaya had been starved into submission. The *Dagh-Register* records that "in Surabaya not more than 500 of its 50 to 60,000 people were left, the rest having died or gone away because of misery and famine".

Despite this drawn-out and debilitating war with Mataram, Surabaya quickly regained its position as one of Java's premier ports. By the latter part of the 17th century the city was again a conduit for the export of rice, salt, sugar, bronze and other products and the Dutch had established a trading post in the city.

By the beginning of the 18th century, the heavy-handed actions of the Dutch had served to alienate the rulers of Surabaya. In 1717 the city rebelled, calling for the Balinese to help their cause. There followed 6 years of vicious conflict which ultimately led to complete defeat, and the death or imprisonment of the rulers of the city. In 1743, the Mataram king was forced to award full sovereignty over Surabaya to the VOC. With Mataram subdued, Surabaya was developed by the VOC into Java's premier port.

Places of interest

The centre of Surabaya is marked by **Jalan Pemuda**. Most of the city's better hotels and the shopping centres for which it seems to have a penchant, are found within walking distance of this road. The immaculately maintained **Grahadi** towards the W end of Jl Pemuda was the residence of the Dutch colonial governor of E Java; today it is still the official residence of the Governor of E Java. Opposite is a rather poor **statue of Soerjo**, E Java's first post-independence governor who was killed during a communist insurrection in Madiun in 1948. Behind him is the stone statue known as **Joko Dolog** (guardian of the young teak forest). This was carved in 1326 as a memorial to the last king of the Singasari Dynasty, and was transferred here from Mojokerto by the Dutch. At the junction of Jl Pemuda and Jl Yos Sudarso is a statue of **General Sudirman** (Soedirman), a military leader during the war of independence (1945-1949) and now immortalized in road names across the nation. He was appointed to command the resistance forces in Nov 1945.

At the N edge of the city is **Kali Mas** or River of Gold, a wharf at which traditional *perahu* moor. Most vessels here are Bugis *pinisi*, better known in the West as **Makassar schooners** (see page 620). It is claimed that these elegant boats are made without a single nail – they are pegged together. Pinisi link the islands of the archipelago, carrying mixed cargoes of lumber, barbed wire, glass, tinned goods, house tiles...just about anything that is relatively water resistant. Although modern cargo vessels are becoming more common, the versatility of the pinisi mean that they remain popular and profitable, and indeed represent one of the largest sailing fleets still operating in the world

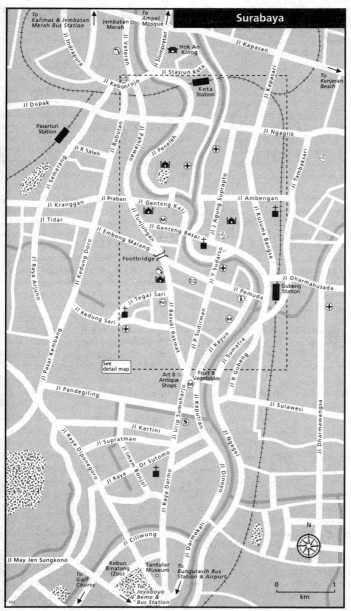

Surabaya

To Kalimas & Jembatan Merah Bus Station
To Ampel Mosque
Jembatan Merah
Jl Slompretan
Hok An Kiong
Jl Kapasan
Jl Indrapura
Jl Veteran
Jl Stasiun Kota
Kota Station
Jl Kebonrojo
To Kenjeran Beach
Jl Kapasari
Jl Dupak
Pasarturi Station
Jl R Saleh
Jl Ngaglik
Jl Bubutan
Jl Pahlawan
Jl Peneleh
Jl Semarang
Jl Tambaksari
Jl Praban
Jl Genteng Kali
Jl Ambengan
Jl Kranggan
Jl Tunjungan
Jl Genteng Besar
Jl Kusuma Bangsa
Jl Tidar
Jl Agung Suprapto
Jl Embong Malang
Footbridge
Jl Kedung Doro
Jl Y Sudarso
Jl Dharmahusada
Gubeng Station
Jl Pemuda
Jl Tegal Sari
Jl Basuki Rakmat
Jl Kedung Sari
Jl Raya Arjuno
Jl P Sudirman
Jl Kayun
Jl Sumatra
See detail map
Jl R Gubeng
Art & Antique Shops
Fruit & Vegetables
Jl Pandegiling
Jl Sulawesi
Jl Pasar Kembang
Jl Urip Sumoharjo
Jl Keputran
Jl Dharmawangsa
Jl Kartini
Jl Raya Diponegoro
Jl Supratman
Jl Imam Bonjol
Jl Ngagel
Jl Dioyo
Jl Raya Dr Sutomo
Jl Raya Darmo
Jl Ciliwung
Jl Darmokali
Jl May Jen Sungkono
N
To Golf Course
Kebun Binatang (Zoo)
Tantular Museum
To Bungurasih Bus Station & Airport
To Joyoboyo Bemo & Bus Station
0   1
km
101

The battle for Surabaya, 1945

The battle for Indonesia's independence lasted 5 years from the end of WW2 (see page 48). Surabaya was the site of the heaviest fighting and so became a symbol of resistance to the re-imposition of Dutch colonial rule. When the Japanese surrendered in 1945, the commander in the area, Vice-Admiral Shibata Yaichiro, ordered his men to give-up their arms not to the Dutch, but to the Indonesian resistance. Soon afterwards, at the end of Oct, two religious associations – the Nahdatul Ulama and Masyumi – announced that defending the fatherland was a Holy War, and in response to the call many thousands of young Muslims flooded into Surabaya. One of the leaders of the movement, Soetomo, broadcast stirring speeches on the local radio, calling the faithful to resist any return of the Dutch.

On 25 Oct, 6,000 British Indian troops were landed to evacuate former Japanese internees. Ranged against this small force were 20,000 Indonesian troops in a newly-formed People's Security Army (Tentara Keamanan Rakyat), and over 100,000 assorted irregular fighters. Faced with the possibility of a massacre of their own troops, the British flew Sukarno, Hatta and Amir Sjarifuddin to Surabaya to arrange a ceasefire. When this broke down, the British commander, Brigadier-General AWS Mallaby was killed. In retribution the British – who had by now brought in reinforcements – mounted an assault on the city. With the use of airpower and their better equipped soldiers, the British defeated the resistance, finally quelling the city after 3 weeks and the death of many thousands of Indonesians. The date of the assault – 10 Nov – is still commemorated as Heroes' Day (*Hari Pahlawan*). But though tactically defeated, the resistance scored a significant strategic victory. As Professor Ricklefs writes in his history of modern Indonesia:

"The battle of Surabaya was a turning-point for the Dutch... for it shocked many of them into facing reality. Many had quite genuinely believed that the Republic represented only a gang of [Japanese] collaborators without popular support. No longer could any serious observer defend such a view".

today. The wharf is on Jl Kalimas Baru, on the eastern side of the Tanjung Perak Port area. Strictly-speaking, photographs can only be taken with permission from the harbour master. Ask at the police post. The wharf is best visited in the morning; boats tend to leave by mid-morning.

South of the port, to the E of the Surabaya River, is **Kampung Arab** or the Kasbah Quarter (it lies off Jl Kyai Mas Mansur). This is the heart of the old city with narrow streets and a bazaar atmosphere. (The Indonesian word for market – *pasar* – is derived from the Arabic *bazaar*.) Among its buildings, the architecturally and historically most important is the **Ampel Mosque**, the oldest mosque in E Java, originally built by Sunan Ampel, one of the nine *walis* (see page 95), in the

15th century. Sunan Ampel died in Surabaya in 1481 and his grave lies within the mosque compound. The site is a popular pilgrimage spot for Indonesians.

South of the Arab quarter is the **Jembatan Merah** or Red Bridge, a strategic site in the Battle of Surabaya waged during Nov 1945 (see box). Close to the bridge, on Jl Slompretan is the Chinese temple **Hok An Kiong**, while just to the N of the bridge is Surabaya's Chinatown. The Hok An Kiong temple is three centuries old and traditional Chinese puppet shows are said to be held here in the middle and end of every month (every full and half moon). South of here is the **Tugu Pahlawan** or Heroes Monument, which stands in the centre of the rather unexciting main city square, opposite the Governor's office on Jl

Pahlawan. It commemorates the thousands of young Muslims who poured into the city and died fighting against British forces during the Battle of Surabaya (see box).

The **Kayun Flower Market** is situated on Jl Kayun, while the **People's Amusement Park** (known as THR) is E of the river on Jl Kusuma Bangsa. Open 1800-2300 Mon-Sun.

The **Kebun Binatang** (or Zoo) is within walking distance of the Joyoboyo bemo station on Jl Setail, but about 3 km from the centre of the city. It is one of the best zoos in Southeast Asia, with a good collection of local and regional animals. Most bemos run to Joyoboyo. Admission 2,000Rp (additional 400Rp for aquarium). Open 0900-1700 Mon-Sun. Opposite the zoo on Jl Raya Diponegoro is the **Tantular Museum**, an ethnographic and archaeological museum with what might be termed an eclectic collection including a steam-powered Daimler motorcycle and neolithic artefacts. Open: 0700-1400 Tues-Thur, 0700-1100 Fri, 0700-1230 Sat. Admission: by donation.

Excursions

Trowulan lies 52 km SW of Surabaya on the Surabaya-Solo road not far from Mojokerto, see page 285. *Getting there*: take a bus from Surabaya's Bungurasih terminal travelling towards Jombang (there are many) and ask to be let off in Trowulan.

Kenjeran is a rather unexciting beach E of Surabaya. *Getting there*: take a bemo, either line (lyn) 'S' (from Joyoboyo) or 'R1' (from Jembatan Merah).

Madura can be visited as a day excursion – best during the *bull racing* season from Aug-Oct (see page 291).

Gresik lies 14 km N of Surabaya and is an ugly industrial satellite town, with one saving grace: it is the site of the grave of Sunan Giri, one of the nine imam (or walis) who are credited with having first brought Islam to Java (see page 95). A staircase leads up past graves of other holy men to the imam's resting place, which is housed inside an attractive double chamber of heavily carved wood. To the left of the imam's grave are the graves of his children. **Festival** *Khol Sunan Giri* (30 Sep), commemorates the death of Sunan Giri. *Getting there*: microlets travel from Surabaya to Gresik, through an unattractive industrial landscape. Get off at a marked turning to the left, on Jl Sunan Giri (ask for *makam Sunan Giri*); horse-drawn carts and ojeks wait at the end of the road to transport visitors and pilgrims the 1½ km to the tomb.

Paciran lies on Java's N coast, 60 km NW of Surabaya. Near here, on a hill top, is the intricately carved gateway of **Sendang Duwur**, named after the Muslim saint Sunan Sendang who was buried here in 1585. It is interesting for its combination of styles – the carving includes Arabic calligraphy alongside Hindu designs. *Getting there*: from the Bungurasih bus terminal, S of town.

Tuban lies 100 km NW of Surabaya on Java's N coast, see page 287. *Getting there*: buses from Bungurasih terminal S of town.

Mount Bromo lies 145 km SE of Surabaya (see page 298).

Tours

Local travel agents offer city tours (about 24,000Rp), trips to Mt Bromo (80,000Rp for day trip), Trowulan and the ancient sites of the Majapahit Kingdom (80,000Rp), as well as to Malang, Madura, Selecta and Batu. *PT Wisata Bahari Mas Permai*, Jl Tanjung Priok 11 (T 25268, F 25559), provide 'traditional' day-long cruises on their *perahu* (schooner). **The East Java Regional Tourism Office**, in association with the provincial agricultural department (Jl Gayung Kebonsari 173, Wonocolo, (S of centre), T 811879), are pushing 'agrotourism': they organize tours of coffee estates, tobacco farms, coconut plantations, sugarcane mills and other similar 'sights'. There are also trips to a teak plantation, 150 km W of Surabaya (see page 251).

Festivals

May: *Anniversary of THR* (Peoples' Amusement Park) (19th), cultural performances and stalls at THR Surabaya Hall. *Anniversary of founding of the city* (3rd) held at Taman Surya, cultural performances and other ceremonies.

Nov: *Heroes Day* (10th), centred around the Heroes Monument, commemorates those who died in the Battle of Surabaya in Nov 1945. Parades and various festivities.

Local information
● Accommodation
Reflecting the status of the city as a business centre, not a tourist destination, there are a good number of mid and upper range hotels, but woefully few decent losmen and homestays.

A+ Hyatt Regency, Jl Basuki Rakhmat 124-128, T 511234, F 521508, a/c, restaurant, pool, best in town, all facilities – at the end of 1993 another 234-rm tower addition was opened making this a hotel on a grand scale.

A Altea, Jl Raya Darmo 68-76, T 69501, F 69204, a/c, restaurant; **A Elmi**, Jl Panglima Sudirman 42-44, T 471571, F 525625, a/c, restaurant, large pool, modern and characterless; **A Garden**, Jl Pemuda 21, T 521001, F 516111, a/c, restaurant, access to pool, the older version of the *Garden Palace*, price incl breakfast; **A Garden Palace**, Jl Yos Sudarso 11, T 520951, a/c, restaurant, rooftop pool, under renovation, price incl breakfast; **A Natour Simpang**, Jl Pemuda 1-3, T 42151, F 510156, a/c, restaurant, central location; **A Sahid Surabaya**, Jl Sumatra 1, T 522711, F 516292, a/c, restaurant.

B Cendana, Jl KBP M Duryat, T 42251, F 514367; **B Jane's House**, Jl Dinoyo 100-102, T 67722, price incl breakfast; **B Majapahit**, Jl Tunjungan 65, T 43351, F 43599, a/c, attractive old building, centrally located, recently undergone limited renovation, cheaper rooms are cramped; **B Ramayana**, Jl Basuki Rakhmat 67-69, T 46321; **B Tanjung**, Jl Panglima Sudirman 43-45, T 42431, F 512290, rather dirty, price incl breakfast; **A Weta International**, Jl Genteng Kali 3-11, T 519494, F 45512/519494, a/c, restaurant, new and efficient, glitzy western-style hotel, central location, TV, hot water, piped muzac etc.

C-D Gubeng Hotel, Jl Sumatera 18 (in front of the *Sahid Surabaya*), a dirty rather squalid place with little to rec it bar its location close to the railway station.

D Ganesha, Jl Prapen Indah 41B, T 818705, price incl breakfast; **D Hamanda**, Jl Cokroaminoto 2, T 67325, a/c.

E Bamboe Denn, Jl Ketabang Kali 6A, T 40333, the best-known travellers' losmen in Surabaya, linked to a language school; small rooms but central and clean, excellent place for information, good value place, basic food available, rec; **E Stasiun**, Jl Stasiun Kota 1, T 20630, next to the Surabaya Kota train station; **C-D Paviljoen**, Jl Genteng Besar 94-98, T 43449, some a/c, old hotel in need of renovation, dark and musty but on the plus side offers reasonable value for money for Surabaya, breakfast incl.

● Places to eat
The *Tunjungan Plaza*, on Jl Tunjungan houses a large selection of restaurants, serving Chinese, Javanese, Japanese and seafood.

Indonesian: ♦♦♦*Rumah Makan Ria*, Jl M Duryat 7 (nr *Hyatt Regency*), Sundanese specialities locally acclaimed, small restaurant, friendly; ♦♦*Antika*, Jl Raya Darmo 1, good Padang food; ♦*Mie Ayam*, Jl Genteng Kali 119, good, cheap food; ♦*Mie Tunjungan*, Jl Genteng Kali 127 (nr intersection with Jl Tunjungan), good, cheap food; ♦*Puri Garden*, Jl Pemuda 33-37 (in the *Delta Plaza*), huge Indonesian menu; ♦*Soto Ambengan*, Jl Ambengan 3, locally renowned for its excellent soto, rec; *Coffee House*, Jl Praban 2 (nr intersection with Jl Tunjungan); *Dewi Sri*, Jl Tunjungan 96-98.

Chinese: *Phoenix*, Jl Mayjen. Sungkono; *Mahkota Restaurant*, Jl TAIS Nasution 23, not just one restaurant but a veritable confection of them, on Floor 1, a Chinese restaurant, Floor 2 a Karaoke and steak place, Floor 3 an Indonesian and international restaurant, and on Floor 4 a private room for goodness knows what.

Japanese: *Hana*, *Altea Hotel*, Jl Raya Darmo 68-76, karaoke.

International: limited choice of restaurants although the big hotels serve international food. ♦♦♦*News Café*, Jl Panglima Sudirman 47-49, this bar-cum-restaurant (hosting live bands) has a small international menu of generally good dishes; ♦♦♦*Café Venezia*, Jl Ambengan 16, old-style villa with lovely grounds, international food and some Japanese and Korean dishes; *Granada Bakery*, intersection of Jl Pemuda and Jl Panglima Sudirman; *Pizza Hut*, *Delta Plaza* – the best salad bar in town (?); *Texas Fried Chicken*, Jl Basuki Rakhmat 16.

Foodstalls: *Kayun Park*, along Jl Kedung Doro and Jl Pasar Genteng.

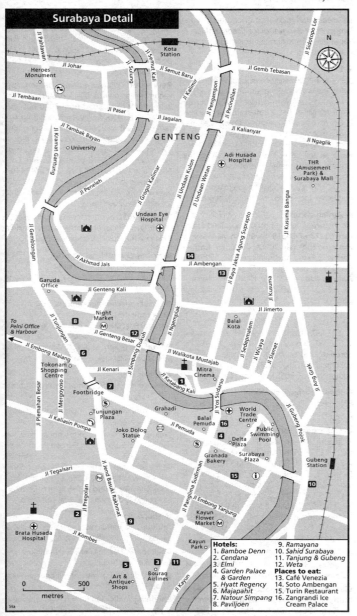

Surabaya Detail

Hotels:
1. Bamboo Denn
2. Cendana
3. Elmi
4. Garden Palace & Garden
5. Hyatt Regency
6. Majapahit
7. Natour Simpang
8. Paviljoen
9. Ramayana
10. Sahid Surabaya
11. Tanjung & Gubeng
12. Weta

Places to eat:
13. Café Venezia
14. Soto Ambengan
15. Turin Restaurant
16. Zangrandi Ice Cream Palace

Ice-cream parlours: *Mon Cheri*, 4th Flr, Tunjungan Plaza; *Zangrandi Ice Cream Palace*, Jl Yos Sudarso 15, stylish but noisy; *Turin*, Jl Embong Kenongo.

● **Bars**
There is a good selection of bars in Surabaya, which are becoming more sophisticated as the city's yuppies grow in number and in wealth. See **Rock Music** in the **Entertainment** section below for bars with live music. *Colors*, Jl Sumatra is a gloomy den in a colonial period building; *Tequila Willies*, Jl Kayon 62 is slicker and less rough at the edges than *Colors* with, as the name suggests, pretensions of Mexican roots; *News Café*, Jl Panglima Sudirman 47-49 (open 1100-0100) is a bar-cum-restaurant with a media theme, local bands occasionally play here.

● **Airline offices**
Air France, T 526134; **Bouraq**, Jl Jend Sudirman 70-72, T 5452918; **British Airways**, Jl Panglima Sudirman 70-72, T 526383; **Cathay Pacific**, Jl Basuki Rakhmat 124-128, T 517543; **Garuda**, Jl Tunjungan 29, T 5457347; **Japan Airlines (JAL)**, T 521733; **KLM**, Jl Yos Sudarso 11, T 520247; **Lufthansa**, T 516355; **Malaysian Airlines**, T 518632; **Mandala**, Jl Raya Diponegoro 49, T 587187; **Merpati**, Jl Urip Sumoharjo 68, T 588111; **Northwest**, T 511870; **Qantas**, T 521880; **Saudia**, T 525802; **Singapore Airlines**, T 519218; **Sempati**, *Hotel Hyatt Regency*, Jl Basuki Rakhmat 124-128, T 525805; **Thai**, Jl Panglima Sudirman 72, T 40681; **United**, T 334528.

● **Banks & money changers**
BNI, Jl Pemuda; Niaga, Jl Tunjungan; Swadesi, Jl Tunjungan 32.

● **Embassies & consulates**
Australia, Jl Pemuda 27-31 (World Trade Centre), T 519123; **Belgium**, Jl Raya Kupang Indah III/24, T 716423; **CIS**, Jl Sumatra 116, T 46290; **Denmark**, Jl Sambas 7, T 575047; **France**, Jl Darmokali 10, T 578639; **Germany**, Taman AIS Nasution 15, T 43735; **India**, Jl Pahlawan 17-19, T 415677; **Japan**, Jl Sumatra 93, T 44677; **Netherlands**, Jl Sumatra 54, T 511612; **UK**, Jl Jemur Sari (S of town) PO Box 310; **USA**, Jl Raya Dr Sutomo 33, T 582287.

● **Entertainment**
Cinemas: *Mitra*, Jl Pemuda 15; *Studio 1-4*, *Tunjungan Plaza*, Jl Basuki Rakhmat (N end).

Classical Javanese dance performances & music: *French Culture Centre*, Jl Darmokali 10-12, T 68639; *Goethe Institute*, Jl Taman

Ade Irma Suryani, T 40368; *Taman Budaya*, Jl Genteng Kali 85, lessons in these arts are also available here; *The People's Amusement Park* or *THR*, E of the river on Jl Kusuma Bangsa, stages performances of wayang, ketoprak, and other dances and drama (open 1800-2300 Mon-Sun).

Rock music: *Colors*, Jl Sumatra, bar and music venue in colonial era building, hosts mostly local heavy metal bands, best from 2300 but open 1800-0200; *Laga*, Jl May Jend Sungkono 107, rather lighter than *Colors*, local bands play cover songs after 2200, open 2000-0200; *Tequila Willies*, Jl Kayon 62, live music and occasional live shows, open 1800-0500, Mon-Sun. Local bands also play live at the *News Café*, Jl Panglima Sudirman 47-49 (open 1100-0100); and *Tavern* (*Hyatt Regency*), Jl Jend Basuki Rachmat (open 1700-0200).

Wayang kulit: performances staged every Sat at the Radio Republic Indonesia station, Jl Pemuda 82-90, studio 2, commencing 2000.

● **Hospitals & medical services**
General Hospital, Jl Dharmahusada 6-8, T 40061; *St Vincentius Hospital*, Jl Raya Diponegoro 51, T 575446.

● **Post & telecommunications**
Area code: 031.
General Post Office: Jl Kebonrojo and Jl Taman Apsari (off Jl Pemuda, nr Joko Dolog).
Wartel (for telephone & fax): *Tunjungan Plaza* (N end of Jl Basuki Rakhmat), open 24 hrs.

● **Sports**
Bowling: *Wijaya Bowling Centre*, Jl Bubutan 1-7 (3rd flr).

Golf: *Yani Golf Club*, Jl Gunungsari (next to *Patra Jasa Motel*, 5 km from city), T 40834.

Swimming: a number of the hotels allow visitors to use their pools, eg *Garden Palace*, Jl Yos Sudarso, 3,000Rp. The *Delta Plaza* on Jl Pemuda (at the back) has a large, usually empty, pool for serious swimmers, 2,500Rp (no shade available). The *Margorejo Indah Sports Centre*, Jl Margorejo (S of town), has a water world.

● **Shopping**
Antiques & handicrafts: Jl Basuki Rakhmat; *Sarinah Craft and Batik Centre*, Jl Tunjungan 7.

Batik: *Batik Danar Hadi*, Jl Diponegoro 184; *Batik Keris*, Jl Tunjungan 12.

Books: *Toko Buku Nasional*, *Tunjungan Plaza*, Jl Basuki Rakhmat.

Shopping malls: Surabaya has an abundance of these. The *Delta Plaza* on Jl Pemuda is said to be the biggest in Southeast Asia; the *Plaza Surabaya*, Jl Pemuda 31-37 must come close; *Apollo Plaza*; *Indo Plaza*; *Surabaya Mall* on Jl Kusuma Bangsa, just S of the THR; *Tunjungan Plaza*, N end of Jl Basuki Rakhmat.

● **Tour companies & travel agents**

Haryono, Jl Pang Sudirman 93, T 41006; *Natrabu*, Jl Dinoyo 40, T 68513; *Orient Express*, Jl Basuki Rakhmat 78, T 43315; *Pacto*, Altea Miramar Hotel, Jl Raya Darmo 68-76, T 69501; *Prima Vijaya Indah Tours*, Delta Plaza, Jl Pemuda 31, T 514399; *Suman Tours*, Jl Yos Sudarso 17, T 510417; *Wiedas Karya Gemilang*, Jl Pucang Rinenggo 1, T 60110.

● **Tourist offices**

East Java Tourism Office, Jl Darmokali 35, T 575448, good range of pamphlets, maps and other information on E Java; **Surabaya Municipal Tourist Development Board**, Jl Gayung Kebonsari 56C, T 832029, only moderately helpful, some maps, open 0700-1500 Mon-Sat; **Tourist Information Centre**, Jl Pemuda 118, T 524499 and Juanda International Airport.

● **Useful addresses**

Immigration Office: Jl Jend S Parman 58A, T 818070.

● **Transport**

793 km from Jakarta, 327 km from Yogya, 89 km from Malang.

Local Becak: banned from much of the city centre. **Bemo**: there are innumerable bemo routes, again some maps mark their routes. There is a flat rate fare of 300Rp. **Bus**: some town maps mark bus routes, 200-400Rp. **Taxi**: metered, with flagfall at 900Rp, 450Rp for every km. *Taksi Zebra*, T 515555/512233. **Car hire**: self drive or with driver from **Avis**, Patra Surabaya Hilton International, Jl Gunung Sari, T 582703.

Air Juanda International Airport is 18 km S of Surabaya. *Transport to town*: irregular number buses into town; taxis cost about 10,000Rp depending on destination. There is a fixed rate schedule; pay at the transport desk outside the arrivals hall. Regular connections on Garuda/Merpati, Sempati and Bouraq with other destinations in Java, Sumatra, Kalimantan, Sulawesi, Bali, Lombok, Nusa Tenggara, Muluku and Irian Jaya (see page 912 for route map).

Train Surabaya has three main railway stations. Gubeng, at the end of Jl Pemuda on Jl Gubeng Masjid, serves Jakarta, Solo, Yogya, Blitar, Malang and Banyuwangi. Some of these trains also stop at Kota station. Pasarturi station on Jl Semarang serves Jakarta via Semarang and other towns on the N route (see timetable, page 917). It is possible to buy a 'combination' ticket – train, ferry, bus – through to Denpasar, Bali 15 hrs. Regular connections with Banyuwangi 7 hrs, Malang 2 hrs, Blitar 5 hrs, Semarang 6½ hrs, Solo 4½ hrs, Bandung 14 hrs and Jakarta 15 hrs.

Road Bus: the new Bungurasih station – the largest, so it is said, in Indonesia – was opened 6 km to the S of the city in 1991. It is at the intersection of Jl Jend A Yani and Jl Let Jen Sutoyo and both town buses and bemos (often via Joyoboyo bus station) link it with the city centre. Regular connections with most destinations in Java; also buses to Denpasar (Bali), Mataram (Lombok), and Sumbawa Besar and Bima (Sumbawa). Local buses run between the Jembatan Merah terminal, in the N of town, and the Bratang terminal in Wonokromo, in the S (250Rp). Night bus companies can be found at Bunurasih Station or on Jl Arjuno and Jl Tidar.

Sea Boat: Surabaya is an important port of call for Pelni ships sailing to towns in Sulawesi, Kalimantan and the islands of Maluku and Nusa Tenggara. In all, 11 Pelni ships dock here on their various fortnightly circuits. (See page 921 for map and schedules.) The Pelni ticket office is on Jl Pahlawan 20, T 21041. There are also numerous unscheduled local cargo vessels sailing to destinations throughout the archipelago – ask the harbour master or simply wander around the Tanjung Perak port for the latest departures. For ferries to Madura see below.

TROWULAN

Trowulan was the site of the capital of the powerful Majahapit Kingdom which reached its zenith in the 14th century. The remains of temples, bathing pools and an artificial lake can be found spread over a wide area and only the major buildings are described below. (The whole archaeological site covers some 100 sq km.) The ruins, most of which have undergone restoration, are built of red brick, making them quite distinctive from other Javanese temple complexes. Because this is an archaeological site, and not a town, there is no accommodation. The nearest town is Mojokerto, 8 km to the N. Here there are some very mediocre places to stay, along with other facilities.

Places of interest A good place to start is the excellent **Museum**, which lies 1 km off the main road to the left, through a red-brick split gate. It houses a wealth of archaeological finds from the area, the majority dating from the Majapahit Period. Fine metalwork and sculpture, well displayed and labelled, give an indication of the sophistication of the society. Admission 200Rp. Open 0700-1600 Tues-Sun. Opposite the museum is the restored **Kolam Segaran**, a large artificial lake, measuring 375m by 175m. Contemporary accounts record that the lake was used as a banquet spot for the entertainment of foreign envoys. At the end of a repast, the precious plates and other tableware would be tossed nonchalantly into the lake to indicate the wealth that the kingdom had at its disposal.

From the lake and museum, continue S for 500m to a crossroads; turn left and a further 2 km along this road is **Candi Bajang Ratu**, a tall slender gateway, with a pyramidal roof. It was built at the beginning of the 14th century and is believed to have been the entrance to a sacred building which has now disappeared. There is some ornamentation on the stepped upper levels. By the Majapa-hit Period, the entrance doorway had become the most important feature of the shrine – a feature which is duplicated in the pura of Bali. Bajang Ratu is the most complete of these gateways, although one of the smaller ones.

A further 1 km on is the unornamented **Candi Tikus**, situated on the left-hand side of the road. The shrine lies below ground level, and is believed to have been a ritual bathing place. The small pavilion set in the middle of the pool represented Mt Penang-gungan (the E Javanese equivalent of Mt Meru), while the surrounding water evoked the sea. The candi was only discovered in 1914 when a plague of rats were found to be nesting in a mound. Upon excavation of the mound, the locals were surprised to discover a temple buried beneath the earth along with the rats; this may be why it became known as Candi Tikus, 'tikus' meaning rat.

Leading off the main road is a narrow lane which runs to **Candi Brahu**, a rectangular temple with cellas projecting from each of its four sides. No decoration remains, and it is at present undergoing restoration. Returning to the main road, and 1.2 km back towards Mojokerto, is a turning on the right to **Candi Wringin**

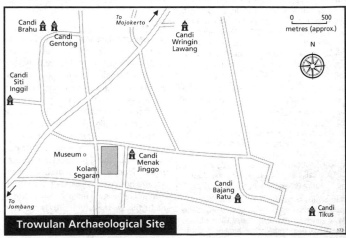

Trowulan Archaeological Site

Tambak fisheries and the perils of over-production

All along the N coast of Java can be seen distinctive *tambak* or fish ponds. Although such ponds are also found on Bali, SW Sulawesi and in NE Java, the N coast of Java is the centre of *tambak* fisheries. Traditionally these fish ponds were dug on the leeward side of protective mangroves, and then used to farm, especially, prawns and milkfish. Salt water, rich with nutrients, is channelled into the ponds along specially dug ditches which, when mixed with river water and rain, produces the brackish conditions in which these fish and prawns thrive. Where production has kept to low intensity traditional methods, the ponds have remained sustainably productive. But in the early 1980s, with prawn prices rising rapidly, farmers turned to the intensive production of tiger prawns. They installed water pumps and used purchased feed to increase production. The protective mangroves, so important as spawning grounds for fish, were removed, and fresh water contaminated with fertilizers and pesticides was channelled from paddy fields into the *tambak*. The high density of prawns led to devastating outbreaks of viral disease, and many farmers who had borrowed money to invest in new technology were bankrupted. The government, to protect the remaining mangroves along the N coast, has now banned the digging of any more ponds. Nonetheless, the *tambak* débâcle represents a lesson in the dangers of over-enthusiastic expansion.

Lawang (so called because a banyan tree – 'wringin' – was found near the gate – 'lawang'). The site is about 200m off the main road and is also known as Candi Bentar because it resembles a temple cut in two, vertically.

● **Accommodation for Trowulan in Mojokerto** Mojokerto, 8 km N of Trowulan, is the nearest large town to the site and accommodation is available although none is particularly rec. But if visitors wish to see the candi at their leisure it may be necessary to be based here. *Padepokan Cahaya Putra*, Trawas, T (0343) 81759; *Swiss Indohotel*, Pacet-Cangar, T (0343) 293285. Cheaper places to stay inc: **C** *Hotel Sriwijaya*, Jl Raya Pacet I, some a/c; **E** *Hotel Tenera*, Jl Cokroaminoto 1, T (0343) 22904.

● **Transport** 52 km from Surabaya, 8 km from Mojokerto. **Local Becak**: some of the sights can be reached on foot, although hiring a becak for a couple of hours is much easier; becak drivers wait for custom on the main road. **Road Bus**: Mojokerto is the nearest large town to Trowulan and buses run here from other main East Java towns incl Surabaya, Jombang, Malang and Kediri. If travelling from Surabaya though, it is not necessary to travel via Mojokerto. Take a bus from Surabaya's Bungurasih terminal travelling towards Jombang (there are many) and ask to be let off in Trowulan.

TUBAN

Tuban is a coastal town, with wide airy streets and a Mediterranean feel. From the W, *tambak* (fish ponds) line the route into this sleepy fishing town and administrative centre (see page 287). Established in the 12th century, by the 16th century Tuban had become an important trading centre with a large Chinese population of merchants and other commercial intermediaries servicing the spice trade between the islands of Maluku and India, the Middle East and Europe. Visitors to the Majapahit Kingdom arrived at Tuban, and Kublai Khan's envoy in the 13th century landed here. The former wealth of this town is reflected in the fine Chinese ceramics which have been found in the vicinity, and in the pageantry of the jousts that were held on the alun-alun (or square) which are recorded in European accounts of the period. The Chinese presence is also reflected in the presence of what is reputed to be the largest Chinese temple in E Java – the **Klenteng Kwan Sing Bio**. This single-storeyed *klenteng*, with rampant dragons over the main entrance, lies to the W of the main square, on the coast, not far from the town centre.

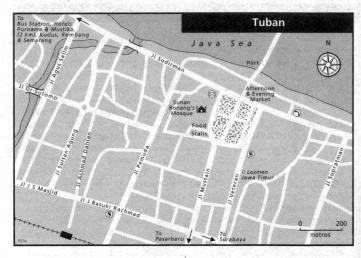

The fine and beautiful **Mesjid Agung Tuban** (Jami'q Mosque) on the grand Alun-alun or main town square honours Sunan Bonang, one of the nine Walis (saints) who introduced Islam to Java (see page 95). The mosque was built in 1894 by the 35th regent of Tuban, Raden Toemenggoeng Koesoemodigdo, and was designed by the Dutch architect Toxopeus. It was renovated most recently in 1986. The **grave of Sunan Bonang**, who is thought to have died in 1525, is situated behind the mosque and has become an important pilgirmmage spot. It was never the intention that Sunan Bonang be buried here: he died in the coastal village of Bonang to the W (see page 260), and his body was being transported to Surabaya where he was to be buried next to his father, Sunan Ampel. But bad weather forced the ship to take refuge at Tuban, where Sunan Bonang ended up being interred. Old porcelain plates are set into the whitewashed walls that surround the tomb and to the right of the entrance way is a trough which, so it is said, was used to water elephants, the preferred mode of transport among the elite of the time. Stalls set up just to the S of the mosque. There is an afternoon and evening market down by the port and jetty near the centre of town, and a daily market off Jl Gadjah Mada, on the inland side of town.

Excursions

Kerek, not much more than a village about 16 km W of Tuban, is one of the last areas where rural households still produce simple batik for home use and local sale. Home production of this type used to be the norm over much of Java: women would make cloth during the agricultural slack season, and then sell a few lengths in local markets. As Michael Hitchcock notes in his book *Indonesian textiles* (British Museum Press: London, 1991), in the late 1980s traditional textiles coloured using natural dyes and hand-spun cotton were still being woven here; blue-black using indigo, yellow with *Cudrania*, bright red with Morinda and *Symplocos fasciculata*, and dark red with *Bruguiera*. *Getting there*: catch a bemo to the market town of Merakurak about 6 km W of Tuban; from here bemos run on to Kerek, about another 10 km W. Alternatively, charter a bemo or ojek.

Weekly tournament (*senenan*) observed by the Dutch in Tuban, Java, in 1599. Note the *gamelan* orchestra playing in the background and the elephant behind the far walls of the arena.

Source: reproduced in Reid, Anthony (1988) *Southeast Asia in the age of commerce*, Yale University Press: New Haven.

Local information

● Accommodation

B-C *Hotel Mustika*, Jl Teuku Umar 3, T 22444, F 21598, some a/c, restaurant, a large, new and rather grandiose hotel on the W edge of town, wide range of rooms some with baths and hot water, others with squat loos and cold water mandis, all are clean but ask to see the full range – suites with 2 bedrooms and 2 bathrooms and a sitting area are good value for groups, the hotel is usually an empty cavernous barn – except when a convention hits town.

C-E *Purnama*, Jl Semarang 1, T 21550, some a/c, restaurant, attractive hotel on a large plot of land overlooking the sea at the W edge of town on the road towards Rembang, rooms are clean and sitting outside in the garden with a brisk sea breeze is a very enjoyable way to spend a hot and lazy afternoon.

E-F *Losmen Jawa Timur*, Jl Veteran 25, T 22312, rooms in an old villa, centrally located, friendly, some with attached bathrooms, older rooms could do with a lick of paint, but overall this is a very atmospheric and pleasant place to stay at the price.

● Places to eat

Foodstalls: the best selection is at the afternoon and evening market down by the port and jetty.

● Banks & money changers

BNI, Jl Bazuki Rachmat 115; Bank Rakyat Indonesia, Jl Veteran.

● Post & telecommunications

Area code: 0356.

Post Office: Jl Sunan Bonang 8 (on town square next to the mosque).

Telephone office: Jl Sudirman.

● Transport

97 km from Rembang, 99 km from Surabaya.

Local Becaks are needed to get around town – it is spread out and hot.

Road Bus: the terminal is on the corner of Jl Sudirman and Jl Teuku Umar, at the NW edge of town. Regular connections with Surabaya, and Semarang via Rembang and Kudus.

MADURA ISLAND

Separated from the mainland by a 3 km-wide strait, Madura is a world apart from Java. The island – 160 km long and 30 km wide – lies off the NW coast and although it is administered as part of the province of E Java, its people regard themselves as Madurese rather than Javanese. Ardent Muslims, and proud of a history of forceful independence, they speak a distinct language and have been partially insulated from the commercialization so evident in Java. Towns are slow-moving and low-key, the landscape is dry, and the people poor by the standards of Java. However, Madura is transformed during the kerapan sapi – or bull racing season (see box, page 291) – when large numbers of tourists are drawn to this backwater of E Java.

Madura is predominantly flat, with a ridge of hills running along the N coast. Most of its 3 million population secure their livelihoods through farming (including growing tobacco), cattle breeding and fishing. Historically there was little economic value to interest the Dutch. Madura became regarded as a source of fine soldiers and also from the late 19th century as a source of salt, in which the colonial authorities maintained a lucrative monopoly. But more than anything else, Madura is famous for its bulls – and certainly they appear healthier-looking than in any other part of Java. Out of the racing season they are put to good use on the land, toning-up their muscles for the big event.

There are three principal towns on Madura: Bangkalan on the W coast and closest to Kamal (the port for Surabaya); Pamekasan, the island's capital in the S-central portion; and Sumenep to the E which offers the greatest concentration of historical sights. The road between the three towns follows the S coast and is relatively quiet and well maintained, passing through small fishing villages notable for their colourful traditional boats moored along the shore.

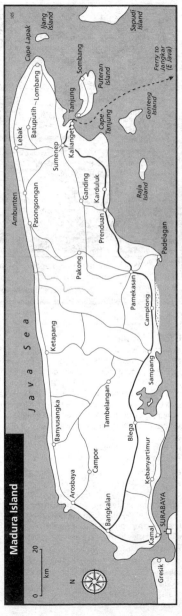

History

Before the 17th century, Madura was a Java in miniature. A number of royal courts or *dalem* controlled the local economy, and these were at the same time the spiritual, cultural and artistic focus of the island. Although today Madura is regarded as being one of the more ardent Muslim areas of Indonesia, the people of the island were not converted to Islam until the 16th century. When Tomé Pires visited Madura in 1512 for example, it was still Hindu, and although local tradition maintains that the conversion of the inhabitants occurred in 1528 when the Prince of Arsobaya embraced Islam, this is likely to have been restricted to the local élite.

Madura was incorporated into the empire of the great Mataram king Sultan Agung during the seige of Surabaya (see page 278) from 1620-1625. By all accounts the campaign for Madura was long and arduous and Agung's army suffered considerable losses. He was forced to devastate the ricelands of the island and also to fight the island's women who joined their menfolk to wage war against the invading army. On finally vanquishing the local forces in 1624, he set about unifying the island, placing it under the control of a single prince with a capital at Sampang. In less than 50 years however, the empire that Sultan Agung had created – and of which Madura was a part – began to fragment.

In 1670 Prince Trunojoyo, buoyed-up by a prophesy that maintained he would be a great hero and that Mataram would fall, travelled to Madura to prepare for revolution. He defeated the local prince and his Javanese soldiers and established a base at Pamekasan on the S coast. By 1671 he had control over the whole island and assembled an impressive army,

Kerapan Sapi (Bull Racing)

Most tourists come to Madura to see the kerapan sapi (bull races) which are staged between Aug and Oct. Bull racing is said to have originated as a simple ploughing contest which, through time, has become institutionalized as an annual festival. The fastest bulls go to stud, on the theory that fast bulls also plough fast.

Like most rural festivals in Southeast Asia, Madura's bull racing occurs after the rice harvest, when farmers – free from the rigours of cultivation – have time to celebrate. However, the demands of tourism mean that today races are staged throughout the year. Associated with the races are parades, dancing and the music of the gamelan orchestra. The bulls are harnessed in pairs and race down a 120m course – taking about 10 secs to cover the distance. The winner is the bull whose legs cross the line first.

Villages and districts compete against one another in knock-out competitions, culminating in the major contest – the Kerapan Besar or Grand Island Championship – which is held in Pamekasan in Sep and preceded by a week of celebrations and ceremonies. Leading up to the big race, bulls are fed up to 50 eggs a day and are dosed up with herbs and various potions of doubtful provenance. It is said they are even given massages and are sung to sleep.

There are bull racing stadiums in Bangkalan, Pamekasan and Sumenep. *Panorama*, the E Java tourist newspaper (Apr 1991), describes the Kerapan Sapi in these terms:

"A folk and home grown enthusiasm which came to existence long ago though lacking the rattle and scarf crew English soccer or the baton twirling beauties of college football as far as the crowd is concerned, its races, district against district, regency against regency even village against village are superbly colorful."

Traditional boats of Madura

Madura is noted for the range and style of its traditional sailing vessels. Particular characteristics of Madurese boats is the boomed triangular sail – the so-called protolateen rig.

The **prahu jaring** (literally, 'fishing net boat') is a heavily-built, single-masted fishing boat with slightly up-turned bow and stern, a triangular sail, and a crew of three. Each village will produce slightly different versions of the boat and they are used for in-shore fishing and the carrying of local cargoes.

The **golekan** is a squat, stubby sea-going boat with twin masts and triangular sails, displacing about 20 tonnes. The name is derived from the Malay word *kolek*, meaning small boat. Today it is rare to see golekan, although they can sometimes be viewed at Bangkalan. In the 1920s the boats were frequent visitors to Singapore, Penang and other regional ports.

The **lis-alis** is a small river or coastal boat ranging from 5 to 10m in length, narrow and elegant, and used for fishing and carrying light general cargoes. Like other Madurese vessels it has a triangular sail, with paired stem- and stern-posts, a projecting keel, and flattened bow and stern.

The **leti leti** is a stubby, sea-going cargo vessel with a short, pointed stern post and a single mast with lateen sail. They were important in serving the trade routes between the islands of Maluku, Nusa Tenggara and Java carrying cattle, salt, rice and simple manufactures.

The **janggolan** was one of the most common of Madurese boats and the word simply means 'transport'. Today they are rarely seen and it is thought that no more are being built – they have been superceded by the smaller lis-alis. Large, sea-going examples exceeded 100 tonnes. They are identifiable by their extended keel, protolateen triangular sail, and decorated flat face between the stern-posts.

Source: Adrian Horridge (1981) *The Prahu: traditional sailing boat of Indonesia*, Oxford University Press;

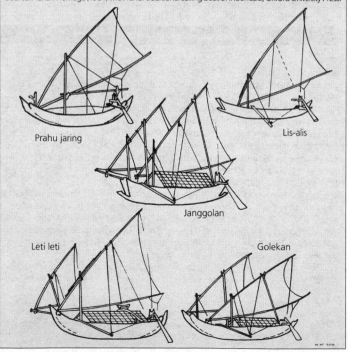

Prahu jaring

Lis-alis

Janggolan

Leti leti

Golekan

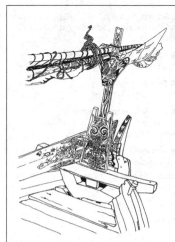

The decoration on the rudder support and sailrest of a *prahu jaring*, partly derived from the Dutch coat of arms, partly from European art nouveau and patterns on the 19th century European manufactures.

Source: Horridge, Adrian (1986) *Sailing craft of Indonesia*, OUP: Singapore.

this history which has given the Madurese a reputation of being a brave and warlike people. Indeed, many of the troops in the Dutch colonial army came from Madura. The Dutch divided the administration of Madura between three royal houses – based at Bangkalan, Pamekasan and Sumenep. These local lords maintained considerable power until the administrative reforms of 1816. By 1887, their influence had been eroded further still until they were reduced to the same status as *bupatis* in Java – mere aristocratic regency figureheads.

● **Transport Local** Two principal roads traverse the island. The main road begins in Bangkalan, runs SE to Sampang (61 km), and then follows the coast to Pamekasan (another 29 km) and Sumenep, a total distance of 154 km. The longer, less well maintained, N route follows the N coast from Bangkalan and after 11 km reaches the village of Arosbaya. Minibuses run regularly between the larger towns. **Sea Boat**: car ferries leave every 30 mins, 24 hrs a day from N of Surabaya on Jl Kalimas Baru (see Surabaya map, city buses 'Pl' and 'C' travel to the ferry dock), docking at Kamal, on the SW coast of Madura, 30 mins later (500Rp, 4,600Rp/car). Minibuses wait at the Kamal dockside to transport passengers to Bangkalan and onward. There are direct buses from Surabaya's Bungurasih terminal through to Sumenep. A daily ferry leaves Sumenep at 0700 for Jangkar (120 km NW of Banyuwangi) 4 hrs (3,400Rp pp).

exploiting the dislike that the local population felt over domination from Java. In 1675, Prince Trunojoyo sailed with his army to the mainland and took Surabaya. By 1677 the rebellion against Mataram was at its height and much of E Java was under rebel control. But with the support of the European troops of the VOC, who sided against Prince Trunojoyo, the rebellion ultimately failed in 1677. Three years later the island was divided into two – W and E Madura and placed under the control of two royal lineages. Later, Mataram ceded E Madura (in 1705), and then W Madura (in 1743) to the Dutch.

But the defeat of Prince Trunojoyo was not to mean that Madura had been pacified. Over the next seven decades Madurese lords would periodically mount campaigns and attack Java. It is

BANGKALAN

Bangkalan is focused on a large central square or *alun-alun*. There is a **small museum** near the square with characteristic Madurese architecture housing ethnographic and historical artefacts including agricultural tools and palm-leaf manuscripts. The bull racing stadium, the centre of activity during **kerapan sapi**, is 1 km out of town on the road S to Kamal.

Excursions

Arosbaya is a small village 11 km NE of town. Nearby, at Air Mata is the royal cemetery of the Cakraningrat family, the lords of Sumenep, who dominated the island during the 17th and 18th centuries. *Getting there*: by minibus from Bangkalan station on the central square.

Festivals
Aug to Oct: *Kerapan Sapi*, traditional bull racing festival (see box, page 291).

Local information
● **Accommodation**
A-D *Ningrat*, Jl H Moh Cholil 113, T 95388, some a/c, best hotel in town, well run, with attractive rooms and bathrooms, rec.

D-E *Wisma Pemda*, Jl Veteran, huge multi-bedrooms making this much cheaper if travelling with 5 or 6 others, central position on the alun-alun.

E *Purnama*, Jl Kartini 19.

● **Post & telecommunuications**
Post Office: Jl Trunojoyo 2.

● **Transport**
16 km N of Kamal, 90 km from Pamekasan.

Road Minibus: the station is on the town square. Regular connections with Kamal, Pamekasan and Sumenep.

PAMEKASAN

Pamekasan is the capital of Madura island, but is still a low key, sleepy town of single-storeyed houses with yellow shutters and attractive white-washed walled alleys. Like Bangkalan, Pamekasan is focused upon a central square in the middle of which is an enigmatic Indonesian monument, in this case looking rather like waving seaweed. Also on the square (Jl Mesjid), is the central **mosque** with its characteristic tiered Javanese roof.

Excursions
Camplong is a beach resort 29 km W of town. It offers visitors a mini amusement park as well as a beach, of sorts; the water here is rather muddy. Traditional boats are picturesquely moored along the shore. *Getting there*: by minibus.

Local information
● **Accommodation**
D-E *Purnama*, Jl Ponorogo 10A, T 81375; **D-E** *Trunojoyo*, Jl Trunojoyo 28, T 81181, some a/c, rooms are reasonably clean, well run.

E *Garuda*, Jl Masigit 1, T 81589, good location right on the square, attractive old house in need of upkeep.

● **Banks & money changers**
Bank Central Asia, Jl Jokotole, will change TCs.

● **Shopping**
Batik: Jl Diponegoro 96.

● **Post & telecommunications**
Area code: 0234.
Post Office: Jl Masigit 3A.

● **Transport**
90 km from Bangkalan, 64 km from Sumenep.

Road Minibus: regular connections with Sumenep, Bangkalan and Kamal.

SUMENEP

Sumenep is the most frequently visited town on Madura, as it offers the most sights of historical interest. These are focused upon the large central square. On the N side of the square is the 18th century **Mesjid Jamik Mosque** with tiered roof, and fronted by a white and yellow washed Madurese gateway. On the opposite side of the square is the street leading to the kraton, Jl Dr Sutomo. On the right-hand side of this street is the badly maintained **Museum Daerah**, with a poorly displayed collection of mainly European pieces, including a carriage. Admission 200Rp. Open Mon-Sun. Opposite, is the 18th century **kraton** built by Panembahan Sumolo, where some of the rooms are open to the public and display a motley collection of Chinese ceramics, krisses, swords, topeng masks, and wayang puppets. Next to the palace is a small water garden or **Taman Sari**. Enclosed by white-washed walls, it contains a clear bathing pool filled with fish. It is said that bathing in the pool will ensure eternal youth.

Excursions
Asta Tinggi The graves of the sultan's family lie 1½ km W of the town.

Pasongsongan Swimming is possible at this mediocre beach NW of Sumenep, home to traditional shipbuilders.

Accommodation F *Coconut Rest House*, welcoming homestay. *Getting there*: by minibus.

Local information
● **Accommodation**
D *Safari Jaya*, Jl Trunojoyo 90 (2 km S of town on road to Pamekasan), T 21989, some a/c; **D-E** *Wijaya I*, Jl Wahid Hasyim 1, T 21532, some a/c, clean rooms and efficiently run; **D-E** *Wijaya II*, Jl Trunojoyo 45-47, T 21433, some a/c, similar standard to sister losmen, *Wijaya I*.

● **Places to eat**
✦✦*Bimba*, Jl Trunojoyo 41, Padang food; *Mawar*, Jl Diponegoro, Chinese; *Wijaya II*, Jl Trunojoyo 45-47, Indonesian.

● **Entertainment**
Bull racing: out of kerapan sapi season, ask the officials at the kraton or museum about staging a bull race.

● **Post & telecommunications**
Area code: 0328.
Post Office: E of the town centre, about 600m from the museum, 1 km from the alun-alun and mosque.
Telekom office: E of town past the Post Office.

● **Shopping**
Batik: the Madurese have a distinctive form of batik, made up of flower patterns of red, purple and blue. Available from *Toko Mashur* (Koleksi Batik Madura), Jl Trunojoyo.

Furniture: several shops in Sumenep sell both antique and new furniture.

● **Sports**
Swimming: pool at *Tampiarto Plaza Hotel*, Jl Suroyo 15, open to non-residents.

● **Transport**
64 km from Pamekasan, 154 km from Bangkalan.

Road Minibus: the station is on Jl Trunojoyo, at the S side of town. Regular connections with Bangkalan, Pamekasan and Kamal.

Sea Boat: see Madura, Transport (page 293). A daily ferry leaves Sumenep at 0700 for Jangkar (60 km N of Banyuwangi) 4 hrs (3,400Rp pp).

PASURUAN

Pasuruan was an independent principality that pre-dated the Dutch occupation of Java. Historical records show that it struggled to maintain its autonomy from more powerful E Java states such as Demak, Surabaya and Mataram during the 16th and 17th centuries – usually losing out in the process. Today Pasuruan, with a population in 1990 of 134,000, is notable mainly for its impressive architecture. The Dutch developed the surrounding area as a centre of plantation crop production (mainly sugar) and the wealth generated is reflected in numerous grand and elegant **mansions** which have so far survived the demolition man's ball. For example, on Jl Kusuma Bangsa, Jl Hassanudin and Jl Raya. Until the 1930s, Java – and especially E Java – was among the world's leading producers of sugar and in fact only Cuba exported more. The main square or Lampangan is dominated by an impressive and beautiful **Moorish-style mosque** on Jl Nusantara – one of the finest in E Java. It has been renovated in recent years.

The **Pelabuhan (Port) Pasuruan** is at the end (surprise, surprise) of Jl Pelabuhan, which runs off Jl Raya, a short walk from the centre of town. Pictureque vessels from all over the Indonesian archipelago dock here – the port is certainly worth exploring for those with some time on their hands.

Local information
● **Accommodation**
There are no places to stay in Pasuruan geared to foreign budget travellers; there are, though, cheap rooms to be found in hotels meeting the needs of travelling Indonesian businessmen.

C *Pasuruan*, Jl Nusantara 46, T 424494, some a/c, set in a large compound set back from the road, central position, clean and spacious rooms with sitting areas outside, no hot water but a professionally managed hotel with charming and enthusiastic staff and some style, rec;

C-E *Wisma Karya*, Jl Raya 160, T 426655, some a/c, an extended old mansion in a central location which is mostly used by Indonesian businessmen and salesmen, the a/c rooms are acceptable although some are dirty – check before booking in.

● **Banks & money changers**

Bank Central Asia, Jl Raya (not far from the train station); BNI, Jl Jend A Yani 13.

● **Entertainment**

Cinemas: *Pasuruan 21*, Jl Raya Pasuruan Indah (behind the Bank Central Asia), modern a/c cinema showing English soundtrack films; *Himalaja*, Jl Nusantara (not far from the Lampangan – main square).

Snooker: play against the local wizards at the Duta Bhakti, Jl Raya Pasuruan Indah (behind the Bank Central Asia).

● **Post & telecommunications**

Area code: 0343.

Post Office: Jl KH Dahlan 1 (close to intersection with Jl Niaga, on the town square or Lampangan).

Wartel (telephone & fax): Jl Alun-alun Timur (on the town square or Lampangan).

● **Transport**

38 km from Probolinggo, 64 km from Surabaya.

Local Bright blue **bemos**, **becaks**.

Train The train station is an old colonial building in the centre of town oin Jl Raya.

Road Bus: the bus terminal is just off Jl Anjas Moro (at the end of Jl Raya), at the E side of town about 1.5 km from the centre. Becaks are available to ferry passengers into town. A/c and non-a/c buses to Yogya, Semarang, Solo, Banyuwangi, Malang, Tretes, Surabaya, Sumenep (Madura), Probolinggo, Madiun, Jember and other destinations in E Java.

PROBOLINGGO

Probolinggo is a commercial town of 131,000 (1990) which doubles up as a Javanese holiday resort. The inhabitants are a mixture of Javanese and Madurese, and most foreign visitors only stop off here en route to Mt Bromo. Probolinggo is noted for the grapes produced in the surrounding area and in honour of the fruit the municipal authorities have created, out of concrete, a giant bunch to record its debt to the humble growth, on the main road into town from Pasuruan. Like every town

in Indonesia this has earned Probolinggo a sobriquet: in this case *Kota Anggur* (Grape Town). More enjoyable still is the port, Pelabuhan Probolinggo, N from the town centre off Jl KH Mansyur – about a 1½ km walk. Brightly-coloured boats from all over Indonesia dock here with their cargoes of mostly dry goods. The northern part of town, centred on Jl Suroyo and the Alun-alun is the administrative heart of Probolinggo; the portion further E on Jl P Sudirman is the commercial heart with the large **Pasar Barde** – a covered market.

Excursions

Candi Jabung lies 26 km E of Probolinggo, about 5 km on from the coastal town of Kraksaan in the small village of Jabung. It was completed in 1354 and – unusually – is circular in plan (although the inner cella is square). It was a Buddhist shrine, built as a funerary temple for a Majapahit princess. The finial is now ruined but was probably in the form of a stupa. The candi is built of brick and was renovated in 1987 – as too was a smaller candi 20m to the W of the main structure. The candi is notable for its finely carved kala head. Visitors should sign the visitors' book – in the first 6 months of 1994 only eight groups made it to Jabung. *Getting there*: minibuses running E towards Sitabundo will stop at Candi Jabung. The village of Jabung is small and the candi rather poorly signposted (in 1994, the sign read 'C-nd-Jabung'). The candi is 500m off the main road, a pleasant walk through fruit groves.

The tiny island **Gili Ketapang** lies 8 km or 45 mins offshore by boat from Probolinggo. No accommodation on the island yet. *Getting there*: by boat from Probolinggo Port (see above), leaving through the day.

Local information
● **Accommodation**

B-D *Ratna*, Jl Raya Panglima Sudirman 16, T 21597, some a/c, a rather gruesome 3-storey structure, rooms in a wide range from non-a/c with shared mandi to a/c rooms with attached showers, clean and with central location but

Candi Jabung

staff are rather surly and uninterested; **B-E** *Tampiarto Plaza*, Jl Suroyo 15, T 21288, F 22103, some a/c, pool, wide range of rooms from fan rooms with shared bathrooms to a/c suites with hot water baths, the best are very good, the cheapest are dark and rather grubby, as with most things you get what you pay for, but even those paying 8,000Rp get to use the pool and the place is quiet.

C-D *Victoria*, Jl Suroyo 1-3 (nr intersection with Jl Raya Panglima Sudirman), T 21461, F 21040, some a/c, old hotel undergoing renovation in mid-1994, more expensive rooms with hot water showers, varied in terms of upkeep and cleanliness, but welcoming management and a reasonable place to spend a night or two; **C-E** *Bromo Permai*, Jl Raya Panglima Sudirman 237, T 22256, F 22256, some a/c, wide range of rooms with varied level of facilities, no hot water but a/c rooms are large, very clean and good value, as are the fan rooms with shared facilities, a 2-storey block around a courtyard with trees and a small pond, situated at the E edge of the commercial district, the same ownership as the *Bromo Permai I* on Mt Bromo so they can book rooms easily – useful in the peak season, rec.

E *Tentrem Hotel*, Jl Raya Panglima Sudirman 61, T 21049, colonial villa converted into a low budget hotel mostly frequented by Indonesians, rooms are cheap, generally dirty, and not very cheerful.

● **Places to eat**
There are numerous warungs and other eating houses along Jl Raya Panglima Sudirman.

● **Banks & money changers**
Bank Central Asia, Jl Suroyo; Bank Rakyat Indonesia, Jl Suroyo; BNI, Jl Suroyo.

● **Entertainment**
Cinemas: *Guntur*, Jl Dr Sutomo, a/c theatre showing English soundtrack films.

● **Post & telecommunications**
Area code: 0335.
Post Office: Jl Suroyo 33.
Wartel (telephone & fax): Jl Jend A Yani.

● **Tourist offices**
Tourist Information: two tour companies facing the bus terminal offer advice for those staying in Probolinggo and travelling up to Bromo. They are not, though, independent.

● **Transport**
99 km from Surabaya, 190 km from Banyuwangi.

Train The train station is on the main square or alun-alun, on Jl KH Mansyur, regular connections on the Mutiara Timur train with Surabaya (2,700-6,000Rp) and on to Yogyakarta (5,000Rp), and Banyuwangi (2,200-5,000Rp) via Jember 9 hrs.

Road Bus: the bus terminal is on the W side of town, about 5 km from the centre, on the road up to Bromo. Bemos whisk bus passengers into town (500Rp), regular connections with Surabaya 3 hrs, Malang 3 hrs and Banyuwangi 4 hrs. Night buses to Denpasar (Bali) 8 hrs and a/c buses to Singaraja, Jakarta, Denpasar and Yogya. **Minibus**: to Cemoro Lawang, 2 hrs (2,500Rp).

ROUTE-WISE: PROBOLINGGO TO BANYU-WANGI 34 km E from **Probolinggo** – to the E of **Paiton** – is a new, large, coal-fired power station built by the Korean firm Hyundai with Japanese assistance. It dominates the coastline at this point and is fuelled with coal shipped in from Kalimantan. Also along this portion of coastline are large sugar estates, rice farms, prawn hatcheries and *tambak* fisheries (see page 287). Inland are the volcanoes which define the area. The uneven railways that run parallel to the road were laid when Dutch controlled sugar estates covered much of the best land; today they are still used to collect and transport the newly-cut cane. At the far NE end of this 'Far East' of Java the road skirts the **Baluran National Park**. The scenery changes quite suddenly from cultivated agricultural land to open savanna forest and teak plantations. For the next 20 km there is scarcely any sign of human settlement. Periodic fires pass through this forest producing, in some areas, a fire 'climax' vegetation featuring trees species which are resistant to light burns. About 20 km N of **Banyuwangi**, travelling S, Bali appears, its golden beaches noticeably more inviting than those of much of the N coast of Java.

MOUNT BROMO

This active volcano stands at 2,329m and is one of the most popular natural sights on Java, lying within the **Bromo-Tengger-Semeru National Park**. The park consists of a range of volcanic mountains, the highest of which (and Java's highest) is Mt Semeru at 3,676m. Mt Semeru is sometimes also called Mt Mahameru, the mountain abode of the Hindu gods. Wildlife in the park includes wild pig (*Sus scrofa*), Timor deer (*Cervus timorensis*), barking deer and leopard (*Pantera pardus*) as well as an abundance of flying squirrels. Perhaps the most distinctive tree is the cemara (*Casuarina junghuhniana*), which

looks on first glance rather like the familiar conifer. It is, however, no relation and grows above 1,400m on the volcanic ash where few other trees can establish themselves.

The local inhabitants of this area are the Tenggerese people, believed to be descended from the refugees of the Majapahit Kingdom, who fled their lands in 928 following the eruption of Mt Merapi. They embrace the Hindu religion and are the only group of Hindus left on Java today.

For many visitors to Indonesia, the trip to Bromo is their most memorable experience. Seeing the sun bathe the crater in golden light, picking out the gulleys and ruts in the almost lunar landscape. Sipping sweet *Kopi manis* after a 0330 start, and feeling the warmth of the sun on your face as the day begins. No wonder the Tenggerese view this area as holy, feeling a need to propitiate the gods. It is hard not to leave feeling the divine hand has helped to mould this inspired landscape. Note that despite the purple prose above, it is possible to visit the crater on a day trip from Probolinggo. The last minibus down the mountain from Cemoro Lawang leaves at 1600. It is also true that during the high season (Jul-Aug) it can be impossibly crowded.

Reaching the crater

From Ngadisari via Probolinggo and Sukapura The easiest access to the park is from the N coast town of Probolinggo, via Sukapura and Ngadisari and then to Cemoro Lawang on the edge of the caldera. The turning from Probolinggo is well signposted. The road starts in a dead straight line and begins to climb slowly through dense forested gulleys of dipherocarps. The road meanders, precariously at times, past fields of cabbage, onions and chillies. At some points a curious, almost coppiced weave of lurid small trees and chopped branch lines the road and divides the fields like trellising. The route becomes steeper and steeper and only first gear seems feasible in the overladen minibuses. After Sukapura the road becomes

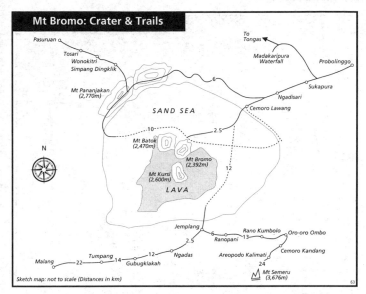

Mt Bromo: Crater & Trails

Pasuruan

Tosari
Wonokitri
Simpang Dingklik

To Tongas
Madakaripura Waterfall
Probolinggo

Mt Pananjakan (2,770m)

Sukapura

Ngadisari
Cemoro Lawang

SAND SEA

N

10
2.5

Mt Batok (2,470m)

Mt Bromo (2,392m)

Mt Kursi (2,600m)

12

LAVA

Jemplang

Rano Kumbolo   Oro-oro Ombo
6
2.5   Ranopani   13

Malang   22   Tumpang   14   12   Ngadas
Gubugklakah

Areopodo Kalimati   Cemoro Kandang
24

Mt Semeru (3,676m)

Sketch map: not to scale (Distances in km)

yet more precipitous. The National Park begins at the village of Ngadisari. The road narrows through here and continues up to Cemoro Lawang where the tourist sellers appear. The throng of ponies let you know you have reached the top.

On arrival in Ngadisari, it is important to obtain a ticket (2,100Rp pp) from the 'tourist information' booth in order to visit the crater's edge. This is the national park entrance fee and the money is used to protect and develop the area. The trip to the caldera is usually undertaken in the early morning in order to watch the sunrise over the volcanoes. To reach the summit for dawn, an early start from Ngadisari is essential, leaving no later than 0330. It is easiest to travel to Cemoro Lawang (from Ngadisari) on one of the 6-seater jeeps, organized by guesthouses in Ngadisari (1,250Rp pp). It takes 20 mins by road from Ngadisari to the outer crater at Cemoro Lawang, and is another 3 km walk from here to the edge of the crater. Either take a pony (it should cost about 10,000Rp per pony for a return trip)

– a 30 mins ride – or walk for about 1 hr along a winding path marked by white boulders (sometimes indistinct in the early morning light) through a strange crater landscape of very fine grey sand, known as *Laut Pasir* or the Sand Sea. Vegetables and other crops are grown in the sand, and it is surprising that it doesn't just get blown or washed away. It is also possible to walk the entire way, about 5½ km, from Ngadisari (4-5 hrs). The final ascent is up 250 concrete steps to a precarious metre-wide ledge, with a vertical drop down into the crater. Aim to reach the summit for sunrise at about 0530. As this is their business, Losmen-owners will wake visitors up in good time to make the crater edge by sunrise, and are also used to arranging transport.

From Tosari via Pasuruan It is also possible to approach the summit from Tosari, on the N slopes of the mountain. Take a minibus from Pasuruan to Tosari (31 km), and from Tosari, walk or take a jeep to the summit, leaving before 0400 to see the sunrise over the crater. The

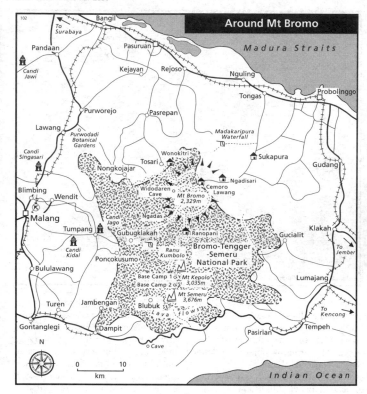

Around Mt Bromo

turn-off for Tosari is about 5 km out of Pasuruan on the road to Probolinggo.

From Ngadas via Malang and Tumpang Finally, visitors can reach Bromo's summit from the W via Malang, Tumpang and Ngadas (see page 274). Entrance fee to National Park: 2,100Rp.

Equipment Take warm clothing as it can be very cold before sunrise. A scarf to act as a mask to protect against the sulphurous vapour and a torch to light the way can also be useful. Avoid opening cameras to change film at the summit; the thin dust can be harmful to the mechanism.

Trekking There are several worthwhile treks in the Bromo-Tengger-Semeru National Park. Ask at your hotel/losmen for information and (in most cases), a map. It is possible to trek from **Cemoro Lawang** to **Ngadas**, or vice versa; from Ngadas, minibuses run down to Tumpang and from there to Malang (see page 274). The trek takes about 4-6 hrs; guides are available but the route is well-marked. For the best view of Bromo, trek to **Mount Penanjakan**, 6 km from Cemoro Lawang.

Best time to visit: during the dry months from May through to Oct and Nov. From Dec to Mar rainfall can be quite heavy. Avoid Mt Bromo on Indonesian public holidays, as it becomes very crowded.

Excursions

Mount Semeru, also known as Mt Mahameru ('seat of the Gods') is Java's highest mountain and lies 13 km (as the crow flies) to the S of Mt Bromo. This route is only suitable for more experienced climbers; a guide and appropriate equipment are also necessary. For more information, enquire at the PHPA office in Malang, Jl Raden Intan 6, T 65100.

Festivals

Feb: *Karo* (movable, according to Tenggerese Calendar) held in Ngadisari and Wonokitri to commemorate the creation of Man by Sang Hyang Widi. Tenggerese men perform dances to celebrate the event.

Dec: *Kasodo* (movable, according to Tenggerese Calendar). This ceremony is linked to a legend which relates how a princess and her husband pleaded with the gods of the mountain to give them children. Their request was heeded on the condition that their youngest child should be sacrificed to the mountain. The couple then had 25 children, but were understandably reluctant to meet their side of the bargain. The mountain continued to erupt periodically to remind the couple of their vow. They finally conceded to the gods' wishes and when the child was thrown into the abyss her voice could be heard chiding the parents for not offering her sooner and requesting that on the night of the full moon in the month of Kasado, offerings should be made to the mountain. The ceremony reaches a climax with a midnight pilgrimage to the crater to make offerings to the gods. Ritual sacrifices of animals, and offerings of vegetables and fruit, are thrown into the crater to appease the gods.

Local information
● **Accommodation**

Accommodation is strung out from Sukapura all the way up to Cemoro Lawang, a distance of about 18 km. Generally the closer one gets to the crater the relatively more expensive rooms become. At Cemoro Lawang itself, rooms are comparatively dear, although the position is incomparable.

At Sukapura: **A** *Grand Bromo*, T (0335) 23103, F (0385) 23142, restaurant, tennis courts, **E** for dorm beds, easily the most sophisticated place to stay on Bromo with all facilities (except a pool) and first class rooms with balconies and views down towards Probolinggo and the coast, it is built along the mountainside about 2 km up out of Sukapura, the most convenient place to stay but also rather inconvenient for Bromo's crater; **C** *Sukapura Permai*, Jl Raya Bromo 135, all rooms with hot showers and attached squat loos, very clean, but not a very convenient location for visiting Bromo's crater, few western visitors stay here, most preferring to carry on up higher to Ngadisari or Cemoro Lawang.

At Ngadisari & Wonotoro: **C-E** *Bromo Permai I*, book at Bromo Permai in Probolinggo (Jl Sudirman 255, T 21626), restaurant, the largest hostel in Cemoro Lawang with a wide range of rooms, the most expensive, almost into our **B** category, are the best available at the crater with good hot water showers, but the cheapest are rather dark and dingy with shared facilities, large restaurant and a great position, check the range of rooms before deciding, **F** for dorm beds; **D** *Bromo Homestay*, Jl Wonokerto, T (0335) 23484, small, clean rooms, some with attached mandi (shared mandis can be very dirty), popular with good information (but reports of surly management and often over-run with noisy tour groups; **D** *Losmen B pk Ida*, Wonotoro, clean rooms but very bare, no hot water and shared squat loos and mandi, little to rec it beyond its cleanliness; **D** *Wisma Ucik*, Wonotoro, basic rooms, rather colourless place; **D-E** *Yoschi's*, Jl Wonokerto 1, 2 km before Ngadisari, T (0335) 23387, restaurant and losmen run by a Dutch woman, married to a Javanese, who speaks good English, this is currently the best place to stay in Ngadisari, some rooms with hot water and attached showers, attractively furnished and designed with bamboo and ikat, the cottages are excellent value, restaurant serves good European and Indonesian dishes using local produce – onions, potatoes, tomatoes etc – and the losmen is a good source of information, highly rec, although the mini zoo is rather sad.

At Cemoro Lawang (a good place to stay for early morning walks): **C** *Lava View Hotel*, same management as the older *Lava View Hostel*, but slightly more upmarket and closer to crater rim, rooms with attached hot water shower, incl breakfast, excellent location and very friendly; **C-F** *Cemoro Indah Hotel and Restaurant*, yards from the crater edge, some rooms with hot water and attached mandi, dirty facilities, limited bedding provided, small breakfasts, not particularly friendly, easily identified by the rearing horse outside the front; **D** *Lava View Hostel*, Cemoro Lawang, T (0335) 23458, a new group of bungalows which opened in Aug 1994, each room has hot water and attached shower, built right on the crater lip in a magnificent position overlooking the caldera, owned and run by the same management as the *Cafe Lava Hostel*; **D-F** *Puty Guest House/Lava Youth Hostel* (formerly the *Cafe Lava Hostel*), T (0335) 23458, offers the cheapest rooms at the caldera, most expensive with attached mandis but no hot water, rooms are all rather small and stuck out round the back, ramshackle but OK, no breakfast available. **Camping**: At Cemoro Lawang, because the area is a national park, it is possible to camp. The camping site is just before the new *Lava View Hostel*, a mere 20m from the lip of the crater. Ask at the National Park information booth close to the *Bromo Permai I* for more details.

At Tosari: **A** *Bromo Cottages*, T (031) 515253, F 511811, restaurant, hot water, tennis courts, great views.

At Wonokiri: **C** *Pendopo Agung*, hot water; **D** *Bromo Surya Indah Homestay*, T 332411, restaurant.

● **Places to eat**
Cemoro Lawang: *Tengger Permai Café*, good value.

● **Banks & money changers**
Bank Rakyat Indonesia, Sukapura; Guesthouses at Ngadisari and Cemoro Lawang (poor rates).

● **Post & telecommunications**
Area code: 0335.
Post Office: Sukapura.

● **Tourist offices**
National Park Information Booth, Cemoro Lawang (nr the *Bromo Permai I*); **Information Offices**: opp Probolinggo bus terminal (not offices as such, but tour companies willing to offer free information – with the hope they might also secure your business).

● **Transport**
2 hrs' drive E of the city of Malang, 3 hrs S of Surabaya and 30 km SW of Probolinggo.

Road Bus/minibus from Probolinggo: the bus station is about 8 km from the railway station (in Probolinggo). So take a bemo to the bus station (300Rp). Regular connections with Sukapura, Ngadisari and Cemoro Lawang, 1 hr to Ngadisari, 1½ hrs to Cemoro Lawang

(1,500Rp to Ngadisari, 1,000Rp more from Ngadisari to Cemoro Lawang) (connections on to Surabaya or Malang). Jeeps at the railway station in Probolinggo go direct to Cemoro Lawang (3,500Rp). The last minibus down the mountain from Cemoro Lawang leaves at 1600. Most losmen and guesthouses will arrange a/c bus connections to Jakarta, Denpasar, Yogyakarta and Lovina Beach (Bali). **Minibus charter from Probolinggo**: for about 60,000Rp, ask at any of the local hotels. **Minibus from Pasaruan** (1½ hrs from Malang and Surabaya): regular minibuses to Tosari (3,000Rp). **Minibus from Malang**: take a bus to Tumpang and change onto a (rather irregular) minibus for the climb up to Ngadas (see page 274). **Bus from Surabaya**: it is even possible to get to Bromo from Surabaya without too much trouble. Take a bus from Surabaya's Bungurasih terminal to Probolinggo and then continue as above.

PASIR PUTIH

Pasir Putih means 'white sand'. Visitors shouldn't get too excited because the sand is, in fact, grey. This is not a very beautiful or a very wild beach resort. The hotels are rather over-priced, the scenery and the bay merely passable, and activities in the area, limited. Mostly frequented by Indonesians, it does not compare with resorts on Bali or elsewhere on Java. Snorkelling is possible, but the reef is degraded; boats are also available for hire.

Festivals
Nov: *Sapp sapp* – traditional chicken race; chickens are released from boats on the water and they try to fly to the shore. The winner is the one that flies the furthest. Animal rights activists might have something to say about it.

Local information
● **Accommodation**
C-D *Sidho Muncul*, Jl Raya Pasir Putih, some a/c, best on the beach with well-kept rooms and small verandahs, located in the heart of the beach – may be the best here, but only the best of a poor bunch; **C-E** *Pasir Putih Inn*, T 81322, some a/c, hotel at W end of beach (Probolinggo end), rather overpriced for what you get – average rooms to go with an average beach resort – but the management have plans to

expand and build new rooms and a pool, with apparently, giant dinosaurs, what more can you say?

D *Bayangkara*, Jl Raya Pasir Putih, T 91083, plain non-a/c rooms with cold water mandis, average from top to bottom; **D** *Hotel Mutiara*, Jl Raya Pasir Putih, non-a/c rooms with cold water mandi, very plain and ordinary with no attempt to introduce any character or atmosphere.

● **Post & telecommunications**
Area code: 0332.

Wartel office (office & fax): *Pasir Putih Inn.*

● **Transport**
105 km from Banyuwangi, 82 km from Probolinggo.

Road Bus: buses travelling along the N coast all stop in Pasir Putih – regular connections with Banyuwangi and Probolinggo as well as other centres on the main E-W route.

SITUBONDO

Situbondo is an orderly, spread-out town of wide streets and low rise buildings. The **mosque** on the Alun-alun is impressive although not historically or architecturally significant. Near the bus station is the new **Pasar Mimbaan Baru** – a market-cum-promenade walkway. The town's rather down-at-heel cinema is also here.

Local information
● **Accommodation**
C-E *Ramayana Hotel*, Jl Sepudi 11A, T 61663, some a/c, best place to stay in Situbondo, although hardly memorable, close to the bus terminal, the a/c rooms are clean with attached bathroom and are very reasonably priced.

E *Hotel Karang Asem Indah*, Jl Raya Sudirman (on the main road entering town from Probolinggo), T 81179, attached bathrooms, cold water, rather run down and abandoned in appearance, rooms verging on the dirty.

● **Banks & money changers**
Bank Rakyat Indonesia, Jl Jend A Yani.

● **Post & telecommunications**
Area code: 0338.

Post Office: Jl Jend A Yani 131 (on the main square).

Wartel office (telephone & fax): Jl Sepudi 7 (nr the bus terminal).

● **Transport**
93 km from Banyuwangi, 103 km from Probolinggo, 34 km from Bondowoso, 67 km from Jember.

Road Bus: the terminal is in the centre of town on the corner of Jl Sepudi and Jl Jawa. Connections with Probolinggo, Surabaya, Jember via Bondowoso, Banyuwangi and Ketapang (for Bali).

BONDOWOSO

Bondowoso is an attractive, and remarkably neat, little town (why are towns in E Java so tidy?) crammed on to the narrow plain of the Sampean River which flows northwards between Mt Raung (3,332m) to the E and Mt Argopuro (3,088m) to the W. The town is only 34 km inland from Situbondo, but because it is off the usual tourist route it receives comparatively few visitors. Nonetheless, it is a gem of a town; friendly, attractive and manageable. The area is also famous for its bull fights, best seen in the village of Tapen (see Excursions).

Excursions
Bull fights are held in the village of **Tapen**, 15 km NE of Bondowoso on the road to Situbondo. The fights are held on Sat and Sun, throughout the year. Fights rarely result in serious injury to the animal – the weaker bull simply runs away. The fights originally served the purpose of improving the breeding stock (see page 291), although the event has gradually evolved into a sport and now into a tourist attraction. *Getting there*: regular buses travel through Tapen which is on the main Bondowoso-Situbondo road.

Ijen Crater is more easily accessible from Bondowoso than any other town (see page 304 for more details on the area and accommodation there). *Getting there*: catch a minibus to Sempol, on the slopes of the volcano, a distance of 52 km. There are direct connections, although it may be quicker to catch a bus to Wonosari on the Situbondo road, and then a minibus from there to Sempol via Sukosari. From Sempol there are minibuses to Kalipahit. From Kalipahit, catch a ojek or charter a bemo to Paltuding. From here it is a 3-km walk to the crater itself.

Local information
● Accommodation
B-D *Palm Hotel*, Jl Jend A Yani 32, T 21505, some a/c, restaurant, pool, the most sophisticated place to stay in town.

C-E *Kinanti Hotel*, Jl Santawi 583A, T 41018, clean rooms at good rates, an excellent budget place to stay.

D-E *Anugerah*, Jl May Jend Sutoyo 12, T 41162, clean and friendly, good value.

E-F *Baru*, Jl Kartini 26, T 21474, very basic.

● Places to eat
♦♦*Puja Rasa*, Jl PB Sudirman, locals maintain that this is the best place to eat in town, serving excellent Indonesian and Chinese dishes.

● Post & telecommunications
Area code: 0332.

● Transport
34 km from Situbondo, 33 km from Jember, 100 km from Probolinggo, 113 km from Banyuwangi.

Road Bus: regular connections with Situbondo and Jember, connections with Probolinggo and Banyuwangi.

MOUNT IJEN

Mount Ijen forms the core of a reserve which spans the slopes and summits of three mountains – Mt Ijen, Mt Merapi (2,800m) and Mt Raung (3,332m). The crater lake at Ijen is a milky blue-green colour. The warm waters are rich in minerals and the dam that holds back the lake was built by the Dutch to protect crop land on the slopes of Mt Ijen. The crater is also mined for its sulphur, which solidifies into huge blocks near the springs that surround the crater lake, steam and volcanic gases hissing from fissures in the rock. About 200 heavily muscled men walk the 17 km up to the crater in the morning, load as much as 75 kg of sulphur into baskets, and then carry this heavy load, slung over their shoulders, back down the mountain. They are paid for the sulphur by weight at a factory outside Banyuwangi and it is then used in the production of medicines and the processing of sugar. Despite the risks – and deaths are common from sulphur inhalation and minor eruptions – the miners are envied by others in their villages. They can earn as much as three times the wages of those who work in agriculture, and the families of the sulphur workers live comparatively well. It is thought that Ijen yields between 9 and 12 tonnes of sulphur a day.

Ijen is an excellent area to explore as there are a handful of mountain villages with homestays. It is possible to bus and trek from E to W, or *vice versa*, from Banyuwangi to Bondowoso. However, the easiest access point is from the W, from Bondowoso (see Excursions, Bondowoso). It is best to hire a guide for the walk to the summit, which takes about 6 hrs each way (34 km round trip). Ask at the tourist board for a recommendation. A third of the path is steep but cobbled; it was constructed by the Japanese during WW2, who needed sulphur for their munitions. Wildlife within the park includes leopard, pig, civet, peafowl and silver leaf-monkey. After a jungle walk, the landscape opens up and the climb is less steep to the crater's edge. The walk down the crater wall to the 175m deep sulphur lake is precipitous.

● Accommodation
Jampit/Kalisat: **C-D** *Arabica Homestay*; *Homestay Kalisat*, hot water, restaurant, trekking and guides. **Sempol**: *Sempol Homestay*; *Pesanggrahan*. **Belawan**: **C-D** *Catimore Homestay*, hot water, swimming pool; *Homestay Blawan*, hot water, restaurant. It is also possible to stay at the post where the trail starts for 10,000Rp, but there is no food available.

● Useful addresses
PHPA (Nature Conservancy) office, Sempol.

● Transport
Bus: there are two main routes up Ijen; one from the W and Bondowoso, and one from the E and Banyuwangi. From the W, take a bus from Bondowoso to Sempol on the slopes of the volcano, a distance of 52 km. The route passes through the towns of Wonosari and Sukosari en route to Sempol. From Sempol, there are minibuses to Kalipahit. From Kalipahit, catch a ojek or charter a bemo to Paltuding.

Note that there seems to be some confusion regarding the availability of public transport to Kalipahit and Sempol, although ojeks should be around. From Paltuding it is a 3-km walk to the crater itself. From the E, take a bus from Banyuwangi to Licin, also known as Jambu Licin. From here it is a 24-km trek although ojeks wait to transport visitors a further 9 km along the road to Sodong.

KALIKLATAK

Kaliklatak is a plantation area on the slopes of Mt Merapi-Ijen-producing coffee, cloves and rubber. Agro tourism tours available, and there are also guesthouses. **Accommodation** *Must* be booked in advance; phone Sugianto on (0333) 24061. *Getting there*: no direct buses; transport arranged after booking, or take a tour.

BALURAN RESERVE

The Baluran Reserve is 40 km N of Banyuwangi, on the E coast and abuts the larger Ijen-Merapi National Park. The reserve of 25,000 ha of wooded savanna supports small populations of monkeys, deer, wild buffalo, leopard, peafowl, green junglefowl and banteng (wild oxen). Naturalist Tony Whitten reports, however, that the reserve is threatened by domestic cattle encroaching on the park, the spread of the introduced tree species *Acacia nilotica* which is invading the grazing grasslands, and by the growth in the numbers of feral water buffalo which are not only competing with the wild banteng but also risk introducing diseases to the wild ungulates. For the visitor, Baluran offers good walks, a pristine 15 km-long sandy beach facing the Bali Strait and good snorkelling. Permission to visit the park can be obtained either through the PHPA office in Banyuwangi or at the *Kantor Taman Wisata Baluran* in Wonorejo, the entrance to the park. Visitors must pay an entrance fee of 2,000Rp. **Accommodation** Guesthouses here can be booked through the PHPA in Banyuwangi, Jl Jend A Yani 108, T 4118, or c/o Taman Baluran, T 68453. There are two places to stay. Bekol is the best base for bird and animal watching; Bama is on

the coast and more suitable for swimming and snorkelling. The two communities are 3 km apart, and visitors pay 4,500Rp pp/night. **NB** that food and other supplies must be taken – there are kitchens for use by visitors, but no shops. Supplies can be picked up in Galean, 2 km before Wonorejo; there are no shops to speak of in Wonorejo. *Getting there*: take a bus from Banyuwangi or Ketapang heading along the coast and ask to be dropped off at the park entrance in Wonorejo. Ojeks and taxis wait there to take visitors to the coast (3,500Rp on an Ojek, 15,000Rp by car).

BANYUWANGI

Banyuwangi, on Java's E coast, is not noted either for its sights or its beauty. Formerly, many tourists were forced to pass through the town as it is near the ferry port for Bali and trains stopped here. Now that a station has been built out at the ferry terminal, 9 km N at Ketapang (See Ketapang entry below), there is no need, and little incentive even to come to Banyuwangi. The **Mesjid Baiturrachman** in the centre of town is worth visiting if visitors have time to kill. There is also a busy market area on Jl Susuit Tubon, near the centre of town.

Local information
● **Accommodation**
C *Blambangan*, Jl Dr Wahidin 4, T 21598, some a/c; **C-D** *Hotel Pinang Sari*, Jl Basuki Rakhmat 116, T 23266, some a/c, hotel on the Ketapang (N) edge of town about 1 km from the bus terminal, excellent rooms, fairly priced with some style and panache, attractive verandahs and garden, attentive service and professional management, rec; **C-D** *Kumala Hotel*, Jl Jend A Yani 21B, T 61287, F 61533, some a/c, an excellent place down a side street, quiet with airy garden, rooms are spacious and immaculate, friendly, professional service, central position, rec.

D *Slamet*, Jl Wahid Hasyim 96, some a/c, own mandis; **D-F** *Hotel Barito*, Jl Dr Sutomo 36, T 21574, some a/c, strangely attractive, weathered, barrack-like hotel, most expensive rooms are small suites which must be the cheapest around, bathrooms could do with some serious scrubbing, but central location, a certain beach hut charm, and value for money make this a possibility.

E *Baru*, Jl Pattimura 82-84, T 21369, own mandi, price incl breakfast (if you can call it that), large clean rooms, friendly management, popular; **E** *Gintangan Homestay*, Gintangan (30 km S of Banyuwangi), an alternative place to stay for those with time on their hands, friendly homestay with a lot to do in the area (on the eco-tourism/cultural tourism front), but hard to reach – from Blambangan terminal in Banyuwangi to Karang Ente terminal (500Rp); Karang Ente to Gladag (450Rp). Gladag to the homestay by becak (500Rp), about 3 km; **E-F** *'AA' (Asia Afrika)*, Jl Dr Wahidin Sudiro Husodo 1 (by the post office), T 21758, run down place with central location but little else to rec it, dirty mandis, grubby rooms, cheap; **E-F** *Anda Losmen*, Jl Basuki Rakhmat 34, T 41441, close to Blambangan bus terminal and to centre of town, rooms are large and clean, some with good attached mandis, hard to beat at the price, rec.

F *Baru Raya*, Jl Dr Sutomo 26, own mandi.

● **Places to eat**

♦♦*Depot Asia*, Jl Dr Sutomo 12 (nr intersection with Jl Jend Sudirman and Jend A Yani) wonderful Chinese-Indonesian food in a/c restaurant incl excellent frog (try the *kodok goreng tempung* – deep fried frogs' legs) and pigeon, as well as superb fish and seafood, ice cold beers, highly rec; *Rumak Makan Sulung* by entrance to railway station – good value; *Samudra*, Jl Jend Sudirman 171; *Sariwangi Bakery*, Jl Jend Sudirman 162 (500m S of Blambangan bus terminal), excellent pastries and cakes; *Wina*, by Blambangan bus terminal.

● **Banks & money changers**

Bank Rakyat Indonesia, Jl Jacksa Agung; BNI, Jl Bantarang 46.

● **Post & telecommunications**

Area code: 0333.

Post Office: Jl Diponegoro 1 (on main square).

Wartel (fax & telephone): Jl Bangka (at the Blambangan bus terminal).

● **Tourist offices**

Head office is at the dock, where ferries arrive from Bali. Branch office, Jl Diponegoro 2, T 41282.

● **Useful addresses**

PHPA office, Jl Jend A Yani 108, T 41118.

● **Transport**

288 km from Surabaya, 194 km from Probol-inggo. Banyuwangi no longer serves as a necessary stopping-off point for people visiting Bali. Ketapang can be reached directly by train and bus. Regular bemos link Banyuwangi and Ketapang. **Local**: Bemos from the ferry terminal to town cost about 400Rp.

Road Bus: Banyuwangi has 2 bus terminals. The Blambangan terminal is at the N edge of town and serves Ketapang (for ferries to Bali) and stops along the N coast to Surabaya and Malang incl Probolinggo. On the S edge of town is the Banjarsari terminal for destinations S of town. **Train** connections with Probolinggo, 7,000Rp.

ROUTE-WISE: BANYUWANGI TO MALANG South of **Banyuwangi**, settlements become more dispersed and forest and plantations more apparent. Rubber trees flank the route. The road then climbs up through a pass between **Mt Raung** (3,332m) to the N and the **Meru Betiri National Park** to the S. There are wonderful views over the plain below. Between **Jember** and **Lumajang** large rice fields, stands of teak, and tobacco are the dominant land uses. Thatched barns used for the drying of tobacco leaf also line the road. Leaving Lumajang for **Malang**, the road passes through a second pass, with **Mt Bromo** to the N. Ahead is the imposing silhouette of **Mt Butak** (2,531m).

KETAPANG

Ketapang is the ferry terminal for Bali and has developed into a thriving little centre that survives for no other reason. There are restaurants and warungs, a train station, large Pertamina distribution centre, tourist information office and one hotel a couple of kilometres to the S. The long line of lorries, their drivers patiently waiting for a space on the ferry testifies to Ketapang's importance as a transport node.

Local information

● **Accommodation**

Only one place to stay at the **B-D** *Manyar Garden Hotel*, Jl Gatot Subroto, T 24741, F 24742, some a/c, 2 km S of Ketapang, this place is pleasant enough but rather overpriced, it is the only hotel here so presumably feels able to push its rates up – try Banyuwangi if possible, places there are better value.

● **Post & telecommunications**
Area code: 0333.
Wartel office (fax & telephone): at the ferry terminal.

● **Tourist offices**
Cabang Dinas Pariwista Daerah, Jl Gatot Subroto, T 41172, the district tourism office, not really geared-up for tourists, not much English spoken, but have information to give, 100m up the road from the ferry terminal towards Banyuwangi (nr car-ferry); **East Java Tourist Information Booth**, at the ferry terminal, can be very useful, or rather useless, depending on who is manning the booth.

● **Transport**
9 km N of Banyuwangi.

Train The station is opp the ferry terminal. Day and night connections with Surabaya's Kota terminal 7 hrs (3,000Rp). Combined bus-train tickets to Denpasar (Bali) cost an extra 3,500Rp (see page 917).

Road Bus: there is a bus station just outside the ferry terminal. Connections with Probolinggo (for Mt Bromo), Surabaya and Banyuwangi.

Sea Boat: passenger and car ferries to and from Gilimanuk on Bali dock at Ketapang. Boats depart every half an hour, 24 hrs a day, 30 mins (8,000Rp for a car and driver, 1,000Rp pp). **NB** If driving to Bali, note that it is not easy to obtain fuel between the ferry terminal at Gilimanuk and Denpasar, so fill up before leaving Java. To get to Ketapang, from Banyuwangi catch a regular minibus from the Blambangan terminal on the N edge of town. Pelni boats dock here on their way to Nusa Tenggara.

GRAJAGAN BAY

Grajagan Bay is situated within the S Banyuwangi reserve, faces W and is renowned for its surfing. The beach is reputed to have one of the longest left breaks in the world, and is a pilgrimage spot for Australian surfers. The reserve itself contains the **alas purwo** (or 'ancient forest') – a collection of rare trees as well as wildlife including leopard, banteng and wild boar. A permit is needed to enter the park, obtainable from the park office near Tegaldlimo or from the PHPA office in Banyuwangi. **Accommodation D** basic huts are available in Grajagan Bay. *Getting*

there: by bus from Banyuwangi to Benculuk, then by minibus to Grajagan.

SUKAMADE AND MERU BETIRI NATIONAL PARK

Sukamade is on East Java's S coast, within the Meru Betiri National Park. Since 1972, this 3 km long stretch of beach has been protected – to allow turtles to lay their eggs. The breeding season stretches from Nov to Mar and seven species lay their eggs on the beach. The most common are the green, hawksbill, snapping and giant leatherback. To see the turtles laying their eggs – between 80 and 180 in a nest – it is first necessary to obtain permission from the PHPA rangers. Loud noises, smoking, lights and flash cameras are not permitted – nor are the turtles allowed to be touched. In early 1994 a tidal wave destroyed much of the beach and inundated several villages, drowning an estimated 200 people. *Best time to visit*: Apr-Oct.

Meru Betiri National Park covers 500 sq km and was declared a reserve in 1972. It represents the last significant area of lowland rain forest in Java. However, the park was really gazetted to protect the last specimens of the once common Javan tiger – a small sub-species of tiger. Although some claim that there may still be a handful of individuals left, most naturalists believe that the Javan tiger is extinct. The park is centred on Mt Betiri (1,223m) and although the tiger may be consigned to the history books it does support leopard, banteng and rusa deer – the latter introduced to the area as prey for the leopards. Four species of turtle also come ashore to lay their eggs along this largely rocky coastline.

● **Accommodation** There are homestays (**E**) available with space for about 50 people and a camping ground at Sukamade. There is also accommodation at the beach (**F**), but no food. The walk from Sukamade to the beach takes 1 hr.

● **Transport** 97 km from Banyuwangi. **Road Bus**: catch a bus from Banyuwangi to Pasanggaran, 2 hrs (1,500Rp); from here there are minibuses to Sarongan (1,500Rp). From Sarongan there is one truck a day in the morning to Sukamade, returning at 0700 (1,000Rp). Alternatively, an ojek to Sukamade costs 8,000Rp. It is also possible to reach Passanggaran via the small market town of Jajag from Banyuwangi. **Accommodation in Jajag** incl the **C-D** *Hotel Suriya*, Jl Yos Sudarso 2, T (0333) 94126, some a/c, pool, very comfortable for such a small place.

JEMBER

Jember is a dispersed, spread-out town with wide, well-planned streets and an airy feel. It is surprisingly busy and sophisticated, and also one of the cleanest town in Java. The reason why it does not feature on most tourist intineraries is that there is, frankly, little obvious to do here. There are no sights or events to entice visitors in large numbers, and people coming here should be ready to take things slowly and be entranced by the everyday and inconsequential. A state-owned plantation company called Perkebunan XXVI have, in the spirit of enterprise, begun organising tours to coconut, rubber, cocoa and sugarcane plantations in the vicinity (see Tours).

Excursions
Watu Ulo is a beautiful beach due S of Jember, about 10 km S of the small market town of Wuluhan. *Getting there*: by bemo to the Ambulu bus terminal and from there a connection to Watu Ulo.

Tours
Perkebunan XXVI, Jl Gajah Mada 249, T 21061, organize tours to coconut, rubber, cocoa and sugarcane plantations in the vicinity.

Local information
● **Accommodation**
B *Bandung Permai*, Jl Hayam Wuruk 38, T 84528, a/c, restaurant, pool, largest hotel in town – or rather on the outskirts of town as it is several kilometres from the centre – ugly 4-storey block with mediocre but comfortable rooms; **B-C** *Safari Hotel*, Jl KH Dahlan 7, T 81882, F 81887, some a/c, quiet garden compound, professionally managed with very clean

rooms and bathrooms, modern but with more character than most such places, good location in town, rec.

C-E *Lestari*, Jl Gadjah Mada 347, T 87920, some a/c, rooms are good but the hotel has a rather inconvenient location (for most) 3 km out of town on the road towards Lumajang and Surabaya, 3-storey building with what looks like strands of telephone wire hanging from the balconies, set down a narrow lane, hot water mandis; **C-E** *Seroja*, Jl PB Sudirman 2, T 83905, F 85580, some a/c, quiet and clean, garden atmosphere, but 2 km from centre of town so not very convenient for those travelling on public transport.

E-F *Kartika*, Jl Trunojoyo 67, T 21057, cheap but dirty, this is a haunt for Indonesians on a tight budget, not travellers.

● **Banks & money changers**
Bank Bali, intersection of Jl Supratman and Jl; **Lippobank**, Jl Diponegoro; **Pertrokoan Trunojoyo Bank Central Asia**, Jl Gatot Subroto.

● **Entertainment**
Cinemas: *Johar 21 Cineplex*, Jl Diponegoro (in the *Matahari Centre*), modern a/c cinema complex.

● **Post & telecommunications**
Area code: 0331.
Post Office: Jl Sudirman (on the main square).
Telephone: Wartel office, Jl Diponegoro 91.

● **Shopping**
Matahari Shopping Centre, Jl Diponegoro.

● **Transport**
33 km from Bondowoso, 67 km from Situbondo, 95 km from Banyuwangi, 70 km from Lumajang.

Local Becaks, town buses, bemos (250Rp).

Train The station is on the northern edge of town.

Road Bus: not content with just one or two terminals, Jember has four, all out of town. The Tawang Alun terminal is the largest, serving Banyuwangi, Surabaya and Probolinggo and is 8 km from town on the road to Surabaya. The Ajung terminal serves Watu Ulo and is in Ambulu, 5 km from town. The Pakusari terminal serves Banyuwangi (although the Tawang Alun terminal has more buses running there) and is 5 km from town. Last, the Arjasa terminal serves Bondowoso and Situbondo and is 6 km from town. Bemos link all the terminals (250Rp).

LUMAJANG

Lumajang is a remarkably clean and tidy town, with an almost Mexican feel. The main market, the Pasar Baru, is at the intersection of Jl Kembar and Jl Jend A Yani. Most activity, commercial and otherwise, is concentrated along Jl Panglima Sudirman.

Local information
● **Accommodation**

C-E *Gadjah Mada*, Jl Panglima Sudirman 42-58, T 81174, some a/c, quiet and peaceful, hot water baths in the more expensive rooms, fan rooms are the real bargain though, clean with large bathrooms, central location, rec; **C-E** *Hotel Lumajang*, Jl Jend A Yani, T 81314, F 83254, some a/c, large compound with rooms built around a courtyard.

● **Banks & money changers**

Bank Bumi Daya, Jl Panglima Sudirman; **Bank Central Asia**, Jl Panglima Sudirman 2.

● **Entertainment**
Cinemas: Jl Panglima Sudirman.

● **Hospital & medical services**
General Hospital, Jl Jend A Yani.

● **Post & telecommunications**
Area code: 0334.
Post Office: Jl Dr Sutomo.

● **Sports**
Swimming: public swimming pool, Jl Jend A Yani.

● **Transport**
52 km from Probolinggo, 128 km from Malang, 70 km from Jember.

Local The main **bemo** terminal is in the centre of town at the intersection of Jl Kembar and Jl Tembus Terminal, close to the Pasar Baru.

Road Bus: the terminal has been relocated 6 km out of town (now imaginatively called the Terminal Baru) on Jl Jend A Yani, the road running N towards Probolinggo. Regular a/c and non-a/c connections with Probolinggo, Malang, Jember, Banyuwangi and Ketapang (for Bali).

Bali

Horizons	310	Pura Besakih and Mount Agung	390
Island information	337	The East	393
Denpasar	345	From Padangbai to Candi Dasa	398
South Bali	349	North from Denpasar to	
The Bukit Peninsula and Nusa Dua	365	Lake Bratan	411
North from Denpasar to Ubud	371	The North Coast: Lovina	
North of Ubud: Gunung Kawi		Beach to Tulomben	416
and Tirta Empul	384	The West	422
North of Denpasar: Gianyar			
to Mount Batur via Bangli	385		

MORE TOURISTS visit Bali than any other place in Indonesia. The island has gained a reputation as the exotic tropical island paradise *par excellence* – a reputation which dates from the early years of this century when artists began to visit the island and record its breath-taking beauty. With its majestic volcanoes, spectacular terraced rice fields, golden beaches, and a rich and colourful culture, Bali is the jewel in the crown of Indonesia's tourism industry. When the author and Bali-lover Miguel Covarrubias and his wife arrived off Bali's north coast on a steamer in 1930, they were enchanted. "We had our first unforgettable glimpse of Bali at dawn," he wrote "when the little KPM steamer approached Buleleng – a high dark peak reflected on a sea as smooth as polished steel, with the summit of the cone hidden in dark metallic clouds".

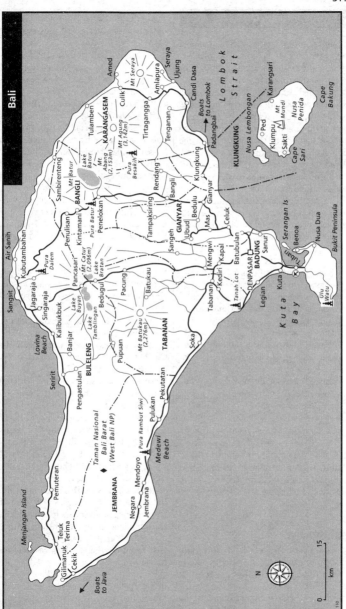

HORIZONS

However, in recent years Bali has suffered from the curse of being too popular, yet somehow the island has retained its beauty, if not always its charm; visitors have reported a change in the welcome they receive. Spontaneous warmth and friendliness have, in some cases, been replaced by a surliness. Perhaps this was inevitable, and it should be stressed that beyond the tourist centres, the Bali of old is still waiting to be discovered. Avoid the main resorts (Kuta and Sanur) during peak season, when hawkers are very persistent and everywhere is crowded. As far back as the 1930s, insightful commentators were predicting what lay in store for Bali. Miguel Covarrubias, for one, in his seminal book, *Island of Bali* (1937) wrote:

"Undoubtedly Bali will soon enough be 'spoiled' for those fastidious travellers who abhor all that which they bring with them. No longer will the curious Balinese of the remote mountain villages, still unaccustomed to the sight of whites, crowd around their cars to stare silently at the 'exotic' long-nosed, yellow-haired foreigners in their midst. But even when all the Balinese will have learned to wear shirts, to beg, lie, steal, and prostitute themselves to satisfy new needs, the tourists will continue to come to Bali to see the sights, snapping pictures frantically, dashing from temple to temple, back to hotel for meals, and on to watch rites and dances staged for them."

The Balinese have traditionally believed that their island belongs to the gods and they are merely custodians entrusted to ensure its well-being.

THE LAND

GEOGRAPHY

Bali is the westernmost island of the chain that make up the Lesser Sundas, and is one of Indonesia's smallest provinces. It covers 5,561 sq km and has a population of 3 million. Like the other islands of the Lesser Sundas, it rises from the deep sea as a series of spectacular volcanic peaks, the highest of which – Mt Agung – exceeds 3,000m.

Separating Bali from Java is the narrow Bali Strait. It is 40-50m deep, and during the last Ice Age when sea-levels were considerably lower than today, Bali would have been connected to the mainland by a land bridge, allowing animals to move freely between the two. To the E, Bali is separated from the next of the Lesser Sunda Islands, Lombok, by the far deeper Lombok Strait. At its deepest, the water depth exceeds 1,300m – and even during the Pleistocene Ice Age the strait would have remained submerged. Wallace's Line, the division between the Asian and Australasian faunal realms, first identified by the great Victorian naturalist Alfred Russel Wallace, passes between the two islands (see page 690). Because of the depth of the water here, the strait is an important passage for nuclear submarines making the trip between the Indian and Pacific oceans.

A feature of life on an island that lies over the spot where two tectonic plates overlap, is great geological instability. One of the most serious earthquakes this century occurred in 1917. During Jan and Feb of that year, a series of tremors hit the E and S regions of the island, followed by the eruption of Mt Batur. When this activity came to an end on 20 Feb, a total of 2,431 temples had been badly damaged – including Pura Besakih on Mt Agung – 64,000 homes had been wrecked, and 1,500 people had died. The inference was clear to every Balinese: the gods were angry. It is partly for this reason that the Balinese have felt it necessary to build temples in great numbers to appease the spirits and therefore help prevent natural catastrophe. In the case of Mt Batur's 1917 eruption, though the lava engulfed the village of Batur, it stopped at the gates to the temple. The villagers took this as a good omen and refused to move, rebuilding their village at the same site. 9 years later, the volcano erupted again,

Bali highlights

Temples The most important and impressively situated temple is *Besakih* on Mt Agung (page 390). *Uluwatu* is perched on a cliff-top on the Bukit Peninsula (page 367), while the coastal temple *Tanah Lot* (page 411) is the most photographed sight on Bali. Other notable temples include *Taman Ayun* at Mengwi (page 413) and *Kehen* at Bangli (page 387).

Other Historical Sights Within easy reach of **Ubud** are *Goa Gajah* or Elephant Cave (page 374), the ancient stone carvings at *Yeh Pulu* (page 375), the mysterious monumental burial chambers of *Gunung Kawi* (page 384), and the holy springs at *Tirta Empul* (page 385). The royal bathing pools of *Tirtagangga* are in the E (page 407). The *Museum Bali* in Denpasar (page 345) has a good collection of ethnographic and archaeological exhibits.

Beaches The main beach resort areas are *Kuta* (page 351), *Sanur* (page 358) and *Nusa Dua* (see page 368); *Candi Dasa* (page 399) and *Lovina Beach* (page 417) are smaller and less developed.

Shopping Bali is a shoppers paradise (see page 338); *fashions* in Kuta (page 353), *craft villages* N of Sanur (page 371), *paintings and crafts* in Ubud (page 372).

Natural sights Among the most notable, is the extraordinary volcanic landscape of *Mount Batur* (page 387); the upland, almost alpine, area centred on *Lake Bratan* (page 414); the *terraced rice fields* of the S and E and the countryside around **Ubud** (page 373); and the *Bali Barat National Park* (page 422).

Sports *Surfing* (see page 343), *white water rafting* (page 379), *snorkeling* (page 342), *golf* (pages 370 and 415) and *diving* (page 342) are the most notable.

Culture & Performance *Balinese dancing* in and around Ubud (page 382), and the traditional *Bali Aga village of Tenganan* (page 400).

this time swamping the temple and leading to one death, an old woman, who died of fright. Nonetheless, the villagers still rebuilt their village on the rim of the volcano – albeit in a safer location – courting possible future disaster.

Despite the devastating effects of periodic earthquakes and volcanic eruptions, Bali has also been blessed by nature in its rich and fertile soils and abundant rainfall. Farmers have exploited this natural wealth by creating terraces on the hillsides, cutting tunnels through the rock to carry irrigation water, and cultivating rice throughout the year (see box).

At the core of the island is a central mountain range consisting of six peaks all exceeding 2,000m. These trap rain clouds and ensure that perennial rivers water the lower slopes. The main expanse of lowland lies to the S of this mountainous interior, and most of the rivers flow S. It is here, on the S slopes and plain, that Bali's famous terraced rice fields are concentrated. Most of the villages or *banjars* are perched on the edge of ridges, surrounded by ricefields. To the N, the lowland fringe is much narrower and the absence of rivers makes the land much drier and more suited to dry land agriculture than intensive wet rice cultivation. The W peninsula, with its poor soils, is yet more arid still.

Despite Bali's unquestioned natural fecundity, the island has begun to feel the effects of over-population. In the 1950s, about 3,000 people were leaving Bali each year to take up places on transmigration settlements in the Outer Islands (see page 427); by the 1960s this had risen to 5,000. It has only been the boom in tourism since the 1970s that has prevented this stream becoming a flood, as tourism has offered young Balinese alternative opportunities outside agriculture.

CLIMATE

Bali is hot and humid, but this is alleviated by ocean breezes and altitude. Annual rainfall averages 2,150mm, the driest months being Aug and Sep and the wet-

---

The gift of water: rice and water in Bali

Among anthropologists, agronomists and geographers, Bali is famous for its system of irrigation. It is a three-fold fascination, bringing together impressive feats of engineering, elaborate social structures, and the guiding hand of religion. (For general background to wet rice cultivation see page 80.)

Most of the 162 large streams and rivers which flow from Bali's mountainous interior have cut deep channels into the soft volcanic rock. This has made it impossible for farmers to dam and channel water for irrigation in the usual way. Instead, they have taken to cutting tunnels through the rock, and constructing elaborate aquaducts and bamboo piping systems to carry the water to the top of a series of terraced rice fields. From here it can flow, with gravity, from paddy field (or *sawah*) to paddy field.

The Balinese have been digging irrigation tunnels in this way for over a thousand years. One tunnel has an inscription recording that it was cut in 944AD. They are dug by professional tunnellers whose main difficulty is not cutting through the soft volcanic rock, but making sure they emerge in the correct place – some are over a kilometre long.

But, these feats of engineering are only half the story. The water then needs to be managed, and the tunnels, weirs and aquaducts, maintained. As American anthropologist Stephen Lansing writes in his book *Priests and Programmers*, "virtually every farmer depends on an irrigation system that originates several kilometres upstream and flows in fragile channels through the lands of many neighbours...". He notes that even a brief interruption of flow will destroy a farmers' crop. To prevent this, every rice farmer is a member of a *subak* or irrigation society. The subak brings together all the farmers who receive water from a common source, and this may include farmers from more than one village. The subak is designed to ensure the equitable distribution of water. Each subak is headed by a *kliang subak* or *penyarikan subak* who can call on his members to police canals, mend dykes and wiers, and generally maintain the system.

Nor does the story of rice and water end with the subak. The subaks, in turn, look to the regional water temple or *pura*, and the head of the pura sets the schedule of planting and harvesting. Subaks are not self-reliant; water control among the farmers of one subak is usually dependent upon those of another. The head of Pura Er Jeruk explained the system to Stephen Lansing in these terms:

There are fourteen... *subaks* all of which meet together as one here. They meet at the Temple Er Jeruk. Every decision, every rule concerning planting seasons and so forth, is always discussed here. Then after the meeting here, decisions are carried down to each *subak*. The *subaks* each call all their members together: 'In accord with the meeting we held at the Temple Er Jeruk, we must fix our planting dates, beginning on day one through day ten'. For example, first *subak* Sango plants, then *subak* Somi, beginning from day ten through day twenty. Thus it is arranged in accordance with water and Pandewasan...".

test, Dec and Jan. Temperatures at sea-level average 26°C (average max 32°C in Mar, average min 29°C in Jul) and vary only marginally through the year; in high-land areas it is considerably cooler, about 20°C. In the wet season the humidity can be oppressive.

There are two seasons: the dry season from May-Oct; and the wet season from Nov to Apr. But this should not deter visitors. Rain tends to fall throughout the year, but it usually comes in short, sharp showers during the afternoon and early evening. If you do get caught in a period of low pressure, the sheer volume of rain can be very limiting and it may be worth considering a move to one of the (usually) drier islands to the E. (See page 337 for best time to visit and climate chart page 36.)

HISTORY

Balinese recorded history begins in the 10th century with the marriage of King Udayana and the E Javanese princess Mahendradatta. In 991 their union resulted in the birth of a son, named Airlangga. He was sent to Java to rule a principality of his father-in-law King Dharmawangsa of Sanjaya. When Dharmawangsa was murdered, Airlangga assumed the throne and for the next 30 years ruled his empire with great skill (see page 82). As a Balinese prince he forged strong links between his island of origin and Java, and in so doing began the pattern of Javanese cultural influence over Bali.

After 1049 when, on Airlangga's death, the kingdom of Sanjaya (or Mataram) was divided, Bali became independent once more. It remained self-governing for the next 235 years until King Kertanagara of the E Javanese dynasty of Singasari invaded in 1284. Kertanagara's domination over Bali was to last only 8 years, when it was invaded by the stronger Majapahit Kingdom of Central Java. Relieved of their Singasari overlords, the Balinese were left to themselves for another 50 years. In 1343, General Gajah Mada, under the flag of Majapahit, conquered Bali,

making the island a Javanese colony. Though the various Balinese principalities revolted time and again against Majapahit overlordship, they were neither individually strong enough nor sufficiently united to resist the weight of Javanese power.

During the 15th century, as Islam filtered into Java, Majapahit began to decline in influence. The last Hindu prince of Majapahit crossed the Bali Strait in 1478, escaping from the Muslim onslaught to the Hindu haven of Bali. He was accompanied by priests, artists and other courtesans – as well as by large numbers of ordinary E Javanese. The prince declared himself King of Bali (his descendants are the rajas of Klungkung) and promptly divided the island up between his various supporters. These later Javanese immigrants are still referred to as *Wong Majapahit* and a shrine for *Batara Majapahit*, or the teachers of Majapahit, can be found in nearly every temple. Some commentators argue that it was because of this wholesale migration of the cream of Javanese artists and craftsmen, that Balinese art today is so strong and prolific. It was on Bali that Java's pre-Islamic artistic accomplishments were preserved.

The Dutch arrival

The Dutch first made contact with Bali in 1597, when a fleet led by Cornelius Houtman landed on the island. His men enjoyed a long sojourn, falling in love with the people and the place. When the expedition returned to Holland, such was the wonder at the stories that the sailors told that another fleet was dispatched, in 1601, with gifts for the hospitable king. The king received these gifts with dignity, and in return presented the captain with a beautiful Balinese girl.

But this initial friendly encounter was not to be the pattern of future contacts. In 1815 Tambora Volcano erupted on Sumbawa (see page 720), and more than 10,000 people on Bali perished in the

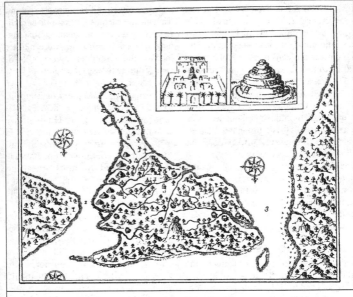

One of the first maps of the island of Bali, Tardieu, c1760.

subsequent famine and plague. This was seen by the Balinese as a taste of things to come. In 1817 a Dutch ship arrived laden with goods to be traded, and in 1826, a trade agreement was signed and the first permanent Dutch representative settled in Kuta. But by then, relations between the Balinese, and what they perceived to be the arrogant, crude and ill-behaved Dutch, were already strained. In 1841, a Dutch ship ran aground and the King of Bali accepted it as a gift. This was the excuse the Dutch needed for intervention.

5 years later, the Dutch sent a large, punitive expeditionary force to conquer N Bali. The attempt failed, but the Dutch, persistent as ever, followed it with another in 1848, and yet a third in 1849. Jagaraga, the capital of the N Balinese Kingdom of Buleleng, was eventually vanquished, but not without considerable losses on both sides. The fact that Bali was divided into various different competing principalities made the Dutch campaign all the easier. Even so, an attack on S Bali at the same time led to the death of the Dutch general, and the Europeans were forced to accept a treaty which left S Bali under Balinese control. This was not the initial intention, and for the next 40 years the Dutch searched for a means of extending their influence from N Bali over the rest of the island.

To do this, the Dutch attacked Lombok in 1894, which was under the control of the E Balinese Kingdom of Karangkasem (see page 324). When Lombok fell, so too did Karangkasem, and then Bangli and Gianyar also accepted Dutch rule. But it was not until the first decade of the 20th century that the final three stubborn, recalcitrant kingdoms of Badung, Tabanan and Klungkung fell to the might of the Dutch.

This last campaign was associated with the arrival in 1904 of a new governor-

The sign of the swastika

Visitors to Bali will notice swastika's intricately carved in stone patterns. This perplexes many people, but it is a sign of Balinese unity, not indicative of supporters of Germany's 3rd Reich.

general, JB van Heutz. He was determined to complete the campaign for Bali, the new Resident of Bali and Lombok recalling that when he first met van Heutz, the governor-general had run "his hand across the principalities of South Bali [saying] no more than 'this all has to be changed'". An expeditionary force sailed from Surabaya in 1906 and, anchoring off the coast of S Bali, began to shell Denpasar's royal palace. The kings remained defiant and the Dutch force had to land in order to subdue the Balinese.

The Balinese king of Denpasar quickly realized that his cause was lost. He announced that anyone who wished could accompany him in a *puputan*, or 'fight to the end'. Most men, and many women as well, heeded their King's call. They dressed in their best clothes (the women wearing men's clothes) and wore their finest gold krisses. The following extract is from Miguel Covarrubias' 1937 book *Island of Bali*:

"At nine in the morning the fantastic procession left the palace, with the Radja at the head, carried on the shoulders of his men, protected by his gold umbrellas of state, staring intently at the road in front of him, and clutching in his right hand his kris of gold and diamonds. He was followed by silent men and entranced women, and even boys joined the procession, armed with spears and krisses. They marched on through what is today the main avenue of Denpasar towards Kesiman, and when they turned the corner, the Dutch regiment was only 300 yards away. The commander, astonished at the sight of the strange procession, gave orders to halt; Balinese interpreters from Buleleng spoke to the Radja and his

followers, begging them anxiously to stop, but they only walked faster. They came within 100 feet, then 70 feet, then made a mad rush at the soldiers, waving their krisses and spears. The soldiers fired the first volley and a few fell, the Radja among them. Frenzied men and women continued to attack, and the soldiers, to avoid being killed, were obliged to fire continually. Someone went among the fallen people with a kris killing the wounded. He was shot down, but immediately another man took his place; he was shot, but an old woman took the kris and continued the bloody task. The wives of the Radja stabbed themselves over his body, which lay buried under the corpses of the princes and princesses who had dragged them over to die upon the body of their king. When the horrified soldiers stopped firing, the women threw handfuls of gold coins, yelling that it was payment for killing them...".

In the battle, the entire court of the King of Denpasar – bar a few wounded women – died. The king himself is said to have adopted the position of *semadi* meditation before falling under a hail of bullets. Following this battle, the same sequence of events was to be repeated at other palaces across Bali. For many Dutch soldiers, what was an overwhelming military victory had the sour taste of moral defeat.

The King of Tabanan to the W, rather than sacrificing his army, came to negotiate with the Dutch. As a symbol of his intentions, he was shielded by a green umbrella rather than the usual gold one. When they took him prisoner, the king cut his own throat with a blunt *sirih* (betel) knife, and the crown prince took an overdose of opium. The last palace to fall was that of Klungkung on 28 April 1908. Again the king chose to die rather than surrender, together with his wives and many members of the court, he was killed in yet another *puputan*. Bali was finally subdued; although the Dutch army remained on the island until 1914. One reason the Balinese were so ready to commit mass suicide rather than surrender to the enemy was their belief that the spirit of a person who died in war would achieve Nirvana.

The problem for the Dutch was how to make the island profitable. One solution was to import and sell opium to the Balinese, particularly the royal families, at great profit to the Dutch. The use of opium was actively promoted and did even more damage to Bali's population than the preceding wars. Van Kol argued strenuously for the ending of the monopoly, writing: "The loss of opium monies will be recompensated by the increasing prosperity of the population whose productive force will no longer be paralysed, and the enormous amounts presently spent on this juice will be used for the purchase of necessities which will increase tax income. Moreover, this will be income to which no tears are attached".

After the Dutch had gained full control of Bali, they set about reorganizing the island so that they could administer it efficiently, with the minimum of fuss. They sent those few members of Bali's royal houses who had survived the various *puputan* into exile and moulded the younger princes into their colonially designated roles. Perhaps even more significantly in the longer term, the Dutch asked the senior priests to simplify the caste system. This was then frozen, removing the flexibility and mobility inherent in the original system. The years of Dutch rule were not happy ones for many Balinese. There was a devastating earthquake in 1917, followed by a plague which decimated the island's rice crop, then an influenza epidemic, and finally the population had to contend with the economic effects of the Depression. As Adrian Vickers says in his book *Bali: a paradise created* "Bali from 1908 to 1942...was an island of social tensions and conflicts for the Balinese".

The Japanese occupation of WW2 did not provide a respite from oppression. Although initially welcomed as liberators, this quickly changed as the Japanese began to target Bali's elite – who were identified with the Dutch – with considerable brutality. The end of the War shifted the conflict to one between the Dutch and their supporters, and the republicans among the island's population. But these periods of confrontation were comparatively mild when compared with the murderous months from Oct 1965 to Feb 1966.

The Communist puputan

During the course of the late 1950s and early 1960s, Bali became one of the strongholds of the Indonesian Communist Party – the PKI. With the failure of the attempted coup in Jakarta at the end of Sep 1965, a wave of violence erupted across the country (see page 50). Nowhere was it more devastating than on Bali. Adrian Vickers in his book *Bali: a paradise created* describes the progress of the massacre:

"They began in the north and west, where the Left was strongest, but by the end of this period the whole of Bali was a landscape of blackened areas where entire villages had beeen burnt to the ground, and the graveyards could not cope with the numbers of corpses. ... The military distanced themselves from the killings. They simply went into each village and produced a list of Communists to be killed, which was given to the head of the village to organize. ... After the initial struggle the killing took on a dispassionate tone. Those identified as PKI dressed in white and were led to graveyards to be executed *puputan*-style."

The numbers killed in this orgy of violence will never be known. One estimate puts the figure at an astonishing 100,000. Rivers were reported to be choked with bodies and the graveyards overflowing with corpses. Today, few on the island will talk about this dark episode, and none with relish.

ART AND ARCHITECTURE

The American anthropologist Margaret Mead, like many other observers ofBalinese life, observed that "everyone in Bali is an artist". This extends from painting and carving, through to the dramatic arts, and into ceremony and ritual. Sometimes the sheer density of artistic endeavour can seem overwhelming. As Noel Coward wrote to Charlie Chaplin in a poem:

As I said this morning to Charlie
There is far too much music in Bali,
And although as a place it's entrancing,
There is also a thought too much dancing.
It appears that each Balinese native,
From the womb to the tomb is creative,
And although the results are quite clever,
There is too much artistic endeavour.

Most of Bali's art and architecture is linked to the 'Javanization' of the island that began in the 10th century with a marriage between two royal houses of Java and Bali (see page 82). However, it was the fall of the Majapahit Empire in the 15th century and the escape of the remnants of the Majapahit court, together with many skilled artisans, that led to the greatest infusion of E Javanese art and architecture. While Java was undergoing a process of Islamization, Bali effectively preserved the Indo-Javanese cultural traditions, though adapting them to accord with existing Balinese traditions.

The Balinese pura

In Bali there are over 20,000 temples – or *pura* – and most villages should have at least three. The *pura puseh*, literally 'navel temple', is the village-origin temple where the village ancestors are worshipped. The *pura dalem* – or 'temple of the dead' – is usually found near the cremation ground. The *pura bale agung* is the temple of the great assembly hall and is used for meetings of the village. There are also irrigation temples, temples at particular geographical sites, and the six great temples or *sadkahyangan*. Finally, there is the mother temple, Pura Besakih.

Balinese pura are places where the gods rule supreme, and evil spirits are rendered harmless. But the gods must be appeased and courted if they are to protect people, so offerings are brought to the site. The buildings that constitute a temple are not as important as the ground, which is consecrated.

The temple complex consists of three courts (two in N Bali), each separated by walls; the front court, or *jaba*, the central court, or *jaba tengah*, and the inner court, or *jeroan*. The innermost court is the most sacred and is thought to represent heaven; the outermost, the underworld; and the central court, an intermediate place. The generalized description of the pura given below accords most closely with newer temples. Old temples, and particularly those on the N coast, tend to show differences in their configuration. **NB** Colonies of longtail macaques inhabit some temple sites; they should not be teased or fed, and certainly not purchased – as has been occurring. Macaques are social animals that suffer if removed from their family group.

The outer court or *jaba* The entrance to the jaba is usually through a *candi bentar*, literally 'split temple' gate. The visual symbolism is clear – if the two halves of the gate are pushed together, closing the entranceway, they would form the shape of a complete candi (see page 90). The split gates may represent the symbolic splitting of the material world, so that the physical body can enter the realm of the spirits. Other art historians maintain that the gates represent duality: male to the right, female to the left.

Within the jaba are a number of structures. In one corner is the *bale kulkul* (*bale* = pavilion, *kulkul* = wooden gong), a pavilion in which hangs a large hollow, wooden, gong or drum. The kulkul is beaten during temple ceremonies and also in times of emergency or disaster – during an earthquake for example. The bale and the kulkul are often decorated. Also within the jaba, it is not uncommon to find a *jineng* – a small barn used to store rice produced from the temple's own fields (*laba pura*).

The central court or *jaba tengah* The entrance leading to the central court is through the *candi kurung*. Like the split gate, and as the name implies, this is also in the form of a candi, but in this case a wooden doorway allows visitors to pass through. In a village pura, the centre of the jaba tengah will be dominated by an open pavilion with a roof of grass or reed.

This is the *bale agung* or village conference hall. There is also often a *bale* for pilgrims who wish to stay overnight in the temple.

The inner court or *jeroan* The entrance to the inner court is through a second, larger, candi kurung called the *paduraksa*. The entrance way is usually guarded by a demon's head and rises up in the form of a pyramid. In larger temples,

Bali Pura

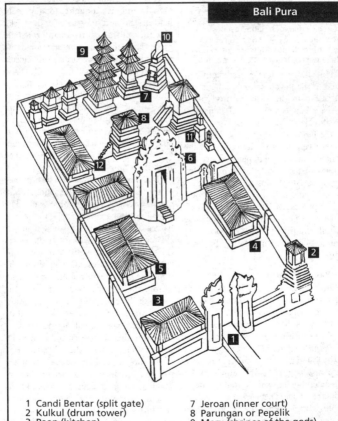

1 Candi Bentar (split gate)
2 Kulkul (drum tower)
3 Paon (kitchen)
4 Bale Gong
   (shed for gamelan orchestra)
5 Bale (resthouse for pilgrims)
6 Paduraksa

7 Jeroan (inner court)
8 Parungan or Pepelik
9 Meru (shrines of the gods)
10 Padmasana (stone throne for sun god Surya)
11 Sanggahs
   (secretaries of the gods)
12 Bale Piasan (sheds for offerings)

there may be three gateways, the central one of which is only opened during ceremonies. Along the back wall of the jeroan are the most sacred of the shrines. These may have multiple roofs – as many as eleven. The greater the number of roofs, the more important the god. Also on the back wall, there is a stone pillar or *tugu*. It is at the tugu that offerings are left for the *taksu*, the god who's job it is to protect the temple and through whom the wishes of the gods are transmitted to the dancer during a trance dance. In the centre of the jeroan is the *parungan* or *pepelik* – the seat of all the gods, where they assemble during temple ceremonies. Finally, along the right-hand wall of the inner courtyard, are two *sanggahs* – *Ngurah Gde* and *Ngurah Alit*. These are the 'secretaries' of the gods; they ensure that temple offerings are properly prepared. (Condensed from: E Utrecht and B Hering (1986) *The temples of Bali*.)

Bali's artistic renaissance

During the early decades of the 20th century, Bali became famous as the haunt of a small community of western artists. They 'discovered' Balinese art and laid the foundations for a significant artistic flowering. Up until that point, art had been produced for the pleasure of the gods and, in some cases, for aristocratic families. Among these early western artists, the most famous were Walter Spies, the son of a German diplomat, and the Dutchman Rudolf Bonnet. Spies, who had first worked for the Sultan of Yogya, arrived in Bali on a short visit and was so taken with the island that he decided to stay. He was also a homosexual, and there seems little doubt that he found Bali less suffocating than Europe. Homosexual activity was accepted as a pursuit among unmarried young men, and the great anthropologist Margaret Mead defended him in these terms when he was tried for homosexuality in 1939. Over the years, Spies recorded Balinese music, collected its art, contributed to academic journals, and established the Bali Museum. He also painted a handful of rich paintings recording in minute detail Bali's natural and cultural wealth. However, Spies was not keen to teach the Balinese.

In contrast, Rudolf Bonnet was more than happy to train and advise Balinese artists in western techniques and to transmit the European aesthetic. In 1936, Bonnet and Spies established the first artists' cooperative – the *Pita Maha* (meaning Great or Noble Aspiration) at Ubud. Balinese artists would bring works to the cooperative and Bonnet and Spies would select those they felt were good enough for sale and exhibition. This naturally led to a trend towards western tastes and Bonnet, particularly, would offer advice to artists as to why their work had been rejected. As the art historian Djelantik writes, in "those years when the prestige of the white man was at its height, Bonnet's word was law and readily accepted". Both Spies and Bonnet remained on Bali until the Japanese occupation from 1941-45. Spies was killed when the ship carrying him to Ceylon was sunk by a Japanese bomb; Bonnet was interned by the Japanese in Sulawesi.

Spies, Bonnet and other western artists visiting Bali viewed the Balinese as innately talented and creative, but failed fully to appreciate – or at least to take note of – the traditional strictures under which most art was produced. Balinese craftsmen worked to strict formulas and there was little room for individual invention. Production was geared to copying existing works, not to creating new ones. As court art was in decline, Spies and Bonnet encouraged Bali's artists to produce for the emerging tourist market. This allowed the Balinese greater artistic freedom, and also led to a change in subject matter; from carving gods and mythical figures, they began to produce carvings and paintings of the natural world and everyday life. At the same time, there was a shift from realism to greater abstraction and expressionism, while the gaudy colours of traditional art were replaced with softer, more natural hues. The birth of Balinese modernism can be directly linked to the influence of this small group of western artists.

Today, art in Bali is predominantly driven by the tourist market. That which sells to foreigners determines production: output is standardized, pieces are small and easily portable, designs are selected which sell well...in short, art is now an industry in Bali.

Balinese painting

Most of the paintings produced by artists in Ubud, Batuan and Penestanan are not 'traditional'. The artists use western materials and methods, and work to an adapted western aesthetic. Yet, Balinese works do have a quality which sets them apart and thus makes them distinctive.

In the past, Balinese painters worked in what has become known as the *wayang* style. Adapted from the wayang kulit or shadow play, figures were painted in profile or three-quarters view, with a strict use of colour. This style of painting was used for Balinese calendars, scrolls for temples and *langse*, and large rectangular works for palaces. Today, most of the few artists still working in the wayang style live near the SE village of Kamasan.

In *Balinese paintings*, the art historian AAM Djelantik divides Balinese painters into seven groups:

❑ The *Traditionalists of Kamasan* mentioned above who continue to paint in the wayang style.

❑ The *Traditional experimentalists of Kerambitan* (20 km SW of Tabanan) who produce wayang-style paintings but use additional colours (like blue and green) and a bolder, stronger style.

❑ The *Pita Maha painters of Ubud* concentrate on realistically reproducing the natural world – fish, birds, frogs, tropical flora – in fresh and vibrant colours.

❑ The *Pita Maha painters of Batuan* produce eclectic paintings; detailed scenes from Buddhist mythology, lively and innovative wayang-style images, and naive-style works – almost caricatures – that depict modern life with humour.

❑ The *Young artists of Penestanan* make up a group initially inspired by the Dutch painter Arie Smit who arrived in Bali in 1956; he took farm boys, and trained them, but also allowed their innate talent to emerge. The resulting works are bold and bright, naive in form, and depict everyday scenes.

❑ The *Academicians* are artists who have received training at western-style art schools in Java. Although the works sometimes employ Balinese or Javanese motifs and even techniques (for example, painting on batik), they are western in inspiration and sometimes abstract.

❑ The *Adventurers* are untrained Balinese artists who have broken away from Balinese tradition, experimenting with new styles and techniques. Their work is diverse and cannot be simply characterized.

Supporting the Balinese handicraft industry

In 1993 a new NGO, *Yayasan Mitra Bali* was established to support the small-scale handicraft producer in Bali from initial production through to the final marketing of the object. It has been estimated that there are 90,000 handicraft producers on the island, and *Yayasan Mitra Bali* is trying to promote an ideal of development which favours balanced social change and eschews the notion that development equals money. The NGO assists producers in selling their work through such international organizations as UK-based OxFam, Shared-Earth and Self-Help Crafts Canada. Most craft producers who sell through shops and other outlets on Bali have to accept a 50%-60% commission (this, it should be added, is roughly the same rate of commission that artists in the West have to accept); *Yayasan Mitra Bali* at the moment takes just 10%, although this is likely to rise soon. One of the NGO's workers,

Agung Alit, explained in *Inside Indonesia* the objectives of his organization: "...more than ideology, more than just words, we offer producers a realistic plan for material and social progress which is not based on exploitation or ecological degradation". The offices of *Yayasan Mitra Bali* are at Jl Sulatri 2, Denpasar, T 224397.

CULTURE

PEOPLE

The original inhabitants of Bali are the Bali Aga, who still live in a handful of communities in the E of the island (see page 406). Since the intrusion of Javanese Hindu-Buddhist people and culture from the 10th century, the Bali Aga have been gradually relegated to a subordinate position. For most visitors today, the culture of Bali means that of the dominant Hindu population.

Despite population growth and considerable modernization, most Balinese still live in villages or *banjar* ranging in size from 200 to several thousand inhabitants. Family compounds or *kuren* are enclosed by high walls and are clustered around a central village courtyard. A kuren will support several families, all eating food from the same kitchen and worshipping at the same family altar. The family gods are paternal ancestors, and descent is patrilineal. The central courtyard is the place where villagers congregate for group activities; for wayang performances, village meetings, and periodic markets. In the past, each village would have been headed by a hereditary prince.

Balinese social structure is stratified in two ways. First, every individual belongs to a ranked descent group or *wangsa* ('peoples'). This system of ordering people is akin to the Indian caste system and was adopted after Javanese rule was established on the island. The nobility are divided into three castes – the *brahmanas* or priests, *satriyas* or ruling nobles, and *wesyas* or warriors. Members of these

three castes are said to be the descendants of aristocrats from the Majapahit Kingdom who settled here towards the end of the 15th century. But 90% of the population, belong to the *sudras* or *jaba*; literally, the outsiders of the court. In addition to belonging to a caste, a Balinese will also belong to a far more egalitarian class structure based upon where a person lives. The *banjar* system of associations is the epitome of this (see page 324).

As dictated by Balinese tradition, a child is not placed on the floor until the 105th day of its life; he or she will be carried until able to stand and walk – never being allowed to crawl, as the Balinese believe this is animalistic. At 210 days (1 Balinese year) the child is given its name. A ceremony occurs to celebrate puberty; first menstruation is followed by a tooth-filing ceremony (often occurring at the same time as the marriage ceremony). From the time of the tooth-filing ceremony, daughters are no longer the father's responsibility. Sons have their marriages financed for them by their fathers. Marriages are still sometimes prearranged among aristocratic families, although increasingly men want to choose their spouses (and *vice versa*) and mixed-caste relationships are occurring.

Language

The Balinese language uses three different forms to indicate the caste, status or social relationship that exists between the speaker and the person being spoken to. High Balinese is used when speaking to superiors who will reply using low Balinese. Low Balinese is also used between friends and equals. Middle Balinese is a form of polite speech used to address strangers and superiors.

Balinese names

Many Balinese names relate to the order of birth. For ordinary (Sudra) people Wayan is usually the firstborn. Made the second, Nyoman the third and Ketut fourth. For higher caste people, the firstborn is often called Raka, Putu or Kompiang, the

The banjar

Every Balinese male is a member of a *banjar*, the basic unit of organization and local government. After marriage, a man is invited to join the banjar. This invitation is in reality a compulsion; if after the third summons the man has not joined, he is declared 'dead' and loses most of his village rights – even the right to be cremated on the village cremation ground. The members of the banjar democratically elect one of their group to act as head (*klian banjar*). He enjoys the status and prestige of being head, and some other minor advantages such as additional rice during group festivities, but no cash payment for his work.

Members of the banjar are bound to assist one another in a variety of tasks. It is, in effect, a cooperative society. In any village there are likely to be a number of banjars, each drawing its members from a geographical neighbourhood. They sometimes own ricefields communally, the production going towards group festivities. Today, money owned through tourist activities – such as staging dances – also goes to the banjar, the society then redistributing it among its members. As Miguel Covarrubias wrote in 1937 (while ignoring the position of women): "Everyone enjoys absolute equality and all are compelled to help one another with labour and materials, often assisting a member to build his house, to prepare his son's wedding, or to cremate a relative".

secondborn Raj, the thirdborn Oka, and the fourthborn Alit. Names can also be indicative of caste; amongst Brahmans you find Ida Bagus for males and Ida Ayu for the females. Amongst the warrior caste, the Satria, Dewa and Anak Agung are common.

RELIGION

Except for small numbers of people in E Java, the Balinese are the only Indonesians who still embrace Hinduism – or at least a variant form of the Indian religion. While across Java and Sumatra, Islam replaced Hinduism, on Bali it managed to persist. Today, 95% of Balinese are still Hindu.

Known as *Hindu Dharma* or *Agama Hindu*, the Balinese religion is an unique blend of Buddhism, Hinduism and pre-Hindu animist beliefs. So, along with the worship of the Hindu trinity of Vishnu, Brahma and Siva, the Balinese also worship deified ancestors or *leluhur*, as well as deities of fertility, of the elements and of the natural world. The whole is suffused with a belief in a transcendental spiritual unity known as *Sang Hyang Widi*.

Reflecting the diverse roots of Balinese Hinduism, there is a corresponding variety of priests and other religious practitioners. There are high-ranking Brahmana priests of both Sivaite and Buddhist persuasions (Buddha is regarded as Siva's younger brother), lower order village priests or *jero mangku*, exorcists, herbal healers, and puppet masters or *dalang*.

The aim of Balinese Hinduism is to reach 'peace of spirit and harmony in the material life' by achieving a balance between philosophy, morals and ritual. The principles of their philosophy or *tattwa* are belief in:

❑ the existence of one God
❑ the soul and the spirit
❑ reincarnation
❑ the law of reciprocal actions
❑ the possibility of unity with the divine.

The three moral rules – or *susila* – of the religion are reasonable enough:

❑ think good thoughts
❑ talk honestly
❑ do good deeds.

Their ritual – or *upacara* – is divided into five areas of sacrifice; ritual for the gods, the higher spirits, the Hindu prophets,

Penjor and janur

Visitors to Bali cannot fail to notice the tall, elegant bamboo poles called *penjor* which bend over the roads, signifying some celebration or festival. Hanging from the slender poles are decorations made out of the yellow leaf of the coconut, known as *janur*. Their design varies enormously, according to the festival and to the place where they are made. So many festivals take place on Bali that there are always penjor to be seen in varying states of decay. Travelling around Bali, visitors may notice arches of palms over the gateway to a house, with janur and banana leaves on either side; this usually signifies a wedding ceremony. Fruit and flowers are placed on (or within) the janur, as offerings to the gods. Any of the following may be seen dangling from the penjor: bananas, pineapples, plastic bags filled with pink liquid, coconuts, carrots, ears of corn and janur; all symbols of fertility. These penjor take about 2 hrs to make and look very beautiful and delicate when first erected; their beauty fades a little as they dry out and turn brown after about 2 days. Janurs are not unique to Bali, and can also be found in parts of Java and North Sulawesi. Reliefs depicting janur on the 9th century Hindu temple of Prambanan, in Central Java, indicate that they have been made for many centuries.

for and on behalf of humans, and sacrifices for neutralizing the negative influences of the natural and supernatural worlds. Praying is also important, for which the devotee requires flowers, incense and *tirta* or holy water. Men sit on the floor with their legs crossed and their hands held together, either at the level of their foreheads (if they are praying to the Supreme God), or at the level of their lips (when praying to Sang Hyang Kala) or resting on their chests (if praying to a dead family member). In Balinese, praying is referred to as *muspa* or *mbakti*. The former means to show respect with flowers, the latter means to worship by means of devotion.

FESTIVALS AND CEREMONIES

There can be few places of comparable size that have more ceremonies and festivals than Bali. The most common are temple anniversary celebrations. Every temple on the island holds an *odalan* once every 210 days, one complete cycle according to the Balinese *wuku* calendar. With more than 20,000 temples, every day is a festival day, somewhere.

The major ceremonies are those of marriage and cremation, both of which are traditionally costly affairs. Also important is tooth-filing. Along with these ceremonies associated with a person's progression through his or her life-cycle, are a vast range of other rites, festivals and ceremonies.

NB The Denpasar Municipality Tourist Office (Dinas Pariwisata Kotamadya Denpasar), Jl Surapati 7, publishes an annual calendar of events listing, day-by-day, Bali's many festivals and their location.

Sesajen

This is not a ceremony, so much as a ritual, but it is so commonplace that it is in some respects the most important religious activity on the island. Three times a day before meals, small woven coconut trays filled with glutinous rice, flowers and salt are sprinkled with holy water and are offered to the gods. They can be seen placed outside the front door of every house.

Eka Dasa Rudra

This is the most important of Bali's festivals and is held, in theory, only once every 100 years at the 'Mother Temple' – Besakih – on Mt Agung. In 1963, the volcano erupted during the festival, killing 2,000 people. As a result, another had to be organized. It took place in 1979 and this

The Balinese calendars: saka and wuku

The Balinese use two traditional calendars, and now have had to add a third, the Gregorian calendar. The Hindu *saka* year is solar and lasts between 354 and 356 days, and is divided into 12 lunar months. But the saka year is 80 years 'behind' the Christian year, so that 1992 AD is saka 1912.

The Balinese also use the Hindu-Javanese 210-day lunar *wuku* year, which operates in parallel with the saka year. But to make things very complicated, the wuku calendar is divided into weeks of 10 days, 10 of which run together so that every day has 10 names according to each of the 10 weeks that it is measured against. Most festivals on Bali are calculated on the basis of the wuku calendar, although some are timed according to the saka year.

time no catastrophe occurred (see page 390 for more details).

Panca Walikrama

This festival is meant to take place once a decade at Besakih temple. However, in practice this has not happened, with only four festivals taking place this century, the last one in 1989.

Odalan

The *odalan* festival celebrates the anniversary of a temple's consecration and is held over about 3 days, every 210 days. This is the festival that visitors to Bali are most likely to see and it includes a great feast to which all the villagers are invited. The villagers prepare for odalan for many days beforehand by cleaning the temple, building altars and awnings, erecting flag poles, and preparing offerings. On the first day of the celebration, women dress in their finest clothes – sarongs, sashes and headdresses – and walk in procession to the temple. On their heads they carry their colourful offerings of fruit and rice cakes, arranged in beautiful and carefully balanced pyramids. The offerings remain at the temple for 3 days during which time they are sprinkled daily with holy water. At the end of this period, the food is taken home again and eaten.

During odalan, the men sit around the compound proudly wearing their krisses tucked into their sarongs. Over the 3 days the temple buzzes with activity; around the entrance locals set up stalls selling food and trinkets, medicine men market cure-alls, cockfights are staged, a gamelan orchestra plays, and in the evenings dance and wayang kulit performances take place. The inner courtyards are reserved for the sacred offerings and here the *pemangku* – or officiating priest – prays in front of the altars.

Marriage

In contrast with western marriages, the traditional Balinese marriage is preceded by the honeymoon – or *ngrorod*. The prospective couple secretly prepare for their honeymoon and, on the day they select, arrange for the abduction of the bride with the complicity of a few close friends. The girl is expected to put up a good fight, but the event is staged. When the parents discover that their daughter has been kidnapped, they send a search party to look for her; again this is for show. During their time in hiding, the couple are expected to consummate their marriage before it happens – an event which is witnessed by the gods. The marriage itself is supposed to occur within 42 days of the abduction, but not before a substantial bride-price has been paid to the parents of the girl. From this point on, the girl becomes part of her future husband's family and relinquishes her own family affiliations. She adopts the groom's ancestral gods to symbolize this. Among aristocratic families marriages were usually pre-arranged (*mapadik*).

The marriage, or *masakapan*, is held on an auspicious day selected by the priest

Kidnapping
(from a Balinese painting)
Source: Covarrubias, Miguel (1937)

Invitations are sent out asking guests to bring certain types and amounts of food. The bride and groom used to have their teeth filed during the ceremony if this had not already been done (see below). While the bride is being prepared for the marriage rite, men – arranged according to status – sit, eat and chew betel nut while being entertained by professional story tellers. The rite varies from area to area, but usually the bride and groom offer food and drink to one another, and then eat together in public; an important symbolic act because in the past only married men and women were allowed to be seen eating food together. In the afternoon, the priest performs a ritual purification and blesses the couple.

Cremation

Cremation is the most important ceremony in the Balinese life-cycle. It is a time for celebration, not sorrow, and is wonderfully colourful. It is also an extremely costly affair, and people will begin to save for their cremation from middle age. Even the poorest family will need to spend about 1 million rupiah, whilst wealthy families have been known to lavish hundreds of millions of rupiah. If there is not enough money saved, families may have to wait years – sometimes more than a decade – before they can hold the cremation of a loved one, thus releasing his or her soul. To avoid the wait, poorer people may be helped out by other members of the village, or they may share in a big ceremony when a number of bodies are cremated together. Another option is to be cremated with an aristocrat who needs a retinue to accompany him to the next life. Towards the end of 1992, the Rajah of Gianyar, 71-year-old Ide Anak Agung Gede Agung, staged an elaborate cremation for his former wife, two stepmothers and two of his late father's concubines: rumour had it that the total cost to the royal house – the richest on Bali – was as much as US$1mn.

Rich people may be cremated soon after they have died, in which case the corpse simply lies in state in the family compound. If there is going to be a considerable time period before cremation, then the body is either buried or mummified first. When enough money has been accumulated, an auspicious day is chosen by a priest for the cremation. The body is disinterred (if buried), the bones collected up, arranged in human form, and draped with a new white cloth. The corpse is carried back to the family compound and placed in a bamboo and paper tower, richly painted and decorated. Here it is adorned with jewellery and cloths decorated with magic symbols. Various rites are performed before the ceremony to awaken and satisfy the soul. An *adegan*, a dual effigy, is carved in palmleaf and sandalwood. On the day before the cremation the effigy is taken in a grand procession to a high priest, accompanied by the dead person's relatives dressed in their finest clothes.

For the cremation itself, a large bamboo tower is built; its size and shape is dictated by the caste of the dead person.

Self-immolation and human sacrifice in a Dutch account of 1633

👣 In 1633 a Dutch expedition visited Gelgel on Bali, and its members witnessed two cremations, one of a queen and another of two princes. In both cases, a number of female slaves and other courtiers also died. The English historian John Crawfurd, quoted the account of the visit and spectacle at some length in his book *The Malay Archipelago* (1820). In the case of the female slaves, each was poignarded:

"Some of the most courageous demanded the poignard themselves, which they received with their right hand, passing it to the left, after respectfully kissing the weapon. They wounded their right arms, sucked the blood which flowed from the wound, and stained their lips with it, making a bloody mark on the forehead with the point of the finger. Then returning the dagger to their executioners, they received a first stab between the false ribs, and a second under the shoulder blade, the weapon being thrust up to the hilt towards the heart. As soon as the horrors of death were visible in the countenance, without a complaint escaping them, they were permitted to fall to the ground...".

In the case of the courtiers and princesses who were cremated with the bodies of the princes, they would not allow anyone of lower status to touch them, and so had to kill themselves:

"For this purpose, a kind of bridge is erected over a burning pile, which they mount, holding a paper close to their foreheads, and having their robe tucked under their arm. As soon as they feel the heat, they precipitate themselves into the burning pile... In case firmness should abandon them... a brother, or another near relative, is at hand to push them in, and render them, out of affection, that cruel office...".

A wooden life-size bull (for men) or cow (for women) is sometimes carved. On the morning of the cremation, friends and relatives are entertained by the family of the deceased and then the body is placed inside the bamboo tower. The village *kulkul* – or gong – is struck, and the construction is carried in a noisy procession (designed to confuse the soul of the departed so that it cannot return to the family home) to the cremation ground by other members of the dead person's *banjar* or village association. The body is roughly handled as it is placed in the tower. At the cremation site, the wooden bull or cow and the corpse are set alight. After the incineration, the ashes are carried off in another raucous procession, to the nearest water, where they are thrown into the wind. The cremation is the most impressive of the Balinese ceremonies, but it is not one where any respect is shown for the corpse. The body is treated like an unclean container; it is the soul that is paramount. To illustrate the point, bodies are poked with sticks to help them burn, and are shown none of the respect evident in the funeral ceremonies of other religions.

Tooth-filing

The practice of tooth-filing was once common across island Southeast Asia. Savages, wild animals and demons have long, white teeth, so filing them down at puberty was necessary to ensure that at death a person would not be mistaken for a wild creature. In some areas of Sumatra this is taken to extremes and every tooth is filed flat; in Bali it is only the front teeth that are filed, although the rationale is the same.

In the past, not only were the front teeth filed, but they were also blackened. In theory, tooth-filing should occur at puberty, but because of the cost of staging the ceremony, it is often delayed until later in life. It is said that filing is necessary to control the six evil characteristics of the human condition, known as *sad ripu*

– passion, greed, anger, confusion, jealousy and earthly intoxication. If someone dies without having had their teeth filed, the priest will often file the teeth of the corpse before cremation. Miguel Covarrubias describes a tooth-filing ceremony he witnessed in the 1930s:

"The operation is performed by a specialist, generally a Brahmana, who knows formulas by which his tools – files and whetstones – are blessed 'to take the poison out of them', to make the operation painless. The patient is laid on a *bale* among offerings, the head resting on a pillow which is covered with a protective scarf, *gringsing wayang wangsul*, one of the magic cloths woven in Tenganan, the warp of which is left uncut. The body is wrapped in a new white cloth and assistants hold down the victim by the hands and feet. The tooth-filer stands at the head of the *bale* and inscribes magic syllables (*aksara*) on the teeth about to be filed with a ruby set in a gold ring. The filing then proceeds, taking from 15 mins to a ½-hr, endured stoically with clenched hands and goose-flesh but without even a noise from the patient..."

DANCE, DRAMA AND MUSIC

Dance

The Balinese are consummate dancers. Everyone dances, and dancing forms an essential element of private and public life accompanying, as Beryl de Zoete and Walter Spies wrote in 1938, "every stage of a man's life from infancy to the grave". Of the various dances, those most often staged for tourists are the masked dance or *topeng*, the monkey dance or *kecak*, and the dance between the witch Rangda and the mythical lion, known as the *barong*. A brief description of the various dances is given below; tourists are normally provided with a printed sheet with information on the dance(s) when they attend a performance.

Kecak – or monkey dance, originates from a trance dance (or *sanghyang*), when a central person in a state of trance com-

Legong costume
Source: Covarrubias, Miguel (1937)
Island of Bali

municates with a god or ancestor. The surrounding chorus of men rhythmically chant *kecak kecak kecak*, which encourages the state of trance and gives the dance its name. The dance itself tells the story of the Ramayana when Sita is abducted by Ravana and subsequently rescued by an army of monkeys (see page 56). The dance is a relatively new creation, having been invented in the 20th century by Walter Spies who combined an ancient dance chorus tradition with an episode from the Ramayana.

Barong or kris dance – is also a trance dance and the epitome of the battle between good and evil. Good, in the shape of the mythical lion *Barong*, fights the evil witch *Rangda*. The witch's spell turns the krisses of the Barong's accomplices against themselves. Inside the barong costume are two men who coordinate their movements much like a Chinese lion dance; indeed, it is thought that the barong dance is derived from the Chinese New Year lion dance. The masks themselves are believed to be infused with magic power, and they are often kept in village temples where they act as patron spirits. Rangda, the personification of evil, has bulging eyes and tusks and is linked to the Indian goddess Durga. Like the barong (the word refers to both the dance and the mask), the mask of Rangda is also revered.

Sanghyang dedari – the Dance of the Holy Angels – is the best known, and possibly the most beautiful of a type of

---

Dance performances on Bali

- **Barong or Kris Dance**
  Batubulan Village, everyday from 0930.
  Puri Saren, Ubud, every Fri from 1830.
  Catur Eka Budi, Jalan Waribang, Kesiman, every day from 0930.
  Sari Wisata Budaya, Jalan By Pass Ngurah Rai, every day from 0930.
  Suwung, every day, 0930-1030.
  Br Abasan, Singapadu, every day, 0930-1030.

- **Kecak Dance**
  Werdi Budaya, Jalan Nusa Indah, everyday from 1830.
  Catur Eka Budi, Jalan Waribang, Kesiman, everyday from 1830.
  Padang Tegal, Ubud, every Sun from 1800.
  Puri Agung, Peliatan, every Thur from 1930.
  Ayodya Pura Stage, Tanjung Bungkak, Denpasar, everyday from 1800.
  Art Centre, Abian Kapas, Denpasar, everyday from 1800.
  Pasar Senggol, Grand Hyatt, Nusa Dua, every Tues from 1900.
  Pelangi Stage, Nusa Dua Beach Hotel, every Sun from 1800.
  Grand Hyatt Bali, every Tues from 1900.
  Br Buni, Kuta, every Sun from 2000.

- **Kecak and Fire Dance**
  Bona Village, every Sun, Mon, Wed and Fri from 1830.
  Batubulan Village, everday from 1830.

- **Legong Dance**
  Puri Saren, Ubud, every Mon and Sat from 1930.
  Peliatan Village, Ubud, every Fri from 1930.
  Pura Dalem Puri, Ubud, every Sat from 1930.
  Pasar Senggol, Grand Hyatt Nusa Dua, every Thur from 1900.
  Hongkong Restaurant, every night from 2000.
  Budaya Stage, Nusa Dua Beach Hotel, every Fri from 2045.
  Grand Hyatt Bali, every Sat from 1900.
  Banjar Tengah Peliatan, Ubud, every Wed from 1930.
  Br Tegal, Kuta, every Tues and Sat from 2000.

- **Shadow Puppet Show**
  Oka Kartini's, Ubud, every Sat from 2000.

- **Tek-tekan Dance**
  Puri Anyar, Kerambitan, on request.
  Puri Agung Wisata, Kerambitan, on request.
  Pasar Senggol, Grand Hyatt Nusa Dua, every Mon from 1900.
  Grand Hyatt Bali, every Mon from 1900.

trance dance known as *Sang* [Lord] *Hyong* [God]. Young girls perform this religious dance of exorcism, designed to rid a community of evil spirits, while a chorus of men and women provide accompaniment. The dancers are often relatives of temple servants and usually have no professional training. They are believed to be possessed by celestial nymphs, and at the end of the performance – traditionally – would walk on hot coals before being brought back to consciousness.

- **Leko and Jangger Dance**
  Puri Anyar, Kerambitan, on request.

- **Ramayana Ballet**
  Pura Dalem Puri, Ubud, every Mon from 2000.
  Puri Saren Ubud, every Tues from 2000.
  Grand Hyatt Bali, every Thur from 1900.
  Br Buni, Kuta, every Mon and Thur from 2000.
  Ubud Kelod, Ubud, every Wed, 1930-2100.

- **Mahabharata Ballet**
  Teges Village, Ubud, every Tues from 1830.

- **Gabor Dance**
  Puri Saren, Ubud, every Thur from 1930.

- **Rajapala Dance**
  Puri Saren, Ubud, every Sun from 1930.
  Ubud Kelod, Ubud, every Tues, 1930-2000.

- **Calonarang Dance**
  Mawang Village, Ubud, every Thur and Sat from 1930.
  Hotel Menara, Ubud, every Fri from 2000.

- **Classical Mask Dance and Legong Dance**
  Banjar Kalah, Peliatan, Ubud, every Thur from 1930.

- **Women's Gamelan and Child Dancers**
  Peliatan Village, Ubud, every Sun from 1930.

- **Sunda Upasunda**
  Puri Saren, Ubud, every Wed from 1930.

- **Baleganjur and Kecak dance**
  Baleganjur procession every afternoon around sunset at **Galleria Nusa Dua**, performed to cleanse the area. Bali's best Kecak dance every Mon, Wed and Fri at the **Nusenglango** Amphitheatre of Galleria Nusa Dua, only 7,500Rp from 1900. Reservations and information: T 771662, T 771663, F 771664.

- **Frog Dance**
  Sanur Beach Hotel from 1930.
  Bebek Mas Restaurant, Kuta, every evening from 2000.
  Penjor Restaurant, Sanur, every Sun from 1900.
  Innercourt Garden of Nusa Dua Beach Hotel, every Tues from 1900.

- **Gebyug Dance**
  'Gurnita Wreksa' Pura Dalem Puri, Peliatan every Mon.

- **Topeng Dance**
  Penjor Restaurant, Sanur, every Sat from 2015.

NB This timetable is subject to change; check beforehand.

The evil witch *Rangda*, enemy of the mythical lion *Barong* in the Barong dance from a
Balinese manuscript
Reproduced in Miguel Covarrubias's Island of Bali, 1937

Legong – a Balinese dance for girls from eight to early teens (although today many tourist dances employ adult performers) which was created at the beginning of the 18th century. This is not a trance dance, but rigorous physical training is needed to perform the movements. Three dancers perform the most popular version, the *legong kraton*, a story taken from the E Javanese classic tale of Prince Panji. In this story, a bird warns the king of the futility of war, which he ignores, and is killed in battle. The dance is regarded as the finest, and most feminine, of Balinese dances and the girls dress in fine silks and wear elaborate headdresses decorated with frangipani and other flowers. The dancers do not speak or sing – the lines of the story are recounted by singers accompanied by a gamelan orchestra. Because of the demands of the dance, girls must be taught – literally physically manipulated – from an early age, so that 'the dance enters their innermost being'.

Topeng – the wayang topeng is a masked dance which, in Bali, recounts stories of former kings and princes. In its purest form, it is performed in silence by a single actor who portrays a series of characters changing his mask each time. Today, he is more likely to be accompanied by a narrator (see page 96).

Jegog – a dance which originates from Jembrana. It is performed by young men and women accompanied by the music of the *jegog* – a bamboo xylophone not unlike the *angklung* of West Java (see box, page 162).

Ramayana ballet – a portrayal of the great Hindu epic (see page 100 and see box, page 56).

Wayang kulit – the famous shadow theatre of Java and Bali in which two-dimensional leather puppets are manipulated, their forms reflected onto a white cloth (see page 100). In Bali, wayang kulit accords, it is thought, more closely with the original Majapahit form than does the Javanese equivalent. This can be seen in the puppets with their elaborate headdresses and costumes, and in the carving of the faces which is similar in style to the low relief carvings on Majapahit temples in E Java.

Gambuh – this is one of Bali's most ancient, and least known, dance dramas. Court tales are enacted in a highly stylized manner by actors dressed in rich costumes and accompanied by a traditional orchestra. Revived from near cultural extinction, *gambuh* is occasionally performed at Pura Desa Batuan in Batuan village, S of Ubud.

Music

Beryl de Zoete and Walter Spies, early foreign residents of Bali, wrote of its music in their paper of 1938 *Dance and drama in Bali*: "Music permeates their life to a degree which we can hardly imagine; a music of incomparable subtlety and intricacy, yet as simple as breathing. Like every other expression of Balinese life, it is easily accessible and at the same time inexhaustible in its interest and variety." It was Walter Spies, an American composer who was captivated when he first heard a recording of Balinese music in the late 1920s in New York, who played a crucial role in detailing and preserving the music of the island. He acted as a patron, wrote a brilliant, seminal book entitled *Music in Bali* (1966), and spread the gospel around the capitals of the world. He even wrote an orchestral work – *Tabuh-Tabuhan* – based on Balinese musical formulas, for which he won a Pulitzer prize in 1936. Such was his love of Bali and its music that what began a short jaunt to the island turned into a life-long love affair.

Like Java, the basis of Balinese music is the gamelan orchestra (see page 101). Sets of gamelan instruments – of which the gongs are regarded as the most important – are usually owned corporately, by the village or *banjar*. Making music is a tightly structured event; the notion of 'jamming' is simply not the Balinese way. Musicians learn their parts and the aim is for an orchestra to produce a perfect rendition of a composed piece. Reflecting this approach, the brilliance of Balinese music is in the whole, which is greater that its constituent parts. There are few superstars; it is the orchestra as a perfectly coordinated unit that determines success.

Experiencing Balinese music, dance and theatre

Most visitors to Bali hear Balinese music or see local dances in the context of their hotels. Although people often assume that such performances cannot be 'authentic', all gamelan and dance groups are regulated by LISTIBIYA, the government arts council. This means that the quality is invariably high, and although pieces are usually condensed to make them more 'acceptable' to tourist audiences, the quality of the performance is rarely affected. However, for a more authentic environment, it is necessary to visit a temple anniversary festival or *odalan* (see page 326).

Performances usually begin in the late afternoon or early evening with a gamelan recital and then continue after dark with dances and shadow plays. Note that visitors should dress and behave appropriately (see Temple etiquette, page 338). The two main music academies are STSI (Werdi Budaya Art Centre) on Jl Nusa Indah in Denpasar; and KOKAR/ SMKI in Batubulan. There is also an annual Bali Arts Festival held from mid-Jun to mid-Jul in Denpasar. See the table for a listing of where to see dances. For information on obtaining recordings of traditional Balinese music (see page 57).

Many villages have a gamelan orchestra; these can often be heard practicing in the evenings on the 'bale banjar', the platform used as a meeting place in the centre of the village.

MODERN BALI

ECONOMY AND TOURISM

Visitors to Bali may leave with the impression that the island's economy is founded on tourism. Certainly, tourism is a crucial element in Bali's economic growth and well-being. Yet over three-quarters of Bali's population still lives in rural areas, and the bulk of the inhabitants depend upon agriculture for their livelihoods. Since the mid-1960s, farmers have turned to the cultivation of high yielding varieties of rice and the use of large quantities of chemical fertilizers. Three-quarters of Bali's riceland now produces two or more crops of rice each year. There has also been a diversification of agricultural production into vegetables and fruit, cloves, vanilla, and livestock.

Outside agriculture, tourism is the next most important industry. The first tourists began to arrive just 6 years after the Klungkung *puputan* (see page 317). In 1914 the Dutch steamship line KPM was publishing brochures with lines like:"You leave this island with a sigh of regret and as long as you live you can never forget this Garden of Eden." Today about 300,000 tourists arrive each year by air, the same number again by sea from Java and Lombok. With a population of 3 million, this means a considerable influx of outsiders – both international and domestic. Given that approaching one half of visitors to Indonesia visit Bali alone, the significance of the island – which accounts for a mere 0.3% of the country's land area – in Indonesia's overall tourist industry is immense.

To serve this influx of visitors, a major building boom has been underway. By 1984, there were already over 9,000 hotel rooms on the island, and the boom continued through the 1980s so that now there are over 20,000. The government has tried to restrict development to buildings no taller than a coconut palm, and has encouraged construction in Balinese 'style'. Although there are not the crude, ungainly high-rise hotels of some other Asian resorts (the only such hotel is the *Bali Beach* on Sanur, constructed before the regulations came into force), the designs do rather stretch the notion of 'traditional' style (particularly those in Nusa Dua and Kuta).

At present, resorts are largely restricted to the S coast, but the government has plans to develop other parts of the island. A projected new road around the island and tourist information centres in each of the island's districts are expected to help the dispersal of tourism to other areas. There is also a plan to develop 'special interest tourism' (or ecotourism), focusing on the island's marine and other natural resources. But although tourism has generated income, jobs and opportunities for Bali's inhabitants, there are those who point to the 'downside' of the industry: cultural erosion, environmental degradation, the undermining of traditional activities, inflation, the growth of crime and drug abuse. But perceptive visitors have been worrying about the impacts of tourism for over half a century. Miguel Covarrubias, who lived on Bali in the early 1930s, wrote that the absence of beggars "is now threatened by tourists who lure boys and girls with dimes to take their pictures, and lately, in places frequented by tourists, people are beginning to ask for money as a return for a service".

Although there is a strong reason to argue that tourism today is little different from the tourism of 20, or even 50-years ago, there are some people – like Balinese anthropologist, Bangkal Kusuma – who see a subtle change in the nature of the industry on the island. From being an industry which drew its life-blood from the maintenance of traditional Balinese culture (or at least what was perceived as 'traditional'), the emphasis is now very much on the McDonaldization of Balinese culture, driven often by investors in

---

Tourism and culture in Bali

👣 One of the areas which has attracted attention among journalists, academics and many tourists who have been to Bali is the relationship between culture and tourism. Bali's tourist industry is unashamedly founded on culture. In a sense, it is the island's culture which is Bali's defining feature. In the 1970s the American anthropologist Philip McKean argued that far from destroying culture, tourism would support, nurture and reinforce culture. Indeed, partly as a result of his work, Bali became an exemplar of how tourism can be managed without undermining culture (see page 22 for a general discussion of the effects of tourism). Arts and crafts appeared to be revivified by the tourism experience, revenue earned widely distributed through the *banjar* system of communal relations, and the Balinese appeared able to separate the sacred from the profane when it came to selling culture to tourists.

The tourism authorities in Bali embraced these views with alacrity. Cultural Tourism or *Pariwisata Budaya* was born in the 1970s. In 1986 the *International Herald Tribune* published an article with the title "Bali: paradise preserved". The article stated:

> "If anything, tourism has pumped more life into the Balinese cultural Renaissance that began earlier this century. There are probably more superb artists and craftsmen in Bali today than at any time in its history."

Putting aside whether 'culture' can be reduced to just artists and craftsmen, this view is being challenged on a number of grounds. Most interesting perhaps is work which has tried to unravel what consistutes 'touristic culture', and what constitutes 'traditional culture' in Bali.

The sociologist Michel Picard wonders whether it is even possible to separate 'tourism' from 'culture' in the case of Bali. Many dances developed for tourists in the 1930s have, over time, become key markers of Balinese, and in some cases of Indonesian, culture. So making a distinction between what belongs to the world of 'tourism' and the world of 'tradition', is impossible. The two have merged. In short, 'cultural tourism' has become 'tourist culture'. As Adrian Vickers has written in his book *Bali: a paradise created*: "This 'culture', expressed in art and religion, is what is promoted in tourist literature, what tourists come to see, and what is eventually accepted by the Balinese themselves as a definition of what is important in their own society." Michel Picard then takes this perspective that tourism is defining culture for the Balinese themselves, one step further when he writes that the Balinese have become "self-conscious spectators of their own culture – taking the growing touristification *cum* Indonesianization of their culture as the very proof of its 'renaissance'".

Jakarta. Kusuma also sees a reduction in the influence of regional tourist authorities and a related rise in that of the national authorities in Jakarta. The latter are now determining the path that tourist development should take on the island; they have perversely placed themselves in the position of identifying 'tradition' for the Balinese people. If this is so, then the challenge for those people who would wish to protect Bali is to carve out a distinctive niche for the island in the context of the nation. In other words to resist the attempts by the 'centre' to determine how tourism in Bali should develop.

Suggested reading

Belo, Jane (edit) (1970) *Traditional Balinese culture*, Columbia University Press: New York. Collection of academic papers, most focusing upon dance, music and drama. Covarrubias, Miguel (1937) *Island of Bali*, Cassell: London (reprinted, OUP: Singapore, 1987). The original treatment of Bali's culture; despite being over 50 years old it is still an excellent background to the island and is highly entertaining. Djelantik, AAM (1990) *Balinese paintings*, OUP: Singapore. Concise history of Balinese painting also covering the major contemporary schools of art. Eiseman, Fred and Eiseman, Margaret (1988) *Woodcarvings of Bali*, Periplus: Berkeley. Eiseman, Fred B (1989 and 1990) *Bali: Sekala and Niskala*, Vol I Essays on Religion, Ritual and Art. Vol II Essays on Society, Tradition and Craft, Periplus: Berkeley. Informative collection of essays giving an insight into the Balinese way of life. Hobart, Angela (1987) *Dancing shadows of Bali: theatre and myth*, KPI: London. Academic book examining the wayang theatre in Bali. Kempers, AJ Bernet (1991) *Monumental Bali: introduction to Balinese archaeology and guide to the monuments*, Periplus: Berkeley and Singapore. New edition of Kempers's 1977 book, with photos and additional 'guide' section; best available. Lansing, J Stephen (1991) *Priests and Programmers: technologies of power in the engineered landscape of Bali*, Princeton University Press: Princeton. An anthropological account of Bali's irrigation system; interesting for rice enthusiasts. McPhee, Colin (1986), *A House in Bali*, OUP: Singapore. An amusing and informed account of Balinese society and the role of music in society by the American composer who visited Bali in 1929. Stuart Fox, David (1982) *Once a century: Pura Besakih and the Eka Dasa Rudra Festival*, Penerbit Citra Indonesia: Jakarta. Tenzer, Michael (1991) *Balinese music*, Periplus: Berkeley and Singapore. Illustrated summary of Balinese music, drawing heavily on Spies's work, best introduction available. Utrecht, E and Hering, B (1987) 'The temples of Bali', *Kabar Seberang Sulating Maphilindo* 18: 161-74. Vickers, Adrian (1989) *Bali: a paradise created*, Periplus: Berkeley and Singapore. Excellent account of the evolution of Bali as a tourist paradise; good historical and cultural background, informed without being turgid.

ISLAND INFORMATION

BEFORE TRAVELLING

WHEN TO GO
● **Best time to visit**
The best time to visit is the dry season between May and Oct when it is slightly cooler and there is less chance of rain. The wet season runs from Nov-Apr when it is hot and humid especially on the coast. At this time of year, Ubud can be cool and it is also wetter than the coast. Accommodation is priciest over Christmas and New Year and several weeks either side, which corresponds with the main holiday period in Australia. A second high season is during Jul and Aug, the northern hemisphere's holiday period. Out of these months accommodation is often cheaper and the island is rather less crowded and frenetic.

GETTING THERE

AIR
Denpasar's Ngurah Rai International Airport is at the S end of the island, just S of Kuta. It is one of Indonesia's 'gateway' cities, with international connections with Australia, Hong Kong, Europe, Singapore, Japan and North America.

● **From Europe**
There are direct flights from Amsterdam, Frankfurt, London, Paris and Rome to Denpasar with Garuda twice a week. In addition KLM operates 2 direct services a week from Amsterdam as does Lufthansa from Frankfurt. Alternatively you can fly direct to Jakarta from most European cities and make an onward connection to Bali; there are many flights between Jakarta and Denpasar, Bali. British Airways fly 4 times a week direct from London to Jakarta; KLM and Garuda each have a daily flight from Amsterdam to Jakarta; Lufthansa has 5 flights and Garuda 3 flights a week from Frankfurt to Jakarta; Air France has 4 flights and Garuda 1 from Paris; Garuda flies twice a week from Zurich. You can also fly from Europe to Singapore and change planes for an onward connection to Bali.

● **From USA**
There are direct flights from Los Angeles to Bali 5 times a week with Garuda.

● **From Asia**
Direct flights to Bali from most capital cities including Hong Kong, Bangkok, Singapore, Taipei, Seoul, Tokyo, Osaka, etc.

● **From Australia and New Zealand**
Direct flights to Bali from Darwin, Cairns, Brisbane, Sydney, Melbourne, Adelaide, Perth and Auckland.

TRAIN
From Jakarta, take the train to Surabaya, a bus to Banyuwangi, and then the ferry to Bali. Alternatively, take the train all the way to Banyuwangi and catch a bus onwards from there. 'All in' train and bus tickets are available in Jakarta.

ROAD
Most long distance bus companies have their offices on Jl Diponegoro and Jl Hasannudin in Denpasar. Regular overnight connections with most destinations in Java, for example to Surabaya, Malang, Yogyakarta, Bandung, Bogor and Jakarta. Examples of prices: a/c buses to Jakarta 30,800Rp; to Yogya 19,600Rp; to Surabaya 10,650Rp. If you are arriving from Java and wish to stay on the N coast, get-off the bus at Gilimanuk (where the ferry docks) and take a bemo to Lovina beach (the price of the bemo is sometimes included in bus/ferry ticket).

SEA
Car ferries every 20 mins from Ketapang, just N of Banyuwangi on Java's E coast, to Gilimanuk on the W tip of Bali 30 mins (1,100Rp). Ferries run every 2 hrs each day from Lembar (Lombok) to Padangbai, near Candi Dasa, 4 hrs (4,500Rp or 6,700Rp; children half price). On arrival in Padangbai, touts beseige visitors to buy tickets on a bemo or shuttle bus to Kuta. There are cheaper public buses to Denpasar. There is a good high-speed catamaran service between Benoa and Lembar (Lombok), 2 hrs (35,000Rp, children half price), a/c, aircraft seats. Buses to Padangbai leave from Denpasar's Batubulan terminal. Cruise liners dock at Benoa Port (T 772521) on the Bukit Peninsula and occasionally at Padangbai. The Pelni ships *Dobonsolo*, *Binaiya* and *Tilongkabila* docks at Padangbai on its 2-week circuit (see schedule page 921). The Pelni office is at Benoa, T 228962. For Lombok, the ferry leaves from Padangbai.

ON ARRIVAL

● **Airport facilities**
24 hrs airport information, T 227825, 235169, 222788, 234606, 234916. The office is situated outside the International departure area. A tourist office with a well-run hotel booking counter offers comprehensive details and prices of up-market accommodation on Bali. Other facilities include money changers, bars, restaurant, shops and taxi counter. Left baggage 3,300Rp/piece/day with no limit on the time.

Accommodation 1 km from the airport (20 mins' walk) **B-D** *Puri Nusantara Cottages Transit Hotel*, Jl Raya Tuban, Kuta, T (0361) 751649, 752996, spotless rooms with private bathroom with fan or a/c, verandahs overlooking attractive gardens, free airport transfers, price incl morning coffee, rec. The airport accommodation service pretends not to know that this place exists in the hopes of steering visitors to more expensive hotels. If you arrive late at night or have an early morning flight, this place is ideal, though the airport transfer service finishes at about 1100, depending on when the driver decides to go home. The *Bali Satwika* is the airport restaurant, good value for such a place. There is a Garuda Reconfirmation office at the International arrivals hall. Open 0800-2100, Mon-Fri, 0900-2100, Sat and Sun. The *Plaza Bali*, at the end of the runway includes craft shops, an art gallery, duty free goods, a Chinese seafood restaurant and a theatre where cultural performances take place. **NB** Porters do not wait to ask whether you would like your baggage carried – they grab it and then demand 500Rp/piece – beware!

Transport to town There are fixed-price taxis from the airport: 8,500Rp to Kuta; 8,500Rp to Legian (12,000Rp to *Oberoi Hotel*); 15,000Rp to Sanur; 10,000Rp to Denpasar. Alternatively, walk out of the airport, past the toll gates, and catch a blue bemo running E to Kuta (500Rp) and from there to Denpasar for connections around the island (see Getting around, page 339). There are several car hire offices at the airport.

● **Airport tax**
Payable on departure – including children – which must be paid in local currency. 25,000Rp on international flights, 7,700Rp on domestic flights.

● **Banks & money changers**
As an international tourist destination, it is easier to change money – either cash or TCs in all major currencies – in Bali than any other spot in Indonesia. All the tourist centres offer money changing facilities at competitive rates. Cash advances can be obtained on Visa cards form **Bank Central Asia (BCA)** in Denpasar.

● **Conduct**
Temple etiquette Visitors are permitted to visit most temples and to attend ceremonies. However, traditional (*adat*) dress is required – a sash around the waist (at some temples a sarong is also required); these are available for hire at the more popular temples, or can be bought for about 1,200Rp (7,000Rp for a sarong). Modest and tidy dress is also required when visiting temples; women should not enter wearing short dresses or with bare shoulders. Do not use flash-guns during ceremonies. Women menstruating are requested not to enter temples. Avoid walking or placing oneself in front of a person praying.

General etiquette As in other countries of Southeast Asia, open displays of emotion – whether anger or affection – should be avoided. Dress modestly and tidily, especially when visiting someone's house or a temple (see above). Try not to point the soles of your feet (the lowest part of the body) at another person, and when gesturing do not point and crook the finger; point the hand and fingers downwards and then motion inwards. The head should not be touched (the holiest part of the body), and the left hand should not be used to give or receive (it is unclean). Although the Balinese have become used to tourists' transgressions, it is polite to adhere to the above rules of conduct.

● **Credit card representatives**
Amex: *Bali Beach Hotel*, Sanur, T 288449; *Galleria Nusa Dua*, Shop A5, T 773334, F 773306.

Diners Club: Jl Veteran 5, Denpasar, T 227138.

Visa & Mastercharge: Bank Duta, Jl Hayam Wuruk 165, Denpasar, T 226578.

● **Emergencies**
Ambulance: T 118.

Police: T 110.

● **Shopping**
Browsing or window shopping can be a stressful experience on Bali – if you express an interest in any goods, expect to be hounded by the sellers. Sales people on the beaches are particularly persistent. Bali has a wide range of goods for sale targeted at the tourist market: a good choice of clothing – ikat, batik and some quality 'fashion' clothes as well as countless T-shirts,

shorts and beachware; brightly-coloured, carved wooden fruit, mobiles, trays and birds; silver jewellery and a scattering of 'antiques'. Carved wooden doors are in plentiful supply and can be dismantled for shipping (packers/shippers can be found in each tourist centre). Ubud and its surrounding craft villages are good places to buy locally-produced handicrafts, while Kuta has the biggest selection of clothing. Always bargain; expect to pay 30%-50% of the asking price except, of course, in fixed-price stores.

Inevitably, much on sale is second-rate and ersatz. This is not a recent development. Miguel Covarrubias when he arrived in Denpasar in 1930 observed that "there are always pretty Balinese girls who sell curios, plainly junk. ...[They] have discovered that the tourists generally prefer hideous statuettes made by beginners or the gaudy weaving dyed with [chemical] anilines to the fine old pieces of wood-carving or to the sumptuous ancient textiles that now rarely find their way into the curio market".

● **Tipping**

The Balinese authorities are trying to prevent the infiltration of tipping, so avoid doing so if you can. You may be forced to use and then, of course, to pay porters at the airport (500-2,000Rp) and the large hotels and restaurants will add 15% to your bill.

WHERE TO STAY

● **Accommodation**

Bali has the best range of accommodation in Indonesia from luxury hotels of the highest standard to comfortable homestays. The degree of competition means that rooms are often very moderately priced. Rates are usually reduced after the peak season; ask for a discount. Peak season is Christmas/New Year and Jul/Aug – hotels can get very full at these times. Accommodation is geared to foreign tastes with, for example, western toilets in most of the cheapest homestays.

Private Villas Ltd, Suite 1102, Windsor House, 19-27 Wyndham St, Hong Kong, T (852) 5251336, F 5377181, have recently started offering short-term rental of about 30 private villas in Bali. Most of these exclusive homes are owned by affluent foreigners who visit Bali for a short time each year. Rental starts at US$280/day. Most villas have private pools and staff provided.

FOOD AND DRINK

DRINK

Water from the tap is not safe to drink.

Ice is government controlled and delivered daily to most establishments.

GETTING AROUND

AIR

Regular domestic connections with Java, Sumatra, Maluku, Sulawesi, Lombok, Nusa Tenggara and Irian Jaya (see page 912 for route map). Flights within Nusa Tenggara may require you to go via Bima with a change of plane (see route map). Examples of fares are as follows: Balikpapan 232,600Rp (daily at 0640); Ende 221,600Rp (daily but you will have to go via Bima with a change of plane); Jakarta 220,500Rp; Yogyakarta 120,400Rp; Manado 372,300Rp (daily at 0640); Mataram 54,000Rp; Sumbawa Besar 95,000Rp (Mon, Wed, Fri and Sun at 0930); Tana Toraja 235,900Rp (Mon, Thur and Sat via Ujung Pandang where you have to change planes); Ujung Pandang 155,600Rp. **NB** Although flights are often 'full' no shows are common and outside peak periods there is little problem finding a flight on the day you want.

BOAT

Boats to Lombok leave from Benoa, see page 367 and Padangbai, see page 397

● **Cruises**

Bali Camar Yacht Charter, T 231591, and *Wakalouka Cruises*, T 262332 and *Island Explorer Cruises*, T 289856, both organize cruises to Nusa Lembongan (see page 363); *Bali Hai*, T 234331, luxurious catamaran day trips to Nusa Penida island for snorkeling and lunch, US$60, dinner cruise US$30; *Golden Hawk*, Jl Sri Kesari 19, Sanur, T 288860, old gaff-rigged ketch (tall ship) for day trips, fishing, snorkeling, lunch and alcoholic drinks, US$68; *Grand Komodo Tours*, Jl Bypass, Sanur, T 287166, F 287165, organize tours to Lombok, Komodo, Flores and Irian Jaya; *P&O Spice Island Cruises*, Jl Let Jen S Parmen 78, Slipi, Jakarta Barat, T 5673401, F 5673403, organize luxury island-hopping cruises between Bali and Kupang (Timor), 2 week round-trip, calling at Komodo, Sumbawa, Flores and Sumba, one way trip about US$2,289, round trip US$4,180, they also organize a 7 day trip from Jakarta to Krakatau, up the E coast of Sumatra and S to the Ujung

	Amlapura	Bangli	Besakih	Candi Dasa	Denpasar	Gianyar	Gilimanuk	Karangasem	Klungkung	Kuta Beach	Lake Batur	Legian	Lovina Beach	Ngurah Rai Airport	Nusa Dua	Singaraja	Tanah Lot
Bangli	26																
Besakih	41	20															
Candi Dasa	13	52	50														
Denpasar	85	47	70	72													
Gianyar	54	16	39	41	31												
Gilimanuk	219	181	201	206	134	165											
Karangasem	–	41	38	13	85	54	219										
Klungkung	38	26	23	27	47	16	181	38									
Kuta Beach	95	57	80	82	10	41	144	95	57								
Lake Batur	50	20	38	71	67	40	135	50	46	77							
Legian	97	59	82	84	12	43	146	97	59	2	79						
Lovina Beach	97	86	106	139	89	102	79	97	112	99	66	101					
Ngurah Rai Airport	98	60	83	85	13	44	147	98	60	3	80	5	102				
Nusa Dua	109	71	94	96	24	55	158	109	71	14	91	16	113	11			
Singaraja	97	79	97	110	78	99	90	97	105	88	59	90	11	91	110		
Tanah Lot	118	80	103	105	33	64	124	118	80	43	100	45	89	46	57	78	
Ubud	67	29	52	54	23	13	157	67	29	33	40	35	106	36	47	95	56

Bali, distances between cities (Km)

Kulon National Park, US$8,869; *PT Motive Bali Tours and Travel*, Jl Sekuta 11, Sanur, T 289435, F 289435, organize all the usual tours around the island and a 'Joy Flight' over Bali in a helicopter, 15-60 mins flight, US$85-195 with 4 passengers (more expensive if less); *Puri Tour*, Jl Padang Galak 7A, Sanur, T (361) 288788, F (361) 287269, organize 10-day pinisi boat cruises from Bali to Flores for US$150/day, all inclusive.

ROAD

● Bemo

Bemos are the cheapest way to get around Bali, although it usually means a trip to Denpasar, the bemo 'node' for most destinations. So, to travel from, say, Kuta to Ubud means getting a bemo from Kuta to Denpasar's Tegal terminal, transferring to Kereneng and then, taking a cross-town trip to the Batubulan terminal, followed by another bemo from there to Ubud. This makes for slow and frustrating travelling and it can be almost as cheap and a lot quicker to charter a bemo (see below) or catch the tourist shuttle bus. It is also worth noting that bemo services are less frequent in the afternoons, and out of the tourist centres are almost non-existent after nightfall. Approx cost of travel is 25Rp/km, with a minimum charge of 100Rp. **NB** Taxi/bemo drivers can be very pushy and find it hard to believe you may be happy to walk. Expect to be asked for double the correct fair, bemo drivers can sometimes be quite unpleasant in their attempts to over-charge you even when they know the correct fair, which you should ascertain in advance. Thefts on bemos are not as frequent as in past years but do still occur. Be wary of gangs pretending to run licenced bemos who pick up unsuspecting travellers, take them to a remote spot and steal their possessions and money. Always use registered bemos which have yellow and black licence plates.

Getting around Bali by bemo

Destination	Denpasar Terminal	Via	Destination	Denpasar Terminal	Via
Agung, Mount	Batubulan	Klungkung	Kuta	Tegal	-
Airport	Tegal	-	Lovina Beach	Ubung	Singaraja
Air Sanih	Ubung	Singaraja	Madewi Beach	Ubung	-
Amlapura	Batubulan	-	Mas	Batubulan	-
Bangli	-	Batubulan	Mengwi	Ubung	-
Banjar	Ubung	Singaraja	Negara	Ubung	-
Batubulan	Kereneng	-	Nusa Dua	Tegal	-
Batur, Mount	Batubulan	-	Padangbai Harbour	Batubulan	-
Bedugul	Ubung	-	Pejeng	Batubulan	Gianyar
Bedulu	Batubulan	Gianyar	Penelokan	Batubulan	Klungkung
Benoa Harbour	Suci	-	Penulisan	Batubulan	-
Benoa Village	Tegal	-	Sangeh	Wangaya	-
Besakih	Batubulan	Klungkung	Sanur	Kereneng	-
Candidasa	Batubulan	-	Singaraja	Ubung	-
Candi Kuning	Ubung	-	Sukawati	Batubulan	-
Celuk	Batubulan	-	Tabanan	Ubung	-
Gianyar	Batubulan	-	Tanah Lot	Ubung	Kediri
Gilimanuk	Ubung	-	Tampak Siring	Batubulan	Gianyar
Goa Gajah	Batubulan	Gianyar	Tenganan	Batubulan	-
Goa Lawah	Batubulan	-	Tirtagangga	Batubulan	Amlapura
Gunung Kawi	Batubulan	Gianyar	Ubud	Batubulan	-
Kehen Temple	Batubulan	Bangli	Uluwatu	Tegal	Pecatu
Klungkung	Batubulan	-			

The **different terminals** are as follows (**NB** Terminals serve other terminals as well as out of town destinations):

Ubung, N of town on Jl Cokroaminoto for trips to N and W Bali including Gilimanuk and Singaraja, Mengwi, Tanah Lot, Bedugul, Negara and Java (see Transport to and from Bali).

Tegal, W of town, nr the intersection of Jl Imam Bonjol and Jl G Wilis, for journeys to S Bali including Kuta, Legian, Sanur, Ngurah Rai Airport, Jimbaran, Nusa Dua and Uluwatu (in the morning).

Suci, nr the intersection of Jl Diponegoro and Jl Hasanuddin for Benoa Port.

Batubulan, 6 km NE of town just before the village of Batubulan on the road to Gianyar, for buses running E to Gianyar, Klungkung, Padangbai, Candi Dasa, Amlapura and Tirtagangga, and N to Ubud, Tampaksiring, Bangli, Penelokan and Kintamani.

Kereneng, at the E edge of town off Jl Kamboja (Jl Hayam Wuruk) has now been replaced as the station for central and E Bali by Batubulan; but bemos do still run from here to the other terminals.

● **Shuttle bus**

Several companies run shuttle bus services to popular destinations on Bali, with onward connections to Lombok and Sumbawa. These are geared to foreign travellers and offer the best value, hassle-free means of getting around. Most will pick you up from and drop you off at your hotel. They will also take you to the airport but are not allowed to pick up passengers from the airport.

One of the most reliable companies is *Perama*, Head Office, Jl Legian, Kuta, T 751551, F 751170. They have regular buses throughout the day to: Kuta, Denpasar Airport, Sanur, Ubud, Kintamani, Lovina, Bedugul, Padangbai, Candidasa, Tirtagangga, Tulamben, Air Sanih. *Perama* can take you to Nusa Lembongan via boat from Sanur. They also offer a service to Bima and Sape on Sumbawa Island, and boat service to Bima, Komodo, and Flores (see page 738).

● **Bicycle/car/motorbike hire**

Available at each resort: bargain hard.

Bicycles Can be hired for about 3,000Rp/day.

Cars For approx 45,000Rp/day from local firms, US$45/day from international companies (eg Avis). **NB** Most hire cars cannot be taken off the island and an international driving licence is officially required (local firms often do not bother with this). Look out for: the condition of the tyres (and the spare), the horn (absolutely essential), windscreen wipers, steering.

Motorbikes Hire costs from 7,000Rp/day. Strictly-speaking, those without an international motorbike licence, should obtain a temporary licence from the Police Station in Denpasar. Applicants need their passport, 3 photographs and their national driving licence; they will also need to undertake a short police driving test (**NB** Few people bother with this).

● **Chartered bemo**

'You want transport' is a much used expression on Bali. Chartering a bemo is easy and often the best way to travel around the island. Expect to pay about 5,000-6,000Rp/hr, 65,000Rp for a full day. Drivers prefer to know your destination, rather than to be hired for half a day or day. **NB** Drivers may try to take you to a craft village as part of the deal.

● **Taxis**

There are now metered radio a/c taxis; (T 289090, 289091, 281919, 759191), the Japanese cars are blue and yellow, with a taxi sign on the roof. Drivers often don't speak English, so insist that the meter is switched on; never agree a fixed price. Minimum fare is 800Rp. Trips within Kuta/Legian are around 2,000-4,000Rp. Kuta to Sanur costs 5,000-6,000Rp. For chartering, it costs about 8,000-10,000Rp/hr by the meter. This is almost certainly a safer bet than bemos now.

● **Tours**

At the last count, the tourist office listed 136 tour companies, usually with little to choose between them. Most provide the same range of tours at competitive prices, although it is worth shopping around before booking. Check the numbers on the tour, whether the guide speaks good English, if entrance fees and meals are included, and whether the car/bus is air-conditioned. Most tour companies are concentrated in the principal tourist centres. Tours include: Lake Batur, volcano and Ubud, Denpasar City, Singaraja and Lake Bratan, Besakih Temple, Amlapura (Karangasem) and the E Coast, Uluwatu and Kuta Beach, Mengwi and Tanah Lot, Lovina and the N Coast; Dance evenings (kecak, legong, sanghyang, barong, Ramayana ballet, wayang); **Nature Trek**; **Shopping Tour**; **Turtle Island and Snorkelling**; **Dolphin Tours**.

There are also a number of 'specialist' tours, see tour entries in each resort.

COMMUNICATIONS

● **Telephone services**
Area code: 0361.

ENTERTAINMENT

● **Media**

The free English language *Bali News* is published once a fortnight and can be found at many hotel desks.

SPORTS

● **Diving**

Diving around Bali is not the best in Indonesia, but the island does have the greatest concentration of dive shops and diving expertise. It is a good place to learn how to dive, but those who have experienced other spots in Southeast Asia or the Pacific may be disappointed. Dive spots include the **Menjangan Marine Park**, an island off the NW tip of Bali, 30 mins by boat (depth 3-50m). Diving here is good, both on the inner and outer reef, although it is not recommended for beginners, as there is too much fragile coral which could be unintentionally damaged. **NB** Divers are contributing to the destruction of the coral in the park, as there are no buoys and the boatmen anchor on the coral. **Tulamben** is the submerged wreck of a US Liberty ship, sunk during WW2 off the NE coast, and is a haven for fish. The coral-covered wreck lies about 50m offshore, so it is a beach dive (10-30m), recommended by one keen diver; **Padangbai**, near Candi Dasa, for 3-20m dives; **Tepekong Island** (depth 15-30m), on the E coast; **Lembongan** and **Nusa Penida Islands**, 2 hrs by boat (depth 3-40m); **Amed**, off the NE coast (depth 3-40m); and the reefs off Sanur and Nusa Dua beaches. With reputable companies expect to pay US$30 for 1 dive, US$80 for an introductory 1-day course, US$250 for a 4-day diving certificate. Most of the larger hotels have dive desks; see relevant sections for addresses of dive shops.

● **Golf**

The Handara Country Club is in a beautiful position just N of Lake Bratan (see page 415). *Bali Golf and Country Club* has opened at Nusa Dua, T 71791 for details. Tee-times from 0630-1600. Green fees US$85-100 for 18 holes. Beautiful sea-side setting. Attractive clubhouse and pool.

● **Mountain biking**

Mountain biking is becoming increasingly popular, as a way of seeing the 'real' Bali, see Tours page 353 and Sport page 386.

● **Surfing**

Kuta Beach was the location upon which Bali's reputation as a surfer's paradise was based. Kuta is a beach break and these days the water is polluted with sewage: about 1 km out is a reef break, a left-hand barrel. However, there are other, better locations. Below is a very brief summary of conditions; far more information can be gleaned from surf shops and places where surfers hang out. Some of the best surfing in Bali is on the Bukit Peninsula. **Uluwatu** about 2 km down a rough track, with a 'world famous' left break; the Peak is a high tide break, Race Track a mid-tide, and Outside Corner a low tide wave. If the current is too strong to reach the cave or onto the reef in front of the cave, make for the beach. Despite its reputation, waves can be few and far between: crowded and over-rated. **Padang Padang** is close to Uluwatu and can be reached along a track or by car/motorbike. The very hollow left is dangerous because of the cliff; very dangerous below mid-tide. Down from Padang Padang is **Bingin**; fast hollow left best at high to medium tides, at low tides it is dangerous and waves can 'suck dry' on the reef; often crowded. **Nyang Nyang**, accessible by track; both left and right. **Suluban**, not far from Jimbaran; the Annual Surf Championships are held here. Minibuses (C1) travel from Kuta to Uluwatu; tracks to the surfing beaches are reasonably well-marked along the road. Other surfing beaches include **Canggu**, near the village of Kerobokan, N on the Legian road (both left and right); and **Medewi** about 75 km W of Denpasar, best above mid-tide. Boards can be hired for about 5,000-10,000Rp/day; repair and other services are also available – see relevant sections for surf shops.

Best time to surf Reasonable throughout the year, although surf is definitely best between Jun and Aug. Between Oct and Apr there are good right-handers at **Nusa Dua** and **Sanur**, the latter only working for 20 days a year.

● **Whitewater rafting**

Down the Ayung River near Ubud includes hotel pick-up, all equipment, insurance and lunch, organized by *Sobek Expeditions*, T 287059 and *Bali Adventure Tours*, T 751292. They also organize mountain biking at Batur, sea kayaking and jungle trekking (see Tours page 353, 360 and 379 for details).

HOLIDAYS AND FESTIVALS

Bali is the festival capital of Southeast Asia; there is a festival every day of the year. With 20,000 temples, each celebrating its anniversary or *odalan* every 210 days (according to the Balinese *wuku* calendar), it is easy to see why (see page 326 for a fuller background to the main ceremonies).

The tourist office supplies a booklet cataloguing the year's festivals, while the *Bali News* (often found in hotel lobbys) lists current events. Both sources of information are extremely useful, as the Balinese calendar, in fact 2 calendars, is complex. The *wuku* calendar which governs most, but not all, festivals is lunar and runs, as noted above, over only 210 days. As a result, festival dates vary dramatically from year to year and a particular festival may be held twice in any one (365-day) year. Locals do not object to tourists being present at most of their ceremonies but they do ask that visitors dress appropriately, with sarong and sash, and behave discreetly (see Temple etiquette, above).

● **Wuku Year Festivals (210-day calendar)**

In 1995 Galungan, Day 1 in the Wuku calendar, was on 27 Dec. In 1996, Galungan fell on 24 Jul; and in 1997 it should fall on 19 Feb.

Day 1: *Galungan*, the most important holiday of the Balinese year. It is a 10-day festival marking the Balinese *wuku* 'New Year' (in fact it comes mid-way through the year, but is usually translated as New Year). It also commemorates the creation of the world by the Supreme God and symbolizes the victory of good over evil. Women make *banten* (offerings of sweets, fruits and flowers) while men make *lawar* (a food made of vegetables and meat). Both are presented as thanksgiving offerings. *Penjors* (a variant of the *janur*, see page 325) are the long bamboo poles which can be seen on the right-hand side of every house entrance, with offerings such as fruit, cakes and flowers hanging from them as symbols of gratitude for the god's gift of life and prosperity. It is said that the offerings are hung on these tall poles so that the gods can see them from their mountain abodes. *Barong* and other dances are traditionally held at this time.

Day 10: *Kuningan*, held 10 days after Galungan and marking the end of the holiday period. It is believed to be the day when the Gods ascend back to Heaven and is a time for honouring the souls of ancestors and saints who have lived their lives in accordance with the customs of their religion. Temple compounds are decorated with flowers and offerings are made.

Day 137: *Saraswati*, commemorates the Goddess of Learning and Knowledge, Batari Dewi Saraswati. All books are given to the Goddess to be blessed and no reading or writing is allowed.

Day 142: *Pangerwesi*, the word means 'iron fence', and the ceremony is dedicated to Shanghyang Pramesti Guru. It is particularly popular in the N.

Day 210: *Penampahan Galungan*, the day prior to Galungan when every Balinese prepares for the big day, slaughtering pigs and chickens and preparing offerings and food. It marks the end of the wuku year.

Recurrent Wuku Festivals In addition to the above wuku festivals, there are also a number of recurrent festival days which are regarded as propitious for making offerings. *Kadjeng-klion* is held every 15 days; *Tumpak*, every 35 days; *Budda-klion*, every 42 days; *Anggara-kasih*, every 35 days; and *Budda-wage*, every 35 days.

● **Saka Year Festivals (354 to 356-day calendar)**

Mar: *Pengerupuk* (movable), the last day of the Balinese year. Purification sacrifices and offerings are made, while priests chant mantras to exorcize the demons of the old year. At night, gongs and cymbals are struck and torchlit processions with *ogoh-ogoh* (large monsters) parade through the streets in order to exorcize the spirits. The spectacle is best in Denpasar, where thousands gather in Puputan Square before the start of the march.

Mar-Apr: *Nyepi* (movable) celebrates the *saka*, solar New Year which is held at the Spring equinox. In the recent past it was a day of silence when everything closed down and no activity was allowed. It is hoped that the evil spirits roused by the previous night's activities will find Bali to be a barren land and will leave the island. People stayed indoors to meditate and pray; there were no fires, no work and no cooking. **NB** Visitors are advised to stay within their hotel compounds from 0500-0500 the following day; the observance of Nyepi is very strict in this regard. **Warning** Independent travellers planning to visit Bali at this time might choose to avoid being on the island during *Nyepi*. Tourists are confined to their accommodation, which in a small guesthouse, means you feel as if you have been placed under 'house arrest' – no swimming in the sea 10 yards from your bungalow, no strolls or other forms of exercise. While most of the taboos surrounding *Nyepi* have fallen by the wayside, the one prohibiting movement in the streets is strictly enforced by the 'religious police' in their green silk sarongs. You may well find yourself surrounded by Balinese having a wonderful time playing rock music, gambling, smoking, watching TV with a house full of guests while you go crazy with boredom. Until recently, *Nyepi* was a day of silence and darkness (no electricity) but in the last 2 years the government has begun scheduling special '*Nyepi Day*' TV programmes.

DENPASAR

Originally called Badung, Denpasar is Bali's capital and has grown in the past 10 to 15 years from a sleepy village to a bustling city. It is situated in the S of the island, about 5 km from the coast. Today, the town has a population of over 300,000 and is Bali's main trade and transport hub, with its central business area centred around Jl Gajah Mada.

Denpasar was once the royal capital of the princely kingdom of Badung, but there is little evidence of its past. **Puputan Square** pays homage to the tragic end of the Rajah and his court in 1906; it is named after the 'battle to the death' – or *puputan* – against a force of Dutch soldiers on the morning of the 20 Sep (see page 317). A monument in the square commemorates the event.

Places of interest

Denpasar is not a particularly attractive town and it contains limited sights of interest for the visitor. The major tourist attraction is easily found, in the centre of town and is a focus for local hawkers. The **Museum Bali** was established in 1931 and is situated on the E side of Puputan Square. The entrance is on Jl Mayor Wismu. The museum, built in 1910, mirrors the architecture of Balinese temples and palaces and is contained within a series of attractive courtyards with well-kept gardens. The impressive collection of prehistoric artefacts, sculpture, masks, textiles, weaponry and contemporary arts and crafts was assembled with the help of Walter Spies, the German artist who made Bali his home. The artefacts on display are apparently only a small proportion of the museum's collection. Labelling could be better and there is no guide to the museum to help the inquisitive visitor. Nevertheless, it gives an impression of the breadth of the island's culture. Admission: adult 200Rp, children 100Rp. Open 0730-1430 Tues-Thur, Sat and Sun, 0730-1130 Fri, T 222680.

Next door to the museum is the new **Pura Jaganatha**, a temple dedicated to the Supreme God *Sang Hyang Widi Wasa*. The statue of a turtle and two nagas signify the foundation of the world. The complex is dominated by the *Padma Sana* or lotus throne, upon which the gods sit. The central courtyard is surrounded by a lily-filled moat with the most enormous carp.

The most important temple in Denpasar from an archaeological perspective is **Pura Masopahit**, down a side street off the W end of Jl Tabanan (the main gateway to the pura faces the main street, but the entrance is down a side road). The temple is one of the oldest in Bali, probably dating from the introduction of Javanese civilization from Majapahit in the 15th century, after which it is named. It was badly damaged during the 1917 earthquake, but has since been partly restored. Note the fine, reconstructed, split gate with its massive figures of a giant and a garuda. Unfortunately, this temple is not open to the public.

The **Werdi Budaya Art Centre** on Jl Nusa Indah was established in 1973 to promote Balinese visual and performing arts. The centre contains an open-air auditorium, along with three art galleries. Arts and crafts are also sold here. Activity peaks during the annual Bali Festival of Art held from mid-Jun for a month. Admission 250Rp. Open 0800-1600 Mon-Sun, closed on holidays.

Excursions

As Denpasar is the transport hub of the island, it is easy to get to most of the main towns, beaches and sights from here.

Festivals

Mid-Jun-mid-Jul: the Werdi Budaya presents an *Annual Arts Festival*, with demonstrations of local music, dance and performance. Hotels or the tourist office will supply a calendar of events.

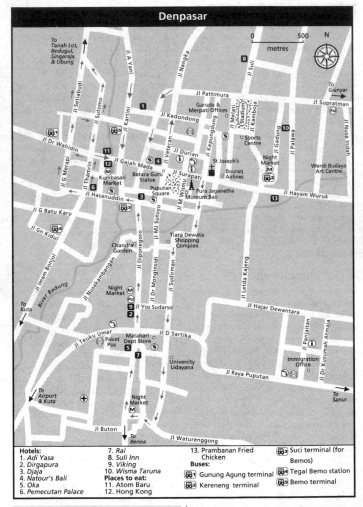

Denpasar

Hotels:
1. Adi Yasa
2. Dirgapura
3. Djaja
4. Natour's Bali
5. Oka
6. Pemecutan Palace
7. Rai
8. Suli Inn
9. Viking
10. Wisma Taruna

Places to eat:
11. Atom Baru
12. Hong Kong
13. Prambanan Fried Chicken

Buses:
1. Gunung Agung terminal
2. Kereneng terminal
3. Suci terminal (for Bemos)
4. Tegal Bemo station
5. Bemo terminal

Local information

● Accommodation

Until the 1950s, Denpasar was the place where most tourists stayed; today it is largely frequented by domestic tourists – foreign visitors either head for the beaches or inland to Ubud. Nonetheless, there is an adequate range of accommodation.

A *Natour's Bali*, Jl Veteran 3, T 225681, F 235347, 75 rm, a/c, restaurant, pool, central location, built in the 1930s, it was the first hotel on Bali, rather frayed now but it does retain some charm.

B-C *Chandra Garden*, Jl Diponegoro 114, T 226425, 38 rm, some a/c, popular with Indonesians, price incl breakfast; **B-C** *Pemecutan Palace*, Jl Thamrin 2, T 223491, some a/c, a reconstruction of a palace which was destroyed here by the Dutch in 1906, rooms are shabby.

C-D *Pura Alit*, Jl Sutomo 26, T 428831, F 288766, some a/c.

D *Dewi*, Jl Diponegoro 112, T 226720; **D-E** *Dharmawisata*, Jl Imam Bonjol 89, T 222186, pool, clean rooms with own mandi.

● **Places to eat**
♦♦*Hong Kong*, Jl Gajah Mada 89, a/c, a tour group stop, wide selection of Chinese dishes, empty fish tanks, some international dishes; *Atom Baru*, Jl Gajah Mada 106-108, Chinese, popular with the locals; *Kakman*, Jl Teuku Umar (half way to Kuta), excellent Indonesian.

Nusa Indah: *Warung Wardani* for cheap, genuine Balinese food, rec; Several *warungs* are to be found within the Kumbasari market.

● **Airline offices**
Bouraq, Jl Sudirman 19A, T 223564; **Garuda**, Jl Melati 61, T 222788; **Merpati**, Jl Melati 57, T 235358; **UTA**, Jl Bypass Ngurah Rai, T 289225.

● **Banks & money changers**
Bank Bumi Daya, JlVeteran 2; **Bank Dagang Negara**, Jl Gajah Mada 2; **Bank Negara Indonesia**, Jl Gajah Mada 20.

● **Embassies & consulates**
Australia, Jl Mohammad Yamin 51, T 235093; **France**, Jl Rayan Sesetan 46, T 233555; **Germany**, Jl Pantai Karang 17, T 288535, F 288826; **Japan**, Jl Pemuda, Renon, T 227628; **Norway**, Jl Jayagiri VII/10, T 234834.

● **Entertainment**
Cinemas: *Wisata Complex*, Jl Thamrin 69, T 423023.

Dance: KOKAR (recently renamed SMKI) is based in Batubulan, it is a conservatory of dance – students perform many different styles of traditional dance, accompanied by a gamelan orchestra. The *Werdi Budaya* Art Centre gives Kecak dance performances every day from 1830-1930.

● **Hospitals & medical services**
Hospitals: *Sanglah Public Hospital*, Jl Kesehatan Selatan 1, T 227911; *Wangaya Hospital*, Jl Kartini, T 222141. 24-hr on call doctor and ambulance, Jl Cokroaminoto 28, T 426393.
Optician: *International Optical*, Jl Gajah Mada 133, T 226294.
Pharmacy: *Apotik Kimia Farma*, Jl Diponegoro 123, T 227812.
Emergency dental clinic: Jl Pattimura 19, T 222445.

● **Places of worship**
Catholic: *Church of St Joseph* on Jl Kepundung (1730, Sat; 0830, 1730, Sun).
Evangelical Church: Jl Melati.
Protestant Church: Jl Surapati.

● **Post & telecommunications**
Paket Pos (packing service & parcel post): Jl Diponegoro 146.
Post Office: Jl Raya Puputan, Renon. Open 0800-1400 Mon-Thur, 0800-1200 Fri, 0800-1300 Sat. *Poste Restante* available here.
Telecommunications centre: Jl Teuku Umar 6.

● **Shopping**
Department stores: *Duta Plaza*, Jl Dewi Sartika, *Tiara Dewata* and *Matahari* both have a good range of goods, incl reasonably priced children's clothes and some handicrafts. The former also has a public swimming pool.

Handicrafts: the *Sanggraha Kriya Asta*, 7 Km E of the centre of town, is a government handicrafts shop, selling batik, jewellery, paintings and woodcarvings. The prices are set and quality is controlled. They will organize free transport to the shop from your hotel if telephoned (T 222942). There are also a number of handicraft shops on Jl Thamrin, and on the 3rd flr of the Kumbasari Market (see Markets, below).

Markets: the biggest market in town (and the biggest on Bali) is the Kumbasari Market, off Jl Dr Wahidin, on the banks of the Badung River. It is a great place to browse, with a range of goods incl textiles and handicrafts.

Textiles: a large selection of textiles is to be found in the shops along Jl Sulawesi.

● **Tour companies & travel agents**
Arha Bali Rafting, Jl Muding Indah 11/4 Kerobakan, T 427446, F 427339, rafting on Klungkung River US$65-75, price incl pick-up from your hotel and lunch; *Ayung River Rafting*, Jl Diponegoro 150B 29, T 238759, F 224236, rafting on Ayung River, US$63, incl hotel pick-up and meal, also mountain cycling and trekking available; *Grand Komodo Tours & Travel*, PO Box 3477, T 287166, F 287165, tours to Komodo and Lombok, from US$390 for 3 days to US$730 for 8 days, incl full board but not air fares; *Bali Vacanza*, Jl Laksamana VI/1.4, T 261576, F 231652, 1 or 2 day trips to Yogyakarta and Lombok; *Waka Experience*, Jl Imam Bonjol No 335 X, T 484085, F 484767, this company offers unique insights into Bali, combining total luxury with great style and cultural sensitivity. They organize Wakalouka Cruises on a catamaran to their idyllic resort on

the island of Lombongan and Wakalouka Land Cruises into the interior by Land Rover, taking in remote rice paddy, ancient quarries and hot springs, and a rustic restaurant in the heart of the rainforest where food is cooked over traditional mud ovens and served on immaculate starched tablecloths, with Italian designer cutlery, US$83 pp covers the day-long trip and incl all the food and drink you want, incl refreshments from the capacious hampers carried on top of the Land Rover, rec; *Bali Safari Rafting*, Jl Hayam Wuruk 88a, T 221315, F 232268, organizes rafting on Telaga Waja River, US$65 incl transfers, buffet lunch, refreshments, insurance.

● **Tourist offices**
Denpasar Tourist Office, Jl Surapati 7, T 223602, open 0700-1400 Mon-Thur and Sat, 0700-1100 Fri, free map, calendar of events and Bali brochure; **Bali Government Tourism Office**, Jl S Parman, T 222387.

● **Useful addresses**
Emergencies: 24-hr helpline, T 228996.
Immigration office: Jl Panjaitan, off Jl Puputan Raya, T 227828.
Police: HQ, Jl Supratman, T 110.

● **Transport**
Local Bemos: the original, rickety and underpowered 3-wheeler bemos travel between the main bemo terminals (300Rp), criss-crossing town. It is also possible to charter these bemos for trips around town. From the terminals – of which there are several – bemos travel to all of Bali's main towns: The **Ubung** terminal, N of town on Jl Cokroaminoto, for trips to W Bali, N Bali and Java; **Tegal**, W of town, nr the intersection of Jl Imam Bonjol and Jl G Wilis, for journeys to S Bali; **Suci**, nr the intersection of Jl Diponegoro and Jl Hasanuddin, for Benoa Port; **Kereneng**, at the E edge of town off Jl Kamboja (Jl Hayam Wuruk) for destinations around town and for Sanur; while **Batubulan**, E of town just before the village of Batubulan on the road to Gianyar, for buses running E and N (see page 340 for more details). **Dokars**: pony-drawn carriages, now on the verge of extinction and/or asphyxiation. **Ojeks**: motorcycle taxis, and the fastest way around town; ojek riders can be identified by their red jackets (500-1000Rp). **Taxis**: there are numerous un-metered cars that can be chartered by the hour or day, or which can be hired for specific journeys. Bargain hard. There are also some metered taxis. *Praja Bali Taxi*, pale blue taxis all operate with meters and make no extra charge for call-out service, T 701111.

Air See page 337 for details.

Road Bemo: these provide transportation from Denpasar's 5 terminals to most places on the island (see page 342). Small, 3-wheeled bemos run between the various terminals (500Rp). **Bus**: bus connections with Java from the Ubung terminal, just N of Denpasar on Jl Cokroaminoto. Express and night bus offices are concentrated nr the intersection of Jl Diponegoro and Jl Hasanuddin, for example, *Chandra Ticketing*, Jl Diponegoro 114, T 226425. Journey time and departure times for night and express buses are as follows: Jakarta 30 hrs (0630-0700), Surabaya 11 hrs (0700 and 1700-2000), Malang 10 hrs (1800-1930), Yogya/Solo 16 hrs (1500-1600), Semarang 15 hrs (1600), Bandung 25 hrs (0700), Bogor 24 hrs (0700), Blitar 15 hrs (1900).

SOUTH BALI

Most visitors to Bali stay in one of the resorts at the S end of the island. Most famous is Kuta, the original backpackers' haven, together with its N extension, Legian. To the S of Kuta is a newly developed zone of hotels and restaurants named Tuban. Further S still is Jimbaran, a small village, as yet unspoilt, with one of Bali's top resorts nearby – *The Four Seasons*, which overlooks Jimbaran Bay – and its new international neighbour, the *Bali Inter-Continental*. Sanur is on Bali's E coast and offers largely middle to upper-range accommodation. Serangan, or Turtle, Island is a short distance offshore. Rather further off the E coast, in the Lombok Strait, are the two islands of Nusa Penida and Nusa Lembongan, offering some accommodation but also accessible on a day trip.

KUTA

The first pub was opened in Kuta in 1930 by an American, Ketut Tantri; in the same decade another American couple opened the first hotel on the beach. Nonetheless, the author and Bali-phile Miguel Covarrubias wrote in 1937 that Kuta and Sanur were "small settlements of fishermen who brave the malarial coasts". It was not until the 1960s that large numbers of western travellers 'discovered' Kuta. Since then, it has grown into a highly developed beach resort with a mind-boggling array of hotels, restaurants and shops. It is no longer a backpackers' haven; most of the cheap losmen have either closed down or moved

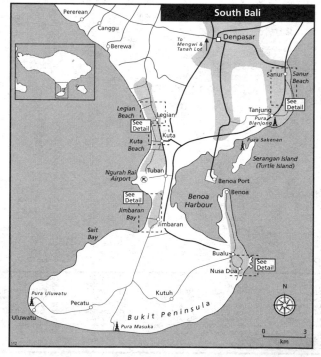

up-market. There is however, a plentiful supply of good middle to high range accommodation here.

Traffic in Kuta frequently comes to a standstill, despite the one-way system. The main drag, containing most of Kuta's

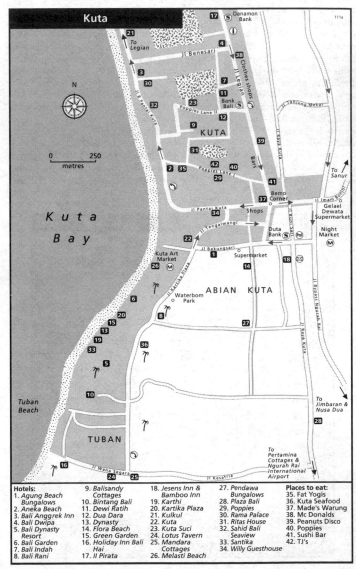

Kuta

Kuta Bay

Tuban Beach

KUTA

ABIAN KUTA

TUBAN

To Legian

Danamon Bank

Il Benesari

Clothes shops

Il Legian

Bank Bali

Poppies Lane II

Bats

Poppies Lane I

Bemo Corner

Shops

Il Pantai Kuta

Il Tegalwangi

Il Bakungsari

Kuta Art Market

Waterbom Park

Supermarket

Duta Bank

Gelael Dewata Supermarket

Night Market

To Sanur

Il Imam Bonjol

Il Raya Kuta

Il Tanjung Mekar

Il Bypass Ngurah Rai

To Jimbaran & Nusa Dua

To Pertamina Cottages & Ngurah Rai International Airport

Il Wana Segara

Il Kesatria

0 250
metres

Hotels:
1. Agung Beach Bungalows
2. Aneka Beach
3. Bali Anggrek Inn
4. Bali Dwipa
5. Bali Dynasty Resort
6. Bali Garden
7. Bali Indah
8. Bali Rani
9. Balisandy Cottages
10. Bintang Bali
11. Dewi Ratih
12. Dua Dara
13. Dynasty
14. Flora Beach
15. Green Garden
16. Holiday Inn Bali Hai
17. Il Pirata
18. Jesens Inn & Bamboo Inn
19. Karthi
20. Kartika Plaza
21. Kulkul
22. Kuta
23. Kuta Suci
24. Lotus Tavern
25. Mandara Cottages
26. Melasti Beach
27. Pendawa Bungalows
28. Plaza Bali
29. Poppies
30. Rama Palace
31. Ritas House
32. Sahid Bali Seaview
33. Santika
34. Willy Guesthouse

Places to eat:
35. Fat Yogis
36. Kuta Seafood
37. Made's Warung
38. Mc Donalds
39. Peanuts Disco
40. Poppies
41. Sushi Bar
42. TJ's

shops, is Jl Legian, which runs N-S (traffic travels one way S). Jl Pantai meets Jl Legian at the notorious 'Bemo Corner' and is the main E-W road to the S end of the beach (with traffic going one way W). The beach road is northbound only.

Kuta Beach is rather unattractive and clinical, offering no shade from trees and fenced off from the road (admission 200Rp). It is because of its accessibility that it is popular with surfers, although better waves can be found elsewhere. It is an excellent spot for beginners and recreational surfers. Boards can be hired on the beach and there are usually locals who will offer their insider's knowledge of surf conditions. Strong and irregular currents can make swimming a little hazardous – look out for the warning notices. The sand is white to the S, but grey further N. Hoards of hawkers are very hassly, selling trinkets and offering hair-plaiting, manicure and massage services. The beach faces W, so is popular at sunset.

Local information
● **Accommodation**

It is advisable to book accommodation during the peak periods of Jul/Aug and at Christmas and New Year, as hotels are often full. There are countless places to stay in Kuta, the list below is not comprehensive; look around when you arrive, or go on recommendations.

L *The Legian*, Jl Kayu Aya, T 730622, F 730623, a/c, restaurant, pool, library, situated on the beach front, 70 suites with sitting and dining areas, simple and sophisticated.

A *Bali Anggrek Inn*, Jl Pantai, PO Box 435, T 751265, F 751766, a/c, restaurant, large pool, facing the beach, average rooms; **A** *Indah*, Poppies Lane II, T 753327, F 752787, pool, central location for shopping, price incl breakfast; **A** *Kulkul*, Jl Pantai, PO Box 97, T 752520, F 752519, a/c, restaurant, pool, on the beach road, well designed hotel with attractive rooms, rec; **A** *Poppies I*, Poppies Lane I, PO Box 378, T 751059, F 752364, a/c, pool, lovely garden, well-run hotel with cottage accommodation, very popular; **A** *Rama Palace*, Jl Pantai, PO Box 293, T 752063, F 753078, on the beach road, a/c, restaurant, pool, standard accommodation; **A** *Sahid Bali*, Jl Pantai, PO Box 1102, T 753855, F 752019, a/c, restaurant, biggest pool on Kuta,

large hotel on the beachfront; **A** *Sol Inn*, 118 Jl Legian, T 752167, F 754372, new 1st-class hotel built in the centre of Kuta, 124 rm, a/c, mini-bar, satellite TV, in-house movie, balcony, en-suite bathroom, pool, Japanese restaurant, Indonesian restaurant, pub, 2 bars, simple but attractive pastel decor; **A-B** *Mutiara*, Poppies Lane I, T 752091, some a/c, attractive pool, nice garden, clean rooms.

B *Agung Cottages*, Jl Raya Legian, T 751147, some a/c, restaurant, good pool, rec; **B** *Aneka Beach*, Jl Pantai, T 752067, F 752892, a/c, pool, on the beach road, 3-storey hotel plus some thatched bungalows, attractive grounds; **B** *Bakungsari*, Jl Bakungsari, PO Box 1044, T 755396, F 752704, a/c, pool, built around a central swimming pool, clean rooms; **B** *Bali Bungalows*, PO Box 371, T 755285, F 751899, a/c, pool, nr *Rama Palace* on the beach road, nice grounds; **B** *Bruna Beach*, PO Box 116, T 751565, F 753201, a/c, on beachfront road, average rooms, price incl breakfast; **B** *Five One Cottages*, behind Poppies Lane I, a/c, small pool, hot water; **B** *Flora Beach*, Jl Bakungsari 13A, PO Box 1040, T 751870, F 751034, a/c, pool, new hotel with attractive pool and clean, well-designed rooms, one of the better of the mid-range hotels; **B** *Kuta Cottages*, Jl Bakungsari, PO Box 300, T 751101, pool, small hotel; **B** *Melasti*, Jl Kartika Plaza, PO Box 295, T 751335, F 751563, a/c, pool, on the beach, may be rather overpriced and living on its reputation, S end of Kuta; **B** *Satriya*, Poppies Lane II, T 752741, pool, hot water, clean rooms, price incl breakfast, rec; **B** *Willy*, Jl Tengalwangi 18, T 751281, F 752641, small, attractive pool, central location in Kuta, attractive rooms, built around a garden, rec; **B-C** *Agung Beach Bungalows*, Jl Bakungsari, T 751263, some a/c, pool, good location S of Jl Pantai; **B-C** *Dewi Ratih*, Poppies Lane II, T 751694, some a/c, small pool, hot water, price incl breakfast.

C *Barong Cottages*, Jl Legian, T 751488, F 751804, a/c, pool, 3-storey accommodation, nice garden, price incl breakfast; **C** *Dewa Bharata Bungalows*, Jl Legian, T 751764, well run, clean rooms with fan, private bathroom with shower and western toilet, attractive gardens with good sized swimming pool, price incl good breakfast and tea all day, *Dewa Bharata Bungalows* in Candi Dasa owned by same people; **C** *Jesen's Inn III*, Jl Bakungsari 19, T 751561, off the main road in a large palm-filled courtyard, rooms in the new wing are best; **C** *Pendawa Bungalows*, Jl Kartika Plaza,

T 752387, down a lane leading away from the beach, just S of the *Kartika Plaza*, set in pretty gardens, the accommodation is spotless and well run, rooms with private bathroom and western toilet; **C** *Sorga Cottages*, off Poppies Lane II, some a/c, good pool, price incl breakfast; **C-D** *Dharma Yudha*, Jl Bakungsari, T 751685, some a/c, friendly, but rooms are rather dark; **C-D** *Lasi Erawati*, Poppies Lane I, T 751665, fan, clean, nice garden, rec; **C-D-E** *Rita's House*, Poppies Lane I, T 751760, F 236021, 12 reasonably priced rooms with fan or a/c and private mandi with western toilet, set around small garden, clean and relaxing.

D *Balisandy Cottages*, Poppies Lane II, T 753344, 2-storey bungalows with private mandi western toilet, fan, set in spacious coconut grove away from the noise of Kuta, attractive decor, very clean and quiet, good value, rec; **D** *Bamboo Inn*, Gang Kresek 1, Jl Bakungsari, T 751935, friendly, clean, but not very close to the beach, price incl breakfast; **D** *Kuta Suci*, just off Poppies Lane II, T 752617, small but clean rooms; **D** *Masa Inn*, Poppies Lane I, T 752606, fan, clean (motorbike hire – 10,000Rp/day); **D** *Sareg*, Jl Pantai Kuta, basic, western toilets, clean, rec; **D-E** *Dua Dara*, Jl Legian, Poppies Lane II, Kuta Beach, T 754031, well run, spotlessly clean simple rooms with fan, private bathrooms with shower and western toilet, attractive small garden with family temple, price incl breakfast and tea all day, safety deposit boxes available, rec.

E *Bali Dwipa I*, Poppies Lane II, price incl breakfast, friendly atmosphere and staff, small rooms but attractive atrium, rec; **E** *Bali Indah Beach Inn*, just N of Poppies Lane II, big clean rooms, own shower, very friendly management, price incl breakfast, rec; **E** *Pension Arka Nini*, Jl Buni Sari 7, very comfortable beds, toilet and mandi in room, price incl good breakfast, friendly management, clean and quiet rooms, despite central location.

● **Places to eat**

Most of the restaurants in Kuta offer a range of food, incl Indonesian and International. For this reason, the listing below is not split into cuisine.

◆◆◆*Bebek Mas*, street-front of *Melasti Beach Bungalows*, Jl Kartika Plaza, T 752750, owned by Dutch chef Wim Hilgers, seafood salad, crab and grapefruit salad, fettucini senora bianca, all rec. Excellent Bebek Betutu (Balinese duck). Pasta night on Mon, Schnitzel night on Wed, Rifsttafel on Thurs, Indonesian buffet on Sun. No a/c and the mosquitoes are bad; ◆◆◆*Edelweiss*, on Jl By-Pass between Kuta and Nusa Dua. Run by

Otto King, previously chef at *Nusa Dua Beach Hotel*, Austrian and international dishes, good steaks; ◆◆*Aromas of Bali*, Jl Legian, vegetarian food in a garden setting; ◆◆*Indah Sari*, Jl Legian, nr Bemo Corner, Indonesian grilled seafood; ◆◆*Kin Khao Thai*, Jl Seminyak 37, authentic Thai food (with Thai chef), reasonably priced, modest portions; ◆◆*Poppies*, Poppies Lane I, attractive garden, good food (mostly international), popular, rec; ◆◆*SC*, Jl Legian, seafood, Chinese; ◆◆*Sushi Restaurant*, Jl Legian, just up from Bemo Corner, good, reasonably priced Japanese food; ◆◆*TJ's*, Poppies Lane I, good Mexican food and excellent margaritas; ◆◆*Un's*, Poppies Lane I, Indonesian, travellers' food, seafood, both only average quality; ◆*Bobbies*, towards Legian, to left of Jl Legian, excellent value food, particularly the pizzas, rec; ◆*Golden Palace International*, Poppies Lane II, good lasagnes, opp here is a small, popular and cheap restaurant (◆), with pizza, fried rice etc and cheap beer; ◆*Made's Warung*, Jl Pantai, the oldest eating establishment on Kuta, serving Asian and travellers' food and still very popular, rec; ◆*Tree House*, Poppies Lane I, travellers' food; ◆*Yunna*, Poppies Lane II, travellers' food, popular; *Burger King*, Jl Legian; *Il Pirata*, Jl Legian, 24-hr pizzaria; *Locanda Fat Yogi*, Poppies Lane I, bakery and Italian restaurant with good pizzas, rec; *Mini's*, Jl Legian, popular Chinese restaurant, with good seafood.

● **Bars**

Kuta probably has the 'best' nightlife on Bali. Most of the bars are to be found on the main road – Jl Legian. *Club Bruna*, Jl Pantai (beach road, see **Disco's**); *Bali Rock*, Jl Melasti; *Lips Bar*, Jl Legian Raya – country and western music; *Sari Club*, Jl Legian; *The Bounty*, Jl Legian, popular Australian drinking-hole, with jugs of Margueritas and videos, happy hours 1800-1900, 2200-2300. Every Tues and Sat a pub crawl leaves *Peanuts*, on Jl Legian at 1830. Arrives at *Casablancas* (Jl Buni Sari – just S of Bemo Corner) at about 2200, where there is often live music. *Hard Rock Café*, expensive drinks, live (good) bands, big crowds, music starts about 2300 and goes on until 0200.

● **Airline offices**

Garuda, *Kuta Beach Hotel*, Jl Pantai, T 754664.

● **Banks & money changers**

Plenty of money changers on Jl Legian and also a handful of banks. Branches of **Lippo Bank** and **Danamon** in *Galael Plaza* (on road into Kuta from Denpasar).

● **Consulates & embassies**
Netherlands, Jl Imam Bonjol 599, T 751094, F 752777.

● **Entertainment**
Balinese performing arts: kecak, legong, Ramayana dance and Balinese music; performances take place at many of the major hotels.

Discos: *Peanut's* (4,000Rp entry fee); *Warehouse* (next door to *Peanuts*), free entry; *Bruna Reggae Pub*, Jl Pantai, live local music starts at 2330 (8,000Rp entry fee); *Spotlights* and *Cheater's*, all on Jl Legian; open-air discos at *Gado-Gado* (closed Mon and Thur) and *Double Six* (open Mon, Thur and Sat), both N of Legian, off Jl Dhyanapura and Jl Legian Cottage. Both these two are open from 2400-0400 (10,000Rp entry fee).

● **Hospital & medical services**
Clinic: Jl Raya Kuta 100, T 753268, 24 hrs on call.

● **Places of worship**
Protestant service: 1000 Sun, Gang Menuh, Jl Legian.

● **Post & telecommunications**
Area code: 0361.
Postal agent: Jl Legian; *poste restante* service.
Post Office: Jl Raya Kuta, S of Jl Bakungsari.
Telecommunications centre: Jl Legian, nr Poppies Lane II.

● **Shopping**
Best buys: Kuta is undoubtedly the best place on Bali to shop for clothing; the quality is reasonable (sometimes good), and designs are close to the latest western fashions, with a strong Australian bias for bright colours and bold designs. There is a good range of children's clothes shops. Silver jewellery is also a good buy (although some of it is of rather inferior quality). In addition, Kuta has a vast selection of 'tourist' trinkets and curios: leather goods, woodcarvings, mobiles, batik. Quality is poor to average.

Children's clothes shops: *Hop on Pop*, Jl Pantai 45; *Kuta Kidz*, Bemo Corner; *Outrageous*, Jl Legian Kaja 460.

Jewellery: several shops on Jl Legian and Jl Pantai. *Shiraz Silver*, on Jl Bunisari, has some attractive silver jewellery.

Leather: leather goods are generally poor quality but cheap and attractive – if you are buying a bag, check the handles are strong. *A-Sodig*, 3 Kuta Theatre St, sells made-to-measure leather jackets and trousers, and has good value boots and shoes.

Men's fashions: shirts at *Aladdin's Cave*, Jl Legian and in several shops around Bemo Corner.

Swimwear & sportswear: Jl Pantai, and from the surfing shops on Jl Legian and Jl Bakungsari.

T-shirts: a multitude of shops along Jl Legian; good designs from *Tony's* on Jl Bakungsari.

Tapes: beware – dodgy cassette tapes sold.

Women's clothes shops: mostly along Jl Legian and Jl Pantai. Lots of lycra, available from *Coconut Tree*, Jl Legian. Outrageous sequined garments from *Dallas*, Jl Legian 496. Batik jump-suits and jackets from *Aladdin's Cave*, Jl Legian; *Bali Design*, good quality cotton fashions.

● **Sports**
Bungy Jumping: *Bali Bungy Co*, Jl Pura Puseh, Legian Kelod, T 752658, open daily 0800-midnight, the first bungy jumping company in Bali – the unsightly 45m metal tower from which jumps are made is clearly seen from quite a long way away, free pick-up service is offered.

Massage: numerous masseurs – with little professional training – roam the beach; more skilled masseurs can be found at hotels or specialist clinics around Kuta.

Surfing: Kuta is famous for its surfing, although the cognoscenti would now rather go elsewhere (see page 343). Surfboards are available for rent on the beach. Surf equipment is available from *The Surf Shop*, Jl Legian; *Amphibia Surf Shop*, Jl Legian; and *Ulu's Shop*, Jl Bakungsari. They will all provide information on currents, tides and latest surfing reports.

Swimming: small pool and spa in historic building, centre of Kuta, opp the Art Market, adult 3,000Rp, child 1,500Rp, towels and lockers for hire.

● **Tour companies & travel agents**
Bali Adventure Tours, Jl Tunjung Mekar, T 751292, F 754334, an organized company owned by long-term Australian resident (the owner of *Yanies Restaurant* in Legian), they can help you with rafting or kayaking trips, mountain biking or trekking, US$40-56, incl pick-up from hotel, lunch and insurance; *Gloria Tours & Travel Services*, Jl Raya Kerobokan 2, T 730272, F 730273, Bali sight-seeing tours, island tours, car rental.

● **Tourist offices**
Government Tourist Information Office, Jl Bakungsari, T 756176, open daily 0800-1300, 1500-1800.

● **Transport**

11 km from Denpasar, 4 km from the airport.

Local Bemos: bemos run from Bemo Corner up Jl Pantai to Legian (200Rp); and from just E of Bemo Corner, to Denpasar's Tegal terminal. Bemos for charter also hang around Bemo Corner. **Bicycle hire**: 3,000Rp/day. **Car hire**: arrange through hotels, or one of the rental agencies in town, approximately 40,000Rp/day; there are also private cars (with drivers) that can be chartered by the hour or day, or for specific journeys. Bargain hard, expect to pay about 50,000Rp/day. Drivers can be found around Bemo Corner. **Motorbike hire**: arranged through travel agents, hotels or from operations on the street, from 7,000Rp/day.

Road Bemo: to Tegal terminal in Denpasar and from there, change to other terminals for next destination (see Local transport page 340). **Shuttle bus**: to most tourist destinations on the island; shop around for best price. **Taxi**: 8,000Rp to the airport.

LEGIAN

It is hard to say where Kuta ends and Legian begins, as the main shopping street, Jl Legian dominates both places. However, Legian is a place and it does have its own identity, even if at first it may not appear so. Like Kuta, Legian is a shopping haven, but the shops are slightly more upmarket, there are less drinking holes and more arts and crafts shops, as opposed to clothing. At the northernmost stretch of Legian is a wide sandy beach with a few hotels dotted along, the most prestigious of which is the *Oberoi*.

Local information
● **Accommodation**

A+ *Oberoi*, Jl Kayu Aya, PO Box 3351, T 730361, F 730791, N end of Legian on a peaceful stretch of sandy beach, surrounded by 15 acres of formal gardens, built in 1972, the *Oberoi* was one of Bali's first luxury class hotels, and has attracted a prestigious clientele over the years, incl David Bowie, John Denver, Art Garfunkel, Mick Jagger, Roman Polanski and Gianni Versace – to name but a few, many of the newer hotels in its category have borrowed features of the *Oberoi*, particularly the stone-walling, thatched alang-alang roofs and the arrangement of accommodation in private villas, or in the case of the *Oberoi*, *Lanai Cottages*, each

Lanai has the expected facilities incl satellite TV, video, stereo, mini-bar, a/c and a luxurious marble finished bathroom, complete with sunken bath, that opens onto a small, walled garden, luxury *Lanai* are also available, twice the size and twice the price, some with private pools, resort facilities incl pool (no paddling pool), health club, beauty salon, boutique, 500m of private beach, tennis, small amphitheatre for regular Balinese performances, 2 restaurants, rec; **L** *Puri Ratih*, Jl Puri Ratih, PO Box 1114, T 751546, F 751549, N of Legian, a/c, restaurant, pool, all suites, with own kitchen, living-room and garden, excellent facilities.

A+ *Bali Imperial*, Jl Dhyanapura, T 754545, F 751545, a/c, restaurant, pools, tennis, Japanese-owned hotel on a beachfront plot, opened 1992 with 121 luxurious rooms and perhaps the most inviting swimming pool in S Bali; **A** *Bali Mandira*, Jl Padma, T 751381, F 752377, a/c, restaurant, large pool, close to sea, free airport pick-up, rec; **A** *Intan Bali Village*, PO Box 1089, Batubelig Beach, T 752191, F 752475, a/c, several restaurants, 2 pools, extensive sports facilities, large central block with some bungalow accommodation; **A** *Kuta Palace*, Jl Pura Bagus Teruna, PO Box 244, T 751433, F 752074, a/c, 5 restaurants, 2 pools, tennis, fitness centre, all facilities, facing the beach, large hotel with 2-storey blocks of accommodation and some family bungalows; **A** *Legian Garden Cottages*, Jl Legian Cottage, T 751876, a/c, pool, quiet except when the *Double Six Disco* is operating; **A** *Pesona Bali*, Jl Kayu Aya, T 753914, F 753915, a/c, restaurant, pool, quiet location with cottage-style accommodation; **A** *Rama Garden Cottages*, Jl Padma, T 751971, F 755909, 30 a/c rm, artistic Balinese decor, mini-bar, private terrace, pool, restaurant.

B *Garden View*, Jl Padma, T 751559, F 753265, a/c, pool, quiet location, a walk to the beach; **B** *Legian Village*, Jl Padma, T 751182, some a/c, pool, popular; **B** *Orchid Garden Cottage*, Jl Pura Bagus Taruna 525, PO Box 379, T 751802, small hotel, attractive gardens, clean; **B-C** *RJ's*, Jl Rum Jungle, T 751922, pool, good value, good food; **B-C** *Three Brothers*, quiet hotel with cottages in a traditional Balinese garden courtyard, attractive and better value than its equivalent in Kuta.

C *Lumbung Sari*, Jl Three Brothers, T 752009, rather squashed in between other developments, cottage with kitchen, (**D**) no fan.

D *Legian Beach Bungalow*, Jl Padma, T 751087, good discount for longer stay;

Legian

To Bali Intan Village
To Puri Ratih
To Denpasar

Pura Petitenget Temple

Jl Oberoi

Jl Raya Seminyak

Jl Kroboka

N

Jl Dhyana Pura

Legian Beach

Jl Double Six

Taxi Stand

Jl Pura Bagus Teruna

Jl Legian

Swiss Consulate

Clinic

Logi Supermarket

Jl Padma

LEGIAN

Clinic

Jl Melasti

To Kuta & Airport

Hotels:
1. Bali Intan
2. Bali Mandira
3. Bali Oberoi
4. Garden View
5. Imperial
6. Kuta Palace
7. La Lucciola
8. Legian Beach
9. Legian Garden
10. Legian Village
11. Oka
12. Orchid Garden
13. Pesona Bali
14. Puri Mangga
15. Rum Jungle Road
16. Three Brothers

Places to eat:
17. Benny's Café
18. Do Drop Inn

0   250
metres

set on a lonely stretch of beach at northern end of Legian, excellent Italian food, interesting and varied menu, good atmosphere, rec, open until 2300; ♦♦♦*Poco Loco*, Jl Padma Utara, terraced Mexican restaurant.

● **Bars**
Do Drop Inn, Jl Legian.

● **Banks & money changers**
Branch of **Lippo** bank and plenty of money changers along Jl Legian.

● **Embassies & consulates**
Switzerland, c/o *Swiss Restaurant*, Jl Pura Bagus Taruna, T 751735.

● **Shopping**
Shopping in Legian is much the same as in Kuta except that clothing shops tend to be slightly more upmarket, and there is more craft for sale.

Handicrafts: a range of 'antiques' and Indonesian fabrics at the N end of Jl Legian.

Swimwear and sportswear: several good shops on Jl Legian and side streets.

● **Tour companies & travel agents**
Perama, Jl Padma, for travel agent services; *Bali Jaran Jaran Kensana, Logi Gardens Hotel*, T 975298, organize pony trekking around Tabanan, daily rate pp US$55, incl hotel pick-up, tuition, buffet lunch, insurance.

D *Oka*, Jl Padma, T 751085, small, clean, but hemmed in by other buildings; **D** *Puri Damai Cottage I*, Jl Padma, T 751965, popular; **D** *Puri Mangga Cottages*, Jl Legian Cottages 23, T 751447, F 753007, good rates for long stays, nice garden; **D** *Sari Yasa Beach Inn I*, Jl Rum Jungle, T 752836, basic but OK rooms.

E *Sri Beach Inn*, with bathroom, quiet.

● **Places to eat**
Benny's, Jl Pura Bagus Taruna, great range of coffee; *Cin Cin*, Jl Dhyana Pura, friendly open-air restaurant on roadside, good salads, emphasis on German dishes, pool for use of clients; *Do Drop Inn*, Jl Legian, steak-house, bar and restaurant; *Koko's Warung*, Jl Pura Bagus Taruna, Indian food; *La Lucciola*, Jl Kayu Aya, spacious open-air building with a vast alang-alang roof,

TUBAN

Tuban is a newly developed area (still not featured on some maps) of luxury hotels, resorts and restaurants, just to the S of Kuta, spread along Jl Kartika Plaza, overlooking sandy beach. Due to the stiff competition in Tuban, it is worth enquiring about promotion rates. Buffet theme nights are also worth finding out about too, they are often very good value and may include entertainment. Facilities are as you would expect with a good choice of pools, sports and recreation facilities.

Most have organized activities and kiddie clubs which makes Tuban very suitable for families. The atmosphere in Tuban lacks the bustle and intimacy of Kuta, the hotels have very good staff and most lobbies have Balinese musicians playing which makes it all very relaxing.

Local information
● **Accommodation**

A+ Bali Dynasty Resort, Jl Kartika Plaza, PO Box 2047, T 752403, F 752402, 225 rm, a 4-star hotel under *Shangri-La* management, set in luscious gardens, a short walk from white, sandy beach, all rooms with a/c, satellite TV, tea and coffee-making facilities, mini-bar, robes and slippers, other facilities incl free-from pool with kiddies section, poolside bar and restaurant, Chinese restaurant, tennis, indoor games room, beauty salon, boutique and disco/karaoke, promotion rates sometimes available, good value food, ideal for families, rec; **A+ Bintang Bali**, Jl Kartika Plaza, T 753292, F 753288, 400 rm, 5-star facilities, attractive lobby overlooking exotic gardens, non-smoking rooms on 3rd floor only, disabled facilities, beauty salon, fitness centre, boutiques, private beach with lifeguard-cum security officer to keep hawkers at bay, pool is complete with a thundering cascade, a hot whirlpool and cold dip, also kiddy pool and swim-up bar, 5 restaurants incl *Coconut Wharf* rec for Italian food, tennis, children's playground, all rooms have a/c, mini-bar, satellite TV, in-house movie, balcony, rec; **A+ Holiday Inn Bali Hai**, Jl Wana Segara 33, T 753035, F 754548, 195 rm, complimentary airport transfer, built in 1992 in style of traditional Balinese architecture, decorated with beautiful carvings and antiques from the owner's private collection, spacious rooms with a/c, fridge, tea and coffee-making facilities, balcony, some non-smoking rooms and disabled facilities, pleasant shady pool with swim-up bar, kiddy pool, tennis, fitness centre, watersports facilities, theme buffets every night (free for under 6s), Ratna Satay terrace has a bar and specializes in satay, live Balinese music plays for sunset; **A Bali Garden**, Jl Kartika Plaza, PO Box 1101, T 752725, F 753851, a/c, restaurant, pool, extensive facilities; **A Bali Rani**, Jl Kartika Plaza, PO Box 1034, T 751369, F 752673, one of the latest additions to the Tuban area, 104 rm, each with a/c, satellite TV, in-house movie, mini-bar, balcony, facilities incl free-from pool and children's pool, Chinese restaurant, French Bakery, pub;

A Green Garden, Jl Kartika Plaza 9, T 754570, 25 comfortable, tiled rooms with wood furniture, a/c, fridge, TV, balcony overlooking small pool with waterfall, good Chinese seafood restaurant; **A Kartika Plaza**, Jl Kartika Plaza, PO Box 3084, T 751067, F 752475, a/c, 5 restaurants, large pool, part of the *Aerowisata* chain, facilities incl squash courts, tennis, fitness centre, huge reception, some cottage-style accommodation; **A Putra Jasa**, Jl Kuta Beach, PO Box 3121, T 751161, formerly *Pertamina Cottages*, 5-star hotel, a/c, satellite TV, mini-bar, restaurants incl the *Borsalino* for Italian food and *Yashi*, a Japanese restaurant, pool, children's pool, good sports facilities, rooms arranged in rather dated villas (4 rm/villa), suites available; **A Santika Beach**, Jl Kartika Plaza, T 751267, F 751260, a/c, restaurants, pools, tennis, rather featureless but pleasant enough.

B Karthi Inn, Jl Kartika Plaza, T 754810, F 751708, dated but comfortable, a/c, TV, pool with sunken bar, open-air Chinese restaurant.

C Mandara Cottages, Jl Kartika Plaza, T 751775, small pool, open-air bathrooms, rec.

● **Places to eat**

Kaisar, Jl Kartika Plaza, Balinese and Indonesian dishes; *Coconut Wharf*, Bintang Bali, Jl Kartika Plaza, poolside Italian restaurant, good pasta dishes, pizza and cocktails, rec; *Croissants de France*, Jl Kartika Plaza, French bakery serves breakfast and snacks 0700-1100; *Kuta Sea Food*, Jl Kartika Plaza, opp Bintang Bali, theatre and restaurant, dancing performances (2200-2100) while you dine – mostly Chinese food steamboat and seafood basket are popular, children's menu available, a definite tourist spot and a little grubby with it; *Bali Sea Food*, Jl Kartika Plaza, next door to Kuta Sea Food, similar in concept, but a bit cleaner, interesting menu features snapper with Thai sauce, Bali fish with Sumatra dressing, free pick-up from hotel offered; *Lotus Tavern*, Jl Wana Segera, open-air restaurant under alang-alang roof, candle-lit after dark, good salads, homemade pasta, wood-oven pizza, friendly atmosphere, pick-up from hotel offered, rec; *Metro Club*, Jl Kartika Plaza, more of a nightclub than restaurant with happy hour from 1600 to 1900, wide range of dishes from Mexican tacos to Indonesian satay.

● **Bars**

O'Brien's Fun Pub, Holiday Inn Bali Hai, a 'sporty' pub, open 1700-0100, happy hour 1800-1900.

● **Banks & money changers**

Bank opp the *Bintang Bali*, money changers along Jl Kartika Plaza and Jl Wana Segara, most hotels change money too but rates are not so good.

● **Entertainment**

Disco: *BB Discotheque*, *Bintang Bali Hotel*, 1900-0200, fashion shows every Tues and Fri; *Waves Discotheque*, *Bali Dynasty Hotel*.

● **Places of worship**

Sunday school for children every Sun 1100, *Kuta Retreat House*, Tuban.

● **Shopping**

Plaza Bali, department store, duty-free shop (selection of perfumes and cosmetics, clothing and pricy liquor), restaurant, venue for Balinese dancing.

● **Sports**

All the big hotels along Jl Kartika Plaza have watersports facilities, pools and tennis courts.

Diving: *Bali Dolphin Divers*, *Bali Garden Hotel*, Jl Kartika Plaza, T 752725, they also provide fishing, parasailing, jetskiing and waterskiing facilities; *OMI Dives*, Kompleks Ruko, Indah Permai Blok C5, Jl By Pass Ngurah Rai, T 757484, F 772982, diving tours locally and on islands, US$65-95 for the day incl 2 tanks, lunch box, instruction and insurance.

Swimming: *Waterbom Park*, Jl Kartika Plaza, T 755676, F 753517, within walking distance of Tuban hotels, open daily 0900-1800, adult 15,000Rp, child 8,000Rp (children under 12 must be accompanied by an adult), over 600m of water slides, restaurant, lockers and towels for hire.

● **Tour companies & travel agents**

Surya Candra, Jl Wana Segara 25x, T 754557, sightseeing around Bali, car rental.

● **Useful addresses**

Immigration: S of town on the road to the airport, Jl Ngurah Rai, Tuban, T 751038.
Police station: Jl By-Pass, Tuban, T 751598.

CANGGU

This area of coastline, only 20 mins N of Legian is slowly being developed and offers peace and rural tranquility, traditional villages untouched by tourism, and frequent ceremonies and festivals at one of its many temples or on the beach. The area features in historical and mythical tales concerning the third king of Bali in the 14th and 15th centuries and his beautiful 'Bangawan Canggu Keris' with magical powers. Particularly important and colourful ceremonies are held at Batu Bulong Temple on the beach of the same name in early Jul and at the end of Aug. This temple, with its sacred spring 'Tirta Empul' features in the Lontar chronicles in the Temple of Batur near Kintanami. There are spectacular sunsets here.

At the moment accommodation consists of three overpriced resort hotels (prices negotiable except during high season) catering to package tourists and one losmen. However, more hotels are nearing completion and more losmen will appear. Some of Denpasar's 'wealthy' have chosen to live in this area and have built large, stylish homes.

Canggu district offers unspoilt, grey sand beaches, with the possibility of excellent surfing (easy 1 to 2m-high waves off left and right-hand reef breaks), as well as swimming. The following beaches are all part of Canggu: Pererean, Banjartengah, Canggu, Tegal Gundul, Padang Linjong, Batu Bulong and Berewa. The villages from which the beaches draw their names are inland and most offer simple homestays, just ask around, local people are very friendly and helpful.

The drive to Canggu is very beautiful as you pass endless lush green paddy fields, coconut and banana palms, cows grazing and only the occasional picturesque, small village full of temples and shrines. It is still very much a rural area, and very peaceful with the sound of the running water from the paddy fields blending with the sound of the waves on the deserted beaches (of course if you stay in a resort hotel with air-conditioning you may miss some of this!).

● **Accommodation Pererean Beach**: a completely undeveloped stretch of beach with only: **D** *Sunset Club Losmen*, 4 new, simple rm with large, attached bathroom with western toilet (one of the bathrooms has 2 papaya trees growing in it!), breakfast and tax not incl, upstairs restaurant (♦) with good views of coast, very peaceful and unspoilt. **Canggu Beach**: hotel will be open by the time this is published.

● **Transport** To reach Canggu you will need your own transport. Follow the main road N from Legian until you pick up signs for Canggu. The beach signposted 'Canggu Beach' is in fact Pererean Beach. To reach 'Canggu Beach' itself turn left at the T-junction in Canggu village and keep going to the beach. If in doubt ask for directions.

BEREWA BEACH

The main temple here is 'Pura Dang Khayangan', there has been a temple here since the 16th century.

● **Accommodation** There are three hotels here which cater primarily for tour groups. Attractive locations beside the sea, they all offer the usual facilities of luxury class hotels: private bathrooms, a/c, TV, poolside bars, etc. Prices should be negotiable off season. Breakfast and tax extra. **A+ Dewata Beach Hotel** (a Best Western hotel), Banjar Berewa, Desa Canggu 80361, PO Box 3271, Denpasar 80032, T (0361) 730263, F (0361) 730290 or any Best Western Office, the grandest of the hotels at this beach, 168 deluxe rm and suites, facilities incl freshwater swimming pool, seasports, beach volleyball, tennis courts and children's playground, restaurants, bars, incl karaoke, theatre for Balinese dances; **A Bolare Beach Bungalows**, PO Box 3256 80, 032 Denpasar, T/F (0361) 730258, probably the best value, rather ornate rooms with a/c, bathroom etc, could do with a little maintainence, facilities incl restaurant, travel agency, car hire, swimming pool etc; **A Legong Keraton Beach Cottages**, PO Box 617, Kuta, T (0361) 730280, F 730285, very ornate rooms, not to everyone's taste, restaurant, swimming pool, free airport transfer.

SANUR

Like Kuta, Sanur was also a malaria-infested swamp which local people, bar a few intrepid fishermen, tended to avoid. In the past, the villages around Sanur had a reputation for producing some of the best dancers and story-tellers, as well as some of the most effective priests and shamans.

In May 1904 the Chinese steamer *Sri Koemala* was wrecked off Sanur and looted by the local Balinese. The Dutch used the failure (and subsequent outright refusal) of the King of Badung to offer compensation for this 'outrage' as justification for blockading the principality. On the 15 September 1906, there followed an armed invasion by the Dutch on the beaches of Sanur, which was unopposed by the peaceful local Brahmanas (the priestly caste). However, an army arrived from Denpasar to confront the Dutch the following morning. Fighting lasted for much of the day, resulting in the death of a handful of Dutchmen and hundreds of Balinese. After the skirmish, the Dutch remained at Sanur for a few days – apparently giving concerts for the local inhabitants – before setting out for Denpasar and the King of Badung's palace. The rest, as they say, is history (see page 317).

Barely two decades after the Dutch military invasion of Sanur, the beginning of another invasion took root: tourism. Hotels sprang up along the beachfront and intrepid travellers from the West began to arrive, enticed by tales of a tropical paradise. Bali's first, and ugliest, international hotel was built here (the *Bali Beach*) but despite considerable development, Sanur remains quieter and more low-key than Kuta, with the most attractive beach on the island and a village atmosphere. The road parallel to the beach is lined with money changers, tourist shops (selling clothing and jewellery), tour companies, car rental outlets and shipping agents.

Places of interest

The **Le Mayeur Museum** is just to the N of the *Bali Beach Hotel* and is named after the famous Belgian artist Adrien Yean Le Mayeur, who arrived in Bali in 1932. He was immediately captivated by the culture and beauty of the island, made Sanur his home and married a local beauty, Ni Polok, in 1935. He died in 1958. The museum contains his collection of local artefacts and some of Le Mayeur's work. The interior is dark and rather dilapidated, making the pieces difficult to view – a great shame

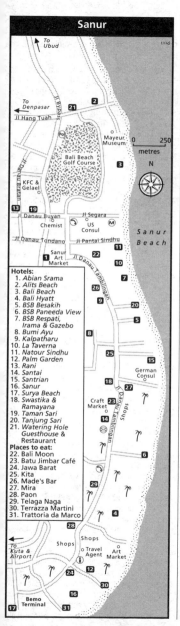

Sanur

To Ubud

To Denpasar
Jl Bypass
Jl Hang Tuah

Po

Mayeur Museum

0   250
metres

N

Bali Beach Golf Course

Jl Danau Buyan

KFC & Gelael

Chemist

Jl Danau Buyan

Jl Danau Tondano

Jl Segara

US Consul

Jl Pantai Sindhu

Sanur Beach

Sanur Art Market

Jl Danau Tamblingan

German Consul

Craft Market

Art Market

Jl Danau Tamblingan

To Kuta & Airport

Shops   Shops

Travel Agent

Art Market

Bemo Terminal

Hotels:
1. Abian Srama
2. Alits Beach
3. Bali Beach
4. Bali Hyatt
5. BSB Besakih
6. BSB Paneeda View
7. BSB Respati, Irama & Gazebo
8. Bumi Ayu
9. Kalpataru
10. La Taverna
11. Natour Sindhu
12. Palm Garden
13. Rani
14. Santai
15. Santrian
16. Sanur
17. Surya Beach
18. Swastika & Ramayana
19. Taman Sari
20. Tanjung Sari
21. Watering Hole Guesthouse & Restaurant

Places to eat:
22. Bali Moon
23. Batu Jimbar Café
24. Jawa Barat
25. Kita
26. Made's Bar
27. Mira
28. Paon
29. Telaga Naga
30. Terrazza Martini
31. Trattoria da Marco

because Le Mayeur's impressionistic works are full of tropical sunlight and colour. Le Mayeur's paintings made a great impression on a number of Balinese artists, including the highly regarded I Gusti Nyoman Nodya. Admission 200Rp. Open 0800-1400 Tues-Thur and Sun, 0800-1100 Fri, 0800-1200 Sat.

To the S of Sanur, on the route to the main road, is the **Pura Blanjong** (on the left-hand side of the road). It houses the **Blanjong Inscription**, an inscribed cylindrical stone pillar, discovered in 1932 and believed to date from 914. The inscription is written in two languages, Sanskrit and Old Balinese, and was carved during the reign of King Kesari, a Buddhist King of the Sailendra Dynasty (who may also have founded the Besakih temple). It supports the view that there was an Indianized principality on Bali at a very early date. The inscription itself, though difficult to decipher, refers to a military expedition.

Excursions

Serangan Island or Turtle Island is, as the name suggests, famous for its turtles which are caught in the surrounding sea, raised in pens, and then slaughtered for their meat – which explains why they are becoming rarer by the year. The formerly common green turtle is now said to be virtually extinct in the area. The beaches on the E coast of the island are best, with offshore coral providing good snorkeling. One of Bali's most important coastal temples is the **Pura Sakenan** in Sakenan village, at the N end of the island. The temple was founded at the end of the 15th century and contains a rare prasada (*prasat*) or stepped stone tower. Stylistically, this is a combination of the Javanese candi and pre-Hindu megalithic stone altar. Like Uluwatu on the Bukit Peninsula, it is constructed of hard coral. Pura Sakenan's *odalan* or anniversary festival, held at Kuningan (the 210th day of the Balinese calendar) is thought by many to be one of the best on Bali. *Getting there*: boats can be chartered from Sanur or from Nusa Dua and Benoa. Usually visitors leave from a jetty just S of Kampung Mesigit and 2 km SW of Sanur. From here there are regular public boats to Serangan Island (600Rp); the problem is that tourists are often forced to charter a boat for far more; share if possible and bargain furiously. It is easier, and often just as cheap, to go on a tour. It is also possible to wade out to the island at low tide.

Nusa Lembongan (see page 363) lies just off the coast. Boats leave every morning for the island from close to the *Bali Beach Hotel*, 1 hr (17,000Rp).

Tours

The major hotels on the beach all have tour companies which organize the usual range of tours: for example to Lake Bratan (where waterskiing can be arranged); to Karangasem and Tenganan, to visit a traditional Aga village; to Ubud; white-water rafting on the Agung River; to the temples of Tanah Lot and Mengwi; to the Bali Barat National Park; to Besakih Temple; the *Golden Hawk* tall ship runs day trips to Lembongan Island (see page 363), as do *Island Explorer Cruises*, Ena Dive Center, Jl Tirta Ening 1, T 287945, F 287945, organize dolphin tours off Nusa Dua and provide watersports equipment, including PADI diving; *Sobek*, the 'adventure' tour company are based in Sanur at Jl Tirta Ening 9, T 287059. They can arrange bird watching and sporting activities (see **Sports**, page 362).

Local information
● **Accommodation**

Accommodation on Sanur is largely mid- to high-range, with 2 large-scale luxury developments – the *Bali Hyatt* and *Bali Beach*. There is some low-budget accommodation here, but not much. There is easy access to beach if staying along Jl Danau Tamblingan and Tanjung Sari. Also down Jl Pantai Karang where the German consul is, or Jl Segara Ayu where you can find the USA consulate.

L *Tanjung Sari*, Jl Tanjung Sari, PO Box 25, Denpasar, T 288441, F 287930, a/c, restaurant, pool, built in the 1960s, 29 bungalows with own

sitting-room and outside pavilion, tastefully decorated, although some rooms are becoming threadbare, rather overpriced, and seems to be living off its reputation.

A+ *Bali Beach*, PO Box 275, Denpasar, T 288511, F 287917, J 320107, N end of the beach, a/c, restaurant, 3 pools, 9-hole golf course, 10-pin bowling, tennis, original international hotel in Bali, built in the 1960s as a showpiece, with the backing of President Sukarno, an ugly high-rise block rather out-of-place now that low-rise designs employing Balinese motifs are all the rage, the more recently built bungalows, to the S, are more attractive, good facilities (the hotel suffered a serious fire in late 1992 but is said to have been repaired); **A+** *Bali Hyatt*, entrance on Jl Tanjung Sari, PO Box 392, T 288271, F 287693, a/c, several restaurants, lovely pool, one of the oldest but still one of the best hotels on the beach, extensive and immaculate grounds, range of sports activities and recently renovated, rec; **A+** *Sanur Beach*, PO Box 3279, T 288011, F 287566, S end of beach, a/c, several restaurants (fish restaurant rec), lovely pool, sports facilities incl fitness centre, attractively decorated rooms in 3-storey block; **A+** *Sindhu Beach*, Jl Danau Tondano 14, PO Box 181, T 288351, bungalow-style rooms.

A *Bali Sanur Bungalows (BSB)* (incl 5 separate developments in Sanur – *Paneeda View*, *Besakih Beach*, *Irama Bungalows*, *Respati Beach* and *Sanur Village Club*), Jl Tanjung Sari, PO Box 3306, T 288421, F 288426, a/c, standard bungalow rooms are poorly lit rooms and slightly claustrophobic as all have well-kept mature gardens with plenty of shade, restaurant, small pools; **A** *Bumi Ayu*, Jl Bumi Ayu, PO Box 1077, T 289101, F 287517, a/c, restaurant (excellent service), pool, inconveniently away from the beach, but attractive mature gardens with plenty of shade – slightly claustrophobic, and well-run, poorly lit rooms, rec; **A** *La Taverna*, Jl Tanjung Sari 30, PO Box 3040, T 288497, F 287126, discounts available, restaurant (rec), pool, rooms are well decorated with traditional furnishings, attractive gardens, small beach front, friendly and obliging staff; **A** *Palm Garden*, Jl Kesuma Sari, T 288299, F 288299, S end of beach, a/c, restaurant, pool; **A** *Santrian*, Jl Tanjung Sari, T 288181, F 288185, a/c, good restaurant, pool, bungalow accommodation, tennis courts, traditional style accommodation amidst large garden; **A** *Sativa*, Jl D Tamblingan, T 287276, a/c, attractive pool, attractively designed with thatched cottage accommodation; **A** *Surya Beach*, Jl Mertasari, T 288833, F 287303, J 5706421, S end of beach, a/c, restaurant, pool, sports facilities, large hotel with 2-storey cottage-style accommodation; **A-B** *Gazebo Cottages*, Jl Tanjung Sari 45, T 288212, F 288300, a/c, restaurant (unimpressive), pool, pleasant rooms, attractive gardens; **A-B** *Swastika Bungalows*, Jl Danau Tamblingan 128, T 288693, F 287526, quiet location set back from road, away from the beach but easy access, simple gardens, popular, central for shops and restaurants.

B *Alit's Beach Bungalows*, Jl Hang Tuah 45, T 288560, F 288766, N end of beach, a/c, pool, large complex of traditional Balinese design, with attractive gardens; **B** *Ramayana*, Jl Danau Tamblingan 130, PO Box 3066, T 288429, a/c, small, family-run hotel, away from the beach, small rooms, noisy; **B** *Santai*, Jl Danau Tamblingan 148, T 287314, some a/c, restaurant, pool, away from beach but better value in this price range, central location; **B-C** *Abian Srama*, Jl Bypass, T 288415, F 288673, some a/c, small pool, bad location, away from the beach, but well-run; **B-C** *Kalpataru*, Jl D Tamblingan, T 288457, some a/c, restaurant, small hotel, rooms are rather hemmed-in, lacking character.

C *Respati Beach Village*, a/c, restaurant, hot water, on the beach front, this resort hotel offers cottages with two units to each, set in a garden with small pool and private beach, rooms nr the street are close to a busy restaurant and tend to be noisy, but this is still a good place to stay, very clean and attractive, rec; **C** *Watering Hole*, Jl Hangtuah 35, T 288289, some a/c, average.

D-E *Hotel Taman Sari*, Jl Danau Buyan, some a/c, good rooms for the price of the cheaper end of what is available here, rate incl breakfast.

● **Places to eat**

Many of the best restaurants on Sanur are concentrated at the S end of the beach, on Jl Bali Hyatt. The 3 big hotels, namely the *Hyatt*, the *Bali Beach* and the *Sanur Beach* all have several good restaurants and many of the smaller hotels have good restaurants, with competitive prices. One reader has suggested that the turnover in all the restaurants on Jl Tanjung Sari is low and therefore, the food is not always fresh.

♦♦♦♦*Kita*, Jl Danau Tamblingan 104, average Japanese food; ♦♦♦*Bali Moon*, Jl Tamblingan 19. Italian, attractive setting in an open-air pavilion, good food; ♦♦♦*Cafe Batu Jimbar*, Jl Tamblingan 152, T 287374, opp Batu Jimbar estate. Pleasant open-air restaurant with a good choice of healthy dishes. The vegetables are grown in their own vegetable garden at Bedugul; ♦♦♦*Made's Bar and restaurant*, Jl Tanjung Sari 51, seafood, Italian, Indonesian, generous portions, good food and atmosphere, rec; ♦♦♦*Paon*, Jl Danau Tamblingan (not far from *Bali Hyatt*), seafood and steaks; ♦♦♦*Tanjung Sari Hotel*, Jl Tanjung Sari, excellent Indonesian and International food (French cook) served in elegant, peaceful surroundings, drinks at candlelit tables on the beach provide a romantic atmosphere; ♦♦♦*Telaga Naga*, nr *Hyatt*, romantic setting in building on stilts overlooking lily pond, classy Szechuan and Chinese food, open evenings only 1830-2300; ♦♦*Mina Garden*, Jl Tanjung Sari. Balinese, Indonesian, Italian and international, Balinese dance, rec; ♦*Jawa Barat*, S end of Jl Bali Hyatt, Indonesian; ♦*Mira*, opp *Hotel Ramayana*, cheap and good value; *Terrazza Martini*, on the beach at the S end, small restaurant serving good Italian food; *Trattoria Da Marco*, on the beach at the S end, Italian, rec.

Supermarkets: *Galael Dewata* is on the By Pass road and has a good range of food and wine, as well as an ice-cream parlour and a *Kentucky Fried Chicken* next door.

● **Airline offices**

All the below have offices in the *Bali Beach Hotel*. **Air France**, T 288511, ext 1104; **Cathay Pacific**, T 288511; **Garuda**, T 288243; **KLM**, T 287577; **Lufthansa**, T 287069; **MAS**, T 288511; **Qantas**, T 288331; **Sempati**, T 288824; **Singapore Airlines**, T 287940; **Thai**, T 288141.

● **Banks & money changers**

There are several along the main street.

● **Embassies & consulates**

France, Jl Sekar Waru 3, T 288090; **Germany**, Jl Pantai Karang 17, T 288826 (0800-1200 Mon-Fri); **Italy**, Jl Padanggalak, T 288372; **Sweden** and **Denmark**, *Segara Village Hotel*, T 288408; **US**, Jl Segara Ayu 5, T 288478.

● **Entertainment**

Dance: the *Sanur Beach Hotel* offers a buffet dinner with Legong (Mon), Ramayana Ballet (Wed), Genggong/frog dance (Sun) all at 1930. The *Tanjung Sari Hotel* has legong dance and gamelan performances on Sat nights. The *Penjor* restaurant (nr the *Bali Hyatt Hotel*) stages legong dance performances on Tues, Thur and Sun 1930-2100, frog dance every Mon 2015, joged dance every Wed 2015 and janger dance every Fri 2015.

Disco: *Rumours*, Jl Sindhu, 2200-0400 (happy hours 2200-0100); *Number One*, Jl Danau Tamblingan, 2000-0300.

Jazz: *Gratan Bar*, *Bali Hyatt Hotel*, live music nightly, 2100-0100; *Olgas Lounge*, *Surya Beach Hotel*, 2000-1200.

Massage: on the beach, or at *Sehatku*, Jl D Tamblingan 23, T 287880, 10,000Rp for a traditional massage.

Sauna/spa: *Sehatku*, Jl D Tamblingan 23, T 287880, 40,000Rp.

● **Hospital & medical services**
Dentist: Dr Alfiana Akinah, Jl Sri Kesari 17.
Doctor: *Bali Beach Hotel* from 0800-1200 daily.

● **Places of worship**
Catholic: church service at *Bali Beach Hotel*, 1800 Sat and *Bali Hyatt Hotel* 1900 Sat (times may vary).
Protestant: Bali Beach, 1800 Sun.

● **Post & telecommunications**
Area code: 0361.
Perumtel telephone service: on the corner of Jl Tanjung Sari and Jl Sindu.
Post Office: Jl Danau Buyan.
Postal agent: Jl Tamblingan 66 (opp *Taverna Bali Hotel*); incl poste restante.
Wartel telephone service: corner of Tanjung and Segara Ayu. Approximate rate to USA and Europe 5,000Rp/minute.

● **Sports**
Diving: *Bali Marine Sports*, Jl Raja Bypass, Blanjong, T 287872, F 287872; *Baruna Watersports* at the *Bali Beach Hotel*, T 288511, *Sanur Beach*, T 288011 and *Bali Hyatt*, T 288271, they are expensive but very professional, with well maintained equipment and very safe procedures; *Oceana Dive Centre*, Jl Bypass 78, T 288652, F 288652.

Golf: 9-hole courses at the *Bali Beach Hotel*, Green fee US$25, club hire US$11.50/ US$16.50, caddy US$1.50.

Jungle skirmish (aka Paintball): *Bali Splat Mas*, T 289073, 2 approx 5-hr sessions a day, US$45/session.

Mountain biking: *Sobek*, organize various trips around the interior, T 287059.

Sea kayaking: with *Sobek*, T 287059.

10-Pin Bowling: at the *Bali Beach Hotel*, 3,500Rp pp/game.

Watersports: equipment available from the bigger hotels or on the beach. Typical prices pp: jet ski US$15/15 mins, parasailing US$10/round; glass bottom boat US$15 (min 2); windsurfing US$8/hr; water skiing US$15/15 mins, deep sea fishing US$240 incl (maximum 6 people for full day).

Whitewater rafting: with *Sobek*, T 287059.

● **Shopping**
Batik: *Popiler*, in Tohpati, 5 km N of Sanur beach, on the road to Batubulan, rec.

Clothing: *Pisces*, Jl Sanur Beach (nr the *Bali Hyatt*) has good designs.

Ikat: *Gego*, Jl Danau Toba 6, ikat and hand-woven fabrics; *Nogo*, Jl Tamblingan 98, high quality ikat made in Gianyar and sold for 14,000Rp/metre for plain colours and 16,000Rp/metre for designs, plus ready-made clothing. They also sell batik.

Jewellery: *Bali Sun Sri*, Jl Bypass Ngurah Rai (out of town) has a wide selection of silver jewellery and good designs; *Pisces*, Jl Sanur Beach (nr *Bali Hyatt*) sells a limited range of contemporary silver jewellery.

Leather & rattan bags: *The Hanging Tree*, Jl Tamblingan.

Tourist trinkets: T-shirts, bags, batik, at the N end of Jl Tanjung Sari.

● **Useful addresses**
Police: Jl By-Pass, T 288597.

● **Transport**
6 km from Denpasar.

Local Bemo: short hops within Sanur limits cost 300Rp. **Bicycle hire**: the *Bali Hyatt Hotel* has mountain bikes for hire. **Car hire**: larger national and international firms tend to be based at the bigger hotels; there are also many smaller outfits along the main road. Big companies charge about 90,000Rp/day, smaller ones about 45,000Rp/day. Note that cars cannot be taken off the island. **Avis**, *Bali Hyatt Hotel*, T 288271 ext 85023; **Bali Car Rental**, Jl Ngurah Rai 17, T 288550; **National**, *Bali Beach Hotel*, T 288511 ext 1304.

Road Bemo: regular connections on green bemos with Denpasar's Kreneng terminal and on blue bemos with Tegal terminal (both 600Rp); also regular connections with the Batubulan terminal, N of Sanur (600Rp). To airport, 15,000Rp. **Taxi**: most hotels will arrange airport transfer/pickup and will charge the same as taxis for the service (15,000Rp).

NUSA PENIDA AND NUSA LEMBONGAN

These two islands off Bali's SE coast in the Lombok Strait are relatively isolated from the 'mainland' and have not experienced the same degree of tourist development. **Nusa Lembongan** the smaller of the two is encircled by beautiful white sand beaches with stunning views of Gunung Agung on Bali, especially at sunset. There is good surfing along the N shore and the surrounding reefs with their clear waters and good visibility offer some of the best snorkelling and diving within easy reach of Bali. You will need to arrange dives with an operator on Bali. These attractions have already caught the attention of both developers and tourists looking for somewhere new. Nonetheless, for the time being it seems that the harvesting of seaweed for export – primarily to Hong Kong for the cosmetics industry – will remain the island's main source of income.

An arid, scrubby island which supports few crops, mainly peanuts, beans and corn; most food has to be brought over from Bali, 12 km distant. Measuring only 4 x 2 km it is easily explored on foot. A pleasant place to stay for a few days: no cars just motorbikes. The main village is Desa Lembongan but most people stay in accommodation along the beach N of Jungut Batu. A tarmac road runs between the two villages, a distance of about 3 km.

At low tide the seaweed beds are worth a visit. There is a track running right round the island which makes a pleasant walk. For a cool, damp interlude you can explore the underground house on the edge of Lembongan village, a network of caves, rooms and passages, bring your own torch; the local kids will offer to act as guides. Boats for rent 5,000Rp/hr, 150,000Rp/day, motorbikes 12,000Rp/day.

The small island of **Nusa Ceningan** can be easily reached from Nusa Lembongan by hiring a boat. There is just one small village, no accommodation, but there are beaches with good surfing, snorkelling and diving; there are sharks in the waters here but they rarely attack.

The far larger sister island of **Nusa Penida** is rugged and barren, with steep cliffs along its S shore and sandy beaches to the N. It has a reputation among the Balinese as a cursed place and criminals and outcasts used to be sent here to live out their days. Perhaps because of its reputation, Nusa Penida has not yet been caught up in the tourist mêlée and there is only basic losmen accommodation available in the main town Sampalan, and the village of Toyapeken where boats from Bali arrive although it might also be possible to persuade a local to take you in at other villages. Ask the *kepala desa* (headman). Most visitors come for the day only.

Tours

Bali Hai Cruises, Benoa Harbour, T 720331, F 720334, operate professionally-run cruises from Benoa Harbour to Lembongan. Under Australian management, the 1-hr crossing is made in a high-tech, fully a/c catamaran – you barely notice you are in a boat. There are three cruise options: A (US$80) sails to a pontoon off Lembongan from where you can snorkel, banana-boat ride, view the reef through a semi-submersible boat and snorkel (extra charge), before buffet lunch served on catamaran deck; B (US$68) sails to beach club on Lembongan, buffet barbecue, relax around pool, snorkel from beach; C (US$38) sunset cruise, buffet and disco/karaoke. Cruise B has the added attraction of being able to visit the island, taking in seaweed farms, Lembongan village and an underground house that was built by a local priest. Cruise A is strictly for those in search of watersports and action, rec. *Wakalouka Cruises*, Benoa Harbour, T 261129, F 261130, 2-hr crossing from Benoa Harbour in state of the art, luxury sailing catamaran to the *Wakanusa Resort* on Lembongan. The trip costs US$78 (free for under 5s) and includes tour of Lembongan village, snorkelling,

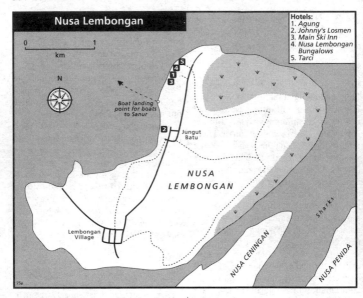

Nusa Lembongan

Hotels:
1. Agung
2. Johnny's Losmen
3. Main Ski Inn
4. Nusa Lembongan Bungalows
5. Tarci

buffet lunch, glass bottom boat to view coral reef, morning and afternoon refreshments, hotel transfers, rec. *Sea Rover*, Jl Segara Werdi 6, Harbour Beno is one of the numerous small companies operating day trips to Lembongan in simple motorboats, the tours cost under US$40, but the experience is downmarket. The *Golden Hawk*, a tall ship of over 100 years old sails from Benoa Harbour to Lembongan for day trips, US$88 for all inclusive trip – pick up from hotel, lunch, snorkel gear, glass bottom boat etc (scuba diving equipment and lessons can be arranged). *Golden Hawk Cruises* operate from Jl Danau Poso 20A, Sanur, T/F 28658. *Island Explorer Cruises*, Jl Sekar Waru 8, Sanur, T 289856, F 289837, organize day trips and an overnight package on sailing yacht and motorboats. Fishing, snorkelling, barbecue lunch provided (US$59-69).

Local information
● Accommodation on Nusa Lembongan
All the accommodation is beside the sea, with fabulous sunset views over Bali and Gunung Agung.

A *Waka Nusa Resort*, booking office Benoa Harbour, T 261129, F 261130, 10 luxury bungalows contained in tiny private garden, simple but artistic decor, alang-alang roofs, polished woods, natural fabrics, pool, restaurant, rec.

C-D *Nusa Lembongan Bungalows* (booking office on Kuta at Jl Pantai Legian, T 53071), price inc breakfast, attractive, clean and spacious rooms; **C-E** *Agung*, good restaurant, clean, thatched-roof bungalows, some with private mandi; **C-E** *Main Ski Inn*, 2-storey bungalows set in garden, upstairs rooms have balconies with sea views, can be noisy due to the restaurant (♦♦) serving good food overlooking the sea; **C-E** *Tarci*, 2-storey bungalows, some with private mandi, restaurant (♦♦) serves good food, beside the beach.

E *Johnny's Losmen*, basic accommodation nr the village.

● Places to eat
Most accommodations have their own restaurant, *Tarci* has a good reputation or try the fish at the *Main Ski Inn*.

● Shopping
Textiles: distinctive weft ikat cotton cloth is produced on Nusa Penida; usually in the form of a red *kamben*.

● Transport

Sea Boat: regular connections to Nusa Penida from either Padangbai or Kesamba, docking nr Sampalan at (respectively) Buyuk or Toyapakeh (the boats from Kesamba are small junks), 1 hr. Locals pay 4,000Rp but the boatmen demand 15,000Rp from foreigners. For Nusa Lembongan they leave every morning from nr the *Bali Beach Hotel* (Sanur Beach) and dock at Jungut Batu. The public boats leave very early from 0500 depending on the tide. It is a 10-min walk from the accommodation N of Jungut Batu to the spot on the beach where the boats come in; no jetty, you wade over to the boat. There are also early morning boats between Nusa Penida and Nusa Lembongan. The best way to get to Nusa Lembongan is with *Perama* who have 2 boats a day from Sanur. Schedules change so check for up-to-date times. Currently boats leave Sanur at 1030 and 1615, and leave Nusa Lembongan at 0900 and 1500. In the off season there may only be 1 boat a day. Crossing takes 1½ hrs, 17,500Rp. *Perama's* shuttle bus service from the popular tourist destinations on Bali, links up with the boats – pick up a copy of their timetable for full details. See page 341 for further information.

THE BUKIT PENINSULA AND NUSA DUA

The Bukit Peninsula extends to the S of Kuta, with just a narrow isthmus connecting it to the mainland. On the W side of the isthmus is Jimbaran Beach, and on the E side, Benoa. The purpose-built resort area of Nusa Dua, created from a barren landscape into a landscaped park of large, international-style hotels lies on the E side, to the S of Benoa. The Bukit Peninsula is a barren, arid, limestone tableland – the Dutch called it Tafelhoek – which rises to 200m. There is a big contrast between the barren landscape here and the lushness of the rest of the S of the island. The soils are sandy and infertile, rainfall is less abundant and highly seasonal, and it was considered such an unpleasant place to live that criminals were once banished here.

In 1969 the Indonesian government commissioned a French consultancy firm to draw up a report on the future development of Bali. The resulting report became the master plan for the island's tourist industry. The plan envisaged that tourist development would be confined to designated resort areas, thus preventing tourists from intruding too much on daily life. Central to this strategy was the creation of **Nusa Dua**: an extraordinary area of large 4- and 5-star hotels and immaculately kept gardens on the E coast of the Bukit Peninsula. Deep bore holes were sunk to provide ample supplies of fresh water, the area was landscaped and replanted, and a highway was built from the airport – the most expensive road ever to have been built on Bali. Although there can be little doubt that the development has isolated the tourists from the locals – a good thing some might maintain – it has also meant that only larger hotels and businesses have benefitted from the tourist dollars. The only way that a Balinese businessman of limited means can set-up in the 'amenity core' of Nusa Dua is by hiring a stall from the Tourist Authority. Even the bulk of the food is imported.

The only 'sight' on the Bukit Peninsula is the **Uluwatu Temple** (see page 367), magnificently positioned on a cliff top overlooking the sea at the SW extremity of the peninsula. Much of the W coast has remained relatively undeveloped because of the steep cliffs. But the excellent surf for which this area is renowned draws large numbers of surfers to the W coast. At the neck of the peninsula is the sandy **Jimbaran Bay**, which is set to become the next target for tourist development.

JIMBARAN

15 mins' drive S of Kuta is the sandy beach of Jimbaran Bay. Although it is sandwiched between the airport and Nusa Dua, the bay was passed by until recently and represented a small enclave of peace surrounded by a activity. But over the last few years developers have moved in, and it may not be long before it is transformed into another bustling resort. Three hotels have already been built and more are planned. At the end of the road down to the bay, on the W road to Uluwatu, is an attractive temple, the **Ulun Siwi Temple**, dating from the 17th century.

● **Accommodation L** *Four Seasons Resort*, T 701010, F 701020, built in 1992 to a design incorporating the best of Balinese pavilion design, voted as one of 'the 10 Healthiest Hotels in the World' by Tatler Travel Guide (UK 1996) and 'No 1 Resort in the World' by Conde Nast Traveler (USA 1996), this is a resort that is hard to beat – the only problem is to summon the will to leave it and see the rest of the island, around 150 beautiful villas, each surrounded by a stone wall, are set on the slope above Jimbaran bay, entered by a traditional courtyard gate, the walled enclosure contains 3 pavilions: 1 free-standing pavilion – an open-air living/dining area, and 2 joined pavilions which contain the sleeping area and a luxurious bathroom with an outdoor shower area and an oversized Victorian bath tub which stands on a solid marble plinth, the sleeping area has a/c and fan, satellite TV and in-house movies, VCR and CD sound system, each villa also has its own plunge-pool and sun-deck, the resort facilities feature beautifully landscaped gardens, 2 pools, outdoor jacuzzi, supergrass tennis courts, spa with sauna, library/lounge, and 2 first-class restaurants incl *PJ's* – a beachside place serving Mediterranean food, specializing in exotic pizza cooked in wood-burning oven; **L-A+** *Bali Inter Continental Resort*, Jl Uluwatu 45, T 701888, F 701777, brand-new neighbour to the *Four Seasons*, total luxury and grandiose style, all the facilities you would expect of a 5-star resort, set in landscaped gardens, overlooking 500m of white sand beach, 3 pools, 3 outdoor jacuzzis, sports centre, spa, 5 restaurants incl a first-class

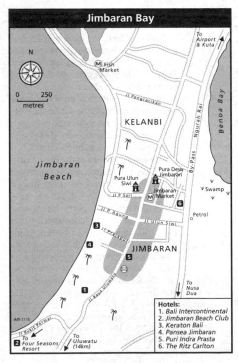

Jimbaran Bay

N

0   250
metres

To Airport & Kuta

Ⓜ Fish Market

Jl Penarcakian

KELANBI

Pura Ulun Siwi

Jl P Sari

Pura Desa Jimbaran

Ⓜ Jimbaran Market

Jl P Aayng

Jl Ulun Siwi

Jimbaran Beach

JIMBARAN

Jl Pratapun

Jl Raya Uluwatu

Ⓟ Petrol

∨ Swamp ∨

To Nusa Dua

Ⓜ IAIS 111b

Ⓑ *To Four Seasons Resort*   *To Uluwatu (14km)*   *Jl Bukit Permal*

By-Pass   *Jl Ngurah Rai*   *Benoa Bay*

Hotels:
1. Bali Intercontinental
2. Jimbaran Beach Club
3. Keraton Bali
4. Pansea Jimbaran
5. Puri Indra Prasta
6. The Ritz Carlton

Japanese teppanyaki bar; **L-A** *Mimpi Jimbaran*, T 701070, F 701074, a small, exclusive development of 14 studios, 4 apartments and 3 villas designed and managed to very high standards, the apartments and villas have kitchens, on a hillside overlooking Jimbaran Bay, with beautiful gardens, restaurant and poolside bar, the villas have their own private pools, monthly rates available, tennis, conference facilities, 15 mins from airport, rec; **A+** *Pansea Jimbaran*, T (20) 752605, F 752220, a/c, restaurants, big pool, first class facilities, price is all inclusive (incl watersport); **A** *Keraton Bali Cottages*, T 753991, F 753881, very attractive traditional Balinese-style bungalows with lovely gardens; **B** *Jimbaran Beach Club*, T (20) 80361; **C** *Puri Indra Prasta*, Jl Uluwatu 28A, restaurant, pool, prices incl breakfast.

● **Transport Road Bemo**: connections with Denpasar's Tegal terminal. **Car hire**: several of the larger car hire companies are in Jimbaran on the Jl By Pass Nusa Dua. **Golden Bird Bali**, Jl Raya By Pass Nusa Dua 4, T 701111, F 701628 offer a range of transport services from car rental (Suzuki jeep, Toyota Kijang) to chauffeur driven cars (Volvo). They are one of the largest car rental companies on the island so they offer good break-down service, insurance etc. *Golden Bird* also manage the blue taxis on the island – amongst the few taxis you will find with meters, rec. **Toyota Rent a Car**, Jl By Pass Nusa Dua, T 701747, F 701741, specialize in Toyota vehicles, namely Kijang, Starlet and Corollas.

BENOA

Benoa consists of a small fishing village called Tanjung Benoa, at the tip of a finger of land extending N from Nusa Dua. Close by is the utilitarian Benoa port, built by the Dutch in 1906 and the main port of call for cruise ships and yachts – this is the place to come for anyone hoping to sign on as crew. The area around Benoa, particularly between Tanjung Benoa and Nusa Dua, is becoming increasingly popular for tourists who want to escape from the excesses of Kuta and Sanur. Benoa has gained a reputation for the quality of its watersports, including diving.

Tours

Tour Devco (T 231592) organize trips on a tall ship to Nusa Lembongan; price incl lunch and watersports equipment. *The Bali International Yacht Club*, T 288391, also organizes yacht and fishing trips to the islands; *Bali Hai Cruises* and *Wakalouka Cruises* specialize in trips to Lembongan Island from Benoa Port (see page 363).

● **Accommodation A** *Puri Tanjung*, T 772121, F 772424; **A+** *Bali Royal*, T 771039, a/c, intimate exclusive suites and an attractive garden; **A+** *Grand Mirage*, T 772147, F 772148, a/c, restaurant, pools, new, big and brash; **A** *Mirage*, PO Box 43, T 772147, F 772148, a/c, restaurant, pool; **A** *Sorga Nusa Dua*, T 771604, F 771143, a/c, restaurant, pool, northernmost accommodation on Benoa peninsular, nice gardens, tennis courts; **B** *Bali Resort Palace*, Jl Pratama, Tanjung Benoa, T 772026, F 772237, to the N of Nusa Dua, a/c, restaurant, pool; **B** *Chez Agung*; **B** *Puri Joma Bungalows*, T 771526, pool, good value; **C-D** *Rasa Sayang*, T 771643, some a/c; **D** *Hasam Homestay*, perfectly adequate clean rooms.

● **Places to eat** There are several on the beachfront opp the hotels, rather overpriced.

● **Transport Road Bemo**: connections with Denpasar's Suci terminal. **Sea Boat**: the *Mabua Express* leaves Benoa twice a day for Lembar (Lombok). Travelling time is 2½ hrs and costs US$13.50-US$27.50, T 261212 for details.

ULUWATU TEMPLE

Pura Uluwatu, also known as Pura Ulu Atu, is considered – despite its small size – one of Bali's *sadkahyangan* – the six most important temples on the island. Entry by donation. Keep clear of the monkeys on the steps up to the entrance. Its full name, *Pura Luhur Uluwatu* literally means 'high headland', an apt name as the temple is spectacularly situated on the S tip of the Bukit Peninsula, perched on a cliff 70m above the sea. The area used to be closed to visitors, and was jealously guarded by The Prince of Badung. The pura's inhospitable location also kept the curious away. Today it is easily accessible.

Pura Uluwatu may have been constructed during the 11th century, although it was substantially rebuilt in the 16th century – and as a result is rather difficult to date. The temple was owned by the Prince of Badung (today's Denpasar) and he alone was allowed to visit

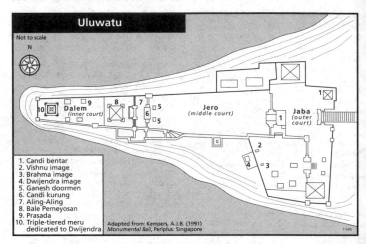

Uluwatu

Not to scale

N

Dalem *(inner court)*

Jero *(middle court)*

Jaba *(outer court)*

1. Candi bentar
2. Vishnu image
3. Brahma image
4. Dwijendra image
5. Ganesh doormen
6. Candi kurung
7. Aling-Aling
8. Bale Pemeyosan
9. Prasada
10. Triple-tiered meru
    dedicated to Dwijendra

Adapted from: Kempers, A.J.B. (1991)
Monumental Bali, Periplus: Singapore

it. Once a year the Prince travelled to Uluwatu to make his offerings, a journey that he made until his death at the hands of the Dutch in 1906 (see page 317). It is said that part of the temple fell into the sea 18 months before the massacre at Denpasar – an event which was therefore prophesied.

Uluwatu has several unusual features; it is built of hard grey coral, which means that the temple's decoration has survived the centuries of weathering remarkably well. Secondly, the *candi bentar* or split gate is shaped in the form of a stylized *garuda* (mythical bird) rather than with smooth sides, as is usual. Also unusually, two statues of Ganesh flank the inner gateway. It was at Uluwatu that the famous Hindu saint, Danghyang Nirartha, is reputed to have achieved *moksa*, or oneness with the godhead.

Entry By donation. Keep clear of the monkeys on the steps up to the entrance.

There are several good **surfing beaches** near Uluwatu, including Bingin, Nyang Nyang (on the S coast) and Padang Padang (just S of Jimbaran Bay) (see page 343). Most involve a walk of up to 2 km down stoney tracks.

● **Accommodation A+** *Bali Cliff Resort*, Jl Pura Batu Pageh, Ungasan, T 771992, F 771993, on cliff to S of Uluwatu, a/c, restaurant, 2 large pools, large hotel perched on a cliff overlooking the Indian Ocean, rather isolated and sterile but all facilities; **D** *Gobleg Inn*, off the track to the beach.

● **Transport** 20 km from Kuta. **Road Minibus**: minibuses (C1) leave from Kuta for Uluwatu; connections with Denpasar's Tegal terminal.

NUSA DUA

Nusa Dua is a 'planned resort', developed with assistance from the World Bank and funds from private developers. The first hotels opened here in 1983. The barren landscape of the Bukit Peninsula has been transformed into a tropical haven: 5-star hotels, beautiful gardens, tennis courts, horse riding and a golf course. The intention was to build a resort which would be isolated from the 'real' Bali and, in so doing, protect the locals from the excesses of international tourism. To make way for the resort, the few farmers who scratched a living from the reluctant soil were unceremoniously turfed out and an enclave created.

The entrance to the resort area is through huge split gates, and the hotels

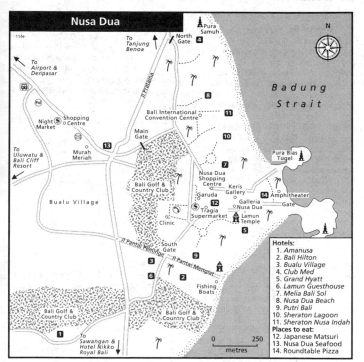

Nusa Dua

To Tanjung Benoa

To Airport & Denpasar

North Gate

Pura Samuh

Badung Strait

Bali International Convention Centre

Night Market

Shopping Centre

Main Gate

Murah Meriah

To Uluwatu & Bali Cliff Resort

Pura Bias Tugel

Nusa Dua Shopping Centre

Keris Gallery

Amphitheater

Bali Golf & Country Club

Garuda

Galleria Nusa Dua

Gate

Bualu Village

Clinic

Tragia Supermarket

Lamun Temple

Il Pantai Pemingge

South Gate

Il Pantai Mengiat

Fishing Boats

Bali Golf & Country Club

Bali Golf & Country Club

To Sawangan & Hotel Nikko Royal Bali

Hotels:
1. Amanusa
2. Bali Hilton
3. Bualu Village
4. Club Med
5. Grand Hyatt
6. Lamun Guesthouse
7. Melia Bali Sol
8. Nusa Dua Beach
9. Putri Bali
10. Sheraton Lagoon
11. Sheraton Nusa Indah
Places to eat:
12. Japanese Matsuri
13. Nusa Dua Seafood
14. Roundtable Pizza

0   250
metres

have been designed in keeping with Balinese traditions (rather loosely interpreted). There are no ugly high-rise blocks here, although the sheer scale of the development can be rather forbidding. Within the resort precinct, reached by roads running through the manicured lawns of the development, are travel agencies, airline offices, banks, a post office, restaurants, art shops, a supermarket, performing arts shows – in short, everything that a western tourist could want. Or at least that is what the consultants thought. What Nusa Dua does not provide is any insight, indeed any sense, of what life in Bali is like. Tourists are sheltered and pampered, but if you wish for more, it is necessary to venture beyond the Bukit Peninsula to Bali proper. On the beach, the surf is gentle along the N shore, but bigger to the S.

Local information
● Accommodation

The hotels below provide a wide variety of sports facilities – waterskiing, windsurfing, scuba diving, fishing, parasailing, horse riding, tennis.

L *Amanusa*, PO Box 33, T 772333, F 772335, latest in the luxurious Aman group, set high above the Badung Straits, away from the concrete of Nusa Dua, with sea views only marred by the towers of the *Hilton*, 'epic' architecture, cathedral-like lobby perfumed by giant vases of tuber rose, accommodation in 35 Balinese style bungalows, 2 dozen roses to welcome guests, a/c, 4-poster bed, CD, satellite TV, minibar, sofa set into bay window, spacious dressing room, marble bathroom with sunken bath overlooking lotus pond, outdoor shower, sunpatio with canopied day bed, some suites with private pools, resort facilities incl the largest swimming pool on Bali, state-of-the-art Italian restaurant, local cuisine at terrace restaurant, complimentary afternoon tea served in terrace bar, library, tennis, mountain bikes, buggy service to beach or golf course, rec.

A+ *Bali Tropic*, PO Box 41, T 772130, F 772131, a/c restaurant, large pool, located at the northern end of the Nusa Dua strip of hotels, on the Benoa peninsula, rooms are in ornate bungalows set within expansive gardens; **A+** *Grand Hyatt*, PO Box 53, T 771188, F 771084, a/c, restaurant, 5 pools, opened Apr 1991, large and very plush, with extensive and elaborate grounds; **A+** *Hotel Nikko Royal Bali*, Jl Raya Nusa Dua Seletan, Nusa Dua Selatan, T 773377, F 773388, a/c, restaurants, pools, tennis, watersports, well designed rooms, highly priced, newest addition to Nusa Dua; **A+** *Melia Bali Sol*, PO Box 1048, T 771510, F 771360, a/c, several restaurants (rec.), large pool, owned by a Spanish chain of hotels, a fact reflected in the design which is rather Mediterranean, good sports facilities; **A+** *Nusa Indah*, PO Box 36, T 771567, F 771908, a/c, 4 restaurants, pool, a recent addition to the Nusa Dua scene, consisting of a large 'U'-shaped block overlooking the beach, huge convention centre attached, gardens in formative stages, rather too large to be in any sense personal; **A+** *Putri Bali*, PO Box 1, T 771020, F 771139, a/c, restaurant, pool, set in attractive landscaped grounds, all facilities, and some cottage-style accommodation; **A+** *Sheraton Lagoon*, PO Box 2044, T 771327, F 771326, attractive development with a pool that competes in size with that of Amanusa; **A+-L** *Nusa Dua Beach*, PO Box 1028, T 771210, F 771229, a/c, 4 restaurants, pool, now owned by the Sultan of Brunei, it recently underwent a US$20mn+ refurbishment, the lavish entrance is through split gates into an echoing lobby with fountains, lush gardens and painstakingly recreated traditional Balinese buildings, good sports facilities, including a new spa centre the new 'palace' extension is for the truly well-healed.

A *Club Med*, PO Box 7, T 771520, F 771831, a/c, 2 restaurants, pool, excellent sports facilities and cultural activities, and also caters well for children.

B *Hotel Bualu Village*, PO Box 6, T 771310, F 771313, a/c, restaurant, pool, away from the beach, but the most peaceful of the hotels in the area.

C *Lamun Guesthouse*, T 771983, F 771985, a/c, nothing to write home about, but the cheapest here.

● **Places to eat**

All the hotels have a range of restaurants serving Indonesian, Balinese, other Asian cuisines and International food. The *Amanusa* has a first class Italian restaurant as well as local cuisine served in their terrace restaurant. Quality is generally good but prices are far higher than anywhere else in Bali – presumably because the management feel they have a captive clientele. *Nusa Dua Shopping Complex* houses some pricey restaurants. There are a few stalls in Buala.

● **Bars**

Players Bar, *Nusa Dua Beach Hotel*, happy hours 1900-2100, games room; *Lila Cita*, *Grand Hyatt*, open 1800-0200, happy hours 1800-2000, good cocktails.

● **Entertainment**

Discos: *Cool Bar*, *Grand Mirage Hotel*, open 2100-2400.

● **Places of worship**

Interdenominational church service at the *Nusa Dua Beach Hotel*, Sun 1730.
Catholic Mass: Bali Sol, Sun 1800.

● **Shopping**

The *Galleria Nusa Dua Shopping Complex* is the largest shopping complex on Bali and has smart clothing boutiques, jewellers, a duty-free store and supermarket. Handicrafts are sold at the *Keris Gallery*. As can be expected, prices are higher than elsewhere on the island, but the quality is good. The complex also boasts the best sports and golf shop in Bali – golf sets available for rent (US$20).

● **Sports**

Diving: *Bali Marine Sports*, Club Bualu, T 771310; *Barrakuda Bali Dive*, Bali Tropik Palace Hotel, T 772130, F 772131; *Baruna Watersports* at the *Melia Bali Sol*, T 771350, *Nusa Dua Beach*, T 771210, *Mirage*, T 772147 and *Nusa Indah*, T 771566.

Golf: 18-hole *Bali Golf and Country Club* (opened 1991, designed by Nelson and Wright), green fee US$65, club hire US$20, cart US$24, T 771791, F 771797.

● **Transport**

27 km from Denpasar, 9 km from airport.

Local Car hire: Avis, *Nusa Dua Beach Hotel*, T 771220 ext 739, and *Club Med*, T 771521. **Taxi**: taxis and hotel cars will take guests into Kuta and elsewhere; prices are high.

Road Bemo: from Jl Pantai in Kuta to Nusa Dua; and regular connections from Denpasar's Tegal terminal.

NORTH FROM DENPASAR TO UBUD

Northeast from Denpasar, the busy road passes through a series of craft villages specializing in the production of wood and stone carvings, and gold and silver jewellery. After 22 km climbing steadily through picturesque paddy fields and past steep-sided ravines, the road arrives at the hill resort and artists' colony of Ubud.

CRAFT VILLAGES ON THE ROAD FROM DENPASAR TO UBUD

A number of craft villages, each specializing in a different craft, line the main road N from Denpasar to Ubud. The concentration of workshops here is extraodinary – much of the products are exported around the world. Most have been centres of production for many years – Miguel Covarrubias in his book *Island of Bali* notes that they had a reputation for the quality of their work in the 1930s. Since then the demands of the tourist industry have caused the mass production of second-rate pieces to become common. Nonetheless there are still some fine works to be found.

Batubulan, 8 km from Denpasar, is a ribbon-like village, stretched out for about 2 km along the road. It is renowned for its stone carving, although the production of carved wooden Balinese screens and doors is very much in evidence. In addition, there is a sizeable pottery industry here. Barong, kecak (fire dance) and kris dances are performed every day (times vary, 0900-1030, 1800-1930) at the N end of the village. One of Bali's principal performing arts academies – KOKAR/SMKI – is based in Batubulan. Just outside Batubulan is the **Taman Burung Bali Bird Park**, open from 0900-1800, T 299352. **Celuk**, 4 km on from Batubulan and 12 km from Denpasar, supports large numbers of gold and silversmiths who sell their jewellery from countless shops and showrooms along the road. Much of the work is inferior, although there are some shops selling slightly better quality jewellery; for example, *Runa*, *Dede's*, Jl Grianyar 18 and *Banjar Telabah*. It is worth bargaining in these shops. Another 4 km N from Celuk is another woodcarving village, **Batuan**. A range of products are on sale although the artists have a particular reputation for the quality of their carved wood panels. Finally, **Mas**, 20 km from Denpasar and 2 km S of Ubud, is a woodcarving village. In the mid-1980s this was the centre of woodcarving in Bali; now the industry is far more dispersed. Nevertheless, some of the finest (unpainted) works are still produced here and it is possible to watch the artists at work. Although there are numerous wood carvers based here, the workshop of *Ida Bagus Tilem* – the *Tilem Gallery* – (T 975099) is recommended. His pieces are expensive, but Tilem's father was an accomplished artist, and his son's work is also highly regarded.

Kemenuh village, about 9 km SE of Ubud, is an important wood carving centre offering a range of pieces including huge mythical beasts, fine art and the usual Balinese objects at more competitive prices than Mas. **Accommodation B** *Sua Bali Lodge*, T/F 32141, Kemenuh village, 6 cottages in large grounds with private facilities, run by Ida Ayu Agung Mas, who has studied in Germany and now teaches at Udayana University, Bali. Her aim is to create the natural atmosphere of Bali in her lodge. The lodge offers language tuition in both Balinese and Indonesian and a unique opportunity to learn about the customs and culture of Bali. The founder set up the lodge with the aim of preserving the local environment and culture. To this end 70% of supplies come from the local village and funds have been given to the village for development and social projects. The lodge recently won first prize in a competition organized by the German Government to reward tourist enterprises worldwide that were social and environmentally responsible.

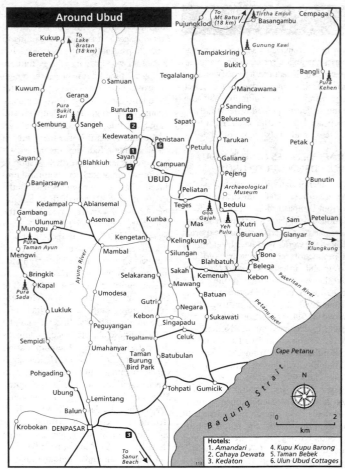

Around Ubud

Hotels:
1. *Amandari*
2. *Cahaya Dewata*
3. *Kedaton*
4. *Kupu Kupu Barong*
5. *Taman Bebek*
6. *Ulun Ubud Cottages*

UBUD

Ubud was one of the more powerful of the principalities that controlled Bali before the Dutch extended their control over the whole island at the beginning of this century. Though primarily an upland rice-growing area it also gained an early reputation for the skill of its artists, particularly for the intricacy of their work. Perhaps it was the latent artistic temperament of the people of Ubud, coupled no doubt with the beauty of the place, that caused many of the entranced western artists to base themselves here. The painter Walter Spies was invited to Bali by the Prince of Ubud, Raka Sukawati, and was so entranced with the place that he settled here – becoming the first of a series of bohemian westerners to make Ubud their home (see page 321). These residents, in turn, attracted such luminaries as Charlie Chaplin, Noel Coward, the

Woolworth heiress Barbara Hutton, and the American anthropologist Margaret Mead. In 1936, Spies, Bonnet (another artist) and the Prince established *Pita Maha*, the first artists' cooperative on the island. Since then Ubud has remained a centre of the arts in Bali, particularly painting, and many of the finest Balinese artists are based here or in the surrounding villages. Because of the influence of Spies, Bonnet and the artists' cooperative, there is a distinct style to much of the work. Paintings tend to be colourful and finely-worked depictions of the natural world.

Ubud is a rather dispersed community, spread over hills and valleys with deep forested ravines and terraced rice fields. A spring near Ubud is the source of *AQUA*, the most popular of Indonesia's bottled waters. For many tourists, Ubud has become the cultural heart of Bali, with its numerous artist's studios and galleries as well as a plentiful supply of shops selling clothes, jewellery and woodcarving. Old-timers feel that the numbers of people staying here has irrevocably changed the town; glitzy bars and restaurants draped in neon are fast spoiling the traditional atmosphere of this once pleasant upland area. However, once away from the two main roads, it is still a relatively quiet place to retreat to. In addition, the villages around Ubud remain unspoilt and it is well worth exploring the surrounding countryside, either on foot or by bicycle. Around Ubud, particularly to the N in the vicinity of Tampaksiring, and to the E near Pejeng and Gianyar, is perhaps the greatest concentration of temples in Bali. The most detailed and accurate guide to these pura is AJ Bernet Kempers's *Monumental Bali* (Periplus: Berkeley and Singapore, 1991).

During the rainy season Ubud gets much more rain than the coastal resorts and can be very wet and much cooler.

Places of interest

Much of the charm and beauty of Ubud lies in the natural landscape. There are few official 'sights' in the town itself – in contrast to the surrounding area (see Excursions). The **Museum Puri Lukisan** is in the centre of Ubud and has been recently renovated. Two of the buildings here contain examples of 20th century Balinese painting and carving (and that of Europeans who have lived here). The third building, to the back of the compound, has a changing exhibition, organized by an artists' cooperative. 50 artists exhibit one or two pieces each; it is a showcase for their work. All work is for sale, but visitors are advised just to look at work here and then to visit the artist's studio, where they will be offered a wider range of work, at discounted prices. Admission 500Rp. Open 0800-1600.

Antonio Blanco, a western artist who settled in Ubud has turned his home into a gallery. The house is in a stunning position, perched on the side of a hill, but the collection is disappointing and includes an array of his 'erotic art', where the frames are more interesting than the actual pictures. Blanco – unlike Spies and Bonnet – has had no influence on the style of local artists. Most people visit his house to meet the man, rather than to see his work. He is an eccentric character who is interesting to talk about Balinese life. He may try to interest you in his recently published autobiography. Admission 500Rp. To get there, walk W on the main road and over a ravine past *Murnis Warung* – the house is immediately on the left-hand side of the road at the end of the old suspension bridge.

The **Museum Neka**, $1\frac{1}{2}$ km from town, up the hill past Blanco's house, six Balinese-style buildings contain a good collection of traditional and contemporary Balinese and Javanese painting as well as work by foreign artists who have lived in or visited Bali. Admission 1,000Rp. Open 0900-1700, Mon-Sun. There is a good art bookshop here and a good restaurant with views over the ravine.

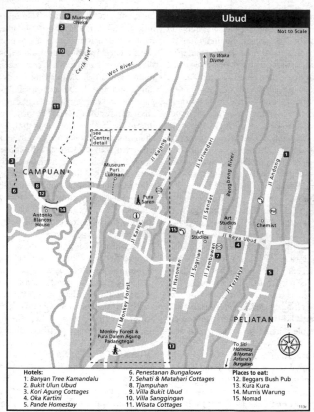

Ubud

Not to Scale

Hotels:
1. Banyan Tree Kamandalu
2. Bukit Ulun Ubud
3. Kori Agung Cottages
4. Oka Kartini
5. Pande Homestay
6. Penestanan Bungalows
7. Sehati & Matahari Cottages
8. Tjampuhan
9. Villa Bukit Ubud
10. Villa Sanggingan
11. Wisata Cottages

Places to eat:
12. Beggars Bush Pub
13. Kura Kura
14. Murnis Warung
15. Nomad

At the S end of Jl Monkey Forest is the forest itself, which is overrun with monkeys. An attractive walk through the forest leads to the **Pura Dalem Agung Padangtegal**, a Temple of the Dead. Admission to forest 500Rp. **NB** Do NOT enter the forest with food – these monkeys have been known to bite and victims will only have 48 hrs to get to Jakarta for a rabies injection. Some tourists have also taken to teasing the animals; it is cruel and dangerous. Back in town on Jl Raya Ubud, opposite Jl Monkey Forest, is the **Puri Saren**, with richly carved gateways and courtyards. West of here behind the Lotus Café is the **Pura Saraswati**, with a pretty rectangular pond in front of it.

Excursions

Sangeh and the **Pura Bukit Sari** are two temples about 25 km W of Ubud, but easier to reach via Mengwi (see page 413).

Craft villages line the route to Batubulan and Denpasar (see page 371).

Goa Gajah or 'Elephant Cave', lies about 4 km E of Ubud, via Peliatan, on the right-hand side of the road and just before Bedulu. The caves are hard to miss as there is a large car park, with an imposing line of stallholders catering for the numerous coach trips. The complex is on the side of a hill overlooking the Petanu River, down a flight of steps.

Hewn out of the rock, the entrance to the **cave** has been carved to resemble the mouth of a demon and is surrounded by additional carvings of animals, plants, rocks and monsters. The name of the complex is thought to have been given by the first visitors who mistakenly thought that the demon was an elephant. The small, dimly lit, 'T'-shaped cave is man-made. It is reached by a narrow passage whose entrance is the demon's mouth. It contains 15 niches carved out of the rock. Those on the main passageway are long enough to lead archaeologists to speculate that they were sleeping chambers. At the end of one of the arms of the 'T' is a 4-armed statue of Ganesh, and at the end of the other, a collection of lingams.

The **bathing pools** next to the caves are more interesting. These were only discovered in the mid-1950s by the Dutch

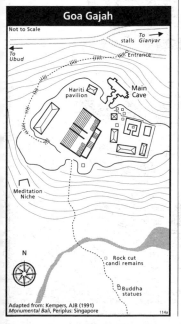

Goa Gajah

Not to Scale

To Ubud

To stalls
To Gianyar

Entrance

Hariti pavilion

Main Cave

Meditation Niche

N

Rock cut candi remains

Buddha statues

Adapted from: Kempers, AJB (1991)
Monumental Bali, Periplus: Singapore
114a

archaeologist JC Krijgsman, who excavated the area in front of the cave on information provided by local people. He discovered stone steps and eventually uncovered two bathing pools (probably one for men and the other for women). Stone carvings of the legs of three figures were uncovered in each of the two pools. These seemed to have been cut from the rock at the same time that the pools were dug. It was realized that the heads and torsos of three buxom nymphs which had been placed in front of the cave entrance belonged with the legs, and the two halves were happily re-united. Water spouts from the urns held by the nymphs, into the two pools.

Stairs lead down from the cave and pool area to some meditation niches, with two small statues of the Buddha in an attitude of meditation. The remains of an enormous relief were also found in 1931 (by Conrad Spies, the painter and Walter Spies's cousin), depicting several stupas. To get there, walk down from the cave and bathing pools, through fields, and over a bridge. The complex is thought to date from the 11th century. Admission 1,050Rp (500Rp extra for camera), children 300Rp. Dress – sarong. *Getting there*: a short ride by bemo from Ubud or from the Batubulan terminal outside Denpasar; alternatively, join a tour.

Yeh Pulu is 2 km E of Goa Gajah, beautifully set amongst terraced rice fields, and a short walk along a paved path from the end of the road. This is a peaceful place, free from crowds and hawkers. It also happens to be the location of the local bath house and laundrette, which has resulted in a profusion of plastic 'Rinso' bags littering the stream. Yeh Pulu is one of the oldest holy places in Bali, dating from the 14th or 15th century. Cut into the rock are 20m of vigorous carvings depicting village life intermingled with Hindu and Balinese gods: figures carrying poles, men on horseback, Krishna saluting, wild animals and vegetation. Originally these would have been plastered over – and perhaps painted – although almost all of the plaster has since weathered away. A small cell cut into the rock at the S end of the reliefs is thought to have been the abode of a hermit – who probably helped to maintain the carvings. The site was 'discovered' by the artist Nieuwenkamp in 1925 when he was sketching nearby. Until 1937 when the site was renovated, water from the overhanging paddy fields

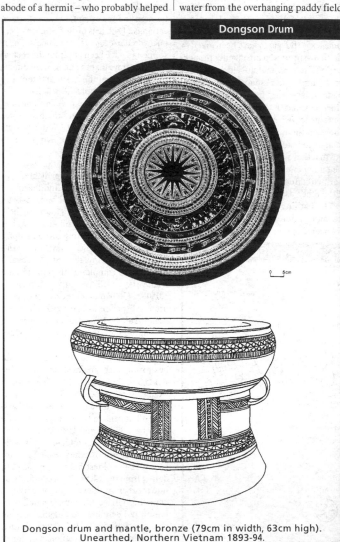

Dongson Drum

0   5cm

Dongson drum and mantle, bronze (79cm in width, 63cm high).
Unearthed, Northern Vietnam 1893-94.

302

Bronze kettledrums of Vietnam

One of the most remarkable and intriguing of metal objects found in Southeast Asia is the bronze kettledrum. These were first produced in Northern Vietnam and Southern China in the 4th century BC and were associated with the Dongson culture. However, they have also been discovered widely distributed across island Southeast Asia – as far E as the island of Alor in Nusa Tenggara and Irian Jaya. In total, around 30 kettledrums have been found in Indonesia. Some of the examples were probably traded from Vietnam; others may have been made in situ. Whatever the case, they are skilfully produced using the lost wax process, wonderfully decorated, and were clearly objects of considerable value and prestige.

Strictly-speaking they are not drums at all but percussion instruments, as they have no membrane. In Indonesia they are known as *nekara*. They consist of a hollow body, open at the bottom, and covered at the top with a metal tympan. In size, they range from 0.4-1.3m in diameter, and 0.4-1.0m in height. The top is often highly decorated with birds, houses, canoes carrying the dead to the afterlife, dancers and drummers. A question which has never been satisfactorily answered is what they were used for. The fact that they are often surmounted by three-dimensional figures of frogs has led some authorities to postulate that they were used to summon rain. Hence their other name: rain drums. Helmet Loofs-Wissowa believes that they were royal regalia – used by chiefs as an indicator of rank and status. Recently a drum was unearthed in East Java with the crouched skeleton of a child inside leading some to suggest that this was a royal burial and the drum was included as an indicator of rank. There is a fine collection of drums in the National Museum, Jakarta (see page 116).

washed over the carvings causing significant erosion. There is also a small bathing pool here. An old lady looks after the small shrine to Ganesh and ensures a donation is placed there.

Bernet Kempers, in his book *Monumental Bali*, interprets the sequence of carvings as follows, beginning at the top. There is an opening piece, followed by five 'scenes':

Opening: a standing man with his arm raised opens the yarn. This is probably Krishna, who as a young shepherd protected his friends from an irate Indra by using Mt Govardhana as an umbrella.

Scene I: a man carries two vessels (probably of palm wine) on a pole over his shoulders and is led by a woman of high status towards a hut where an old woman waits at a pair of double doors.

Scene II: here, an old woman rests in a cave while a man, to her left, approaches with a hoe over his shoulder. Behind him sits an ascetic dwarf with a turban. On the far right is a demon with fangs and a large sacrificial ladel.

Scene III: surrounded by trees, a man on a horse gallops towards two figures, with weapons raised, who are attacking a bear (?) while a fourth man advances from behind. In the lower right corner a frog with a sword fights for his life against a large snake.

Scene IV: two men, their hunting trip completed and successful, carry a pair of dead bears on a pole.

Scene V: a woman holds a horse's tail while two monkeys play on her back. She is either trying to restrain the horse and rider, or they are helping to pull her up a hill.

Admission 550Rp. Dress – sarong and sash (for hire at site). Open – it is probably possible to visit this site at any time, as there are no 'entrance gates'. At the beginning of the path there is a restaurant, and close by is the **E** *Lantur Homestay*.

Getting there: Yeh Pulu is 350m off the main Ubud-Gianyar road just S of the Tampaksiring turning, and is signposted to Bendung Bedaulu. Bemos from Ubud will drop passengers at the turning; it is an easy walk from there to the site.

The road north from Bedulu

400m N of Bedulu, is the small, poorly labelled, **Purbakala Archaeological Museum**, consisting largely of a collection of sarcophagi, neolithic tools and Hindu relics. About 200m further N still is the **Pura Kebo Edan** or 'Mad Bull Temple', a rather ramshackle and ill-kept temple. Among the monumental weathered stone figures in the courtyard is a 0m-high statue of Bima dancing on a corpse, its eyes open, protected under a wooden pavilion. The figure – sometimes known as the 'Pejeng Giant' – is renowned for its 'miraculous' penis, pierced with a peg or pin (used to stimulate women during intercourse, a feature of sexual relations across the region; see page 555). Snakes curl around the figure's wrists and ankles, and his face is covered by a mask, attached with ribbons around the back of the head. Although the figure was thought to be an image of Bima – and it is in all likelihood demonic – it is

probably more accurately interpreted as an incarnation of Siva. Admission by donation. Dress: sarong. **Pura Pusering Jagat** (the 'Navel of the World' Temple), is 50m off the main road, a short distance N from Kebo Edan. **Pura Panataran Sasih** lies another 250m N in Pejeng and is thought to date from the 9th or 10th century. This temple was the original navel pura of the old Pejeng Kingdom. The entrance is flanked by a pair of fine stone elephants. Walk through impressive split gates to see the **'Moon of Pejeng'** (*sasih* means 'moon'). It is housed in a raised pavilion towards the back of the compound and is supposedly the largest bronze kettledrum in the world (see box). In Balinese folklore, the drum is supposed to have been one of the wheels of the chariot that carries the moon across the night sky. The wheel fell to earth and was kept (still glowing with an inner fire) in the temple. It is said that one night a man climbed into the tower and urinated on the drum, extinguishing its inner fire, and paid for the desecration with his life. Visitors should on no account try to climb the tower for a better look at the drum. The drum is believed to date from the 3rd century BC, although no-one is absolutely sure – certainly, it has been housed here for centuries though. It may be a Dongson drum from Vietnam or it may be a later example produced elsewhere. The fine decoration on this incomparable piece of bronze work was first recorded – in a series of brilliantly accurate drawings – by the artist WOJ Nieuwenkamp in 1906 (although it was mentioned in a book by the blind chronicler GE Rumphius published in 1705). A collection of 11th century stone carvings are also to be found here. Admission by donation. Dress – sarong. *Getting there*: by bemo from Ubud or from the Batubulan terminal outside Denpasar.

Tours

Bird watching: walks around Ubud with *Bali Bird Walks* (possible sightings include Java Kingfisher, Bar-winged Prinia,

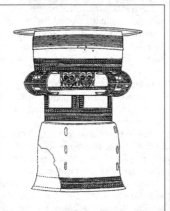

The Moon of Pejeng
After Nieuwenkamp's original drawing

Black-winged Starling, Java Sparrow, Scarlet-headed Flowerpecker), T 975009, based at the Beggar's Bush pub, Tjampuhan, Ubud, US$28, including lunch and shared use of binoculars.

Day tours around the island: 10,000-30,000Rp.

Mountain biking: downhill all the way back from Mt Batur (90,000Rp) and Jungle Mountain trekking (85,000Rp) both with *Sobek Expeditions* (see below).

Whitewater rafting: down the Ayung River with *Sobek Expeditions* (T 287059, F 289448) US$57, for a 3-4 hrs trip and lunch or with *Bali Adventure Tours*, T 751292, see page 353.

Local information

● Accommodation

Ubud has a wide choice of good value, clean and generally high quality accommodation in often romantic and well-designed bungalows. Except in the more expensive hotels, breakfast is incl in the rates. Must book ahead in peak seasons. **NB** Some hotels are marked in the 'Around Ubud' map (page 372).

L *Amandari*, Kedewatan, T 975333, F 975335, NW of town, restaurant, pool, the ultimate hotel, set above the Ayung River, among paddy fields, excellent service (personal staff for each of the 29 bungalow-suites), beautiful rooms each protected by high walls and with its own private garden, magnificently positioned pool and excellent food, one honeymooner called it 'Heaven on Earth', rec; **L** *Kupu Kupu Barong*, Kedewatan, T 975478, F 975079, NW of town, restaurant, pool, stunning position overlooking the Ayung River, superb service and rooms. No children under 12 years old; **L** *Pita Maha*, Jl Sanggingan, Campuhan, T 974330, F 974329, opened Dec '95, the sophisticated sister of the *Hotel Tjampuhan* has 24 self-contained, traditional 'bales (villas), the architect is a member of the Ubud royal family and the quality of workmanship meets regal standards especially in stone masonry and woodcarving, stunning views over the Oos River valley and to Mt Agung, all villas are the ultimate in luxury, very spacious with king-size beds, a/c, fan, minibar, satellite TV, CD, bathroom adjoining exotic garden, indoor and outdoor living areas, spectacular spring-water pool lapping over the edge of the ravine, open-air pavilion restaurant with ravine views, complimentary sarong and 'brem barong' drink – come here to be pampered, rec; **L-A+** *Banyan Tree Kamandalu*, Jl Tegallalang, Banjar Nagi, T 975825, F 975851, 5 mins from Ubud centre (complimentary shuttle service), 58 luxurious, self-contained villas, built in traditional Balinese style, surrounded by rice fields overlooking the Petanu River valley, villas are complete with a/c, fan, fridge, satellite TV/in-house movies, CD player, 4-poster bed, deluxe bathroom with open-air Bale Benjong shower, top of the range villas have private pools and jacuzzi, the large main pool is free form with a swim-up bar and paddling pool attached, herbal spa is one of the new additions to the hotel – couples can go together if they like for Indonesian/new age massage, good new restaurant, *Saffron*, with top chef specializing in spicy Asian food as well as high class international cuisine, rec.

A+ *Waka di Ume*, Jl Sueta, Desa Sambahan, T 96178, F 96179, a few kilometres above Ubud set amongst rice paddies, recently completed, it is as its brochure says "a very different resort" designer-primitive style – natural fabrics, copper, slate, bamboo 'alang-alang', bleached wood, and antiques artistically mixed with primitive farming tools, spacious rooms, white muslin draped 4-poster, fan only, white bath robes, bamboo slippers, luxurious marble bathroom, roof top restaurant serves genuine Balinese food, cascading swimming pool set amongst palms, stone statues and tropical flowers, overlooking the rural valley, meditation chapel with music/TV/library, sauna, steam baths, traditional massage, an oasis of tranquility, rec; **A+-L** *The Chedi Ubud*, Desa Melinggih Kelod, Payangan, Gianyar, T 975963, F 975968, a/c, restaurant, pool, health spa, library, new hotel with 65 rooms, quietly sophisticated, exquisite views, private garden and walkways, located N of Ubud village; **A** *Cahaya Dewata*, Kedewatan, in-between the *Amandari* and *Kupu Kupu Barong* (out of town), T/F 975495, excellent restaurant, pool, rec; **A** *Dewi Sri*, Jl Hanoman, Padangtegal (nr the intersection with Jl Monkey Forest), T 975300, F 975005, pool, 2-storeyed beautiful thatched bungalows amid the rice fields, well-run, rec; **A** *Padma Indah Cottages*, Campuan, T 975719, F 975091, a/c, restaurant, pool, cottages could sleep 4, attractive cottages but badly managed; **A** *Pringga Juwita*, off Jl Raya Ubud (by *Miro's restaurant*), T/F 975734, pool, fan, hot water, lovely grounds, well designed rooms, price incl breakfast, rec; **A** *Siti Bungalows*, Jl Kajeng 3, T 975699, F 975643, restaurant rec, very peaceful, 4-poster beds; **A** *Taman Bebek*

Villas, 2 km S of *Amandari Hotel* on Sayan-Ubud Rd, T/F 975385, 8 1-or 2-bedroomed bungalows, with sitting areas and kitchenettes, a family-style homestay set in a beautiful garden above the Ayung River; **A** *Tjampuhan*, Jl Raya Campuhan, PO Box 198, Gianyar, T 975368, F 975137, at W end of Jl Raya Ubud, over the river and up the hill, this hotel was originally the artist Walter Spies' home, restaurant, small spring-fed pool, stunning setting on the side of a ravine, watery gardens (complete with frogs), bungalows built in layers up the ravine, romantic rooms with old wooden beds and pleasant sitting areas, plans afoot to revitalize its faded elegance, in the meantime the 'Raja' rooms are the best; **A** *Ulun Ubud*, Sanggingan, T 975024, F 975524, simple restaurant, pool, traditional Balinese style, attractive position on steep hillside facing the Campuan River, people work at the bottom of the gorge chipping out stones for carving, women carry the rocks on their heads up to the road; **A** *Villa Bukit Ubud*, by Neka Museum, Sanggingan, T 975371, F 975787, restaurant with good views and good value food, good pool, pleasant a/c bungalows on edge of ravine, Balinese thatch roofs and surprising suburban comfort inside, a/c, hot water, good for families, rec; **A** *Villa Sanggingan*, just of S of Neka Museum, Sanggingan, T 975389, F 975639, pool, breakfast room, rooms away from road are quieter; **A-B** *Oka Kartini*, Jl Raya Ubud, T 975193, F 975759, pool, small hotel with friendly staff, rooms are a little over-elaborate but thoughtfully designed, rooms with a/c in **A** price range, pleasant bar with marble tables and art gallery next door, rec.

B *Fibra Inn*, Jl Monkey Forest, T 975451, F 975125, pool, good rooms and open-air bathrooms, hot water, rec; **B** *Pertiwi Bungalows*, Jl Monkey Forest, T 975236, F 975559, restaurant, pool, lovely rooms, open-air bathroom, rec; **B** *Pringga Juwita Inn*, off Jl Raya Ubud and next to *Pringga Juwita Water Garden Cottages*, T/F 975734, bungalows in pleasant garden on edge of rice fields; **B** *Sehati*, Jl Jembawan 7, T 975460, lovely cool rooms overlooking a leafy ravine, bathrooms with hot water and western toilet, rec; **B-C** *Artini*, hidden cottage, new, attractive rooms set amongst rice paddies off Jl Hanoman, same ownership as *Artini I* and *II*, bathrooms with hot water and western toilet; **B-E** *Matahari Cottages*, Jl Jembawan, T 975459, more expensive rooms are well-designed and secluded, some hot water, rec.

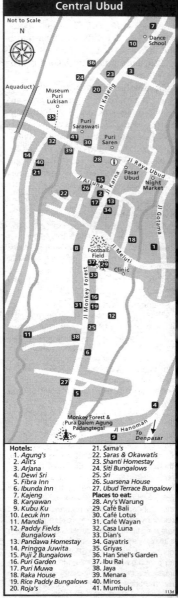

Central Ubud

Not to Scale

N

Aquaduct)

Museum Puri Lukisan

Dance School

Puri Saraswati

Puri Saren

Puri Ubud

Pasar Ubud

Night Market

Football Field

Clinic

Monkey Forest & Pura Dalem Agung Padangtegal

To Denpasar

Jl Kajeng
Jl Raya Ubud
Jl Karna
Jl Arjuna
Jl Gotama
Jl Meluti
Jl Monkey Forest
Jl Hanoman

Hotels:
1. Agung's
2. Alit's
3. Arjana
4. Dewi Sri
5. Fibra Inn
6. Ibunda Inn
7. Kajeng
8. Karyawan
9. Kubu Ku
10. Lecuk Inn
11. Mandia
12. Paddy Fields Bungalows
13. Pandawa Homestay
14. Pringga Juwita
15. Puji 2 Bungalows
16. Puri Garden
17. Puri Muwa
18. Raka House
19. Rice Paddy Bungalows
20. Roja's
21. Sama's
22. Saras & Okawatis
23. Shanti Homestay
24. Siti Bungalows
25. Sri
26. Suarsena House
27. Ubud Terrace Bungalow
Places to eat:
28. Ary's Warung
29. Café Bali
30. Café Lotus
31. Café Wayan
32. Casa Luna
33. Dian's
34. Gayatris
35. Griyas
36. Han Snel's Garden
37. Ibu Rai
38. Jaya
39. Menara
40. Miros
41. Mumbuls

113d

C *Kori Agung*, Penestanan-Campuan, T 975166, a little out of town, off the main road, but lovely rooms with verandah, cold water showers only, rec; **C** *Kubu Ku*, Jl Monkey Forest, at the end of the road, set in the middle of paddy fields with lovely rooms; **C** *Mandia*, 30m off Jl Monkey Forest, T 870571, lovely garden atmosphere, rec; **C** *Penestanan Bungalows*, Campuan, T 975604, F 975603, small pool, a little out of town, set scenically on a hill overlooking paddy fields, good rooms, hot water; **C** *Puri Garden*, Jl Monkey Forest, T 975395, lovely water garden, good rooms, fan, rec; **C** *Siddhartha's Shelter*, Penestanan Kaja (Campuan), T 975748, W of town, set among paddy fields; **C** *Wisata Cottages*, Campuan, nr Neka Museum, T/F 950177, pool, lovely position with views over paddy fields; **C-D** *Bali Breeze*, Jl Hanoman, accommodation is in thatched cottages ('pondok'), the larger can sleep 6, with balcony and patio, lovely garden and views over paddy fields, attached cold water shower, free tea and coffee, room rate incl breakfast, rec; **C-D** *Nuriani Guesthouse*, just off Jl Hanoman, T 975346, 12 clean, attractive rooms, small garden, bathrooms with hot water and western toilet, upstairs rooms have views of rice paddies; **C-D** *Pondok Impian*, Jl Hanoman, comes rec by several visitors, the wok has an excellent reputation; **C-D** *Ubud Terrace Bungalows*, Jl Monkey Forest, T 975690, situated in a quiet grove, friendly management, attractive decor, private bathrooms with hot water and western toilet, upstairs rooms have good sunset views.

D *Agungs*, off Jl Raya Ubud (by *Nomad's restaurant*), friendly owner, but rooms are a little overpriced; **D** *Dewangga*, off Jl Monkey Forest (by the football field), attractive setting, nice garden, good rooms, open-air bathroom, friendly staff, breakfast incl, rec; **D** *Ibunda Inn*, Jl Monkey Forest, T 870571, 2-storeyed thatched houses with baths, hot water; **D** *Kajeng*, Jl Kajeng 29, T 975018, rooms with verandahs overlooking a ravine and duck pond, clean with attractive open-air mandis; **D** *Karyawan*, Jl Monkey Forest, lovely gardens, clean, rec; **D** *Lecuk Inn*, Jl Kajeng 15, open-air mandi, incl breakfast, friendly people, big rooms with a terrace, attractive setting by river and lovely gardens; **D** *Paddy Fields*, off Jl Monkey Forest (opp *Café Wayan*), attractive position overlooking rice paddy, good breakfast, friendly owners, rec; **D** *Pramesti Cottages*, Jl Monkey Forest, 3 attractive 1- or 2-rm cottages set in garden with pond, each room with balcony and small terrace, set back from the street in a rural setting – you hear the frogs at night – hot water and breakfast incl, rec; **D** *Rice Paddy Bungalows*, convenient central location in Jl Monkey Forest, modern rooms, clean, upstairs rooms have views over rice paddies; **D** *Sama's*, off Jl Raya Ubud (by *Miro's restaurant*), wonderful position among paddy fields, 3 rm, clean, charming owner, rec; **D** *Shanti Homestay*, Jl Kajeng 5, new homestay, friendly; **D** *Sri*, Jl Monkey Forest, T 975394, very clean, rec; **D-E** *Ibu Arsa*, Peliatan, (E of town), older rooms are rather dark, the newer rooms are characterful with attractive open bathrooms, friendly, rec; **D-E** *Nyoman Astana's Bungalows*, Peliatan (next to *Siti Hotel*), attractive cosy rooms (the newer ones are more expensive) with attached bathrooms and hot water, beautiful quiet garden, price incl a generous breakfast, excellent value for money, rec; **D-E** *Rona's*, Peliatan, T 976229, popular and now has a restaurant and beauty parlour where you can have a petal bath and massage; **D-E** *Suarsena House*, Jl Arjuna, clean and central, more expensive rooms with large bathrooms.

E *Alit's*, Jl Monkey Forest, nice garden, clean rooms, friendly; **E** *Anom*, Jl Arjuna, central, only 3 rm, but good; **E** *Arjana*, Jl Kajeng 6, T 978233, quiet, clean rooms, good bathrooms, rec; **E** *Budi*, off Jl Monkey Forest (by the football field), 3 rm, clean, fan, good value, rec; **E** *Kubu Roda*, off Jl Raya Ubud (by *Miro's restaurant*), 3 rm, fan, friendly owners; **E** *Pandawa Homestay*, Jl Monkey Forest, good value, big rooms; **E** *Pande Homestay*, Peliatan, (E of town), friendly, clean; **E** *Puji 2*, Gg Arjuna (off Jl Monkey Forest), private bathroom – shower and western toilet, mosquito nets, large breakfast incl, comfortable and the cheapest around; **E** *Puri Muwa*, Jl Monkey Forest, T 975046, well-decorated rooms; **E** *Raka House* (off Jl Meluti – nr the football field), 3 or 4 rm, rec; **E** *Roja's*, Jl Kajeng 1, attractive bungalows, well kept garden, rec; **E** *Sara's*, off Jl Monkey Forest (next to *Okawati's restaurant*), mandi, verandah and large breakfast, good value, rec; **E** *Sukerti*, Jl Bima, Banjar Kalah (nr intersection with Jl Raya Ubud), clean and very friendly.

● **Places to eat**

Food in Ubud is good, particularly international food. Most restaurants serve a mixture of Balinese, Indonesian and international dishes.

◆◆◆◆*Saffron*, Banyan Tree, Kamandalu, good quality spicy Asian food, interesting menu, rec.

***Café Lotus**, Jl Raya Ubud, overlooks lotus ponds of Puri Saraswati Palace, international (particularly Italian), pleasant situation and good atmosphere (closed Mon); ***Café Wayan**, Jl Monkey Forest, international, some seafood, very popular, delicious desserts, Balinese buffet on Sun evenings, tables arranged in a series of outdoor kiosks, rec; ***Han Snel's Garden Restaurant**, Jl Kajeng, N of Jl Raya Ubud, very attractive setting and charming owners, generous, though pricey, servings (closed Sun), rec; ***Tjampuhan Hotel restaurant**, W end of Jl Raya Ubud, Indonesian and international, pleasant ravine-side setting; **Ary's Warung**, Jl Raya Ubud (opp the temple complex), international and Indonesian food served in relaxed, occasionally bohemian atmosphere, with musical accompaniment, frequented by the Ubud cognoscenti, rec for food but rather close to the main street; **Bumbu**, Suweta No 1, pleasant terrace off the main drag, good value food, excellent presentation, friendly service, rec; **Café Bali**, Jl Monkey Forest (bottom end of football field), international, attractive setting, rec; **Café Roni**, 23 Tebasaya, good tomato soup! **Casa Luna**, Jl Raya Ubud, opp Museum Puri Lukisan, good range of International dishes, rec; **Dian's**, Jl Monkey Forest, well-cooked range of dishes, pleasant place for a drink; **Gayatri's**, Jl Monkey Forest, inexpensive and good for children, rec; **Ibu Rai**, Jl Monkey Forest (next to the football field), Balinese and international, rec; **Jaya Restaurant**, Jl Monkey Forest, good reasonably priced Indonesian and western food; **Mumbul's Garden Terrace**, Jl Raya Ubud (close to the *Puri Lukisan Art Museum*), T 975364, for excellent salads, international and Balinese food, timing for serving dishes erratic, rec; **Nomad**, Jl Raya Ubud, T 975131, international and Balinese incl Balinese duck and suckling pig, good guacamole; **Nuriani Restaurant**, Jl Hanoman, T 975558, excellent reasonably priced Indonesian and western food with pretty views over the paddy fields especially at sunset, rec; **Pondok Tjampuhan**, next to *Blanco's House*, pizza, Indonesian, Chinese, good position overlooking ravine; **Ubud Raya**, Jl Raya Ubud (E end), Javanese, Japanese and international, rec; Bagus Café, Jl Raya Ubud, Peliatan (SE of the centre), Balinese specialities; Griya's, Jl Raya Ubud, barbecued chicken is rec, but poor service; Kura Kura, Jl Monkey Forest (at the end, nr Jl Padangtegal), Mexican; Lilies, Jl Monkey Forest, rec; **Miro's**, in garden set above Jl Raya Ubud, generous helpings and beautiful presentation, good food at very reasonable price, candle-lit at night, very atmospheric, rec; **Murni's Warung**, overlooking ravine at W end of Jl Raya Ubud, at the Ubud end of the old suspension bridge, Indonesian and international (mostly American), an old-time favourite, good service, but food is not special (closed Wed); **Yudit Restaurant and Bakery**, Jl Monkey Forest, pizzas and good bread, rec.

● **Bars**
Beggar's Bush, nr *Hotel Tjampuhan*, W of town on Jl Raya Ubud, English pub (some food); *Salzbar*, Jl Monkey Forest, live music on Tues and Thur; *Nomad*, Jl Monkey Forest, open late.

● **Banks & money changers**
Numerous money changers will change cash and TCs and offer rates similar to banks.

● **Entertainment**
Artists' colonies: Ubud has perhaps the greatest concentration of artists in Indonesia, exceeding even Yogya. Many will allow visitors to watch them at work in the hope that they will then buy their work. The *Pengosekan Community of Artists* is on Jl Bima.

Dance: there are numerous performances every day of the week; most begin at between 1900 and 2000 and cost 5,000Rp. A board at the *Bina Wisata Tourist Centre*, Jl Raya Ubud (opp the palace), lists the various dances, with time (most performances start at 1930 or 2000), location and cost (almost entirely 7,000Rp). There are almost nightly performances at the *Puri Saren* at the junction of Jl Raya Ubud and Jl Monkey Forest. Performances incl legong, Mahabharata, barong, kecak, Ramayana ballet and wayang kulit (7,000Rp).

Massage: *Mentari Massage Service Centre*, No 1 Anoman St, professional massage, not a 'beach-rub', very popular, book in advance (T 974001).

Videos: there is a very popular *Video Bar* on the far side of the football field on Jl Monkey Forest. Two shows a night of western films. Laser disc videos at *Menara Restaurant*, Jl Raya Ubud.

● **Post & telecommunications**
Area code: 0361.
Perumtel (for fax, telex & international telephone): Jl Andong (close to intersection with Jl Raya Ubud) and Jl Raya Ubud (nr *Nomad bar and restaurant*), or on the road to Petulu, at the E end of Jl Raya Ubud.
Postal agents: *Nominasi*, Jl Monkey Forest 67 and Jl Raya Ubud. **NB** they sometimes charge very high 'service charges'.

Post Office: Jl Jembawan 1 (road running S off Jl Raya Ubud, opp Neka Gallery); poste restante.

● **Shopping**

Ubud offers a good range of crafts for sale.

Batik & ikat: *Ibu Rai* travel agent nr *Lilies restaurant* on Jl Monkey Forest; *Kunang Kunang*, Jl Raya Ubud. *Lotus Studio*, Jl Raya Ubud.

Books: *Ubud Bookshop*, Jl Raya Ubud (next to *Ary's Warung*) for a good range of English language books on the region; *Ubud Music*, Jl Raya Ubud, selection of English language books and local music; *Ganesha Bookshop*, Jl Raya Ubud, nr Post Office, good selection of second-hand English language books as well as new; *Book Exchange*, 3 on Jl Monkey Forest, 1 on Jl Gotama.

Clothing: *Bali Rosa*, on Jl Raya Ubud, towards Campuan, for accessories (bags, belts, beaded pumps) rec; *Balika*, Jl Monkey Forest for fashion clothing; *Hare Om*, Jl Monkey Forest for well-designed but expensive hand-painted silk scarves and shirts; *Lotus Studio* for unusual designs and great hats; the market on the corner of Jl Raya Ubud and Jl Monkey Forest offers a range of 'travellers' clothes – T-shirts, batik etc; *Mutiara Art Company*, Jl Raya Ubud, good value batik shirts, mostly rayon but some cotton too, interesting designs, rec.

Jewellery: there are a number of shops along Jl Raya Ubud. Good designs but the quality is not always very high – it looks better than it feels.

Paintings: Ubud painters have a distinctive style, using bright colours and the depiction of natural and village scenes (see page 322). There is a large selection of paintings to be found in the town and galleries are concentrated along the E section of Jl Raya Ubud. It is possible to visit the artists in their homes; enquire at the galleries.

Pottery: nr the post office, just off Jl Raya Ubud.

Shoes: *Bali Rosa*, Jl Raya Ubud, for 'pumps'; *Hare Om* for a range of individually designed suede shoes.

Wind chimes: shop specializing in wind chimes at the end of Jl Monkey Forest in the paddy fields – worth a visit.

Woodcarving: concentrated on the Peliatan road out of town. The so-called 'duck man' of Ubud (Ngurah Umum) is to be found on the road to Goa Gajah, with a selection of wooden fruits and birds. Recommended shop nr the *Bamboo restaurant*, off Jl Monkey Forest, facing the football field.

● **Sports**

Mountain biking: see tours, page 379.

Swimming: some hotel pools are open to non-residents; the *Andong Inn*, Jl Andong 26A; Champlong Sari Hotel, 3,000Rp; *Okawatis restaurant*, Jl Monkey Forest, 2,500Rp; *Ubud Village*, Jl Monkey Forest, 3,000Rp (for the day; you can come and go as you like).

Whitewater rafting: see tours, page 379.

● **Tour companies & travel agents**

Double check airline tickets bought here; there have been complaints that despite assurances that flights are confirmed, on reaching the airport, visitors have found they are not. *Cahaya Sakti Utama*, Jl Raya Ubud, T 975131, F 975115; *Ibu Rai*, Jl Monkey Forest 72, T 975066, rec; *Kurnia*, Jl Raya Ubud, T 975020 for buses to Lombok and around Bali, tours and car rental; *Nominasi*, Jl Monkey Forest 67-71, T 975065.

● **Tourist offices**

Bina Wisata, Jl Raya Ubud (opp the Puri Saren). Good for information on daily performances but otherwise not very helpful.

● **Useful addresses**

Police: on the road to Petulu, E end of Jl Raya Ubud.

● **Transport**

Local Bicycle hire: bicycles are the best way to get about (apart from walking); there are several hire places on Jl Monkey Forest, 3,000Rp/day. **Car hire**: hire shops on Jl Monkey Forest, 40,000Rp/day plus insurance for Suzuki 'jeep'; 50,000Rp/day for larger Toyota Kijang. **Motorbike hire**: several outfits on Jl Monkey Forest, from 10,000Rp/day.

Road Bemos: bemos leave from the Pasar Ubud in the centre of town, at the junction of Jl Monkey Forest and Jl Raya Ubud; regular connections with Denpasars' Batubulan terminal (700Rp). **Bus**: there are occasional 'shuttle' (in fact not as regular as the name implies) buses to Kuta, the Ngurah Rai Airport (4,000Rp), Candi Dasa, Padangbai, Sanur, Denpasar. Details are available at the travel or tour agents. **Taxi**: taxis congregate at the Pasar Ubud in the centre of town.

NORTH OF UBUD: GUNUNG KAWI AND TIRTA EMPUL

4 km E of Ubud is the small town of Bedulu, close to which are the sights of Goa Gajah and Yeh Pulu (see page 374). 10 km N of Bedulu, on the road to Lake Batur, shortly after the village of Tampaksiring off the main road on the right hand side, are two popular tourist destinations: the temples of Gunung Kawi and Tirta Empul. By continuing N from here, the road runs up a steep-sided valley to Mt Batur and the town of Penelokan.

GUNUNG KAWI

Gunung Kawi, literally the 'Mountain of the Poets', is one of the most impressive, and unusual, temples in Bali. A steep rock stairway, with high sides leads down to the bottom of a humid, tree-filled, ravine. At the bottom lies the temple. The whole complex was literally hewn out of the rock during the 11th century, when it was thought to have been created as the burial

Gunung Kawi

Not to scale

Queen's Tombs

Entrance

Royal Tombs

Pura

Main cloister

Pakerisan River

Tenth Cloister

Second cloister

Third cloister

Adapted from: Kempers, AJB (1991)
Monumental Bali, Periplus: Singapore

temple for King Anak Wungsu and his wives, who probably threw themselves on his funeral pyre. Visitors descend 315 steps to a massive rock archway, and from there to the nine tombs which face each other on either side of the Pakerisan River. These two rows of candis, four on the S side and five on the N, were cut out of the rock. It is believed that the five on the N bank of the river were for the King and his four wives, whilst the four on the S bank may have been for four concubines. They resemble temples and are the earliest traces of a style of architecture which became popular in Java in the following centuries. As such they may represent the precursor to the Balinese *meru* (see page 412). Balinese mythology maintains that Empu Kuturan, a royal prince, carved these shrines with his fingernails. Over the years there has been disagreement over the function of the candis. The art historian C Lekkerkerker in 1920 postulated that the corpses were left in the cells to be eaten by wild animals, picked-over by birds, and to putrify and degenerate. Rather later, Bernet Kempers argued that they were not tombs at all, but merely symbols of death.

East of the five candis on the far side of the river is a cloister of various courtyards and rooms, also carved out of the rock. They were created for the Buddhist priests who lived here (perhaps reflecting its Buddhist origins, visitors are asked to remove their shoes before entering). Still farther away, on the other side of the river, is the so-called 'tenth tomb'. The local people call this tomb 'the priest's house' and it was not discovered by western archaeology until 1949 when Krijgsman revealed the site. The tenth tomb is, in all likelihood, a monastery and consists of a courtyard encircled by niches. To get to the tenth tomb take the path across the paddy fields that runs from the rock-hewn gateway that leads down into the gorge; it is about a 1 km walk. Admission 1,000Rp. Dress – sash or sarong required. There is accommodation close by in

Tampaksiring eg *Gusti Homestay*. Tampaksiring also has a number of good jewellery workshops.

● **Transport Road Bemo**: connections with Denpasar's Batubulan terminal or from Ubud to Tampaksiring. It is about a 3 km walk from here, passing Tirta Empul (see below), although bemos also make the journey to the temple site.

TIRTA EMPUL

Tirta Empul is 2 km N of Tampaksiring, 1 km on from Gunung Kawi. The temple is one of the holiest sights on Bali and is a popular pilgrimage stop, evident by the maze of trinket stalls that has to be negotiated on the way out of the complex.

Tirta Empul is built on the site of a holy spring which is said to have magical healing powers. In the past, barong masks were bathed here to infuse them with supernatural powers during the dance. Originally constructed in 960, during the reign of Raja Candra Bayasingha, the temple is divided into three courtyards, and has been extensively restored with little of the original structure remaining – bar a few stone fragments. The outer courtyard contains two long pools fed by 30 or more water spouts, each of which has a particular function – for example, there is one for spiritual purification. The holy springs bubble up in the inner courtyard. During the *Galungan Festival* (see page 343), sacred *barong* dance masks are brought here to be bathed in holy water. Admission 1,050Rp (500Rp extra for a camera).

● **Transport Road Bemo**: take a bemo from Denpasar's Batubulan terminal or Ubud towards Tampaksiring. The temple is 2 km N of the town centre; either walk or catch a bemo. From here it is a 1 km walk to Gunung Kawi (see above).

NORTH OF DENPASAR: GIANYAR TO MOUNT BATUR VIA BANGLI

East of Ubud is the royal town of Gianyar, which has little of interest to attract the tourist. 15 km N of Gianyar, at the foot of Mt Batur, is another former royal capital, Bangli, with its impressive Kehen Temple. A further 20 km leads up the slopes of Mt Batur to the crater's edge – one of the most popular excursions in Bali. Along the rim of the caldera are the mountain towns of Penelokan and Kintamani, and the important temples of Batur and Tegen Koripan. From Penelokan, a road winds down into the caldera and along the W edge of Lake Batur. It is possible to trek from here up the active cone of Mt Batur (1,710m), which thrusts up through a barren landscape of lava flows. North from Penulisan, the road twists and turns for 36 km down the N slopes of the volcano, reaching the narrow coastal strip at the town of Kubutambahan.

GIANYAR

Gianyar is the former capital of the kingdom of Gianyar. During the conquest of Bali, this principality sided with the Dutch and so escaped the massacres that accompanied the defeat of Denpasar, Klungkung and Pemetjutan. In the centre of Gianyar, on Jl Ngurah Rai, is the **Agung Gianyar Palace**, surrounded by attractive red-brick walls. It is not normally open to the public, but the owner, Ide Anak Agung Gede Agung, a former politician and the rajah of Gianyar, does let visitors look around his house if asked. The bemo station is 5 mins walk to the W of the palace, also on Jl Ngurah Rai. Traditionally regarded as Bali's weaving centre, there is only a limited amount of cloth on sale these days. Gianyar's other claim to fame is that it is said to have the best *babi guling* (roast suckling pig) on the island.

Local information
● **Accommodation**
B *Agung Gianyar Palace Guesthouse*, within the Palace walls.

● **Entertainment**

Dance: at 1900, every Mon and Thur, a cultural show incl dinner is staged at the *Agung Gianyar Palace*, T 93943/51654.

● **Sports**

Mountain biking: down into the volcano on the 'Batur Trail', organized by *Sobek Expeditions*, T 287059 (US$45 incl lunch), pickup from all the resorts.

● **Tourist offices**

Gianyar Tourist Office (Dinas Pariwisata), Jl Ngurah Rai 21, T 93401. The office provides

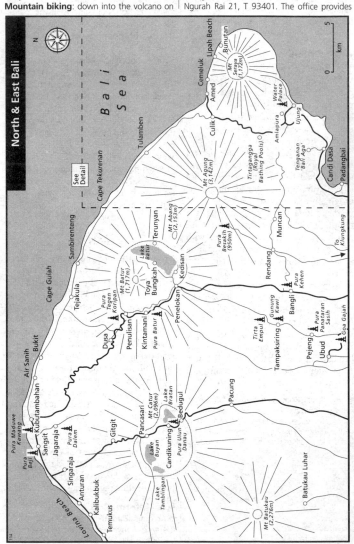

visitors with pamphlets on sights in the regency.

● **Transport**
27 km from Denpasar.

Road Bemo: regular connections with Denpasar's Batubulan terminal.

BANGLI

Bangli is a peaceful, rather beautiful town and the former capital of a mountain principality. Never the strongest of Balinese kingdoms, it capitulated to the Dutch in the middle of the 19th century. Bangli's principal claim to fame is the **Pura Kehen**, probably founded in the 13th century. There is some dispute over the true origin of the temple as inscriptions within the compound have been dated to the 9th century. Nonetheless, Pura Kehen is one of Bali's more impressive temples. It is the second largest on Bali and is built on the side of a wooded slope. Elephants flank the imposing entrance, leading up to three terraced courtyards, through finely carved and ornamented gateways decorated with myriad demons. The lower courtyard is dominated by a wonderful 400 year old *waringin* tree (*Ficus benjamina*) with a monk's cell built high up in the branches. It is here that performances are held to honour the gods. The middle courtyard houses the offertory shrines, while the topmost courtyard contains an eleven-tiered *meru* with a carved wood and stone base. The elaborate woodwork here is being beautifully restored and repainted by craftsmen. In the wall below, guides will point out the old Chinese plates cemented into it. Curiously, some of these depict rural England, with a watermill and mail coach drawn by four horses. Admission by donation. The temple is about 1 km N of town on the back road to Besakih and Penelokan.

● **Accommodation** *Jaya Giri Homestay*, by the Pura Kehen. **E** *Losmen Dharma Putra*, room rate incl breakfast, a good, friendly, family-run losmen.

● **Transport Road Bemo**: from Denpasar's Batubulan terminal.

MOUNT BATUR

The spectacular landscape of Mt Batur is one of the most visited inland areas on Bali. Despite the hawkers, bustle and general commercialization, it still makes a worthwhile trip. The huge crater – 20 km in diameter – contains within it Lake Batur and the active Mt Batur (1,710m), with buckled lava flows on its slopes. The original **Mount Batur**, which first erupted centuries ago, must have been immense. In 1917, an eruption killed over 1,000 people and destroyed 65,000 homes and more than 2,000 temples. The lava flow stopped at the foot of the village of Batur's temple, which the local people took as a good omen and continued to live there. In 1926, the village of Batur, and its temple, were completely destroyed by another eruption. This time the village moved to a safer site. In Aug 1994 Mount Batur erupted again, after 18 years of dormancy. The eruption was not a major event; it lasted for a period of 5 days and ash was deposited on the village of Kintamani about 6 km away. The volcano's shape tells a geological tale of great violence though – making more recent eruptions minor by comparison, notwithstanding the lives lost. The double caldera, with one caldera lying within the second, "is the product of two cataclysmic eruptions each of which would certainly have destroyed large parts of Bali", as Graeme Wheller, a geologist, says in an article in *Inside Indonesia*. The older explosion occurred between 40,000 and 100,000 years ago; the more recent, some 23,500 years ago. Perhaps it is the constant battle with combative nature which has made the inhabitants of the area less welcoming, and more surly, than those of other parts of the island. It is dangerous to generalize, but many visitors leave the slopes of Mt Batur with a sense of relief.

Lake Batur in the centre of the caldera is considered sacred, and is thought to be the fountain-head of the water that flows into Bali's rice fields. A local legend recounts that the Goddess of the Crater

Lake, Dewi Danu and her male counterpart, the God of Mt Agung, rose from the depths of the lake and extended their power over the lands and waters of Bali. Dewi Danu and the God of Mt Agung are complementary; female and male, and occupy the two highest peaks on the island, Agung and Batur.

A steep road winds down the crater side and then through the lava boulders and along the W shore of Lake Batur. There are hot springs here and paths up the sides of Mt Batur, through the area's extraordinary landscape. **Treks** begin either from **Purajati** or **Toya Bungkah** (a 4 and 6 hrs round trip respectively), or around the lake (guides are available from Ged's, see below). Boats can be hired from the village of **Kedisan** on the S shore of Lake Batur – be prepared for the unpleasant, hard-line sales people here – or from Toya Bungkah, to visit the traditional Bali Aga village (see page 406) of **Terunyan** and its cemetery, on the E side of the lake. Terunyan's customs are different from Tenganan (see page 400) – but these differences can only be noted during festival time, which tend to be rather closed affairs. The cemetery is interesting for those of a morbid disposition: the corpses are left to rot in the open air.

On the W rim of the crater are two villages, Kintamani and Penelokan. Large-scale restaurants here cater for the tour group hoards. The area is also overrun with hawkers selling batik and woodcarvings – some so vociferously as to scare the most hardened visitor. **Penelokan**, is perched on the edge of the crater and its name means 'place to look'. About 5 km N of here, following the crater rim, is the rather drab town of **Kintamani**, which is a centre of orange and passionfruit cultivation. The town's superb position overlooking the crater makes up for its drabness. Ged's trekking is based here; they can advise on the best walks in the area and provide a guide for the more dangerous routes up to the crater rim.

Just S of Kintamani is **Pura Batur**, spectacularly positioned on the side of the crater. This is the new temple built as a replacement for the original Pura Batur which was engulfed by lava in 1926. Although the temple is new and therefore not of great historical significance, it is in fact the second most important temple in Bali after Pura Besakih. As Stephen Lansing explains in his book *Priests and programmers* (1991), the Goddess of the Crater Lake is honoured here and symbolically the temple controls water for all the island's irrigation systems (see page 314). Ultimately therefore, it controls the livelihoods of the majority of the population. A 9-tiered meru honours the goddess and unlike other temples it is open 24 hrs a day. A virgin priestess still selects 24 boys as priests who remain tied as servants of the temple for the rest of their lives. The most senior is regarded as the earthly representative of the goddess, with whom he is magically linked.

Pura Tegeh Koripan is the last place on the crater rim, on the main road 200m N of Penulisan. 333 steep stairs lead up to the temple which stands at a height of over 1,700m above sea-level next to a broadcasting mast. The temple was first visited by a European at a relatively early date – a scientist, Dr J Jacobs, climbed up to the temple in 1885. However, after that first visit, the local population forcibly kept foreigners away from the temple and it was only in 1918 that the archaeologist Nieuwenkamp managed to gain admission and become its second western visitor. The temple contains a number of highly weathered statues, thought to be portraits of royalty. They are dated between 1011 and 1335. Artistically they are surprising because they seem to anticipate later Majapahit works. The whole place is rather run down at the moment, though there are some signs that repairs are being attempted. Admission 1,000Rp. Open Mon-Sun. *Getting there*: catch a bemo running N and get off at Penulisan.

NB Numerous visitors have written to us saying how unfriendly the villages of this area are. They report a distinct lack of hospitality, an oppressive and unpleasant air – even palpable hostility.

● **Accommodation** On Lake Batur: C-D *Under the Volcano*, good restaurant, clean rooms, friendly management; **D** *Segara Bungalow*; **D** *Surya Homestay*, great position; **D** *The Art Centre*, (or *Balai Seni*), Toya Bungkah, quite old but still a good place to stay; **F** *Mountain View*. **Penelokan**: **B-D** *Lake View Homestay*, basic but good views over the lake; **C-D** *Gunawan Losmen*, clean, private bathroom, fantastic position. **Kintamani**: **C** *Puri Astina*, large clean rooms; *Losmen Sasaka*, stunning views over the crater and lake. **Toya Bungkah**: **F** *Nyoman Pangus Homestay*, the accommodation here is fine, but the food is poor value, with small portions, rather unfriendly – like the village.

● **Places to eat** *Segara*, in Kedisan, across road from boat jetty, serves excellent lake fish, clean, friendly staff.

● **Transport Road Bemo**: from Denpasar's Batubulan terminal to Bangli and then another to Penelokan. Some bemos drive down into the crater to Kedisan and Toya Bungkah. **Bus**: regular coach services from Denpasar (2-3 hrs).

ALTERNATIVE ROUTE FROM UBUD TO MT BATUR

If you have your own transport and are starting from Ubud, you can turn left at the end of Ubud's main street and take the back road heading N. This leads through an almost continuous ribbon of craft villages, mainly specialising in woodcarving, with pieces ranging in size from chains of monkeys to full size doors and 2m high *Garudas*. There are good bargains to be found in this area off the main tourist track.

The road, its surface not too good in places, climbs steadily through rice paddies and then more open countryside where cows and goats graze, before eventually arriving at the crater rim – 500m W of Penelokan.

From Mt Batur to the N coast From Penulisan the main road runs down to the N coast which it joins at Kubutambahan. It is a long descent as the road twists down the steep hillsides and there are many hairpin bends.

If exploring the NE coast, a very pleasant alternative is to take the minor road which turns directly N just short of a small village called Dusa. The turning is not well signed – ask a local to make sure you are on the right road.

This is a steep descent but the road is well made and quiet. The road follows ridges down from the crater of Mt Batur, with steep drops into ravines on either side. The route passes through clove plantations and small friendly villages with stupendous views to the N over the sea. Behind, the tree-covered slopes lead back up to the crater.

The road eventually joints the coast road near Tegakula. Turn left, NW, for Singaraja and Lovina, and right, SE, for the road to Amlapura – for description see page 405.

PURA BESAKIH AND MOUNT AGUNG

The holiest and most important temple on Bali is Pura Besakih, situated on the slopes of Bali's sacred Mt Agung. Twinned with Mt Batur to the NW, Agung is the highest mountain on the island, rising to 3,140m. It is easiest to approach Besakih by taking the road N from Klungkung, a distance of 22 km. However, there are also two E-W roads, linking the Klungkung route to Besakih with Bangli in the W and Amlapura in the E. Although little public transport uses these routes, they are among the most beautiful drives in Bali, through verdant terraced rice paddys.

BESAKIH

Pura Besakih is not one temple, but a complex of 22 puras that lie scattered over the S slopes of Mt Agung at an altitude of about 1,000m. Of these, the central, largest and most important is the Pura Penataran Agung, the Mother Temple of all Bali. It is here that every Balinese, whatever his or her clan or class, can come to worship – although in the past it was reserved for the royal families of Klungkung, Karangkasem and Bangli. The other 21 temples that sprawl across the slopes of Mt Agung surrounding the Mother Temple are linked to particular clans. Mount Agung is an active volcano, and last erupted in 1963 killing 2,000 people. Graeme Wheller, in an article in *Inside Indonesia* published at the end of 1994, claims that "Gunung Agung is a disaster waiting to happen – again". The 1963 explosion, in his view, is set to repeat itself with even greater human repercussions. The population is now considerably denser and the scale of investment much greater. He claims that not only would thousands be at risk but the tourist industry would be devastated for months afterwards. There are three observatory stations that monitor the state of the mountain, but these are very poorly equipped and under-funded. When – it is

not considered to be a question of 'if' – the mountain does erupt, it could be with very little warning. The traditional *lontar* manuscripts (see page 416) sometimes name the mountain *To Langkir* meaning Uppermost Man, or 'The Abode of the Gods' and the area has been a sacred spot for several centuries.

The **Pura Penataran Agung**, which most visitors refer to as Pura Besakih, is dedicated to Siva and was probably a pre-Indic terraced sanctuary. An indication that the pura is of great antiquity and

Pura Besakih

Pura Pangubengan
Pura Tirtha
Pura Paninjoan
Pura Gelap
Pura Batu Madeg
Pura Kiduling Kreteg
Pura Ratu Panyarikan
Pura Ratu Pande
Pura Panataran Agung
Pura-Pura Padharman
Pura Ratu Pasek
Pura Dukuh Segening
Suci
Pura Jenggala
Bancingah
Pura Basukian
Pura Merajan Kanginan
Mandapa Kesari Warmadewa
Pura Banua Kawan
Pura Merajan Selonding
Pura Goa
Pura Ulun Kulkul
Pura Bangun Sakti
Pura Manik Mas
Pura Dalem Puri
Candi Bentar (Split Gate)
N
Car Park
To Pura Pasimpangan (5 km)
IMS 114d

The 1979 festival of Eka Dasa Rudra at Pura Besakih

The once-a-century Eka Dasa Rudra is the most important Hindu festival in Indonesia. It is held when, according to the Hindu *saka* calendar (see page 326), the year ends in two zeros. However, it can also be held when natural, political or economic calamity or disturbance is such that one needs to be called. Such was the case in 1963 (saka 1884), when it was deemed necessary to hold the festival following the events of the Indonesian revolution (1945-1949). An Eka Dasa Rudra had not been held for several centuries, and it was widely felt that one was due. Indeed, so many years had elapsed that the Balinese had forgotten, in large part, how to hold the festival and had to re-invent the celebration. However, shortly before the great sacrifice, scheduled for 8 Mar, Mt Agung began to erupt, leading to extensive death and destruction. Perhaps it was fortunate that saka 1900 (1979AD) was to fall only 16 years later, allowing the Balinese to atone for any wrongs that might have been committed.

Eka Dasa Rudra is not just one festival, but a series of many. The most important is the purification sacrifice, or *Taur Eka Dasa Rudra*, which occurs on the last day of a saka century – saka 1900 fell, for example, on 28 March 1979. The magnificence of the Eka Dasa Rudra can be imagined by magnifying immeasurably the colourful every-day festivals held in Bali's smaller temples; offerings on a massive scale, flowers in great piles, and janurs and colourful banners fluttering from the temple's shrines. During the course of the festival large numbers of animals were brought up to Besakih for sacrifice – about 60 species in all. It was not a reassuring sight for conservationists, as among the creatures were tiger cubs and rare eagles. President Suharto made an appearance at the ceremony and, unlike 1963, it ended with no incident or eruption. DS Fox writes at the back of his book about the festival *Once a century: Pura Besakih and the Eka Dasa Rudra Festival* (1982):

"It is impossible to imagine the Balinese world in another 100 years able to support an Eka Dasa Rudra as extravagant as the 1980 [sic] festival: Will there still be baby tigers and eagles for the animal sacrifices? Will the Balinese still be willing to spend millions of man-hours weaving a spectacle of such scale? Will the tenacity of Balinese culture survive the severe pressures of 21st century life?"

pre-dates the arrival of Hinduism in Bali is the use of Old Indonesian and Old Balinese to name some of the gods that are worshipped here. Since then, it has seen many changes. It seems that the temple was enlarged during the reign of King Dharmavangsa (1022-1026). But the most significant changes occurred after 1343 when Gajah Mada of the Majapahit Kingdom of Java, sent a force to subdue the 'infamous and odious' ruler of Bali. With the victory of the Majapahit army, viceroys were sent from Java to rule the island. A descendant of one of these men established himself as the Prince of Gelgel, and this royal family became closely associated with Besakih, making it their ancestral *pura*. The *merus* were probably added at this time.

Temple layout

From the entrance gate, it is a 10 mins walk up to the temple, past a long row of souvenir stalls. Although it is possible to walk up and around the sides of the temple, the courtyards themselves are only open to worshippers. It is the spectacular position of this pura, rather than the quality of its workmanship, which makes it special: there are views over fields to the waters of the Lombok Strait.

Pura Besakih consists of three distinct sections (for general background to

Balinese temple layout see page 319). The entrance to the forecourt is through a *candi bentar* or split gate, immediately in front of which – unusually for Bali – is a *bale pegat*, which symbolizes the cutting of the material from the heavenly worlds. Also here is the *bale kulkul*, a pavilion for the wooden split gongs. At the far end of this first courtyard, are two *bale mundar-mandir* or *bale ongkara*, their roofs supported by single pillars.

Entering the central courtyard, almost directly in front of the gateway, is the *bale pewerdayan*. This is the spot where the priests recite the sacred texts. On the left-hand wall is the *pegongan*, a pavilion where a gamelan orchestra plays during ceremonies. Along the opposite (right-hand) side of the courtyard is the large *bale agung*, where meetings of Besakih village are held. The small *panggungan* or altar in front and at the near end of the bale agung is used to present offerings to the gods. The similar *bale pepelik* at the far end is the altar used to present offerings to the Hindu trinity – Vishnu, Brahma and Siva. These gods descend and assemble in the larger *sanggar agung* which lies in front of the bale pepelik.

From the central courtyard, a steep stone stairway leads to the upper section, which is arranged into four terraces. The first of these terraces in the inner courtyard, is split into an E (right) and W (left) half. To the right are two large *merus*; the meru with the 7-tiered roof is dedicated to the locally venerated god Ratu Geng, while the 11-tiered meru is dedicated to Ratu Mas. The 3-tiered *kehen* meru is used to store the temple treasures. On the left-hand side is a row of four merus and two stone altars. The tallest meru, with seven tiers, is dedicated to Ida Batara Tulus Sadewa. Up some steps, on the second terrace is another 11-tiered *meru*, this one dedicated to Ratu Sunar ing Jagat or Lord Light of the World. There are also a number of bale here; the bale in a separate enclosure to the left is dedicated to Sira Empu, the patron god of blacksmiths. Up

some more stairs, to the third terrace is yet a further 11-tiered meru, dedicated in this instance to Batara Wisesa. On the final terrace are two *gedongs* – covered buildings enclosed on all four sides – both dedicated to the god of Mt Agung.

At the back of the complex there is a path leading to three other major puras: **Gelap** (200m), **Pengubengan** (2.5 km) and **Tirta** (2 km). There are over 20 temples on these terraced slopes, dedicated to every Hindu god in the pantheon. Guides available (about 2,000Rp). **Best time to visit** Early morning, before the tour groups. Admission by donation (ignore the vast sums that are claimed to have been donated). Open from 0800, Mon-Sun.

Festivals

There are a total of 70 festivals held in and around Pura Besakih each year, with every shrine having its own festival. The two most important festivals are occasional ceremonies: The *Panca Wali Krama* is held every 10 years, while the *Eka Dasa Rudra* is held only once every 100 years and lasts for 2 months. In fact, two Eka Dasa Rudra festivals have been held this century (see box above for explanation).

Jan: New moon of 7th lunar month.

Mar/Apr: *Nyepi* (movable, full moon of 10th lunar month), the Balinese Saka new year, a month-long festival, which is attended by thousands of people from all over Bali, centering on the triple lotus throne (see page 344).

● **Transport** 22 km from Klungkung, 60 km from Denpasar. **Road Bemo/minibus**: regular minibuses from Klungkung; from Denpasar catch a bemo from the Batubulan terminal to Klungkung and then get a connection on to Besakih (via Rendang). But bemos are irregular for this final leg of the journey and it makes more sense to charter a bemo for the entire trip or rent a car or motorbike (chartering a bemo makes good sense in a group).

THE EAST

The greatest of the former principalities of Bali is Klungkung and its capital still has a number of sights which hint at its former glory. East of here is the resort of Candi Dasa and 3 km outside Candi Dasa, the ancient Bali Aga village of Tenganan. The road then cuts inland and runs NE to Amlapura (Karangkasem), with its royal palace (40 km from Klungkung). 7 km inland and N from Karangkasem are the royal bathing pools of Tirtagangga. From here the road continues N following the coast all the way to Singaraja (almost 100 km from Amlapura). Few tourists make the drive, which is peaceful and very beautiful, passing black sand beaches and coconut groves, see page 420.

KLUNGKUNG

Klungkung was the centre of another of the numerous principalities that made up Bali before the Dutch conquest of the island. It was also the oldest and most powerful, and the last to fall to the Dutch. It was not until 1908 that Dewa Agung of Klungkung had a force sent against him – in this case, under the pretext that he had been 'insolent'. Like the kings of Denpasar and Pemetjutan, the Dewa Agung opted to fight and die rather than surrender. Another *puputan* or 'fight to the death' took place (see page 317) in the main street in Klungkung, and the King and his entire family were killed by the Dutch forces. On the side of the road approaching from Ubud are a series of tunnels, bored by the Japanese occupying army in WW2.

The **Puri Smarapura** was once the symbolic heart of the kingdom of Klungkung. All that remains of this palace on Jl Untung Surapati are the gardens and two buildings; the rest was destroyed in 1908 by the Dutch during their advance on the capital and the ensuing *puputan*. The **Kherta Ghosa** or Hall of Justice, built in the 18th century by Ida Dewa Agung Jambe, was formerly the supreme court of the kingdom of Klungkung. It is famous for its ceiling murals painted in traditional, wayang style, with vivid illustrations of heaven (towards the top) and hell (on the lower panels). As a court, the paintings represent the punishment that awaits a criminal in the afterlife. The murals have been repainted several times this century. Miguel Covarrubias describes the nature of traditional justice in Bali in the following terms:

"A trial must be conducted with the greatest dignity and restraint. There are rules for the language employed, the behaviour of the participants, and the payment of trial expenses. It is interesting that the court procedure resembles that of cockfights in its rules and terminology. On the appointed day the plaintiff and the defendant must appear properly dressed, with their witnesses and their cases and declarations carefully written down. ... When the case has been thoroughly stated, the witnesses have testified and the evidence has been produced, the judges study the statements and go into deliberation among themselves until they reach a decision. ... Besides the witnesses and the material evidence, special attention is paid to the physical reaction of the participants during the trial, such as nervousness, change of colour in the face, or hard breathing."

The Kherta Ghosa was transformed into a western court by the Dutch in 1908, when they added the carved seats, as they found sitting on mats too uncomfortable. It is said – although the story sounds rather dubious – that one of the Rajahs of Klungkung used the Kherta Ghosa as a watch tower. He would look over the town and when his eyes alighted on a particularly attractive woman going to the temple to make offerings, he would order his guards to fetch her and add the unsuspecting maid to his collection of wives.

Adjoining the Kherta Ghosa is the **Bale Kembang** (or Floating Pavilion), originally built in the 18th century, but extensively restored since then. Like the Kherta Ghosa, the ceiling is painted with murals; these date from 1942.

Further along the same road, just past a school, is the attractive **Taman Gili** also built in the 18th century. This consists of a series of open courtyards with finely carved stonework, in the centre of which is a floating pavilion surrounded by a lotus-filled moat. Admission 1,000Rp. To the E of the main crossroads in the centre of town – behind the shopfronts – is a bustling **market**, held here every 3 days and considered by many to be the best market on Bali and also a large monument commemorating the *puputan* (see page 317).

Excursions

Goa Lawah or 'bat cave', is one of the state temples of Klungkung. There are tunnels here which are reputed to lead as far as Pura Besakih. As the name suggests, the temple is overrun by bats and corresponding smells. *Getting there*: take a bemo heading for Padangbai or Candi Dasa.

Nusa Penida and **Nusa Lembongan**: boats leave for these two islands from Sanur, Kusamba in E Bali, and Benoa. Boats leave Padangbai for Nusa Penida only.

Local information
● **Accommodation**
E *Ramayana Palace*, Jl Diponegoro (E edge of the town on road to Candi Dasa), T 21044, restaurant.

● **Post & telecommunications**
Area code: 0366.

Post Office: to the W of the Kherta Ghosa.

● **Shopping**
Textiles: although good examples are not easy to find, Klungkung is the centre of the production of royal *songket* cloth, traditionally made with silk but today more often from synthetics. The cloth is worn for ceremonial occasions and characteristically features abstracted floral designs, geometric patterns, wayang figures and animals. It takes 2 months to weave a good piece.

● **Transport**
Road Bemo: regular connections with Denpasar's Batubulan terminal and points E – Besakih, Amlapura, Candi Dasa (500Rp).

The road runs on to the SE from Klungkung and reaches the coast after 8 km at the fishing village of Kusamba, from where there are boats to Nusa Penida. On the beach are huts and shallow troughs used in salt production. The fishing fleet consists of hundreds of brightly painted outrigger craft with triangular sails, which operate in the Lombok Strait (similar to the *lis-alis* of Madura, see page 292). They are fast and manoeuvrable, and can make way in even the lightest breezes.

REGENCY OF KARANGASEM

An area of great beauty dominated by Gunung Agung (3,140m), Bali's highest and most sacred volcano, Karangasem is also one of the most traditional parts of Bali and one of the most rewarding areas to explore.

During the 17th and 18th centuries Karangasem was the most powerful kingdom on Bali. Its sphere of influence extended to western Lombok, and the cross cultural exchanges which resulted endure to this day. During the 19th Century, the regency cooperated with the Dutch thus ensuring its continued prosperity.

The massive eruption of G Agung in 1963 devastated much of the regency and traces of the lava flows can still be seen along the NE coast, particularly N of Tulamben.

There are traditional villages rarely visited by tourists where unique and ancient forms of dance and music are still a part of village life. Any of the following villages are worth exploring, especially at festival time: **Bugbug**, **Perasi**, **Jasi**, **Ngis**, **Timbrah**, **Bungaya**, **Bebandem** and **Asak**. The main festivals are held at the time of the full moon, the appearance of *penjors* lining the roads is an indication of a forthcoming celebration; ask around for details. One important festival is *Usuba*

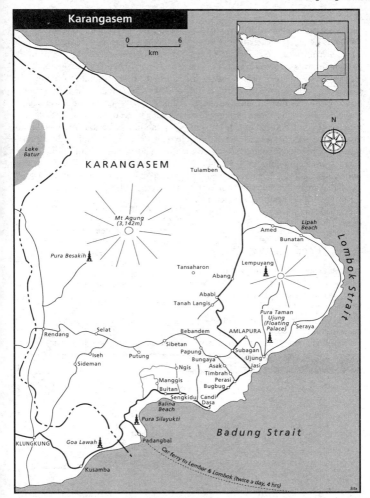

Sumbu, an agricultural ceremony held in some of the above villages between the months of May and Aug. Another important festival takes place in Jun/Jul at these villages to pay tribute to the village ancestors; other festivals take place in Jan/Feb and Mar/Apr. These festivals often last for several days and are accompanied by sacred dances and traditional music with the performers dressed in exquisite ritual dress. The heirarchy and ritual life of some of these villages dates back to the days of the Bali Aga, the original people of Bali. While perhaps not quite as fascinating as the village of Tenganan, these villages have retained an authenticity which Tenganan has lost due to the impact of tourism.

● **Transport**

While you can reach most of these villages by public bemo it is better to hire a car. There are many scenic backroads which climb up into the hills offering spectacular views when the weather is fine; be warned that some of these minor roads are in dreadful condition with numerous, huge potholes. The road leading up from Perasi through Timbrah and Bungaya to Beban-dem is especially scenic and potholed. A much better road with outstanding views leads W from Amlapura to Rendang; en route you pass through an area famed for its salak fruit and in the vicinity of Mun-can you will find beautiful rice terraces. From Rendang you can continue on up to Pura Besakih.

PADANGBAI

Padangbai has a beautiful setting over-looking a crescent-shaped bay with golden sand beach, colourful *jukung* (fishing boats) and surrounded by verdant hills. This is the port for ferries to Lombok and boats to Nusa Penida (see page 363) and is a hive of excitement when ferries arrive

and depart. When there are no ships call-ing, the town is quiet and relaxed. It is one of the best deep-water harbours in Bali, and many tankers ride at anchor in the approaches. There are beaches on either side of the town. Walking S from the pier and bus station follow the road until you come to a tatty sign on the left indicating the rough, steep path that leads up and over the hill to **Pantai Cecil**, 400m ap-proximately, 15 mins' walk. This is a beau-tiful, undeveloped white sand beach surrounded by grassy hills, the perfect setting for a quiet swim or evening stroll. There are two beachside warungs.

Local information
● **Accommodation**

The most attractive rooms are in town. However, the best location is to the N along the bay where rooms and bungalows are surrounded by gar-dens and coconut groves and are quieter; they are in need of refurbishment, though, and are overpriced for what they offer.

B-D *Puri Rai* (formerly *Rai Beach Inn*), 7 Jl Si-layukti, T 41385/6/7, F 41386, has attempted to go upmarket but rooms are very overpriced, rather spartan and unattractive, rooms and 2-storey bungalows (these have drab, plywood

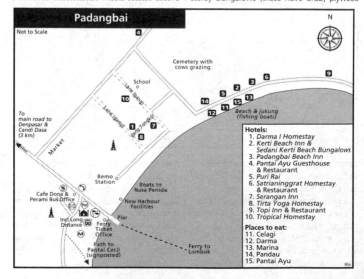

Padangbai

Not to Scale

To main road to Denpasar & Candi Dasa (3 km)

Cemetery with cows grazing

School

Lane (gang)

Lane (gang)

Gang Tongki

Market

Bemo Station

Cafe Dona & Perami Bus Office

Incl Long Distance

Ferry Ticket Office

Path to Pantai Cecil (signposted)

Boats to Nusa Penida

New Harbour Facilities

Pier

Ferry to Lombok

Beach & jukung (fishing boats)

Hotels:
1. Darma I Homestay
2. Kerti Beach Inn & Sedani Kerti Beach Bungalows
3. Padangbai Beach Inn
4. Pantai Ayu Guesthouse & Restaurant
5. Puri Rai
6. Satrianinggrat Homestay & Restaurant
7. Serangan Inn
8. Tirta Yoga Homestay
9. Topi Inn & Restaurant
10. Tropical Homestay

Places to eat:
11. Celagi
12. Darma
13. Marina
14. Pandau
15. Pantai Ayu

floors and easy access for mosquitoes), with fan or a/c, private mandi with western toilets but not always toilet seats!, restaurant (♦♦).

D *Pondok Serangan Inn*, Jl Segara, T 41425, clean, modern, 1st floor rooms with fan, private mandi, western toilet, attractive, 1st floor balcony seating area with views of town and sea, pot plants and family shrine, rec; **D** *Topi*, E side of bay, restaurant, isolated position, clean and comfortable basic rooms but creaky floors and thin walls makes for little privacy; **D-E** *Darma I Homestay*, Jl Silayukti Gang Tongkol No 6, T 41394, in town, well run, very clean, modern rooms with private mandi and western toilet, fan and mosquito nets, 1st floor balcony seating area with lovely sea views, good value, rec; **D-E** *Jati Wangi Inn*, Melanting 5 (owner at l Wayan Wista nr market), clean, cool, friendly; **D-E** *Kerti Beach Inn*, Jl Silayukti, T 41391, outside town with garden, rooms are basic and need redecorating, private mandi with western toilets, fan; **D-E** *Padangbai Beach Inn*, Jl Silayukti, one of the best locations, outside town, set in large grounds, but rooms are fairly basic, the more expensive rooms with private mandi and western toilet are okay, but the cheaper rooms are pretty grim with private squat toilet and shared shower; **D-E** *Pantai Ayu Guesthouse*, Jl Silayukti, T 41396, set on a hill overlooking Padangbai and the sea with fabulous views and flower filled garden, well run, clean but rooms are a little older than some, private bathrooms, western toilets, 3rd floor restaurant (♦♦), rec; **D-E** *Satrianinggrat*, Jl Silayukti No 11, T 41517, outside town, in quiet garden location with pleasant view of coconut grove, behind restaurant, 4 new rooms with private mandi (no wash basin), western toilet, fan, not particularly well built, somewhat overpriced; **D-E** *Sedani Kerti Beach Bungalows*, cottages and plain rooms on the beach front.

E *Tirta Yoga Homestay* (opp *Darma I Homestay*), Jl Silayukti Gang Tongkol, T 41415 (after 2000), set in pretty, small garden with shrine, clean rooms with fan, private mandi, western toilet, new rooms are good value, older rooms smelt damp; **E** *Tropical Homestay*, Jl Silayukti 1A, T 41398, good (new) rooms, attractive courtyard, friendly staff, choice of breakfast, quite noisy, rooms with fan, private mandi, western toilet.

● **Places to eat**
All offer Indonesian and western food.

♦♦*Pandan*, not by sea but set in pretty gardens backing onto coconut grove; ♦♦*Pantai Ayu*, Jl Silayukti, on the beach, also 3rd floor restaurant in guesthouse with fabulous views over Padangbai and sea, see accommodation, great seafood, moneychanger; ♦♦*Topi Inn*, upstairs, with views; *Marina Restaurant* has lovely sea views, several small warungs along sea front.

● **Post & telecommunications**
Area code: 0363.

● **Transport**
Road Bemo: Padangbai is 2½ km off the main coastal road; connections with Denpasar's Batubulan terminal (2,000Rp), Candi Dasa (500Rp) and Amlapura (1,000Rp). **Bus**: from the bus station you can catch long distance buses W to Java and E to Sumbawa and Lombok.

Sea Boat: ferries for Lembar on Lombok leave daily, every 2 hrs and takes 4-5 hrs, 4,800Rp, 9,300Rp in 1st class (children half price). The busiest departure is 0800 which is not a problem if one of the 2 large ultra-modern ferries is doing that sailing; otherwise try to get on as early as possible to secure a decent seat. Boats also depart for Nusa Penida (3,000Rp, local price; tourists pay 15,000Rp).

FROM PADANGBAI TO CANDI DASA

For many people Bali is at its best and most rewarding away from the tourist centres. Along the road leading from Padangbai to Candi Dasa there are several hotels and bungalow-style accommodation which offer peace and quiet in secluded settings with beautiful sea views. (The rice paddies in these parts sprout an interesting selection of scarecrows in different styles!) Breakfast is included in the price except at the luxury hotels.

BALINA BEACH

Balina Beach lies midway between Padangbai and Candi Dasa (approximately 4 km from the latter) adjacent to the village of Buitan, which runs this tourist development as a cooperative for the benefit of the villagers. It is a slightly scruffy black sand beach with a definite tourist feel to it. Sengkidu village and beach 2 km further E have more charm. Sometimes there are strong currents.

The village of Buitan has a public telephone and several small warung/restaurants and shops; the road to the beach and the accommodation is signposted. Perhaps the highlight of this village is the large advertisement promoting the advantages of artificial insemination in pig breeding.

At present there are two upmarket accommodations; the simpler, cheaper places seem to have disappeared.

Local information
● Accommodation

A-B *Balina Beach Bungalows (Pondok Pantai Balina)*, Balina Beach, Manggis, Postal reservations: *PT, Griyawisata Hotel Management,* Wijaya Grand Centre Blok G No 20-21, Jl Darmawangsa Raya, Jakarta 12160, T 41002/3/4/5, F 41001, 42 Balinese style bungalows set in large, tropical gardens with beautiful sea views, each bungalow has a private, western style bathroom with hot water and fan or a/c, and a verandah, the bungalows are set in the grounds away from the sea, restaurant (♦♦), bar and café overlooking the sea, small swimming pool, sea sports, snorkelling, scuba diving, fishing and sailing can be arranged, tours, car/motorbike hire, currency exchange, the most attractive of the 2 accommodations at Balina Beach, but other places offer better value; **A-B** *Puri Buitan*, Balina Beach, Manggis, Postal reservations: PO Box 3444, Denpasar 80034, T/F (0361) 223718, T (at hotel) (0363) 41021, 34 rm in a featureless modern hotel, rooms are functional, lacking in character, but clean, with fan or a/c, private western style bathrooms, deluxe rooms have a sea view, restaurant (♦♦) overlooking the smallish pool, access to pebbly beach, not particularly attractive, or good value.

SENGKIDU VILLAGE

2 km W of Candi Dasa, is an authentic Balinese village as yet unravaged by tourism. The pretty backstreets lead down to the sea and beach along which a hotel and five bungalow accommodations have so far been built. If arriving by bemo, ask the driver to let you off in the centre of the village by the temple and sign for *Candi Beach Cottage*. Follow the signpost to the right of the temple; the track leads to the beach and accommodation, 400m. Surrounded by coconut groves and tropical trees, Sengkidu offers an attractive alternative to Candi Dasa and is more pleasant and more interesting than Balina Beach. The village itself has a number of shops, fruit stalls and a temple where local festivals are celebrated; foreigners are welcome to participate if they observe temple etiquette and wear the appropriate dress, otherwise they can watch.

Local information
● Accommodation

A *Candi Beach Cottage*, reservations: PO Box 3308, Denpasar 80033, T 41234, F 41111, luxury hotel set in large, scenic tropical gardens, in a quiet location beside sea with access to beach, offering everything you would expect from a hotel in this class, popular with tour groups, elegant rooms with a/c, minibar, satellite TV, IDD telephone, private bathrooms, private terrace or balcony, seaside restaurant (♦♦-♦♦♦), bar, large swimming pool, children's pool, tennis courts, fitness centre, games room, etc, scuba diving, snorkelling, tours, money exchange, car rental, medical clinic; **A-B** *Anom Beach Bungalows,*

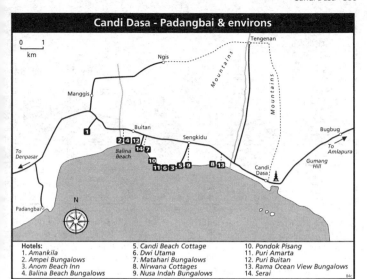

Candi Dasa - Padangbai & environs

Hotels:
1. Amankila
2. Ampei Bungalows
3. Anom Beach Inn
4. Balina Beach Bungalows
5. Candi Beach Cottage
6. Dwi Utama
7. Matahari Bungalows
8. Nirwana Cottages
9. Nusa Indah Bungalows
10. Pondok Pisang
11. Puri Amarta
12. Puri Buitan
13. Rama Ocean View Bungalows
14. Serai

T/F (0361) 233998, 18 bungalows and rooms, attractively decorated, with fan or a/c, some with mini-bar, private bathroom with hot water, small pool, seaside restaurant (♦♦), access to beach, airport transfer available, watersports, tours, car hire, very overpriced, the grounds are not particularly attractive, the rooms do not face the sea.

C-D *Pondok Bananas (Pisang)*, T 41065, family-run, set in a large coconut grove beside the sea with access to beach, very peaceful and secluded, 400m beyond the other accommodations, might suit an artist or writer looking for long-term accommodation, 4 spotless rm/bungalows built to a high standard in Balinese style, with private modern bathrooms with hot water, incl a 2-storey bungalow with downstairs living area and upstairs bedroom.

D *Puri Amarta (Amarta Beach Bungalows)*, T 41230, 10 bungalows set in large, attractive gardens beside the sea and beach, well-run and very popular, liable to be full even off-season with many guests returning year after year, bungalows face the sea and are very clean with private bathroom, western toilet, good breakfast incl in price, restaurant (♦♦) beside sea; **D-E** *Dwi Utama*, T 41053, 6 very clean rm, not facing sea, with fan, private bathroom, shower and western toilet, beachside restaurant (♦-♦♦),

access to good, small beach, well-tended, small garden, peaceful, good value; **D-E** *Nusa Indah Bungalows*, Sengkidu, signposted and reached via a separate track to the left of the temple, set in a peaceful location beside the sea, amidst coconut groves and rice paddies, 7 clean, simple bungalows facing the coconut grove with private mandi, western toilet, fan, verandahs with seating, access to small, rocky beach, beachside restaurant (♦♦).

● **Places to eat**

Several ♦♦ restaurants along this road: *Dwi Utama* (in addition to its beachside restaurant) and shop which also acts as a Post Office; *Baliarsa Restaurant*. See also under accommodation.

CANDI DASA

Candi Dasa is smaller, more intimate and offers better value for money than the main seaside resorts of Bali. It also provides an excellent base from which to explore the sights of E Bali.

The gold and black sand beach has been badly eroded, washed away by the sea due to the destruction of the reef for building materials, despite the unsightly concrete groynes and piers, which were

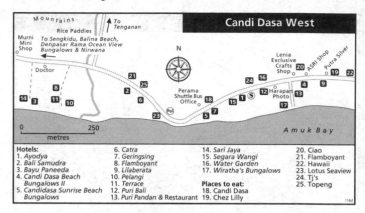

Candi Dasa West

Mountains
Rice Paddies
To Tenganan
Murni Mini Shop
To Sengkidu, Balina Beach, Denpasar Rama Ocean View Bungalows & Nirwana
Doctor
N
Lenia Exclusive Crafts Shop
ASRI Shop
Putra Silver
Perama Shuttle Bus Office
Harapan Photo
Amuk Bay

0 — 250 metres

Hotels:		14. Sari Jaya	20. Ciao
1. Ayodya	6. Catra	15. Segara Wangi	21. Flamboyant
2. Bali Samudra	7. Geringsing	16. Water Garden	22. Hawaii
3. Bayu Paneeda	8. Flamboyant	17. Wiratha's Bungalows	23. Lotus Seaview
4. Candi Dasa Beach Bungalows II	9. Lilaberata		24. Tj's
5. Candidasa Sunrise Beach Bungalows	10. Pelangi	**Places to eat:**	25. Topeng
	11. Terrace	18. Candi Dasa	
	12. Puri Bali	19. Chez Lilly	
	13. Puri Pandan & Restaurant		

constructed to prevent this happening. However, the lack of beach has saved Candi Dasa from over development. Even so, it is at its best off season. There is no surf, so swimming is safe. **Candi Dasa temple** is on the opposite side of the road from the lagoon. There are good walks in the area, either round the headland E to a deserted black-sand beach, only possible at low tide, or up over the hills to Tenganan. You can also climb Gumang Hill, by following the main road out of town to the E, for spectacular views of the surrounding countryside and across the strait to Lombok. The small temple at the top of the hill is the site of a major festival every 2 years at the time of the full moon in Oct (see below).

Candi Dasa gets its name from the temple on the hill overlooking the main road and the fresh water lagoon; the ancient relics in this temple indicate that there has been a village on this site since the 11th century. The word 'dasa' means 10 and refers to the 10 holy teachings of the Buddhist 'Tripitaka'. There are in reality two temples, one dedicated to Siva and the other to Hariti, giving rise to an unusual situation whereby one site serves both Hindus and Buddhists. Childless couples come here to pray to Hariti for children.

Traditionally fishermen in these parts have gone out fishing each day from 0400 until 0800, and again in the afternoon from about 1430 until 1800. Although most people on Bali fear the sea as a place of evil spirits and a potential source of disaster, those who live near the sea and earn their living from it consider it a holy place and worship such sea gods as *Baruna*. The boats they use, *jukung*, are made from locally grown wood and bamboo which is cut according to traditional ritual practice. The day chosen for cutting down the tree must be deemed favourable by the gods to whom prayers and offerings are then made, and a sapling is planted to replace it. Carved from a single tree trunk without using nails and with bamboo outriders to give it stability, the finished boat will be gaily coloured with the characteristic large eyes that enable it to see where the fish lurk. The design has not changed for thousands of years; it is very stable due to the low centre of gravity created by the way the sail is fastened. These days there are fewer fish to catch and many fishermen augment their living by taking tourists out snorkelling on the reef. *Jukung* cost about 850,000Rp.

Excursions

Tenganan 3 km N of Candi Dasa, the village of Tenganan is reputed to be the

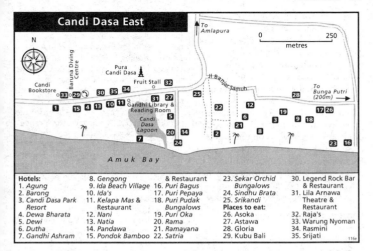

Candi Dasa East

To Amlapura

0   250
metres

To Bunga Putri (200m)

Baruna Diving Centre

Pura Candi Dasa
Fruit Stall

Candi Bookstore

Gandhi Library & Reading Room

Candi Dasa Lagoon

Amuk Bay

Hotels:
1. Agung
2. Barong
3. Candi Dasa Park Resort
4. Dewa Bharata
5. Dewi
6. Dutha
7. Gandhi Ashram
8. Gengong
9. Ida Beach Village
10. Ida's
11. Kelapa Mas & Restaurant
12. Nani
13. Natia
14. Pandawa
15. Pondok Bamboo
16. Puri Bagus & Restaurant
17. Puri Pepaya
18. Puri Pudak Bungalows
19. Puri Oka
20. Rama
21. Ramayana
22. Satria
23. Sekar Orchid Bungalows
24. Sindhu Brata
25. Srikandi

Places to eat:
26. Asoka
27. Astawa
28. Gloria
29. Kubu Bali
30. Legend Rock Bar & Restaurant
31. Lila Arnawa Theatre & Restaurant
32. Raja's
33. Warung Nyoman
34. Rasmini
35. Srijati

oldest on Bali – and is a village of the Bali Aga, the island's original inhabitants before the Hindu invasion almost 1,000 years ago (see box). The walled community consists of a number of longhouses, rice barns, shrines, pavilions and a large village meeting hall, all arranged in accordance with traditional beliefs. Membership of the village is exclusive and until recently visitors were actively discouraged. The inhabitants have to have been born here and then to marry within the village; anyone who violates the rules is banished to a neighbouring community. Despite the studied maintenance of a traditional way of life, the inhabitants of Tenganan have taken the decision to embrace the tourist industry. It is in fact a very wealthy village, deriving income not only from tourism but also from a large area of communally owned and worked rice paddys and dryland fields.

Tenganan is one of the last villages to produce the unusual **double ikat** or *geringsing*, where both the warp and the weft are tie-dyed and great skill is needed to align and then weave the two into the desired pattern (see box). The cloth is woven on body-tension (back-strap) looms with a continuous warp; colours used are dark rust, brown and purple, although newer pieces suffer from fading due to the use of inferior dyes. Motifs are floral and geometric, and designs are constrained to about 20 traditional forms. It is said that one piece of cloth takes about 5 years to complete and only six families still understand the process. Note that much of the cloth for sale in the village does not originate from Tenganan. *Admission to village*: by donation, vehicles prohibited. *Getting there*: it is possible to walk the 3 km to Tenganan; take the road heading N, 1 km to the W of Candi Dasa – it ends at the village. Alternatively, walk or catch a bemo heading W towards Klungkung, get off at the turning 1 km W of Candi Dasa and catch an *ojek* up to the village. Tours to Tenganan are also arranged by the bigger hotels and the tour agents on the main road. Bemos run past the turn-off for the village from Denpasar's Batubulan terminal.

About 13 km SW of Candi Dasa is the temple and cave of **Goa Lawah** (see page 394). *Getting there*: regular bemos run along the coast.

Boats leave for **Nusa Penida** from Padangbai (see page 396).

The royal bathing pools of **Tirtagangga** (see page 407) and the town and palace of **Amlapura** (see page 405) are both within easy reach of Candi Dasa.

Three small islands with coral reefs are to be found: 30 mins by boat from Candi Dasa. They make a good day trip for snorkelling or diving. Samuh village cooperative keeps goats on the largest of these islands. Every 6 months the goats are transported back to the mainland by boat. Quite a sight if you are lucky enough to witness it. *Getting there*: most hotels and losmen will arrange a boat for the day.

Local information
● **Accommodation**

There are many very reasonably priced accommodations available. Most accommodation is sited adjacent to the beach on the seaward side of the main road. At the eastern end of Candi Dasa, where the main road bends to the left, a small road (Jl Banjar Samuh, there is no name sign but there are many signs indicating accommodations incl *Puri Bagus* and *Genggong*) leads off on the right lined with accommodation on the seaward side. Known as Samuh village, this slightly rural area is perhaps the most attractive place to stay. Expect power cuts if you visit during the rainy season unless yours is one of the many accommodations which have their own generators. Most include breakfast in their rates. Most hotels with swimming pools allow non-residents to use their pools for a charge of 6,000Rp pp.

L *Amankila* (outside Candi Dasa) (reservations through *Amanusa* at Nusa Dua T 21993, F 21995), reservations T 71267, F 71266, opened mid-1992, one of the Aman group of hotels, highly luxurious with 35 guest pavilions amongst coconut and frangipani trees on a hill with great views over the Lombok Strait, stunning swimming pool on 3 levels, sandy beach with beach club and pool, library, impeccable service, hard to beat and possibly the most remarkable of the Amen hotels on Bali – but prices to match.

A+ *Puri Bagus* (E of lagoon), T 51223, F 52779, a/c, restaurant, pool, good rooms and attractive open-air bathrooms, but overpriced, shadeless pool area; **A+** *Serai*, Buitan, Manggis, Karangasem 80871, T 41011, F 41015, a luxury class hotel set in a coconut grove beside the sea in total seclusion, 58 rm (superior, deluxe and suites), a good location but the decor is rather functional, large swimming pool, restaurant, boutique, satellite TV, airport transfer; **A** *Candi Beach Cottages*, T 51711, F 52652, a/c, pool, tennis, 2 km W of town so quieter with better beach, but inconvenient for restaurants, bars and Candi Dasa's other facilities, but good rooms; **A** *Rama Ocean View*, T 51864, F 51866, a/c, restaurant, pool, on the road into Candi Dasa about 1 km from the town 'centre', tennis and fitness centre, good pool, overpriced catering mainly to tour groups, restaurant (♦♦♦); **A-B** *Ida Beach Village*, Jl Banjar Samuh, postal address: PO Box 3270, Denpasar, T 41118/9, F 41041, designed as a Balinese village, each bungalow is built in traditional style and set in its own small, private courtyard, very attractive rooms with a/c, hot water, telephone and western-style bathroom, some 2-storey bungalows with downstairs living room, swimming pool and access to beach, beachside restaurant (♦♦), rec; **A-B** *Kubu Bali Bungalows*, T 41532, 41256, F 41531, these bungalows have a breathtaking location extending up the hill behind the *Kubu Bali* restaurant with spectacular seaviews, each attractively furnished bungalow has a western bathroom with hot water, a/c, refrigerator, telephone and ceiling fan, and a verandah with seating, set in extensive, beautiful, tropical water gardens with live gamelan music playing all day, there is a coffee shop and swimming pool set high on the hill with the same inspiring views, you will need to be fairly fit to reach the topmost suites, ♦♦♦ restaurant located on the high street, with the *Baliku Restaurant* beside the sea just across the main street, airport transfer available, highly rec; **A-B** *Nirwana Cottages*, Candi Dasa Beach, Sengkidu, Amlapura 80871, T (0361) 36136, F 35543, situated outside Candi Dasa on the S side, 300m from the main road down a dirt track, 12 spotless bungalows built in the traditional Balinese style offering peace and tranquility, set in a coconut grove beside a quiet beach with beautiful sea views, a/c, hot water, house phone, deluxe rooms with refrigerator, large swimming pool with sunken bar, transport to/from airport available on request, seasports and tours available by arrangement, car hire, *Seaside Restaurant* (♦♦), no music in order to preserve the peaceful atmosphere here, owned by a German married to a Chinese who run this place to the highest standards at very reasonable prices, highly rec; **A-B** *Park Resor*, Jl Banjar Samuh, PO Box 01, Manggis 80871,

T/F 204440, a rather unattractive hotel catering mainly to tour groups, the 28 rather dark rooms face each other away from the sea, a/c, hot water, fridge, TV, pool, beach access; **A-B** *Water Garden*, PO Box 39, T 35540, restaurant, pool, individual cottages, set on the hillside in lovely gardens, each cottage has its own verandah overlooking a private lily pond, simple rooms (with hot water) but very attractively laid out, rec.

B *Candi Dasa Beach Bungalows II*, Jl Raya Candi Dasa, T 35536, F 35537, a/c, 2 restaurants, pool, 2-storey blocks, set in beautiful garden, views from rooms vary, beach here is only so-so, food rec; **B** *Samudra Indah*, T 35542, F 35542, a/c, pool, on the S edge of town, nice pool, comfortable but featureless rooms with hot water; **B-C** *Dewa Bharata Bungalows* (also has branch in Kuta, see Kuta section), T 41090, 41091, F 41091, popular, located in the centre of town beside the sea, 24 attractive bungalows in well-tended tropical gardens, rooms with a/c or fan, hot water, private bathrooms with western toilets, swimming pool beside the sea, open air, reasonably priced, beachside restaurant (♦♦) with beautiful sea views offering western, Indonesian and Chinese food; **B-C** *Puri Oka*, T 41092, F 41093, small pool, simple but attractive rooms, with attached bathrooms and hot water, very pleasant restaurant overlooking the sea, the tiny beach here evaporates at high tide and there is no swimming – although outrigger trips can be arranged to the islands off-shore for snorkelling, very overpriced; **B-D** *Puri Pudak* (E of lagoon), T 41978, well-designed, clean bungalows, with fan, private bathrooms, some with hot water, attractive garden, beside sea but with no direct access which is a major drawback, a little overpriced; **B-D** *Sindhu Brata* (beside lagoon), T 41825, some a/c and hot water, clean with private bathroom, set in large attractive garden beside the sea with beach, ♦♦ restaurant with sea views.

C *Pondok Bamboo*, T 41534, F 41818, in centre of town beside the sea, average rooms all with private bathroom, western toilet, some with hot water, new swimming pool and sea side restaurant with grand sea views should be finished late 1996; **C-D** *Bayu Paneeda Beach Inn*, T 41104, peaceful location to W of town beside the sea with fabulous sea views, bungalows with private bathrooms (western toilet) and fan, deluxe rooms with a/c and baths with hot water, restaurant ♦♦ with good sea views;

C-D *Genggong Cottage*, Jl Banjar Samuh, T 41105, 12 rooms set in large gardens with beach, rooms are clean but simple with fan, private mandi, western toilet and shower, 2 rooms have hot water, rooms are overpriced but you are paying for the beach, a rare asset in Candi Dasa; **C-D** *Ida's*, T 41096, this place consists of just 5 bungalows set in a large coconut grove beside the sea with access to its own small beach (due to the contours of the land and the direction of the sea current, less of the sandy beach was lost at Ida's following the destruction of the coral reef). Ida's was the second homestay to open in Candi Dasa in 1975, 2 large 2-storey bungalows and 3 smaller single storey bungalows beautifully built in the traditional Balinese style with rattan floors, bamboo walls and screens, mosquito nets and private bathrooms. An underground stream in the garden supplies fresh water. In the gardens are 2 old rice barns brought here from a nearby village and rebuilt to provide a traditional style rest area for guests. The 50 coconut palms produce 600 coconuts in 2 months; there is a local saying 'Coconuts have eyes' meaning that a falling coconut will not hit you!, manager/owner is Ida Ayu Srihati and her German husband both of whom have lived in the USA for many years, and are an excellent source of local knowledge; Ida herself is related to the klungkung royal family, highly rec, reservations advisable; **C-D** *Kelapa Mas*, PO Box 103, Amlapura 80801, T 41047, located on the eastern edge of town in a beautiful, large, traditional Balinese garden with a shrine, beside the sea with its own small area of beach, spotless bungalows, some overlooking the sea, with private bathrooms, western toilets, deluxe rooms with a/c, bathtubs, hot water, library and secondhand book shop, ♦♦ restaurant offering excellent food incl seafood, Balinese specialities and performances of the Legong Dance on certain evenings, English language Indonesian newspapers can be read in the lobby, excellent value, rec; **C-D** *Matahari Beach Bungalows* (formerly *Sunrise Beach Bungalows*), Buitan, Manggis, Postal address: PO Box 287, Denpasar 80001, T 41008/41009, signposted from the main road, follow a steep path down the hill for about 50m, beautiful setting in a large coconut grove beside the sea, with a beach suitable for swimming though occasionally there is a current, and offering complete seclusion, 11 fairly attractive bungalows and rooms with private bathroom, western toilet, fan, very clean, some large family rooms with 3 beds, several of the cheapest rooms have a shared ceiling so your neighbours will probably hear your every movement, breakfast incl, meals available if required, Ketut, the owner, speaks good English and is very helpful, he used to be in the tourist industry so is knowledgeable about Bali; **C-D** *Sekar Orchid Beach Bungalows*, Jl Banjar Samuh, PO Box 113, Candi Dasa, Bali 80851, T 41086, 8 attractive rooms with private bathroom, western toilet, some with hot water and bathtub, fan, set in large, pretty gardens beside the sea with a beach except at high tide, very well run and spotlessly clean, safety deposit box, Wendy the Javanese owner has lived in England and Germany and speaks both languages, a very secure accommodation which is an important consideration given the growing number of thefts from tourist bungalows in Candi Dasa, rec; **C-E** *Barong*, Jl Banjar Samuh, T 41127, set in attractive gardens beside the sea, simple rooms with large comfortable bamboo beds, fan and in the cheaper rooms minimal furniture and weatherbeaten, 'no maintenance' private bathrooms open to the skies with western toilets, you can listen to the waves crashing at night or hear the magical frog chorus at the start of the rainy season, you might even find a frog in your bathroom!, the more expensive rooms face the sea and have enclosed bathrooms, be mindful of security as there have been thefts, good breakfast.

D *Agung Bungalows*, T 235535, good value for location in centre of town, situated beside the sea with access to beach, basic bungalows with private bathroom (western toilet), set in large gardens with coconut palms; **D** *Bunga Putri* (E of lagoon), at the N end of the bay, past the fishing boats, restaurant, peaceful undeveloped setting, good rooms, rec; **D** *Puri Amarta Beach Inn*, clean, average; **D** *Puri Pandan*, PO Box 126, Amlapura 80801, T 41541, rooms average, bathrooms better than average with hot water; **D** *Srikandi* (E of lagoon), T 53125, clean rooms but rather close together, popular, new restaurant (♦♦) beside sea serving Indonesian and western food; **D-E** *Ampel Bungalows*, Manggis Beach, T 41209, 6 km from Candi Dasa, just off the main road in a peaceful, rural setting overlooking rice paddies and the sea, 4 simple, very clean bungalows, with private mandi, western toilet and verandah with seating, the black sand beach is 5 mins' walk as is Balina Beach with a selection of restaurants, price incl breakfast, very friendly owners, signposted from the main road shortly after the *Amankila Hotel*; **D-E** *Dutha Cottages*, Jl Banjar Samuh, T 41143/5, 10 rm beside the sea but

with no direct access, fairly basic but clean, with private mandi, western toilet, shower, set in coconut grove with pretty gardens; **D-E** *Nani Beach Inn*, Jl Banjar Samuh, simple rooms with private mandi, western toilet, shower, set in coconut grove; **D-E** *Pandawa Homestay* (just E of lagoon), T 41929, closely spaced bungalows with fan and private bathroom, some with hot water, access to sea via tiny beach; **D-E** *Pepaya Bungalows*, Jl Banjar Samuh, T 41567, clean, simple rooms with fan and attractive private bathroom, western toilet, set in large gardens but not beside the sea, attached to the *Asoka Restaurant*; **D-E** *Ramayana*, Jl Banjar Samuh, T/F 41778, 3 very clean, simple but attractive bungalows with private mandi, western toilets, shower, verandahs with outside seating and hammocks, run by Made and his British wife Deborah who also have a house nr Amed available to rent (price **D** or slightly more if all meals incl), the owners have some land also nr Amed where they plan to build some reasonably priced bungalows, beside the sea with access to small beach where the local fishermen land their catch and keep their boats, Deborah can arrange for you to accompany them on a night fishing trip, Deborah also sells local handicrafts, good value; **D-E** *Satria* (E of lagoon), attractive rooms, nice bathrooms, good value, but not on the beachside, popular with local Balinese men.

Gandhi Ashram, overlooking the lagoon at eastern end of town, this ashram is run according to Gandhian principles and guests follow strict codes of behaviour, by invitation to those who are genuinely interested in Gandhi's teachings, there are bungalows and more basic rooms, this was the first homestay to open in Candi Dasa, run by Ibu Gedong Oka.

D-E The following are all situated outside of town to the W in a peaceful setting with access to the sea, well-sited for visits to Tenganan. Inland there are beautiful views of rice terraces and mountains, with possibilities for walks. These rice paddies are communal land owned by Tenganan village; you can watch the villagers rhythmically working the fields as if living in a different age, adjacent to but oblivious of the tourist world across the road. They all offer similar accommodation consisting of basic bungalows with private bathrooms and western toilets, fan, at similar prices, and in descending order of preference: *Terrace Beach Bungalows*, nice setting beside beach; *Taruna Homestay*, rooms could do with redecoration, good sea views, tea and coffee available all day; *Flamboyant Bungalows*, beside sea, rooms could do with redecoration, tea available all day; *Sari Jaya Sea Side Cottage*, T 41149, average rooms in attractive gardens beside the sea; *Pelangi Homestay*, T 41270, bungalows set in attractive gardens, not beside the sea but with easy access via adjacent accommodation.

● **Places to eat**

There are a variety of well-priced restaurants dotted along the main road with similar menus; seafood is the best bet. Most restaurants cater to perceived European tastes which can be disappointing for anyone who likes Indonesian food. Many of the above accommodations have restaurants, often with sea views. The following are also rec though quality and ingredients can vary enormously from day to day; you might have a delicious meal one day, order the exact same dish the next day and be very disappointed.

◆◆◆*Kubu Bali*, good seafood and Chinese and Indonesian specialities.

◆◆*TJ's Café*, Mexican, good food, friendly, rec; ◆◆*Legend Rock Café*, western and Indonesian; ◆◆*Pandan*, on the beach, daily Balinese buffet, reasonably priced international food, rec; ◆◆*Raja's Restaurant and Cocktail Bar*; ◆◆*Kelapa Mas*, good value and sometimes excellent food; ◆◆*Astawa*, popular though you are paying for the decor.

◆*Rasmini Warung*, a genuine warung serving simple Indonesian food and the best Nasi Campur in town though quality varies from day to day, excellent value.

Several restaurants incl *Kelapa Mas*, *Bali Tropical* and *Astawa* offer dance performances and gamelan recitals in the evenings.

● **Banks & money changers**

There are several money changers offering reasonable rates.

● **Entertainment**

Dance: Balinese dance performances staged nightly at 2100 at the *Pandan Harum* nr the centre of town. Many restaurants offer performances of Balinese dance and gamelan music in the evenings, see under **Places to eat**. The best performances are at the newly opened *Lila Arnaud* which has been designed as a theatre with a proper stage, prices incl dinner. Several places have nightly shows of western films on video; best of these is *Raja's* whose Australian owner imports the latest films.

● **Post & telecommunications**

Area code: 0363.

Postal agent: opp the *Candi Dasa Beach Bungalows*.

● **Shopping**

Asri, fixed price store for film, food and medicine.

Crafts: *Geringsing*, on the main road, sells double ikat cloth from Tenganan and other Balinese arts and crafts. *Lenia*, T 41174, a good place to see ATA baskets, these baskets are made from a locally grown vine which is much more durable than rattan, water resistant, it is claimed these baskets can last for up to 100 years, *Lenia* also has a stall selection of Sumba blankets and other quality crafts.

● **Sports**

Diving: *Stingray Dive Centre*, *Puri Bali Homestay*; *Baruna Watersports*, *Puri Bagus Hotel*, T (0361) 753820/751223, F 753809/752779, prices start from US$40 for 1 dive PADI course (4 days), US$300. Also available fishing and watersports.

Snorkelling: rent snorkels from hotels and charter a boat to go out to a reef.

● **Tour companies & travel agents**

Several travel agents book tours, reconfirm tickets and sell bus tickets to major destinations in Java.

● **Transport**

Local Bicycle, motorbike and car hire from hotels, losmen and from shops along the main road.

Road Bemo: regular connections with Denpasar's Batubulan terminal (2,000Rp), Amlapura (500Rp) and Klungkung (500Rp). **Shuttle bus**: more expensive, but quicker, shuttle buses link Candi Dasa with Denpasar, Ubud, Kuta, Lovina and Kintamani (4,000-10,000Rp).

AMLAPURA (KARANGASEM)

At one time Amlapura, capital of the Regency of Karangasem, was the seat of one of the most powerful states in Bali. Today, this may be hard to believe – it is a quiet and attractive town, with wonderful views of Gunung Agung from its clean landscaped streets. Little happens here. Earthquakes which accompanied the massive eruption of Gunung Agung in 1963 caused much damage and in order to protect the

The Bali Aga: the original Balinese

In pre-history, Bali was populated by animists whose descendants today are represented by the Bali Aga, literally 'Original Balinese'. The Aga are now restricted to a few relic communities in N and E Bali, particularly in the regency of Karangkasem. Most have been extensively assimilated into the Hindu-Balinese mainstream. Miguel Covarrubias visited the Aga village of Tenganan in the 1930s, a village which even then was extraordinary in the extent to which it was resisting the pressures of change. He wrote:

"The people of Tenganan are tall, slender and aristocratic in a rather ghostly, decadent way, with light skins and refined manners. ...They are proud and look down even on the Hindu-Balinese nobility, who respect them and leave them alone. They live in a strange communistic... system in which individual ownership of property is not recognized and in which even the plans and measurements of the houses are set and alike for everybody".

Even today, a distinction is still made between the Bali Aga and the *Wong Majapahit*. The latter arrived from Java following the fall of the Majapahit Kingdom at the end of the 15th century.

In former years, the Aga were probably cannibalistic. It has been said that Aga corpses used to be washed with water which was allowed to drip onto a bundle of unhusked rice. This was then dried and threshed, cooked, moulded into the shape of a human being, and served to the relatives of the deceased. The eating of the rice figure is said to symbolize the ritual eating of the corpse, so imbibing its powers.

town from future devastation the name of the capital was changed from Karangasem to Amlapura to confuse the evil spirits who had wreaked this havoc. Several palaces are to be found in Karangasem, the most accessible being the **Puri Agung**, or Puri Kanginan, to the E of the main N-S road, Jl Gajah Mada. The last king of Karangasem was born at the Puri Agung. Entrance to the palace is through tall gateways. To the S are a cluster of buildings, which would have been offices and artist's workshops. Another gateway takes the visitor out of this first compound and a door to the S leads into the major part of the palace. A pillared building faces S onto a *bale Kembang* or floating pavilion. The buildings are all rather run-down, and are eclectic architecturally with European, Balinese and Chinese elements and motifs. There are interesting photographs from the early part of this century and some rather tatty furniture. Admission 200Rp. Open 0800-1700 Mon-Sun. There is a **market** to the S of the palace; the stallholders seem strangely reluctant to bargain.

Excursions

The ruined water palace of **Ujung** is very beautiful in its romantic decrepitude. It lies 8 km S of town towards the coast and was built by the last King of Karangasem. The hills of Lombok can be seen from the site which is in a beautiful position at the edge of the sea with the huge volcanic cone of Mt Agung inland. Most of the buildings were destroyed during an earthquake in 1963. The palace must have been splendid in its time. Now, you can wander among the large lotus ponds, still part full, and explore the ruined pavilions. The bridges leading over the water to the old temple have all collapsed, and columns lean at crazy angles. Parts of the balustrades, their intricate carvings still intact, litter the ground. Although the rice terraces and steps up to the central pavilion above the ponds are intact, the palace has the air of

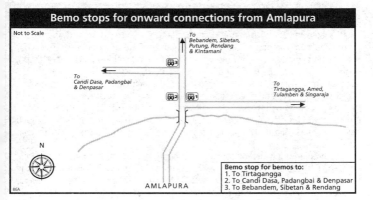

Bemo stops for onward connections from Amlapura

Not to Scale

To Bebandem, Sibetan, Putung, Rendang & Kintamani

To Candi Dasa, Padangbai & Denpasar

To Tirtagangga, Amed, Tulamben & Singaraja

N

AMLAPURA

Bemo stop for bemos to:
1. To Tirtagangga
2. To Candi Dasa, Padangbai & Denpasar
3. To Bebandem, Sibetan & Rendang

86A

an ancient lost city. No crowds or hawkers – suitable for those with fertile imaginations. There are plans to have the palace restored. *Getting there*: bemos leave from the station near the market (S of the palace).

Tirtagangga These royal bathing pools are 7 km N of town (see next page).

Bebandem This village is the scene of an important cattle market held every 3 days, as is usual with Balinese markets. On market day stalls are set up selling everything from medicines to sarongs. Ironsmiths take up their positions along the main road producing cockfighting spurs, keris knives, farm tools etc. The animals start their journey to the village at dawn, often on foot, and the activity is over by 0900. *Getting there*: by bemo from Amlapura, 500Rp.

Local information

● **Accommodation**

E *Homestay Sidha Karya*, Jl Hasannudin; **E** *Lahar Mas Inn*, Jl Gatot Subroto 1, small, friendly people; **E** *Losman Kembang Remaja*, 200m along the road to Bebandem outside of town, T 21565, fairly basic rooms with private mandi, squat toilet, few westerners stay here.

● **Places to eat**

♦♦*RM Surabaya*, adjacent to the market, good Chinese and Indonesian dishes, popular with local expats, good value; *Pasar Malam*, nr the main market serves good local food. Restaurants close early at about 2100.

● **Banks & money changers**

Bank Rakyat Indonesia, Jl Gajah Mada.

● **Post & telecommunications**

Area code: 0363.

Post Office: Jl Gatot Subroto 25.

● **Transport**

Road Bemo/minibus: the bemo terminal is on Jl Kesatrian. Regular connections with Denpasar's Batubulan terminal and to Manggis, Culik, Padangbai, Klungkung, Tirtagangga and Singaraja. See map on this page – above, for bemo stops outside the main town for onward connections.

TIRTAGANGGA

7 km NW of Amlapura is the site of the royal bathing pools of Tirtagangga. Built in 1947 by the last king of Amlapura, they were badly damaged by the earthquake of 1963 but have since been restored. The pools occupy a stunning position on the side of a hill, overlooking terraced ricefields. At harvest times the fields are full of people gathering the golden rice, and carrying it on poles back to the villages to dry. The complex consists of various pools (2 of which visitors can swim in), fed by clear mountain streams with water spouting from fountains and stone animals. It is popular with local people as well as visitors and is a peaceful place to retreat to except at weekends and holidays when young Balinese arrive en masse on their motorbikes. Admission

Cloth as art: Ikat in Southeast Asia

Ikat is a technique of patterning cloth characteristic of Southeast Asia and is produced from the hills of Burma to the islands of Eastern Indonesia. The word comes from the Malay word *mengikat* which means to bind or tie. Very simply, either the warp or the weft, and in one case both, are tied with material or fibre so that they resist the action of the dye. Hence the technique's name – resist dyeing. By dyeing, retieing and dyeing again through a number of cycles it is possible to build up complex patterns. Ikat is distinguishable by the bleeding of the dye which inevitably occurs no matter how carefully the threads are tied; this gives the finished cloth a blurred finish. The earliest ikats so far found date from the 14th-15th centuries.

To prepare the cloth for dyeing, the warp or weft is strung taut on a frame. Individual threads, or groups of threads are then tied tight with fibre and leaves. In some areas wax is then smeared on top to help in the resist process. The main colour is usually dyed first, secondary colours later. With complex patterns (which are done from memory, plans are only required for new designs) and using natural dyes, it may take up to 6 months to produce a piece of cloth. Prices are correspondingly high – in Eastern Indonesia for example, top grade cloths can easily exceed 1,000,000Rp ($500), and ritual cloths considerably more still. Today, the pressures of the market place mean that it is more likely that cloth is produced using chemical dyes (which need only one short soaking, not multiple long ones as with some natural dyes), and design motifs have generally become larger and less complex. Traditionally, warp ikat used cotton (rarely silk) and weft ikat, silk. Silk in many areas has given way to cotton, and cotton sometimes to synthetic yarns. Double ikat, where incredibly both the warp *and* the weft are tie-dyed, is produced in only one spot in Southeast Asia: the village of Tenganan in Eastern Bali.

Warp ikat:	**Weft ikat:**
Sumatra (Bataks)	Sulawesi (Bugis)
Kalimantan (Dayaks)	NE Java
Sulawesi (Toraja)	E Sumatra
East Nusa Tenggara (Savu,	Bali
Flores, Sumba, Roti)	Burma (Shans)
	Thailand
Double ikat:	Laos
East Bali	Cambodia

500Rp, plus 2,000Rp to swim in the upper pool, 1,000Rp in the lower pool, children half price. Open Mon-Sun.

Excursions

There are many walks in the hills around Tirtagangga; the scenery is superb and there are several traditional villages worth visiting: *Abadi*; *Tanah Lingis* with its interesting music group which sings in rhythms imitative of a gamelan orchestra, this musical form originated in Lombok and on Bali is found only in Karangasem; *Budakling* with a Buddhist tradition that pre-dates the arrival of Hinduism on Bali, this village also produces good quality gold and silver pieces. There are spectacular walks up Mt Agung one of which starts from the village of *Tanaharon*.

About 8 km NE of Tirtagangga is temple *Pura Lempuyang* situated at an altitude of 1,060m, it is one of the more important temples on Bali; it is a steep climb, make an early start to avoid the heat and enjoy the views before the clouds roll in. All these villages have traditional festivals during the year. Your accommodation can help you plan walks.

Local information

● **Accommodation**

As you follow the main road out of town up the hill towards Tulemben you come first to *Puri Sawah Bungalows and Restaurant.* Further up the hill you come to *Kusumajaya Inn* and finally *Prima Bamboos Homestay;* of these two accommodations *Prima* offers better, cleaner, newer, more attractive rooms, with slightly better views, at lower prices than Kusumajaya. The other accommodations are in Tirtagangga. All incl breakfast in their price.

B-C *Puri Sawah* (formerly *Rice Terrace*), PO Box 110, Amlapura 80811, T 21847, run by Liz from Guernsey and her Balinese husband Made, the 2-storey bungalow was built to a very high standard to accommodate friends and family visiting from the UK, the upstairs bungalow is decorated very tastefully in Balinese style with a balcony offering glorious views over the rice paddies, private bathroom with squat toilet, the attractive downstairs bungalow has private bathroom with hot water, bath and western toilet, 2 additional simpler bungalows are due to be built, the ✦✦ restaurant offers excellent Indonesian and western food and is well known for its filled baguettes, you can even get baked beans on toast!, the owners have land nr Amed which they will be developing, highly rec; **B-D** *Tirta Ayu Homestay*, within the water garden itself, rather overpriced for unexciting rooms, though the one most expensive room is attractive with a large attractive bathroom, a great position, rooms are clean with private bathrooms, western toilet set around lovely, very peaceful gardens, 2-3 times a month there is a Holy Water Ceremony in the grounds of the water gardens in the afternoon, ask owner for information, price incl access to the water gardens and swimming pools, restaurant (✦✦✦) overlooking water gardens with cool breezes (see below).

C-D *Kusumajaya Inn*, T 21250, rooms in need of refurbishment, no fans, 1 rm with hot water, all rooms with private bathroom and western toilet, set in pretty gardens with grand views over the rice paddies to the distant sea, this view is shared by the functionally decorated, but reasonably priced restaurant (✦✦), trekking available, there are 99 steps up to the Inn from the road, it is a hard slog if you are not fairly fit; **C-E** *Prima Bamboos Homestay and Restaurant*, T 21316, F 21044, 7 rm, well run, clean, set in immaculate gardens with bamboo windchimes, terrific views of rice paddies and the coast, all rooms with fan, private mandi with

western toilet, outside verandahs to enjoy the view, very peaceful, restaurant (✦✦), climbs of Mt Agung and other treks can be arranged, owner is a keen chess player, rec.

D-E *Dhangin Tamin Inn*, PO Box 132, Amlapura 80811, T 22059, rooms are attractive, very clean but rather dark, set around a pretty courtyard, all with private mandi and western toilet, fan, safety deposit box available, restaurant (✦); **D-E** *Pondok Batur Indah*, in same ownership as *Rijasa*, 500m from town centre by foot following a path through paddy fields (ask for directions at *Rijasa*), 1½ km by road, 4 basic rm with private mandi, views; **D-E** *Pondok Wisata Dau*, T 21292, reached across paddy fields just above the water palace in a peaceful setting, modern house with 3 clean, new but featureless rooms, only 1 with private mandi, squat toilets, if there is no one at home ask at *Rama Tirtagangga Restaurant* in town nr the entrance to the water palace; **D-E** *Rijasa Homestay and Restaurant*, T 21873, clean but drab and basic rooms with private mandi (western toilet), set round simple gardens, owner can provide a map and information about local walks, restaurant (✦) the *Nasi Campur* has been rec, off season prices negotiable.

● **Places to eat**

✦✦*Good Karma*, same ownership as *Good Karma Bungalows* at Amed, just outside the pools, friendly people, food rec; ✦✦*Tirta Ayu restaurant*, T 21697, an open-air restaurant within the water garden, with a fabulous position overlooking the pools and the terraced paddy fields beyond; ✦*Kusumajaya Inn and Prima*, on the hill with great views over the whole panorama down to the sea, good spot for lunch. **Rijasa**: *Nasi Campur* has been rec.

● **Post & telecommunications**
Area code: 0363.

● **Transport**
Road Minibus/bemo: connections with Amlapura, Culik, Kubu, Singaraja. From Denpasar's Batubulan terminal catch a bemo to Amlapura and get off at the intersection just before Amlapura (see map, page 407) to catch a connection up the hill to Tirtagangga. Tirtagangga is easily reached by public bemo as a day trip from Candi Dasa (where there is a much better choice of budget price accommodation), 30 mins door to door. *Getting there*: Candi Dasa to Amlapura, 500Rp, ask to be let off at the turning for Tirtagangga (see map). Amlapura to Tirtagangga, 300Rp. There are many bemo, you won't have to wait long.

AMED

For peace and quiet, this area on the E coast, N of Tirtagangga has much to offer. The drive from Culik via Amed to Lipah Beach is quite spectacular especially on the return journey with Mt Agung forming a magnificent backdrop to the coastal scenery. Numerous coves and headlands, with colourful fishing boats completing the vista, offer endless possibilities for walks and picnics. At present most of the accommodation lies beyond Amed at Lipah Beach, reached along a dreadful, pot-holed road. Lipah Beach itself is an extremely average grey sand public beach with litter. The area became popular because of the good snorkelling and diving available here. However, at present the accommodation is overpriced; own transport is essential. New accommodations are appearing along the coast road leading from Culik to Lipah Beach, some with spectacular hillside locations with grand views of Mt Agung. This is an area to watch as new accommodations will appear; several Balinese/British families have bought land here with a view to developing more reasonable bungalow accommodation.

● **Accommodation A-B** *Coral View Villas* (in same ownership as *Hidden Paradise Cottages* next door, below, same address and T/F), 19 bungalows in attractive garden beside sea, new with attractive decor, private bathrooms, hot and cold water, fan or a/c, seaside bar and restaurant (♦♦-♦♦♦), swimming pool, children's play area; **A-B** *Hidden Paradise Cottages* (at Lipah Beach), PO Box 121, Amlapura, Bali, T (0361) 431273, F (0361) 423820 and (0363) 21044, 16 bungalows in attractive gardens beside public beach, with private bathrooms (western toilets), with fan or a/c, hot water, swimming pool, restaurant (♦♦-♦♦♦), diving and snorkelling, transport available; **C** *Kusumajaya Beach Inn*, Amed Jemeluk (also spelt Cemeluk), Amlapura (same ownership as *Kusumajaya* at Tirtagangga), nr Amed in unspoilt rural setting beside sea, more attractive location than Lipah Beach, new Balinese-style bungalows in large, slightly unkempt gardens, with private bathrooms, shower, western toilet, fan, restaurant (♦♦) overlooking the sea with beautiful views, staff can be less than helpful, rec; **C-D** *Good*

Karma Beach Bungalows, Dusan Selang, Amed, Amlapura (at Lipah Beach), owner is planning to change name to *Pala Karma Beach Bungalows*, set in rather scrubby garden beside public beach, more expensive bungalows have attractive new decor, private bathrooms with shower and western toilets, cold water, fan, cheaper bungalows are very close together and have squat toilets, restaurant (♦♦) overlooking sea; **C-D** *Pondok Vienna Beach Bungalows* (Lipah Beach), 1 Wayan Utama, PO Box 112, Amlapura 80801, Bali, bungalows in beachside garden setting with fan, private bathrooms (western toilet) and cold water, restaurant (♦♦), watersports available.

WEST OF AMLAPURA

For those in search of peace and seclusion and pleasant walks amongst the cool hills – this area fits the bill.

Putung 21 km by road W of Amlapura, 10 km W of Bebandem. *Getting there*: can be reached via bemo from Amlapura to Bebandem (500Rs) change to a bemo heading for Selat, ask to be dropped at the turn off for Putung 1 km before Duda village, then it is about a 2 km walk. Much easier by car. **Accommodation C-D** *Pondok Bukit Putung*, T (0366) 23039, reservations: PT Griyawisata Hotel Management, Wijaya Grand Centre Blok G No 20-21, Jl Darmawangsa Raya, Jakarta 12160, F (021) 720 4065, set admidst stunning mountain scenery with magnificent views from its perch on the edge of a cliff to the coast and sea, bungalows with private bathroom, western toilet, good walks in the cool mountain air, 750m above sea level, (♦♦) restaurant.

Sideman In the hills 10 km N of Klungkung with beautiful scenery and views of rice paddies. There is a weaving factory where you can buy good quality cloth woven in the traditional manner. **Accommodation B** *Sideman Homestay*, superb views from these attractive but expensive bungalows with private bathroom, western toilet, (♦♦-♦♦♦) restaurant.

Abian Soan A small peaceful village 4 km W of Amlapura. *Getting there*: take a bemo bound for Rendang and get off after

$2^{1}/_{2}$ km (300Rs). By car follow the road to Rendang for $2^{1}/_{2}$ km from the turn-off outside Amlapura. **E** *Homestay Lila*, simple bungalows with private bathrooms, in a pretty location set amidst rice paddies on the northern fringe of the village, look for the signpost.

15 km NW of Denpasar is the town of Kapal. Shortly after Kapal, in the village of Bringkit, the road branches; W for Tanah Lot and Gilimanuk, and N for Lake Bratan, Singaraja and Lovina Beach. The coastal temple of Tanah Lot is 10 km off the main road and is a popular tourist attraction. The other arm of the fork runs N for 2 km to Mengwi (with its impressive temple complex). Continuing N, the road climbs through breathtaking terraced paddy fields to Lake Bratan, one of three crater lakes that fill part of a massive caldera. Mount Catur lies to the N of the lake and is the highest peak in the area at 2,096m.

KAPAL

The meru-making town of Kapal is best-known for its red-brick **Pura Sada** which lies just S of the main road, past the bend near the market place (it is signposted). The pura is an important shrine of the former dynasty of the kingdom of Mengwi. Inside the enclosure is an unusual 10m-high *prasada* or *prasat* (possibly explaining its name 'Pura Sada'), similar in style to Javanese candis, and dedicated to the king's ancestors. An earthquake in 1917 all but destroyed the prasada and the *candi bentar* or split gate. In 1949, it was carefully restored by local craftsmen. The sculptures that decorate the prasada were all carved after 1950.

● **Transport** 15 km from Denpasar. **Road Bemo**: regular bemos from the Ubung terminal, just NW of Denpasar.

TANAH LOT

The coastal temple of **Tanah Lot**, perched on a rock at the edge of the shore-line and 30 km NW of Denpasar, is probably the most photographed sight in Bali. The temple is one of the *sadkahyangan* – the six holiest shrines – and is said to have been built after the Hindu saint Danghyang

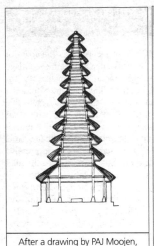

After a drawing by PAJ Moojen, 1926

The Balinese pagoda: the meru

Perhaps the most characteristic feature of Balinese architecture is the *meru*. These are multi-tiered (but always odd in number) pagoda-like towers made of wood and coir thatch. As the name suggests, they symbolize the cosmic Hindu-Buddhist mountain, Mt Meru (as do candis and prasada/prasats). The underworld is represented by the lower section, the world of men by the middle section, and the heavens by the towering, tapering roofs. There are clear stylistic links between merus and the brick candis of Java, as well as with similar buildings in Nepal. Whether the idea of making the upper portions from perishable materials was introduced from Java is not clear. Certainly, there are structures today in Java which consist only of a base, indicating that there may have been an upper portion of wood or thatch.

Nirartha spent a night here and subsequently suggested that a temple be constructed on the spot.

The temple itself is small, and hardly remarkable artistically, with 2-tiered merus and several other pavilions. What makes it special, and so popular, is its incomparable position. Built on a rock outcrop just off the coast, it can only be reached at low tide. The surrounding rocks are said to be inhabited by sea-snakes but this does nothing to deter the hoards of visitors who clamber over the rocks and stroll along the beach. The profusion of trinket stalls, warungs and hawkers can be over-powering, detracting from the overall ambience of the location, but it is still well worth the visit, particularly in the late afternoon, when the sun sets behind the temple (and photographers line-up to catch the moment). There are good coastline walks S from Tanah Lot. Admission by donation. Facilities here include a money changer, restaurant and post office.

At the beginning of 1994 plans were announced to build a 5-star hotel, a complex of luxury apartments and a golf course within 2 km of Tanah Lot. This announcement came despite a ruling by the supreme Hindu body in Indonesia, the Parisada Hindu Dharma, that construction within 2 km of any of the six *sadkahyangan* was prohibited. The announcement resulted in public demonstrations against the development, although pessimists argue that with the well-connected Bakrie Group behind the project, it is unlikely that even large-scale protests will have any effect. A local anthropologist, Bangkal Kusuma, maintains that the developers, in collusion with irrigation officials, cut off water to the rich rice lands needed for the complex and forced the owners of the land to sell their holdings.

● **Accommodation   A+** *Nirwana Resort*, scheduled to have opened by early 1996, after much protest from the islanders, who believe it will despoil the holy ground around Tanah Lot; **B** *Bali Wisata Bungalows*, Yeh Gangga Beach, T 261354, a/c, restaurant, saltwater pool, a dozen small bungalows close to rice paddies, the beach on one side and a pura on the other, 1 hr walk from Tanah Lot along the beach; to the cognoscente: Bali as it used to be – quiet, relaxed, peaceful, only drawback is that the currents here are too strong for swimming in the sea, rec; **C** *Dewi Sinta*, some a/c, restaurant, hot water, attractive position overlooking rice fields, close to the walkway to Tanah Lot.

● **Post & telecommunications Area code**: 0361.

● **Transport** 30 km from Denpasar. **Road Bemo**: connections with Denpasar's Ubung terminal, N of town to Kediri (500Rp) and then another from Kediri to Tanah Lot (300Rp); be sure to leave Tanah Lot by 1400 in order to catch a connecting bemo from Kediri back to town. The turning for the temple is 20 km NW of Denpasar on the road to Negara and Gilimanuk. From here it is a 10 km drive down a lovely road through paddy fields to the sea.

MENGWI

Mengwi on the road N from Kapal towards Lake Bratan and Singaraja, is an unremarkable market town, save for the **Pura Taman Ayun**; take the turning to the right opposite the colt station to get there. This impressive temple, with its classic design, lawns and ponds is free from crowds and hawkers, making it worth the visit. It was built for the founder of the Mengwi Kingdom in 1634. Surrounded by a moat, it consists, characteristically, of a series of three courtyards. The tallest gate leads into the back courtyard, where there are two rows of *palinggih-palinggih* or shrines for visiting deities on the N and E sides, each with ornate pillars and beautifully carved doors. On the W side are a number of *bales* or pavilions. The courtyard also contains a stone altar (*paibon*) with reasonable relief carvings. To the left of the main entrance there is a poor 'Museum of Complete Cremation' (admission by donation).

Excursions Sangeh nutmeg forest is 15 km N of Mengwi (it is also known as 'monkey forest' because of the many monkeys found here) and is the sight of the **Pura Bukit Sari**. The temple was built at the beginning of the 17th century by the son of the King of Mengwi as a meditation temple. Today it is a *subak* (or irrigation) temple. *Getting there*: although the forest and temple are closest to

Mengwi it is difficult to get there on public transport except by returning to Denpasar's Ubung terminal and taking another bemo N (600Rp) – which means a total journey of nearly 40km. With private transport, it is easy to take the road E towards Kedampat.

Pura Luhur is an isolated mountain temple situated on the slopes of Mt Batukau (or 'shell' mountain), amidst tropical forest. *Getting there*: it is not easy to reach by public transport – it is best to charter a bemo from Denpasar or Mengwi, turning N at Tabanan. The final climb is steep. On the way, visit the **hot springs** at **Penatahan**. The natural hot springs of **A+** *Yeh Panes*, Jl Batukaru, Desa Penatahan, T 262356, is a spa resort, with simple chalets, wooden floors and balconies, standing on a hillside overlooking swimming pool and spa area. The spa comprises a series of nine enclosed hot-spring rock pools with jacuzzi jets. Massage available. Towels and lockers for hire. Open air restaurant overlooking river. Tennis courts. Lunch and use of spa is US$48 per person. If you stay at the resort, use of the spa and breakfast is included in the room rate.

Pura Yeh Gangga is an attractive temple 15 km from Mengwi off the road N to Lake Bratan. Unusually, the base of the merus are constructed of stone, rather than wood, with porcelain set into the walls. A stone inscription discovered within the compound can be dated to 1334. *Getting there*: take a bemo running N towards Lake Bratan from Mengwi or Denpasar's Ubung terminal and ask to be let off just after the village of Bereteh (and before Kukup). Take the turning to the left and walk through the village of Paang to Perean, where the pura can be found (a walk of about 1½ km).

● **Transport** 18 km from Denpasar. **Road Bus**: connections with Denpasar's Ubung terminal; buses turn off the main road to Gilimanuk at Bringkit, and fork N. Alternatively, big buses travel the main road from Denpasar to Gilimanuk from Denpasar's Ubung terminal; ask to be let off at the turning to Mengwi and Bedugul (in the village of Bringkit); bemos wait at this junction and run N.

LAKE BRATAN AND LAKE BUYAN

The beautiful, almost alpine, Lake Bratan is surrounded by the crater walls of the now extinct volcano, Mt Catur. This is a peaceful spot to visit, with cool evenings and away from the hassle of the beach resorts. Because of the altitude, it is much cooler here than at the coast. There are attractive walks around the lake and boats can be hired. On its W shore is the stunningly positioned and mystical, **Pura Ulun Danau Bratan**, which seems to almost float on the water (indeed, in the 1970s it was at risk of sinking beneath the rising waters of the lake). The temple, set in well kept gardens, was built in 1633 by the King of Mengwi to honour the Goddess of the Lake who provides water for irrigation. Along with the temple at Lake Batur (see page 387), the Pura Ulun Danau Bratan, is the most important of the various irrigation temples on Bali. Restaurant within the temple gardens for lunch and snacks. Toilets: 200Rp. Outside the walls of this Hindu temple is a stupa with seated Buddha images in its niches, revealing Bali's Buddhist roots. Admission 500Rp plus 200Rp to park. Open 0800-1900 Mon-Sun.

South of Candikuning, on the S lip of the crater is the small town of **Bedugul**. There is a good permanent fruit, vegetable, flower and spice market here everyday. Near Bedugul, at an altitude of 1,240m, the road passes the **Bali Botanical Gardens**. North from Lake Bratan, the road crosses the floor of the crater and as the road climbs up over its N walls, **Lake Buyan** comes into sight. This is another lake of great natural beauty and is the proposed site of a national park. Curious platforms about 50m from the shore are used by the locals for fishing. To get to the lake, stop the bemo by the entrance to *Lake Buyan Cottages* (there is a barrier on the left hand side, travelling N), just before the road starts to climb out of the crater. There is a small surfaced road, passing a dilapidated temple on the right, to a car park where drinks are sold and fishing-rods are for hire. From here, it is possible to walk around the lake, if the level is not too high. There are no watersports, so it is very peaceful. Coffee is grown on the hillsides around the lake.

Just 2 km N of Lake Bratan is the site of the Handara Kosaido Country Club and golf course, voted one of the world's 50 most beautiful courses (see below for details).

Excursions

Air Terjun Gitgit lies about 15 km N of Lake Bratan, near the village of Gitgit. A path leads to this waterfall which is quite impressive during the wet season. Admission on main road 500Rp, 15 mins walk to the falls. *Getting there*: take a bemo heading for Singaraja.

Local information

● Accommodation

Near Lake Bratan NB It is important to be dropped off **at** your hotel, otherwise you may have quite a walk. Hotels listed are divided into three, with southernmost places listed first.

Bedugul: A *Pacung Mountain Resort*, Jl Raya Baturiti Pacung, T 21038, F 21043, 9 km S of Bedugul on the main road with view over steep valley and terraced rice fields, beneath the peaks of Batukaru and Pohen mountains, 27 small but comfortable rooms arranged on steep valley side, linked by walkways and steps, a/c, satellite TV, en-suite bathroom, resort facilities incl heated pool (a consideration at this altitude), jogging track, gift shop, restaurant very popular with passing coach tours, good value buffet lunch, rather quiet in the evening, rec; **B** *Bukit Permai*, T 23663, on left of road at lip of crater before road descends into Bedugul, cottage-type accommodation, some rooms have fireplaces, but they smoke badly, compelling occupants to open windows and lose any benefit of the warmth, well-kept garden, excellent views towards Denpasar – awkward for lake visits without own transport; **B** *Bedugul*, T 21197, canteen-like restaurant, bland resort hotel, very popular with day trips, plain rooms, all have view across the lake, noisy during the day, watersports and curio shops; **D** *Strawbali*,

T 23467, on main road by turn-off for *Bedugul Hotel*, small rooms, noisy during the day, excellent view towards Denpasar but not close to the lake.

If you get dropped off at Bedugul market there are 3 cheaper places to stay, all within 10 mins walk of lake, but no view of lake. **D** *Ibu Hadi*, T 23497, restaurant, new building, clean rooms, very steep staircase, rec; **D** *Mawar Indah*, T 21190, small, simple rooms, scrub garden (both the above are down the road with the Botanical Garden gateway); **D-E** *Sari Artha Inn*, just after market on left, noisy, but convenient location for transport and lake, no lake view.

Candikuning: on reaching the lakeshore for the first time, there are 2 similar places to stay. Stop the bemo/bus here. **C-D** *Ashram Guesthouse*, T 22439, F 21101, some a/c, restaurant (not rec), some hot water, tennis court, best for views of lake, friendly staff, set on old paddy terrace, over 100 steps to rooms at back, well kept gardens, very relaxing, rec; **C-D** *Lila Graha*, restaurant, cottage type rooms, shady gardens, overlooks lake, above road.

Pancasari: bemo station here, approximately 2 km beyond temple. **A** *Handara Country Club*, entrance on right just before village, T 28866/88944, some bungalows, tennis, fitness centre, golf course, beautiful location, but rather overpriced; **A** *Pancasari Inn*, T 53142, just N of *Handara Country Club* on left hand side, tennis, no lake views, last place to stay before road climbs out of the crater; **B** *Bukit Mungsu Indah* (before Bedugul, at Baturiti), price incl breakfast; **A+** *Lake Buyan Cottages*, T 21351, F 21388, N of Lake Bratan, luxurious cottages with own kitchens and lounge, small pitch and put course, immaculate gardens, views across Lake Buyan.

● **Places to eat**

In Bedugul close to market: *Ananda*, *Bogasari* and warungs.

Closer to the lake: *Ashram Guesthouse*, *Lila Graha* or *Taliwang Bersaudara* (simple Lombok restaurant), good value, views across lake; *Perama Ulundanu*, in temple complex, lunch only, although they might be persuaded to open for dinner.

● **Sports**

Golf: *Handara Country Club*, 18 holes, designed by the Australian golfer Peter Thomson; green fees 90,000Rp, clubs for hire, T 28866.

Watersports: there are 3 locations to hire boats: 1) temple complex (pedalo 7,500Rp/30 mins, circuit of lake in motorboat (15 mins) 4 people 14,000Rp, 5 people 17,500Rp; 2) layby next to *Ashram Guesthouse*, rowboat 7,500Rp/30 mins; 3) *Bedugul Hotel* offers jet-skiing (US$10/15 mins), waterskiing (US$10), parasailing (US$10), and motorboats (US$15/30 mins).

● **Transport**

53 km from Denpasar, 35 km from Mengwi.

Road Bemo: to Singaraja from Pancasari 1,000Rp – it should be possible to flag down passing bemo rather than wait for them to fill up. Regular 'express' bemos leave from Denpasar's Ubung terminal (2-3,000Rp) for Singaraja (see below), passing through Bedugul and Lake Bratan *en route*, 1½ hrs.

To the W of Lake Buyan lies **Lake Tamblingan** and a little further W still is the village of **Munduk**. This beautiful area lies 500m-1,500m above sea-level and is part of a new scheme where visitors can stay in simple bungalows and can learn the ways of the Balinese people. **Accommodation** is at **Puri Lumbung** (a *lumbung* is a Balinese rice barn and the houses have been built in a similar way). Visitors can learn anything from carving a wooden door frame to cooking a Balinese meal. Weaving, music playing (and the making of the instruments), learning about traditional medicines or repairing a fishing net are all part of the 'cultural experience'. For more information write to Puri Lumbung, Balai Pendidikan dan Latihan Pariwisata Bali (BPLP), Kotak Pos 2, Nusa Dua, Bali 80363.

THE NORTH COAST: LOVINA BEACH TO TULOMBEN

The N coast is a different world from the rest of Bali. Fewer rivers water this side of the island and rainfall is less; as a result the lushness of the S is replaced by savanna forest. The road from Lake Bratan is a long and twisting descent through clove and coffee groves. Singaraja, the former Dutch capital of Bali and Nusa Tenggara, remains an important local town but has little to entice the visitor. 11 km W from here is the resort of Lovina Beach. The road continues W following the N coast all the way to Gilimanuk (and the ferry for Java). The road E from Singaraja passes a number of important temples built in distinctive N Balinese style (see excursions, Lovina Beach below). Although few people take the road along the N coast eastwards and then S to Amlapura, the drive is very beautiful and peaceful, passing black sand beaches and coconut groves. The distance from Singaraja to Amlapura is almost 100 km. Beautiful walks can be taken in the hills behind Singaraja with views over the coast to the sea. Some of the best mangoes and durians are grown in this region. In season the growers sell them from big baskets by the roadside. Although still hard and unripe they will ripen to become delicious.

SINGARAJA

Singaraja is the capital of the regency of Buleleng and was the original Dutch capital of Bali and the other islands of Nusa Tenggara. During this period, it was a relatively important harbour and trading post, but has since declined in significance.

On Jl Veteran, next door to the tourist office, is the **Gedong Kirtya**, a manuscript library founded by the Dutch in 1928 when it was named the Kirtya Liefrinck van der Tuuk. It contains Bali's best collection of palm leaf illustrated books or *lontars* which record local myths, magic formulas, literature and dances. Many were taken from the palace in Lombok during the Dutch campaign at the beginning of this century. Some of the Lombok manuscripts originated in Java, from where they were rescued during the disintegration of the Majapahit Empire. The palm leaves are cut into lengths of about 50 cm and then incised with a sharp blade and the incisions filled with a mixture of soot and oil to accentuate the marks. They are then bound together using lengths of cord and protected between two wooden boards.

Excursions

Singaraja is the most convenient base for visiting the sights of the N coast, E of town. Accommodation however is very limited and most visitors base themselves elsewhere (eg Lovina Beach or Air Sanih, which is more peaceful). The temples of the N are interesting for their distinct N style of architecture; in general they are artistically 'busier', exhibiting much more elaborate and dense carving. For details on excursions, see page 417. Bemos travelling E leave from Singaraja's Kampung Tinggi terminal.

Local information
● **Accommodation**
B-D *Wijaya*, Jl Sudirman, T 21915, a/c, range of good accommodation.

D-E *Duta Karya*, Jl Jend A Yani, T 21467, some a/c, adequate.

E *Garuda*, Jl Jend A Yani 76, T 41191, price incl breakfast; **E** *Gelarsari*, Jl Jend A Yani, T 21495; **E** *Sakabindu*, Jl Jend A Yani, T 21791

● **Airline offices**
Garuda, Jl Jend A Yani (next to *Hotel Duta Karya*), T 41691.

● **Hospitals & medical services**
General Hospital, Jl Ngurah Rai, T 41046.

● **Post & telecommunications**
Area code: 0362.
General Post Office: Jl Gajah Mada 158; poste restante service.

● **Shopping**
Textiles: Singaraja is known for its finely detailed ikat cotton and silk weft ikat; there are 2 factories in town producing the cloth.

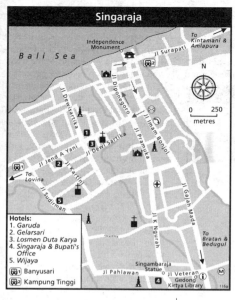

Singaraja

Hotels:
1. Garuda
2. Gelarsari
3. Losmen Duta Karya
4. Singaraja & Bupati's Office
5. Wijaya

Banyusari
Kampung Tinggi

● **Tour companies & travel agents**
Nitour, Jl Jend A Yani.

● **Tourist office**
At Jl Veteran 23, T 61141. Brochures and local map. Open 0700-1400 Mon-Sat.

● **Transport**
78 km from Denpasar, 11 km from Lovina Beach.

Road Bus: Singaraja has 2 bus stations, Kampung Tinggi at the E edge of the town on Jl Surapati for destinations to the E (Kubu, Amlapura and Kintamani); and Banyuasri on the W edge at the intersection of Jl Jend Sudirman and Jl Jend A Yani for destinations S and W of the town (Denpasar, Lovina, Gilimanuk and Bedugul). Bemos link the 2 terminals. Night buses leave from the Banyuasri terminal at 1700 for Surabaya (bus companies have their offices at Taman Lila, Jl Jend A Yani 2).

LOVINA BEACH

Lovina Beach, an 8 km stretch of grey sand, is the name given to three beaches which merge into one another. From E to W, they are Anturan, Kalibukbuk and Temukus. Lovina has been the latest section of Bali's coastline to be developed for tourism and it has already become a mini-resort. The beach itself is quite narrow, with calm but murky waters close in to the shore, and reasonable snorkelling on the reef just off-shore. Hawkers make relaxation on the beach a near impossibility. The most popular outing is an early morning boat trip to see the **dolphins** cavorting off the coast (16,000Rp, with coffee and snack) for a 90 mins 'tour'. Unfortunately, there are too many boats now, and the dolphins are badly hassled.

At present, Lovina remains largely a backpackers' resort, although there are a handful of mid-range hotels with a/c and swimming pools and yet more are under construction. But there are no large-scale hotels.

Excursions

Pura Beji is situated just N of the main coastal road 8 km E of Singaraja and nearly 20 km from Lovina Beach, near the village of **Sangsit**. The temple is dedicated to the rice goddess Dewi Sri and belongs to the local *subak* or irrigation society which is served with the task of managing and allocating water resources among its members (see page 314). The association of rice, water and religion reflects the dependence of rice cultivation upon an adequate and constant supply of water, and of people upon rice for their survival. Visitors are likely to be mobbed by the local children. *Accommodation*: **A-D** *Berdikara Cottages*, T (0362) 25195, some rooms with a/c and hot water, private bathroom with western toilets, attractive gardens with fruit trees, with open air theatre for dance performances, price includes breakfast, bar restaurant, long stay guests are offered lessons in Balinese dancing and hand weaving;

they may also eat the fruit growing in the garden. *Getting there*: take a bemo to Singaraja and then another from Singaraja's Kampung Tinggi terminal.

Jagaraga village is 13 km SE from Singaraja, 24 km from Lovina Beach, and 4 km inland from the coast road. The village has two claims to fame. In 1849 the Dutch wiped out virtually the entire settlement in what has come to be known as the **Pura Dalem** – a Temple of the Dead – which has reliefs depicting, for example, Model 'T' Ford motorcars being held up by bandits. Dutchmen being eaten by crocodiles, and aeroplane dogfights. Admission – suggested donation comparatively overpriced at 1,000Rp. *Getting there*: if travelling independently, turn right off the main coast road 1 km beyond Sangsit, and then travel S for 4 km to the village of Jagaraga. Getting to the village is more difficult by public transport; take a bemo to Singaraja and then another travelling E from Singaraja's Kampung Tinggi terminal; get off 1 km past Sangsit – from there either walk the 4 km or wait and hope for a lift.

Pura Maduwe Karang is situated in the village of Kubutambahan, 12 km E of Singaraja, 23 km from Lovina Beach and on the main coast road. Like Pura Beji, the temple of Maduwe Karang is dedicated to ensuring a bountiful harvest, though not of irrigated rice, but of dry land crops. An interesting relief here is of an official (some people maintain that the cyclist is the artist WOJ Nieuwenkamp (1874-1950) who played such an important role recording Bali's artistic heritage) riding a bicycle, found in the base of the temple wall. *Getting there*: by bemo to Singaraja and then another from Singaraja's Kampung Tinggi terminal.

Air Terjun Gigit is a waterfall 11 km S of Singaraja, worth visiting in the wet season (see page 414). *Getting there*: catch a bemo to Singaraja and then one heading towards Lake Bratan.

Travelling W along the N coast The road follows the flat, narrow coastal strip all the way to Gilimanuk. After 10 km a left turn leads to the Buddhist monastery and hot springs at Banjar. 2 km on is Seritit. Turning S, the road starts climbing into the central mountains through spectacular terraces of rice paddies.

Lovina Beach

To Singaraja

ANTURAN

N

0   250
metres

Bali Sea

KALIBUKBUK

Pura Segara

Spice Dive

TEMUKUS

To Gilimanuk

Hotels:
1. Aditya
2. Angsoka
3. Astina
4. Bali Lovina Beach Cottages
5. Baruna Beach Cottages
6. Krisna
7. Lila Cita Beach
8. Mandhara
9. Pulestis
10. Puri Tasik Madu
11. Purnama Homestay
12. Rini
13. Samudra
14. Susila Beach Inn, Nirwana & Manggala Homestay
15. Toto

116b

There are many picturesque villages on this quiet road. if you take the right fork at Pupuan, the road contours along the narrow mountain ridges and eventually descends through villages and clove plantations to reach the main road along the S coast at Pekutatan, not far from the surfing beach at Medewi, see page 343.

Local information
● Accommodation
Most hotels are situated on the central beach area of Kalibukbuk and rates incl breakfast and tax. **NB** Mosquitoes are bad at night; not all bungalows provide nets. Telephone numbers are within the Singaraja area code.

Anturan Beach: C *Baruna Beach Cottages*, PO Box 149, (situated closer to Singaraja than Lovina, about 2 km SE of the former), T 23745, F 22252, some a/c, pool, private mandi, some rooms overlook beach which is not great for swimming, rooms nicely appointed in thatched 'traditional' bungalows, attractive gardens, pool small but clean, reasonable food; **D** *Lila Cita Beach*, superb position on the beach, but dingy rooms; **E-F** *Mandhara Cottages*, T 23476, price incl a good breakfast, quiet place, relaxed atmosphere.

Kalibukbuk Beach: A-B *Bali Lovina Beach Cottages*, T 41385 or T 33386 (Denpasar), some a/c, pool, bungalows, hot water, rather overpriced, rates incl breakfast; **B-E** *Angsoka*, T 41841, some a/c, restaurant, pool, overpriced, dark and drab; **C-D** *Permata*, T 41653, good value; **C-D** *Rini*, clean, big room, fan, own mandi, depressing cheaper rooms, rather overpriced; **D** *Nirwana*, clean but no mosquito protection, nice rooms overlooking a garden, rather overpriced; **D** *Pulestis*, gaudy but big clean rooms; **D-E** *Manggala Homestay*, basic, fan; **E** *Astina*, very clean accommodation but no mosquito protection, some private mandis, dark rooms, but good value and run by friendly people; **F** *Arjuna*, small basic rooms with fan; **F** *Purnama Homestay*, small, friendly, average rooms.

Temukus Beach: B-D *Aditya*, PO Box 134, T 41059, some a/c, pool, clean, hot water and baths; **C-D** *Puri Tasik Madu*, towards Temukus, T 21585, restaurant, dark but characterful with 4-poster beds but nasty furniture, friendly owners; **D** *Krisna*, clean, big rooms, good value; **D** *Samudra*, PO Box 15, some a/c, hot water; **E** *Toto*, 4 or 5 rm, noisy bungalows nr the road, better ones on the beach, good value; **F** *Susila*

Beach Inn, T 61565, price incl breakfast, friendly people but basic accommodation.

● Places to eat
Many of the restaurants at Lovina serve good, and reasonably priced, seafood.

Bali Pub, good fresh fish, rec; *Ciri Warung*, next to *Khi Khi restaurant*, on non-beach side of the road, excellent Balinese food (*nasi campur*); *Wina restaurant*, excellent Chinese and Indonesian food, rec. *Puri Jaman Lorina*, excellent food, good value.

● Banks & money changers
On the main road.

● Entertainment
Live music: at *Wina's* and *Malibu*.

Videos: evening showings at *Malibu* and *Wina's*, both popular.

● Post & telecommunications
Postal agent on main road.

● Sports
Boat tours: organized by the *Bali Lovina Beach Cottages*.

Diving: trips to Menjangan Island are easily organized from here (see page 422). *Spice Dive*, Kaliasem, US$45-60 for 2 dives all incl; introductory training and 1 dive US$45; 5 day certification course US$230. *Spice Dive* also arrange offshore snorkelling trips (25,000Rp). Seems the best company on Lovina, with well maintained equipment and helpful, friendly staff. *Lovina Marine Resort* and *Bali Lovina Beach Cottages* organize diving expeditions.

Fishing: most hotels and losmen offer fishing trips (7,000Rp).

Sailing: boats available for hire.

Snorkelling: average snorkelling just off the beach (5,000Rp); better marine life at Menjangan Island (25,000Rp for a day trip with *Spice Dive*). Equipment available from the *Bali Lovina Beach Cottages*.

Swimming: at the *Bali Lovina Beach Cottages*, 5,000Rp to non-residents.

● Tourist office
The police station doubles as a tourist information office; they supply a map but little else.

● Transport
11 km from Singaraja.

Local Car/motorbike/bicycle hire from several of the hotels; for example *Rambutan* have motorbikes for hire.

Road Bus: from Denpasar's Ubung terminal catch an express bus to Singaraja, 1½-2 hrs. The bus stops at Singaraja's Banyuasri terminal, from where there are regular buses to Lovina. There are also regular buses and minibuses from Gilimanuk, taking the N coast route, 1½ hrs (buses from Java will drop passengers off at Gilimanuk to catch a connection to Lovina – sometimes incl in the cost of the ferry and bus ticket). **Shuttle bus**: range of prices, 9,000Rp to Kuta.

EAST FROM SINGARAJA

Air Sanih lies 17 km E of Singaraja, on the coast. It has become quite a popular tourist spot because of its spring-fed swimming-pool. However it has retained its local village atmosphere and is, as yet, unspoilt by mass tourism; the glistening black-sand beaches remain almost empty. The main season for visitors here seems to be Jul and Aug.

● **Accommodation A** *Ciliks Beach Garden*, T (0362) 243833, one very large, very beautiful, luxury bungalow with marble floor, very tastefully decorated, mosquito net, attractive bathroom with hot water and squat toilet, beside the sea with verandah and garden, and a separate pavilion for relaxing, offers complete privacy, traditional fishing boat available for hire; **A-E** *Puri Sanih Bungalows*, some a/c, restaurant, pool. The most expensive modern bungalows are right on the beach and have their own bathrooms, the cheapest accommodation is atmospheric but decrepit (rooms on the 2nd flr have lovely views of the sea), immaculate gardens, tour groups catered for, largest place to stay on Air Sanih; **C** *Graha Ayu*, 2 bungalows, new and attractive with fan, private bathroom with shower and western toilet, price incl breakfast, unfortunately on the wrong side of the road from the beach and with no immediate access to beach once you cross the road; **D** *Sunset Graha Beach*, restaurant. On a hill above Air Sanih, the restaurant has a good view of the sea, but the bungalows are set behind, facing a rather neglected garden. Large, rather kitsch rooms, with grandiose bathrooms, reasonably priced; **D** *Tara Beach Inn*, 4 bungalows with shower and western toilet, 2 older thatched bungalows with squat toilet, all basic but with nice location beside sea, listen to the waves crash against the shore, beautiful sunsets, owners' dogs and children can be noisy, pub and restaurant, Australian co-owner sometimes lives in the treehouse in the garden.

● **Places to eat** ✦✦✦*Archipelago Restaurant*, on hill overlooking Air Sanih is more upmarket. **Warungs**: there are several warungs opp the *Puri Sanih Bungalows*, offering reasonably priced local and western food, good cheap nasi campur and mie goreng at first small restaurant, in shop, as you enter Air Sanih from the W, on right side of road.

● **Cultural centres** *Osho Abheeshu Meditation & Creative Centre*, F (0362) 21108, daily meditation programme creativity course US$25 for 1 day.

Continuing E from Air Sanih, the road follows the coast, rounding Cape Sanih, with good views out to sea. 11 km from Air Sanih, a minor road turns inland, climbing the steep ridges to Mt Batur's crater rim at Penulisan, see page 388 for this route.

There are no set piece sights along this coast; the beauty lies in the natural scenery. The road passes through small rural villages, the land is much drier here and there are none of the rice terraces, so prevalent elsewhere.

Sambirenteng is a village on the coast, with some accommodation. The **Les waterfall** is about 6 km from here and is worth a visit. **Accommodation B** *Alamanda*, bookable through a German travel agent – *Pike Travel*, Uwi Siegfriedsen, Ostersielzung 8, 25480, Friedrichstadt, T 494881 930633, F 494881 930699, booking rec, restaurant, right on the edge of the sea, 12 back-to-nature bungalows on stilts, set amongst coconut palms. Lovely, clean rooms with western bathrooms and friendly service. German owned, and also a dive centre, equipped with full sub-aqua gear. Snorkeling on the reef just off the beach. Diving offered at Tulamben, Ulami, Amed, Menjangan and Nusa Penida as well as at Alamanda. Includes night dives, introductory dives available for 125,000Rp. Prices for 2 dives at each site, 95,000Rp-135,000Rp depending on site.

Further E the land becomes more arid and the road skirts the lower slopes of Mt

Batur and the huge Mt Agung, punctuated by 20-30m wide dry water courses which have cut channels into the barren volcanic rock. **Tulamben**, an established dive centre, attracts divers because of the wreck of the American Liberty ship which sank just 40m from the shore; lying in shallow waters it offers good snorkelling as well. The location is very scenic with Mt Agung towering to the W of the deep blue seascape, though the beach consists of grey/black pebbles with some litter. **Accommodation A+-B** *Mimpi Resort Tulamben* (Reservations: Kawasan Bukit Permai, Jimbaran, Denpasar 80361, T (0361) 701070, F 701074), sister resort to *Mimpi Jimbaran*, new, beautifully designed complex of cottages with private courtyards and cheaper rooms set in glorious, landscaped gardens with fabulous views of Mt Agung which provides a spectacular backdrop especially at sunset, well-equipped diving facilities offering PADI courses, the wreck of the American Liberty ship lies just 400m along the beach from the hotel, 40m out from the shore, snorkelling in fron of the hotel and climbs of Mt Agung can be arranged, large freshwater swimming pool fed by underground spring, this is also used to teach novice divers, restaurant (♦♦♦) with sea views, the beach itself is pebbles, rec; **B-C** *Paradise Palm Beach Bungalows* (Reservations: *Friendship Shop*, Candi Dasa, T (0363) 41052, good setting beside sea (pebble beach) with attractive gardens, but rather overpriced reflecting its location as a mecca for divers, 20 rm, 4 with a/c and hot water, all rooms with private bathroom (western toilet and shower) and fans, diving arranged at sites off E and N Bali, prices from US$30 for one dive at Tulamben up to US$85 at Nusa Penida and Menjangan Island; **D** *Ganda Mayu Bungalows and Restaurant* (♦♦), 8 bungalows ranging from rather basic to attractive depending on price, all with private bathroom (western toilets) and fan, situated beside the sea with beachside restaurant, diving can be arranged, the cheapest place to stay at Tulamben.

Leaving Tulamben on the main road to Amlapura another accommodation is being built on a hillside beside the sea with fabulous views, and more development will surely follow.

The road surface improves here and leaves the coast to thread its way between Mt Agung and Mt Seraya, back to Tirtagangga (see page 407) and Amlapura (see page 405).

THE WEST

The W of Bali is the least visited part of the island; most visitors merely pass through en route between the E of Bali and Java. In a number of respects the W is atypical: the area is far less rich agriculturally, it remains the least populated part of the island, there are no historic sights to match those of the E, and there is a strong Muslim representation with settlers from Madura, Java and Sulawesi. At the W tip and 134 km from Denpasar is Gilimanuk, the ferry port for Java. Completely encompassing the port and much of the W is the Bali Barat National Park.

GILIMANUK

Gilimanuk is the departure and arrival point for the ferry that runs between Bali and Java. There is no reason to stay here unless forced to; it is only a transit point. 3 km S of Gilimanuk is **Cekik** and the headquarters of the Bali Barat National Park. For archaeologists, Gilimanuk is important as the site of a bronze/iron age burial ground excavated in the 1960s and 1970s, thus providing evidence of prehistoric settlement on Bali.

Excursions

The **Bali Barat** (or W Bali) **National Park** was established as recently as 1984, and covers over 75,000 ha straddling both the dry N coast and the forested, tropical S. The Bali white mynah or *jalak putih Bali* (*Leucopsar rothschildi*), one of the rarest birds in the world, is found here, mostly confined to Menjangan Island. It is a small white bird, with black tips to its wings and tail, and a streak of blue around its eye (easily confused with the black-winged starling, which has wholly black wings and tail). Only 50 still exist in the wild although there are thousands in captivity. A programme to re-introduce captive birds back into the wild has begun, although trapping is still a problem. One captive bird recently released promptly reappeared for sale at the Jakarta bird market.

The wild Javan buffalo (*Bos javanicus*) is also present in small numbers. Other less rare animals include monkeys, leopard, civets and the rusa, barking and mouse deers. The PHPA office for the Bali Barat National Park is in Cekik. Permits and information on trails can be obtained from the office (permits are also available from the Forestry Department, Jl Suwung, Denpasar, and from Labuan Lalang). **NB** Guides are obligatory. Accommodation is available in the park but it is very basic.

● **Accommodation E** *Kartika Candra*.

● **Transport** 134 km from Denpasar, 88 km from Singaraja. **Road Bus**: regular connections with Denpasar's Ubung terminal. Connections with Singaraja via Lovina Beach. **Sea Ferry**: regular connections throughout the day with Ketapang on Java, ferries leaving every 15-30 mins during the day and less regularly at night, 25 mins (450-550Rp). **NB** During Indonesian holidays and at weekends there may be a long wait for a boat.

LABUAN LALANG (Teluk Terima)

Labuan Lalang, also known as Teluk Terima, is the most convenient base for visits to Menjangan Island (see below, Excursions). **Accommodation** Basic losmen accommodation.

Excursions

Pulau Menjangan lies just off Bali's N coast and is part of the Bali Barat National Park. It offers the best diving to be found around Bali and boats can be chartered to the island from Labuan Lalang. Fins and masks are available but diving equipment must be hired from a dive shop at one of the major beach resorts. The island, fringed with mangroves, is very beautiful and home to the rare Java deer and Bali white mynah. There are no losmen on the island and camping is not permitted.

Pemuteran B-C *Pondok Sari Beach Bungalows and Dive Centre*, Desa Pemuteran Gerokgak Singaraja 81155, T/F (0362) 92339, modern, attractively decorated bungalows, beautiful setting on the beach – good sunsets (more expensive bungalows face the sea). The owner organizes hiking trips to **Taman Nasional Bali Barat**, rec. Located at *Pondok Sari Beach Bungalows* is *Reef Seen Aquatics Dive Centre*, manager Chris Brown is British and a PADI instructor. He is very conservation minded and has launched the 'Turtle Project' to save the endangered local species. There are safe dives off the beach as well as further afield, and he operates to high standards; not always the case in the Bali/Lombok area. *Getting there*: easily reached by public bus from Singaraja, 1½ hrs (1,500Rp); buses run from 0700-1700.

● **Transport Road Bemo**: connections with Gilimanuk/Cekik. Take a bus from Denpasar's Ubung terminal to Gilimanuk and then catch a connection on. From Singaraja, take a bemo from the Banyuasri terminal, running W towards Gilimanuk.

NEGARA

Negara is the capital of the regency of Jembrana and is an attractive town with wide avenues and elegant horse-drawn carriages. The town is best known for the *mekepung* or **bullock races** which are held here between Jul and Oct. The sport was introduced by migrants from the island of Madura where the *kerapan sapi* (bull races) are the main form of entertainment (see page 291). Information on Negara's bull races can be obtained from the Bali Tourist Office on Jl S Parman in Denpasar. Races normally take place after the rice harvest. Negara is also a convenient base from which to visit **Jembrana**, to hear the Gamelan Jegog.

● **Entertainment** Gamelan Jegog is a giant bamboo orchestra. These huge gamelan of 10 perform *Jegog Mebarung*, where several orchestras compete against each other in a frenzy of energy and sound; it is also a visually impressive event. Ask around for the time of a performance – there are no regular scheduled performances.

Excursions

Medewi Beach is situated 22 km E of Negara, about 4 km from the village of Pulukan. Medewi is a black sand beach and is good for surfing. Some accommodation here. No other facilities. *Getting there*: take a bus running E towards Denpasar and ask to be let off at *Pantai Medewi*. **Accommodation A-C** *Medewi Beach Cottages*, Pantai Medewi, Pekulatan, T 0365 40029, F 0365 41555, a/c, restaurant, pool (entrance 5,000Rp for non-residents), basic rather dark rooms, but clean; **B-D** *Balian Beach Club* S of Medewi, down the coast, restaurant, 200m from a beach which is good for surfing; **E** *Ana*, Jl Ngurah Rai 75, T 65; **E** *Indraloka*, Jl Nakula 13; **E** simple losmen, shared mandi.

Rambut Siwi Temple is about 8 km W of Medewi off the main coast road, at the top of a cliff overlooking a black sand beach. This is the main temple for the area and large scale celebrations take place every full moon. This is a wonderful place to watch the sun blazing down across the Bali Strait over Java.

● **Transport** 100 km from Denpasar, 34 km from Gilimanuk. **Road Bus**: regular connections with Gilimanuk and Denpasar's Ubung terminal.

Sumatra

Horizons	424	**Southern Sumatra**	482
Island information	429	'The Minang Homeland:	
Northern Sumatra	432	Bukittinggi and surroundings	488
Medan	432	The Riau Archipelago	497
The Route North: Medan to Bukit		The Riau islands to Pekanbaru and	
Lawang and Banda Aceh	440	Bukittinggi	507
The West Coast: Bunda Aceh to		The West Coast	511
Sidikalang	449	The Mentawi Islands	517
The Route South from Banda Aceh		Padang South to Sungai Penuh	520
to Sidikalang down the West Coast	450	Padang to Jambi and Palembang	523
The Route South: Medan to Lake		Palembang to Bengkulu	532
Toba via Brastagi	451	Muaraenim to Bandar Lampung,	
The Route North	460	Bakauheni and Java	537
Lake Toba South to			
Padangsidempuan	461		

THE ISLAND of Sumatra straddles the Indian Ocean and the Java Sea. It stretches from the city of Banda Aceh at its northern tip, over 1,750 km to Bakauheni at its S extremity. In area it is twice the size of Britain or one third larger than Japan. The name Sumatra is thought to derive from one of the 13th century trading ports on the island's NE coast – Samudra, Sanskrit for 'ocean'.

Sumatra has a surface area of nearly 475,000 sq km, making it the fourth largest island in the world. It is relatively sparsely settled, with around 40 million inhabitants. Population densities here are less than one tenth those on neighbouring Java, although some areas – such as Lampung province – are beginning to suffer the effects of overcrowding.

Although Sumatra does not have the historical and archaeological sights that distinguish Java, it does offer magnificent natural landscapes. There are over a dozen ethnic groups who speak some 20 different dialects. Among these are the peripatetic Minangkabau of W Sumatra (see page 483), the Christian Bataks of N Sumatra (see page 462) the Ferrant Muslins of Aceh, and the tribal peoples of the islands of Nias (see page 476) and Mentawi (page 517). The forests, mountains, rivers and coasts of Sumatra provide trekking and rafting opportunities, some of the finest national parks in the country, and pristine beaches.

Sumatra is also crucial to the Indonesian economy. It was in N Sumatra that Indonesia's first commercial oil well was sunk in 1871, and over 60% of the country's total production comes from the island and the waters around it. Sumatra also acts as a 'safety valve' for Java's 'excess' population. About 60% of Indonesia's transmigrants – 4 million people – have been resettled on Sumatra, mostly in the S (see box).

THE LAND

GEOGRAPHY

A range of mountains – the Bukit Barisan – forms a spine running down Sumatra's W edge. Many of the 93 peaks exceed 2,000m, the highest point being Mt Kerinci at 3,805m. Like Java, Sumatra also has a string of active volcanoes, and the bowl that forms Lake Toba in N Sumatra was

formed after a massive volcanic eruption. This occurred 100,000 years ago, and was probably the greatest explosion in geological history – causing over 1,500 km of rock to be blown into the sky.

To the W of the Bukit Barisan is a narrow ribbon of lowland – rarely more than 20 km wide – on which towns such as Padang and Sibolga cling tenaciously. Offshore, to the W, are the ethnologically fascinating Nias and Mentawi islands. To the E there is a wide expanse of mostly swampy lowland. Sumatra's largest rivers – such as the Musi, Hari and Rokan – cut through this lowland, carrying large quantities of silt and sediment to the coast, which is advancing at rates as high as 90m a year. As it advances, so Sumatra is enveloping the inshore islands that constitute the Riau archipelago.

In general, the soils of Sumatra are poorer than those of Java and agriculture is correspondingly less productive. The lowlands of the E suffer from extensive waterlogging, and development is difficult. In the foothills, farmers have to contend with soils that are heavily leached and although the land may support thick forest, fertility quickly declines when it is cleared for agriculture. Tree crops have fared relatively well on these former forest lands and Sumatra is a significant exporter of natural rubber and palm oil. However, the area of Sumatra with the greatest agricultural potential is in the vicinity of the city of Medan. Here, the volcanic soils are fertile and the Dutch colonial administration successfully promoted the cultivation of such estate crops as tea, tobacco, coffee and sisal.

CLIMATE

Sumatra is bisected by the equator which runs through the island, just N of Bukittinggi. Daytime temperatures vary little through the year – the annual range is only 1.4°C at sea-level. Far more important is rainfall in determining the seasons. The wettest part of the island is the narrow W coast plain and the W foothills of the Bukit

Barisan. Here rainfall averages about 4,000 mm/year, but rises to 6,000 mm/year in the town of Bengkulu, as rain-filled clouds blown in over the Indian Ocean release their load before being forced up and over the Bukit Barisan. In central, E and N Sumatra rainfall is lower, ranging from 2,500 mm to 3,000 mm/year. To put these figures into perspective, average rainfall in Padang – some 4,500 mm – is seven times higher than the figure for rainy London.

There is rain throughout the year in Sumatra, but it is heaviest N of the equator between Oct and Apr, and S of the equator from Oct to Jan. The 'dry' season – a relative concept in this part of the world – is during Jun and Jul. Monthly rainfall graphs for Medan and Padang are on pages 433 and 512 respectively.

HISTORY

Pre-Colonial kingdoms: Srivijaya, Melayu and Aceh

Sumatra does not have as rich a history as Java, but one great empire did evolve here – Srivijaya, or 'Glorious Victory'. **Srivijaya** was possibly the greatest of all Southeast Asia's maritime empires. Founded during the 7th century, it aggressively expanded its influence so that by the 9th century Srivijaya controlled all Sumatra, W Java, the E portion of Borneo and the Malay Peninsula as far N as S Thailand. In total, Srivijaya was the dominant power in the area for 350 years, from 670-1025, finally dissolving in the 14th century. With its capital at Palembang on the Musi River in SE Sumatra, Srivijaya was in a strategic position to control trade through the two most important straits in Southeast Asia: the Melaka Strait between the Malay Peninsula and Sumatra, and the Sunda Strait between Sumatra and Java. (Archaeologists have presumed that with Sumatra still accreting eastwards, over a thousand years ago Palembang must have been significantly closer to the coast.) Palembang offered exhausted seafarers an excellent

harbour and repair facilities, and an ample selection of recreational activities. In this last respect, the city acted in a manner not unlike latter-day Bangkok during the Vietnam War.

In order to exploit its position, the rulers of Srivijaya built up an impressive fleet with which they suppressed piracy in the Strait of Melaka. This gave traders the confidence to forego the more arduous – but safer – overland route across the Kra Isthmus. In a rather less humanitarian fashion, the fleet also forced all shipping passing through the strait to pay exorbitant taxes – an element of Srivijayan foreign policy which infuriated seafarers. With their stranglehold on trade that flowed through the region, Srivijaya's wealth and power expanded.

The Arab geographers Ibn Khurdadhbih (writing in 846) and Abu Zaid (writing in 916) record the custom of Srivijayan Maharajas 'communicating with the sea'. Each day, the Maharaja would propitiate the ocean by throwing a gold bar into the water, saying "Look, there lies my treasure" – and in so doing demonstrating his debt to the waters. When the Maharaja died, the gold bars would be dredged from the river bed and distributed to the royal family, military commanders, and to the ruler's other subjects. Foreign accounts of Srivijaya – and these are the only records that historians have to draw on – paint a picture of a kingdom of almost mythical wealth.

However, for an empire of such apparent size and wealth, there was – until very recently – surprisingly little physical evidence of its existence. Few temples, inscriptions, or fine art survives. Why this should be so has concentrated scholars' minds ever since the French archaeologist George Coedès identified Palembang as the capital of the empire in 1918. Some have argued that the lack of physical evidence is an indication that Srivijaya was, in fact, a kingdom of little consequence. However, most historians and archaeologists find this hard to believe. It may be that the politico-religious amalgam of indigenous symbols and Hindu-Buddhist legitimacy required few physical monuments; or because this portion of Sumatra is so swampy and unstable, that much of the evidence has simply been lost or merely overlooked. Buildings were constructed of wood, and most edicts were probably recorded on *lontar* palm paper – neither would have survived the intervening years in such a hot and humid environment. Recent work in Palembang has, however, helped to shed some light on the problem. Indonesian and French archaeologists have uncovered several tonnes of artefacts from multiple sites in the city and demonstrated that Palembang was, indeed, the capital of Srivijaya. They argue that the conundrum is not hard to solve: the archaeology of Sumatra has simply been ignored.

The beginning of the end for Srivijaya's Empire came in 1025 when an Indian fleet set sail and sacked the ports along the E Sumatran coastline, including the capital. The motivation for the

Transmigration: 'a matter of life and death'

Transmigration is the government sponsored movement and resettlement of people from Java and Bali to the Outer Islands. President Sukarno said in the 1950s that transmigration was a 'matter of life and death for the Indonesian nation'. In believing this, he was emulating the Dutch who thought that the only way to solve what they saw to be Java's chronic overpopulation problem and resultant poverty, was by moving surplus people from Java to the Outer Islands. Since 1950, this process of resettlement has been known as 'transmigration', and the scheme has become one of the largest social engineering projects in the world. In total, nearly 7 million people have been plucked from Java and Bali and deposited in newly-built villages across the archipelago – in Sumatra, Kalimantan, Sulawesi, Nusa Tenggara and Irian Jaya.

Of these transmigrants, over 60% have been settled in Sumatra, and most of these in Lampung province. Lampung was chosen by the Dutch as the site for the first of the country's transmigration settlements (at that time called *kolonisasi*) in 1905, when 155 families were moved to Gedong Tataan District. Since then, hundreds of thousands have followed. For the Indonesian government, the transmigration scheme has had multiple objectives: to ease population pressure on Java, improve the standard of living of those being settled, promote regional development in the Outer Islands, raise agricultural output, and secure sensitive frontier areas.

But the scheme has also drawn severe criticism from environmentalists and human rights activists. They claim that it has led to massive deforestation and has displaced indigenous people from land that is rightfully theirs. The fact that the indigenous inhabitants of Irian Jaya and Kalimantan are ethnically, religiously and linguistically distinct from the settlers has led to accusations of 'Javanization' and 'ethnocide'. The construction of settlements in politically volatile areas such as E Timor and along the Irian Jaya-Papua New Guinea border lends some support to the notion that transmigration is being used as a political and military tool to unify the country.

It is also true that some of the settlements appear to have transferred the problems of Java to the Outer Islands. Lampung province now has a population of over 6 million, and during the 1970s and 1980s population growth averaged over 4% a year. As a result, deforestation and erosion have become severe problems and the province itself has now been designated a source area for transmigrants. The problem has come full circle.

action has been linked to Srivijaya's exploitation of merchants – of which those of S India's Chola Kingdom were among the more numerous. By the 14th century, this former great empire had vanished from the historical landscape.

Following the destruction of Srivijaya, the rival **Melayu** Kingdom based not far from Jambi in S Sumatra came to prominence. Archaeological remains uncovered at Muara Jambi (see page 523) indicate that Melayu was influential from the late 11th to the late 13th centuries, but dated back to the 7th century. In 1278, the E Javanese Singasari Dynasty (see page 83) launched an expedition against Melayu and kidnapped a royal princess. She was married to a Singasari prince, and their son Adityavarman returned to his mother's homeland to become ruler. But, in the mid-14th century, Adityavarman decided to move his capital from the lowlands of S Sumatra into the Minang highlands of W Sumatra. It is presumed that Adityavarman made this move to insulate his kingdom from the attentions of the more powerful Javanese empires with whom relations were deteriorating.

By the 14th century a number of Muslim trading states had also arisen along the coastline facing the Strait of Melaka. Within 200 years, Islam had spread all the way down the coast and was beginning to make an impact on the N coast of Java. Of these sultanates, the greatest was Aceh, which reached the zenith of its influence during the reign of Sultan Iskandar Muda (see page 443). But, just at the time that Aceh seemed set to become a great empire, the European powers began to exert their influence over Sumatra.

The colonial period in Sumatra

The European powers first established footholds on Sumatra in the 17th century. The Dutch built a fort at Padang on the W coast in 1663, and the British at Bengkulu in 1685. But these were far from secure and hardly substantive. Both the Dutch and the British were periodically expelled by local raiders as well as by one another and by a third European power, the French.

It was Sumatra's wealth in pepper, tin, gambier and, rather later, in coffee, which attracted settlers and traders to the island. With no significant indigenous power to offer a bulwark against outside intervention, it became an international free-for-all. The British, Americans, Dutch and the French were all pressing various claims to the island and its wealth. However, it was the Dutch who emerged as the dominant influence. In 1824, the British renounced their various claims to Sumatra in return for the Dutch doing the same in Malaya, and Bengkulu and Melaka were effectively 'swapped'.

But striking an accord with the British did not mean that Sumatra was under Dutch control. Much of the interior had yet even to be explored, let alone brought under effective administration. To do this, the Dutch had to wage a succession of wars during the 19th and into the 20th century. Among these, the most bitterly fought were the 'Padri' Wars of the early 19th century, focused on W Sumatra (see page 486), and the Acehnese resistance which dates from 1873, and continues – in another form – today (see page 444). It was not until 1910 that the Dutch could claim to have brought all Sumatra under their authority.

ISLAND INFORMATION

BEFORE TRAVELLING

TOURS

● **Tourist information**

There are tourist information offices in major tourist centres, and regional offices (*Dinas Pari-wisata*) in the regional capitals. In the main, the offices are poorly organized in comparison with Java and the staff are not very helpful.

WHEN TO GO

● **Best time to visit**

The rainy season extends from Oct to Apr, to the N of the Equator and from Oct to Jan to the S. Road travel during the dry season is quicker and easier, but overland travel in the wet season is fine on the (largely) all-weather Trans-Suma-tran Highway. The most comfortable time to travel is during the onset of the rains (Sep-Oct) when temperatures have cooled but showers have not become torrential. Most tourists visit between Jun and Oct, so travelling out of those months is relatively quiet and hotel rates can often be bargained down.

HEALTH

Parts of Sumatra – the Riau and Mentawi islands particularly – have a serious malaria problem. Take adequate precautions to protect against malaria (note that chloroquine-resistant strains are now common), and also avoid insect bites in general (see page 901).

MONEY

All bigger towns provide exchange rate facilities. Cash seems to get a better rate than TCs'. There are still some towns where there are no banks at all, and hotels provide unattractive rates of exchange. Travellers leaving for Samosir Island in the middle of Lake Toba, for example, are advised to change money in either Medan or Prapat. For those going to the Nias or Mentawi islands, sufficient money should be changed in Sibolga or Padang respectively.

GETTING THERE

The usual 'route' through Sumatra begins (or ends) at Medan, and takes in Lake Toba, Bukittinggi and Padang. From Padang, most travellers then catch the ferry or a plane to Jakarta. The more adventurous can proceed overland to the S tip of Suma-tra where there are ferries from Panjang or Bakauheni, across the Sunda Strait, to Merak on Java, 3 hrs from Jakarta. The other main en-try/exit point is via Pekanbaru and the Riau Islands.

AIR

Most visitors arrive at Medan, on the W coast of Sumatra which offers international connec-tions with Penang, Singapore, and Kuala Lum-pur. It is increasingly popular to fly to Batam (Riau Islands) which is just 30 mins' ferry ride away from Singapore (see page 502). There are also international connections between Singapore and Pekanbaru, and domestic connections with Jakarta from all Sumatran provincial capitals. Padang is also an international gateway airport.

BOAT

There is a twice weekly 'international' ferry linking Penang (Malaysia) with Belawan (Medan's port), 14 hrs. Hydrofoils and high-speed catamarans also make the crossing, daily. The *Selesa Ekspres* runs a twice weekly high-speed service from Lumut on Peninsular Malaysia to Medan (Lumut-Medan Wed and Sun, Medan-Lumut Tues and Sat). There are also ferries from Port Klang, Kuala Lumpur, to Medan's Belawan Port, but again only twice weekly (KL-Medan Tues and Thur, Medan-KL Mon and Wed). An alternative route into or out of Indonesia is to catch a regular ferry or hydrofoil from Singapore's Finger Pier to Batam or Bintan islands in the Riau archipelago. From there it is possible to catch a boat – fast or very slow – to Pekanbaru, up the Siak River on the Sumatran 'mainland'. But, the most common domestic sea-borne entry/exit point is Bakauheni on Sumatra's S tip; hourly ferries link Bakauheni with Merak, W Java. The Pelni ship *Rinjani* docks at ports on Sumatra's E coast every fortnight, while the *Kerinci* does the same on the W coast. From Tanjung Pinang on Bintan Island, there are regular ferries to Pekanbaru (see page 507). For more informa-tion on these travel alternatives see the Transport section at the end of the relevant town/city entry.

ON ARRIVAL

● **Conduct**

Sumatra is home to a number of ethnic, religious and cultural groups. Being polite and unruffled works wonders at all times. In the N, the province of Aceh is one of the most strictly Islamic in Indonesia and the same is also true of Padang. Particular care should be taken to dress conser-vatively (women should wear bras, long

Sumatra: good buys

Bandar Aceh: Achenese daggers (*rencong*) and jewellery.
Bandar Lampung: traditional textiles including 'ship cloths'.
Bukittinggi: silver and gold jewellery.
Lake Toba, Brastagi and Bukittinggi: Batak handicrafts, including Batak calenders, carved spirit figures, traditional textiles, carved buffalo horn, and basketry.
Medan: for antiques and textiles from all over Sumatra.
Nias & Mentawi islands: ethnographic pieces, mostly woodcarvings.
Padang: hand woven *songket* cloth, embroidery, jewellery including fine silverwork and 'primitive' art from Mentawi Islands.
Palembang: lacquerware and traditional Palembang textiles.

skirts/trousers and shirts with sleeves) and to respect Islamic laws. In W Sumatra, there are also some additional rules of conduct that should be observed (see page 487).

● **Shopping**
Local and regional handicrafts, textiles, jewellery and other works of art are the best and most distinctive buys in Sumatra (see box). Genuine antiques are rare: if a salesperson tries to sell a 'very old and very rare' work of art it is probably a fake.

WHERE TO STAY

● **Accommodation**
In parts of Sumatra, such as the Riau Islands, the term *losmen* to describe a guesthouse is not used – *penginapan* is employed instead. During the 'off' season – Nov to May – hotels often have low occupancy rates and prices can be bargained down.

FOOD AND DRINK

The town of Padang in W Sumatra is the home of Padang food – *makan padang* – now available just about everywhere in Indonesia but best sampled in its place of origin. A large selection of usually hot and spicy food is brought to the table and customers pay for whatever they eat (see page 487).

GETTING AROUND

AIR

Merpati, Garuda, Mandala and SMAC all operate in Sumatra. All provincial capitals and other major towns are served by these carriers (see route map, page 912).

TRAIN

There is a limited rail network in S Sumatra, although some routes are only for freight. The only regular passenger service used by travellers is that linking Bandar Lampung, Palembang and Lubuklinggau.

BUS

Transport is the main mode of long-distance travel. It is often a cultural experience in itself. Buses are crammed with people, animals and their belongings. Space is limited, seats are designed with small bottoms and narrow hips in mind – except in the VIP coaches – and delays and breakdowns are common. In the rainy season, the problems and delays become even more severe. But, steady improvements to the 2,500 km Trans-Sumatran 'Highway' (a misnomer – over large sections it is more like a village road, one and a half lanes wide) which runs down the entire island from Banda Aceh in the N to Bakauheni in the S, is making road travel much faster and more comfortable. It used to take 20 hrs from Prapat to Bukittinggi, now it takes 13 hrs. Roads off the Trans-Sumatran Highway are still generally poor, and in the rainy season delays of 2 days are not unknown while floodwaters subside. Travelling through the Bukit Barisan, or along the W coast is still quite slow, with average speeds of 40-50 km/h, as the road follows every turn of the mountain. 'Coach travel stories' are becoming a thing of the past and there are 'full' a/c, VIP or express buses plying all the major routes. The most highly regarded private bus companies are **ALS** and **ANS** although so-styled Tourist Buses are probably the most comfortable and, some argue, the safest.

OTHER LAND TRANSPORT

● **Taxi**
An alternative way to travel between towns is by chartered long-distance taxi. Shared taxis can be similar in price to buses. See town entries for addresses.

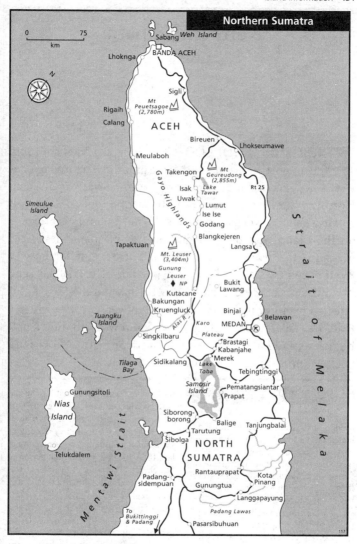

Northern Sumatra

Northern Sumatra

FOR THIS GUIDEBOOK, Sumatra has been split into two: northern and southern Sumatra. The divide does not correspond with any administrative division. Northern Sumatra consists of only two provinces: Aceh and North Sumatra. North Sumatra is the most populous province on the island with over 10 million inhabitants. The city of Medan is the 'gateway' to Sumatra. The Special Territory of Aceh encompasses the far north portion of the island. The 3½ million Acehnese are ardent Muslims and the area is still affected by a low intensity separatist movement. Few visitors take the road north; most head southwest to the Batak highlands and Lake Toba, both in North Sumatra. Nias Island is also administered as part of North Sumatra.

MEDAN

Medan, on the E of Sumatra, is the island's largest city with well over 2 million inhabitants. It is big, hot, noisy, congested and dirty with only a few havens of greenery – for example, Merdeka Square. Yet, travellers entering Indonesia from Malaysia will have to pass through Medan.

It is the third most important entry point after Jakarta and Bali. Most visitors try to keep their stay as short as possible. But the accommodation has improved in range and quality over the years, and there is a good selection of reasonable restaurants. Some visitors even profess to liking Medan.

Medan was established in 1682 as a trading centre and there is still some evidence of a graceful and rather less frenetic past. In 1886 the Dutch made it their regional capital, but even as recently as 1942 it had a fairly modest population of less than 100,000. During the period of Dutch rule, economic development was more marked in N Sumatra than in any other region outside Java. The volcanic soils of the surrounding area are rich and the land was rapidly cleared for plantation agriculture. Medan developed from little more than a village to become the administrative hub of an agriculturally-based export economy, and large quantities of tea, rubber, coffee and tobacco were funnelled through Belawan – Medan's port – to the Strait of Melaka and from there to markets in Europe. To fuel this economic growth, the Dutch used immigrant Chinese labourers, and even today Medan has one of the largest Chinese populations in Indonesia.

Medan remains the most important commercial centre in Sumatra, handling many of N Sumatra's natural resource exports. Among the most important are rubber, palm oil and, of course, petroleum. As in so many other towns in Southeast Asia, a disproportionate share of the wealth of Medan is controlled by an entrepreneurial Chinese community. The inequalities between the ostentaciously wealthy and the depressingly poor are all too obvious.

PLACES OF INTEREST

The greatest concentration of **colonial buildings** is to be found along Jl Jend A Yani (which becomes Jl Balai Kota) and around Merdeka Square. Few still perform their original functions as the headquarters of plantation companies, European clubs, and stately hotels. At Jl Jend A Yani 105, to the S of Merdeka Square, there is a rather rundown and romantically decrepit **quasi-colonial/quasi-Chinese mansion** with a peacock-topped entrance arch; this was built by a wealthy Chinese businessman named Tjong A Fie. Other notable buildings include the **Bank of Indonesia** (formerly the De Javaamsche Bank), the **Balai Kota**, **Jakarta Lloyd** and the offices of the **British Council** (once the headquarters of the English plantation company Harrisons and Crosfield). The central **Post Office**, built in 1911 and unchanged since then, is at Jl Bukit Barisan 1, overlooking Merdeka Square. Another road with historical buildings is the garden-like Jl Jend Sudirman (Polonia quarter), SW of the town square.

The attractively decayed **Mesjid Raya** or **Grand Mosque**, with its fine black domes and turquoise tiles can be found at the corner of Jl Sisingamangaraja and Jl Mesjid Raya. The mosque was built in 1906 in 'Moroccan' style by Sultan Makmun Al-Rasyid, and designed by a Dutch architect. The marble came from Italy, the chandelier from Amsterdam, and the stained-glass from China. In the grounds is a small enclosed plot containing the tombs of the sultans of the Istana Maimun Palace (see below), and a fairy-tale style minaret. Admission by donation.

To the W of the mosque, set back from the road on Jl Brig. Jen. Katamso, is the **Istana Maimun** – also known as the **Istana Sultan Deli**. This impressive building was designed by a Dutchman (some say an Italian) and constructed in 1888 as one element in a complex that included the Grand Mosque. It is eclectic architecturally, embracing Italian, Arab, and Oriental styles. Inside are photographs of the various sultans and their wives, and a poor oil painting of the Sultan Deli himself who built the palace. The interior includes a few pieces of Dutch furniture and the Sultan's throne. His descendants continue to live in one wing of the Palace. Admission by donation. Open daytime.

Scattered throughout the city are a large number of shrines, churches, temples, pagodas and mosques. The plain **Chinese pagoda**, just off Jl Pandu, not far from the railway line (near No 2), contains a jumbled array of Buddhas, Chinese deities and ancestor tablets, and is permeated with the smell of burning incense. At the SW edge of the city is the

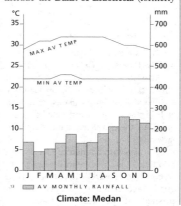

°C / mm

MAX AV TEMP

MIN AV TEMP

J F M A M J J A S O N D

13   AV MONTHLY RAINFALL

Climate: Medan

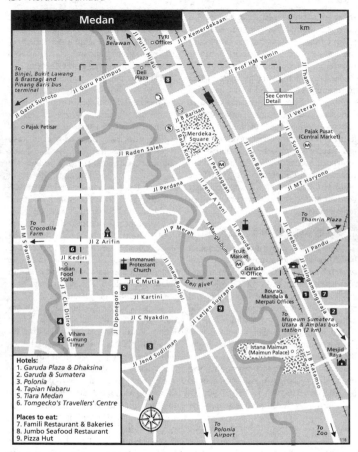

Medan

To
Belawan
Jl Putri Hijau
TVRI
Offices
Jl P Kemerdekaan
0   1
km

To
Binjei, Bukit Lawang
& Brastagi and
Pinang Baris bus
terminal
Jl Guru Patimpus
Deli
Plaza
Jl Prof HM Yamin
Jl Thamrin

Jl Gatot Subroto

Pajak Petisar
Jl B Barisan
Merdeka
Square
Balai Kota
See Centre
Detail
Jl Veteran
Pajak Pusat
(Central Market)
Jl Dr Sutomo
Jl MT Haryono

Jl Raden Saleh
Jl Perdana
Jl Perniagaan
Jl Jend A Yani
Jl Irian Barat

To
Crocodile
Farm
Jl M S Parman
Jl Z Arifin
Jl Kediri
Indian
Food
Stalls
Jl Cik Ditiro
Immanuel
Protestant
Church
Jl Imam Bonjol
Jl Diponegoro
Jl C Mutia
Jl Kartini
Jl C Nyakdin
Jl P Merah
Deli River
Jl Mangkubumi
Jl Pemuda
Fruit
Market
Garuda
Office
Jl Letjen Suprapto
Jl Pandu
Jl Cirebon
Jl Sisingamangaraja
To
Thamrin Plaza
Bourag,
Mandala &
Merpati Offices
Familí Restaurant & Bakeries

Vihara
Gunung
Timur
To
Museum Sumatera
Utara & Amplas bus
station (2 km)
Mesjid
Raya

Hotels:
1. Garuda Plaza & Dhaksina
2. Garuda & Sumatera
3. Polonia
4. Tapian Nabaru
5. Tiara Medan
6. Tomgecko's Travellers' Centre

Places to eat:
7. Famili Restaurant & Bakeries
8. Jumbo Seafood Restaurant
9. Pizza Hut

Istana Maimun
(Maimun Palace)
Jl B Katamso
Jl Jend Sudirman
To
Polonia
Airport
To
Zoo
118

Vihara Gunung Timur, at Jl Hang Tuah 16, just W of Jl Cik Ditiro. This building is the largest Chinese pagoda in Medan. Set in a peaceful area, the entrance is flanked by two guardian lions. Filled with lanterns, incense and demons, the temple is a rewarding retreat from the bustle of the city. **NB** No photography is allowed in the pagoda and remove shoes before entering the inner sanctuary with its Buddha statues. **Candi Hindu** at Jl H Zainul Arifin 130, is an Indian temple serving Medan's large South Asian community and has been re-cently renovated and expanded. The **Immanuel Protestant Church**, built in 1921 in Art-Deco style, can be found at Jl Diponegoro 25, while the **Roman Catholic Cathedral of the Immaculate Conception** at Jl Pemuda 1 was constructed in 1929. Strangely, the entrance is flanked by military mines and shells.

The **Museum Sumatera Utara**, at Jl HM Joni 51, is an extensive building with an equally extensive – though of variable quality – collection of artefacts. Not surprisingly, it specializes in those of N

Sumatran origin and upstairs has some fine wood and stone-carvings from the Nias Islands. Unfortunately it is ill-lit and poorly maintained, with little useful explanatory detail. Admission 400Rp. Open 0800-1700 Tues-Sun. The **Bukit Barisan Museum** at Jl H Zainul Arifin 8, displays a decaying selection of Sumatran tribal houses and arts and crafts as well as military paraphernalia. Admission: by donation. Open 0800-1300 Mon-Thur and Sat. Rather further out of downtown Medan, travelling S towards Prapat is the **Taman Margasatwa Zoo** (Kebun Binatang) on Jl Katamso. It imprisons a miserable selection of poorly kept regional wildlife in a small park. Admission 500Rp, 750Rp Sun and hols. Open Mon-Sun.

One of the greatest attractions of Medan are its markets, known locally as *pajak*. The huge **Central Market** or *Pajak Pusat* (Pajak Sentral) – in fact an agglomeration of various markets selling just about everything – is located close to Jl Dr Sutomo. It is renowned for its pickpockets. Safer is the **Pajak Petisar**, on Jl Rasak Baru, just off Jl Gatot Subroto. It is a fruit and vegetable market in the morning (0600), that later develops into a general market, selling clothes, food, and general merchandise. The **Pajak Ikan Lama** (Old Fish Market) is a good place to buy cheap batik, other types of cloth, and assorted garments. It is on Jl Perniagaan, close to Jl Jend A Yani. Visitors may see live fruit bats strung up for sale – lucky ones could have the chance to eat them too.

EXCURSIONS

Asam Kumbang Crocodile Farm is 5 km from the city, off Jl Kampung Lalang, at Asam Kumbang Village. It is the largest crocodile farm in Indonesia, with over 2,000 of the beasts. The crocodiles are hatched, reared and made into bags. This is not a place for animal lovers: dirty and over-crowded, chained monkeys, animals in small cages. *Getting there*: by town bus (*bis damri*) from Jl Balai Kota. Ask for *Asam Kumbang* and take a becak the final few kilometres.

Binjei, Brastagi and the Orang Utan Rehabilitation Centre at Bukit Lawang are all accessible as day trips from Medan. 22 km W of Medan on route 25 is **Binjei**, famed for its fruit – and especially its rambutans and durians. The best time to visit is when they are in season, Jul-Aug. It is possible to reach **Brastagi** (see page 451) and the **Orang Utan Rehabilitation Centre** at Bukit Lawang (page 440) from here (about 3 hrs). *Getting there*: regular buses and minibuses travel down Jl Gatot Subroto, which becomes Jl Binjei, leaving from the Central Market, 45 mins (500Rp). Bukit Lawang can be visited as a long day trip.

Bandar Baru, on the road to Brastagi, is Medan's red light district – in fact a red light town. Bandar Baru is a vast collection of hotels and brothels, serving the city's male population, who can be seen driving out in convoy, in their darkened windowed cars on a Sat night. **NB** Indonesia does have AIDS.

TOURS

Tour companies have offices in most of the larger hotels and organize half day city tours, and day tours to Brastagi and to the orang utans at Bukit Lawang. Longer overnight tours to Lake Toba and to the Nias Islands are also offered by most tour agents. *Pacto Tours* run raft adventures down the Alas River from Medan (5 days, US$499; 13 days, US$1,299) (see page 454); *Edelweiss* also organize rafting and trekking tours.

FESTIVALS

Mar-May: *Medan Fair* is held between Mar and May each year at the Taman Ria Amusement Park on Jl Gatot Subroto. There are also permanent cultural exhibits at the park.

Apr (movable): *Idul Fitri* (Islamic holy day), Muslims descend on the Maimun Palace in traditional dress to mark the end of the fasting month of Ramadan – very colourful.

Medan Centre

Hotels:
1. Danau Toba
2. Dharma Deli
3. Dirga Surya
4. Irama

Places to eat:
5. Kohinoor
6. Lyn's Bar

LOCAL INFORMATION

● Accommodation

A+ *Novotel Soeichi*, Jl Cirebon 76A, T 561234, F 572222, a/c, restaurant, pool, new 246-room hotel with all facilities including tennis court, business centre, fitness centre and executive floor, good for businessmen, French general manager, professional; **A+-A** *Danau Toba*, Jl Imam Bonjol 17, T 557000, F 530553, a/c, several restaurants, good pool, good range of facilities, too large to be personal (259 rm) and some recent visitors have reported that the management is none too helpful; **A** *Dirga Surya*, Jl Imam Bonjol 6, T 552662, F 549327, a/c, restaurant, modern, but with a Chinese ambiance; **A** *Tiara Medan*, Jl Cut Mutia, T 516000, F 510176, a/c, restaurant, pool, tennis, squash, new and lavish, most stylish hotel in town with 188 rm, rec; **A-B** *Dharma Deli*, Jl Balai Kota 2, T 557744, F 544477, a/c, restaurant, pool, colonial-style hotel in centre of town, reasonable rooms and service, attractive gardens and some original decor, rec; **A-B** *Garuda Plaza*, Jl Sisingamangaraja 18, T 716255, F 714411, a/c, restaurant, small pool, health club, large, modern hotel with 154 rm, close to Maimun Palace and the mosque.

B *Pardede*, Jl Ir H Juanda 14, T 543866, a/c, 115 rm, restaurant, small pool; **B** *Polonia*, Jl Jend Sudirman 14, T 535111, F 519553, a/c, restaurant, pool, not very central but nr the airport and recently renovated, good sports facilities; **B** *Sri Deli*, Jn SM Raja 30, T 713571, a/c, some rooms provide good views of the city, friendly management, rec; **B-C** *Angkasa*, Jl Sutomo 1, T 322555, a/c, restaurant, pool, featureless hotel, average rooms; **B-C** *Dhaksina*, Jl Sisingamangaraja 20, T 720000, F 740113, some a/c, own bathroom, dark rooms, unfriendly service; **B-C** *Garuda*, Jl Sisingamangaraja 27, T 717733, some a/c, clean, but rather imposing and grim, nr mosque; **B-C** *Kenanga*, Jl Sisingamangaraja 82, T 712426, F 716399, some a/c, not particularly clean dorm (**F**).

C-D *Sumatera*, Jl Sisingamangaraja 35, T 721552, F 721553, some a/c, price incl breakfast, clean, good value, though lacking in any local character.

D *Legundri*, Jl Kirana 22 (nr Medan Plaza), T 521924, some a/c, clean, but for shared bathroom rather expensive; **D** *Zakia*, Jl Sipiso-Piso, T 722413, across from Mesjid Raya, bath and fan, clean and quiet (except when the faithful are called to prayer!), helpful staff and just 3 mins from where the 'ferry bus' drops off; **D-E** *Shahiba Guesthouse*, Jl Armada 3, T 718528, friendly place with a range of rooms, satellite TV, but next to a factory and rather musty, some rooms with mandi, not far from the Mesjid Raya, S off Jl Sisingamangaraja.

E *Melati*, Jl Amaluin 6, T 516021, some a/c, musty rooms with shared bathrooms; **E-F** *Tapian Nabaru*, Jl Hang Tuah 6, T 512155, quite a trek from the city centre, we have had rather conflicting reports on this place from 'friendly, quiet and clean' to 'bad place, dirty linen and bed bugs', a useful night market is situated nearby, just off Jl Zainal Arifin.

F *Irama*, Jl Palang Merah 112-S, T 326416, good base for travellers just arriving in Indonesia, central location, with information on destinations in Sumatra incl Nias Island, friendly but rooms dark and dingy – toilets too!; **F** *Losmen Berlin Baru*, Jl Hindu 3, gloomy, dark, dingy, only as the very last of resorts; **E** *Sarah's Guesthouse*, Jl Pertama 10, T 719460, friendly, with good information, 10 mins from bus station, close to *Shahiba Guesthouse*, rec.

● **Places to eat**
Medan is better served with decent and reasonable restaurants than it is with hotels.

Indonesian: ♦♦*Angelo's Café*, Jl Jend A Yani 29; ♦♦*Garuda IV*, Jl Gajah Mada; ♦♦*Famili*, Jl Sisingamangaraja 21B, specializes in Padang food; ♦♦*Jumbo*, Jl Putri Hijau 8, seafood; ♦*Garuda*, Jl Palang Merah (nr the railway crossing), excellent and inexpensive food.

Other Asian cuisines: ♦♦♦*Angkasa Hotel*, Jl Sutomo 1, good Chinese food; ♦*Kohinoor*, Jl Mesjid 21, excellent N Indian dishes, there is now a second restaurant at Jl Sisingamangaraja 23; ♦♦♦*Polonia Hotel*, Jl Jend Sudirman 14, excellent Chinese; ♦♦♦*Yokohama*, Jl Nibung Raya 58, best Japanese in town; ♦♦♦*Danau Toba Hotel*, Jl Imam Bonjol 17, Japanese; ♦*Rumali*, Jl Palang Merah 1 Col Sugiono 2, wide selection of Minang and Padeng foods, friendly, rec.

Foodstalls: *Selat Panjang* behind Jl Pandu has stalls selling Chinese (and seafood) and Indonesian favourites. **Jl Semarang** off Jl Pandu also has quantities of foodstalls which really get wokking in the evening. ♦*Surya Food Centre*, Jl Imam Bonjol 6, lots of open-air stalls open till late, seafood, rec. The new shopping plazas, such as **Deli Plaza** and **Thamrin Plaza** have good, cheap 'food centres'. **Indian food** can be found at the foodstalls on Jl Jenggala, Jl Cik Ditiro and Jl Pagaruyung.

International: ♦♦*Kentucky Fried Chicken*, five of these scattered around town, mostly in the shopping complexes; ♦♦*Lyn's*, Jl Jend A Yani 98A, steaks and other Western dishes, like *Tip Top* mostly frequented by Westerners and Westernized Indonesians; ♦♦*Pizza Hut*, Jl Jend Sudirman; ♦♦*Tip Top*, Jl Jend A Yani 92, an old favourite among Medan's small band of expats, with some tables outside, it also serves Chinese and Indonesian food and icecream, rec.

● **Bars**
Lyn's Bar, Jl Jend A Yani 98A.

● **Airline offices**
Bouraq, Jl Brig Jend Katamso, T 552333; **Cathay Pacific**, Tiara Hotel, Jl Cut Mutia, T 526088; **Garuda**, *Dharma Deli Hotel*, Jl Balai Kota 2, T 516400; *Hotel Tiara Medan*, Jl Cut Mutia, T 538527 and Jl Suprapto 2, T 516066; **KLM**, *Dharma Deli Hotel*, Jl Balai Kota 2, T 515266; **Mandala**, Jl Brig Jend Katamso 37E, T 538183; **Malaysian Airlines (MAS)**, *Danau Toba Hotel*, Jl Imam Bonjol 17, T 519333; **Merpati**, Jl Brig Jend Katamso 41, T 514102; **Sempati**, Tiara Hotel, Jl Cut Mutia, T 537800; **Singapore Airlines**, *Polonia Hotel*, Jl Jend Sudirman 14, T 325300 and *Dharma Deli Hotel*, Jl Balai Kota 2, T 327011; **SMAC**, Jl Imam Bonjol 59, T 537760; **Thai**, *Dharma Deli Hotel*, Jl Balai Kota 2, T 510541.

● **Banks & money changers**
NB If travelling from Penang to Medan via Belawan Port, it is advisable to change money in Georgetown (Penang) before departure – the exchange rate is much better than in Medan. There are numerous banks in Medan, all fairly internationally-minded. There are also a number of money changers on Jl Katamso.

Bank Central Asia, Jl Bukit Barisan 3 (will provide cash advances on Visa card); **Bank Dagang Negara**, Jl Jend A Yani 109; **Ekspor Impor**, Jl Balai Kota 8; **Bank Negara Indonesia**, Jl Pemuda 12; **Bank Duta**, Jl Pemuda 9.

● **Embassies & consulates**

Belgium, Jl Pattimura 459, T 520559; Denmark, Jl Hang Jebat 2, T 323020; Germany, Jl Let. Jend Parman 217, T 520908; India, Jl Uskup Agung Sugiopranoto 19, T 510418; Japan, Jl Suryo 12, T 510533; Malaysia, Jl Diponegoro 11, T 518053; Netherlands, Jl Rivai 22, T 519025; Norway, Jl Zainul Arifin 55, T 510158; Singapore, Jl T Daud 3, T 513134; Sweden, Jl Hang Jebat 2, T 511017; UK, Jl Jend A Yani 2, T 518699; USA, Jl Imam Bonjol 13, T 322200.

● **Entertainment**

Cultural performances: are held twice a week at the *Bina Budaya* on Jl Perintis Kemerdekaan.

Discos: the *Xanadu* at the *Dirga Surya Hotel*, Jl Imam Bonjol 6; *Le Cartier*, Jl Ir H Juanda 14; *Dynasty* at *Danau Toba Hotel*, Jl Imam Bonjol 17.

Nightclubs: *Bali Plaza*, Jl Kumango 1A.

● **Hospitals & medical services**

Clinics: *Bunda* (24 hrs), Jl Sisingamangaraja.

Hospitals: *Herna Hospital*, Jl Majapahit 118A, T 515397; *St Elizabeth's Hospital*, Jl Haji Misbah 7, T 512455.

● **Post & telecommunications**

Area code: 061.

General Post Office: Jl Bukit Barisan 1 (on Merdeka Square).

Perumtel: Jl Putri Hijau 1 (nr GPO) for fax, telex, telegraph and international telephone.

● **Shopping**

Antiques: Jl Jend A Yani is the main shopping area, with the largest concentration of 'antique' shops. Beware of fakes: old Batak artefacts are cunningly mass produced. There are few real antiques for sale these days. Shops incl *Borobudur Art Shop*, at No 32; *ABC Art Gallery*, No 50; *Rufindo*, No 56; *Toko Bali*, No 68.

Books: English language books are thin on the ground. The best bet for newspapers and magazines is to try the gift shops at one of the luxury hotels – like the *Tiara Medan*.

Plazas: *Sinar Plaza* and *Deli Plaza*, both on the corner of Jl Putri Hijau and Jl Guru Patimpus; *Thamrin Plaza* on Jl Thamrin.

Textiles: Jl Jend A Yani III, which runs off Jl Jend A Yani has a number of textile outlets. Browsing through the markets can be rewarding – either the massive Central Market or the Old Fish Market; the latter is the best place to buy batik (see Places of interest, above). Both *Batik Semar* and *Batik Keris* are to be found on Jl Z Arifin.

● **Sports**

Golf: *Nicotiana*, Jl Karya, nine holes. *Polonia*, nr the airport, nine holes. *Tuntungan*, 30 mins towards Brastagi, excellent 18 hole course.

Hash House Harriers: this throw back to British colonial days in Malaya is alive and kicking in Medan (and elsewhere in Southeast Asia). A jog with knobs on, it involves a 'hare' laying a trail for the pursuing 'hounds' to follow, and then a bout of often heavy drinking. There are two clubs in Medan which run every Mon and alternate Tues and Sun. There is a small entrance fee and all are welcome. Runs begin and end at *Lyn's Bar*, Jl Jend A Yani 98A.

Health clubs: *Danau Toba Hotel*, *Polonia Hotel* and *Tiara Hotel*.

Swimming: *Dharma Deli Hotel*, Jl Balai Kota 2.

Tennis: *Danau Toba Hotel*, Jl Imam Bonjol 17, *Tiara Hotel*, Jl Cut Mutia.

Ten-pin Bowling: *Marati Bowling*, Jl Gatot Subroto 2.

● **Tour companies & travel agents**

Concentration on Jl Brig Jend Katamso. *Asri Nusantara*, Jl Jend S Siswomiharjo 50B, T 325754; *Edelweiss*, Jl Irian Barat 47, T 517297; *Mutiara*, Danau Toba Hotel, Jl Imam Bonjol 17, T 327000; *Natrabu*, Jl Ir H Juanda Baru 52B, T 26810; *Nitour Inc*, Jl Prof HM Yamin 21E, T 23191; *Pacto*, Jl Brig Jend Katamso 35G, T 510081, F 513669; *Trophy*, Jl Brig. Jend Katamso 33D, T 514888; *Eka Sukma Wisata Tour & Travel*, Jl Sisingamangaraja 92A, T 720964.

● **Tourist offices**

Medan Tourist Office (Kanwil Pariwisata), Jl Alpalah 22, T 554677. Unhelpful and out of town. **North Sumatran Tourist Office** (Dinas Pariwisata), Jl Jend A Yani 107, T 538101. Helpful; maps and other information. Open 0730-1430 Mon-Thur, 0730-1200 Fri, 0730-1330 Sat. There is also a tourist information booth at the airport, but it's not always open and the information available is very limited.

● **Useful addresses**

Immigration office: Jl Jend A Yani 74.

PHPA: Jl Sisingamangaraja, Km 5.5, T 523658.

Police station: Jl Durian, T 520453.

● **Transport**

66 km from Brastagi, 176 km from Prapat/Lake Toba, 349 km from Sibolga, 728 km from Bukittinggi, 819 km from Padang, 594 km from Banda Aceh.

Local Becak, sudaco, mesin becak (motorized becak), bis damri (150Rp), metered taxi and kijang – if it moves, it can be hired. It is amazing how some of the mesin becaks keep going. **Car hire**: National Car Rental (*Dharma Deli Hotel*), Jl Balai Kota 2, T 327011; **Avis** (Nitour), Jl Prof HM Yamin 21E, T 532191. **Taxis**: can be rented by the day; ask at your hotel or T 524659, T 520952.

Air Medan's international Polonia Airport is 3 km S of the town. **Transport to town**: a taxi to the city centre costs 7,000Rp, 5,000Rp to Jl Sisingamangaraja. Expensive, but probably the best option. Bus from Pinang Baris terminal (in direction of Amplas terminal) get off at traffic lights on Jl Juanda, airport is 500m on right (500Rp). Regular connections with Mandala, Garuda/Merpati and Sempati with most Sumatran destinations incl Padang, Banda Aceh, Batam, Pekanbaru and Nias; several flights a day to Jakarta and other Indonesian towns beyond Sumatra (see route map, page 912). Passengers should ensure they have a confirmed seat.

Road **Bus**: women should expect a certain amount of unwelcome attention at the bus terminals. Medan has two new, main bus terminals: Amplas and Pinang Baris. **Amplas terminal** is on Jl Medan Tenggara VII about 5 km S of the city centre and serves all destinations S of Medan inc Bukittinggi, Prapat and Lake Toba (4 hrs), Jakarta, Jambi, Pekanbaru, Palembang and Sibolga. Get there by yellow oplet running S (250Rp). The **Pinang Baris terminal** is on Jl Pinang Baris (off Jl Gatot Subroto), about 9 km NW of the city centre and serves Banda Aceh and other destinations N of Medan including Bukit Lawang (leaving every 30 mins); buses to Brastagi 2 hrs, also leave from the Pinang Baris terminal. Get to the terminal by orange or green microlet running along Jl Gatot Subroto (500Rp). **Blue Timur 'taxis'** (in fact minibuses) for Binjei leave regularly from Jl Kumango which is parallel to Jl Perniagaan, N of the tourist office (500Rp). For Bohorok and Bukit Lawang, see page 440. **Taxi**: most of the taxi companies are located at Jl Sisingamangaraja 60-107.

Train The station is on Jl Prof M Yamin. There is a limited rail network around Medan but few use it.

Sea Boat Medan's port, Belawan, is 26 km N of the city. Town buses for Belawan leave from the intersection of Jl Balai Kota and Jl Guru Patimpus, near the TVRI offices. The Pelni vessels *Kerinci* and *Kambuna* call at Belawan on their fortnightly circuits (see page 921 for route schedule). Pelni's office is at Jl Kol Sugiono 5, T 518899.

International connections There is not much difference in price between flights and ferries. **Air International connections**: Medan is a 'gateway' city and there are daily connections with Penang, Kuala Lumpur and Singapore. There are also weekly connections with Bangkok and with Vienna and Amsterdam (on Garuda). MAS, Silk Air, Garuda/Merpati and Sempati all operate international flights. **Boat** Ferry connections with Penang (Malaysia) every day except Mon, 6 hrs (M$89-96). The fare incl bus transfer to Medan. In Georgetown, Penang's capital, tickets are available from *Silver Econ Travel*, 436 Lebuh Chulia, and at other travel agents. The *Express Bahagia* and *Selasa Express*, two high speed catamarans, leave Belawan (Medan's port) for Penang every day except Mon at 1330, 4-5 hrs (80,000Rp, M$90). Boats return from Penang every day except Sun. *Selasa's* office in Medan is at Jl Sisingamangaraja 92A, T 720954. Free transfer to port. *GSA* operate a hydrofoil between Belawan and Penang, every Tues, Thur and Sun 0900, 4½ hrs (68,350Rp). Tickets from *Sukma Travel*, Jl Brig. Jend Katamso 62A, T 516045. Free transfer to port. The vessel returns from Penang on Mon, Wed, Fri and Sat, also at 0900. Tickets available from *Happy Holidays*, Lbh. Chulia, T 629222. *GSA* are considering adding Langkawi (Malaysia) to their destinations.

THE ROUTE NORTH: MEDAN TO BUKIT LAWANG AND BANDA ACEH

The Trans-Sumatran Highway runs W from Medan to Binjei, a distance of 22 km. At Binjei, a minor road continues NW to Bukit Lawang and the Orang Utan Rehabilitation Centre, while the main highway turns N for the fast 600 km journey along the E coast past plantations, rice fields and swamps, to Banda Aceh. Few people travel this long road N but the appearance of bucolic tranquility is rewarding. Stops could include the important natural gas town of *Lhokseumawe, Bireuen* – a provincial market town – or *Sigli*, famed for its strict adherence to Islam. All three towns have a reasonable selection of losmen, and the first some good hotels, but little else. From Bireuen, a road cuts S and inland to Takengon and Lake Tawar, and from there into the Gunung Leuser National Park, before linking up with the Medan-Lake Toba road.

BUKIT LAWANG

Bukit Lawang is a small community on the edge of the **Gunung Leuser Reserve** (see page 457), an area of stunningly beautiful countryside. Just outside the village is the famous **Orang Utan Rehabilitation Centre**, established in 1973 – and fast developing into one of Sumatra's most popular tourist destinations. The work of the centre is almost entirely supported now by revenue from tourism. The orang utan (*Pongo pygmaeus*) is on the verge of extinction throughout its limited range across island Southeast Asia, and the centre has been established by the World Wide Fund for Nature to rehabilitate domesticated orang utan's for life in the wild (see page 548 for more information on these apes). The problem is that there is a ready black market for cuddly orang utans. In Medan they sell for US$350. But when young, friendly animal grows up into a powerful, obstreperous adult ape they are often abandoned. These sad crea-

tures – or some of them at least – end up at Bukit Lawang. The usual immediate problem for these exiles from nature is malnutrition. Fed on a diet of food such as pizzas and beer, they are deficient in many essential nutrients. The centre puts them on a diet of milk and bananas, partly because these foods are highly nutritious and partly because it is so monotonous they will be keen to forage for themselves. Between 1973 and 1993 the centre has rehabilitated 179 animals. Another 35 have died at the centre. In total, the Gunung Leuser National Park probably supports about 2-3,000 apes; the carrying capacity of the park, though, is nearer 8,000. Fee for entrance to park: 400Rp.

Seeing the orang utans The entrance to the reserve is a 30 mins walk from the village following the Bohorok River, which then has to be crossed by boat. Visitors can see the apes during feeding times (0800-0900 and 1500-1600), although these do sometimes change, so check at the PHPA office in Bukit Lawang. Guides can be hired from the PHPA office for 1, 2 or 3 day treks of varying difficulty; visitors have reported seeing gibbons, monkeys, orang utans etc. All visitors must obtain a permit from the PHPA office (1 day: 4,200Rp; 2 days: 4,500Rp) before entering the park. The office is Open 0700-1500 Mon-Sun. **NB** Passport must be shown before a permit is issued. Leave Bukit Lawang 45 mins before feeding for the walk and river crossing. Afternoons are more crowded, especially at weekends; it is best to stay the night and watch a morning, weekday, feed if possible. Next door to the PHPA office is a Visitors Information Centre, with an informative slide show in English on Mon, Wed and Fri at 2000; films on orang utans 3 nights a week, study room, a display, and small collection of relevant literature.

Excursions Hiking is the best way to experience the forest and see the wildlife. The visitors centre has handouts and maps of hiking trails. Hikes, with obligatory guide, range from 1 day to 1 week and cost 20,000Rp pp for a 1 day hike, 25,000Rp pp/day for a 2 day hike, and 25,000Rp+ pp/day for a 3-5 day hike. Minimum three people, all inclusive. It is possible to hike to Brastagi in 3 days. Note that this is an arduous trek requring fitness and good hiking boots; check the credentials of guides carefully – many lack experience. Some people have marvellous treks, followed by friendly orang utans which allow themselves to be petted (hardly aiding their rehabilitation); others see nothing. During the rainy season (roughly Aug-Dec) there can be very heavy downpours: a good waterproof can be essential.

There are a number of **caves**. For the Bat Cave (500Rp) take a torch and non-slip shoes; it is not an easy climb, a guide is recommended (5,000Rp) in the vicinity of Bukit Lawang, along with **rubber processing plants** – ask at the visitors centre for a handout and map.

Floating down the Bohorok River on an inner tube has become a popular excursion. Tubes can be hired (1,000Rp/day) in the village for the 12 km (2-3 hrs) journey to the first bridge. There is public transport from the bridge back to Bukit Lawang. **NB** There have been drownings – beware of whirlpools and low branches.

● **Accommodation** About 20 or so losmen line the Bohorok River up to the crossing-point for the reserve. Each year one or two more open, and the quality of those operating also seems

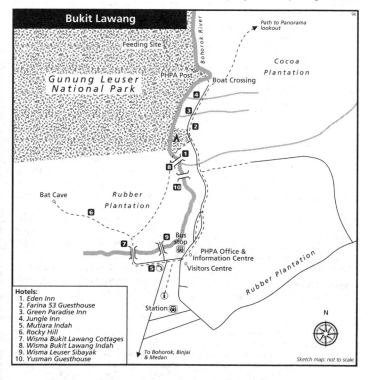

Bukit Lawang

Bohorok River

Path to Panorama lookout

Feeding Site

Cocoa Plantation

Gunung Leuser National Park

PHPA Post

Boat Crossing

Bat Cave

Rubber Plantation

Bus stop

PHPA Office & Information Centre

Visitors Centre

Rubber Plantation

Station

N

Hotels:
1. Eden Inn
2. Farina 53 Guesthouse
3. Green Paradise Inn
4. Jungle Inn
5. Mutiara Indah
6. Rocky Hill
7. Wisma Bukit Lawang Cottages
8. Wisma Bukit Lawang Indah
9. Wisma Leuser Sibayak
10. Yusman Guesthouse

To Bohorok, Binjai & Medan

Sketch map: not to scale

Orang utan illustrated on a Bank of Indonesia 500Rp note

to change month to month. **D** *Wisma Leuser Sibayak*, T 20774, restaurant (see below), popular, the more expensive rooms are a better bet, being cleaner; **E** *Wisma Bukit Lawang Cottages*, mandis shared between 2 rm, simple rooms and charming management, attractive garden and good food; **F** *Bukit Lawang Indah*, shared bathroom, clean, good food; **F** *Eden Inn* (15 mins walk' from PHPA office, lovely views over the river); **F** *Green Paradise Inn* (20 mins' walk from PHPA office); **F** *Jungle Inn* (25 mins' walk from PHPA office), good food, worth the walk, friendly and quiet, atmospheric, very popular with travellers, good value, rec; **F** *Mutiara Indah*, (en route to *Bukit Lawang Cottages*) quiet and secluded, very friendly, rec; **F** *Rocky Hill*, the most secluded of the places to stay, past the *Bukit Lawang Cottages* en route to Bat Cave, adjacent to the forest and a rubber plantation, 4 huts and no electricity (paraffin lamps supplied); **F** *Yusman Guesthouse*, basic rooms with mosquito nets, shared bathroom, friendly, although the food is mediocre, rec. **Camping**: free camping ground about a 15 mins walk upriver towards the crossing-point for the reserve.

● **Places to eat** Travellers' food at losmen; good at *Leuser Sibayak*, good vegetable dishes and excellent fruit salad, large portions; *Jungle Inn* and *Yusman*. Handful of warungs.

● **Banks & money changers** Losmen will change money, but rates are poor so it is best to bring sufficient cash.

● **Tourist offices** Visitors Information Centre (nr the minibus stop), free maps and advice on hiking. Open 0900-1500 Mon-Sat, 1000-1500 Sun. They also sell a useful booklet on the Park and its wildlife and flora (12,000Rp).

● **Transport** 87 km from Medan. **Road Bus**: direct buses now leave from Medan's new Pinang Baris terminal, every 30 mins (3 hrs, 1,300Rp). From Brastagi catch a bus to Medan and get off when it reaches route 25; from here, catch a regular bus to Bukit Lawang (see above). There is one direct bus each day from Brastagi to Bukit Lawang via Medan; the bus doing the return trip leaves Bukit Lawang at 0530, 4 hrs. The road deteriorates over the final 10 km to Bukit Lawang. **Taxi**: for hire in Medan, 2 hrs.

LHOKSEUMAWE

This coastal town is extremely important for Indonesia's economic development, but is rarely visited by tourists. It has become one of the key administrative and processing centres for the country's natural gas and petroleum industry and is consequently thriving and relatively wealthy. The massive P T Arun natural gas 'train' is nearby, while the town virtually lies in the shadow of a large urea fertilizer plant built as one of a series of rather poorly thought-through ASEAN Industrial Projects or AIPs. It was completed in 1984 and still operates at a loss, producing fertilizers that could be bought more cheaply on the international market.

Because of all this investment, and Lhokseumawe's role as the district capital of N Aceh, it has a good range of accommodation and other facilities. On the other hand, it is rather short in the local charm department. The extraction of this natural wealth from Aceh and its investment elsewhere, particularly in Java, is one of the factors that has fuelled the Acehnese secessionist movement. The province has one of the country's highest gross provincial products, but at the same time a high level of poverty indicating that the wealth is being creamed-off and invested elsewhere.

Excursions The **Samudera Pasai** is the graveyard of a former Islamic kingdom of Sumatra, 18 km E of town. **Ujung Blang** is the nearest decent beach to town.

● **Accommodation A-C** *Lido Graha International*, Jl Raya Medan-Banda Aceh, T 22266, F 22555, a/c, roof top-pool, another hotel built to provide for the needs of visiting oil men, 60 rm, a large rambling place, comfortable enough but rather ersatz; **A-C** *Meutia*, Jl Medan-Banda Aceh, T 21164, F 22986, a/c, 54 well appointed rm with a good range of facilities for a district town – built to meet the needs of visiting oil executives; **C-D** *Dewi Plaza*, Jl Pase 52, T 21442, some a/c; **D-E** *Wisma Kuta Karang Baru*, Jl Pang Lateh 8, T 22492; **F** *Farina 53*, clean and friendly.

● **Post & telecommunications Area code**: 0645.

● **Transport** 274 km from Banda Aceh. **Bus**: regular a/c and non-a/c bus connections with Banda Aceh to the N and Medan to the S.

BANDA ACEH

Banda Aceh, at the N extremity of Sumatra, has a population of 75,000 and is the capital of the Special Region or *Daerah Istimewa* of Aceh (the only other is Yogyakarta). It has been plagued by political turmoil ever since the Dutch began to exert their influence over the area in the late 19th century. The discovery of large reserves of natural gas in the 1960s has helped to make the province one of the richest in Indonesia, but the failure to unite the population behind the central government means the fruits have often not filtered down to the average man or woman. The bulk of the population are still farmers and even though much of the province is mountainous and inaccessible,

Aceh maintains a healthy rice surplus.

Aceh grew to prominence as an Islamic trading centre during the 16th century. The sultanate's wealth was based upon the pepper trade and several expeditions were sent to Melaka to try and dislodge the competing – and infidel – Portuguese. They failed in each instance. Aceh reached the height of its power during the reign of the brilliant Sultan Iskandar Muda (1607-1636) when the city became a cultural and economic centre, controlling the entire W coast of Sumatra as well as a substantial proportion of the E coast and parts of the Malay Peninsula. Iskandar Muda enthusiastically promoted Islam in his kingdom (first introduced by Arab traders during the 9th or 10th centuries) and it is said that when two drunken Acehnese were brought to him he had them executed by pouring molten lead down their throats. His military forces included a regiment of cavalry mounted on Persian horses, an elephant corps, and a navy of heavy galleys. Iskandar was constantly worried about his successor and even had his own son killed because he could not trust him. Following Iskandar's death, and with a fall in pepper prices and the growing power of the Europeans, Aceh gradually declined in influence.

Although by all accounts Iskandar Muda was absolutely ruthless, his reign saw a flowering of Acehnese arts. For example, a tradition of goldsmithing was established as a result of the discovery of mines to the W and the city became famous for the quality of its gold jewellery and dagger hilts. Today, gold ornamentation is still highly valued; brides wear cloths known as *songket* (see page 529), which have gold woven into them, and belts of gold called *simplaih*.

The Acehnese have displayed a long-standing penchant for resisting externally imposed authority. This thirst for autonomy means that Aceh feels almost like a nation apart. The Dutch lost large numbers of soldiers during the Aceh War

The Aceh War (1873-1878)

The Dutch found quelling the sultanate of Aceh to be their most difficult military task on Sumatra – something which in a sense they never achieved. In 1873 the Dutch mounted an expeditionary force of 3,000 men to confront the sultan and his army. Within weeks the force had retreated, its commander killed in the shadows of the city's mosque. The Dutch reacted to this humiliation by collecting together a force of 10,000 men, supported by 4,300 servants and coolies. They captured the city within 2 months, although not before losing several thousand men – mainly from cholera. The Dutch announced the abolition of the sultanate and the annexation of Aceh. But the resistance was far from subdued and the Dutch military were forced to continue to wage a low intensity war against the rebels until 1903.

(1873-1878) which never succeeded in completely quelling local resistance (see box). Even since independence, Aceh has continued to demonstrate its distaste for central rebellion. In 1953 there arose a vigorous rebellion over the role of Islam, and this rumbled on until 1962. There remains the impression that the authorities have only a tenuous hold over this diverse and fiercely independent province.

In the summer of 1990 there were widespread reports of increased activity by the rebel Aceh Merdeka (Free Aceh) guerrillas, and accusations of a heavy-handed military response, with summary arrest of suspects, torching of villages, and beatings. It should be stressed that few of these reports have been confirmed, although there is little doubt that Aceh remains a 'problem' area for the government and Amnesty International in 1993 estimated that 2,000 civilians have been unlawfully killed – some in public executions – since 1989. Few visitors will see any evidence of rebel activity, although buses are sometimes stopped at military roadblocks on the main road N (particularly at night). **NB** Tourists should remember that Aceh is possibly the most staunchly Muslim region in Indonesia and women should dress very modestly; even so, be prepared for some minor difficulties.

Places of interest

Much of Banda Aceh's glorious past was destroyed when the Dutch invaded the town in 1874, including the Sultan's Palace and the Great Mosque. Banda Aceh is a small provincial capital and can be explored on foot, with most of the sights of interest found S of the centre of town.

A good place to start a tour of the sights is the **Mesjid Raya Baiturrahman**, or Great Mosque, at the intersection of Jl Perdagangan and Jl Balai Kota. The mosque was built by the Dutch in 1879 to replace the one that they had destroyed during the assault on 14 April 1873. The commander of the Dutch forces, J H R Kohler was killed in the attack and a plaque marks the spot where he fell. The black-domed and white-walled mosque, with its gardens and ponds, is an island of peace in the city. Open to non-Muslims: 0700-1100, 1330-1600 Mon-Sun. Remove shoes, women should be veiled, dress appropriately. Behind the mosque and to the W is the **Chinese quarter** and the **market** with jewellery and handicrafts for sale.

SE of the mosque, down Jl Alauddin Mahmudsyah, is the **Aceh Museum** which displays a range of local artefacts, but unfortunately there is little explanatory information. Admission 200Rp. Open 0900-1300, 1500-1800 Tues-Thur, 0830-1200 Fri and Sat. In the same compound as the museum is a black-stained **rumah Aceh**, a model of a traditional Acehnese aristocrat's house. Here too are the graves of a number of 18th century sultans of Aceh. Right next to the museum, in the grounds of part of the University Iskandar Muda, is the **tomb of Sultan Iskandar Muda** himself (1607-1636).

Further S still on Jl T Umar, is the site of **Gunungan**, a palace and enclosed pleasure garden built during the 17th century – possibly by Sultan Iskandar Muda. It is said to have been built by the Sultan for one of his queens who wished to be able to take an evening stroll – forbidden at that time. The grounds also contain a cake-like, white structure with stairs running up the side. There have been a number of theories as to the use and symbolism of this weird artificial

mountain. Some argue that it was an observatory; others, a topographic map of the queen's homeland to make her feel less homesick; still others, the cosmic mountain, Mt Meru; or perhaps even an altar to Agni, the Hindu god of fire. The art historian Jacques Dumarçay believes all these to be wrong and argues that it is a phallic symbol – he notes that the name of the park, Ghairah, means ardour, love or passion, and believes the rest to be self-explanatory.

On the other side of the road is the immaculately kept **Kher Khoff**, which contains the graves of 2,200 Dutch soldiers killed fighting the Acehnese be-

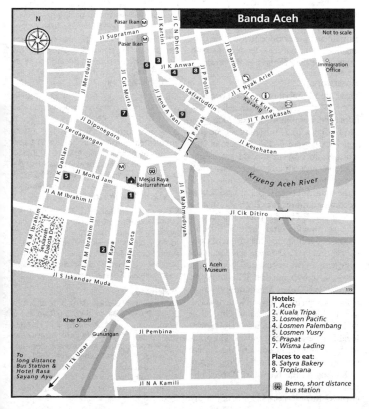

Banda Aceh

Not to scale

Hotels:
1. Aceh
2. Kuala Tripa
3. Losmen Pacific
4. Losmen Palembang
5. Losmen Yusry
6. Prapat
7. Wisma Lading

Places to eat:
8. Satyra Bakery
9. Tropicana

Bemo, short distance bus station

tween the late 19th century and early 20th century. Among them is the grave of J H R Kohler, killed while storming the Mesjid Raya. Admission free (although the grave-yard keeper may expect a 'donation'). Open 0800-1200, 1400-1700 Mon-Sun.

The park on the other side of Jl Sultan Iskandar Muda contains **Seulawah** – 'Golden Mountain' (RI-001) – a **Dakota DC3**, belonging to Indonesian Airways. Bought in 1948, it was Indonesian Airways' first plane, purchased with donations from people in Aceh Province and was intended to break the Dutch blockade. Facing onto the park are a number of fine examples of Dutch colonial architecture.

The **Pasar Ikan** (Fish Market) is worth a visit in the morning. It is at the N end of Jl Jend A Yani, at the intersection with Jl Supratman by the bridge crossing the Kreung Aceh. The market extends along both banks of the river N and S of the bridge.

Excursions

There are a number of beautiful **beaches** to the W of Banda Aceh. Travelling SW from town, **Lampuuk** beach is 13 km away and **Lhoknga** 18.5 km. There is good surf here, but beware of the dangerous cur-rents. Swim only in modest swimsuits. There is snorkeling off-shore, for which you will have to hire a boat. Further on still is the beautiful beach area of **Lho'seuda**. **Accommodation**: the **E** *Pondok Wisata Mitabu* and **E** *Pondok Wisata Darlian* are both at Lhoknga and there is little to choose between them. In a different cate-gory entirely is **C-D** *Taman Tepi Laut Cottages* with stylish rooms and bungalows. *Getting there*: by bemo from Jl Diponegoro.

Cut Nyak Dhien Museum is 33 km E of Banda Aceh in the town of Krueng Raya. The building is a replica of Cut Nyak Dhien's house, an Acehnese heroine who fought bravely in the Aceh War. The origi-nal house was burnt down by the Dutch. *Getting there*: by bemo from Jl Diponegoro.

Sabang on the **Island of Weh** can be reached from Pelabuhan Malahayata (Krueng Raya), a port 33 km E of the city

(see page 447). *Getting there*: by bemo from Jl Diponegoro.

Tours

Tours to sights in the surrounding country-side and to Sabang (see page 447) are ar-ranged by *Krueng Wayla* and by *Tripa Wisata*.

Local information
● **Accommodation**

Many of the budget-priced hotels are on Jl Jend A Yani but quite a few seem to cater for locals only (tourists may be given the cold shoulder). In addition, because Banda Aceh is not a popular tourist destination accommodation at the lower end is comparatively expensive – the very cheap-est places to stay are around double the price that they are elsewhere.

A-B *Kuala Tripa*, Jl Mesjid Raya 24, T 21879, F 21790, a/c, restaurant, pool, best in town, good value, all modern facilities, 40 rm.

B-C *Rasa Sayang Ayu*, Jl Tk Umar 439, S of the centre, nr the bus station, T 22846, a/c, 40 rm, restaurant, big clean rooms; **B-C** *Sultan*, Jl Pan-glima Polim 127, T 23581, F 31770, a/c, clean and comfortable with 60 rm.

C-D *Prapat*, Jl Jend A Yani 17, T 22159, some a/c, clean, popular and rather better managed than others in this category.

D *Losmen Yusry*, Jl Mohd Jam 1, T 23160, attached mandis and reasonably clean; **D-E** *Los-men Palembang*, Jl Khairil Anwar 51, T 22044, some a/c and some rooms with private mandis; **D-E** *Wisma Lading*, Jl Cut Mutia 9, T 21359, some a/c, attached mandi, apparently designed by a blindfolded architect.

E *Aceh*, Jl Mohd Jam 1, T 21354, some a/c, colonial and rather decrepit, but excellent position facing the mosque, the most atmospheric place to stay if not the cleanest; **E** *Losmen Pacific*, Jl Ahmad Yani 22, T 31364, just about the cheapest place around, but still comparatively expensive, clean rooms with shared facilities.

● **Places to eat**

Indonesian: ◆◆*Garuda Baru*, Jl Jend A Yani 30-41; ◆◆*Ujong Batee*, Jl Krueng Raya, out of town, wide array of Acehnese and excellent seafood, rec; ◆◆-◆*Rindang Café*, Jl Balai Kota, excellent outdoor café with extensive menu and good fruit drinks; ◆*Minang Surya*, Jl Safiatud-din, good Padang food; ◆*Satyva*, Jl Khairil An-war 3, bakery, good for breakfast; ◆*Sinar Surya*, Jl Jend A Yani (by the night market), Minang food.

Chinese: ♦♦*Tropicana*, Jl Jend A Yani 90-92, considered by locals to be the best Chinese restaurant in town, in fact in all of Sumatra, despite an element of home town exaggeration, it does serve excellent Chinese food (and ice cream) and is very popular with Banda's Chinese population – a good sign, rec; ♦*Warung Surabaya*, Jl Khairil Anwar 32, satay.

International: ♦♦♦*Kuala Tripa*, Jl Mesjid Raya 2, also serves Chinese and seafood.

Foodstalls: there are a number of cheap warungs along Jl Cik. Ditiro; also try the stalls in Penayong, Chinatown. There is a night market on the junction of Jl Jend A Yani and Jl Khairil Anwar, where good, cheap Indonesian and Chinese food can be found.

● **Airline offices**
Garuda Merpati, *Hotel Sultan*, Jl Panglima Polim 127, T 22469.

● **Banks & money changers**
Bank Negara Indonesia 1946, Jl A H K Dahlan; Bank Dagang Negara, Jl Diponegoro; Bank Bumi Daya, Jl Cut Mutia.

● **Entertainment**
Very little nightlife because of strict adherence to Islam. The stadium sometimes stages bullfights.

Disco: *Kuala Tripa*, Jl Mesjid Raya 24.

● **Hospitals & medical services**
Hospital: Jl T Nyak Arief, T 22616.

● **Post & telecommunications**
Area code: 0651.

General Post Office: Jl T Angkasa.

Telephone office: Jl T Nyak Arief 92.

● **Shopping**
Antiques: Dutch, Acehnese and Chinese antiques to be found on Jl Perdagangan.

Handicrafts: there is a government handicraft shop on Jl S R Safiatuddin 54. The Pasar Aceh (market) near the mosque is a good place to browse.

Jewellery: shops line Jl Perdagangan, and they will copy most things.

● **Tour companies & travel agents**
Kreung Wayla, Jl Safiatuddin 26, T 22066; *Nustra Agung*, Jl Diponegoro, T 22026; *Sastra*, Jl Jend A Yani, T 22207; *Tripa Wisata*, Kuala Tripa Hotel, Jl Mesjid Raya 24, T 21455; *Natrabu*, Beurawe Shopping Centre, T 32243.

● **Tourist offices**
Aceh regional tourist office, Jl Cik Kuta Karang 3, T 23692. Good for maps and other information; surprisingly well organized. Open 0730-1430, Mon-Thur, 0700-1100 Fri and 0730-1100 Sat.

● **Useful addresses**
Immigration Office: Jl T Nyak Arief 82, T 23784.
Police: Jl T Nyak Arief, T 21125.

● **Transport**
594 km N of Medan, 112 km from Sigli, 218 km from Bireuen.

Local Bus: the Stasiun Kota (short-distance bus station) is by the mosque. Frequent service around town; just hail one from the side of the road. **Becak mesin**: (motorbikes with sidecarts). **Bemos**: leave from Jl Diponegoro for the beaches at Lhoknga, Lampuuk and for the ferry to Sabang. **Labi-labi**: (minibuses) for short distances. 200Rp around town. **Taxis**: metered.

Air The airport is nearly 20 km from town (12,000Rp by taxi). Daily connections on Merpati with Medan, and from there to other destinations in and beyond Sumatra (see route map, page 912).

Road Bus: the Terminal Bus Seuti is SW of town on Jl Tk. Umar. Regular a/c and non-a/c bus connections with Medan and down the W, Indian Ocean coast to Meulaboh and onward to Sidikalang. The road to Medan is fast and good (although some bus drivers appear to have no sense), 12 hrs. The major bus companies (*ATS*, *Kurnia*, *Melati* and *ARS*) have their offices on Jl Mohd Jam.

SABANG AND THE ISLAND OF WEH

Under Dutch rule, this small island of 150 sq km – inhabited at that time only by fishermen – was developed into an important bunkering depot. Steamships and liners from around the world docked here to replenish their stocks of coal and fresh water. Indeed, up until WW2, Sabang was a more important port than Singapore. However, as diesel replaced steam, so the island became redundant. During WW2, the Japanese took over the island and reminders of the 3½ year occupation can still be seen in the gun emplacements that dot the island's cliffs.

In 1970, **Sabang** – the main town on Weh with 25,000 inhabitants – was declared

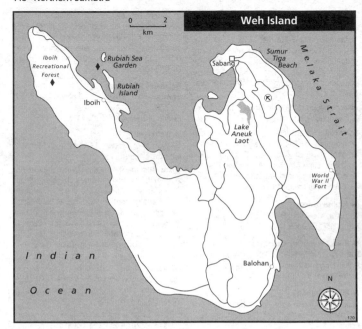

Weh Island

Iboih Recreational Forest

Rubiah Sea Garden

Sabang

Sumur Tiga Beach

Melaka Strait

Rubiah Island

Iboih

Lake Aneuk Laot

World War II Fort

Indian Ocean

Balohan

N

0   2
km

a duty-free port and it seemed that it would once again become a centre of commercial activity. These plans came to nothing when the port's duty-free status was abruptly terminated in 1986. Since then, the Island of Weh has developed into a modest beach resort, the population hopeful that great times may come again.

Sabang hit the news most recently – and tragically – in Jan 1996 when one of the ferries linking the island with the mainland foundered. The *Gurita* was crowded with people returning home for Ramadan and over 300 drowned.

Places of interest The best reason to visit Weh is for the snorkelling, diving, swimming and palm-lined beaches – and for the peace and quiet. Beaches include **Patai Sumur Tiga** (Three Wells Beach) on the NW coast where high tide leaves little sandy area, **Paradise Beach** and **Lovers Beach** (the latter is probably the best).

The **Rubiah Sea Garden**, a 2,600 ha marine reserve, provides excellent visibility and a wealth of sea life, although the coral is being gradually destroyed by fishermen, illegally using dynamite. The marine reserve is centred on Pulau Rubiah, on the W of Sabang Bay, and is accessible from the village of Iboih, on the W of the island and 23 km from Sabang. **NB** Getting across to Rubiah can be difficult, as currents are very strong. Divers have been known to drift a long way from the beach. Just outside Iboih is the small **Iboih Recreational Forest** (1,300 ha), a tropical forest reserve with good walks and a smattering of wildlife (for example, wild boar). Also accessible from Iboih is **Mount Merapi**, a small semi-active volcano with hot springs on its slopes. Boats can be chartered to explore the **caves** along the coast of the W peninsula.

The island is dotted with abandoned WW2 **guns and fortifications** and there is also a Chinese temple – **Tua Peh Kong Bio** – the most northerly in Indonesia.

● **Accommodation** There are a handful of losmen in Sabang and one at Iboih (with several more under construction – when they are completed other facilities, like water, are likely to be stretched); it is also possible to stay in surrounding villages. **Holiday: D-E** *Holiday*, Jl Perdagangan Belakang 1, T 21131, quiet and more relaxing than other losmen in town with 30 rm; **D-E** *Pulau Jaya*, Jl TK Umar 17, T 21344, some a/c, the largest of the losmen with clean rooms, popular; **E-F** *Irma*, Jl TK Umar 3, T 21128, just 15 rm, good, clean place with café downstairs, a valuable source of information, rec; **E-F** *Sabang Marouke*, Jl Seulawah 1, T 21139, small, quiet family style place with 9 rm. **Iboih Beach: E-F** *Iboih*, situated at the beach of the same name, on the W limb, 10 mins' walk from bus stop, over undulating path, restaurant with basic food, basic accommodation; **F** *Fatima Bungalows*, the rooms here are very good value, although the food is rather dull; **F** *Mama's*, produces probably the best food on the beach.

● **Places to eat** There are a number of Padang and Chinese restaurants in Sabang. The *Dynasty* on Jl Perdagangan serves the best Chinese cuisine.

● **Post & telecommunications Area code**: 0651. **Post Office**: Jl Perdagangan (next to the Post Office).

● **Sports Snorkelling and diving**: equipment is hired out by the *Stingray Dive Centre* at the *Losmen Pulau Jaya* (T 21265), in town, cheaper equipment is available at Iboih.

● **Useful addresses Immigration Office**: Jl Seulawah, T 21343. **Police Station**: Jl Perdagangan, T 21306.

● **Transport Local** Taxi, bemo and motorbike. Fishing boats can be chartered for trips to the smaller islands for snorkelling and fishing. **Air** There are daily flights by SMAC from Banda Aceh. **Boat** A daily ferry leaves from Krueng Raya (Pelabuhan Malahayati), about 33 km E of Banda Aceh, at about 1430-1500 each day 2½ hrs (3,900-5,500Rp). Ferries depart from We for Krueng Raya at 0900. To get to Krueng Raya, take a bemo from Jl Diponegoro in Banda Aceh 45 mins. Passengers should aim to arrive 1 hr before departure. The ferry docks at Balohan, on the S coast of Weh, from where there are minibuses and taxis to take passengers the 10 km N to Sabang town. In Banda Aceh, the ferry office (PASDP) is at Jl Gabus (Lam Prit), T 21377.

THE WEST COAST: BANDA ACEH TO SIDIKALANG

For adventurous travellers there is now the possibility of continuing on from Banda Aceh S down the W coast of Sumatra to Sidikalang, and from there to Lake Toba – a route which over the last couple of years has become increasingly popular. Changes in hotels and other facilities are rapid. The road is much improved and the journey takes about 24 hrs by bus. There are isolated and rarely visited beaches along the coast, which bear the full brunt of the surf rolling in off the Indian Ocean.

Accommodation On the W coast: except for Meulobah, Tapaktuan and Sidikalang, only basic losmen accommodation and homestays are available. Many of the losmen are brothels, so staying with families is recommended wherever possible.

Women Although this is a beautiful part of Sumatra, female travellers have reported a considerable amount of hassle. Where possible it is advisable to travel with a male companion, and always dress very modestly, keeping well covered.

THE ROUTE SOUTH FROM BANDA ACEH TO SIDIKALANG DOWN THE WEST COAST

Banda Aceh (see page 443). Buses run direct from Banda Aceh to Meulaboh, the next large town on the W coast travelling S, 8 hrs.

Lamno Losmen accommodation available; the beaches along the 40 km of coast S from Lamno to Calang are very beautiful. The hiking is excellent and the local people friendly.

Rigaih (near Calang) **C-D** *Dieter's Beautiful Place* aka *Camp Europa* and *Dieter's Farm* (F 0651-32139) is an excellent losmen, highly recommended by those travellers who have stayed there. It is run by a German – Dieter – who has built a small number of stilt houses in the forest just inland from a stupendous beach with wonderful clear blue sea and excellent swimming. The place could be criticized though for being a little pricey and visitors have also complained that the food is rather lacklustre (4 meals and drinks are included in the room rate).

Calang 140 km S of Banda Aceh, a 2½ hr trip by minibus. Losmen accommodation available.

Anda Losmen accommodation available, although reported to be noisy.

Meulaboh The **C-E** *Hotel Mutiara*, Jl Teuku Umar 157, T 21531, some a/c, provides slightly more sophisticated accommodation than in other towns and villages along the W coast route. It is worth paying the extra. Meulaboh is a district administrative centre and so is relatively well-endowed with facilities. Cheaper losmen include the **E-F** *Losmen Erna* and **E-F** *Losmen Pelita Jaya*, both on Jl Singgahmata. Ferries run from the harbour (worth a wander) to the off-shore island of Simeulue. Buses from here to Tapaktuan with one change, and N to Banda Aceh.

Tapaktuan This bustling small town has a good daily market and a recommended losmen, the **E** *Bukit Barisan*, Jl Merdeka 37 with clean rooms, a bargain. Also recommended is **E-F** *Losmen Jambu*, another excellent place to stay with an inexpensive Padang-style café attached; breakfast, including fresh donuts can be bought across the road. The beaches to the N and S, stretching over 40 km or so, are very beautiful. There are also jungle walks, waterfalls and hot springs all within walking distance. Many travellers choose to break their journey for several days here. However, the bulk of the trip between here and Meulaboh is unremarkable and taking a bus or hitching is rec (4-7 hrs). Buses available from the station 1 km out of town all the way to Sidikalang, 6 hrs.

Bakungan Losmen accommodation available.

Kruengluck A small village; homestays available.

Glombang A small village on the Alas River. No losmen as yet, but travellers do stay with local families. From here there is (said to be) a boat every Thur to Kutacane (see page 455).

Sidikalang A larger town with a range of accommodation available. Buses from here to Lake Toba, Brastagi and elsewhere (see entry page 455).

Buses down the W coast

From/to	Price (Rp)	Journey time (hrs)
Banda Aceh to Calang	6,000	2½
Calang to Meulaboh	4,000	2
Meulaboh to Tapaktuan	6,000	4-7
Tapaktuan to Sidikalang	-	6
Prices and journey times, 1996.		

THE ROUTE SOUTH: MEDAN TO LAKE TOBA VIA BRASTAGI

From Medan there are two routes S. The Trans-Sumatran Highway runs S and then begins to climb into Sumatra's mountainous spine. The road winds its way upwards through a succession of hairpin bends, bus conductors clambering onto the roofs of their vehicles to spy out the competition: if there is a bus in front they will drive like the wind to overtake and catch any fares; if there is no other bus in sight they will dawdle to maximize their pick-up rate. After 68 km the road reaches the hill resort of Brastagi, established by the Dutch in the Karo Batak Highlands. The alternative route S passes through Tebingtinggi (76 km from Medan) to Pemangtangsiantar (another 52 km). From Brastagi, the N route passes through the Karo Batak market town of Kabanjahe before linking up with the S route and arriving at Lake Toba. Taking the road that skirts the N shore of Lake Toba, the route passes through Merek and Sidikalang. Travelling N from here, it is possible to reach Banda Aceh via Kutacane, the Gunung Leuser National Park and the Gayo Highlands (including Takengon). Travelling W from Sidikalang it is possible to then travel N all the way to Banda Aceh along the W coast road (see page 449).

BRASTAGI (BERESTAGI)

Brastagi, or Berestagi, is a hill resort town, lying 1,300m above sea-level on the Karo Plateau among the traditional lands of the Karo Batak people. It was established by the Dutch in the early 20th century as a retreat from the heat and humidity of the lowlands and was frequented by Dutch planters from Sumatra's E coast, and by planters, businessmen and officials from British Malaya. The surrounding area is dotted with tea and coffee plantations and market gardens, growing temperate fruit and vegetables.

Places of interest

The town does not have many specific sights of interest, but its position, surrounded by active volcanoes, is memorable. Unfortunately, Brastagi has a rather uncared for feel, and it is dirty and featureless. There are plans afoot to revive the resort as a tourist destination; cleaning it up would be a good way to start. Nonetheless, Brastagi is a good place to cool off after the heat and bustle of Medan, and play a little golf, hike, or go riding.

For those without the time to visit the Batak villages outside Kabanjahe (see Excursions), there is a Batak village of sorts – **Paceren** – just outside town on the road to Medan, 100m past the *Rose Garden Hotel*. It is rather run down and dirty, with a few Batak houses interspersed with modern houses, however it is in some respects more authentic than those which have been preserved, showing how living

Brastagi

Not to Scale

Hotels:
1. Bukit Kubu
2. Ginsata
3. Losmen Sibayak
4. Rose Garden
5. Rudang
6. Sibayak International
7. Wisma Sibayak
Places to eat:
8. Eropa

Karo Batak architecture

The Karo Batak build the greatest variety of traditional or *adat* houses of all the Batak groups. Houses are always aligned according to religious criteria, and are usually divided by roof type and by differences in the body of the structure. Most distinctive and common is the gabled hipped roof, where the high-peaked, (traditionally thatched) roof – surmounted by buffalo horns – slopes steeply down below the projecting gable. The houses are either built on massive wooden pillars sunk into the ground (*rumah pasuk*), or resting on stone blocks (*rumah sangka manuk*) – to resist rotting (like the Toba Batak houses).

Extending from the front and the rear are bamboo platforms where food is prepared and provisions stored. Young couples also meet here in the evening. As many as eight families may live in a single house, and there are no interior divides to ensure privacy. Two families will share a cooking hearth so that houses commonly have four hearths. The roof area is used to store tools and fuelwood.

Rectangular rice barns or *sapo page* are always built at right angles to the main dwelling house. They rest on stone blocks to protect against damp and are entered from above. Today traditional rice barns are rarely built. Peculiar to the Karo Batak are skull houses or ossuaries (*geriten*) used to store the bones of dead ancestors. These buildings are usually square in plan, and like the main dwelling usually feature a gabled hipped roof. Poorer families unable to afford the cost of building a dedicated skull house, keep the bones of their ancestors in the roof area of the main house. Traditional houses are no longer being built in the Karo area, and as older houses are replaced, so these wonderful *rumah adat* are becoming rarer.

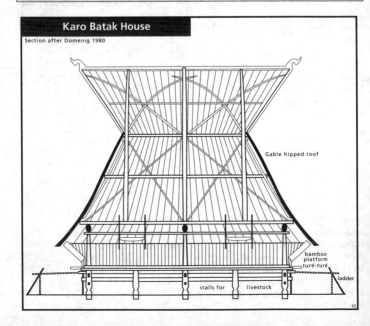

Karo Batak House

Section after Domenig 1980

Gable hipped roof

bamboo platform *turé-turé*

ladder

stalls for livestock

communities are adapting to the changing world. There is no admission fee, although the children will shout 'rupiah, rupiah'. There is a fresh fruit and vegetable **market** opposite the monument at the N end of Jl Veteran.

Excursions

For a map of the surrounding area see page 456.

Kabanjahe meaning 'Ginger garden', is 12 km S of Brastagi and easily accessible by bus. It is a local market town of some size and is especially worth visiting on Mon – market day. From here it is possible to walk to traditional villages of the *Karo Batak* people (see below). *Getting there*: regular buses from the station on Jl Veteran.

Karo Batak villages are to be found dotted all over the hills around Brastagi. But note that the more traditional villages are not accessible by road and must be reached on foot; to visit these communities it is recommended to hire a guide (ask at your hotel or the tourist centre). Two villages which can be visited with relative ease from Kabanjahe are Lingga and Barusjahe – both can be reached by microlite from Kabanjahe. This ease of access has inevitably resulted in rather 'touristy' villages. **Lingga** is about 4 km NW of Kabanjahe and is a community of about 30 Batak longhouses; it is a friendly village. Tourists must pay an 'entrance fee' of 300Rp at the Tourist Information Centre in the main square, then are free to roam. **Barusjahe** is slightly more difficult to get to and as a result is marginally more 'traditional', but can still be reached by microlite from Kabanjahe. Some of the wooden houses are over two centuries old and the soaring roofs are particularly impressive. *Getting there*: for Lingga and Barusjahe, catch a bus from the bus station on Jl Veteran to Kabanjahe, and from there a microlite or bemo onwards. In Kabanjahe they leave from the intersection of Jl Pala Bangun, Jl Veteran and Jl Bangsi Sembiring. If hoping to visit more remote villages hire a guide in town (ask at your hotel or the tourist centre). It can make sense to charter a bemo for the day – a great deal more ground can be covered.

There are waterfalls at **Si Piso Piso**, 24 km from Kabanjahe, on the N side of Lake Toba, good views from a gazebo at the top of a hill over the 120m falls and towards Lake Toba. **Accommodation**: recent visitors have reported nice accommodation at Si Piso Piso. *Getting there*: catch a bemo to Merek and ask for the falls.

It is possible to **hike** through spectacular countryside all the way to Bukit Lawang from Brastagi in 3 days. However, the government is anxious about visitors disturbing this culturally sensitive area and trekkers should take the time and care to organize trips properly. Ask in town at the *Sibayak Guesthouse* or at the *Rafflesia Tourist Information Service*, Jl Veteran 84 for up-to-date information on trekking. There are numerous 'guides' offering treks to Bukit Lawang; note that this is a difficult and demanding trek requiring a degree of fitness and good walking boots. **NB** Many of the 'guides' have little experience, check their credentials carefully. Most people trek this route in the other direction, from Bukit Lawang to Brastagi (see page 440).

Mount Sibayak lies NW of Brastagi at 2,095m and can be climbed in a day, but leave early for the best views (and to avoid rain). Take the trail from behind Gundaling Hill, asking at your hotel for directions before setting-out. Guides can be easily found (again, ask at your hotel), a map of the route is available from the *Tourist Information Office*, and it is advisable to wear good walking shoes and take a sweater as it can be chilly. About 2-3 hrs to the summit, along a logging road, quicker if you take a bemo to Semangat Gunung, in the Daulu valley. Over the summit, the descent is down 2,000 plus steps, to Hot Water and Sulphur Springs (entrance fee charged). The sulphur is collected by local people and is used as medicine and as a pesticide.

Tours

Tour companies arrange **canoe or raft trips** along the **Alas River** (to the NW of Brastagi (see the map on page 456 and the entry on page 458). The journey passes through the **Gunung Leuser Nature Reserve** with traditional villages and tropical rainforest. A 5 day trip should cost about 125,000Rp, all inclusive. Alternatively, take a jungle trek (with a guide) through the reserve – a 3 day trek costing about 63,000Rp. Ask for details at the *Sibayak Guesthouse*. More expensive 4-6 day White Water Rafting trips are organized by *Pacto Tours* (in association with *Sobek Expeditions*, USA). Contact *Pacto*, Jl Surabayu 8, T 3848634.

Local information
● Accommodation

A *Sinabung Resort*, Jl Kolam Renang, T 91400, restaurant, pool, new 100-rm hotel with golf, tennis, health centre, sauna, disco, satellite TV ... we haven't been able to confirm whether this amounts to more than a long string of facilities, but on paper it should be the swishest place to stay; ˙ **A** *International Sibayak*, Jl Merdeka, T 20928, a/c, restaurant, pool, comfortable, well-appointed rooms and good sports facilities.

B *Brastagi Cottages*, Jl Gundaling, T 20888, a/c, restaurant, large rooms, big garden, hot water, great views; **B** *Bukit Kubu*, Jl Sempurna 2, T 20832, basic restaurant with average food, colonial-style grandeur, old wing has the best rooms, hot water, fabulous views, cheap golf and tennis facilities, with management which can be rather surly; **B** *Danau Toba*, Jl Gundaling, T 20946, a/c, pool; **B** *Rose Garden*, Jl Picaran, T 20099, a/c, pool, hot water.

C *Kolam Renang*, Jl Kolam Renang, restaurant, large garden.

D *Rudang*, Jl Picaran, T 20921, restaurant, pool, bungalow-style accommodation nr the *Bukit Kubu Hotel*, attractive setting.

E *Ginsata*, Jl Veteran 79, restaurant, mandi, friendly management, close by is the slightly cheaper *Ginsata Guesthouse*.

F *Dieng*, Jl Udara 27, colonial house with rather run-down rooms, but friendly management and good information, rec; **F** *Losmen Sibayak*, Jl Veteran 119, popular, good source of information, bag store room, bicycle hire, tours avail-

able, average rooms some with baths, rec; **F** *Wisma Sibayak*, Jl Udara 1, popular place and good source of information, sister losmen to *Sibayak*, and better, with dorm beds, tasty food, very well managed, tours, bikes for hire, rec.

● Places to eat

Some of the hotels have quite decent restaurants. **♦♦***Eropa*, Jl Veteran 48G, International and Chinese; **♦♦***Sehat*, Jl Veteran 134, good Chinese, friendly service; **♦***Irfan*, Jl Veteran 79, Padang food.

Foodstalls: there are many open-air warungs serving good, fresh food, using the temperate fruit and vegetables grown in the surrounding countryside; *Jl Veteran* has the best selection. The market nr the monument just off Jl Veteran sells fresh fruit and vegetables.

● Banks & money changers

Money can be changed at the bigger hotels or at the *Sibayak Guesthouse*, Jl Veteran 119. However, rates are poor and it is advisable to arrive with enough cash for your stay here.

● Hospitals & medical services

Health centre: Jl Veteran 30.

● Post & telecommunications

Area code: 0628.

Post Office: Jl Veteran (by the monument at the top of the road).

● Shopping

Antiques and handicrafts: sold in several shops along Jl Veteran.

● Sports

Golf: nine hole course (very short) at the *Bukit Kubu Hotel*, Jl Sempurna 2. Clubs for hire.

Horse riding: ask the men and boys, who are to be found with their horses waiting for custom around the more expensive hotels.

Pool/snooker: pool hall at Jl Veteran 52.

Swimming: public pool on Jl Sempurna, opp the *Bukit Kubu Hotel*.

Tennis: *Bukit Kubu Hotel*, Jl Sempurna 2.

● Tourist offices (unofficial)

Tourist Information Service, Jl Gundaling No 1. Information on hotels and rather overpriced tours. *Sibayak Guesthouse*, Jl Veteran 119, is a good source of travellers' information. There is also the **Rafflesia Tourist Information Service** at Jl Veteran 84, in the middle of the road.

● Transport

68 km from Medan, 147 km from Prapat.

Local Bicycle hire: from the *Losmen Sibayak* and *Wisma Sibayak*. **Car hire**: from *Rafflesia Tourist Information Service* at Jl Veteran 84. **Dokars**: for short local journeys.

Road Bus: the bus station is to the S of Jl Veteran. Regular connections with Medan 2 hrs, Prapat – changing at Kabanjahe – 3½ hrs, Bukit Lawang 4 hrs, Sidakalang 3 hrs and Sibolga 9 hrs. Alternative route to Samosir Island: catch a bus to Kabanjahe, then to Seribudolok and from there to Haranggaol, on the N side of Lake Toba. Ferries leave from Haranggaol for Tuk Tuk and Ambarita on Samosir every Mon and Thur at 1300 and 1500. **Taxi**: share taxis sometimes run to Medan; ask at the *Sibayak Guesthouse*, or at the *Rafflesia Tourist Information Service*.

SIDIKALANG

This is a small, unremarkable town which serves an important 'linking' function. From here it is possible to travel N, along the valley of the Alas River to Kutacane and the Gunung Leuser National Park, and from there to Takengon and the Gayo Highlands, and finally to Banda Aceh at the northern tip of Sumatra. Alternatively, it is possible to travel W to the coast and then N along the coast, again to Banda Aceh (see page 449 for a summary of the W coast route).

● **Accommodation** A range of hotels and losmen is available including the **D-E** *Hotel Merapi*, small, basic rooms, some are dirty so ask to see the rooms available before checking-in, insects galore.

● **Transport Bus**: regular connections with Pangururan, Kutacane and Brastagi.

PEMANGTANGSIANTAR

Pemangtangsiantar, better known simply as **Siantar**, is the second largest city in N Sumatra and has built its wealth on the tea, tobacco, rubber and oil palm cultivated in the surrounding countryside. Most visitors simply pass it by on the route from Medan to Lake Toba. The **Museum Simalungun** is at Jl Sudirman 20 and has a reasonable ethnographic collection of Simalungun Batak artefacts, which are poorly displayed and explained. There are also some colonial exhibits. Admission small donation. Open

0800-1200, 1400-1700 Mon-Sat. The **Central Market** on Jl Merdeka is rather gloomy but large and bustling, while the **Siantar Zoo** has a poorly kept collection of Sumatran wildlife.

● **Accommodation B** *Siantar*, Jl W R Supratman 3, T 21091, F 21736, a/c, restaurant, pool, colonial hotel with garden, 80 good rooms, hot water, friendly, tennis court, rec; **E** *Garuda*, Jl Merdeka 33, shared mandi and dirty; **F** *Delima*, Jl Thamrin 131.

● **Banks & money changers** Bank Rakyat Indonesia, on the corner of Jl Sudirman and Jl Merdeka.

● **Post & telecommunications Area code**: 0622. **Post Office**: Jl Sutomo 2.

● **Shopping** Batak handicrafts, incl *ikat* cloth, are on sale at the central market.

● **Tour companies & travel agents** C V *Titipan Kilat*, Jl Merdeka 24.

● **Transport** 128 km from Medan, 103 km from Brastagi, 48 km from Prapat. **Bus**: there are two bus stations. Stasiun Sentral for Medan. Stasiun Parlusan for Prapat 1¼ hrs, Sibolga, Bukittinggi, Kabanjahe and Brastagi (changing at Kabanjahe) 3 hrs.

KUTACANE AND THE GUNUNG LEUSER NATIONAL PARK

Kutacane is the main town and service centre for the magnificent Gunung Leuser National Park and is situated in the heart of the Alas Valley. The land around the town is intensively farmed, but the forested hills of the reserve can be seen in the distance. There is accommodation here, guides and other services for trekking.

The **Gunung Leuser National Park** is perhaps the finest conservation area in Indonesia, and certainly one of the most important parks in Southeast Asia. It covers 850,000 ha of tropical rainforest and other habitats in the provinces of N Sumatra and Aceh. The wide range of ecological zones, from alpine meadows among the peaks of the Bukit Barisan, to brackish-water swamps, makes this a critical conservation area. In total, the park is estimated to support some 500

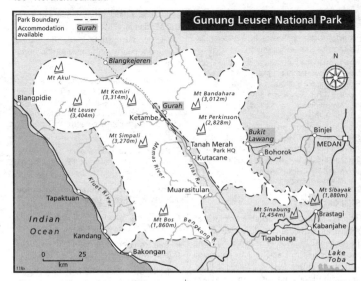

Gunung Leuser National Park

Park Boundary
Accommodation available — *Gurah*

Blangkejeren
Mt Akul
Blangpidie
Mt Kemiri (3,314m)
Mt Bandahara (3,012m)
Gurah
Ketambe
Mt Leuser (3,404m)
Mt Perkinson (2,828m)
Mt Simpali (3,270m)
Bukit Lawang
Binjei
MEDAN
Tanah Merah Park HQ
Kutacane
Bohorok
Mamas River
Alas R.
Kluet River
Muarasitulan
Mt Sibayak (1,880m)
Tapaktuan
Mt Sinabung (2,454m)
Brastagi
Indian Ocean
Mt Bos (1,860m)
Bengkong R.
Kabanjahe
Kandang
Bakongan
Tigabinaga
Lake Toba

0   25
km

species of birds, and 3,500 species of plants (of Sumatra's total recorded flora of 8,500 species). Fauna include tiger, rhino, gibbon, elephant and orang utan.

The park was gazetted in 1980, to become one of Indonesia's first five National Parks and is named after Gunung Leuser in Aceh Province which rises to a height of 3,455m, and is the second highest mountain in Sumatra. Although the park was not created until 1980, parts of the area that now make up the park were established as wildlife reserves and sanctuaries by the Dutch as early as the 1930s. The important step that the Indonesian government took in 1980 was to recognize the importance of the whole area and amalgamate a series of reserves into one extensive park.

Flora

Among the park's flora is the famous Rafflesia, which bears the largest bloom of any plant in the world (see page 490); the carnivorous *Nepenthes* or pitcher plant; the giant tulang tree (*Koompassia excelsa*) which has wood so hard that it is impervious even to chainsaws; and

countless species of broad-leaved *Dipterocarp*, the tree which, more than any other, defines the lowland tropical forest of Malesia. The importance of preserving ecologically viable areas of tropical forest like that of Gunung Leuser lies in the extreme species diversity that exists. In terms of the number of species found in an average hectare of forest, the forests of island Southeast Asia are even more diverse than those of the Amazon Basin. In a single hectare of Gunung Leuser's forest, botanists can expect to identify over 150 species of tree – yet each of which will be represented by between just one and three individual plants. Forest formations found in the park, and some of their notable flora, are:

● **Beach and swamp forest** (wild nutmeg, Myristica sp; camphor, *Dryobalanops aromatica*).

● **Lowland rainforest** (Rafflesia; wild figs, Ficus sp., an important jungle larder and of which there are 70 species); lianas; rotans – for rattan; Dipterocarps.

● **Submontane forest** (at 1,000-1,500m).

Trekking in Gunung Leuser National Park: check list

- Light, long-sleeved shirts and trousers
- Good walking boots
- Leach socks
- Waterproof
- Sleeping bag (temperatures at altitude fall markedly at night)
- First aid kit
- Food for all, including the guide(s)
- Tent and plastic ground sheet

NB Most accidents in the park occur when crossing rivers.

- **Montane or moss forest** (above 1,500m; lichins; Nepenthes).

- **Subalpine meadows or blangs** (relatives of temperate, northern hemisphere plants like primroses, gentians and strawberries).

Fauna

130 species of mammal have been recorded in the park, a quarter of all the species found in Indonesia. Most are rats, bats and squirrels. Of the primates, there is a large population of around 5,000 orang utan (see page 548) living in the park, the white handed gibbon (*Hylobates lar*) and black siamang (*Hylobates syndactylus*) with their distinctive calls which can be heard over a distance of 1 km or more, two species of macaques, two species of leaf monkey, the slow loris and the lutung (*Presbytis cristata*). Among the nine species of wild cat, the tiger is becoming increasingly scarce and is rarely seen. Also found is the clouded leopard (*Neofelis nebulosa*), the golden cat (*Felis temmincki*), and the marbled, flat-headed, leopard and fishing cats. Other carnivores include wild dogs and the sun bear (*Helarctos malayanus*). In general, the large carnivores are reclusive, tending to hunt at night, and are rarely seen.

The best known of the park's herbivores is the elephant (see page 550) and the Sumatran rhinoceros (see page 522). Sadly, the numbers of Sumatran rhino in the park have halved over the last 10 years due to poaching and it is on the verge of extinction not only in Gunung Leuser, but across its natural range. Other plant-eaters are deer, including the large sambar deer (*Cervus unicolor*), wild pigs, and the serow or mountain goat.

Birds

To date, 325 species of bird have been recorded in the park. There are seven species of hornbill whose distinctive cry and flight are often heard and seen (see page 551). These include the rhinoceros hornbill with its outrageous beak (*Rhinoplax vigil*). Other notable birds are the argus pheasant, five species of kingfisher, the crested serpent eagle, laughing thrushes, various parrots, warblers, flycatchers and others. Perhaps the best local name for a bird is that given to the woodpecker, which is known as *tok tok perago*.

Reptiles and amphibians

Tortoises and turtles (some, in the Alas River, growing to 30 kg in weight), monitor lizards and a small population of false ghavials (a type of crocodile) in the Besitang River are all found in the reserve. The snake population include pythons, king cobras, kraits, rat snakes and the black cobra.

NB The above summary of the Gunung Leuser National Park's flora and fauna is condensed from Mike Griffith's excellent booklet *Leuser National Park* (1992, World Wide Fund for Nature).

Gateways to the park

Most visitors to the park enter at the **Orang Utan Rehabilitation Centre** in **Bukit Lawang** (see page 440). However, the best access point to the park is **Kutacane**.

Excursions

Day hiking trails are easily accessible from Kutacane and it is possible to see a good range of wildlife. However park regulations insist that a guide be used. Trails range from easy saunters through the forest to more demanding **overnight treks** to the summits of the mountains in the area. Below is a summary of the main treks. Check at the park HQ for more details. Trekking information is also available in Brastagi and Bukit Lawang. Guides, and porters for longer treks, can be hired at the Park HQ.

Gurah and Ketambe lie on different banks of the Alas River. Ketambe is a research centre, 20 km N of Kutacane, at the entrance to the park. Around Gurah there is a network of trails. One of the best begins at Lawe Gurah and leads to a hot spring and salt lick frequented by tigers, serow, leaf monkeys and other fauna. The walk is a leisurely 1½-2 hrs. After 30 mins or so the track arrives at a camping ground. Here, cross the river – and after another 1 hr the trail reaches the hot springs. A great place to relax. Rejuvenated, it is possible to continue up the river bed, taking the first tributary off to the left – which leads to an attractive waterfall. There is a network of trails around the visitors' centre and some hikers choose to stay overnight at the hot springs. Orang utans, hornbills and other wildlife are present in the area.

Gunung Kemiri rises to 3,314m and can be climbed in 5-6 days. The trail begins at Gumpang, which is situated at an altitude of 740m. The path follows a ridge and climbs up through pristine lowland tropical rainforest, through submontane forest, and up on to some of the finest alpine meadows or *blangs* found in Sumatra. The view from the rocky summit, over a series of peaks, is spectacular. There is a camp site 300m below the summit.

Gunung Leuser, after which the park is named, reaches a height of 3,404m and can be climbed in 10-14 days. Although the ascent is a long one, the walk is not arduous. The trail begins at the village of Angasan, 3-4 hrs walk W of Blangkejeren (see below), where homestays are available. The first 4 days of the trek are through lowland rainforest; only on the fifth day does the path steepen and pass into submontane and montane forest, and then onto alpine meadows. There are again spectacular views from the summit.

Gunung Perkison, which rises to 2,828m, lies on the eastern border of the park's boundaries. The trail begins at Lawe Harum which is close to Tanah Merah and the Park HQ. Again the ascent is not very demanding as the route passes through lowland forest and then into submontane and moss forest. The Rafflesia flower can sometimes be seen growing at the side of the path at an altitude of about 1,200m.

Tours

One of the best ways to experience the park is by **rafting down the Alas River**. Tour companies in Medan (see page 435) and in Brastagi (see page 454) can arrange such trips, as can the Tourist office in Kutacane. Mr Maraengg at the Wisma Rindu Allam can organize trekking and accommodation in Ketambe.

Local information
● **Accommodation**

In Kutacane: C *Brudihe*, Jl Cut Nyak Dhien, a/c, restaurant; D *Layant Manas*, *Wisma Wisata* (next to the tourist office), E *Losmen Maroon*, clean, shared facilities; F *Wisma Rindu Allam*; F *Paddy Field Guesthouse*, ask for Alec at the tourist information office.

In Ketambe: E-F *Ketambe Guesthouse*, on the right as you enter the village, basic, oil-lamp lit bungalows, central communal area, basic food and drink available, rec. Other guesthouses incl: F *Family Guesthouse*; F *Pondok Wisata Ketambe*, smart new wooden huts and useful source of information, perhaps a trifle overpriced; F *Sada Wisata*, good restaurant attached, better than average rooms, pleasant and good value. It is also possible to stay in the *Visitors' Centre*.

In the park: The park authorities run a few

lodges; availability can be checked at the park HQ at Tanah Merah. Note that visitors need to take their own food and supplies.

● **Useful information**

Park headquarters: are situated at Tanah Merah, 5 km N of Kutacane. Guides and porters can be hired for trekking here. Guides are also available for hire at Ketambe although we have received reports that their rates are very high. **Tourist Information office**, across road from *Rindu Allam Guesthouse* in Kutacane. **Permits** available in Ketambe and Kutacane. 2,000Rp/day plus 2,500Rp insurance.

● **Transport**

Kutacane is about 150 km NW of Brastagi.

Road Bus: regular connections with Sidikalang and Brastagi (6 hrs). Buses also run N from here to Blankejeren and less frequently further N still to Takengon and the Gayo Highlands.

Sea Boat: every Thur there is a boat from Glombang, to the W, up the Alas River to Kutacane.

BLANKEJEREN

Blankejeren is a small town at the northern end of the road which follows the valley of the Alas River through the Gunung Leuser National Park (see page 455). Until recently, continuing N from here to reach Takengon and Lake Tawar, and from there Banda Aceh, was only for the very adventurous. Although this is still a route reserved for those who have time on their hands and are willing to accept a degree of discomfort, there are now slow buses which run all the way to Takengon. The road is gradually being improved so transport is likely to improve.

There is excellent **trekking** around Blankejeren in pristine forest scenery. It is no longer necessary to obtain a permit, and there are many good day treks in the area.

Excursions

The village of **Kedah**, 10 km or so from Blankejeren, is the home village of one of the area's best known guides: Mr Jally. **Accommodation**: available at **E** *Mr Jally's Tobacco Hut*, nice bungalows, room rate inc all 3 meals. From here there is excellent trekking with stupendous mountain scenery and rainforests. For a 2-night trek, all meals inc, expect to pay about 25,000Rp. Gibbons, Orang utan and other wildlife often seen. Other than Mr Jally, good guides inc Mr Muhmudin and Mr Muhamad Naen. Daily rates are 10,000Rp/person. *Getting to Kedah village*: catch a bus from Blankejeren to Penosan, a 10 km journey; from Penosan, walk to Kedah.

Tours   Contact M R Hardiannsyah through the *Wisma Mardhatthila* for tour and trekking information. He is knowledgeable and enthusiastic. Also see **Excursions**, above.

● **Accommodation**   **F** *Wisma Mardhatthila*, basic losmen accommodation, friendly and sparse, washing facilities on the roof, very reasonable.

● **Places to eat** *Happy Travelled*, excellent little restaurant with good menu at the Ketambe end of the main square.

● **Transport** About 140 km from Takengon. **Road Bus**: regular buses run N from Sidikalang, Kutacane (5 hrs via Ketambe) and the Lake Toba area. From Brastagi, catch a bus to Kutacane, and then catch another bus on to Blankejeren. Infrequent buses do now make the journey further N still to Takengon (6-7 hrs) where there are regular connections with the main NS east coast highway and Banda Aceh and Medan. This section of the road is currently being upgraded and the bus service should become more regular.

THE ROUTE NORTH

BLANKEJEREN TO TAKENGON (APPROX 140 KM)

There are no large towns on the road N from Blankejeren to Takengon. However, there are sufficient places to stop en route to hike the entire way. Now that there are also occasional buses that make the trip (one a week, on a Fri, at last report), it is also possible to part-hike, part-bus the trip. Below is a list of the main villages from S to N with amenities available. **NB** During the rainy season, or after storms, buses may not run and hiking can be very arduous. Basic Indonesian is very useful if undertaking this trip without a guide.

Blankejeren   (See above.)

Rikit Gaib   20 km from Blakejeren. An easy walk along a flat gradient.

Godang   8 km from Rikit Gaib. A more demanding up-hill trek.

Ise Ise   42 km from Godang. The path/road here is good, and being improved, but it is still prone to being washed away or made impassable during wet weather. Some hikers have stayed with the road gangs working on the project – the long hike can be very arduous in hot weather. It is also easy to hitch a lift on the lorries that are helping to build the road. This is the 'wildest' part of the route with the forest intruding on both sides. Monkeys, snakes and the occasional tiger are seen and it is recommended by locals that hikers walk only during hours of good daylight (ie not at dusk or day break). Ise Ise is a small hamlet situated near a river (good for washing) with one friendly losmen.

Lumut   10 km from Ise Ise. The track to Lumut is mostly downhill. There are daily buses to Takengon from Lumut and places to stay.

Uwak   10 km from Lumut. The walk from Uwak to Takengon takes about 2 days (with a stop in Isak), but is not very pleasant, and nor therefore recommended. Daily buses to Takengon run from Uwak and there are places to stay.

Isak   25 km from Lumut. Daily buses to Takengon and places to stay.

Takengon   25 km from Isak. See below for more information.

TAKENGON

The upland areas of Aceh Province are difficult to reach and rarely visited by tourists. Takengon is the most important town in the Gayo Highlands. Because of its upland location, Takengon enjoys cool temperatures – around 70°C year-round, chilly at night. Norman Lewis, in his book *An empire of the east: travels in Indonesia*, describes his arrival in Takengon in glowing terms: "The view of Lake Tawar was of extreme charm.... enclosed in a coronet of low, pointed mountains which were mantled as if in velvet of the deepest green". It is beautifully situated at 1,000m in the Bukit Barisan, on the shores of Lake Tawar. Unfortunately, the town itself – a recent creation – is rather unattractive with a mixed population of indigenous Gayo and immigrants from other parts of Sumatra and beyond.

The hills and valleys surrounding Takengon offer a number of attractive **hiking trails**. A road also circles Lake Tawar (50 km in total) and it is possible to hire a boat to explore the creeks and bays. Ask at your hotel for further information.

● **Accommodation B** *Renggali*, Jl Bintang, 2 km S of town, T 21144, best hotel in town built on a spit of land on the lake shore with 28 large rm – some with magnificent views – a rambling place ideal for those who romanticize about finding a forgotten castle in the wilds, but are willing to put up with slowish but friendly service, charming gardens, rec; **C-E** *Triarga Inn*, Jl Pasar Inpres, T 21073, small hotel with 25 small and dirty rooms, to be avoided if possible although other (better) places tend to be booked out; **D** *Danau Tawar*, Jl Leber Kader 35, T 21066, in the centre of town close to the main town mosque, good value; **E** *Batang Ruang*, Jl Mahkama 5, T 21524, clean rooms with friendly, helpful management.

● **Post & telecommunications Area code**: 0643. **Post Office**: Jl Lebe Kader.

Lake Toba illustrated on a Bank of Indonesia 1000Rp note

● **Transport** 96 km from Bireuen. **Road Bus**: connections N with Bireuen 3½ hrs, Sigli 6 hrs, and Banda Aceh 8 hrs. There is accommodation available in Sigli at the **E-F** *Losmen Paris*, close to the bus station so convenient for a stop-over, clean and reasonable rooms, nearby restaurants on the town square. Buses run down the E coast to Medan, but those going S to Kutacane and Lake Toba tend to run only during the dry season. However the road is being improved and a year round service is likely to be inaugurated soon.

LAKE TOBA

Lake Toba and the surrounding country-side is among the most beautiful in South-east Asia. This vast inland lake lies 160 km S of Medan and forms the core of Batak-land in both a legendary and a geographical sense. 87 km long and 31 km across at its widest point, the lake covers a total of 1,707 sq km and is the largest inland body of water in Southeast Asia. From the lake-shore town of Prapat, ferries leave for the island of Samosir, one of Sumatra's most popular destinations.

Lake Toba was formed after a massive volcanic explosion 75,000 years ago, not dissimilar – although far more violent – to the one that vaporized Krakatau in the late 19th century. The eruption of Toba is thought to have been the most powerful eruption in the last million years. Michael Rampino and Stephen Self of New York University and the University of Hawaii respectively believe that it could have triggered the onset of the last ice age by lowering northern hemisphere temperatures by 3-5 °C for a year. This would have allowed snow to lie year-round in many areas, so reflecting light and lowering temperatures still further, turning a 'volcanic winter' into an ice age. It is not only one of the highest lakes in the world at 900 m above sea-level, but also one of the deepest at 529m. The area is now volcanically dormant, the only indication of latent activity being the hot-springs on the hill overlooking Pangururan (see page 472). One problem that the authorities are having to face is a mysterious drop in the lake's water level. Between 1984 and 1986 it dropped by between 0.6 and 1.4m – if it drops much further, then there will not be a sufficient head of water to run the two hydropower plants downstream on the Asahan River, and this in turn will compromise the operation of the massive aluminium smelter at Kuala Tanjung.

The cool climate, pine-clothed mountain slopes, the lake, and the sprinkling of church spires gives the area an almost alpine flavour. After Medan or Padang, it is a welcome relief from the bustle, heat and humidity of the lowlands. Lodged in the centre of the lake is Samosir Island – a long-time haven for backpackers.

PRAPAT (PARAPAT)

Prapat, also known as Parapat, is a small resort on the E shores of Lake Toba frequented by the Medan wealthy, and increasing numbers of Asian tourists from beyond Indonesia. It was established by the Dutch in the 1930s, although today most Western visitors merely breeze through *en route* to Samosir Island. There are stunning views over the lake, but unfortunately, and like so many tourist suc-

---

The Bataks of North Sumatra

The Bataks of North Sumatra inhabit the highland areas centred on Lake Toba, and most villages are situated at about 1,000m above sea-level. There are usually said to be six Batak groups: the *Toba Batak* in the centre, the *Karo* and *Simalungan* in the N and NE, the *Pakpak* or *Dairi* in the NW, and the *Angkola* and *Mandailing* (the latter are largely Muslim) in the S. Each group lives in a particular part of the highlands, and although they are distinct in linguistic and ritual terms, they share many common values and traditions. The word Batak is a derogatory Muslim term meaning 'pig-eater'. This six-fold division is misleading insofar as it imposes unity on groups of people who probably have little sense of themselves as belonging to such wider designations as 'Karo' or 'Toba'.

The two Batak groups visitors are most likely to come into contact with are the *Toba Batak* – concentrated on Samosir Island and to the S of Lake Toba – and the *Karo Batak*, who live in the vicinity of Brastagi and Kabanjahe. The *Toba Batak* are considered to be more 'aggressive' and demonstrative and number about one million. The much 'younger' *Karo Batak* are more gentle, hospitable, and traditional and number around 250,000. In total there are about 3 million Batak in this part of Sumatra.

Because the Batak homeland is in such a moutainous and inaccessible area, the people were largely insulated from Western contact until the late 19th century.

The 'discovery' of the Batak The first European to mention the Batak was the Venetian trader Nicolo di Conti in the early 15th century who wrote that the 'Batech' ate human flesh, kept heads as valuable property and used skulls as coinage. The first detailed account of the Batak was provided by the Englishman William Marsden in his *History of Sumatra* published in 1783. He described a people who, to the great surprise of the 'civilized' world, possessed a sophisticated culture and a system of writing. His account also fleshed-out the stories of Batak cannibalism, titillating dinner party guests all over Europe. But it was not until the early 19th century that Batakland began to be explored in a comprehensive manner. Lake Toba was not discovered until 1853.

Although the Batak remained isolated from Western scrutiny until the 19th century, their culture and language shows distinct outside influences. For example, over 150 words in the *Karo Batak* language are Tamil in origin, while various rituals and some elements of Batak art also appear to show links with the Indian sub-continent. With the opening up of Batakland to Dutch and German missionaries, many converted to a mystical form of Christianity. Only the *Karo Bataks* have maintained their traditional animist beliefs in anything close to their original form.

Batak architecture and economy The most immediately distinctive element of Batak life are their traditional houses or *rumah adat*. The *Karo Batak* build houses with 'hipped' gabled roofs (see box, page 452), while the better known dwellings of the *Toba Batak* have 'saddleback' roofs with dramatic projecting gables (see box,

cess stories in Southeast Asia, uncontrolled development has diminished the attractiveness of the town.

There are few sights in Prapat. The best **beaches** are a little way out of town – but easily walkable – like those at Ajibata village, about 1 km S of Prapat. Sat is market day when Bataks selling local handicrafts and 'antiques' converge on the town and particularly on the market area at **Pekan Tigaraja**, close to the ferry dock for Samosir. A smaller market

see page 470). An average village rarely contains more than 10 houses, built close together. For the inhabitants, their community is regarded as the 'navel' of the world. In areas where inter-tribal warfare was prevalent, stone fortifications are also sometimes present (for example in Simanindo, see page 471).

Economically, the Batak traditionally pursued a diverse subsistence system, growing dry and wet rice, maize, taro, potatoes and a wide range of other crops. They also raised cattle and pigs, while Batak horses were very highly regarded for their speed and endurance (although the Batak themselves did not ride). Hunting and gathering contributed a further important element to their diets.

Cannibalism among the Batak More than anything else, the reputation of the Batak in the W was coloured by their cannabalism, which continued among the Toba and Pakpak into the 20th century. However, cannibalism was not common, only occurring during warfare and as a punishment for certain crimes. The German geographer and physician Franz Junghuhn, who lived among the Toba Batak for 18 months between 1840-1841, witnessed only three cases. His two volume account of the Bataks is one of the best and most thoughtful descriptions of Batak life and society. He describes cannibalism as follows:

"When an enemy is captured the day is set upon which he should be eaten. Then messengers are sent to all allied chiefs and their subjects inviting them to be present at the feast. ... The captive is now bound to a stake in an upright position. ... Then the chief of the village in which the ceremony takes place draws his knife, steps forward and addresses the people. ... It is explained that the victim is an utter scoundrel, and in fact not a human being at all...At this address the people water at the mouth and feel an irresistible impulse to have a piece of the criminal in their stomachs...All draw their knives. The radja [chief] cuts off the first piece...He holds up the flesh and drinks with gusto some of the blood streaming from it. ... Now all the remaining men fall upon the bloody sacrifice, tear the flesh off the bones and roast and eat it. ... The cries of the victim do not spoil their appetites. It is usually 8 or 10 minutes before the wounded man becomes unconscious, and a quarter of an hour before he dies."

Bataks and the modern world With the intrusion of the modern world into Batakland, so Batak society and economy has been encouraged to adapt to new pressures and incentives. Cash crops such as coffee and vegetables are grown for the market, many Batak have entered higher education and have attained important posts in the Indonesian army, while tourism has also brought the Batak in contact with the wider world. Given these pressures, it is surprising how far Batak traditional society and life has managed to survive. Traditional rules (*adat*) of land ownership are still usually maintained, the clan (*marga*) system appears as strong as ever, and Batak arts are still vigorously pursued if, in part, only for the tourist trade.

Recommended reading Sibeth, Achim (1991) *Living with Ancestors – the Batak, peoples of the Island of Sumatra*, Thames & Hudson: London.

is also held here on Thur. The bright, rust-red roofed church above the town sits in well cared for gardens, with views over the lake. On Sun, services have as many as eight to 10 hymns.

Excursions Samosir Island with its Batak stone chairs and tables and *rumah adat*, is only a 30 mins boat trip from Prapat. *Getting there*: regular ferries (see page 468); or charter a speedboat to visit the sights (40,000-80,000Rp).

Festivals Jun/Jul: *Danau Toba Festival* (movable), held over a week. Hardly traditional, but there are various cultural performances and canoe races on the lake.

● **Accommodation** Most of the more expensive hotels are on the lakefront. Cheaper accommodation is concentrated along Jl Sisingamangaraja. For those on a lower budget, the accommodation on Samosir Island is without doubt better and cheaper; there are no 'luxury' hotels on Samosir. **NB** During Indonesian public holidays and sometimes at weekends, it is a good idea to book ahead. **B** *Danau Toba International*, Jl P Samosir 17, T 41583, set on the side of the hill, overlooking the lake, modern and plush; **B** *Danau Toba International Cottages*, Jl Nelson Purba, T 41583, on the lake, with good watersports facilities and comfortable rooms but in need of refurbishment; **A** *Natour Prapat*, Jl Marihat 1, T 41012, F 41019, a/c, restaurant, Dutch-built pre-war hotel in attractive position overlooking the lake, with its own beach; **A-B** *Niagara*, Jl Pembangunan 1, T 558877, F 555880, a/c, restaurant, pool, golf and tennis, new hotel on hillside above the lake, well appointed rooms and excellent sports facilities; **A-B** *Patra Jasa*, Jl Siuhan, T 41796, F 41536, a/c, restaurant, pool, 4 km N of town overlooking the lake, with own golf course and lovely grounds; **B** *Tarabunga Sibigo*, Jl Sibigo 1, T 41665, portentous place, over large and charismatically challenged; **C** *Astari*, Jl P Samosir 9, T 41219; **C** *Toba*, Jl P Samosir 10, T 41073; **C** *Wisma Danau Toba*, Jl P Samosir 3-6, T 41302, one of the best hotels in this price category; **D** *Budi Mulya*, Jl P Samosir 17, T 41216, clean rooms and well-run; **E** *Sinar Baru*, Jl Josep 45, rec; **E-F** *Sing-*

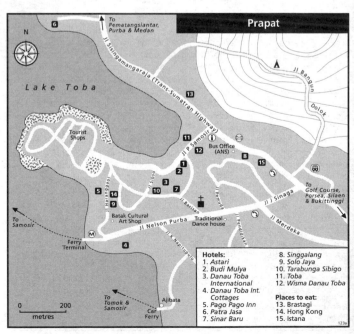

Prapat

Hotels:
1. Astari
2. Budi Mulya
3. Danau Toba International
4. Danau Toba Int. Cottages
5. Pago Pago Inn
6. Patra Jasa
7. Sinar Baru
8. Singgalang
9. Solo Jaya
10. Tarabunga Sibigo
11. Toba
12. Wisma Danau Toba

Places to eat:
13. Brastagi
14. Hong Kong
15. Istana

0   200
metres

123a

galang, Jl Balige 20, up the hill on the Trans-Sumatran Highway (Jl Sisingamangaraja), good sized, clean rooms with shared facilities; **D-E** *Soloh Jaya*, Jl Haranggoal 12, new hotel with good views, the more expensive rooms are large and good value, this is one of the three hotels that will open up for late-night bus arrivals. Beware of dirty rooms; **E** *Trogadero*, Jl Haranggaol (50m up street from ferry dock), a new place set on the lake shore that comes recommended, very clean rooms with attractive terraces and sitting areas, attached restaurant; **F** *Andilos*, at the bus station, shared mandi, dirty, PEEPHOLES in bedrooms, definitely not rec; **F** *Pago Pago Inn*, Jl Tigaraja 2, clean rooms, popular, shared mandi. **Camping**: there is a free camping ground on Jl Bangun Dolok, off Jl Sisingamangaraja, but it is a long walk up a steep hill.

● **Places to eat** There are many cheap restaurants along Jl Sisingamangaraja. ✦✦*Brastagi*, Jl Sisingamangaraja 55, Indonesian; ✦✦*Hong Kong*, Jl Haranggaol 1, good, cheap Chinese and Indonesian, rec; ✦*Istana*, Jl Sisingamangaraja 68, Indonesian.

● **Banks & money changers** Rates are poor in Prapat, but even worse on Samosir. It is best to arrive with sufficient cash for your stay, although that may present risks in itself. **Bank Rakyat Indonesia**.

● **Entertainment Batak cultural shows**: held on Tues and Sat nights at the *Batak Cultural Centre*, Jl Josep 19, at 2100 (2,000Rp). The more expensive hotels (eg *Natour Prapat*) also sometimes organize cultural shows. **Disco**: *Danau Toba International*, Jl P Samosir 17.

● **Hospitals & medical services Hospital**: Jl P Samosir.

● **Post & telecommunications Area code**: 0625. **Post Office**: Jl Sisingamangaraja 90. **Telephone**: from the Warpostel, Jl Sisingamangarja 72 (opp the Post Office).

● **Shopping Batak handicrafts, batik and woodcarvings**: try the shops along Jl Siantar and Jl Sisingamangaraja. Jl Haranggaol also has an array of rather tacky souvenir shops. There is a market at Pekan Tigaraja near the ferry jetty, held on Sat and a smaller one on Thur. A good place to buy batik and Batak handicrafts.

● **Sports Golf**: there is a course 2 km out of town off the road to Balige, with clubs for hire. There is also a 9-hole course at the *Patra Jasa Hotel*, 4 km N of town, on Jl Siuhan. **Riding**:

enquire at better hotels. **Water-skiing**: on Lake Toba, surely one of the most dramatic places in the world to ski. Enquire at the more expensive hotels. **Watersports**: water-scooters and pedal boats can be hired on the waterfront.

● **Tour companies & travel agents** *Dolok Silao*, Jl Sisingamangaraja 113, T 41467; *Goraharaja*, Jl Sisingamangaraja 87; *PT Andilo Nancy* (opp bus terminal), T 41548, not rec, irresponsible drivers; *Dolok* and *Goraharaja* also have offices at the ferry dock for Samosir Island.

● **Tourist offices** Pusat Informasi (tourist centre), Jl P Samosir, under the archway that welcomes visitors to the town. Little information available. **Batak Cultural Centre**, Jl Josep 19 (for information on Batak cultural events).

● **Useful addresses Police Station**: Jl Sisingamangaraja.

● **Transport** 147 km from Brastagi, 176 km from Medan, 509 km from Bukittinggi. **Local** Bemo and various forms of water transport. **Road Bus**: most people arrive in Prapat from Medan on one of the regular buses that travel the route via Tebingtinggi, 4 hrs. The main bus terminal is on Jl Sisingamangaraja – aka the Trans-Sumatran Highway – a modest trek from the centre of town. Some express buses stop at bus agencies. There are also buses to Brastagi (some go via Kabanjahe – the most convenient 'tourist bus' to Brastagi leaves Prapat daily at 0830), Bukittinggi 13 hrs, Padang 15 hrs, Palembang, Jambi, Pekanbaru, Bukit Lawang and even Jakarta. The two largest tour agencies in Prapat, *Andilo Nancy* and *Dolok Silau* (see **Tour companies & travel agents**) also run tourist minibuses to Bukittinggi, Brastagi, Bukit Lawang and Medan. **Car**: several companies in Medan will transport passengers to Prapat; contact one of the major hotels in Medan. **Boat** Prapat is the main 'port' for Samosir Island and ferries leave the town from the jetty on Jl Haranggaol for Samosir every hour or so, 30 mins (800Rp), the last leaving at 1730. The last ferry back to Prapat from Samosir departs at 1630. Most ferries dock at Tuk Tuk on Samosir, although some continue N to Ambarita, while others dock at Tomok. Check before boarding. **Long-distance taxi**: an efficient taxi company can be found under the entrance arch to the piers (also bookable through the Tourist office). Non a/c taxi to Bukittinggi, approx 240,000Rp.

NB Arriving in Prapat after dark makes it difficult to reach Samosir the same day. The only ferry operating after 2000 is the car ferry from Ajibata to Tomok (last ferry leaves 2100).

SAMOSIR ISLAND

Samosir Island, 40 km long and 20 km wide, is not really an island at all, but a peninsula. It is attached to the mainland at Pangururan, although a canal dug by the Dutch cuts through the slender isthmus. An eruption 75,000 years ago thrust Samosir up from the lake bed and the peak contains lake sediments on its summit. The island's highest point at 1,657m above sea-level is 750m above the surface of the lake, or more than 1,250m above the lake bed.

In all, Samosir covers 640 sq km. With a large number of traditional Batak villages, fine examples of *rumah adat* or traditional houses (see box, page 470), cemeteries, churches, enigmatic stone carvings, good swimming, hiking, cheap accommodation, and few cars, it has proved a favourite destination for travellers. Surrounded by the lake and mist-cloaked mountains, it is one of the most naturally beautiful and romantic spots in Southeast Asia.

But, Samosir is not the out-of-the-way, laid-back place that it once was. The locals have grown accustomed to tourists and sometimes treat them with disdain. A building boom is underway and this will no-doubt further reduce the mystery of the island. However, it is still a memorable place.

Local information

● Accommodation & other information

Accommodation is concentrated on the Tuk Tuk peninsula, and at Tomok and Ambarita, although there are basic guesthouses scattered right across the island. The cheaper losmen are in the **E-F** range, more expensive losmen and hotels, **C-E**. Rooms with a lake view are usually double the price of those without. Camping is also easy on Samosir. Food on the island is good and cheap and there are a number of warungs in Tomok, Ambarita and on the Tuk Tuk Peninsula. Note that flight reservations cannot be confirmed on Samosir – it is necessary to visit Prapat.

● Banks & money changers

Rates of exchange on Samosir are poor, even worse than in Prapat although the larger hotels and some travel agents will change TCs and cash. There is also a money changer (again, offering poor rates) in Ambarita.

● Post & telecommunications

Area code: 0645.

Post Office: Ambarita.

● Transport

Local A road in a reasonable state of repair follows the coast, running anti-clockwise from Tomok to Pangururan. There is also a road which runs around the S portion of the island, but it is rougher and is currently being improved. **Bus**: a minibus service runs about every 20 mins in the morning between Tomok and Ambarita, and then on to Pangururan; the service runs less frequently in the afternoons. Note that the bus does not take the route that skirts around the lakeshore on the Tuk Tuk peninsula – it cuts straight across the neck of the peninsula. From Pangururan, a less frequent service operates to the interior village of Roonggurni Huta. An occasional service has begun operating in the S part of the island between Tomok and Naing-golan, and then on to Pangururan. **Car**: the more expensive hotels have kijangs for charter. **Boat**: there is a cruise around the N portion of the island on Wed, Fri and Sun which leaves from Tuk Tuk and Ambarita. It includes a visit to the hot springs on Mt Belirang (6,000Rp) (see page 472). Boats also carry passengers up and down the island during daylight hours – simply wait at a dock for the first vessel, state your destination, and make sure the fare is agreed in advance. **Bicycle hire**: from many of the guesthouses and hotels in Tuk Tuk a recommended way to see the island, 5,000-8,000Rp/day. **Foot**: this is one of the most enjoyable ways to see Samosir. Walking across the island takes 2 days, with an overnight stop at Roonggurni Huta in the highland interior (see box, page 468). **Motorcycle hire**: from Tuk Tuk, or from men found around the hotels or guesthouses. A driving licence is not required. Expect to pay about 20,000Rp/day. This is a recommended way to see the island although accidents are all too frequent on the narrow roads. There are also other hiking trails across the island; ask at your hotel or losmen.

Road **Bus**: buses arrive at Pangururan on the W side of the island from Medan, Brastagi, Sibolga and Sidikalang. **NB** There have been a number of reports of travellers having to pay an extra 'commission' when booking onward bus

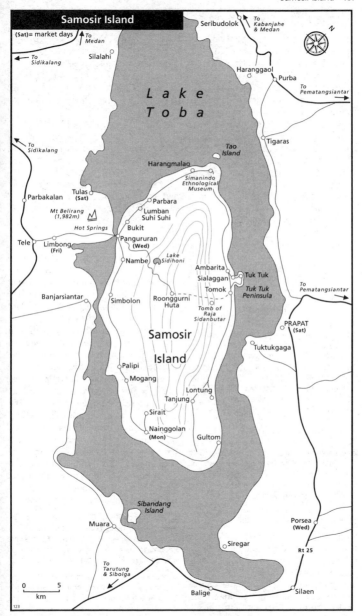

Samosir Island

(Sat)= market days

To Medan

To Sidikalang

Seribudolok

To Kabanjahe & Medan

N

Silalahi

Haranggaol

Purba

To Pematangsiantar

L a k e
T o b a

To Sidikalang

Tao Island

Tigaras

Harangmalang

Simanindo Ethnological Museum

Parbakalan

Tulas **(Sat)**

Parbara

Mt Belirang (1,982m)

Lumban Suhi Suhi

Hot Springs

Bukit

Tele

Limbong **(Fri)**

Pangururan **(Wed)**

Nambe

Lake Sidihoni

Ambarita

Tuk Tuk

Banjarsiantar

Simbolon

Roonggurni Huta

Sialaggan

Tomok

Tuk Tuk Peninsula

To Pematangsiantar

Tomb of Raja Sidanbutar

PRAPAT **(Sat)**

Samosir Island

Tuktukgaga

Palipi

Mogang

Lontung

Tanjung

Sirait

Nainggolan **(Mon)**

Gultom

Sibandang Island

Porsea **(Wed)**

Muara

Siregar

Rt 25

To Tarutung & Sibolga

Balige

Silaen

0   5
km

123

Hiking across the central highlands

Hiking across Samosir's central highlands is one of the most rewarding ways to see the island. The distance from E to W is only about 20 km as the crow flies, but the route is a steep and circuitous climb of 750m, making the real walking distance about 45 km. It is just possible to walk the route in a long day if tackling the hike from W to E (ie from Pangururan to Tomok), but it is best to stay overnight at the interior village of Roonggurni Huta to recuperate from the climb. There are a number of homestays here which charge about 5,000Rp for a bed.

The hike from Roonggurni Huta to Tomok or *vice versa* is about 29 km: 10 hrs if walking uphill, 6 hrs down. There are also trails to Ambarita and (longer still) to Tuk Tuk, although these are less well marked. From Roonggurni Huta to Pangururan it is a less steep 17 km, about 3 hrs walking. There is also a bus service for the terminally exhausted between Pangururan and Roonggurni Huta. It is probably best to climb from W to E as this misses out the steep climb up to Roonggurni Huta from Tomok. Catch a bus to Pangururan and set off from there. A map marking the hiking trails and giving more details about the routes is available from the *Gokhon Bookshop* in Tuk Tuk.

tickets through agents on Samosir. Note that due to the timings of the buses (most leave Prapat early in the morning) it is difficult to reach Bukittinggi without spending at least one night in Prapat. **Long-distance taxi**: it is expensive chartering taxis from Samosir; better to charter from the mainland – see the **Transport** section of Prapat.

Boat Most visitors get to Samosir by ferry from Prapat. The ferry leaves about every hour, 30 mins (800Rp). It stops at Tomok and Tuk Tuk and also at Ambarita. The first ferry from Prapat leaves at 0930, from Samosir at 0730. The last departs Prapat at 1730, Samosir at 1630. It is also possible to charter a 'special' boat for rather more (1,500-2,000Rp). The car ferry service from Ajibata, just S of Prapat (see map page 464) to Tomok runs rather later, until 2100. Ferries also link Tuk Tuk and Ambarita with Haranggaol on Lake Toba's N shore, but these only run on Mon and Thur. They leave Haranggaol for Samosir at 1300 and 1500; check in your hotel for the time of journeys in the other direction. To/from Haranggaol, there are buses to Seribudolok, then to Kabanjahe and finally to Brastagi and Medan.

TOMOK

Positioned just to the S of the Tuk Tuk Peninsula, this was a traditional Batak village and remains the main landing point for day visitors from Prapat. It contains some fine high prowed **Batak houses** and **carved stone coffins, elephants** and **chairs**. Walking from the jetty inland,

there is a path lined with souvenir stalls which winds up a small hill. Half way up is the **Museum of King Soribunto Sidabutar**, housed in a traditional Batak house, containing a small number of Batak implements and photographs of the family. Admission by donation.

Walking a little further up the hill on from the mass of stalls and taking the path to the right, there is a carved stone coffin, the **King's Coffin**, protected by what remains of a large but dying *hariam* tree. The Sarcophagus contains the body of Raja Sidabutar, the chief of the first tribe to migrate to the area. The coffin is surrounded by stone elephants, figures, tables and chairs. Further up the main path, past the stalls, is another grave site with stone figures arranged in a circle. The **church services** at the town and elsewhere on Samosir, are worthwhile for the enthusiasm of the congregations.

● **Accommodation B** *Toba Beach*, S of Tomok, T 41275, good rooms, quiet position on the lakeside, but expensive for Samosir; **F** *Roy's* (in a Batak village, just outside town), good information and friendly management; **F** *Silalahi*, friendly.

● **Places to eat** There are a number of warung in and around the village, eg *Islam* and *Roy's*. *Toba Beach Hotel* has a good restaurant serving Indonesian and international dishes.

• **Shopping** This is the main landing point for day-trippers from Prapat, so there are a large number of souvenir stalls selling Batak handicrafts and 'antiques'.

• **Tourist offices** Roy's Tourist Information.

• **Transport Road Bus**: in theory, every 20 mins to Panguruan and all stops along the route. **Foot** 1 hr to Tuk Tuk, 1½ hrs to Ambarita. **Boat** Car ferry connections with Prapat approx every hour (800Rp) until 2100.

TUK TUK PENINSULA

Tuk Tuk is located almost at the tip of the Tuk Tuk Peninsula about 5 km from Tomok. This is really just a haven for tourists: there is nothing of cultural interest here. There are hotels and losmen scattered right across the Tuk Tuk peninsula, lining the road that skirts the lake shore. But in spite of rapid development it is still a peaceful spot, with good swimming.

Excursions Cross-island hike to Pangururan (see box, see page 468).

Tours Every Wed, Fri and Sun a cruise sets out to tour the N part of Samosir including a stop at the hot springs on Mt Belirang (see page 472). Ask at your hotel or losmen for information.

• **Accommodation** There are 50 or so places in Tuk Tuk, from very simple affairs to large, comfortable hotels. The more expensive accommodation is in the **C-D** range. Cheap losmen/huts are available in our **F** range. Hotels and losmen will commonly offer a wide range of rooms, in terms of size, location (view of lake) and facilities (hot water). Prices vary accordingly. In order from the S to the N around the peninsula, the following are rec: **B** *Toledo Inn*, N tip of peninsula, T 41181, large restaurant, one of the oldest hotels on the island on the lakeshore; **B** *Toledo Inn II*, nr new *Ambarita Hotel*, standard restaurant (good soups) with slow service, quiet and clean rooms, with hot water; **B-C** *Slintong's* in the centre of the peninsula, T 41345, restaurant; **B-D** *Carolina's*, S end, T 41520, good restaurant, very popular, with a range of rooms, more expensive Batak-style cottages and rooms with hot water showers and some with lovely views over the lake, and a relaxed feel to the place, an old favourite but still rec; **C** *Toledo Dua*, newer version of *Toledo*, lovely rooms with balcony overlooking lake, clean bathrooms, breakfast incl, transport back to Prapat,

rec; **C-D** *Rumba*, centre of Tuk Tuk, restaurant (see below), run by Swiss lady and her Batak husband, 4 rm with bathrooms en suite, clean and quiet; **D** *Duma Sari*, S end; **E** *Matahari* in the centre, popular place with an established reputation; **E** *Romlan*, S end, on the lakeshore, among the best of the cheaper places to stay; **E** *Smiley's* on the S neck of the peninsula; **F** *Abadi*, N end, basic but remains popular among those on a tight budget; **F** *Christina's*, N section of isthmus; **F** *Endys*, chalets on the beach; **F** *Mafir*, S end, restaurant with good food, clean guesthouse; **F** *Tony's*, N end, large and expanding – excessively; *Murni*, N end.

• **Places to eat** Most visitors tend to eat at their hotels. *Carolina's* good Western food; *Endys*, nr Toledo, rec; *Gokhon Bookshop*, see below; *Juwita's*, small restaurant serving Indonesian food, as hot as you like it, special requests taken the day before, Hedi the cook speaks good English and is very friendly; *Bagus Bay*, good food; *Rumba*, centre of Tuk Tuk, Indonesian and European food incl spaghetti, pizza, freshly baked bread and cakes, and traditional Swiss specialities like Rosti, Wienerschnitzel and fondu, rec; *Tabo*, on S neck of Tuk Tuk, vegetarian restaurant and bar, run by a Batak and his German wife, home produced wholesome food, using fresh herbs and vegetables from their garden, wholemeal bread, yoghurts, tofu etc, information board, comments book and games provided, traditional massage offered; there are a number of other warungs serving basic Indonesian and travellers' food.

• **Entertainment** *Bagus Bay Bookshop* has a 'cinema' which shows 2 English language films a day and a TV with BBC news.

• **Shopping Books**: *Gokhon Bookshop* and Library offers a postal service and a small café. Daily baking of brown bread, birthday cakes on request, friendly owners. *Bagus Bay Bookshop*. **Crafts**: there are a number of craft shops on Tuk Tuk, but they are expensive; there is a better, cheaper selection in Tomok.

• **Tour companies & travel agents** *PT Andilo Nancy*, *Goraha Tour* and *Bukit Santai Travel and Tours*.

• **Transport Road Bus**: walk to the main road to catch one of the buses running between Tomok and Pangururan, in theory every 20 mins. **Boat** Ferry connections with Prapat about every 30 mins (800Rp). **Foot** 1 hr to Tomok and Ambarita.

Toba Batak architecture

The traditional soaring roofed houses of the *Toba Batak* are among the most characteristic sights in Indonesia. These *rumah adat* or *jabu* are rectangular buildings raised-up on piles which rest on stone bases to prevent rotting. The houses are entered through a trap door which can be locked.

Typical of the *Toba Batak* houses are the enormous saddleback roofs, sloping dramatically towards the centre, and surmounted at either end with buffalo horns (the horns are real, but the head is carved from *ijuk* wood). The gables extend much further at the front of the house than they do at the back, and the gable at the front is richly decorated with carvings of animals, birds and mythical creatures. The rear gable is left unadorned. Originally covered in thatch, corrugated iron has become increasingly common in recent years. The roof area is used for storage while that beneath the house is used to corral livestock. The houses are built of wood and rope, and are held together with wooden pegs – no nails are used in construction.

Of the Batak groups, the *Toba Batak* decorate their houses most profusely. Carvings are concentrated on the two side walls, but particularly on the front gable. Only the colours white, black and red are used; these symbolize the three kinship groups, the three realms of the Batak cosmos, and the three hearthstones. Black is obtained from charcoal, white from lime, and red from red earth. Formerly, the blood from killed enemies was also mixed with the red earth. At the ends of the side beams of many Toba Batak houses are large carvings of animal heads called *singa*, from the Sanskrit word for lion. These mythological creatures, tongues extended, serve a protective function.

A number of families – up to 12 – will live in each *jabu*, and traditionally each would have its own hearth at the front of the main living area. European influence means that today most cooking is done in extensions added onto the back of the building. Many traditional rice barns or *sopo* have been converted in recent years into dwellings – they can be identified by the working area mid-way between the ground and the main dwelling area.

AMBARITA

The pretty town of Ambarita is an hour's walk from Tuk Tuk along the lake shore travelling N. It has more to offer in the way of sights than Tuk Tuk, but a less extensive range of accommodation. As the number of losmen grows, so Ambarita is losing its former quiet and peaceful image.

There are several **megalithic complexes** in the vicinity of town which also has a hospital (of sorts), a market, and a post office. The most important of the megalithic complexes is near the jetty at **Siallagan village**. It consists of a group of 300 year old stone chairs and a table where village disputes were settled. A stone figure mysteriously occupies one of the seats. Admission: by donation. Facing the complex is a row of well preserved **Batak houses**. Also here is the **tomb of Laga Siallagan**, the first chief of Ambarita. There is another group of stone chairs close by where criminals and other unfortunates were killed and then eaten. The last such occurrence was at the beginning of this century. Tour guides delight in recounting the gory details.

Tours Every Wed, Fri and Sun a cruise sets out to tour the N part of Samosir including a stop at the hot springs on Mt. Belirang (see page 472). Ask at your hotel or losmen for details.

● **Accommodation** No accommodation in Ambarita itself; these are in the vicinity of the town. **C** *Sopo Toba*, T 41616, 2 km N of the town, large place occupying quiet position out of town, with

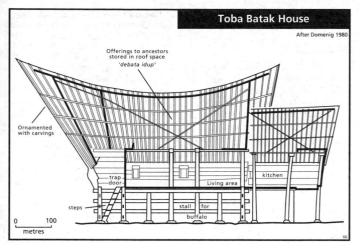

Toba Batak House

After Domenig 1980

Offerings to ancestors stored in roof space 'debata idup'

Ornamented with carvings

trap-door

Living area

kitchen

steps

stall for buffalo

0 100 metres

66

own beach created out of a concrete waterfront; **E** *Sony's*, between Ambarita and Tuk Tuk, 20 mins' walk to Ambarita, bathroom, large clean rooms, friendly, rec; **E-F** *Gordon's*, 4 km N of the town, popular, maintaining standards well; **F** *Barbara's*, T 41230, 4 km N of the town; **F** *Le Shangri-La*, 7 km N of the town, very secluded (a problem when getting back in the evenings as bemos are often full), with clean, spacious bungalows, good value, rec; **F** *Rohandy's*, on the lakeshore nr town, well-run and popular with good food; **F** *Tuk Tuk Tinbal*, lovely position between Tuk Tuk and Ambarita.

● **Banks & money changers** Bank Lainggolan, Bank Rakyat Indonesia.

● **Hospitals & medical services** Clinic: in town.

● **Post & telecommunications** Post Office: Jl Besar 39.

● **Shopping** There is a concentration of craft shops and stalls in the vicinity of Siallagan village.

● **Tourist offices** Golden Tourist Information Centre.

● **Useful addresses** Police station: in town.

● **Transport Road** Bus: in theory, regular connections every 20 mins with Tomok and all stops to Pangururan. **Boat** A number of ferries from Prapat dock each day, both scheduled and chartered. **Foot** 1 hr to Tuk Tuk, 7 hrs to Simanindo at the N tip of the island.

SIMANINDO

Simanindo is at the N tip of Samosir. The house of a former Batak chief, Raja Simalungun, has been restored and turned into an **Ethnological Museum** (*Huta Bolon Museum*) containing an assortment of Batak, Dutch and Chinese artefacts which are reasonably displayed. Admission 500Rp. Open Mon-Sun. Close by is a well preserved **fortified Batak community**, with fine examples of richly carved Batak houses. Batak dancing shows are staged at 1030 and 1115, Mon-Sat and at 1130 on Sun. Admission 3,000Rp. This is the best maintained of the various 'preserved' communities on Samosir.

Just offshore from Simanindo is the small 'honeymoon' island of **Tao**. There are secluded and rather expensive bungalows on the island for those who really do wish to be alone. Day trippers can visit Tao for a swim and a meal – 10 mins boat ride.

● **Accommodation** *Boloboloni's*.

● **Transport** 15 km N of Ambarita. **Road Bus**: regular connections with Ambarita and Tuk Tuk, and onwards to Pangururan. **Boat** Ferries connect Simanindo with Tigaras, N of Prapat, leaving every 1½ hrs between 0630 and 1430. The ferry between Ambarita and Haranggaol also sometimes stops here (see page 468), as do various lake cruises (see page 469). **Foot** 7 hrs to Pangururan, 7 hrs to Ambarita, 7¾ hrs to Tuk Tuk.

PANGURURAN

Pangururan, the capital of Samosir, is on the W coast, close to the point where the island is attached to the mainland by a small bridge. There is not much in town. Most people visit the town on the way to the **hot springs** on Mt Belirang.

Excursions The **Mt Belirang hot springs** or *air panas* are 1 hrs walk from town (2½ km). The sulphurous gases and water have killed the vegetation on the hillside, leaving a white residue which can be seen from Samosir. Cross the stone bridge and turn right (N). They are about a third of the way up Mt Belirang (also known as Mt Pusuk Buhit). It is too hot to bathe at the point where it issues from the ground, but lower down there are pools where visitors can soak in the healing sulphurous waters. It is said that bathing here three times will cure scabies. There are separate bathing pools for men and women and some warungs nearby for refreshments. There is even accommodation (for those with severe scabies). Views of the lake are spoilt by uncontrolled, unattractive development and even the spring site itself leaves rather a lot to be desired: plastic pipes and moulded concrete make it look, in places, more like a plumber's training site.

Cross-island hike to Tomok Pangururan is probably the best place from which to set out to hike across the island (see page 468).

Simarmata village lies between Pangururan and Simindo and is one of the best preserved working communities in the N part of the island. It contains fine Batak houses, save for the corrugated iron roofs, and a large monument to the deceased King and Queen of Simarmata.

● **Accommodation D** *Wisata*, Jl Kejaksan 42, T 41150; **F** *Barat Guesthouse*, restaurant, popular.

● **Places to eat** *Barat Guesthouse* has an international menu.

● **Transport Road Bus**: buses leave Pangururan for Medan, Brastagi, Sidikalang (at 0700 and 1600; rather scary switchback road) and Sibolga in the morning (0700-0900). Regular connections with Simanindo, Ambarita, Tuk Tuk and Tomok. Buses at 0500, 1200, 1700 to Ronggurni Huta. **Boat** No boats leave from Pangururan for Prapat. **Foot** 7 hrs to Simanindo; 10-12 hrs across the island to Tomok.

HARANGGAOL

This is a small, sleepy town on Lake Toba's north-eastern shore. Few tourists visit the town, but there is an excellent **market** on Mon and Thur – when there are boat connections with Samosir – and good walks in the surrounding countryside. If visitors wish to experience the wonder of Toba, without the crowds at Prapat and on Samosir, then this is the place to come.

Excursions Hiking in the surrounding countryside is highly recommended.

There are boat connections on Mon and Thur with **Samosir Island**, and all the sights of historical and cultural interest that the island has to offer (see page 466).

● **Accommodation C** *Haranggaol Hotel*, situated in town rather than on the lake shore, but the best place to stay; some rooms with hot water, large eating area, used to catering for tour groups. **D** *Segumba Cottages*, Bali-style cottages situated 3 km out of town in a beautiful, quiet position, some rooms with mandi, rec. **E** *Losmen Horison*, basic losmen located on the lake shore, some rooms with mandi, food available.

● **Transport Road Bus**: Haranggaol lies off the main bus route so it can take a time to reach the town. There are bus connections from Kabanjahe (easily accessible from Brastagi) to Seribudolok, and from there bemos run to Haranggaol. Getting to or from Prapat to Haranggaol is not easy; it involves three changes of bus and usually takes 8 hrs to cover the 50-odd km. Taking the ferry is easier (see below). **Ferry** A ferry connects Haranggaol with Tuk Tuk and Ambarita on Samosir Island on Mon and Thur. From Samosir there are many ferry boats making the crossing to Prapat.

LAKE TOBA SOUTH TO PADANGSIDEMPUAN

Travelling SW from Lake Toba, the road reaches the administrative and marketing centre of Tarutung, 107 km from Prapat. Here the road divides; the Trans-Sumatran Highway continues S along the Bukit Barisan towards Bukittinggi, while another road turns W towards the coast and the port of Sibolga. The road descends spectacularly from the Bukit Barisan to the narrow coastal plain, a total distance of 173 km from Prapat. Sibolga is the main departure point for the 'Stone Age' Nias Island with its megalithic culture and some of the best surfing in Southeast Asia. 88 km S of Sibolga and 215 km from Prapat is Padangsidempuan, an important local town and the best base from which to visit the archaeological site of Padang Lawas.

SIBOLGA

Sibolga is not a town to linger in. Most visitors stay here merely *en route* to Prapat and Lake Toba from Bukittinggi, or as the transit point for Nias Island. The route into town on the Trans-Sumatran Highway is spectacular – descending steeply from the Bukit Barisan range of mountains to the narrow coastal strip. A visit to the **harbour** is worthwhile – it is a colourful place and visitors can watch large quantities of fish being unloaded and dried.

Excursions Pandan Beach is 10 km from Sibolga. It is sandy and palm-fringed, with a refreshing un-commercialised air. *Getting there*: regular oplet connections from the terminal on Jl Sisingaman-garaja.

● **Accommodation** Hotels in Sibolga have a reputation for being dirty and uncomfortable. There are an assortment on Jl Jend A Yani and Jl Mesjid, including: **C** *Tapian Nauli*, Jl S Parman 5, T 21116, best hotel, but out of town to the N, nr the immigration office, a/c, quiet, colonial-style with balconies; **C-E** *Indah Sari*, Jl Jend A Yani 27-29, some a/c, better-managed and maintained than most hotels with large sitting room, serves tea and breakfast; **D-E** *Pasar Baru Inn*, Jl Suprapto 41, best of the cheaper places to stay, more expensive rooms with a/c, but all clean, efficiently managed; **F** *Sudimampir*, Jl Mesjid 98, small rooms, squalid.

● **Places to eat** ♦♦*Rejeki*, Jl Brig. Gen. Katanuso 40 (opp Bank Dagang Negora).

● **Banks & money changers** Bank Dagang Negara, Jl Jend A Yani (end of the road), good rates.

● **Post & telecommunications** Post Office: Jl Dr F L Tobing.

● **Tour companies & travel agents** *P T Simeulue*, Jl Pelabuhan 2; *P T Idapola*, Jl S Parman 34, T 21646; *P T Perlani*, Jl Letjen 57.

● **Transport** 173 km from Prapat, 381 km from Bukittinggi. **Local Becak**: 500Rp around town. **Road Bus**: the bus station is on Jl Sisin-gamangaraja. Regular connections with Medan 8 hrs, Bukittinggi 10 hrs, Padang 12 hrs and Prapat 3-5 hrs. Local buses leave from the same terminal for Padangsidempuan, Barus and else-where. *ALS*, *Makmur* and *Bintang Udara*, 3 of the major bus companies have their offices on Jl Sutoyo. There is also a daily tourist bus to Medan, perhaps the most comfortable of the services. **Sea Boat**: Sibolga is the main depar-ture point for Nias. Boats leave every day except Sun from the dock at the end of Jl Horas. Details can be obtained from the travel agents listed above. Departures for Gunungsitoli daily except Sun, for Telukdalam on Mon, Wed and Fri. The *Lawit* also docks at Sibolga having stopped at Gunungsitoli (Nias), and returns a few hours later to Padang and from there to Tanjung Priok (Jakarta's port), see route schedule page 912. Pelni office is at Jl Pelabuhan 46, T 21193.

PADANGSIDEMPUAN

Padangsidempuan is an uninteresting town situated in the Bukit Barisan and lies on the Trans-Sumatran Highway at an important crossroads: highways run N to Lake Toba, NW to Sibolga, S to Bukit-tinggi and Padang, and E to the lowlands, Tebingtinggi and, eventually, Medan. It is a halfway point between Prapat and Bukit-tinggi, but unfortunately does not have good accommodation. Usually known simply as Sidempuan, the town is the best base from which to visit the 10th-14th century ruins at **Padang Lawas** (see below).

Excursions Padang Lawas – meaning Great Plain – lies over 70 km E of Padangsidempuan. To archaeologists, the ruins here are the most interesting in Sumatra. So far, 26 temples scattered over 1,500 sq km along the course of the Barumun River have been discovered. Archaeological work did not begin until after WW2, and the area has still to be properly researched. The monuments date from the 10th to 14th century, and are probably linked to an ancient Hindu-Buddhist kingdom called Panai.

The main concentration of ruins is at the village of Portibi, near Gunungtua. The surrounding area is a dry, almost treeless landscape, carpeted with *alang alang* grass and whipped by a dry wind. The temples are known as *biaros*, or sanctuaries, and only a few are easily accessible: Biaro Bahal I, II, III, Pulo, Bara, Si Topayan and Si Pamutung. Each is surrounded by a wall, the inner courtyard containing the principal shrine, surrounding minor shrines, and stupas. Statuary is limited, and generally in poor condition, while reliefs are also few in number. Given that rudimentary excavations have revealed no evidence of large-scale habitation, it would seem that the biaros were funerary/ceremonial in function. An alternative explanation is that they lay on an important Trans-Sumatran trad-

ing route linking the W and E coasts of the island. It is at this point that the mountains which form a spine down Sumatra are least imposing, and there are rivers flowing E from the plain which could have been used as convenient arteries of communication. A day at least is needed to explore the area, and because of the heat it is worth taking water along. **Accommodation** There is a restaurant just outside the temple complex entrance where it is possible to stay the night on a mat. *Getting there*: take a bus from the large regional centre of Padangsidempuan to the market town of Gunungtua, 72 km to the E. From there, catch an oplet or a mesin becak to the turnoff to the temple site, 15 km in all.

● **Accommodation C** *Natama*, Jl Sisingamangaraja 100, T 22305, a/c, billed as a 2-star hotel; **C-E** *Samudra*, Jl T Umar 60A, grubby, noisy hotel with more life in the beds than among the staff; **C-E** *Danau Marsabut*, outside town on the road to Siporok, dirty and poorly maintained.

● **Post & telecommunications Area code**: 0634.

● **Transport** 88 km from Sibolga, 215 km from Prapat, 293 km from Bukittinggi. **Road Bus**: regular connections with Sibolga, Prapat and Bukittinggi. The buses from Bukittinggi stop outside town; catch an oplet into the centre. Connections with Gunungtua (for the Padang Lawas ruins).

The main temples at Padang Lawas

Biaro Si Pamutung The largest and most important of the shrines, near the confluence of the Panai and Barumun rivers. The temples are constructed of brick and are similar in style to 9th-10th century Central Javanese shrines. The staircase on the main tower, which faces E, is flanked by two crocodiles with human features.

Biaro Bahal I Located in the village of Bahal, near Portibi, this is regarded as the most beautiful of the Padang Lawas ruins. The 13m-high brick built tower rises from a lotus cushion and is surmounted with a garland. Yakshas and makaras in relief are still in evidence, although the original life size figures which flanked the doorway have disappeared.

Biaro Pulo Situated on a hill, but only the ruins of the main tower remain. Five highly unusual reliefs of dancing figures were found here in a good state of repair, and are now on display in the National Museum, Jakarta.

NIAS ISLAND

Nias Island is part of the series of submarine peaks which run down the W coast of Sumatra and which include the Mentawi, Batu and Simeulue islands. Nias is 125 km long and about 40 km wide, with a land area of 4,772 sq km. It is separated from the Sumatran mainland by 110 km of occasionally rough sea. The W coast is rocky and inhospitable, while the E coast is more accessible, with natural harbours and a more gently shelving shoreline. The interior of the island remains thickly forested.

The population of Nias is now about 500,000 and the capital of the district is Gunungsitoli, in the N. The island is usually divided into three regions: N, Central and S Nias. These divisions reflect important differences in language, culture, and art and architecture. There are two main reasons to visit Nias: for surfers, to experience the waves at Lagundi Bay; and for non-surfers, to see its unique culture which has evolved over several thousand years, apparently in isolation from developments elsewhere in Southeast Asia. In Jul 1994 the Indonesia Open International Surfing Championship was held on Nias, confirming the island's place as Indonesia's surfing Mecca.

Nias was first mentioned in Arab and Persian geographies of the 9th century, and over a long period the island was raided for slaves by stronger Sumatran states. Europeans began marking the island on their charts in the 16th century, and the Dutch established a trading post here in the 17th century as part of their efforts to control the spice trade. In the 18th century the British established a

Nias Island

toehold in the N part of the island. The presence of Europeans led to the spread of Christianity, and now the majority of the population are Christian, although there are significant numbers of Muslims in the port towns.

Culture

The Nias culture presents something of a conundrum to anthropologists. There are clear links in linguistic and cultural terms with the Bataks of the mainland, and yet the Niha – as the inhabitants of Nias are known – do not have a tradition of writing nor of cannibalism (although headhunting was prevalent). There are also distinct differences between the Niha of the southern, Central and northern regions of the island. Niha society is divided into three groups: nobles or *si'ulu*, who were viewed as descendants of supernatural beings, commoners or *sato*, and slaves or *sawuyu*. The financing or sponsoring of feasts and the commissioning of sculptures and jewellery were – and still are to an extent – crucial in determining a person's status. By erecting a stone monument, a noble legitimated his position and made him eligible to join his deified ancestors in the upper world. With the spread of Christianity, so traditional beliefs and rituals have disappeared – the last traditional funeral for example occurred in 1914.

Niha settlements in the S are the most impressive and also the most visited. Villages consist of two rows of raised houses or *omo*, facing a paved stone courtyard which may be several 100m long. Formerly villages were surrounded by a palisade, and within that a sharpened stake-filled ditch. Now that internecine warfare has been eradicated, the fortifications have been allowed to fall into disrepair. The central street which separates the two rows of houses is known as the *ewali* and it is equally divided into two by a central stone pavement or *iri*. The centre of the village contains the chief's house (*omo sebua*), a meeting house (*bale*), and an assembly square (*gorahua newali*). The latter should be beautifully paved

Adu or ancestor figure from Nias;
note the gun
Adapted from: Hersey, Irwin (1991) *Indonesian primitive art*, OUP: Singapore

and surrounded by stone benches and other megaliths. It is here that village rituals, dances and other activities are held. The 2m-high stone pyramid used for stone-jumping (see below) is erected near the square.

Villages show that although the culture of Nias may popularly be considered 'primitive' or 'Stone Age', the inhabitants had a genius for design. There are village baths or *hele* with running water, sometimes even private baths for noblewomen. The houses of chiefs are particularly impressive, being richly decorated with polished wood panelling called *hagu laso*, recording the possessions of the present and former occupants of the house.

The Niha people are most famous for their **megalithic culture**. Formerly, archaeologists believed that this indicated

The earthquake-proof houses of Nias

The houses of the three cultural regions of Nias share certain common features: they are raised off the ground, they are wooden, and all have high 2-sided roofs. To defend against attack, the house support posts were 2 to 3m high, and entry was up a moveable ladder and through a trapdoor. A family's heirlooms were kept in a windowless room, situated in the heart of the house.

The houses of Nias are also uniquely designed to withstand the constant earthquakes that affect the area: the support posts are aligned both vertically and obliquely, and rest on stone slabs. This gives houses the flexibility and strength to resist earth tremors. The size of a house is determined by the number of posts (*ehomo*) wide it is: a commoner's house is usually four posts wide; a chief's house, six.

There are significant differences between houses in the N, Centre and S. In the N, houses are – almost uniquely in Southeast Asia – oval in form, and are wider than they are long. In the Centre and S, they are rectangular, and longer than they are wide. In the S, the villages are encircled by defensive walls, protecting them from attack from rival villages; these were usually absent in the Centre and N. Within the house, a distinction is drawn between a communal front section and private rear quarters. Livestock are kept beneath the house.

The oval houses of the N are no longer built and modern, Malay-style houses are the norm. In the S, traditional houses of an adapted form are still constructed but they are gradually being replaced by Malay-style dwellings. It is in the Centre that the tradition of house construction is strongest.

close links with India, and particularly with the Naga of Assam. Latterly, there has been a tendency to play down possible outside influences and stress local origins. In every village there are stone benches or *daro daro* (erected as seats for the dead), beneath which human skulls are sometimes kept. Benches are also found by bathing places, and in the forests and hills. They are not just resting places of the dead; they are also for the living, and are starkly unadorned, bar a few symbolic shapes such as the rosette. Memorial stones are also widespread, as are idols (often phallic) made of wood, stone and clay. An idol was made whenever someone died, except when that person left no male descendants.

Woodcarving is a widespread traditional art form in Nias. In fact, the carvings of Central Nias are regarded as among the finest in Southeast Asia. Christianity however has had a marked effect on production. Ancestor or *adu* figures for example are rarely seen or made; missionaries discouraged production and most were either destroyed or taken off the island and placed in museums before WW2.

The Niah are not only renowned for their megalithic material culture, but also for their **dances**, and particularly for their '**stone-jumping**' – *fahombe*. A stone pedastal or *batu hombo* in the middle of the square that separates the two rows of houses in a Nias village was vaulted by acrobatic warriors, often with a sword in their hand, in preparation for battle. Warriors would spring from a smaller launching stone. The columns are 2-2.5m high and 0.5m wide – in the past they were also topped-off with pointed sticks to galvanize the competitors. Today, stone-jumping is enacted for tourists and important guests.

Economy

The economy of the Niha is based upon the cultivation of wet and dry rice (although this was only introduced in the late Dutch period), sago, maize and a wide variety of other crops and vegetables. Meat is eaten rarely, except during festivals, when large quantities of pork are consumed. Pigs are slaughtered in front of the house of the feast-giver; they are stabbed, their skin singed, and they are then cut up for distribution. The parts of the pig are allocated according to strict rules; the head goes to the foremost chief. In addition to livestock and crops, forest products also represent an important element in the Niha diet. Apes, civets, birds and turtles, tubers and wild fruits, insects and snakes are all consumed. Mice, however, are avoided because they are said to contain the souls of the ancestors, while women are forbidden to eat monkeys because a Niha legend recounts how a woman once turned herself into a monkey.

Today the economy of Nias is based upon the export of natural products such as rubber, pigs and *nilam* (pachouli) and – increasingly – upon tourism. Cash earned through the integration of Nias into the wider Indonesian economy is used to acquire prestige consumer goods and also to send children to the 'mainland' for higher education.

Where to go

For the visitor, S Nias is probably the more rewarding part of the island to visit. The N was raided by the Acehnese for slaves, and much of their material culture was destroyed in the process. The S has the greater cultural integrity, and more 'traditional' villages. It is also the S where the island's best surfing beaches are to be found. The isolated central portion of the island also contains a number of abandoned villages with monumental stone sculptures.

Cross Island Trek

It is possible to trek and bus all the way from Gunungsitoli to Telukdalam, or *vice versa*, staying in villages *en route*. Basic Indonesian is required, and a certain degree of patience and fortitude. From Gunungstitoli take a bus S to Tetehasi and from there walk to Siofabania. The next village is Hilimbowo where there are ex-

amples of traditional architecture and stone megaliths. An hour's walk further on is Lahusa Idanotae (again with traditional houses and megaliths), and another hour still, Orahili Gomo. It is possible to continue southwards all the way to Telukdalam visiting, in turn: Tetegewo, Helezalulu, Lahusa, Lawinda, Hilizoroilawa, Hilinaurato Mazings, Hilizalootono, Bawolahusa, Bawaganowo, and Hilinamoniha before reaching, finally, Telekdalam. **Accommodation** can be arranged through the *Kepala desa* (head of the village) in each village.

Conduct The inhabitants of Nias are even more sensitive to 'inappropriate' dress than most Indonesians. Except at the beach resorts of Lagundi and Jamborai, women should wear long skirts/trousers, a bra and shirt, and men should wear shirts.

Recommended reading Feldman *et al* (1990) *Nias, tribal treasures: cosmic reflections in stone, wood and gold*, Volkenkundig Museum Nusantara: Delft.

WARNING Malaria is a problem on Nias as some chloroquine-resistant strains have appeared. It is also recommended that visitors have a cholera inoculation. Nias has an unfortunate reputation for being a haven for tricksters and thieves. Be wary, but always be polite.

● **Banks & money changers** Exchange rates are poor in Gunungsitoli, it is better to change money before leaving the mainland.

● **Transport Local** There is a fairly extensive road network on the island; the problem is that it is in a poor state of repair. There are buses, bemos and jeeps as well as the odd motorcyclist who might offer a ride. Expect to average 25 km/hr on buses. Bicycles can be hired in tourist destinations. **Air** Binaka airport is 12 km S of town. There are flights from Medan to Gunungsitoli by SMAC. There is also a weekly SMAC flight, on Wed, between Padang and Gunungsitoli. **Sea Boat**: there are boats from Sibolga to Gunungsitoli every day except Sun, leaving at 1100 and 2000, 7-9 hrs (9,500-13,500Rp). The return boat leaves at 0700, but again not on Sun. There are also ferries to Telukdalam (on Mon, Wed and Fri at 1900, arriving at 0700

Fahombe or `stone-jumping' in Nias illustrated on a Bank of Indonesia 1000Rp note

(11-16,000Rp, 12 hrs). Ferries to Gunungsitoli leave from Pelabuhan Baru (New Harbour), those for Telukdalam from Pelabuhan Lama (Old Harbour) (8,500-22,500Rp). *P T Perlani*, Jl Letjen 57 and *P T Pelni*, Jl S Parman 34, both in Sibolga have information on departures. The Pelni ship the *Lawit* also docks at Gunungsitoli once a fortnight on a loop between Padang and Sibolga, before returning to Jakarta. In addition there are usually several cargo ships which leave for the island each week – cheaper, but can be uncomfortable.

GUNUNGSITOLI

Gunungsitoli, on Nias' E coast, is the capital of the island, and much like any other Indonesian town. There is not much to see and the town has a poor selection of hotels. From the town there are many paths and attractive walks, and oval-shaped northern-style houses can be seen in the vicinity of the town. Ask at the tourist office for information. From town, it is possible to walk to Siwahili and Sihareo, and from these two villages to Tumori and Danaha, before reaching the *Miga Beach Hotel*. This hike takes 1 day.

● **Accommodation D-E** *Gomo*, Jl Sirao 8, T 21926, some a/c, the cheap rooms are dirty and dark; **E** *Wisata*, Jl Sirao 2, T 21858, restaurant, all that can be said is that the rooms are relatively clean; **E** *Wisma Soliga*, 4 km out of town, Chinese restaurant, clean rooms and helpful management, best place to stay.

● **Airline offices** SMAC, Jl Lagundri 47, T 21010.

● **Banks & money changers** Rates are poor and only US$ and A$ TCs are accepted. **Bank Negara Indonesia**, Jl Pattimura; **Bank Rakyat Indonesia**, Jl Gomo 1.

● **Hosptials & medical services Hospital**: Jl Ciptomangunkusumo, T 21271.

● **Post & telecommunications Post Office**: Jl Hatta 1. **Telephone Office**: Jl Hatta 7.

● **Tourist offices** Tourist Information Office, Jl Sukarno 6 (nr the dock).

● **Transport** 80 km from Telukdalam. **Air** The airport is 19 km out of town. Flights from Medan on Merpati and SMAC. **Road Bus**: daily connections with Telukdalam 4-10 hrs from the terminal on Jl Diponegoro depending on the state of the road and weather. **Sea Boat**: the port is 2 km N of town. Daily ferry connections (except Sun) with Sibolga (see page 478). The ferry company, *P T Idapola*, has an office at Jl Sirao 8. Pelni have an office on Jl Jend A Yani, on the waterfront. They also sell tickets for boats to the mainland.

TELUKDALAM

This is the second biggest town on Nias, and the entry point for those wishing to visit the S. There is nothing in town except for a church. Surfers head W for 12 km to Lagundi Bay (see below). Visitors wishing to see the traditional S Nias villages could use Telukdalam as a base.

Excursions Bawamataluo (Sunhill) is a traditional village about 14 km NW of Telukdalam. Approached up a 480-step flight of stone stairs, the village contains impressive soaring-roofed houses, megaliths, funerary tables, woodcarvings, and a magnificent chief's 'palace'. The village was built in 1888 as a defensive measure against the Dutch who had attacked and sacked the previous village. The main *omo sebua* or chief's house is said to be the oldest in Nias, although it was built barely a century ago. The house is richly decorated with woodcarvings, depicting family heirlooms, ritual feasts – even a Dutch steamship. These carvings are designed to link the present with the past, and thereby assure the living a link with their deified ancestors. The position of each carving is tightly prescribed. Images of the village founders – *adu* figures – used to occupy the two carved chairs outside the house; like most *adu* figures, missionaries had these destroyed. Though still inhabited, the house has been turned into a museum. Admission by donation. Bawamataluo is the most accessible of the traditional villages, so is fairly touristy. Stone-jumping (*fahombe*) exhibitions are put on for tourists – expect to pay around 15,000Rp (see page 476). Nonetheless, for the budding anthropologist, it is a definite 'must'. *Getting there*: by minibus from Telukdalam.

Hilisimaetano is another traditional village, although it is considerably 'newer' than Bawamataluo. It lies 16 km from Telukdalam. Again, there is a fine collection of 140 *rumah adat* (traditional houses), megalithic stone benches, chairs and other stone and woodcarvings. *Fahombe* (stone-jumping) is performed on Sat (see page 477). **Accommodation** **E** *Losmen Mawan*. *Getting there*: by minibus from Telukdalam.

Treks It is possible to walk from Bawamataluo to Hilisimaetano visiting, en route, the villages of **Siwalawa**, **Onohando**, **Hilinwalo** and **Bawogosali**. There are also treks to other, less visited, villages. Most have megalithic complexes and, as always, the more remote the village the friendlier the villagers. *Getting*

there: on foot, but hire a guide in town (ask at your hotel).

● **Accommodation** B-C *Sorake Beach*, Jl Sorake, a/c, restaurant, pool, 73 rooms in this new hotel, the tip of the mass market iceberg which some local tourist officials hope will soon hit Nias, tennis court, hot water, TV, what more could one want? We can't confirm its quality though; **D** *Ampera*, Jl Pasar, clean rooms; **D** *Effendi*, best in town; **E** *Sebar Menanti*; **E** *Wisma Jamburae*, clean rooms.

● **Banks & money changers** Money changer at Jl Jend A Yani 4. Very poor rates offered.

● **Transport Road Bus**: there are daily bus connections with Gunungsitoli, 4-10 hrs. **Sea Boat**: ferry connections with Sibolga on Mon, Wed and Fri (see page 478); also daily boat connections with Gunungsitoli (again, except Sun). The Pelni vessel *Lawit* calls here once a fortnight from Tanjung Priok and Padang, before continuing onto Sibologa, Padang and Tanjung Priok (see route schedule page 921).

LAGUNDI (LAGUNDRI) BAY

Lying 12 km from Telukdalam, Lagundi Bay was an important port until Krakatau exploded and destroyed it in 1883. Now there are just two villages here – Lagundi and Jamborai. Since the late 1970s, the area has taken on a new life and become a surfer's paradise.

Surfing enthusiasts maintain that Lagundi has the most perfect reef right-hander on earth – although the surf can be inconsistent. The waves at Lagundi Bay are powerful and the coral is close to the surface, so it is not recommended for beginners. There are boards for hire on the beach. Other than surfing and swimming, there is not much to do here, except walking and visiting surrounding villages (see below).

Excursions It is possible to visit the **traditional Nias villages** of **Hilisimaetano** (20 km N) or **Bawamataluo** (17 km) from Lagundi (see above).

● **Accommodation** Losmen are concentrated at Jamburai village. They are basic and charge similar rates – our **F** range. Food is almost universally poor. However, there are plans afoot to develop Lagundi into something more up-market. A/c hotels are planned and land use and land ownership disputes are bound to material-ize as speculation intensifies.

Some losmen owners insist that their guests also eat all their meals at the losmen (if room rates are very cheap this is usually the reason). Check whether rates incl meals or not; there have been reports of disputes over this. It is best to look at a number before making a decision, as stand-ards change very fast. Among the more popular, at the last count, were *Ama Soni, Yanti, Jam-burai* and *Friendly*. But try and obtain a per-sonal recommendation from a recent visitor in Sibolga or Telukdalam.

● **Places to eat** There are a handful of warungs serving basic Indonesian and travellers' food and, sometimes, superb seafood. Most people eat at their losmen.

● **Transport** 12 km from Telukdalam. **Road Bus & ojek**: Lagundi is 6 km off the road from Telukdalam. It can be reached by bus or oplet (both irregular), or by hitching a lift on the back of a motorcycle. Oplet drivers regularly over-charge. If coming from Gunungsitoli by bus ask to be let off at the junction with the road to Lagundi. Ojeks wait here to take passengers the final 6 km.

Southern Sumatra

FOR THIS GUIDEBOOK, Sumatra has been split into two: southern and northern Sumatra. This division does not correspond with any administrative division. Southern Sumatra consists of six provinces: West Sumatra, Riau, Jambi, Bengkulu, South Sumatra and Lampung. West Sumatra with a population of 4 million is the home of the Minang people. The hill town of Bukittinggi and the provincial coastal capital of Padang are the province's best known settlements; the 'Stone Age' Mentawi Islands lie offshore. Riau Province with 3.4 million inhabitants is situated to the east of West Sumatra, and includes the islands of the Riau archipelago. The oil town of Pekanbaru on the Siak River is the provincial capital. South of Riau is another resource-rich but rarely visited province, Jambi, and south of here the province of South Sumatra with its capital, Palembang, situated on the Musi River. Bangka and Belitung islands off South Sumatra's east coast are being developed into tourist resorts. Far more imposing scenically is small Bengkulu province which encompasses the Bukit Barisan and a narrow coastal strip of lowland; the capital, also named Bengkulu, is one of the most attractive towns in Sumatra. Finally, densely settled Lampung province is the gateway to Java, its capital of Bandar Lampung overlooking the Sunda Strait.

THE MINANGKABAU OF WEST SUMATRA

The Minangkabau people are concentrated in the upland areas of W Sumatra province and number about 4 million. They are known throughout Indonesia for their business acumen and peripatetic habits: there are Minangs, as the Minangkabau are usually known, scattered right across the Indonesian archipelago from Aceh to Irian Jaya, and every town has its Minang or Padang restaurant run by a Minang family. They are also beloved by anthropologists for their unique matrilineal society. One Minang poem dating at least from the early 19th century, even exhorts mothers to teach their daughters "to judge the rise and fall of prices". Important Minang towns include the hill towns of Bukittinggi, Payamkumpuh and Batusangkar, which lie near the centre of the Minang homeland or *darek*, and the coastal provincial capital, Padang.

History

The origins of the Minang Kingdom are hazy, although Adityavarman (r 1356-1375), who had links with Majapahit (see page 84), seems to have been influential in unifying the state. Power was based upon gold which was mined in the Minang highlands. During the 14th and 15th centuries when Minangkabau power was at its height, the kingdom's influence extended over much of central Sumatra.

Early European explorers searched unsuccessfully for the ancient city of 'Menangkabu', thought to be the source of the wealth and gold of Malesia – the mythical and unimaginably rich Golden Khersonese. When Stamford Raffles visited the area at the beginning of the 19th century, he was immensely impressed by the Minangkabau Kingdom, believing the technology of agriculture and the level of civilization to be superior to that of Java. However by the time the Dutch began to establish a presence in the 18th century, Minangkabau was already in decline. The gold mines had been worked out by the

Pencak silat: martial art of West Sumatra

Pencak silat is a martial art that originated in West Sumatra and is now practiced in various forms throughout Indonesia and also in Malaysia. Using the feet as well as the hands, Minanagkabau males are expected to become proficient in this deadly art before they can be said to have become men. It has been adapted into a dance form and can be seen along with other dances in Bukittinggi and Padang.

1780s, and the old royal order was being undermined by new sources of wealth: coffee, gambier and pepper. A Hindu kingdom between the 12th and 14th centuries, the Minang turned increasingly to Islam as the religion's influence gradually filtered S from Aceh, in the N. This culminated in the Padri Wars between 1820 and 1837 which pitted the traditionalists against a new breed of Muslim fundamentalists.

Minangkabau matrilineal society

Each Minangkabau *sa-buah-parui* or clan, the smallest unit of traditional 'government', traces its lineage from a common female ancestor. Titles, wealth and family names are all passed down through the female line. Men are given the responsibility of looking after the family's heirlooms, but it is the women who keep the keys. It is felt by many that the tendency for Minang men to leave the village and go *merantau* – or walkabout – is because of the dominant role that women play. In the view of many anthropologists, centrifugality has been part of the historical process in Minangkabau society – and a process which is culturally determined. Many Minang feel that it is improper, for example, for young men to stay in their mother's house. E M Loeb, in his 1935 book *Sumatra: its history and people*, describes a system that might warm the heart of many a Western woman:

"According to Minangkabau adat, a man

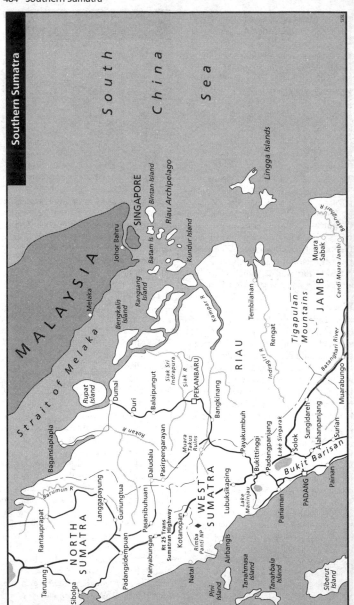

neither gains possession of a woman by marriage nor a woman a man. By the payment of a certain price the woman rents the services of her husband at night. The husband then can sleep with his wife in her bilik, the small sleeping room of the family house, or else with the men in the men's house... The Minangkabau man has no rights over his wife other than demanding that she remains faithful to him. He cannot ask her to make clothes for him... The woman on the other hand, can always demand that her husband come to visit her from time to time and fulfil his marital obligations".

But this interpretation of male migration has been challenged. More recent studies have associated *merantau* not with matrilineality but with egalitarianism. In this context, the only way that a Minang man can accumulate status in a world where everyone is equal, where sharing is the norm, and where everyone in a community is king, is by migrating. It is also true that the process of 'modernisation' is undermining Minang traditions, and thus undermining the role of women. Today, a visitor staying with a 'modern' Minang might be hard put to discern the matrilineal traditions which preoccupy anthropologists.

Architecture

To the visitor, the most obviously distinctive element of the Minangkabau is their magnificent architecture. The traditional wooden house or *rumah adat* – literally, 'customary house', also known as *rumah gadang* or 'big house' – is raised off the ground and surmounted by an impressive curved roof, the gables soaring upwards at either end like the horns of the buffalo which they are said to represent. These houses are similar in design to the traditional houses of the

---

Islam versus tradition: the Padri Wars (1803-1838)

By the beginning of the 19th century, fundamentalist Muslims, or *Padris* – named after the Acehnese port of Pedir where pilgrims left for the journey to Mecca – were impatient for the Minangkabau to abandon their traditional beliefs and embrace the true, and pure, Islamic path. This probably stemmed from the return of three *hajis* – or pilgrims – from Mecca, where they had witnessed the violent overthrow of the holy city by the puritanical Wahhabi in 1803. Among the aspects of Minang culture which they most opposed were gambling, drinking, the taking of betel and opium, and the continued influence of matriarchal customs. The most influential of the Padris was Imam Bonjol (1772-1864), immortalized today in road names across the country.

To impose their beliefs, the Padris resorted to force, killing and imprisoning those who resisted their religious reform movement. By 1815, they had killed most of the Minangkabau royal family and imposed their will over the Minang homeland. They were even beginning to convert the Batak. However, their religious war was not won: in 1821 the few remaining members of the Minang royal house signed a treaty and surrendered their kingdom to the Dutch. This marked the beginning of the Padri War which lasted until 1838. The Dutch saw the contest as a battle between *adat* or traditional law and Islamic law, and between traditional Minang leaders and the new breed of Muslim leaders.

The traditional Minangkabau *adat* chiefs joined forces with the Dutch to fight their common enemy, the Padris. The Dutch had to virtually blockade W Sumatra before they were victorious – capturing the leader Imam Bonjol in 1837. Today, although the Minang are ardent Muslims – a legacy of the Wars – traditional pre-Islamic beliefs still exert a strong influence. In particular, the Minangkabau have stubbornly clung to the matrilineal *adat* organization of their society.

Toraja of Sulawesi (see page 636), although they are now, sadly, seldom built.

One side of the interior of the house is taken up by a row of small sleeping cubicles, in front of which is a large meeting room. The house is flanked by a pair of rice barns. Traditionally, both the house and the rice barns were deeply and colourfully carved. In a village, each compound of houses will usually be inhabited by one matrilineal line, with a separate structure (*surau*) for the men and boys, along with one or more rice barns.

Language

The Minang language is similar to Bahasa Indonesia, and the two are mutually intelligible. However, the vowels 'a' and 'e' commonly become an 'o' in Minang so that *apa* (what) becomes *apo*, *kemana* (where) becomes *kamano*, and the numbers *dua* (2) and *tiga* (3), *duo* and *tigo* respectively.

Minang cuisine

Another feature of W Sumatra is Minang food – known throughout Indonesia as *Makan Padang*, after the capital of the province. It tends to be chilli hot, although some of the dishes are mild. On taking a seat in a restaurant, an assortment of bowls of food are brought to the table – and the customer only pays for what he or she eats. Distinctive dishes include *rendang* (a dry beef curry cooked in coconut milk, spices and chilli), *pangek ikan* (fish cooked in coconut milk with chilli and spices), *panggang ikan* (fish roasted over an open fire), *kalio* (beef or chicken rendang where some of the juice remains), and cassava leaves in coconut milk (somewhat like spinach). Although not characteristically Minang, sweet fresh W Sumatran coffee (*kopi manis*) is also delicious.

Conduct amongst the Minangkabau

Like most Indonesians, the majority of Minang people are Muslims – and staunchly so. It is also regarded as polite to offer food to neighbours – even in a restaurant and sitting next to complete strangers. The offer will invariably be refused. Further, it is considered rude to stand with hands on hips, to point a finger at an adult, or to sit with legs crossed. And finally, it is regarded as extremely impolite to touch a person's head.

Chief's house and rice barn, West Sumatra
Source: Wallace, Alfred Russel (1896) *The Malay Archipelago*, Macmillan: London

THE MINANG HOMELAND: BUKITTINGGI AND SURROUNDINGS

On the route S from Sibolga and Lake Toba, the Trans-Sumatran Highway crosses the Equator at the town of Bonjol – indicated by a globe and a sign at the side of the road. From here Batakland becomes Minangkabau country – about 450 km S of Lake Toba. 50 km further S from Bonjol is the popular hill resort of Bukittinggi.

BUKITTINGGI

Bukittinggi – meaning High Hill – is one of the most attractive towns in Sumatra and has many places of interest in the immediate vicinity. The town is situated at 1,000m, encircled by volcanoes, and the climate is cool and invigorating. Like the Minang people in general, the inhabitants of Bukittinggi are relaxed and welcoming, making it a very popular place to stay.

Bukittinggi is the cultural centre of the Minangkabau people. It supports a university, zoo, museum, a good market, and yet is small and accessible. Many travellers arrive here, and after the trials of the road and such towns as Sibolga, seem very reluctant to leave. Compared with some other resort towns, it is clean (by Sumatran standards) and reasonably well organized. The core of the town is Jl Jend A Yani, marked at one end by a clock tower and the other by a statue of a turbaned man mounted on a rearing horse – the Padri hero, Imam Bonjol (see page 486). Along this road are concentrated many restaurants and tour and travel companies, as well as the cheaper travellers' hotels.

Places of interest

The geographic and functional centre of Bukittinggi is marked by a strange-looking **clock tower** at the S end of Jl Jend A Yani, the town's main thoroughfare. The Jam Gadang or 'Great Clock' as it is known, was built by the Dutch in 1827. It is a veritable Sumatran 'Big Ben' and has a Minangkabau-style roof perched uneasily on the top. The **central market** is close to the clock tower. Although there is a market every day of the week, market day is on Wed and Sat (0800-1700) when hoards of Minangkabau men and women descend on Bukittinggi. The market – in fact there are two markets, the Upper Market (*Pasar Atas*) and Lower Market (*Pasar Bawah*) – covers an enormous area and sells virtually everything. Good for souvenirs, handicrafts, jewellery, fruit, spices and weird foods.

The N end of Jl Jend A Yani runs between two hills. On top of the hill to the W is **Fort de Kock**, built by the Dutch in 1825 as a defensive site during the Padri Wars (see page 486). Very little of the fort remains apart from a few rusting cannons and a moat. The centre of the decaying fortifications is dominated by a water tower. However, the views of the town and the surrounding countryside are worth the trip (although trees are beginning to obscure the view). To the E, and linked by a foot-bridge, on the other side of Jl Jend A Yani, is Bukittinggi's high point, **Taman Bundokandung** – 'Kind-Hearted Mother Park'. The park contains both a museum and a zoo. The **Bukittinggi zoo** is hardly an object lesson in how to keep animals in captivity, but it does have a reasonable collection of Sumatran wildlife, including orang utans and gibbons. Strangely, there is also an exhibit of stuffed animals (perhaps former inmates?) and the skeleton of a whale. Admission to fort and zoo: 1250Rp. Open 0730-1700 Mon-Sun, closed over lunch on Fri for prayers. Within the zoo is a **museum** – established in 1935 and the oldest in Sumatra. The collection is housed in a traditional *rumah adat*, or Minangkabau clan house, embellished with fine woodcarvings and fronted by two rice barns. The museum specializes in local ethnographic exhibits, including fine jewellery and textiles, and is one of the best arranged in Sumatra. There are also some macabre stuffed and deformed buffalo calves here. Admission 300Rp. Open 0730-1700, Mon-Sun, closed over lunch on Fri for prayers.

To the SW of the town is the spectacular **Ngarai Canyon**, 4 km long and over 100m deep. A road at the end of Jl Teuku Umar leads down through the canyon past the back entrances to the Japanese tunnel system. A path leaves the road at a sharp bend (there is a snack bar here serving tea etc.) and continues to a bridge at the foot of the chasm and steep steps on the opposite side of the canyon. Follow a road through a village and across paddy fields until you eventually arrive at **Kota Gadang**. Many small silversmiths sell their wares throughout the village. The walk takes about 2 hrs, but is very beautiful and rewarding. From Kota Gadang, either retrace your steps, or catch an oplet back into town from Koto Tuo, 1 km to the S of the village.

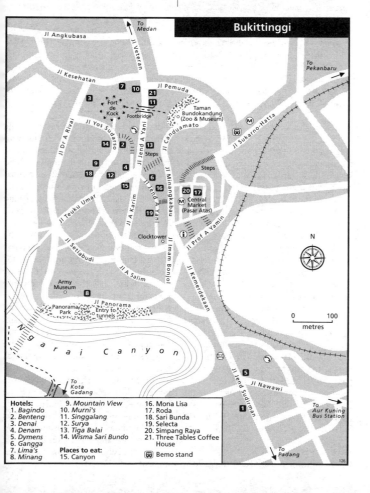

Bukittinggi

Hotels:
1. Bagindo
2. Benteng
3. Denai
4. Denam
5. Dymens
6. Gangga
7. Lima's
8. Minang
9. Mountain View
10. Murni's
11. Singgalang
12. Surya
13. Tiga Balai
14. Wisma Sari Bundo

Places to eat:
15. Canyon
16. Mona Lisa
17. Roda
18. Sari Bunda
19. Selecta
20. Simpang Raya
21. Three Tables Coffee House

Bemo stand

Rafflesia arnoldi: the largest flower in the world

🔍 The rafflesia (*Rafflesia arnoldi*), named after Stamford Raffles, is the largest flower in the world. The Swedish naturalist Eric Mjoberg wrote in 1930 on seeing the flower: "The whole phenomenon seems so amazing, so unfamiliar, so fantastic, that we are tempted to explain: such flowers cannot be real!". Stamford Raffles, who discovered the flower for Western science one hundred years earlier during his first sojourn at Bengkulu, noted that it was "a full yard across, weighs fifteen pounds, and contains in the nectary no less than eight pints [of nectar]...". The problem is that the rafflesia does not flower for very long – only for a couple of weeks, usually between Aug and Dec. Out of these months there is usually nothing to see. The plant is in fact parasitic, so appropriately its scent is more akin to rotting meat than any perfume. Its natural habitat is moist, shaded areas.

Almost as monstrous, but far less well known, is the massive *Amorphophallus titanum* (a giant aroid lily) discovered for Western science by the Italian explorer Odoardo Beccari in 1879 in W Sumatra. When he reported that this flower was 2m tall no-one believed him; he had to wait until a tuber of the plant, a full 2m in circumference, bloomed at Kew Gardens, London in 1889. *A titanum's* close relative *A decus-silvae* has a stalk almost 4.5m tall and makes Sumatra truly the island of giant flowers.

Also at the S edge of town and overlooking the canyon is **Panorama Park** (admission 300Rp), a popular weekend meeting place for courting couples. Monkeys in these gardens provide entertainment. Within the park is the entrance to a **maze of tunnels** excavated by the Japanese during the Occupation, with ammunition stores, kitchens and dining rooms. Guides gleefully show the chute where dead Indonesian workers were propelled out into the canyon to rot. Admission 500Rp. Opposite the park, on Jl Panorama (formerly Jl Imam Bonjol), is the **Army Museum** (*Museum Perjuangan*) which contains military memorabilia from the early 19th century through to the modern period. There are some interesting photographs of the disintering of the army officers assassinated by the PKI during the attempted coup of 1965 (see page 50), as well as exhibits relating to Fretilin – who continue to fight for the independence of E Timor (see page 784). Admission by donation. Open 0800-1700 Sat-Thur, 0800-1100, 1300-1700 Fri.

Excursions

One of the attractions of Bukittinggi is the wide array of sights in the surrounding area. Below are the main excursions, although there are also additional hikes, waterfalls, traditional villages, lakes and centres of craft production. Tour companies will be able to provide information on these other sights. Note that sights around the nearby town of Batusangkar are listed in the box on page 492.

Lake Maninjau lies about 35 km to the W of town (see page 496). *Getting there*: for the modestly energetic, take a bus from Bukittinggi's *stasiun bis* to Lawang. From Lawang walk the 4 km to **Puncak Lawang** (**Lawang Top**) at the lip of the crater and 1,400m up – a spectacular view. **NB** Check there is no mist before departing. The walk down to the lake starts at Lawang, a stunning descent of 1,000m which should take about 2 hrs, and ends up at the hamlet of Bayur, 4 km N of Maninjau village. Alternatively, catch a bus straight to Maninjau village on the lake shore, navigating 44 hairpin bends on the way down (2 hrs). The last bus leaves Maninjau village for Bukittinggi at between 1600 and 1700, later on market days. A direct bus to Padang leave Maninjau at 0630, 3½ hrs.

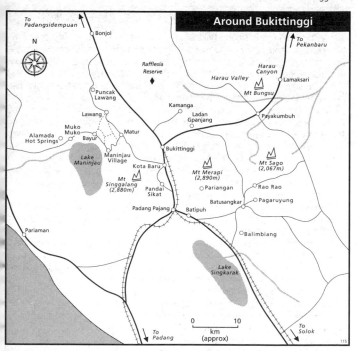

Around Bukittinggi

Batang Palupuh, situated 12 km N of town, is a reserve for the monstrous *rafflesia* flower (see box). *Getting there*: catch a bus to Batang Palupuh on the Trans-Sumatran Highway, or take an oplet and then walk to the reserve (30 mins). A guide from the village will point the flower out for a small fee.

Kota Baru is a rather unattractive town 10 km S of town on the main road to Padang, redeemed only by the fact that it has a good **market**. The villages surrounding Kota Baru often hold **bullfights** (in fact buffalo fights) on Tues and Sat at 1700 – for example, at Panyalarun (14 km) and Padang Lawas (10 km). There are also fights only half an hour from Bukittinggi – touts will try to sell tours for 4,000Rp, but it is possible to go by public transport for 500Rp, and pay a 500Rp entrance fee. The bulls fight one another rather than a

matador, and the ring is formed by the spectators rather than by a protective fence. The buffaloes are believed to be possessed by the spirit of their owners, so that it is they who are in combat, not their animals. *Getting there*: by bus from Aur Kuning terminal.

Pandai Sikat is one of a number of villages specializing in traditional craft production. It is situated 13 km S of town at the foot of Mt Singgalang, just off the road to Padang Panjang, and is a cloth and woodcarving centre. The carvings tend to use natural motifs (trees, animals, flowers etc), as does the famous *songket* cloth (see page 529) that is produced here. About 1,000 women weave richly patterned cloth. Note that the warp may be rayon, imported from Japan, and only the weft, cotton or silk. *Getting there*: by bus to Kota Baru from Aur Kuning terminal and then

Places of interest around Batusangkar: the Minang Darek

The Minang highlands around Bukittinggi constitute the *darek*, or the core of the Minang Homeland. Many of the most interesting sights lie to the SE of town, in the area around the cultural centre of Batusangkar. Seeing these sights is easiest on a tour from Bukittinggi (see Tours, page 493). Travelling by local transport is time-consuming and often cramped, although it is not difficult: take a bus to Batusangkar and then catch a bemo from the station close to the market in Batusangkar.

The road to Batusangkar, after the turn-off at Padang Panjang (which has some fine examples of *rumah adat* along the main street), is breathtaking. Like Bukittinggi, **Batusangkar** is located on an upland plateau, surrounded by terraced rice fields and mountains. The town of Batusangkar, although it is regarded as one of the three centres of Minang culture, is not particularly attractive. It has a mediocre market and an array of souvenir shops. However, there is much to see in the vicinity (see below). Accommodation *Pagaruyung*, Jl Parak Juar 4. *Getting there*: take a bus to Padang Panjang and then another local bus to Batusangkar.

● **Rao Rao** is a traditional mining village off the road between Padang Panjang and Batusangkar. Most of the houses now have corrugated iron roofs, but there are a handful wih tiles or thatch.

● **Pagaruyung** lies 5 km E of Batusangkar, and is the site of a Minangkabau **sultan's palace** – in effect a very large traditional Minang house – now a museum. In 1815 during the Padri War (see page 486), Muslim radicals slaughtered nearly all the sultan's family. Unfortunately, the original palace was destroyed during WW2, and this is a reconstruction. Beneath the wooden cladding it is made of concrete, and the dimensions and lay-out of the original palace have been altered to accord with its

walk the final 2 km (or take a bemo). Other craft villages include **Desa Sunga**, 17 km S of town, which specializes in brasswork; and **Sungaipua**, on the slopes of Mt Merapi, which specializes in metalwork (knives, swords).

Mount Merapi is an active volcano to the SE of town which stands at a height of 2,891m and last erupted in 1979. The difficult climb to the summit takes 4-6 hrs. Enquire at the Police Station in Kota Baru for more information. Register here before ascending and ask for directions; the route is indistinct in places (it is sensible to take a guide – although see the warning below). Start very early as mist envelopes the mountain by 1100. Wear warm clothes: it is cold on the summit. The ground around the crater is loose and hikers should keep away from the lip. On Sat nights, locals from Bukittinggi make the ascent to be at the top for the sunrise; following them is the easiest way to reach the summit. *Getting there*: catch a bus to Kota Baru from the Aur Kuning terminal (first departure 0500), and then hike. **N** The mountain was closed to climbers fo. 2½ years in the early 90s because of the risk of volcanic activity, and has only recently opened again. Nonetheless, check at your hotel before leaving. Also be aware that some 'guides' lack any training whatsoever and may not even be familiar with the mountain. In Mar 1995 two British hikers were lost on the mountain and we have also received a letter from another climber abandoned by his guide for 4 days.

Mount Singgalang to the SW of Bukittinggi stands at a height of 2,878m and offers a less arduous climb than Mt Merapi. The trail starts at the village of Pandai Sikat, and the climb takes about 4-5 hrs. Start early, as mist often descends over the mountain later in the day. *Getting there*: take a bus to Kota Baru from the Aur Kuning terminal and then walk the 2 km to Pandai Sikat (or take a bemo).

Kamanga Cave is an impressive cave

new function as a museum. Admission 300Rp. Close by are some ancient stone slabs inscribed in Sanskrit. *Getting there*: by bus to Batusangkar and then a bemo from the station near the market in Batusangkar (250Rp).

● **Balimbiang** is situated 10 km S of Batusangkar. It is a 'traditional' village, where some of the 300 year old *rumah adat* – built without nails – have been opened-up to visitors (the owners, very sensibly, making sure they make a profit). *Getting there*: by bus to Batusangkar and then a bemo from the station near the market in Batusangkar.

● **Pariangan** is a less visited, and more peaceful, traditional Minang village. It nestles in a small valley on the slopes of Mount Merapi at an altitude of 850m, surrounded by ricefields. It is thought to be one of the original Minang villages – inscriptions found here certainly date it to the 14th century reign of King Adityavarman – and it is one of the few villages where *surau* quarters for men and boys are still in use (see page 486). It is one of the most beautiful and friendly villages in the Minang highlands but has lost some of its charm, as the old mosque is being replaced by a new one. *Getting there*: by bus towards Batusangkar and ask to be let off at the track for Pariangan, about 7 km E of Batipuh; the track leads uphill to the villages.

● **Lake Singkarak** is a 20 km-long lake to the SW of Batusangkar and about 30 km S of Bukittinggi. It does not compare with the beauty of Lake Maninjau, but the swimming is refreshing and there are several hotels for those who wish to stay longer. **Accommodation B** *Singkarak Sumpur*, on the N shore, T 82529, F 82103, a/c, restaurant, pool, sports facilities, 38 rm, best on the lake; two hotels on the E shore (**D**), including the *Jayakarta*, are not good value, but are cheaper. *Getting there*: by bus from Bukittinggi, or by bemo from Batusangkar and Balimbiang.

15 km E of Bukittinggi. It is said to have been used as a haven from which rebels fighting against the Dutch during the 19th century carried out their raids. A number of stone statues commemorate the heroes of the movement. The cave is 1,500m deep, with the usual array of stalacmites and stalactites. *Getting there*: by bemo to the village of Kamanga and then walk.

Harau Canyon is a 'nature' reserve of 300 ha encircled by 100m-high canyon walls, 47 km NE of Bukittinggi. It's rather disappointing, dirty and crowded. The walk from here to Lamaksari is enjoyable, through rice fields. Admission small charge. *Getting there*: the entrance to the reserve lies only 3 km off the main Bukittinggi-Pekanbaru road; take a bus from the Aur Kuning terminal running NE, through the market town of Payakumbuh (33 km), and get off at the village of Lamaksari (another 11 km); it is a 3 km walk from here.

Tours

There are a range of tours organized to Lake Maninjau, Batusangkar, Lake Singkarak and other sights around Bukittinggi. Tours tend to take one of three routes: the Minangkabau tour, featuring many different places which are representative of the Minangkabau culture, past and present (including Batusangkar, Pagaruyung, and Lake Singkarak), the Maninjau line (including Kota Gadang and Lake Maninjau), and the Harau Valley line (including Mt Merapi and the Harau Valley). Most tour/travel agents organize these day-long tours for about 20,000-25,000Rp; they are also sometimes arranged by hotels and losmen. A man named 'Barta' can be found at the *Three Tables Coffee House*, he organizes a range of treks which have been recommended. Good lunch included. Tours to watch the waterbuffalo fights can also be arranged. Treks to the Harau Valley are organized by 'Efi' at the Blues Club, if enough people can get together. This costs about US$20/day (4 day trek) but comes rec. Tour operators also organize tours further afield – for example, 10-day trips to the Mentawai Islands (see page 517). Bear in mind that it can take up to 3 days to get to Siberut Island, Mentawi, so a 10-day tour becomes, effectively, only 7-days.

Local information
● Accommodation

Most of the travellers' hotels and guesthouses are concentrated along the N end of Jl Jend A Yani. Quieter, smaller and often cleaner homestays are located on the hills either side of Jl Jend A Yani. As Bukittinggi makes the transition from traveller's stop-over to tourist destination so new hotels.

A *Pusako*, Jl Sukarno-Hatta 7, PO Box 69, T 321110, F 21017, a/c, restaurant, pool, new hotel with 185 rm and all facilities, low rise block modelled – very approximately – on traditional lines, best in town and part of the Aerowisata chain; **A** *Novotel* has recently opened (T 31122, F 31123) but we have had no further information.

B *Denai*, Jl Rivai 26, T 32920, F 23490, restaurant, best in town, well-run and quiet, some separate bungalows, popular, but undergoing renovation at present; **B** *Dymens*, Jl Nawawi 3, T 21015, F 21613, some a/c, excellent restaurant, comfortable, on the S edge of town nr the bus station; **B** *Wisma Sari Bundo*, Jl Yos Sudarso 7A, T 22953, well-run, with small but comfortable rooms, rooms above parking space can be noisy, rec.

C *Bagindo*, Jl Sudirman 41-45, T 23100, S of town not far from the bus station, clean but inconvenient location; **C-D** *Lima's*, Jl Kesehatan 34, T 22641, restaurant (slow service), clean and popular, good value; **C** *Marmy's Homestay*, Jl Kesehatan 30, friendly, up-market homestay; **C** *Minang*, Jl Panorama 20, T 21120, private bathrooms, great views over the canyon, a little way out of town so very quiet, rooms are rather variable in quality but staff very friendly – no restaurant.

D-E *Benteng*, Jl Benteng 1, T 21115, F 22596, restaurant, peaceful hotel overlooking the centre of town, well-managed and popular with some ambience, rec; **D-E** *Mountain View*, Jl Yos Sudarso 3, T 21621, good views, friendly management, peaceful (although the construction of a large new hotel nearby during 1996

may well have changed its characterization, rec. All the guesthouses listed below are of similar price and quality, with little to choose between them. **E** *Denam*, Jl Yos Sudarso 4, T 21333, clean and simple, food available, free tea and coffee, quiet, rec; **E** *Gangga*, Jl Jend A Yani 70, T 22967, some with attached mandi, popular, good value although we have received reports that the rooms are becoming rather grubby; **E** *Kartini*, this place comes rec by recent visitors, it is friendly, clean and the room rate inc a good breakfast, the owner, Erwin, also offers tours of the local area; **E** *Murni's*, Jl Jend A Yani 115, popular, clean rooms; **E** *Nirwana*, Jl Jend A Yani 113, T 21292, popular budget place; **E** *Surya*, Jl Teuku Umar 7, T 22587, off the main road and quieter than other guesthouses; **E-F** *Asheika Chalik*, Jl Minangkabau (at the top of the steps), basic but clean, simple food also available.

F *Pelita*, Jl Jend A Yani 17, T 22883; **F** *Singgalang*, Jl Jend A Yani 130, T 21576, clean, airy and pleasant place to stay; **F** *Tiga Balai*, Jl Jend A Yani 100, T 21824, one of the better of the cheap places to stay, but like the *Gangga* reports of creeping grubbiness.

● Places to eat

Bukittinggi is renowned for the quality of its food. The town has many excellent foodstalls selling sate, gulai soup and other specialities. Like the guesthouses, most of the restaurants are concentrated along Jl Jend A Yani, particularly the popular travellers' restaurants.

Indonesian: ◆◆◆*Sari Bunda*, Jl Yos Sudarso 31, also serves Chinese and seafood, lovely setting – outdoor eating in garden area, with good view for sunsets, roast duck cooked with cloves and coconut and the *Kankung* hotplate are particularly good, rec; ◆◆*Famili*, Jl Benteng 1, nr the *Benteng Hotel*, perched on the hillside with good views and excellent food with friendly management, rec; ◆*Roda*, Pasar Atas (Upper Market), Blok C-155, good, Padang food; ◆*Selamat*, Jl Jend A Yani 19, good Padang food; ◆*Simpang Raya*, Jl Lantai 2, nr Pasar Atas, popular Padang restaurant, part of the chain, better food at lunch than at night, good views.

Other Asian cuisine: ◆*Asean*, Jl A Karim 6A, good Chinese; *Selecta*, Jl Jend A Yani 3, Chinese; ◆*Mona Lisa*, Jl Ahmad Yani 58, good Chinese food, fresh juice, fruit salads, very popular.

International: ◆◆◆*Dymens Hotel*, Jl Nawawi 3, Indonesian, Chinese, Japanese, International; ◆◆–◆◆◆*Harau Cliff Café* (formerly the *Mexico Restaurant*), Jl Jend A Yani 134, new owners and a new name but still a place to be rec – steaks and cold beers in a friendly, relaxed environment; ♦♦*Canyon Coffee Shop*, Jl T Umar, good good with guided walks in the canyon; ♦♦*Coffee Shop*, Jl Jend A Yani 105, tables on street, usual range of travellers' dishes; ♦♦*Jazz and Blues Coffee Shop*, Jl Jend A Yani, good value with music thrown in, rec; ♦*Three Tables Coffee House*, Jl Jend A Yani 142, serves travellers' food and good standard Indonesian food, popular.

Foodstalls: the best foodstalls are found in and around the market area; sate, fruit, Padang dishes etc.

● **Airline offices**

Garuda and Merpati, *Dymens Hotel*, Jl Nawawi 3.

● **Banks & money changers**

Banks close at 1100 on Sat. Many of the tour and travel companies will change money. **Bank Negara Indonesia 1946**, 3rd flr, Pasar Atas; **Bank Rakyat Indonesia**, Jl Jend A Yani 3 (in the shadow of the clock tower); **P T Enzet Corindo Perkasa**, Jl Minangkabau 51 (moneychanger).

● **Entertainment**

Minangkabau dances: including *Pencak silat* (see page 483), a traditional form of self-defence, can be seen performed at **Medan Nan Balindung**, Jl Khatib Suleiman 1, at 2030 every day except Thur (admission 5,000Rp). Another venue is the **Hoya Kota Wisata**, Pasar Banto Building, shows at 2030 on Thur and Sat only.

Minangkabau traditional arts (music, song, dance and silat): **Saayun Salankah**, Jl Lenggogeni 1A, on Wed, Thur and Sat at 2030.

● **Hospitals & medical services**

Hospital: *Dokter Achmad Mochtar Hospital*, Jl Rivai (opp the *Denai Hotel*).

● **Post & telecommunications**

Area code: 0752.

General Post Office: Jl Jend Sudirman (opp *Dymens Hotel*), on the S edge of town.

Branch Post Office: on Clock Tower Square.

Telephone Office: Jl Jend A Yani.

● **Shopping**

Bukittinggi has a good selection of shops selling handicrafts and antiques, and has a particular reputation for its silver and gold jewellery. The shops are concentrated on Jl Minangkabau (close to the Central Market) and along Jl Jend A Yani. The most enjoyable way to shop is in the **Central Market** on Wed or Sat (see above, Places of interest). If interested in buying **jewellery**, it is worth visiting the Kota Gadang silversmithing village (see above, Places of interest), which specializes in producing silver filigree.

Book exchange: 3 on Jl Jend A Yani.

● **Tour companies & travel agents**

Concentrated along Jl Jend A Yani. They incl: *Dymens Travel Agency*, *Dymens Hotel*, Jl Nawawi 3, T 22904; *Maju Indosari Travel Bureau*, Jl Muka Jam Gadang 17, T 21671; *Gangga Tours and Travel*, Jl Jend A Yani 70; *Nintrabu*, Jl Jend A Yani 100; *Batours*, Jl Jend A Yani 105; *Travina Inti*, Jl Jend A Yani 107, T 21281; *Mitra Wisata*, Jl Jend A Yani 99, T 21133.

● **Tourist offices**

Bukittinggi Tourist Office, Jl Byekh Bantam 1, J1. Muka Jani Gadang (by the clock tower), T 22403. Provides some information and will arrange tickets and tours (incl individual tour, eg hire of driver and minibus). Open 0800-1400 Mon-Thur, 0800-1100 Fri, 0800-1230 Sat.

● **Transport**

108 km from Padang, 381 km from Sibolga, 508 km from Prapat, 174 km from Pekanbaru. **Local** Bukittinggi is a small enough (and cool enough) town to wander around on foot. However, there are **bemos** and **bendis** – romantic 2-wheeled horse-drawn carts – for longer trips. **Oplets**: from the bus station at Aur Kuning, 3 km SE of town, for excursions. **Motorbike hire**: from most tour/travel companies for about 17,500Rp/day. **Mountain bike hire**: ask at your hotel or losmen (4,000Rp/day).

Road Bus: the station is at Aur Kuning, 3 km SE of town. Regular connections with Padang 2-3 hrs, Sibolga 11 hrs, Prapat 14 hrs – though it can take as much as 17 hrs – (bus/ferry tickets available for Samosir Island, book 2-3 days in advance at tour operators, can collect from hotels. **NB** The bus may not connect with the last ferry to Samosir, which means a late night arrival at Prapat and a limited choice of hotels (see Prapat accommodation). Medan 20 hrs, Pekanbaru 6 hrs and Jambi 22 hrs. *JASTRA* (*Jawar Sumatera Transport*) run a direct service between Bukittinggi and Jakarta, 30 hrs and 90,000Rp. No toilets but said to be relatively comfortable and safe. Most of the bus companies have their offices at the station inc *ANS* and *JASTRA*. Tickets are also available from travel agents (see above) but beware of buying tickets from touts roaming hotels and guesthouse; the bus is unlikely to be 'air-conditioned, express and very, very comfortable'. Early morning buses to Padang leave from the clock tower. Tourist buses for Toba/Samosir (Prapat) leave in the early morning, about 0730, and sometimes pick up from hotels. *Transport to town*: travellers arriving at Aur Kuning are sometimes encouraged to take a 'taxi' into town; there are regular oplets plying the route between Aur Kuning and town for a fraction of the price. **Chartered minibus**: for comfort, a minibus to Prapat (for Samosir Island) is an attractive option, 12 hrs (200,000Rp for whole bus). **Taxi**: taxis can be hired, even as far as Medan. Ask at one of the tour offices (see above).

LAKE MANINJAU

Lake Maninjau is one of the most beautiful natural sights in Sumatra, rivalling Lake Toba: it is a huge, flooded volcanic crater with 600m-high walls. Maninjau village lies on the E shore of the lake (see map page 491). The area supports a fair amount of wildlife, and the lake is good for swimming, fishing and waterskiing. There are also hiking trails through the surrounding countryside. Because the lake is some 500m above sea level it is cool even during the day and can be chilly at night. The range of hotels and restaurants has expanded considerably in recent years, and some repeat visitors maintain it has lost at least some of its former charm.

Excursions   From Maninjau village, a worthwhile walk or bicycle ride is around the N edge of the lake to the village of **Muko Muko**, 16 km in all (buses also ply the route). Just before Muko Muko there are the **Alamada Hotsprings** (rather small and insignificant), an excellent fish restaurant, and a hydropower station. The total distance around the lake is about 50 km – 20 km on a good road, 30 km is a dirt track. It is also possible to hike up to, or down from, **Lawang Top** (**Puncak Lawang**), on the crater lip (see page 490 for more details).

For walks above the lake to the lip of the crater (for those who hanker after a view), see the Lake Maninjau entry on page 490.

● **Accommodation**   Hotels and guesthouses are strung out over a kilometre or so along the lake shore running N from Maninjau village. **C** *Maninjau Indah*, Maninjau village, T 61018, F 61257, a/c, pool, 17 rm, relaxing place, excellent for a lengthy stop and vegetate, a lack of upkeep and investment is beginning to show; **B-C** *Pasir Panjang Permai*, 1 km from the village on the lakeside, T 61022, F 61255, restaurant, tennis, 15 rm, hot water, lake views, best of the upmarket places, rec; **F** *Amai Guesthouse*, situated at the S edge of the village, T 61054, Dutch-era mansion with good lake views and some ambience; **F** *Beach Guesthouse*, on the lake, friendly, mountain bikes for hire (4,000Rp), slightly over-priced; **F** *Homestay Pillie*, Jl Hudin Rahmani 91, S of Maninjau village, good food, clean and the most popular of the budget places to stay, ample information available on surrounding area; **F** *Café 44*, 750m N of Maninjau village, down a track towards the lake shore, this is really a restaurant but there are also some lakeside huts, friendly, cheap and clean, dug out canoe and inner tubes for use on the lake, rec. **Bayur**: **E** *Riah Danau* much like the *Bayur Permai* – peaceful, relaxing and friendly; **E-F** *Bayur Permai*, lovely, peaceful place 3 km or so N of Maninjau on the lake, friendly with good food, bemos into and out of Maninjau stop at 1900, but the walk is not far, rec; **F** *Rizal Beach*, beautiful position, only 4 rm.

● **Places to eat**   ♦♦-♦♦♦*Alamada Hotsprings restaurant*, excellent fish; rec; ♦♦*Bobo*, Maninjau village, excellent Indonesian food, rec; *Café 44*, on the lake shore N of Maninjau village, good food and atmosphere, popular (also some accommodation, see above).

● **Banks & money changers**   Bank Rak Yat Indonesia, Jl SMP (a short distance N of the bus stop). Will change US$, TCs and cash.

● **Post & telecommunications   Area code**: 0752. **Post Office**: Jl Muara Pisang (facing the police station and not far from the bus stop). **Telephone Office**: Jl SMP (next to the bus stop). International calls can be made from the office.

● **Transport**   35 km W of Bukittinggi. **Local** Bicycles can be hired from many losmen; they are an excellent way to get around the lake. **Road Bus**: regular buses from Bukittinggi to Maninjau village, negotiating 44 bends down from the crater lip to the lake (1 hr). Two buses/day also run from Muko Muko on the NW side of the lake to Padang (2-3 hrs).

THE RIAU ARCHIPELAGO

Insular Riau – or *Kepulauan Riau* – is made up of more than 3,000 islands, scattered in a belt stretching 700 km from the Sumatran mainland, NE to the Natuna and Anambas islands. A third of the Riau islands are uninhabited and many do not even have names. The other two-thirds have a total population of just over 400,000 and include Batam – which is fast turning into Singapore's industrial backyard – and Bintan, the biggest in the group. Bintan played a pivotal role in Malay history with the founding of the Riau-Johor Empire there in the 16th century. Many of the Riau islands have beautiful deserted beaches, although Batam is a far cry from the palm-fringed paradise it is sold as.

PEOPLE

The Riau islands were first settled in the second millennium BC by proto-Malays who were later displaced by successive streams of Malay migrants. The *Orang Laut* (Sea Gypsies) were among the islands' earliest inhabitants, but the Malays are the ethnic majority in insular Riau, followed by descendants of Bugis seafarers (originally from S Sulawesi, see page 617). There are also many Chinese (mainly in the towns), Bataks (from the Sumatran mainland) and Minangkabaus (from W Sumatra). One Riau island serves as a Vietnamese refugee camp. The islands are predominantly Islamic, but Buddhism and Christianity are also practised. The traditional games of Riau reflect the dominant Malay culture: they include *gasing* (spinning tops), flying kites, and the martial art *pencak silat* (see page 483).

HISTORY

The Riau islands are strategically located on the shortest sea route between China and India at the S end of the Straits of Melaka. From the beginning of the first millennium AD, important seafaring kingdoms grew up in the area, exploiting the islands' location; Riau's rajahs control-led regional trade in gold, silk, spices and porcelain. Bintan was even important enough to merit a visit from Marco Polo in 1202. By the 15th century, with the rise of the Melakan sultanate, the Straits had become the trading crossroads of the Orient. But to the Chinese and Arab traders, insular Riau was one sprawling navigational nightmare. Many boats sank on Riau's reefs and the hundreds of scattered islets made perfect pirates' dens. Today it is possible to wander along beaches and pick up fragments of Ming Dynasty porcelain, which are still being washed ashore from wrecked Chinese junks which sank over 400 years ago.

When the Portuguese took Melaka and forced the sultan to flee S he re-established his kingdom in Johor and when the Portuguese destroyed the Johor capital in 1526, it was uprooted again and moved to Bintan. Throughout the 16th and 17th centuries, the sultanate's capitals alternated between Johor, Bintan and Lingga, to the S. In the 18th century the Buginese, displaced by the Dutch from their homelands in S Sulawesi, arrived in Riau and soon came to dominate the Malay court. The two main centres of power were Penyenget Island (off Bintan) and Lingga Island. Dutch influence increased after the defeat of the Portuguese in Melaka in 1641 and the sultans gradually lost their hold on trade and then their independence.

The Riau-Johor Empire was already disintegrating when the British ousted the Dutch from both Melaka and Riau and in 1812, following a succession crisis prompted by the death of Sultan Mahmud, the kingdom split in two. Mahmud's eldest son, who was recognized by the British, went to Singapore to become the Sultan of Johor. His younger son, supported by the Buginese and the Dutch, became the Sultan of Lingga-Riau. This division of the Riau-Johor Empire was formalized with the signing of the Treaty of London between the Dutch and the British in 1824.

MODERN RIAU

The islands of Batam and Bintan have had their fortunes revived by Singapore's decision to transfer the republic's cumbersome land and labour-intensive industries to Riau. At the same time, both islands are being turned into resort islands catering for the Singapore market. Despite sometimes environmentally savage redevelopment, there are still long stretches of deserted beaches on Bintan. It is also possible to get away to tiny, untouched islands, with good beaches and coral. The Riau islands are a great escape from Singapore – Bintan's beaches and Tanjung Pinang's rickety backstreets could not be a greater contrast to ultra-modern Singapore, just 2 hrs away. They are also a good stepping stone between Singapore and Sumatra.

Best time to visit The monsoon season from Oct-Feb brings an average of 250 mm of rainfall each month. Mar-Sep is drier and the best time to visit the islands.

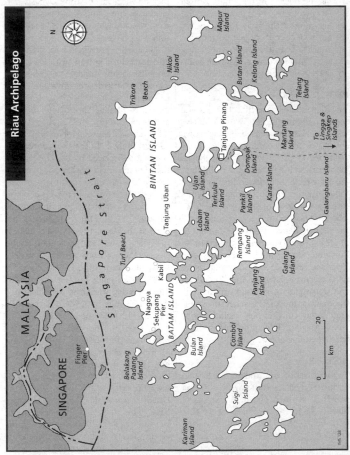

Riau Archipelago

Health warning Malaria is rife in the Riau Archipelago. It is important to take preventative medication (see page 901).

BATAM ISLAND

Batam, at 415 sq km, is 2-thirds the size of its rich N neighbour, Singapore. Today it has a population of 100,000 but is planned to increase 20-fold within a few years. Since Singaporean speculators started venturing across the Strait (see box, page 501) new towns, factory sites and a port have sprung up where a few years ago there was only jungle. Batam is no longer a beautiful island; most tourists pass through quickly, *en route* to Singapore or other islands in the archipelago and Sumatra. But Batam is a popular getaway for Singaporeans, and there are a number of beach resorts, designed for weekenders, which are fairly quiet during the week.

The main town, **Nagoya** (formerly Lubuk Baja) has nothing to offer visitors other than a few hotels, restaurants, shops and banks.

Tours

For an island bereft of sights, there are a remarkable number of travel agencies offering round-the-island tours. One typical itinerary reads: "You will visit a modern Chinese temple in Nagoya, eat a delicious seafood lunch, proceed to Smiling Hill where you can have a panoramic view of the Singapore skyline and Batu Ampar Industrial Estate. You are then at leisure to explore the Duty Free Shop."

Local information
● Accommodation

Top-end beach-side accommodation is over-subscribed and over-priced during weekends – big discounts are on offer during the week. Singaporeans and expatriates comprise the majority of the clientele. **NB** Hotels are priced in Singapore dollars, although rupiah are acceptable.

Nagoya: **A** *Holiday*, Jl Imam Bonjol Blok B, No 1, T 458616, a/c, restaurant, clean, popular with Singaporeans; **A** *Horisona*, Complek Lumbung Rezeki Blok E, T 457111, F 57123, a/c, restaurant, recently refurbished, central, popular

karaoke bar, ticketing service for ferries to Singapore and Tanjung Pinang.

B *Batam Jaya*, Jl Raya Ali Haji, T 458707, F 458057, a/c, restaurant, pool, large, ugly hotel, but well-equipped, disco, massage centre and in-house travel agent.

Around the Island: **A+** *Batam Fantasy Resort*, Tanjung Pinggir, Sekupang, T 22850, a/c, restaurant, pool, well designed (the rooms actually face the sea), good range of sports facilities.

A *Batam Island Country Club*, Tanjung Pinggir, Sekupang, T 22825 (Bookable in Singapore, T 2256819), a/c, restaurant, pool, view over the straits towards Singapore, one of Batam's first hotels on an ugly private beach, duty-free shop, tennis courts and a golf driving range, chalets; **A** *Batam View*, Jl Hang Lekir, Nongsa, T 453740, F 453747, a/c restaurant, pool, luxurious, but characterless, on a hill overlooking a featureless beach (with no waves), full range of facilities including a golf driving range, quiet during the week; **A** *Hill Top*, Jl Ir. Sutami 8, Sekupang, T 22391, F 22211, a/c, restaurant, pool, 5 mins from the ferry terminal, recently upgraded; **A** *Turi Beach Resort*, Nongsa, T 321543 (bookable in Singapore, T 7322577, F 7333740), a/c, restaurant, pool, well-equipped rooms, full range of facilities (including golf course), timber-built traditional-style chalets and the best beach on Batam, rec; **A** *Wisma Persero Batam*, Jl Kuda Laut, Batu Ampar, T 58281, a/c, restaurant, pool, full range of facilities, pleasant garden.

D *Setia Budi Chalets*, Nongsa Beach (between *Batam View Beach Resort* and *Turi Beach Resort*), restaurant (see below), simple beachside chalet accommodation – one of the very few places catering for budget travellers, organizes excursions to islands and fishing trips.

● Places to eat

The Riau seafood speciality is the *gong-gong* shellfish, which lives in a twisting, tapered shell, is served with a sweet chilli sauce and which is said by locals to have aphrodisiacal properties. Riau is also known for its *ikan bilis*, or anchovies.

Nagoya: ♦♦*Pagi Sore*, Block B, Jl Imam Bonjol, 2, Padang food, rec; ♦♦*Palapa*, Pulat Perbelanjaan, Blok 1, Komplek Bumi Indah, No 8, upmarket coffee shop, Muslim food; ♦♦*Tunas Baru*, 3rd Flr, Blok E (blue block), Jl Nagoya 42, seafood, the oldest established restaurant in town.

Around the island: ♦♦*Rejeki*, Pantai Batu Besar, nr Nongsa, *klong*-style jetty with open-sided dining areas, seafood, chilli crabs and deep-fried crispy sotong, particularly pleasant at high tide, muddy at low tide, rec; ♦♦*Setia Budi Seafood*, Nongsa Beach, fresh seafood in pleasant open-sided restaurant overlooking the beach; *Batam Punggur*, Pantai Telaga Punggur (4 km from Kabil), another *klong*-style seafood restaurant which is also not at its best at low tide, its seafood is said to be the best on the island.

Foodstalls: *Batama Food Centre*, Blok C, Nagoya; *Shangri-La Food Centre*, 2 km from Sekupang on road to Nagoya, good selection of Malay/Indonesian and Chinese stalls.

● **Airline offices**
Garuda, 2nd Flr, Persero Bldg, Jl Kuda Laut, Batu Ampar, T 458864; **Merpati**, Pertokoan Pribumi, Jl Teuku Umar 6, Batu Ampar, T 58963.

● **Banks & money changers**
Nagoya: Bank Bumi Daya, Bank Dagang Negara, Bank Rakyat Indonesia, Bank Duta and Bank Lippo. There are money-changing

facilities at Sekupang ferry terminal, in Nagoya and at major hotels. Singapore currency is widely used.

● **Entertainment**
Karaoke is popular, mainly for the benefit of visiting Singaporeans. Almost every big hotel has a disco. *Studio 21*, in Nagoya, is a cinema complex (four theatres) with the latest Hollywood releases.

● **Post & telecommunications**
Area code: 0778.

● **Shopping**
Handicrafts/batik: *Aloha Souvenirs*, 1 Blok B, Jl Imam Bonjol, Nagoya; *Batik Danar Hadi Solo*, Pusat Pembelanjaan, Sekupang; *Duty-free shop*, Sikupang ferry terminal; *House of Batam Fiesta*, 12 Blok H, Jl Sultan Abdulrachman, Nagoya; *Utami Souvenir and Batik Shop*, Sekupang ferry terminal.

Duty-free goods are also available from hotel shops around the island.

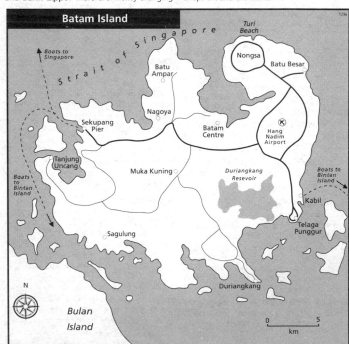

Batam Island
Turi Beach
Boats to Singapore
Strait of Singapore
Nongsa
Batu Besar
Batu Ampar
Nagoya
Sekupang Pier
Batam Centre
Hang Nadim Airport
Tanjung Uncang
Boats to Bintan Island
Muka Kuning
Duriangkang Resevoir
Boats to Bintan Island
Kabil
Sagulung
Telaga Punggur
N
Duriangkang
Bulan Island
0   5
km

Batam – Singapore's industrial zone and holiday playground

🐛 Until 1990, most Singaporeans had only heard of Batam because of Radio ZOO, a rock music station operating from Riau. Now it has become their latest holiday playground. Batam is also the buzzword on the lips of Singapore industrialists and the pace of developments on the island in the early 1990s has had transnational investors scrambling for their atlases. In the course of a few months, Singapore's private sector achieved more than Batam's inert bureaucracy managed to achieve in decades.

The surge of speculative money that flooded into Batam in the early 1990s was spearheaded by the huge Batam Industrial Park, a Singapore-Indonesian joint venture. BIP provides foreign investors with the industrial equivalent of a package tour. The park's management takes care of everything, from immigration clearance to the supply of cheap labour – at wage-rates four times cheaper than in Singapore. Foreign companies using Batam as an export base can even retain 100% ownership for 5 years – something they are not allowed to do anywhere else in Indonesia.

On a clear day in Batam, Singapore's skyscrapers shimmer on the horizon, 20 km to the NW across the Strait of Singapore. The tourist literature, which is designed with the lucrative Singapore market in mind, describes Batam as "a microcosm of Indonesia's rich cultural heritage" – in reality you learn a lot more about Singapore and Singaporeans on Batam than you learn about Indonesians.

When the Singapore government joined hands with Jakarta and the state government of Johor (Malaysia's southernmost state) to form the so-called 'Growth Triangle', the Singapore press called it a 'vision of mutual gain'. While Batam and Johor get investors' dollars and development, the claustrophobic island republic gets a hinterland with cheap land and labour. By the time Indonesia has shipped in workers from over-populated Java and pumped water across from nearby Bintan Island, Singapore will have 2-million workers on its doorstep, living in model industrial towns in a duty-free export processing zone. Batam will also be plugging directly into Singapore's power network and telecommunications system. In short, the island is becoming the ultimate insurance policy for Singapore's future industrial growth.

● **Sport**

Golf: Turi Golf Club at Nongsa has 18-hole and 9-hole courses.

● **Tour companies & travel agents**

Hanita Wisatama, Sekupang ferry terminal, T 321429, reservations and ticketing; *Natrabu*, Batam Jaya Hotel, Jl Raja Ali Haji, Nagoya, T 58787; *Persero Baram*, Wisma Persero Batam, Jl Kuda Laut, Batu Ampar, T 58281; *Pinang Jaya*, 14 Blok H, Jl Sultan Abdulrachman, Nagoya, T 458585; ticketing and tours around Riau islands; *Turi Citramas Wistata*, Turi Beach Resort, Nongsa, T 321323.

● **Tourist offices**

Tourist Information Centre at Sekupang ferry terminal.

● **Transport**

Local **Car hire**: Turi Travel, *Turi Beach Resort*, T 21543, big range of vehicles for hire incl limousines, jeeps and even Austin Princess London taxis, from S$12.50/hr. **Pinang Jaya**, 14 Block H, Jl Sultan Abdurachman, Nagoya, T 58585, self-drive from S$12.50/hr. **Taxis**: from Sekupang port around the island. Taxis can be chartered for about 15,000Rp/hr.

Air Hang Nadim Airport is on the E side of the island. Regular connections on Garuda/Merpati with Medan, Pekanbaru, Padang, Palembang, Banda Aceh, Bandung, Pontianak and Jakarta.

Sea Regular connections with Bintan Island from Sekupang, the main port on the NW of the island, and from Kabil, on the E side of the island. There are regular boats from Sekupang to Bintan (19,000Rp) and regular speedboat services (and fishing boats) from Kabil to Bintan 30-75 mins (8,800-12,500Rp). (For those travelling between Bintan and Singapore, there is a direct service, bypassing Batam, see page 507). It is also possible to catch boats to Pekanbaru from Sekupang, several hundred kilometres up the Siak River in Sumatra. Boats leave at 0830, before the banks open, although S$ are accepted. Buses to Bukittinggi meet the boat for onward connections (see page 511 for more details on the journey). A much faster, although perhaps less interesting option is to take one of the express boats to Tanjung Buton/Selat Panjang, on the coast of the Sumatran 'mainland'. (The 0930 departure is probably the most convenient.) The journey, with stop-offs at various seedy-looking ports, takes just 4 hrs and at Tanjung Buton/Selat Panjang travellers either have the choice to take a bus onward to Pekanbaru (another 3 hrs) or a speedboat up the Siak River. **International connections**: a/c high-speed passenger ferries run between Sekupang and Singapore's Finger Pier 30 mins (S$20) and there is a twice-daily service to Johor. Services run in daylight hours. Regular connections with Singapore; contact Singapore shipping companies for schedules: *Dino*, T 2214916; *Yang Passenger Ferry Service*, T 2239902; *Inasco Enterprises*, T 2240698; *Sinba Shipping*, T 2240901; *Indo-Falcon Shipping*, T 2203251.

BINTAN ISLAND

Bintan Island is about $2\frac{1}{2}$ times the size of Singapore and was the capital of the Malay sultanate of Riau-Johor in the 16th century. Little remains of the old sultanate except a few disappointing relics on Penyenget Island, just offshore from Bintan's capital, Tanjung Pinang.

The focus for the majority of visitors now lies on the northern shore of Bintan. The *Bintan Beach International Resort*, a Singaporean company, has leased the entire N shore, and development is under way, creating several hotels, sports facilities, restaurants etc. A 'wildlife sanctuary' and an 'agro-tech park' are being created, as is a marina and other 'leisure facilities', but it is all in the formative stages. Bintan Resort Management have been at pains to create a sound infrastructure; a reservoir was created, and the water is drinkable, the roads are excellent and the electricity supply reliable.

Tanjung Pinang

The seaward side of insular Riau's capital is built out on stilts over what, at low tide, is a rat and mosquito-infested mudflat. But above the mud, the narrow piers – or *pelantar* – teem with life and have a maze of alleyways leading off on each side to residential pile houses. The older part of town is found around the piers; this is the interesting area to explore. The night's catch is carried down the old pier (Pejantan II) to the **fish market** on Jl Pasar Ikan every morning. There are stalls and coffee shops lining the piers, which are good places to sit and watch life go by; there is a hectic bazaar at the town end of the piers.

The **pasar malam** (night market) around *Hotel Tanjung Pinang* on Jl Pos is also a lively spot in the early evening.

Excursions

Sungei Ular (Snake River) is on the other side of the harbour from Tanjung Pinang. The narrow river winds its way through mangroves to *Jodoh Temple* – the oldest Chinese temple in Riau, built as a refuge by Buddhist monks in the late 18th century. Murals on the walls depict unpleasant visions of hell. *Senggarang* is the old Bugis stilt village Tanjung Pinang's *kampung ayer* – which today is predominantly Chinese. *Bayan Island*, in the middle of the harbour, has been earmarked for an ambitious marina and hotel project. *Getting there*: boats leave from the end of either jetty.

Penyenget Island – covering only $2\frac{1}{2}$ sq km – is just offshore, facing Tanjung Pinang. Once the centre of the Riau-Johor sultanate, the island is littered with relics, most of them in the NW corner. The island can be walked around in 1-2 hrs. From the jetty, turn right and the road runs past most of the sights of interest. The unusual and beautifully kept yellow mosque, the *Mesjid Raya Sultan Riau* – which houses a library of antique Islamic texts – was built in 1818, and is said to be cemented together with egg-white mortar. There are a few ruins of an old fort,

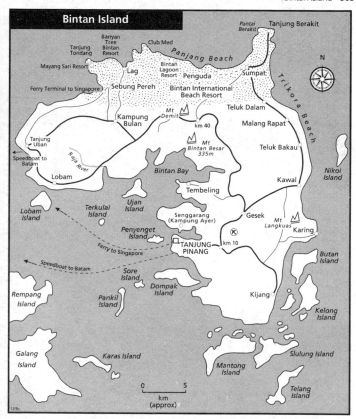

Bintan Island

(map labels:)

Pantai Berakit
Tanjung Berakit
Banyan Tree Bintan Resort
Tanjung Tondang
Club Med
Panjang Beach
Mayang Sari Resort
Lag
Bintan Lagoon Resort
Penguda
Sumpat
N
Ferry Terminal to Singapore
Sebung Pereh
Bintan International Beach Resort
Teluk Dalam
Trikora Beach
Kampung Bulan
Mt Demit
km 40
Malang Rapat
Tanjung Uban
Mt Bintan Besar 335m
Teluk Bakau
Speedboat to Batam
Raja River
Bintan Bay
Kawal
Nikoi Island
Lobam
Tembeling
Terkulai Island
Ujan Island
Senggarang (Kampung Ayer)
Gesek
Mt Langkuas
Karing
Lobam Island
Penyenget Island
TANJUNG PINANG
km 10
Butan Island
Ferry to Singapore
Sore Island
Speedboat to Batam
Dompak Island
Kijang
Rempang Island
Pankil Island
Kelong Island
Galang Island
Karas Island
Mantong Island
Slulung Island
Telang Island

0   5
km
(approx)

and further round is the ruined *Kerjaan Melayu Palace*, also built at the beginning of the 19th century in a blend of Javanese and Dutch styles, but abandoned in the early 1900s. In the centre of the island, on the way back to the jetty, are the *tombs of Rajah Ali Jaji*, who wrote the first Malay grammar and compiled a dictionary (classical Malay is still spoken on Penyenget), and Engku Peteri Permaisuri, a Bugis princess who received the island of Penyenget as her dowry from Sultan Mahmud. She ruled until her death in 1844. The descendants of the Riau-Johor royal family still live in pile houses on the S side of the island; most are fishermen. *Getting there*: regular sampans to the island leave from the end of the old pier (Pejantan II) (500Rp).

The **Riau Kandil Museum** is 2 km E of town on Jl Bakarbatu. The museum contains an eccentric but impressive array of historical artefacts – ceramics, manuscripts, *kris*, and guns. Nothing is catalogued, and the curator's explanations are delightfully confusing. Open on demand. *Getting there*: ojek (300Rp).

The **Regional Houses of Parliament** are in a traditional Riau-style house (*rumah lipat kijang*) at Batu Lima (5th Mile).

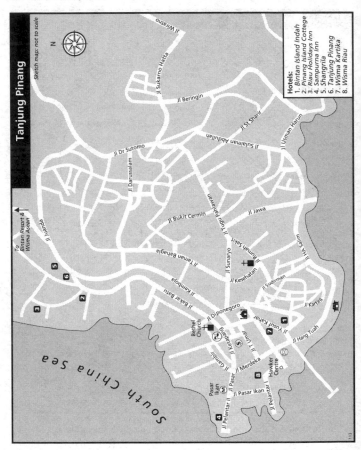

Tanjung Pinang

Sketch map: not to scale

Hotels:
1. Bintan Island Indah
2. Pinang Island Cottege
3. Riau Holidays Inn
4. Sampurna Inn
5. Shangrila
6. Tanjung Pinang
7. Wisma Kartika
8. Wisma Riau

South China Sea

To Bintan Resort & Wisma Asean

It is decorated with symbolic carvings of flowers (prosperity), bees (mutual understanding) and various other emblems.

Trikora Beach is a long stretch of palm-fringed beach, 45 km NE of town on the quiet E side of the island. The beach is safe for swimming and the water is clear, although most of the coral on the nearby reefs is dead. The road to Trikora passes through the picturesque fishing kampung of *Teluk Kawal*. Offshore are Mapor, Nikoi and Merapas, islands which can be reached by hired boat (either from the kampung or from the resort). The beach itself is a little way off the road. The road, which follows the beach, leads N to **Tanjung Berakit**, where there are more good beaches. *Getting there*: the best way to explore the beach is to hire a motorbike in town (see Local transport). Taxi 2,500Rp pp; mini-buses can be chartered for 60,000Rp/day. Yasin (see Accommodation) leaves the *pasar malam* in Tanjung Pinang for Trikora every morning at 1100 (4,000Rp). **Accommodation B** *Trikora Country Club*, Km 37 Teluk Bakau,

F 24456 (bookable in Singapore, T 2216421, private transport to Trikora can be arranged through *Wisma Kartika*, Tanjung Pinang), a/c, restaurant, pool, pleasant, low-key resort on a steep hill overlooking the sea, with private beach and shady coconut palms, tennis court and boat for snorkeling expeditions, best value resort in Riau, but prices go up on the weekends, rec; **E** *Yasin Guesthouse*, all food incl, beach-side Kampung-style chalets, very friendly on a pleasant stretch of beach, seasonally invaded by sandflies – from Jul-Oct, there is a sea breeze which keeps them away, rec; **C** *Riau Beach Resort*, Teluk Bakau, 175 atap-roofed chalets. **Places to eat** ♦♦*Rumah Makan Pantai Trikora*, Km 39, Jl Teluk Bakau, fresh seafood on a genuine bamboo fishing klong, a little further out from the *Country Club*, rec. On Sun there are stalls selling sate and grilled fish along one stretch of beach.

Panjang Beach is on the N coast. There is some reasonably good coral offshore. This area is now known as the **Bintan Beach International Resort** – see local information for facilities available.

Mount Bintan Besar is Bintan's highest (335m) peak and can be climbed in about 3 hrs. From the top there are good views over Bintan and the surrounding islands of the archipelago. *Getting there*: it is not easy to reach Kampung Sekuning at the foot of the hill. It is 60 km from town and buses do not go directly to the village. Take an ojek from town (see Local transport, below).

Other islands Tanjung Pinang can be used as the jumping-off point for visits to other islands in the archipelago, although there are no regular boat services. They include **Singkep Island**. The capital is Dabo, on the SE coast which is mildly interesting for its markets. Out of town are some lovely white sand beaches. **Accommodation E** *Wisma Sri Indah*, Jl Perusahaan, clean; **E** *Wisma Gapura Singkep*, Jl Perusahaan. Good foodstalls around town and in the market. Post Office and telephone office available (out of town) towards Sunggai Buluh), bank on Jl Penuba, with good rates. *Getting there*: SMAC fly to Singkep. Daily ferries to Daik on Lingga Island and to Tanjung Pinang, irregular ferries to Jambi (Sumatra). **Penuba Island** is a tiny island between Lingga and Singkep, with some beautiful beaches both at Tanjung Dua, on the N coast and Penuba on the S. Basic accommodation (**F**) in Penuba near the mosque. **Lingga Island** was home of the last Riau sultanate. Some ruins of the old palace remain, some distance from Daik, the main town and ferry port. A guide is needed to find these ruins in the jungle. Other points of interest on Lingga are a cemetery, a mosque and Gunung Daik, some of which it is possible to climb. **Accommodation F**, near the ferry. *Getting there*: regular ferries from Dabo, on Singkep Island and some connections with Tanjung Pinang. Ask at the tourist information kiosk at the harbour or at *Infotravel* (on Jl Samudra) about boats. The nearest deserted islands from Bintan are **Terkulai Island** (W of Tanjung Pinang; 20 mins by speedboat) and **Sore Island** (SW of Tanjung Pinang; 20 mins by speedboat). Both have good beaches and, like Penyenget, are littered with shards of Ming Dynasty porcelain.

Festivals

5th month of the lunar calendar: *Bak Chang* (Meat Dumpling Festival) (movable) celebrated with dragon boat races between different Hakka Chinese clans around Tanjung Pinang.

Local information
● **Accommodation**

Cheapest homestays in Tanjung Pinang are concentrated in the alleyways enclosed by Jl Merdeka, Jl Samudra and Jl Yusup Kahar. On arrival at the harbour, expect to be bombarded with suggestions about where to stay.

L *Banyan Tree Bintan*, the most exclusive of the new resorts, 40 individual villas with their own jacuzzi and swimming pools; **L** *Bintan Lagoon*, Bintan Resort, Panjang Beach, part of Sedona chain, T (Singapore) 339-1368, F 339-

1551, 400 rm and no-expense-spared facilities, inc 11 restaurants and excellent sports facilities.

A-B *Mayang Sari Beach Resort*, Bintan Resort, Tanjung Tondang, T (Singapore) 339-1368, F 339-1551, 56 chalets, with another 140 under construction, in a coconut grove, restaurant, good location for proximity to watersports centre and seafood restaurant; **A** *Sampurna Inn* (formerly *Sampurna Jaya International*), Jl Yusuf Kahar 15, T 21555, F 21269, a/c, restaurant, biggest and supposedly smartest – hotel in Tanjung Pinang, 3-star facilities (incl 'the mini beautifully garden for your relaxes').

B *Bintan Island Indah*, Jl Bakar Batu 22, T 21946, F 23616, a/c, restaurant, almost new next door to *Sri Santai Seafood*, very clean and new – the best value in town; **B** *Pinang Island Cottages*, 133 Komplek Rimba Jaya, T 21307, F 22888, a/c, restaurant, pleasant newish complex on the outskirts of town; **B** *Riau Holiday Inn*, Jl Pelantar II 53, T 22644, F 21394, a/c, restaurant (bookable in Singapore, T 7375735, F 7330163), organizes marine sports (incl waterskiing, *Apocalypse Now*-style, through the mangroves up Snake River) and trips around the island, built out on stilts off Jl Pelantar II (the old pier), beer garden, interesting location, attracts big tour groups from Singapore; **B** *Shangri La Hotel and Island Resort*, Jl Gudang Minyak, T 22202 (bookable in Singapore, T 2925889, F 2983978), a/c, restaurant, good location on the seaward side of town, in-house videos in all rooms, breakfast incl; **B** *Wisma Asean*, Jl Gudang Minyak, T 22161, F 21162, breakfast incl and big discounts during the week; **B** *Wisma Kartika*, 3.5 Km Jl MT Haryono, T 22446, a/c, restaurant, sister hotel to the *Trikora Country Club* (above), pleasant, well managed; **B** *Wisma Riau*, Jl Yusuf Merdeka 8, T 21023, a/c, restaurant, reasonable hotel opp *Sampurna Inn*, on the hill, sometimes smells a bit like a hospital, expect to be woken for prayer regularly – the town mosque is on the opp corner, breakfast incl.

C *Tanjung Pinang*, Jl Pos 692, T 21236, F 21379, a/c, all rooms have attached bathrooms, reasonable value for money, central location, next to the Kabil pier.

D *Surya*, Jl Bintan, T 21811, a/c, restaurant, clean, good coffee house attached.

F *Bong's Homestay*, Lorong Bintan II 20 (behind Jl Merdeka), cheap and friendly, very similar to *Johnny's*, next door, dormitory or rooms; **F** *Jaafar's Guesthouse*, Lorong Bintan II, nr *Bong's*, similar set-up; **F** *Johnny's Guesthouse*,

Lorong Bintan II 22 (behind Jl Merdeka), probably the most popular of the budget places, clean and friendly, breakfast incl; popular getaway for Singaporeans, mountain bike hire.

● **Places to eat**
Food is neither cheap nor particularly good in Tanjung Pinang, nor is it that good. There are a few Chinese coffee shops where the coffee is wonderful, but the food very average. ♦♦♦*Panorama Kelong Seafood Restaurant*, on western point of Bintan Resort, it sits on stilts, with seating for 100, some a/c available; ♦♦*Teluk Keriting Seafood Centre*, Jl Usman Harun 16. (*Getting there*: ojek from Jl Merdeka, 400Rp.) rec.

Foodstalls: *Pasar Malam*, around the *Tanjung Pinang Hotel*, has a number of stalls in the evening selling seafood (mud crabs, *sotong* (squid), prawns etc.) and satay. Also on sale: *gong-gong* – Riau's aphrodisiacal shellfish. Night stalls at the bus station compound off Jl Teuku Umar; during the day there are pavement cafés next to the market on the corner of Jl Teuku Umar and Jl Terat I.

● **Airline offices**
Sempati, Jl Bintan 9, T 21612; SMAC, Jl A Yani, 5 km out of town, T 22798.

● **Banks & money changers**
Bank Dagang Negara, Jl Teuku Umar, next to the bus station; Bank Rakyat Indonesia, Jl Teuku Umar, on the other side of the bus station. Money changers on Jl Merdeka, where some shops also change money.

● **Post & telecommunications**
General Post Office: Jl Hang Tuah (extension of Jl Merdeka).

● **Shopping**
Handicrafts: *Lasmin Art Shop*, Jl Tugu Pahlawan 12, Kampung Kolam; *Toko Batik Gloria*, Jl Temiang; *Batik Prima*, Jl Mawar. There are souvenir shops in the market area next to the cinema (and indoor stadium) on the corner of Jl Teuku Umar and Jl Terat I.

There is also a souvenir shop opp the travel agents on Jl Samudra, next to the harbour.

● **Sports**
The new *Bintan Resort* provides a great range of sport. The *Mana Mana Beach Club*, on the NW point is a **watersports** centre. Several 18-hole **golf** courses are under construction.

● **Tour companies & travel agents**
Bintan Panorama, 50A Jl Bakar Batu, T 21894,

F 22572, services *Bintan Island Resort*; water-sports and fishing; *Infotravel*, Jl Samudra 12, next to the harbour-master's office, between the jetty and Jl Merdeka, mainly a ticketing agency, schedules for ferries to Java/Sumatra and advice on how to get to other islands; *Toko New Oriental*, Jl Merdeka 61, T 21614, ferry tickets to Batam and Singapore; *Netra Service* (Jaya Travel Bureau) Jl Samudra 8, T 21882; *Pinang Jaya*, Jl Bintan 44, T 21267; *Zura Abadi Travel Bureau*, Jl Samudra 6.

● **Tourist offices**
Tourist Information Office on the main jetty, next to the immigration point.

● **Useful addresses**
Immigration Office: ferry jetty.

● **Transport**
Local The bus station is on Jl Teuku Umar. **Taxis**: Bintan's taxis were on the vintage, with 1950s Fords and Chevrolets and a number of ex-NTUC Singapore taxis. They can be chartered for around 40,000Rp/day. **Ojek**: the easiest way to get around is by ojek (public motorcycle), 200Rp around town. Motorbike hire: check at hotels, or rent an ojek (without the driver) along Jl Merdeka for 20,000-25,000Rp/day.

Air Kijang airport is 15 km SE of Tanjung Pinang. Regular connections on Sempati with Jakarta and Pekanbaru and on SMAC with Batam, Dabo (Singkep Island), Bangka Island, Jambi and Pekanbaru. *Transport to town*: by bus (800Rp) by taxi (1,500Rp).

Sea Boat: an efficient Catamaran service now runs between the Tanah Merah Ferry Terminal in Singapore and Bandar Bentan Telani Terminal at Bintan Resort, 3 a day, 45 mins, S$54 adults, S$32 children, T (Singapore) 345 1210. The Pelni vessel *Awu* calls here on its fortnightly circuit between Java, Sumatra and Kalimantan (see route schedule, page 921). **Speedboats**: to Kabil (Batam) leave hourly (0800-1700) from the jetty off Jl Pos/Pasar Ikan next to the *Tanjung Pinang Hotel* (8,000-10,000Rp). There are many ticket agents along the pier. There are daily boats from Tanjung Pinang to Pekanbaru (15,000-20,000Rp). The trip can take 2 days, with long stops at island ports along the way. Passengers are advised to take food (see page 511). There are less regular connections with Jakarta and Dumai (Sumatra) (fortnightly), Medan and Jambi, Pontianak and many other destinations elsewhere in Indonesia. Schedules from Pelni office, or from the various shipping agencies to be found near the entrance to the main pier.

THE RIAU ISLANDS TO PEKANBARU AND BUKITTINGGI

An alternative route into Sumatra is by ship from the Riau Islands, up the Siak River, to the wealthy oil town of Pekanbaru, 160 km from the coast. From Pekanbaru, a road runs W through the humid and swampy Riau lowlands to the foot of the Bukit Barisan. About 70 km from Pekanbaru the road passes the turn-off for the Srivijayan ruins at Muara Takus, before beginning the climb upwards, passing through Payakumbuh before reaching the popular hill resort of Bukittinggi, a total of 174 km from Pekanbaru.

PEKANBARU

Pekanbaru is the regional capital of Riau province, and was founded in 1784. Located on the Siak River, 160 km from the coast, it is the administrative centre of the oil industry in the area. Oil was discovered just prior to WW2, although the Japanese were the first to exploit the resource (see box). Over 85% of Riau province's GDP is generated by petroleum and natural gas production, an industry which is dominated by Caltex Pacific Indonesia Company (CPI). CPI has helped to build the Riau University, sports facilities, 52 schools, the Pekanbaru airport and roads to Dumai and Duri.

Much of the area surrounding Pekanbaru remains a wilderness of forest and swamp. Although criss-crossed by pipelines and dotted with oil rigs, the activity of oil exploration and production has not, seemingly, adversely affected the wildlife. Indeed, the companies are so worried about the effects that roads might have on access to the forest by spontaneous settlers that they helicopter in the equipment, creating an isolated island of activity in the jungle. This is one of the few areas with reasonable numbers of Sumatran rhinoceros, tigers and other rare Sumatran animals. More of a threat than the oil industry is the settlement of transmigrants (see page 427). During the government's third 5 year plan (1980-1984), over 100,000 transmigrants arrived on settlements in Riau province.

Riau exhibits many of the features of a 'dual' economy: on the one hand there is the high technology, capital intensive oil sector; and on the other traditional, low technology, agriculture. The two seldom interact, and animist tribes such as the Sakai and Kubu (perhaps 10,000 individuals) have only marginally benefited from all the wealth that has been generated.

Places of interest

Pekanbaru is a featureless town with little charm or colour. Well-maintained and wide streets, impressive government buildings and opulent commercial offices bear testimony to the wealth generated by the oil industry. Few tourists visit here except in transit. Boats arrive and depart from the river dock for the Riau archipelago, an alternative route into or out of Sumatra from Singapore.

Although there are a number of worthwhile excursions from Pekanbaru, sights in the city itself are few and far between. The **Mesjid An Nur**

Excursions

Muara Takus is an archaeological site $2\frac{1}{2}$ km outside a village of the same name and about 80 km W of Pekanbaru. These Buddhist Srivijayan ruins, were probably built between the 9th and 11th centuries. Four buildings have been uncovered: *Candi Tua, Candi Bungsu, Candi Pelangka* and the *Mahligai Stupa. Getting there*: the ruins are off the inter-provincial bus routes and can only be reached easily by taxi, private car, or on a tour (US$40 pp, see below).

Siak Sri Indrapura is an historic town downstream on the Siak River, 125 km by road NE of Pekanbaru. The sultanate of Siak Sri Indrapura was founded in 1723 and there have been 12 sultans, the last surrendering his position in 1949. The stark white, gothic-style *Asseriyah Hasyimlah Palace* was built in 1889 and contains various pieces of royal regalia. Also notable is the *Royal Graveyard* (Makam Kota Tinggi) and the *Mesjid Raya*. There

Pekanbaru

To Siak, Duri & Dumai

To Siak Sri Indrapura

Siak River

Mesjid An Nur

Jl Juanda   Jl S Budi

Jl Riau

Jl S S Qasyim

Jl Dr Sutomo

Jl T Umar

Jl Gatot Subroto

Jl Melati

Jl Teratai

Jl Jend A Yani

Jl Sisingamangaraja

Jl H Tuah

Jl Jend Sudirman

Jl Diponegoro

N

Jl Warsito

Jl Pepaya

Jl Pattimura

Jl Pelalar

To Bukittinggi & Muaro Takus

Jl Nangka

0   250
metres

To Airport & Museum

Hotels:
1. Anom
2. Indrapura
3. Linda
4. Mutiara Panghegar
5. Riau
6. Sri Indrayani
7. Tommy's Guesthouse

Places to eat:
8. New Holland Bakery

is basic accommodation at the **E** *Peninga-pan Harmonis*, although the town is easily visited on a day trip. *Getting there*: by regular minibus from Pekanbaru's Pasar Lima Puluh terminal at the N end of Jl Sultan S Hasyim 2½ hrs, or charter a taxi, take a tour (US$40), go by speedboat down the river 2 hrs, or take a ferry.

The **Sabanga Elephant Training Camp** is 135 km from Pekanbaru, 19 km from Duri. *Getting there*: by charter taxi or on a tour; buses go to Duri from the Loket terminal on Jl Nangka.

A **boat trip along the Siak River to the Riau Islands** might be viewed as an (over-night) excursion – it certainly can be an adventure. The number of logs being floated down the river makes it clear that considerable deforestation is occurring – with or without official consent. There are also a number of settlements along the route, established by pioneer agricultu-ralists who have used the river as an artery of access and have cut small plots out of the forest for cultivation (see Transport to and from Pekanbaru for further details).

Tours

Local companies offer day tours around the 'sights' of the city (US$15), to Siak Sri Indrapura (US$40), Muara Takus

---

Black gold: Indonesia's oil industry

Indonesia is the only Asian member of the Organization of Petroleum Exporting Countries (OPEC), and production averages about 0.5 billion barrels/year. In the peak years of the early 1980s when oil prices were over US$35/barrel, exports of oil and gas were generating US$20bn/year in foreign exchange earnings.

Acehnese chronicles of the 17th century record that oil naturally bubbled to the surface at Perlak in N Sumatra. People at the time saw this as evidence of God's special blessing on the area. James Bontius, a scientist and one of the first Europeans to write about the diseases of the East Indies in 1629, thought oil to be an excellent cure for *beri beri* and was appalled that it should be wasted as lighting oil. But the commercial exploitation of oil had to wait another 250 years until 1871, when the first well was sunk in N Sumatra. By the outbreak of WW2, production was 55 million barrels/year.

Indonesia's breakthrough into the big league of producers came with the discovery of the huge Central Sumatran Minas field by Caltex just before WW2. Oilmen say that the initial productive well (now a tourist sight) was drilled by a Japanese army corporal. Between 1938 and 1969, production of oil rose five-fold, doubling again between 1969 and 1977. More importantly, the value of exports rose by a factor of nearly 45 between 1969 and 1981 – from US$0.4bn to US$18.2bn.

Some of the revenue generated by the oil boom was pumped back into the economy. After the first oil price rise of 1973, teachers' pay was quadrupled and civil servants' salaries doubled. More important in the longer term, over 6,000 schools were built each year, roads were extended into the more remote areas of the country, and fertilizer prices were subsidized, allowing Javanese farmers to become self-sufficient in rice production. But large sums were also lost through increased corruption and investment in what some economists view as prestige 'white elephants' such as the Krakatau steel works (see page 139) and the aircraft manufacturer, IPTN (page 157).

Despite the expansion of oil and gas production and exploration to other parts of Indonesia, Sumatra – and particularly Riau province – remains the biggest producer, yielding over 60% of total output. The problem for the Indonesian government is that with prices weak and exports declining in volume as domestic needs increase, it is unlikely that oil will ever play such a significant role again.

(US$40) and to the elephant training camp at Sabanga (US$40). See Excursions for background and Travel agents (below) for addresses.

Local information
● Accommodation
A-B *Indrapura*, Jl Dr Sutomo 86, T 36233, F 56337, a/c, good restaurant, pool; **A-B** *Mutiara Panghegar*, Jl Yos Sudarso 12A, T 32526, F 23380, a/c, good restaurant, pool, tennis, best hotel in Pekanbaru, professionally managed with well appointed rooms, nr the Siak River and slightly out of town; **A-B** *Sri Indrayani*, Jl Dr Sam Ratulangi 2, T 31870, F 21509, a/c, tennis.

B *Tasia Ratu*, Jl K H Hasyim Ashari 10 (off Jl Jend Sudirman), T 33225, F 25912, a/c, central, average rooms for the price.

C *Badarussamsi*, Jl Sisingamangaraja 175, T 22475, a/c, restaurant; **C** *Riau*, Jl Diponegoro 34, T 22986, restaurant; **C-D** *Anom*, Jl Gatot Subroto 3, T 22636, a/c, restaurant, popular with Chinese visitors, central, good value; **C-D** *Yani*, Jl Pepaya 17 (nr bus station), T 23647, some a/c, price incl breakfast, private mandi, pleasant atmosphere; **C-E** *Linda*, Jl Nangka 133 (opp bus station), T 22375, some a/c, cheaper upstairs rooms are clean, convenient for buses, rec.

F *Tommy's*, Gang Nantongga, nr bus station, small and rather cramped but cheap.

● Places to eat
The cheap restaurants and foodstalls are on Jl Jend Sudirman, nr the central market, and along the market's inner streets.

Bakeries: *Big M*, Jl Jend Sudirman 143; *New Holland*, Jl Jend Sudirman 155.

Indonesian: ✦✦✦*Indrapura Hotel*, Jl Dr Sutomo, good hotel restaurant serving Indonesian, Chinese and international dishes; ✦✦✦*Mutiara Panghegar*, Jl Yos. Sudarso 12A, some locals maintain this hotel restaurant is the best in town, also serves International and Chinese food; ✦✦*Sari Bunda 88*, Jl Gatot Subroto, Padang food; ✦*Mitra Sari*, Jl Sisingamangaraja, tasty Padang food.

International food: ✦✦*Kota Piring*, Jl Sisingamangaraja, some cheaper Indonesian food; ✦✦*Ky-Ky*, Jl Jend Sudirman, steaks and Indonesian food.

Other Asian cuisines: ✦✦*Gelas Mas*, Jl H Sulaiman, Chinese and International; ✦✦*Jumbo*, Jl Juanda. Chinese, particularly good seafood; ✦✦*Medan*, Jl Juanda, large menu of Szechuan, Mandarin and International food, rec.

● Airline offices
Sempati, *Hotel Mutiara*, Jl Yos Sudarso 12A, T 21612; **SMAC**, Jl Sudirman 25, T 23922; Garuda/Merpati, Jl Jend Sudirman 343, T 21575.

● Banks & money changers
Bank Bumi Daya, Jl Jend Sudirman. Bank Central Asia, Jl Jend Sudirman; Ekspor Impor, Jl Jend A Yani.

● Entertainment
Cinema: Dewi Santika, Jl Jend Sudirman 306, a/c, modern, comfortable.

● Hospitals & medical services
General Hospital: Jl Diponegoro 2.

● Post & telecommunications
Area code: 0761.

General Post Office: Jl Jend Sudirman 229.

Telkom: Jl Jend Sudirman 306A (next to the Dewi Santika Cinema) for fax, international telephone and telex/telegraph services.

● Shopping
Antiques: *Rezki Utama*, Jl Sisingamangaraja 12, carvings from the Nias Islands, Chinese porcelain, krisses, wayang puppets.

● Tour companies & travel agents
Inti Angkasa, Jend Sudirman 37, T 21074; *Kotapiring Kencana*, Jl Sisingamangaraja 3, T 21382 (Pelangi Air reps); *Cendrawasih Kencana*, Jl Imam Bonjol 32, T 21915; *Setia*, Jl Karet, T 22331.

● Tourist offices
Riau Provincial Tourist Office (Dinas Pariwisata Propinsi Riau), Jl Gajah Mada 200 (unmarked, in new white government building). Some useful pamphlets.

● Transport
174 km from Bukittinggi, 158 km from Dumai. **Local** No becaks. **Oplets/microlets**: the station is next to the long-distance bus terminal on Jl Nangka, in front of the Pasar Cik Puan (125 Rp). Unmetered **taxis**.

Air Simpangtiga Airport is 8½ km S of town. Merpati, Sempati, Garuda, SMAC and Pelangi Air all fly out of Pekanbaru. International connections with Singapore, Melaka and Kuala Lumpur. Domestic connections with Batam, Jakarta, Medan, Tanjung Pinang and Palembang. *Transport to town*: taxis to the town centre cost 7,000Rp, there is no public transport. *Airport facilities*: Post Office, money changer and a souvenir shop in the departure lounge selling stuffed frogs and what look like badly baked baguettes.

Road Bus: the long-distance Mayang Terurai terminal is at Jl Nangka 92 on the S edge of town, next to the Pasar Cik Puan. Microlets go there from the city centre (ask for 'Loket'). Regular connections with Bukittinggi 6 hrs, Padang, Bandung, Yogya, Aceh, Palembang, Jakarta 34 hrs, Medan and other destinations. Bus companies such as *ANS* (T 22065) have their offices at the terminal. Local and intra-provincial buses go from the Pasar Lima Puluh terminal at the N end of Jl Sultan Syarit Hasyim. **Minibus**: regular connections with Bukittinggi and Padang 7 hrs.

Sea Boat: Pekanbaru 'port' is at the end of Jl Saleh Abbas, the northward continuation of Jl Jend A Yani Microlets from the centre of town are marked 'Boom Baru' although it is an easy walk. Numerous companies have desks and sell tickets along Jl Saleh Abbas. Regular connections with Tanjung Pinang, Batam Island and other stops in the Riau archipelago (including Selat Panjang, Moro, Tanjung Batu and Tanjung Balai). The boats thread their way along the Siak River to Silat Panjang, and then enter the Melaka Strait and islands of the Riau Archipelago. Most are Conradian cowboy operations, with overloaded boats, smuggling of goods, drunk captains and frequent groundings. Take food along. Slow boats take 18-36 hrs (16,000-21,000Rp), fast boats rather less (38,000-43,000Rp). An alternative is to take a bus to Tanjung Buton/Selat Panjang on the coast (3 hrs) from where there are speedboats to Batam (4 hrs), see page 501.

International connections: **Air** With Singapore, Melaka and Kuala Lumpur. **Boat** Regular ferries from Singapore (Keppel Ferry Terminal) to Batam, 30 mins, and from there to Sumatra (on the Siak River), 3-5 hrs, then a bus to Pekanbaru, 3 hrs, total journey about 9 hrs. For travellers in no hurry, this is an attractive way to arrive in Indonesia.

THE WEST COAST

The Trans-Sumatran Highway continues S from Bukittinggi through the town of Padang Panjang (19 km), before descending steeply to the narrow coastal plain and the provincial capital of Padang, a total distance of 108 km. Off the W coast are the undeveloped and thickly forested Mentawi Islands, anthropologically interesting and offering good trekking. Travelling S from Padang – along the coastal lowlands for much of the way – it is 236 km to the small district capital of Sungai Penuh, lodged in the centre of the Kerinci-Seblat National Park. After climbing into the Bukit Barisan and before reaching Sungai Penuh, the road passes Mt Kerinci, the highest peak in Sumatra (3,805m). From Sungai Penuh, buses run E to Bangko through the narrow Batang Merankin Valley, and from there to Jambi (410 km). There are also buses which continue S along a poor road to Muko Muko and Bengkulu.

PADANG

Padang, with a population of 400,000, is the capital of the small province of W Sumatra (Sumatera Barat) and the largest town on Sumatra's W coast. Lying on the narrow plain between the Bukit Barisan and the Indian Ocean, it supports a university (Universitas Andalas), an impressive array of regional government and private offices, and an enormous cement plant with an annual capacity of nearly 5 million tonnes. The romantic mist which hangs over the hills is in fact dust and smoke from the plant.

The town is also hot and very, very wet – with annual rainfall of 4,500 mm (seven times greater than London's annual rainfall, four times more than New York). Moisture-laden clouds blow in from the Indian Ocean and are forced to deposit rain on the coastal lowlands – and on Padang – as they rise over the peaks of the Bukit Barisan.

The black, red and yellow flag – similar to the German flag – which can be seen flying from offices and along roads throughout the city, is the Minangkabau or W Sumatran provincial flag. It is said that when civic dignitaries from the German town twinned with Padang arrived on an official visit, they were overcome by the effort to welcome them. No one was brave enough to tell the truth.

NB Padang is a very Muslim and conservative town. Women should dress modestly.

Places of interest

The **Adityavarman Museum** is at Jl Diponegoro 10. Housed in a large traditional Minangkabau house and flanked by two rice barns, the museum has a limited display of cultural objects (textiles, tools and antiques), poorly arranged and catalogued. Admission 200Rp. Open 0800-1800 Tues-Thur, Sat and Sun, 0800-1100 Fri.

Padang has some **Dutch colonial buildings** in the Padang Baru area, and a **Chinese Buddhist temple** in Chinatown or Kampung Cina. Chinatown, which lies between Jl Dobi, Jl Pondok and Jl Cokroaminoto, also contains a number of older colonial buildings as well as traditional Chinese herbalists. It is one of the more interesting areas of Padang to wander around. The modern and rather drab **central mosque** is at Jl Imam Bonjol 1.

The **main market** or Pasar Raya covers a large area between Jl Pasar Baru and Jl M Yamin. It is certainly worth walking through, especially if looking for traditional textiles.

Padang beach is rather dirty and has a strong undercurrent – not recommended for swimming (see Excursions, below, for other beaches). Foodstalls line the seafront and it receives an on-shore breeze in the evening, making it a good place to sit and watch the sunset.

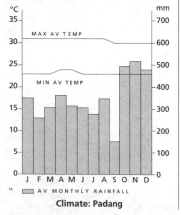

Climate: Padang

Excursions

Air Manis is a fishing village, 5 km to the S of town. The beach here is popular with locals and crowded at the weekend; the surf can be strong and swimming dangerous. A local legend tells of an unfaithful son, Malin Kundang, who left his family to seek his fortune. When he returned to Air Manis by sea a rich man, he was so ashamed by the shabby appearance of his mother he refused to greet her. Falling to her knees, she prayed that God punish her son; a wind rose and the boat carrying Malin sank drowning all on board. **Accommodation E** *Papa Chilli-Chilli. Getting there*: walk, or catch a bemo, to the coast at the mouth of the Batang Arau River and then take the ferry boat to the other side. From there it is a 45 mins walk to Air Manis, through a Chinese cemetery overlooking the sea. Alternatively, catch a bemo straight to the beach. From Air Manis it is possible to walk further S to **Padang Port** and **Teluk Bayur**; from there, regular bemos run back into town.

Bungus Beach lies 22 km S of Padang. At one time this was the most romantic beach in the area; it has now been disfigured by the construction of a wood processing enterprise. The plant is a joint S Korean/Indonesian venture and uses timber from the Mentawai Islands, contributing to the islands' rapid deforestation. There is an attractive 7 km walk from Bungus, S, to the – at present – isolated and peaceful **Telur Sei Pisang Beach**. The Japanese International Cooperation Agency and the Indonesian government are thinking of developing the area as a tourist destination. Offshore from Bungus Beach are a number of small, uninhabited, **palm-fringed coral islands**, including **Sirandah** – peaceful, with excellent snorkelling and sandy beaches. Unfortunately most of the coral is dead, although the fish remain resplendent. To visit the islands, hire a boat for the day either through one of the hotels or – cheaper – from the shop five doors down from the *Losmen Carlos* (11,000Rp pp). **Accommodation C** *Carolina Beach Re-*

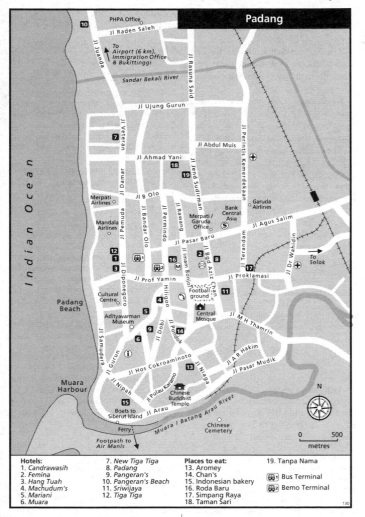

Padang

Hotels:
1. *Candrawasih*
2. *Femina*
3. *Hang Tuah*
4. *Machudum's*
5. *Mariani*
6. *Muara*
7. *New Tiga Tiga*
8. *Padang*
9. *Pangeran's*
10. *Pangeran's Beach*
11. *Sriwijaya*
12. *Tiga Tiga*

Places to eat:
13. Aromey
14. Chan's
15. Indonesian bakery
16. Roda Baru
17. Simpang Raya
18. Taman Sari
19. Tanpa Nama

Bus Terminal
Bemo Terminal

sort, Pasar Laban Km 20, T 27900, rec; **D** *Bungus Beach Hotel*, good position but rather overpriced, slow service; **E** *Losmen Carlos*, arranges trips to the islands; **E** *Losmen Carlos*, arranges trips to the islands. *Getting there*: by bemo, 1 hr.

Off-shore Islands Idyllic palm-fringed tropical islands including Pisang Besar Island, Padang Island and Bintangur Island lie offshore from Padang. All have good snorkeling, and are very peaceful. Pisang Besar Island is the closest – 15 mins by outrigger from Muara Harbour at the mouth of the Batang Arau River. Further information on how to reach the islands is available from the Tourist Information Office. *Getting there*: by chartered boat from Muara Harbour, 15-30 mins (10,000-15,000Rp).

The **Kerinci-Seblat Nature Reserve** lies S of Padang, and stretches nearly 350 km down to the tip of Sumatra (see page 520).

Bukittinggi and the surrounding sights are only 108 km away (see page 488). *Getting there*: regular bus connections from the city terminal, 2 hrs.

The **Taman Hutan Raya Bung Hatta** is a botanical gardens situated in the mountains on the road to Solok, 20 km from Padang. The reserve covers 70,000 ha of the Bukit Barisan; among its flora is the rafflesia flower (see page 490). Good views of the coast 700m below. *Getting there*: by bus from the city terminal, heading E towards Solok.

Festivals

Jul: *Tabut* (movable), Islamic festival commemorating the martyrdom of Mohammad's two grandchildren Hasan and Husain. Symbolic coffins and models of *Bouraq*, the mythical winged horse who carried them into paradise, are paraded through the streets to the accompaniment of music and dancing and are then cast into the sea.

Aug: *Independence Day* (17th: public holiday). A carnival, parades and exciting boat races on the Batang Arau River are held on Independence Day; events extend 1 week either side of the 17th.

Local information

● **Accommodation**

A+ *Bumi Minang*, Jl Bundo Kandung 20-28, T 37555, F 37567, a/c, restaurant, pool, new *Sedona Hotel* which recently opened in centre of town with 164 rm, swimming pool, fitness and business centres, and tennis courts, in terms of facilities and level of comfort the best in town although the Minang-style roof seems somewhat contrived on a place of this size; **A** *Pangeran's Beach*, Jl Ir H Juanda 79 (out of town on the road to the airport), T 51333, F 54613, a/c, restaurant, pool, the smartest hotel in town, well-managed, with good rooms, its location on the beach means it is quiet but suffers from an inconvenient location;

A-C *Pangeran's*, Jl Dobi 3-5, T 32133, F 27189, a/c, popular hotel and best in the city centre, 65 rm.

B *Femina*, Jl Bgd. Aziz Chan 15, T 21950, 34388, a/c, small hotel, centrally located with friendly and efficient management and good rooms, rec; **B** *Muara*, Jl Gereja 34, T 35600, F 31163, a/c, restaurant, pool, new hotel with 42 rm, international 'style' but really only provincial standard, popular for office parties; **B-C** *Wisma Mayangsari*, Jl Jend Sudirman 19, T 22647, a/c, price incl breakfast but food is reputedly very poor, clean and convenient for the airport, rec.

C *Machudum's*, Jl Hiligoo 45, T 32283, some a/c, colonial hotel, centrally located, now rather down-at-heel, friendly management and ambience still make it one of the more attractive places to stay, rec; **C** *Mariani*, Jl Bundo Kandung 35, T 34134, F 25410, a/c, restaurant, unattractive decor but efficiently-run, rec; **C-D** *New Tiga Tiga*, Jl Veteran 33, T 22173, some a/c, N of town and out of city centre, quiet with comfortable rooms but indifferent food, luggage store (5,000Rp/week); **C-D** *Padang*, Jl Bgd. Aziz Chan 28, T 31383, some a/c, set in gardens with range of rooms some with a/c and attached bathrooms.

D *Candrawasih*, Jl Pemuda 27, T 22894, some a/c rather grubby; **D** *Hang Tuah*, Jl Pemuda 1, T 26556, some a/c, unattractive 'new' hotel nr bus station, rooms are adequate with hot water and satellite TV; **D** *Immanuel*, Jl Tanah Beroyo 1, T 23917, quiet location towards S of town, reasonable rooms; **D** *Jakarta*, Jl Bgd. Olo 55, T 23331, close to the bus terminal; **D** *Tiga Tiga*, Jl Pemuda 31, T 22633, opp the bus terminal, unimpressive restaurant, a favourite with backpackers, rooms are bare but clean, some with attached mandis.

E *Sriwijaya*, Jl Alanglawas 1/15, T 23577, quiet location away from main road, clean.

● **Places to eat**

Padang is the place to sample Padang food (see page 487); there are a number to choose from on Jl Pasar Raya. A large assortment of bowls are brought to the table, and the bill is calculated according to the quantity eaten. Hot and spicy beef *rendang* is probably the most characteristic Padang dish. Try, if you dare, Sate Padang – made with boiled cow's intestines, skewered and grilled, served with a curry sauce.

Bakeries: *Aromey*, Jl Miaga 275; *Indonesian*, Jl Nipa 47, nr the harbour, excellent cakes and pastries, rec; *Tulip's*, Jl Pondok 139.

Chinese: several noodle houses along Jl Niaga. ♦♦♦*Apollo*, Jl Hos. Cokroaminoto 36, locals maintain this is the best Chinese in town.

Ice-cream: *Chan's*, Jl Pondok 94, Chinese and International food, live music.

Indonesian: ♦♦*Mariani*, Jl Bundo Kandung 35, also serves Chinese and International food; *Taman Sari*, Jl Jend A Yani 23. Javanese food, rec.

International: ♦♦*3M*, Jl Damar 69, breakfasts, sandwiches, omelettes, pasta.

Padang: ♦♦*Bak Haji*, Jl Permindo 61A, rec; ♦♦*Kartini*, Jl Pasar Baru 24; ♦♦*Purnama*, Jl Pasar Raya 111-117; ♦♦*Roda Baru*, Jl Pasar Raya 6; ♦♦*Serba Nikmat*, Jl Dobi 12, rec; ♦♦*Simpang Pauk*, Jl Pasar Baru 34F; ♦♦*Simpang Raya*, Jl Bgd. Aziz Chan 24; ♦♦*Simpang Raya*, Jl Bundo Kandung 3-5; ♦♦*Simpang Raya*, Jl Pasar Baru 34; ♦♦♦*Surya*, Jl Pasar Baru 38; ♦♦♦*Tanpa Nama*, Jl Rohana Kudus 87, rec.

Seafood: ♦♦*Nelayan*, Jl Hos. Cokroaminoto 34; ♦♦*Sari*, Jl Thamrin 79.

● **Airline offices**
Garuda and **Merpati**, Jl Jend Sudirman 2, T/F 31850; **Mandala**, Jl Pemuda 29A, T 32773, F 33814; **Pelangi**, Jl Diponegoro 13, T 54516; **Sempati**, *Pangeran's Beach Hotel*, Jl H Juanda 79, T 51612, F 55366; **Silk Air**, Jl Hayam Wuruk 16, T 38122, F 38120; **SMAC**, Jl Sudirman 2, T 55367.

● **Banks & money changers**
Bank Negara Indonesia 1946, Jl Dobi 2; **Bank Dagang Negara**, Jl Bgd Aziz Chan 21; **Bank Bumi Daya**, Jl Jend Sudirman 2A; **Citra Setia Prima** (money changer), Jl Diponegoro 5.

● **Entertainment**
Cinema: *New Raya* (film) *Theatre*, Jl Pasar Baru (nr the market), a/c, comfortable, films with English soundtrack and Indonesian subtitles.

Cultural Centre (Taman Budaya) on Jl Diponegoro. Dances, plays and exhibitions are regularly held here. Open 0900-1400.

● **Hospitals & medical services**
General Hospital: Jl Perintis Kemerdekaan, T 22355.

● **Places of worship**
Catholic Church: *St. Joseph's*, Jl Gereja 43.

Protestant Church: Jl Bgd. Aziz Chan.

● **Post & telecommunications**
Area code: 0751.

General Post Office: Jl Bgd. Aziz Chan 7 (nr clock tower).

Telephone Office: corner of Jl Ahmad Dahlan and Jl Khatib Sulaiman.

● **Shopping**
Antiques: *Sartika*, Jl Jend Sudirman 5, specializes in Sumatran and Mentawi ethnographic pieces, both souvenirs and antiques rather overpriced.

Basketry: Jl Pasar Raya and Jl Imam Bonjol.

Books: *Budi Daya*, Jl Prof M Yamin, Blok D II/4; *Lari Anggrek*, Jl Permindo.

Department stores: *Matahari*, Jl Yamin 3M, large, swish, a/c department store.

Jewellery: shops on Jl Prof M Yamin and Jl Pasar Baru.

Shopping centres: a number of new a/c plazas have opened inc *Ambacang Plaza*, Jl Bondo Kandung 18, *Damar Plaza*, Jl Damar 42A.

Textiles: cheap cloth is sold in the central market, at the corner of Jl Pasar Raya and Jl Prof M Yamin; several specialist textile shops along Jl Imam Bonjol – some sell *kain songket* (see page 529).

Woodcarving: several shops along Jl Pasar Raya and Jl Imam Bonjol.

● **Sports**
Pool: Pool Hall, Jl Pondok 151.

Swimming: non-residents can use *Pangeran's Beach Hotel* at Jl Ir H Juanda 79 (5,000Rp).

● **Tour companies & travel agents**
A number are located opposite the long-distance bus terminal: *Desa Air*, Jl Pemuda 23B, T 23022; *Nitour*, Jl Hiligoo 4C, T 21163, F 22175; *Tunas Indonesia*, Jl Pondok 86C, T 31661, F 32806; *Pacto*, Jl Tan Malaka 25, T 37678, F 33335; *Natrabu*, Jl Pemuda 23B, T 37442, F 23410.

● **Tourist offices**
Tourist Information Office, Jl Khatib Sulaiman 22 (the N extension of Jl Jend Sudirman), T 55711, open 0700-1400 Mon-Thur, 0700-1100 Fri and 0700-1230 Sat. Useful range of maps and helpful staff. (**NB** It is about 3 km N of the town centre and is poorly marked and easily missed. Take an orange *bis kota* or bemo N.) **Dinas Pariwisata**, junction of Jl Gurun and Jl Samudera, little English spoken and little information to offer. **Regional Tourist Office**, Jl Jend Sudirman 43, T 34251.

● **Useful addresses**
Immigration Office: Jl Khatib Sulaiman,

T 25113 (for visa extension).

Nature Conservation Office (PHPA): Jl Raden Saleh, T 25136.

Police: Jl Prof M Yamin.

● **Transport**

108 km from Bukittinggi, 246 km from Sungai Penuh. **Local Buses** (*bis kota*) **and bemos**: travel along fixed routes, setting off from the oplet terminal on Jl Prof M Yamin, next to the central market. **Dokars**, also known as **bendis**: horse-drawn carts; rows of them are to be found at the central market. **Taxis**: new taxis with meters; some unmetered for charter. **Oplets**: run from the oplet terminal on Jl Prof M Yamin, between Jl Pemuda and Jl Olo. **Motorcycle hire**: check with your hotel or at the Information Office (see below).

Air Tabing Airport is 7 km N of town. International connections on Garuda with Singapore, and on Sempati with Kuala Lumpur. Daily domestic connections on Merpati and Mandala with Jakarta, and on Merpati with Medan, Palembang and Pekanbaru; and three connections a week with Batam. There is also a SMAC flight on Wed to Gunungsitoli (Nias). *Transport to town*: hire a taxi (8,000Rp – fixed fare) or go out onto the main road and catch an orange *bis kota* (town bus) – it runs to the market area, close to a number of hotels. Taxis are expensive and unmetered from the airport; apparently the air force who run the airport have an 'arrangement' with the taxi drivers and do not allow the new, cheaper metered taxis to pick up passengers – although they can be dropped off.

Road Bus: the station, *Lintas Andalas*, is on Jl Pemuda close to the junction with Jl Prof M Yamin. Regular connections with Bukittinggi 3 hrs, Sibolga, Pekanbaru 6 hrs, Bengkulu 14 hrs, Prapat 16 hrs, Medan 20 hrs, Palembang 24 hrs, and Jakarta 48 hrs. *ANS* has an office at the bus terminal and at Jl Khatib Sulaiman, T 26689.

Sea Boat: the modern and comfortable Pelni ship *Lawit* runs on a 2-week circuit between Jakarta and Padang 27 hrs, including other stops in Sumatra, Java and Kalimantan (see route schedule page 921). It docks at Padang's port, Teluk Bayur, which is 7 km S of town. Book tickets at travel agencies or at Pelni's office at Teluk Bayur, Jl Tanjung Priok 32, T 33624. The ship also docks at Surabaya, Ujung Padang, Balikpapan, Pantoloan, Toli Toli, Tarakan Sibolga and Gunungsitoli (Nias) (see route map, page 922). The Pelni 'pioneer' vessel *Baruna Dwipa* also operates a fortnightly circuit calling at Engano en route for Jakarta. Boats also leave from Teluk Bayur to the Mentawi Islands (see page 519. **Taxi**: chartered taxis are available just N of *Machudum's Hotel* on Jl Hiligoo.

International connections Air: connections on Merpati, Sempati and Pelangi with Singapore and Kuala Lumpur.

THE MENTAWI ISLANDS

The Mentawi group of islands lie about 100 km off the W coast of Sumatra and are part of the same chain as Nias to the N. The name *Mentawi* is derived from the local word *si manteu* which means a 'man' or 'male'. The group consists of four islands – **Siberut**, **Sipora**, **Pagai Utara** (N Pagai) and **Pagai Selatan** (S Pagai). All the islands are inhabited but only Siberut is visited by significant numbers of tourists. The primary reason to visit Mentawi is to see a culture and people who have remained relatively unscathed by the 20th century.

A few years ago, visiting the Mentawi Islands was an adventure; now there are tours from Padang and Bukittinggi – 10 days for US$100. Even so, the number of visitors is still relatively small: the W Sumatran Regional Tourist Office in Padang estimated that in 1989, only 1,000 tourists visited these islands.

Fauna

For the same reason that the inhabitants of the Mentawi Islands are unique among the peoples of Indonesia, so too is some of the fauna. The archipelago was separated from the mainland about 500,000 years ago, an event which isolated the islands and allowed the wildlife to evolve independently. As a result there are a surprising number of endemic species. In 1980 the then World Wildlife Fund reported that 60% of mammal species were endemic and 15% of plant species including four species of primate: the black gibbon (*Hylobates klossii*), the Mentawi macaque, the long-tailed *joja* (*Presbytis potenziani*) and the pig-tailed langur (*Simias concolor*). Appreciating the supreme importance of the islands' flora and fauna, UNESCO formally recognized Siberut Island as a National Biosphere Reserve in 1981. Sadly, the Indonesian government has only gazetted two protected areas of 90,000 ha in total, and logging and development is fast eroding the archipelago's environment.

History

The indigenous inhabitants of the Mentawi Islands are Austronesians, descendants of the original inhabitants of Southeast Asia. As the islands lie off the main trading routes, they were cocooned from the wider world until after WW2. Not even the influx of Hindu civilization and, later, that of Islam, broke upon the shores of these islands. The Dutch claimed the Mentawi group in 1864 and established a limited presence in 1904, but did little to integrate the population into the wider cash economy. Large-scale conversion to Christianity only began with increased missionary activity in the 1950s. As many as 60% of the population are now nominal Christians, although animism still plays an important role in their lives.

Economy and culture

There are several different tribes in Mentawi, among them the Sakkudei, Sarareiket and Simatalu. The Sakkudei live in the most remote and inaccessible regions, and a few still cling tenaciously to their traditional life-styles. These beautiful people tattoo their bodies, and wear loin cloths and elaborate head-dresses. They hunt with bows and poisoned arrows and live in communal long houses or *uma*, sheltering 5-10 families. The chief of the community is the *rimata*, and his right-hand man the shaman or *sikerei*. Transport through the thick forest is by dug-out canoe along rivers.

Traditionally, their subsistence needs were met through hunting and gathering in the rich forests which even today – and despite considerable deforestation – make-up the majority of the islands' land area. The pressures of modern day life have led to a decline in hunting and gathering and a corresponding rise in agricultural activities: rice, sago, taro, fruit trees and other crops are all cultivated. But to supplement their diet, the inhabitants still eat such diverse natural products as wild boar, deer, monkey, beetle larvae and fish.

Siberut Island (Mentawi)

As tourists and mainland Indonesians increase their presence on the islands, it is inevitable that traditional ways of life will disappear. Most alarmingly for those who would wish to preserve the Mentawi way of life, the islands have now been designated as a transmigration site for landless Javanese (see page 427) and settlement was scheduled to begin in 1992. Tourists should be aware that most of the guides come from Bukittinggi and have little understanding of Mentawi language and customs. An organization has been established to press for the better protection of Siberut's people and environment. For more information write to SOS Siberut, 36 Matlock Court, 46 Kensington Park Rd, London W11 3BS, UK (T 071-727-4118).

Orientation

Most boats from Sumatra land at the town of Muarasiberut, at the S end of Siberut Island's E coast. There is one losmen here, and a restaurant. The other main town on Siberut is Sikabaluan, which lies to the N of Muarasiberut, also on the E coast. There is no accommodation at Sikabaluan, although homestays are available.

Trekking

There are a number of traditional villages within hiking distance (1-8 km) of Muarasiberut. More remote villages can only be reached by first taking a chartered longboat inland; ask on arrival. Note that living conditions are very basic and the walking can be hard. **NB** When trekking, be sensitive to locals; share your meals and try not to overwhelm, if in a large group.

Tours

Tours to the Mentawi Islands can be arranged through tour companies in Bukittinggi (see Travel agents, Bukittinggi) and Padang. Bukittinggi offers a wider range of tours and agents. Ensure your guide speaks Mentawi. An alternative is to hire a guide in Mentawi; this is usually cheaper and allows a trek or tour to be designed according to your own preferences. Groups are usually smaller too (see below). In Padang, tour agents incl *P T Desa Air*, Jl Pemuda 23B, T 23022, F 33335 and *Pacto*, Jl Pemuda 1, T 27780. Tours vary a great deal in price, from US$100 to US$330, depending on what is provided. They should incl trekking and canoe trips, and take the visitor through virgin forest and to what are rather condescendingly referred to as 'primitive' villages. Note that tours from Bukittinggi can take 3 days to reach Mentawi, so a 6 day tour is in effect only a 3 day tour.

Travelling independently

Independent travel is not advised for those without some Indonesian language. In the past it was necessary to register first at the police station in Padang before leaving, to obtain a permit or *surat Jl*. Recent information maintains that this is no longer required. However, check first at the Regional Tourist Office in Padang – they also provide a list of recommended guides and other useful information.

On arrival in Muarasiberut, tourists should register at the police station there. Porters and guides can be hired in Muarasiberut. The restaurant opposite the hotel in Muarasiberut is a good place to find out about guides, porters and other trekkers. Supplies can be bought from the restaurant, although they are cheaper elsewhere. Guides will be able to arrange a boat upriver and buy supplies as well as clear the trip with the police. The boat upriver costs about 80,000Rp one way, depending on the destination. The villages around Muarasiberut tend to be new Indonesian villages; it is necessary to travel upriver to see the 'real' Mentawi, so neither Muarasiberut nor Sikabaluan make good bases. Visitors should expect to spend a week on Mentawi to get a good taste of local life.

What to take:

● trekking equipment (good walking shoes, waterproof, warm clothing).

● waterproof bags.

● cigarettes or salt (for leeches).

● toiletries.

● plasters.

● mosquito repellent and a net (malaria pills are essential).

● food and cooking equipment.

● barter goods (cigarettes, tobacco and pens).

● rupiah notes in small denominations sufficient for stay; about US$150 for a week (there are no money changing facilities).

Useful words:

Anai loita – hello
Annaikaimei – goodbye
Masurabagata – thank you
Kasai anin – what is your name?
Mita – go on/let's go.

Local information

● **Accommodation**

The only losmen at Muarasiberut, is the grandly named **E** *Hotel Surat Izin Pengusahan*, although doubtless more will shortly appear. Trekking accommodation is in the homes of missionaries or with local headmen. Transmigrant villages are, by definition, less 'local' in character, try and stay in villages or homes of locals if possible for a taste of Mentawi life. Gifts of pens and tobacco are essential. There is a homestay at Masilot Beach, a boat trip from Muarasiberut (a return boat to Masilot Beach costs about 60,000Rp – snorkelling is good here).

● **Transport**

Local This is expensive as there is no public transport and **private boats** must be chartered.

Sea Boat: boats leave for Muarasiberut (the capital of Siberut Island) from Teluk Bayur (Padang's port) 3 times a week. They usually leave at 1900 and arrive at 0600 the next morning. One of the services stops at Sikabaluan, also on Siberut, but 60 km N. The return boat leaves at 1900 on Tues and Fri, again via Sikabaluan. The service is *P T Rusco Lines*, Jl Batang Arau 31, T 21941 (offices at Teluk Bayur, Padang's port). Tickets can be booked through travel agents (15,000-20,000Rp). It is also possible, though expensive, to charter a boat. On arrival at Muarasiberut it is necessary to take a boat to shore. **NB** During the rainy season (Oct-Jan) seas can be rough and departures may be delayed.

PADANG SOUTH TO SUNGAI PENUH

Sungai Penuh lies 236 km S of Padang in the Bukit Barisan. The road S along the coast via Tapan is much improved; so too is the interior road via Alahanpanjang and Surian. Accommodation is sparse. There are basic losmen in Painan, but the best place to stay en route is the *Camelia*, on the beach, clean and friendly, 8 km outside Painan on the road to Indrapura. From Tapan the road runs S through Muko Muko all the way to Bengkulu.

SUNGAI PENUH

Sungai Penuh is a small, rather unexciting district capital, 236 km S of Padang. Cinnamon trees are cultivated in the valleys and foothills around the town. When mature, the trees are cut down and the bark stripped off and then dried in the sun before being sold. Few tourists stop here, but those interested in Sumatran wildlife can use Sungai Penuh as a base to explore the large **Kerinci-Seblat Nature Reserve** which surrounds the town (see below). In Pondok Tinggi, the old part of town, is the **Mesjid Agung**, a mosque built in 1874, in pagoda-style and decorated with Dutch tiles and carved doors and columns. Across the street is one of the town's few remaining **rumah panjang** – traditional wooden longhouses up to 200m in length which were occupied by members of a single clan or *marga*. Most residents have moved into Javanese-style houses which are regarded as a sign of modernity.

Excursions

Lake Kerinci is situated about 5 km to the SE of town in a beautiful upland valley nearly 750m above sea-level and surrounded by 2,000m peaks. *Getting there:*

bus to Sanggaranagung or by hired motorbike or bicycle.

Mount Kerinci lies to the N of town and at 3,805m, is the highest peak in Sumatra. It can be climbed in 2 days, with 1 night spent at a hut part way up at 3,000m. The trail to the summit is about 16 km. The best base from which to climb the mountain is the small town of **Kersik Tuo** where accommodation is available in homestays (**E**). The Eco-Rural cooperative on Jl Raya, to which all homestays and guides belong, can provide guide services for climbing the mountain. Another popular trek is to the 10 km mountain lake of **Gunung Tuju** (Seven Mountain Lake) 50 km from Sungai Penuh, said to be the highest freshwater lake in Southeast Asia at 1,996m and so named because it is encircled by seven mountains. The climb to the lake takes about 2-3 hrs along a steep path through forest. It is also one of the least disturbed. The Eco-rural Coop charges about 30,000Rp pp/day for its tours. *Getting there*: regular buses and bemos run from the station in the market area in Sungai Penuh. Visit the Nature Conservation Office (PHPA) in Sungai Penuh on Jl Arga Selebar Daun 11 for a permit (which may be unnecessary), advice and information.

Kerinci-Seblat National Park is named after two of the highest mountains in Sumatra: Mt Kerinci (3,805m) and Mt Seblat (2,385m). The reserve stretches almost 350 km from Padang S to Bengkulu and covers almost 15,000 sq km straddling four provinces – making it the largest park in Sumatra. It accounts for a large segment of the mountainous spine of Sumatra, the Bukit Barisan, and supports a wide variety of wildlife including tigers, tapirs, elephants, Sumatran rhinoceros, sun bears, clouded leopards, semiang, five species of hornbill and the endemic short-eared rabbit (*Nesolagus netscheri*). There are no orang utans, but there have been many reported sightings of the *orang pendek* (a hairy 1½m tall and immensely strong hominid), the *cigau* (half lion, half tiger) and *kuda liar* (wild horses). The vegetation is primarily lowland, hill and montane tropical forest, with alpine vegetation on the higher slopes. Guides can be hired in Sungai Penuh and in Kersik Tuo (see Mt Kerinci excursion). Visit the Nature Conservation Office (PHPA) in town for permits, advice and information, or the PHPA offices in Padang or Bengkulu. *Best time to visit*: Jan-Mar and May-Nov, when it is driest in the valley enclave around Sungai Penuh; road travel out of these months may be difficult. Note that the mountainous areas of the reserve are wet year-round.

Kerinci-Seblat Reserve

Small and hairy: the Sumatran rhinoceros

Although not as rare as its Javan brother (see page 143), the Sumatran, or lesser 2-horned rhino (*Didermoceros sumatrensis*) is severely endangered. It was once widespread through mainland and island Southeast Asia but has now been hunted to the point of extinction; there are probably less than 1,000 in the wild, mostly in Sumatra but with small populations in Borneo, Peninsular Malaysia and Vietnam. Only on Sumatra does it have a chance of surviving. The situation has become so serious that naturalists have established a captive breeding programme as a precaution against extinction in the wild. The species has suffered from the destruction of its natural habitat, and the price placed on its head by the value that the Chinese attach to its grated horn as a cure-all. Should the Sumatran rhino disappear so too, it is thought, will a number of plants whose seeds will only germinate after passing through the animal's intestines.

The Sumatran rhino is the smallest of all the family, and is a shy, retiring creature, inhabiting thick forest. Tracks have been discovered as high as 3,300m in the Mount Leuser National Park. It lacks the 'armoured' skin of other species and has a soft, hairy hide. It also has an acute sense of smell and hearing, but poor eyesight.

Local information

● **Accommodation**

D *Busana*, Jl Martadinata, T 122, attached bathrooms with mandi, hot water brought to rooms, friendly and popular with tour groups, best in town; **D-E** *Mata Hari*, Jl Basuki Rahmat, good source of information.

F *Jaya*, basic.

● **Post & telecommunications**
Area code: 0748.

PHPA office, Jl Argo Selebar Daun 11.

● **Transport**
236 km from Padang, 410 km from Jambi. The road S from Padang to Sungai Penuh is newly resurfaced and relatively good.

Local Mr Bukari, owner of the *Busana Hotel*, will arrange car charter for 50,000Rp/day.

Air Occasional SMAC connections with Jambi.

Road Bus: the bus station is in the market area. Bus connections with Jambi via Bangko 12 hrs, and an overnight bus to Padang along bad roads, 10-12 hrs. There are also buses running S to Bengkulu via Muko Muko about 12 hrs; note that the road is poor.

TAPAN

This small town marks the beginning of the new, improved road S from Sungai Penuh to Bengkulu, following the narrow coastal strip between the ocean and the Bukit Barisan. The town itself has nothing of note to recommend it, but it does offer basic accommodation.

● **Accommodation E** *Wisma Kebehan*, Jl Talang Bungo Tapan (2 km S of town on the Bengkulu road), food available; **E-F** *Matahari*, situated 3 km E of town on the road to Sungai Penuh.

● **Transport Road Bus**: connections with Sungai Penuh, Muko Muko 2 hrs, Bengkulu 10 hrs and Padang 6½ hrs.

MUKO MUKO

This is the largest settlement on the long stretch of road between Sungai Penuh/Tapan and Bengkulu and is a good place to stop. The town overlooks the coast and sea and there are the remains of **Benteng (Fort) Anna Victoria** built between 1798 and 1810 to root around. Also here is the grave of an English youth who met an untimely end aged 18 in 1776. Swimming is not recommended for women because of the likely unwarranted attentiont – few foreigners come through here, let alone stop for a swim.

● **Accommodation E-F** *Losmen Muko Muko Putri*, Jl Prof Doktor Hazairin 1 (facing the main square nr the bridge).

● **Transport Road Bus**: connections with Tapan 2 hrs, Sungai Penuh, Padang 8-9 hrs and Bengkulu 8 hrs.

PADANG TO JAMBI AND PALEMBANG

From Padang, the Trans-Sumatran Highway turns inland and climbs into the Bukit Barisan. The drive is beautiful, passing through the town of Solok after 59 km, and gradually descending to the humid plain. The road then turns SE into the province of Jambi, before arriving at Muarabungo, 295 km from Padang. This small, nondescript roadside town lies at an important junction. The Trans-Sumatran Highway continues S, while another main road cuts E for the 212 km trip to the provincial capital of Jambi, a gruelling 507 km from Padang. Travelling S from Jambi across marshy terrain, the road passes into the province of S Sumatra before reaching the important city of Palembang, about 260 km from Jambi. To the NE of Palembang are the islands of Bangka and Belitung, formerly important tin mining areas and now emerging as tourist centres.

JAMBI

Jambi, with a population of about 300,000, is the capital of the province of the same name. It is a featureless town and the city centre occupies a relatively small area on the Batanghari River, near the port. There are a few old shophouses still standing on Jl Sam Ratulangi. Boats sail from here for Batam Island, Tanjung Pinang (on Bintan Island) and, occasionally, Jakarta and Singapore, negotiating the river for over 150 km to the sea (see below). Modest freighters can navigate as far inland as Jambi.

The **Museum Negeri Jambi** is on Jl Prof Dr Sri Soedewi Masjahun Sofwan 4 km from the centre of town and has a small but interesting collection of ethnographic and archaeological pieces from the surrounding area. Admission 200Rp. Open 0900-1600. There is a sprawling **street market** on Jl Ir. Sutami, Jl Wahid Hasyim and Jl Supratman. **Speedboats** can be hired from close to the bridge on Jl Sultan Taha, at the intersection with Jl Ir. Sutami, for trips along the river.

In the Telanaipura area of town (to the W of the city centre), opposite the Governor's Office, is the **Mayang Mengurai Park** which contains a reconstruction of a traditional Jambi house, along with traditional costumes of the area. Also in this part of town is an **art and craft workshop** run by the PKK Women's group, known as PKK Batik Art.

Tours

Companies are beginning to run trekking tours to visit the Kubu people of Jambi (also known as *sukuanak dalam*. They are among SE Asia's last hunter-gatherers and are now 'protected' in a reserve of 28,703 ha. Fortunately access is difficult, although they are becoming objects of tourist fascination as well as targets for government 'development' programmes (see box).

Excursions

Candi Muara Jambi is a complex of restored temples 25 km E of the city, on the left bank of the Batanghari River (downstream). They are part of the largest archaeological site in Sumatra and are believed to date from the 7th-13th centuries and to be associated with the Melayu Kingdom (see page 428), a rival of Srivijaya. They were first researched by Captain S C Cook in 1810. The chronicles record 35 structures here, although only 9 large brick-built structures have been excavated and restored stretching over nearly 2 km, E to W. They have little decorative detail, consisting of stupas and shrines surrounded by brick walls with steps leading up into plain, square cellas. The best of the artefacts have been carted-off to the National Museum in Jakarta. **Candi Gumpung**, one of the larger temples, yielded a statue of Prajnaparamita regarded as among the finest examples of East Javanese-style carving. In addition, excavations uncovered a wealth of Chinese ceramics showing the degree to which the area was integrated into a wider international trading network. Open 0800-1600 Mon-Sun (including small site

The Kubu: remnant hunter-gatherers of Sumatra

🐾 The Kubu are among Southeast Asia's last, and best-known, hunter-gatherers. The name 'Kubu' does not refer to a homogeneous tribal group, but to a disparate and culturally diverse series of groups who inhabit the foothills of the Bukit Barisan in the vicinity of Palembang and Jambi. Like other hunter-gatherers, the Kubu were probably never isolated from other populations. They traded forest products such as wild animal skins, *damar* (forest resins), benzoin and camphor with settled agriculturalists and had close economic and social relations with other peoples.

Hunting and gathering is often perceived as the most 'primitive' of subsistence strategies. But recent research has shown that agriculturalists have sometimes turned to hunting and foraging when opportunity allowed. Likewise, hunter-gatherers have taken up agriculture when necessary. Because of the need to be highly mobile, the Kubu live in small groups where hierarchy is based on relative age, and class divisions are rare. Often, small groups will operate from fixed base camps, although some Kubu are highly mobile. Like many other tribal groups, the Kubu are under threat of cultural extinction. Over the decades, and pre-dating the modern era, they have been gradually absorbed into neighbouring groups such as the Minangkabau of W Sumatra. More recently, the Indonesian government has endeavoured (not always very successfully) to teach Bahasa and draw the Kubu into the mainstream of the country's economic and social life.

museum with a small collection of ceramics and incomplete statuary). *Getting there*: by speedboat from close to the bridge on Jl Sultan Taha, 1hr; or by waterbus bound for Muara Sabak. It is best to go on a Sun when there are scheduled boats – much cheaper than chartering one.

Festivals

Jan: *Pekan Persona Budaya Jambi (Jambi Cultural Festival)* (6th-12th), a jamboree of cultural festivities created to raise the profile of Jambi and its people, and timed to coincide with the anniversary of the founding of the province on 6 January 1957. Events include *bidar* (long boat) races, traditional dances and songs, and local food specialities.

Local information
● Accommodation

No budget accommodation, because few travellers visit Jambi. However, there is a reasonable selection of mid-range hotels serving local businessmen. The *Jambi River View Resort*, a three star hotel, is due to open in mid-1993 and will be the best hotel in town.

B-C *Abadi*, Jl Jend Gatot Subroto 92-98,

T 24054, F 23065, a/c, restaurant, 'best' in town, rooms in the old wing are musty and dark, better in the new extension, service is enthusiastic rather than slick; **B-C** *Surya*, Jl Husni Thamrin 48, T 25399, a/c, like a multi-storey carpark, hotel on 1st flr; rooms in the new wing are slightly better.

C-D *Kartika Jaya*, Jl Dr Sutomo 32, T 22690, a/c, dark rooms, but better than expected given hotel's run-down appearance; **C-D** *Makmur*, Jl Cut Nyak Dien 14, T 22324, some a/c, friendly, darkish rooms, rather out of centre of town; **C-D** *Pamalayu*, Jl Jend Gatot Subroto 100, T 22588, a/c; **C-D** *Pinang*, Jl Dr Sutomo 9, T 22324, some a/c, unfriendly, basic accommodation for the price; **C-D** *Sederhana*, Jl Dr Sutomo 46A, T 22786, some a/c, central location, clean rooms but a little musty and windowless rooms.

● Places to eat

Jambi specialities are served at the *Pinang Merah Restaurant*, Jl Prof Dr Sri Sudewi.

Bakery: *French Modern Bakery*, Jl Husni Thamrin 46.

Chinese: *Aneka Rasa*, Jl Empu Gandring; *Terkenal*, Jl M Asa'at 124, large menu, rec.

Indonesian: *Ayam Yogya*, Jl Abdul Muis 58, good chicken dishes; *Safari*, Jl Dr Wahidin.

Padang food: several restaurants in the town centre, nr the market.

● **Airline offices**
Merpati, Jl Damar 55, T 22184. **Garuda**, Jl Dr Wahidin 95, T 22041. **SMAC**, Jl Orang Kayo Hitam 26, T 22804.

● **Banks & money changers**
Bank Danamon, Jl Dr Sutomo 21; Bank Dagang Negara, Jl K H Wahid Hasyim 8-12.

● **Hospitals & medical services**
General Hospital: Jl Jend Suprapto, T 22364.

● **Post & telecommunications**
Area code: 0741.

General Post Office: Jl Sultan Taha Syaifuddin 5.

Telephone Office: Jl M Taher.

● **Shopping**
Antiques: *Pasar Cindera Mata*, Jl Pinang Masak 14.

Books and maps: *Media Agung Bookshop*, Jl Jend Gatot Subroto Blok A No 1 (nr *Abadi Hotel*).

Handicrafts: handicraft centre at *Sanggar Batik dan Kerajinan*, Jl Prof Dr Sri Soedewi Masjchun, 4 km from the centre of town; also outlet at Jl Jend Sudirman 32A; *PKK Batik Art*, run by a women's group in the Telanaipura area of town is good for art and crafts.

● **Sports**
Swimming: large public swimming pool (*Kolam Renang Tepian Ratu*), Jl Slamat Riyadi (3 km from town centre). Open 0800-1700 Mon-Sun.

● **Tour companies & travel agents**
Mayang, Jl Hayam Wuruk 7, T 25450; *Jambora Kencana*, Jl Jend Gatot Subroto, T 23926.

● **Tourist offices**
Provincial Tourist Office, Jl Basuki Rachmat 11 (about 5 km S of town), T 25330. Get there by oplet (250Rp) or taxi. Little English spoken, some brochures.

● **Useful addresses**
Immigration Office: Jl Dr Sam Ratulangi 2.

● **Transport**
507 km from Padang, 260 km from Palembang.

Local No becaks. **Colts** (150-250Rp), **dokars**, **taxis**, **oplets**. **Speedboats**: can be hired nr the bridge on Jl Sultan Taha, nr the intersection with Jl Ir. Sutami (upstream from the Port Administration Office).

Air Sultan Taha Airport is 6 km S of town, off Jl Jend Sudirman. Taxis to the centre of Jambi cost 4,500Rp; oplets also go past the airport (250Rp). Regular daily connections on Merpati with Jakarta, Palembang Batam, and Pangkalpinang. SMAC operate flights to Sungai Penuh.

Road Bus: the Simpang Karwat long-distance bus terminal is 3½ km SW of town, at the intersection of Jl Hos. Cokroaminoto and Jl Prof M Yamin. Colts run there from the city centre (150Rp), a/c express bus companies have their offices on Jl Mr Assa'ad (*ACC* at No 60 and *Jaya Bersama* and *ALS* at No 64), which runs off Jl Jend Gatot Subroto, not far from the *Abadi Hotel*. Buses to major Sumatran towns and to Jakarta 30 hrs, Bali, Bandung and Sungai Penuh.

Sea Boat: boats leave from the docks on the river near the centre of town, Boom Batu and Boom Rakit. Daily boats to Kuala Tungka; slow ferry 12 hrs (4,000-6,000Rp); speedboat 4 hrs (15,000Rp). Also ships/boats to Batam Island and Tanjung Pinang (Bintan Island); journey time varies but averages 48 hrs (25,000Rp). Occasional departures for Singapore and Jakarta. The best source of information about departures is the Kantor Administrator Pelabuhan (Port Administration Office) at Jl Sultan Taha 4, on the river front, or ask around the various offices at Jl Sultan Taha 2 (Pelabuhan Jambi). *Pelni* have an office at Jl Sultan Taha 17, T 23649.

PALEMBANG

For years there has been debate in archaeological circles about Palembang's status. Was it really the capital of Srivijaya, the greatest maritime empire in Southeast Asian history, as George Coedès postulated in 1918? If so, why did the city reveal so little in the way of artefacts to indicate as much? Some scholars maintained that Coedès was wrong all along; others that the low lying, swampy land, had simply enveloped what remained. The conundrum is now, it seems, solved. Work by Indonesian archaeologists in collaboration with the French scholar Pierre-Yves Manguin have uncovered a wealth of evidence in and around the city. As Manguin writes, it was due "to an amazing neglect for Sumatran archeology" that these sites had been left un-excavated for so long. It seems that Coedès, prescient as ever, was correct all the time and Palembang was the former capital of magnificent Srivijaya (see page 426).

The Dutch developed Palembang as an administrative centre serving the tin mines of Bangka Island and the plantations of the surrounding area. In more recent years, the city has emerged as the administrative oil export hub of S Sumatra and has a population of about 750,000. Palembang sprawls across both banks of the Musi River, about 80 km from the sea, the two halves of the town linked by the Ampera Bridge. Palembang's commercial core, central shopping district and most of the sights are on the N bank, in Seberang Ilir.

Places of interest

The heart of the city is marked by the 1960s built **Ampera Bridge** which spans the Musi River and links Palembang's two halves: Seberang Ulu (upstream, S) and Seberang Ilir (downstream, N). The river is 500m wide at this point, and in total is about 600 km long. There are good views of the city from the bridge.

Within sight of the bridge, on its N side, down Jl Jend Sudirman, is the elegant **Mesjid Agung** or **Grand Mosque**, with its fine minaret. The mosque was built in 1738 by Sultan Mahmud Bandaruddin I, and has recently been restored. Across Jl Merdeka is the ugly **Monumen Perjuagan Rakyat Sumatera Bagian Selatan** (sensibly known as MONPERA) which commemorates the 1947 'Battle of Five Days and Nights' when the Dutch succeeded in wrenching control of the oil and coal fields around Palembang away from republican rebels. Behind this, on Jl Sultan Mahmud Bandaruddin II and almost on the river is the **Museum Budaya Sultan Mahmud Bandaruddin**. The museum was renovated in 1991 (the building dates from 1826) and contains a small collection of local and European pieces (the provincial museum is better, see Excursions). In the grounds is a fine stone Srivijayan Buddha, along

with a new arts and crafts market. The grounds of the museum are an important excavation site: 55,000 artefacts have been uncovered dating back to the Srivijaya period. Open 0800-1230, 1330-1600 Mon-Thur and Sat; 0800-1100, 1330-1600 Fri. The city's tourist office occupies the ground floor of the museum.

Immediately to the E of the Ampera Bridge, on the N bank of the Musi, is the **Pasar 16 Ilir**, a maze of streets, stalls and houses reaching down to, and over, the river (see Shopping). This is Palembang's **Chinatown** and among the streets are some Chinese temples (eg **Klenteng Kwa Sam Yo** on Jl Sungai Lapangan Hatal and the river). Another attractive and interesting area to explore is N of the river and W of Jl Jend Sudirman. Here, among the winding streets are numerous **rumah limas** – traditional Palembang houses – with their distinctive roof decoration, far more attractive than the sterile example at the Provincial Museum (see below). Jl Datuk M Akib is a particularly good place to view them.

Excursions

Museum Negeri Propensi Sumatera Selatan is a large museum, 5½ km N of town at Jl Srivijaya 1. It has rooms exhibiting traditional houses, ceremonies, technology, and arts and crafts of S Sumatra. At

Stone megalith showing a warrior riding on a elephant with a bronze dongson drum strapped to his back. Museum Negeri Propensi Sumatera Seletan

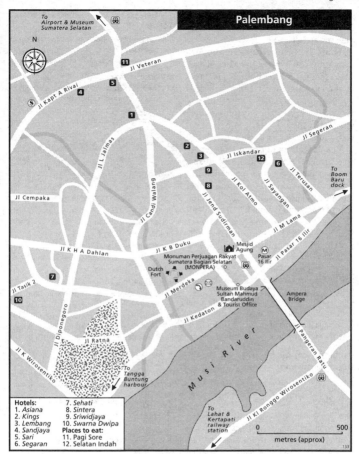

Palembang

Hotels:
1. Asiana
2. Kings
3. Lembang
4. Sandjaya
5. Sari
6. Segaran
7. Sehati
8. Sintera
9. Sriwidjaya
10. Swarna Dwipa

Places to eat:
11. Pagi Sore
12. Selatan Indah

the back are two traditional **limas houses**, said to be 300 years old. They have been rebuilt four times and although originally held together with bamboo pegs are now nailed in place and incorporate much new material. Most interesting is a collection of megaliths from Lahat District and two Srivijayan stone Buddhas, under a protective awning outside the museum. Of the megaliths (see page 533), note the wonderfully rounded elephant with a rider and a Dongson drum (*batu purbakala*) on its back

(see page 377). Admission 200Rp. Open 0800-1200, 1330-1600 Tues-Thur and Sat; 0800-1200 Mon; 0800-1100, 1330-1600 Fri. *Getting there*: take a kijang or town bus travelling N on Jl Jend Sudirman (which becomes Jl Kol H Barlian) towards 'Km 12'; ask for 'Museum' and alight just past Jl Srivijaya – the museum is a 30 km walk off the main road.

Hutan Wisata Puntikayu are public gardens opened in 1991, 7 km from the city centre continuing N from the turn-off for the museum along Jl Kol H Barlian. *Getting there*: by kijang or town bus running towards 'Km 12'.

Boats can be hired close to the Ampera Bridge to explore the **Musi River**. The usual trip passes houseboats, takes in the Pasar 16 Ilir, and then proceeds into the countryside. Expect to pay about 5,000Rp/hr. The city tourist office recommend that visitors contact them beforehand.

The **Megaliths in Lahat District** are an overnight excursion from Palembang; it takes a day to reach the plateau and at least a day to view the sculptures and megaliths. The megaliths are scattered over the highland Pasemah Plateau about 260 km W of Palembang (see page 532). *Getting there*: direct bus to Pagaralam, 7 hrs; some of the megaliths are within walking distance from the town.

Festivals

Aug: *Independence Day* (17th), *Bidar* (boat) races on the Musi in the morning, each boat carrying as many as 40 oarsmen. Commercial firms sponsor boats and village teams compete.

Local information
● **Accommodation**
A *King's*, Jl Kol. Atmo 623, T 310033, F 310937, a/c, restaurant, central location, comfortable rooms, but over-priced; **A-B** *Lembang*, Jl Kol Atmo 16, T 313476, F 352472, a/c, restaurant, new, large, centrally located hotel with no character; **A-B** *Sanjaya*, Jl Kapt A Rivai 6193, T 350634, F 313693, a/c, restaurant, pool, central location, good facilities but cheaper rooms are poor for the price.

B *Swarna Dwipa*, Jl Tasik 2, T 313322, F 28999, a/c, restaurant, pool, hotel on the W edge of town; quiet location in gardens with average rooms but friendly management, rec.

C *Sari*, Jl Jend Sudirman 1301, T 313320, a/c, restaurant, average rooms, popular with Indonesians, price incl breakfast; **C-D** *Sehati*, Jl Dr Wahidin 1, T 350338, some a/c, large rooms with separate sitting area, rather musty; **C-D** *Sintera*, Jl Jend Sudirman 38, T 354618, some a/c, a little run down, but central, not far from Ampera Bridge; **C-D** *Sriwidjaya*, Jl Let. Kol. Iskandar 31, T 355555, some a/c, central,

rooms are poorly maintained and dark, price incl breakfast.

E *Asiana*, Jl Jend Sudirman 45, popular, simple but clean rooms; best of a poor bunch; **E** *Segaran*, Jl Segaran 207C, popular, rooms are grubby.

● **Places to eat**
Chinese: **♦♦***Kings Hotel*, Jl Kol. Atmo 623, rather characterless restaurant, but serves good Chinese; **♦♦***Selatan Indah*, Jl Let. Iskandar, locals maintain this is the best Chinese restaurant in Palembang.

Indonesian: **♦♦***Sudi Mampir*, Jl Merdeka, one of the best places to sample Palembang food which is served like Padang food – you only pay for what you eat; **♦***Sari Mulia*, Jl Jend Sudirman 589, excellent soup 'kitchen'; **♦***Suwito*, Jl Demang Lebar Daun, good sate; *Pagi Sore*, Jl Jend Sudirman, Padang food.

Other Asian cuisine: *Har*, Jl Tustam Effendi, Indian Muslim food.

Foodstalls: on Jl Jend Sudirman, W side, N from the Pasar Cinde. Cheap restaurants concentrated here as well.

● **Airline offices**
Garuda, Jl Kapt Ravai 20, T 312204; Mandala, *Sanjaya Hotel*, Jl Kapt Rivai 6193, T 350634; Merpati, *Sanjaya Hotel*, Jl Kapt Rivai 6193, T 310675; Deraya, Jl Jend Sudirman 2954D, T 353700 (for Pangkal Pinang, Bangka Island).

● **Banks & money changers**
Bank Central Asia, Jl Kapitan Rivai 22; Ekspor-Impor, Jl Rustan Effendi 81; Bank Rakyat Indonesia, Jl Kapitan Rivai 15.

● **Hospitals & medical services**
Hospital Caritas: Jl Jend Sudirman (at intersection with Jl Kapt A Rivai).

● **Post & telecommunications**
Area code: 0711.

General Post Office: Jl Merdeka 5.

Post Office: Jl Kapt A Rivai 63.

Telephone Office: Jl Jend Sudirman. **Telekom office**, Jl Merdeka (next to GPO).

● **Shopping**
Antiques: *Mir Senen*, Jl AKBP. BM Amin (Selero) 39.

Jewellery: traditional designs available at the Pasar 16 Ilir.

Lacquerware: Palembang has a reputation for its lacquerware, a technique which was introduced by Chinese craftsmen. Shops incl *Mekar Jaya*, Jl Slamet Riyadi 45A.

Cloths of gold and silver: kain songket

The characteristic cloth of coastal Sumatra is *songket*. This covers a wide range of types but perhaps most immediately recognizable is *kain songket* (literally, songket cloth), where supplementary gold and silver yarns are woven into plain cloth. Among the centres of production are Padang, Palembang and the towns around Bukittinggi. Floral motifs are most common, and the metallic yarn is usually woven into a cloth made from a mix of cotton and silk. In the past, 14-carat gold thread was used to embellish the cloth; today, new supplies of such thread are no longer available. Instead, weavers resort to removing the yarn from old pieces of cloth, using threads thinly coated in metal, or even weaving the patterns with plaited copper wire.

Fine pieces of kain songket were regarded as family heirlooms. They were indicative of wealth and envoys to the court of Aceh were presented with ornately wrought sarongs, headcloths and scarves. Wearing the richest examples – known as *songket lupus* – clearly marked a person's position in society. In some pieces, for example those made in the villages around Bukittinggi where they are also known as *kain balapak*, the metallic yarn is so thickly interwoven that the underlying silk or cotton cloth is barely visible. Kain songket were an essential part of the bride price, and were also exchanged on the birth of a child or during circumcision ceremonies.

Textiles: Palembang is a centre of *songket* weaving (see box); *jumputan pelangi* is a tie-dyed cloth unique to Palembang. Shops incl: *Songket Palace*, Megaria Shopping Centre, Jl T P Rustam Effendi; *Sumatra Shopping Centre*, Pasar 16 Ilir; *Shopping Centre*, Jl Kol. Atmo 623; *Taras*, Jl Merdeka; *Cek Ipah*, Jl Ki Gede Lng Suro 141, 30 Ilir; and in the *Pasar 16* Ilir; *Danar Hadi*, Jl Veteran 8001B for batik.

Woodcarving: *H Azis*, Jl Jend Sudirman No Gang Pakis.

● **Sports**
Golf: **Palembang Gold Club** is on Jl AKBP Cek Agus, N of the city centre, run by the state oil company Pertamina. Green fee for non-members: 15,000Rp, 25,000Rp on Fri, Sun and public holidays. Caddy fee: 3,000Rp. Clubs for hire.

Swimming: large public pool, *Lumban Tirta*, on Jl Kapt A Rivai ('kampus'). Admission 1,250Rp, 1,750Rp Sun and public holidays. Open 0800-1930 Mon-Sun.

● **Tour companies & travel agents**
Ista Travel, Jl Jend Sudirman 53F, T 350800, *Santra*, Jl Kapt A Rivai 6193, T 310675.

● **Tourist offices**
Palembang City Tourist Office, Jl Sultan Mahmud Badaruddin II (ground flr of the Museum Budaya), T 358450, some useful maps and information; **South Sumatra Tourist Office**, Jl Bay Salim 200, T 357348, not very help-

ful; **Parpostel Tourist Office**, Jl Rajawali 22, T 311345, unhelpful.

● **Useful addresses**
Immigration Office: Jl Memet Sastrawirya Palembang.

● **Transport**
260 km from Jambi, 247 km from Bengkulu, 202 km from Lahat.

Local Becaks. Town **buses** travel fixed routes (200Rp). **Kijangs/oplets** (200Rp). Unmetered **taxis**. **Ferry boats**: cross the river from Tangga Buntung Dock (200Rp).

Air Sultan Mahmud Badaruddin II Airport is 12 km N of town. *Transport to town*: unmetered taxis for 10,000Rp or walk onto the main road, 2 km away, to catch a minibus (350Rp). Palembang is a Sumatran travel hub, with regular connections with Jakarta (several daily), Bandar Lampung, Batam, Bengkulu, Jambi, Padang, Medan, and Pangkal Pinang; also connections with Dumai.

Train Kertapati station is 4 km SW of town, close to the Musi River. From the station, take an oplet going to Warna Kuning (150Rp) – they cross the river and then run along Jl Merdeka and Jl Sudirman to the centre of the city. Daily trains to Tanjungkarang, 10 hrs (18,000-28,000Rp); buses leave from here for Bakauheni and Jakarta. Connections with Lubuklinggau (10,000-14,000Rp), where there are bus connections to Padang and Lampung 9 hrs (12,000-20,000Rp).

Road Bus: the city's main bus terminal is on Jl Kl Ronggo Wirosentiko, not far from the southern end of the Ampera Bridge. There is also a terminal – the Tujuluh terminal – on Jl Iskandar, in the centre of the city. Express and a/c bus offices are scattered over the city; there are a number on Jl Kol. Atmo (eg *Hidup Baru* and *Lorena*, a short distance N from the *King's Hotel*; *C V Manila* on Jl Kapt Cek Syeh 200 (off Jl Jend Sudirman); *ANS* at Jl Diponegoro 100; *Putra Remeja* at Jl Veteran 6887F and *Continental* at Jl Veteran 156 (just off road near intersection with Jl Jend Sudirman); *ALS* also on Jl Veteran, T 20640. Regular connections with Medan, Jambi 4 hrs, Jakarta 24 hrs, Padang, Bukittinggi, Pekanbaru, Medan, Aceh, Bogor, Bali, Yogya and Solo.

Sea Boat: *Wisin Tour*, Jl Veteran 173C, T 21811 run daily fast boats from Boom Baru Dock to Muntok on Bangka Island, 3 hrs. Depart 0830; depart Muntok for return trip 1300. *K M Bahari Express* and *K M Adiyasa* also run boats to Muntok from Boom Baru at 0930 and 1000 daily, respectively. A slower ferry leaves daily from Tangga Buntung Harbour for Muntok, 13 hrs.

BANGKA ISLAND

Bangka Island – shaped rather like a seahorse – lies to the NE of Palembang and is separated from the mainland by the 20 km-wide Bangka Strait. It covers an area of about 11,500 sq km and has a population of about ½ million. The capital is Pangkal Pinang on the E coast; its most important port, Muntok, is on the NW coast. Formerly Bangka's wealth was founded on tin; today, as tin declines in importance, the island is turning to tourism. But Bangka is not on the travel itinerary of most western visitors – it remains a holiday resort catering mainly to Asian tourists.

The attraction of Bangka to visitors today are the island's sublime white-sand **beaches**, concentrated on the NE coast. Among the most popular are Hakok Beach and Matras Beach, both about 35 km N of Pangkal Pinang, past the town of Sungailiat.

The capital, **Pangkal Pinang**, has a population of about 100,000, and in the town there are a few remnants of Dutch colonial architecture to serve as reminders of the past. But sights are few and far between. There is a small **mining museum** at the intersection of Jl Jend A Yani and Jl Depati Amir, and a **Chinese temple**, built in the 1830s, on Jl M H Muhidir.

The town of Muntok, on the W coast of Bangka and 125 km from Pangkal Pinang was the original capital of the island (until 1913) and is the main ferry point for boats to Sumatra. The **lighthouse** and **fort** in the harbour area were built at the beginning of the 19th century, while in town there is a 150 year-old **mosque** and an early 19th century **Chinese temple**.

Local information
● **Accommodation**

In Pangkal Pinang: **C** *Sabrina*, Jl Diponegoro, T 22424, a/c, hot water, inc breakfast, rec.

B-D *Menumbing*, Jl Gereja 5, T 22991, a/c, restaurant, pool, best in town.

C-D *Bukit Shofa*, Jl Mesjid Jamik 43, T 21062, some a/c, mandi.

D *Penginapan Srikandi*, Jl Mesjid Jamik 42, T 21884, fan and mandi, friendly management.

E *Losmen Maras*, Jl Sudirman.

On the beaches: **A** *Parai*, T 92335, bookable from Jakarta T (021) 356025, F 356383, a/c, restaurant, pool, bungalow accommodation.

B *Romodong*, on the N tip, bookable from Jakarta T (021) 560415, F 594469, or from Pangkal Pinang, T 21573 a/c, restaurant (with good seafood), attractive gardens and cottage accommodation.

● **Places to eat**
Excellent seafood (several restaurants in Pangkal Pinang) and a large selection of Chinese stall food.

● **Airline offices**
Sempati, Jl Kapt Sulaiman Arif 41, T 21796; Merpati, Jl Jend Sudirman 31, T 22077.

● **Post & telecommunications**
Area code: 0717.
Post Office: Jl Jend Sudirman.

● **Sports**
Swimming: pool at *Menumbing Hotel*, open to non-residents, 2,500Rp.

● **Tour companies & travel agents**
Duta Bangka Sarana (DBS), Jl Jend Sudirman

10, Pangkal Pinang, T 21698, F 22300; *Priaventure*, Jl Jend Sudirman 10, Pangkal Pinang, T 351002.

● **Useful addresses**

Immigration office: Jl Taman Ican Saleh 2, T 21774.

● **Transport**

Local Infrequent **bus** services around the island, and between Pangkal Pinang and Muntok. **Cars** can be chartered.

Air The airport lies 6 km S of Pangkal Pinang. Taxis available to town (6,000Rp) or to the beaches (16,000Rp). Regular daily connections on Merpati with Jakarta and Palembang; Sempati have two connections a week with Batam, and Singkep. Deraya offers connections with Belitung Island, Singkep and Batam as well as with Palembang. *DBS* at Jl Jend Sudirman 10 will book tickets on Merpati and Deraya.

Sea Boat: twice daily ferry connections with Palembang's Tangga Buntung Harbour leave from Mentok on the W coast (and 125 km from Pangkal Pinang) 13 hrs (6,000Rp). Jetfoils also run between Muntok and Palembang, leaving Muntok twice daily in the early afternoon, 3 hrs (20,000Rp). There are some ferries which go to Kayu Arang, on the N coast and only an hour from Pangkal Pinang (and closer to the best beaches). A Pelni ship visits Muntok every 2 weeks on its circuit between Jakarta and Medan via Batam (Pelni office, Muntok, T 22743).

BELITUNG ISLAND

This is Bangka's smaller sister island, 80 km off Bangka's SE coast. Belitung covers an area of 4,000 sq km and has a population of about 175,000. Like Bangka, its wealth was founded on tin, and it is now turning to tourism as an alternative source of revenue as the tin mining industry declines. The capital of Belitung is Tanjung Pandan.

Bangka Island

The best beaches are found to the N of the capital. Tanjung Kelayang, 25 km N, is probably the best. *Getting there*: by bus from Tanjung Pandan to Tanjung Binga; and then change for Tanjung Kelayang.

Local information

● **Accommodation**

A *Biliton Beach Hotel*, Belitung's first international hotel is due to open in 1994, with 300 rm, a beach front location, large pool and tennis, T 788011 or F 88106 for details, part of the Aerowisata chain of hotels.

In Tanjung Pandan: **B-C** *Martani*, Jl Yos Sudarso, T 432, some a/c, clean rooms, well-run; **D** *Wisma Dewi*, Jl Srivijaya, some a/c, old house with ambience, clean rooms and friendly.

At Kelayan Beach: **D** *Kelayang Beach*.

● **Transport**

Air Daily connections on Merpati with Jakarta; two connections a week with Palembang and Bandar Lampung. Deraya fly to Pangkal Pinang.

Sea Boat: two ferry connections a week travel with Pangkal Pinang, 10 hrs (14,000Rp).

PALEMBANG TO BENGKULU

The road W from Palembang crosses the swampy plain and meets up with the Trans-Sumatran Highway at Muaraenim, 159 km away. From here it is only 43 km to Lahat where a minor road leads to Pagaralam and the megaliths of the Pasemah Plateau. Continuing NW from Lahat for 158 km, the Trans-Sumatran Highway reaches the junction town of Lubuklinggau. From here the Highway continues N towards Padang, while another road runs W. It crosses the Bukit Barisan and descends to the peaceful, and relatively unspoilt, town of Bengkulu – the capital of Bengkulu Province – and 268 km from Lahat. About 100 km offshore from Bengkulu is the remote and untouched island of Enggano.

PAGARALAM

Pagaralam is a small market town about 60 km SW of Lahat, set in the middle of the upland Pasemah Plateau which lies at

---

Bangka's tin mines

Bangka is part of a series of tin deposits which run from the lower hills of Burma, through Thailand and Peninsular Malaysia, to the islands of Belitung and Bangka. Between them, these deposits account for the bulk of world tin production. However, tin was not mined in Bangka until 1709 and today the rich alluvial deposits which attracted the Dutch have been nearly exhausted. The tin content of the ore has declined from 70% to 20%, or less.

The Dutch East India Company reached an agreement with the Sultan of Palembang over the exploitation of the tin ores of Bangka in 1755, and by the 19th century it had become one of the Dutch colonial government's most lucrative sources of revenue. However, the locals proved both unproductive and unwilling workers, and the mining firms – like those in British Malaya – began to employ Chinese indentured labourers. Conditions on the 'coolie' ships that brought these men from the over-populated and famine afflicted provinces of S China were sometimes little better than the vessels that took black slaves to the Caribbean. The death rate occasionally exceeded 50% just on the journey from Guangdong (Canton). The miners then had to endure hazardous and appalling working and living conditions.

At the beginning of the 20th century, the steam tin dredger revolutionised production and led to a dramatic improvement in working conditions. It also had the effect of putting the smaller (often Chinese-run) operations out of business, leading to the concentration of mining activity among a handful of large companies.

about 600m above sea level. Its single claim to fame are the megaliths that lie scattered over the surrounding countryside, particularly in the paddy fields lining the road to Manna (many bemos run along this road) and on the slopes of mounts Dempo and Gumai. They include obelisks, massive enigmatic carved figures of warriors, some carrying Dongson drums (see page 377), others riding on elephants or struggling with buffalo and some with helmets and swords. It is thought they were carved during the first centuries AD, although archaeologists' knowledge of their origins and meaning remains limited. The best and most accessible example lies in the beautiful gardens of a mosque, 3 km from town on the road to Mirasa. There is a good example of one of the megaliths in the Provincial Museum in Palembang (see page 527). A number of these massive stone carvings can be seen, literally, in among the houses of Pagaralam. Simply ask for directions. Better examples lie outside the town (see Excursions). In addition to the stone carvings, a series of subterranean chambers have been discovered, lined with stone slabs and decorated with red, yellow and black paintings. They are assumed to have been burial chambers although no bones have been found.

Excursions Megaliths The best concentrations of the finest megaliths are to be found in the vicinity of the villages of Muara Pinang (7 km from town) and Tegur Wangi (15 km from town). *Getting there*: easiest by chartered bemo.

● **Accommodation D** *Dharmakarya*, garden atmosphere; **D** *Losmen Mirasa*, Jl Major Ruslan, T 21266, friendly and helpful management with knowledge of surrounding area and megaliths (a guide from here charges US$10/day – worthwhile), good rooms and food.

● **Transport** 260 km from Palembang, 60 km from Lahat, 328 km from Bengkulu (9 hrs). **Road Bus**: Pagaralam lies off the Trans-Sumatran Highway; there are direct bus connections with Palembang, 7 hrs and Bengkulu, 5 hrs. A direct bus to Lampung leaves daily at midday.

BENGKULU

Bengkulu is the capital of Bengkulu province, the smallest province in Sumatra with 1.2 million inhabitants. Although few tourists visit the town, it is one of the most attractive in Sumatra. Bengkulu retains a large proportion of its colonial architectural inheritance and has not (yet) been scarred by insensitive redevelopment. Attractive wooden houses with raised porches, verandahs and elaborate fretwork still grace much of the town.

Bengkulu was originally known as *Bencoolen*. The English E India Company established a trading post here in 1685, building York Fort near Muara Air to protect their claim (of which nothing remains). For nearly 150 years, Bengkulu remained Britain's only colony in Southeast Asia. By the 18th century – and despite the population being periodically decimated by malaria – the port had become an important centre for the pepper trade. However, with the downturn in the pepper market in the 19th century, the town lost its economic *raison d'être*, and became a backwater. Perhaps because of the undemanding nature of administration in Bengkulu, the British Residents dispatched to the colony turned their attention to the surrounding countryside instead. Both Sir William Marsden (1771-1779) and Sir Stamford Raffles (1817-1824) were Residents of Bengkulu and both contributed significantly to contemporary knowledge of Sumatra. In 1824 the British and Dutch signed the Treaty of London, exchanging Bengkulu for Melaka and rationalizing their spheres of influence in the region.

In contemporary Indonesia, Bengkulu has acquired a degree of fame in being the town where Sukarno was placed under house arrest between 1933 and 1942, the Dutch no doubt believing that being such a quiet and inaccessible town it was the perfect place to 'lose' him.

Places of interest

Overlooking the sea on Jl Benteng is **Fort**

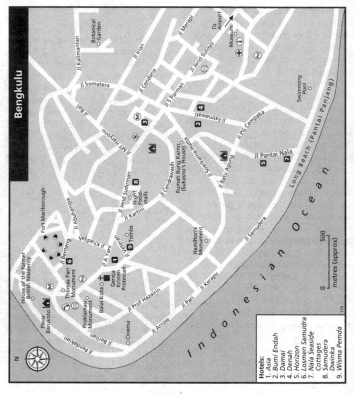

Marlborough or Benteng Marlborough. Dating from 1715 and approached through massive walls, it is an impressive and well-maintained piece of history – reputedly the strongest fort constructed by the British in the E after George Fort in Madras. Graves of British soldiers can be found here and there are reasonable views from the ramparts. Sukarno was incarcerated in Fort Marlborough when he was banished into internal exile by the Dutch in 1933; his bare quarters are marked. Despite the size of the fort's defences, it was twice overwhelmed, in 1719 by local rebels and in 1760 by the French. Malaria also took its toll and few soldiers or administrators made it back to Britain. Admis-

sion 250Rp. Open 0800-1400 Mon-Thur, 0900-1100 Fri, 0800-1200 Sat (**NB** It is also often open out of these official hours).

Just up the hill from the fort is the **Pasar Barukoto**, a large covered market. It faces onto a **classical British monument** built by Stamford Raffles – who was Resident from 1817-1824 – to a previous Resident, **Thomas Parr**. Parr was stabbed to death and then decapitated by disatisfied Bugis officers in 1807. The monument and market overlook **Chinatown** or *Kampung Cina*, which includes many of the town's older colonial buildings, among them the overgrown, though protected, ruins of the former **British Residency** (1760). Within sight of the Parr

Monument is the **Proklamasi Monument**, in the centre of a large, grassed square. Behind this is the elegant **Balai Kota** (the current Governor's residence), at the intersection of Jl Jend A Yani and Jl Ir Indra Caya.

A 5 mins walk from the Parr Monument, on Jl Veteran which runs off Jl Jend A Yani, is the orange corrugated iron-roofed **Gereja Kristen Protestan** or Protestant Church. Behind the church and in the compounds of the surrounding government offices, are the unloved tombs and graves of British and Dutch colonists, distorted by earthquakes.

On Jl Sukarno-Hatta, a 10 mins walk from the town centre, is a stark-white **mosque** designed, apparently, by Sukarno. At each of its four corners stand slender minarets, and the main body of the building is surmounted by five domes. A short distance S from the mosque is **Sukarno's house** – or Rumah Bung Karno – where he lived with his wife and children for part of the time of his period of internal exile in Bengkulu. The house has been turned into a museum and displays assorted Sukarno memorabilia. Admission 250Rp. Open Tues-Thur 0800-1400, Fri 0800-1100 and Sat 0800-1200.

Pantai Panjang or 'Long Beach' (7 km in all) begins about 1 km from Kampung Cina, and runs along the S coast. It is a romantic place to wander in the evenings, and interesting in the morning, when the fishing boats come in. Reasonable swimming, but surf and currents can be strong. Some accommodation is available (see below).

Excursions

Dendam Tak Sudah Lake and Botanical Gardens lie 8 km E of town. The rare water orchid *Vanda hookeriana* grows on its banks. *Getting there*: accessible only on foot or by 4WD.

Bengkulu was something of a base for naturalists during the 19th century. Stamford Raffles, while he was Resident, decided that as there was so little else to do he would turn his attention to the 'great volume of nature' in Sumatra. He discovered the magnificent, even monstrous, **Rafflesia flower** – the largest in the world (see page 490). The flower can be found growing in two locations off the road running E towards Palembang – outside Tabapenanjung and Kepahiang. They usually flower between Jul and Aug, for a few weeks only. Check at the PHPA Office, Jl Mahoni 11 before venturing out. *Getting there*: by bus from the Terminal Panorama.

Curup is a hill town 63 km NE of Bengkulu on the main road over the Bukit Barisan to Palembang. About 19 km E of Curup town is the active Mt Raba. Rising to a height of 1,937m, its 12 craters smoulder menacingly. A road runs from the foot of the mountain. *Getting there*: bus towards Palembang.

The **megaliths of Pagaralam** are to be found near the small market town of Pagaralam about 60 km SW of Lahat, over the Bukit Barisan, and 328 km from Bengkulu. In and around the town are numerous megaliths (see page 533). Accommodation available. *Getting there*: the trip really requires an overnight stay in Pagaralam; direct buses from Bengkulu, 5 hrs; taxis from Bengkulu to Pagaralam cost 90,000Rp one way.

Festivals

Jul: *Tabot* (movable): extends over 10 days and celebrates the martyrdom of Hussin and Hassan, two of Mohammad's grandsons. Effigies of Bouraq, a winged horse, are carried in procession with music and dancing. One of the most colourful and extravagant festivals in Sumatra.

Local information

● **Accommodation**

In town: **B** *Garden Inn*, Jl Kartini 25, T 21952, a/c, pool, best hotel in town, friendly management, attractive situation, central, rec; **B-C** *Dena*, Jl Fatmawati 29, T 21981, a/c, comfortable, but slightly out of town and overpriced.

C *Asia*, Jl Jend A Yani 922B, T 21901, a/c, restaurant, large rooms, central location; **C-D** *Samudera Dwinka*, Jl Jend Sudirman 246, T 21604, some a/c, friendly and central, price incl breakfast, rec; **C-D** *Wisma Pemda*, Jl Veteran 1 (at the end furthest from Jl Jend A Yani), T 20562, a/c, peaceful location, good value, price incl breakfast.

D *Bumi Endah*, Jl Fatmawati 29, T 21665, a/c, out of town centre, average rooms.

E *Losmen Hayani*, Jl S Parman 5, T 20718, out of town nr General Post Office, attractive colonial house, average rooms; **E** *Surya*, Jl K Z Abidin 26 (Chinatown), T 21341; **E** *Wisma Kenanga*, Jl Let. Kol. Santoso, T 21709, attractive colonial house with only average rooms.

F *Damai*, Jl K Z Abidin 18 (Chinatown), T 21439, some rooms with attached mandi; **F** *Losmen Samudera*, Jl Benteng 213, T 21231, in the shadow of Fort Marlborough, dirty rooms.

On the beach (4 km from town): **A-B** *Horizon* (formerly the *Pantai Nala Samudra*), Jl Pantai Nala 142, T 31722, a/c, pool, best available beach accommodation but rather characterless.

C *Nala Seaside Cottages*, Jl Pantai Nala 133, T 21855, restaurant, bungalows on the beach, attractive but basic amenities for the price.

● **Places to eat**
There are a number of restaurants along Jl Jend Sudirman (which becomes Jl Suprapto), incl *Pak Liha* at No 215 and *Simpang Raya* at 380A (serving Padang food). There are many foodstalls on the same road, some with excellent and cheap seafood. The *Citra*, also on Jl Jend Sudirman, serves Chinese and Javanese food. There is a **bakery** (the *New Holland*) at Jl Suprapto 85.

Foodstalls: the night stalls on Jl Sudirman sell good seafood.

● **Airline offices**
Garuda, Jl Jend A Yani 922B, T 21119; Merpati, *Samudera Dwinka Hotel*, Jl Jend Sudirman 246, T 42337.

● **Banks & money changers**
Bank Central Asia, Jl Suprapto 150; Bumi Daya, Jl Indra Caya; Ekspor Impor, Jl Suprapto.

● **Entertainment**
Cinemas: two a/c cinemas on Jl Jend Sudirman.

● **Hospitals & medical services**
General Hospital: Jl Padang Harapan, T 31919.

● **Post & telecommunications**
Area code: 0736.

General Post Office: Jl S Parman 111 (S edge of town).

Perumtel: Jl Suprapto 155 for long distance telephone calls.

Post Office: Jl Jend A Yani 38 (facing the Parr Monument) and more central than the GPO.

● **Shopping**
Handicrafts: rattan products and the local batik *besurek*. There is a handicraft shop between the Nala Seaside Cottages and Pantai Nala Samudra.

● **Sports**
Golf: *Lampangan Golf Course* on Jl Rustandi, SE of town, open to non-members.

● **Tourist offices**
Bengkulu Tourist Office, Jl Pembangunan 14, T 21272, out of town; not really geared to tourists.

● **Useful addresses**
Immigration Office: Jl Padang Harapan.

PHPA: Jl Mahoni 11 (for permits to local National Park).

● **Transport**
560 km from Padang, 460 km from Palembang.

Local The inter-provincial and local **bus** station is Terminal Panorama, about 7 km from town; get there by **bemo** from the central market. Bemos run fixed routes around town (150Rp), or they can be chartered.

Air Kemiling Airport is 14 km from town. Connections on Merpati with Jakarta, Bandar Lampung, Batam, Palembang, Jambi, Medan, and Padang. *Transport to town*: by taxi, 10,000Rp; or walk out onto the road and catch a bus or bemo.

Road Bus: the Terminal Panorama is 7 km E of town; regular bemos link it with the central market. *Citra Rafflesia*, Jl M T Haryono 12 operate a/c and non-a/c buses to Jakarta 22 hrs, Padang 24 hrs, Palembang 16 hrs and other destinations in Java and Sumatra. *Indah Tour and Travel*, Jl M T Haryono 14 and *Citra Travel Agent*, Jl Suprapto 88 also arrange bus transport. *Sriwijaya Express*, Jl Bali 36 operate buses to Muko Muko and Sungai Penuh.

Sea Boat: there are weekly boats to Enggano Island from Baai Harbour about 15 km S of town. The Pelni ship *Baruna Dwipa* also docks here on its fortnightly circuit between Padang and

Jakarta; it also calls at Enggano Island. The Pelni office is at Jl Khadijah 10, T 21013.

ENGGANO ISLAND

Enggano Island is about 100 km off the W coast of Sumatra, and is one of the least visited spots in Indonesia. There is excellent snorkeling, peaceful villages and jungle walks. It is said the name *Enggano* is derived from the Portuguese for 'disappointment'; they had hoped it would be clothed in valuable clove trees – it was not.

● **Accommodation** E-F *Losmen Apaho*, Malakoni, the only official place to stay although locals will allow visitors to stay in their homes – ask the *kepala desa* (village headman) on arrival.

● **Transport Boat** Irregular connections with Bengkulu's Baai Harbour about 15 km S of town. Alternatively, boats can be chartered at Bintuhan, a port to the S of Bengkulu near the border with Lampung province. The Pelni vessel *Lawit* also calls here on its fortnightly circuit between Java, Sumatra and Kalimantan (see route schedule page 921).

(see route schedule page 921)

MUARAENIM TO BANDAR LAMPUNG, BAKAUHENI AND JAVA

Muaraenim is an important crossroads, linking Palembang, Bengkulu, Bandar Lampung and destinations to the N. From Muaraenim the Trans-Sumatran Highway runs S through monotonous countryside into Lampung province and the provincial capital of Bandar Lampung, almost 400 km away. Another 90 km S of here is Bakauheni, the port where ferries cross the Sunda Strait – passing Krakatau – to Merak in W Java.

BANDAR LAMPUNG

Tanjungkarang, a hillside administrative centre and **Telukbetung**, the port 5 km to the S, are the twin cities of Lampung province and have recently been amalgamated and renamed **Bandar Lampung**. Telukbetung was almost entirely destroyed by the tidal wave which followed the eruption of Krakatau. Bandar Lam-

Caripaksa: sanctioned kidnapping

One of the more surprising cultural features of the Lampungese is *caripaksa* – the sanctioned abduction of women for marriage. Although most women find their partners by more normal means, *caripaksa* is still common in rural areas. Becky Elmhirst's research in Tiuh Baru showed that 20% of women were married in this way.

Caripaksa operates in the following way: a young man, with the help of male accomplices, will abduct – effectively kidnap – an unwilling young woman and then imprison her in his parents' house. Though the girl's family may often come and protest, even threaten violence, local *adat* (see the box on page 55) means that ultimately they must accept their daughter's marriage. The *kepala desa* (headmen) of Tiuh Baru did maintain that if a girl is adamant she does not wish to marry she can go home, but such is the shame brought upon the girl and her family that very few opt out in this manner:

"I was married in 1989, I was 18. He was some sort of distant relative. I was grabbed as I was coming out of the house. I didn't want to marry him. I cried. Who wouldn't cry! I couldn't go home again. My parents were very angry. They came and threw stones at his house."

It is partly because of the risks of *caripaksa* that so many unmarried girls from Tiuh Baru travelled to the Javanese town of Tengarang to work in a garment factory. There they were safe from the young men of their home region.

pung is the main bus and train terminus for travellers arriving from, or leaving for, the N of Sumatra. The train and bus stations are both in Tanjungkarang.

Today Lampung is one of the poorest provinces in Indonesia, a consequence – in part – of the numbers of transmigrants who have been settled here from Java (see box, page 427). Annual population growth was over 5% in the 1970s, and now the province has more than 6 million inhabitants, a degraded environment, and severe poverty. It is claimed only one in 10 of Lampung's inhabitants were born in the province.

Places of interest

As a major transit point, there is a good range of accommodation, but few sights. The **Provincial Museum** is situated on Jl Teuku Umar, and has a small collection of local *kain tapis* – or 'ship cloths' (see box below) – and archaeological and ethnographic pieces. Open 0800-1230, 1330-1600 Mon-Thur and Sat; 0800-1100, 1330-1600 Fri.

Excursions

Pasir Putih is the closest good beach to the city, situated 16 km S on the road to Bakauheni. Rather further afield is **Merak Belantung**, 43 km S of town; this is a beautiful sandy beach, good for swimming, with facilities for windsurfing. Accommodation available. *Getting there*: bus to Panjang and then on towards Bakauheni.

Mount Rajabasa lies about 80 km S of Bandar Lampung and close to Bakauheni. A scenic road runs around the S slopes of this dormant volcano. The route to Mt Rajabasa passes through **Canti**, where it is possible to take the ferry to the small islands of **Sebuku** and **Sebesi**, or to charter a boat to **Krakatau** (3 hrs) (see page 144).

Pugung Raharja Archaeological Park is situated about 40 km NE of town. This fortified town is thought to date from the 12th to the 17th century, and among the remains are megaliths and stepped temples. It was discovered in the 1950s by transmigrants who had moved to the area. There is a small museum 1 km from the site. *Getting there*: the site is about 2½ km N (left) off the main road; catch a bus running towards Sribawono and alight after the road crosses the Sekampung River; then walk.

Way Kambas National Park and Elephant Reserve occupies 1,300 sq km expanse of low-lying land bordering the Sunda Strait and Java Sea. The park was first delimited as a Protection Forest by the Dutch in 1924, who upgraded its status to a Game Reserve in 1937. It was finally declared a National Park in 1982 – making it one of the oldest protected areas in Indonesia. Even so, much of the area has been partially logged over the years and only some one fifth remains as forest. It is best known for its large population of elephants – about 250-300 – and its elephant training school. Fauna also includes a number of primates including macaques, gibbons, langurs and siamangs, as well as other large mammals such as small populations of tapir, Sumatran tiger, wild dog, Sumatran rhino, clouded leopard and honey bear. 300 species of bird have been identified, among them the rhinoceros hornbill and white-winged duck. Bird-watching trips on the Kanan River are popular. The park office is at Tridatu, about 10 km N of Jepara; permits are issued here. The Elephant Training Camp is the most popular tourist attraction and is situated at Kadang-sari. **Accommodation D** *Way Kanan Resort*, Way Kanan, 13.5 km into the Park on the Way Kanan River. Basic accommodation in chalet huts. Mosquito nets provided. Bring your own food and drink. No cooking facilities. In the early morning you can see wild deer and wild pig wondering through the resort. Herds of wild elephants have also been known to visit. *Getting there*: by vehicle (30 mins). Take an ojek (motorbike taxi) from the park entrance (7,500Rp one way). Boat trips can be arranged through the PHPA war-

Bandar Lampung

Jl Sam Ratulangi

Jl Imam Bonjol

Jl Tamin

Jl Srikresno

Jl P Antasari

Jl Kota Raja

TANJUNG-KARANG

Jl Agus Salim

Jl Pinang

Jl Hayamwuruk

W Away

Jl Katamso

Jl Dr Harun

Jl R Sutioso

Jl Kartini

Jl Raden Intan

Jl Ri Said

Jl Mas Mansur

Jl S Parman

Jl A Yani

Jl Sudirman

Jl Perintis Kemerdekaan

Jl Jend Gatot

Jl Cendana

Jl Dr Amir Hamzah

Jl Way Sekampung

Jl Diponegoro

Jl Emir M Nur

Jl Rasuna Said

Jl Dr Susilo

Jl Dewi Sartika

Jl Cutmutiah

Jl W Monginsidi

Jl Cipto Mangunkusumo

Jl Basuki Rahmat

Jl Akhmad Dahlan

Jl Salim Batubara

W Balahu

TELUKBETUNG

Jl WR Supratman

Jl Tenggiri

Jl Kembung

Lampung Bay

Hotels:
1. Arinas
2. Indra Palace
3. Kurnia City
4. Kurnia Dua
5. Losmen Gunungsari
6. Marcopolo
7. Penginapan Berkah
8. Ria
9. Sahid Krakatau

0   500
Meters

den. Expensive at 75,000Rp for a short trip, but well worth it just to see the abundance of bird life.

Bukit Barisan Selatan National Park straddles the southernmost section of the Barisan range of mountains and includes 120 km of coast. A road runs W from Bandar Lampung to the town of Kota Agung (about 80 km), on the edge of the park. Fauna include Sumatran tigers, elephants, honey bear, rhinoceros, pigs, pheasant as well as some rare flora including the famous rafflesia flower (see page 490). *Getting there*: the easiest entry point into the park is via Kota Agung (accommodation available); regular buses from Bandar Lampung, 2½ hrs.

Tours

Tours can be arranged to most of the sights around Bandar Lampung (see Travel agents).

Local information
● **Accommodation**

Most of the top and mid-range accommodation is in what was formerly Telukbetung, on Lampung Bay; while lower-range losmen are concentrated in Tanjungkarang, 5 km to the N. Regular bemos link the two towns.

In Telukbetung: **A** *Indra Palace*, Jl W Monginsidi 70, T 62766, F 62399, a/c, rooms are well appointed, situated outside the town on a hill with good views but inconvenient; **A** *Sheraton*, Jl W Monginsidi 175, T 46666, F 46690, a/c, restaurant, pool, good sports facilities incl tennis and fitness centre, top class, low-rise hotel set around a swimming pool – best in town with 107 rm; **B** *Marcopolo*, Jl Dr Susilo 4, T 62511, F 54419, a/c, restaurant, large pool, set on the hill with good views and friendly management, best of the mid-range hotels; **B** *Sahid Krakatau*, Jl Yos Sudarso 294, T 46589, F 63589, a/c, restaurant, pool, on the beach; **B-C** *Arinas*, Jl Raden Intan 35A, T 66778, a/c, hot water, the most recent addition, comfortable; **C-D** *Andalas*, Jl Raden Intan 89, T 63432, some a/c, comfortable but characterless; **C-D** *Kurnia City*, Jl Raden Intan 144, T 62030, some a/c, restaurant, pool, tennis courts, rather noisy location but central with good range of facilities; **D** *Kurnia Dua*, Jl Raden Intan 75, T 52905, F 55512; **E** *Losmen Bahagia Raya*, Jl Bawal 72, small rooms, rather dark and dirty.

In Tanjungkarang: numerous, generally poor quality accommodation on Jl Kota Raja; **E** *Losmen Gunungsari*, Jl Kota Raja 21; **E** *Penginapan Berkah*, Jl Kota Raja 19; **D-E** *Hotel Ria*, Jl Kartini, T 53974, some a/c.

● **Places to eat**

An abundance of Padang food restaurants here – even more than usual – but also some excellent Chinese, seafood and European food too – the Sheraton and Sahid Krakatau both have good, but expensive, restaurants.

International: ♦*Cookies Corner*, Jl Kartini 29, good burgers and salads, as well as Chinese and Indonesian food.

Padang: *Begadang II*, Jl Diponegoro, also serves other Indonesian food, rec; ♦♦*Simpang Raya*, Jl Diponegoro 18, rec.

Foodstalls: ♦Jl Yos Sudarso in the evenings; ♦*Pasar Mambo*, S end of Jl W Monginsidi, evening stalls selling excellent seafood and Chinese food.

● **Airline offices**

Garuda, *Marcopolo Hotel*, Jl Dr Susilo 4; **Merpati**, Jl Kartini 90, T 63419.

● **Post & telecommunications**
Area code: 0721.

Post Office: Jl Hasanudin 41.

Telephone Office: Jl Majapahit 1.

● **Shopping**

Textiles: Lampung is best known for its fine traditional textiles (see box). Good examples are harder and harder to find though; try the *Lampung Art Shop*, Jl Kartini 12 (Tanjungkarang).

● **Tour companies & travel agents**

Femmy, Jl Dempo 35, T 42593; *Sahid Gema Wisata*, Sahid Krakatau Hotel, Jl Yos Sudarso 29A, T 46589.

● **Tourist offices**

Jl Kotaraja 12, T 51900, English speaking and helpful.

● **Transport**

90 km from Bakauheni.

Local Bus, **minibus** and **bemos** (200Rp around town): buses and bemos run between Telukbetung, Tanjungkarang and the main Rajabasa bus terminal, N of town. Both intra and inter-provincial buses leave from Rajabasa. Bemos can also be chartered (about 8,000Rp/hr). **Car rental**: Avis at the *Sheraton Hotel*. **Taxis**: hang around the more expensive hotels.

Ship cloths and tapis: textiles of Lampung

Some of the finest examples of weaving Indonesia has ever produced are the 'ship cloths' of Lampung. Sadly, fine pieces are no longer woven, and can only be seen in museums and private collections. The principal motif is usually a ship, or a pair of ships, geometrically interpreted and symbolizing death and the afterlife. This motif is complemented by animals, houses, umbrellas, banners and other designs. The pattern is produced using a supplementary coloured weft woven into a plain, unbleached, cotton ground.

Usually, two types of ship cloth are identified. The *palepai* was produced by the aristocratic Kroe families of Lake Ranau, and are more often called *kain kroe*. These were traditionally used during important transitional ceremonies such as birth, death and circumcision, and were hung on the wall of the wife's side of the house. In this instance, the ship symbolizes not just death, but more generally the progress from one stage of life to the next. As the function of these pieces as ceremonial objects has declined, so too has their quality. Many of the pieces on sale today are second-rate. The second type of ship cloth is the *tampan*. These were produced more widely across Lampung and were not associated solely with higher class families. They were commonly exchanged as gifts, and motifs and designs are less constrained by convention.

However, the most ostentatious Lampung textiles were the glorious gold and silver embroidered *tapis* sarongs worn as ceremonial cloths by women. Tapis began to be made after Chinese technology of sericulture and embroidery were introduced by traders in the 14th century. The gold and silver thread is a cotton or silk yarn, wrapped around with gold or silver leaf; it must be embroidered using couching stitches because the process of sewing would damage it. Fine pieces might take a year to make and weigh 5 kg. It is still possible to buy *tapis*, although decoration tends to be simpler and the work less fine.

Air The airport is at Branti, 24 km N of the city. Taxis run passengers into town. Regular connections on Merpati with Jakarta, Palembang, Jambi and Padang.

Train The station is on the N side of town. Two trains a day leave for Palembang at 0800 and 2030, 9 hrs. From Palembang there are trains to Lubuklinggau, or buses to various other Sumatran destinations (see Palembang). If intending to travel straight on by train to Lubuklinggau, get off at Prabumulih – the Lubuklinggau train stops here.

Road Bus: the Rajabasa terminal lies 10 km N of town. Constant minibuses run there from town. Bus companies have their offices at the terminal and a/c and non-a/c buses leave for Palembang, Jambi 30 hrs, Padang 36 hrs, Bukittinggi 38 hrs, Sibolga 48 hrs, Medan 60 hrs, Banda Aceh 72 hrs and Jakarta – via the ferry at Bakauheni – 8 hrs. Buses to Bakauhani ferry terminal leave regularly from the station.

BAKAUHENI

Bakauheni, situated at Sumatra's SE tip, is the ferry port for Java. Ferries ply the 27 km-wide Sunda Strait to Merak every hour or so, within sight of Krakatau (see page 144). There is little here, although the 90 km trip N to Bandar Lampung passes through attractive scenery.

● **Transport** 90 km from Bandar Lampung. **Road Bus**: from the terminal to Bandar Lampung 2 hrs. **Sea Boat**: regular car ferries link Bakauheni with Merak, W Java. Times of departure vary through the year, but normally there are between 15 and 30 crossings/day (fewer at night), 2 hrs (22,750Rp/car, 1,550-2,050Rp pp). Passengers should be ready for a hot and crowded crossing – there are three classes, and it is worth paying extra for first class. Buses and share taxis wait at the ferry terminal to take passengers on to the main Rajabasa bus terminal in Bandar Lampung, or to the city centre.

Indonesian Borneo: Kalimantan

Horizons	542	Central Kalimantan	579
Banjarmasin and South Kalimantan	568	Balikpapan and East Kalimantan	581
Tanjung Puting National Park and		Pontianak and West Kalimantan	599

KALIMANTAN is a huge, thinly populated territory of swamps, jungle, mountains and rivers. Borneo, of which Kalimantan forms the major part, has always held a mystical fascination for westerners – it was a vast isolated, jungle-covered island, where head-hunters ran wild, and which, if romantic myths were to be believed, was rich in gold and diamonds. It is the third largest island in the world (after Greenland and New Guinea) and is divided between three countries: Indonesia, Malaysia and Brunei. Kalimantan's 549,000 sq km (nearly 30% of Indonesia's total land area) has just 5% of the country's population (about 9.5 million), most of which is concentrated in a handful of coastal cities. The interior is populated by various Dayak tribes, whose villages are scattered along the riverbanks.

HORIZONS

The name Borneo is thought to be a European mispronunciation of Brunei. This was not entirely the Europeans' fault, for as John Crawford points out in *A Descriptive Dictionary of the Indian Isles* (1856), the name is "indifferently pronounced by the Malays, according to the dialect they happen to speak – Brune, Brunai, Burne or Burñai". The sultanate itself became known as 'Borneo Proper', and its capital as Brunei Town. Crawfurd concluded that "the name of the town was not extended to the island by European writers, but by the Mohamedan navigators who conducted the carrying trade of the archipelago before the advent of Europeans". Borneo Proper was first visited by Europeans in the early 16th century, most

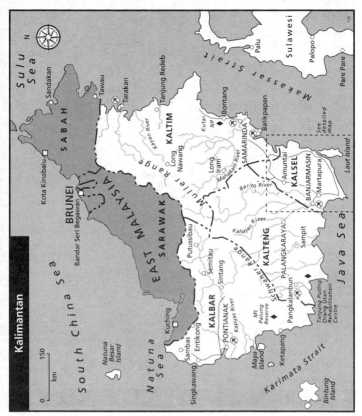

notably by Antonio Pigafetta, the official chronicler on the Portuguese explorer Ferdinand Magellan's expedition, which called in on the Sultan of Brunei in 1521 (see page 551). The Ibans of Sarawak maintain that the name Borneo derives from the Malay *buah nyior*, meaning 'coconut', while the Malays had another, less well-known name for the island: Kalimantan. This, according to Crawfurd, was the name of a species of wild mango "and the word... would simply mean 'Isle of Mangoes'". This was the name chosen by Indonesia for its section of the island; for some reason, it is generally translated as 'River of Diamonds'– probably because of the diamond fields near Martapura in the S (see page 573).

THE LAND

Three countries have territory on Borneo, but only one of them, the once all-powerful and now tiny but oil-rich sultanate of Brunei, is an independent sovereign state in itself. It is flanked to the W by the Malaysian state of Sarawak and to the E by Sabah, formerly British North Borneo, and now also a Malaysian state. Indonesian Borneo, occupies about three-quarters of the island.

GEOGRAPHY

During the Pleistocene period, Borneo was joined to mainland Southeast Asia, forming a continent which geologists know as Sundaland. The land bridge to mainland Asia meant that many species – both flora and fauna – arrived in what is now Borneo before it was cut off by rising sea levels. Borneo is part of the Sunda shelf. Its interior is rugged and mountainous and is dissected by many large rivers, navigable deep into the interior. The two biggest rivers are in Kalimantan: the Kapuas flows W from the centre of the island, and the Mahakam flows E. About half of Borneo's land area however, is under 150m – particularly the swampy S coastal region. About half of Indonesia's total swampland is in Kalimantan.

Borneo's highest mountain, Gunung Kinabalu in Sabah (4,101m) is often declared the 'highest mountain in Southeast Asia'. Despite this claim being repeated so many times that it has taken on the status of a truth, it isn't: there are higher peaks in Indonesia's province of Irian Jaya and in Myanmar (Burma). Kinabalu is a granite mound called a pluton, which was forced up through the sandstone strata during the Pliocene period, about 15 million years ago. The highest peak in Kalimantan is Gunung Rajah (2,278m) in the Schwaner Range, to the SW. The mountain ranges in the W and centre of the island run E-to-W and curve round to the NE. Borneo's coal, oil and gas-bearing strata are Tertiary deposits which are heavily folded; most of the oil and gas is found off the NW and E coasts. The island is much more geologically stable than neighbouring Sulawesi or Java – islands in the so-called 'ring of fire'. Borneo only experiences about four mild earthquakes a year compared with 40-50 on other nearby islands. But because there are no active volcanoes, Borneo's soils are not particularly rich.

Kalimantan itself is divided into four provinces. South Kalimantan (or Kalimantan Selatan) is ubiquitously referred to as **Kalsel** and is the smallest of the four; it is the most accessible from Java and is also the highlight of most tourists' visits to Kalimantan. To the W is Central Kalimantan (Kalimantan Tenggah) which is known as **Kalteng**. It is a vast province with a very small population; few foreign tourists venture here – its only real tourist attraction is a remote orang utan rehabilitation centre near the

---

River roads

In Borneo, rivers are often the main arteries of communication. Although roads are being built, linking most main towns, many Dayak (tribal) longhouse communities are only accessible by river. Rivers are the mediators that divide forest dwellers from coastal settlers and this is usually expressed in terms of upriver, or *hulu* and downstream, or *hilir*. The two terms are not just geographical; they also reflect different lifestyles and economies, different religions and cultures. In Borneo, to be *hulu* is to set oneself apart from the Malay peoples of the lowlands and coasts.

Contrary to many assumptions, the tribal *hulu* peoples were never entirely isolated and self-reliant. From early times, there was a flourishing trade between the coasts and the interior. Upriver tribal peoples would exchange exotic jungle products like rattan, benzoin, camphor, skins, hornbill 'ivory', precious stones and rare dyes for products that they could not obtain in the forest – like iron, salt, dried fish (now, tinned fish), betel and gambier. They also bartered for prestige objects like brass gongs, large ceramic Chinese pots, and Dutch silver coins. Many of these prestige objects can still be seen in the longhouses of Borneo and have become precious heirlooms or *pusaka*.

swampy S coast. East Kalimantan (Kalimantan Timur) is known as **Kaltim** and is the richest of the four provinces because of its timber, oil and gas resources. Its main attraction is the Mahakam River which penetrates deep into the interior from the provincial capital, Samarinda. West Kalimantan (Kalimantan Barat) –

20/20 vision: Kalimantan bushfires

1994 saw a repeat of the bushfires in Kalimantan of 1982-3, 1987 and 1991. The 1982-3 outbreak was the most serious, affecting 3.6 million ha of forest (an area equivalent to that of Belgium) although some estimates put the area affected in 1994 at around 5 million ha. Fires of this nature have always been a feature of the island, and of Sumatra. Shifting cultivators and foresters have traditionally cleared land in the dry season through firing, a much more efficient approach than clearing by hand. Bushfires also sometimes naturally occur, and many forests in Southeast Asia where there is a pronounced dry season are adapted to periodic burning (so-called fire climaxes). The blazes reach temperatures of 600C, roasting the subsoil and killing root systems and micro-organisms to depths of more than 2m. Experts believe some of the worst fires have coincided with areas where there are underground coal deposits, suggesting that some of these have been set alight; the coal smoulders for years and is virtually impossible to extinguish.

The media has tended to report the fires in terms of the effects that they have had on air quality in Singapore and Kuala Lumpur (where most journalists happen to be based), and the problems they cause airliners trying to land in poor visibility. In KL the almost seasonal nature of the fires has led locals to call the effects simply 'the haze', almost as if it were as natural as the 'wet season'. At the end of Sep 1994, at Shah Alam, 15 km from KL, pollution levels reached an index of '500'-'300' is defined by the authorities as 'hazardous', and visibility was down to 400m. In Singapore the reading (based on a different index) was 142, when anything above 100 is defined as 'unhealthy'. The *Straits Times* ran an editorial entitled 'Give Us Back Our Day'. Street traders were doing a brisk business in face masks and there were widespread reports of eye irritation, asthma attacks, headaches and breathing difficulties. Although the root of the problem is clearly the fires themselves, their effect is combined with car exhaust and other local emissions to produce the haze.

But it almost goes without saying that the main effects are felt in Kalimantan itself. The fires have killed wildlife, created treeless landscapes where the first rains of January cause rapid overland flow and erosion, and have undermined the livelihood strategies of those Dayaks (and others) who rely on the forest.

The question which has occupied people is why have the fires apparently become so much more severe. One explanation is that the climate has become considerably drier. This appeals to those who see the root cause as global environmental change – global warming, the greenhouse effect. Possibly more likely though is that deforestation has lowered the ability of the land to retain moisture. Another explanation, popular with government officials, is that the main culprits are shifting cultivators who traditionally burn the forest to create clearings for agriculture (*ladangs*). If this is true, then it is more likely that the culprits are not the Dayaks (tribal peoples) but those immigrants to Kalimantan who are unskilled in the art of swiddening. Those who prefer a natural explanation say the fires are a result of the periodic dry periods associated with changes in the El Niño Southern Oscillation. In an effort to prevent future bushfires on the scale of 1994's, President Suharto outlawed the clearing of land by fire in April 1995.

or **Kalbar** – is, like neighbouring Kalteng, visited by few tourists. It is cut off from the rest of Kalimantan by the mountainous, jungled interior and can only be reached by air – although some E coast tour operators offer 2-week trans-Borneo treks. The longest river in Indonesia, the 1,243 km-long Kapuas, reaches far into the interior from Kalbar's capital, Pontianak.

Tourists usually come to Kalimantan in search of two things: jungle and jungle culture – the Dayak forest tribes. It sometimes comes as a shock that loggers have beaten them into the jungle, particularly in the more accessible areas along the coasts and rivers. For quite long distances on either side of the riverbanks, the primary forest has all been 'harvested'. Kalimantan's powerful rivers (the Kapuas, Mahakam and Berito) have been the arteries of commerce and 'civilization'; the riverbanks are lined with towns and villages as far as they are navigable. Missionaries and traders have also beaten tourists into the tribal interior. Many Dayak tribes have been converted to Christianity and most have completely abandoned their cultures, traditions and animist religion. The majority of upriver people – apart from those in the remoter parts of the Apo Kayan in Kaltim – prefer to wear jeans and T-shirts and many have relatively well-payed jobs in the timber industry.

In the neighbouring Malaysian state of Sarawak (which can now be reached overland from Pontianak), tribal culture is much more intact and more readily accessible. Despite Sarawak's notorious logging industry, its national parks are better geared to cater for 'ecotourists' than Kalimantan's and the state's tourism infrastructure is more developed. That said, it is still possible to visit traditional longhouses in Kalimantan (in the hills of Kalsel and the upper reaches of the Mahakam and Kenyah rivers in Kaltim) – and trek through tracts of virgin rainforest. But trips to these areas take time and cost money. There are several experienced adventure tourism companies in Kalimantan – mostly based in Balikpapan and Samarinda. They categorize their tours into 'comfortable', 'safari' and 'adventure'. There are also a number of tour operators and travel agents around the world dealing with adventure tours to Kalimantan. Most have direct dealings with tour companies in Banjarmasin, Balikpapan and Samarinda.

CLIMATE

Borneo has a typical equatorial monsoon climate: the weather usually follows predictable patterns, although in recent years it has been less predictable – a phenomenon some environmentalists attribute to deforestation and others to periodic changes to the El Nin_-Southern Oscillation. Temperatures are fairly uniform, averaging 23-33°C during the day and rarely dropping below 20°C at night, except in the mountains, where they can drop to below 10°C. Most rainfall occurs between Nov and Jan during the NE monsoon; this causes rivers to flood, and there are many short, sharp cloudbursts. The dry season runs from May to Sep. It is characterized by dry S-easterly winds and is the best time to visit. Rainfall generally increases towards the interior; most of Borneo receives about 2,000-3,000 mm a year, although some upland areas get more than 4,000 mm. Note that there are significant variations in the pattern of rainfall across Kalimantan; see page 1050 for a graph of monthly rainfall and temperature in Balikpapan (see page 581).

FLORA AND FAUNA

Borneo's ancient rainforests are rich in flora and fauna, including over 9,000 species of flowering plant, 200 species of mammals, 570 species of birds, 100 species of snake, 250 species of fresh water fish and 1,000 species of butterfly. The theory of natural selection enunciated by Victorian naturalist Alfred Russel Wallace (see page 690) – while that other great Victorian scientist Charles Darwin was coming to similar conclusions several thousand miles away – was influenced by Wallace's observations in Borneo in the 1850s and 1860s.

Flora

As late as the middle of the 19th century, the great bulk – perhaps as much as 95% – of the land area of Borneo was forested. Alfred Russel Wallace, like other Western travellers was enchanted by the island's natural wealth and diversity: "ranges of hill and valley everywhere", he wrote, "everwhere covered with inteminable forest". But Borneo's jungle is disappearing fast – some naturalists would say that over extensive areas it has disappeared – and since the mid-1980s there has been a mounting international environmental campaign against deforestation. The campaign has been particularly vocal in Sarawak but other parts of the island are also suffering rapid deforestation, notably Sabah and also Indonesia's province of E Kalimantan. Harold Brookfield, Lesley Potter and Byron state in their hard-headed book *In place of the forest* (1995):

"Concerning those large areas of forest that have been totally cleared and converted to other uses or that lie waste [in Borneo], we can state only that there is nothing to be gained from bemoaning the past. A great resource has been squandered, and the major part of the habitat of a great range of plant and animal species has been destroyed. Moreover, this has been done with far less than adequate economic return to the two nations [Malaysia and Indonesia] concerned."

How extensive has been the loss of species as a result of the logging of Borneo's forests is a topic of heated debate. Brookfield *et al* in the volume noted above suggest that there "is very little basis in firm research for the spectacular figures of species loss rates that appear not infrequently in sections of the conservationist literature and that readily attract media attention." But they do admit that the flora and fauna of Borneo is especially diverse with a high degree of endemism and that there has been a significant loss of biodiversity as a result of extensive logging. It has been estimated that 32% of terrestrial mammals, 70% of leaf beetles, and 50% of flowering plants are endemic to Borneo – in other words, they are found no where else.

The best known timber trees fall into three categories, all of them hardwoods. Heavy hardwoods include *selangan batu* and *resak*; medium hardwoods include *kapur*, *keruing* and *keruntum*; light hardwoods include *madang tabak*, *ramin* and *meranti*. There are both peat-swamp and hill varieties of meranti, which is one of the most valuable export logs. *Belian*, or Bornean iron wood (*Eusideroxylon zwageri*) is one of the hardest and densest timbers in the world. It is thought that the largest belian may be 1,000 years or more old. They are so tough that when they die they continue to stand for centuries before the wood rots to the extent that the trunk falls. On average, there are about 25 commercial tree species per hectare, but because they are hard to extract, 'selective logging' invariably results in the destruction of many unselected trees.

The main types of forest include: **lowland rainforest** (mixed dipterocarp) on slopes up to 600m. Dipterocarp forest is stratified into three main layers, the top one rising to heights of 45m. In the top layer, trees' crowns interlock to form a closed canopy of foliage. The word 'dipterocarp' comes from the Greek and means 'two-winged fruit' or 'two [di]-winged [ptero] seed [carp]'. The leaf-like appendages of the mature dipterocarp fruits have 'wings' which makes them spin as they fall to the ground, like giant sycamore seeds. Some species have more than two wings but are all members of the dipterocarp family. It is the lowland rainforest which comes closest to the Western ideal of a tropical 'jungle'. It is also probably the most species rich forest in Borneo. A recent study of a dipterocarp forest in Malaysia found that an area of just

50 ha supported no less than 835 species of tree. In Europe or North America a similar area of forest would support less than 100 tree species. The red resin produced by many species of dipterocarp, and which can often be seen staining the trunk, is known as *damar* and was traditionally used as a lamp 'oil'. Another characteristic feature of the trees found in lowland dipterocarp rainforest is buttressing – the flanges of wood that protrude from the base of the trunk. For some time the purpose of these massive buttresses perplexed botanists who arrived at a whole range of ingenious explanations. Now they are thought – sensibly – to provide structural support. Two final characteristics of this type of forest are that it is very dark on the forest floor (explaining why trees take so long to grow) and that it is not the inpenetrable jungle of Tarzan fantasy. The first characteristic explains the second. Only when a gap appears in the forest canopy – after a tree falls – do light-loving pioneer plants get the chance to grow. When the gap in the camopy is filled by another tree, these grasses, shrubs and smaller trees die back once more.

Many of the rainforest trees are an important resource for Dayak communities. The jelutong tree, for example, is tapped like a rubber tree for its sap ('jungle chewing gum') which is used to make tar for waterproof sealants – used in boatbuilding. It also hardens into a tough but brittle black plastic-like substance used for *parang* (machette) handles.

Montane forest occurs at altitudes above 600m, although in some areas it does not replace lowland rainforest until considerably higher than this. Above 1,200m mossy forest predominates. Montane forest is denser than lowland forest with smaller trees of narrower girth. Moreover, dipterocarps are generally not found while flowering shrubs like magnolias and rhododendrons appear. In place of dipterocarps, tropical latitude oaks as well as other trees that are more characteristic of temperate areas, like myrtle and laurel, make an appearance.

The low-lying river valleys are characterized by **peat swamp** forest – where the peat is up to 9m thick – which makes wet-rice agriculture impossible.

Heath forest or *kerangas* – the Iban word meaning 'land on which rice cannot grow' – is found on poor, sandy soils. Although it mostly occurs near the coast, it is also sometimes found in mountain ranges, but almost always on level ground. Here trees are stunted and only the hardiest of plants can survive. Some trees have struck up symbiotic relationships with animals – like ants – so as to secure essential nutrients. Pitcher plants (Nepenthes) have also successfully colonised heath forest. The absence of birds calls and other animal noises make heath forest rather eerie, and it also indicates their general biological poverty.

Along beaches there are often stretches of **casuarina forest**; the casuarina grows up to 27m, and looks like a conifer, with needle-shaped leaves. **Mangrove** occupies tidal mud flats around sheltered bays and estuaries. The most common mangrove tree is the *bakau* (*Rhizophora*) which grows to heights of about 9m and has stilt roots to trap sediment. Bakau wood is used for pile-house stilts and for charcoal. Further upstream, but still associated with mangrove, is the *nipah* palm (*Nipa fruticans*), whose light-green leaves come from a squat stalk; it was traditionally of great importance as it provided roofing and wickerwork materials.

Mammals

Orang utan (*Pongo pygmaeus*) Walt Disney's film of Rudyard Kipling's *Jungle Book* made the orang utan a big-screen celebrity, dubbing him "the king of the swingers" and "the jungle VIP". Borneo's great red-haired ape is also known as 'the wild man of the jungle', after the translation from the Malay: orang (man), utan (jungle). The orang utan is endemic to the tropical forests of Sumatra and Borneo.

The 'Oran-ootan' as remembered by an early European visitor.

Source: Beeckman, Daniel (1718) *A voyage to and from the island of Borneo*, London

The Sumatran animals tend to keep the reddish tinge to their fur, while the Bornean ones go darker as they mature. It is Asia's only great ape; it has four hands, rather than feet, bow-legs and has no tail. The orang utan moves slowly and deliberately, sometimes swinging under branches, although it seldom travels far by arm-swinging. Males of over 15 years old stand up to 1.6m tall and their arms span 2.4m. Adult males (which make loud roars) weigh 50-100 kg – about twice that of adult females (whose call sounds like a long, unattractive belch). Orang utans are said to have the strength of seven men but they are not aggressive. They are peaceful, gentle animals, particularly with each other. Orang utans have bluey-grey skin and their eyes are close together, giving them an almost human look. Males develop cheek pouches when they reach maturity, which they fill with several litres of air; this is exhaled noisily when they demarcate territory.

Orang utans are easily detected by their nests of bent and broken twigs, which are woven together, in much the same fashion as a sun bear's, in the fork of a tree. They always sleep alone. Orang utans have a largely vegetarian diet consisting of fruit and young leaves, supplemented by termites, bark and birds' eggs. They are usually solitary but the young remain with their mothers until they are 5 or 6 years old. Two adults will occupy an area of about 2 sq km. They can live up to 30 years and a female will have an average of three to four young during her lifetime. They mainly inhabit riverine swamp forests or lowland dipterocarp forests.

Estimates of the numbers of orang utan vary considerably. One puts the figure at 10,000-20,000 animals; another at between 70-100,000 in the wild in Borneo and Sumatra. Part of the difficulty is that many are thought to live in inaccessible and little researched areas of peat swamp. But this is just a very rough estimate, based on one ape for each 1½ sq km of forest. No one, so far, has attempted an accurate census. What is certain is that the forest is disappearing fast, and with it the orang utan's natural habitat. The black market in young apes in countries like Taiwan means that they fetch US$350 in local markets – a ready incentive to local hunters. In 1991, six baby apes were discovered, by chance, in a crate labelled 'live birds' at Bangkok's Don Muang Airport. They had diarrhoea and were severely dehydrated. The customs officers only opened the crate because it seemed suspiciously heavy for a box of birds.

Proboscis monkey (*Nasalis larvatus*) The proboscis monkey is an extraordinary-looking animal, endemic to Borneo, which lives in lowland forests and mangrove swamps all around the island. Little research has been done on proboscis monkeys; they are notoriously difficult to study as they are so shy. Their fur is reddish-brown and they have white legs, arms, tail and a ruff on the neck, which gives the appearance of a pyjama-suit. Their facial skin is red and the males have grotesquely enlarged, droopy noses; females' noses are shorter and upturned. The male's nose is the subject of some debate among zoologists: what ever else it does, it apparently increases their sex-appeal. To ward off intruders, the nose is straightened out, "like a party whoopee whistle", according to one description. Recently a theory has been advanced that the nose acts as a thermostat, helping to regulate body temperature. But it also tends to get in the way: old males often have to resort to holding their noses up with one hand while stuffing leaves into their mouths with the other.

Proboscises' penises are almost as obvious as their noses – the proboscis male glories in a permanent erection, which is probably why they are rarely displayed in zoos. The other way the males attract females is by violently shaking branches and making spectacular – and sometimes near-suicidal – leaps into the water, in which they attempt to hit as many dead branches as they can on the way down, so as to make the loudest noise possible. The monkeys organize themselves into harems, with one male and several females and young – there are sometimes up to 20 in a group. Young males leave the harem they are born into when the adult male becomes aggressive towards them and they rove around in bachelor groups until they are in a position to form their own harem.

Proboscis monkeys belong to the leaf monkey family, and have large, pouched stomachs to help digest bulky food – they feed almost entirely on the leaves of one tree – the *Sonneratia*. The proboscis is a diurnal animal, but keeps to the shade during the heat of the day. The best time to see them is very early in the morning or around dusk. They can normally be heard before they are seen: they make loud honks, rather like geese; they also groan, squeal and roar. Proboscis monkeys are good swimmers; they even swim underwater for up to 20m – thanks to their partially webbed feet. Males are about twice the size and weight of females. They are known fairly ubiquitously (in both Malaysian and Indonesian Borneo) as 'Orang Belanda', or Dutchmen – which is not entirely complimentary. In Kalimantan they also have other local names including *Bekantan*, *Bekara*, *Kahau*, *Rasong*, *Pika* and *Batangan*.

Other monkeys found in Borneo include various species of leaf monkey – including the grey leaf monkey, the white-fronted leaf monkey, and the red leaf monkey. One of the non-timber forest products formerly much prized was bezoar stone which was a valued cure-all. Bezoars are green coloured 'stones' which form in the stomachs of some herbivores, and in particular in the stomachs of leaf monkeys. Fortunately for the leaf monkeys of Southeast Asia though, these stones – unlike rhino horn – are no longer prized for their medicinal properties. One of the most attractive members of the primate family found in Borneo is the tubby slow loris or *kongkang*. And perhaps the most difficult to pronounce – at least in Dusun – is the tarsier which is locally known as the *tindukutrukut*.

Elephant Borneo's wild elephants pose a zoological mystery. They occur only at the far NE tip of the island, at the furthest possible point from their Sumatran and mainland Southeast Asian relatives. No elephant remains have been found in Sabah, Sarawak or Kalimantan. Zoologists speculate that they were originally introduced at the time of the Javan Majapahit Empire, in the 13th and 14th centuries. It is known that some animals were introduced into Sabah – then British North Borneo – by early colonial logging concerns. But it is certain that there were already populations established in the area. Another theory has it that one of the sultans of Sulu released a small number of animals several centuries ago. The difficulty with this explanation is that experts find it difficult to believe that just a handful of elephants could have grown to the 2,000 or so that existed by the end of the last century. Some zoologists speculate that they were originally introduced at the time of the Javan Majapahit Empire, in the 13th and 14th centuries. Antonio Pigafetta, an Italian historian who visited the Sultanate of Brunei as part of Portuguese explorer Ferdinand Magellan's expedition in Jul 1521, tells of being taken to visit the sultan on two domesticated elephants, which may have been gifts from another ruler.

It is possible, however, that elephants are native to Borneo and migrated from the Southeast Asian mainland during the Pleistocene when sea levels were lower and land-bridges would have existed between Borneo and the mainland. Their concentration in NE Borneo could be explained by the presence of numerous salt-licks between the Sandakan and Lahad Datu areas of Sabah. This would make the present population a relic of a much larger group of elephants. Borneo's male elephants are up to 2.6m tall; females are usually less than 2.2m. Males' tusks can grow up to 1.7m in length and weigh up to 15 kg each. Mature males are solitary creatures, only joining herds to mate. The most likely places to see elephants in the wild are the Danum Valley Conservation Area and the lower Kinabatangan basin, both in Sabah.

Rhinoceros The 2-horned Sumatran rhinoceros, also known as the hairy rhinoceros, is the smallest of all rhinos and was once widespread throughout Sumatra and Borneo (see page 522). The population has been greatly reduced by excessive hunting. The horn is worth more than its weight in gold in Chinese apothecaries, and that of the Sumatran rhino is the reputedly the most prized of all. But the ravages of over-hunting have been exacerbated by the destruction of the rhino's habitat. Indeed, until quite recently it was thought to be extinct

on Borneo. Most of Borneo's remaining wild population is in Sabah, and the Malaysian government is attempting to capture some of the thinly dispersed animals to breed them in captivity, for they remain in serious danger of extinction.

Other large mammals include the **banteng**, a wild cattle known as the *tembadau* in Sabah. These are smaller than the *seladang* of Peninsular Malaysia, and are most numerous in lowland areas of eastern Sabah where herds are encountered on country roads. The **bearded pig** is the only member of the pig family found in Borneo and is a major source of meat for many Dayak groups. Of the **deer family**, Borneo supports two species of barking deer or *kijang*, and the Greater (*npau*) and Lesser mouse deer. The latter barely stands 30 cm (one foot) tall.

Birds

Hornbill There are nine types of hornbill on Borneo, the most striking and biggest of which is the rhinoceros hornbill (*Buceros rhinoceros*) – or *kenyalang*. They can grow up to 1.5m long and are mainly black, with a white belly. The long tail feathers are white too, crossed with a thick black bar near the end. They make a remarkable, resonant "GERONK" call in flight, which can be heard over long distances; they honk when resting. Hornbills are usually seen in pairs – they are believed to be monogamous. After mating, the female imprisons herself in a hole in a tree, building a sturdy wall with her own droppings. The male bird fortifies the wall from the outside, using a mulch of mud, grass, sticks and saliva, leaving only a vertical slit for her beak. She remains incarcerated in her cell for about 3 months, during which the male supplies her and the nestlings with food – mainly fruit, lizards, snakes and mice. Usually, only one bird is hatched and reared in the hole and when it is old enough to fly, the female breaks out of the nest hole. Both emerge looking fat and dirty.

The 'bill' itself has no known function, but the males have been seen duelling in mid-air during the courting season. They fly straight at each other

* Kenyalang, hornbill image
From Roth, Henry (1896) *The Natives of Sarawak and British North Borneo*, Truslove & Hanson: London

The Iban Hornbill Festival

One of the main Iban festivals is *Gawai Kenyalang*, or the Hornbill Festival. The *kenyalang* – a carved wooden hornbill – traditionally played an important part in the ceremony which preceded head-hunting expeditions, and the often ornate, brightly painted images also made appearances at other *gawais*, or festivals. The kenyalang is carved from green wood and the design varies from area to area. A carved hornbill can be about 2m long and 1m high and is stored until a few days before the festival, when it is painted, bringing the carving to life. It is carried in procession and offered *tuak* (rice wine), before being mounted on a carved base on the *tanju*, the longhouse's open verandah. As the singing gets underway, the kenyalang is adorned with specially woven *pua kumbu* (see page 565) and then raised off the ground to face enemy territory. Its soul is supposed to attack the village's enemies, destroying their houses and crops.

and collide head-on. The double-storeyed yellow bill has a projection, called a casque, on top, which has a bright red tip. Most Dayak groups consider the hornbill to have magical powers and the feathers are worn as symbols of heroism. In tribal mythology the bird is associated with the creation of mankind, and is a symbol of the upper world. The hornbill is also the official state emblem of Sarawak. The best place to see hornbills is near wild fig trees – they love the fruit and play an important role in seed dispersal. The helmeted hornbill's bill is heavy and solid and can be carved, like ivory. These bills were highly valued by the Dayaks, and have been traded for centuries. The third largest hornbill is the wreathed hornbill which makes a yelping call and a loud – almost mechanical – noise when it beats its wings. Others species on Borneo include the wrinkled, black, bushy-crested, white-crowned and pied hornbills.

Reptiles

Crocodiles The largest populations of estuarine crocodiles are found in the lower reaches of Borneo's rivers. However they have been so extensively hunted that they are rarely a threat – although people do very occasionally still get taken.

HISTORY

Archaeological evidence from Sarawak shows that *Homo sapiens* was established on Borneo at least 40,000 years ago. The outside world may have been trading with Borneo from Roman times, and there is evidence in Kaltim (E Kalimantan) of Indian cultural influence from as early as the 4th century. Chinese traders began to visit Borneo from about the 7th century – they traded beads and porcelain in exchange for jungle produce and birds' nests. By the 14th century, this trade appears to have been flourishing, particularly with the newly formed Sultanate of Brunei. The history of the N coast of Borneo is domi-

Piracy: the resurgence of an ancient scourge

In Feb 1992, the International Maritime Bureau convened a conference on Piracy in the Far East Region in Kuala Lumpur, Malaysia. The IMB had become alarmed at the increase in piracy and by the fact that attacks were becoming more ferocious. The number of ships arriving in Singapore that had suffered pirate attacks doubled to 61 in 1991. In 1994 the IMB recorded 90 pirate attacks worldwide. Of these, 48 were in Southeast Asian waters. Some ships just suffer hit-and-run attacks; other pirates hijack entire vessels, whose cargo is removed and the ship resold under another name. On 2 May 1991, for example, the *Hai Hui I*, a Singapore-registered ship bound for Cambodia was attacked and relieved of its cargo in the Strait of Singapore. The pirates seized 400 tonnes of electronics, motorcycles and beer. Most attacks took place in the Strait of Melaka, in the Riau Archipelago, to the NW of Sarawak in the South China Sea, and around Sabah.

Many modern pirates use high-speed boats to escape into international waters and avoid capture by racing from one country's waters into another's. Cooperative international action offers the only way to successfully patrol the shipping lanes. Following the IMB conference, a Regional Piracy Centre was set up in Kuala Lumpur.

But while modern shipping companies might consider the rise in piracy a new and dangerous threat, there is nothing new about piracy in Southeast Asian waters. For centuries, pirates have murdered and pillaged their way along the region's coasts, taking hundreds of slaves as part of their booty. As far back as the 6th century, pirates are thought to have been responsible for the destruction and abandonment of the ancient Hindu capital of Langkasuka, in the NW Malaysian state of Kedah. Piracy grew as trade flourished: the Strait of Melaka and the South China Sea were perfect haunts, being on the busy trade routes between China, India, the Middle East and Europe. Most of the pirates were the Malay Orang Laut (sea gypsies) and Bugis who lived in the Riau Archipelago, the Acehnese of N Sumatra, the Ibans of the Sarawak estuaries and – most feared of all – the Illanun and Balinini pirates of Sulu and Mindanao in the Philippines. The Illanuns were particularly ferocious pirates, sailing in huge *perahus* with up to 150 slaves as oarsmen, in as many as three tiers. The name *lanun* means pirate in Malay.

nated by the Sultanate of Brunei from the 14th-19th centuries. The Europeans began arriving in the East in the early 1500s, but had little impact on N Borneo until British adventurer James Brooke arrived in Sarawak in 1839. From then on, the Sultan's empire and influence shrank dramatically as he ceded more and more territory to the expansionist White Rajahs and to the British North Borneo Chartered Company to the N.

To the S, in what now comprises Kalimantan, it was a similar story. A number of small coastal sultanates grew up (see respective provincial history sections), many of which were tributary states of Brunei, and most of which are thought to have been founded by members of the Brunei nobility. The upriver Dayaks were left largely to themselves. In the 16th century, following the conversion of Banjarmasin to Islam, the religion was embraced by these other sultanates. The Dutch, who first tried to muscle-in on Banjarmasin's pepper trade in the late 1500s, were unsuccessful in establishing themselves in Kalimantan until 1817 when they struck a deal with the Sultan of Banjarmasin. In return for their support in a succession dispute, he ceded to Holland the sultanates he considered under his control. Their claim was never recognized and from the very beginning of their intervention in Indonesia, the Dutch found Kalimantan a difficult proposition.

Konfrontasi

🐾 The birth of the Federation of Malaysia on 31 August 1963 was not helped by the presence of heckling spectators. The Philippines was opposed to British North Borneo (Sabah) joining the federation because the territory had been a dependency of the Sultan of Sulu for over 170 years until he had agreed to lease it to the North Borneo Chartered Company in 1877. But Indonesia's objection to the formation of the federation was even more vociferous. In Jakarta, crowds were chanting "Crush Malaysia!" at President Sukarno's bidding. He launched an undeclared war against Malaysia, which became known as *konfrontasi* – confrontation.

Indonesian armed forces made numerous incursions across the jungled frontier between Kalimantan and the two new East Malaysian states; it also landed commandos on the Malaysian peninsula and despatched 300 saboteurs who infiltrated Singapore and launched a bombing campaign. Sarawakian Communists fought alongside Indonesians in the Konfrontasi and there were countless skirmishes with Malaysian and British counter-terrorist forces in which many were killed. Sukarno even managed to secure Soviet weapons, dispatched by Moscow "to help Indonesia crush Malaysia". Konfrontasi fizzled out in 1965 following the Communist-inspired coup attempt in Indonesia, which finally dislodged Sukarno from power.

CULTURE

PEOPLE

Borneo's population is still pretty sparse by Asian standards, but compared with the state of affairs only two centuryies ago it has grown enormously. Anthony Reid in his book *Southeast Asia in the age of commerce* (1988) estimates that the total population in 1800 was just 1,500,000. The vast majority of Borneo's population is concentrated in the narrow coastal belt; the more mountainous, jungled interior is sparsely populated by Dayak tribes. It has been suggested that there was a long lasting hostile relationship between the tribal peoples of the interior and the settled coastal populations – explaining why only those people living along the main rivers like the Kapuas and Barito in Kalimantan ever converted to Islam.

Whereas the word 'native' has taken on a derogatory connotation in English – it tends to smack of colonial arrogance towards indigenous people – this is not the case in Borneo, particularly in Sarawak and Sabah. Borneo's 200-odd Dayak tribes are the indigenous people; they are generally fairly light-skinned with rounded facial features and slightly slanted eyes, although physical characteristics vary from tribe to tribe. Their diverse anthropological backgrounds have defied most attempts at neat classification. In Sabah and Sarawak, Dayaks are known by their individual tribal names – except in the case of the Orang Ulu, a collective term for upriver groups. Kalimantan's tribespeople are simply labelled Dayaks, however: few outsiders ever refer to their separate tribal identities, although there are many different groups and subgroups. (See below for a short summary of the major groups.) Today, Dayak cultural identity is strong, and upriver tribespeople are proud of their heritage.

Dayak groups are closely-knit communities and many traditionally live in longhouses. Many Dayaks are shifting cultivators. Most are skillful hunters but few made good traders – historically, that was the domain of the coastal Malays and, later, the Chinese. While Dayak communities are represented in all state and provincial governments in Borneo, they only have one province of their own –

The palang – the stimulant that makes a vas diferens

One of the more exotic features of upriver sexuality is the *palang*, or penis pin, which is the versatile jungle version of the French tickler. Traditionally, women suffer heavy weights being attached to their earlobes to enhance their sex-appeal. In turn, men are expected to enhance their physical attributes and entertain their womenfolk by drilling a hole in their organs, into which they insert a range of items, aimed at heightening their partner's pleasure on the rattan mat. Tom Harrisson, a former curator of the Sarawak Museum, was intrigued by the palang; some suspect his authority on the subject stemmed from first-hand experience. He wrote: "When the device is put into use, the owner adds whatever he prefers to elaborate and accentuate its intention. A lively range of objects can so be employed – from pigs' bristles and bamboo shavings to pieces of metal, seeds, beads and broken glass. The effect, of course, is to enlarge the diameter of the male organ inside the female." It is said that many Dayak men, even today, have the tattoo man come and drill a hole in them as they stand in the river. As the practice has gone on for centuries, one can only assume that its continued popularity proves it is worth the agony.

Kalimantan Tengah (Central Kalimantan), with its capital at Palangkaraya. The Dayaks lived in self-sufficient communities in the interior until they began to come under the influence of Malay coastal sultanates from the 14th and 15th centuries. Some turned to Islam, and more recently, many have converted to Christianity – due to the activities of both Roman Catholic and Protestant missionaries (see page 562). Few Dayaks – other than those in the remoter parts of the interior – still wear their traditional costumes. Most have abandoned them in favour of jeans and T-shirts.

Dayaks throughout Borneo have only been incorporated into the economic mainstream relatively recently – although they have always traded with settled 'down river' people (see box on page 544). Relations with coastal groups were not always good, and there was also constant fighting between groups. Differences between the coastal peoples and inland tribes throughout Borneo were accentuated as competition for land increased. The situation was aggravated by a general movement of the population towards the coasts. There was constant rivalry between tribes, with the stronger groups taking advantage of the weaker.

Today however, Dayak groups have relatively good access to education and many now work in the timber and oil and gas industries, which has caused out-migration from their traditional homelands. This has completely changed the lifestyles of most Dayak communities, who used to live in what some anthropologists term 'primitive affluence'. With a few exceptions, everything the people needed came from the jungle. There was an abundance of fish and wild game and building materials; medicine and plant foods were easily obtainable. Jungle products such as rattan, tree resins, edible birds nests were traded on the coast for steel tools, salt, brass gongs, cooking pots and rice wine jars from China. Villages are now tied to a coastal cash culture and western subculture.

Kalimantan's Dayak groups

The coasts of Kalimantan are dominated by Malays – a broad term which includes Muslim Dayaks – and the Malays make up about three-quarters of the population. Many originally migrated to Kalimantan from the Malay peninsula, the Riau islands and from Sumatra and they embraced Islam in the 15th century, following the conversion of the ruler of Banjarmasin.

Main Dayak groups in Kalimantan

NAME(S)	MAIN DISTRIBUTION	ESTIMATED POPULATION	LIVELIHOOD	SOCIETY
Penan (also Punan, Ol, Basap, Bukit, Bukat, Bekatan)	Central Kalimantan	12,000	Hunter-gatherers	Egalitarian society
Kayan (also Bahau, Busang)	Central and E Kalimantan (Kayan Basin, near the Mahakam and Mendalam Rivers)	27,000	Settled agriculturalists	Stratified society: * aristocrats * ordinary villagers * slaves
Kenyah	Central and E Kalimantan	40,000	Settled agriculturalists	Stratified society
Ga'al (also Segai, Long Glat, Modand, Menggai)	Central and E Kalimantan	5,000	Settled agriculturalists	Stratified society
Kelabit-Murut (also Apo Duat, Lun Dayeh, Lun Bawang)	NE Kalimantan	40,000	Shifting cultivators	Stratified society
Meloh (also Memaloh)	W Kalimantan (Kapuas Basin)	12,000	Shifting cultivators	Egalitarian society
Iban	W Kalimantan (Kapuas Basin)	500,000-550,000	Shifting cultivators	Egalitarian society
Bidayuh groups (Land Dayaks)	W Kalimantan	100,000	Settled agriculturalists	Egalitarian society
Malayic Dayaks	W and S Kalimantan	-	Settled agriculturalists	Egalitarian society
Barito groups	S Kalimantan	350,000	Shifting cultivators	Egalitarian society
Kadazan (also Dusun)	Border areas of E Kalimantan	400,000 (incl the majority in Sabah)	Settled agriculturalists; cattle raisers; shifting cultivators	Egalitarian society

NB Many formerly shifting cultivating Dayaks have embraced settled agriculture, and the trend away from shifting cultivation is continuing.

Source: Rigg, Jonathan (1996) (edit) *Indonesia: the human environment*, Singapore: Didier Millet.

The Kalimantan Dayaks can be broadly grouped by region. Kalsel (S Kalimantan) and Kalteng (Central Kalimantan) groups are collectively known as the **Barito River Dayaks** and include the '**Hill Dayaks**' of the Meratus mountains, NE of Banjarmasin. The **Ngaju** live in Kalteng; they were the first Dayak group in Kalimantan to assert their political rights, by lobbying (and fighting) for the creation of Kalteng in the 1950s. The province was later separated from Kalsel, which was dominated by the strictly Islamic Banjarese. Other Dayak groups in Kalteng include the **Ma'anyan**

and the **Ot Danum**, who live along the rivers on either side of the Schwaner Range.

The main groups living in E Kalimantan are the **Kayan** and **Kenyah** who live in the Apo Kayan region and near the Mahakam River. They are also found on the Mendalam River in W Kalimantan. Almost all Kayan and Kenyah have converted to Christianity (most are Protestant). These two closely related groups were the traditional rivals of the Ibans and were notorious for their warlike ways. Historian Robert Payne, in his history *The White Rajahs of Sarawak* described the

---

Traditional Banjarese architecture – high ridged roofs

Before the demise of the Banjar sultanate in 1860, the big houses, called *bubungan tinggi*, with their characteristic high, sharply pointed roofs (*bunbungan* means 'the ridge of the roof' and *tinggi* means 'tall'), were the homes of royalty, the high aristocracy and important state officials. All the older Banjar houses, dating back to the time of the sultanate, have disappeared, although there are several, scattered around the province, dating to the early 1900s. The nearest to Banjarmasin are at Kampung Melayu Laut and in Teluk Selong village. Increasingly, the traditional Banjar house-style is being adopted and readapted by modern architects – in Banjarmasin, the governor's official residence and the Mahligai Pancasila (Palace of the Five Principles) next door, being good examples. They are on Jalan Jend Sudirman, facing the river – as all good Banjar houses should be.

Traditional (and modern) *bubungan tinggi* houses are known for their decorative woodwork, all carved in belian, or ironwood – better known in Kalimantan as *kayu ulin*. The most distinctive decorative features are the 'wings', which continue the line of the eaves upwards, crossing at the ridgeline. Typically, these wings were carved with stylized hornbill figures, a design which originates in pre-Islamic times. According to ancient Dayak belief, the hornbill embodies the gods of the upper world. Other common decorative themes include floral and geometric designs on the woodwork in and around the house as well as Arabic calligraphy. Many other patterns were also used including pineapples (representing success in life), mangosteens (whose pure white soul is enclosed in a dark and scruffy shell), bamboo shoots (symbolic of perceptiveness) and twisted rope (representing the family bonding of those who live inside). Today traditional woodcarving skills are still practised, although it is a dying art.

Kayans of the upper Rejang as "a treacherous tribe, [who] like nothing better than putting out the eyes and cutting the throats of prisoners, or burning them alive". They probably originally migrated into Sarawak from the Apo Kayan district in E Kalimantan (see page 596). Kenyah and Kayan raids on downriver people were greatly feared, but their power was broken by Charles Brooke, just before he became the second White Rajah, in 1863. The Kayans had retreated upstream above the Pelagus Rapids on the Rejang River, to an area they considered out of reach from their Iban enemies. In 1862 they killed two Sarawak government officers at Kanowit and went on a killing spree. Charles Brooke led 15,000 Ibans past the Pelagus Rapids, beyond Belaga and attacked the Kayans in their heartland. Many hundreds were killed.

The Kenyahs and Kayans are very different from other tribal groups, have a completely different language (which has ancient Malayo-Polynesian roots) and are class-conscious, with a well-defined social hierarchy. Traditionally their society was composed of aristocrats, noblemen, commoners and slaves (who were snatched during raids on other tribes). One of the few things the Kayan and Kenyah have in common with other Dayak groups is the fact that they live in longhouses, although even these are of a different design, and are much more carefully constructed, in ironwood. Many have now been converted to Christianity.

In contrast to their belligerent history, the Kenyahs and Kayans are much more introverted than the Ibans; they are slow and deliberate in their ways, and are very artistic and musical. They are also renowned for their parties; visitors recovering from drinking *borak* rice beer have their faces covered in soot before being thrown in the river. This is to test the strength of the newly forged friendship with visitors, who are ill-advised to lose their sense of humour on such occasions.

The **Bahau**, who are related to the Kayan, live in the upper Mahakam region, upriver from Long Iram; the majority are Roman Catholics. The other groups living in the upper Mahakam area include the **Modang** (they are mainly Catholic and are a subgroup of the Kenyah who migrated S), the **Bentian** and the **Penihing**. **Tanjung** Dayaks live in the middle reaches of the Mahakam; some remain animist although large numbers have converted to Christianity (both Roman Catholic and Protestant). The other main group on the middle Mahakam are the **Benuaq** – Tanjung Isuy (see page 595) is a Benuaq village, for example. They are also Roman Catholic.

In addition, there are a few **Murut** groups (the **Tidung** and the **Bulungan** to the NE). The Murut live in NE Kalimantan as well as around Tenom and Pensiangan in the SW of Sabah, and in the Trusan Valley of N Sarawak. Some of those living in more remote jungle areas, retain their traditional longhouse way of life – but many Murut have now opted for detached kampong-style houses. *Murut* means 'hill people' and is not the term used by the people themselves. They refer to themselves by their individual tribal names.

The Nabai, Bokan and Timogun Murut live in the lowlands and are wet-rice farmers, while the Peluan, Bokan and Tagul Murut live in the hills and are mainly shifting cultivators. They are related to Kalimantan's Lun Dayeh people, although some of the tribes in the S Philippines have similar characteristics too. The Murut staples are rice and tapioca, they are known for their weaving and basketry and have a penchant for drinking *tapai* (rice wine). They are also enthusiastic dancers and devised the *lansaran* – a sprung dance floor like a trapeze. The Murut are a mixture of animists, Christians and Muslims and were one of the last tribes to give up head-hunting.

The **Kelabits** who live in the highlands at the headwaters of the Baram River, are closely related to the Kelabit-Murut and the Lun Dayeh and Lun Bawang of interior Kalimantan. The Kelabit-Murut are distinct culturally and linguistically from the Murut of NE Kalimantan. Of all the tribes in Sarawak, the Kelabits have the sturdiest, strongest builds, which is usually ascribed to the cool and invigorating mountain climate. They are skilled hill-rice farmers and the highland climate also allows them to cultivate vegetables. Kelabit parties are also famed as boisterous occasions, and large quantities of *borak* rice beer are consumed – despite the fact that the majority of Kelabits have converted to Christianity. They are regarded as among the most hospitable people in Borneo.

Painted panel from a Dayak coffin of a 'Ship of the Dead'. Note the gongs and cannon

Adapted from: Hersey, Irwin (1991) Indonesian primitive art, OUP: Singapore

Deep in the forested interior of all the provinces, but mostly around the Apo Kayan, there is a very small population of nomadic **Penan**, who are related to the Punan, Bukat, Bukit, Bekatan and Ot, most of whom are now settled agriculturalists.

The **Penan** are perhaps Southeast Asia's only remaining true hunter-gatherers live mainly in the upper Rejang and Limbang areas of Sarawak, but there is also a small population in the Apo Kayan. They are nomads and are related – linguistically at least – to the Punan, former nomadic forest-dwellers. Groups of Penan hunter-gatherers still wander through the forest in groups to hunt wild pigs, birds and monkeys and search for sago palms from which they make their staple food, sago flour. The Penan are considered to be the jungle experts by all the other inland tribes. Because they live in the shade of the forest, their skin is relatively fair. They have a great affection for the coolness of the forest and until the 1960s were rarely seen by the outside world. For them sunlight is extremely unpleasant. They are broad and much more stocky than other river people and are extremely shy, having had little contact with the outside world. Most of their trade is conducted with remote Kayan, Kenyah and Kelabit longhouse communities on the edge of the forest.

In the eyes of the West, the Penan have emerged as the 'noble savages' of the late 20th century for their spirited defence of their lands against encroachment by logging companies. But it is not just recently that they have been cheated: they have long been the victims of other upriver tribes. A Penan, bringing baskets full of rotan to a Kenyah or Kayan longhouse to sell may end up exchanging his produce for one bullet or shotgun cartridge. In his way of thinking, a bullet will kill one wild boar which will last his family 10 days. In turn, the buyer knows he can sell the same rotan downstream for many times more than the value of a bullet. Penan still use the blowpipe for small game, but shotguns for wild pig.

The **Kadazans** are the largest ethnic group in neighbouring Sabah (comprising about a third of the population), and are also to be found in border areas of E Kalimantan. They are a peaceful agrarian people with a strong cultural identity. Formerly, they were known as 'Dusuns', meaning 'peasants' or 'orchard people'. This name was given to them by outsiders, and picked up by the British. Most Kadazans call themselves after their tribal place names. Most Kadazans used to live in longhouses; these are rare now, and most live in Malay-style houses.

All the Kadazan groups share a common language (although dialects vary) and all had similar customs and modes of dress (see below). Up to WW2, many Kadazan men wore the *chawat* loin cloth. The Kadazans used to hunt with blowpipes, and in the 19th century, were still head-hunting. Today, however, they are known for their gentleness and honesty. The Kadazans traditionally traded their agricultural produce at large markets, held at meeting points, called *tamus*. The Kadazan used to be animists, and were said to live in great fear of evil spirits; most of their ceremonies were rituals aimed at driving out these spirits. The job of communicating with the spirits of the dead, the *tombiivo*, was done by priestesses, called *bobohizan*. They are the only ones who can speak the ancient Kadazan language, using a completely different vocabulary from modern Kadazan. Most Kadazans converted to Christianity during the 1930s, although there are also some Muslim Kadazan.

The big cultural event in the Kadazan year is the **Harvest Festival** which takes place in May. The ceremony, known as the *Magavau* ritual, is officiated by a high priestess, or *Bobohizan*. These elderly women – who wear traditional black costumes and colourful headgear with feathers and beads – are now few and far between. The ceremony culminates with offerings to the *Bambaazon*, or rice spirit.

Skulls in the longhouse: heads you win

Although head-hunting has been largely stamped out in Borneo, there is still the odd reported case, once every few years. But until the early 20th century, head-hunting was commonplace among many Dayak tribes, and the Iban were the most fearsome of all. Following a head-hunting expedition, the freshly taken heads were skinned, placed in rattan nets and smoked over a fire – or sometimes boiled. The skulls were then hung from the rafters of the longhouse and they possessed the most powerful form of magic.

The skulls were considered trophies of manhood (they increased a young bachelor's eligibility), symbols of bravery and they testified to the unity of a longhouse. The longhouse had to hold festivals – or *gawai* – to appease the spirits of the skulls. Once placated, the heads were believed to bring great blessing – they could ward off evil spirits, save villages from epidemics, produce rain and increase the yield of rice harvests. Heads that were insulted or ignored were capable of wreaking havoc in the form of bad dreams, plagues, floods and fires. To keep the spirits of the skulls happy, they would be offered food and cigarettes and made to feel welcome in their new home. Because the magical powers of a skull faded with time, fresh heads were always in demand. Tribes without heads were considered spiritually weak.

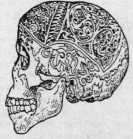

Today, young Dayak men no longer have to take heads to gain respect. They are, however, expected to go on long journeys (the equivalent of the Australian aborigines' Walkabout) – or *bejalai* in Iban The one unspoken rule is that they should come back with plenty of good stories, and, these days, as most berjalai expeditions translate into stints at timber camps or on oil rigs, they are expected to come home bearing video recorders, TV sets and motorbikes. Many Dayak tribes continue to celebrate their head-hunting ceremonies. In Kalimantan, for example, the *Adat Ngayau* ceremony uses coconut shells, wrapped in leaves, as substitutes for freshly cut heads.

Dayak decorated human skull
Adapted from: Hersey, Irwin (1991)
Indonesian primitive art, OUP: Singapore

After the ceremonies Catholic, Muslim and animist Kadazans all come together to play traditional sports such as wrestling and buffalo racing. This is about the only occasion when visitors are likely to see Kadazan in their traditional costumes. Belts of silver coins (*himpogot*) and brass rings are worn round the waist; a colourful sash is also worn. Men dress in a black, long-sleeved jacket over black trousers; they also wear a *siga*, colourful woven head gear. These costumes have become more decorative in recent years, with colourful embroidery.

Dayak communities in Kalbar (W Kalimantan) include the **Iban**. But the Iban are far better known as the largest tribal group in E Malaysia than they are in Kalimantan. The Iban are usually stereo-typed as an out-going people who extend a warm welcome to visitors. Iban women are skilled weavers; even today a girl is not considered eligible until she has proven her skills at the loom by weaving a ceremonial textile. The Ibans love to party, and during the Gawai harvest festival (Jun), visitors are particularly welcome to drink copious amounts of *tuak* (rice wine) and dance through the night.

The Iban are shifting cultivators who originated in the Kapuas River basin of W Kalimantan and migrated into Sarawak's Second Division in the early 16th century, settling along the Batang Lupar, Skrang and Saribas rivers. By the early 19th century, they had begun to spill into the Rejang River valley. It was this growing pressure on land as more and more migrants settled in the river valleys that led to fighting and headhunting (see page 561). Probably because they were shifting cultivators, the Iban remained in closely bonded family groups and were a classless society. Historian Mary Turnbull says "they retained their pioneer social organization of nuclear family groups living together in longhouses and did not evolve more sophisticated political institutions. Long-settled families acquired prestige, but the Ibans did not merge into tribes and had neither chiefs, *rakyat* class, nor slaves."

The Ibans joined local Malay chiefs and turned to piracy – which is how Europeans first came into contact with them. They were dubbed 'Sea Dayaks' as a result – which is really a misnomer as they are an inland people. The name stuck, however. Rajah James Brooke of Sarawak (one of the famous 'White Rajahs') had great admiration of them; he once described the Iban as "good-looking a set of men, or devils, as one could cast eye on. Their wiry and supple limbs might have been compared to the troops of wild horses that followed Mazeppa in his perilous flight." The Iban have a very easygoing attitude to love and sex (best explained in Redmond O'Hanlon's book *Into the Heart of Borneo*.) Free love is the general rule among Iban communities which have not become evangelical Christians, although once married, the Iban divorce rate is low and they are monogamous. Groups related to the Iban include the **Seberuang**, **Kantuq** and **Mualang**.

There are also several '**Land Dayak**' groups in Kalbar, related to the **Bidayuh** of Sarawak. In the 19th century, Sarawak's European community called the Bidayuh 'Land Dayaks' – mainly to distinguish them from the Iban 'Sea Dayak' pirates. The Bidayuh are concentrated in W Kalimantan (as well as Sarawak, W of Kuching). They were virtually saved from extinction by the White Rajahs of Sarawak. Because the Bidayuh were quiet, mild-mannered people, they were at the mercy of the Iban head-hunters and the Brunei Malays who taxed and enslaved them. The Brookes afforded them protection from both groups.

Most live in modern longhouses and are dry rice farmers. Their traditional longhouses are like Iban ones, but without the *tanju* verandah. The Bidayuh are Borneo's best traditional plumbers, and are known for their ingenious gravity-fed bamboo water-supply systems. They are bamboo-specialists, making everything from cooking pots and utensils to finely carved musical instruments (see page 564) from it. Among other tribal groups, the Bidayuh are renowned for their rice wine and sugar cane toddy. Henry Keppel, who with Rajah James Brooke fought the Bidayuhs' dreaded enemies, the Sea Dayaks, described an evening spent with the Land Dayaks thus: "They ate and drank, and asked for everything, but stole nothing."

Another of the groups which lives along Kalimantan's coasts are the **Bugis** ('Sea Gypsy') people, originally from S Sulawesi (see page 617). They are famous shipbuilders and their schooners are still made in Kalsel (S Kalimantan) (see page 571).

RELIGION

Apart from the coastal groups, many of whom converted to Islam, the inland tribes remained animist until the arrival of Europeans . The religion of all the Dayak tribes in Borneo boiled down to placating spirits, and the purpose of tribal

The tree of life

According to the religion of the Ngaju Dayak of Kalimantan – known as Kaharingan – the life-giving essence of everything is stored up in the Water of Life which, itself, is contained within the Tree of Life. Visual representations of the Tree of Life are found engraved on such things as bamboo containers. The aerial roots, depicted as daggers (*duhung*) or spears (*rawayang*) drip the Waters of Life. In the knots of the tree are small containers or pots within which is stored the rain of prosperity (or knowledge), known as *ujan sangkalemu*. A large tap root, sometimes drawn as a big pot (*balanga*), is the main store for the Waters of Life. In the branches of this mythical tree are two creatures: Didis Mahandera and Rowang Riwo, both of whose saliva has great power. Their identity is not known – some people maintain that one is a civet. In the uppermost branches of the tree are two hornbills whose cry is said to endow rain with the power of life. The Tree of Life itself pierces and connects the three worlds. The roots reside in the Underworld, the main trunk in the earthly world, and the branches in the Upperworld. It is the Water of Life which flows through the tree which connects the three worlds and which gives life to men and women.

totems, images, icons and statues was to chase bad spirits away and attract good ones, which were believed to be capable of bringing fortune and prosperity. Head-hunting (see page 561) was central to this belief, and most Dayak tribes practiced it, in the belief that freshly severed heads would bring blessing to their longhouses. Virtually everything had a spirit, and complex rituals and ceremonies were devised to keep them happy. Motifs associated with the spirit world – such as the hornbill (see page 552) – dominate artwork and textiles and many of the woodcarvings for sale in art and antique shops had religious significance. Islam began to spread to the tribes of the interior from the late 15th century, but mostly it was confined to coastal districts or those areas close to rivers like the Kapuas and Barito where Malays penetrated into the interior to trade. Christian missionaries arrived with the Europeans but did not proselytize seriously until the mid-19th century. The Dutch, particularly, saw missionaries fulfilling an adminstrative function, drawing the tribal peoples close to the Dutch and, by implication, away from the Muslim Malays of the coast: it was a policy of divide and rule by religion

means. Both Christianity and Islam had enormous influence on the animist tribes, and many converted en-mass to one or the other. Despite this, many of the old superstitions and ceremonial traditions, which are deeply ingrained, remain a part of Dayak culture today.

The traditional beliefs of Kalimantan's Dayaks is formalized in the *Kaharingan* faith, which, despite the in-roads made by Christianity and Islam, is still practiced by some Mahakam and Barito river groups. The religion became a focus of Dayak cultural identity when Kalteng split from Kalsel province in the late 1950s, and the Indonesian government recognizes it as an official religion, bracketing it (absurdly) with Balinese Hinduism. Kaharingan revolves around spirit and ancestor worship and is characterized by complex sets of rites and rituals, particularly those relating to death and burial. Several months after the initial funeral, a body is exhumed and cleaned and placed in a *sandung* (mausoleum), which is finely carved and decorated, alongside the remains of the deceased's ancestors. The Dayaks believe that after death, a person will join the spirit world. All the different Dayak groups have different variations on this faith.

DANCE, DRAMA AND MUSIC

Dance

Dayak tribes are renowned for their singing and dancing, and the most famous is the hornbill dance. In her book *Sarawak*, Hedda Morrison writes: "The Kayans are probably the originators of the stylized war dance which is now common among the Ibans but the girls are also extremely talented and graceful dancers. One of their most delightful dances is the hornbill dance, when they tie hornbill feathers to the ends of their fingers which accentuate their slow and graceful movements. For party purposes everyone in the longhouse joins in and parades up and down the communal room led by one or two musicians and a group of girls who sing." On these occasions, drink flows freely. With the Ibans, it is *tuak* (rice wine), with the Kayan and Kenyah it is *borak*, a bitter rice beer. After being entertained by dancers, a visitor is under compunction to drink a large glassful, before bursting into song and doing a dance routine themselves. The best guideline for visitors on how to handle such occasions is provided by Redmond O'Hanlon in his book *Into the Heart of Borneo*. The general rule of thumb is to be prepared to make an absolute fool of yourself, throwing all inhibition to the wind. This will immediately endear you to your hosts.

Music

Gongs range from the single large gong, the *tawak*, to the engkerumong, a set of small gongs, arranged on a horizontal rack, with five players. An engkerumong ensemble usually involves between five and seven drums, which include two suspended gongs (*tawak* and *bendan*) and five hour-glass drums (*ketebong*). They are used to celebrate victory in battle or to welcome home a successful head-hunting expedition. The Bidayuh also make a bamboo gong called a *pirunchong*. The *jatang uton* is a wooden xylophone which can be rolled up like a rope ladder; the keys are struck with hardwood sticks.

The Bidayuh, make two main stringed instruments – a 3-stringed cylindrical bamboo harp called a *tinton* and the *rabup*, a rotan-stringed fiddle with a bamboo cup. The Kenyah and Kayan play a 4-stringed guitar called a *sape*. It is the most common and popular lute-type instrument, whose body, neck and board are cut from one piece of softwood. It is used in Orang Ulu dances and by witch doctors. It is usually played by two musicians, one keeping the rhythm, the other the melody. Traditional sapes had rotan strings, today they use wire guitar strings and electric pick-ups. Another stringed instrument, more usually found in Kalimantan than Sarawak, is the *satang*, a bamboo tube with strings around the outside, cut from the bamboo and tightened with pegs.

One of the best known instruments is the *engkerurai* (or *keluri*), the bagpipes of Borneo, which is usually associated with the Kenyahs and Kayans. It is a hand-held organ in which four vertical bamboo pan-pipes of different lengths are fixed to a gourd, which acts as the wind chamber. Simple engkerurai can only manage one chord; more sophisticated ones allow the player to use two pipes for the melody, while the others provide an harmonic drone. The Bidayuh are specialists in bamboo instruments and make flutes of various sizes; big thick ones are called branchi, long ones with five holes are kroto and small ones are called nchiyo.

CRAFTS

Textiles The Benuaq Dayaks of the Mahakam are known for their *ikat* weaving, producing colourful pieces of varied designs. They are woven with thread produced from pineapple leaves. While traditional costumes are disappearing fast, it is still possible to find the *sholang*, colourful appliqué skirts, which have black human figures and dragon-dogs (*aso/asok*) sewn on top. The traditional sarong worn by Dayak women is called a *ta-ah*, which is a short, colourful, patchwork-style material.

Tribal tattoos

Tattooing is practiced by many indigenous groups in Borneo, but the most intricate designs are those of the upriver Orang Ulu tribes. Designs vary from group to group and for different parts of the body. Circular designs are mostly used for the shoulder, chest or wrists, while stylized dragon-dogs (aso), scorpions and dragons are used on the thigh and, for the Iban, on the throat. Tattoos can mean different things; for the man it is a symbol of bravery and for women, a good tattoo is a beauty-feature. More elaborate designs often denote high social status in Orang Ulu communities – the Kayans, for example, reserved the aso design for the upper classes and slaves were barred from tattooing themselves at all. In these Orang Ulu groups, the ladies have the most impressive tattoos; the headman's daughter has her hands, arms and legs completely covered in a finely patterned tattoo. Designs are first carved on a block of wood, which is then smeared with ink. The design is printed on the body and then punctured into the skin with needles dipped in ink, usually made from a mixture of sugar, water and soot. Rice is smeared over the inflamed area to prevent infection, but it usually swells up for some time.

The weaving of cotton *pua kumbu* is one of the oldest Iban traditions, and literally means 'blanket' or 'cover'. The weaving is done by the women and is a vital skill for a would-be bride to acquire. There are two main methods employed in making and decorating pua kumbu: the more common is the *ikat* tie-dyeing technique (see page 529), known as *ngebat* by the Iban. The other method is the *pileh*, or floating weft. The Ibans use a warp-beam loom which is tied to two posts, to which the threads are attached. There is a breast-beam at the weaving end, secured by a back strap to the weaver. A pedal, beneath the threads, lowers and raises the alternate threads which are separated by rods. The woven material is tightly packed by a beater. The material is tie-dyed in the warp.

Because the pua kumbu is made by the warp-tie-dyeing method, the number of colours is limited. The most common are a rich browny-brick-red colour and black, as well as the undyed white sections; blues and greens are used in more modern materials. Traditionally, pua kumbu were hung in longhouses during ceremonies and were used to cover images during rituals. The designs and patterns are representations of deities which figure in Iban myths and are believed to protect individuals from harm; they are passed down from generation to generation. Such designs, with deep spiritual significance, can only be woven by wives and daughters of chiefs. Other designs and patterns are representations of birds and animals, including hornbills, crocodiles, monitor lizards and shrimps, which are either associated with worship or are sources of food. Symbolic representations of trees, plants and fruits are also included in the designs as well as the events of everyday life. A typical example is the zigzag pattern which represents the act of crossing a river – the zigzag course is explained by the canoe's attempts to avoid strong currents. Many of the symbolic representations are highly stylized and can be difficult to pick out.

Beadwork Like the Orang Ulu of Sarawak, the upriver tribes in Kalimantan are known for their beadwork, which decorates everything from betelnut containers to baby-carriers.

Among many Kenyah, Kayan, Bidayuh, and Kelabit groups, beads have long been symbols of status and wealth; necklaces, skull caps and girdles are handed down from generation to generation. Smaller glass – or plastic – beads (usually imported from Europe) are used to decorate baby carriers, baskets, headbands, jackets, hats, sheaths for knives, tobacco boxes and handbags. Beaded baby carriers are mainly used by the Kelabit, Kenyah and Kayan and often have shells and animals' teeth attached which make a rattling sound to frighten away evil spirits. Rounded patterns require more skill than geometric patterns, the quality of the pattern used to reflect the status of the owner. Only upperclasses are permitted to have beadwork depicting 'high-class' motifs such as human faces or figures. Early beads were made from clay, metal, glass, bone or shell (the earliest have been found in the Niah Caves.) Later on, many of the beads that found their way upriver were from Venice, Greece, India and China – even Roman and Alexandrian beads have made their way into Borneo's jungle. Orang Ulu traded them for jungle produce. Tribes attach different values to particular types of beads.

Woodcarvings Many of Borneo's tribal groups are skilled carvers, producing everything from huge burial poles to small statues, masks and other decorative items and utensils. The Kenyah's traditional masks, which are used during festivals, are elaborately carved and often have large protruding eyes. Eyes are always emphasized, as they are to frighten the enemy. Other typical items carved by tribal groups include spoons, stools, doors, walking sticks, *sapes* (guitars), ceremonial shields, tops of water containers, tattoo plaques, and the hilts of *parang ilang* (ceremonial knives.) The most popular Iban motif is the hornbill, which holds an honoured place in Iban folklore (see page 551), being the messenger for the sacred Brahminy kite, the ancestor of the Iban. Another famous Iban carving is the sacred measuring stick called the *tuntun peti*, used to trap deer and wild boar; it is carved to represent a forest spirit. The Kayan and Kenyahs' most common motif is the *aso*,

a dragon-like dog with a long snout. It also has religious and mythical significance. The Kenyah and Kayan carve huge burial structures, or *salong*, as well as small ear pendants made of hornbill ivory. The elaborately carved masks used for their harvest ceremony are unique.

Small carved statues, or *hampatong*, are commonly found in handicraft shops. They are figures of humans, animals or mythical creatures and traditionally have ritual functions. They are often kept in Dayak homes to bring good luck, good health or good harvests. They are divided according to the Dayak cosmology: male figures (human and animal) are associated with the upper world, female figures (human and animal), with the lower world while hermaphrodite figures symbolize the middle world. Large hampatong are associated either with death or headhunting, while others, usually placed as a totem outside a village, will serve as its protector. Another group of large hampatong are the *sapundu*, to which sacrificial victims were tied before being put to death – the victims used to be slaves; no buffalo are used.

Hats Kalimantan's Dayak hats are called *seraung* and are made from biru leaves; they are conical and often have colourful *ta-ah* patchwork cloth sewn onto them, or they might be decorated with beads. The Kenyah – like their relations across the Sarawak border – wear distinctive grass-plaited caps called *tapung*.

Weapons The traditional Dayak headhunting knife is called a *mandau*. It is a multi-purpose knife with practical and ritualistic uses. The different tribes have different-shaped mandau blades, which are made of steel; their handles are carved in the shape of a hornbill's head from bone. Human hair was traditionally attached to the end of the handle. Other Dayak weapons include the *tombak* hunting spear, made from ironwood, with a steel tip. The *sumpit*, or blowpipe, was used for hunting, but now plays a largely ceremonial rôle during rituals and festivals. The Dayak battle shield (*kelbit*) is made from cork, and is shaped like an elongated diamond.

Blowpipes Blowpipes are usually carved from hardwood – normally belian (ironwood.) The first step is to make a rough cylinder about 10 cm wide and 2.5m long. This rod is tied to a platform, from which a hole is bored through the rod. The bore is skillfully chiselled by an iron rod with a pointed end. The rod is then sanded down to about 5 cm in diameter. Traditionally, the sanding was done using the rough underside of *macaranga* leaves. The darts are made from the *nibong* and wild sago palms and the poison itself is the sap of the *upas* (Ipoh) tree (*Antiaris toxicari*) into which the point is dipped.

Basketry A wide variety of household items are woven from rotan, bamboo, bemban reed as well as nipah and pandanus palms. Basketry is practised by nearly all the ethnic groups in Borneo and they are among the most popular handicrafts. A variety of baskets are made for harvesting, storing and winnowing paddy as well as for collecting and storing other items. The Penan are reputed to produce the finest rattan sleeping mats – closely plaited and pliable. The Kayan and Kenyah produce four main types of basket. The *anjat* is a finely woven jungle rucksack with two shoulder straps; the *kiang* is also a rucksack-type affair but with a rougher weave and is stronger and used for carrying heavier loads; the *lanjung* is a large basket used for transporting rice; while the *bakul* is a container worn while harvesting rice, so that the pannicles drop in. The *bening aban* is the famous baby carrier; it is woven in fine rattan, has a wooden seat and is colourfully decorated with intricate beadwork.

Many of the native patterns used in basketry are derived from Chinese patterns and take the form of geometrical shapes and stylized birds. The Bidayuh also make baskets from either rotan or sago bark strips. The most common Bidayuh basket is the *tambok*, which is simply patterned and has bands of colour; it also has thin wooden supports on each side.

BOOKS ON BORNEO

Bock, Carl (1985, first published 1881) *The headhunters of Borneo*, OUP: Singapore. Bock was a Norwegian naturalist and explorer and was commissioned by the Dutch to make a scientific survey of southeastern Borneo. His account, though, makes much of the dangers and adventures that he faced, and some of his 'scientific' observations are, in retrospect, clearly highly faulty. Nonetheless, this is an entertaining account.

Chapman, F Spencer: *The jungle is neutral*. An account of a British guerrilla force fighting the Japanese in Borneo — not as enthralling as Tom Harrisson's book, but still worth reading.

Charles, Hose (1985, first published 1929) *The field book of a jungle wallah*, OUP: Singapore. Hose was an official in Sarawak and became an acknowledged expert on the material and non-material culture of the tribes of Sarawak. He was one of that band of highly informed, perceptive and generally benevolent colonial administrators.

Hanbury-Tenison, Robin (1980) *Mulu, the rain forest*, Arrow/Weidenfeld. This is the product of a Royal Geographical Society trip to Mulu in the late 1970s; semi-scholarly and useful.

Harrisson, Tom (1959) *World within*, Hutchinson: London. During the Second World War, explorer, naturalist and ethnologist Tom Harrisson was parachuted into Borneo to help organize Dayak resistance against the occupying Japanese forces. This is his extraordinary account.

Keith, Agnes (1969) *Land below the wind*, Ulverscroft: Leicester. Perhaps the best-known English language book on Sabah.

King, Victor T (edit) (1992) *The best of Borneo travel*, Oxford University Press: Oxford. A compilation of travel accounts from the early 19th century through to the late 20th. An excellent companion to take while exploring the island. Published in portable paperback.

O'Hanlon, Redmond (1984) *Into the heart of Borneo*, Salamander Press: Edinburgh. One of the best recent travel books on Borneo. This highly amusing and perceptive romp through Borneo in the company of poet and foreign correspondent James Fenton, includes an ascent of the Rejang River and does much to counter the more romanticized images of Bornean life.

Payne, Robert: *The white Rajahs of Sarawak*. Readable account of the extraordinary history of this East Malaysian state.

Payne, Junaidi *et al*: *Pocket guide to birds of Borneo*, World Wildlife Fund/Sabah Society.

Payne, Junaidi *et al*: *A field guide to the mammals of Borneo*, World Wildlife Fund/Sabah Society. Good illustrations, reasonable text, but very dry.

SOUTH KALIMANTAN
(KALIMANTAN SELATAN – KALSEL)

South Kalimantan or Kalsel is the smallest and most densely populated of the four provinces in Indonesian Borneo: it has a population of 2.6 million. The population density is about 60 per sq km – low by Javanese standards, but high in comparison with Kalimantan's other sparsely populated provinces. Kalsel used to include all of Central Kalimantan (Kalteng), until the latter's predominantly Dayak population won administrative autonomy from the Muslim Banjarese. The Banjarese are descended from a mixture of Dayak, Sumatran Malay, Javanese and Buginese stock – although their dialect is close to classical Malay.

The timber industry is an important source of revenue for Kalsel, although it is not as important as in E Kalimantan. Much of the logging has been along the coast and on either side of the main road to Balikpapan. There has been increasing concern voiced over the pace of deforestation and about the frequent and damaging forest fires; however, about 50% of the province's 3.7 million ha is still officially forested. The area between the road and the coast, the *Pegunungan Meratus* (the Range of 100 Mountains), which forms the backbone of the state, is still covered in primary forest – it is too remote even for loggers.

To the W of this range is the Barito River which has its headwaters deep in the interior. The coastal area is low lying and swampy: the name of the provincial capital, Banjarmasin, derives from the Javanese term 'saline garden'. Kalsel's coasts are dominated by riceland – where high yielding varieties have been successfully introduced. The hybrid strains have been named after Kalsel's main rivers, the Barito and Negara. Over the past 50 years most of these ricefields have been reclaimed from the tidal swamps. Paddy seedlings are planted in the swamps during the dry season, and in the wet season they flood to a depth of 2-3m. This *padi air dalam* (deep water paddy) is harvested from boats. These swamplands are also home to another oddity: the swimming buffalo of S Kalimantan. Herds of water buffalo paddle from one grazing area to another, sometimes swimming long distances. Farmers build log platforms (called *kalang*) as resting places for their buffalo (which are known as *kalang* buffalo). In recent years the unchecked spread of water hyacinth has begun to threaten their grazing grounds.

Best time to visit Kalsel is during the dry season from Jun to Sep.

History Legend has it that a kingdom centred on the SE corner of Borneo was founded by Ampu-jatmika, the son of a merchant from India's Coromandel coast who settled in the area in the 12th century. He called it Negara-dipa. It became a vassal state of Java's Hindu kingdom of Majapahit in the 13th century and from then on, the city retained close cultural and trade links with Java, which led to its conversion to Islam in the 1540s. The city of Banjarmasin was founded by the Hindu ruler Pangeran Samudera (The Prince from the Sea) in 1526; it was he who first embraced Islam, changing his name to Pangeran Suriansyah in the process.

The Banjarese sultanate – which continued through a succession of 22 rulers – was the most important in Borneo (other than Brunei, on the N coast) and its tributary states included all the smaller sultanates on the W and E coasts of the island. However, in 1860, after several years of political turmoil, the Dutch abolished the sultanate altogether, and installed its administrative headquarters for all of what is now Kalimantan, in Banjarmasin. This sparked the 4 years Banjarmasin War against the Dutch occupiers; long after the uprising was put down, the Dutch presence was deeply resented. The hero of the guerrilla struggle against the Dutch was Pangeran Antasari (his name immortalized in many Kalimantan street names), who was born in the nearby city of Martapura. He unified the Banjarese, the Dayaks and the Buginese against the Dutch and had a 100,000 guilder price on his head. He died in 1862, having evaded capture, and 106 years later was proclaimed an Indonesian national hero.

BANJARMASIN

Like several other cities in Asia, Banjarmasin has been dubbed 'The Venice of the Orient'. It might be an over-worked cliché, but if there is one city that deserves the epithet, it is Banjarmasin, the capital of Kalsel. The number of tourists visiting Banjarmasin is growing fast; an estimated 30,000 every year, mostly from Java and Bali. There is plenty to see in Banjarmasin, and much of the sightseeing can be done from a *klotok* (a motorized gondola): a Banjar proverb goes '*Sekali jukung didayuh, haram balabuh*' – 'once you start paddling, don't dock'.

The city grew up at the confluence of the Barito and Martapura rivers – at a point where the Barito is over 1-km wide – about 22 km upstream from the sea. In 1991 the city had a population of 444,000, making it the largest urban centre in not just Kalimantan, but the whole of Borneo. (In 1930 it had a population of just 66,000, but this still made it the largest town on the island.) Banjarmasin is dominated by its waterways: most of its population lives in pile houses and floating houses (*lanting*) on the sides of the Martapura, Barito, Kuin and Andai rivers along and around which the city is built. These rivers – and the canals which link them – are the focus of day-to-day life in Banjarmasin. The waterways are alive with people bathing, swimming, fishing and washing their clothes; they clean their teeth in them, squat over them and shop on them.

Although Banjarmasin may be the largest urban centre in Borneo, it does not exude wealth in the same way that other cities do. Periodic outbreaks of cholera,

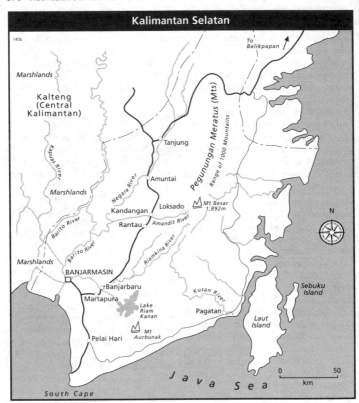

Kalimantan Selatan

and a shortage of drinking water in the dry season means that wealthier potential inhabitants tend to live elsewhere – such as at Banjarbaru/Martapura some 40 km away (see **Excursions**).

Places of interest

The imposing **Sabila Muhtadin Mosque** (Grand Mosque), built in 1980, dominates the city's waterfront. Every Fri 15,000 Muslims gather for prayer in its cool marbled interior; about 98% of Banjarmasin's population is Muslim. The Banjarese became Muslims when the local prince, Pangeran Samudera, converted to Islam around 1540, after which he became

known as Pangeran Suriansyah. The city has more mosques per head of population than anywhere else in Indonesia – about one for every 40 families. Mosques, and their smaller equivalent *surau*, line the city's waterways – their domes and minarets, standing out among the parabola satellite dishes and television aerials on the skyline.

NB Muslim sensitivities should be observed in Banjarmasin – women should dress modestly and should avoid smoking in public.

The highlight of most peoples' visit to Banjarmasin is the **Pasar Terapung** (floating market) which lies on the W

The Hill Dayaks of Kalsel – a fragile culture

👣 The Hill Dayak tribal areas of the Pegunungan Muratus have a fragile culture which is being eroded as groups of trekkers venture further into remote areas. Tour operators stress that westerners should be particularly sensitive to cultural traditions and respect tribal customs. (Although there are many differences between the Muratus Dayak people and the tribal groups in Sarawak, visitors may wish to refer to the basic ground rules of longhouse etiquette, see *House rules*, page 606). Johan Yasin, the most experienced tour operator in Banjarmasin (see below) tells of tourists on trekking expeditions who have swapped T-shirts for tribal handicrafts and heirlooms. On another occasion, a European doctor began handing out western medicines liberally; while drugs are in short supply and are much needed, it seems he was too generous and managed not only to put the local *balian* (shaman) out of business, but completely undermined his authority and social standing in the community.

outskirts of town on the Barito River. Unlike floating markets elsewhere in the region – notably Bangkok's – this is far from being a tourist-showpiece. The market is big and very lively – perhaps because sellers can actively pursue buyers, paddling after them in their sampans and canoes (*jukung*) or chasing them in their *klotoks*. The market includes a floating clinic (*posyandu*) and floating pharmacy; as well as jukung-vendors selling rice, fish, fruit and vegetables, there are floating boutique shops, hardware shops, supermarkets, petrol stations and soup stalls. There is even a floating parking attendant, taking 50Rp from each of the stall-holders. There are also delightful floating tea shops; these little covered sampans have their front sections covered in plates of sticky rice, doughnuts, cakes and delicacies which customers draw up alongside and spear with a long harpoon-rod handed over by the tea-man. When the sun comes up, the *tanggui* – the famous wide-brimmed Banjar hat – comes into its own as marketeers shelter from the heat under its lofty rim.

The floating market starts early (0400) and finishes early (0900-1000) – but there is little point getting there much before 0700. By 0600 it is just light enough to see, so the river trip down the canals to the market, as Banjarmasin is awakening, is fantastic.

En route to the floating market, from town, in Kuin village, is the **Grave of Pangeran Samudera** (see page 569). Next to the floating market and along the canals there are *pengger gajian* – small family-run **sawmills** – making sawn timber for the construction industry and for construction of Bugis schooners (see page 620). The main schooner-building yards – in riverside dry docks called *alalak* – are just upstream from the floating market at the confluence of the Barito and Andai rivers. But the best place to see the schooners is at the **Pelabuhan Lama** (Old Harbour) on the Martapura River, not far from the town centre. The Orang Bugis, who still build their beautiful sailing ships in the traditional manner, live in little pockets along the Kalsel coast (there is another boat-building yard at Batu Licin on the coast, 225 km E of Banjarmasin). The schooners, with their sweeping bows and tall masts are known as *perahu layar* – sailing boats. These days, most of them have powerful engines too, so they are commonly known as PLMs (*parahu layar motor*). At the 1989 World Expo' in Vancouver, Canada, a Bugis schooner sailed over from Banjarmasin carrying skilled boatbuilders and the materials to build another one. It was completed within the year and was one of the stars of the show. When the boatbuilders

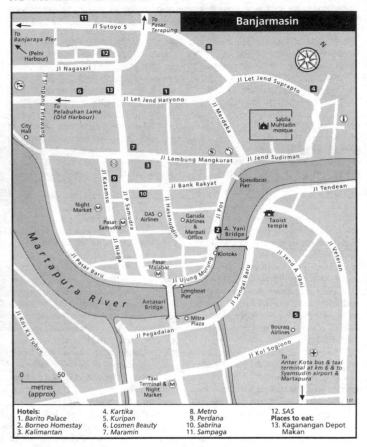

Banjarmasin

Hotels:

1. Barito Palace	4. Kartika	8. Metro	12. SAS
2. Borneo Homestay	5. Kuripan	9. Perdana	**Places to eat:**
3. Kalimantan	6. Losmen Beauty	10. Sabrina	13. Kaganangan Depot
	7. Maramin	11. Sampaga	Makan

came home to Indonesia, they were welcomed as national heroes and received medals from President Suharto. The schooners are still in frequent use as trading vessels and most have a crew of about 30, living in quarters at the stern. On the opposite bank of the Barito River to the floating market there are several large plywood factories, one of which belongs to President Suharto's daughter, Batuti.

Pulau Kembang (Flower Island, but better known as 'Monkey Island' because of the troops of monkeys found here) is just downriver from the floating market, in the middle of the Barito. Do not touch the big male long-tailed macaques: these 'rajahs' can be vicious. The island gets rather overcrowded on weekends; donation on arrival (around 500Rp). *Getting there*: often included at the end of a tour to the floating market; alternatively take a klotok from under A Yani Bridge. About 12 km further down the Barito River is **Pulau Kaget**, also in the middle of the river. The river around the island is one of the best places to observe the proboscis monkey (*Nasalis larvatus* – see page 549) which are active on the shoreline at dawn and dusk. The local name for these is the *kera Belanda* – the monkey that looks like a Dutchman. The trip takes 1½-2 hrs return.

Excursions

Martapura and the Cempaka Diamond Fields are the focus of Kalsel's gemstone-mining industry, about 40 km SE of Banjarmasin. The diamond fields are near the village of Cempaka, 10 km from Martapura. There, labourers dig 5m-deep shafts using techniques little changed in over a century, extending tunnels from the bottom of the shafts. The stoney mud is handed to the top in bamboo baskets and then sifted and swilled in flowing water in the hope of striking lucky. If other precious stones are found in the pan, it is taken as an indication that a diamond is nearby. Many large diamonds have been unearthed at Cempaka over the past 150 years; the biggest was the 167.5-carat *Intan Trisakti* diamond, found in 1965. In 1990 a 48-carat diamond was found and was named *Intan Galuh Pampung*.

Diamonds are traditionally believed to be benevolent spirits with characters like virtuous virgins and are treated by the miners with similar respect; they refer to them as *Galuh*, or 'Princess'. A rigorously observed code of social conduct is in force in the diamond field so that nothing is done to frighten or offend 'her' in case 'she' refuses to appear. This includes the barring of sour-tasting food (said to be craved for by pregnant women), the banning of whistling (a vulgar means of attracting a girl's attention) and smoking is also taboo in case it offends Galuh. Other precious metals and stones mined at the site include gold as well as sapphires and amethysts. Cempaka is one of at least six diamond-mining villages in the area.

Around 30,000 people are employed in the gemstone industry, both in the mines and at Martapura. The latter is the gemstone cutting and polishing centre and there are many shops selling stones of all qualities. The best of Martapura's jewellery shops is *Kayu Tangi*, Jl Sukaramail 4/J; it is the only one where stones are guaranteed. They have a good selection of precious and semi-precious stones, from diamonds to rough-cut lapis lazuli, but it is still important to bargain. Although this is the best shop in Kalsel for stones, they are not well finished and will probably require recutting and re-polishing. There is a **polishing factory** next door (closed Fri) and many stalls selling semi-precious stones, beads and jewellery – including *manik manik* stone necklaces – in the **Pasar Niaga** market (some shops close Fri).

There is a vast and very colourful vegetable market next to Pasar Niaga (Mon-Sun, but the Fri market is the biggest). Behind the vegetable market is a building with shops where silversmiths make rings. *Getting there*: see below.

NB When to visit Martapura's Diamond Fields are shut on Fri, as are the stone-cutting and polishing workshops; most jewellery shops do, however, stay open on Fri. Fri is also the best day to see the Martapura market in full swing.

Lambung Mangkurat State Museum, housed in a dubious modern interpretation of a traditional Banjar-style building at Banjarbaru, near Martapura, has historical and cultural displays on Kalsel. On the ground floor there is a life-size, ulin-wood (belian/ironwood) *tambangan* boat (the traditional Banjar river boat, in use from the 17th century to the 1950s). Admission 200Rp. Open 0830-1400 Tues-Sun; closes early on Fri (1100) and Sat (1300). *Getting there*: taxi (30,000Rp round trip), minibus (1,200Rp) or bus (800Rp), both from the intercity bus terminal or speedboat (10,000Rp) from the Dermaga Pier in front of the Grand Mosque. Cempaka can be reached from the bemo terminal in Martapura (take green minibuses to the Diamond Fields).

Around Banjarmasin

(map labels)

Bugis Schooner Building Yards

Sawmills

Pasar Terapung (Floating Market) Ⓜ

Grave of Pangeran Samudera

Kuin River

Andai River

0   500
metres

N

Pulau Kembang (Monkey Island)

Barito River

Governor's Office

Ⓜ Fish Market

City Mayor's Office

Pelabuhan Lama (Old Harbour Bugis Schooners)

See Detail

Pekapuran Canal

To Martapura

Sea Port

Kelayan River

Martapura River

138

Jungle trekking and white-water rafting The best area for trekking is in the Meratus Dayak – or Hill Dayak – country around Loksado (on the Amandit River) and Mt Besar (1,892m), 190 km NE of Banjarmasin in the *Pegunungan Muratus* range. From Loksado, it is possible to run the rapids on the Amandit by bamboo raft – there are many stretches of white water, of different grades of difficulty. There are more than 30 longhouses – or *balai* – in and around Loksado, where trekkers can stay overnight. There are also caves in the area. The Kalsel tourism office produces a detailed list of treks between villages, with distances and approximate timings. To the SE of Banjarmasin, at the S end of the range, there are jungle trails around Lake Riamkanan, accessible from Martapura/Awang Bankal. It is necessary to take guides to both these areas (see Tours, below); few people speak English. **Essential equipment**: mosquito repellent, a torch and a sleeping bag (temperatures drop sharply at night).

Tours

Prices listed below are those of Johan Yasin; he undercuts bigger tour operators' prices substantially. **Banjarmasin waterways**: 1½ hrs, 7,500Rp pp. **Floating market**: 3 hrs, 12,500Rp (for groups of two or more). **Kaget Island**: 5 hrs, 20,000Rp (for groups of two or more). **Martapura and Cempaka**: 15,000Rp. **Tanjung Puteh Orang Utan Sanctuary** (Central Kalimantan): 3-4 days, 650,000Rp pp (cost includes flight to Pankalanbun, SW Kalimantan). **Trekking tours**: typical 5-days trek to Loksado and Mt Besar areas NE of Banjarmasin, involves rafting and trekking through Hill Dayak areas, staying overnight in longhouses (*balai*), (roughly 200,000Rp). Shorter 1-2 days jungle tours to Lake Riamkanan (nestled into the S end of the Pegunungan Muratus range, 100 km SE of Banjarmasin), 75,000Rp/day. Johan Yasin and Pujo Santoso are small highly rec operations. More expensive but good tours can be organized through the travel agents *Adi Angkasa* and *Arjuna*.

Festivals

Traditional Banjarese wedding ceremonies take place on Sundays, in the auspicious month before Ramadan. Tourists are always welcome at these celebrations and do not require invitations. Traditional dances (such as the *hadrah* and *rudat*, which have Middle Eastern origins) are performed during wedding festivities.

Mar/Apr: *Mappanre Tassi Buginese Fishermens' Festival* (movable, but usually around mid-month) 7 days festival on Pagatan beach (S of Batu Licin on the SE coast, 240 km E of Banjarmasin) in which local Buginese fishermen sacrifice chickens, food and flour to the sea. Dancing and traditional songs, boat races and tug-of-war competitions. The festival climaxes on the last day. It is possible to stay overnight in the village where there are several losmen; enquire at tourist office or with tour operators as to how best to get to Pagatan. *Ramadan* (movable) throughout the Islamic fasting month, when Banjaris break *puasa* after sundown, they indulge in local delicacies. Every day from 1400-1800, in front of the Grand Mosque, the Ramadan Cake Fair is held, where people come to sell cakes for the evening feast. Traditional Banjari cakes are made from rice flour, glutinous rice, cassava and sago. Most are colourful, sweet and sticky.

Aug/Sep: *Aruh Ganal* – 'the big feast' (movable) is the Hill Dayak harvest festival. (Another smaller harvest festival, *Aruh Halus*, is held in Jun, to celebrate the first of the twice-yearly rice crop). Dancing all night from around 2000-0800; celebrated in the Hill Dayak longhouses in the Loksado and S Hulu Sungai districts. *Boat races* (17 Aug). Teams compete in traditional *tanabangan* rowing boats on the river in front of the mosque – the course is from the government office to the Grand Mosque.

Local information
● **Accommodation**

A *Barito Palace*, Jl Haryono MT 16-20, T 67300, F 2240, a/c, restaurant, pool, formerly the best hotel in town, but recent letters indicate a sharp down-turn in fortunes: it has become, in one guest's view, "dingy, characterless, lacking a bar, and very bad value"; **A** *Kalimantan*, Jl Lambung Mangkurat, T 66818, F 67345, a/c, restaurant, pool, very smart, new hotel in central location, standard rooms are small but well appointed, and this is in all respects superior to the *Barito Palace*, rec.

B *Maramin*, Jl Lambung Mangkurat 32, T 68944, F 3350, a/c, restaurant, mid-market hotel in central location, avoid rooms on the top flr as they are close to the noisy *Matt's Disco and Karaoke*; **B** *Nabilla Palace* (formerly *Fabiola*), Km 3.5 Jl Jend A Yani, T 52707, a/c, restaurant, out of town, on the airport road, good range of facilities incl tennis courts; **B** *Sampaga*, Jl May Jend Sutoyo S 128, T 52480 (on the N outskirts of town, but plenty of becaks available), a/c, restaurant, very clean rooms with big windows looking out onto a long verandah, rec.

C *Kartika*, Jl Pulau Laut 1, T 52325, a/c, restaurant, clean enough rooms, but the bathrooms leave a bit to be desired; **C** *Kuripan*, Jl Jend A Yani 126, T 53313, a/c, very smart looking new hotel with interesting architecture and sculptured front desk, but rooms average, difficult to get transport into town because it is on a one-way street; **C** *Metro*, Jl May Jend Sutoyo S 26, T 52427, some a/c; **C** *Perdana*, Jl Brig Jend Katamso 3, T 68029, a/c, restaurant, airy, bright and clean, good range of rooms, rec; **C** *Sabrina*, Jl Bank Rakyat (Jl Samudra end) 21, T 54442, a/c, restaurant, clean, but some rooms a bit dark and pokey, some triple rooms; **C** *SAS*, Jl Kacapiring 2, T 53054, some a/c, restaurant, traditional Banjari house in quiet location, but rooms a bit dark, breakfast incl, rec.

D *Rahmat*, Jl Jend A Yani 9, T 54429, fan-cooled rooms only (economy rooms do not even have a fan).

F *Beauty*, Jl Haryono MT 174, T 4493, a/c, does not live up to its name, but it is cheap and clean; **F** *Borneo Homestay*, Jl Pos, T 66545 123, F 66418, run by Johan and Lina Yasin, very simple accommodation right next to the river (adjacent to A Yani Bridge), the friendliest homestay/hotel in Borneo, rec.

● **Places to eat**

One of the best known Banjar foods is *soto banjar*, a duck egg soup; roast duck also appears frequently on Banjarmasin menus. This is thanks to the celebrated Alabio duck, which is thought to be related to the Peking Duck, discovered at the village of Alabio in 1927. Kalimantan is the biggest producer of ducks and duck eggs in Indonesia. Alcohol in Kalsel has a 40% tax imposed upon it; this is an attempt to cut down the problem of alcoholism amongst the young in Banjarmasin.

Indonesian: ♦*Cendrawasih*, Jl P Samudra 65, simple but excellent Padang food, good selection of seafood incl spicy roast fish and turtle eggs; ♦*Corner Garden*, Jl Hasanuddin 1, T 52488, seafood speciality is fried lobster in butter sauce, good crab curries, rec; ♦*Kaganangan Depot Makan*, Jl P Samudra 16, seafood, freshwater fish and sate (300Rp/stick).

Other Asian cuisine: ♦♦*Golden Lotus*, Jl Veteran 61, (nr the 150-year-old Tempat Ibadai Tri Dharma Suci-Nurani Taoist temple), big Chinese restaurant – popular for big Chinese functions for the Chinese community, big menu, speciality sapo with sticky sauce; ♦♦*Hakone*, Arjuna Plaza, Jl Lambung Mangkurat 62, Japanese restaurant, upstairs from *Rama Steak House* (see above), private rooms and a huge menu; ♦♦*Lezat Baru*, Jl Pang Samudra 22, part of a small chain of restaurants, with branches in Samarinda and Balikpapan, huge Chinese menu with a good choice of seafood, specials incl oysters done 10 different ways; ♦♦*Shinta*, 3rd Flr, Arjuna Plaza, Jl Lambung Mangkurat 62, Chinese restaurant attached to a nightclub and disco, private rooms, open until 0200.

International: ♦♦♦*Rama Steak Corner*, Arjuna Plaza, Jl Lambung Mangkurat 62, very cosy restaurant with soft lighting, imported Australian steaks double cost of local ones.

Food centres: *Grand Palace* is an upmarket, a/c food centre in *Mitra Plaza*, on the S side of Antisari Bridge, good views over the river. There are several good buffet-style restaurants incl: ♦*Hero Fast Food*, cheap, high quality local dishes – curries etc; ♦*Japanese Corner*; *Home Bakery*, pastries, cakes.

Warungs: in night market, off Jl Lambung Mangkurat, open to 0100.

Bakeries: *Minseng Bakery*, nr corner of Jl Pasar Baru and Jl Samudra, good selection of cakes and ice creams.

● **Airline offices**

Bouraq, Jl Jend A Yani 343, 4 km out of town, T 52445; **DAS**, Jl Hasanuddin 6, T 52902; **Garuda/Merpati**, Jl Hasanuddin 31, T 54203.

● **Banks & money changers**

Bumi Daya, **Dagang Negara** and **Negara** are along Jl Lambung Mangkurat; **Rakyat** is on Jl P Samudra. Money-changer in the back of *Adi Angkasa Travel*, Jl Hasanuddin 27.

● **Entertainment**

Cinemas: *Studio 21* (3 screens), *Mitra Plaza*, S side of Antisari Bridge. There are several other cinemas around town incl: *Banjarmasin*, *President* and *Ria* theatres.

● **Hospitals & medical services**

Hospitals: *Suaka Insan*, Jl Pembangunan (on the N side of town), best in Banjarmasin, with wards and private rooms.

● **Post & telecommunications**

Area code: 0511.

Post Office: on the corner of Jl Lambung Mangkurat and Jl Samudra.

● **Shopping**

Antiques: Jl Kacapiring II 10, T 4386. The home of Mr Ilmiyanto is an antiques supermarket without parallel in Kalimantan. It is a real treasure trove, anything purchased there can be professionally exported to your home country. The contents of the house – in a quiet suburban area of Banjarmasin – incl ancient Chinese ceramics, rare, beaded Dayak baby-carriers (which sell for up to 400,000Rp), Dayak statuettes, masks, blowpipes, spears, knives, drums, basketware and canoe paddles as well as coins and precious and semi-precious stones, rec.

Handicrafts: Hill Dayak handicrafts, basketware and semi-precious stones from the Martapura mines. Many of the shops have good selections of Dayak knives (*mandau*) from Central Kalimantan; in S Kalimantan, these knives are just called *parang*. One of the more unusual items on sale are the Dayak war canoes/death ships, intricately carved from rubber. There are several art shops on Simpang Sudimampir and Pasar Malabar (nr Antisari Bridge), bargain.

Jewellery/precious stones: *Gloria Jewellery*, Junjung Buig Plaza, Lt I/48, for those who do not have time to go to Martapura, expensive selection; *Toko Banjar Baru*, Jl Sudimanpir 61.

Sasirangan tie-dyes – from the shaman to the shop shelves

The bright Banjar cloth is called *sasirangan* and was traditionally believed to hold magical powers capable of driving out evil spirits and curing illnesses. The cloth could be made only by shamans – it was *pamali* (taboo) for common people to make it – and was designed to cure specific medical problems, from headaches to malaria. It was tailor-made by the shaman for specific customers and was known as *kain pamintan*, or 'the cloth that is made to order'. Patterns had particular significance to the spirit world, and dragons, bamboo shoots, rocks and waves, lotus and sun motifs were prescribed like drugs at a pharmacy. Colours were also important: the most common ones were yellow, green, red and purple. The afflicted person's medical prescription was then worn as a headcloth (*laung*) by men and a scarf (*serudung*) by women, who would also wear sasirangan blouses. Babies swung in sasirangan hammocks and children wore sasirangan sarungs to protect them from disease.

When pharmaceuticals arrived in Banjarmasin, the shamans began to go out of business and with their demise, the sasirangan faded into obscurity. Realizing that the art form had all but disappeared, local women enthusiastically began to revive the dying art in the 1980s. Within a few years, hundreds of tiny cottage industries had sprung up across the town and in a bid to popularize the material, sasirangan shirts and blouses were presented to celebrities. The cloth was traditionally coloured with natural dyes: yellow came from turmeric root, brown from the areca nut and red from the *karabintang* fruit; today chemical dyes are used. Sasirangan is made by a lengthy tie-dye procedure, involving several dyeing stages, interspersed with intricate tying and stitching sessions. A simple sasirangan with basic motifs can take up to 4 days to produce, while complex ones are said to take several months.

Streetside jewellers around Pasar Malabar can be seen cutting and polishing agate and amethyst (among other stones), the stones are rarely of high quality.

Markets: *Pasar Malabar* is next to Antasari Bridge (on the opp side of the river from *Mitra Plaza*), handicraft stalls and jewellers; *Pasar Samudra* on Jl Samudra/Jl Pangeran, mainly textiles, good for sarungs and mosquito nets.

Shopping centres: *Jujung Buik Plaza* (under *Kalimantan Hotel*), more expensive jewellery shops and boutiques, *Svensons* and supermarket; *Mitra Plaza*, on the S side of Antisari Bridge is a modern shopping centre with a supermarket which is the best place to stock up on provisions before treks and upriver expeditions.

Textiles/Batik: *Batik Semar*, Jl Hasanuddin 90, mainly imported Javanese batiks; *Toko Citra*, Km 3.5 Jl Jend A Yani (towards the airport, nr *Nabilla Palace hotel*), best place in town for Sasirangan tie-dyes (see below).

● **Tour companies & travel agents**
Adi Angkasa, Jl Hasanuddin 27, T 53131,
F 66200; *Arjuna*, Ground Flr, Arjuna Plaza, Jl Lambung Mangkurat 62, T 65235, F 64944; *Johan Yasin*, *Borneo Homestay*, Jl Pos 123, T 66545, F 66418; *Pujo Santoso*, Jl Nagasari 80, T 53023.

● **Tourist offices**
Dinas Pariwisata Kalimantan Selatan, Jl Panjaitan 23, T 2982; the Kalsel provincial tourist office is the best organized in Kalimantan, it produces some reasonably informative literature.

● **Transport**
Local Bajaj: congregate around Pasar Malabar (off Jl Samudra); 1,000-1,500Rp, to anywhere in town; or chartered for 3,000Rp/hr. **Bemos**: yellow bemos leave from in front of the *Minseng Bakery* nr the corner of Jl Pasar Baru and Jl Samudra. They follow fixed routes, but go all over town (250Rp to any destination). Bemos can also be found on the corner of Jl Bank Rakyat and Jl Hasanuddin, in front of the *Corner Steak House*. **Boat**: for travelling on the waterways, the best place to hire a klotok is from under A Yani Bridge or Kuin Cerucuk (also known as Kuin

Pertamina), to the NW side of town on the Kuin River. Motorized klotoks (which can hold up to 8 or 10 passengers) cost about 5,000Rp/hr; paddle-powered ones cost around 3,000Rp/hr. Speedboats are hired for around 30,000Rp/hr and leave from the Dermaga speedboat pier nr the Grand Mosque. **Ojeks and becaks**: congregate around *Mitra Plaza*. **Taxis**: the city taxi terminal is on Jl Antisari, next to the main market.

Air Syamsudin Noor Airport is 27 km E of town. Regular connections on Garuda, Merpati, Sempati, Bouraq, Asahi and DAS with most major Indonesian cities incl Jakarta, Surabaya, Balikpapan, Palangkaraya, Yogyakarta and Semarang. **Transport to town**: 11,500Rp (non-a/c), 14,000 Rp (a/c) by taxi, 1,000Rp by minibus to the intercity bus terminal.

Road Bus: Intercity buses leave from the Terminal Taksi Antar Kota at Km 6. Overnight buses (a/c and non-a/c) to Balikpapan leave at 1600-1700, 12 hrs. Overnight buses direct to Samarinda leave at the same time, 15 hrs. **Taxi**: taxis around Kalsel leave from the Terminal Taksi Antar Kota at Km 6.

River Boat: passenger boats leave for destinations upriver from Bajaraya Pier, at the far W end of Jl Sutoyo. The boats are double-deckers which, for trips beyond Palangkaraya, are equipped with beds (which can be rented for 1,000Rp) and even warungs. Behind the warungs there is a small prayer room and toilets and mandi. Those travelling long distances upriver should reserve beds the day before. Boats have signs next to them indicating their departure times. Most leave in the morning around 1100; ticket office open 0800-1400. *Getting to Bajaraya pier*: bemos (250Rp) or bajaj (2,500Rp) from Pasar Malabar. Palangkaraya, 24 hrs (5,100Rp), Muara Teweh, 48 hrs (12,000Rp) and Puruk Cahu, 60 hrs (13,000Rp). In the dry season big passenger boats cannot make it to Muara Teweh and Puruk Cahu; it is necessary to disembark at Pendang and take speedboats and motorized klotoks further upriver, 3 hrs (10,000Rp to Muara Teweh and 8 hrs, 6,000Rp to Puruk Cahu). Pelni passenger ferries leave Banjarmasin's Trisakti terminal (on the Barito River) for other destinations in Indonesia. The *Karakatau* leaves for Pangkalanbun (for Orang Utan Sanctuary – see page 579) every fortnight, 18 hrs. The Pelni vessels *Kelimutu*, *Sirimau* and *Tidar* also call here on their fortnightly circuits. See route schedules, page 921. Pelni office, Jl Laks E Martadinata 192, T 3171. **Bugis schooner**: to Java, enquire at Kantor Syahbandar Pelabuhan I, Jl Barito Hilir at Trisakti dock. **Speedboat**: regular connections with Palangkaraya (and other upriver destinations) from the Dermaga pier in front of the Grand Mosque. Most leave from 0900-1100, 5 hrs (20,000Rp).

CENTRAL KALIMANTAN
(KALIMANTAN TENGAH – KALTENG)

The vast province of Kalteng is most easily reached from Banjarmasin, but few tourists go there; it is the domain of Dayaks and loggers. It is Borneo's Dayak heartland, and the province was created in the late 1950s when the Dayak tribes sought autonomy from the Muslims of Banjarmasin. It covers nearly 154,000 sq km and has a population of 1.4 million. The N part of Kalteng is particularly remote, and is fringed by the mountains of the Schwaner and Muller ranges. The S part of the state is nearly all marshland with virtually impenetrable mangrove swamps which reach inland as far as 100 km.

PALANGKARAYA

This provincial capital was built virtually from scratch in 1957 and in 1991, at the time of the last census, had a population of 100,000. It has little to offer the tourist. There is a small state **museum** (on Jl Cilik Riwut, 2 km from town, open: Tues-Sun 0800-1200, 1600-1800) containing some Dayak heirlooms; mostly brass and ceramic jars. The only real tourist attraction here is the Tanjung Puting Orang Utan Rehabilitation Centre (which is still 8-10 hrs by road).

● **Accommodation** **C** *Dandang Matingang*, Jl Yos Sudarso 11, T 21805, a/c, restaurant, best in town, with multi-lingual staff. Out of town, but rec: **C** *Adidas*, Jl A Yani 90, T 21770, a/c; **C-D** *Melati Halmahera*, Jl Halmahera 24, T 21222, some a/c, quiet; **D-E** *Yanti*, Jl A Yani 82A, T 21634, some a/c, very clean; **D-E** *Mina*, Jl Nias 17, T 22182, some a/c, pleasant staff, clean rooms; **E** *Laris*, Jl Darmasugondo 78, clean, but noisy location.

● **Places to eat** *Rumak Makan Aluminum*, Jl Halmahera, excellent fish; *Depot Makanan Sampurna*, Jl Jawa 49, good range of fish dishes.

Foodstalls: night market on Jl Halmahera and Jawa near the docks.

● **Airline offices** DAS, Jl Milono 2, T 21550; Bouraq, Jl A Yani 84, T 21622; **Merpati**, Jl A Yani 69A, T 21411; **Sempati**, Jl A Yani 4, T 21612.

● **Post & telecommunications** **Area code**: 0514.

● **Tour companies and travel agents** *Patas*, Jl A Yani 52, T 23307.

● **Tourist office** Jl Parman 21, T 21416, English speaking, informed staff.

● **Transport** The town can be reached by river from Banjarmasin; canals, cut by the Dutch in the late 19th century, connect the Barito, Kapuas and Kahayan river systems. **Air** Regular connections with Banjarmasin, Sampit and Pangkalanbun on Bouraq and Balikpapan and Surabaya (Java) on Sempati. Merpati flies these routes too. **Road Bus**: connections with Pulang Pisau and Kuala Kapuas. **River Boat**: boats travelling downstream leave from Rambang Pier, tickets are available from here. To Banjarmasin, the fast boat takes 6 hrs, the slow boat takes 18 hrs (travelling past Pulang Pisau and Kuala Kapuas en route). Boats travelling upstream to Tewah leave from Dermaga Flamboyan (or Flamboyant Pier). Any journeys beyond Tewah require chartering a boat.

TANJUNG PUTING NATIONAL PARK AND ORANG UTAN REHABILITATION CENTRE

The 300,040 ha Tanjung Puting National Park was founded by Dr Birute Galdikas in the early 1970s in an area with a wild population of orang utans, see page 548. The park straddles several forest types, including swamp forest, heath forest and lowland dipterocarp rainforest. The unusual heath forest is found in the northern area of the park where stunted trees, many with under-sized leaves, grow on impoverished white-sand soils. The swamp forest is concentrated in the central portion of the park and many of the trees here are adapted to periodic flooding with stilt roots.

The orang utan centre is smaller and less touristy than Sepilok in Sabah, Malaysia and Bukit Lawang in Sumatra (see page 440) but has the same mission: to look after and rehabilitate orang utans orphaned by logging or rescued from captivity. In addition to the orang utans, there is a large population of other fauna in Tanjung Puting, including proboscis monkeys (see page 549), crab-eating macaques, clouded leopards, false gharial crocodiles, monitor lizards and over 200 species of bird. There are two main stations in the park; **Camp Leakey** is the main research centre; **Tanjung Harapan** was set up in the late 1980s as an overflow centre – it is the one visited by most tourists. At Camp Leakey, orang utans are fed at 1500, 1600 and 1700. There is an ongoing Proboscis monkey research programme at Natai Lengknas, within the park.

Permits

A police permit must be obtained in **Pangkalanbun** before making the 25 km road trip to Kumai where visitors should obtain a park permit (no charge) from the Conservation Office (PHPA Office). (A photocopy of the police letter and a photocopy of the first page of your passport is required to secure the park permit). Permit costs 2,500Rp/day.

NB Anyone who is sick is strictly barred from entering the centre. Visitors should also note that malaria is rife in this region and that anti-malarial drugs are essential.

Tours

Tours to the park are organized from Banjarmasin (see page 574). *Trekforce Expeditions* in London (0171 8248890) organize 2 week conservation/scientific expeditions, where participants assist in the programme.

Park information

● **Accommodation**
C *Hotel Rimba* (nr Tanjung Harapan), restaurant; *Andika Hotel* or *Blue Kecubung Hotel* (both **B-C** with a/c), Kumai. Minibus from Pangkalanbun to Kumai (7,500Rp).

E-F *PHPA* provide basic accommodation at Tanjung Harapan, just inside the park on the Sekonyer River. Most visitors stay on the Kelotok houseboats, hired from Kumai.

● **Transport**
Air Regular *Bouraq* and *DAS* flights from Banjarmasin to Pangkalanbun, 2 hrs (100,000Rp).

DAS also flies to Pangkalanbun from Palangkaraya (100,000Rp) and Pontianak (100,000Rp). *Merpati* flies daily to Pangkalanbun from Semarang (change here, if coming from Jakarta) and Bandung (3¼ hrs). Transport to Pangkalanbun by taxi from airport (9,500Rp).

Sea Boat: it is also possible to take a Pelni passenger boat from Banjarmasin to Pangkalanbun; the boat leaves twice a month. Tanjung Puting is 4 hrs up the Sekonyer River from Kumai. Kelotoks can be hired at Kumai from around 75,000-100,000Rp/day. The boats *Garuda I & II* – sleep 6 and 10 people respectively and are the best-kitted out of the Kumai Kelotoks. The boatman running the *Garuda* boats is called Ha Baso and can be contacted at Jl HM Idris 6, Kumai Hulu. It is necessary to bring food and water upriver unless you stay at *Hotel Rimba*. River water must be thoroughly boiled before drinking.

EAST KALIMANTAN
(KALIMANTAN TIMUR – KALTIM)

With its economy founded on timber (it produces 70% of Indonesia's sawn timber exports), oil, gas and coal, Kaltim is the wealthiest province in Kalimantan. Its capital is Samarinda, the launch-pad for trips up the Mahakam River. Balikpapan is bigger than Samarinda and is the provincial transport hub; it is an ugly oil town. The province covers an area of 211,400 sq km – more than six times the size of The Netherlands – and has a population of 1.9 million. It is the second largest province in Indonesia after Irian Jaya.

Archaeological digs on the E Kalimantan coast have uncovered stone 'yupa' poles with Sanskrit inscriptions, suggesting Indian cultural influence possibly dating back to the 5th century or even earlier. The province's first substantial settlement was founded by refugees from Java in the 13th century, who fled from the Majapahits. They founded the kingdom of Kertanegara ('the lawful nation' – which later became known as Kutai). This kingdom is believed to have been an important centre on the trade route between Java and China. The word 'Kutai' is thought to have been the term used by Chinese traders, who knew it as 'the great land'. The imaginative Chinese traders also gave the Mahakam River its name; *Mahakam* means 'big river'.

Following Banjarmasin's conversion to Islam, Kutai also embraced the faith in 1565 and became an Islamic sultanate. It came into conflict with neighbouring kingdoms – most notably the Hindu kingdom of Martapura, on the Mahakam River. Their disputes were settled by a royal marriage which forged an alliance between the upriver kingdom and the Islamic sultanate. In the 17th century, hostilities broke out again and Kutai defeated and then absorbed the kingdom of Martapura. The first Buginese settlers arrived from Sulawesi in 1701. As piracy in the Sulu Sea grew worse in the 18th century, Kutai's capital was moved inland and was finally transferred to Tenggarong on the Mahakam in 1781. Kutai remained intact as a sultanate until 1960.

BALIKPAPAN

At night, from the dirty beach along Balikpapan's sea front, the clouds are periodically lit up by the orange glow of flares from the offshore rigs in the Makassar Strait. There are several big offshore fields and the town is the administrative headquarters for Kaltim's oil and gas industry. The support staff of Pertamina, the Indonesian national oil company, live mainly on Gunung Dubb, in Dutch colonial villas dating from the 1920s and overlooking the refinery. Unocal and Total, US oil companies, have their residential complexes on the opposite hill, on Pasir Ridge, overlooking the town. At the last census in 1991, Balikpapan was recorded as having 309,000 inhabitants, up from 92,000 in 1961. The largest group are the Javanese who make up 35-40% of the population, followed by Bugis (25-30%) and Banjarese (20%).

The foreign oil workers live like kings in Balikpapan which is a soulless town: it is strung out untidily along several kilometres of road. It was established early this century as an oil town, and to a

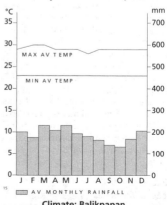

Climate: Balikpapan

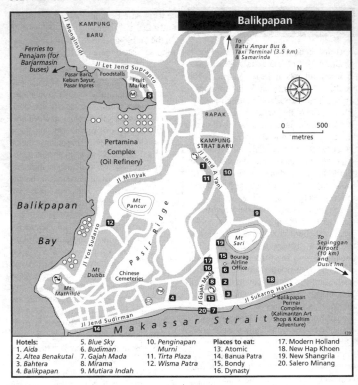

Balikpapan

Hotels:
1. Aida
2. Altea Benakutai
3. Bahtera
4. Balikpapan
5. Blue Sky
6. Budiman
7. Gajah Mada
8. Mirama
9. Mutiara Indah
10. Penginapan Murni
11. Tirta Plaza
12. Wisma Patra

Places to eat:
13. Atomic
14. Banua Patra
15. Bondy
16. Dynasty
17. Modern Holland
18. New Hap Khoen
19. New Shangrila
20. Salero Minang

significant extent remains one. Some attempt has been made in recent years to create a business district and this has begun to bear fruit around the bottom of Jl Jend A Yani, next to the smart *Altea Benakutai Hotel*. The new shopping centre at the T-junction at the end of Jl Jend A Yani will help towards the creation of a commercial centre. Apart from some excellent arts and crafts shops and some good restaurants and hotels, Balikpapan has little to offer tourists; it is a transit camp for visits to Samarinda and the Mahakam River or for Banjarmasin, to the S.

Excursions

The best **beaches** are to the N of Balikpapan at Tanah Merah and Manggar (3 km from town). These tend to become crowded at weekends.

Tours

There are three big agents (*Kaltim Adventure* and *Musi Holidays* and *Tomaco*) which operate tours, mainly up the Mahakam River (see page 591) as well as more unusual treks around the Apo Kayan (see page 596) and trans-Borneo treks to Putussibau and Pontianak in Kalbar. On the whole these agents are more expensive than the smaller (but often equally efficient) companies at Samarinda. *Kaltim Adventure Tour* has two houseboats at Samarinda for Mahakam trips as well as five full-time guides and cooks. Tours include: 3-15 days Mahakam trips; Long Apung/Apo Kayan tours; Kutai Game

Balikpapan's streetnames – selamat jalan-jalan

🐌 The Kota Madya (Municipal Office) in Balikpapan has a lot to answer for. In late 1991 it unilaterally declared that more than half the streets in town were to be renamed. But it went one step further than just changing the names: it swapped them round too. Balikpapan's hoteliers, restaurateurs and businessmen all had to print new cards, tourists (and guidebook writers) became hopelessly lost and even Kijang taxi drivers where unable to tell people where they were. To compound the problem, the municipal office failed to print a new town map.

The most important changes concerned the T-junction at the S end of town. Jl P Antisari, Jl May Jend Sutayo and Jl May Jend DL Panjaitan were all changed to just one road name: Jl Jend A Yani. The fact that there was already an important road called Jl Jend A Yani did not bother the municipal office: its name was changed to Jl Jend Sudirman – which now stretches along the coast from W to E, also encompassing the old Jalan Gajah Mada. To confuse matters further, Jl Dondang, which cuts between the old Jl Jend A Yani and the new Jl Jend A Yani, was renamed Jl Gajah Mada – for what town could be without one? The road further to the E, towards the airport, which used to be called Jl KS Tubun, is now Jl Sukarno Hatta.

The nightmare of Balikpapan's urban nomenclature does not end there. Because the locals are so confused, they have taken to using both names. This will ease in time, but until then, a typical conversation between a lost tourist and a bewildered local might go something like this:

"Excuse me, where is the *Benakutai Hotel*?"
"It's over there on Jl Jend A Yani."
"But I thought that was Jl Antisari."
"Yes, it is."

The only comforting irony was that the municipal office managed to embroil itself in the mess. Those wishing to complain should contact the municipal officer on Jl Jend Sudirman – formerly Jl Jend A Yani.

NB For more detail on Indonesia's street names, see page 49.

Reserve and overland 15-days treks from Balikpapan to Pontianak, rec; *Musi Holidays*, variety of package tours, mainly up the Mahakam River, rec; *Tomaco*, biggest, most professional and most expensive tour agent in town, has a new houseboat in Samarinda with a/c cabins to accommodate 12, also several other smaller boats. Tour prices 15% off published rates for walk-in tourists, rec. See page 121 for Jakarta head offices.

Local information
● **Accommodation**

A+ *Dusit Inn*, Jl Jend Sudirman, T 20155, F 20150, a/c, restaurants, pool, the most luxurious hotel in town, set in extensive gardens overlooking the Makassar Strait, 191 rm, fitness centre, business facilities, fine for those with transport or willing to use taxis, but with a 15 min drive to the centre of town a trifle inconvenient for those who like (or have) to walk.

A *Altea Benakutai*, Jl Jend A Yani, T 31896, F 31823, a/c, restaurants, pool, very smart, international-class hotel, mainly used by oil industry workers, good service and wide range of facilities, helpful representative office at airport.

B *Bahtera*, Jl Jend Sudirman 2, T 22603, F 31889, a/c, restaurant, nothing special, but adequate; **B** *Balikpapan*, Jl Erry Suparjan 2, T 21490, a/c, restaurant, clean hotel and reasonable value, satellite TV, disco, sauna and massage parlour; **B** *Blue Sky*, Jl Let Jend Suprapto 1, T 22268/35895, a/c, restaurant, pool, Balikpapan's second-best hotel, new and modern with good range of facilities incl in-house videos, satellite TV, sauna, billiards and Japanese

Shiatsu massage, rec; **B** *Mirama*, Jl AP Pranoto 16, T 22960/33906, a/c, restaurant, big hotel, clean, be wary of the lift which periodically jams between flrs; **B** *Wisma Patra*, Jl Prabumulih (off Jl Minyak), T 33011, a/c, restaurant, pleasant out-of-town location on top of the steep hill overlooking the Pertamina complex, detached bungalows as well as rooms, tennis court.

C *Budiman*, Jl Jend A Yani, T 22583/36030, a/c, a little run-down but although the rooms are grubby, the hotel is not as dingy as many other local hotels in the same (or higher) bracket; **C** *Gajah Mada*, Jl Jend Sudirman 14, T 23019/34634, a/c, breakfast incl, satellite TV, unmarried couples might be a little circumspect here, the Muslim management has been known to ask to see marriage certificates!, the rooms on the seaward side, at the back of the hotel are the nicest, there is a very pleasant balcony running along the back of the hotel on both flrs, rec; **C** *Mutiara Indah*, Jl May Jend Sutoyo 65, T 22925, a/c, restaurant, hardly the 'pearl' its name suggests, its 'cottages' look more like prison complexes, but the rooms are spotless and the hotel well maintained; **C** *Piersa*, Jl Sepinggan Bypass, T 23048, a/c, restaurant, out of town towards the airport, but with few guests it is a quiet retreat, clean and empty; **C** *Tirta Plaza*, Jl Jend A Yani, a/c, recently refurbished; **C-D** *Aida*, Jl Jend A Yani 1/12, T 76123/21006, sister hotel to its namesake in Samarinda, popular with budget travellers.

D *Surya*, Jl Karang Bugis, T 21580, a/c, clean enough and seems reasonable value, but offers a half-hourly room rate.

E *Penginapan Murni*, Jl S Parman 1, very basic; **E** *Penginapan Sinar Lumayan*, Jl Jend A Yani 1A/49, very basic.

● **Places to eat**
Indonesian: ♦♦*Salero Minang*, Jl Gajah Mada 12B, fresh and tasty Padang food.

Other Asian: ♦♦*Atomic*, Jl Sutoyo/Jl Dondang 3/10, mainly seafood and Chinese; ♦♦*Lezat Baru*, Pasar Baru Blok A, Jl Jend Sudirman 1, Komplek Pertokoan, part of a small chain of restaurants, huge Chinese menu with a good choice of seafood, specials incl oysters done 10 different ways; ♦♦*Mahakam*, Blue Sky Hotel, Jl Let Jend Suprapto 1, Chinese and European cuisine, seafood and steaks, popular with expatriates; ♦♦*New Hap Khoen*, Jl Jend Sudirman 19, huge Chinese menu, good seafood selection, specialities incl crab curry, chilli crab and *goreng tepung* (squid fried in batter), rec;

♦♦*Paradise*, Komplek Pantai Mas Permai, Jl Jend A Yani, huge restaurant and huge menu with Chinese, European and Japanese dishes, mostly seafood, fish grill outside, built on stilts out over the sea on a dirty stretch of beach.

International: ♦♦♦*Banua Patra*, Jl Jend Sudirman 39, T 23746, smart – and snooty – seafront restaurant run by rig supply company, imported steaks and European *haute cuisine* as well as selection of Indonesian, Korean and Japanese dishes; ♦♦♦*Bondy*, Jl Jend A Yani 7, one of the best restaurants in town, entrance through bakery with enticing smell of fresh pastries, past the fast-food area, to the rear where it opens into a large 2-storey open-air restaurant, built around an open courtyard, European and local food, mixed grill very good and local and imported steaks, vast selection of sundaes and ice creams, very popular with locals, rec; ♦♦♦*Tenggarong Grill*, Altea Benakutai Hotel, Jl Jend A Yani, international, steaks and seafood, popular with expatriates; ♦♦*Modern Holland*, Jl Jend A Yani 2, bakery with small restaurant attached serving local and imported steaks, good ice creams; ♦♦*Sampan*, Altea Benakutai Hotel, Jl Jend A Yani, coffee shop with Chinese, Indonesian and international selection, rec.

Seafood: ♦♦*Dynasty*, Jl Jend A Yani 10/7, Chinese food and seafood, huge menu, deep-fried crab claws, prawns fried with rambutan, shellfish, sate, rec; ♦*New Shangrila*, Jl Gunung Sari Ilir 29, seafood and Chinese dishes, speciality *kangkung asap* and deep-fried crab claws.

Foodstalls: there are stalls in the new Balikpapan Permai complex on the road to the airport, more at the vegetable market (Kebun Sayur) – the Chinatown of Balikpapan.

● **Airline offices**
Asahi, Jl Jend A Yani 41, T 22044/222301; **Bouraq**, Jl Jend A Yani, (close to *Hotel Budiman*), T 23117; **Garuda**, Jl Jend A Yani 19, T 22300; **Merpati**, Jl Jend Sudirman 29, T 22380/24477; **Sempati**, Altea Benakutai Hotel, Jl Jend A Yani, T 31896/31612.

● **Banks & money changers**
Bank Dagang Negara, Jl Jend A Yani; **Bank Duta**, Jl Jend Sudirman 26 (nr *Altea Benakutai Hotel*), probably the best place for foreign exchange; **Bank Negara Indonesia**, Jl Jend Sudirman 30; **Bank Rakyat**, Jl May Jend Sutoyo.

● **Entertainment**
Cinemas: there are 3 big cinemas, all showing recent Hollywood releases; the biggest and best is on Jl Sudirman.

Discos: the best known nightclub in town is the *Altea Benakutai Hotel's* **Black Orchid Disco** (known locally as 'The BO'); nearby is the *Sabatini; The Club*, nr the airport also has a disco.

● **Hospitals & medical services**
Hospitals: *Pertamina*.

● **Post & telecommunications**
Area code: 0542.
Post Office: Jl Jend Sudirman.

● **Shopping**
Balikpapan has a vast array of arts and crafts shops and is probably the best place in Kalimantan to buy Dayak handicrafts; 'antiques' may not, however, be as old as they first appear. A new shopping centre (to be opened by mid-1993) has been built right on the seafront at the bottom of Jl Jend A Yani.

Arts and crafts: *Bahati Jaya Art Shop*, Jl May Jen Sutoyo 9, good range of tribal arts and crafts and antiques; **Borneo Art Shop**, Jl Jend A Yani 34/03, one of the best selections of handicrafts, Dayak antiques, ceramics, gemstones and coins; **Kalimantan Art Shop**, Blok A1, Damai Balikpapan Permai, Jl Jend Sudirman 7, the undisputed king of Balikpapan's antiques, and Dayak arts and crafts shops, textiles, beads, porcelain etc, proprietor Eddy Amran is friendly and knowledgeable; **Susila Art Shop**, Jl Jend A Yani 11 (nr *Dynasty Restaurant*), small, but good selection of Dayak pieces and ceramics; **Syahda Mestika**, Jl Jend A Yani 147, vast selection of tribal arts and crafts, Chinese porcelain and antiques. There are also a large number of arts and crafts shops above the vegetable market (Kebun Sayur/Pasar Inpres) on Jl Let Jend Suprapto at the N end of town. Many stalls also sell stones from Martapura (incl *manik manik* stone necklaces) and antique jewellery.

Batik: *Iwan Suharto Batik Gallery*, Hotel Benakutai, Jl Jend A Yani, T 31896, excellent selection of very original batik paintings (traditional and modern), much of it is by batik artists on Java, but incl some interesting batiks with Dayak designs.

Newspapers: a good selection of national and international English-language publications are on sale in the *Altea Benakutai Hotel* shop, incl the *Jakarta Post*, the *Singapore Straits Times*, *USA Today*, *The International Herald Tribune*. Elsewhere in Kaltim, English-language newspapers are hard to come by.

● **Tour companies & travel agents**
Kaltim Adventure Tour, Blok C-1/1 Komplex Balikpapan Permai, Jl Jend Sudirman, T 31158, F 33408; *Musi*, Jl Dondang (Antasari) 5A, T 24272, F 24984; *Natrabu*, Jl Jend A Yani 58, T 22443; *Tomaco*, Hotel Benakutai, Jl Jend A Yani, T 22747.

● **Tourist offices**
Tourist Information Office, Seppinggang Airport, T 21605, unpredictable opening hours, but *Altea Benakutai Hotel* representative office is usually staffed and can help with immediate queries.

● **Transport**
Local Bemo: all trips around town cost 300Rp, the bemos take a circular route around town, down Jl Jend A Yani, Jl Jend Sudirman and past the Pertamina complex on Jl Minyak. They can be hailed at any point; shout 'STOP!' when you want to alight. **Ojeks**: 1,000Rp minimum charge.

Air Sepinggang Airport is 10 km from Balikpapan. *Airport facilities*: a post office, souvenir shop, money-changer and restaurant and an international telephone which takes major credit cards. **Transport to town**: fixed price taxis (7,500Rp), buying ticket in airport terminal, or direct to Samarinda (55,000Rp). Regular connections on Garuda, Merpati, Sempati and Bouraq airlines with most major cities in Indonesia such as Samarinda, Banjarmasin, Pontianak, Jakarta, Semarang, Tarakan, Ujung Pandang, Yogyakarta, and Pangkalanbun. **International connections**: (via Pontianak) with Singapore.

Road Bus: regular long-distance bus connections with Samarinda and Banjarmasin. *CV Gelora* express buses to Samarinda leave every 30 mins from 0530-2000 from Batu Ampar terminal at Km 3.5 on Samarinda road, 2 hrs. Buses to Banjarmasin also leave from the Batu Ampar terminal or from Penajam, on the other side of the bay. Boats cross to Penajam from Pasar Baru at the N end of town on Jl Monginsidi (2,000Rp). *Getting to Batu Ampar terminal*: take a Kijang taxi to Rapak, the junction with the Samarinda Rd (300Rp). From Rapak, taxis leave for Batu Ampar when full (300Rp); alternatively an ojek costs 500-700Rp. **Taxi**: saloon taxis also go to Samarinda from Batu Ampar bus terminal; one car takes up to 7 people (5,000-6,000Rp pp). It is also possible to charter an a/c taxi to Samarinda (60,000Rp), T 35555.

Sea Boat: the Pelni ships *Tidar, Umsini* and

Kambuna dock at the harbour to the W of the city centre, off Jl Yos Sudarso, and call at Tarakan, Toli-Toli, Ujung Pandang, Surabaya and Tanjung Priok (Jakarta) – among other ports – on their 2-week circuits (see route map, page 922). The Pelni office is at Jl Pelabuhan (off Jl Yos Sudarso), T 22187.

SAMARINDA

Kaltim's capital, 120 km N of Balikpapan, is one of Kalimantan's main tourism centres – it is the gateway to the interior, up the Mahakam River and to the remote Dayak areas of the Apo Kayan, near the border with Sarawak. The town, however, is short on tourist attractions: the only real 'sight' is the Mahakam River itself. Samarinda is a bustling modern town and has grown rich from the proceeds of the timber industry (see box). The town was founded by Buginese seafarers from S Sulawesi in the early 1700s and became the capital of the Kutai sultanate. It is 40 km from the coast at the head of the splayed Mahakam estuary. The river is navigable by large ships right up to the town – only the recently-built bridge across the Mahakam prevents them going further upriver. In 1991 it had a population of 335,000, a figure approaching five times that of 1961 when the city was recorded as having 70,000 inhabitants. The rapid growth of Samarinda is based squarely of natural resource exploitation. The town produced almost three-quarters of E Kalimantan's plywood in the early 1990s and was reputed to have one of the world's highest densities of plywood factories and sawmills. This output has since declined because of a shortage of logs, and a stiff export tax on sawn timber.

Unlike some other cities in Indonesian Borneo, like Balikpapan, the Banjarese are still the largest ethnic group, making up perhaps 40% of the population (with 30% Javanese, 10% Bugis and 10% Chinese).

Places of interest

It is well worth chartering a boat to cruise around the **Mahakam River** for an hour. On the left bank, at the E end of town, is the harbour, where the elegant Bugis schooners dock (see page 619). Kampung Sulili, further downriver from Samarinda is built out over the river on stilts and backed by a steep hillside; there are lively scenes all along the riverbank. Small boats can be hired from any of the countless jetties behind the Pasar Pagi (Morning Market) for around 5,000Rp/hr.

Excursions

Mahakam River, see page 591.

Kutai National Park, 120 km N of Samarinda is a 200,000 ha area of primary forest. The World Wide Fund for Nature (WWF) believes it contains at least 239 species of bird. It is also home to a population of wild orang utans (around Teluk Kaba) and proboscis monkeys. The park was first gazetted as a protected area before the Second World War but has found itself gradually diminished in size as the government has allowed portions to be logged. At the beginning of the 1980s 60% of the remaining protected area was devastated by a vast forest fire (see page 545). Kutai park is reached via **Bontang**, which lies on the equator. Bontang is the site of a large liquified natural gas plant. Nearby, at Kuala Bontang, there is a Bajau fishing kampung built out on stilts over the water. **Accommodation in Bontang C** *Equator Hotel*, PT Pupuk Kaltim (Persero Complex), Loktuan, Bontang Utara (owned by Pupuk Kaltim fertilizer company) T J3845286, a/c, restaurant. **Accommodation in the park** There are a number of rangers' posts in the park with basic accommodation and food. There is one on Teluk Kaba and others along the Sengata River (5,000Rp/night; 3,000Rp/ meal). **Permits/guides**: it is necessary to acquire a permit from the Conservation Office (PHPA Office) in Bontang (no charge). The office can advise independent travellers on their itinerary and organize boat trips to the park; it will also provide guides (10,000Rp/day) and help charter boats.

Getting there: most people visit the park on an organized tour (see below). Regular buses, 3 hrs (3,000Rp) and passenger boats (10,000Rp) from Samarinda to Bontang. Tour agencies sometimes fly tourists into Bontang (45 mins flight from Balikpapan). From Bontang (Lok Tuan or Tanjung Limau harbours) the park can be reached by speedboat in 30 mins. Hiring boats can be expensive for the inde-

Deforestation in Kalimantan – the chainsaw massacre

At Balikpapan's Sepinggang airport, on the road leading into town, there is a huge billboard saying 'Welcome to Balikpapan'; the words superimposed on a picture showing caterpillars clearing logs out of the jungle. It might be intended to signify development and progress, but it leaves a graphic, striking – and, as it turns out, accurate – first impression of E Kalimantan. From Balikpapan, the road to Samarinda winds through hills affording panoramic views over the denuded landscape: virtually the whole area has been deforested, leaving only scrubland and secondary forest. Few trees are higher than 10m tall, other than the occasional towering *Kompassia*, whose wood is too brittle for commercial use, and scattered palms. The sky is often hazy from smoke as shifting cultivators clear the remaining vegetation for their *ladangs* (farms).

Originally E Kalimantan had 17.3 million ha of forest. Most of this has been divided up; 3.6 million ha is protected forest, 2 million ha is classed as forest reserve and 10.3 million ha is classed as 'productive forest'. East Kalimantan is Indonesia's biggest timber-producing province; most of which goes to supply the thriving downstream wood processing industries. Round-log exports were banned in 1985 in an effort to increase the value of wood exports, but this did little to slow the rate of felling. Logging directly employs around 10,000 people in the province, and downstream industries another 40,000.

Sawmills manufacture plywood, chipboard, furniture and veneer. About 40% of the wood products produced in E Kalimantan go to supply the domestic market. But plywood exports alone earn the province US$250mn a year. For every cubic metre of Meranti hardwood bought by the wood processing industry, the buyer is legally required to pay a premium of US$10 which is put towards replanting projects. Whether this actually happens or not is another matter – although the government has reportedly come down hard on timber companies shirking their environmental responsibilities. However, distances in Kaltim are so huge that the Forestry Department cannot hope to police the timber industry adequately, either to collect premiums or to prevent illegal logging. Logging companies also wield considerable influence both locally and in Jakarta, and few officials are willing to become embroiled in a dispute which they have little chance of winning. The other problem is that most silviculturists believe it is impossible to replant a rainforest. This has not stopped scientists from trying: 36 km from Balikpapan, just off the Samarinda Rd, is the Tropen Bosch/Wana Riset Forest Research Institute, which has had some measure of success in trying to propagate dipterocarps. But most of the species that are replanted on cleared land are fast-growing trees which critics say 'mine' the soil of nutrients.

Such is the scale and pace of deforestation in E Kalimantan that some tribal groups have taken the law into their own hands – much as their brethren in E Malaysia has done. In Aug 1995 one group outside Samarinda, in a probably futile attempt to save their last remaining patch of forest, blocked the route of the tractors and purloined the keys. In other cases, logging camps have been attacked.

The tough life of a turtle

Historically, green and hawksbill turtles have been hunted for their meat, shells and their edible eggs (a Chinese delicacy). They were a favourite food of British and Spanish mariners for centuries. Japanese soldiers slaughtered thousands of turtles for food during WW2. Dynamite fishermen are also thought to have killed off many turtles in Indonesian, Malaysian and Philippines waters in recent years.

Malaysia, Japan, Hong Kong, Japan and the Philippines, where green turtle meat and eggs are much in demand, are all signatories of the Convention in International Trade in Endangered Species (CITES), and trading in sea turtles has been proscribed under Appendix 1 of the Convention since 1981.

In his book *Forest Life and Adventures in the Malay Archipelago*, the Swedish adventurer and wildlife enthusiast Eric Mjoberg documents turtle egg-hunting and shell collecting in Borneo in the 1920s. He tells of how the Bajau would lie in wait for hawksbills, grab them and put them on the fire so their horny shields could be removed. "The poor beasts are put straight on the fire so that their shield may be more readily removed, and suffer, in the process, the tortures of the damned. They are then allowed to go alive, or perhaps half-dead into the sea, only to come back again after a few years and undergo the same cruel process." The Bajau, he says, used an 'ingenious contrivance' to hunt their prey. They would press pieces of common glass against their eyes 'in a watertight fashion' and would lie face-down on a piece of floating wood, dipping their faces into the water, watching for hawksbills feeding on seaweed. They would then dive in, armed with a small harpoon and catch them, knocking them out with a blow to the head.

pendent traveller.

Tours

About 15,000 tourists travel up the Mahakam River annually. The vast majority go on organized tours which can be tailored to suit all budgets. Most tours are prohibitively expensive for groups smaller than two; the costs fall dramatically the more people there are. Tour agents usually require a deposit of 50% upon booking. There are some excellent tour companies in Samarinda and three major ones in Balikpapan (see page 574) offering similar deals. There are also more adventurous trekking trips to the Apo Kayan (see page 596) and 3-4 days package deals to the Kutai National Park, N of Samarinda (see above) for about 450,000-500,000Rp for groups of four to six people (including full board and travel).

Unlike neighbouring Sarawak, upriver tours on the Mahakam of less than a week's duration will not get far enough upstream to reach traditional longhouses. 3-4 days tours cost about US$300 per head for four to six people and travel to Lake Jempang and Tanjung Isuy. 5-9 days tours continue upriver to Tunjung, Bahau and Kenyah Dayak villages W of Long Iram, they cost from US$400-800 per head for four to six people. A 14 days tour reaches Long Baun or beyond. **Apo Kayan Tours**: all tours to the Apo Kayan area include the return flight from Samarinda to Long Ampung. Few are shorter than 6 days, most are about 9-10 days. Most tours involve a mixture of trekking and river trips by longboat and canoe, visiting Long Nawang and nearby longhouses and waterfalls. Some even throw in a day's hunting with local Dayaks. Tours cost around US$700-900 for groups of four to six.

Cisma Angkasa is an experienced tour agent specializing in adventure tourism along Mahakam River and Apo Kayan. The company owns four well fitted double-decker river boats (a/c cabins) and

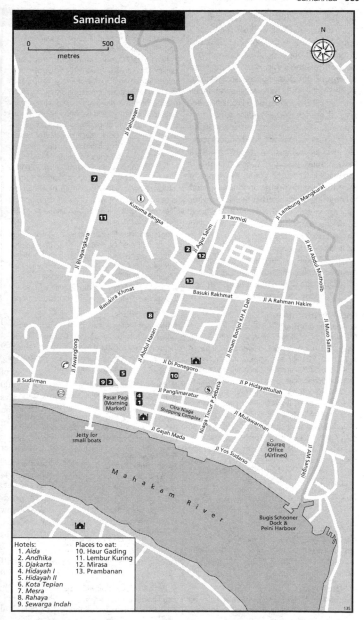

Samarinda

0 — 500
metres

N

Jl Pahlawan

Kusuma Bangsa

Jl Tarmidi

Jl Lambung Mangkurat

Jl Bhayangkara

Jl Agus Salim

Jl KH Abdul Mutholib

Basukira Khmat

Basuki Rakhmat

Jl A Rahman Hakim

Jl Muso Salim

Jl Awanglong

Jl Abdul Hasan

Jl Di Ponegoro

Jl Imam Bonjol KH A Dah

Jl P Hidayattullah

Jl Sudirman

Jl Panglimaratur

Niaga Timur P Sebatik

Jl Mulawarman

Pasar Pagi
(Morning Market)

Citra Niaga
Shopping Complex

Jetty for
small boats

Jl Gajah Mada

Jl Yos Sudarso

Bouraq
Office
(Airlines)

Jl AM Sangaji

M a h a k a m   R i v e r

Bugis Schooner
Dock &
Pelni Harbour

Hotels:
1. *Aida*
2. *Andhika*
3. *Djakarta*
4. *Hidayah I*
5. *Hidayah II*
6. *Kota Tepian*
7. *Mesra*
8. *Rahaya*
9. *Sewarga Indah*

Places to eat:
10. Haur Gading
11. Lembur Kuring
12. Mirasa
13. Prambanan

supplies mosquito nets. Can arrange tours to destinations well off the beaten track (including trans-Borneo treks) and caters for all budgets (cheaper tours use public transport), rec. *Ayus Wisata* is an adventure tourism specialist (Jakarta, T 749155, F 7491560). Has good boats with a/c cabins and bunks as well as experienced guides, rec. *Freelance guides* tout around hotels looking for tourists wanting to go upriver. Some are good, others terrible: it is advisable to stick to those with tourist guide licences. (When planning a trip with a freelance guide, ask them to trace the intended route on a map; it soon becomes apparent whether they know what they are talking about). Many of the good guides in Samarinda contract out their services to tour companies. An average daily rate for a freelance guide should be about 30,000Rp. Suriyadi is a recommended freelance guide who can be contacted through the *Hidaya Hotel* or through *Anggrek Hitam* tour company.

Local information
● **Accommodation**
B *Kota Tepian*, Jl Pahlawan 4, T 32513, a/c, restaurant, good facilities; **B** *Mesra*, Jl Pahlawan 1, T 21011, F 21017, a/c, restaurant, pool, Samarinda's top hotel – at the top of a hill, golf course and tennis, good bar, rooms, suites and cottages, rec; **B** *Sewarga Indah*, Jl Jend Sudirman 11, T 22066, F 23662, a/c, restaurant, clean and reasonable, souvenir shop downstairs.

C *Djakarta*, Jl Jend Sudirman 57, a/c, average; **C** *Hidayah I*, Jl KH Mas Temenggung, T 31408, a/c, restaurant, next to the morning market and the *Aida*, friendly staff, average rooms, pleasant balcony overlooking the street; **C** *Hidayah II*, Jl KH Halid 25, T 21712, some a/c.

D *Aida*, Jl KH Mas Temenggung, a/c, next to morning market and *Hidayah I*, popular with budget travellers; **D** *Andhika*, Jl H Agus Salim 37, T 22358, some a/c, clean enough; **D** *Rahayu*, Jl KH Abul Hasan 17, T 22622, clean and best of the budget options, shared bathroom; **D** *Sukarni*, Jl Panglima Batur 154, T 21134, some a/c, very basic.

● **Places to eat**
Indonesian: ♦♦*Haur Gading*, Jl Pulau Sulawesi 4, T 22456, beautifully decorated with ikats, baskets and Dayak handicrafts, soft lighting, does not fill up until after 2000, freshwater fish (*ikan mas*) and saltwater – *ikan bawal, terkulu, bandeng* and kakap, also Mahakam River prawns, rec; ♦*Depot Handayani*, Jl KH Abul Hasan 11, curries, Padang style; ♦*Gumarang*, Jl Jend Sudirman 30, extraordinary menu which incl cow brain gravy, cow foot gravy, cow lung gravy, sliced lung, raw leaves and potatoes, spicy *tongkol* fish wrapped in banana leaf rec; ♦*Lembur Kuring*, Jl Bhayangkara (next to cinema), small, basic but tasty selection of curry dishes; ♦*Mirasa*, Jl H Agus Salim 18/2 (opp *Andhika Hotel*), good *nasi campur* curries, specializes in grilled fish and chicken; ♦*Prambanan*, Jl H Agus Salim 16, grilled fish and chicken; ♦*Rumah Makan Banjar*, Jl KH Abul Hasan 19, cheap and cheerful restaurant with simple menu, curries; ♦*Sari Bundo*, Jl KHM Halid 42, simple but tasty Padang food.

Other Asian: ♦♦*Lezat Baru*, Jl Mulawarman 56, part of a small chain of restaurants, huge Chinese menu with a good choice of seafood, specials incl oysters done 10 different ways, rec; ♦♦*Sari Rasa*, Jl H Agus Salim 26, offers Chinese, Japanese and European dishes with a good line in seafood, pleasant ambience but rather empty.

● **Airline offices**
Bouraq, Jl Mulawarman 24, T 41105; **DAS**, Jl Gatot Subroto 92, T 35250; **Garuda**, Jl Jend Sudirman 57, T 22624; **MAF**, Jl Ruhui Rahayu, T 23628; **Merpati**, Jl Sudirman 23, **Sempati**, Jl Imam Bonjol (agency only), T 38607.

● **Banks & money changers**
Bank Bumi Daya, Jl Irian 160; **Bank Dagang Negara**, Jl Mulawarman 66; **Bank Negara Indonesia**, Jl Pulau Sebatik 1 (corner with Jl Batur); **Bank Rakyat**, Jl Gajah Mada 1 (across from the post office).

● **Entertainment**
Disco: *Blue Pacific Disco*, Kaltim Bldg, Citra Niaga, there are 5 discotheques in the building, and this is the best, lively music, good atmosphere and no cover charge; *Tepian Mahakam*, Jl Untung Suropati, T 34204, floating discotheque – which plays a mixture of chart hits and traditional Indonesian love songs – is in the bowels of a barge moored next to the bridge on the Mahakam, restaurant on top, rec, cover charge 5,000Rp (weekdays), 7,500Rp (weekends).

● **Post & telecommunications**
Area code: 0541.
Post Office: Jl Awang Long/Jl Gajah Mada.

● **Shopping**

The **Pasar Pagi** (morning market) is in the middle of town and is busy most of the day; the area around the modern **Citra Niaga** shopping complex, between Jl Yos Sudarso and Jl P Batur is particularly lively in the evenings with musicians, fortune-tellers and quack doctors and dentists. Samarinda has many small arts and crafts shops, mostly selling Dayak bits and pieces; there are 1 or 2 good ones, but the selection is not as good as Balikpapan. Always bargain and be suspicious of 'antiques'. **Dewi Art Shop**, Jl Awang Long 19, T 21482, antiques and tribal arts and crafts, especially good selection of statues and sculptures; **Fatmawati**, Jl Kesuma Bangsa 2, good selection of semi-precious stones and rings. Other art shops are located along Jl Martadinata (**Berhati Jaya**, **Kings of Dayak Primitive Art Shop** and **Sutra Borneo Art Shop**); Jl KH Agus Salim (**Armarta Art Shop**, **Dan Daman Art Shop** and **Permata Sinar**); Jl P Batur (**Hollywood** and **Syachran**).

● **Tour companies & travel agents**

Anggrek Hitam, Jl Yos Sudarso 21, T 22132, F 23161; **Ayus Wisata**, Jl H Agus Salim 13B, T 22644, F 32080; **Cisma Angkasa**, Jl Imam Bonjol 10/27, T 21572, F 22700; **Dayakindo**, Jl Bhayangkara.

● **Tourist offices**

Kantor Pariwisata, Jl Ade Irma Suryani 1 (off Jl Kesuma Bangsa), T 21669, poorly organized and badly informed: visitors are best advised to get their information from travel agents.

● **Useful addresses**

Pelni office: Jl Yos Sudarso 40/56, T 41402.

● **Transport**

Local Minibuses: like in Balikpapan, these are called taxis. Red ones go anywhere in town and congregate around Mesra Indah Komplex, 300Rp. Green ones go to Sungai Kunjang (for upriver trips and express buses to Balikpapan), 400-500Rp. **Ojeks**: congregate around the Pasar Pagi (Morning Market); 300-400Rp around town (can be chartered for 2,000-3,000Rp/hr).

Air The airport is on the NE outskirts of town. Regular connections on Bouraq, Merpati, Sempati, Garuda and Asahi airlines with Balikpapan, Banjarmasin, Berau, Tarakan, Surabaya, Jakarta, Yogyakarta, Semarang. Other less regular connections incl Bandung and Ujung Pandang. Asahi also flies to Datah Dawai on the upper Mahakam and both Asahi and Merpati fly to Long Ampung in the Apo Kayan (see page 598).

Road Bus: to Balikpapan 2 hrs and Tenggarong 1 hr leave from Seberang on the outskirts of town on the S bank of the river. The terminal can be reached by green taxis (see above) or by boat – a pleasant trip from the Pasar Pagi; the station is immediately behind the ferry terminal. Buses to Bontang leave from the Segeri bus terminal on the N side of town. **Taxi**: to Balikpapan leave from Sungai Kunjang (5,000-6,000Rp pp). Taxis to Bontang leave from Terminal Segeri (7,000Rp pp).

Sea Boat: Sapulidi speedboat from end of Jl Gajah Mada (nr the Post Office), T 23821. Terminal Feri, Jl Sungai Kunjang is the launch-pad for Mahakam River tours. To get there, take a 'taxi A' – green minibus (500Rp). The Pelni vessel *Leuser* calls here on its fortnightly circuit between ports in Java, Sulawesi and Kalimantan. See route schedule page 921.

THE MAHAKAM RIVER

The 920 km-long muddy Mahakam is the biggest of Kaltim's 14 large rivers; it is navigable for 523 km. There are three main stretches. The lower Mahakam runs from Samarinda, through Tenggarong to Muara Muntai and the three lakes; these lower reaches are most frequently visited by tourists. The middle Mahakam stretches to the W from Kuara Muntai, through Long Iram to Long Bagun – where public river-boat services terminate. The upper Mahakam, past the long stretch of rapids, runs from Long Gelat into the Muller Range: only a few adventure tours go this far. Most tours reach the upper Mahakam by plane (Asahi Airways flies to Data Dawai airstrip at Long Lunuk). The Mahakam's riverbanks have been extensively logged, or turned over to cultivation. Visitors wishing to reach less touristed destinations along the river should have plenty of time on their hands, and if on organized tours (see above), they should also have plenty of funds at their disposal. Many tourists just enjoy relaxing on the decks of the boats as they wind their way slowly upriver: one of the most important pieces of equipment for a Mahakam trip is a good long book.

One of the first Western explorers to venture up the Mahakam was Carl Bock (1849-1932). Though born in Oslo he went to England as a young man, and from there to the Dutch East Indies collecting biological specimens for the collection of Arthur Hay, the Marquis of Tweeddale and president of the Zoological Society. Unfortunately, while frantically pillaging the flora and fauna of Sumatra, his patron died. A stroke of good fortune gave him a new mission: in Batavia (Jakarta) he met Governor-General Van Lansberghe who asked him to mount an expedition to 'Koetai' (Kutai) and venture up the Koetai or 'Mahakani' river. He agreed, but immediately found a problem: no one would accompany him – even when the wages were so high they 'amounted to a positive bribe' – because of the fear of cannibals. But perseverance and the governor-general's deep pocket allowed him to proceed and, accompanied by the Sultan of Kutai himself, he ventured upstream. In a sense, the expedition was a bit of a let-down: he met no headhunters in 6 months, nor did he find the celebrated *Orang Buntut* – the 'Tailed People' who were supposed to be the missing link between apes and humans. Nonetheless, he wrote up the account of the journey – with a literary flourish which did more for sales than his scientific credibility – that was published, in Dutch, in 1881. The book was also translated into English and published as *The headhunters of Borneo* (available as a 1985 reprint from Oxford University Press).

Today, when they are taking time out from their cultural performances for tourists, the Mahakam's Dayaks are not the noble savages, dressed in loin cloths and hornbill feathers, that some of the tourist literature might paint them as. Longhouses are quite commercialized; tourists are likely to be asked for money for photographs. Most villages on the lower and middle reaches of the river have been drawn – economically and socially – into the modern world over the past century. Although the traditional Kaharingan religion is still practised in some areas (see page 563), many upriver Dayak groups have been converted to Christianity. This is all in marked contrast to neighbouring Sarawak, where the upriver tribespeople maintain their traditional lifestyles to a much greater degree.

The reason for this can be traced back to the policy of Sarawak's successive Brooke governments – the White Rajahs of Sarawak who attempted to protect the Orang Ulu (the upriver tribes) from the warring Ibans and Chinese traders. Other than attempting to stamp out 'social vices' such as head-hunting, they

Traditional East Kalimantan house illustrated on a Bank of Indonesia 500Rp note

A ceramic inheritance

Family wealth and status in Borneo was traditionally measured in ceramics. In the tribal longhouses upriver, treasured heirlooms include ancient glass beads, brass gongs and cannons and Chinese ceramic pots and beads. They were often used as currency and dowries. Spencer St John, the British consul in Brunei, mentions using beads as currency on his 1858 expedition to Gunung Mulu. Jars (*pesaka*) had more practical applications; they were (and still are) used for storing rice, brewing *tuak* (rice wine) or for keeping medicines. Their value was dependent on their rarity: brown jars, emblazoned with dragon motifs, are more recent and quite common while olive-glazed *dusun* jars, dating from the 15th-17th centuries are rare.

Chinese contact and trade with the N coast of Borneo has gone on for at least a millennium, possibly two. Chinese Han pottery fragments and coins have been discovered near the estuary of the Sarawak River and from the 7th century, China is known to have been importing birds' nests and jungle produce from Brunei (which then encompassed all of N Borneo), in exchange for ceramic wares. Chinese traders arrived in the *Nanyang* (South Seas) in force from the 11th century, particularly during the Sung and Yuan dynasties. Some Chinese pottery and porcelain even bore Arabic and Koranic inscriptions – the earliest such dish is thought to have been produced in the mid-14th century. In the 1500s, as China's trade with the Middle East grew, many such Islamic wares were traded and the Chinese emperors presented them as gifts to seal friendships with the Muslim world, including Malay and Indonesian kingdoms.

were largely left undisturbed. In Kalimantan, the Dutch colonial government did nothing to discourage the activities of Muslim and Christian missionaries, traders and administrators.

Best time to visit Sep-Oct, before the rainy season starts; this coincides with rice-planting rituals and the Erau festival (see below). Harvesting festivals are held Feb-Mar. During the dry season (Jul-Sep), many of the smaller tributaries and shallow lakes are unnavigable except by small canoes; during the height of the wet season (Nov-Jan), many rivers are in flood and currents are often too strong for upriver trips.

The Lower Mahakam: Samarinda to Muara Muntai

Tenggarong, the last capital of the Sultanate of Kutai, is the first major town (40 km) upriver from Samarinda. The highlight of a visit to the town is the **Mulawarman Museum**. It is housed in the Dutch-built former sultan's palace – his old wooden one, which was exquisitely furnished, burned to the ground in the mid-1930s. The museum contains a recreation of the opulent royal bed chamber, a selection of the sultan's *krisses* (see page 118), clothes and other bits and pieces of royal regalia as well as his collection of Chinese ceramics. There are also replicas of the stone stelae bearing Sanskrit inscriptions dating from the 4th or 5th centuries. There is a poor display of Dayak arts and crafts, although there are some woodcarvings in the grounds – notably the tall Dayak *belawang* pole (with a carved hornbill on top) in front of the museum. Open Tues-Sun 1000-1400. Admission 500Rp. **NB** A Dayak cultural show is often staged in the museum on Sundays.

Near the museum is the **royal cemetery**, containing graves of the founder of Tenggarong, Sultan Muslidhuddin and his descendants. There are several cheap losmen in town (two on Jl Diponegoro, near the pier and two over the bridge on Jl Sudirman) a few simple restaurants and a good arts and crafts shop – the

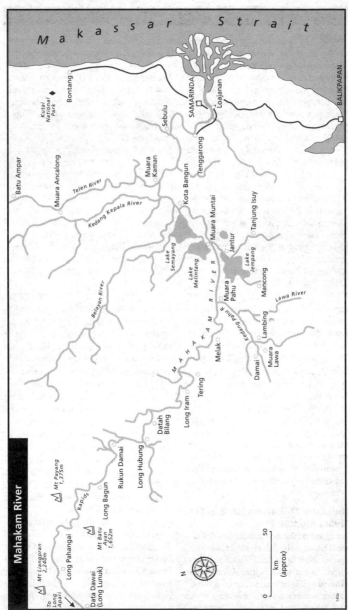

Mahakam River

Karya Indah Art Shop on Jl Diponegoro. The *Erau Festival* is held here at the end of September. Dayaks congregate in their traditional costumes. Dancing and ceremonies take place (Tenggarong can also be reached by road from Samarinda, see below).

Upriver tours pass through the villages of Muara Kaman and Kota Bangun before reaching **Muara Muntai**, a village built out over the riverbank on ironwood stilts. The lakes of **Semayang**, **Melintang** and **Jempang** lie to the W and SW of Kota Bangun, about 6-7 hrs upriver from Tenggarong. The lakes are known for their freshwater dolphins and other wildlife in the area include proboscis monkeys. The Dayak village of **Tanjung Isuy** is on the Mancong River, which feeds into Lake Jempang, the most southerly of the three main lakes; it takes about 2½ hrs to reach the village from Muara Muntai. Tanjung Isuy is quite touristy. It is, however, the best place on the Mahakam to witness traditional dance performances in full costume; these are included in most tour packages. **NB** It is necessary to report to the police post on arrival. **Accommodation** Most visitors stay at the longhouse which the villagers have rejected in favour of detached kampung houses, strung out along the riverbank. It is possible to visit the **Mancong longhouse**, about 10 km from Tanjung Isuy; 3 hrs walk (one-way); 2½ hrs canoe (one-way); 15,000Rp (return) by hired motorcycle.

The Middle and Upper Mahakam

Along the Mahakam, W of Muara Muntai, are many modern Dayak villages where the traditional Kaharingan religion is still practised. Funerals are particularly interesting affairs, involving the ritual sacrifice of water buffalo. Several more traditional villages are within reach of **Melak** (all are accessible by motorcycle). These villages become increasingly traditional the further W you go, towards Long Bagun, although some villages and tribal groups have embraced Christianity. Only a few

public river-boats go beyond **Long Iram**. There are losmen in Long Iram and a small restaurant. Few tours reach this point; it is possible to go further upriver, but this usually involves chartering a longboat which is expensive. Upriver from Long Iram is the domain of the Tunjung and Benuaq Dayaks and a substantial number of Kenyah who have spilled over from the Apo Kayan. The scenery becomes increasingly dramatic, towards Long Bagun; there are many villages and it is always possible to stay somewhere. Past the long stretch of rapids to the W of Long Bagun, is the upper Mahakam, which runs SW and then twists N to its headwaters in the Muller Range, on the Sarawak border. It is possible to fly from Samarinda to **Long Lunuk** (Data Dawai airstrip), well to the SW of the rapids, and then continue upriver by longboat.

Tours

Most people travel up the Mahakam River on an organized tour, either from Samarinda (see page 588) or from Balikpapan (page 582).

Festivals

Sep: *Erau festival* (23-28) in Tenggarong – traditionally celebrated at the coronation of a new Sultan of Kutai – used to go on for 40 days and nights. Today it lasts for 5 days. Festivities include traditional Dayak dances, where the different tribes dress in full costume (including the impressive Hudoq dance, designed to frighten spirits, diseases, rats, wild boar, monkeys and birds away from the rice crops) and sporting events such as *behempas* (where men fight with braided whips and rattan shields), *sepak takraw*, (top spinning), *lomba perahu* (boat races) and blowpipe competitions. Following the final *ngulur naga* ceremony – in which a large colourful dragon is floated down the Mahakam – the festival degenerates into a water-fight (water in which the dragon has swum is lucky water and should be shared – in bucketfuls). Dayak rituals are performed during the festival, including

The longhouse – prime-site apartments with river view

Most longhouses are built on stilts, high on the riverbank, on prime real estate. They are 'prestigious properties' with 'lots of character', and with their 'commanding views of the river', they are the condominiums of the jungle. They are long-rise rather than high-rise however, and the average longhouse has 20-25 'doors' (although there can be as many as 60). Each represents one family. The word *long* in a settlement's name – as in Long Iram or Long Nawang – means 'confluence' (the equivalent of *kuala* in Malay), and does not refer to the length of the longhouse.

Behind each of the doors – which even today, are rarely locked – is a *bilik*, or apartment, which includes the family living room and a loft, where paddy and tools are stored. In Kenyah and Kayan longhouses, paddy (which can be stored for years until it is milled) is kept in elaborate barns, built on stilts away from the longhouse, in case of fire. In traditional longhouses, the living rooms are simple atap roofed, bamboo-floored rooms; in modern longhouses – which are designed on exactly the same principles – the living rooms are commonly furnished with sofas, lino floors, a television and an en suite bathroom. All biliks face out onto the *ruai*, or gallery, which is the focus of communal life, and is where visitors are usually entertained. Attached to this there is usually a *tanju* – an open verandah, running the full length of the house – where rice and other agricultural products are dried. Long ladders – notched hardwood trunks – lead up to the tanju; these can get very slippery and do not always come with handrails.

the *belian* healing ceremony (where shamans cast out evil spirits causing sickness) and *mamat*, the ceremony which traditionally welcomed heroes back from war and headhunting expeditions and during which a buffalo is slaughtered.

Local information

● Transport

Road *Taksi kota* (colts) run from Sungai Kunjang (Samarinda) to Tenggarong, 1 hr.

River Boat: travelling by public transport gives visitors more contact with locals, and it costs a fraction of the price of a package tour (staying in losmen and longhouses en route) but these boats are much less comfortable than the big houseboats operated by tour companies. Regular connections from Sungai Kunjang in Samarinda to all settlements upriver to Long Bagun (in the wet season) and Long Iram (in the dry season). Boats leave from Sungai Kunjang in the early to mid-morning, Kota Bangun, 9 hrs, Tanjung Isuy, 14 hrs, Muara Muntai, 12 hrs, Melak, 24 hrs, Long Iram, 30 hrs, Long Bagun, 40 hrs. It is possible to charter a longboat anywhere along the river for a cruise; for about 30,000-60,000Rp/hr.

THE APO KAYAN

This remote plateau region borders Sarawak and is the most traditional tribal area in Kalimantan. The inaccessible mountains and rapids have made the Apo Kayan non-viable from a commercial logger's point of view, and the jungle is largely intact. The region has suffered from outmigration in recent decades and the tribal population has shrunk to a fraction – perhaps just a tenth – of what it was in the early 1900s. This migration has been spurred by the availability of well-paid work in the timber camps of Sarawak and E Kalimantan, combined with the prohibitive cost of ferrying and portering supplies from downriver. Since the late 1980s the airstrip at Long Ampung has been served by commercial airlines – opening the area up and bringing the cost of freight and passenger fares down.

The Apo Kayan is divided into the Kayan Hulu (upriver) and Kayan Hilir (downriver) districts. The former has a much higher population (about 5,000)

The massacre at Long Nawang

One-hundred years and three months after James Brooke was proclaimed Rajah of Sarawak, the Japanese Imperial Army invaded the country. On Christmas Day 1941, when Rajah Vyner Brooke was visiting Australia, they took Kuching; a few days earlier they had occupied the Miri oilfields. Japanese troops, dressed for jungle warfare, headed upriver. They did not expect to encounter such stiff resistance from the tribespeople. The Allies had the brainwave of rekindling an old tribal pastime – head-hunting, which successive Brooke administrations had tried to stamp out. Iban and Orang Ulu warriors were offered 'ten-bob-a-knob' for Japanese heads, and many of the skulls still hanging in longhouses are said to date from this time. The years of occupation were marked by terrible brutality, and many people fled across the border into Dutch Borneo – now Kalimantan. The most notorious massacre in occupied Sarawak involved refugees from Kapit.

Just a month after the Japanese invasion, a forestry officer stationed on the Rejang heard that a group of women and children from Kapit were planning to escape across the Iran Range into Dutch territory. He organized the evacuation, and led the refugees up the rivers and over the mountains to the Dutch military outpost at Long Nawang. The forester returned to Kapit to help organize resistance to the Japanese. But when the invading forces heard of the escape they dispatched a raiding party upriver, captured the Dutch fort, lined up the fifty women and ordered the children to climb into nearby trees. According to historian Robert Payne: "They machine-gunned the women and amused themselves by picking off the children one by one... Of all those who had taken part in the expedition only two Europeans survived."

and the vast majority are Kayan (see page 557), most originally from Sarawak, driven upriver by Iban raids. Nearly all of them have converted to Christianity – most are Protestant. Until the 1920s the Kayan were the sworn enemies of Sarawak's Iban: in 1924 the Sarawak Brooke government convened a peace conference in Kapit (on the Rejang River) which was attended by Dayak groups from both sides of the border. This formally put a stop to upriver and cross-border headhunting raids.

During WW2, many Europeans in the coastal towns of E Kalimantan made their way upriver to what they considered the relative safety of Long Nawang, deep in the Apo Kayan, in the face of Japanese occupation. The Japanese troops followed them upriver and many were killed, having been forced to dig their own graves. Among those shot was a group of women and children – refugees from Kapit in Sarawak (see page 597).

Most tours to the Apo Kayan involve trekking and canoe trips from Long Ampung to Long Nawang and visits to longhouses in the area such as Nawang Baru and Long Betoah and W of Long Ampung, along the Boh River, to Long Uro, Lidung Panau and Long Sungai Barang. **Accommodation** It is possible to stay in these longhouses but it is important to bring gifts (see box, page 606). Independent travellers should pay around 6,000Rp/night to the longhouse headman. Visitors should bring a sleeping bag (it gets cold at night) and essential equipment includes insect repellent and a torch.

● **Transport Air** The only realistic way of getting to the Apo Kayan is by air. Connections (on Wed and Sun) to Long Ampung from Samarinda on Merpati and Asahi 1½ hrs (100,000Rp). Flights into Long Ampung can carry 21 passengers, but on departure they can only carry 10 passengers, due to a short airstrip. Organized package tours to the Apo Kayan with big tour companies are more expensive, but your flight out is guaranteed. *Kaltim Adventure* (based in Balikpapan) undertakes to charter a helicopter if its tourists cannot get onto a flight. *Missionary Aviation Fellowship (MAF)* also flies Cessna aircraft to longhouses in the interior, incl Long Ampung. But MAF is not a commercial airline and should not be treated as one. It does not have a concession from the government to operate on a commercial basis and also has an agreement with Merpati that it will not poach passengers. It is a religious, non-profitmaking organization servicing remote communities; it will only agree to fly tourists out of Long Ampung in the case of emergencies or in the unlikely event of planes being empty. Once in Long Ampung, MAF may consider requests for flights further into the interior; prices vary depending on whether they are scheduled or non-scheduled flights. Write in advance to: MAF, Box No 82, Samarinda with details of where and when you intend to go. MAF flies to about 5 airstrips in the remote parts of the Apo Kayan.

TARAKAN

The oil-island of Tarakan, with 81,000 inhabitants in 1991, has little to offer the tourist, besides being a hopping-off point to neighbouring Sabah.

● **Accommodation B** *Tarakan Plaza*, Jl Yos Sudarso, T 21870, a/c, restaurant, best in town, with helpful, friendly staff; **C** *Nirama*, Jl Sudirman, T 21637, a/c and hot water; **D-E** *Taufiq*, Jl Sudarso 26, T 21347, some a/c, rather basic but OK; **F** *Jakarta*, Jl Sudirman 112, T 21704.

● **Places to eat** *Ikan bakar* (barbecued fish) is good here. **✦✦***Kepeting Saos*, Jl Sudirman, excellent crab dishes; **✦***Antara*, Jl Yos Sudarso, good *ikan bakar;* **✦***Bagi Alam*, Jl Yos Sudarso; **✦***Turi*, Jl Yos Sudarso, good *ikan bakar.* **Chinese**: **✦✦***Bulungan Restoran*, Tarakan Plaza Hotel; **✦✦***Phoenix*, Jl Yos Sudarso.

● **Airline offices** Bouraq, Jl Yos Sudarso 8, T 21248; **DAS**, Jl Sudirman 9, T 51612; **Garuda**, Jl Sebengkok 33, T 21130; **MAF,** Jl Sudirman 33, T 51011; **Merpati,** Jl Yos Sudarso 8, T 21875; **Sempati**, Tarakan Plaza Hotel, Jl Yos Sudarso 8, T 21871.

● **Banks & money changers** Jl Yos Susdarso, for TCs and cash.

● **Post & telecommunications Area code**: 0551.

● **Tour companies & travel agents** *Angkasa*, Jl Sebengkok 33, T 21130; *Aruis*, Jl Sudarjo V/19, T 21240; *Nusantara Raya Sari*, Jl RE Martadinata; *Tam Jaya*, Jl Yos Sudarso, T 21250.

● **Transport Local Colt**: around town cost 300Rp. **Air** Regular connections on Bouraq, Merpati, Sempati and DAS with Balikpapan and Samarinda. **Sea Boat**: the Pelni office is at the main port, at the S end of Jl Yos Sudarso. Regular passenger boat connections with Samarinda and Balikpapan. **International connections with Malaysia Air** Regular connections on Bouraq and MAS every Mon with Tawau in Sabah 35 mins. **Sea Boat**: regular passenger boat connections with Tawau in Sabah. The Pelni ship *Leuser* calls here; the Pelni office is at the port (see route schedule, page 665).

WEST KALIMANTAN
(KALIMANTAN BARAT – KALBAR)

Because it is cut off from Kalimantan's other provinces, Kalbar attracts few tourists. It occupies about a fifth of Kalimantan's land area (146,800 sq km), most of which is very flat. The **Kapuas River** is Indonesia's longest at 1,243 km and runs through the middle of the province, E to W. Its headwaters, deep in the interior, are in the Muller range, which fringes the NE and E borders of Kalbar.

The Kapuas River is navigable for most of its length, which – as with the Mahakam River in E Kalimantan – has allowed the penetration of the interior by merchants and missionaries over the past century. There are small towns all along the river, and the surrounding forest has been heavily logged. For tourists, the Kapuas is less interesting to travel up than the Mahakam River, and pales in comparison with the rivers in neighbouring Sarawak. Because few foreign visitors make the trip however, the Kapuas River is certainly not 'touristy'. To the N, the province borders Sarawak, and the E end of this frontier runs along the remote Kapuas Hulu mountain range. The SE border with Central Kalimantan province, follows the Schwaner Range. About two thirds of W Kalimantan's jungle (a total of about 9.5 million ha) is classed as 'production forest'; most of the remaining 3 million ha is protected, but it is such a large area that it is impossible to guard against illegal loggers. The timber industry is the province's economic backbone, but Kalbar is also a major rubber producer.

HISTORY

At about the time Java's Hindu Majapahit Empire was disintegrating in the mid-1300s, a number of small Malay sultanates grew up along the coast of W Kalimantan. These controlled upriver trade and exploited the Dayaks of the interior. When Abdul Rahman, an Arab seafarer-cum-pirate decided to set up a small trading settlement at Pontianak in 1770, he crossed the paths of some of these sultans. This prompted the first Dutch intervention in the affairs of W Kalimantan, but they did not stay long, and for the next 150 years, their presence there was minimal: Borneo's W coast ranked low on the colonial administration's agenda. A gold rush in the 1780s brought Hakka Chinese immigrants flooding into the Sambas area. Their descendants – after several generations of intermarriage with Dayaks – make up more than 10% of W Kalimantan's population today, most living in Pontianak. In the 19th century, the Dutch were worried about the intentions of Rajah James Brooke of Sarawak as he occupied successive chunks of the Sultanate of Brunei. In response, the Dutch increased their presence but any threat that Brooke posed to Dutch territory never materialized. During WW2, the people of Kalbar suffered terribly at the hands of the Japanese Imperial Army, who massacred more than 21,000 people in the province, many at Mandor in Jun 1944.

CULTURE

People

West Kalimantan's 3.9 million inhabitants are concentrated along the coasts and rivers. Malay Muslims make up about 40% of the inhabitants, Dayaks account for another 40%, Chinese 11% and the remainder include Buginese (originally from Sulawesi) and Minangkabau (originally from Sumatra). West Kalimantan has also received large numbers of transmigrants (see page 427) from Java. Most were originally resettled at Rasau Jaya, to the S of Pontianak, but many have come to the metropolis to find work as labourers – others have simply resorted to begging. Tribal people also come to Pontianak from settlements upriver on the Kapuas; they have usually fared better than the transmigrants and a number hold important jobs in the provincial administration.

Tourism

In 1986 only 5,000 foreign tourists arrived in Kalbar; by 1990 this had quadrupled and, following the opening of the Entikong border crossing on the Sarawak frontier, the number of tourists rose again by around 50%. The vast majority of these tourists were curious Malaysians; westerners account for less than a tenth of Pontianak's tourist arrivals – according to provincial government statistics, a maximum of around 2,000 pass through a year. The main reason for this is that the province is rather lacking in 'tourist objects' and receives little attention in the national tourism promotion literature. True, Kalbar has jungle and rivers and Dayaks and offshore islands – but these can also be found in countless other more accessible places in Indonesia.

English is not widely spoken in Kalbar: visitors are advised to learn some basic Bahasa – particularly those heading upriver. The tourist literature produced by the provincial tourism office waxes lyrical about Kalbar's many beautiful islands just offshore and the national parks. But besides being written in rather opaque English, it also fails to mention that few of these have any facilities for tourists and most are extremely difficult to get to. Visitors who want to immerse themselves in Dayak culture and visit traditional longhouses will not find much of interest in Kalbar; only a few tribal groups still live in longhouses on the uppermost reaches of the Kapuas River and its tributaries.

PONTIANAK

Living in Pontianak is like a European living in a city called 'Dracula' – the name literally translates as 'the vampire ghost of a woman who dies in childbirth'. Apparently, hunters who first came to this area heard terrible screams in the jungle at night and were so scared by them that they dubbed the area 'the place that sounds like a *pontianak*'. But modern Pontianak is no ghost town. It is a thriving, prosperous town with a population at the last census in 1991 of 387,000 – a third of whom are Chinese – and a 'parabola' on almost every rooftop. (Other ethnic groups are Melayu [26%], Bugis [13%] and Javanese [12%]. Dayaks make up just 3% of the population.) These satellite dishes pick up television stations from around the region as well as blue movie channels from the United States and are no small investment: 3m-diameter dishes cost about 1.5 million rupiahs (US$750) while the big 4m ones cost up to 3 million rupiahs.

The confluence of the Kapuas and Landak rivers, where the Arab adventurer Abdul Rahman founded the original settlement in 1770, is a strongly Malay part of town. This area, which encompasses several older kampungs, is known as Kampung Bugis. The commercial heart of Pontianak, is on the left bank of the Kapuas, around the old Chinese quarter. The other side of the river is called Siantan and is distinguished only by its bus terminal, a few rubber-smoking factories (whose choking smell permeates the air) and the pride of Pontianak: the equator monument.

Like other cities in Kalimantan, Pontianak derives much of its wealth from timber – there seem to be scores of plywood factories and sawmills close to the city. The second string to Pontianak's economic bow, so to speak, is Siam orange production, of which it is Indonesia's largest grower.

Places of interest

The **Musium Negeri** – the state museum – at the southern end of Jl Jend A Yani, contains good models of longhouses and a comprehensive display of Dayak household implements including a collection of tattoo blocks, weapons from blowpipes to blunderbusts, one sad-looking skull, masks, fishtraps and musical instruments. There are examples of Dayak textiles, ikat (see page 408), songket (see page 529) and basketry. There is also a model of a Malay house and a collection of typical

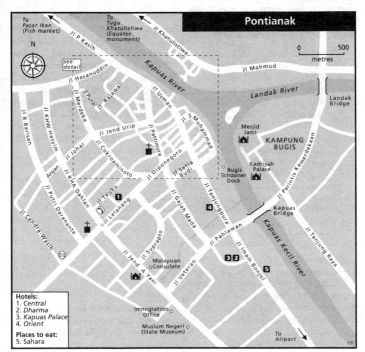

To Pasar Ikan (Fish market)

To Tugu Khatulistiwa (Equator monument)

Jl P Kasih

Jl Khatulistiwa

N

0   500
metres

Kapuas River

Jl Mahmud

see detail

Jl Hasanuddin

Landak River

Landak Bridge

Jl Usman

Jl B Barisan

Jl KHW Hasyim

Jl Merdeka

Jl Punai

Jl Rajawali

Jl Johar

Jl Cokroaminoto

Jl Pattimura

Jl S Muhammad

Jl Jend Urip

Mesjid Jami

KAMPUNG BUGIS

Anyan

Jl KH A Dahlan

Jl Diponegoro

Jl Setia Budi

Bugis Schooner Dock

Kadriyah Palace

Jl Perintis Kemerdekaan

Jl Teuku

1

Jl Lelanang

Jl Gajah Mada

Jl Tanjungpura

4

Kapuas Bridge

Jl Putri Daranante

Jl Cendra Wasih

Jl Pahlawan

Kapuas Kecil River

Jl Tanjung Raya

Jl Supapto

Jl Jend A Yani

Malaysian Consulate

Jl Veteran

3 2

Jl Imam Bonjol

5

Hotels:
1. Central
2. Dharma
3. Kapuas Palace
4. Orient

Places to eat:
5. Sahara

Immigration Office

Musium Negeri (State Museum)

To Airport

household implements. The Dayak and Malay communities are represented in the huge relief-sculptures on the front of the museum. But there is absolutely nothing on or in it acknowledging the presence of the large Chinese population – other than some Chinese ceramics. Nor, unfortunately, are any of the objects labelled in English. Open 0900-1600 Mon-Sun, 0900-1100 Fri. *Getting there*: oplet from Kapuas Indah Covered Market (400Rp). Just past the museum is the huge whitewashed W Kalimantan governor's office. There is a replica Dayak longhouse near the museum, off Jl Jend A Yani, built in 1985 to stage a Koran-reading contest.

The ironwood *istana* or *kraton* – **Kadriyah Palace** – was built at the confluence of the Landak and Kapuas rivers by the town's Arab founding father, Abdul Rahman, shortly after he established the trading settlement. The palace was home to seven sultans; Sharif Yusof, son of the seventh, looks after it today. His uncle married a Dutch woman whose marble bust is one of the eccentric collection of items which decorate the palace museum. Among the fascinating array of odds and ends are two 5m-tall decorated French mirrors, made in 1923; these face each other across the room and Sharif's party trick is to hold a lighter up to create an endless corridor of reflected flames. There is also a selection of past sultans' *bajus* and *songkoks*, a jumble of royal regalia, including two thrones and tables of Italian marble and a photograph of the sixth sultan and his heir, who were murdered by the Japanese in a mass killing during WW2. Admission by donation, about 500Rp. Open 0900-1730.

The **Mesjid Jami** (mosque) – which is

next to the palace – was built shortly after the founding of the city in the late 1700s, although it has been renovated and reconstructed over the years. It is a beautiful building with tiered roofs, standing at the confluence of the two rivers, with its lime-green turret-like minarets and its bell-shaped upper roof. The Kapuas riverbank next to the mosque is a pleasant place to sit and watch life on the river – the elegant Bugis schooners berth at the docks on the opposite bank. The sky over the mosque and palace is alive with kites flown by the children in Kampung Bugis.

Over the Landak Bridge and past the stinking Siantan rubber smokehouses, which line the right bank of the Kapuas, is the **Tugu Khatulistiwa** (Equator Monument), standing at exactly 109 degrees, 20 mins E of Greenwich. During the Mar and Sep equinoxes, the column's shadow disappears, which is an excuse for a party in Pontianak. In 1991, the old belian (ironwood) equator column was encased in a new architectural wonder, a sort of concrete mausoleum where it is intelligently hidden from the sun. There is a new 6m-high column on top.

The heart of the city, around **Kapuas Indah** indoor market, is an interesting and lively part of town. There are a number of *pekong* (Taoist temples) around the market area; the oldest, **Sa Seng Keng**, contains a huge array of gods. The **Dwi Dharma Bhakti Chinese Temple** on Jl Tanjungpura is notable for its location in the middle of the main street.

The **Pasar Ikan** (Fish Market), downriver from town, on Jl Pak Kasih, is a great place to wander in the early morning; the stallholders are just as interesting as the incredible variety of fish they sell.

Excursions

Tourist facilities are limited outside Pontianak – and so are tourist sights. Some areas along the NW coast – including offshore islands – can be visited in day-long excursions from Pontianak, and these have been listed under the separate sections below. Package excursions are operated by the two main travel agents in Pontianak (see below).

Tours

Pontianak's two main tour operators offer city tours and short package tours along the W coast to Singkawang and Sambas regencies as well as offshore islands. Longer upriver trips on the Kapuas can be arranged, as can adventure tours with jungle trekking and white-water rafting. *Insan* offers one particularly adventurous whitewater rafting trip to rapids on the Pinoh River.

Festivals

Jan: *West Kalimantan anniversary* (1st), commemorating its accession to the status of an autonomous province in 1957. Folk art exhibitions and dance.

Sep: *Naik Dango* (21st) (rice storage) festival, when the sun is directly overhead at noon.

Nov: *Trans-Equator marathon*; in the past this has been a full 42 km event; from 1992 it has become a quarter marathon (10 km).

Local information
● **Accommodation**

B *Kapuas Palace* (formerly *Kapuas Permai*), Jl Imam Bonjol, T 36122, a/c, restaurant, large

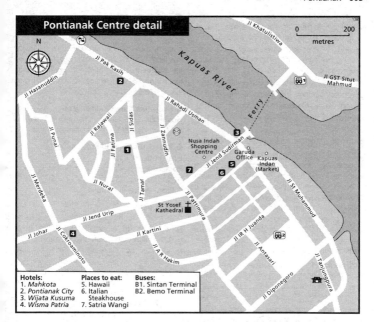

Pontianak Centre detail

0   200
metres

St Yosef Kathedral

Hotels:
1. Mahkota
2. Pontianak City
3. Wijata Kusuma
4. Wisma Patria

Places to eat:
5. Hawaii
6. Italian Steakhouse
7. Satria Wangi

Buses:
B1. Sintan Terminal
B2. Bemo Terminal

pool, modern low-rise hotel in spacious grounds with good range of facilities, located quite a long way from the market area, rooms and cottages; **B** *Kartika*, Jl Rahardi Usman, T 34401, F 38457, a/c, good location on the river, next to the docks and the market area, rooms facing the river rec; **B** *Mahkota*, Jl Sidas 8, T 36022, F 36200, a/c, restaurant, pool, newest, smartest best hotel in Pontianak, with full range of facilities incl tennis courts, a billiard room and a good bar, rooms small but well appointed, rec; **B** *Pontianak City*, Jl Pak Kasih 44, T 32495, a/c.

C *Central*, Jl Cokroaminoto 232, a/c and hot water, quite new and clean; **C** *Dharma*, Jl Imam Bonjol 10, T 34759, a/c, restaurant, once Pontianak's top hotel, now run down; **C-D** *Orient*, Jl Tanjungpura 45, T 32650, some a/c, friendly.

D *Wijaya Kusuma*, Jl Musi 51-53, T 32547, some a/c, restaurant, on the grimy side, but passable, good location on the riverfront, opp Kapuas Indah Indoor Market and the warungs, popular with budget travellers; **D** *Wisma Patria*, Jl Hos Cokroaminoto 497 (Jl Merdeka Timur), T 36063, a/c, restaurant, sprawling overgrown home-stay, without much charm,

rooms average but popular with tourists and friendly staff, automatic 'teh/kopi' wake-up call at 0630.

● **Places to eat**

Indonesian: ♦*Beringin*, Jl Diponegoro 115, Padang food, rec; ♦*Sahara*, Jl Imam Bonjol, Padang food; ♦*Satria Wangi*, Jl Nusa Indah II 11A, Chinese food with Indonesian, rec by locals.

Other Asian: ♦♦*Gajah Mada*, Jl Gajah Mada 202, big Chinese-run restaurant, with a land-scaped interior offering very high quality food, particularly seafood and freshwater fish, speci-alities incl: *jelawat* (W Kalimantan river fish), *hekeng* (chopped, deep-fried shrimp), *kailan ca thik pow* (thinly sliced salted fish), crab *fu yung* and sautéed frog, rec; ♦♦*Nikisa*, Jl Sisingaman-garaja 108, sophisticated Japanese restaurant, the most upmarket in Pontianak, shabu-shabu buffet, sukiyaki, teriyaki burgers and an inter-national selection – mainly imported steaks, set lunch/dinner, rec by locals; ♦♦*Pinang Merah Restoran*, Disko dan Singing House, Jl Kapten Marsan 51-53 (behind Kapuas Indah), down the alleyway past the *Wijaya Kusuma Hotel*, very cool and pleasant place for a drink in the early evening, on wooden walkway next to the river, seafood and Chinese dishes; ♦*Hawaii*, Jl Satria 79-80 (across the road from Nusa Indah Plaza), also branch at Jl Gajah Mada 24, a/c restaurant serving Chinese dishes and seafood, specialities: *puyung hai* (crab or prawn omelette with spicy peanut sauce) and chicken steaks, rec.

International: *Bali Palace*, Jl Imam Bonjol 402, European, Japanese and Indonesian food; ♦♦♦*Italian Steak House*, Jl Nusa Indah III 109, Japanese, Chinese, as well as Italian; ♦*KFC*, Jl Gajah Mada.

Seafood: ♦*Corina*, Jl Tanjungpura 124, simple seafood menu.

Foodstalls: *Bobo Indah*, opp the *Wijaya Kusuma Hotel* next to the colourful cinema hoardings. There are also some stalls next to the river. In the mornings there are hawker stalls selling breakfast fishballs and *mee kepitang* (noodles and crab) along Jl Nusa Indah II. In the evenings, on the S side of Jl Diponegoro there are lots of hawker stalls selling cheap Chinese, Padang and Batawi (Jakarta) food.

Coffee shops (*warung Kopi*): appear to be the hubs of Pontianak social life. They serve not just good coffee, but also snacks such as *pisang goreng* (deep fried banana) and local patisseries.

Fruit market: at the top of Jl Nusah Indah next to St Yosef Katholik Kathedral, excellent selection, incl jeruk oranges from around Tebas, N of Singkawang. Their greeny-yellow appearance makes them look rather unappetizing but they are very sweet. Good durians when in season in Jul and Aug.

Out of town: ♦♦*Sea Food Garden*, Kakap, about 30 mins drive W of Pontianak, on the coast, in a village famous for its seafood, local farm crabs, lobsters, shrimps and fish, rec by locals.

● **Bars**
Corner Bar, round the corner from Pontianak Theatre and next to *Bandung Indah* fastfood restaurant, bamboo and brick open-sided bar with good atmosphere.

● **Airline offices**
Bouraq, Jl Tanjungpura 253, T 32371; **DAS**, Jl Gajah Mada 67, T 34383; **Garuda/Merpati**, Jl Rahadi Usman 8A, T 34142; **Sempati/Deraya**, Jl Sisingamangaraja 145, T 34840.

● **Banks & money changers**
There are several banks along Jl Tanjungpura (incl **Bank Dagang Negara** and **Bank Duta**); **Safari Money-changer**, Jl Tanjungpura 12 (and Jl Nusa Indah III 57).

● **Entertainment**
Cinemas: several in town, most of them screening the latest Hollywood releases with a few kung-fu movies. They are owned by a Jakarta businessman who has virtually put the old Pontianak Theatre out of business, Top Flr, Kapuas Indah Indoor Market; 4 cinema halls. Nusa Indah Plaza, Jl Nusa Indah; 7 cinema halls.

● **Hospitals & medical services**
Hospitals: *Dr Sudarso Hospital*, Jl Adisucipto; *Sei Jawi Hospital Centre*, Jl Merdeka Barat.

● **Post & telecommunications**
Area code: 0561.
Post Office: Jl Rahadi Usman 1 and Jl Sultan Abdurrakhman 49.
Telkom office: Jl Tenku.

● **Shopping**
Due mainly to its large Chinese population, Pontianak is full of gold shops. There are a number of art and craft shops selling Dayak handicrafts, porcelain, textiles (incl *ikat* and *songket*) and antiques, but the selection is limited in comparison with Balikpapan and Samarinda. *Borneo Art Shop*, Blok VII, Jl Nusa Indah I 27; *Fariz Art Shop*, 3 Blok C, Pasar Nusa Indah I, good selection of old ikats; *Koperasi Kerta*, Jl Adisucipto 187; *Leny Art Shop*, Jl Khattulistiwa (at the roundabout opp the equator monument), interesting collection of antique Dayak pieces – incl stone axes, medicine boxes, knives, ikat, basketware and Chinese ceramics – and not forgetting a few model equator monuments (also branch at 1A Blok D, Jl Nusa Indah III).

Batik: good batik shop in *Nusa Indah Plaza* on Jl Tanjung Pura.

Markets: *Piska Centre* (Kapuas Indah Indoor Market), opp *Wijaya Kusuma Hotel*, uninteresting selection of cheap clothes and goods.

Maps: *Juanda Baru Toko Buku*, Jl Hos Cokroaminoto 232.

● **Sports**
Golf: course at Siantan Hulu and a driving range at Jl Haryono.

● **Tour companies & travel agents**
Ateng, Jl Gajah Mada 201, T 32683, F 36620, rec; *Citra Tour & Travel*, Jl Rahadi Usman, T 36436; *Insan Worldwide Tours & Travel (ITT)* Jl Tanjungpura 149; *Jambore Express Tour*, Jl Pahlawan 226, T 36703.

● **Tourist offices**
The Department of Posts and Telecommunications (Parpostel), Jl Sutan Syahril 17,

T 39444, has information on travelling around Kalbar, not much English spoken; **Tourist Information Office** at the airport (and at Entikong border crossing); **Tourist Promotion Office** (Kalbar), Jl Achmad Sood 25, T 36712.

● **Transport**

Local Bus (*bis kota*): around the Pontianak area leave from Sintian terminal on the N side of the river (regular ferries cross the river from Jl Bardan to the terminal, 200Rp). **Ojeks:** good way to see the sights. The easiest place to pick up an ojek is along Jl Tanjungpura; short trips cost 300-400Rp or chartered for 3,000Rp. **Oplets:** leave from Jl Kapten Marsan in front of the Kapuas Indah Indoor Market, next to the warungs; special demarcated routes to most destinations around town. Also oplet stations on Jl Sisingamangaraja and Jl Teuku Cik Ditiro. **Taxis** (saloons): congregate around *Dharma Hotel* on Jl Tanjungpura, 6,500Rp/hr.

Air Supadio Airport is 20 km from town. Taxis from airport into town cost 10,000Rp. Regular connections on Garuda, Merpati, Sempati and Bouraq with most major destinations in Indonesia such as Jakarta, Medan, Balikpapan, Ketapang, Sintang, Putu Siban and Pangkalanbun.

Road Bus: long-distance buses (*Kirana, Sago* and *SJS* – on Jl Sisingamangaraja – bus companies) leave from Batu Layang terminal at Km 8 on the Sambas road. Tickets can be bought at the bus station. Regular buses to Singkawang 3½ hrs, Sambas, Sintang (on the Kapuas River) 10 hrs, Meliau, Tayan, Sekadan and Ngabang. *Getting to Batu Layang:* ferry to Sintian terminal and *bis kota* (city bus) from Sintian terminal (200Rp) or oplet (200Rp). **Car hire**: available from *Citra Tour & Travel.* **Long distance taxis**: available from the taxi office by the *Kartika Hotel.*

Sea Boat: a/c express launches bought from Sibu in Sarawak leave for Ketapang (S of Pontianak) daily at 0900. Tickets for Malindo and Kita express boats sold at *Insan Worldwide Tour & Travel.* *Bandong,* Kalbar's ungainly big river cargo barges, go from near the *Hotel Wijaya Kusuma,* Pontianak to Putusibau (4 days, 3 nights) from Sep to Apr when the water level is high. The Pelni ships *Lawit, Sirimau, Awu* and *Bukitraya* call at Pontianak on their fortnightly circuits through Java, Sumatra, Sulawesi and Kalimantan. See route schedule, page 921. There are also regular connections with Montok, Kijang, Dumai and Mahayati. Pelni office: Jl Pelabuhan 2, T 34133.

International connections Air With Kuching (Sarawak) on MAS (Mon, Thur) and Singapore (Tues, Thur, Sat); although it is much cheaper to fly to Batam Island and then take the half-hour boat trip to Singapore from Sekupang (see page 501). **Road Bus**: the border is open 0600-1800 W Indonesian time (0500-1700 Malaysian time). Many buses ply the route between Pontianak and Kuching, 6-9 hrs (M$34.50, 35,000Rp for luxury tour bus). *SJS Executive Bus* at Jl Sisingamangaraja 155 (Pontianak) is recommended. Note that this is classified as a gateway 'port' of entry so visas are not required for citizens of those countries which are permitted visa-free entry to Indonesia.

THE NORTHWEST COAST

SINGKAWANG

Singkawang was originally settled by Hakka Chinese in the early 1800s and was the main town servicing the nearby gold rush shanty at Mantrado. It is now an important farming area and is named after a local turnip. In 1991 the town had a recorded population of 85,000.

Excursions About 7 km S of Singkawang there is a **pottery** village where replicas of antique Chinese ceramics are fired in a big kiln. **Pasir Panjang** beach is 17 km S of Singkawang. **Accommodation C** cottage-style beach-side hotel, a/c, restaurant, pool, facilities include tennis court and watersports.

Pulau Randayan is a 12 ha island with good coral; facilities are being developed on the island and it is possible to stay overnight. Trips to the island are organized by Mr Sukartadji, owner of the *Palapa Hotel* in Singkawang. *Getting there*: 2 hrs by boat from Pasir Panjang.

Pulau Temajo is 60 km S of Singkawang (off the coast from the village of Sungai Kunyit), an island with white sand beaches and good coral. There is some accommodation available on the island. *Ateng Tours & Travel* in Pontianak (see page 605) can advise on the best way to get there; the company also runs 1-day package tours to the island costing 25,000Rp, including transport, food and

---

Visiting longhouses: house rules

The most important ground rule is not to visit a longhouse without an invitation... people who arrive unannounced may get an embarrassingly frosty reception. Tour companies offer the only exception to this rule, as most have tribal connections. On arrival, visitors should pay an immediate courtesy call on the headman (known as the *tuai rumah* in Iban longhouses). It is normal to bring him gifts; those staying overnight should offer the headman a cash gratuity. The money is kept in a central fund and saved for use by the whole community during festivals. Small gifts such as beer, whisky, batik and food (especially rice or chicken) go down well. It is best to arrive at a longhouse during late afternoon after people have returned from the fields. Visitors who have time to stay the night generally have a much more enjoyable experience than those who pay fleeting visits. They can share the evening meal and have time to talk... and drink. Visitors should note the following:

❑ On entering a longhouse, take off your shoes.

❑ It is usual to accept food and drink with both hands. If you do not want to eat or drink, the accepted custom is to touch the brim of the glass or the plate and then touch your lips as a symbolic gesture; sit cross-legged when eating.

❑ When washing in the river, women should wear a sarong and men, shorts.

❑ Ask permission to take photographs. It is not uncommon to be asked for a small fee.

❑ Do not enter a longhouse during *pantang* (taboo), a period of misfortune – usually following a death. There is normally a white flag hanging near the longhouse as a warning to visitors.

---

skin-diving equipment.

● **Accommodation B** *Mahkota*, Jl Diponegoro 1, T 31244, a/c, restaurant, pool, sister hotel to *Mahkota* in Pontianak with equally good range of facilities; **C** *Palapa*, Jl Ismail Tahir 152, T 31449, a/c, restaurant, clean; **D** *Kalbar*, Jl Kepol, T 21404, a/c; **D-E** *Duta Putra Kalbar*, Jl Diponegoro 32, T 31430, some a/c, clean and adequate; **E** *Khatulistiwa Plaza*, Jl Selamat Karman 17, T 31697, adequate.

● **Places to eat** *Diponegoro*, Jl Diponegoro (Padang food) and 2 Chinese restaurants, *A Hin* and *A Sun*, next door to each other on Jl Diponegoro.

● **Transport** 143 km N of Pontianak. **Road Colt**: regular connections with Pontianak's Sintian terminal, 3½ hrs.

THE KAPUAS RIVER

The first European to venture up the 1,243 km-long Kapuas River was a Dutchman, Major George Muller, who reached the site of present-day Putussibau in 1822 and who lent his name to the mountains to the E. 4

years later, while attempting to cross these mountains, from the upper Mahakam to the Kapuas, he had his head taken by Dayaks. The Dayaks of the upper Kapuas were themselves terrorized by Iban headhunters, mostly from the Batang Lupar in Sarawak – although some Iban settled in the area to the N of the Kapuas. Few Dayak communities – except those in more remote areas – live in traditional longhouses or observe tribal rituals today. Those who did not turn to Islam – under the influence of the coastal Malays – converted to Christianity: there is a large number of Roman Catholic and Protestant evangelists working throughout the Kapuas basin. Christians (mainly Catholics) make up about 28% of Kalbar's population.

There is still a lot of gold-panning along the Kapuas – using *palong dulang* pans – and larger operations have turned some areas of jungle into a moonscape. Many Dayaks are also employed in the logging industry. Although it is possible to take a *bandung* barge all the way up the river from Pontianak (4-5 days to Putussibau, 40,000Rp), most tourists opt to travel to Sintang by road, which branches off the coast road from Sungai Pinyuh, 50 km NW of Pontianak. A road is being built between Sintang and Putusibbau.

Pah Auman, between Pontianak and Ngabang (120 km from Pontianak, *en route* to Entikong) is the nearest village to Kamung Saham longhouse (12 km by road). This 30-door Kendayang (or Kenatyan) longhouse is one of the most traditional longhouses remaining in Kalbar, despite the fact that it is not particularly remote. Tourists are under the impression that the further they go into the interior, the further they will get from civilization – but in that, Kalbar is not like neighbouring Sarawak. **Accommodation** It is possible to ask the Kepala's (headman's) permission to stay overnight in the Kendayang longhouse. *Getting there*: any E-bound bus from Pontianak's Batu Layang bus station (3,500Rp).

The area N of the Kapuas River was a focus of the *Konfrontasi* – the brief war between Indonesia and Malaysia between 1963 and 1965 (see page 554). The W Kalimantan Communist Party was also very active in the area in the late 1960s, before being crushed. While tourists heading into remoter areas upriver are no longer shadowed by soldiers, it is still necessary to report to the local police station on arrival.

Sintang (245 km, 8 hrs E of Pontianak) is at the confluence of the Kapuas and Melawi rivers. About 18 km from town is Mt Kelam – 'Dark Mountain' – which at 900m affords good views of the surrounding plains and rivers. Guides can be hired in Sintang (2 hrs walk to the summit). Sintang is a mainly Chinese town, founded by traders dealing with the Dayaks of the interior. On the upper reaches of the Melawi – and its tributary, the Pinoh – there are some traditional Ot Danum (upriver) Dayak groups (the

equivalent of Sarawak's Orang Ulu), notably the Dohoi on the upper Melawi. The two rivers begin in the Schwaner Range. **Accommodation C** *Sasean Hotel*, Jl Brig Jend Katamso on the river; **D-E** *Flamboyan*, some a/c and some baths. *Getting there*: regular buses from Pontianak's Batu Layang bus station (9,000Rp). There are regular passenger boats leaving Sintang for Putussibau (35,000Rp). MAF flies between Sintang and Putussibau (68,000Rp).

From **Semitau** – half way between Sintang and Putussibau – it is possible to visit Sentarum, Luar and Sumpa lakes. The lake area is predominantly settled by the Ibans, who originally came upriver from the Batang Lupar in Sarawak; other tribal groups include the Maloh Dayaks (famed for their skill as silversmiths and goldsmiths) and the Kantuq.

Putussibau is the last noteworthy settlement on the Kapuas before the Muller range, which divides the watersheds of the Kapuas and Mahakam (in E Kalimantan). In the 1800s, when Chinese traders first visited the upper Kapuas, the settlement was frequently raided by Iban headhunters from the Batang Lupar in Sarawak. The Malays along the upper Kapuas are mainly Dayaks who converted to Islam. Despite Putussibau's remoteness, few Dayaks in the area live in traditional longhouses, the exception being the Taman Kapuas Dayaks. Two Taman Kapuas longhouses are accessible from Putussibau: Melapi I and Semangkok, the latter being more traditional; it is possible to stay overnight at both (see House Rules, page 606). Longboats for expeditions further upriver are prohibitively expensive to charter (roughly 60,000Rp/hr; 100,000Rp/hr with rapids); regular passenger boats connect main towns. **Accommodation** *Harapan Kita Bersama Losmen* and *Marisa Hotel* (both **E**, both grotty).

SOUTH OF PONTIANAK

There are few tourist attractions in the southern **Ketapang** regency, except for the

Entikong's fiscal advantages

For thousands of years tribal people have travelled freely across the ill-defined Kalimantan/Sarawak jungle frontier on the so-called *jalan tikus* – 'mouse trails'. Finally, 25 years after the *Konfrontasi* ended – the 2 year war between Indonesia and Malaysia – the first official border crossing point between the two countries opened. The steel barrier at the Entikong frontier post was dismantled in 1991, and the 400 km road between Kuching and Pontianak declared open. While many Malaysians have visited Pontianak for the first time, most of the traffic has been in the other direction. This was thanks to the strange decision to make Entikong the only exit point in Indonesia where Indonesians should not have to pay any *fiskal* – the exit tax of 250,000Rp. This has been a welcome boon to Pontianak's tour companies who have attracted huge business since 1991 – not just from the city's wealthy Chinese population, but from Java and Sumatra too. They now route all their international tours through Kuching instead of Jakarta. It makes sense for families on pilgrimage to Singapore, Hong Kong or China: a family of four, for example would save 1 million Rp. Pontianak travel agents say shopping tours to Singapore have become big sellers.

90,000 ha **Mount Palung Wildlife Reserve**, which encompasses most forest types and contains a wealth of flora and fauna, including orang utans and proboscis monkeys. It is difficult – and expensive – to get to and is mainly a scientific research centre; there are, however, basic facilities at nine camps within the park.

Permits must be obtained from the Conservation Office (PHPA) in Pontianak (at Jl Abdurrahman Saleh 33). Tourists wishing to visit the reserve should contact Mr Tan Yong Seng, director of *Ateng Tours & Travel*, whose company can organize the tortuous travel arrangements.

Sulawesi

Horizons	609	Toraja	634
Island information	616	Southeast Sulawesi	656
Ujung Pandang	616	Pendolo to Palu	658
Ujung Pandang to Toraja		Palu to Manado	671
via Pare Pare	627		

FORMERLY KNOWN AS the Celebes, Sulawesi is the third largest of the so-called Greater Sundas, with a land area of 189,216 square kilometres and a population of 13 million. The first use of the name by a European was by the Portuguese apothecary, secretary and accountant Tomé Pires who, in his journals written at the beginning of the 16th century, referred to the north tip of the island as **Punta de Celebres**. The origin of the word, though, is the subject of dispute. Some people have argued it is derived from the Bugis word *selihe* meaning 'sea current', some that it is an amalgamation of *sula* ('island') and *besi* ('iron'), and still others that it is taken from *si-lebih* ('the one with more islands'). The modern name's origin is not disputed: it means 'Island of Iron' (*Sula-besi*), referring to the rich deposits of nickel-iron ore in the centre of the island. This ore furnished the iron – it was called Luwu iron – for the laminated krisses of Majapahit, famous across the region for their strength.

HORIZONS

A glance at any map of Sulawesi immediately highlights the island's strangest attribute: its shape. Variously described as looking like an orchid, a deformed spider, giant crab and mutant starfish, the island's four 'arms' radiate from a mountainous core. Despite covering an area nearly as great as Britain, no place is more than about 40 km from the sea.

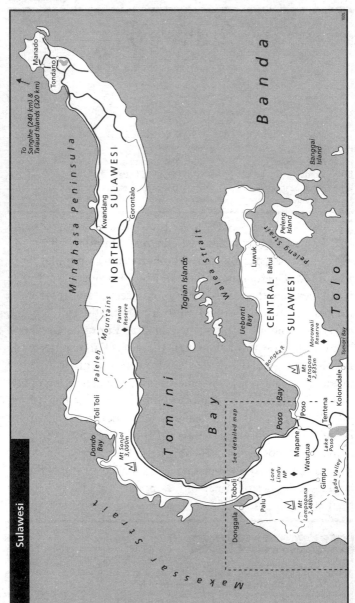

Sulawesi

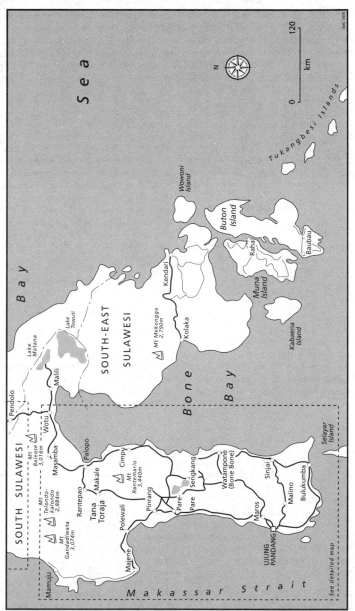

Sulawesi is divided into four provinces: N, S, Central and SE. Combined, they have a population of nearly 13 million. Most people visit the island to see the Toraja of S Sulawesi; their funeral ceremonies, cliff burial sites and soaring-roofed houses make this culture one of the most fascinating in the world. Ujung Pandang, Sulawesi's largest city and unofficial capital, is the usual port of entry. Manado on the N tip of the island offers some of the best diving in the country and is also becoming increasingly popular. However, with improving transport, other areas are becoming more accessible.

THE LAND

GEOGRAPHY

Sulawesi's strange shape is linked to its geological evolution. Studies have shown that the island is composed of two distinct halves – an E and a W portion. These only collided 15 million years ago when the process of continental drift – or tectonics – caused them to be thrust together. Like Java, Bali and Sumatra, Sulawesi is geologically unstable – altogether, the island has 11 active volcanoes, concentrated in the Minahasa area and N of Toli Toli.

But despite these complicated geological origins, Sulawesi is characteristically an island of uplands cut through by deep rift valleys with short, fast-flowing rivers. Beyond a narrow coastal fringe, there are few areas of lowland and most of the island is above 450m in altitude. The highest peak is Mt Sonjol in the S (3,225m), although mountains throughout the four provinces exceed 2,500m in height.

Because of Sulawesi's mountainous character, overland communications are difficult, and it has only been since the late 1980s that an all-weather road has linked the N and the S. Even transport by sea is dangerous because of the treacherous reefs which ring the island. The generally inhospitable nature of the island, and in particular its inaccessibility and

poor soils, led the English colonial envoy John Crawfurd to write of the indigenous inhabitants that "no one nation among them has emerged from the savage state to subjugate its neighbours, and take the lead in the march to civilization" (1820).

CLIMATE

Seasonal variations in rainfall are less pronounced in Sulawesi than in many other parts of Indonesia. The wettest months are from Dec to Feb, and the driest are Aug and Sep. Because of the mountainous landscape however, there are great differences in total rainfall between different areas. For example, while Manado in the far N has annual rainfall of 3,352 mm and Ujung Pandang in the far S, 3,188 mm; Palu in the centre receives only 533 mm. As so much of the island is upland, temperature differences can be pronounced. In the Rantepao area for example, temperatures at night regularly fall to below 10°C.

FLORA AND FAUNA

Because Sulawesi has diverse geological origins, encompasses a range of ecological zones, and because of the role that mountain barriers have played in restricting the migration of animals, the island has a fauna and flora which is not only quite unlike any other, but is also highly varied within the island itself. For example, there are seven species of macaques occupying different parts of the island, and two species and nine sub-species of carpenter bee. It is, in short, a naturalist's dream come true.

Of the 127 mammal species, an incredible 79 (62%) are endemic (ie found nowhere else); if bats are excluded, this rises to 98%. Even among birds, 88 of the 328 species so far identified are endemic to the island. The same degree of endemism is also true of amphibians, reptiles and insects. Alfred Russel Wallace, the Victorian naturalist, wrote down his first ideas on evolution after visiting Manado in N Sulawesi, and his letters to Charles

A Noah's ark: endemic animals of Sulawesi

Curly-tusked babirusa (*Babyrousa babyrussa*): as the name suggests – it means 'pig-deer' – naturalists have found this animal hard to classify. Described first by Piso in 1658, they are usually grouped with pigs but have no near common ancestor because they have evolved in isolation for 30 million years. Most distinctively, the upper canines grow through the animal's lips and curl upwards towards the head. Confused early naturalists thought these tusks were used to hook onto trees when the animal was exhausted; now the received wisdom is that they are used as sparring weapons when males fight during the breeding season.

Anoa (*Bubalus depressicornis* and *B quarlesi*): these are both dwarf buffalo – about the size of a large dog – but are the largest indigenous mammals on Sulawesi. They are renowned for their ferocity and have not been tamed for captivity despite attempts by the Torajans and others.

Bear cuscus (*Phalanger ursinus* and *P celebensis*): these animals look rather like sloths and are related to the possums of Australia. They are arboreal and use their prehensile tails as a fifth limb.

Black-crested macaques (*Macaca nigra*): there are four species of macaque found in Sulawesi, but only *M nigra* has been studied by scientists. They are arboreal, foraging in the upper canopy, and live in groups of up to about 50.

Large-eyed jumping tarsier (*Tarsius spectrum*): this is one of the world's smallest primates, with a body length of not more than 10 cm and a weight of 100g. They are nocturnal and form long-standing monogamous relationships. A new species, *Tarsius Diana* has recently been discovered.

Maleo (*Macrocephalon maleo*): perhaps Sulawesi's most famous animal, this bird incubates its eggs in holes dug in the sun-baked ground (see page 684).

Red-knobbed hornbill (*Rhyticeros cassadix*): like other hornbills, the red-knobbed hornbill incubates its eggs in hollow trees (see box, page 552). They are solitary, monogamous birds and are only rarely seen in flocks.

Source: Whitten, AJ *et al* (1988) *The ecology of Sulawesi*, Gajah Mada University Press: Yogyakarta. Whitten, Tony and Whitten, Jane (1992) *Wild Indonesia*, New Holland: London.

Darwin in England prompted Darwin to publish the *Origin of species*.

Given the uniqueness of Sulawesi's fauna, conservation takes on particular importance. The IUCN Red Data Books record that 19 species are endangered; but because of the generally poor knowledge of the island and its wildlife, the true figure is probably much higher. For example, the Caerulean paradise flycatcher (*Eutrichomyias rowleyi*) was discovered in 1873 by the German ornithologist AB Meyer. Since then not a single example has been captured, and it is not even known whether the original specimen was male or female. The reason why so much of Sulawesi's unique fauna is threatened is due not so much to hunting as to habitat loss. Tony Whitten reported at the end of the 1980s that 67% of productive wet lowland forest (ie 'rainforest') had disappeared; today it must be three-quarters or more.

HISTORY

The pre-colonial history of Sulawesi was focused upon the coastal regions of the S. Among a number of trading kingdoms which developed between the 13th and 15th century were the Bugis kingdoms of Luwu, Bone, Wajo and Soppeng and, most importantly, the Makassarese

Billiards: Indonesian style

The basic rule of the game is to pot the balls in numerical order, 1-15. Score points to the value of each ball you pot. Each turn you must always 'play' the lowest value ball left on the table (except for the initial break).

The Break. 1. Play the white from anywhere along the baulk line, there is no 'D'. 2. Any value ball may be pocketed, no foul for more than one ball being pocketed, all count to your score.

Subsequent visits. 3. You must play the lowest value ball left on the table, but you can cannon it on to balls of higher/lower value and pot these. More than one ball can be potted, there is no foul as long as you first hit the lowest value ball. 4. Your turn ends when you fail to pot a ball.

Fouls. 5. If you pot the white (direct or in-off another ball). Score: minus the value of the last ball the white hit before going into the pocket. If no ball touched then score minus the value of the ball you were aiming for. 6. If you hit a ball other than that of the lowest value when you first play the white. Score: minus the value of the highest ball you touch. 7. You don't hit any ball with the white. Score: minus the value of the lowest ball remaining on the table.

Penalty. 8. After any foul shot the lowest value ball is placed on the 'black spot', and the next player plays the white anywhere from the baulk line. Should another ball be directly in front of the 'black spot' this is moved to either side cushion. 9. If a player is snookered and feels they cannot hit the object ball, they call a miss and the white is returned to the baulk line, the object ball is moved to the black spot. Score: minus the value of the ball placed on the black spot.

The game is won when the difference between the player with the highest score and the player with the second highest is greater than the value of points remaining on the table. In many halls 3 or 4 players may play. In this case the turns rotate, but a player drops out as soon as they are unable to overhaul the leading score. The first player to drop out first three times is responsible for paying for the next series of games. In some cases the winner of the game is paid 1,000Rp by each other player.

A great way to pass a rainy afternoon or evening!

Kingdom of Gowa. Both the Bugis and the Makassarese had a reputation across the archipelago for fearlessness in battle.

At the beginning of the 16th century, Gowa, in alliance with the Bajau or sea nomads (not to be muddled with the Bugis – see box), began to emerge as the dominant power in the area. They extended their influence over the neighbouring Bugis kingdoms and the commercial capital, Makassar, became an important trading centre. By the 17th century there were Dutch, English, Arab, Malay, Chinese and Indian seafarers striding the streets of Makassar and doing business in spices, slaves, birds' nests, Dammar resin, sandalwood and products of the sea such as trepang (edible sea cucumbers), pearls, shark's fin and ambergris (a waxy substance secreted by whales and used in perfumes).

Gowa was the last of the great kingdoms of Indonesia to accept Islam (at about the same time that European traders were beginning to establish godowns and factories there). In 1605 the King of Gowa accepted Islam, and when the subordinate kings of the Bugis states failed to follow suit, he staged a number of religiously-inspired military campaigns (1608-1611). By the second decade of the 17th century, Gowa was at the head of the greatest Muslim trading empire in Southeast Asia.

Although the Dutch had established a trading post in south Sulawesi as early as 1609, they were never satisfied with the Gowa sultanate's tendency to allow the smuggling of spices from the Moluccas. By 1615, the VOC had closed down their trading post and limited military action had begun. Despite peace agreements in 1637, 1655 and 1660, conditions were brewing towards a major confrontation between Gowa and the Dutch.

Appreciating the military power of Gowa, the Dutch forged an alliance with the Bugis prince Arung Palakka of Bone. Like other Bugis leaders, Arung Palakka resented the domination of Gowa. In 1660 the Dutch attacked Gowa with the support of Arung Palakka and his men and forced Sultan Hasanuddin to sign a peace treaty. Sultan Hasanuddin chose to ignore the treaty, and in 1666 the VOC mounted a second expedition of 21 ships with Arung Palakka again in support. As the Dutch had hoped, the vassal Bugis kingdoms of Bone and Soppeng joined in the campaign against the Makassarese and after a year of hard fighting on both land and sea, Sultan Hasanuddin was forced to capitulate and sign the Treaty of Bungaya on 18 November 1667. Again, Hasanuddin chose to ignore the treaty, forcing the Dutch to mount a third, and final, campaign against the duplicitous Sultan in Apr 1668. By Jun 1669, the Sultan of Gowa and his armies were finally vanquished. The great days of Makassarese trading power were at an end.

Following the Dutch victory, Arung Palakka – upon whom the Dutch had depended for their success – became the *de facto* king of S Sulawesi. By all accounts, his rule was authoritarian and heavy-handed, depending more on military might than consultation and conciliation. The historian of Indonesia, RC Ricklefs maintains that Arung Palakka's rule led to large numbers of Bugis and Makassarese fleeing Sulawesi. He writes: "They took to their ships like marauding Vikings in search of honour, wealth and new homes. They intervened in the affairs of Lombok, Sumbawa, Kalimantan, Java, Sumatra, the Malay Peninsula and even Siam". Arung Palakka finally died in 1696.

Minahasa in N Sulawesi was first visited by Europeans in 1524 when Magellan's fleet anchored there. Shortly afterwards in the 1560s, Portuguese missionaries were successful in converting the population to Christianity and in 1568, Indonesia's oldest church – the Evangelical Church of Minahasa – was founded. The Spanish, from their colony in the Philippines, exerted control over Minahasa until 1643 when their attempt to place a half Spanish king on the throne led to the Minahasans turning to the Dutch for support.

In the interior, contact between the European powers and the various local groups was virtually non-existent. The Torajans, for example, were not brought under Dutch administrative control until the 20th century. After WW2, Dutch attempts to cling onto the East Indies led to greater bloodshed in Sulawesi than anywhere else in the archipelago. Even after independence in 1950, there were strong movements in the S and N for greater regional and religious autonomy. By 1958, only the larger towns of the S remained under government control, and between 1958 and 1961 there was a regional rebellion in Minahasa (see page 673).

ISLAND INFORMATION

● **Getting around**

Road Not long ago, Sulawesi enjoyed a reputation for having some of the worst roads in Indonesia, particularly in Central Sulawesi between Palopo and Palu. However, the Indonesian government has allocated considerable funds to improving and upgrading the 2,500 km-long Trans-Sulawesi Highway, the road is now surfaced from Ujung to Manado.

Boat Because of the poor state of much of Sulawesi's road system, the traditional mode of transport was boat. Local *prahu* (see page 620) still link much of the island and travel by ship and boat can be an alternative, more comfortable, and sometimes quicker, means of getting from A to B.

UJUNG PANDANG

Ujung Pandang, lying on the W coast of Sulawesi's S peninsula, is the hot and rather ramshackle capital of the province of S Sulawesi, and the *de facto* capital of the island. Until 1971 it was called Makassar, after the people who live in the area – the Makassarese.

Makassar was the port and commercial hub of the powerful trading sultanate of Gowa which dominated the area between the 13th and 15th centuries. The skilled sailors who operated out of Makassar – the Bajau 'sea nomads' – were instrumental in enabling the sultanate to control the lucrative trade in spices from the Moluccas. Makassar became one of the great entrepôts of Southeast Asia and traders from India, China and Europe would gather here to buy produce. The kings of Gowa did not accept Islam until 1605, and a Dutch visitor of 1607 remarked on the continued use of penis balls and the tendency for lower class women to roam the city with bare breasts. Less than 40 years later when the French priest Alexandre de Rhodes published his account of the Orient, he noted that women in Makassar were clothed from head to foot so that "not even their faces can be seen".

Gowa's position as the most powerful trading kingdom in eastern Indonesia finally came to an end in 1669 when Sultan Hasanuddin signed a peace treaty with the Dutch after 60 years of intermittent warfare (see page 615). The Sultan was forced to give up control of the fort of Ujung Pandang, which became the core of a new, colonial, city.

As Sulawesi's main port of entry and exit, Ujung Pandang is visited by considerable numbers of tourists. But there is not a great deal to see in this characterless city with a population of over 750,000, and most visitors merely pass through *en route* to Tana Toraja and elsewhere. Accommodation for budget travellers is

The original bogeymen – the Bugis of South Sulawesi

The Bugis were, and remain, coastal adventurers from S Sulawesi. They became renowned throughout the region for their sailing skills and fearlessness. Often likened to the Vikings, the appearance of an elegant Bugis schooner (see page 620) offshore would strike fear into coastal communities. Reports of fleets of Buginese boats plundering the islands around Java date back to the beginning of the 16th century, and when the Portuguese captured Melaka in 1511, a large Bugis fleet is said to have been sent to ward off the impertinent newcomers. Bugis wealth was not just founded on violence however; they were also skilled businessmen and controlled much of the trade between the islands of the Malay world.

Such was the Bugis' success in imposing their will across Southeast Asia, that by the early 18th century they controlled the sultanates of Johor, Kedah and Perak on the Malay Peninsula, and had established their own kingdom or *negeri* at Selangor near present day Kuala Lumpur. Their success inevitably brought the Bugis into conflict with the colonial powers, and by the late 18th century the Dutch and English between them had ejected the Bugis from Malaya. Befitting their role as the scourge of the archipelago, the English word bogey, or bogeyman, is derived from bugis (see page 619).

poor, a situation partially rectified by the presence of some excellent seafood restaurants.

Places of interest

Benteng (fort) Ujung Pandang was built in 1545 during the reign of Tuni Pallanga, the 10th Sultan of Gowa, overlooking the sea. When the city was captured by the Dutch in 1667 it was renamed Fort Rotterdam by the victorious Dutch admiral Speelman. The Indonesian independence hero **Prince Diponegoro**, now immortalized in virtually every town, was incarcerated here for 27 years. His cell in the SW corner of the fort is unmarked, although a statue of the 19th century independence hero on horseback stands outside the fort (his grave is on Jl Diponegoro – see below). Admission 500Rp. Open 0800-1600 Tues-Sun.

Within the precincts of the substantially remodelled fort are 13 buildings; 11 built by the Dutch and the remaining two by the Japanese. Among them is the **Ujung Pandang State Museum**. One half contains a diverse collection of coins, photographs and ceramics; the other, ethnographic artefacts, models of Torajan houses and elaborate Dutch and local

sailing vessels. The collection continues upstairs, with agricultural implements, weaving technology, and examples of traditional textiles and dress. Admission 200Rp. Open 0800-1330 Tues-Thur, 0800-1030 Fri, 0800-1230 Sat-Sun. Also found here is the **Conservatory of Dance and Music**, the **National Archives**, and the **Historical and Archaeological Institute**. The tourist office in the fort gateway has map handouts, plus leaflets in French, German and Dutch. The town bus No 6 which runs between the Central Market and Perumnas, along Jl Rajawali, stops by the fort.

Northeast of Fort Rotterdam, on Jl Diponegoro is the **Tomb of Prince Diponegoro** (see page 192) along with his genealogy chart. He challenged the Dutch in Java for 5 years during the early part of the 19th century, finally being arrested in 1830 and exiled to Manado; from there he was transferred to Ujung Pandang where he spent the remaining 27 years of his life in Fort Rotterdam.

North of the fort, are a number of **Chinese temples** on (or near) Jl Sulawesi, the earliest of which dates from the early 18th century. Just W of here, off

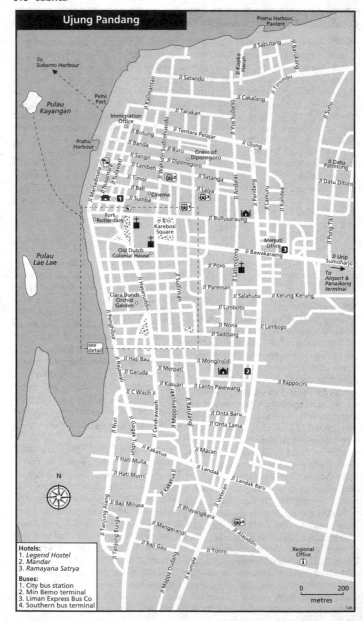

Ujung Pandang

Hotels:
1. Legend Hostel
2. Mandar
3. Ramayana Satrya

Buses:
1. City bus station
2. Min Bemo terminal
3. Liman Express Bus Co
4. Southern bus terminal

Prahu Harbour, Paotere

To Sukarno Harbour

Pulau Kayangan

Pelni Port

Prahu Harbour

Pulau Lae Lae

Immigration Office

Jl Kalimantan
Jl Satando
Jl Kopko Harun
Jl Sabutang
Jl Baru Kang
Jl Tinumbu
Jl Cakalang
Jl Tarakan
Jl Yos Sudarso
Jl Suju
Jl Butung
Jl Tentara Pelajar
Jl Ujung
Jl Banda
Jl Buru
Jl Datu Patimung
Jl Sangir
Jl Diponegoro
Grave of Diponegoro
Jl Datu Ditoro
Jl Lembeh
Jl Wahidin Sudirohusodo
Jl Timor
Jl Satanga
Jl Nusantara
Jl Sulawesi
Jl Pandang
Jl Lamuru
Jl Bali
Jl Laiya
Jl Andalas
Jl Kandea
Cinema
Jl Sumba
Jl Bullusaraung
Jl Martadinata
Fort Rotterdam
Karebosi Square
Jl Pong Tiki
Merpati Office
Jl Urip Sumoharjo
Jl Hasanuddin
Old Dutch Colonial House
Jl Bawakaraeng
To Airport & Panaikang terminal
Jl Sudirman
Jl Latimojong
Jl Poso
Clara Bundt Orchid Garden
Jl Pareman
Jl Salahutu
Jl Kerung Kerung
Jl Penghibur
Jl Limboto
Jl Nona
Jl Lambogo
Jl Saddang
Jl Haji Bau
Jl Monginsidi
Jl Rajawali
Jl Merpati
Jl Rappocini
Jl Garuda
Jl Kasuari
Jl Lanto Pasewang
Jl C Wasih II
Jl Mappanyukki
Jl Cendrawasih
Jl Ratulangi
Jl Onta Baru
Jl Nuri
Jl Onta Lama
Jl Gagak Tubun
Jl Kakatua
Jl Macan
Jl Hati Mulia
Jl Landak
Jl Hati Murni
Jl Kakatua II
Jl Landak Baru
Jl Baji Minasa
Jl Veteran
Jl Tanjung Alang
Jl Bhayangkara
Jl Tanjung Bunga
Jl Mangerangi
Jl Alauddin
Jl Baji Gau
Jl Mappa Oudang
Jl Tonro
Jl Kumala
Regional Office

N

0   200
metres

Bogeymen and antimacassars

Two words of Sulawesi origin have entered the English language: bogey or bogeyman, and antimacassar.

Antimacassar Beginning in the 17th century, macassar oil – a hair dressing – began to be exported from Makassar to Europe. It later became the generic term for all hair oils of Eastern origin. As men slicked with the oil, greased sofas and chair backs all over Europe and North America, so antimacassars were produced to soothe the ruffled sensibilities of house-proud wives. These ornamental coverings are rarely seen today in the West although they are in widespread use in aeroplanes and the Chinese also have a penchant for them.

Bogey, Bogeymen The word bogey was first used in 1836 and is a semi-proper name for the devil. The word is derived from Bugis, the name given to the feared pirates and traders of S Sulawesi (see box, page 617). Thackeray wrote "The people are all naughty and bogey carries them all off" and even today, parents in Europe and North America still invoke the bogeyman at bedtime, warning that if children misbehave the bogeyman might come and snatch them away. In 1865 the word was bastardized once again into bugbear, a hobgoblin reputed to devour naughty children.

Jl Martadinata is one of the three harbours where boats are loaded and unloaded with every conceivable merchandise. Further N still, at the edge of the city and 3 km from the centre, is **Paotere Harbour**. *Pinisi* schooners, a smaller version of the famous island-linking bugis schooners, can be seen berthed here (see page 620). Wiry men laden with sacks and timber climb the narrow planks to load the boats with cargo. Admission: 350Rp. Get there by bemo (G) from the Central Market, or Damri bus N3.

Running S from Fort Rotterdam is the seafront road, **Jl Penghibur**. During the cooler evening hours, scores of *soto* carts and other stalls set-up along the road S from the *Makassar Golden Hotel* to sell cheap food to promenading locals. Not far away at Jl Mochtar Lofti 15, is the residence of **Clara Bundt**. An avid collector of marine life, her house is now a museum displaying a collection of **seashells and corals**. Many of the beautiful shells are also for sale. Behind the house, the garden is filled with orchids and roses (*best time to visit*: Mar-Sep). **NB** The rather run-down house looks locked; walk through the garage to reach the shell collection and garden. Open Mon-Sun.

The **Sutera Alam Silk Factory** at Jl Onta 47 is one of the best places to watch women laboriously spinning and weaving silk in a range of vibrant colours. This goes on upstairs, while the ground floor is a shop, selling a good range of silks, both plain and patterned, by the metre. Dyeing is done in the central courtyard. The **Pasar Sentral** (Central Market) is a huge market, up Jl Cokroaminoto and just to the N of Jl Ramli, currently undergoing major renovation.

Excursions

Old Gowa lies S of town and was the administrative centre of the once powerful Sultanate of Gowa (see history, page 613). Sights of interest here include a number of tombs and a 'palace', spread over several square kilometres; they are not particularly exciting architecturally but are historically significant. About 8 km S of Ujung Pandang, just before the archway welcoming visitors to Sungguminasa, a road to the left leads to Old Gowa and its sights. The **Syech Yusuf Mosque** is a short distance off the main road. Next to the mosque are some tombs and graves; the grave of *Syech Yusuf* (1626-1694) is sacred

The Pinisi schooner of Sulawesi

One of the most evocative sights in Indonesia is that of a *bugis* or *pinisi* schooner. In the past, these boats carried cargo to all the main ports of the region. But the elegant boats that can be seen today docked at Ujung Pandang, Surabaya, Balikpapan, Sunda Kelapa (Jakarta) and other ports across Indonesia are in fact modelled on western schooners of the 19th century. The design of the boat has continually changed as advances have been incorporated – *pinisi* only refers to the current design. They weigh from 120-200 tonnes, have a ketch rig of seven sails, and twin rudders. When fully loaded – usually with water resistant cargoes such as timber – the decks are virtually awash.

Today, many *pinisi* are also fitted with a 10-cylinder Mercedes engine – which costs almost as much as the boat itself – and which gives the vessels an average speed of 8-12 knots. But, despite these advances in design, the schooners are still built without plans, using handsaws and traditional tools. Instead of metal nails and bolts, 30 cm-long pegs of ironwood (*belian* or *kayu ulin*) are used to bind the *pajala* hull together below the waterline. The problem for shipyards in Southern Sulawesi is that there is almost no ironwood left – forcing shipwrights to use inferior alternative woods. The best boats are said to be made in Banjarmasin (see page 571) where ironwood is still plentiful. Despite competition from alternative forms of marine transport, Indonesia's *pinisi* fleet remains one of the largest surviving fleets of sailing craft in the world.

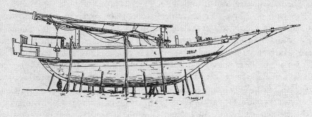

Source: Horridge 1981, with thanks.

The famous *pinisi* schooner illustrated on a Bank of Indonesia 100Rp note

to Muslims and an important pilgrimage spot. Yusuf was a 17th century religious scholar who left Gowa on a pilgrimage to Mecca in 1644 and never returned to Sulawesi alive. Instead he settled in Banten, W Java in 1671 where, with the support of a force of fierce Makassarese soldiers, he was instrumental in organizing resistance against the Dutch. He was captured in 1682, and exiled first to Ceylon and then to the Cape of Good Hope. To the consternation of Muslim purists, supplicants come here and make offerings hoping to have their wishes granted by Yusuf, who is also known as Tuanta Salamaka or 'Our Lord who grants us blessings'. Also here is Yusuf's wife's tomb – which is a pilgrimage spot for women having difficulty bearing children. Another 1 km along this road, on a bend, is the **Katangka Mosque**, claimed to be one of the oldest mosques in Sulawesi (although to the untutored eye it seems remarkably modern). It is surrounded by the pyramidal tombs and **graves of the Gowa royal family**. Continue for another 100m and turn right to reach **Tamalate**, a second royal graveyard. Set on a slight hill, the enclosure includes the *tomb of Sultan Hasanuddin* (1629-1670) who fought against the Dutch from 1666 to 1669 when weight of VOC arms finally prevailed. To the right of the enclosure is the *Tempat* (literally 'place') *Pelantikan* or Inauguration Stone, on which the Sultans were crowned. It is said that the original ancestors of the royal family descended to earth on the stone, and the coronation ceremony bestowed divine right of kingship.

Back on the main road, 3 km S of here, is **Sungguminasa**, the former seat of the sultans of Gowa. Facing the square is the **Istana Ballampoa**, a wooden palace on stilts, built in 1936. It is now a **museum**, housing a rather tatty collection of national costumes, a backstrap loom, family trees, photographs and other artefacts. The **Treasure Room** is kept locked; to see the royal regalia (or *pusaka*) inside ask at the bupati's office, across the square in front of the palace. *Getting there*: take a town bus (*bis damri*) No 2 (via Panakukang), No 4 (along Jl Veteran) or No 5 (along Jl Candrawasih), or a microlet. Becaks wait at the end of the road to take visitors to the tombs.

The **hill resort of Malino** lies 70 km E of Ujung Pandang, past Sungguminasa, at an altitude of 1,050m, on the slopes of Mt Bawakaraeng (also known as Mt Lompobatang). The best day to visit is Sun – market day – when traders from the surrounding hills bring produce to sell here. There are good walks through the surrounding forests. *Takkapala Waterfall* is 4 km S of town, with swimming pools. **Accommodation** In basic hotels/losmen. Guides are available in town for longer treks and to climb Mt Bawakaraeng which rises to 2,876m. *Getting there*: take a bus running towards Sinjai or charter a car.

Offshore Islands There are a number of beautiful islands off Ujung Pandang, easily accessible as day trips from the city. **Lae Lae Island** is 3 km offshore and is populated by Makassarese fishermen. Tiny **Samalona Island** is a 45 mins boat ride across the harbour and is one of the best places to go on a day trip from Ujung Pandang. It is a popular local resort with swimming, snorkelling (much of the coral has been damaged by dynamite fishing), fishing and waterskiing (admission to the island 2,000Rp). The island is rather dirty. Snorkelling equipment is available for hire on the island. **Accommodation C** (more at weekends), *Pulau Samalona* have house boats and chalets, T 22417, F 312838 for reservations. **Barrang Lompo Island** is rather further afield and offers excellent snorkelling; many of the shells on sale at Clara Bundt's museum in Ujung Pandang are pillaged from the reefs around Barrang Lompo. Simple accommodation available. **Getting to the islands**: boats for all three of these islands (should) leave from the dock just N of the *Makassar Golden Hotel* on Jl Pasar Ikan. However, these public boats are rather thin on the ground and visitors have reported travelling out to the islands to find there is no way back until the next day. Private boats can be chartered, approx. 25,000Rp for a half day.

Kayangan Island is a different sort of island entirely. It is really just an overgrown club with discos, bars and a great deal of noise and activity. *Getting there*: boats leave every hour from the pier in front of Fort Rotterdam, 30 mins (3,500Rp), the last vessel departing at about 1600.

Caves at Taman Purbakala Leang Leang are 42 km NE of Ujung Pandang, and 14 km from Maros. **Maros** is a riverside town 28 km N of Ujung Pandang. Great rafts of bamboo can be seen being floated down the Maros River, which flows through the town. In Maros, a turning to the right is signposted to Bantimurung, the road snaking through impressive karst scenery, clothed in thick forest. After 8 km, turn left by a mosque; a further 6 km along this rough road is the *Taman Purbakala Leang Leang* (caves and archaeological park). Here there are a series of caves (two of which are easily accessible – *Pettae* and *Pettakere*), with prehistoric hand prints and paintings of deer and ox. There is also a small museum. Admission 500Rp. *Getting there*: take a bemo or bus from Ujung Pandang's Sentral terminal to Maros, 45 mins; from Maros catch another bemo running E towards Bantimurung and alight after 8 km at the turn-off for the park – bemos travel down this side road for the final 6 km to the caves; becaks also wait at the intersection.

Bantimurung Falls lie 41 km NE of Ujung Pandang on the road to Bone and are hard to miss – the entrance is marked by a monstrous archway in the form of a concrete monkey. The impressive falls cascade over a smooth rock surface, and a spectacular number of butterflies fill the air over the plunge pool. Alfred Russel Wallace came here in 1856 and was astounded by the myriad of butterflies. However, the numbers are dwindling as local boys use nets to catch protected species to sell to unscrupulous tourists. The whole area is rather ruined by an over-enthusiastic use of concrete, with grottos, bridges and concrete animals disfiguring the area. There is a swimming pool and restaurant. About 1 km above the falls is *Gua Mimpi* or Dream Cave. **Accommodation D-E** *Wisma Bantimurung*. Admission 2,000Rp to the falls area, incl entrance to the associated caves. There is a display of butterflies revealing that more than 200 species have been found here (admission: 750Rp). *Getting there*: take a bemo from Ujung Pandang's Sentral terminal to Maros, 45 mins, or a Damri bus from the Central Market and then a bemo from Maros to Bantimurung, 30 mins. Alternatively, charter a taxi (25,000Rp), or book a tour (60,000Rp).

Tours

Most tour companies run city tours, day trips to Bantimurung (60,000Rp), Malino (80,000Rp) and to the off-shore islands. Overnight tours are also available to Toraja (about US$200 for 4 days/3 nights), and to the megaliths of Central Sulawesi (US$400 for 8 days/7 nights).

Festivals

Apr (1st): *Anniversary of Ujung Pandang*, most events and cultural shows occur in the week before the anniversary. A formal ceremony is held in the square on the 1st.

Jun (1st): *Cleansing of Royal Regalia and Heirlooms*, one chance in the year for the public to get a good view of the royal regalia.

Jul (17th-23rd): *South Sulawesi Cultural Festival*, an arts festival of both traditional and contemporary arts and culture. Exhibitions, tournaments, parades, dancing.

Aug (17th): *Pelra Race*, traditional Buginese/Makassarese boats start from here in a race to Sunda Kelapa, Jakarta. (19th): *Makassar Regatta*, international yacht race.

Ujung Pandang Centre

Hotels:
1. Celebes
2. Kenari
3. Losari Beach Guesthouse
4. Losari Beach Inn
5. Makassar
6. Makassar Gate Beach
7. Makassar Golden
8. Makassar Royal Inn
9. Marannu City & Tower
10. Pondok Delta
11. Pondok Suanda
12. Purnama
13. Sentra
14. Surya Inn
15. Victoria Panghegar
16. Widhana
17. Wisata Inn
18. Wisma Amala
19. Wisma Tiatira
20. Wisma Venus Golden

Places to eat:
21. Aroma Labbakkang
22. Sulawesi Ayam Goreng

Local information
● Accommodation

Ujung Pandang has a good range of mid- and upper-bracket accommodation. Losmen for budget travellers are thin on the ground and often dirty.

A+ Sedona Makassar, new 229-room high-rise hotel on the waterfront, due to open in 1996 or 1997. All facilities envisaged incl swimming pool, fitness and business centres and satellite TV; **A+-A Marannu City & Tower**, Jl Hasanuddin 3-5, T 315087, F 321821, a/c, restaurant, very dirty pool, available for use by non-residents (7,000Rp), fitness centre, ugly hotel block in city centre with 400 rooms each with attached bathroom; TV, mini bar, hot water, comfortable enough but barely an ounce of charm;

A Celebes, Jl S Hasanuddin 2, T 320770, F 320769, new hotel with poor rooftop restaurant, central location, but not rec; **A Kenari**, Jl Yosef Latumahina 30, T 874250, F 872126, a/c, restaurants, excellent value, friendly and helpful staff, clean rooms, good location, rec; **A Makassar Gate Beach**, Jl Pasar Ikan 10, T 325791, F 316303, a/c, restaurant, satellite TV, situated in the heart of the city, this well-run hotel is a haven in an otherwise frenetic city, views over Ujung Pandang Bay, the best place to stay for those not on a budget; **A Makassar Golden**, Jl Pasar Ikan 50, T 314408, F 320951, a/c, restaurant, pool (not open to non-residents), best hotel in town, with great position on the seafront, attractive pool, the deluxe rooms are in separate bungalows (rec) on the waterfront, the standard rooms are rather grim, the super cool lobby is rec for a coffee break if walking about town, beer though is expensive, good view from terrace cafe, gloomy restaurant; **A Marannu Garden**, Jl Baji Gau 52, T 852244, F 873606, a/c, restaurant, large pool with no shade, inconvenient location S of the city, bungalows have little character, tennis; **A Victoria Panghegar**, Jl Jend Sudirman 24, T 311556, F 312468, a/c, restaurant, pool, on main road, away from seafront, comfortable, well managed, no smoking rooms available, rec.

A-B Losari Beach, Jl Penghibur 3, T 326062, F 319611, new hotel catering mostly to local businessmen, cheaper rooms are in our '**B**' category, a/c, excellent position on the seafront close to Fort Rotterdam, ugly furnishings but comfortable enough simple rooms, restaurant.

B Delia Orchid Park, Jl Urip Sumaharjo Km 6, T 324111, a/c, out of town, in garden compound with orchids and birds; **B Makassar City**, Jl Chairil Anwar 28, T 317055, F 311818, a/c, restaurant, central location with good amenities, but characterless; **B Makassar Sunset** (formerly Pasanggrahan Makassar), 297 Somba Opu (overlooks sea), T 854218, run down; **B Marina Inn**, Jl Haji Bau 30, T 82324, F 84255, 4 rm, all with ensuite bathrooms, newly fitted out and spotless, friendly but unobtrusive staff, ample Dutch breakfast incl, owned by the people who represent Tunas Indonesia Tour, bookable at the airport, from the Tunas desk; **B Pondok Delta**, Jl Hasanuddin 43S, T 312711, F 312655, a/c, small hotel, large rooms, friendly; **B Venus Golden**, Jl Botolempangan 17, T 24995, a/c, no restaurant but next to Aroma Labbakkang, medium-sized new hotel, very clean, helpful staff, cool lounge area, quiet; **B Wisata Inn**, Jl Sultan Hasanuddin 36-38, T 324344, F 312783, some a/c, immaculate, medium-sized businessmens hotel with rooms set around courtyard, peaceful, central location, friendly, strongly rec.

B-C Makassar Royal Inn, Jl Daeng Tompo 8, T 322903, F 328045, a/c, 30 rm, very clean, in quiet backstreet close to Pantai Losari with evening foodstalls nearby, rooms have attached bathrooms, some with hot water, friendly staff and good value for Ujung, rec.

C Losari Beach Inn, Jl Pasar Ikan 10, T 24363, F 6303, attractive position overlooking the sea, rooms could be cleaner; **C Oriental**, Jl WR Monginsidi 38A, T 83558, some a/c, ramshackle and grubby, but cheap a/c rooms; **C Pondok Suanda Indah**, Jl Hasanuddin 12, T 312857, new, clean and good; **C Ramayana Satrya**, Jl G Bawakaraeng 121, T 322165, convenient for the bus station, but far from the town centre and seafront, but convenient for those planning going direct from the airport to Toraja without going into town centre; **C Tiatira**, Jl Dr Sutomo 25, T 311301, a/c, hot water, friendly, price incl breakfast, popular with locals; **C Widhana**, Jl Botolempangan 53, T 22499, some a/c, hot water; **C Wisma Amala**, Jl Arif Rate 6, T 854709, small hotel, clean, price incl breakfast.

D Purnama, Jl Pattimura 3-3A, T 323830, central location, dark and dirty, not good value; **D Sentral**, Jl Bulusaraung 7, noisy and dirty.

E Legend Hostel, Jl Jampea 5, T 320424, restaurant, helpful staff, clean rooms, good source of information for travellers; **E Mandar Inn**, Jl Anuang 17, rooms with bathrooms, prices incl tea and coffee, no windows in some rooms, very friendly atmosphere, with informative staff, one of whom speaks good English and can advise on places to go and modes of transport, rec.

F Aman, Jl Mesjid Raya, opp the mosque, popular, but small rooms and unpleasant bathrooms.

● **Places to eat**

Although not everyone likes Ujung Pandang, few would argue that it offers delicious, inexpensive seafood. The local speciality is ikan bakar – barbecue grilled fish.

Indonesian: ◆◆◆-◆◆**Ayam Goreng Ratu Muda**, Jl Ranggong 5, serves, believe it or not, ayam goreng, but also excellent Chinese cuisine and seafood dishes, reasonable prices, popular with locals; ◆◆**Aroma Labbakkang**, Jl Chairil Anwar 25, T 324520, excellent seafood restaurant with ugly grotto exterior, frequented by the Ujung Pandang Chinese community, rec (closed some lunchtimes); ◆◆**Asia Baru**, Jl Salahutu 23, good seafood and Indonesian (delicious jackfruit stew); ◆◆**Empang**, Jl Siau 7, seafood and Indonesian, popular; ◆◆**Sulawesi Ayam**

Goreng, on corner of Jl Hasanuddin and Jl Ince Nurdin, popular, with some tables outside, amongst the barbecue smells, chicken and fish; ♦♦*Surya*, Jl Nusakembangan 16, crab is their speciality, but they also serve prawns, squid and fish and other Chinese dishes; above *Galael's supermarket*, on Jl Hasanuddin there is a cheap ♦*self-service* restaurant serving a range of good Indonesian dishes.

International: there is little to offer in the way of western food although the large hotels have coffee shops and restaurants serving international cuisine. There are several bakeries/pastry shops and ice-cream parlours (the one in front of the *Golden Makassar Hotel*) and a *KFC* above *Galael's supermarket* on Jl Hasanuddin.

Foodstalls: the best place to eat cheaply in the evening is along the waterfront, where hundreds of stalls set up to serve the local community. There are also some good fish warungs opp the fort entrance on Jl Jend A Yani, and some warungs serving Chinese-style dishes along the promenade nr the *Makassar Golden Hotel*.

● **Bars**
Café Taman Safari, Jl Penghibur (corner of Jl Haji Bau), fine position on the seafront close to a Bugis fishing community, cold beer and views of the sun setting make this one of the best places to while away an early evening.

● **Airline offices**
Bouraq, Jl Veteran Selatan 1, T 83039; **Garuda**, Jl Slamet Riyadi 6, T 322543, office hours 0730-1630 Mon-Fri, 0730-1300 Sat, 0900-1200 Sun; **Mandala**, Jl Irian 2A, T 317965; **Merpati**, Jl G Bawakaraeng 109, T 24114; **Sempati**, *Makassar Golden Hotel*, T 311556.

● **Banks & money changers**
Bank Dagang Negara, Jl Nusantara 147-149; **BNI**, Jl Sudirman; **Bumi Daya**, Jl Nusantara 70-72; **Rakyat Indonesia**, Jl Slamet Riyadi.

● **Entertainment**
Cinema: *Benteng Theatre*, Jl Ujung Pandang; *Studio 21*, Jl Dr Ratulangi (nr intersection with Jl Lanto Dg Pasewang), a/c cinema showing occasional western films.

Karaoke bars: *Irani*, S end of Jl Somba Opu.

● **Post & telecommunications**
Area code: 0411.
General Post Office: Jl Andi Pangerang Petta Rani, E of town.
Post Office: Jl Slamet Riyadi 10.
Telephone: small Wartel office just S of *Victoria Panghegar Hotel*.

Wartel: Jl Bawakaraeng 84 (for fax, telegrams and telephone).

● **Sport**
Golf: *Makassar Golf Club*, 14 km N of town off the road to the airport, open to non-members, clubs for hire.

Swimming: the *Victoria Panghegar* and *Marannu City* hotels both allow non-residents to use their pools, 7,000Rp (although neither are very good), as does the inconveniently located *Marannu Garden*, S of town, where there is a large, often empty, pool.

Tennis: court available for use by non-residents at the *Marannu Garden Hotel*, Jl Haji Bau 52.

Windsurfing: there is a club facing Fort Rotterdam; boards for hire.

● **Shopping**
Antiques: shops along Jl Somba Opu and Jl Pasar Ikan. Good antique buys are still to be had in Ujung Pandang, but these are outnumbered by the fakes on sale.

Baskets: Jl Tinumbu. Shops along Jl Nusantara and Jl Kakatua sell rattan and bamboo.

Ceramics: N end of Jl Somba Opu.

Gold & silver: several shops along Jl Somba Opu.

Market: Jl Sultan Alauddin, good local baskets.

Silk: *Sutera Alam*, Jl Onta 47 (see page 619), 18,000Rp/m (plain), 27,500Rp/m (patterned).

● **Tour companies & travel agents**
Ceria Nugraha, Jl Usman Jafar 9, T 22482, F 311848; *Libra Golden Star*, *Victoria Panhegar Hotel*, Jl Sudirman 26, T 312841, F 312468; *Mattappa Tours*, Jl Pattimura 16-18, T 323932, Pelni dates/movements on board in office (saves trip further N); *Nitour*, Jl Lamaddukelleng 2, T 217723; *Pacto*, Jl Jend Sudirman 56, T 83208; *Pan Travel*, T 323272, open 0800-1600; *PT Aksa Utama Tour and Travel*, Artis Bldg, Jl G Lompobattang 3, T 22417, F 312838; *Suita Tours*, Jl Sultan Hasanuddin 22A, T 323274, F 326160.

● **Tourist offices**
Dinas Pariwisata, Jl Urip Sumoharjo 269, open 0700-1400 Mon-Thur, 0700-1100 Fri, 0800-1300 Sat; **Kanwil Pariwisata**, Jl Andi Pangerang Petta Rani, T 317128, inconveniently located E of the city centre, some handouts, open 0800-1400 Mon-Thur, 0800-1100 Fri, 0800-1300 Sat.

● **Useful addresses**
Immigration Office: Jl Sultan Alauddin 34A, T 83153.

● **Transport**
70 km from Malino, 155 km from Pare Pare, 180 km from Bone (Watampone), 328 km from Rantepao.

Local Becaks: known as *tiga roda*, they are available all over town and are single seaters. **Bemos**: locally known as *pete pete*, 300-400Rp around town; the main terminal is by the central market, appropriately named 'Sentral'. Bemos from here to most destinations. **Bicycles**: mountain bikes for hire from *Legend Hostel*, Jl Jampea 5. **Metered taxis**: flagfall 800Rp, or hired for the day through your hotel for about 80,000Rp. **Town buses** (bis damri): run set routes, most setting off from the Sentral terminal (200Rp): No 1 to Daya, No 2 to Sungguminasa via Jl Panakukand, No 3 to Batangase and the airport via the toll road, No 5 to Sungguminasa via Jl Cendrawasih, No 6 to Perumnas via Jl Rajawali. Bus No 4 leaves from the Pannampu Market along Jl Veteran to Sungguminasa.

Air Ujung Pandang's Hasanuddin Airport is 23 km N of the city centre (30 mins drive). Regular connections by Merpati/Garuda, Sempati and Bouraq with numerous destinations including daily direct flights to Ambon, Balikpapan, Biak, Denpasar, Jakarta, Jayapura, Solo, Kupang, Samarinda, Maumere, Surabaya and Ternate. Within Sulawesi, there are connections with Gorontalo, Kendari, Manado, Palu, Maumere and Tana Toraja (for Rantepao). **Transport to town**: taxi from airport to town 14,300Rp; booth is on the left as one exits from the terminal. **NB** The drivers charge an extra 4,000Rp if taxis are shared and they need to make a second drop-off. The best bus to town is the one marked 'Patas', a limited express bus. The slower City bus (bis damri) No 3 goes past the airport entrance from the Central Market (on the toll road) – it is a 500m walk from the road to the airport. For both buses, stand on the same side of the road as the airport for the journey to town. Bemos running between Ujung and Daya also pass in front of the airport entrance. For transport to the airport, catch the *Patas* bus from outside the *Mattappa Travel Agent*, on Jl Pattimura (though the agent knows nothing about it). If taking the town bus be advised that it is very slow and to leave enough time. *Airport facilities*: a money changer, information desk (poor) and hotel booking counters. Check the local newspaper *Pedoman Rakyat* for flight details out of Ujung Pandang for the week ahead. **Accommodation near the airport**: **C** *Hotel Aplat*, just a ½ km from the airport, saving a 23 km ride into town if catching a connecting flight the following day, but noisy, dirty and generally run down, so don't expect the Ritz.

Road Bus: the Panaikang Terminal for long-distance buses is at the E edge of town on Jl Urip Sumoharjo just past, '45 University. Regular bemos run between the terminal and the Sentral bemo station in the city centre. There are plenty of food stalls and shops to stock up on fruits, water, biscuits, etc for the journey. Pelni information is available at this bus station. Regular connections with Tana Toraja 10 hrs, Bone Bone 4 hrs, Pare Pare, Sengkang 5 hrs, Soppeng 4 hrs, Bulukumba, Selayar, Palopo and other major destinations in S Sulawesi. There are also buses to Bajoe, where nightly ferries depart for Kolaka in SE Sulawesi. *Liman Express*, Jl Laiya 25, T 315851, and *Litha*, Jl G Merapi 160 run buses to Toraja via Pare Pare; *PIPOSS*, Jl Buru 10A operates buses to Palopo; while *Cahaya Bone*, Jl Andalas 37, T 24225, have a service to Bone (departs 0800 town centre, Ujung Pandang (office) 0830 Panaikang). *Damri* Bus (departs 2100) for Manado (75,000Rp). **NB** *Liman Express* and *Cahaya Bone* are convenient because they both have offices in the town centre, 5 mins walk E from the bemo station. But by taking the time to visit the Panaikang bus station (300Rp by bemo) it is possible to scout around all the private companies at the back of the terminal and book a numbered seat; 600Rp well spent.

Sea Boat: Ujung Pandang is a major port and a good place to catch a ship or boat; 9 Pelni ships stop here – there are 5 trips a fortnight to Jakarta and 6 to Surabaya (see route schedule, page 921). The **Pelni** Office is at Jl Laks E Martadinata 38, T 317965. **Kalla Lines** run a

	Time	a/c	Ekonomi
	hrs	Rp	Rp
UJUNG PANDANG to:			
Rantepao	8-10	14,500	10,000
Pare Pare			5,500
Sengkang	5		4,600
Soppeng	4		5,000
Palopo		14,500	
Kolaka			10,000
Bone			5,000

Selected bus fares

ship which follows a 2 week loop stopping at Jakarta, Surabaya, Balikpapan, Tarakan, Pantoloan and Ternate. The Kalla Lines office is at Jl Jend Sudirman 78, T 82464. Ships leave from the Pelabuhan Sukarno to the N of town. Pinisi schooners also run regularly between Ujung Pandang's Paotere harbour and most other ports in Sulawesi and beyond; simply ask around.

UJUNG PANDANG TO TORAJA VIA PARE PARE

The road from Ujung Pandang runs N for 28 km to the riverside town of Maros. Here it divides, one route running NE through Bantimurung to the capital of

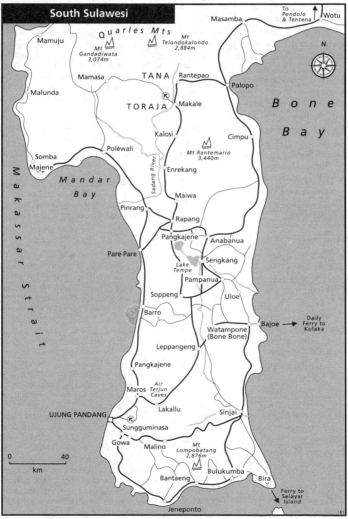

South Sulawesi

the former Bugis Kingdom of Bone – Watampone – 180 km from Ujung. Continuing N from Watampone, the road passes through the attractive silk weaving town of Sengkang and then follows the coast N to Palopo. The more usual route runs N from Maros up the coast, usually out of sight of the sea, but on occasions passing through small fishing villages with attractive clapboard houses on stilts, before reaching the port of Pare Pare, 155 km from Ujung Pandang. From here, the road turns inland and threads its way upwards between limestone crags and past ricefields – scenically stunning, but exhausting by bus. 156 km from Pare Pare the road reaches the district capital of Makale and, 18 km N from Makale, the town of Rantepao – in the heartland of the Toraja. From Rantepao, the road turns E and descends spectacularly to the coastal town of Palopo, a distance of 62 km, where it meets up with the road from Sengkang.

PARE PARE

Pare Pare is S Sulawesi's second city with a population of 100,000 – although it feels more like a market town. The 'city' runs eel-like up the coast and for much of its length is only two or three streets wide. The centre is marked by the **Monumen Rakyat Pejuang**; a statue of a man, staff in hand, pointing into the distance and standing on a map of Indonesia.

Primarily a trans-shipment point for inter-island cargoes, Pare Pare is a quiet town. Visitors usually only come here as a stopping-off point between Ujung Pandang and Rantepao, in Tana Toraja; it is also a good port to catch a passage to Kalimantan (see below). The small **La Bangenge Museum** is 2 km S of town in Bacukiki sub-district; it has a small collection of local enthnographic pieces. Get there by becak. There is an attractive, provincial, multi-domed **mosque** on Jl Hasanuddin.

• **Accommodation** C *Gandaria*, Jl Bau Massepe 171, T 21093, some a/c, clean, though small, rooms, pleasant courtyard and open-air restaurant; **D** *Tanty*, Jl Hasanuddin, T 21378, rather over-priced, but rooms are clean enough; **E** *Siswa*, Jl Baso Dg Patompo 3, T 21374, attractive colonial façade, appears to have improved recently, good value.

• **Places to eat** Good, fresh, grilled seafood – particularly the excellent *ikan bakar* – is one reason to visit Pare Pare. The food is grilled in front of the restaurants, and there are a number just N of the central statue on Jl Baso Dg Patompo: ♦♦*Asia*, Jl Baso Dg Patompo 25, also serves Chinese food; ♦*Monas*, Jl Baso Dg Patompo 33; ♦*Sedap*, Jl Baso Dg Patompo 21, good fish; ♦*Sempurna*, Jl Bau Massepe, good Indonesian and Chinese food.

• **Entertainment Cinema**: *Pare Theatre*, Jl Bau Massepe (nr *Gandaria Hotel*).

• **Banks & money changers** Bumi Daya, Jl Baso Dg Patompo 17 (Amex, US$, TCs).

• **Post & telecommunications Post Office**: Jl Karaeng Burane 1 (S of the central statue, corner with Jl Bau Massepe). **Wartel** (international telephone, telegrams, fax): Jl Sultan Hasanuddin 53.

• **Transport** 155 km from Ujung Pandang, 173 km from Rantepao. **Road Bus**: the new(ish) bus terminal is 3 or so km S of the city centre. Buses to Rantepao 6 hrs, Ujung Pandang 3 hrs, Bone Bone, Soppeng, Majene, Palopo, Masamba and Sengkang 3 hrs. **Sea Boat**: regular ships call at Pare Pare and is the best port in Sulawesi to catch ships to Kalimantan. Shipping agents are concentrated in two areas of town, 10 mins walk apart: on Jl Andi Cammi (the road running parallel to Jl Bau Massepe but one closer to the sea) and on Jl Sulawesi (just N of the central statue). Rates and length of journey vary according to the vessel; shop around – some of the ships are barely seaworthy. Boards outside the agents list destinations and arrival and departure dates. Regular ports of call in Kalimantan incl Balikpapan 1-2 days (20,000Rp), Samarinda 2 days (20,000Rp), Nunukan 2-3 days (40,000-50,000Rp) and Tarakan. Ships also call at other ports in Sulawesi (eg Toli Toli, 40,000Rp) and Surabaya, Kupang and Dili among others. The Pelni vessels *Tidar* and *Leuser* call here on their fortnightly circuits between Sulawesi, Java and Kalimantan (see route schedules page 921). Pelni have their office at Jl Andi Cammi 130, T 21017.

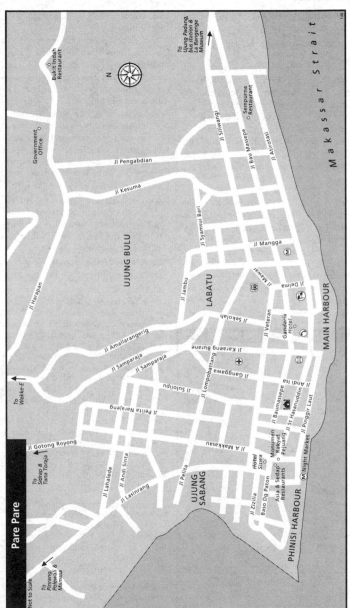

Pare Pare

Not to Scale

Makassar Strait

UJUNG BULU

LABATU

UJUNG SABANG

MAIN HARBOUR

PHINISI HARBOUR

To Wekke-E

To Sidrap & Tana Toraja

Jl Gotong Royong

To Pinrang, Polewali & Mamasa

To Ujung Padang, bus station & La Bangenge Museum

Bukit Indah Restaurant

Government Office

Jl Harapan

Jl Pengabdian

Jl Kesuma

Jl Siliwang

Sempurna Restaurant

Jl Bau Massepe

Jl Attotasi

Jl Syamsul Bari

Jl Mangga

Jl Jambu

Jl Mawar

Jl Delima

Jl Sekolah

Jl Veteran

Gandaria Hotel

Jl Amallarangerig

Jl Samparaja

Jl Samparaja

Jl Karaeng Burane

Jl Lompobattang

Jl Sulolipu

Jl Ganggawa

Jl Andi Isa

Jl Pinggir Laut

Jl Pelita Narjeng

Jl A Makkasau

Jl Baumassepe

Jl St Hasanuddin

Monumen Rakyat Pejuang

Jl Lahalede

Jl Andi Sinta

Jl Pelita

Hotel Siswa

Jl Zizilia

Baso Dg Paton

Asia & Sedap Restaurants

Night Market

Jl Lasinrang

WATAMPONE (BONE BONE)

Watampone was the former capital of the Bugis Kingdom of Bone, and it is still popularly known as Bone Bone. During the 16th century, the city emerged as the main rival to the kingdom of Gowa based near Ujung Pandang, and it was not subdued by its more powerful neighbour until 1611. Gowa pressured Bone into a subordinate relationship, and also forced the king to embrace Islam. This left an enduring distrust and dislike between the two great powers of Sulawesi, and when the Dutch began to undermine Gowa, they found a willing ally in the brilliant and ruthless Prince Arung Palakka of Bone (see page 615). It was with the help of Arung Palakka's army – by all accounts one of the most fearsome any Indonesian power has ever raised – that the Dutch finally conquered Sultan Hasanuddin of Gowa in 1669. From 1669 until his death in 1696, Arung Palakka was the most powerful man in all Sulawesi. Bone continued to be an important trading centre until the beginning of the 19th century.

'Bone', as it is called by everyone, is a friendly, sleepy town, useful as a stopping-off point to and from Kendari. Despite its charm, there are few obvious reasons to make a detour to stay here. The **Bola Soba** was built in 1890 as the residence of Baso Pagiling Abdul Hamid; it now houses the offices of the Department of Education. The **Museum Lapawawoi**, with a small collection of ethnographic pieces, is on the main square and is worth a visit. Open Mon-Sun 0800-1400. Bone Bone's port, **Bajoe**, is 4 km E of town.

Excursions Mampu caves lie 34 km NW of Watampone, and are said to be the largest in S Sulawesi. *Getting there*: a minibus to Uloe and then a bemo to the caves (ask for *Gua Mampu*).

Festivals Apr (6th): *Anniversary of Bone Regency*, entertainments and traditional dancing.

- **Accommodation B** *Wisata Watampone*, Jl Jend Sudirman 14, T 21362, F 22367, a/c, restaurant, pool, modern, clean but featureless, overpriced for such a town and location, forecourt still looks like a building site, poor value; **C** *Mario Pulana*, Jl Kawerang 16, T 21098, some a/c, price incl breakfast, gloomy rooms, disinterested, unhelpful staff who seem less than keen to accept tourists, *Rio Rita* is much more welcoming, avoid; **C** *Rio Rita*, Jl Kawerang 4, T 21053, some a/c, attached mandi, small hotel, attractive, price incl breakfast, comfortable sitting area, best value in town, rec; **D** *Losmen Nacional*, Jl Masjid Raya 86, large building set in middle of unkempt garden, close to shops, restaurants and Raya Mosque; **D** *Wisma Cempaka*, Jl Biru 36, T 21414, medium size place with 26 rm.

- **Places to eat** Several restaurants along Jl Mesjid. ♦♦*Rumah Makan Ramayana*, Jl Masjid Raya 4, good size portions, clean, more Chinese style, rec; ♦♦*Rumah Makan Setia Budi*, Jl Beringin 89. **Foodstalls**: selection of *Kaki lima* operate from nr the clocktower, very difficult to find a beer.

- **Entertainment** Play pool with locals in one of the many halls nr Jl Beringin (pot order 1 to 15, see page 614).

Watampone

Hotels:
1. Losmen Nacional
2. Maria Pulana
3. Rio Rita
4. Wisata Watampone

Places to eat:
5. Ramayana
6. Setia Budi

● **Transport** 180 km NE of Ujung Pandang. **Local Bemo**: around town for 150Rp. Bejaks from hotel to Bemo station 500Rp. Bemo to Bajoe 500Rp. **Road Bus**: connections with Ujung Pandang 6 hrs, Pare Pare, Sengkang and Rantepao 8 hrs. The road from Bone to Sengkang is very poor. Company fares: Ujung Pandang (5,000Rp), Kendari (incl ferry) (19,000Rp), Palopo (7,000Rp), Bontosunggu (7,500Rp). Other bemo/bus fares: Bone-Bulukumbu 3 hrs (5,000Rp); Bone-Sengkang (bemo) 3 hrs (2,000Rp). *Cahaya-Ujung Pandang* (minibus company), Jl Veteran 167, T 21348. The bemo station is on Jl Agus Salin. Many buses drop passengers off at their hotels. **Sea Boat**: there are nightly ferries departing 2000 from Bajoe, Bone Bone's port, to Kolaka in SE Sulawesi, 8 hrs (5,100-9,500Rp). Bemos run regularly between the town and the port, 4 km to the E.

SENGKANG

Sengkang is a Bugis town and the capital of Wajo district with one of the most attractive settings in Southern Sulawesi, close to the shores of Lake Tempe. The town is a good base to explore the surrounding countryside. There are some excellent walks in the gentle hills behind the town, and relaxing boat trips can be taken on Lake Tempe but other than walking and exploring around Lake Tempe, there is little to keep visitors here. Some people with time on their hands resort to playing video games with the local children. The market is nothing special, a filthy food area and poor fruit selection. Sengkang and nearby villages are also highly regarded for their silk weaving (see box).

But undoubtedly the main attraction of Sengkang is **Lake Tempe**. Although at different times of year the water level of the lake can vary by as much as 3m, it is generally shallow and more like a marsh over large areas than an open expanse of water. In these shallower areas, the 'lake' is interpenetrated by a multitude of channels and provides good breeding grounds for water birds. (But note that because the boats are powered, birdwatching is not usually very rewarding. For those wishing to birdwatch, it is recommended that they make special arrangements.) One of the most interesting and remarkable features of the lake are the floating gardens where crops are anchored by wig-wam shaped bamboo poles. These also act as feeding grounds for fish which congregate around the gardens. Three hotels in town organize boat trips on the lake (the *Apadi*, *Pondok Eka* and *Al'Salam*) at a standard rate of 15,000Rp. **NB** It is hard to organize such an outing independently, and it is best to go early in the morning or evening as there is no shade except at the floating houses (see below). The boat, with outboard motor, sets out from the river, 5 mins walk from the bemo station, and then proceeds upstream passing stilt houses belonging to the fishermen who earn their livelihoods on the lake. Once on the lake, the boats usually visit one of the floating villages moored off shore and consisting of houses built on bamboo rafts. Swimming from these houses is recommended. Occasionally, large iguanas can be seen at the lake edge. For the more adventurous it is possible to cross the lake (2 hrs) and then trek up into the hills on the far side.

Buginese textiles of Sengkang

It is said that 4,700 women weave nearly 500,000 sarongs a year on back-strap looms in the Sengkang area. This is the only place in Indonesia where silk is produced in large quantities. Imported yarn tends to be used for the warp, and local yarn for the weft. Chemical, aniline dyes have replaced natural dyes to a large extent but traditional Buginese designs are still much in evidence. These include plaids, checks and stripes. The distinctive zig-zag pattern – known as *bombang* or wave pattern – is produced using a warp ikat technique. Also popular are floral designs picked out using a supplementary metallic weft.

Sengkang

To Bone & Ujung Pandang

Jl A Yani

Radio Mast

Jl Pahlawan

Museum

Jl Kartini

Jl Kenanga

Supermarket

Jl Mesjid Raya

Risman-Putra Office

Jl Jawa

Central Market

Cinema

Sejahtera

Bemo Station

Jl Andi Nalingkaan

Jl Sudirman

To Palopo

Boats to Lake Tempe

Sketch map

Hotels:
1. Al'Salam I
2. Al'Salam II
3. Apada
4. Asoka Inn
5. Pondok Eka
6. Wisma Ayumi
7. Wisma Bukit Nusa Indah
8. Wisma Dan Herawaty
9. Wisma Lamaddukkelleng

Places to eat:
10. Romantis
11. Tomudi

Excursions Trekking in the hills on the far side of Lake Tempe from Sengkang. Arrange for a boat to take you across the lake (2 hrs) and set out from there. Ask at your hotel for further information on routes.

Paddle boats from fishermen in the villages along the lake shore near Sengkang. It is then possible to venture on to the lake to **birdwatch** rather more discretely and, during the right season, to see the lotus flowers which stand up to 2m above the lake's surface. The boats are hired out for about 4,000Rp/hr. *Getting there*: to reach the fishing villages take a bemo from the station on Jl Agus Salin (500Rp).

A **boat trip** downriver to **Salotangah** is worthwhile. The village on the lake consists of about 20 stilt dwellings and the journey there and back takes about 2½ hrs. *Getting there*: hire a boat from town, about 15,000Rp, or through your hotel, about 20,000Rp. The advantage of paying the extra is that hotel-arranged trips usually include tea in one of the

fishermen's houses. Another possibility is to go to the pier in the village of **Tempe**, 3 km outside Sengkang (look out for the large mosque). Here boats are available for charter even more cheaply.

Sempang is a silk-weaving town 6 km outside Sengkang where the process can be easily seen. *Getting there*: by bemo from the Bemo station.

Tours Boat tours on Lake Tempe are the most popular thing to do in Sengkang (see above for description). The *Apada, Pondok Eka* and *Al'Salam* hotels all offer boat tours.

Festivals Aug (3rd week): *Tempe Lake Festival*, annual fishing boat races.

● **Accommodation C** *Asoka Inn*, Jl Latenri-vali 3, T 21526, spacious lounge with comfortable sofas, rooms at the front are cleanest, owned by ex-regional government official (now based in Ujung Pandang), close to museum and bank, good for hill walks; **D** *Al'Salam II*, Jl Emmy Saelan 8, T 21278, some a/c, restaurant (rec), family run hotel with rooms located around peaceful communal lounge, 8 new rm on 1st flr have a view of sorts (cheaper rooms are dark), beware of low door frames to bathrooms, good size rooms with attached mandi/shower, central location, helpful and reliable guide, Zubaer, speaks good English, French and German, very popular, best in town, although they do tend to over-push their tours, rec; **D** *Apada*, Jl Durian, restaurant, the house of a Buginese aristocrat transformed into a hotel with traditional atmosphere, the rooms are clean, location inconvenient for bemo station and restaurants, set in residential area close to police station; **D** *Pondok Eka*, Jl Maluku 12, T 21296, rickety looking traditional wooden house, relaxing verandah, 2 mins walk from the bemo station, noisy when there is a film showing next door, but good value and welcoming; **D** *Wisma Lamaddukkelleng*, Jl Kenango, T 21157, wooden building in poorly kept grounds, next door to the mosque, owner is a CB radio ham, overpriced, on outskirts of town; **E** *Al'Salam I*, Jl A Nalingkaan, opp the bemo station exit, same owner as *Al'Salam II*, but dirty, if you end up here by mistake transfer to *Al'Salam II*; **E** *Wisma Ayumi*, Jl A Yani 13, T 21009, close to museum, in residential part of town, colonial house with spacious, clean rooms and attached mandi, rec; **E** *Wisma Bukit Nusa Indah*, Jl Lamungkace Toaddamang 12, T 21448, good location on the side of a hill, view across town and lake, awkward to get to by Bejak because of its hill position, but as a result the only place in town with a decent view (just below 'Pasanggrahan Hirawati' and radio tower); **E** *Wisma Dan Herawaty*, Jl A Yani 20, T 48482.

● **Places to eat** Several small restaurants, with good food at very reasonable prices. **◆◆***Romantis*, Jl Petta Rani, excellent Indonesian; **◆◆***Tomudi*, Jl Andi Oddang, chicken a speciality; *Al'Salam II Restaurant*, people come every evening to eat here from other hotels, excellent shrimps when in stock, and good fruit juices, caters for western tastes, excellent coffee, cold beers, continental breakfast.

● **Shopping Silk**: Sengkang is a centre of silk production, (see box). Hand-woven silk is becoming harder to find, but there is plenty of machine-made cloth. The *Mustaquiem* factory on Jl A Panggaru is the best known but seems to be rather over-priced now; local guides are the best source of information on other weaving factories in the area. **NB** Depending on the stage of silk production, visits can be more or less interesting.

● **Transport Road Bus**: the terminal is in the town centre; regular connections with Ujung Pandang and Pare Pare. The best service is provided by *Steven Bus Co* which departs at 0900, 1000, 1400, 1800 and travels via Pare Pare (6,000Rp); Watampone, 3 hrs (2,000Rp), very poor road; Palopo, 3 hrs (4,000Rp), good road. There are no direct buses to Rantepao. It is necessary to catch a bus to Lawawoi, and there change to a bus for Rentepao. Buses will pick passengers up from their hotels. **NB** Only bemo minibuses travel to Ujung Pandang via the central route through Camba and Bantimurung; the road is poor and the trip is very uncomfortable, although the scenery more spectacular.

TORAJA

The mountainous N region of S Sulawesi is inhabited by the Toraja. The name is probably taken from the Buginese words, *to ri aja* – meaning 'those people in the highlands upstream'. The Sa'dan Toraja live in the basin of the Sa'dan River at an altitude of 900-1,200m, in the administrative district of Tana Toraja (often known by its acronym Tator). They number about 320,000. The capital and largest town in the area is Makale, although Rantepao, a local market town about 17 km to the N, has developed into the main tourist base. It is to visit Toraja that most visitors venture to Sulawesi.

It is not hard to understand why this remote area should have become such a tourist attraction: cool and refreshing weather; breathtaking scenery of limestone cliffs sharply contrasting with lush valleys and terraced rice fields; and a people who live in extraordinary boat-shaped houses, spend their savings on elaborate funeral ceremonies, and place their dead in holes carved into the limestone cliffs. All this contributes to make Toraja one of the highlights of any trip to Indonesia.

HISTORY

Local mythology maintains that the Toraja originated from the island of Pongko'. It is said that 8 boats set sail from Pongko' and were driven by a storm onto the shores of S Sulawesi. Following the Sa'dan River upstream, the original ancestors arrived after a long and eventful journey in the area

The buffalo: symbol of wealth and power

Buffalo are the most highly prized animals in Torajan society. Wealth is measured in terms of buffalo – it is often said of a rich or important man "He has a lot of buffalo". Buffalo are also associated with men, while pigs are linked with women. Even today, riceland is not valued in terms of its yield but according to the buffalo standard – in other words, how many buffalo were sacrificed at the funeral of the field's previous owner. As Toby Alice Volkman writes in her book *Feasts of honour*: "Buffalo, in short, are symbols of the person, his land and ancestors, and his wealth and power".

Buffalo come with different colourings, hair swirls, horn shapes and eyes, and each of these factors is taken into account in the valuation of an animal. A buffalo with the right colour configuration can command a very high price. The most valuable are piebalds – but with white heads and black bodies – pink spots and blue eyes, known as *bonga*. They can be sold for as much as 6-7 million rupiahs (US$3,000-3,500). A standard slate grey buffalo, in contrast, sells for only 1-2 million rupiahs, while an all white animal is only worth 200,000 rupiahs (US$100). Also prized are long legs and horns. Buffaloes with black bodies are thought to be very strong and good for fighting.

The buffalo and their horns are status symbols; a buffalo is given as a bride price, as well as gifts at funerals. They are rarely put to work in the fields but are cosseted and pampered, bathed and polished, even their genitals rubbed, until it is time to present them for a sacrifice. Generally, a woman's funeral warrants the slaughtering of an additional animal – in payment for the milk she has provided for her children. Depictions of buffalo are prominent on Torajan houses and rice barns. Buffalo heads adorn the *tulak somba*, whilst stylized low relief images are often carved on doors of rice barns, on interior doors within the homes, or on the shutters of graves. They act as guardians, to ward off evil spirits.

nowknownas Toraja.

Whatever the true origins of the Torajans, they remained isolated from the outside world for considerably longer than the Buginese and Makassarese of the coast. They experienced an unhappy period of occupation during the 17th century, when fierce Buginese warriors – aided and abetted by the Dutch East Indies Company – invaded their land and ransacked their sacred burial sites. Naturally, the Toraja were incensed by this desecration and after a period of 7 years, they rebelled, slaughtered the interlopers and regained control of the area. Little information leaked out of their inaccessible highland home until the 20th century. The French Jesuit priest, Nicolas Gervaise, mentions the Toraja at the end of the 17th century, and the White Raja James Brooke also wrote of the 'Turajah' in the mid-19th century – but both were second-hand reports.

Two Swiss scientist-explorers, the Sarasins, together with a Dutchman, Van Rijn, were the first Europeans to cross the lands of the Toraja from coast to coast in 1902. However, even they failed to discover the Torajan heartland. It was not until 1905 that the Dutch finally decided it was time to extend their control into the highlands and to subdue these 'primitive' people. Among the Torajan leaders, only Pong Tiku resisted the Dutch for long. Fighting a guerrilla campaign, he and his men frustrated the Dutch for two years, finally succumbing to their enemy's far greater firepower in Oct 1906. An old woman, Ne'Bulaan, remembers when she first saw the Dutch: "I was just a girl, and then they came, thorns on their feet and smoke pouring from their mouths! Waduuh, I was scared". Pong Tiku was awarded with the title 'National Hero' in 1960.

On achieving supremacy in the highlands, the Dutch abolished slavery and, in 1913, sent the first missionaries of the Dutch Reformed Church into the area. But conversions were few: by 1930, only 1,700 Torajans had been converted to Christianity (1% of the population), and in 1950 when Indonesia attained independence, the figure had risen to just 10%. Today however, over 80% are nominal Christians – mostly Protestants – although traditional beliefs and practices still exert a pervasive influence, most clearly evident in their elaborate funeral ceremonies. This rapid spread of Christianity since independence is said to have been driven by the Torajan's fear of *to sallang* – Muslims.

CULTURE

Traditional society and religion

The Toraja world consisted of three classes of people: nobles or *to parengnge'* (literally, 'to carry a heavy load'), commoners or *makaka*, and – formerly – slaves, or *kaunan*. Slavery was common until the beginning of this century and there are numerous accounts of women being plucked from their fields and houses and sold into slavery. Even visiting the market demanded a protective escort, and many villages were surrounded by earthern and stone ramparts, and connected to neighbouring villages by underground passageways. People even sold their own brothers 'like buffalo or vegetables'.

The traditional 'religion' of the Toraja is called *Aluk to Dolo*, meaning Ceremonies of the Ancestors. It is based around the complementary elements of life and death, E and W, sunrise and sunset, morning and afternoon, and right and left (known to anthropologists as 'complementary binary opposition'). These contrasting elements are reflected in house architecture and the timing of rituals. Rituals associated with rice, and therefore life, are held in the mornings, people will face E and wear light clothes; while funerals are held after noon, people will face W and wear black. 'Rituals of the East' are known as *rambu tuka'* which means 'smoke ascending', and are concerned with life-giving events. They include rice rituals, rituals of exorcism to heal the sick, birth rituals, the first haircut, circumcision, teeth-filing, body decoration, weddings – even growth, prosperity and the rising of the sun. 'Rituals of the West' or *rambu solo*, which means 'smoke descending' are concerned with death, decrease and the setting sun.

Village and house

Among the many notable features of Torajan culture and life are their stunning peaked houses. Many are anything from 1 to 3 centuries old, although the bamboo roofs are changed every 50 years or so. Houses are known as *banua*, or, if the house is the 'ancestral seat' of an important family, as *tongkonan* – a name derived from the word *tongkon*, which means 'to sit'.

The village Torajan villages or *tondok* have changed since the Dutch pacified the highlands at the beginning of this century. Before then, villages were built on ridges or at the top of hills to provide protection against attack. The Dutch encouraged communities to relocate in the valleys, and few of these newer villages have the defensive ramparts that were such a feature of earlier settlements. A village will often consist of a line of houses, facing a line of rice barns. The residence or *tongkonan* is the 'mother' house, while the rice barn or *alang* is the 'father' house. The latter is a miniature copy of the former. Tradition requires that the roof-lines of both are aligned N-S, a requirement which gives Torajan villages a certain orderliness.

Another important division is between the two ritual grounds that every village must have: to the W is an area reserved for burial rites and associated with death; to the E is an area associated with life, crops, livestock and the general well-being of the community. Villages should also have a rock face burial ground – although given the shortage of such sites, this may be shared with another village.

The house The Torajan house bears some resemblance to the houses of the Batak (see page 470), the Niha of the Nias Islands (page 475), and the Minangkabau (page 483). The shape resembles a boat, and this is said to symbolize the boats that brought the original inhabitants to Sulawesi (see above).

Torajan houses are raised off the ground on sturdy piles. The area between the piles, below the living quarters, is known as the *bala bala* and was originally used to stable buffalo. Today it is more commonly used for the storage of farm implements. A steep staircase leads from the E side of the house into the home. There are three rooms. The back room or *sumbung* is the sleeping quarters of the head of the household and his wife and small children. Valuables and important heirlooms are also stored here. Unmarried girls sleep in the front room or *tangdo'* (sometimes *sondong*). While the central room or *sali* is the main living and eating area, and is also used as the sleeping area for young, unmarried men. The hearth is positioned on the E side of the *sali* – the E, and food, both being associated with life. The Torajans never sleep with their feet pointing towards the W, as this is the direction of death.

The N gable of the house – facing the rice barn – is one of the most sacred parts of the house, particularly the triangular upper part, which is sometimes called the *lindo puang* or 'face of the lords'. The Torajans believe that this is where the gods enter the house and it is here that heirlooms are hung during important rituals. In the case of *tongkonan*, the lindo puang is protected by the overhang of the roof, which is known as the *longa*. The *tulak somba* are the posts at either end of the more important houses, which support the roof ends, and are often elaborately decorated with geometric patterns, buffalo horns, carved images of buffalo heads (known as *kabongo* and images of the *katik* bird.

The rice barn or *alang* faces the home. It is like a house in miniature, but all the

Tongkonan: Toraja House

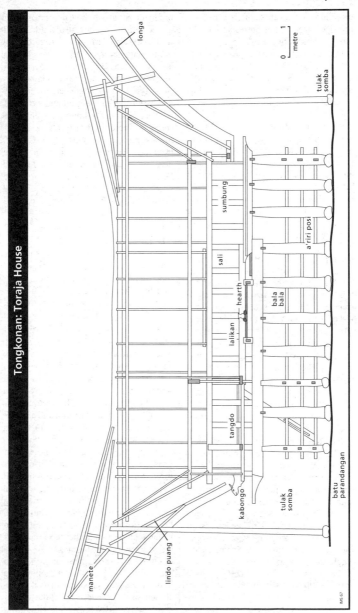

IMS 67

directions are reversed. This is because the rice barn neither belongs to one binary element, nor the other (see note on complementary binary opposition, page 635). It contains both the rice seed for the next year's crop and traditionally, human skulls. The rice barn is therefore a mediator, where life and death meet, and so its orientation is inverted. In western culture the classic mediator is New Year's Eve – neither 1 year nor the next – when, for example, officers serve their men, reversing roles. In Thailand and Laos, New Year – or Pimai – usually falls in mid-Apr, but again it represents a period when people can take liberties, dousing one another with water. The impressive piles supporting the structure are round, unlike those of the house which are rectangular. The wood of these piles is polished, to prevent mice from climbing up into the granary. The platform below the storage area is used for sitting and socializing as well as for sleeping during festivals. The inner walls of the barn and the ceiling of the sitting area are traditionally decorated with geometric patterns and scenes from everyday life. The area of ground between the house and the rice barn is known as the *parampa* and is used to dry rice or coffee, as a space for children to play, men to stage cock-fights and women to work (for instance, at weaving).

The house represents a microcosm of the Torajan world. Like the houses of the Batak and Minangkabau, it can be divided into three sections: the roof and gables represent the Upper World of gods and spirits; the central living area, the Middle World of men and earthly concerns; while the *bala bala* represents the Under World. A central post, known as the *a'riri posi'* (or navel post) connects the whole structure with the earth.

The Torajan death ritual

The Toraja people are probably best known in the W for their elaborate death

or funeral ritual – the *aluk rambe matampu'* – which transports the soul of the deceased to the next life. This elaborate ceremony is the major event in the life cycle of a Torajan and the costs of mounting an *aluk rambe matampu'* can be financially crippling for the family concerned. Rituals vary according to the rank and wealth of the dead person: for a noble, an elaborate ceremony is required, lasting up to 7 days; for a commoner, a more modest event, extending over only 1 or 2 days. Unless the deceased is given an appropriate funeral, he or she is unable to become an active ancestor and watch over the rice and the family group. The Torajans accept the ephemeral nature of life:

> "We are as the phantoms of this world,
> the apparitions of this region,
> as the wind that blows along the house."

The aluk rambe matampu' consists of three stages, which are adhered to whatever the status of the deceased: first the wrapping of the corpse and lamentation, then the funeral ritual and the associated slaughter of animals, and last the entombment of the corpse in a rock grave.

The wrapping and lamentation After a person dies, they are dressed in ceremonial clothes and placed on a chair in the southern-most room of the house. Several days later, the corpse is cacooned in multiple layers of funeral shroud and a kapok blanket and then transferred to the W side of the central room. The body remains in the house until the second phase. This may involve a wait of anything from 6 months to 6 years – indeed, in 1985, it was reported that there was one dead person still waiting to be buried who had died during the Japanese occupation. During this period of waiting, the death is not acknowledged; the deceased is referred to simply as the 'sick one'.

Over the subsequent months and years, considerable sums of money have to be amassed, relatives informed, a site chosen for the construction of the temporary houses needed to stage the ritual, and

Torajan mortuary effigies (tau tau)

🐋 *Tau tau* means 'little person' and refers to the wooden, life-sized, effigies of the deceased, which are to be found on stone galleries carved out of the cliffs, or on wooden hanging galleries, positioned close to burial vaults. Tau tau images are only commissioned following the death of wealthy people or nobles. Some (lesser) tau tau – known as *tau tau lampa* – are made out of bamboo and cloth, but they are rare. Full tau tau are carved from the durable wood of the jackfruit tree (*nangka*) and are repaired every 25 years or so. An event known as *Ma'nene* is performed sometime between Jul and Sep, when the tau tau's clothing is replaced.

A living jackfruit tree is cut to provide the wood for the carving. The lemon-yellow wood is treated with coconut oil over several weeks to stain it to the colour of the Torajan skin, and then a specialist sculptor ritually carves the image. The body is made of several pieces which are moveable – rather like a puppet – and during the funeral ceremony the figure may be manipulated. As the tau tau is a 'living' representation of the deceased, great attention is paid to detail. Traditionally, the head was carved with almond-shaped eyes and finely formed features. Under the sarong, sexual organs are carefully carved – the male penis always erect. The clothing also helps to establish the identity of the deceased. In modern images, the figure is almost an exact representation of the deceased.

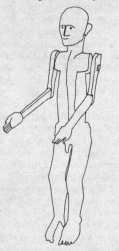

A problem that has arisen in recent years is the stealing of tau tau images. As demand for these aesthetically pleasing carvings has increased in the West, so the incentive to raid cliff face galleries has likewise increased. The spread of Christianity may also have played a role, reducing the traditional fear of these spirit-imbued figures. Today many are duplicates – the originals having disappeared during the night, doubtless to be sold to collectors.

Tau tau with atriculated arms, 1-2m high, wood.

agreement reached on suitable contributions of buffalo. In addition, the rice has to have been harvested before the ceremony can commence. The following description of the second phase of the ceremony only applies to the *Dipirai* – the most elaborate of the ceremonies. It should also be noted that because most Torajans are now nominal Christians, the traditional ceremony is becoming increasingly rare.

The funeral and ritual slaughter The houses for the funeral ceremony are constructed to form a square around the *rante*

(the place chosen for the funeral rites). Older *rante* may have megaliths standing in them. In the centre of the rante stands the *lakkean* or 'corpse tower'. The tower is several storeys high and is surmounted with a roof similar in style to that of the Torajan house. A bier – or *sarigan* – is also constructed in the shape of a miniature house.

The second phase is heralded by the transferring of the body from the house to the floor of the rice barn. At this stage, a buffalo is sacrificed – preferably one with a white head and black body. The *tau tau* – a representation or portrait of the deceased (see box) – is held by the sculptor, who manipulates it, and precedes the body in procession to the rice barn.

After 2 days, the corpse is transferred to the bier and a colourful procession – known as the *mapalao* – moves off in the direction of the *rante* or funeral field. Upon arrival, the body is paraded around the central *lakkean* three times and is then transferred to a platform, where other family members sit.

From this point, the festivities get into full swing. Buffalo fights, dances, parades and kick fights (*sisepak*) take place (although kick fights have been officially banned). Funerals are important social events. As Torajans explain, "if there were no funerals, none of us would ever get married". The next day, the guests (dressed in black) are formally received and the slaughtering of the animals begins. Buffalo are slaughtered in a central area on the ceremonial field in front of the guests. This is not for the faint-hearted; the entire central area becomes awash with blood and gore, staring buffalo heads, bones, hooves, entrails and dung. The pigs are often slaughtered out of sight, and are then carried in for dismemberment, after having been singed over an open fire. In the past, the crowd would attack the animal alive and dismember it – this practice was banned by the Dutch. Each animal, as it is slaughtered, is registered in a notebook and a value placed against the gift. The value of buffalos is determined by an appraisal of a combination of factors: size, condition, horn shape and colour configuration. Single-coloured black/grey buffalo are the least highly valued at between 500,000Rp and 3,000,000Rp. A piebald pink and white animal may fetch anything up to 10,000,000Rp though. After offerings to the ancestors, the meat is shared out among the guests, palm wine (*tuak*) contained in bamboo is passed around, more dancing takes place and buffalo – and cock-fights (also banned) – are organized.

The entombment Several days later, after all the sacrifices have taken place and debts recorded, the guests start to leave, carrying their meat with them strung onto bamboo poles. A small procession of close family then accompanies the corpse to its final resting place with its ancestors (this stage is known as *mapeliang*). These resting places are traditionally burial vaults carved out of the limestone cliffs. Family members climb bamboo ladders and clear out a place in the vault to make room for the corpse. The body is placed in the tomb head first, with its feet towards the door; thus easing the passage of the soul to the next world (the *Tondok Bombo*, or Land of the Souls). Then the *tau tau* of the deceased is placed with the other mortuary effigies in a gallery on the cliff face. At this point a black chicken is released at the burial site, symbolizing the release of the soul.

Visiting a funeral ceremony

It is not difficult to find out where and when ceremonies are due to occur; local guides make it their business to discover where they are taking place and hotel staff are also often well informed. Jul and Aug is the most active funeral period as this coincides with the long Indonesian holiday and is the period when Torajans living away from home can return to their villages. If you are visiting a ceremony and are invited into the guests' enclosure, it is usual to bring a small gift – several packets of cigarettes for example. Visitors are generally welcomed at such events, but they should dress modestly and be sensitive to the occasion.

The burial chamber

There are four kinds of burial place in Tana Toraja. The oldest burial places are the *erong*, which date back about 500 years. These are beautifully carved wooden sarcophagi, which were placed at the base of cliffs. They were made in the shape of boats, houses or animals; possibly signifying different ranks of the deceased. Heirlooms and other valued possessions were placed in the erong along with the corpse. In the 17th century, marauding Buginese working for the Dutch East India Company invaded Tana Toraja and plundered these sacred burial sites (see page 634). When, after 7 years of occupation, the Buginese were ejected, the Toraja abandoned the erong system of burial as too vulnerable.

Instead, they began to cut tombs – known as *keborang batu* – high-up in inaccessible limestone cliff faces. This new form of burial was made possible due to the metal-working skills the Torajans had acquired during the Buginese occupation, enabling them to make iron chisels and other metal tools. They now placed their dead, along with their valuables, in these catacombs, safely sealed behind wooden doors. Only by climbing high up the vertical cliff face could these graves be plundered.

The most recent burial method to emerge is the *burial 'house'*. These are associated with the pacification of the area in the 20th century and, also, a simple lack of cliff space. An example of these ground-level tombs can be seen at Ke'te Kesu' (see page 644).

Finally, there are the *'tree graves'* of babies who die before their first tooth is cut. The corpse is taken to an *antolong* tree (also known as *kayu mate*, literally 'dead wood'), and placed in a cavity hollowed out of the trunk. The hole is covered with fibres from the sugar palm, a dog and pig slaughtered, and the tree allowed to grow around the baby's body (see Kembira excursion, page 645).

Further reading Crystal, Eric (1985) "The soul that is seen: the tau tau as shadow of death", in: Jerome Feldman (edit) *The eloquent dead: ancestral sculpture of Indonesia and Southeast Asia*, UCLA: Los Angeles. Well illustrated article. Kis-Jovak, JI *et al* (1988) *Banua Toraja: changing patterns in architecture and symbolism among the Sa'dan Toraja, Sulawesi*, Royal Tropical Institute: Amsterdam. Wonderful black and white photo-essay with informative text. Nooy-Palm, Netty (1986) *The Sa'dan Toraja: a study of their social life and religion – rituals of the east and west*, Foris: Dordrecht. Dense but informative anthropological work. Volkman, Toby A (1985) *Feasts of honour: ritual and change in the Toraja highlands*, University of Illinois Press: Urbana. Readable account – part academic, part personal – of an anthropologist's stay in Toraja.

ECONOMY

In the past, the Toraja economy was founded on the cultivation of wet rice (see page 80) in the upland valleys that dissect the area. Rice is still the pre-eminent subsistence and ritual crop, although other activities are taking on increasing importance. The rice cycle lasts 6 months and in addition to white rice, black rice (*nasi hitam*) and red rice (mixed with coconut milk for sweets) are also cultivated. Other crops include maize, cassava and vegetables, while the raising of livestock, both for sale and ritual purposes, is also important.

Since the late 1970s, tourism has played an increasing role in the local economy. As ever, there are those who view this with concern, maintaining it is undermining local customs, and those who welcome it as a healthy diversification of economic activity. Many younger Torajans have moved away to Ujung Pandang, partly because of the lack of agricultural land and partly because they no longer want to farm. Paradoxically, this exodus has probably helped to keep Torajan traditions alive – the migrants send money home to finance funeral ceremonies and return for important ceremonies. When a migrant dies away from home, he will often be transported back to be buried with his ancestors.

Best time to visit: during the dry season, Mar-Nov. During the wet season, Dec-Feb, it may be difficult to get to the more out-of-the-way sights, although those close to the main roads are accessible. Room rates are also considerably lower. Night time temperatures range between 15°C and 23°C, daytime temperatures, 20°C to 32°C.

Tana Toraja entrance fee: foreigners entering Tana Toraja now have to pay an entrance fee of 3,500Rp.

MAKALE

Makale is the largest town in the Toraja region and the administrative capital of the district of Tana Toraja. Most tourists choose to stay in Rantepao, 17 km to the N, which has a much more extensive tourist infrastructure. However, there are a number of hotels and losmen in Makale

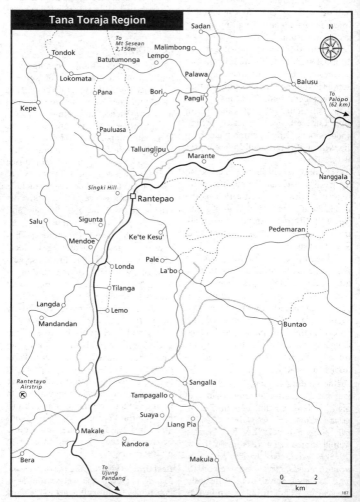

Tana Toraja Region

N

To Mt Sesean 2,150m

Sadan
Malimbong
Tondok
Batutumonga
Lempo
Palawa
Lokomata
Pana
Bori
Pangli
Balusu
Kepe

To Palopo (62 km)

Pauluasa
Tallunglipu
Marante
Nanggala

Singki Hill
□ Rantepao

Salu
Sigunta
Ke'te Kesu'
Pedemaran
Mendoe
Pale
Londa
La'bo
Tilanga
Langda
Lemo
Buntao
Mandandan

Rantetayo Airstrip ⊗

Sangalla
Tampagallo
Suaya
Liang Pia
Makale
Kandora
Bera
Makula

To Ujung Pandang

0   2
km

which are cheaper and some visitors also prefer the less touristic atmosphere. The heart of the town is arranged around a large – and sometimes empty – artificial lake. The **Pasar Umum** (General Market) is at the end of Jl Pasar Baru. The pig market is held on Mondays.

Excursions
Most of the sights in the area are equally accessible from Makale and Rantepao, and some are considerably closer to Makale (see Excursions Rantepao).

Local information
● **Accommodation**
A *Marannu City*, Jl Pongtiku 116-118 (1 km N of town), T 22221, F 22020, restaurant, pool, tennis courts, best hotel in Makale with good facilities but little character, rooms have a/c, TV, hot water and mini bars; A *Sahid Toraja*, Jl Raya Gettengan 1 Mengkendek, T 22444, F 22167, 12 km S of Makale, a/c, restaurant, pool, tennis, Torajan style houses.

E *Batupapan*, Jl Pongtiku (2 km N of town); E *Wisma Bungin*, Jl Nusantara 35, T 22255, central, nr the lake, clean rooms with bathrooms, rec; E *Wisma Puri Artha*, Jl Pongtiku, T 22047, N of town, basic.

F *Losmen Merry*, Jl Muh Yamin 168, T 22013, rudimentary rooms, nr bus offices. The main road has changed its name from Jl Pongtiku to Jl Nusantara – most of the hotels have yet to acknowledge the change.

● **Post & telecommunications**
Area code: 0423.
Perumtel (international telephone, telegram & fax): Jl Pongtiku 8 (N of town).

● **Hospitals & medical services**
Hospitals: *Fatima*, Jl Pongtiku 103.

● **Transport**
17 km from Rantepao, 79 km from Palopo, 156 km from Pare Pare, 333 km from Ujung Pandang.
Local regular bemo connections with Rantepao (500Rp).
Air See Transport to and from Rantepao, page 650.
Road Bus: regular connections with Rantepao 40 mins, Pare Pare and Ujung Pandang. Also buses to Poso and Palu 36 hrs, Tator, Watampone, Polmas and Pinrang. Most of the bus

companies have their offices on Jl Ikhwan, off the central square. Note that most buses for Ujung Pandang and other points S leave from Rantepao and may be full by the time they arrive in Makale, so it is best to reserve a seat.

RANTEPAO
This rather ramshackle market town is utterly overshadowed by the beautiful countryside and villages which surround it. It has become a 'tourist centre' because it is undoubtedly the best base from which to explore the surrounding area. The four roads into town meet at a roundabout, where there is a miniature tongkonan (Torajan house). The central market has some handicrafts, textiles and 'antiques' for sale (see shopping).

The only sight that Rantepao itself has to offer is the weekly **pig and buffalo market**, held on Wednesdays, a few kilometres N of town. The pig market, when 100s of animals are brought in from the surrounding villages, is the more lively; the buffalo market is rather slower. To get to the market, take either one of the direct market bemos or a vehicle running towards Sa'dan and Lempo.

Excursions
Getting around the sites of Toraja Because the sites of interest around Rantepao are scattered over a wide area, it is easiest to charter a car or bemo for the day (see Local transport). Public bemos do travel along most roads, but it is often a time-consuming business getting from one sight to the next. It is also possible to hire motorbikes and bicycles in town (see Local transport). However, many visitors find that the best way to see the sights, and experience the surrounding countryside, is on foot. The climate is cool enough to make walking very pleasant, roads are rarely busy, and most sights are less than 10 km from Rantepao. Note that local drivers – understandably – often insist it is only possible to see the sights of the area with a guide; this is not true. By buying a good map and asking questions it is quite possible to explore the area. *Admission to*

Trekking around Rantepao

One of the best ways to see and experience the Torajan highlands is to go on an organized trek for several days. There are a number of local guides in Rantepao who will arrange and lead trekking expeditions. There are few losmen outside the main towns, the exception being the village of Batu Tumonga, to the NW of Rantepao, where there are five, and Mamasa. Outside these two villages, expect to stay with the *kepala desa* (headman), the local teacher, or with another family. **NB** That it is usual to bring small gifts for your host (soap, cigarettes etc). Horses can sometimes be hired to carry baggage (10,000Rp/day). Most treks explore the hills, valleys and villages to the W of Rantepao. Expect to pay US$60/day for two, all inclusive (local guides hired independently of tour companies will be cheaper). The best time to trek is between Mar and Nov. Treks, with approximate length, include:

Rantepao–Sesean–Rantepao: 2 days/1 night
Rantepao–Sesean–Dende–Rantepao: 3 days/2 nights
Bittuang–Mamasa: 3 days/4 nights
Ulusalu–Pangala–Rantepao: 4 days/3 nights
Mamasa–Ulusalu–Rantepao: 5 days/4 nights

Trekking companies *Eskell*, Jl Pongtiku, T 21344, F 21500, and *Ramayana Satrya*, Jl Pongtiku, T 21336, F 21485 are both recommended. There are also many private guides who can be hired for about $15-25/day. Ask at your hotel or visit the Tourist Office in Rantepao and ask for a recommendation.

Suggested equipment Good walking shoes, hat, sweater for the nights, sleeping roll, sleeping bag, food for lunches, water (or a means of boiling, or sterilizing it), mosquito repellent, gifts for your hosts.

villages: most villages expect visitors to make a donation of about 1,000Rp before they intrude into their communities.

Southeast from Rantepao

Ke'te Kesu' is the first stop travelling S from Rantepao; take the left-hand turn about 1 km S of town and continue for another 4 km to the village. Ke'te Kesu' has perhaps the finest collections of **tongkonan** (see page 636) in the Rantepao area. If visitors do not wish to hire a car or have limited time this is one site worth visiting which has a cross section of all aspects of Toraja village life; it can be reached on foot (1 hr) from Rantepao (take first left out of town going S, by *Rantepao Lodge*. The central of the larger houses contains a small museum. Walk behind the village and down a slope to see the tomb of a village chief (with a very life-like *tau tau*) and, further on, some hanging graves with

fine carving and cliff graves. **NB** The modern *tau tau* noble with orange robes, glasses and umbrella, in the glass display case. The family tomb is a modern concrete structure. *Getting there*: bemos run along the road to this village.

Londa is a burial site about 5 km S of Rantepao, and 1 km off the main road. There is a series of caves here containing coffins and bones with rows of *tau tau* effigies (see page 639) overhead. All *tau tau* have been placed in a cage to prevent theft. They are rather gloomy caves, full of bones, but it is a popular attraction, firmly on the tour group route. Guide with lamp 1,000Rp (or cunningly use the light of others). A path leads from Londa to Tilanga, and from there on to Lemo. But it is not well marked – ask along the way.

Tilanga, a natural spring and swimming-pool, lies 9 km S of town, also off the main road. It is busy at weekends and rather dirty. A path leads from here to Lemo, and also N to Londa – ask for directions.

Lemo lies 1 km off the main road, the turning is a little further S from Londa and about 9½ km from town. This is a superbly positioned burial site overlooking paddy fields. It is best to come here early in the morning before the crowds arrive, when the sun illuminates the rock face with its rows of *tau tau* effigies and graves hewn out of the cliff face. A path leads up and around the limestone outcrop to other, less impressive, grave niches. Follow the path to the left along the cliff face, past further 'common' graves (no *tau tau*), and back across the paddy fields. On the other side of the paddy fields from the cliff face is a *tau tau* carver workshop open for visitors. There is also a group of Tongkonan, but better examples of the houses can be seen at Nanggala. A path leads from Lemo N to Tilanga and from there to Londa – ask directions. **NB** Paths are slippery, and some of the steps are steep.

Suaya lies about 8 km E of Makale, up a steep and winding (deteriorating) road (negotiable by car). This was a noble burial site, and some of the coffins are said to be 500 years old. Attractively decrepit white *tau tau* effigies occupy niches in the rock face here. At the base of the cliff is the grave of a noble daughter who left the village and married a Muslim; as a convert she could not be buried in the cliff. A building houses what can be best described as *objets mort* – very weathered boat and buffalo coffins containing skeletal remains. A steep climb to the right of the effigies leads up to a viewpoint from where it is possible to look up and down the beautiful valley. There is a beautiful 1-hr walk up the valley beyond the graves to the Sangalla-Makale road. The ponds which can be seen in the middle of the paddy fields are a couple of metres deep. They are stocked with young fish at transplanting, and at harvest time the grown fish are given to the labourers as part of their payment. There are no bemos to Makale from here; it is necessary to walk a couple of kilometres toward Tampangallo.

Liang Pia lies E of Suaya. There are baby graves here (see page 641), set in bamboo forest. If you carry on walking past the entrance you come out on the road near the Buntu Kalando Museum (2 km).

Tampangallo is one of the most atmospheric spots in Toraja. (Negotiable by car or on foot across paddy fields from Suaya.) Turn off the road almost 1 km E of Suaya and travel about 500m down a track (negotiable by car). This limestone cave grave, set in a verdant rice valley, contains some wonderful decaying 300 year-old boat coffins, some of which may originally have been stored in hanging graves, and a quantity of skeletal remains. There are also some new *tau tau* effigies here.

The **Sarapang** baby grave is to be found 200m before Tampangallo, down a track running off the road. If a baby dies before cutting his or her teeth they are buried in cavities hollowed out of living tree trunks (see page 641).

Buntu Kalando Museum lies a short distance further E on the Suaya-Kembira road. It houses a small collection of ethnographic artefacts from Toraja. There is a restaurant here.

For the **Kembira** child grave, continue on from the museum to a 'T' junction; turn left and it is a short distance away. Along the path leading to the grave, villagers sell local spices and flavourings – vanilla, cinnamon, nutmeg, cocoa and pepper – at grossly inflated prices. The path, 200m in all, leads through a bamboo grove to a buttressed tree in which families have hewn-out niches for their dead children. These are then pegged over with a fibre curtain and the tree is allowed to grow around the corpse (see page 641). **Accommodation** Just S of Sangalla on the right hand side of the road coming from Makale, is the **E** *Kalembang Homestay*, well kept gardens, hamlet owned by noble family who still live in the confines, remote but recommended as a base for walking and seeing the sites in the region. *Getting there*: take a bemo from the bridge on the northern outskirts of Makale (10 km).

Getting to the sights SE of Rentapao
Most of these sights lie within walking distance of the main Rantepao-Makale road; bemos run constantly along the road. Fares range from 250Rp (to Marante) to 1,500Rp (to Lempo). Bemos also run E from Makale to Kembira and then N to the market town of Sangalla before looping westwards back to the main road, coming out opposite the hospital N of Makale (9 km from Kembira). Admission to sites 1,250Rp (each site).

Northeast from Rantepao
Marante is 5 km E from Rantepao and 500m off the main road, set in a beautiful valley. There are some rather untidy cliff and cave graves here and some heavily carved *tongkonan*. Follow the path past the cliff graves and the bridge to a small group of traditional houses. From here, the path returns quickly to the main road. Admis-

sion 1,250Rp. *Getting there*: regular bemos run along this road.

The turn-off for **Nanggala** is 7 km further E (12 km in all from Rantepao). The village is 1.8 km along the rough road, which makes for a pleasant walk. This village contains a great swathe of beautifully carved rice barns facing two houses, one said to be 500 years old. Near the entrance are two clumps of bamboo used by bats to roost during the day. Admission 1,500Rp. *Getting there*: regular bemos from Rantepao pass the turn-off for Nanggala.

North and northwest from Rantepao
Pangli, 8 km due N from Rantepao, contains a house grave and *tau tau* effigies. At this point the road forks; one route runs NW, while the main road continues due N. An alternative to taking the main road N is to trek along the path from **Tallunglipu**, just N of Rantepao, to **Bori** (where there are some huge *rante* stones), 6 km in all from Rantepao, and from there to the road running E-W, which is only 1½ km from Pangli.

Palawa is a hamlet 2 km N from Pangli on the main road, and 500m off the road (9½ km in all from Rantepao). Palawa consists of a wonderful double row of *tongkonan* and rice barns, with stacks of buffalo horns, dense carving and carved life-size buffalo heads. Although many of the families have set up small souvenir stalls selling cloth, woodcarvings and jewellery, few tourists make it out here and the primary source of income is still agriculture. Admission 500Rp. On the track to Palawa, about 200m before the village, is a group of neglected **megaliths**.

To'karau is a village another 1 km on the 'main' road N. A periodic market is held here.

Sa'dan is a market centre a further 4 km N. The town is an important ritual centre and has emerged in recent years as a centre of weaving. The cloths are made for the tourist market using imported

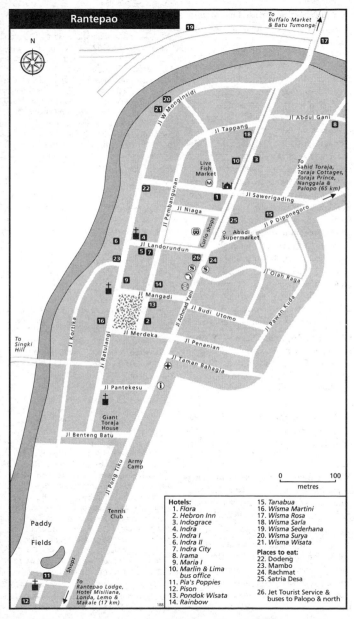

Rantepao

To Buffalo Market & Batu Tumonga

Jl W Monginsidi

Jl Tappang

Jl Abdul Gani

Jl Pembangunan

Live Fish Market

To Sahid Toraja, Toraja Cottages, Toraja Prince, Nanggala & Palopo (65 km)

Jl Sawerigading

Jl Niaga

Curio shops

Abadi Supermarket

Jl P Diponegoro

Jl Landorundun

Jl Olah Raga

Jl Achmad Yani

Jl Mangadi

Jl Budi Utomo

Jl Pawan Kuda

Jl Kortika

Jl Ratulangi

Jl Merdeka

Jl Penanian

To Singki Hill

Jl Taman Bahagia

Jl Pantekesu

Giant Toraja House

Jl Benteng Batu

Army Camp

Tennis Club

Paddy Fields

Shops

To Rantepao Lodge, Hotel Misiliana, Londa, Lemo & Makale (17 km)

Jl Pong Tiku

0   100
metres

Hotels:
1. Flora
2. Hebron Inn
3. Indograce
4. Indra
5. Indra I
6. Indra II
7. Indra City
8. Irama
9. Maria I
10. Marlin & Lima bus office
11. Pia's Poppies
12. Pison
13. Pondok Wisata
14. Rainbow

15. Tanabua
16. Wisma Martini
17. Wisma Rosa
18. Wisma Sarla
19. Wisma Sederhana
20. Wisma Surya
21. Wisma Wisata

Places to eat:
22. Dodeng
23. Mambo
24. Rachmat
25. Satria Desa

26. Jet Tourist Service & buses to Palopo & north

yarn and chemical dyes, but maintaining traditional designs and motifs (see shopping, below).

Taking the W fork at Pangli the road leads to **Deri** where it deteriorates into little more than a track. Many treks start here. **Lempo** has an attractive group of *tongkonan*. There is also a homestay here. **Batutumonga** is one of the higher points in the region; there are magnificent views over Rantepao and Makale. Take a bemo to the village, and walk down the valleys to Rantepao. Or walk from Batutumonga to **Tikala** (well signposted, about 1½ hrs), and from there catch a bemo back to Rentepao. En route to Tikala the path passes **Pana** where there are some baby graves. **Accommodation** There are four places to stay in Batutumonga: **E** *Batutumonga Homestay*, in forest, has excellent views; **E** *Mama Siska Homestay*, rec. **E** *Mentiratiku*, rooms with attached bathrooms, very clean, restaurant; **E** *Landorundun*, wooden homestay. **Avoid** the *Betani Homestay*, several bad reports.

Getting to the sights N and NW from Rantepao Bemos run from Rantepao through Pangli and on to Palawa, To'karau and Sa'dan with the road threading its way along a beautiful rice valley.

Trekking to Mamasa: it is possible to trek westwards to the Mamasa Valley. The journey takes about 3 days (see page 653).

Tours

Marthen Madoi at Wisma Tanabua on Jl Diponegoro organizes 7 day tours to N Sulawesi. For **treks** in the surrounding countryside, see box, page 644.

Rafting tours are becoming increasingly popular. Tour companies arrange trips on the Sa'dan and Maulu rivers. Day tours cost US$65, 3 day tours US$255. **Toranggo Buya**, Jl Pongtiku 48, T 21336 is one company which operates rafting trips.

Local information
● Accommodation

A+-A *Marante Highland Resort*, Jl Jurusan Palopo, PO Box 52, Rantepao, T 21616, F 21122, restaurant, pool, satellite TV, minibar, babysitting, car and mountain bikes for hire, situated 4 km outside Rantepao amidst rice fields, over 110 rooms in Toraja-style bungalows, beautifully situated and well run, probably the best of the new 'luxury' hotels that have opened in the area; **A** *Misiliana*, PO Box 01 (3 km S of town), T 21212, F 21512, restaurant, pool, large, new hotel with good amenities, comfortable rooms; a large new hotel, the **A** *Sahid Toraja*, has recently opened in Rantepao; **A** *Toraja Cottages*, Desa Bolu, Paku (3 km E of town), T 21089, F 21369, restaurant, pool, quiet location out of town, set on the side of a hill in attractive gardens; **A** *Toraja Prince* (3 km E of town), T 21304, F 21369, pool, new hotel with well appointed rooms; **A-B** *Indra*, Jl Dr Ratulangi, T 21583, F 21547, a/c, restaurant, very clean, all 19 rooms have private bathrooms, hot water and TV as well as sitting area overlooking central garden, curio and bookshop, opp *Indra I*, the best of the 'Indra chain'.

B *Hebron Inn*, Jl Pembangunan, T 21519, the best of the hotels in this range, clean and peaceful, well managed, rec; **B** *Pondok Torsina* (50m off main road, 500m S of town), T 21293, restaurant, pool, hot water, set among rice fields, large, clean rooms; **B** *Rantepao Lodge*, Jl Pao Rura (1.5 km S of town), T 21248, restaurant, good rooms and beautiful setting but beyond easy walking distance of town.

C *Indra I*, Jl Landorundun 63, T 21163, F 21547 restaurant, hot water, 14 clean and comfortable rooms with attached bathrooms, with an attempt at 'traditional' decor; **C** *Indra City*, Jl Landorundum 63, T 21060, F 21547, next to *Indra I*, 14 rooms set around a courtyard all with private bathrooms and hot water; **C** *Maria II*, Jl Pongtiku (S of town), popular; **C** *Pison*, Jl Pongtiku 8, T 21344 (just off main road, S edge of town, about 15 mins' walk from the centre), restaurant, very popular, good food, clean rooms with hot water and attached bathrooms and balconies, friendly service, quiet location, good value, rec; **C** *Pondok Wisata*, Jl Pembangunan, new hotel, large clean rooms; **C-D** *Tanabua*, Jl Diponegoro 43, T 21072, restaurant, clean, but the rooms are dark.

D *Irama*, Jl U Abdul Gani 2, T 21371, restaurant, basic but clean; **D** *Maria I*, Jl Dr Ratulangi 23, T 21165, some hot water, quiet, simple room, nice garden, (although only the more expensive rooms face onto it) rec; **D** *Pia's Poppies*, Jl Pongtiku (just off main road S edge of town), T 21121, restaurant, hot water, strange grotto-like bathrooms, the hotel has character and is friendly, overlooking rice fields, not very central but therefore peaceful, price incl breakfast, rec; **D** *Rainbow*, Jl Pembangunan (corner with Jl Mangadi), quiet rooms with attached bathrooms, tea and coffee but no breakfast incl in room rate; **D** *Wisma Martini*, Jl Dr Ratulangi 62, T 21240, tidy garden, purple veranda, peaceful and friendly, albeit a little worn now, rec; **D** *Wisma Wisata*, Jl Monginsidi 40 (next to *Wisma Surya*), T 21746, clean rooms with attached mandi, attractive position overlooking the river and a peaceful garden, rates incl breakfast, rec.

E *Flora*, Jl Sesan 25, T 21210, small losmen nr the mosque, rooms are clean but noisy; **E** *Marlin*, Jl Mappanyuki 75, restaurant, basic but clean, motorbike hire; **E** *Rosa*, Jl Pahlawan, T 21075, on the outskirts of town on the road to Sa'dan, quiet rooms with mandis in garden surroundings, rec; **E** *Sarla*, Jl Mappanyuki 83; **E** *Sederhana*, Jl Suloara 110, T 21011, room rate incl breakfast, lies outside town, over the bridge to the N, attractive setting and quiet, friendly owners; **E** *Surya*, Jl W Monginsidi 36, T 21312, next to the river, with garden and attractive views.

F *Palawa*, Jl Mappanyuki 81.

● **Places to eat**

Most hotels have their own restaurants. Local specialities include black rice (*nasi hitam*), fish and chicken cooked in bamboo (*piong*), and palm wine (*tuak*). ✦✦✦*Setia Awan*, Jl Mappanyuki, the restaurant of the *Wisma Pasadena*, prices are a little higher than in some other restaurants, but the food is good with Torajan specialities like fish cooked in bamboo, also popular with locals, which is a good sign; ✦✦✦*Tamu Pub & Restaurant*, Jl Mappanyuki, for Torajan specialities order 2 hrs ahead; ✦✦✦*Indograce*, Jl Mappanyuki (facing *Marlin Hotel*), popular place serving Chinese, Indonesian and Torajan specialities; ✦✦*Indra I*, Jl Landorundun 63, good hotel restaurant, rec; ✦✦*Mambo*, Jl Dr Ratulangi (facing *Wisma Maria I*), usually packed with tourists which perhaps explains the excruciatingly slow service, average Indonesian and international dishes, good breakfasts; ✦✦*Marendeng Restaurant* (within *Indra Hotel*), red checked table cloths, atmospheric location overlooking river and Singki Hill, evening

'shows'; ✦✦*Mart's Café and Restaurant*, Jl Dr Ratulangi 44a (facing the football pitch), open 0700-2200, clean restaurant with good and well priced food, excellent place for breakfast, the Indonesian owner studied in Ireland of all places so speaks good English; ✦✦*Pia's Poppies*, Jl Pongtiku, unbelievably slow service and over-ambitious menu; ✦✦*Pison*, Jl Pongtiku 8, good Indonesian/Chinese food, with Torajan specialities, rec; ✦*Central Market*, for cheap warung food, Indonesian and Torajan; ✦*Dodeng*, Jl Pembangunan 30 (on the market square), good Indonesian/Chinese menu incl Torajan specialities like buffalo meat and palm wine; ✦*Satria Desa*, Jl Diponegoro 15, basic Indonesian dishes; *Rachmat*, Jl Achmad Yani, large and central, geared to tour groups, Indonesian/Chinese.

● **Airline offices**

Merpati, *Rantepao Lodge*, Jl Pongtiku (S of town).

● **Banks & money changers**

Danamon, Jl Achmad Yani (next to Post Office); **Rakyat Indonesia**, Jl Achmad Yani; **Raya Eka Abadi**, Jl Achmad Yani 102.

● **Post & telecommunications**

Area code: 0423.

Perumtel: Jl Achmad Yani (next door to Post Office).

Post Office: Jl Achmad Yani 111. Poste Restante available.

● **Sport**

Rafting: on the Sa'dan and Maulu rivers, see **Tours**.

Swimming: the small pool at the *Toraja Cottages* is open to non-residents (3,000Rp).

● **Shopping**

Rantepao has a selection of shops selling crafts and some antiques. Most are concentrated in the town centre on Jl Achmad Yani, and on the ground floor of the central market. Crafts include hats, basketry, carved wooden statues, model tongkonan, and bamboo containers. Antiques include weavings and carved house panels.

Book Exchange: one on Jl Mangadi.

● **Tour companies & travel agents**

Jet Tourist Service, Jl Landorundun 1, T 21145, guides speak English, French or Italian, approx rates: guide 30,000Rp/day; trek 40,000Rp/day; vehicle and driver 60,000Rp/day; *Ramayana Satrya*, Jl Pongtiku, T 21615, F 21485.

● **Tourist offices**

Rantepao Tourist Office, Jl Achmad Yani, T 21277, free maps but little else, open 0730-1400 Mon-Sun. However, they do recommend guides which is 'safer' than taking a chance with one of the freelance guides. Expect to pay the guides about 30,000-35,000Rp/day. Note that they do not give out information of where ceremonies are occurring. This may be because they feel un-guided tourists are a hazard (which the visual evidence shows to be true in too many cases); or it may be because they do not wish to put the area's guides out of business.

● **Transport**

17 km from Makale, 62 km from Palopo, 173 km from Pare Pare, 350 km from Ujung Pandang.

Local Bemos: the 'station' is behind the central market. **Bicycle hire**: about 3,000-5,000Rp/day. **Car hire**: from 45,000Rp/day. **Chartered bemos**: can be picked up anywhere and cost about 10,000Rp/hr. **Motorbike hire**: about 25-30,000Rp/day from *Jet Travel*, *Celebes Travel* and *Wisma Tanabua*. To hire cars, motorbikes or bicycles ask at your hotel.

Air Pongtiku airport is just N of Makale and 21 km S of Rantepao. It is spectacularly built along a mountain ridge. Daily flights to Ujung Pandang. **Transport to town**: minibuses wait for the daily flight to take passengers to Rantepao (5,000Rp). (Drivers earn much of their income mainly in commissions from the hotels, so it is sometimes necessary to be very insistent.) Merpati have their office in the *Rantepao Lodge*, S of town. **NB** Fog is a problem at Pongtiku airport and it is not uncommon for planes to be unable to land, and the return flight to be cancelled. In addition, the flights are regularly over-booked in the tourist season, particularly the return flight to Ujung Pandang – the shortness of the runway and the altitude means that only eight seats are filled on the flight and it must be one of the few airports where both the passengers as well as their luggage are weighed-in. The office also sometimes fails to register reservations made through other Merpati offices (it is not on-line). It is best to allow for a day extra in Ujung Pandang, if connecting with an onward flight.

Road Bus: buses leave from outside the bus offices N of and around the market on Jl Mappanyuki. **Litha and Co**, Jl Mappanyuki (ground floor of the Central Market) is the largest bus operator running vehicles between Rantepao and Ujung Pandang, incl a/c buses with reclining seats. Regular connections with Palopo 2 hrs,

Selected bus fares			
	Time hrs	a/c Rp	Ekonomi Rp
RANTEPAO to:			
Ujung Pandang	8	14,500	10,000
Pendolo	10		20,000
Tentena	11½		20,000
Poso	12½		20,000
Palu	18-24		25,000
Gorontalo			55,000
Manado			65,000
1995 fares quoted.			

Ujung Pandang 9 hrs, Pare Pare 6 hrs, Watampone, Pendolo 10 hrs, Poso 12½ hrs, Tentena 11½ hrs and Palu 18-24 hrs. **Damri bus**: Pendolo, Tentena, Poso (Mon, Tues, Thur, Sun), Palu. For the windy journey S to Pare Pare and Ujung Pandang, try to get a seat on one of the larger buses, not on the cramped and uncomfortable minibuses. For Gorontalo and Manado change buses at Palu. Bus offices are concentrated along Jl Mappanyuki.

THE MAMASA VALLEY

Mamasa lies to the west of Rantepao and to the north of Polewali. It could be described as Tana Toraja 15 years ago, although the people here would probably resent being characterized as such. Nonetheless, both geographically and culturally there are clear parallels between Mamasa and Rantepao: both lie in rich upland rice valleys surrounded by handsome peaks and offer superlative hiking possibilities; and the people of both areas have converted to Christianity (the first Dutch Protestant missionaries only arrived in Mamasa in 1927), traditionally built impressive **tongkonan** houses (see page 636), and are linguistically very closely related with their cousins to the east. (For more detail on the arts and culture of the Toraja people see page 635.) But because the Mamasa Valley is more difficult to reach, especially during the wet season (there is no air service to Mamasa) most visitors tend to opt for the Rantepao area. This means that Mamasa has retained more of a frontier quality; it also

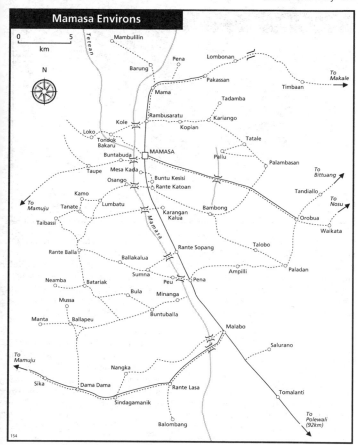

Mamasa Environs

0 5 km

N

Mambulilin
Tetean
Pena
Lombonan
Barung
Pakassan
To Makale
Timbaan
Mama
Tadamba
Rambusaratu
Kariango
Kole
Loko
Kopian
Tatale
Tondok Bakaru
MAMASA
Pallu
Palambasan
Buntabuda
To Bittuang
Taupe
Mesa Kada
Buntu Kesisi
Osango
Rante Katoan
Tandiallo
Kamo
Lumbatu
Karangan Kalua
To Nosu
To Mamuju
Tanate
Bambong
Orobua
Taibassi
Waikata
Rante Balla
Rante Sopang
Ballakalua
Talobo
Neamba
Batariak
Sumna
Ampilli
Paladan
Mussa
Peu
Pena
Minanga
Manta
Ballapeu
Bula
Buntuballa
Malabo
Salurano
To Mamuju
Nangka
Sika
Dama Dama
Rante Lasa
Tomalanti
Sindagamanik
To Polewali (92km)
Balombang

154

means, of course, that the luxuries of Rantepao are less available – although one new, up-market hotel has opened. Note that nights in the Mamasa area are cool, and sometimes downright cold. It is always possible to buy a blanket if you arrive unprepared, though (see **Shopping**, below).

When Harry Wilcox made the overland journey from Makale to Mamasa in the 1940s it was a truly isolated place. In his book *Six moons in Sulawesi* (1949) he records how one of his local companions, Timbu, grunted disparagingly, "Ignorant people here, Tuan. They don't know how to plant rice. Dogs would plant it as well." Then, even more shocking, another companion, Massang, added "These people don't make *tuak* (palm wine). They are not able. Truly fools, these people." Sugar in Mamasa sold for 300 cents a kilo; in Makale it cost just 100 cents, although rice and salt were both cheaper as there were local supplies of both. Nonetheless, Wilcox found Mamasa "more adulterated than Makale by alien blood and faith. Bugis people, with their mosques and

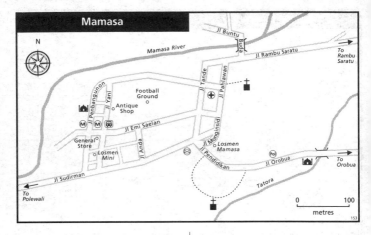

Mamasa

To Rambu Saratu

To Orobua

To Polewali

0 — 100 metres

goats, were everywhere. Many local Torajas, too, have been converted to Islam; one in every ten Torajas in the province (of South-West Toraja) is a Muslim now. Of the other nine, two are Christian and seven heathen." It was, in the 1940s, surprisingly also a larger town than Makale – because it was a Dutch administrative centre. This has now changed, largely because of the influence of the tourist industry in the Rantepao area.

MAMASA TOWN

This small town, with a population of, apparently, 2,000 (all sources seem to quote this figure although it may simply have become the accepted truth through endless repetition) is the base from which most visitors explore the surrounding countryside. The town, at 1,160m, is set in the upper reaches of the Mamasa Valley at the point where the Tetean and Mamasa rivers meet. Impressive mountains surround the settlement and although the area can be shrouded in mist for many days during the wet season, in the dry season the air is clear and cool. There are a good number of guesthouses, and information on where to go and how can be gleaned from guestbooks and evening talks with other travellers. It is worth spending some

time here before venturing out overnight into the countryside.

The only sight in town is the **market**, sandwiched between Jalan Jend A Yani and Jalan Penbangunon. This is the best place to see a good range of Mamasa blankets (see **Shopping**, below).

Excursions

There are a number of sights – traditional *adat* houses or *tongkonan*, *tedong-tedong* burial sites, traditional weaving villages and wonderful vistas – within a day's trek of Mamasa town. See **Hiking in the Mamasa Valley**, below.

Local information
● **Accommodation**

Until recently Mamasa only offered basic guesthouse accommodation. However as the road here from Polewali is gradually upgraded and communication becomes easier so bigger investors are being attracted to the undoubted charms of the area. Already a hotel has opened and more are bound to follow. For the present, guesthouse quality changes rapidly as new places open and others fall into somnolent disrepair. The comments below, in other words, may have been rendered obsolete by the passage of time.

A-B *Mamasa Cottage*, Kole (4 km N of Mamasa town, see surrounding area map), the first of what is likely to become a mini-rush of more up-market places to stay, for the present undoubtedly the most comfortable place to stay with hot water and spacious, well-designed room in beautiful surroundings.

E *Losmen Mini*, Jl Jend A Yani, popular place with range of rooms, the ones upstairs are much more cheery and airy and therefore also more expensive, friendly, noisy, family atmosphere, good place to scout out information on trekking; **E** *Mamasa Guesthouse*, this place has only opened recently and has been built to a good standard, rooms are airy and fresh and the management, with the enthusiasm that comes from starting a new business, are energetic and keen to please; **E** *Wisma Mamasa*, an old Dutch house on the top of the hill just on the fringe of town, one of the original guesthouses in the area and still attracting some custom although more for its incomparable position than for its cleanliness and luxury; **E-F** *Losmen Marapan*, Jl Jend A Yani, another older guesthouse but seems to have maintained a reasonable standard of cleanliness.

● **Entertainment**

Dances: it is sometimes possible to witness traditional dancing. The most distinctive dances of the area are the *Bulu Londong*, a war dance, and the *Simbong*.

● **Shopping**

As in the Rantepao area, the people of Mamasa are accomplished weavers and there is a flourishing *sambu* blanket-making industry in Mamasa. Blankets are sold on the street corner or at the market. Most are dyed using aniline (chemical) dyes, although some people report that traditionally dyed examples are still available: look for the duller, more sombre-coloured blankets.

● **Useful addresses**

Area code: 0428.

Post Office: Jl Jend Sudirman

● **Transport**

92 km from Polewali, 184 km from Pare Pare, 339 km from Ujung Pandang.

Road Bus: bemos link Mamasa with Polewali (5 hrs travelling up to Mamasa, rather less going down, but getting quicker as the road is upgraded). To get to Mamasa from Ujung Pandang, there are some direct express buses, which are the quickest and most comfortable way of reaching, or leaving Mamasa. Alternatively take a bus to Pare Pare and then a connection onto Polewali (some buses go straight through). From Polewali catch a bemo to Mamasa. There are hotels in Polewali if stuck there for the night. **Foot**: it is possible to trek from Rantepao to Mamasa (see above).

Hiking in the Mamasa Valley

Road transport is pretty limited in this area and the best way to get around, thank goodness, is still by foot. There are also some rather moth-eaten ponies for hire. There are numerous paths criss-crossing the region, linking villages and markets. The map here should only be taken as a rough guide to the area; the best way to plan a route is to give yourself a few days in Mamasa town to ask other hikers where they have been and the state of the various tracks. Losmen/hotel owners also sometimes keep guestbooks and can also offer advice. Remember that it is cold at night, can be extremely wet, and facilities in the surrounding villages are basic. Simple supplies for trekking are available in Mamasa town and it is a good idea to take some small gifts along.

In the last few years it has become possible to hire motorcycles in Mamasa to explore the countryside. This is best during the dry season, and it also restricts riders to the few vehicle-friendly roads in the area. Bemos also ply these roads, so it is possible to walk out and ride back.

Villages and sights in the valley

The villages and sights below are ordered according to how far they are (in hiking distance) from Mamasa. It is possible to visit villages on a series of day treks, returning to Mamasa town each evening. Use the map to work out an appropriate route.

The main sights of interest – bar the incomparable highland countryside – are the traditional villages with their fine *tongkonan* (*adat* houses) and the *tedong-tedong* burial sites. The *tongkonan* are similar to those found in the Rantepao area (see page 636). The *tedong-tedong* grave sites, though, are distinctive. Coffins, carved in the shape of buffalo heads, are placed in open sided mini-houses, almost like rice barns without walls.

Southwest of Mamasa, west of the Mamasa River

Taupe (3 km): a traditional village with *tongkonan* and a grave site set in the midst of the forest. **Osango** (5 km): this is what a geographer might call a dispersed settlement rather than a village. Nonetheless there are some *tongkonan* and also a two-centuries old *tendong-tedong* burial site. **Tanate** (8 km): a village that specializes in the weaving of *sambu* blankets (see Mamasa, Shopping) and there is also a cave grave site. **Taibassi** (9 km): *sambu*-weaving village. **Rante Balla** (11 km): traditional *sambu*-weaving and handicraft centre; also has some fine *tongkonan*. **Ballakalua** (13 km): a fine traditional village with *tongkonan* also specializing in the weaving of *sambu* blankets. **Minanga** (14 km): *tedong-tedong* grave site. **Buntuballa** (15 km): a fine traditional village with impressive *tongkonan* and grave site and also good views. **Bula** (16 km): traditional village. **Ballapeu** (18 km): traditional village. **Mussa** (19 km): view point with outstanding vista up the Mamasa valley back to Mamasa town.

Southeast of Mamasa, east of the Mamasa River

Mesa Kada (2 km): hot springs where it is possible to bathe. **Buntu Kesisi** (2.5 km): *tongkonan*. **Rante Katoan** (3 km): traditional village with *tongkonan* and hot springs. **Rante Sopang** (9 km): a traditional village on the 'main' road S of Mamasa so has its fair share of visitors. The inhabitants have taken advantage of this by transforming themselves into a weaving and handicraft centre. **Orobua** (9 km): the *tongkonan* in this traditional village are particularly fine and well-maintained Paladan (12 km): a *tedong-tedong* burial site in a spectacular position. **Malabo** (18 km): a *tedong-tedong* grave site. **Tomalanti** (23 km): hot springs.

Northwest of Mamasa, west of the Mamasa River

Loko (4 km): a well-preserved traditional village with fine *tongkonan*. **Kole** (4 km): ancient *tongkonan* and hot springs. The new *Mamasa Cottages* are here (see Accommodation, Mamasa Town). **Barung** (8 km): a fine traditional village with grave site, *tongkonan* and good views. **Mambulilin** (9 km): a steep walk to a waterfall.

Northeast of Mamasa, east of the Mamasa River

Rambusaratu (3 km): the ancient *tongkonan* here is reputed to be the largest in the Mamasa Valley and to be three centuries old. It was a clan chief's house and visitors are welcomed inside – although a small donation is requested. **Kopian** (6 km): *tedong-tedong* burial site. **Kariango** (7 km): *tedong-tedong* grave site. **Tatale** (8km): traditional village with good *tongkonan* and *tedong-tedong* burial site. **Pallu** (8.5 km): traditional village with *tongkonan* and good views.

The Mamasa-Rantepao Trek

This trek should take 3 full days, but may take longer if some in the party are unfit or if you crawl from your sleeping bags like reluctant maggots after 0900. Nights are spent in traditional villages with basic facilities. It is best to take a sleeping bag along (cold at night), although some trekkers do survive wrapping themselves in layers of *sambus* (blankets). The villages are listed here as if trekking from Mamasa to Rantepao (west to east). See the 'Around Mamasa' map for the route from Mamasa as far as Timbaan.

Timbaan (night one, 26 km from Mamasa).

Paku (night 2, 24 km from Timbaan).

Bittuang (either night 3 or bus from there the final 22 km to Makale. Bittuang is 16 km from Paku).

NB Check details of the trek with those in Mamasa or Rantepao before setting out.

PALOPO (LUWU)

Palopo is a quiet coastal town, sandwiched on a narrow slice of lowland between Bone Bay and the S Sulawesi Highlands. It is useful as a stopping-off point on the

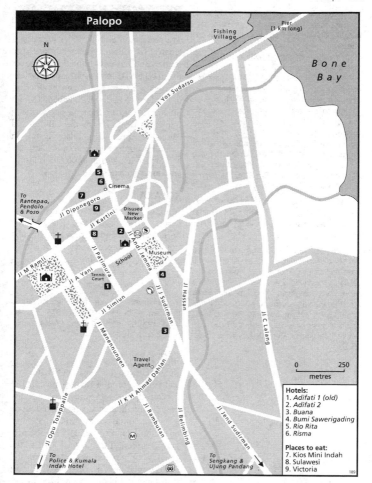

Palopo

N

Fishing Village

Pier (1 km long)

B o n e B a y

Jl Yos Sudarso

To Rantepao, Pendolo & Poso

Cinema

Jl Diponegoro

Jl Kartini

Disused New Market

School

Museum

Jl M Ramli

Jl A Yani

Jl Simiun

Tennis Court

Jl Patimura

Jl Andi Jemma

Jl Sudirman

Jl Hassan

Jl C Lalang

Jl Manenmungen

Jl K H Ahmad Dahlan

Travel Agent

Jl Opu Tosappaile

Jl Rambutan

Jl Belimbing

Jl Jend Sudirman

To Police & Kumala Indah Hotel

To Sengkang & Ujung Pandang

0   250
metres

Hotels:
1. *Adifati 1* (old)
2. *Adifati 2*
3. *Buana*
4. *Bumi Sawerigading*
5. *Rio Rita*
6. *Risma*

Places to eat:
7. Kios Mini Indah
8. Sulawesi
9. Victoria

189

arduous journey between Central Sulawesi and Toraja. There is a **museum** on Jl Andi Jemma, which was formerly a palace. It contains a modest, but interesting collection of local ethnographic artefacts and some Asian ceramics. Admission 2,000Rp. Fishing boats, ferries and *pinisi* schooners dock at the long pier reaching out into the bay. Most places in Palopo (except for the bemo station) are within easy walking distance of each other and it is easy to get around town.

- **Accommodation C-D** *Adifati 2*, Jl A Jemma 86, T 21467, some a/c, clean, 2-storey, overlooking small garden, all rooms have own seating outside, those at the front a bit noisy, spacious lobby with crimson sofas, office has a good wall map, no restaurant, best not to confuse this place with the *Adifati 1* around the corner which is a dump, ask for *Adifati* next to the mosque, not tennis courts, good value, rec;

D *Buana*, Jl KH Ahmad Dahlan 89, T 22164, compact hotel, close to market and bemo station, friendly and helpful staff; **D** *Bumi Sawerigading*, Jl Jend Sudirman 2, T 21033, close to museum, don't be put off by tatty exterior, on main road, Telkom office opp; **D** *Kumalah Indah*, Jl Opu Tosapaille 77, T 22488, some a/c, no restaurant, on outskirts of town, clean, spacious, but seemingly reluctant to take foreigners or only to make the most expensive rooms available despite others being unoccupied; **D** *Risma*, Jl A Jemma 14, T 21178, small new building, well kept gardens, but noisy when film showing next door; **D-E** *Adifati 1*; **D-E** *Palopo*, Jl Kelapa 2, T 21789, only stay here if you wish to be by bemo station; **E** *Rio Rita*, Jl A Jemma 10, old wooden building, very dirty.

● **Post & telecommunications Area code**: 0471. **Post Office**: next door to BNI. **Wartel Office**: Jl Jend Sudirman, no IDD, phone cards available.

● **Transport Road Bus**: buses to Rantepao 3-4 hrs, Ujung Pandang 8 hrs and N to Tentena, Poso and Palu. Bemos to Rantepao 2½ hrs (2,000Rp), wonderful views and scenery, but a windy road; Sengkang (4,000Rp). **Sea Boat**: for those with an adventurous turn of mind, it is well worth walking out onto the pier; boats regularly leave for Maluku, about a 7 day journey. Regular connections with Malili and Kolaka (SE Sulawesi).

SOUTHEAST SULAWESI

The province of SE Sulawesi, with a population of 1.4 million, is very rarely visited by tourists and has only limited facilities for the traveller. The provincial capital is Kendari on the E coast; Kolaka, on the W coast, is the ferry port for S Sulawesi. Off SE Sulawesi's S tip are the large and formerly influential island kingdoms of Buton and Muna. The province is relatively rich in natural resources with nickel mines, asphalt and timber. It is also an important transmigration settlement area (see page 427).

KOLAKA

A minor port and transit point for S Sulawesi. Ferries from Bajoe, Watampone's port, dock here and there is accommodation for those forced to stay overnight.

● **Accommodation E** *Alkaosar*, Jl Jend Sudirman 20; **E** *Rahmat*, Jl Kadue 6, own mandi; **F** *Pelita*, Jl Repelita 56.

● **Transport** 173 km from Kendari. **Road Bus**: regular buses to Kendari, 3½ hrs. **Sea Boat**: nightly ferries to Bajoe (Watampone's port) 8 hrs (5,100-9,400Rp).

KENDARI

Kendari lies on the E coast of SE Sulawesi and is the capital of the province. It was developed by the Japanese as a military base during their occupation of Indonesia when the capital was moved from Baubau on Buton Island to Kendari. As the provincial capital, it is endowed with all the usual paraphernalia of government and has a population of over 100,000. The town is strung-out, ribbon-like, over several kilometres.

Excursions Moramo Waterfall which cascades down seven terraces, is 50 km S of town. The pools at each level make for pleasant swimming. *Getting there*: by bus (1¾ hrs) from the Madonga terminal.

Tours *Alam Jaya*, Jl Konggoasa 50, T 21729, organizes 5-7 day trips around SE Sulawesi; *BPU*, Jl Konggoasa 48 will organize boat and car trips around the area.

● **Accommodation** At present, accommodation is rather expensive, with few cheap places for travellers to stay. **A** *Kendari Beach*, Jl Hasanuddin 44, T 21988, a/c, restaurant, out of town and expensive, but the only upmarket place in town, attractively positioned overlooking the bay, with tennis courts; **C-D** *Armins*, Jl Diponegoro 55 and Jl Diponegoro 75, some a/c; **E** *Cendrawasih*, Jl Diponegoro, best place for budget travellers.

● **Airline offices** Merpati, Jl Konggoasa 29, T 21729.

● **Banks & money changers** It is advisable to change TCs before travelling to SE Sulawesi.

● **Post & telecommunications Area code:** 0401. **Post Office:** Jl S Ratulangi 79.

● **Tourist office** On the hill behind the harbour, T 21764.

● **Transport** 173 km from Kolaka. **Air** The airport is 35 km N of town. **Transport to town:** minibus 30 mins (4,000Rp), or share a taxi service for 5,000Rp/person. Regular connections on Merpati with Ujung Pandang. **Road Bus:** regular connections with Kolaka 3½ hrs from the Wawotobi terminal, 7 km from town (regular bemos into town for 150Rp). From Kolaka, there are ferries to Ujung Pandang (see above). **Sea Boat:** a daily ferry leaves for Muna and Buton Islands (see below). The Pelni ship *Tilongkabila* making its fortnightly circuit between Sulawesi and the islands of Nusa Tenggara, including Bali, also docks here (see route schedules, page 921).

BUTON AND MUNA ISLANDS

Buton and Muna islands lie side by side, off the SE tip of SE Sulawesi, separated from one another by the narrow Buton Strait. Buton is the larger and more important of the two covering nearly 6,500 sq km with a population of over 400,000, while Muna has a land area of 4,900 sq km and over 200,000 inhabitants. They are administered as separate districts. The largest town is **Baubau**, at the SW corner of Buton Island, and overlooking the straits to Muna, with a population of about 50,000.

During the 16th and 17th centuries, Buton was a powerful local sultanate, making vassal states of several neighbouring islands, including Muna. Sir Francis Drake in the *Golden Hind* sailed past Muna and Buton before being blown off course towards Nusa Tenggora (see page 42). The Dutch made contact with Buton in 1690, and were on friendly terms with the sultanate during the VOC's confrontation with Gowa. It was off Buton in 1666 that the Dutch admiral Speelman devastated the Makassarese fleet, leading to the downfall of Gowa.

Places of interest In **Baubau**, the new **Wolio Kraton**, and a 16th century **mosque** within it are worth visiting. The kraton contains an eclectic collection of local and colonial artefacts. The hilltop **fort** was built by the Dutch in the early part of the 17th century. About 10 km outside Baubau is **Nirwana Beach** with good swimming; popular at weekends.

Raha is the capital of Muna Island. The main attractions here are **horse-fighting** – a practice which seems to have been part of an ancient local ritual – and the **caves** near Bolo (9 km from Raha), which contain prehistoric paintings. Horse-fighting is best seen at the village of Latugo (24 km from Raha), and can be arranged at a day's notice. The fight involves two riderless stallions, who are shown mares before the contest in order to agitate them. The stallions do battle until one loses heart and gallops away, at which point another animal is brought forward to fight the victor. If the fight gets vicious, the horses are prised apart. It is necessary to acquire permission from the National Archaeological Research Centre in Jakarta to visit the caves. The caves themselves are quite inaccessible, as they are high up – it is best to take a guide. Paintings include images of sailboats, hunters, the sun, deer and other animals.

● **Accommodation** In Baubau: **D** *Liliyana*, Jl Kartini. In Raha: **D** *Andalas*, comfortable, price incl breakfast, other food can be arranged, bemo available for charter; **E** *Tani*, price incl breakfast.

• **Transport Air** 2 connections a week on Merpati with Ujung Pandang. **Sea Boat**: a daily ferry leaves from Kendari at 1400 for Buton and Muna islands docking, in order, at Raha 7 hrs and Baubau 15 hrs. The return ferry leaves from Baubau at 1300 and Raha at 2300. The Pelni ships *Kerinci*, *Rinjani*, *Ciremai* and *Tilongkabila* also call at Baubau (see route schedules, page 921). The Pelni office is at Jl Yos Sudarso 19, T 188.

PENDOLO TO PALU

From Palopo, the road runs NE along the coastal plain to Wotu, where it turns N into the mountains and towards Lake Poso. Just S of Lake Poso, the road passes from the province of S Sulawesi into Central Sulawesi. This road used to be very bad; now it is surfaced all the way to Palu. The climb up from Mangkutana to Pendolo passes through some of the most beautiful, unspoilt rainforest in Sulawesi; try and make this journey in daylight. 1 hr N of Mangkutana there is a spectacular waterfall, most buses will stop here for 5 mins. The only delays that are likely on this route will be caused by landslides during heavy rains, however the local authorities are quick and efficient at clearing the road. The forest and hills suddenly end, and the road continues straight, like a Roman road to Pendolo, at the S end of Lake Poso. A daily ferry leaves here for Tentena on the N shore.

Lake Poso Region

Lake Poso

This ancient, upland lake, at 600m above sea-level, covers over 32,000 ha and is the third largest lake in Indonesia (after Toba and Towuti, the latter also in Sulawesi). Lake Poso is famed for its clear waters and for its rare fauna. 67% of species so far identified in Lake Poso are endemic – they are found nowhere else – and some are already thought to have become extinct. Early travellers to the lake reported seeing estuarine crocodiles (*Crocodylus porosus*) – some exceeding 5m in length – although they now seem to have been hunted to extinction.

The road between Pendolo and Tentena is surfaced, but the forest has suffered from logging, and clearing for agriculture. From Tentena the road continues N. About 25 km out of Pendolo a road runs E to the rarely visited town of Kolonodale. From Tentena the road continues N to the port of Poso, and from there follows the coast to Toboli. At Toboli, on the E side of Sulawesi's N 'limb', the road cuts inland to cross the narrow 20 km-wide mountainous spine to the W side and the capital of Central Sulawesi, Palu. 34 km N of here is the formerly important port of Donggala.

PENDOLO

Pendolo is a small town on the S shores of Lake Poso. Swimming is very pleasant here. There is a daily boat from here N to Tentena – following an ancient trade route between Central Sulawesi and Toraja. This is the most relaxing way to make the journey N, but the boat quite frequently breaks down, then it's 2 hrs to Tentena by bemo (2,000Rp).

● **Accommodation** Most people choose to stay in the larger town of Tentena, on Lake Poso's N shores, rather than in Pendolo, however, the setting is more beautiful at Pendolo, especially at dawn when a thin mist hangs just above the lake. **NB** When the lake is high, the losmen by

the jetty can become flooded. Lake water can reach the *Danau Poso Hotel*. **C** *Mulia*, new complex 1 km out of town towards Tentena, restaurant (very poor) and bar, comfortable accommodation on white sandy beach, private mandi but no hot water, not convenient for those who wish only to spend 1 night and then catch ferry (N) or bus (S), although they do pick up/drop off at the bus station and boat dock, pleasant place to rest up for few days; **E** *Danau Poso*, Jl Pelabuhan, 2-storey building opp *Damri* bus office, short walk to lakeside and jetty, rooms have balcony overlooking main street; **E** *Pamona Indah Losmen*, on lake, 5 mins walk W from jetty, just off main street, Jl Pelabuhan; **E** *Sederhana*, Jl Pelabuhan; **E** *Victory Wisma*, to the right of jetty, similar setting to the *Masamba*, slightly newer building; **E** *Wisma Masamba*, Jl Pelabuhan, friendly old building to left of jetty, have breakfast in dining area on stilts over clear lake, very small, cramped mandis, rec.

● **Places to eat** *Caya Bone*, next to *Damri* office. There are a few simple warungs on the main road, which close early.

● **Tourist office** Useful office next to mosque, worth a visit for map of the area, and photos of various local sights. A new grave site has been found by local farmers just beyond Bone on W shore lake road.

● **Transport Road Bus**: buses ply (very slowly) N to Tentena 6 hrs, and S to Palopo. The journey to Rantepao takes about 10 hrs. **Damri bus**: to Rantepao, Mon, Wed, Thur, Sat 0300, Sun 0800 (20,000Rp). There is a through bus to Ujung Pandang, Tues, Fri, Sun 0300. Connections with Palu, Mon, Tues, Thur, Fri, Sat 2000 and Wed, Sat 1000 (2,500Rp). **NB** There could be delays in either direction due to landslides. Also there may be a problem getting a seat, so it is recommended to book a seat in Poso, and board in Pendolo. If heading S the price is the same (ie, a bemo from Poso to Tentena and a boat to Pendolo). **Sea Boat**: daily departures to Tentena, 0800, 3 hrs (2,000Rp); return boat leaves Tentena at 1600, strong winds whip across the lake later in the day; because of this the boat may need to stop at a coastal village on the return, therefore it could take 4 hrs.

KOLONODALE

This small town on the rarely visited E coast of Central Sulawesi is the best base for trips into the magnificent **Morowali**

Nature Reserve (see Excursions, below). It also provides easy access to **Tomori Bay**. The town has few facilities for tourists and is only for those who really want to be off the traveller's trail.

Excursions The Morowali Nature Reserve covers over 225,000 ha of Central Sulawesi to the N of Kolonodale, including extensive stands of virgin tropical rainforest, pristine coastline, beautiful rivers and islands in Tomori Bay. Originally tagged as a potential site for transmigration settlements, the untouched environment and rich flora and fauna fortunately drove the government to gazette it as a national park in the 1980's after Operation Drake had visited the area. Ranging from sea level (or rather sub-sea level) to 2,630m, it encompassed a huge range of environments: highland rainforests, dry grasslands, mangroves and lowland evergreen rainforest. The park's fauna include the pig-deer or babirusa, the anoa (see page 613) and the maleo bird (see page 684). Along the Morowali River, there is excellent bird and butterfly life; the black orchid is also found in Morowali. The mystical **Ranu Lake** (2-3 hrs from Kayu Poli) is the home of the legendary white crocodile. The park is inhabited by the Wana, who are hunters and shifting cultivators. In total there are thought to be 5,000 Wana living within the park, most of whom inhabit remote and inaccessible highland areas. There are, though, about 100 settled in the lowlands of Ranu and Kayo Poli who regularly interact with visitors to the park. NGO groups recommend that visitors who come into contact with the Wana should not give sweets to children, nor packets of cigarettes (which tend to find their way to children), nor to distribute medicines indiscriminately. **Accommodation** None available as yet but the coastal Bajo people and the interior Wana tribe do sometimes offer homestays; **Kayu Poli** is a Wana village on the banks of the River Morowali, where it may be possible to stay (4 hrs walk from the Ranu River). A minimum of 5 days (4 nights) is recommended, this will cost in region of 500,000Rp for two people (all incl). *Permits*: obtainable from the PHPA subseksi Morowali in Kolonodale. Note that it is currently illegal to enter the park without a guide or permit. *Best time to*

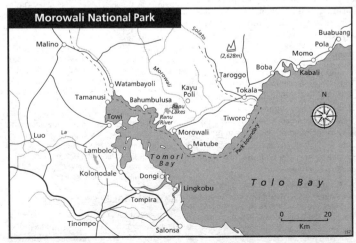

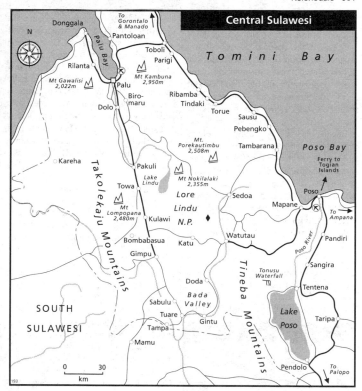

Central Sulawesi

visit: during the dry season, Oct to Feb. *Guides*: are available in Kolonodale (see **Tours**, below, and reference to Friends of Morowali). *Getting there*: on a tour or by boat (2 hrs); there are also MAF flights to Tokala Atas and Beteleme, both outside the park's NE boundary.

Tours Friends of Morowali (*Sahabat Morowali*) in Kolonodale, are a local conservation group concerned for the reserve and the welfare of the Wana people. They can help organize a visit to the park and will arrange permits, boat travel, basic food and accommodation in Wana villages; '*Jabar Lahadji*' in Kolonodale (Jl Jend A Yani 154) speaks good English and is very knowledgeable.

● **Accommodation** E *Sederhana*, Jl Yos Sudarso 13, on the waterfront, good source of information for trips to the Morowali Nature Reserve – Jabar Lahadji, who runs **Friends of Morowali**, can be contacted from the losmen; *Tomorindah*, located in the forest.

● **Transport Air** MAF flies irregularly from Tentena to Kolonodale. **Road Bus**: buses leave daily from Pendolo 4 hrs, Tentena 6-7 hrs and Poso 10 hrs. **Boat** The Pelni ship *Tilongkabila* travels fortnightly from Ujung Pandang to Kolonodale, via Kendari before continuing on to Gorontalo, Bitung and the Sangihe islands (see route schedule, page 921). The reserve is another 2-3 hrs by boat from Kolonodale. 'Johnsons' dug out canoes with outboards can be hired for around 30,000Rp (one way). It is advisable to take a guide from Kolonodale. **NB** Arranging a guide in Tentena can be costly.

TENTENA

Tentena is a small town situated on the N shores of **Lake Poso**. It has a cool and invigorating climate and a reasonable range of accommodation, making it the best stopping-off point between Palu and Toraja. A **210m wooden bridge** crosses the river Poso, which flows out of the lake at this, its northern-most and narrowest extremity. Eels – which migrate as elvers from the sea 50 km away – and carp are trapped below the bridge. The largest eel caught measured 1.8m and carp weighing as much as 20 kg are also netted. Tentena was a centre of missionary activity in the area when two Dutch priests, Dr AC Kruyt and Dr Adriani, set up operations here in 1895. It still supports the oldest **Protestant church** in the province.

Excursions The **Saluopa waterfall** lies 12 km E of Tentena and is a popular and impressive excursion. Just before you reach the falls there is a homestead with a visitors' book. Tea, coffee and fresh fruit

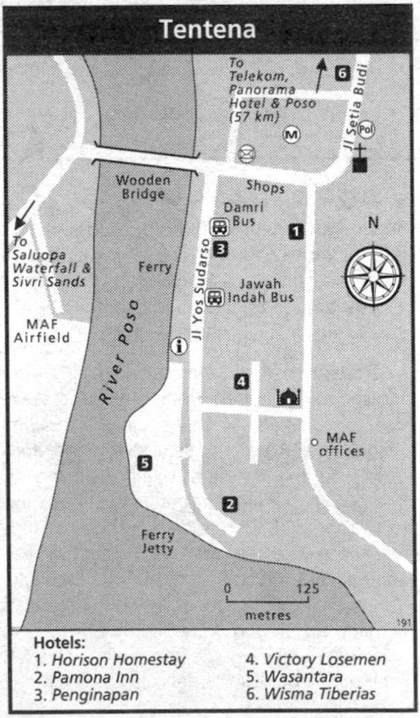

Tentena

To Telekom, Panorama Hotel & Poso (57 km)

Jl Setia Budi

Wooden Bridge

Shops

Damri Bus

To Saluopa Waterfall & Sivri Sands

Ferry

Jawah Indah Bus

Jl Yos Sudarso

N

MAF Airfield

River Poso

MAF offices

Ferry Jetty

0   125
metres

Hotels:
1. *Horison Homestay*   4. *Victory Losemen*
2. *Pamona Inn*   5. *Wasantara*
3. *Penginapan*   6. *Wisma Tiberias*

are available for a donation. You can walk up either side of the falls, which is in fact a series of 12 steps/terraces. *Getting there*: take a bemo from by the wooden bridge to Tonusu. The turn off for the falls is just beyond the village, the driver will usually take you to this point, 1,000Rp. There is then a 1-hr walk through cultivated land and paddy fields before entering the forest.

Lore Lindu National Park Tentena is one of the best spots to organize **treks** into the Lore Lindu National Park to see the **megaliths** of the **Bada Valley** (see page 665). Ask at the *Pamona Indah* for information. Ignore guides who say you can not go on MAF flights; more often than not this is a ploy to hire them to 'guide' you to the valley. Check at the office at the airfield for availability; a waiting list and schedule is clearly displayed here. More knowledgeable guides can be hired in Gintu, though they are not necessary; the local villagers and farmers can direct you to all main megaliths.

Caves The limestone hills around Tentena, and along the shores of Lake Poso, are rich in caves, most of which are not as exciting as the tourist literature tries to make out. Most famous – in relative terms – is **Pamona Cave** near the Theological School, a series of caves running deep into the mountainside (it is said that no one has yet reached the end, or at least has returned to tell the story). Closer to town, near the offices of the Protestant church, are a number of caves with skulls and crude coffins.

Lake trips It is possible to charter boats in Tentena to venture out onto the lake (15,000Rp/hr), or to travel to Bancea and the **Bancea Orchid Reserve** on the W shore, where there are 50 species of orchid. The water on this side of the lake is beautifully clear.

● **Accommodation** Most hotels are on, or overlook the Poso River. **C** *Sivri Sands*, on W shore of lake, 18 km from Tentena, take a bemo from wooden bridge heading for Toindse, simple wooden cottages on stilts beside the lake, white sand beach, new and therefore clean, remote, no other facilities within walking distance; **D** *Pamona Inn*, on lakeside, T 21245 best restaurant in Tentena, don't be put off by state of the ceiling, selection of Chinese and Indonesian dishes, none of the rooms have a good view, rooms in new wooden block clean but gloomy, older block at back has smaller, noisy rooms (TV full volume below), close to the ferry jetty and enclosed children's boating area with giant ducks, tours of the region can be arranged from here; **D** *Panorama*, 2 km from town centre, awkward to get to and from since there are no town bemos, high up on the hill with views across town and river; **D** *Victory Losmen*, T 21392, restaurant poor value, new and clean, sister hotel in Pendolo, located behind restaurant of same name, popular, good value; **D** *Wasantara*, by lake, T 21345, no restaurant, best views of lake and river from economy rooms 1, 2 and 3, modern building set in unkempt gardens, rooms at back overlook river, possible to swim from here, beware of strong current when lake full, peaceful and private, within walking distance of all other amenities in Tentena, rec; **E** *Horison Homestay*, Jl Setia Budi 6, T 21038 located on quiet street at back of town, easy walk from bridge, colourful garden, all rooms have veranda, new block at back; **E** *Penginapan*, basic rooms, central location, good view of bridge, next to the Damri bus office; **E** *Wisma Tiberias*, basic rooms, on main road nr Police.

● **Post & telecommunications Post Office**: close to bridge on edge of market. **Telekom Office**: Jl Kartini 25, T 21001.

● **Useful addresses Police Station**: next to white church which dominates centre of town.

● **Tourist office** Quite informative, when the local officer is present.

● **Transport** 57 km S of Poso, 77 km N of Pendolo. **Air** MAF (Missionary Aviation Fellowship) operates an irregular service to Palu, Gintu (Tues and Fri, 35,000Rp) – in the Bada Valley – Kolonodale and other, even more remote, destinations in Sulawesi. **NB** MAF is not a commercial airline and may decline to take passengers. **Road Bus**: connections N to Poso 1½ hrs (1,500Rp), Palu 10 hrs and S to Pendolo 6 hrs, Rantepao and Ujung Pandang; also buses E to Kolonodale. Long distance buses tend to leave from outside their offices, most of which can be found along Jl P Sumatera. *Jawa Indah* and *Damri* have their offices close to *Losmen Victory*. It is potentially difficult to guarantee a seat on long distance buses to Rantepao or Palu since few passengers get off mid way. If travelling further N, take a local bemo to Poso, and buy a ticket here from one of the many bus companies (1,500Rp, a scenic drive leaving the lake). **Sea Boat**: to Pendolo, on the S shores of the lake (the best way to travel S); departs at 1600, 3-4 hrs (2,000Rp).

POSO

Poso is the largest town in the area and the capital of the district of Poso. The people of the area are largely Christian, converted at the beginning of this century by a very patient member of the Dutch Reformed Church. With the completion of the Trans-Sulawesi Highway, Poso has become an important transport centre for visitors, providing a smattering of budget hotels. The town is divided by the Poso River. On the eastern side is the older commercial centre with a few hotels close to the port, and pleasant, quiet streets. The western side of the river has many newer offices and shops as well as most bus offices, and the central market. In addition to a selection of beaches close to the town (the beach in the town itself is filthy), there are a variety of routes the traveller can take; E by bus to Ampana and Tanjung Api Reserve, W to Palu, S to Tentena and Lake Poso, and N by ferry to the Togian Islands.

Excursions

Toini beach is 10 km W of town in a tranquil location. There is a restaurant here with a dining area over the sea. The end of the restaurant pier is a good location for swimming. No accommodation. *Getting there*: flag down bemo by main market (500Rp). Get off by sign for *Toini Seafood Restaurant*.

Maranda 40 km W, hot springs and waterfall. *Getting there*: by bemo (1,500Rp).

Matako beach, 25 km E. *Getting there*: by bemo (1,000Rp).

Tombiano 40 km E, small atolls and limestone caves.

Lore Lindu (see below) and **Morowali Reserve** (see page 660).

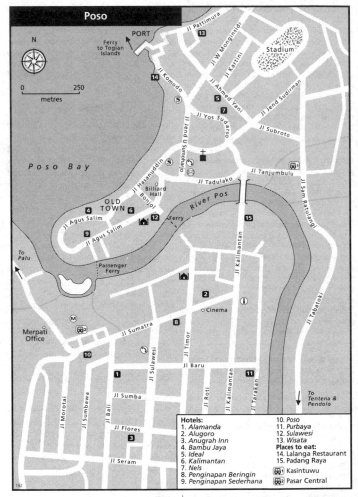

Poso

Hotels:
1. Alamanda
2. Alugoro
3. Anugrah Inn
4. Bambu Jaya
5. Ideal
6. Kalimantan
7. Nels
8. Penginapan Beringin
9. Penginapan Sederhana
10. Poso
11. Purbaya
12. Sulawesi
13. Wisata
Places to eat:
14. Lalanga Restaurant
15. Padang Raya
🚌1 Kasintuwu
🚌2 Pasar Central

Tours

Agents will organize trips to the Morowali Reserve, Lore Lindu and the Togian Islands (see page 667).

Local information

● Accommodation

C-D *Bambu Jaya*, Jl Agus Salim 106, T 21886, some a/c, restaurant currently closed, suites downstairs off gloomy corridor, 'best in town'

but very run down, simple rooms (surprisingly clean) with very small mandis, good views from upstairs open-air balcony across the bay, quiet location.

D *Anugrah Inn*, Jl Samosir 1, T 21820, close to market and bus offices in western side of town, off the main road; **D** *Wisata*, Jl Pattimura 33, T 21379, small hotel with rooms arranged around large central hall, pleasant garden at back, close to the port, quiet with views across the bay, rec.

E *Alugoro*, Jl P Sumatra 20, excellent new hotel behind bus company offices, simple covered veranda with central open lounge, rec; **E** *Ideal*, Jl Ahmed Yani 64, T 21841; **E** *Kalimantan*, Jl Agus Salim 18, T 21420, simple small hotel with rooms arranged around central breakfast area, close to mosque on side street convenient for Post Office and banks, rec; **E** *Nels*, Jl Yos Sudarso, T 21013, old building on leafy side street close to banks and port; **E** *Penginapan Beringin*, Jl P Sumatera 11, T 21851, close to bus offices, noisy location; **E** *Penginapan Sederhana*, Jl Agus Salim 25, T 21228, small old house, pleasant veranda, clean rooms; **E** *Purbaya*, Jl P Tarakan 46, close to tourist office, cheap and simple.

● **Places to eat**

Not a good range, best in town is *Lalanga Restaurant*, Jl Komodor, close to port, new restaurant, open air on stilts over bay, good seafood, but some portions small, popular at w/e, friendly waitresses.

● **Airline offices**

Merpati, Jl Subang, T 21274.

● **Banks & money changers**

Bank Dagang Negara, Jl Hasanuddin 13; Negara Indonesia 1946, Jl Yos Sudarso.

● **Post & telecommunications**

Post Office: Jl Tadulako.
Telekom: Jl Jend Urip Sumoharjo 4.

● **Tour companies & travel agents**

Aksa Utama, Jl Yos Sudarso 10, T 386; *Rajawali Ashhab*, Jl Sumatra 16a, T 21274 (Merpati agent).

● **Tourist offices**

Information on all the places of interest and how to reach them is clearly displayed here. The local tourist officer, Amir Kiat, is bound to track you down soon after your arrival; he is extremely helpful and understanding.

● **Transport**

57 km N of Tentena.

Local Bemos: all over town, no fixed routes, but link all the commercial centres, just state destination when boarding, 350Rp. **Minibus**: for local towns leave from the Kasintuwu Terminal (Jl Tanjumbulu) for destinations S and E. Pasar Central Terminal (Jl Sumatera) for westerly destinations. **Passenger ferry**: across the Poso River (100Rp), hard to find (see Map) but very convenient. Service stops at 1700.

Air: The airport is out of town – ask at the Merpati office to arrange transport. Merpati flies to Manado (240,000Rp, Sat, Sun); Ujung Pandang (196,800Rp, Sun) and may provide a service to Palu and Luwuk.

Road Bus: direct bus to Ujung Pandang (*Litha* and *Alam Indah*) departs 2000 daily, 20 hrs, via Pendolo, Palopo, Sengkang, Pare-Pare (25,000Rp). Night bus N to Palu departs 2200, 8 hrs. *Alugoro Bus*, Jl P Sumatra 20, is one of the better companies serving Palu (7,000Rp). An a/c day bus costs 10,000Rp. To Ampana, 5 hrs (5,500Rp); Ampana to Pagimana, 7 hrs (12,000Rp). *Jawa Indah Bus*, Jl P Sumatra 71, T 21560.

Sea Boat: night ferry Pagimana to Gorontalo, 10,000Rp (Mon, Wed, Fri; departs 2200). Ferry to Togian Islands (see page 667), Mon and Thur. Irregular boats to Ujung Pandang and Bitung (for Manado).

TANJUNG API RESERVE

The Tanjung Api Reserve includes the coast and waters NE of Ampana. The reserve is home to a number of endemic Sulawesi mammals including the babirusa, tarsier and macaque (see page 613). The name Tanjung Api means Fire Cape. This romantic name is probably associated with the natural seepages of gas that work their way up through the fissured rock and bubble to the surface offshore. There are walks in the forest that works its way down almost to the shore. **NB** The local waters are rough between Dec and Feb and the journey to the Reserve by boat can be uncomfortable. **Accommodation** Nothing is available in the Reserve, the nearest place to stay is Ampana, where there are several losmen. Simple shelters have recently been built in Reserve, suitable for camping. Good trekking in Reserve, take all food and shelter. *Getting there*: take a bus to Ampana, 5 hrs (5,500Rp) and from Ampana docks, charter a boat, approx 1 hr (25,000Rp return). Or, take horse and cart to Labuan village and then walk.

LORE LINDU NATIONAL PARK

The Lore Lindu National Park covers 229,000 ha of upland in Central Sulawesi between Palu and Lake Poso. Ranging between 300m and 2,610m above sea-level – which marks the summit of Mount Rorakatimbu – the park is mainly composed of montane forest, with the upland Lake Lindu in the NW corner. The area is renowned for the massive and enigmatic **megalithic statues** and '**cisterns**' that lie scattered over the Bada, Besoa and Napu valleys (copies stand outside the Central Sulawesi Museum in Palu), and for its exceptional range of bird (especially) and animal life. 19 species of waterfowl have been identified on Lake Lindu including the spotted tree duck (*Dendrocygna guttata*) and the little pied cormorant (*Phalacrocorax melanoleuca*), and in the montane forests that characterize the national park there are flocks of such insectivorous birds as the Sulawesi leaf warbler (*Phylloscopus sarasinorum*), the mountain white-eye (*Zosterops montana*) and citrine flycatcher (*Culicicapa helianthea*). Lake Lindu is not only notable for its endemic species of fish and molluscs but also because this is the only place in Indonesia where the parasite which causes schistosomiasis is to be found – making the lake a favourite haunt of both epidemiologists and naturalists.

The strange megaliths were erected by a people who have long-since disappeared and possibly date from the first millennium AD – archaeologists are still unsure. They are found in a number of spots in Central Sulawesi, but are most numerous in and around Lore Lindu. They are 'worked' stones, in the form of giant urns, menhirs, vats, stone blocks, statues and mortars. These are decorated with faces, lizards, figures and monkeys. What use they were put to is not certain although it has been postulated that they were burial chambers. They show a remarkable resemblance to the 'jars' of the Plain of Jars in Laos, although no connection between the two cultures has been identified. The greatest concentration of megaliths is near Gintu, at the S edge of the park.

Organizing a trip to Lore Lindu Few, though increasing, numbers of visitors make it to this remote spot and it is easiest to venture here on a tour (see below). Those intending to visit the park independently are recommended by the Tourist Office in Palu to first check-in at the PHPA Office also in Palu on Jl Moh Yamin for advice, although this is not strictly necessary. Guides can be found in Gimpu and Tentena and treks of 6 days or more link the two towns. Horses can also be hired, either to carry bags or to ride. The megaliths are in the vicinity of Gintu (for instance, on the Sepe Plateau),

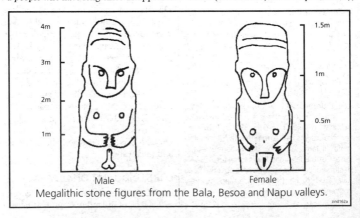

Megalithic stone figures from the Bala, Besoa and Napu valleys.

and an additional, local guide needs to be employed here as the statues are difficult to find. *Best time to visit*: at the driest time of year from Jun to Aug.

Tours Palu is the main base for specialist tours to Lore Lindu; *Katriall Utama*, in Palu, is a specialist operator. Treks can also be mounted from Tentena; for instance, from the *Pamona Indah Hotel*, on the lakeshore.

● **Accommodation** There are homestays/losmen in Gintu, Gimpu and Tentena, and it is sometimes possible to stay in locals' homes in Tuare. But outside these towns it is necessary to sleep in the open – often on covered bridges along with villagers away from home.

● **Transport Air** MAF (Missionary Aviation Fellowship) flies to Gintu and Tentena from Palu. **NB** MAF is not a commercial airline and may decline to take passengers. **Road Bus**: from Palu's Masomba terminal to Gimpu, 8 hrs (poor road); there are also regular buses from Tentena to Masomba.

TOGIAN ISLANDS AND TOMINI BAY

With the advent of a regular ferry service from Poso and Gorontalo the Togian Islands have become one of the newest destinations for the visitor to Sulawesi. As yet the beaches and small atolls have not been spoilt by litter and other pollution. They have some of the best water visibility in Sulawesi and are the ultimate secluded island paradise. Unfortunately the local fishermen have picked up the iniquitous habit of using dynamite and poison (cyanide) to fish (practices which seem to have come from the Philippines), which has already destroyed sections of the coral reef. Local villagers also catch large numbers of sharks, and sell their fins to Chinese traders for about US\$60/kg. Nevertheless they offer the best snorkelling in Sulawesi. The mangrove has been cleared and small hotels and homestays have been built on Badudaka (Wakai) and Waleakodi (Dolong). To get the best out of the islands you can either hire your own canoe (hard and hot work), or get taken to your own island for the day.

Because of the richness of the fauna here and its high rate of biodiversity there is currently a campaign being orchestrated by Jatna Supriatna to have the area declared a national park. At the moment, apparently because there is little sense of local community solidarity, the population are not reacting to the gradual destruction of the habitat – and their livelihoods.

● **Accommodation Waiki** (on N coast of Badudaka Island): there is no beach at Waiki itself, only verandas at hotels; consequently there is limited privacy. It is necessary to rent a boat from the hotels to get to the beaches, and the reef for snorkelling. Motorboat to atolls 20,000Rp, return (with collection at pre-arranged time). Canoe hire 4,000Rp. **B-E** *Togian Islands Hotel*, all incl of 3 meals, restaurant on stilts, calm surroundings, gift shop, edge of tranquil village, this hotel is the main driving force behind the development of the area at present; **D** *Kaderi beach*, 3 cottages and restaurant, completed Jul 1994, managed by *Togian Islands Hotel*, price incl all meals and transport; **D** *Taipi Island*, 3 cottages, owned by *Togian Islands Hotel*, price incl all meals and transport, paradise, whole island to yourselves; **E** *Bolilanga Indah Losmen*, Katupat Island, all meals incl; **E** *Indah Losmen*, Tongkabo Island, all meals incl; **E** *Sederhant Losmen* and *Surya Losmen*.

● **Transport Sea Ferry**: from Poso departs Mon and Thur 2200, goes via islands and on to Gorontalo; return boats leave Gorontalo Mon and Fri evenings. From Poso to Ampana, 6 hrs (6,000Rp); to Waiki, 4 hrs (9,000Rp); to Katupat and/or Tongkabo, 1 hr (10,000Rp); to Dolong, 3 hrs (12,500Rp); to Pagimana (15,000Rp); to Gorontalo, 9 hrs (20,000Rp). It costs 1,000Rp for any leg by boat between islands. Tickets can be purchased on the boat, pay extra for a cabin (9-10,000Rp). **NB** Times above do not take into account the time spent at each port of call, for example if returning to Poso it is quicker to leave the ferry at Ampana and take the bus into Poso.

PALU

Palu, with a population of 150,000, is the capital of the province of Central Sulawesi. Located on the S shores of Palu Bay, it is sandwiched between two ranges of mountains running N-S. Because it lies in

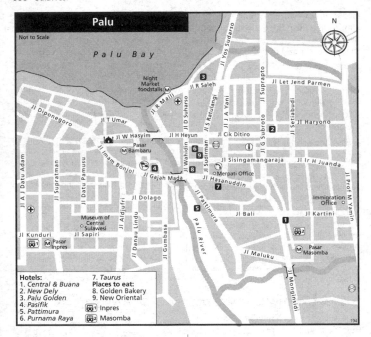

Hotels:
1. Central & Buana
2. New Dely
3. Palu Golden
4. Pasifik
5. Pattimura
6. Purnama Raya
7. Taurus
Places to eat:
8. Golden Bakery
9. New Oriental
🚌1 Inpres
🚌2 Masomba

the rain shadow, rainfall here is very low –
only 600 mm – making the Palu valley one
of the driest spots in Indonesia.

Palu is usually only visited as a rest
stop on the arduous overland route N to
Gorontalo and Manado, and S to Rantepao and Ujung Pandang. The Palu
River neatly divides this dispersed town
into two.

Places of interest
The **Museum of Central Sulawesi** is at Jl
Sapiri 23. It houses a reasonable display of
model traditional houses and assorted local ethnographic artefacts. Outside the
museum stand replicas of the megaliths of
Lore Lindu (see page 666). Admission
200Rp. Open 0900-1600 Tues-Thur, 0900-
1530 Fri and Sat, 0900-1200 Sun. The
central market, **Pasar Bambaru**, is N of Jl
Imam Bonjol, between Jl Teuku Umar and
Jl Hr Dg Pawindu. It is a rather characterless, modern, concrete affair. More

interesting are the **alleys** running E off Jl
Teuku Umar. The sprawling **Pasar Masomba** is SE of town, off Jl Monginsidi.

Excursions
Donggala lies 34 km N of Palu and is a
small, formerly important, port which has
fallen on hard times since being eclipsed
by other ports in Central Sulawesi. The
road to Donggala runs along the W shoreline of Palu Bay past fishing villages and
mangroves. With the hills rising up on
either side it could almost be a loch in the
Scottish highlands. Donggala is quiet and
peaceful, the port picturesque, with cloves
drying on the pavements. **Accommodation** The most popular place is the **C-
D** *Prince John Dive Resort* (formerly
Milano Beach Cottage), 1½ km on past
Douggala, next to the village of Tanjung
Karang, the owners are well known, a German expatriate, Peter, and his Indonesian
wife Maureen, the more expensive rooms

are private bungalows, all on stilts with superb views across the bay (with own bathrooms and veranda), the cheaper rooms are simple, with communal bathrooms, but price includes all 3 meals, meals are served on a communal basis, excellent vegetables, plus a bonus of different snacks in the morning and afternoon, clean white sand beach, very good snorkelling, limited coral, but wide range of fish, also possible to windsurf and scuba dive, deep sea fishing can be arranged with Peter, all your onward travel arrangements can be arranged by Maureen, saving you tiresome journeys into Palu, rec as a good retreat to recharge midway through Sulawesi. *Getting there*: take a kijang from the Inpres terminal at the SW corner of the Inpres market, just S of Jl Kunduri, 40 mins (1,000Rp). Share taxis also travel between the two towns (1,250Rp), leaving from Jl Imam Bonjol, not far from the intersection with Jl Teuku Umar (10,000Rp each way, 4 people, worth it to avoid the hassle). Donggala station is S of the port; walk or catch a dokar into town. For the *Prince John Drive Resort* take a taxi or dokar to the resort (1-hr walk through Donggala, up steep hill to resort) – expect to pay 2-5,000Rp. But the easiest way is to go to *Milano Ice Cream* (T 23857, F 23256), in centre of Palu which is owned by Peter and Maureen and arrange transport there.

Excursions

Kamarora Forest lies 55 km from Palu. It is a good place for bird watching. Camping facilities available. *Getting there*: 2 hrs by car (taxi hire available).

Tours

Palu is the base for specialist tours to the **Lore Lindu** and **Morowali National Parks** (see page 665). Recommended are the well-organized tours of *Katriall Utama*. A 5-day all-inclusive tour costs US$400-$450 (1-4 people). Treks to visit the hilltribes of Central Sulawesi are organized by the *Milano Restaurant*, Jl Hasanuddin 2.

Local information
● **Accommodation**

A *Palu Golden*, Jl Raden Saleh 1, T 21126, F 23230, a/c, pool (usually empty), the characterful though run-down Palu Beach has been demolished and replaced by this nondescript structure, 'best' in town with comfortable rooms, tour groups stay here, discounts are often available.

B *Wisata*, Jl S Parman 39, T 21175, F 22427, a/c, clean, well-run hotel, even has a fitness centre – of sorts.

C *Pattimura*, Jl Pattimura 18, T 21775, restaurant; **C-D** *Central*, Jl RA Kartini 6 (behind Warpostel office), T 22418, a/c, immaculate new hotel run by Warpostel, price incl breakfast, rec.

D *Buana*, Jl RA Kartini 8, T 21475, some a/c, clean, pleasant atmosphere, walking distance from Masomba bus terminal, rec; **D** *New Dely*, Jl Tadulako 17, T 21037.

E *Kemajuan*, Jl Cokroaminoto 57 (nr the Pasar Baru), T 21479, basic; **E** *Pasifik*, Jl Gaja Mada 99, T 22675, good clean rooms, best on airy top floor, the most popular budget hotel in Palu, rec; **E** *Penginapan Karsam*, Jl Dr Suharso 50, T 21776, rather dirty, attached mandis; **E** *Purnama Raya*, Jl Dr Wahidin 4, T 23646, with mandis, basic, but clean, rec; **E** *Taurus*, Jl Hasanuddin, rooms and mandis could be cleaner.

● **Places to eat**

♦*Andalas*, Jl Raden Saleh 50, good Padang food; ♦*Golden Bakery*, intersection Jl Hasanuddin and Jl Dr Wahidin, good cakes; ♦*Meranu Setiabudi*, Jl Setia Budi 44, excellent Chinese/Indonesian and seafood; ♦*New Oriental*, Jl Hasanuddin II, great Chinese food.

Foodstalls: one of the most pleasant places to eat or drink is at the stalls which setup on the seafront, just W of the *Palu Golden Hotel* on Jl Raja Moili. With the onshore breeze, view and wicker chairs it is very civilized and cheap.

● **Airline offices**

Bouraq, Jl Juanda 87, T 22995; **Garuda** and **Merpati**, Jl Hasanuddin 71, T 21172.

● **Banks & money changers**

Concentrated on Jl Jend Sudirman, Jl Imam Bonjol and Jl Hasanuddin. **Ekspor Impor**, Jl Hasanuddin.

● **Hospitals & medical services**

Hospital: Jl Dr Suharso 33, T 21270.

● **Post & telecommunications**
Area code: 0451.
General Post Office: Jl Jend Sudirman 15-17.
Warpostel: Jl RA Kartini 6, T 23411, international telephone, telegram and fax.

● **Tour companies & travel agents**
Aksa Utama, Jl Hasanuddin 33, T 21295; *Ambas Corporation*, Jl Hasanuddin 21b, T 21820; *Bemagy Travel*, Jl Cik Ditiro 9, T 21529; *Celebes Citra Wisata*, Jl Hasanuddin 11, T 24986; *Katriall Utama*, Jl Hasanuddin 10, T 23236, F 23017; *Rajawali*, Jl SIS Aldjufri 12B, T 21095; *Wisata Gautama Putra*, Jl Sis Aldjufri 10a, T 52334.

● **Tourist offices**
Central Sulawesi Tourist Office, Jl Cik Ditiro 32, T 2175, open 0800-1400 Mon-Thur, 0800-1100 Fri, 0800-1300 Sat, handouts available and they will also help with organizing treks to Lore Lindu National Park and the Bada Valley (see page 665). Jl Raja Moili 103, T 21793.

● **Useful addresses**
Immigration Office: Jl RA Kartini, T 21433.
PHPA Office: Jl Moh Yamin.

● **Transport**
Local Microlets: 250Rp around town.

Air Palu's Mutiara airport is 7 km SE of town. Regular daily connections on Merpati or Bouraq with Ujung Pandang, Gorontalo, Manado Toli Toli and Luwuk, and 4 flights a week to Poso. There is an information and hotel booking counter at the airport. Taxis to town, 5,000Rp.

Road Bus: the long-distance Masomba terminal is between Jl Monginsidi and Jl TG Pagimpuan. Regular connections with Gorontalo 24 hrs, Manado 36 hrs, Rantepao 24 hrs, Ujung Pandang, Soppeng, Watampone, Sengkang, Palopo, Pare Pare, and Poso 8 hrs. Bus companies have their offices at Masomba terminal and bemos travel constantly between the terminal and the town centre. In addition, *Bina Wisata Sulteng*, Jl SIS Aldjufri 12B, run buses S to Ujung Pandang and Rantepao. Minibuses to Rantepao are operated by *Modern* on Jl Pramuka (near intersection with Jl Jend Sudirman) 18 hrs. Regular connections with Poso 7 hrs and Tentena from bus offices on Jl Raden Saleh (eg *Alugoro* at No 48) and Jl S Parman (eg *Jawa Indah* at No 5). Buses from these offices also travel along the E 'leg' of Sulawesi to such rarely visited towns as Bunta, Luwuk and Ampana. The roads N to Gorontalo and Manado and S towards Palopo are slow, although much improved in recent years and being further upgraded.

Sea Boat: larger vessels, including the Pelni ships *Kambuna*, *Umsini* and *Tidar*, dock at Pantoloan on the E shores of Palu Bay (see route schedules, page 921). Pelni office is at Jl Gaja Mada 86, T 21696. Get to Pantoloan by bus from the Masomba terminal.

PALU TO MANADO

From Palu, the road crosses Sulawesi's N limb to the E shore at Toboli and then follows the coast N to the attractive town of Gorontalo. Before Gorontalo, a road crosses the mountainous spine of the island to the small, out-of-the-way port of Toli-Toli. From Gorontalo, the road cuts across to the N coast and runs E to the provincial capital of Manado. The coral reefs off Manado offer some of the finest diving in Southeast Asia, and there are a large number of worthwhile excursions from the city. It is also a transport hub for air and sea connections with Maluku and Irian Jaya. Off Sulawesi's N coast are the rarely visited Sangihe and Talaud islands.

TOLI-TOLI

This small town on the N coast of Sulawesi's northern 'leg' is a locally important port but because it lies off the main trans-Sulawesi highway is not on the itineraries of most visitors. The mountainous spine further serves to isolate the town from the rest of the island and when the first 5-year development plan, *Repelita I*, was introduced in 1969 the town was still inaccessible by land.

Excursions Batu Bangga Beach offers the best swimming in the area; it lies 12 km N of town. *Getting there*: bemos runs N along the coast.

Lutungan Island lies only 1 km off the coast and is said to be the site of the tomb of one of the former kings of Toli-Toli. The surrounding waters offer reasonable snorkelling and swimming. *Getting there*: boats can be chartered from town; ask at your hotel.

● **Accommodation** *Anda*, Jl H Mansyur 27; *Nirmala*, Jl Jend Sudirman; *Salamae*, Jl Jend A Yani.

● **Tour companies & travel agents** *Alia Dirgantara Travel Service*, Jl Suprapto 69.

● **Transport Air** Merpati operate one return flight a day to Palu. **Road Bus**: buses link Toli-Toli with Palu, Gorontalo and Manado; the trip is arduous. **Sea Boat**: the Pelni ships *Kambuna* and *Leuser* call at Toli-Toli on their fortnightly circuits (see page 921 for route schedules). The Pelni office is on Jl Yos Sudarso. Smaller ferries also operate between Toli-Toli and Donggala (Palu), Manado and Bitung.

GORONTALO

A peaceful, low-rise, low-key and friendly town with bendis, houses with verandahs, fretwork and wicker chairs. Few 'sights' as such, but a perfect place to rest-up on the overland route between Palu and Manado. Unlike so many other towns in Indonesia it has not yet suffered the scourge of the Redevelopment and Shopping Centre Disease. There are some wonderful examples of **Dutch provincial architecture** – the hospital on Jl Jend A Yani and the Mitra Cinema at Jl S Parman 45 (Art Deco) for example. The **Pasar Satya Pradja** is at the intersection of Jl S Parman and Jl MT Haryono. More interesting is the **Pasar Sentral** with its narrow alleys, at the intersection of Jl Pattimura and Jl Dr Sam Ratulangi. Gorontalo has two small harbours – bigger ships dock at Kwandang, 45 km NW. To get to the smaller and closer **Pelabuhan Kota** (literally 'Town Port') take a bemo from the Pasar Sentral.

Excursions Kwandang is a port 45 km NW of Gorontalo. Shortly before the town there are two **forts**, a short walk from the main road. *Getting there*: by bus from the Andalas terminal.

Panua Reserve lies about 100 km W of Gorontalo, on the coast near Marisa. This is one of the spots where the rare and extraordinary maleo bird (*Macrocephalon maleo*) nests – although uncontrolled egg collection has substantially reduced the number of nesting adults (see page 684). *Getting there*: by bus from the Andalas terminal.

● **Accommodation B** *Saronde*, Jl Walanda Maramis 17, T 21735, some a/c, biggest hotel in town, charming owner with good English, set around courtyard, range of rooms, rec; **C** *Indah Ria*, Jl Jend A Yani 20, T 21296, some a/c, central, friendly, clean, price incl all meals, rec;

C-D *Wisata*, Jl 23 Januari 19, T 21736, some a/c, range of rooms, rec; **E** *Penginapan Sinar Utama*, Jl Dr Sam Ratulangi 33B, nr market and bemo station, thin walls, dark but clean and homely; **E** *Teluk Kau*, Jl S Parman 42, T 21785, rather shabby and down-at-heel; **E** *Wisma Budi Utomo*, Jl Budi Utomo 24, T 21564, clean and well run, rec; **F** *Penginapan Teluk Kau*, Jl S Parman 44, wonderful wooden villa, but rooms are dark and dirty, they will not always take foreigners.

● **Places to eat** ♦*Brantas*, Jl Hasanuddin 5, bakery and reasonable Indonesian dishes; ♦**Foodstalls**, cheap and good, set up on Jl Pertiwi in the evenings.

● **Airline offices** Bouraq, Jl Jend A Yani 34, T 21070; **Merpati**, *Hotel Wisata*, Jl 23 Januari 19, T 21736.

● **Banks & money changers** Bank Dagang Negara, Bank Rakyat Indonesia and BNI all on Jl Jend A Yani nr the intersection with Jl MT Haryono.

● **Post & telecommunications Area code**: 0435. **General Post Office**: Jl Jend A Yani 14. **Perumtel**: Jl 23 Januari 35.

● **Shopping Basketware**: local baskets can be bought at the Pasar Sentral. **Krawang embroidery**: a speciality of the area. Shops along Jl Jend Suprapto.

● **Transport Local Bemos**: the main terminal is at the Pasar Sentral, at the N end of Jl Dr Sam Ratulangi, nr the intersection with Jl Pattimura. Frequent departures for the long-distance Andalas bus terminal. 200Rp around town. **Horse-drawn bendis**: 2,000Rp/hr for touring around town. **Microlets**: can be chartered for approximately 4,000Rp/hr for touring around town and the harbour. **Air** Jalaluddin airport is 32 km NW of town. Regular daily connections by Merpati or Bouraq with Palu, Manado, Ujung Pandang and to Ternate and Ambon in Maluku. Minibuses wait to take passengers to town, 45 mins (3,500Rp). The road between Gorontalo and the airport passes through the charming town of Limboto 30 mins (4,000Rp). **Road Bus**: the long-distance Andalas terminal is on the outskirts of town; get there by regular bemo from the Pasar Sentral. Regular connections with Manado 12 hrs and Palu 24 hrs. **Sea Boat**: the main port is at Kwandang, 45 km NW of town, on the N shores of this 'leg' of Sulawesi. The Pelni ship *Umsini* stops here (see route map page 921).

Pelni office, Jl 23 Januari 31, T 20419. There are regular buses to Kwandang from the Andalas terminal.

MANADO

Looking out from the 'beach' front over Manado Bay, it is easy to understand why travellers such as Alfred Russel Wallace thought the area so beautiful: the two peninsulas curling around like crab claws, and Bunaken Island, the volcanic cone of Manado Tua, and the other islands, shimmering in the distance. However, for people arriving here after travelling through the quiet towns of Central and N Sulawesi, Manado is something of a culture shock – the city centre is brash, noisy and fast-paced. It is as if the influence of the nearby Philippines has filtered in across the Celebes Sea to transform the city.

Manado has a population of 275,000 and is the capital of the province of N Sulawesi. The area around Manado is known as Minahasa, and was a separate province until 1964, when it was combined with Gorontalo to form N Sumatra. Although rather featureless, it is – by Indonesian standards – visibly wealthy. This wealth is built primarily on cloves, but also on coconuts, nutmeg and coffee. The area is now being targeted for rapid tourist growth; the airport runway is being lengthened to take wide-bodied jets, and the big hotel chains are moving-in.

History

In the 16th century, Minahasa consisted of a number of small, independent states including Gorontalo, Limboto and the Talaud and Sangihe islands. The Spanish and Portuguese were already calling at ports in the area in the 1500s, and by the middle of the 16th century missionaries were having considerable success converting the population to Christianity. The Dutch concluded a treaty with the chiefs of Minahasa in 1679, heralding nearly 300 years of close association between the Christians of the area and the colonial government. Among the various peoples of the East Indies, the Dutch felt a greater affinity for the Minahasans than with almost any other group. This led to a proportionately greater role in the Dutch civil service and army, a rapid development spread of education and health facilities – in which Church schools were at the forefront – and a more pervasive 'westernization' of culture.

It was this close association which played a part in encouraging rebels in N Sulawesi to join with the PRRI – the Revolutionary Government of the Indonesian Republic – in the Permesta rebellion of 1958 and challenge the authority

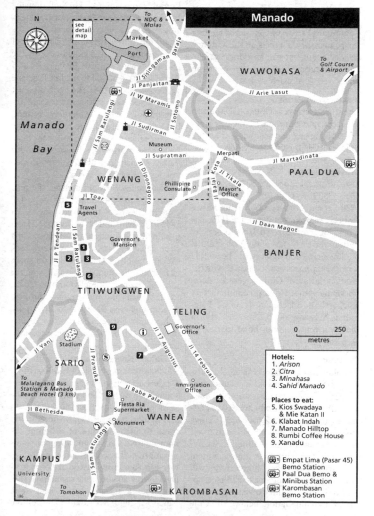

Manado

Hotels:
1. *Arison*
2. *Citra*
3. *Minahasa*
4. *Sahid Manado*

Places to eat:
5. Kios Swadaya & Mie Katan II
6. Klabat Indah
7. Manado Hilltop
8. Rumbi Coffee House
9. Xanadu

1. Empat Lima (Pasar 45) Bemo Station
2. Paal Dua Bemo & Minibus Station
3. Karombasan Bemo Station

of President Sukarno and his associates. The two centres of this rebellion against Jakarta were W Sumatra and N Sulawesi. Sukarno demanded harsh reprisals against the rebels, and in Feb 1958 the Indonesian airforce bombed Manado. By mid-May the army had overwhelmed the rebels in Gorontalo and in late-Jun recaptured Manado. The US, anxious about Sukarno's association with the Indonesian Communist Party even considered sending troops to assist the rebels; in the end they decided not to, but sent arms instead. The rebellion stuttered on until 1961 when the rebels were finally defeated.

Places of interest

There are few places of interest in Manado – most people come here for the incomparable diving and snorkelling, and for the sights outside the city (see below, Excursions). The **North Sulawesi Provincial Museum** is on Jl WR Supratman (S of town) and has a moderate collection. Open 0800-1330 Tues-Thur, 0800-1030 Fri, 0800-1230 Sat and Sun. The **Ban Hing Kiong Chinese temple** is at the end of Jl Panjaitan, in the centre of town. It was originally built in the early part of the 19th century, but has since been renovated. The temple is neither impressive nor unusual, with the requisite array of Chinese temple paraphernalia – incense, a predominance of gold, red and black, and lanterns. **Pelabuhan Manado**, off Jl Suprapto, also in the town centre, might be of interest to ship and port lovers.

Excursions

Bunaken Sea Garden is Manado's greatest attraction. It is a magnificent underwater park with crystal clear waters, named after Bunaken Island which lies 8 km offshore (for full entry, see page 683). *Getting there*: Most of the major hotels and travel agents can arrange snorkelling, scuba diving, or just viewing from a glass bottom boat, trips to Bunaken; however you will end up being part of an excursion organized by one of the three dive resorts listed under accommodation, below. All of the resorts have people meeting each flight at the airport, they offer free transfer to and from airport. They all visit the same set of dive sites in the Marine Park, and lunch on one of two islands.

Excursions south from Manado

Tomb of the nationalist leader Imam Bonjol is to be found 8 km S of Manado. Just before the town of Pineleng, there is a small paved road to the left which winds uphill for 2 km to this tomb of a native of W Sumatra, who was exiled here by the Dutch after his capture during the Padri Wars (see page 486). He died in Pineleng on 6 November 1864. The tomb does not begin to match the stature of the man. Admission by donation. *Getting there*: by minibus from the Karombasan terminal either to Kali (which passes the tomb) or the more frequent service towards Tomohon, walking the last 2 km up the hill from the main road (ask for *makam Imam Bonjol*).

Continuing S from Pineleng, the road winds upwards (there are said to be 135 corners) between two volcanoes – Mt Lokon (1,589m) and Mt Mahawu (1,311m) towards the hill village of **Kinilow**. On a clear day, there are stunning views back over the city, with Bunaken and the other islands in the distance. 12 km on from the turn-off for Imam Bonjol's tomb and 20 km from Manado the road reaches Kinilow. **Accommodation D** *Indraloka*, T 64, pool, rather down-at-heel. *Getting there*: regular departures from Manado's Karombasan terminal.

Kakas Kasen is another hill town which almost merges with Kinilow and is a more attractive, horticultural centre. Villages on this upland plateau – known as Minahasa – are almost 100% Christian and small communities have not one, but three to five churches of different denominations. On Sun mornings, streams of smartly dressed Minahasans file to worship. **Accommodation B** *Lokon Resting Resort*, T 203, new, clean and peaceful, discounts available. Paths lead from Kakas Kasen up **Mt Lokon**. The volcano

Around Manado

has recently stopped erupting, making it possible to climb to the summit in half a day, returning by following the lava flow back to the road. **Mt Mahawu** is a spectacular smoking volcano; it is possible to walk right around the crater rim. Check at the tourist office in town for the latest news. Climbing the volcano from Kakas Kasen should not take more than half a day. *Getting there*: regular departures from Manado's Karombasan terminal.

Tomohon is 25 km from Manado and 700m above sea-level. It is rather a shabby town notable as the centre of missionary activity in the area and for perhaps the finest bendi horses in Indonesia. *Getting there*: regular departures from Manado's Karombasan terminal.

Lake Linau lies almost 1 km off the road from the village of *Lahendong* and 32 km S of Manado. Sulphurous odours tell the story: steam roars out of vents in the ground and muddy water bubbles noisily – it is not very spectacular, and is spoilt by discarded rubbish. *Getting there*: regular departures from Manado's Karombasan terminal to Lahendong, and then walk the final 1 km.

Continuing S, some 37 km from Manado, is **Sonder** – the centre of clove production in the area. Clove trees can be seen growing at the side of the road (sparsely leaved, and rather like eucalypts): the smell of the spice drying permeates the air. *Getting there*: regular departures from Manado's Karombasan terminal.

Kawangkoan cave complex – one of a series – lies just N of Kawangkoan, over a bridge (there is another just S of Tanggari). They were dug on the orders of the Japanese to store and protect supplies and ammunition from Allied bombing. For a small gratuity someone in the restaurant opposite will provide a torch (to illuminate the bats). This is only interesting for those who dream of being on the set of a Harrison Ford film. *Getting there*: regular departures from Manado's Karombasan terminal.

Watu Pinabetengan is a large boulder which lies 3 km beyond the village of Pinabetengan, on the lower slopes of Mt Rindengan. On it are as yet undeciphered pictographic carvings. It was at this spot that the 17 chiefs of the Minahasa tribes met to discuss important matters. During the full moon, ceremonies and sacrifices are still held. It is disappointing – graffiti obscures the dim carvings and the stone itself has been set in concrete and an ugly pavilion built over it. *Getting there*: catch a bus to Kawangkoan from Manado's Karombasan terminal, and from there a bemo to Pinabetengan village. It is a pleasant 2½-km walk uphill to the site. A path behind the stone leads down into a ravine to some **hot springs**.

The town of **Langoan** lies S on the main road from Kawangkoan, some 54 km from Manado. From here bemos run N to **Kakas** on the S shores of **Lake**

Tondano, and from there link the various communities that line the beautiful W shores of the lake. From Tondano at the N extremity of the lake there are bemos to Airmadidi (see Excursions SE from Manado, below), and from there back to Manado's Paal II terminal.

Excursions southeast from Manado

Airmadidi lies 19 km SE of Manado. It is proudly touted as the **kenari nut** capital of Indonesia (kenari nuts are tropical almonds from which the oil is usually extracted; they are also used as shade trees in the cultivation of nutmeg (see page 797). There is a big copra factory in Airmadidi, and some examples of *waruga* (see below). Tourists usually stop here to visit the **Taman Anggrek** or **orchid garden**, which has a reasonable collection of orchids (disappointing out of season). Admission by donation. The garden is on the Manado side of Airmadidi, just past the 6 km marker. *Getting there*: by bemo from the Paal II terminal.

Mount Kalabat is a 1,995m-high volcano NE of Airmadidi. It can be climbed in 4-6 hrs. Popular with university students from Manado who climb during the night and watch the sun rise. *Getting there*: take a bemo to Airmadidi from the Paal II terminal.

Taman Purbakala Waruga is a cemetery in **Sawangan**, 24 km from Manado, and 50m off the main road. It contains 144 upright megalithic sarcophagi or *waruga*, with prism-shaped lids, each of which would have been used by one family. They were assembled here from surrounding villages in 1817 and the oldest is believed to date from the 10th century. The ancient Minahasans 'buried' their dead above ground to stop the smell of the rotting corpses reaching the earth god Makawalang – an event which would have led to earthquakes. It is speculated that corpses were placed upright in the *waruga* because this is the way the foetus was thought to form in the womb and so this is the way a dead person should enter the

Megalithic sarcophagi or *waruga* at Sawangan

afterlife. The massive stone chambers and lids are decorated with crude carvings – some depicting 17th century figures in frock coats. Just outside the cemetery is a small museum containing artefacts retrieved from the sarcophagi – bronze bracelets, ceramics from China and spear heads. Admission by donation. *Getting there*: take a bemo to Airmadidi from the Paal II terminal, and then another from Airmadidi to Sawangan.

Tondano lies S from Sawangan, 36 km from Manado, on the N shores of **Lake Tondano**. The area is still volcanically active and many villages on the lake shore have hot springs and public baths. Hot water is even piped through bores sunk 75m into Lake Tondano's bed. In Tondano town, a number of hotels/losmen offer thermal hot water (eg *Asri, Kanopasu* and the *Tamaska Hijau Homestay*). The Minahasa tourism office is out of town on the road to Tomohon. *Getting there*: bus from Manado's Paal II terminal to Airmadidi and then an onward bemo to Tondano.

Remboken is situated on the W shore of Lake Tondano, almost 50 km S of Manado. From Tondano, bemos run down both shores of the lake, linking the various lakeside communities. The W shore is particularly attractive. Just N of Remboken (49 km from Manado) is a lakeside **Taman Wisata** (tourist garden) with accommodation (**C**), hot swimming baths and restaurant. Very popular with locals at the weekend. Continuing S from Remboken, the road leads to **Kakas** on the S edge of the lake. From here bemos run to **Langoan**, and from there N back to Manado's Karombasan terminal (see Excursions S from Manado, above). *Getting there*: by bemo from Manado's Paal II terminal to Airmadidi and then an onward bemo to Remboken.

Excursions east of Manado

Tangkoko Batu Angus National Park is a comparatively small reserve covering just 8,867 ha of tropical rainforest, encompassing the peaks of Tangkoko (1,109m), Batuangus and Duasaudara, in the eastern part of Bitung. Duasaudara, the highest of the peaks at 1,351m is a dormant volcano that last erupted in 1839. Tangkoko was first established as a forest reserve

Tangkoko Batu Angus National Park

Selected large mammals and birds of Tangkoko Batu Angus Nature Reserve, showing which are endemic and which are exploited by humans.

English name	Scientific name	Endemic	Hunted
Anoa	Bubalus depressicornis	Y	Y
Sulawesi pig	Sus celebensis	Y	Y
Javan rusa	Cervus timorensis	N	Y
Crested black macaque	Macaca nigra	Y	Y
Bear cuscus	Phalanger ursinus	N	Y
Babirusa	Babyrousa babirussa	Y	Y
Maleo	Macrocephalon maleo	Y	Eggs
Tabon scrubfowl	Megapodius cumingii	N	Eggs
Red junglefowl	Gallus gallus	N	Y
Red-knobbed hornbill	Aceros cassidix	Y	Y
Sulawesi tarictic hornbill	Penelopides exarhatus	Y	N

Source: O'Brien and Kinnaird in *Oryx* 30(2) 1996

in 1919. The Reserve is home to several endemic species (see page 613), including the large-eyed jumping tarsier (*Tarsius spectrum*), the anoa or dwarf buffalo, bear cuscus, Sulawesi hornbill, black macaques, yaki (*Macaca nigra*), taon bird (*Rhiticeros cassidiz*), and the extraordinary and endangered maleo bird (see box, page 684). Being a fairly small reserve, the chances of seeing an abundance of wildlife are high and because it covers a wide range of habitats for such a small area the flora and fauna are rich. But the area surrounding the park is settled and the wildlife is under threat. In 1989 the Mackinnons estimated there were 15,000 crested black macaques in Tangkoko; in 1996, Timothy O'Brien and Margaret Kinnaird reckoned there were just 3,100, and predicted the disappearance of the species there. Trails into the park lead from Danowudu, where there is also a campsite. Admission to park 750Rp/day. En route to Batuputih (sometimes confusingly referred to as Tangkoko), the road passes through Danowudu where there is a trail through a small (5 ha) protected reserve of rainforest containing around 30 rare species of bird. **Accommodation** Stay at Batuputih (get park permit here), where there are five homestays (**E**), including *Mamma Rosa* and *Ranger's Homestay*; from here you can hire a forest ranger (10,000Rp), rec, and go

on early morning and evening walks in the forest. Hiking boots are not necessary, trails are well defined. There is a black sand beach nearby with excellent snorkelling. Tour companies in Manado also run tours here. *Getting there*: take a bus from Paal II terminal in Manado towards Bitung, get off at Girian (1,500Rp), from here get another bus or jeep to Batuputih (2,000Rp), road can be difficult. **A** *The Kungkungan Resort* is on the coast just N of the port of Bitung, run by an American, this small 'boutique' resort built out over the sea offers excellent service in an idyllic setting, good diving – although perhaps not as spectacular as Bunaken. *Getting there*: by bus from Paal II terminal in Manada to Bitung.

Tours

A number of tour companies in Manado offer roughly the same range of tours (all prices are for a group of 3-4 people). **City tours** (US$12, half day); **highland/Minahasa tour** to Tomohon, Kawangkoan, Remboken, Sawangan (US$32); **Tangkoko Batu Angus National Park** (US$45); **Bunaken sea garden** (US$35 snorkelling, US$65 diving).

Festivals

Jul: *Bunaken Festival*, assorted cultural and sporting festivities; not a traditional event but created by and for the tourist industry.

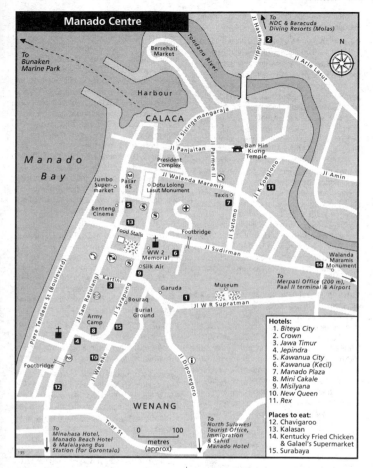

Manado Centre

To NDC & Baracuda Diving Resorts (Molas)

To Bunaken Marine Park

Bersehati Market

Tondano River

Jl Hasanuddin

Jl Arie Lasut

N

Harbour

CALACA

Manado Bay

Jl Sisingamangaraja

Jl Panjaitan

Jl Parmen II

Ban Hin Kiong Temple

President Complex

Jumbo Super-market

Pasar 45

Dotu Lolong Lasut Monument

Jl Walanda Maramis

Jl K Soegoro

Jl Amin

Taxis

Benteng Cinema

Food Stalls

Footbridge

WW 2 Memorial

Silk Air

Jl Sudirman

Jl Sutomo

Walanda Maramis Monument

To Merpati Office (200 m), Paal II terminal & Airport

Garuda

Museum

Pier Tendean St (Boulevard)

Jl Sam Ratulangi

Kartini

Jl Sarapung

Bouraq

Burial Ground

Jl W R Supratman

Army Camp

Jl Wakeke

Pol

Footbridge

Jl Diponegoro

WENANG

Toar St

0   100
metres (approx)

To Minahasa Hotel, Manado Beach Hotel & Malalayang Bus Station (for Gorontalo)

To North Sulawesi Tourist Office, Immigration & Sahid Manado Hotel

Hotels:
1. Biteya City
2. Crown
3. Jawa Timur
4. Jepindra
5. Kawanua City
6. Kawanua (Kecil)
7. Manado Plaza
8. Mini Cakale
9. Misilyana
10. New Queen
11. Rex

Places to eat:
12. Chavigaroo
13. Kalasan
14. Kentucky Fried Chicken & Galael's Supermarket
15. Surabaya

Local information
● Accommodation

Manado has a lack of cheap accommodation, but some good mid-range hotels. The new 4-star **A+-A** *Boulevard Hotel* on the sea front was scheduled to have opened in late 1995 or 1996 and on doing so should have become the town's ritziest place. **A+** *Sedona Hotel Manado*, a new beach front hotel with 257 rooms due to open in 1996. It will be located 25 km from the city (and 39 km from the airport) on a large 20 ha site on Tateli Beach so is a place for those who want a relaxing seaside holiday and do not intend to explore the city. All facilities.

A *Kawanua City*, Jl Sam Ratulangi 1, T 67777, F 65220, a/c, restaurant, coffee shop, pool, money changer, dull modern hotel, central location, not rec for the tourist, pretensions of grandeur totally unfulfilled; **A** *Manado Beach Hotel*, Tasik Ria, 18 km S of town centre, T 67001, F 67007, 200 rm, restaurant, coffee shop, pool, sunken poolside bar, watersports, relaxing palm gardens and white sand beach but poor location for anyone hoping to do more than lie on a beach and sip cocktails, low occupancy rate of 50% shows it is struggling – discounts available.

B *Hotel New Queen*, Jl Wakeke 12-14, T 65979, F 65748, immaculate small hotel, winner of Governor's trophy for cleanest hotel in Manado for 6 years, full a/c, restaurant, central, but off main roads, good value when compared to other top range in town; **B** *Manado Plaza Hotel*, Jl Walanda Maramis 1, T 51124, F 62940, situated in grubby shopping/cinema complex, noisy, shabby rooms, poor value, large restaurant, fitness centre, travel agent *Trampil Tours*; **B** *Sahid Manado*, Jl Babe Palar Manado 1, T 51688, F 63326, situated in the hills behind the town centre, good views across bay, restaurant, coffee shop, swimming pool (open to non-residents, 4,000Rp), friendly and helpful staff, but a rather soulless modern business class hotel; **B** *Tulip Airport Hotel*, 1½ km from airport, a/c, only worth considering if flying next day; **B-C** *Malalayang Indah*, Jl Raya Malalayang, 5 km S of town, T 61523, F 61525, wooden cottages set in well kept mature gardens, some a/c, restaurant, peaceful location on the waterfront.

C *Arison*, Jl Sam Ratulangi 85, T 64739, some a/c, clean maze of corridors and whitewashed bannisters, plenty of house plants help create tranquil feel, compact, clean rooms, breakfast only; **C** *Biteya City*, Jl WR Supratman 11, T 66598, new hotel on hill behind Garuda office (close to museum), comfortable rooms, some a/c with good views across town, breakfast only, friendly staff, pleasant small hotel slightly off beaten track, quiet; **C** *Minahasa*, Jl Sam Ratulangi 199, T 62059, some a/c, restaurant (order evening meals in advance), popular old villa with character, plenty of communal seating areas, quiet veranda at back overlooking small garden, friendly with good service, price incl morning and afternoon tea; **C** *Yuta*, Jl Santu Joseph 2, T 52153, F 63857, a/c, restaurant, snorkelling rental, simple, small, mid-range hotel; **C-D** *Malinda*, Jl Garuda 29, T 52918, some a/c; **C-D** *Wisma Charlotte*, Jl Yos Sudarso 56, T 62265, F 65100, well-run, N of town centre, price incl breakfast.

D *Citra*, Jl Sam Ratulangi XVIII 12, T 63812, simple, plain rooms, clean, homely shady veranda on 1st flr, new relaxing area on roof with views of sunset, in quiet lane off Jl Sam Ratulangi, rec; **D** *Jawa Timur*, Jl Kartini 5, T 51970, small central hotel in quiet side street, spotless rooms, rooms downstairs open onto TV lounge, close to GPO, Telekom and Pelni offices, rec;

D *Jepindra*, Jl Sam Ratulangi 33, T 64049, a/c, central for all facilities, bathrooms shabby and indifferent water supply, price incl breakfast (boiled egg, chocolate sandwich, coffee), cheerful and helpful staff, rec; **D** *Mini Cakale*, Jl Korengkeng 40, T 52942, clean good value, shady sitting area, some rooms overlook tiny garden, noisy rooms at the front; **D** *Misilyana*, Jl Sarapung 11, T 63445, pleasant old house with heavy wooden furniture and porcelain, dark cool rooms, owner speaks good Dutch and English, central, but on busy corner, name derived from the first letters of the owner's 4 daughters; **D-E** *Kawanua (Kecil)*, Jl Sudirman II 40, T 63842, F 61974, some a/c, restaurant and lounge in open air central courtyard, slightly difficult to find: down alley next to footbridge opp hospital on Jl Sudirman, selection of second-hand paperbacks and snorkels available at reception.

E *Crown*, Jl Hasanuddin 28, T 66277, F 52511, dirty budget hotel; **E** *Rex*, Jl Kol Soegiono 3, T 51136, F 67789, spotless new hotel, no frills, tiny white tiled cell-like rooms, communal washing facilities, central, convenient for ferries to Bunaken Island, no restaurant, limited lounge area, best budget hotel in town, good security, rec.

F *Jakarta Jaya*, Jl Hasanuddin 25, T 64330, small rooms, but cheap, price incl breakfast; **F** *Keluarga*, Jl Jembatan Singkil, small rooms, thin walls, noisy, basic – and cheap.

Diving accommodation: B-D *Nusantara Diving Centre* (NDC), Molas, T 63988/63955, F 60365/60368, 7 km N of Manado, new large a/c rooms, half open air bathrooms with mini verdant garden, fan cooled bungalows or fan cooled rooms, large bathrooms, discount available in off-season (high season: Jun-Sep and Christmas), restaurant serves excellent buffet nightly, bar by restaurant, next to the jetty, this was the first diving centre in N Sulawesi (estab 1975) and is widely recognized for its professionalism and knowledge of local conditions. The Centre received the 'Kalpataru Award' in 1985 (the highest honour for environmental work in Indonesia), the success of NDC and popularity of diving in the region is largely attributable to the work of Loky Herlambag, the owner of NDC. He has brought together a friendly and dedicated group of people who together make NDC one of the most relaxing places to dive anywhere in the world, rec. SSI Open Water Diving Course: 6 days, full board (US$580-745). Certification from the USA;

Snorkelling: (min 2 persons), US$30/day; Scuba dive: US$60 (2 dives), both include lunch, boat, equipment (extra for BC and regulator). **B-D** *Barracuda Diving Resort*, Molas (office Jl Sam Ratulangi 61), T 54288, F 64848, 8 km N of town, bungalows on hillside with views of Manado and Mt Lokon or local style cottages on stilts, no view, overlooking mangrove, high ceiling, open air dining block and bar by the jetty. This is the newest dive resort in the region, it lacks the friendly welcome of NDC, but is still a pleasant place to stay. Scuba tuition is available. New quick, fibreglass boats, but they have little deck space for relaxing when you're not in water. Snorkelling: (min 3 persons), US$35/day; Scuba dive: US$65 (2 dives), both include lunch, boat, equipment (extra for BC and regulator). Deep sea fishing is also available. *Getting there*: take bemo to Tuminting (250Rp), change to oplet which runs as far as Molas village. **B** *MU-REX* (Manado Underwater Exploration), (office Jl Jend Sudirman 28), T 52116, Desa Kalasey, the smallest of the three scuba operators, friendly attention, attractive bungalows in gardens on the sea front, but inconvenient for visiting Manado town centre.

● **Places to eat**

Minahasan food is spicy hot. Specialities incl *rintek wuuk* or *RW* – pronounced 'air way' (dog), *paniki* (fruit bat), field rat, *bubur manado* (a local congee) and *kenari* (coconut crab). There are a range of restaurants stretched out along Jl Sam Ratulangi from the centre of town.

Chinese: ◆◆◆*Xanadu*, Jl Sam Ratulangi II 88, T 63022, smart, lanterns and linen table cloths, dimly lit, a/c, rec for seafood; ◆◆*Klabat Indah*, Jl Sam Ratulangi 211, T 62405, ornate bamboo entrance flanked by giant Chinese vases, seafood, limited menu (on quiet evenings hit and miss as to what fresh fish available, accept what they have), excellent Ikan Mas Goreng and kangkung rebus; ◆◆*Manado Hilltop*, T 66581, buffet, large restaurant catering for groups, panoramic view of bay, close to N Sulawesi Tourist office; ◆◆*Rumbi Coffee House*, Jl Sam Ratulangi 356, seafood, large selection of dishes, bamboo walls, thatch roof, open air, opp Fiesta Ria Supermarket; ◆*Chavigaroo*, Jl Sam Ratulangi 63, tasty fish, open kitchen at front, watch your meal being prepared, rec.

Indonesian: ◆◆◆*Cakalang* (in *Kawanua City Hotel*), Jl Sam Ratulangi 1, also serves Chinese and International, ambitious menu, disappointing seafood, small portions (nouvelle cuisine?), comfortable location, overlooking pool;

◆◆◆*New Queen Hotel*, also serves International, overpriced menu, bar; ◆◆*Surabaya*, Jl Sarapung 33, T 62562, also serves Chinese, popular with comprehensive menu, but most dishes have canteen, formula blandness, good cold fresh fruit juices (very sweet); ◆*Kalasan*, Jl Sudirman 9, tasty cheap Javanese food; ◆*Solo*, Jl Sam Ratulangi 192, open air, sate and chicken specialities; *Kios Swadaya* and *Mie Katan II* (next to Isuzu garage), Jl Sam Ratulangi, they also serve Minahasan, both very popular with local students, good value.

Jl Sudirman also has a number of good, cheap and very popular **warungs** – eg those just N from the *Kawanua Kecil Hotel*; stalls set up in the evenings on Jl Sudirman nr the intersection with Jl Sam Ratulangi. On the same stretch of road is the ◆◆*Sate House*, seafood, sate and squeaky clean; ◆*Dua Raya*, Jl Piere Tendean 84, good Chinese; *Kentucky Fried Chicken/Svensen's Ice Cream*, Jl Sudirman 73. There are also good moderate priced places on Jl Dr Sutomo, eg *Andalas Fast Food*, *Kios 18*, *Kios Nasi Kuning Sederhana*.

● **Airline offices**

Bouraq, Jl Serapung 27B, T 62757; Garuda, Jl Diponegoro 15, T 51544; Merpati, Jl Balai Kota 1, Mon-Fri 0730-1630, Sat 0830-1500; Silk Air, Jl Sarapung 5, Mon-Fri 0830-1630, Sat 0830-1300.

● **Banks & money changers**

Bumi Daya, Jl Dotulolong Lasut 9; Central Asia, Jl Dotulolong Lasut 6; Ekspor Impor, Jl Sudirman 47; Indra Arta Money Changer, Jl Sam Ratulangi 1 (in the *Kawanua City Hotel*); PT Haji La Tunrung, Jl Korengkeng 40 (money changer close to *Hotel Mini Cakale*); Rakyat Indonesia, Jl Sudirman.

● **Entertainment**

Cinemas: *Benteng*, Jl Sam Ratulangi (opp the *Kawanua City Hotel*); *Plaza* (4 screens), *President*, President Complex, Jl Piere Tendean.

Discos: *Ebony*, 2200-0200, *Plaza Hotel*; *Maramba*, Wed and Sat, *Manado Beach Hotel*.

● **Post & telecommunications**

Area code: 0431.

General Post Office: Jl Sam Ratulangi 21.

Perumtel: Jl Sam Ratulangi 4 (open 24 hrs).

Warpostel: Jl Walanda Maramis 81.

● **Shopping**

Manado's shopping district is crammed into a small area delineated by Jl Sudirman, Jl Dr Sutomo and Jl Sam Ratulangi. Within this quarter there are tailors, opticians and shopping complexes.

Clothing: *Makmur* and *Ramayana* department stores on Jl Walanda Maramis, cheap, reasonable quality.

Krawang embroidery: a Gorontalo speciality, available at *Krawang*, Jl Walanda Maramis and *UD Kawanua*, Jl Balai Kota 1/30 (a private house).

Souvenirs: *Bunaken Souvenir Shop*, Jl Sam Ratulangi 178.

Supermarkets: *Galael's*, Jl Sudirman 73; *Jumbo*, Jl Suprapto 1.

Tailoring services: fast and cheap, many available throughout the city.

Textiles: shops along Jl Dotulolong Lasut.

● **Sport**
Diving: off-season diving (during rainy season) can be cheaper – it's worth bargaining. *Barracuda Dive Club* have been recommended (US$50 for 2 dives, equipment and lunch, after bargaining).

Golf: *Wenang Golf Club*, Jl AA Maramis (airport rd), T 51599, 9 holes, 18 tees, Chinese restaurant and driving range. Green Fee 25,000Rp; club rental 25,000Rp, caddie 5,000Rp. *Getting there*: take airport bound Oplet (Lapangan) from Paal 2 terminal (350Rp).

Swimming: *Kawanua City Hotel* open to non-residents (3,500Rp); *Sahid Manado Hotel*, 4,000Rp non-residents, poolside bar, restaurant.

● **Tour companies & travel agents**
Metropole, Jl Sudirman 135, T 51333, F 66445; *Pandu Express*, Jl Sam Ratulangi 190, T 56188, F 51487; *Pola Pelita Express*, Jl Sam Ratulangi 113, T 60007, F 64520, ask for Rico Taramen, he has good English and an understanding of tourist interests and needs; *Wina Mulia Jaya Tours*, Jl Jend Sudirman 106, T 65227.

● **Tourist offices**
Manado Town Tourist Office, Jl Ahmad Yani Sario; **North Sulawesi Tourist Office**, Jl 17 Augustus, T 64299, open 0800-1400 Mon-Thur, 0800-1100 Fri, 0800-1300 Sat, rather out of town; catch a bemo going to Jl 17 Augustus and get out at the large new Governor's office (ask for the Dinas Pariwisata), it is off the road (signposted), down towards the sea, very helpful, worth the effort, there is also a counter at the airport, again very helpful, plenty of info on

range of accommodation in town; **Parpostel Tourist Office**, Jl Diponegoro 111, T 51723; easier to get to, but not as useful.

● **Useful addresses**
Immigration Office: Jl 17 Augustus, T 63491.
PHPA: Jl Babe Palar 68, T 62688.

● **Transport**
Local Bemos/buses: there are no fewer than 4 bemo/minibus terminals serving different local towns (see map for locations of terminals). The central Pasar 45 terminal (Terminal Empat Lima) serves Tuminting and also has constant bemos travelling to the other three terminals; the Karombasan terminal serves Pineleng, Tomohon, Sonder, Kawangkoan, Langoan, and Tondano; the Paal II (Paal Dua) is the terminal for Airmadidi, Bitung and the airport (from Airmadidi there are buses to Tondano); and the Malalayang terminal for Tanawangko (from here there are buses to Tomohon) and also for long distance buses to Kotamobagu, Gorontalo, and the rest of Sulawesi (eg Palu, Ujung, etc). 250Rp for any journey in town, look at sign hanging in window for destination, not on roof. **Bendis**: horse-drawn carts – about 300Rp for 2 people, or they can be chartered for about 5,000Rp/hr. **Mikrolets**: 200-250Rp around town. **Oplets**: 200Rp around town, or chartered for about 3,000Rp/hr. **Taxi**: some are metered (white, marked cars). 750Rp flagfall. Metered taxis are good and reliable, get your hotel reception to call for taxi if you need one. For unmetered taxis, agree price before boarding. Taxis can be chartered for about 6,000Rp/hr (T 52033 for taxi service).

Air Manado's Sam Ratulangi Airport is 13 km NE of town. Regular daily connections on Merpati or Bouraq with Ujung Pandang, Gorontalo, Palu, Ternate and Ambon. Less regular flights to Biak, Jayapura, Luwuk, Poso and Sorong. **Transport to town**: no fixed rate taxi counter, but still easy to get into town; there are two options but allow at least 30 mins for either option. If you have a lot of baggage, take a taxi, about 5,500Rp to hotels in centre of town; alternatively take an oplet from the airport car park exit to Terminal Paal 2 (350Rp); change oplets there for town centre (Pasar 45) (250Rp). Useful visitors information counter at airport. **International connections** with Davao (Philippines): departs Wed, Sat; returns Thur, Mon; and Singapore (Silk Air): Mon, Thur, returns same day. Garuda is considering stopping in Manado on flights between Nagoya (Japan) and Bali.

Road Bus: the long distance Malalayeng terminal lies 30 mins SW of the centre of town (250Rp by bemo from Pasar 45 or Karombasan terminals). All the bus companies have their offices here. It is best to visit the terminal a day before travelling to organize tickets. Most buses leave early morning or evening. Many buses from Gorontalo tend to arrive after midnight, if you want to avoid extortionate taxi fares there is a hotel left out of the bus station, 5 mins walk, **B-C** *Kolongan Beach Hotel*, views over the sea. Regular connections with: Ujung Pandang, daily, 1600 (75,000Rp); Gorontalo (13,500Rp); Palu (35,000Rp); Poso (45,000Rp); Palopo (65,000Rp) (*Tomohon Indah*, T 55767). Change in Palopo for Rantepao (regular buses and bemos onwards). The *Golden Barcelona* bus company runs a/c buses to Gorontalo, departing 1700, 8 hrs (17,500Rp with meal). To get to Toli-Toli, take a bus to Gorontalo, 24 hrs, then a boat.

Sea Boat: Manado's main port is Bitung on the other side of this leg of Sulawesi and 55 km E of the city. The Pelni ships *Kerinci, Kambuna, Umsini, Ciremai* and *Tilongkabila* dock here (see route schedules, page 921). The Pelni Office is at Jl Sam Ratulangi 7, T 62844. *Kalla Lines* run a ship which also follows a 2 week loop stopping at Jakarta, Surabaya, Ujung Pandang, Balikpapan, Tarakan, Pantoloan and Ternate. The Kalla Lines office is at Jl Sam Ratulangi 100. For further information on unscheduled ship departures from Bitung visit the AGAPE/TERATAI at Bitung port. There are also two smaller ports in Manado itself. Close to the Pasar 45 terminal, off Jl Suprapto, and in the heart of town is Manado Port (Pelabuhan Manado). Ship offices line Jl Rumambi which leads to the port. Ships/boats leave from here for Palu, Toli Toli, Ternate, Sangir, Talaud, Pare Pare, Ambon and elsewhere. Finally, Singkil port is 1 km N of the city centre; boats from here go to Sangihe and Talaud. Get to the port by bemo from Pasar 45 terminal.

BUNAKEN NATIONAL MARINE PARK

The **Bunaken National Marine Park** (8 km offshore), is the principal destination for the majority of visitors to Northern Sulawesi. The park (75,265 ha), encompasses the five islands of Bunaken, Manado Tua (Old Manado), Montehage, Siladen and Nain. Each island is surrounded by mangrove and white sand beaches with coral reef flats (3m), dropping off to steep reef walls. The water temperature averages 28°C throughout the year, and visibility of up to 30m is common. The park has a wide range of corals and fish: marine biologists regard Bunaken as being within one of the richest and most diverse coral ecosystem zones in the world. There are over 20 different recognized dive spots within the Marine Park and of the more spectacular marine life there are barracuda, dolphins, colubrine sea snakes, killer whales, and hawksbill turtles. If your time is limited the following dives are recommended. Of course no sitings of pelagics etc can be guaranteed. *Liang Cove*, on the S side of Bunaken island, is where the majority of day trip boats (diving, snorkelling, glass bottom) come for lunch, consequently there is a

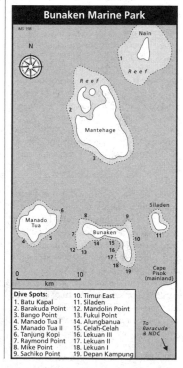

Bunaken Marine Park

Dive Spots:	
1. Batu Kapal	10. Timur East
2. Barakuda Point	11. Siladen
3. Bango Point	12. Mandolin Point
4. Manado Tua I	13. Fukui Point
5. Manado Tua II	14. Alungbanua
6. Tanjung Kopi	15. Celah-Celah
7. Raymond Point	16. Lekuan III
8. Mike Point	17. Lekuan II
9. Sachiko Point	18. Lekuan I
	19. Depan Kampung

The extraordinary maleo bird

The maleo (*Macrocephalon maleo*) is a member of the small Megapode family of birds which build mounds to incubate their eggs. It is only found in Sulawesi. The bird is about the size of a domestic hen, with striking black and white plumage, and a bald skull. It has been argued that this is to keep its brain cool when it is on hot, exposed beaches. The Megapodes are the only birds – other than the Egyptian plover – which do not incubate their eggs with their bodies. Instead the maleo uses hot beaches, or land near hot springs or volcanic vents. The maleo digs a hole in the ground and buries its enormous – relative to its body weight – eggs in the sand to incubate. They also dig false pits to confuse predators. After 3 months the single egg hatches and then the chick struggles upwards, through the sand, for 2-3 days. The large size of the egg enables the chick to fly immediately upon emerging from the sand. Unfortunately for the maleo, their eggs are a delicacy and as a result their numbers have diminished. The national parks service have begun to hatch the eggs themselves to maintain the population – a strategy which has had some success.

choice of places to eat and shop. Good snorkelling, canoes to rent from small boys, 5,000Rp. Unfortunately a lot of litter gets washed ashore here from the mainland. *Lekuan I, II & III*: common starter and refresher dives. Shallow reef flats, dropping off to steep walls. Sheltered, limited current. *Fukui Point*: sloping coral garden, good samples of lettuce coral, and giant clams (15m), also good for schooling fish, jacks, manta rays and pelagics. *Sachiko Point*: wall dive, small cave at 5m, turtles. *Celah Celah*: good for night dive (10-20m), colourful sponges and plant growth, sleeping fish and hermit crabs. *Siladen*: for the first dive of the day (particularly as a lunch spot), explore the small island between dives, sleepy paradise. *Ship wreck*: in the bay opposite the *Barracuda Diving Club* (30-45m), Dutch cargo vessel sunk during WW2.

● **Accommodation** For dive centres and more information on accommodation and tours see Accommodation in the Manado entry. Accommodation within the marine park is available at two locations. **In the vicinity of Bunaken village**: D-E *Daniel's Homestay* is the best (Jl Stadion Klabat 15, T 66317), on the NE side of the island, generous meal servings, some rooms with veranda and private mandi. **At Liang Cove on the S side of the island**: has about six homestays along the beach front. **D-E** *Hardin's Homestay* is the best (to the left of the central pier), book through *Utama Aman Travel Agency*, Manado, T 63441, the more expensive rooms are bamboo cottages on hillside with excellent views across the bay, cheaper rooms include all meals, rooms are small, with a veranda. It is also possible to arrange an overnight stay on *Manado Tua* from here.

● **Transport Sea Boat**: there is a daily public boat from Bunaken at 0700, 1 hr (2,500Rp). This vessel picks up from several points depending upon tides and demand; arrange pick-up the night before. Return boat leaves 1500 from Pasar Bersehati (close to Tondano River).

THE SANGIHE AND TALAUD ISLANDS

These are two of 77 islands that comprise the district of Sangihe Talaud, which has a total population of over 260,000. **Tahuna**, on Sangihe Besar, is the capital. The islands were discovered by the Dutch in the 18th Century. The economic mainstays of the area are farming and fishing, with the primary crops being coconut, nutmeg and cloves. The principal attraction of the islands are its **white sand beaches** and magnificent **sea gardens**.

Festivals Jan (end of month): *Menulude*, a ceremony of Thanksgiving.

● **Accommodation** *Nasional*, Jl Makaampo 58; *Tagaroa*, Jl Malahasa 1; *Veronica*, Jl Raramenusa 16, T 79.

● **Shopping Handicrafts**: ebony carvings and fine embroidery from Batunderang on Sangihe Besar.

● **Transport Air** Manado to Naha (21 km from Tahuna or Sangihe Besar), depart 0900, Mon, Wed, Fri, Sat (105,000Rp), and to Melang-guane (on Karakelang Island, part of the Talaud group), Mon and Sat only (140,200Rp). Flights return the same day to Manado. **Sea Boat**: boats leave from Pelabuhan Manado and also from Pelabuhan Singkil, about 1 km N of Manado's city centre (take a bemo from Pasar 45). The Pelni ship *Tilongkabila* docks at Tahuna and at Lirung on its fortnightly circuit through Sulawesi and Nusa Tenggara (see page 921 for route schedule).

West Nusa Tenggara: Lombok and Sumbawa

West Nusa Tenggara	686	The Northwest Coast and	
Lombok	688	Mount Rinjani	709
Horizons	689	Central Lombok and the West	712
Island information	694	South Lombok and the	
Ampenan – Mataram –		South Coast	715
Cakranegara	696	**Sumbawa**	717
Lombok's West Coast	700	Horizons	717
The Gilis	704	Sumbawa Besar to Bima-Raba	722

Travelling E from Bali into West Nusa Tenggara, rainfall lessens and the dry season becomes markedly longer. This transition continues all the way along the island arc of the Lesser Sundas, but it is travelling from Bali, through Lombok, and into Sumbawa, that the change in climate and landscape are most pronounced. From a biogeographical perspective, it is on Sumbawa that Alfred Russel Wallace's observation that Nusa Tenggara marked the division between the Asian and Australasian faunal realms becomes most obvious (see page 690).

Lombok, though drier than Bali, is nonetheless rich agriculturally – particularly on the central plain where irrigated rice is cultivated. The island supports three-quarters of West Nusa Tenggara's population of 3.4 million, yet covers only one quarter of the province's land area. Sumbawa, in contrast, is far less developed. It is dry and infertile and supports just ¾ million people.

What is surprising about West Nusa Tenggara is that although it enjoys better communications and a higher income than East Nusa Tenggara, infant mortality rates and levels of literacy are lower in the W. It is a sensitive issue because it addresses differences between religions: some commentators put this variation down to the differing influences of Islam and Christianity. They highlight the role of Church schools and hospitals in the E, and also the liberating influence of Christianity for women.

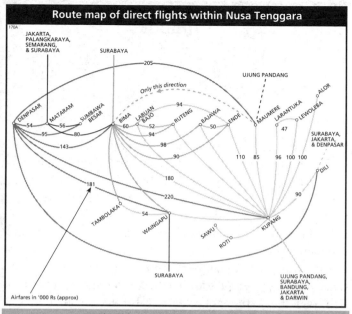

Route map of direct flights within Nusa Tenggara

Airfares in '000 Rs (approx)

Island-hopping in Nusa Tenggara

Travel through Nusa Tenggara involves a great deal of island hopping, as well as intra-island travel. For information on transport through and between islands see the pages listed below. Sections on transport to & from individual towns are listed, as usual, at the end of the town entries. **NB** There are multiple ways of skipping through Nusa Tenggara, by air, bus, boat, ship and ferry, or any combination of these. Working out the best way given different budgets and schedules needs careful thought:

Inter-island transport	Page(s)	Intra-island transport	Page(s)
Bali-Lombok:	337	Bali:	339
Lombok-Bali:	694	Lombok:	695
Lombok-Sumbawa:	694,721	Sumbawa:	717
Sumbawa-Komodo:	726,731		–
Sumbawa-Flores:	726	Flores:	729,735-737
Komodo-Flores:	731		–
Flores-Timor:	744,750,751,776		–
Flores-Lembata:	753		–
Timor-Alor:	754,776		–
Timor-Lembata:	753		–
Timor-Rote:	776,779		–
Timor-Savu:	780		–
Sumba-Flores:	765,770		–
Sumba-Timor:	765		

Lombok

T HE CIRCULAR island of Lombok stretches 80 km from north to south and 70 km from east to west, making it only slightly smaller than its more illustrious neighbour, Bali. However, although there has been a tendency to view Lombok as 'Bali twenty years ago' – or Bali 'before the fall' – there are in fact major differences between the two islands embracing geography, climate, culture and religion. Lombok is drier, it is predominantly Muslim, and it is artistically less rich; the Hindu temples are mediocre imitations of those on Bali, even the textiles are unremarkable in comparison. What Lombok does have to offer is a unique culture, a beautiful landscape, the magnificent Mt Rinjani and a far less frenetic, pressured atmosphere than its better-known sister.

Lombok highlights

Temples The **Mayura Water Palace and Gardens** (page 697) is the largest temple complex on Lombok; other significant historical sights include **Taman Narmada** (page 712) and **Suranadi** (page 713).

Beaches The main beach resort area is **Senggigi** (page 700), while the **Gilis** (page 704) and **Kuta** (page 715) cater largely to budget travellers.

Natural sights Mount Rinjani dominates the island and can be climbed in 3-4 days (page 709).

Culture and performance Traditional villages in the centre (page 712) and S (page 715).

Sports Diving and snorkelling off the Gilis (page 704).

Shopping Traditional **ikat textiles** from Pringgasela (page 714) and from workshops in Mataram (page 696) and **basketry** from Kota Raja (page 713).

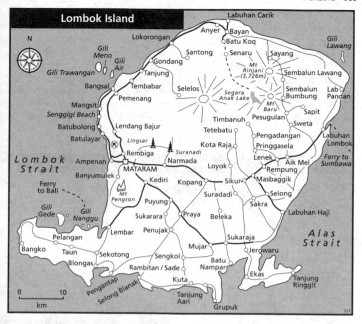

Lombok Island

Labuhan Carik

Lokorongan · Anyer · Bayan · Batu Koq · Gili Lawang

Gili Meno · Gili Air · Gondang · Santong · Senaru · Sayang

Gili Trawangan · Tanjung · Mt Rinjani (3,726m) · Sembalun Lawang

Bangsal · Tembabar · Selelos · Segara Anak Lake · Sembalun Bumbung · Lab Pandan

Mangsit · Pemenang · Mt Baru · Sapit

Senggigi Beach · Lendang Bajur · Timbanuh · Pesugulan

Batubolong · Tetebatu · Pengadangan · Sweta

Batulayar · Lingsar · Suranadi · Kota Raja · Pringgasela · Labuhan Lombok

Lombok Strait · Ampenan · Rembiga · Narmada · Lenek · Aik Mel · Ferry to Sumbawa

Banyumulek · MATARAM · Loyok · Rempung · Masbaggik

Ferry to Bali · Mt Pengson · Kediri · Kopang · Sikur · Selong

Gili Gede · Gili Nanggu · Puyung · Suradadi · Sakra · Labuhan Haji

Sukarara · Praya · Beleka

Pelangan · Lembar · Penujak · Sukaraja · *Alas Strait*

Bangko · Taun · Sekotong · Mujar · Jerowaru

Blongas · Sengkol · Batu Nampar · Ekas

Rambitan / Sade · Kuta · Tanjung Ringgit

Pengantap · Selong Blanak · Tanjung Aan · Grupuk

0   10
km

Horizons

Nonetheless, Lombok has been earmarked for tourist development over the next decade, on the pretext that it is in a position to emulate Bali's success. Whether the development plans will ever come to fruition is another matter and for the time being it remains a relatively quiet alternative. Although there are a number of first-class hotels along the beaches (and several more under construction), away from these tourist areas, Lombok is still 'traditional' and foreigners a novelty. It is also a poor island; the famines of the Dutch period and the 1960s remain very much in the collective consciousness (see below).

Most visitors to Lombok stay on Senggigi Beach, on the W coast and just N of the capital Mataram, or on the 'Gilis', a small group of islands N of Senggigi. The S coast, around Kuta, is more dramatic with beautiful sandy bays set between rocky outcrops. At present the road to Kuta is poor and accommodation consists of basic bungalows. However, plans are afoot to make Kuta a focus of future tourist development (see below). There are also a handful of towns inland with accommodation.

THE LAND

GEOGRAPHY

The name Lombok is Javanese for 'chilli pepper'. The island is divided into three *kabupaten* or districts – W, E and Central. The capital Mataram has become fused with the former royal city of Cakranegara, forming a rather sprawling town along the main E-W road. In 1991 the population of Lombok was 2.5 million, the majority of whom are Muslim Sasaks.

Covering 4,700 sq km, Lombok is dominated by the magnificent volcano

Mt Rinjani which rises to 3,726m – making it the highest peak in Indonesia outside Irian Jaya. A hard, 3 day climb to the crater can be organized (see Tours). The island's main crop is rice, which is primarily cultivated in irrigated paddy fields on the fertile central plain. Like Bali, irrigation is regulated through a supra-village organization, the *subak* (see page 314). Other crops include cassava, cotton, tobacco, soyabean, areca nuts, chilli peppers, cinnamon, cloves, vanilla and coffee. Lombok is also an important exporter of frogs' legs. Because of the rapid increase in the population of Lombok, there has been an associated increase in the pressure on the environment. Forests are now reduced to degraded secondary growth, over-grazing is commonplace, and erosion serious. To try to offset the decline in the fortunes of agriculture, there has been some attempt to diversify

Wallace's line

In his book *The Malay Archipelago*, published in 1869, the great Victorian naturalist Alfred Russel Wallace wrote: "If we look at a map of the Archipelago, nothing seems more unlikely than that the closely related chain of islands from Java to Timor should differ materially in their natural productions". During his travels he noted the "remarkable change...which occurs at the Straits of Lombock, separating the island of that name from Bali; and which is at once so large in amount and of so fundamental a character, as to form an important feature in the zoological geography of our globe". Wallace was struck by the change in the faunal composition of Bali and Lombok – two islands separated by a strait only a few kilometres wide. The former was dominated by animals of Asian origin, and the latter of Australasian – Wallace's Indo-Malayan and Austro-Malayan regions respectively.

The first reference to Wallace's 'line', as it became known, is contained in a letter he wrote to Henry Bates who had just returned to London from his South American travels, in January 1858. Since then, numerous zoogeographers and naturalists have offered their own interpretations, all highlighting the change in fauna but postulating various different 'lines'. Even Wallace changed his mind: his original line had Sulawesi in the Austro-Malayan region, by 1880 he had decided the island to be anomalous, and then in 1910 he drew his line to the east of Sulawesi, placing it in the Indo-Malayan region. The other lines proposed include Weber's line (1894), Lydekker's line (1896) and an updated Weber's line (1904), of which the last has received the greatest recognition.

The validity of Wallace's line rests on the distribution of animals through the island arc of the Lesser Sundas. Botanists have found little to lead them to similar conclusions. For example, the majority of East Asian mammals – like the elephant and rhinoceros – do not extend beyond Bali. Likewise, over 80% of reptiles, amphibians and butterflies in Sulawesi are of western origin. But some naturalists have stressed the importance of ecology in determining the faunal composition of the islands of the Lesser Sundas. The Oxford zoologist W George has summed up this view by writing that Wallace's line "marks the division between a rich continental fauna associated with high rainfall, forests and varied habitats and an impoverished fauna associated with low rainfall, thorn scrub and restricted habitats".

However, perhaps most remarkably, Wallace 'predicted' the theory of plate tectonics and continental drift when he wrote that the distribution of animals "can only be explained by a bold acceptance of vast changes in the surface of the earth".

the economy. The island's main export is now pumice, although seaweed and sea cucumber are harvested for the Asian market and tourism is rapidly becoming a major source of revenue.

CLIMATE

Lombok is drier than Bali, but wetter than the islands to the E, and receives an annual rainfall of 1,500-2,000 mm. The dry season spans the months from May to Jul, the hot rainy season from Nov to Mar when downpours can be quite severe and prolonged. The W is considerably wetter than the rest of the island, receiving rain even during the dry season. The E, N and S are noticeably more arid.

HISTORY

It seems that the Sasak population of Lombok converted to Islam during the 16th century when either Sunan Giri or possibly Senopati, two of the nine Muslim saints (see page 95), arrived from Java. Local legend has it that epidemics only began to afflict Lombok after the introduction of Islam and that it was by turning to Islam Waktu Telu that further epidemics were prevented. At this time – although the history is sketchy to say the least – it seems that Lombok was ruled by a series of Sasak princes who spent their time fending off successive invasions from Sumbawanese, Makassarese and Balinese attackers.

In the 17th century, the Balinese king of Karangasem invaded W Lombok and attempted to annex the island. He failed, and it was not until 1740 that the Balinese established a stronghold in the W. Even then, the independently-minded Sasaks of the E managed to maintain their autonomy until the 19th century. Nonetheless, the Balinese – as the dominant group – imposed their culture on the Sasaks. They became the ruling caste, occupied all the positions of authority, and stipulated for example, that while a Balinese man could marry a Sasak woman, a Balinese woman was prohibited from marrying a Sasak man. The Balinese overlords also attempted to control the economy of the island: if a Sasak man died without leaving any male children, all his lands were automatically confiscated. Given the harshness with which the Sasaks were treated by their rulers, it is no wonder that they rebelled on a number of occasions, and when the chance offered itself, asked the Dutch to come to their rescue.

The Dutch In 1894, the Dutch resident of N Bali succeeded in persuading his superiors in Batavia to mount an invasion of Lombok as a prelude to an invasion of S Bali. The pretext for the invasion was that the local Sasaks had requested Dutch assistance in ridding themselves of their Balinese overlords. General Vetter was put in charge of the invasion force and he landed his troops on the S coast. Negotiations with the Balinese and the Sasaks broke down, and the former attacked the bivouacked Dutch. General Van Ham, the second in command, along with 100 other soldiers were killed and the Dutch withdrew to the coast where they built further fortifications. Reinforcements were sent to bolster Vetter's force, which in the Dutch view had been a victim of 'sinister treachery' on the part of the Balinese. With their Sasak allies, the Dutch set about attacking and looting every town and village in S Lombok. Mataram was taken apart, literally stone by stone – even the trees were cut down. On the 18 November 1894 Vetter shelled and destroyed the palace at Cakranegara. The Crown Prince Ktut and several thousand Balinese defenders were killed in the attack, while the Dutch lost only 460 men – 246 of whom died of disease. As was later to be the case during the Dutch campaigns in Bali, rather than surrender, the Balinese chose to die in a *pupatan* or 'fight to the death' (see page 317). The King of Cakranegara was sent into exile, where he died 6 months later, and when the treasure house of the palace was opened it yielded, to the delight of the Dutch, 230 kg of gold, 7,299 kg of silver and three caskets of jewels.

For the Sasaks and the remnant Balinese population of Lombok, the years of Dutch rule from 1900 to 1940 were not happy ones. Indeed, the Dutch period on Lombok represents, in the eyes of many historians, an object lesson in the excesses and inequities of colonial rule. The Dutch taxed everyone heavily, not just the peasants, but also the landlords and the aristocracy. The latter passed the costs of their taxation on to their tenants, who therefore had a double burden to bear. It has been estimated that over a quarter of a farmer's rice harvest – which was already barely sufficient to ensure subsistence – was forfeited in taxes. There was a consequent sharp deterioration in conditions in the countryside and by the 1920s a class of marginalized paupers had been created where previously there was none. Meat and rice consumption fell, malnutrition became widespread, and when harvests failed, famine ensued. Farmers were forced to eat their seed grain and an island which should have produced a surplus of food was afflicted with endemic famine. Historians believe Lombok's condition was rooted in the nature of the colonial system itself.

Even after the Dutch had withdrawn and Indonesia had achieved independence, life on Lombok remained difficult. Famines became almost a way of life, and in 1966 many thousands died of starvation after a particularly poor harvest. The inhabitants of Lombok, and of the other islands of Nusa Tenggara, talk of lapar biasa, literally 'normal hunger' (akin to the 'hungry season' in Africa). Even the introduction of new rice technology in the early 1970s helped little – the rice was devastated by the brown plant hopper (known by entymologists as the BPH). To try and ease these pressures, the government has been settling people elsewhere in the archipelago as part of the transmigration scheme (see page 427) – 42,000 were moved between 1973 and 1983. But, this out-migration of Lom-

Islam Waktu Telu

On Lombok, it is thought that there are still a handful of adherents of Islam Waktu Telu. A figure of 1% of the population (25,000 people) is quoted, but this seems unlikely. Waktu Telu is a mixture of Islam and ancestor and spirit worship. Because the religion is not considered one of the five 'official' religions of Indonesia (they are Islam, Hinduism, Buddhism, Catholicism and Protestantism), the adherents of Islam Waktu Telu have been ignored and – at times – even persecuted. In 1919-1920 the Waktu Telu rebelled against what they saw to be an unholy coalition between the Dutch and members of the rival religion, Islam Waktu Lima. Orthodox Muslims regard Waktu Telu as a travesty of the teachings of the Prophet and between 1927 and 1933 one fervant Islam Waktu Lima missionary travelled the island breaking-up idols and converting the population to orthodox Islam. Now that many Sasaks are almost embarrassed to admit they are believers of Waktu Telu, it is likely that before the century is out, the religion will have been consigned to the history books. This is not just because the religion is unpopular, but also because while it is possible for a Sasak to convert to orthodox Islam, a Sasak is only a Waktu Telu by birth, and cannot convert from orthodox Islam to Waktu Telu. Like the giant panda, Islam Waktu Telu is on an evolutionary dead-end.

The ceremonies and festivals of the religion focus upon the stages of a person's life, and upon the natural world – particularly that connected with agricultural production. Adherents to Waktu Telu only obey the central tenets of Islam – namely, belief in Allah and Mohammad as his prophet.

bok's inhabitants has not stemmed the growth of the island's population. Unlike many other areas of Indonesia, the country's family planning programme has had only a marginal effect on Lombok. Analysts maintain that the strong Muslim beliefs of the majority of Sasaks has prevented the adoption of family planning methods, and fertility rates remain high, as does infant mortality.

CULTURE

PEOPLE

The largest ethnic group are the Muslim Sasaks, the original inhabitants of Lombok, who maintain their unique language, dress and customs. There is also a significant population of Hindu Balinese who survived the Dutch invasion of 1894 (see below), along with smaller groups of Chinese, Sumbawanese, Buginese and Makassarese. Most of the Balinese and the other 'immigrant' groups are concentrated in the W, and it is in this area that Balinese *pura* are interspersed with Islamic mosques.

The Sasaks embrace two forms of Islam: the traditional – and now virtually 'extinct' – *Islam Waktu Telu* (see page 692) and the more orthodox, and more popular, *Islam Waktu Lima*. The 'traditional' marriage ceremony in Lombok is very similar to that of Bali where the bride-to-be is kidnapped by the groom and his accomplices (see page 326). The *kawin-lari* or runaway marriage is known in Sasak as *merari*.

ARTS AND CRAFTS

In comparison to neighbouring Bali, Lombok is not nearly as rich in terms of artistic achievement. Distinctive ikat cloth is still produced on the island, although even this is suffering from a decline in quality as weavers turn out material at an ever-faster rate to satisfy burgeoning tourist demand. Traditionally, Sasak women were expected to weave a trousseau of about 40 pieces of cloth. Some of these are believed to be imbued with magical powers and they are important in ceremonies during the life cycle, for example during circumcision

---

Lombok's crafts

- **Banyu Mulek** (6 km from Mataram): a village specialising in earthenware products.
- **Beleka** (10 km E of Praya): baskets, bags, cases and other goods made from reeds and rotan (rattan).
- **Getap** (1 km E of Cakranegara): a village of blacksmiths where swords, knives and other objects are cast.
- **Loyok Kutaraja** (40 km E of Mataram): furniture and woven goods.
- **Masbaggik** (44 km E of Mataram, see page 713): earthenware bowls and pots, now produced with the marketing and technological help of a New Zealand NGO.
- **Penjanggik** (4 km E of Praya): a weaving village producing hand-woven cloth distinct from that at Sukarara.
- **Penujak** (5 km S of Praya, see page 715): earthenware bowls and pots, now produced, as at Masbaggik, with the marketing and technological help of a New Zealand NGO.
- **Pringgasela** (50 km from Mataram, see page 714): a weaving village, although many of the hand-woven cloths are no longer made to traditional designs.
- **Sayang-Sayang** (1 km N of Cakranegara): lacquered boxes made from palm leaves.
- **Senanti** (73 km from Mataram): wood carvings.
- **Sukarara** (25 km from Mataram, see page 715): traditional, and some not so traditional, hand-woven textiles.

and tooth-filing. Such *kain umbak* are unremarkable, coarse weave cloths, often striped. Lombok's basketwork is also highly regarded, and finely worked baskets are probably one of the best, and most distinctive, products of the island.

TOURIST DEVELOPMENT: THE NEXT DECADE

Since the late 1980s, Lombok has undergone considerable change and it is likely to see much more in the next few years. The Indonesian government views Lombok as a nascent Bali, and the Lombok Tourism Development Corporation has been established to oversee an expansion in hotels and other facilities. In 1995, 308,200 tourists visited Lombok, of who 167,250 were foreigners. This latter figure is up from a mere 44,850 in 1988, so do not expect to find a pristine island untouched by the hand of international tourism.

Virtually all the developments – built and planned – are along the coast, particularly on the W side of the island. A large proportion of the coastline from Senggigi to Bangsal has already been bought by speculators or hotel groups and has been fenced-off.

One constraint to these plans is Lombok's limited infrastructure. Rural roads are paved but generally poor, the airport can only accommodate small planes, and telecommunications capacity is limited. Nonetheless, *Sheraton* opened a large luxury hotel on Senggigi in late 1991 and *Heritage* completed a development on the W coast in 1992. In the last few years a second *Sheraton* has opened, an *Oberoi* and a *Holiday Inn*, while 15 other luxury developments are planned, under discussion or slated for development. Kuta, on the S coast, has been the focus of plans that have changed this quiet stretch of coastline into an international resort with marinas, golf courses and several luxury hotels. The *Novotel Lombok* is scheduled to open here at the end of 1996. Old Lombok hands view the changes with horror and trepidation.

ISLAND INFORMATION

Health Warning Malaria exists on Lombok particularly in the north in rural areas, as does Cholera and Hepatitis B. The government has initiated Health programmes to combat these diseases but visitors should take malaria prophylactics and appropriate precautions (see page 903).

GETTING THERE

AIR

Selaparang Mataram Airport lies N of Mataram and 20 mins S of Senggigi Beach. Multiple daily connections on Merpati with Denpasar. Regular connections (on **Merpati**) with destinations in Java, Sumatra and most towns in Nusa Tenggara, including Sumbawa Besar and Bima-Rabar (Sumbawa); Labuanbajo, Bajawa, Ende and Maumere (Flores); Waingapu and Waikabubak (Sumba); and Kupang (W Timor). **Sempati** is the only airline to offer direct connections with Jakarta. *Airport facilities*: a money changer (for US$ TCs only and cash), information office, and hotel booking counter. **Transport to town**: fixed-fare taxis to Senggigi Beach (7,500Rp). **International connections**: in 1995 **Silk Air** and Indonesia's **Sempati** launched a joint four times weekly service between Lombok and Singapore. Work is just beginning on the upgrading of Lombok's airport so that it will be able to take 747 services though this is not expected to be completed until well into the next century.

ROAD
● Bus
Shuttle buses from Bali, and buses to major destinations in Java, and also E to Sumbawa. *Damai Indah*, Jl Hasanuddin 17, Cakranegara (for Bali and Surabaya); *Karya Baru*, Jl Pejanggik, Mataram (for Surabaya, Bandung and Jakarta). A/c buses travel from Mataram to Bima (on Sumbawa) via Sumbawa Besar. Companies that operate this route include *Tirta Sari*, *Langsung Jaya* and *Mawar Indah*, all with offices on Jl Pejanggik. From Mataram to Sumbawa Besar, 6½ hrs (9,000Rp), to Bima (9,000-10,000Rp). Most buses leave from the Sweta terminal in Cakranegara.

SEA
● Catamaran
Mabua Express operate a daily round trip from Benoa (Bali) to Lembar on a new a/c boat with

aircraft seats and 'in-flight' video. A comfortable, clean and efficient service, 2½ hrs, (40,000Rp second class; first class is not really worth it). Departs Benoa 0800 and 1430, returns from Lembar 1130 and 1730. Price on ticket includes bus transport to any destination not further than Senggigi on Lombok and Kuta on Bali. Often runs extra sailings according to demand. Booking advised at Benoa harbour (T/F 72370) or Lembar (T 35895, F 37224). Office at Jl Langko 11A, T 21655, Mataram and on Senggigi Beach (opposite turning to *Senggigi Beach Hotel*). Bemos link Lembar with the Sweta bus terminal and with Mataram and Ampenan.

● **Ferry**

Ferries sailing every 2 hrs from 0400-2000, link **Lembar** (22 km S of Mataram on the W coast) with Padangbai, near Candi Dasa on Bali 4-5 hrs (5,000Rp) arrive ½-hr early for a seat. **Accommodation at Lembar** There are several losmen offering basic accommodation near the port. Popular with backpackers. **E** *Serumbung Indah*, T 37153, 2 km N of the port on main road, basic rooms with shared mandi. From Lembar, bemos run to Mataram, Ampenan and the Sweta bus terminal, E of Mataram (for onward connections) beware of over-charging – should cost around 1,500Rp; for other destinations, it is easier to charter a bemo (for example, a large proportion of the people arriving at Lembar head straight for Bangsal, to catch a boat to the Gilis); a chartered bemo to Bangsal costs about 30,000Rp, **NB** Hang on to your luggage and bargain hard: the drivers here are tough negotiators. There are three ferry crossings each way every day between Labuhan Lombok on Lombok's E coast and Poto Tano on Sumbawa's NW coast, 1 hr 50 mins (2,500Rp). The *Pelni* ships *Binaiya*, *Auru* and *Sirimau* call at Lembar on their fortnightly circuits through Java, Kalimantan, Sumatra, Sulawesi and the islands of Nusa Tenggara – see route schedules, page 921. The Pelni office is in Ampenan, Jl Industri 1, T 37212.

　　Gili Nanggu 1 hr by chartered fishing boat from Lembar (25,000Rp but only 20,000Rp for the return), offers the perfect restful hideaway. There is only one place to stay by the sea, **C** *Istana Cempaka*, Reservations: Jl Tumpang Sari, Cakranegara, Lombok, T 22898, very attractive bungalows on beach with private mandi, price incl breakfast, restaurant serves good freshly caught fish: very friendly Balinese owner who does not want to develop the island. It takes 30 mins to walk around the island. Reasonable snorkelling. There is also basic losmen accommodation (**E** in the village for 15,000Rp).

WHERE TO STAY

● **Accommodation**

Unlike Bali, it is unusual for losmen and bungalows to include breakfast in their room rates. In general, accommodation is less good value than Bali and bungalows have not been as attractively designed. **NB** It is **essential** to book well in advance at peak seasons, especially in the Christmas/New Year period.

GETTING AROUND

Lombok's main artery is the excellent road running E from Mataram to Labuhan Lombok. There is now a paved road to Lembar and Praya, and to Bangsal in the N. Most of Lombok's roads are paved, but the secondary roads are not well maintained and car travel can be slow and uncomfortable. This is likely to change over the next few years as tourism expands.

BUS

Minibuses (called bemos here) and colts are the main forms of inter-town and village transport. It is a good cheap way to get around the island and, unlike Bali, frequent changes of bemo are not necessary to get from A to B. However, they can be crowded and beware of being over-charged – check with other travellers before boarding. The transport hub of Lombok is the Sweta terminal, 2 km E of Cakranegara (see page 700). *Perama* run a reliable bus service geared to foreign travellers connecting the following places: Bali, Mataram, Senggigi, Bangsal, Kuta Lombok, Tetebatu. They have offices in all these places and also on Gili Air and Gili Trawangan. Head office (Kuta, Bali): T 0361 751551, F 751170.

OTHER LAND TRANSPORT

● **Hiring**

Greatest selection and availability at Senggigi Beach. Generally the cost of hiring transport is higher than on Bali and the vehicles are not as good. Check everything works before you set off, including the windscreen wipers, and the spare tyre. **Cars**: from 35,000-60,000Rp/day; **Bicycles**: 5,000Rp/day; **Motorbikes**: 7,000-10,000Rp/day.

● **Cidomos**

These are the Lombok equivalent of the *dokar*, a 2-wheeled horse-drawn cart. The word is said to be an amalgamation of *cikar* (a horse cart), dokar and automobile (because they now have pneumatic tyres). In the W cidomos are gradually being replaced by bemos, but in the less developed C and E they remain the main mode of local transport and are more elaborate, with brightly coloured carts and ponies decked out with pompoms and bells.

COMMUNICATIONS

● **Telephone services**
Area code: 0364.

ENTERTAINMENT

● **Sports**
A variety of **watersports** are available on Senggigi Beach (see page 703). Day trips can be made to the 'Gilis', for the best snorkelling and diving. Several diving companies are listed in the Mataram section.

Golf: *Golong Golf Course* (E of Narmada), 9 holes, charmingly informal. Green fee: 10,000Rp. Office: Jl Langko 27, Mataram, T 22017.

● **Tours**
Most tour companies have their offices in Mataram, although there are also some at Senggigi. They tend to run variations on the tours described below:

Southern tour To Sukarara (weaving village), Penujak (pottery village), Kuta Beach, Sengkol and Rambitan ('traditional' Sasak villages), Narmada (summer palace) and the Lingsar Temple, 30,000-50,000Rp/person.

Northern tour Landang Bajur Market, Bali Kuku temple, Pusuk, Sendang Gile and Senaru ('traditional' Sasak village), 40,000-50,000Rp/person.

Gili Air tour To a Chinese cemetery, Bangsal Beach and Ledang Bajur Market, Gili Air (for snorkelling), and Batubolong, 40,000-60,000Rp/person.

Tetebatu tour To Narmada, Loyok (rattan village) and Tetebatu, 27,500Rp/person.

Mount Rinjani Trek up Mt Rinjani (1-3 nights), approximately 250,000Rp/person.

Komodo Island 3/4 days, 750,000Rp (all inclusive).

● **Alternative tours**
Environmental Forum, Jl Pejanggik 10B, Cakranegara. This agency specializes in arranging stays in traditional Sasak villages so that visitors can experience village life and customs at first hand.

AMPENAN – MATARAM – CAKRANEGARA

The Mataram 'conurbation' is not the most attractive town in Indonesia, sprawling from Ampenan on the W coast, inland to Mataram and then to the former royal capital of Cakranegara. The three towns have a combined population of about 250,000. They have a rather drab and bedraggled feel, and the few remaining Dutch-era buildings in the Ampenan port area are ramshackle and unloved. Cakranegara was the site of the battle between the Balinese king of Lombok and the Dutch in 1894, during which the palace was badly shelled (see below and page 697). As the capital of the province of Nusa Tenggara Barat, Mataram has a large number of grand government buildings and banks – rather out-of-place in a town of this size.

Places of interest

Most of the conurbation's few sights are in Cakranegara, in the E of town. The description below runs from W to E.

The **West Nusa Tenggara Provincial Museum** is in Ampenan on Jl Banjar Tilar Negara, at the W end of town. It houses a collection of assorted regional textiles and krisses. Admission 200Rp. Open 0800-1400 Tues-Thur, 0800-1100 Fri, 0800-1300 Sat-Sun. Travelling E into Mataram, there are a number of **weaving factories** producing ikat cloth, although rarely in traditional designs. *Rinjani Hand Woven* on Jl Pejanggik was established in 1948 and tends to produce cotton textiles for the Balinese market, using motifs from Sulawesi, Bali and the other islands of Nusa Tenggara as well as Lombok. Behind the shop is a large weaving operation where the various processes can be seen. There are also a number of other factories in this area of town: *Slamet Riyadi Weaving* (which produces Balinese-style cloth) is on Jl Tenun, a narrow back street near the Mayura Water Palace (see below), while the well-known *Sari*

Kusuma is at Jl Selaparang 45, in Cakranegara.

To the E, the **Mayura Water Palace and Gardens** and associated Pura Mayura just N of Jl Selaparang were built in 1744 by the Balinese king of Lombok. The Gardens contain a water lily-filled lake, with a floating pavilion – the *Bale Kembang* – set in the centre. The king would conduct audiences here, and originally there were tiers of wooden benches for officials of different grades. These were destroyed in 1894 during the Dutch assault on Cakranegara and have not been replaced, the *Bales Wedas* within the Palace was used to store weapons. Admission 500Rp. Open 0700-1700. Across the road to the E of the Gardens is the Balinese **Pura Mayura**, also known as the **Pura Meru**. This temple was built in 1720 by Anak Agung Made Karang and is dedicated to the Hindu trinity – Siva, Vishnu and Brahma. It is composed of three courtyards symbolizing the cosmos. The innermost contains three symbolic Mt Merus, aligned N-S; the central court, two pavilions with raised platforms for displaying offerings; and the outermost, a hall containing a large ceremonial drum. The 11-tiered meru is dedicated to Siva, and the 9-tiered merus to the S and N, Brahma and Vishnu respectively. Admission by donation. Open Mon-Sun.

Right at the E edge of the town is Lombok's main **market** (see shopping), next to the Sweta bus terminal on Jl Selaparang. Also here is the Cakranegara **bird market**. **Horse racing** takes place at the Selakalas track, on Jl Gora, N of the Water Palace, twice a week on Thur and Sun from 0800-1200 and at festivals. The ponies are ridden bare-back by young boys.

Excursions

Mount or **Gunung Pengsong** lies about 6 km S of Mataram. There is a small Hindu shrine at the summit and, on clear days, good views over to Bali and Mt Agung and to Mt Rinjani. Japanese solders hid here during WW2. *Getting there*: by chartered bemo or cidomo.

Bangko-Bangko This sandy beach is 63 km from Mataram, past the harbour of Lembar, on the SW tip of the island. It is a long drive on a poor road. There is sometimes surf here: this is a reef break. There is limited accommodation in bungalows and food. *Getting there*: hiring a car is the best way. On the way to Bangko-Bangko, the road passes **Taun**, a white sandy beach (42 km from Mataram) and **Labunan Poh**, (55 km from Mataram) a coastal village from where it is possible to reach **Gili Poh** (good for snorkelling) and **Gili Gede** (a traditional Sasak island). **Gili Nanggu** is another tiny, but very attractive, island in this group (Accommodation: **D** for a double beach hut). *Getting there*: motorboats depart from Lembar (20 mins trip).

Tours

For the range of tours on offer, see page 696, Information for travellers.

Festivals

Apr (16th): *Anniversary of Mataram* is marked by parades and performances.

Jun: *Pura Meru festival.*

Aug (17th): *Independence Day.*

Oct (5th): *War memorial.*

Nov/Dec (15th day of the 4th month of the Balinese lunar calendar): *Pujawali* held at Pura Meru in Cakranegara, at Pura Kalasa (Narmada) and at Pura Lingsar (N of Cakra). The Pujawali ceremony is followed 3 days later by the *ketupat war*, when participants throw *ketupat* (steamed rice wrapped in palm leaves) at one another.

Dec (17th): *Anniversary of West Nusa Tenggara* is celebrated with dance and wayang kulit performances.

Local information
● **Accommodation**
Ampenan: **B** *Nitour (Wisma Melati)*, Jl Yos Sudarso 4, T 23780, a/c, comfortable rooms, small garden, breakfast on verandah, rather overpriced; **E** *Horas*, Jl Koperasi 65, T 31695, very clean; **E** *Wisma Triguna*, Jl Koperasi 76, T 31705, restaurant, basic large rooms with

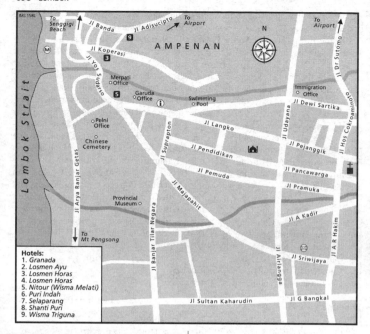

Hotels:
1. Granada
2. Losmen Ayu
3. Losmen Horas
4. Losmen Horas
5. Nitour (Wisma Melati)
6. Puri Indah
7. Selaparang
8. Shanti Puri
9. Wisma Triguna

private bathrooms with western toilet, could do with redecoration but good source of trekking information, set around large courtyard garden.

Mataram: there are several cheap losmen on Jl Pancawarga. **C-D** *Puri Indah*, Jl Sriwijaya, T 37633, good value hotel in central Mataram with pool and restaurant, rooms with private bathroom, shower, western toilet, some rooms a/c and TV; **D** *Wisma Giri Putri*, Jl Pancawarga 29, T 33222, some a/c, attractive house, clean rooms.

Cakranegara: **B** *Granada*, Jl Bung Karno, T 22275, F 23856, a/c, restaurant, pool, best hotel in the area, attractive tropical gardens and aviary, good rooms with adequate services; **B-D** *Handika*, Jl Panca Usaha 3, T 33578, F 35049, some a/c, reasonable restaurant, poor breakfast but excellent in price, rooms are standard but clean, rates negotiable, central location, friendly staff, the hotel organizes car rental and tours; **C** *Mataram*, Jl Pejanggik 105, T 23411, some a/c, price incl breakfast; **C-E** *Ayu*, Jl Nursiwan 20, T 21761, set around attractive courtyard, rooms with mandi, more expensive bungalows with western toilet and a/c, Balinese owner;

D *Selaparang*, Jl Pejanggik 40-42, T 32670, some a/c, clean, reasonable rooms; **E-F** *Shanti Puri*, Jl Maktal 15, T 32649, restaurant, best of the budget places, good value and surprisingly swish for a place in this price category, cheapest rooms with shared facilities.

● **Places to eat**

♦*Cirebon*, Jl Yos Sudarso 113, Ampenan, Chinese and seafood, very popular; ♦*Flamboyant*, Jl Pejanggik 101, seafood, with attractive ambience; ♦*Sekawan*, Jl Pejanggik 59, seafood and Chinese, good portions, tasty; ♦*Warungs*, opp *Astiti Guesthouse* in Cakranegara. Each warung has a different speciality and you sit inside a tent at a long wooden table. Friendly place, delicious food, rec. There are several warungs along Jl Yos Sudarso, in Ampenan. *Kentucky Fried Chicken*, Cakra Plaza, Jl Pejanggik; *Selaparang*, Jl Pejanggik, next to Rinjani's Weaving.

● **Airline offices**

Merpati, Jl Pejanggik 40-42, T 22226 (next to the *Selaparang Hotel*); there is also a Merpati office at Jl Yos Sudarso 4 (next to the *Nitour Hotel*).

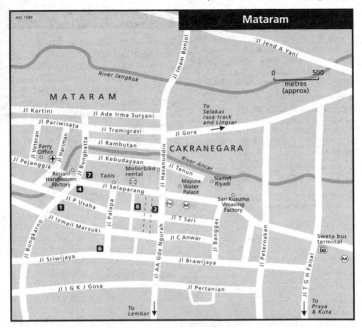

Mataram

To Selakas race track and Lingsar

To Lembar

To Praya & Kuta

● **Banks & money changers**
Bank Central Asia, Jl Pejanggik 67, Mataram;
Bank Rakyat Indonesia, Jl Pejanggik 16; Bank
Negara Indonesia, Jl Langko 64. Money
changers on road into Ampenan from Senggigi.

● **Hospitals & medical services**
Hospitals: General Hospital, Jl Pejanggik 6,
Mataram, T 21345.

● **Post & telecommunications**
Area code: 0364.
General Post Office: Jl Majapahit Taman,
Mataram T 21345.
Perumtel telephone exchange: Jl Pejanggik;
Post Office: Jl Langko 21, Ampenan.
Telephone office: Jl Langko.

● **Shopping**
Antiques: there are a number of shops in Ampenan on the road N towards Senggigi, most with
rather poor quality merchandise. Despite the layer
of authentic dust, virtually none of the pieces on
sale is antique. The original shop on this strip was
Sudirman, Jl Yos Sudarso 88; close by is Hary
Antiques, Jl Saleh Sungkar Gg Tengiri 2.

Baskets: the market next to the Sweta bus

terminal (E of town) on Jl Selaparang sells local
products, incl baskets.

Handicrafts: Lombok Asli, Jl Gunung Kerinci
36 (nr the University); Pandawa, Jl Ismail Marzuki; Sidhu Putra, Jl Gora 36, Cakranegara.

Supermarket: Galael's, Cakra Plaza Blok B, Jl
Pejanggik; Mataram Supermarket, Jl Pejanggik 139B, well stocked, competitive prices.

Textiles: Rinjani Hand Woven, Jl Pejanggik
46, good value cotton (15,000Rp/m) and silk
(40,000-60,000Rp/m) ikat. Other weaving
shops incl Sari Kusuma, Jl Separang 45 and
Slamet Riyadi, Jl Tenun.

● **Sports**
Diving companies: Corona, Jl Dr W Rambige,
Mataram; Rinjani, Jl Pemuda, Mataram,
T 21402; Satriavi, Jl Pejanggik 17, Mataram,
T 21788.

Horse racing: every Sun at Selagalas village, 4
km from Mataram.

● **Tour companies & travel agents**
Bidy Tours, Jl Ragigenep 17, T 22127; Environmental Forum, Jl Pejanggik 10B; Mavista, Jl Pejanggik Complek, Mataram,

T 22314; *Nominasi*, Jl Dr Wahidin 3, T 21034; *Peramaswara*, Jl Pejanggik 66, T 22764; *Putri Mandalika*, Jl Pejanggik 49, T 22240; *Saka-tours*, Jl Langko 7-8, T 23114; *Satriavi*, Jl Pejanggik 17, T 21788; *Setia*, Jl Pejanggik; *Wisma Triguna*, Jl Adisucipto 76, Ampenan, T 21705 for 3 or 4 day hikes to the summit of Mt Rinjani.

● **Tourist offices**
Regional tourist office for West Nusa Tenggara, Jl Langko 70, T 21866, maps and brochures available, open 0700-1400 Mon-Thur, 0700-1100 Fri, 0700-1200 Sat, friendly and helpful.

● **Useful addresses**
Immigration Office: Jl Udayana 2, T 22520.

● **Transport**
Local There is a one-way road system linking the three towns of the 'conurbation'. **Bemos**: run across the city, travelling E down Jl Langko/Pejanggik and Selaparang to the Sweta bus terminal and W down Jl Pancawarga/Pendidikan and Jl Yos Sudarso (200Rp) to Ampenan. **Car hire**: available from **Avis**, *Nitour Hotel*, Jl Yos Sudarso 4, T 26579; CV Metro, Jl Yos Sudarso 79; **CV Rinjani**, Jl Bungkasno; **CV Surya**, Jl Raya senggigi. **Dokars**: for short journeys around town; should cost about 250Rp/person. **Motorbike hire**: 12,000-15,000Rp/day. Several in town.

Road Bemo/bus: the Terminal Induk Sweta, Lombok's transport hub, is on Jl Selaparang at the E edge of Cakranegara (2 km E of Mataram). Regular buses and bemos from here to Labuhan Lombok (and on to Sumbawa), Bangsal (for the Gilis), Tanjung, Keruak and Bayan. Bemos wait on Jl Salah Singkar to pick up passengers for Senggigi Beach (see local transport for bemo routes in town).

Most visitors to Lombok stay either at Senggigi Beach or on the 'Gilis'. Senggigi Beach stretches over 8 km from Batulayar to Mangsit. The road from Mataram to Bangsal winds through impressive tropical forest in the foothills of Mt Rinjani. A strategically placed 'coffee house' offers fabulous views of the surrounding countryside from the highest point on the road. Travelling further N along the coast from Mangsit, the road reaches Bangsal, the 'port' for boats to the Gilis.

SENGGIGI

Lombok's principle beach resort, **Senggigi**, lies 12 km N of Mataram on the island's W coast. The beach overlooks the famous Lombok Strait which the English naturalist Alfred Russel Wallace postulated divided the Asian and Australasian zoological realms (see box, page 690). The sacred Mt Agung on Bali can usually be seen shimmering in the distance. Hotels and bungalows are in fact found over an 8 km stretch of road and beach from Batulayar Beach in the S, to Batubolong, Senggigi, and Mangsit beaches, to the N. Mangsit is quieter and less developed, although there are a number of hotels under construction and land speculation is rife.

Many visitors express disappointment with Senggigi Beach itself which is rather tatty, overdeveloped and not very attractive. There are many hotels catering largely for the package tour trade; these are not always particularly well-managed, or maintained. Their rates are highly negotiable off season. Many of the best guesthouses on Lombok are Balinese owned, and as prices on Bali rise inexorably, they no longer seem as overpriced as they once did.

Some regular visitors recommend avoiding Senggigi and staying at one of the beaches further N which are still quiet and undeveloped and offer beautiful, windswept beaches with lovely views across the Lombok Strait to Gunung

Agung on Bali and superb sunsets. They are also at present free of the hawkers that so mar a visit to Senggigi itself.

In the mornings between 0800 and 1100 hundreds of brightly coloured fishing boats return to the beach. The fishermen leave at 0500 and use traditional methods of fishing eschewing nets for a length of string with 30 hooks; when the string feels heavy they know it is time to haul it in. If the wind is onshore they fish off Mangsit, if the wind is offshore they fish off Senggigi beach.

2 km S of Senggigi, on a headland, is the **Batubolong Temple**. Unremarkable artistically (particularly when compared with the temples of Bali), it is named after a rock with a hole in it (*Batu Bolong* or 'Hollow Rock') found here. Tourists come to watch the sun set over Bali – devotees, to watch it set over the sacred Mt Agung.

Each evening an informal **beach market** sets-up on the beach in front of the Senggigi Beach Hotel; vendors lay out their wares (textiles, T-shirts, woodcarvings and 'antiques'); heavy bargaining is required – these people really know how to sell.

Tours

Day trips to the Gilis; for example, on the *Studio 22 – Anthea Wisata* catamaran (US$20/head), Jl Lazoardi. *Nazareth Tours* and *Satriavi* both organize treks up Mt Rinjani (see page 709).

Local information
● **Accommodation**

The accommodation on 'Senggigi' is spread out for several kilometres along the main beach road and extends N to Kerandangan Beach, Klui Beach and Mangsit. All the hotels and guesthouses are easily accessible by bemo from Mataram. The better hotels have generators for when the mains power fails, which it does quite often. **NB** The telephone numbers in the Senggigi area have recently changed. Those listed are thought to be correct at going to press.

A+ Sheraton, Jl Raya Senggigi Km 8, PO Box 1154, T 93333, F 93140, a/c, restaurant, free-form pool, largest and newest addition to Senggigi, facilities incl tennis courts, fitness centre and jacuzzi set into an attractive pool on beach-front.

A *Ida Beach Cottages*, PO Box 51, T 93013, a/c, restaurant, pool, ornate rooms set on the side of the hill overlooking the sea, hot water; **A** *Lombok Intan Laguna*, PO Box 50, T 93090, a/c, restaurant, attractive pool, most exclusive hotel on Senggigi until being recently displaced by the Sheraton, good sports facilities; **A** *Senggigi Beach*, PO Box 2, T 93339, F 93185, a/c, restaurant, pool,

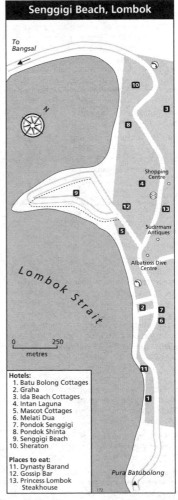

Senggigi Beach, Lombok

Hotels:
1. Batu Bolong Cottages
2. Graha
3. Ida Beach Cottages
4. Intan Laguna
5. Mascot Cottages
6. Melati Dua
7. Pondok Senggigi
8. Pondok Shinta
9. Senggigi Beach
10. Sheraton

Places to eat:
11. Dynasty Barand
12. Gossip Bar
13. Princess Lombok Steakhouse

large, well-run hotel, in prime position, with extensive grounds, greater competition should improve it, overpriced; **A-B** *Graha*, T 93400, a/c, restaurant, watersports available, hot water, price incl breakfast.

B *Mascot Cottages*, PO Box 100, T 93365, a/c, restaurant, large but rather dark rooms with hot water; **B** *Pacific Beach Cottages*, PO Box 36 (N of Senggigi), T 93027, a/c, restaurant, shadeless pool, a bit tatty.

C *Asri Beach Cottages*, Jl Senggigi, T 93075, the rooms in the new block are reasonable, those in the older 2-storeyed bungalows are dirty and in poor condition; **C** *Batu Bolong Cottages*, Batubolong Beach, T 93065, restaurant large, clean rooms but nothing special, rooms on the beach are more expensive; **C** *Pondok Senggigi*, T 93273, restaurant, traditional huts in garden compound, good value but wrong side of the road for the beach, loud music might disturb some.

D *Atithi Sanggraha*, Jl Senggigi, Batu Layar (S of Senggigi), T 93070, average; **D** *Melati Dua*, Jl Raya Senggigi Km 13, T 93288, clean, popular; **D** *Pondok Rinjani*, PO Box 76, T 93274, 93170, basic accommodation in central Senggigi, set in large garden with 2 enormous live turkeys, private bathrooms with shower and western toilet, could do with a little redecoration, price does not incl breakfast, restaurant (♦♦), you might be disturbed by loud music from *Pondok Senggigi*.

E *Astiti*, next to mosque, T 93041, ceiling fan, en suite mandi, price incl breakfast, some noise from mosque, otherwise quite peaceful; **E** *Pondok Shinta*, Senggigi, T 93012, probably the cheapest place to stay in Senggigi, catering for backpackers, basic rooms, some with private mandi, squat toilets, would benefit from redecoration, friendly, good value, price incl breakfast; **E** *Siti Hawa Pondok*, Jl Raya Senggigi 999, Batu Layur, 4 km S of Senggigi, T 95414, budget accommodation by sea, price incl breakfast and tea all day, bicycles for hire, Indonesian dinner with family, Siti Hawa's husband is a New Zealander and runs a programme to help 'poor village people' from the hostel, guests are welcome to become involved.

Berbintang (5 km N of Senggigi Beach), new development; *Seaside Cottage* (5 km N of Senggigi Beach), new development.

Heading N from Senggigi the first beach is **Kerandangan** where the Park Royal Group is due to build a luxury hotel.

A+ *Hilberon*, N of Klui Beach, Austrian owned, well-managed luxury hotel in attractive grounds beside quiet beach, restaurant; **A+** *Holiday Inn*, T 93444, F 93092, Mangsit, brand new, spacious and well designed, offering everything you would expect from this hotel chain incl an arrow on the ceiling of each room to indicate the direction of Mecca; a/c, fabulous large bathrooms, satellite TV, tea and coffee making facilities in each room, minibar, shopping arcade, water sports, tennis, fitness centre, children's playground, swimming pool, restaurants and outdoor cultural performance stage, set in 5 ha of tropical gardens, convention facilities; **A** *Bunga Beach Cottages* (at Klui Beach just N of Mangsit), PO Box 1118, T 93035, F 93036, 14 large, very attractive, a/c thatched cottages set in colourful, tropical gardens with swimming pool, beside the sea, excellent restaurant (♦♦♦), helpful French co-owner, Anja, in residence, reservations essential at all times of the year for this very select, superbly run 'hotel', highly rec; **A** *Lombok Dame Indah Cottages*, Lendang Guar, Pemenang Barat, 12 km N of Senggigi 83352 (PO Box 1128), T 93246/93247, F 93248, cottages with bath, pool, restaurant, tours, snorkelling and diving available, on opposite side of road to beach, on a hillside overlooking the Lombok Strait, traditional style Sasak bungalows, well furnished, quiet hotel; **A-C** *Santai Beach Bungalows*, Mangsit, T/F 93023, attractive, well-managed thatched bungalows built in the Sasak style, tastefully furnished with fan, private bathroom with western toilet and shower, set in a coconut grove beside the sea, restaurant (♦♦♦); **C** *Windy Beach Cottages*, Mangsit, PO Box 1116 Mataram, Lombok 83126, T 93191/93192, F 93193, 14 attractive traditional style thatched bungalows with fan, private bathroom with shower/bath, western toilet, some with hot water, set in large gardens amidst a coconut grove beside the sea, restaurant (♦♦) offering good Indonesian, Chinese and Western food, can arrange tours in their own vehicles, car hire available, well-managed, Windy's husband is a Scotsman from Lerwick in the Shetland Isles. They are also the local *Perama* shuttle bus agent, rec; **C-D** *Pondok Damai*, Mangsit Beach Inn, (reservations address: Jl Bangau 7, Cakranegara 83231), T 93019, 15 attractive thatched bungalows set in beautiful gardens with assorted fruit trees, beside the sea, private bathrooms featuring an indoor garden with shower and western toilet, fan, TV, restaurant (♦♦) beside the sea, rec.

● **Places to eat**
There are not many independent restaurants on Senggigi – most eating places are attached to hotels. However, with the recent and continuing rapid expansion in accommodation there should be an accompanying increase in the number of restaurants. ♦♦*Café Wayang*, on main road in Senggigi, a branch of the one in Ubud, Bali, building has character (complete with family of mice in the rafters!), but service not up to full speed yet; ♦♦*Dynasty*, large open-air restaurant, overlooking the sea on the road to Senggigi, Indonesian and International; ♦♦*Gossip*, Jl Lazoardi (nr Senggigi Beach Hotel), live music, good food (particularly seafood) although limited menu, rec.

● **Banks & money changers**
Senggigi Beach Hotel has a bank on site with exchange facilities for non-residents.

● **Post & telecommunications**
Area code: 0364.

● **Shopping**
Pacific supermarket on the main road has everything from food to T-shirts, film and gifts at reasonable prices.

● **Sports**
The *Sasak Gardens* is the centre for watersports, with parasailing, waterskiing, windsurfing, sailing.
Diving: *Baruna Watersports*, *Senggigi Beach Hotel*, T 23430; *Rinjani* have a branch at the *Intan Laguna Hotel*.
Snorkelling: around Senggigi beach, masks for hire (2-3,000Rp/day).

● **Tour companies & travel agents**
Anthea Wisata, Jl Lazoardi, T 21572; *Bunga Tours* at *Bunga Beach Cottages*, T 93035, F 93036, guide Ayang has excellent English; *Mavista* at *Mascot Cottages*, T 23865; *Nazareth Tours*, T 21705 (in Ampenan); *Satriavi*, *Senggigi Beach Hotel*.

● **Useful addresses**
Police: opp *Ida Cottages* (N end of beach).

● **Transport**
12 km from Mataram.
Local Various forms of transport can be hired from travel agents along the main road. **Car hire**: 35,000-60,000Rp/day, both self-drive and with driver. *Kotasi*, Jl Raya Senggigi on main street nr *Senggigi Beach Hotel* turning, T 93058. **Bicycle hire**: 5,000Rp/day. **Motorbike hire**: 10,000Rp/day.

Road Bemo: bemos wait on Jl Salah Singkar in Ampenan to pick-up fares for Senggigi Beach and N to Mangsit. There are regular bemos linking Ampenan with Mataram, Cakranegara and the main Cakra bemo terminal between 0600-1800, 350Rp fare.

BANGSAL

The coast road N from Senggigi is slow, it steeply switchbacks its way over headlands and past some attractive beaches. There is some surf on this part of the coast, mainly reef breaks, surfed by the locals on wooden boards.

Bangsal is just off the main road from Pemenang, and is little more than a tiny fishing village. However, as it is also the departure point for the Gilis, there are a couple of restaurants here which double up as tourist information centres, a ferry booking office, a money changer and a diving company. There is a charge of 2,000Rp/vehicle to drive down to Bangsal from Pemanang on the main road.

● **Accommodation** E *Kontiki Bangsal Beach Inn*, traditional cottages nr beach.

● **Tourist information** *Kontiki Coffee Shop* is an informal information centre with a particularly helpful man who will advise on boat crossings; *Perama Tourist Service* (nr the beach) provides bus and ferry connections with the Gilis, Senggigi and Lembar, and all towns on Bali. They also organize tours on Lombok (US$8-US$14) as well as an excellent 7-day boat tour from Bangsal to Labuanbajo (Flores) via Moyo Island (Sumbawa) and Komodo; 200,000Rp all inclusive. **NB** This tour is considerably cheaper in the opp direction, ie Labuanbajo to Bangsal – only 80,000Rp. This tour then returns to Bangsal from Labuanbajo along the same route. A worthwhile alternative to travelling overland; 8 people minimum.

● **Transport** 28 km from Mataram. **Road Bemo**: regular connections from Mataram or the Sweta terminal in Cakranegara; take a bemo heading for Tanjung or Bayan. Bemos stop at the junction at Pemenang, take a dokar the last 1 km to the coast (about 200Rp/person). From Pelabuhan Lombok there are no direct bemos; either charter one (20,000Rp) or catch a bemo to the Sweta Terminal in Cakranegara and then another travelling to Bayan/Tanjung. From the port of Lembar, it is easiest to club together with other passengers and charter a bemo to Bangsal (20,000Rp). **Bus**: regular connections with Lembar with *Perama Tour*, who have an office by the pier and sell all-in bus/ferry tickets to most destinations in Bali (Kuta, Sanur, Ubud, Lovina, Candi Dasa). **Sea Boat**: a new high speed boat service with Padangbai on Bali is supposed to be operating, but service is erratic. Regular ferries and boats to the Gilis (see Transport in Gilis).

THE GILIS

These three tropical island idylls lie off Lombok's NW coast, 20-45 mins by boat from Bangsal. Known as the Gilis or the Gili Islands by many travellers, this only means 'the Islands' or 'the Island Islands' in Sasak. Most locals have accepted this western adaptation and will understand where you want to go.

With the development of Bali into an international tourist resort, many backpackers have moved E and the Gilis are the most popular of the various alternatives. This is already straining the islands' limited sewerage and water infrastructures. During the peak months between Jun and Aug Gili Trawangan becomes particularly crowded.

The attraction of the Gilis resides in their golden sand beaches and the best snorkelling and diving on Lombok – for the amateur the experience is breath-taking. However, the coral does not compare with locations such as Flores, Maluku and N Sulawesi: large sections are dead or damaged (perhaps because of dynamite fishing). There is little to do on the islands except sunbathe, swim, snorkel or dive, or go for walks. Nonetheless, one visitor remained here for 8 weeks and professed to having a 'wild time'. **NB** Be careful swimming away from the shore as there are strong currents between the islands. **Warning** Malaria may exist on these islands so be sure to take precautions.

The largest of the three islands – and the furthest W from Bangsal – is **Gili Trawangan**. It is the most interesting island because of its hill in the centre; there are several trails to the summit and excellent views over to Mt Rinjani on Lombok from the top. **NB** Give the cows a wide berth. In the opposite direction, you can watch the sun set over Mt Agung on Bali. There is a coastal path around the island, which takes about 2½ hrs to walk. Originally a penal colony, it now supports the greatest number of tourist bungalows. These are concentrated along its E coast, as are a number of restaurants (serving good seafood) and bars. For lone travellers seeking company, this is the best island. Snorkelling is good off the E shore, particularly at the point where the shelf drops away near *Blue Marlin Dive Centre* and at the N end of the beach near *Sudi Mampir Bungalows*. But, Gili Trawangan is in danger of ruining itself (like so many other tropical island idylls in the region). Indeed, for some, it already has. This is a brash, loud, over-developed piece of Nusu Tenggara Timur; those looking for peace and quiet are strongly recommended to try Gili Meno or Gili Air.

Rumours abound regarding Gili Trawangan and its future, notably that the island has been bought by a Japanese consortium who plan to develop it as a centre for upmarket tourism and build a golf course. Informed opinion is that the cost and scale of the infrastructure required to support this is sufficiently great that nothing will happen for a good few years. Other rumours concern a lack of planning permission for certain bungalows which has led to some being razed to the ground; as is usually the case, the reality is not as sensational as the rumours might lead one to believe and it is unlikely that travellers will be disadvantaged by any of the rumours currently doing the rounds.

There is concern on the part of local elders that Gili Trawangan might be becoming too 'Kuta-esque'. The mushrooming of stalls selling tourist items, sarongs etc, along the beach area near the boatlanding, and restaurants featuring noisy, alcohol-ridden party nights, undermine the peace of this beautiful island and threaten local standards of morality.

The most 'luxurious' accommodation is found in the developed area of the island behind the restaurants; locals already refer to it being like Kuta, although this is an exaggeration. Here you can find modern air-conditioned rooms with western bathrooms; unfortunately you lose the peace and beauty associated with a small, relatively undeveloped island as the accommodation is hidden behind the noisy restaurants away from the beach. To find a tropical paradise visitors have to accept more basic facilities at the outer edges of the developed areas. Here guests can hear the waves lapping against the shore and the birds singing, watch truly inspirational sunrises and sunsets from the peace of their verandahs and believe they are in paradise. Room rates triple at some of the more upmarket places in the high season. Even off-peak rooms can become scarce so it is worth arriving on the island early. Gili Trawangan offers the best choice of restaurants of the three 'Gilis', and many people consider that it has the best snorkelling.

Inland from the tourist strip is the original village where life goes on almost as usual, a world apart from the tourists and therefore interesting to stroll through. Further inland there are scattered farms in amongst the coconut groves that dominate the interior, and pleasant walks.

Gili Meno, between Trawangan and Air, is the smallest of the islands, and also the quietest and least developed. The snorkelling off Gili Meno – especially off the NE coast – is considered by some to be better than Trawangan, with growths of rare blue coral.

Gili Air is the eastern most island, lying closest to Bangsal. It has the largest local population, with a village in the centre of the island. The island takes about an hour to walk around. As the local population is Muslim, visitors should avoid topless sunbathing. The government is keen to develop the island sympathetically and to this end is donating 'useful' trees as part of its plan to keep the island green and beautiful. This year young mango trees have been dispatched to Gili Air; last year coconut seedlings were being planted all over the island. Despite the number of bungalows, it remains the most peaceful place to stay. Snorkelling is quite good off the island. **NB** There are mice on the island, so shut food away.

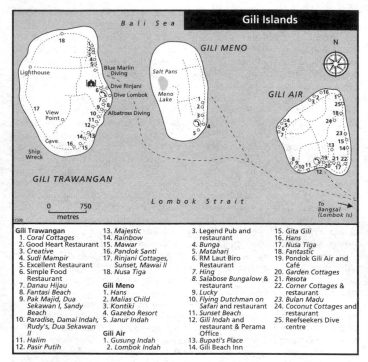

Gili Islands

Bali Sea

GILI MENO

Lighthouse

Blue Marlin Diving

Salt Pans

Dive Rinjani

Dive Lombok

Meno Lake

GILI AIR

View Point

Albatross Diving

Cave

Ship Wreck

GILI TRAWANGAN

Lombok Strait

To Bangsal (Lombok Is)

0   750
metres

Gili Trawangan
1. Coral Cottages
2. Good Heart Restaurant
3. Creative
4. Sudi Mampir
5. Excellent Restaurant
6. Simple Food Restaurant
7. Danau Hijau
8. Fantasi Beach
9. Pak Majid, Dua Sekawan I, Sandy Beach
10. Paradise, Damai Indah, Rudy's, Dua Sekawan II
11. Halim
12. Pasir Putih
13. Majestic
14. Rainbow
15. Mawar
16. Pandok Santi
17. Rinjani Cottages, Sunset, Mawai II
18. Nusa Tiga

Gili Meno
1. Hans
2. Malias Child
3. Kontiki
4. Gazebo Resort
5. Janur Indah

Gili Air
1. Gusung Indah
2. Lombok Indah
3. Legend Pub and restaurant
4. Bunga
5. Matahari
6. RM Laut Biro Restaurant
7. Hing
8. Salabose Bungalow & restaurant
9. Lucky
10. Flying Dutchman on Safari and restaurant
11. Sunset Beach
12. Gili Indah and restaurant & Perama Office
13. Bupati's Place
14. Gili Beach Inn
15. Gita Gili
16. Hans
17. Nusa Tiga
18. Fantastic
19. Pondok Gili Air and Café
20. Garden Cottages
21. Resota
22. Corner Cottages & restaurant
23. Bulan Madu
24. Coconut Cottages and restaurant
25. Reefseekers Dive centre

Local information

Security: When leaving your accommodation take sensible precautions and make sure you lock both the door to the bathroom and the front door. As most bathrooms have no roofs, a favoured way for thieves to gain entry is over the bathroom wall and into your room via the bathroom door.

● **Accommodation**

Many bungalows are upgrading the standard of their rooms; of the more basic ones there is often little difference – they tend to charge the same rates, and the huts are similar in design and size, attractively built out of local materials, in a local style, mostly raised on stilts. Mosquitoes can be a problem at certain times of year, mosquito nets are routinely provided. Rates tend to be 12,000/15,000Rp attached/outside mandi with breakfast, 17,500/20,000Rp with all meals though very few offer all meals these days. Free tea and coffee is usually available all day. Friendliness and the cleanliness of the mandis tends

to be the deciding factor. **NB** During the peak months between Jun and Aug it can be difficult to get a room, so arrive early in the day. There are only two upmarket hotels, both on Gili Meno. **NB** In 1994 a number of bungalow operations were forced to close by the authorities; there are constant rumours of other such actions on the part of the authorities.

Gili Trawangan (25 bungalows and rising, mostly along the E coast): **NB** Development is rapid here, so tips from travellers are probably your best bet. Unless otherwise stated all bungalows have private mandis with squat toilets. **B-D** *Danau Hijau*, modern bungalows with western bathrooms in built-up area; **B-D** *Fantasi Beach*, perhaps the most upmarket of the bungalows with spring beds, modern rooms and bathrooms, though in the built-up area away from the sea, good breakfast; **C-D** *Dua Sekawan I* and *Sandy Beach Bungalows*, both offer modern rooms with western bathrooms, good breakfast, can be noisy as it is situated in the built-up area; **C-D** *Pak Majid* has just been rebuilt to provide modern, attractive rooms with private bathrooms, western toilet and fan, in the built-up area of the island; **C-E** *Dua Sekawan II*, en suite mandi, toilet and shower, avoid old building, new bungalows are noisy – disco next door; **D** *Creative*, one bungalow has a western toilet, others with private or shared mandis; **D** *Halim*, on beach, nice bungalows, friendly, rec; **D** *Santigi Bungalows*, on beach, outside mandi; **D** *Trawangan Beach Cottages*, on beach, outside mandi, noisy; **D** *Wisma Mountain View*, on beach, attached mandi; **D-E** *Coral Cottages*, at the quieter northern edge of bungalow development nr to good snorkelling, if you are looking for a western toilet 2 of the bungalows have squat toilets raised on concrete to seat height! – not a huge success but perhaps better than nothing; **D-E** *Nusa Tiga*, one of the best locations on its own at the N end of the island set in large gardens with 3 colourful 'tame' parrots, some of the beds are due for 'bed heaven', excellent breakfast, private mandi with squat toilet, the water here is very saline, good value; 15-min walk from the bars, owner organizes 'all you can eat' Indonesian buffets; **D-E** *Pondok Santi*, set in a peaceful coconut grove at the southern end of the island, well made bungalows with western toilets, during the rainy season the coconut palms block out some light so the bungalows are damper with more mosquitoes, 20-min walk to the best snorkelling, joint owner is from Australia; **D-E** *Rainbow Cottages*, in a quieter area to the S, joint owner is from Holland; **D-E** *Rudy's Bungalows*, off beach, some attached mandis; **D-E** *Sudi Mampir*, one of the best locations with each bungalow facing the sea and memorable views of the sunrise over Gili Rinjani in a quiet area; **D-E** *Mawar II* (4 bungalows), **D-E** *Rinjani Cottages* (4 bungalows), **D-E** *Sunset* (10 bungalows), are all on the western side of the island to take advantage of the splendid sunsets featuring Gili Agung on Bali as a breathtaking backdrop, very peaceful, all offer similar accommodation and have their own small restaurants, it's about a 40-min walk into 'town' for other restaurants and shopping, or take a dokar; **E** *Simple Bungalows*, off beach, simple.

Gili Meno (11 bungalows): Meno has a reputation as a mosquito haven, so choose your accommodation carefully. **A** *Gazebo Resort*, office: Jl Majapahit 1, Mataram (booking: Bali T 88212, F 88300), a/c, classiest hotel on the Gilis, lovely bungalows with wooden floors and attractively decorated, rec; **B** *Bougenvil Resort*, T 27435, rooms with a/c, bathroom with hot water, minibar, satellite TV, pool, ♦♦♦ restaurant; **B** *Indra Cemana*; **D** *Janur Indah Bungalows*; **D** *Kontiki*, southern end of bungalows, with mandi and meals; **D** *Malia's Child*, nice bungalows, rec; **D** *Matahari Bungalows*.

Gili Air: quieter than Trawangan. To make the most of this 'paradise' island it is best to stay in one of the bungalows dotted around the coast within sound and sight of the sea. There is also accommodation inland from the point where the boats land on the S coast but this location does not offer sea views. Several of the bungalows are owned by Europeans married to Indonesians and these tend to be the better run and more attractive. In the village there are several small shops which sell basic provisions and fruit. The price of accommodation doubles or more in the high season; some greedy and unscrupulous owners turn travellers away in the morning knowing that by late afternoon accommodation seekers will be so desperate that they will pay quite outrageous prices. **B** *Bulan Madu Beach Cottage and Restaurant*, the entire cottage, owned by a German, is available to rent, restaurant with good yoghurt drinks, not quite as well looked after as it used to be; **B** *Hans Cottages*, T/F 34435, the most upmarket accommodation on the island, though maintenance might become a problem as the property ages, 24 rooms, private bathrooms with western toilets and attractive indoor gardens, fan or a/c, some with hot water, the deluxe rooms are built of brick which does not breathe as well in this tropical climate as the more attractive, cheaper thatched rooms, well sited beside the beach with gardens and a fine view of Mount Rinjani on Lombok – the gardens are slightly marred by the half-built swimming pool currently awaiting planning permission which may not be forthcoming! Restaurant (♦♦♦), many European dishes, the giant clams that sometimes appear on the menu are a protected species and should not have been caught, let alone eaten, reefseekers (see under Diving) try to buy these clams from the fishermen and release them back into the sea; **B** *Gili Beach Inn*, E coast; **B** *Melati Gili Indah*, PO Box 1120, T 36341, F 37328, the next most upmarket accommodation consisting of bungalows with private bathrooms and western toilets, some rather dark, set in rather shaded and gloomy grounds, restaurant, though quite pricey, is very average, the owner, Pak Aji, is Kepala Desa of the 'Gilis' which are now self-governing, and is a keen conservationist which bodes well for future development on the islands; **C-D** *Coconut Cottages and Restaurant*, T 35365, 7 attractive bungalows with private bathrooms, 2 with western toilet, fan, mosquito nets, large attractive bamboo beds; very well run, set in flower-filled gardens amidst a coconut grove 30 m from the beach where you can watch the sun rise over Mount Rinjani on Lombok, in early 1996 26 mango trees arrived, donated by the government (see above) nr the best area for snorkelling, offers a book exchange, Elaine, the owner's wife, is from Scotland, restaurant (♦♦♦), good food, will organize special Sasak dinners by prior arrangement, rec; **D** *Fantastic Bungalows*, on E side of island (best swimming and snorkelling here), 6 well-run bungalows with own (clean) mandi, price incl good breakfast, rec; **D** *Pino's Cottages*, one of the first places you come to going up E coast, run by German lady, own mandi, electricity (occasional) in some bungalows, restaurant on the beach with reasonable food, rec; **D** *Pondok Gili Air Bungalows and Café*, attractive, clean bungalows with private mandis and squat toilets, in attractive garden, well run by very friendly and helpful Australian lady, Dee, own generator and uses bottled water for making tea, can arrange delicious Sasak dinners with one day's notice, offers a book exchange, rec; **D** *The Flying Dutchman on Safari*, brand new, well-run bungalows, built by the Dutch owners, Jan and Vincent, offering new bathrooms with squat toilets, fed by fresh spring water, new beds with good mattresses, mosquito nets, hammock on verandah, gardens with banana trees, restaurant and bar, good sunset views, rec.

The best of the remaining bungalows are: *Gusung Indah Bungalows; Salabose Bungalows* (one of which has a western toilet), good sunset views; *Pena; Gita Gili*, good breakfast; *Gili Air Santay*, good bungalows with and without attached showers, all with electricity, excellent food, 500m E of the boat 'dock' and situated inland; *Bupati's Place*; *Nusa Tiga*, inland from the E coast, German owner.

● **Places to eat**
A number of restaurants serving excellent seafood, particularly fish; 'specials' or the 'chalkboards', will tell you what is the fresh catch.

Gili Trawangan: *Excellent Restaurant* (♦♦), good food, rec; ♦*Simple Food*, limited menu but large helpings, friendly and enthusiastic owners, rec. Many of the accommodations in the built-up area feature restaurants, some with barbecue facilities, the number of customers should indicate which are best.

Gili Air: many of the restaurants cater primarily to western tastes and the 'Indonesian' food is often disappointingly bland. There have been some cases of food poisoning caused by eating fish which was not gutted prior to being stored. Restaurants and bungalows with the best food are: *Corner Restaurant and Bungalows, Coconut Cottages, Pondon Gili Air* and *Nusa Tiga Bungalows* (all ♦♦), *Hans Cottages* (♦♦♦), and *Il Pirata* (♦♦♦), run by an Italian couple in a thatched building designed in the shape of a boat, good, though pricey, Italian food.

● **Banks & money changers**
It is best to change money before leaving the 'mainland' as rates are more expensive on the islands, although the *Wisma Mountain View* on Trawangan will change TCs ($US, $A, Sterling, DM, $HK) and cash at not far off the best rates on Lombok.

● **Post & telecommunications**
There is a post box at the *Gili Indah Hotel* on Gili Air, where the boat docks. Letters *do* get through, but there are no stamps available on the island.

Area code: 0364.

● **Sports**
Diving: whilst the diving here may not be quite as good as that in some other parts of Indonesia, it is ideal for less experienced divers as many of the dives are no deeper than 18m and the waters are calm. Best diving conditions are late April through August. **Warning** It is advisable not to dive if taking Larium as a malaria prophylactic. *Reefseekers*, postal address: Jl Koperasi 81, Ampenan 83111, Lombok, T 34387 (fax due). This is the outstanding dive centre on Lombok. Members of PADI International Resort Association No 2979, they offer a full range of courses to PADI Divemaster. Run by Ernie and Kath from England who have over 23 years experience, they operate to the highest safety standards and welcome inspections of the equipment and compressors by prospective divers. Experienced divers must bring their certificates and preferably their log books. *Reefseekers* are also very involved in conservation and are members of the Cousteau Society doing research into local ecosystems. Through their conservation survey work they have discovered new and exciting dive sites. All dives are guided. Because of their strict adherence to the highest safety standards this is an ideal place for nervous divers and beginners. Ernie is also working with Newcastle University researching local growing conditions, soil analyses etc, to determine the best crops and plants for the island. *Blue Marlin Dive Centre*, head office: Gili Trawangan, T 24503, counters on Gili Air, Jl Raya Senggigi Beach,

Senggigi Palace Hotel, Jl Koperasi 81, Ampenan, Lombok, PADI courses up to Divemaster Course, courses start at US$25 for an introduction to scuba diving with one dive, up to US$299 for the PADI Open Water Course. Resident English instructor. This is the best dive centre on Gili Trawangan. *Albatross Dive Center*, Jl Raya Senggigi, Km 8, PO Box 1066, Mataram 83010, T 93399, F 93388. Also at the *Sheraton Hotel*, Senggigi Beach, PADI courses up to Open Water (US$350) and Advanced Diver (US$240). There are also many other dive shops. If taking an introductory dive course check that the instructor speaks acceptable English (or Dutch, German etc).

Fishing deep sea and night fishing available from tour companies and *Albatross Diving* (see under Diving for address), approx costs US$200-300.

Massage: sometimes available at *Rudi's*, a restaurant set back from the beach, near where the ferry docks.

Snorkelling: masks and fins are for hire from many of the losmen (2,000Rp/day for each). The snorkelling off Gili Trawangan is marginally the best.

● **Transport**
Sea Boat: regular boats from Bangsal to the Gilis wait until about 16 people have congregated for the trip to the islands, 1 hr (5,000Rp). Boats can also be chartered for the journey, 1 hr (1,600Rp) to Gili Trawangan, 30 mins (1,500Rp) to Gili Meno, 20 mins (1,200Rp) to Gili Air. In the morning there is rarely a long wait but in the afternoon people have had to wait several hours. An alternative is to buy a combined bus and boat ticket with one of the shuttle bus companies. *Nomad* charge: 8000Rp Mataram-Gilis; 8500Rp Senggigi-Gilis; 15,500Rp Padangbai-Gilis; 16,500 Candi Dasa-Gilis; 21,000Rp Kuta, Bali-Gilis. Boats leave from 0700 onwards. The shuttle bus companies offer boats between the islands for 3,000-4,000Rp. **Gili Air** boats are blue, **Gili Meno** are yellow, and **Gili Trawangan** are red and white. *Rinjani Tours* at the *Trawangan Beach Cottages* book seats on the catamaran from Lembar to Padangbai (Bali). From Senggigi, boats sail to the Gilis frequently throughout the day, 7,000Rp to Gili Trawangan. To get to Bali, catch the 0730 boat to Bangsal and book the connecting bus to Lembar and ferry to Bali there.

Following the coast N from Pemenang and Bangsal, the road passes the turn-off for Sir Beach (about 2 km N of Pemenang). This NW coast is little touched by tourism and there are several 'traditional villages' where the more adventurous tour companies take visitors. The best-known of these is Bayan at the foot of Mt Rinjani's northern slopes and about 50 km from Pemenang. Mount Rinjani at 3,726m dominates N Lombok.

Siri Beach is down a dirt track to the left which passes through coconut plantations and reaches this deserted long, narrow strip of soft, white sand on a headland looking across to Gili Air. Take all food and drink: no facilities here. This is worth a visit to get away from the crowds. *Getting there*: take a bemo running N from Pemanang – the walk to the beach is about 2 km from the road.

BAYAN

This is a traditional Sasak village and the birthplace of Lombok's unique Muslim 'schism' – *Islam Waktu Telu* (see page 692). There is a mosque here which is believed to be 300 years old. Some authorities postulate that when the Muslim 'saint' Sunan Giri (or possibly Senopati) arrived on Lombok he landed here, and so Bayan was the first village to be converted to Islam. The village is the jumping-off point for climbs up Mt Rinjani (see below). No accommodation. **Transport** 50 km from Pemenang. **Road Bemo**: connections with the Sweta terminal in Cakranegara. From Bayan bemos run up to Batu Koq. Bemos also run E from here along the very scenic coastal road to Labuan Lombok. From the looks of surprise it is clear that few *orang putih* make this (long) journey.

MOUNT RINJANI

Visitors who have made the effort invariably say that the highlight of their stay on

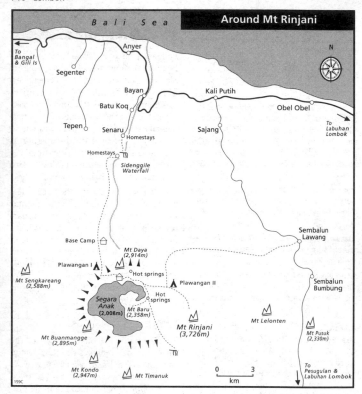

Around Mt Rinjani

Lombok was climbing Mt Rinjani. It is certainly the most memorable thing to do on the island. The views from the summit on a clear day are simply breathtaking. The problem is that the ascent requires 3 days (although some keen climbers try to do it in 2) and few tourists are willing to sacrifice so much time. There is the additional problem that not only is the summit often wreathed in cloud, but views down to the blue-green lake within the caldera are also often obscured by a layer of cloud which lies trapped in the enormous crater.

Mount Rinjani is the second highest mountain in Indonesia outside Irian Jaya – rising to an altitude of 3,726m. The volcano is still active but last erupted some time ago – in 1901. The mountain, and a considerable area of land surrounding the mountain totalling some 400 sq km, has been gazetted as a national park. Beyond this there is a further 760 sq km of forest and scrub which is also protected to varying degrees. The location of Lombok between the Asian and Australasian zoo geographic realms is reflected in the presence of a number of birds of Australian origin – including the highly distinctive sulphur-crested cockatoo. Mount Rinjani is believed by locals to be the seat of the gods, in particular Batara, and although Lombok is ostensibly Islamic, each year during the *Pakelem* ceremony gold offerings are carried up to the mountain and tossed into the lake. There are also regular pilgrimages of local Sasak (Waktu Telu) priests to the summit each full moon.

The climb There are two routes up Mt Rinjani. The easiest and more convenient begins about 2 km to the W of the village of Bayan, on the way to Anyer. The track leads upwards from the road to the small settlement of **Batu Koq** and from there, 1 km on, to another village, **Senaru**. Tents, equipment and guides or porters can be hired in either of these two settlements (ask at the losmen); accommodation is available (see below). It is recommended that trekkers check in at the conservation office in Senaru before beginning the ascent. A guide is not essential as the trail is well-marked from Senaru to the crater rim; however, suitable climbing gear is required (see below). From Senaru, the trek to the summit takes about 2 days, or 10 hrs solid climbing. On the trek up, the path passes through stands of teak and mahogany, then into pine forest and lichin. There are stunning views from the lip of the crater down to the beautiful blue-green and mineral rich lake, **Segara Anak** (Child of the Sea), below. A third day is needed to walk down into the caldera. The caldera is 8 km long by 5 km wide.

On the E side of the lake is **Mt Baru** (New Mountain), an active cone within a cone that rose out of the lake in 1942. It can be reached by boat and the climb to Mt Baru's summit, through a wasteland of volcanic debris, is rewarded with a view into this secondary crater. Along the base of the main crater are numerous hot springs – like **Goa Susu** (Milk Cave – so called because of its colour) – which are reputed to have spectacular healing powers; bathing in them is a good way to round-off a tiring descent.

An alternative and more difficult route up the mountain – but some climbers who have done both claim is the more interesting – is via **Sembalun Lawang**, **Sembalun Bumbung** or **Sapit** on the mountain's eastern slopes. There is accommodation here (see below) and guides are also available but there is a shortage of equipment for hire. There is food available to buy for the trek but the range of victuals is not as good as in Senaru. To get to Sembalun Bumbung, take a bus from Labuhan Lombok. For details on Sapit, see page 714. The climb to the crater takes about 9 hrs. For ambitious climbers who intend to reach the true summit of Mt Rinjani – rather than just the caldera – this is the better of the two routes. **NB** This alternative route is less well marked. A guide is recommended to show climbers the route to the second rim.

Round trip taking in both sides of the mountain: because each side of Rinjani offers its own character a recommended alternative is to climb up the eastern flank and down the western. To do this, go to Senaru to rent equipment and buy supplies (the choice is best here), return to Anyer or Bayan and take a bemo or ojek to Sembalun Lawang. (Start early, bemos to Sembalun Lawang are rare after 1600.) Hire a guide and porter in Sembalun Lawang and stay the night. The next day the guide can show the route to the second rim (6-7 hrs); from here the climb to the summit (3-4 hrs) and then down into the caldera (3 hrs), and from there up to the first rim and back down to Senaru (6-7 hrs) is well marked and the guide is not needed.

Best time to climb: from May to Nov, during the dry season when it is less likely to be cloudy. Do not attempt the climb during the rainy season as the trail can be treacherous. **Recommended equipment**: water, sweater and coat, foam camping roll, sleeping bag, tough walking shoes, food/supplies, firewood (there is increasing evidence of climbers chopping down trees within this National Park in order to light a fire). *Please* take all your litter with you. **NB** Some climbers have complained of the poor quality of some of the equipment hired in Senaru; check it carefully. **Guides**: cost about 7,500Rp/day. A tent and/or sleeping bag hired for the guide would be greatly appreciated; it's cold on the mountain. **NB** The climb, though not technically difficult, is arduous and climbers should be in reasonable physical condition.

Tours The most convenient way to climb Rinjani is by booking a place on a 'tour'. Several tour operators in Mataram (see page 697), Senggigi (page 701) and on the Gilis organize climbs, about 150,000-250,000Rp/person.

Festivals Dec (2nd week): *Pakelem*, offering feast on Segara Anak to ask for God's blessings.

● **Accommodation** It is possible to stay at Batu Koq and Senaru, as well as at Sembalun Lawang if making the climb from the E. Senaru has the best selection of (basic, all **E**) losmen and new ones seem to open almost every month. **Senaru**: *Bale Bayan Guesthouse*, clean and friendly, the owner speaks reasonable English and German, rec; *Pondok Senaru*. **Batu Koq**: *Segara Anak Homestay* has been rec, price incl breakfast and supper; *Guru Bakti*, good bungalows especially those at the rear which offer superb views down the valley, price incl breakfast. On the SE slopes of Rinjani at the village of **Sapit** is the **D-F** *Hati Suci Homestay*, peaceful and highly rec, a good base for climbing the mountain. **Sembalun Lawang**: **E** *Diriam Guesthouse*, very helpful and friendly place, the owner speaks some English and can help arrange the trek although equipment is in short supply and may not be available, rec.

● **Camping** There are trekkers' camp-sites at various positions up the mountain – the corrugated shelters are rather dilapidated and the litter is bad.

● **Transport Road Bemo**: for the more usual N route, take a bemo from the Sweta terminal to Bayan, and then a second bemo from Bayan to Senaru. Alternatively, walk from Bayan. For the E route, take a bemo from Labuhan Lombok to Sembalun Bumbung; for transport to Sapit, see page 714. **Taxi**: a taxi from Bangsal to Senaru should cost about 30,000Rp.

CENTRAL LOMBOK AND THE WEST

Lombok's excellent main road runs for 74 km, E to W; from Mataram to Labuhan Lombok – the small port where ferries leave for Sumbawa. Most of these places can be visited on a day trip from Senggigi Beach; there is little accommodation available. East of Mataram (and 10 km from Cakranegara) is the town of Narmada with its rather down-at-heel 'pleasure garden'. A little way NE of here is Lingsar, the site of the Waktu Telu Temple. 7 km to the N of Narmada is the cool hill town of Suranadi set at 400m above sealevel (where there is a hotel). About 25 km E of Narmada, a road to the N (just after Sikur) leads up the lower slopes of Mt Rinjani, through Kota Raja, to a second hill resort, Tetebatu.

NARMADA

The **Taman Narmada**, or terraced 'pleasure garden' opposite the bemo station, was built in 1805. There are various spring-fed pools here, one of which is open to the public for swimming (admission to pool 300Rp). The gardens are supposed to be a scale model of the upper slopes of Mt Rinjani, including a replica of the holy crater lake, *Segara Anak*. The whole ensemble was laid out by King Anak Gede Karangasem of Mataram when he was too old to climb the real thing. A Hindu Balinese temple is situated above the bathing pools. The gardens are a popular picnic spot for Indonesians, but sadly are poorly maintained and rather dirty. There are, however, good bargains available within the grounds for T-shirts, (3,000Rp each). Dance performances are held here (1,500Rp). Admission to garden 200Rp. Open 0700-1800 Mon-Sun.

Festivals Nov/Dec: *Pujawali*, an annual festival held in conjunction with the *Pekalem* festival on Mt Rinjani, (when pieces of gold are thrown into the crater lake) once a year there is a 'duck-chasing' festival at Taman Narmada. Ducks are released onto the lake and at a signal from the leader of the ceremony boys plunge in to collect the birds. They are allowed to keep any ducks they catch.

● **Transport** 11 km E of Mataram. **Road Bemo**: regular connections with the Sweta terminal in Cakranegara.

LINGSAR

The **Waktu Telu Temple**, also known as the Lingsar Temple, was originally built in 1714, and then rebuilt in 1878. Both Hindu Balinese and Muslim Sasaks come to worship here, and there are compounds dedicated to each religion. It is particularly favoured by adherents of Lombok's unique Islam Waktu Telu religion – although their numbers are rapidly dwindling (see page 692). A lake here is said to contain holy fish, but seems rather too dirty to sustain any kind of marine life. Admission 1,000Rp. Open 0700-1800. Dress modest, sash required.

Festivals Nov/Dec: *Pujawali*, a 7-day festival, culminating in the two religions, the Muslims and Hindus, staging mock battles in the lower courtyard where they throw rice cakes (or *ketupat*) at one another.

● **Transport Road Bemo**: take a bemo from the Sweta terminal in Cakranegara to Narmada, and change here for Lingsar. If driving oneself, there is a more direct back route along a minor road from Cakranegara to Lingsar.

SURANADI

Set at an altitude of 400m, this is the site of one of Lombok's holiest temples – **Pura Suranadi**. The site was chosen by a Hindu saint who led settlers here while in a trance. Suranadi is the name of a celestial river in Hindu mythology and the temple is situated at the source of a mountain spring. Ornate Balinese carvings decorate the shrine. In the courtyards of the temple are several holy springs; the large black eels living in the pools fed by the springs are sacred and catching them is forbidden. For a small donation, the keepers will bang on the walls of the pools and throw hard-boiled eggs into the water to attract the eels from their dark lairs.

● **Accommodation B-C** *Suranadi*, Jl Raya Suranadi, PO Box 10, T 23686, a/c, restaurant, tennis, hot water, Lombok's original colonial hotel, now refurbished and with a new wing, friendly, with a slightly murky, spring-fed, swimming pool also used by many local people, rec.

● **Transport** 7 km N of Narmada, 18 km from Mataram. **Road Bemo**: from the Sweta terminal in Cakranegara to Narmada, and then change to another travelling N to Suranadi (500Rp).

TETEBATU

Tetebatu is a tiny village on the slopes of Mt Rinjani. There is very little to do here, except enjoy the beautiful scenery and visit the surrounding villages. The presence of the *Wisma Soedjono* here at the end of the road has made Tetebatu into something of a mountain 'retreat' for westerners. There are good walks in the surrounding countryside, a number of which start from the *Wisma Soedjono*, ranging from short ambles to half or full day trips. For the longer walks you need to arrange a guide. Even a short walk can be most rewarding. Walking down towards the rice paddies, is like entering a different world. The maze of narrow paths which connect the paddies provides a fascinating, yet discreet, insight into rural life in central Lombok. There is a good vantage point on a low hill for watching the people and their animals at work and play in the fields.

Excursions The villages in this part of Lombok are well worth exploring, and this is best done by hiring a car or motorcycle. **Kota Raja** is a market town 7 km S of Tetebatu noted for its handicrafts, particularly basketwork. **Loyok**, just off the road to Tetebatu, is known for its bamboo crafts and palm leaf boxes while **Pringgasela**, E of Kota Raja, is a centre for ikat weaving (see below). **Lendang Nangka** is a traditional Sasak village 7 km E of Kota Raja; while **Masbaggik**, on the main road just to the E of the turn-off for Kota Raja and Tetebatu is a pottery-making town. There are other craft villages in the central highlands area.

● **Accommodation C-D** *Wisma Soedjono*, some a/c, restaurant (cheap-medium) slow service, large pool, occupies a lovely position looking out over paddy and pineapple fields and the S slopes of Mt Rinjani, the owners speak English and hire out motorbikes for visiting the surrounding countryside. There is a variety of accommodation, including some 'traditional' Sasak houses along the side of the hill; **E** *Wisma Dewi Enjeni*, 2 km S of Tetebatu, lovely views, price incl breakfast.

● **Transport** 11 km N of the main road linking Mataram with Labuhan Lombok. **Road Bemo**: from the Sweta terminal in Cakranegara to Paok Motong and then another bemo to Tetebatu (1,500Rp).

PRINGGASELA

East of Kota Raja is this small weaving village, where traditional back-strap looms have not yet been displaced by more advanced technology, and where natural rather than artificial (chemical aniline) dyes are still in use. As there is accommodation available in Pringgasela, this is an good place to experience the 'real' Lombok.

● **Accommodation** Family-run homestay. Suhaidi (better known as 'Eddie') can arrange tours and trekking. **D** *Sasak House Homestay*, friendly, shared mandi.

● **Transport Road Bemo**: from the Sweta terminal in Cakranegara to Rempung (1,000Rp) and then a dokar to Pringgasela (300Rp) or from Labuhan Lombok (600Rp).

SAPIT

Sapit is a small Sasak village on the SE slopes of Mt Rinjani, with views W towards the mountain and E over the sea to Sumbawa. Set amidst rice paddies, it is one of the most relaxing places to unwind and also makes a good base for climbing Mt Rinjani (see Excursions, below).

Excursions Mount Rinjani is a 3-5 day excursion from Sapit (see page 709); guides are available in the village and charge about 10,000Rp/day.

● **Accommodation D-F** *Hati Suci Homestay*, restaurant, bungalow and dorm accommodation, clean and professionally run, stunning views, peaceful, breakfast incl, tours/treks organized, highly rec.

● **Transport Road Bus**: regular buses from the Sweta terminal in Cakranegara to Pringgabaya (1,000Rp); from Pringgabaya catch a bemo to Sapit (1,000Rp). Total journey time 2½-3 hrs. From Labuhan Lombok, take a bus to Pringgabaya and then a bemo to Sapit.

LABUHAN LOMBOK

Labuhan Lombok is the small ferry port for Sumbawa. It is little more than a fishing village and most tourists are only too happy to catch the first ferry out.

● **Accommodation E** *Losmen Muanawar*, basic; **E-F** *Lima Tiga*, new losmen, very clean and well-run when it opened, shared mandi, price incl breakfast, the best place to stay here, rec.

● **Places to eat** ◆*Warung Kelayu*, close to the *Lima Tiga* losmen, good value local food.

● **Transport** 74 km from Mataram. **Road Bemo**: from the Sweta terminal in Cakranegara (2½ hrs by chartered bemo). **Sea Boat**: there is a ferry linking Labuhan Lombok, with Poto Tano on Sumbawa's W coast, 6 departures each day, each way (0700-1730), 1½ hrs (2,000Rp).

SOUTH LOMBOK AND THE SOUTH COAST

From Cakranegara, a good road runs 26 km SE to the market town of Praya. 3 km before Praya is the small village of Puyung, and 2 km S of here the popular weaving village of Sukarara. Turning S from Praya, the road reaches the pottery-making village of Penujak after 5 km and continues S to Sengkol. This area is one of the centres of Sasak culture with a number of traditional villages. It is a poor part of the island, with low grade agricultural land and abandoned paddies. The road ends at the quiet beach and fishing village of Kuta, 32 km from Praya and 58 km from Mataram.

SUKARARA

Sukarara is a small **weaving village** SE of Mataram. The weavers here still use traditional backstrap looms but the workshops along the main road are now geared to tourists and the quality is indifferent, with artificial dyes in widespread use. Traditional Lombok designs are still produced – in particular cloth inter-woven with gold and silver thread – but it is becoming increasingly difficult to find finely-worked, quality cloth. **Transport** 25 km from Mataram. **Road Bemo**: from the Sweta terminal in Cakranegara bound for Praya; get off at Puyung, 3 km N of Praya. From here either walk or hire a dokar for the 2-km ride to the village.

PENUJAK

Penujak is a **pottery-making village** 5 km S of Praya on the road to Kuta. The New Zealand government has been providing aid to support and develop the craft since 1988, in particular through improving design, technology and marketing. Both traditional pottery forms such as the *gentong* (storage jar), *kaling* (water jar) and *periuk* (cooking vessel) along with designs produced purely for the tourist market are on sale. A major problem the industry has faced is adapting to a market where size/weight and fragility are both serious impediments to increased sales. Other important pottery-making villages include **Rungkang** and **Masbaggik** in E Lombok, and **Banyumulek** to the S of Mataram. The latter two villages also receive support from the New Zealand project.

The road splits at Penujak. One branch leads on to the S coast of Silungblanak where there is a good sandy beach. The other road goes on to Kuta. **Transport Road Bemo**: from the Sweta terminal in Cakranegara to Praya; change in Praya and catch another travelling S to Penujak (900Rp).

SADE

The area S of the town of Sengkol to Kuta Beach is one of the centres of Sasak culture and there are a number of 'traditional' Sasak villages here. The best known is Sade where women, realizing their potential as a tourist attraction, still wear traditional Sasak dress. Also here, there are some of the few remaining examples of Sasak architecture, including the tall-roofed, thatched, *lumbungs* (rice barns). But, Sade is firmly on the tour bus circuit and although the villagers have made a conscious effort to maintain 'tradition' for the foreign visitors, the economy is geared as much to tourism as to agriculture. Women frantically sell textiles while the children hustle. **Transport Road Bemo**: from the Sweta terminal in Cakranegara to Praya; change here and catch another travelling S towards Kuta.

KUTA BEACH

Kuta Beach, also sometimes known as Putri Nyale Beach, is situated amongst the most spectacular coastal scenery on Lombok; rocky outcrops and cliff faces give way to sheltered sandy bays, ideal for swimming and surfing.

Kuta itself has a stretch of beautiful white sand on Lombok's S coast in a bay with a little fishing village at its head. There is a substantial fishing fleet of sailing boats with brightly decorated dugout hulls and outriggers. There are no 'sights' and few facilities here, apart from the simple bungalows along the coast road, some of which have restaurants attached.

The beach is the focal point of a strange annual festival, called the *Bau Nyale* (see Sumba, page 767 for similar event), when thousands of seaworms come to the surface of the sea. Local people flock here to witness the event, and it is becoming quite a popular tourist attraction. See below for details.

Still a quiet place to stay, with basic accommodation and a poor road linking it with Mataram, Kuta has been earmarked for future development. A plan for a 'Putri Nyale Resort' has been published, envisaging the construction of multiple luxury hotels, two golf courses, lagoons, craft villages and an international size airport... Whether it will come to anything is another matter, but the Lombok Tourism Development Corporation has big ideas for Kuta.

The coast road continues E from Kuta. After 2 km a dirt track turns off to **Seger Beach** where the West Nusa Tenggara Tourist Office has a large fenced-off administration complex. There are a couple of white sand sweeping bays here: no facilities. Several kilometres further on again, past low-lying swampy land is the fine beach at **Tanjung Aan**. **NB** There is no shade on any of these beaches, just basic scrub. The track bends round to the S and ends at **Grupuk (Desert) Point**.

Festivals Feb/Mar (on the 19th day of the 10th month of the Sasak lunar calendar): *Nyale ceremony*, several days before the ceremony "the rain comes down cats and dogs with lightning and thundering thunder bolts". Calm weather follows and thousands of mysterious sea worms called Nyale fish (*Eunice viridis*), 'hatch' on the reef and rise to the surface of the sea off Kuta. According to the legend of Putri Nyale, the episode is linked to the beautiful Princess Nyale who drowned herself here after failing to choose between a bevy of eligible men. The worms are supposed to represent her hair, and celebrations are held each year to mark her death. Traditionally, this was a time

for young people to find a partner for marriage and it is still an occasion when the usual strictures controlling contact between the sexes are eased. The worms are scooped from the sea and eaten.

● **Accommodation** Bungalows are rather unattractive, made of clapboard with linoleum floors, squashed together and facing away from the sea. Rooms are usually very small (mostly clean), up on stilts. In short, Kuta gives the air of a downmarket European holiday camp. They are all of similar standard and mostly in our **D** range, although cheaper rooms do come down in price to our **F** category. The bungalows are strung out along the beach road a short distance from the village: *Anda*; *Lockatoo Cottages*; *Mandalika Seaview Cottages*; *Maria Homestay*; *Mascot Cottages*; *Pondok Sekar Kuning*; *Rinjani Agung Beach*; *Segara Anak*, restaurant, basic style but friendly staff; *Tanjung Aan Hotel*.

● **Places to eat** Restaurants are attached to several of the above places to stay incl *Rinjani Agung Beach*; *Florida*; *Auda*; *Cockatoo Inn*, good spring rolls, popular with tour buses; *Segara Anak*, popular; *Bamboo*, nr the village.

● **Transport** 32 km from Praya, 54 km from Mataram. **Road Bemo**: from the Sweta terminal in Cakranegara (Mataram) to Praya and then a second from Praya to Kuta. *Perama* shuttle bus service next door to *Segara Anak Hotel*. Public bemos also connect Kuta with Lahbuan Lombok (for ferries to Sumbawa).

WEST OF KUTA

There is now a sealed road running W of Kuta as far as Selong Blanak. Along the way there are several good beaches, all quite deserted. Few bemos, so most people get here by private or chartered transport.

● **Accommodation** **D-E** *Selong Blanak Cottages*, clean and well run, rooms with private mandi, restaurant (♦♦), the deserted beach is about 2 km away and free transport is provided. *Getting there*: the occasional bemo runs to Selong Blanak from Praya, 1,000Rp.

EAST OF KUTA: EKAS

● **Accommodation** **D** *Laut Surga Cottages*, restaurant, popular with surfers, this remote place several kilometres S of Ekas is set on a pretty, secluded beach. *Getting there*: by boat from Awang. In the dry season it is possible to drive there via Jerowaru.

Sumbawa

S UMBAWA'S landscape is harsh and dry with rugged, boulder-strewn hills, scrubby vegetation and a bright searing light. When the mist hangs over the land in the early mornings, the island looks almost like a moonscape. There are a handful of oases of cultivation – for example, around Dompu, to the east of the island – but generally Sumbawa is infertile and population densities here are markedly lower than the richer islands of Lombok and Bali to the west.

Horizons

The island runs E-W for 280 km but varies in width from as little as 15 km, to 90 km at its widest point. Like the rest of Nusa Tenggara, Sumbawa is volcanic in origin, most clearly illustrated when Mt Tambora erupted in 1815 to devastating effect, killing an estimated 12,000 people (see page 720).

Even though Sumbawa covers nearly 16,000 sq km its population remains just 1 million. The island is divided into three districts: Sumbawa, Dompu and Bima. In fact, Sumbawa is really two islands – joined by a thin isthmus – in one. Locals refer only to the western half as 'Sumbawa'; the E is Bima. It is said that when the first ever marriage occurred between the royal houses of Sumbawa and Bima in 1929, the bride and groom could only communicate with one another in Dutch, such had been the degree of mutual ignorance. Sumbawa Besar has been influenced by its neighbours to the W, with a language reminiscent of Sasak, whilst Bima looks to the E, with a language more akin to that spoken in Flores.

Islam was introduced to Sumbawa in the early 17th century when the King of Bima became a Muslim, and thus a Sultan. The Dutch did not exercise control over the island until the early part of the 20th century, and this lasted barely a single generation before the Japanese invaded. Today, the royal court of Bima still survives, but in an impoverished state. The two main towns on Sumbawa are Sumbawa Besar, to the W, and Bima-Raba in the E.

● **Transport** The Trans-Sumbawa highway is excellent, and made-up all the way from Poto Tano (the port on the W coast, serving Lombok) to Sape (on the E coast, serving Komodo and Flores). There are 'direct' buses from Mataram (Lombok) via Sumbawa Besar and Dompu to Bima-Raba (see page 700). *Jawa Baru* run direct buses all the way from Surabaya to Bima-Raba, a crippling 2 night/1 day journey (42,000-46,000Rp).

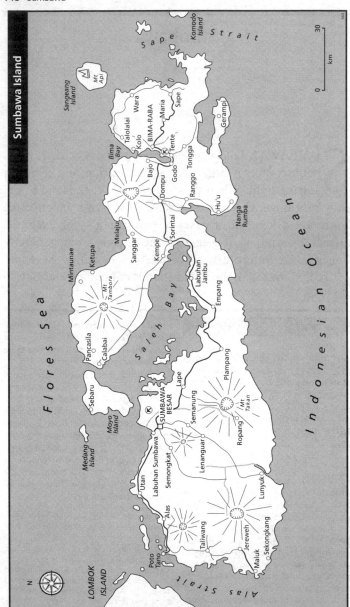

Sumbawa Island

ALAS

Alas was once the main port for Lombok; now ferries leave from Poto Tano, 22 km to the S and 10 km off the main road. There is little reason to stay here, but there are losmen available if travellers get stranded (Poto Tano has no accommodation).

- **Accommodation** E *Anda*, Jl Pahlawan 14, T 169; **E** *Selamat*, Jl Pahlawan 7, T 26; **E** *Telaga*, Jl Pahlawan.

- **Transport** 22 km from Poto Tano. **Road Bus**: connections with Sumbawa Besar, Poto Tano and Taliwang.

TALIWANG

Taliwang lies to the S of Alas; people travelling further S to the surfing beach at Maluk may have to stay overnight here, but there is little reason to extend a stay.

- **Accommodation** E *Hamba*, Jl Sudirman 64, T 8; **E** *Taliwang*, Jl Sudirman, some rooms with shower, English speaking management; **E-F** *Tubalong*, Jl Sudirman 11, T 18.

- **Places to eat** ♦*Taliwang Indah*, good value dishes.

- **Transport** 40 km from Alas, 40 km from Maluk. **Road Bus**: bus connections with Poto Tano and Alas and onward to Sumbawa Besar; trucks take travellers further S to Maluk.

MALUK

Maluk is a beach, reputed to have good surf, on Sumbawa's W coast, S of Taliwang. **NB** The coral is just below the surface and surfing can be hazardous – this is only for the most adventurous of surfers.

- **Accommodation** There are no losmen as yet, but visitors have stayed in the local village. Ask the *kepala desa* (headman) for permission. In addition, there are no warungs for food, so take your own.

- **Transport** 95 km S of Poto Tano. **Road Bus**: from Poto Tano, catch a bus S to Taliwang 45 km, and from here a truck to Maluk 40 km. From Sumbawa Besar, catch a bus from the Bawah terminal to Taliwang 114 km and then a truck onwards. **Sea Boat**: a more direct route to Maluk is from Labuhan Haji on Lombok's E coast, 1½ hrs.

SUMBAWA BESAR

This dusty, quiet town on the N coast of the island is really only a stop-over on the way E to Bima-Raba and the island of Komodo, or W to Lombok. It is small enough to walk around, and is very friendly – the locals are inclined to invite visitors back to their houses. Sumbawa Besar is the capital of the district of Sumbawa and a former royal capital.

Places of interest

Sumbawa Besar's main sight is a large wooden palace on Jl Sudirman, at the E side of town. The **Istana Tua**, known locally as *Dalam Loka* ('Old Palace') is raised off the ground on 99 wooden pillars and was extensively renovated in 1985. Built a century earlier in 1885 by Sultan Mohammad Jalaluddin III, it is now an empty shell, but is impressive nonetheless. It is due to metamorphose into a museum, although the pieces to stock the museum have yet to materialize. Admission by donation. Open 0600-1800 Mon-Sun. An abandoned **Dutch fort** is visible from the palace, situated on the hill overlooking the town. Next to the palace is the modern and uninspired **Mesjid Nurul Huda**.

Not far from the post office on Jl Yos Sudarso is a poorly maintained Balinese temple, **Pura Agung Girinatha**. A short walk E of here, on Jl Cipto, is the very ordinary **Seketeng Market**.

Excursions

Kencana Beach 10 km W of town, offers snorkelling. **Accommodation D-E** *Kencana Beach Inn*, Karang Teruna Beach, 10 km W of town (book through *Tambora Hotel* in town). Snorkelling and diving equipment available for hire, free transfer from *Tambora Hotel*. *Getting there*: by bemo (500Rp).

Moyo Island is just accessible as a day trip, although it is best to stay overnight. The S area of the island is a national park and lies just to the N of Sumbawa Besar. Rich in wildlife, with particularly good snorkelling off the S coast, it is being considered for 'hunting safaris'. Contact the PHPA office in Sumbawa Besar (see below) before visiting the island. *Best time to visit*: Jun-Aug. **NB** No snorkelling equipment available for hire on Moyo, the *Kencana Beach Inn* (see above) organizes day trips to the island, and supplies snorkelling equipment. **Accommodation L** *Amanwana*, Moyo Island, T (0371) 22333, F (0371) 22288 reservations c/o *Amanusa*, Nusa Dua, Bali, T 71267, F 71260), a remarkably luxurious 'tent' hotel. The first so-called 'Aman Hideaway', 'tents' are large chalets with canvas roofs, a/c, king size beds, divans and large bathrooms, the hotel has a restaurant, bar, lounge and library and rates include all food and drink and most activities, surely one of the most civilized ways to camp on this pristine island. Alternatively there is much cheaper accommodation available in PHPA bungalows, **F**. *Getting there*: there are three ways to reach the island. From Labuhan Sumbawa, sailing boats can be chartered for the 3-4 hr journey (75,000Rp each way). Alternatively, go to Labuhan Sawo, much closer to Moyo, and charter a local boat for 10,000-15,000Rp. Get to both Labuhan Sawo and Sumbawa by bemo

(200Rp) from the Seketeng market in Sumbawa Besar. It is also possible to reach Moyo from Kencana Beach, 10 km W of Sumbawa Besar. The *Kencana Beach Inn* has a speedboat which can be chartered, 1½ hrs (200,000Rp) and a slower launch, 3 hrs (80,000Rp). Bemos run to Kencana Beach from Sumbawa Besar (500Rp).

Mount Tambora is 2,800m high and is best known for the eruption of 5-15 July 1815, which killed tens of thousands and made the following summer one of the coldest ever. It is said that the paintings of JMW Turner (1775-1851) reflect the magnificent fiery sunsets that the eruption brought on. *The Fighting Téméraire* is one such painting, of which Thackeray wrote: "The old Téméraire [the second ship of the line after Nelson's Victory at Trafalgar] is dragged to her last home by a little, spiteful, diabolical steamer. A mighty red sun, amidst a host of flaring clouds, sinks to rest on one side of the picture, and illumines a river that seems interminable, and a countless navy that fades away into such a wonderful distance as never was painted before." Unfortunately, however, *The Fighting Téméraire* was painted in 1839, 14 years after Mount

Sumbawa Besar

Hotels:
1. Losmen Indra
2. Losmen Saudara
3. Losmen Suci
4. Tambora

Places to eat:
5. Rakun Jaya

Not to Scale

Tambora erupted. Still, it makes a pleasing story.

There are two coloured lakes in the caldera. To climb the mountain really requires a 2-3 days excursion. A guide is essential – they can be hired at Pancasila; the police also recommend that trekkers register at their station in Calabai before setting out. The track is often difficult to follow, through thick forest. Wear trousers and long-sleeved shirts (to avoid leeches) and a sturdy pair of walking boots. There are freshwater streams en route, but they are not always easy to find, so take a supply of water and some food. Thick vegetation gives way to pine forest and then a volcanic landscape on the approach to the rim of the volcano. Cloud cover is often bad, making for disappointing views from the summit. It is possible to climb down a precipitous slope into the caldera, where there is a lake. *Getting there*: charter an early morning boat from the harbour in Sumbawa Besar to Calabai (60,000Rp), where there is accommodation; then take an ojek or dokar the 15 km to Pancasila; this is the start of the climb.

Tours

Tours can be organized to surrounding villages for buffalo races, to off-shore islands (including Moyo), and to trek to the summit of Mt Tambora (2,820m) (see above). The *Tambora Hotel* will organize 3-day treks to the summit of Mt Tambora, and Abdul Muis and Stephen Annas are recommended as guides (both contactable through the hotel). The *Kencana Beach Inn* (see excursions) organize trips to Moyo.

Local information
● **Accommodation**

B-E *Tambora*, Jl Kebayan 2, T 21555, F 21624, some a/c, best hotel in town, less than 1 km from airport, well-run, clean rooms, quiet, price incl breakfast, rec.

E *Losmen Saudara*, Jl Hasanuddin 50, T 21528, rather dark rooms, attached mandi; **E** *Suci*, Jl Hasanuddin 57, T 21589, restaurant, courtyard with open air restaurant, some rooms rather dirty, friendly staff.

F *Losmen Indra*, Jl Diponegoro 48A, T 278, basic, attached mandi.

● **Places to eat**
Stalls and warungs around the Bawah bus terminal on Jl Diponegoro and at the Pasar Seketeng on Jl Dr Cipto. Restaurants on Jl Hasanuddin and Jl Kartini; nothing of culinary excellence. ♦♦*Tambora Restaurant* (at hotel of same name), Jl Kebayan 2; ♦*Rakun Jaya*, Jl Hasanuddin 53, Indonesian; ♦*Usfa Warna*, Jl Kartini 16, Chinese and seafood.

● **Airline offices**
Merpati, Jl Garuda 2, T 21416.

● **Banks & money changers**
BNI, Jl Kartini 10, US$ cash only.

● **Hospitals & medical services**
Hospitals: *General Hospital*, Jl Garuda (W edge of town).

● **Post & telecommunications**
Area code: 0371.
General Post Office: Jl Yos Sudarso 6A.
Perumtel (international telephone, telex, telegram & fax): Jl Yos Sudarso (opp Post Office).

● **Sports**
Diving & snorkelling: snorkelling equipment available from the *Kencana Beach Inn*; they also claim to have diving equipment for hire now, but check at the sister *Tambora Hotel* in town for availability beforehand.

● **Tour companies & travel agents**
Tarindo Wisata, Jl Hasanuddin 80, T 21026; *Tirta Martan*, Jl Garuda 88.

● **Useful addresses**
PHPA Office: Jl Candrawasih 1A, T 21446 (W, just past the *General Hospital*).

● **Transport**
70 km from Alas, 92 km from Poto Tano, 250 km from Bima-Raba.

Local Bemos: the station is in front of the Seketeng Market on Jl Dr Cipto. **Dokars** (known as *cidomos*): 200Rp.

Air The airport is only 2 km W of the town centre. There are 'taxis', but it is easy to walk, or catch a bemo. Regular connections on Garuda/Merpati with Denpasar, Jakarta, Mataram, Surabaya, Ujung Pandang and Yogyakarta.

Road Bus: there are two bus stations. In the heart of town on Jl Diponegoro is **Terminal Bawah**. Connections from here W to Utan, Alas,

Mount Tambora and the year without summer

The eruption of Mt Tambora is overshadowed in most people's minds by the much more famous Krakatau (see page 144). But the sheer destructive power of Tambora was, in fact, far greater. Indeed, volcanologists believe it to be the most powerful eruption in the last 10,000 years. Around 150 cubic kilometres of volcanic material were ejected; the figure for Krakatau was a comparatively measly 18 cubic km. 117,000 people are thought to have died as a result of the eruption – as against 36,000 for Krakatau.

Tambora blew its top in April 1815 – beginning on 5 April and culminating in a series of eruptions from the evening of the 10th through to the 15th. The explosions were heard as far away as Yogyakarta, where the Sultan, fearing attack, readied an army to mount a defence of his city. Much of Java was plunged into darkness for 3 days and ash settled as far as 1,300 km away. The mountain itself shrunk from its pre-eruption height of 4,200m to 2,800m, and a massive caldera was created.

But Mt Tambora was not just a natural phenomenon of mind-stretching proportions. It was also a human catastrophe. The local princedoms of Pekat and Tambora were annihilated, not a single resident surviving the event. As a consequence, the Tambora language became extinct. Around 10,000 people are thought to have died in the initial eruption. The blanket of ash, which averaged around 50-60 cm deep but in places reached over 1m, destroyed crops over a wide area. The local economy was reduced to nought and famine ensued. Drinking water became polluted with ash and hundreds of people died, if not of the explosion and famine, then of fevers brought on by drinking dirty water. These secondary effects lead to the death of perhaps another 37,000 people. Sumbawa's population declined from 170,000 before the event to 86,000 after.

In 1819, JC Vetter visited Tambora and reported, some 4 years after the eruption, a scene of devastation. Although rice was being grown again by 1820, in 1821 CGC Reinwardt reported that he had great problems reprovisioning his ship such was the dearth of foodstuffs. In 1824, Papekat was still, according to Schelle and

---

Taliwang and to Poto Tano port (for Lombok). There are direct buses from Mataram (Lombok) to Sumbawa Besar and onward to Bima-Raba. For Bima-Raba, Dompu and other destinations E of Sumbawa Besar, buses leave from **Terminal Brangbara** on Jl Sultan Kaharuddin on the E edge of town. Buses to Bima-Raba leave roughly hourly, 0600-1200; there is also a night bus at 2130, 7-8 hrs (5,000Rp). **NB** Buying a ticket from the touts who visit the hotels will cost an extra 1,000Rp; the advantage is that you will be picked up from your hotel.

Sea Boat: there is a ferry linking Labuhan Lombok, on Lombok's E coast, with Poto Tano on Sumbawa's W coast, 6 departures each day, each way (0700-1730), 1½ hrs (2,000Rp). There are regular buses from Poto Tano to Alas, and then onward to Sumbawa Besar and Bima-Raba.

SUMBAWA BESAR TO BIMA-RABA

The road E from Sumbawa Besar runs through a boulder-strewn, arid landscape and after just over 100 km reaches the coast, passing the picturesque fishing village of Labuhan Jambu. Wood and tile houses are elevated on stilts, with traditional boats hauled up on the beach or moored along the shore. Tour parties sometimes stop here; the regular bus will stop, but it won't wait. From here the road follows the coast before cutting inland to Dompu. The surfing beach of Hu'u lies 40 km to the S of Dompu. From Dompu the road continues E to Sumbawa's main town, Bima-Raba.

Tobias, two Dutch officials, a "desolate heap of rubble". When E Francis sailed past Tambora in 1831, well over a decade-and-a-half since the event, he looked through his field glasses and reported an "horrendous scene of devastation", going on to explain with a touch of poetic licence that "in its fury the eruption...[had] spared, of the inhabitants, not a single person, of the fauna, not a worm, of the flora, not a blade of grass". Fifteen years after Francis' visit, the naturalist Heinrich Zollinger surveyed the area and reported abandoned rice fields and a flora which was much more impoverished, he hazarded, than that which existed before the eruption. It seemed the event had changed the very nature of the area's vegetation and he suggested that rainfall was markedly less. Even beyond Sumbawa the effects were pronounced. Lombok and Bali suffered severe famines as the harvest failed. How many people died on Bali and Lombok is not known. Estimates vary from well over 100,000 down to around 10,000. 25,000 is regarded as a conservative figure. Ironically, a few years on from the eruption, Bali was reporting record rice harvests as the ash began to improve soil fertility.

But perhaps the most remarkable effect of the eruption of Mount Tambora was the effect it had on the northern hemisphere's climate. The summer of 1816 in Europe and North America was particularly cold and wet. In the USA's corn belt, virtually the entire crop was lost; livestock across the northeastern United States died of cold; the wine harvest in France was the latest ever recorded – and records go back over 500 years; there were June frosts in New England; in Switzerland, people resorted to eating famine foods like moss, cats and sorrel, such was the state of the harvest; and it has even been suggested that outbreaks of cholera in places like Bengal, Nepal and Russia were linked to the eruption of Tambora. 1816 became known as the Year Without Summer. At the time no one linked Mt Tambora's eruption with the extraordinary weather that followed it. In the 1960s Hubert Lamb developed his 'dust-veil index', which measures the amount of climate-changing particles in the air. The index is based on the Krakatau explosion which has a figure of 1,000. Mt Tambora's index is 4,200.

Adapted from: Boers, Bernice de Jong (1995) "Mount Tambora in 1815: a volcanic eruption in Indonesia and its aftermath", *Indonesia* 60: 37-59.

DOMPU

Dompu is the capital of Dompu district and en route between Sumbawa's two principal towns, Sumbawa Besar and Bima-Raba. Surfers making their way S to the beach at Hu'u (see below) may have to change buses here and possibly stop-over for the night.

- **Accommodation E** *Anda*, Jl Jend A Yani, T195; **E** *Bala Kemar Cottages*, Jl Merdeka 82, Empang, only accommodation on the main road, half way between Sumbawa Besar and Dompu, just W of Empang, restaurant, big rooms but no fans, ensuite mandi; **E** *Karijawa*, Jl Sudirman T230; **E** *Losmen Ati*; **E** *Manura Kupang*, attractive garden location.

- **Transport** 40 km from Hu'u. **Road Bus**: regular connections with Bima-Raba and Sumbawa Besar. Onward buses to Hu'u.

HU'U

A surfing beach popular with Australians since the late 1980s who come here on 'package tours' and stay in surf camps. The surf is best in Apr, although the resort is most crowded during Jul and Aug.

- **Accommodation B-C** *Primadona Lakey Cottages and Restaurant*, Lakey Beach, Jl Nanga Doro, Dompu, Sumbawa Hu'u, T (0373) 21168, 21384, 21585, one of the newest places in Hu'u, set right on the beach, private bathrooms with western toilet, some rooms have satellite TV; **D** *Bobby's Surf Camp*; **D** *Mona Lisa*, some with attached mandi; **E** *Lestari*, some with attached mandi.

- **Transport** 40 km from Dompu. **Road Bus**: direct morning buses to Hu'u from Terminal Bima in Bima (4,500Rp). Otherwise catch a bus from either Bima or Sumbawa Besar to Dompu, and from here a connection S to Hu'u.

BIMA-RABA

Bima-Raba, also known as Raba-Bima, are twin towns (Raba and Bima or, if you like, Bima and Raba) separated by about 3 km. Most of the activity is centred on Bima. This is where the hotels and losmen are to be found, where the port is located, and from where buses leave for Sumbawa Besar and Lombok/Bali. The bus terminal for Sape (and from there to Flores) is in Raba, as well as the central post office. Constant bemos link the two towns. *Dokars* here are called *ben hurs* – and it really is due to the film (it must have made quite an impact on the population of Bima-Raba). The half-starved, large dog-sized animals that masquerade as horses would not have passed muster in Roman days. On the *ben hurs* 'don't eat too much' is often written in Bimanese (an Austrone-sian language), reflecting the desolate nature of the island, the formerly frequent famines and the concern of its inhabitants for food security.

The inhabitants of the town refer to themselves as Dou Mbojo, or 'People of Mbojo', and the name Bima is thought to be taken from the Hindu epic poem the Mahabharata in which one of the heroes is named Bhima. Traditionally, society was stratified into four classes: the royal family, nobles, commoners, and slaves. Today, though, Bima-Raba is a multi-ethnic place with settlers from Flores and Timor, Chinese including Cantonese and Hokkien, Arabs from southern Arabia, Makassarese and Bugis from Sulawesi, and Javanese – along with some Europeans called *'Dou Turi'*. (Although this means tourist it is also used for expatriates.)

Places of interest

Bima's principal sight is the **Sultan's Palace** which faces onto the main square, at

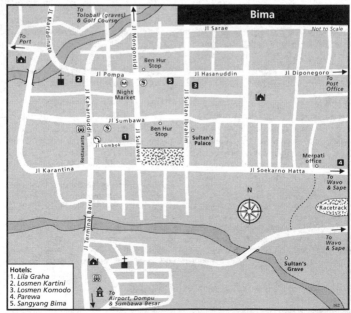

Hotels:
1. *Lila Graha*
2. *Losmen Kartini*
3. *Losmen Komodo*
4. *Parewa*
5. *Sangyang Bima*

the E edge of the town centre. Built in 1927, it has been converted into a museum that houses a dismal collection of weapons, baskets, farm implements and other assorted paraphernalia. Traditional dances are irregularly performed here. The Bimanese Sultanate was swept to one side after the Revolution, and almost disappeared from sight. However, the predilections of tourists, as well as a government policy to promote regional cultures as part of an attempt to strengthen national culture, has led to a resurgence in interest in Bima's royal roots. Admission by donation. Open 0700-1800 Mon-Sun. The **central market** is in the heart of town between Jl Sultan Kharuddin and Jl Sulawesi. Stall food is available here. Climb up the hills behind the Terminal Bima, or to the S of Jl Soekarno-Hatta for views over the town and bay. One of the Sultans has his grave here (ask for *makam sultan*).

Excursions

Lawata Beach 3 km S of town on the road to Dompu and Sumbawa Besar, hardly deserves to be called a beach. Locals come here for the sunsets. *Getting there*: by *ben hur* or walk.

Kolo on Bima Bay to the N of town is visited for its snorkelling. *Getting there*: boats can be chartered from Bima port, or cadge a lift on one of the regular boats, 1 hr (1,000Rp).

Maria lies 30 mins outside Bima-Raba, on the road to Sape and is notable for its traditional wood and tile rice barns (*lengge*) massed on the overlooking hill. The local residents are often characterized – wrongly – as belonging to some unspecified hill 'tribe'. They are, in fact, lowland Bimanese although their hillside residence means that they do, reportedly, speak some of the Wawo language. (They live quite close to the upland Dou Wawo.) Anthropologist Michael Hitchcock, who has worked in Bima, wonders what the people of Maria make of the pejorative 'hill tribe' label. Given that it brings tourists and money, possibly with gratitude. *Getting there*: by

bus from Kumbe terminal in Raba.

Climbing Mt Tambora to the NW of Bima-Raba is a 3-day excursion (see page 720). *Getting there*: there is usually one bus a day to Calabai from the Bima station.

Tours

Grand Komodo run recommended tours from Bali to Komodo (see page 730), but it is possible to sign on in Bima-Raba. They also arrange tours to sights around the town. Their office in Bima is at Jl Soekarno-Hatta, T 2812, F 2018. *Komodo Tours*, as well as the *Parewa Hotel* (which also has a boat for charter to Komodo) have minibuses for charter to explore the surrounding countryside.

Local information
● Accommodation

B *Sangyang Bima*, Jl Sultan Hasanuddin 6, T 2788, F 2017, a/c, pool in new extension, well-run, but rooms only average for the price.

C-D *Lila Graha*, Jl Lombok 20, T 2645, some a/c, central, noisy, with poor rooms, price incl breakfast; **C-D** *Parewa*, Jl Soekarno-Hatta 40, T 2652, some a/c, this building was to be a cinema but the owner couldn't get the licence, and it shows – there are no outside windows, it seems to have deteriorated since our last visit: dirty, poor food, indolent staff, price incl breakfast.

D *Sonco Tengge Beach Hotel*, Jl Sultan Salahuddin, T 2987, 1½ km from town on road to Dompu, alternative to being in town, rooms are clean, beach is nothing to speak of, get there by *ben hur*.

E *Losmen Kartini*, Jl Pasar 11, T 2072, shared mandi, upstairs rooms are more airy, a little grubby, central, nr market; **E** *Losmen Komodo*, Jl Sultan Ibrahim (next to Sultan's Palace), T 2070, shared mandi, simple but fine, rec; **E** *Putera Sari*, Jl Soekarno-Hatta 7 (nr intersection with Jl Sultan Hasanuddin), T 2825, acceptable rooms, shared mandi; **E** *Viva*, Jl Soekarno-Hatta (nr intersection with Jl Sultan Hasanuddin), T 2411, reasonable rooms, shared mandi.

● Places to eat

♦♦*Lila Graha*, Jl Lombok 20, Chinese, Indonesian, seafood; *Ariana*, Jl Martadinata (on road to harbour); *Parewa Modern Bakery and Ice Cream*, Jl Lombok.

● Airline offices

Merpati, Jl Soekarno-Hatta 60, T 2697.

● **Banks & money changers**
BNI, Jl Sultan Hasanuddin, US$ cash only.

● **Post & telecommunications**
Area code: 0374.
General Post Office: Raba (get there by mini-bus from Bima, 150Rp).

● **Transport**
250 km from Sumbawa Besar, 45 km from Bima-Raba.

Local Bemos: run between the two bus termi-nals and through both Bima and Raba (150Rp).

Air Mohammad Salahuddin airport is 20 km S of town, outside Tente and on the Trans-Sum-bawa highway. Regular connections by Garuda/Merpati with Bali, Lombok and other destinations in Nusa Tenggara. Bemo taxis into town cost 8,500Rp, although it is easy to walk out onto the main road and wait for a bus.

Road Bus: Bima-Raba has two bus stations. **Terminal Bima** is at the SW edge of Bima town on Jl Terminal Baru. Buses from here for all points W – Dompu, Hu'u, Sumbawa Besar, Lombok, Bali and Surabaya. The **Kumbe terminal** for Sape (the port for Komodo and Flores) is in Raba town, 5 km from Bima. Regular minibuses to Sape. Bemos run constantly between the two terminals through Bima and Raba. Bus compa-nies such as *Jawa Baru*, *Bima Indah* and *Surya Kencana* have their offices on or nr Jl Kharuddin, between the market and Terminal Bima.

Sea Boat: Bima's harbour is walking distance from Bima town. The Pelni ships *Binaiya* and *Tilongkabila* dock here on their 2-week circuits through Java, Kalimantan, Sulawesi and Nusa Tenggara (see route schedules, page 921). The Pelni office is at Jl Martadinata (also known as Jl Pelabuhan) 103, nr the docks.

SAPE

Sape is the usual place to stay, while wait-ing for the ferry to Komodo Island and Flores. The port itself – Labuhan Sape – is about 4 km from Sape town. Most of the population are not Bimanese at all, but Bugis – the famed seafarers from Sulawesi. Nothing happens in Sape, but staying here does make it easier catching the 0800 ferry. The accommodation is some of the poorest in Indonesia.

Excursions Labuhan Sape (Sape Port) is 4 km from town and can be reached on foot or by *ben hur*. There is boat building along the road, fishing boats landing their catch in the morning, and a mosque with a lighthouse-style minaret.

● **Accommodation** Basic and of uniformly poor quality, losmen are all found on Jl Pela-buhan, on the seaward side of town. Because it is usually necessary to stay the night in Sape to catch the ferry, the town is a 'choke point' and accommodation is sometimes in short sup-ply between the peak months from Jul to Sep. An alternative is to stay in Bima and catch an early bus to Sape. New losmen are opening here and the hope is that the challenge of some competition may improve standards. **F** *Friend-ship*, dirty, small rooms, dark with uncomfort-able beds; **F** *Give*, dirty; **F** *Ratnasari*, new, cleanish (for Sape), the best of a very bad bunch. **E-F** *Mutiara*, right by the dock; one of the newer losmen and at the last count the best of a very poor bunch.

● **Places to eat** *Hovita*, Jl Pelabuhan, friendly, cold beer, good fish (if asked in advance), rec; *Surabaya*, next to *Losmen Give*.

● **Post & telecommunications Post Office**: Jl Pelabuhan 34. **Wartel**: Jl Pelabuhan (between *Losmens Give* and *Ratnasari*).

● **Tourist offices** Komodo Tourist Centre, between Labuhan Sape and Sape town, only marginally useful, but some information on Komodo.

● **Transport** 45 km from Bima-Raba. **Road Bus**: the station is on the seaward side of town, although buses will drop passengers off nr the losmen. Regular connections with Raba's Kumbe terminal, 1½ hrs. From Kumbe, bemos run to Bima town and then on to the Bima terminal for buses W (see page 726). **Sea Boat**: the ferry for Komodo 6½ hrs and Labuanbajo 10 hrs leaves from the port 4 km E of town daily at 0800. *Ben hurs* whisk passengers from Sape town to the port for 150Rp (inflated on morning of ferry departure). The ferry also takes motor-cycles, cars (77,400Rp), goats (2,000Rp) and buffalo (4,000Rp); buying tickets the night be-fore means you miss the scrum on the morning of departure. The boat ride between Sape and Komodo is uneventful; but between Komodo and Labuanbajo the ferry weaves between bar-ren, mangrove wreathed islands. At certain times of year, the currents which converge here cause impressive up-wellings and depressions in the sea.

East Nusa Tenggara and East Timor

East Nusa Tenggara	729	**Timor**	771
Komodo	730	West Timor	773
Flores	733	Roti	778
Labuanbajo to Ende	737	Savu	779
Ende to Larantuka	745	Dili	788
Lembata	752	East from Dili to Los Palos	792
Alor	753	South from Dili to Maubessi	793
Sumba	755		

UNTIL RECENTLY, East Nusa Tenggara was, in Indonesian terms, at the very edge of the world. Overland communications were slow, and occasionally impossible, and few visitors had the time, or the inclination, to brave the system. As recently as 1974, two Indonesian economists, Makaliwe and Partadireja found they were able to write that East Nusa Tenggara was "...a society rather remote from the nation's centre, where small farmers work their plots according to their traditions... Most of the adult population will seldom or never hear a radio, see a film, send or receive letters, or read daily newspapers...". This has all changed. Improvements in the road system and the spread of commercial life has brought most of the population of these islands in touch with the centre.

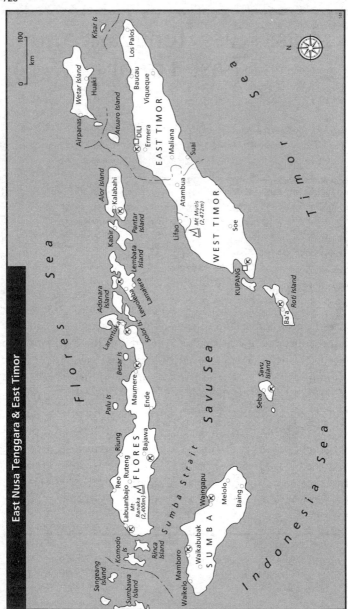

East Nusa Tenggara & East Timor

Horizons

East Nusa Tenggara and East Timor are considerably drier than the islands to the W, and the further E, the more arid it becomes. Compared with other areas of Indonesia, it is dry and barren, more like Australia than the jungle-clad tropics. Rainfall averages only 800-900 mm in E Flores, Alor and E Sumba, and the dry season stretches over 7 months, from Apr to Oct. The lack of rain is compounded by the geography of the islands. They are long and thin, and rivers tend to be short and fast-flowing. This makes it difficult to utilize the water for agriculture. East Nusa Tenggara is not one of Indonesia's industrial powerhouses. The province's main exports are coffee, fish and sandalwood.

Christianity has made greater inroads into the provinces of Nusa Tenggara and East Timor than anywhere else in Indonesia. Islam had scarcely penetrated these remote islands before the Portuguese arrived in the 16th century, and the population were therefore more amenable to conversion. Today, 90% of the population is Christian, and Christianity is one of the few forces which binds together a geographically dispersed population, made up of no less than 37 ethnic groups with different histories and cultural traditions.

Health warning
Malaria is a serious problem in parts of Nusa Tenggara with the recent emergence of the potentially fatal *P falciparum* as the dominant strain. *P falciparum* can be fatal.

Areas affected include Komodo, along the N coast of Flores, including Riung, Maumere, Labuhanbajo, the island of Roti and Timor. Larium (Melfoquine), the most effective anti-malarial drug believed to be 95% effective, causes side effects in 22% of people who take it. Of these a very small minority (the manufacturers claim 1 person in 10,000) suffer serious problems including fits, manic depression and panic attacks. Last year 11 British travellers died from malaria contracted in Africa and Asia.

Transport in East Nusa Tenggara
Travelling through the islands of East Nusa Tenggara and East Timor, particularly Flores (see page 735 for more information), used to be difficult enough to deter all but the most adventurous visitor. Now the islands are readily accessible, and surfaced all-weather roads link the main towns of the province. This has meant that in the peak tourist months from Jul to Sep, accommodation may become very stretched. There is essentially only one road through Flores, so visitors travel along a very tightly defined route; choke points include Labuanbajo (the port for the ferry to Komodo and Sumbawa) and Bajawa, both on Flores.

Language
Bahasa Indonesia is useful in Nusa Tenggara and East Timor, but not essential if travellers stick to the main route through the islands.

Komodo

THE NATIONAL PARK

The principal reason people come to Komodo is to see the illustrious Komodo dragon (see page 731). But there is more to Komodo than giant lizards – there is also good trekking, swimming and snorkelling. The island is a national park and visitors must register and pay an entrance fee of 1,000Rp on arrival at the village of Loh Liang. The park covers 170,000 ha, and is made up not just of Komodo Island, but also Rinca and a number of other surrounding islets. The highest peak on this barren and rugged spot is Mt Satalibo (735m).

After the luxuriant vegetation of Bali, Komodo can come as a bit of a shock. The islands of the Komodo archipelago are dry and rainfall is highly seasonal. For much of the year, therefore, the grasslands are burnt dry, interspersed with drought resistant savanna trees such as the distinctive lontar palm (*Borassus flabellifera*) (see page 779). In contrast the seas are highly productive and the irridescent blue of the water, set against the dull brown of the islands, provides a striking backdrop.

Despite the other attractions of Komodo, it is the dragons which steal the show. They are easily seen, with Timor deer (their chief natural prey) wandering amongst them.

NB Visitors are only allowed to walk

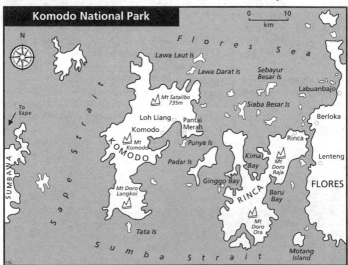

alone along marked trails. Those wishing to hike off the trails and see the dragons in a more natural setting, must hire a guide. This is not just to generate income for the wardens: there have been fatalities (see box).

Excursions

Rinca Island can be reached from Komodo. There are dragons here too, as well as wild horses and good snorkelling. PHPA accommodation available. *Getting there*: by chartered boat from Loh Liang, about 60,000-100,000Rp for the day.

Park information
● **Accommodation**
The only accommodation is in the **E** *PHPA bungalows* at Loh Liang which have a capacity of about 40, rooms are often dirty and poorly maintained, and there is a rat problem, during peak months (Jul-Sep), rooms are often unavailable and visitors must resort to sleeping in the dining-room.

● **Camping**
There is a camp ground at Loh Liang.

● **Sports**
Boats: Speedboats are also available.

Diving: there is said to be some equipment for hire.

Snorkelling: good snorkelling.

● **Transport**
Air Merpati flies to both Labuanbajo (see page 739) and to Bima (page 726); the former is closer to Komodo. From either town it is then necessary to catch the ferry (see below). The rich and famous arrive direct by helicopter.

Indonesia's living dinosaur: the Komodo dragon

The Komodo dragon (*Varanus komodoensis*), a massive monitor lizard, is the largest lizard in the world and can grow to 3m and weigh over 150 kg. They are locally called *ora* and were not discovered by the West until 1911. In total there are estimated to be about 3,000-4,000 of them. About 2,000 live on Komodo Island, with significant numbers also on Rinca (750) and on Flores. Of all the large carnivore species, the *ora* has the most restricted range – and the fossil evidence so far does not indicate that they lived anywhere beyond this small area of Nusa Tenggara Timur. They are strictly protected and cannot be exported live to zoos or, for that matter, dead to museums.

Like other animals, the size of the Komodo dragon has been grossly exaggerated. Major PA Ouwens, the curator of the Botanical Gardens at Buitenzorg (Bogor), Java, who first scientifically described the animal and collected the type specimen in 1912, was informed by the Governor of Flores that specimens of over 7m existed; these were almost certainly over-estimates or mis-identified estuarine crocodiles. Even the celebrated British television zoologist David Attenborough, during his 1957 visit to the island succumbed to exaggeration, claiming to have seen a dragon "a full twelve feet" in length. The largest accurately measured dragon was one exhibited at the St Louis Zoological Gardens in 1937 reported as measuring 10 ft 2 ins and weighing 365lbs. The extreme size of the Komodo dragon is thought to be due to it having evolved on these isolated islands, insulated from competition by other carnivores. The same is true of other reptiles – for example, the Galapagos iguana.

Young lizards, less than 4 years old, are remarkably fast moving, and are said to be able to outrun a dog over short distances. The reptiles live on carrion of goat, deer and even eat carcasses of their own kind. Although primarily carrion eaters, they will also prey on deer and pigs and have even been known to kill water buffalo. They are also voracious feeders, consuming 80% of their body weight in a single day. They have been known to kill and eat people: a Swiss baron – admittedly a frail 80-year old – was killed in 1979 and there has been another reported fatality since. Flesh is torn from the carcass with teeth and claws and swallowed whole.

Sea Boat: there are now two ferries plying between Flores and Sumbawa via Komodo, leaving both Sape and Labuanbajo daily at 0800. The journey from Sape takes 6½ hrs; from Labuanbajo, 3½ hrs. The ferry cannot dock at Komodo; small boats come alongside to take passengers to the PHPA office to register. It is possible to charter a boat for a 2 day trip to Komodo from Sape (about 400,000Rp). But some of the boats are said to be unreliable and currents in the Sape Strait are strong. Locals recommend going through one of the tour companies in Bima for safety's sake (see page 725) or from Labuanbajo (see page 738). It is cheaper to hire a boat from the nearer port of Labuanbajo, a 1 day trip should cost 75,000Rp. Before chartering a boat, visit the Komodo Park offices in Sape or Labuanbajo for advice.

Flores

FLORES stretches over 350 km from east to west, but at most only 70 km from north to south. It is one of the most beautiful islands in the Lesser Sundas. Mountainous, with steep-sided valleys cut through by fast-flowing rivers, dense forests and open savanna landscapes, Flores embraces a wide range of ecological zones. One of the local names for the island is *Nusa Nipa* or 'Serpent Island', because of its shape.

Horizons

On 12 December 1992 at 1330 an **earthquake** measuring 7.2 on the Richter scale struck eastern Flores. Over 1,500 people were killed by the quake and associated *tsunami* (tidal wave), many in the districts of Sikka, Ende and E Flores and their respective capitals of Maumere, Ende and Larantuka. Islands off the N coast where the wave struck were devastated – particularly Pulau Babi where 700 out of a total population of 1,000, died. One fisherman was quoted as saying: "The second [tidal] wave was as high as a coconut tree. The waves were hot, like lava." Low-lying islands were literally swamped as the *tsunami* washed over them, destroying everything in their paths. In Maumere it is thought that over 40% of the town was destroyed by the quake and similar levels of devastation have been reported for Ende. However, reconstruction has been rapid and most hotels in the two district capitals survived relatively unscathed.

THE LAND

GEOGRAPHY

Unlike neighbouring Sumbawa, the deep volcanic soils here are fertile; the problem is that in most areas the unreliable and highly seasonal rainfall makes agriculture difficult. Strangely, the area of the island with the highest density of population is also among the driest: the district of Sikka (Maumere). Here population densities can exceed 600 people/sq km, and even the 1930 census recorded a population of over 100,000. Because of the population pressure, farmers have cleared forested slopes right up to the watersheds, causing severe problems of erosion and land degradation. Conservation measures such as terracing were introduced by the Dutch, but in general these have proved ineffective. It has only been when farmers have owned their land that they have seen the economic sense of investing time and money protecting the land and soil.

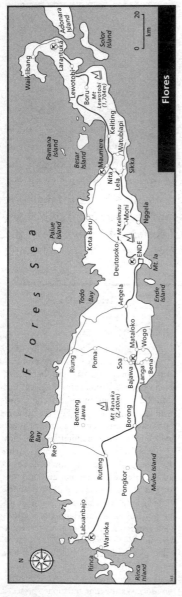

HISTORY

Flores' history is sketchy. It appears that Chinese mariners first made contact with the island – perhaps as early as the 12th century – to trade in sandalwood. As Flores lay on the trading route to Timor (sandalwood) and the Moluccas (spices), Portuguese chroniclers also noted the existence of the island in the 16th century. Dominican missionaries built a stone fort and church on Solor, just off Flores' E coast, in 1561, and later one at Larantuka. So enthusiastic were the Dominican friars in their proselytizing that by 1599 there were thought to be 100,000 Roman Catholics in E Flores, laying the foundations for Flores' Roman Catholic complexion. The sandalwood traders from Melaka and Macao who based themselves here also began inter-marrying with local women, creating a group of *mestizos* (half castes).

By the time the Portuguese were in decline as a power in the archipelago at the beginning of the 17th century, they had established settlements at Solor, Ende and Sikka. The Dutch, seeing little of value on Flores, concentrated their attentions elsewhere. As a result, although they established a mission at Ende in 1670, Portuguese religious influence over Flores continued to remain strong (see box, page 751). It was not until 1859 that Portugal officially ceded all its claims to Flores to the Dutch. And this was only agreed on the understanding that Flores would remain Roman Catholic.

CULTURE

PEOPLE

In total, the island covers an area of 14,300 sq km, and supports a population of 1.5 million. The majority of the population is Roman Catholic, but pre-Christian animist beliefs still exert a considerable influence even among those who are nominally Christian. There are five major ethnic groups on the island: the Manggarai,

Ngada, Sikka, Ende and Larantuka. In general, while the inhabitants in E and central Flores are Papuan-Melanesian, those in the W are Malay. The mountainous terrain and the difficulties of communication have effectively isolated these various groups from one another until fairly recently.

ISLAND INFORMATION

CONDUCT

Flores is a conservative island – short skirts and vests are not appropriate; dressing in such a manner is considered impolite.

ACCOMMODATION

There is a shortage of accommodation and people travelling alone may find it hard to find single rooms; they may be encouraged to share, particularly in Moni, Riung and Bajawa. Late arrivals may be offered floor space. Blankets are also at a premium (essential if you have no sleeping bag). **NB** An earthquake in Dec 1992 caused serious damage in Maumere and Ende, and in surrounding towns and villages. Reconstruction is complete and there is no shortage of rooms – bar the usual pre-earthquake high season bottlenecks (see page 733).

The textiles of Flores

Because Flores' geography has made contact between the island's peoples difficult, a number of distinct textile traditions have evolved. Three broad types stand out: the textiles of Manggarai to the W, those of Ngada in the centre, and the cloths of Ende, Sikka, Lio and Larantuka to the E.

Manggarai textiles show stylistic links with both Bima (Sumbawa) and south Sulawesi. Predominant colours are red, blue and green, and designs may be either bold and simple, or complex and minutely worked. Geometric motifs are the norm, and it is unusual for these to be interlinked. The best cloths have a tapestry weave border design along the edge. Unlike other areas of Flores, the designs of Manggarai are produced by weaving, not by dyeing the warp (*ikat*).

Ngada textiles from central Flores can be found on sale at the market in Bajawa. Women's sarongs and men's shawls are made from rough home-grown and home-spun cotton, dyed red and blue, with an elementary ikat design. The more expensive and harder to find weft ikat *kain kudu* have horse motifs and are traditionally part of a woman's dowry.

The textiles of the E are the richest and show a range of influences, from Sumba, Solor, and even Europe and India. They are made using the warp ikat technique (see page 408) and feature geometric, animal and floral motifs. If weavers are Muslim, the animal designs have been reduced to geometric shapes. Cloths from **Lio** villages (eg Nggela and Jopu, see pages 745 and 745) are finely patterned, with yellowish-brown designs on a dark red or blue ground. The motifs, often floral, are contained within parallel bands. It is also possible today to find cloth decorated with aeroplanes, cars, ships, and even teapots. The warp ikat from **Sikka** (see page 748) is probably the most immediately attractive of Flores' textiles to the Westerner. Cloth is made from thick, handspun cotton, and the ikat designs are bolder. Sikka ikat is a grey weave on a dark blue, almost black, background, although reddish hues are also common. Motifs are usually natural – flowers, chickens, crabs.

Across the island, it is increasingly difficult to find quality cloth made using natural dyes and handspun cotton. It is more usual to see cloth coloured using synthetic dyes and made from commercially-spun cotton.

To build in pairs: the Ngadhu and Bhaga of Flores

Much of the art of the Lesser Sundas is based upon maintaining balance between opposites: between male and female, old and young, living and dead, white and black. This concern for harmony is reflected in the cult altars of Bajawa where *ngadhu* represent the male ancestors of the clan, and *bhaga* the female ancestors.

Ngadhu are known in some areas of Flores as *ndaru* and elsewhere as *peo*. The *bhaga* is also known as *sao heda*. *Ngadhu* consist of a carved wooden post surmounted by a conical thatched roof, usually about 2-3m in height. The *bhaga* is built to resemble a miniature house with dimensions of around 3-4m, again with a thatched roof and usually standing on a raised platform. The *bhaga* is often used as the cooking site during important rituals and the two are constructed as a pair, usually positioned close together outside the house of the prominent clan that commissioned their erection. Clans undertake this task as an indicator of their position in society, and also usually after a sign has been received from the ancestors of that clan.

There seems to be some disagreement among specialists as to the timing of construction. Some authorities maintain that the female *bhaga* must always be built before its male counterpart. The explanation for this is said to relate to the pattern of courtship: men court women, not the other way around, so that the female must be in place ready for the male to make his advance. Other specialists argue quite the reverse, and state that only when the *ngadhu* post has been planted in the ground can the construction of the *bhaga* begin. It is possible that both groups are correct, and that there are regional differences across this part of Flores.

The male post is carved from the wood of a particularly hard tree (the *sebu* or *hebu* tree) which is dug out of the ground, roots and all. Should any sprouts later appear from roots left in the ground, then danger beckons for the clan. Various rites are observed before a tree is selected. For example, a spear plunged into the ground must remain upright as it would be demeaning for a man to fall over in public. Having selected a tree, it must be dug in the afternoon between 1500 and 1600. The tree is then carried back to the village by four men, to great celebration. These festivities exclude women of child-bearing age and young girls, as it is believed that they might be in danger of being raped by the tree. The tree is placed close to its female companion and buffaloes and pigs are slaughtered. The post is then carved over a three day period – from the top down (face, body and then legs). During the construction of the *ngadhu* those men involved must have no contact with women and observe various sexual and bathing prohibitions. At the end of the carving period, the post is 'planted' in the ground and yet further fesitivities and sacrifices ensue. The end of the work is marked by the naming of *bhaga* and the *ngadhu*. The names chosen are usually those of the ancestors of the clan that commissioned the construction.

Conversion to Christianity, inevitably, is changing these traditions and many clans no longer bother with *bhaga* and *ngadhu*, although weathered examples can be found in many villages. Presumably, in a few decades, they will have become objects of veneration in the museums of Indonesia, their cultural function and role lost.

Transport in Flores

Travelling by road in Flores was, until fairly recently, a nightmare. However the Trans-Flores Highway is now almost complete and though hardly comfortable, travel is quite bearable. The road twists and turns, and rises and falls, through at times breathtaking scenery. It is these contortions that the road must endure to cross Flores' rugged landscape which makes travel slow – expect to average 25-30 km/hr, less in the wet season. The Highway is made up almost all the way from Labuanbajo in the E to Larantuka in the W with the exception of one section over the mountains between Ruteng and Bajawa, which is in the process of being rebuilt. But despite the improvements in communications, overland travel is still exhausting and it is best to stay overnight in at least three towns on the journey across the island. Buses travel along the main routes, while open trucks with seats (known as *bis kayu*) ply the secondary roads. In most towns, buses will pick-up and drop-off passengers from their losmen/hotels. It is best to book your seat the day before travel with a bus agency or through your losmen (who may take a commission). This ensures you get a seat and avoid the very uncomfortable back seat. Be prepared for a 2-hr drive around town, whilst the driver picks up passengers.

A note about flights There seems to be some problem with booking Merpati flights out of Ende, either back to Denpasar or on to Kupang. To get around this difficulty, it is advisable to fly out of Maumere, where the office seems to be more switched on and are contactable by telephone.

LABUANBAJO TO ENDE

Labuanbajo at the western tip of Flores is the ferry port for Komodo Island and Sape (Sumbawa). From here the Trans-Flores Highway works its way eastwards through a fragmented and mountainous landscape to the hill town of Ruteng, 125 km away. Nearly 40 km N of Ruteng is the small port of Reo. Continuing on the Trans-Flores Highway from Ruteng, the road runs E and then turns S towards the coast, before climbing again to another hill town – Bajawa – a distance of 130 km. The district of Bajawa is best known for the strange thatched cult 'houses' which can be found in the surrounding villages. With a good range of accommodation, Bajawa is one of the best places to stop-off on a journey through Flores. From Bajawa, the road deteriorates, although it is in the process of being improved. The route passes through a rock-strewn, almost African savanna-like landscape, before reaching the coast after about 100 km, which the road follows for the final 30 km to the port of Ende.

LABUANBAJO

Labuanbajo, or Bajo, is really just an over-grown fishing village. Like Sape on Sumbawa, the town is little more than a transit point for catching or disembarking from the ferry. But there the comparison ends. There is good accommodation here, some excellent restaurants, and reasonable beaches, with offshore snorkelling. The town is stretched out along one road which runs from the dock, along the seashore, and then S towards Ruteng. **Pramuka Hill**, behind the town, offers good views over the bay, especially at sunset.

Excursions Waicicu Beach lies 15 mins by boat N of town. It offers good snorkelling and diving (snorkel equipment is for hire from the *Bajo Beach Hotel*). **Accommodation E** *Waerama Beach Resort*, PO Box 3, T 86554, run down, with dirty washrooms and rats, approachable by road or boat, a kiosk in town organizes free transport, the *Waerama* lies between Labuanbajo and Waicicu; **E** *Waicicu*, relaxed atmosphere, all meals incl in price, difficult to get a single room – 2 or 3 to a room, popular place.

Komodo It is possible to charter a boat for the day to see the dragons; expect to pay about 75,000Rp (see Rinca, below for details).

Rinca Island is part of the Komodo National Park and even closer to Labuanbajo. It also has a small population of Komodo dragons. PHPA accommodation available. *Getting there*: boat charter, 60,000Rp for a day trip (1½ hrs each way). Ask at the PHPA booth in town about boat charter; the *Bajo Beach* and *Mutiara Beach Hotels* both have vessels for charter. **NB** Not all the boat charterers are reliable. Check before paying by insisting on seeing the vessel and by talking to other visitors.

Tours *Perama Tours* have boats for charter to Komodo and Rinca, 30,000Rp for 2 days. They provide snorkelling equipment but it is poor quality. They also run a 7-day boat tour from Labuanbajo to Bangsal (Lombok) stopping at Komodo and Moyo Island (Sumbawa) en route, 80,000Rp (it is much more expensive in the opposite direction, from Labuhan Lombok – 250,000Rp) all inclusive. The tour then returns from Bangsal to Labuanbajo along the same route. 8 people maximum. **NB** Check out boat before agreeing to tour; some boats are overloaded and pretty uncomfortable – we have received reports that *Perama* have been overloading their boats, picking up passengers along the way; *Mutiara Beach Hotel* organize a 4-night tour. *Waicicu Beach Hotel* organize a 2-day boat trip to Sape, via Rinca Island and Komodo (with snorkelling stops) and a visit to 'Flying Fox Island'. Average 8 people per boat, good service and food, 30,000Rp, or 40,000Rp if stopping at Sape.

● **Accommodation** Hotels and losmen stretch out along the main street running S (to the right as the ferry docks from Sape). **B-D** *Gala Hill Resort* (toward *Waerama Beach Hotel*), 1 km from town, some rooms with hot water and a/c, good restaurant, big rooms with ensuite bathrooms, superb position overlooking the sea, friendly, helpful staff, good place to rest up; **C** *Pede Beach*, 2 km S of town; **E** *Bajo Beach*, T 41009, central, clean, well run, car, boat and snorkelling equipment (2,500Rp/day) for hire, price incl breakfast, rec; **E** *Gardena*, on the main street perched on a hill with good views over towards Komodo, bungalows with attached showers but basic toilets, food is good but portions small, tours arranged to Komodo and Rinca, and through Flores, good source of information; **E** *Sony and Chez Felix*, friendly homestays on hill overlooking bay, 15-20 mins walk from the dock – walk through the town, past the bank and turn left, another 150m; **E** *Wisata*, past bridge on road to Ruteng, T 41020, excellent restaurant, one of the few hotels with its own generator, which means a fan all night, and the only normally functioning restaurant, rooms are clean with showers attached, pretty garden, well run and maintained, good value, highly rec; **E-F** *Mutiara Beach*, Jl Pelabuan 31 (opp *Bajo Beach*), T 41039, restaurant, basic rooms, attached mandi; **F** *Chez Felix*, S end of town, up a hill, some with attached bathrooms, good clean, light rooms, family run establishment, speaking English; **F** *Sony Homestay*, opp *Chez Felix* S of town on a hill with good views, rooms have attached bathrooms.

● **Places to eat** ♦*Bajo Beach Hotel*, good food, friendly; ♦*New Tenck Nikmat* (on the main road, between Post Office and *Bajo Beach Hotel*), attractive, with friendly ambience, good fish, rec; *Banyuwangi*, past the bank, Indonesian.

● **Airline offices** Merpati, E of town, towards airport.

● **Banks & money changers** BNI, main road (150m towards Ruteng from *Bajo Beach Hotel*), will change US$ cash and TCs.

● **Post & telecommunications Post Office**: main road, next to *Sanjei Losmen*. **Telkom office**: S of town, nr the PHPA office.

● **Tour companies & travel agents** *Varanus*, *Waerana Beach Resort*.

● **Tourist information** Available from the PHPA information booth, on the main street opp

Gardena Hotel. They can provide information on Komodo and Rinca islands.

● **Transport** 125 km from Ruteng, 255 km from Bajawa, 380 km from Ende, 528 km from Maumere. **Local** The *Bajo Beach* and *Mutiara Beach Hotels* both have vehicles for hire to explore the surrounding countryside. **Air** The airport is 2 km from town. Daily connections on Merpati with Denpasar, Kupang and other destinations in Nusa Tenggara. **NB** Flights are often booked well ahead during the peak season (Jul-Sep). **Road Bus**: there is no bus station; buses cruise the hotels and losmen picking up passengers. Connections with Ruteng, 4 hrs and Bajawa, 13 hrs. *Sinar 99* run a packed, but relatively efficient service; *Komodo* run buses to Ruteng. As yet, no through buses to Ende. **Sea Boat**: daily ferries leave at 0800 for Sape (Sumbawa) 10 hrs via Komodo 3$\frac{1}{2}$ hrs. Buses meet the ferry from Sape/Komodo and take passengers straight on to Ruteng. Boats travel frequently between Labuanbajo and the Gilis (Lombok) (see page 704). The Pelni vessel *Binaiya* docks at Labuanbajo on its fortnightly circuit through the islands of Nusa Tenggara (see route schedule page 921). **Warning** These boats are not always reliable or seaworthy. Security is a problem.

RUTENG

Ruteng is a market town at the head of a fertile valley. It is a peaceful, pleasant spot to stop en route through Flores. This upland area – the town is 1,100m above sea level – is a centre of coffee cultivation and it gets chilly at night. Despite being predominantly Catholic, the practice of **whip fighting** or *caci* is still practiced, particularly during wedding festivities. Opponents flail each other, the scars being regarded as honourable and, apparently, beautiful by local women. Most weddings are held during the peak tourist months from Jun to Sep; ask at hotels and losmen for information on weddings. **NB** Try to be invited; turning-up unannounced and uninvited is bad manners and not recommended.

Excursions Pongkor, 45 km SW of Ruteng and **Lambaleda**, 50 km to the NW are two traditional villages worth visiting. Lambaleda is a weaving centre. *Getting*

there: trucks (*bis kayu*) run from Ruteng to Pongkor (2 hrs) and to Lambaleda via Benteng Jawa. Alternatively, explore the route N to **Reo** – regular trucks make the journey, through spectacular scenery (see below).

● **Accommodation C-E** *Dahlia*, just off Jl Motang Rua (main road), T 21377, restaurant, most sophisticated losmen in town, clean and efficiently-run, rec; **D-E** *Agung II*, Jl Motang Rua, T 21835, in centre of town; **E** *Agung I*, T 21180, N of town on road to Reo, quiet and popular, big rooms, rec; **E** *Manggarai*, Jl Adisucipto, T 21008, the more expensive rooms are large, clean and with own mandi; **D-E** *Sindha*, Jl Yos Sudarso, close to *Manggarai*, T 21197, good restaurant, some recently added rooms provide bathrooms, TV and a balcony; **F** *Homestay Florensa*, Jl Ahmad Yani 23, T 21793, about 2 km out of town, clean rooms and good value, breakfast incl.

● **Places to eat** Ruteng is not renowned for the quality of its food. There are several warung in the bus station and market area, and losmen also serve meals. Dog, known as 'RW', is available in some places. **Chinese**: good restaurant about 20m up the road from the *Hotel Dahlia*.

● **Post & telecommunications Post Office**: Jl Baruk (S side of town).

● **Transport** 125 km from Labuanbajo, 130 km from Bajawa, 255 km from Ende. **Air** The airport is on the outskirts of town; bemos meet flights. Daily connections on Merpati with Denpasar, Kupang and other destinations in Nusa Tenggara. **Road Bus**: the station is on the W side of town, a short walk downhill from the centre. Regular connections with Labuanbajo 4 hrs, Bajawa 6 hrs, Ende 12 hrs and N to Reo 2 hrs. Also buses to other local destinations. *Komodo Bus* and *Nusa Indah* (for Labuanbajo) both have their offices on Jl Amenhung; *Agogo* (for buses to Ende) is at Jl Yos Sudarso 4.

REO

A small town on the N coast, is off the Trans-Flores Highway and therefore rarely visited by tourists.

● **Accommodation E** *Losmen Nisang Nai*, Jl Pelabuhan, outskirts of town, towards Kedindi; **F** *Telukbayar*, Jl Mesjit 8, bit grim.

● **Transport** 38 km from Ruteng. **Road Bus**:

regular connections with Ruteng; the road is reasonable. **Sea Boat**: there are said to be infrequent boats from Reo to Labuanbajo and also to Riung. It might be possible to hitch a lift to other ports in Flores, and mixed cargo boats bound for Surabaya also sometimes stop here.

BAJAWA

This hill town is the capital of the Ngada District at 1,100m above sea level and has a pleasant climate, with fresh days and chilly nights. It is a predominantly Christian area but is best known for its thatched cult altars known as *ngadhu* and *bhaga* (see Excursions and box). Bajawa town makes a pleasant and logical stop on the Trans-Flores route. The **Inpres market** sells traditional textiles – blankets from Bajawa and ikat from Ende and Kelimutu.

Excursions The surrounding villages are interesting to visit to see their cult houses. **Langa**, 7 km S of town, has a fine collection of *ngadhu* and *bhaga* (see box). *Getting there*: the village lies 2½ km off the main Trans-Flores road towards Ende; bemos are sometimes available for the short trip from the turnoff. It is also possible to walk from Bajawa to Langa (about 5 km).

Bena is a village 19 km S of town, past the turn off to Langa and en route to Monas. It is the ceremonial centre of the area. Entry to village: 500Rp plus 500Rp for camera. *Getting there*: buses leave from the market in Bajawa, 1½ hrs (1,000Rp).

Wogo lies about 20 km E of Bajawa and has a collection of rather neglected megaliths just beyond the village. **Accommodation** There is a Christian mission at nearby Mataloko which will provide accommodation for visitors. *Getting there*: take a bus from the market in Bajawa to Mataloko which is on the main road to Ende (¾ hr) and then walk the final 100m or so to Wogo.

Tours 'Lucas' from the *Hotel Sunflower* arranges tours to the village of **Bena** (1,000Rp for transport, entrance fee and a good meal in the evening, cooked by his wife), good value.

● **Accommodation NB** During peak months between Jul and Sep, losmen may be full, although space will be found somehow and somewhere. All prices below incl a simple breakfast. **D** *Kembang*, Jl Martadinata 18, T 21072, featureless building, but good large rooms and mandis, rec; **E** *Dagalos*, Jl A Yani 70, with mandi, excellent food but dingy rooms, friendly family; **E** *Dam*, Jl Gereja, T 21145, on quiet street nr church, mostly frequented by Indonesians; **E** *Kambera*, Jl Eltari 9, T 21166, restaurant on 1st floor, small rooms, popular, friendly and helpful, if a little (and charmingly) disorganized, rec; **E** *Korina*, Jl A Yani, T 21162, friendly management; **E** *Losmen Anggrek*, Jl Let Jend Haryono 9, T 21172, good restaurant, clean, with attached mandi, good value; **E** *Losmen Johny*, Jl Gajah Mada, T 21079, rather grubby, attached mandi; **E** *Melati Virgo*, Jl May Jend D1 Panjaitan, T 21061, good value, rec; **E-F** *Nusatera*, Jl Eltari, T 21357, more expensive rooms are big and bright with own mandi, eager manager; **F** *Kencana*, Jl Palapa 7, T 21155, on quiet track not far from the market and bus station, attached mandi; **F** *Sunflower*, off Jl Basuki Rahmat A Yani, T 21230, clean, nice views of the valley from balcony.

● **Places to eat** *Losmen Kambera* has a popular, though disorganized, restaurant serving good food. Also try the *Kasih Bahagia* and the *Wisata*, both nr the entrance to the market.

● **Airline offices** Merpati, Jl Budi Utomo/Pasar Rahmat (by market).

● **Banks & money changers** BNI, Jl Boulevard (aka Jl Soekarno-Hatta), will change TCs and cash in most major currencies.

● **Post & telecommunications General Post Office**: Jl Boulevard (aka Jl Soekarno-Hatta). **Perumtel** (telephone & telegraph): Jl Boulevard/Soekarno-Hatta (nr **Bank Rakyat Indonesia**).

● **Shopping Textiles**: Bajawa blankets and ikat from Ende and Kelimutu are available from the Inpres market (see box, page 735).

● **Tourist information** The *Carmellya Restaurant* has plenty of information for travellers and several good maps of the area.

● **Transport** 130 km from Ruteng, 255 km from Labuanbajo, 125 km from Ende. **Air** The airport lies 30 km N of town, nr Soa. Minibuses bring passengers into Bajawa. Connections on Merpati with Denpasar, Kupang and other destinations in Nusa Tenggara. **Road Bus**: the terminal is in the heart of town, nr the market. Regular connections with Ruteng 6 hrs; also to Labuanbajo 11 hrs, Ende 5 hrs and Riung. Buses cruise the losmen looking for passengers. *Sinar 99* operates buses to Labuanbajo via Ruteng and has its office at Jl Martadinata 8. No direct buses to Maumere (yet), but by catching a morning bus to Ende it is possible to get the 1700 connection from there to Maumere. **Truck**: (*bis kayu*) to Bena, Langa, Mataloko (see excursions) and other surrounding towns leave from the terminal next to the market.

RIUNG (NANGAMESE)

Riung, or more accurately Nangamese (Riung is the name of the sub-district, Nangamese is the largest town, although most people now also call the town Riung) is a small town on Flores' N coast, due N of Bajawa. The people of the area are largely Muslim fishermen and Catholic farmers who grow rice and corn.

The **Seventeen Island National Park** offers superb snorkelling as well as a small population of monitor lizards closely related to the famous Komodo dragons, but rather smaller (see page 731).

● **Accommodation D-E** *Dwi Putra Losmen*, good source of information, basic but friendly; **E** *Mandiri*, basic rooms, nr the market.

● **Shopping Textiles**: local textiles can be bought for about 80,000Rp for a reasonable quality piece. Fine examples will cost considerably more, while there are always 'tourist' pieces available for somewhat less.

● **Tourist information** At PHPA office, near *Tamri Beach Homestay*, good local information.

● **Transport** 120 km from Bajawa. **Road Bus**: buses leave from Bajawa and take an agonizing and slow 9 hrs, via Soa. **Sea Boat**: occasional boats from Reo and Maumere.

ENDE

Ende is the largest town on Flores with 66,000 inhabitants, and is the capital of the district of Ende. The town is sited in a spectacular position on the neck of a peninsula, surrounded by mountains. To the S is the distinctive Mt Meja (Table Mountain), and on the other side of town is Mount Ia, a dormant volcano that last erupted in 1969. The Portuguese had established a settlement here as early as the 17th century and it then became a popular posting with the Dutch. In Dec 1992 the town was devastated by an earthquake, with an estimated 40% of buildings destroyed (see page 733). However, it is still an attractive place to visit, with a friendly

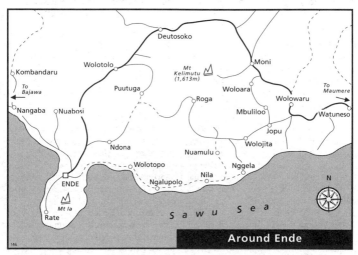

Around Ende

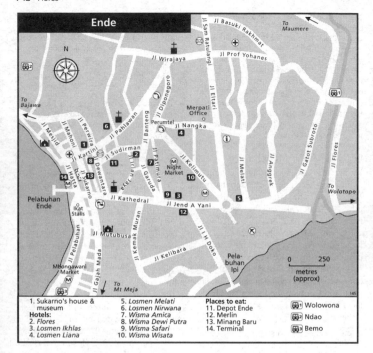

Ende

1. Sukarno's house & museum
Hotels:
2. *Flores*
3. *Losmen Ikhlas*
4. *Losmen Liana*
5. *Losmen Melati*
6. *Losmen Nirwana*
7. *Wisma Amica*
8. *Wisma Dewi Putra*
9. *Wisma Safari*
10. *Wisma Wisata*
Places to eat:
11. *Depot Ende*
12. *Merlin*
13. *Minang Baru*
14. *Terminal*
🚌1 Wolowona
🚌2 Ndao
🚌3 Bemo

atmosphere; the evenings see groups of local youths collecting on street corners to play guitars and sing.

Places of interest

Ende is best known in Indonesia as the spot to which Sukarno was exiled by the Dutch between 1934 and 1938. **Sukarno's house** and **museum**, is on Jl Perwira. It has a poor collection of photographs, and little else. The museum is only likely to be of interest to Sukarno acolytes and students of modern Indonesian history. Open mornings (but variable).

In town, the **Mbongawani market** on Jl Pelabuhan is colourful with traditional healers selling local cures, and a good range of textiles also on sale (see Shopping, below). There is a night market, **Pasar Potulando**, on Jl Kelimutu. For good views of the town and bay, climb **Mt Meja**, about a 1½ hrs walk, starting from

the market; walk S on Jl Gajah Mada and turn left towards Waniwona village.

Excursions

Mount Ia To climb to the crater of this dormant volcano takes about 2 hrs, and affords good views of the town and bay. *Getting there*: catch a bemo to Rate village from the central market and ask for directions.

Mount Kelimutu is too far to reach in a single day except by chartered vehicle; it is better to spend the night in Moni (see page 745). However, the *Wisata* and *Dewi Putra* hotels both have vehicles for charter (60,000Rp and 75,000Rp respectively) for a day trip to Kelimutu with a *very* early departure.

Nangalala Beach lies 13 km W of Ende. The beach has reasonable swimming and is popular at weekends with locals. *Getting there*: catch a bemo from the central market bound for Nanga-panda or Nangaroro and get off at the Km 13 marker.

Nuabosi, 9 km NW of Ende, offers wonderful views of the town; there is also a *rumah adat* (traditional clan house) here. *Getting there*: catch a bemo from the central market.

There is a **pleasant walk** along the coast from the Wolowona bus terminal on the edge of town (constant bemos travel there from the town centre) E to **Wolotopo**, about 6 km. Wolotopo has some *rumah adat* (traditional houses) and weaving. It is beautifully positioned.

Ngalupolo is a village a further 7 km E of Wolotopo (see above). It has some *rumah adat*, ikat weaving, ivory tusks and gold jewellery on show (donation required for display). *Getting there*: there *should* be a daily boat at 0700 (except Fri) from Pelabuhan Ipi in Ende to Ngalupolo, which then returns in the afternoon. It is possible to walk from town to the port, or catch a bemo heading E.

Nggela is a coastal weaving village E of Ende (see page 745). There are homestays here. *Getting there*: 4-5 hrs from Ende by *bis kayu* (truck) from the Wolowona terminal (1 departure/day). Boats leave from Pelabuhan Ipi (outside Ende) every morning roughly between 0600 and 0700. To get to Pelabuhan Ipi, enter the airport and walk across the runway. Continue through the village (an interesting visit in itself) to the beach and harbour. It is not possible to return the same day by boat, as the boat only waits 15 mins and it is an hours walk from the coast to Nggela. To return the same day, take a bus via Moni.

Tours

There are as yet no good tour agents in Ende, but the *Dewi Putra* and *Wisata* hotels have cars for charter to Kelimutu, and surrounding villages. The Dewi Putra tour visits local villages, beaches and the surrounding countryside – bargain hard.

Local information
● **Accommodation**

All losmen and hotels incl a simple breakfast in the room rate; most are out of the centre of town.

C-D *Dewi Putra*, Jl Dewantara, T 21465, some a/c, restaurant, noisy downstairs, quieter upstairs, clean, and unlike all other losmen it is central, rec, the manager's brother organizes tours (see above); **C-D** *Flores*, Jl Sudirman 28, T 21075, some a/c, restaurant, new and sparklingly clean; **C-E** *Nirwana*, Jl Pahlawan 29, T 21199, some a/c, on hill above town but still quite central, earthquake of '92 forced management to renovate this establishment, it was in need of it; **C-E** *Wisata*, Jl Kelimutu 68, T 21368, some a/c, clean, attached mandi, range of rooms – the most expensive are extensive.

E *Amica*, Jl Garuda 15, T 21683, quiet street, rather dark, attached mandi; **E** *Ikhlas*, Jl Jend A Yani, T 21695, good restaurant, small clean rooms with verandahs, some rather dark, some with attached mandi, but popular with travellers and well-run, good source of information, good value, rec; **E** *Losmen Liana*, Jl Kelimutu 15, T 21078, totally destroyed in the 1992 earthquake, this is a newly built losmen of 4 rm, price incl breakfast, communal mandi and wc, a fan can be borrowed on request, Johnny Jongeneelen, who runs it, is a cheerful, helpful person who can organize air, boat and bus tickets; **E** *Safari*, Jl Jend A Yani, T 21499, villa with large clean rooms and attractive garden and restaurant area, rec.

F *Melati*, Jl Gatot Subroto, T 21311, reasonably clean with attached mandi, and a raised area for sipping tea and coffee.

● **Places to eat**

♦♦*Terminal Restaurant*, Jl Hatta 70 (by the old terminal kota), good fish and lobsters plus Indonesian favourites; ♦*Adi Putra*, Jl Kemakmuran 30, good Indonesian food in attractive shuttered house, nr mosque; ♦*Depot Ende*, Jl Sudirman 6, good cheap Indonesian and Chinese; ♦*Merlin*, Jl Jend A Yani 6, Indonesian, good, simple food; ♦*Saiyo*, Jl Benteng 7, very good Padang food; ♦*Minang Baru*, Jl Sukarno (nr Cathedral), excellent Padang food, also sells textiles. The *papaya* in the market is delicious.

Bakeries & coffee shops: Jl Kemakmuran (nr *Flores Theatre*).

● **Airline offices**

Merpati, Jl Nangka, T 21355.

● **Banks & money changers**

BNI, Jl Jend Sudirman (up hill from *Depot Ende Restaurant*), will change cash and TCs in major currencies; **Bank Rakyat Indonesia**, in *Hotel Dewi Putra*, Jl Dewantara, open am only.

● **Entertainment**

Cinemas: *Flores Theatre*, Jl Kemakmuran 1 – occasionally shows western movies.

● **Hospitals & medical services**

Hospitals: Jl Mesjid.

● **Post & telecommunucations**

General Post Office: Jl Sam Ratulangi (inconvenient, out of town).

Perumtel: Jl Kelimutu 5 (international telephone, telegraph & fax).

Post Office: Jl Dewantara 4.

● **Shopping**

Books: *Toko Nusa Indah*, Jl Kathedral 5 (just up the hill from the Cathedral).

Tailors: for making-up new clothes and mending, Jl Sukarno, nr Cathedral.

Textiles: Ende is a good place to buy local ikat from Ende, Kelimutu, Moni and elsewhere (see box, page 735). Salesmen and women visit the losmen, and congregate at the end of Jl Pelabuhan (nr Jl Hatta and the port). For a sarong, expect to pay 15,000-30,000Rp, depending on quality. There is also a good range on sale at the *Minang Baru Restaurant*, including Sumba blankets.

● **Tourist offices**

Tourist 'desk', **Kantor Bupati**, Jl Eltari (nr intersection with Jl Nangka), very helpful man running the desk; useful pamphlet and map on sights around Ende and practicalities.

● **Transport**

54 km from Moni, 147 km from Maumere, 284 km from Larantuka, 125 km from Bajawa, 255 km from Ruteng. **NB** The road to Maumere was badly damaged during the Dec 1992 earthquake; it is now open but in poor condition; expect delays during the rainy season.

Local Bemos: ply the main roads, routes are marked over the roof (200Rp). Most link the town bus terminals, Ndao and Wolowona. The bemo terminal is by the Pasar Mbongawani, nr the centre of town.

Air Ende's Ipi airport is on the SE edge of town; bemos to the centre cost about 1,500Rp, although it's only a 50m walk to the main road where there are frequent public bemos for 200Rp. It is a 5-10 mins walk from the airport to the closest of the losmen. Daily connections on Merpati with Denpasar, Kupang and other destinations in Nusa Tenggara.

Road Bus: Ende has two bus terminals. Ndao terminal is for Bajawa 5 hrs, Ruteng 10 hrs and other destinations to the W. It is situated on the NW side of town, off Jl Imam Bonjol and 1 km from the centre. Wolowona terminal is for buses to Wolowaru 2¼ hrs, Moni/Kelimutu 2¾ hrs, Maumere 6 hrs, Larantuka 10 hrs, and other destinations to the E and is at the end of Jl Gatot Subroto, 4 km from the town centre. Constant bemos link both terminals and the town centre. Buses from Bajawa and Maumere drop passengers off at losmen if requested. A minibus leaves the Ikhlas Losmen every night at 1700, going all the way to Labuanbajo. *Agogo* bus company runs a service to Ruteng and Maumere and has its offices at Jl Pelabuhan 28.

Sea Boat: the Pelni ship *Binaiya* docks at Ende twice on its 2-week circuit between Semarang and Dili and calling at ports in Nusa Tenggara (see route schedule, page 921). The Pelni office is at Jl Kathedral 2, T 21043. There is also a weekly ferry service to Waingapu (Sumba) on Wed pm continuing on to Savu (10-15,000Rp). **NB** At different times, depending upon the state of the tides, the *Binaiya* docks at either of Ende's two ports – Pelabuhan Ende at Jl Hatta 1 in the heart of town, or the new Pelabuhan Ipi to the S-E. Check at the Pelni office. There is also a weekly ferry on Wed to Kupang, and it is sometimes possible to hitch a lift on a freighter.

ENDE TO LARANTUKA

For the first 45 mins out of Ende the road rises spectacularly up through a limestone gorge, with worryingly precipitous drops. After 50 km the road reaches the town of Moni, the logical base for trips to the stunning crater lakes of Mt Kelimutu. From Moni the road descends to the coast and the town of Maumere, a distance of 93 km. The coral gardens near Maumere offer some of the best snorkelling and diving in Indonesia. Continuing E from Maumere, the last leg of the Trans-Flores Highway runs 137 km to the port of Larantuka. This was one of the centres of Portuguese missionary activity in Flores, and remains among the most obviously Christian towns on the island.

KELIMUTU AND MONI

Mount Kelimutu, with its 3-coloured crater lakes, is one of the highlights of Flores. The first foreigners to climb the volcano were the Dutchmen Le Roux and Van Suchtelen in 1915. The lakes are at 1,640m and their colours have changed over the years, as the chemicals and minerals in the waters have reacted. In the 1970s they were red, white and blue; now they are, rather less spectacularly, maroon (almost black), iridescent green, and yellow-green. Local villagers believe that the lakes are the resting places for souls called by Mutu (Kelimutu): young people are destined for one lake, old for another, while witches and evil people go to the third. On a clear morning, the view of the crater lakes and the surrounding mountains is simply unforgettable.

The nearby village of Moni (alt 600m) has become the main tourist base from which to visit Mt Kelimutu. *Getting to Mt Kelimutu*: reaching the summit used to require an early morning/late night trek of 8 km. This is not advisable, as the path is difficult to see in the dark, and it means leaving Moni around 0200; today there is a truck which takes people up to the summit at about 0400, in time for the sunrise, 1 hr (overpriced at 3,000Rp). Ask at your losmen to check on departure time and make it known that you wish to be picked-up. The truck will also take passengers down again, although the 8-km walk is easy enough and very worthwhile (the road to the summit is 12 km, but the well marked path – Jl Potong (Jl Shortcut) – only 8 km). The path takes you past hot springs and a waterfall – good for a dip. *Ojeks* (motorcycle taxis) will also take people to the top (5,000Rp). Having reached the viewing spot on the summit, everyone waits for the dawn and hopes that it will be clear. Entrance fee to volcano: 1,000Rp. **NB** It is cold, both at the summit and on the open truck; take a sweater (at least). Also note that it is often cloudy and it may be necessary to wait a few days for a clear morning.

Moni (at 600m above sea level) is a friendly village with beautiful walks in the surrounding area and excursions to local villages (see below). The **market** on Tues mornings on the playing field is worth seeing.

Excursions Wolowaru is situated on the main Ende-Maumere road, 11 km from Moni. This is a bigger town than Moni but has not developed into such a tourist base for climbing Mt Kelimutu. It is worth visiting on market days (Mon, Wed and Sat) when there is a reasonable range of ikat on sale (see page 735). **Accommodation** Includes: **D** *Losmen Kelimutu*, T 20, clean, some attached mandis. The *Jawa Timur* is a popular restaurant stop for buses travelling through the town; it has good food. *Getting there*: by *bis kayu* from Moni, or on a bus from Ende or Maumere.

Jopu is a weaving village 4 km from Wolowaru, producing weft ikat (see page 735). The various processes involved in producing ikat are on view to visitors (see page 408). *Getting there*: take a *bis kayu* to Wolowaru and then a bemo to Jopu.

Nggela 15 km from Wolowaru on the same road as Jopu, this weaving village has become over-touristed. However ikat is on sale and production processes are on view (see page 408). The locals employ rather pushy sales tactics. There are hot springs and a couple of homestays here. *Getting there*: take a *bis kayu* to Wolowaru, and a bemo to Nggela; there is also a daily boat (except Fri) to Ende from the beach, which is a steep 2-km descent from Nggela, 2½ hrs, only recommended for the hardy, as it is easy to fall out of the small canoe, which transports you from shore to boat. Alternatively, the walk is very beautiful, through paddy fields and along the beach (take a short cut from Wolojita and take plenty of water to drink).

● **Accommodation** Accommodation is quite poor in Moni and rooms are often in short supply. **D** *Bungalow Hotel* (10 mins walk from Moni village on road to Ende), clean and attractive, rec; **E** *Sao Ria Wisata*, does not come rec, rooms are dirty and the management unfriendly; **E-F** *Palm Homestay*, out of town just off the road to Wolowaru, single and double bungalows with and without attached mandi, good transport information, excellent buffet dinner, breakfast incl; **F** *Amina Moe*, two parts to this establishment, the older part is on your left on entering the village from Ende, the newer part is further down the road, also on the left, rooms in newer part are particularly good, comfortable communal sitting-room and attractive balcony with bamboo chairs, friendly establishment, excellent, very good value, evening meal available, price incl breakfast and tea/coffee, rec; **F** *Daniel*, cold water, shared mandi, friendly and popular; **F** *Friendly*, best of the low price range.

● **Places to eat** **♦♦***Kelimutu*, down road from *Sao Ria Wisata Hotel*; **♦***Ankermi*, good views and music, food unexceptional; Chinese restaurant on main road into Moni from Maumere, friendly owners, good food; **♦***Moni Indah*, next door to *Daniel Homestay*, good and cheap.

● **Transport** 11 km from Wolowaru, 54 km from Ende, 93 km from Maumere. **NB** It can be difficult to get out of Moni in the high season; you may have to hitch a lift on a truck travelling to Nggela on market day. **Road Bus**: regular connections with Ende 2¼ hrs, book tickets 24 hrs in advance, otherwise standing room only,

Wolowaru 2¾ hrs and Maumere, 3½ hrs. Getting out of Moni can sometimes be difficult as the buses passing through the town are often full; it may be necessary to catch a *bis kayu* to Wolowaru and wait for the bus there.

MAUMERE

Maumere, with a population of about 50,000, is a rather featureless, disorganized town: as if a small town suddenly had pretensions of being large and was not sure how to cope. Most people come here to dive and snorkel in some of the best sea gardens in Indonesia, and to explore the sights around the town.

It is possible to walk around Maumere in a morning. The central **market** is just that – central – with a good selection of ikat cloth on sale (see Shopping). The **port** (Pelabuhan Maumere), usually quiet, is 5 mins walk to the NW; on the way there the road passes **Maumere Cathedral**. In Dec 1992 an earthquake devastated Maumere, destroying almost half of the town. Within a year, the effects of the event were hard to discern (see page 733).

Excursions

Waiara and Sao Wisata Beaches lie 12-13 km E of Maumere. There is good swimming and the sea off the coast is a marine park and offers superb snorkelling and diving – or at least it did until the Dec 1992 earthquake. The coral has been badly damaged, especially off Sao Wisata Beach. The most seriously affected coral gardens are those in shallow waters. Experts are currently surveying the damage but preliminary indications are that some of the deeper dive sites still offer excellent diving. Two dive clubs are based here and run dive boats out to the reefs (see Accommodation and Sports). It is easiest to reach the reef by booking a place on one of these dive boats (US$25 – see Sports). *Getting to the beaches*: by bemo from the Terminal Timur (500Rp). It is also possible to reach the marine park by chartering a boat from Keliting (9 km E, take a bemo from Terminal Timur) for about 50,000Rp/day.

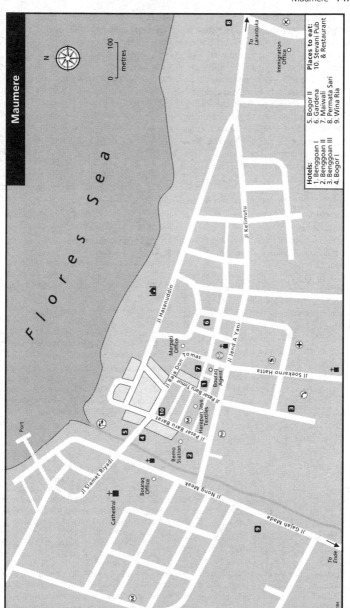

Maumere

Flores Sea

To Larantuka

Immigration Office

Hotels:
1. Benggoan I
2. Benggoan II
3. Benggoan III
4. Bogor I
5. Bogor II
6. Gardena
7. Maiwali
8. Permata Sari
9. Wina Ria

Places to eat:
10. Stevani Pub & Restaurant

Jl Kelimutu

Jl Hasanuddin

Merpati Office

Jl Raja Don Tomas

Bouraq Agent

Jl Jend A Yani

Jl Soekarno Hatta

Jl Pasar Baru Timur

Harapan Jaya Textiles

Jl Pasar Baru Barat

Bemo Station

Port

Jl Slamet Riyadi

Bouraq Office

Cathedral

Jl Nong Meak

Jl Gajah Mada

To Ende

There are regular boats crossing between the islands out on the reef and Keliting on market days (Wed and Fri). Homestays available on Permaan Island, and local guides (but little English) 10,000Rp/day.

Ladalero houses the only museum on Flores, the **Blikan Blewut Museum**. It is situated 9 km from town, on the road to Ende. A cluttered, mixed, yet interesting display of ethnographic exhibits, textiles and ceramics assembled by the local Seminary (Societas Verbi Divini). The Seminary suffered heavy damage during the earthquake, but the museum is still open to visitors. Admission by donation. Open 0730-1400 Mon-Sat, 1000-1400 Sun. *Getting there*: take a bus from Terminal Barat (250Rp).

Nita is about 2 km from Ladalero and 11 km from Maumere. The 'Rajah' here has a collection of old elephant tusks and other memorabilia. *Getting there*: take a bus from Terminal Barat (500Rp).

Sikka is a weaving village 25 km S of town. It is possible to buy ikat here at reasonable prices (check at *Harapan Jaya* for comparison – see Shopping) and see some of the multiple stages of the ikat process – something like 35 in all (see page 408). If on a tour, all the stages may be demonstrated. There is also an attractive **Portuguese church** at Sikka, white with green fretwork, built in 1800. *Getting there*: take a bus from Terminal Barat.

Watublapi is another, less frequently visited, weaving village, 11 km S from Geliting (which lies just E of Maumere, on the main trans-Flores road). Nearby is Bliran Sina Hill from where there are views N to the Flores Sea and S to the Sawu Sea. *Getting there*: take a bus from Terminal Timur.

Wodong lies 25 km E of Maumere. There are two places to stay here, good snorkelling, and it is the best base from which to climb **Mt Egon** (see page 750 for further details). *Getting there*: take a bus or bemo from the Lokaria terminal to Wodong.

Tours

Day tours from Maumere to Sikka weaving village, the Ladalero museum and Nita; or to Geliting Market and Watublapi weaving village. Some hotels and shops have cars and drivers for charter. *Hotel Maiwali*, minibus to Wairara Beach (8,000Rp), Sikka weaving village (25,000Rp), Ladalero (8,000Rp), Kelimutu (75,000Rp 1 day leaving at 0300; 125,000Rp 2 days with 1 night in Moni). *Harapan Jaya*, a textile shop on Jl Moa Toda has a car for hire (50,000Rp/day around town, 100,000Rp to Kelimutu). *Wina Ria Hotel* can arrange boats for snorkelling (60,000Rp). *Sea World* at Wairara Beach also organize tours to Sikka, Kelimutu and elsewhere (see accommodation).

Local information
● **Accommodation**

Because Maumere is a popular diving area, it features on many tour itineraries and consequently hotel rates are overpriced; nowhere here is particularly rec.

B-D *Maiwali*, Jl Raja Don Tomas, T 21220, some a/c, comfortable, quiet and clean.

C *Permata Sari Inn*, 2 km from town, T 21171, on the beach, quite nice bungalows but definitely overpriced.

D *Benggoan III*, Jl KS Tubun, T 21284, some a/c, featureless hollow building, but rooms are fine, price incl breakfast; **D** *Flora Jaya*, Jl Raja Don Tomas, homely atmosphere, small rooms, price incl breakfast; **D-E** *Gardena*, Jl Pattirangga 5, T 21489, some a/c, 5 mins from town centre on quiet side street, popular with Indonesian officials.

E *Benggoan I*, Jl Moa Toda, T 21041, some attached mandis, dirty and overpriced; **E** *Losmen Benggoan II*, Jl Raya Centis (by market), T 21283, dirty, overpriced; **E** *Losmen Bogor II*, Jl Slamet Riyadi 4, T 21137, thin walls, shared mandi, lacklustre management, edge of town; **E** *Naga Beach*, 10 km W of town, T 21605, 50m from the beach, clean bungalows with shared mandi, very friendly, good value, price incl breakfast. *Getting there*: bemo 5 from *Losmen Bogor II* or from Pasar Baru; **E** *Wina Ria*, Jl Gajah Mada, T 21388 (about 5-10 mins walk out of town on road to Ende), shared mandi but large rooms, very clean, garden, rec.

F *Homestay Varanus*, Jl Nong Meak, friendly,

nice garden, good value, rec; **F** *Losmen Bogor I*, Jl Slamet Riyadi, rather dirty, shared mandi.

Dive Clubs at Waiara, 12 km from town: **B** *Flores Sao Wisata*, Waiara Beach, T 21555, (Jakarta) T 370333, F 3809595, better of the 2 dive centres, good equipment, **A**/day if diving; **B-C** *Sea World*, Jl Nai Noha, Km 13, PO Box 3, T 21570, some a/c, attractive cottages, price incl breakfast.

● **Places to eat**
Concentrated nr the market on Jl Raya Centis (aka Jl Pasar Baru).

♦♦*Sarinah*, Jl Raya Centis, Chinese, excellent seafood, rec; ♦♦*Stevani's Pub and Restaurant*, Jl Raya Centis (nr intersection with Jl Raja Don Tomas), seafood, open air pavilions in garden, good range of meals and karaoke in the evenings.

♦*Andika*, Jl Raya Centis, simple Indonesian bakso, soto etc; *Saiyo*, Jl Raya Centis, padang food; *Surya Indah II*, Jl Raya Centis.

● **Airline offices**
Bouraq, Jl Nong Meak, T 467 (also agent on Jl Moa Toda, next to *Benggoan I losmen*); **Merpati**, Jl Raja Don Tomas, T 347.

● **Banks & money changers**
BNI, Jl Soekarno-Hatta (behind and to the side of the Kantor Bupati), will change TCs and cash in major currencies.

● **Entertainment**
Karaoke: *Maiwali Hotel*, Jl Raja Don Tomas.

● **Hospitals & medical services**
Hospitals: *General Hospital*, Jl Kesehatan, T 21118.

● **Post & telecommunications**
Area code: 0380.

General Post Office: Jl Pos 2 (on the square nr the Kantor Bupati).

Perumtel: Jl Soekarno-Hatta (200m from Jl Jend A Yani) (international telephone & telegram).

● **Shopping**
Textiles: excellent range of ikat from all over Nusa Tenggara on sale at *Harapan Jaya*, Jl Moa Toda (market area, opp *Losmen Benggoan I*). Reasonable prices (but not bargains): ikat from Roti and Sabu, Ende (50,000Rp), Sumba (250,000Rp), Larantuka and Lembata (100-200,000Rp), Manggarai (nr Ruteng) (50,000Rp), West Timor (150,000Rp), Sikka (25,000Rp). Also textiles next door at Subur Jaya.

● **Sports**
Diving: although the earthquake of Dec 1992 is now history, the effect of the earthquake on the area's sea life is still evident. Large stands of coral were destroyed and these will take years to recover. Although other sections of reef, remarkably, appear to have survived intact, regular visitors report that the diving is still not back to its pre-earthquake best. Expect to pay approx. US$70/day; best to stay at one of the dive clubs (see accommodation).

Snorkelling: it is possible to book a place on *Sao Wisata's* dive boat, US$25 with equipment, lunch and drinks provided.

● **Tour companies & travel agents**
Astura, Jl Yos Sudarso, T 21498; *Floressa Wisata*, Jl Jend A Yani, T 21242; *Sikka Permai*, Jl Pasar Lama, T 21236.

● **Tourist offices**
Kantor Pariwisata, Jl Wairklau, T 21562, to get there, walk along Jl Gajah Mada towards Ende, turn right after the Perusahaan Umum Listrik, and walk 400m – the office is just past the Kantor Statistik, 10-15 mins in total from town centre, useful booklet, little English spoken.

● **Useful addresses**
Immigration office: Jl Kom A Sucipto, T 21151 (slip road to airport).

Police: Jl Jend A Yani, T 21110.

● **Transport**
82 km from Wolowaru, 93 km from Moni, 147 km from Ende, 137 km from Larantuka. **NB** The road to Ende was badly damaged during the Dec 1992 earthquake; it is now open but in poor condition; expect some delays during the rainy season. Travelling E from Maumere to Larantuka the road is good and the countryside particularly beautiful.

Local Bemos: the bemo station is by the market on Jl Jend A Yani in the centre of town. Bemos criss-cross the town linking the two bus terminals, Barat and Timur (or Lokaria) (200Rp). Ensure you know the correct cost of a fare before boarding, as overcharging has been known.

Air Maumere's Waioti Airport is 2 km E of the town centre, off the road towards Larantuka. Taxis to the town centre (3,000Rp) or walk the 750m to the main road and catch a bemo (200Rp). Regular connections by Merpati and Bouraq with Jakarta, Denpasar, Bima and Kupang, and towns in Kalimantan and Sulawesi.

Road Bus: Maumere has two bus terminals; **Terminal Barat** on Jl Gajah Mada for destinations to the W, incl Wolowaru 3 hrs, Moni 3½ hrs and Ende 6 hrs; and **Terminal Timur** (also known as Terminal Lokaria) E of town on Jl Larantuka for eastern destinations incl Larantuka 4 hrs and Wodong. Buses link the two terminals and the town centre (200Rp). Buses arriving in Maumere drop passengers off at their losmen/hotels. *Agogo* (for Ende, Moni and Wolowaru) has its offices on Jl Jend A Yani; *Sinar Remaja* on Jl Pattirangga, and *Sinar Agung* (for Larantuka and Ende) on Jl Gajah Mada by the Terminal Barat. Losmen/hotels will also usually book tickets.

Sea Boat: the Pelabuhan Maumere is a 5-10 mins NW from the town centre. The Pelni ship *Binaiya* docks here on its 2 week circuit between Surabaya and Dili calling at ports in Sulawesi and Nusa Tenggara (see route schedule, page 921). The Pelni office is next to *Losmen Bogor II* on Jl S Pranoto (aka Jl Slamet Riyadi), just over the bridge on the road to the port. Irregular mixed cargo vessels leave here for Ende, Reo, Riung, Kupang, Larantuka and Surabaya.

WODONG

Wodong is a small village 25 km E of Maumere, en route to Larantuka. There are two excellent, though basic, places to stay here (see **Accommodation**, below), good snorkelling, and it is also convenient as a base from which to trek to Mt Egon (see **Excursions**, below). The two losmen hire out masks and flippers, can arrange fishing trips and excursions to offshore islands. Those looking for a place to enjoy the landscape of Flores away from the masses, this is a good place to stay for a few days.

Excursions

Mount Egon (1,703m) is an active volcano, visible from Wodong. The trek to the summit takes 3½-4½ hrs and is well worthwhile. From Blitit (see *Getting there*, below, for information on reaching Blitit), follow the gravel track until it reaches a roadside, concrete water culvet and a rocky ford. Here is the first of a series of stone cairns marking the way to the summit. The route passes from scree into dry grassland, and from grassland into savanna scrub forest, with eucalyptus pre-

dominating. The path through the forest is clear enough; it emerges into more open landscape after about 2 hrs. From here the summit is visible, and it is about another hour's walk to the top. Near the peak, old tubes – now lying in disuse – laid by the Japanese during their occupation of Indonesia for sulphur extraction – are visible. A path leads around the crater edge, and another snakes its way into the caldera. The caldera lake, though, has dried out. From the crater lip there are superb views – on a clear day – over the sea towards Pulau Besar. **NB** Take ample water and some food for the trek. *Getting there*: take a bemo to Blitit, at the end of the surfaced road (it is also possible to arrange a pickup after descending from Mt Egon). Ask the owners of the *Wodong Homestay* or *Flores Froggies* if they will make the necessary arrangements.

- **Accommodation**   **E-F** *Wodong Homestay*, this new place (1995), with just 10 bungalows, is situated on the beachfront, friendly atmosphere, clean shared mandis, good food, basic but cosy, a dormitory has recently been built – (**F**, rec); **E-F** *Flores Froggies*, run by a French couple, attractive bungalows on the beachfront, as one might expect the travellers' and Indonesian food comes rec, friendly, the bungalows have attached mandis, dormitory accommodation also available, rec.

- **Sports Diving, snorkelling** and **fishing**: the two losmen can arrange diving with the *Sea World Club* outside Maumere; they also hire out masks and flippers and can arrange fishing trips.

- **Transport** 25 km from Maumere.

Bus: regular connections with Larantuka and Maumere. From Maumere, take a bemo or bus from Terminal Lokaria to Wodong (500Rp).

LARANTUKA

The small town of Larantuka is the district capital of E Flores, with a population of 25,000. It is strongly Christian, with a remarkable Easter celebration showing Portuguese origins (16th century). Particular devotion is shown to the Virgin Mary, a statue of whom was reportedly miraculously washed-up on the shore

The old Catholics of Larantuka

In 1613 a Dutch ship, the *Half Moon*, anchored off Solor and bombarded the Portuguese fort there, forcing the 1,000 strong population to surrender. Two of the Dominican friars – Caspar de Spiritu Santo and Augustino de Magdalena – asked that rather than withdraw to Melaka with the rest of the population, they be landed at Larantuka. Here they set about building another mission and by 1618 they had established more than 20 missions in the area. However, as the Portuguese lost influence so the Roman Catholics of Larantuka became isolated. The raja of the area took the title 'Servant of the Queen of the Rosary' and the church's devotional objects – chalice, cross, statues and so on – became part of local *adat* or tradition. Christianity became fossilized: the few Dutch Protestant ministers were sent smartly packing when they unsatisfactorily answered questions about Mary, Mother of Jesus, and visits by Portuguese Roman Catholic priests were few and far between.

Even so, the Roman Catholic rites and beliefs inculcated by the original Dominican friars were handed down through the generations. Devotees were taught to say their prayers in Latin and old Portuguese, and to wear robes like those of 17th century *penitentes*, with pointed hoods. When the Roman Catholics of Larantuka were finally 'rediscovered' by the Dutch priest, Father C de Hesselle in 1853 he was amazed to see the population keeping to a tradition over 2 centuries old. The most remarkable of these ceremonies is the Easter parade, replete with a rudely-hewn cross carried in procession (see Festivals).

here. On 8 September 1887, Don Lorenzo Diaz Viera de Godinho II consecrated the entire town to the Virgin. The town's name means 'on the way', and its strategic position made it a locally important port – Magellan's chronicler Francesco Antonio Pigafetta records passing here in 1522 on the expedition's voyage home from the Spice Islands (Maluku).

The **Chapel of the Virgin Mary**, in the centre of town, houses the sacred statue of the Virgin (see Festivals). On Sat, the Mama Muji pray in ancient Latin and Portuguese, distorted to such a degree that it is unintelligible even to students of the language (see box). There are also prayers said each evening. There are a number of other churches in town including the century-old **Cathedral of Larantuka** and the **Chapel of Christ** (Tuan Ana Chapel). The old **docks** are also worth visiting. Larantuka was fortunate to survive the earthquake, which devastated much of eastern Flores, relatively unscathed.

Festivals *Easter* (movable), the sacred statue of the Virgin is washed and dressed on Maundy Thursday (the water, in the process, becoming Holy Water with healing powers). In the afternoon the statue is kissed (the *Cio Tuan* ceremony) by the townspeople and other pilgrims, while the streets are cleaned and prepared for Good Friday. On the afternoon of Good Friday, the statue is taken to the Cathedral, where a statue of Jesus from the Chapel of Christ joins it. Following the service at about 1900, the statues are paraded through the town in a candle-lit procession. There are numerous other festivities during Holy Week.

● **Accommodation D** *Fortuna*, Jl Diponegoro 171, T 21140, 2 km NE of town, private bathroom; **D** *Tresna*, Jl Liker, T 21072, some private mandis, food served, best hotel in town; **D-E** *Rulis*, Jl Yos Sudarso 36, T 21198, rather scruffy, popular.

● **Places to eat** The *Rumah Makan Nirvana* is one of the best places to eat in Larantuka.

● **Airline offices** Merpati agent, Jl Diponegoro 64.

● **Transport** 137 km from Maumere. **Air** Gewayan Tana airport is 12 km N of town. 2

flights/week on Merpati from Kupang and on to Lewoleba and Lembata. **Road Bus**: regular connections with Maumere's Terminal Timur, 4 hrs. **Sea Boat**: a ferry leaves Larantuka port (5 km from town on road to Maumere) on Mon and Fri at 1400 for Kupang (12,500Rp). It is usually packed, although the captain sometimes allows tourists to sleep behind the wheelhouse or on the roof; making for a wonderful panorama of the stars and far more comfortable than on deck. Return ferry from Kupang departs Thur and Sun. A twice-daily ferry also connects Larantuka with Lewoleba, 4 hrs (4,400Rp).

LEMBATA

Lembata is a small island to the E of Flores, famous for its traditional whaling communities. The largest town on the island is **Lewoleba**, situated on the W coast. There is a spectacular **weekly market** held in Lewoleba each Mon; Lembata ikat is available.

Lerahinga Beach offers good snorkelling as well as excellent views of the imposing Gunung Ile Ape. *Getting there*: by bemo from the market in Lewoleba; most bemos travel all the way to the beach, otherwise it is a 1-km walk.

The traditional **whaling village of Lamalera** is on Lembata's S coast. The population trace their origins to Lapan Batan, an island between Lembata and Pantar. Unlike many of the other villages on Lembata which are land-based and rely on maize, rice and sweet potatoes, the population of Lamalera relies on fishing, and particularly whaling (see box). Until the late 1980s, Lamalera was so far off the beaten-track that virtually no one ventured there; the village has now become

Lamalera's whaling

The whaling season runs from Apr to Sep when the great whales migrate through the area to the rich southern oceans, and the villagers set out in man-powered boats in search of sperm whales (*ikan paus* – 'pope fish'), sharks, manta rays and other large denizens of the deep. The boats belong to village clans, or sections of clans, and have been constantly repaired and rebuilt over the centuries. They are said to be modelled on the ships that brought the original inhabitants from Lapan Batar.

The animals are killed using hand-thrown harpoons, the harpooner literally launching himself off the boat to plunge the iron as deeply as possible into the whale. Because, like Eskimos and a handful of other people, the hunters of Lamalera are traditional, they have been exempted from the world-wide ban on whaling. It is thought the two villages who still hunt whales only kill 20-30 a year; hardly a threat to the population. The meat is divided traditionally among families in the village, and the women then barter a portion for agricultural products and other goods. Only the teeth of the sperm whales are traded beyond the island.

Sadly, but perhaps predictably, insensitive tourists seem to have already made an impact: there have been reports that whalers have stopped rowing mid-ocean and demanded additional payment. It is also true that modernization, perhaps accelerated by tourism, has made traditional whaling increasingly rare. Before long this account will be one of history.

part of the travellers' itinerary. Even the tour company *Natrabu* runs a tour to Lamalera from Kupang. To go along with the whalers as a paying passenger will cost about 15,000Rp.

● **Accommodation In Lewoleba**: **D** *Losmen Rejeki I & II*, helpful owners, excellent food, shared mandi. **In Lamalera**: **F** *Mr Guru Ben's Homestay*, the room rate incl all meals and tea throughout the day, superb view from the rear of the house over the whaling beach, excellent value.

● **Banks & money changers** The *Losmen Rejeki I & II* will change US$ cash.

● **Shopping Textiles**: Lembata ikat (see page 735) is produced in villages across the island; available from Lewoleba market.

● **Transport Air** Lewoleba airport is 3 km from town. Merpati has 2 flights/week from Kupang to Lewoleba via Larantuka, returning the same day to Kupang. **Road**: During the dry season trucks run from Lewoleba to Puor, a 6-km walk from Lamalera. **Sea Boat**: 2 ferries/day from Larantuka to Lewoleba, 4 hrs (4,400Rp). There is also a boat from Larantuka to Lamalera every Fri departing at 0900, 6 hrs (5,000Rp). The same vessel leaves Lamalera for Lewoleba each Mon at 0800, 4 hrs (3,000Rp) returning the same evening. This boat is scheduled to allow villagers to get to the weekly market at Lewoleba (see above). The Kupang-Larantuka ferry calls at Lewoleba on Mon and Fri, returning to Larantuka before continuing on to Kupang on Tues and Sat.

ALOR

The rugged island of Alor is E of Lembata and is 100 km long and 35 km wide at its widest point. The capital, **Kalabahi**, is on the W coast and the island has a population of about 150,000. The various tribes of the island – Nedebang, Dieng, Kaka and

The Moko drum currency debâcle

Before the 19th century, bronze *moko* drums were traded and used as bride price. They are related to the Dongson drums of northern Vietnam (see page 377), although no exact equivalent has ever been found there. The older examples of *moko* also show similar decoration to their presumed Vietnamese prototypes, although newer examples have Chinese and Indian inspired floral motifs. How these drums came to Alor is not known, but they have also been discovered elsewhere in the Indonesian archipelago (see Bali, page 378).

Around 1900, imitation brass *moko* began to be made in large quantities in Gresik, Java and exported to Alor. They created chaos in a monetary system which owed its stability to there always being a limited number of *moko* in circulation. In 1914, in an attempt to stabilize the *moko*, the Dutch introduced coinage and forbad all use of the drums in transactions, except in tax payments. This exemption was designed to take *moko* out of circulation; some 1,660 drums were acquired, and then melted down.

Bride price in Alor is still sometimes paid using *moko*. The cheapest drum, and thus presumably the cheapest wife, is said to cost about 150,000-200,000Rp. The oldest drums are the most valuable, and through time and their association with powerful people, drums are thought to acquire powers of their own. Such drums are rarely traded, but remain within the family.

Mauta – practice shifting cultivation (see page 33), although as land becomes scarcer, so they are being forced to become settled agriculturalists. Most of the population are Christian.

Alor illustrates, in microcosm, the enormous diversity of Indonesia's people. There are seven major language groups spoken on the island, representing some 50 languages in all – or one language for every 3,000 inhabitants. Sir Francis Drake in the *Golden Hind* sailed past Alor, having been blown off course towards Wetar, E of Alor (see page 42).

● **Accommodation In Kalabahi**: **C-D** *Pelangi Indah*, Jl Diponegoro 34, some a/c, private mandis but no hot water, clean and neat with tasty food, a good little hotel; **D-E** *Adi Dharma*, on the waterfront, owner speaks English and is a good source of information; **D-E** *Melati*, on the waterfront.

● **Shopping Textiles**: Alor ikat; some are rather inferior, but there are villages on Alor still producing high quality cloth, so look around.

● **Transport Air** Alor's Mali airport is 28 km from Kalabahi. Connections on Merpati with Kupang, Larantuka, Lewoleba, Rote and Denpasar. **Sea Boat**: 1 ferry/week from Kupang to Kalabahi, leaving Kupang on Mon and returning from Kalabahi on Tues (12,000Rp). The Pelni vessel *Binaiya* calls here on its fortnightly circuit through Nusa Tenggara (see route schedule page 921.

Sumba

THE OVAL ISLAND of Sumba is noted for its megalithic tombs (mainly in the W), fine ikat cloth (mainly in the E) and horseback-fighting festivals. It is divided into two administrative districts covering a land area of 11,052 sq km: the regencies of E and W Sumba. Their capitals are Waingapu and Waikabubak respectively. The island lies outside the volcanic arc that runs through Java and the other islands of Nusa Tenggara. The generally subdued relief presents a startling contrast to Java, Bali and Flores.

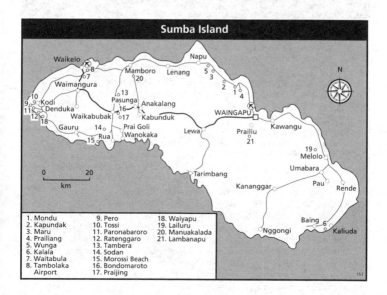

Sumba Island

1. Mondu	9. Pero	18. Waiyapu
2. Kapundak	10. Tossi	19. Lailuru
3. Maru	11. Paronabaroro	20. Manuakalada
4. Prailiang	12. Ratenggaro	21. Lambanapu
5. Wunga	13. Tambera	
6. Kalala	14. Sodan	
7. Waitabula	15. Morossi Beach	
8. Tambolaka	16. Bondomaroto	
Airport	17. Praijing	

Horizons

Though Sumba is only 300 km long and 80 km wide, the two regencies of E and W Sumba are environmentally very different. While the E of the island is generally dry (annual rainfall 674 mm) and barren, the W is considerably wetter (1,826 mm), and consequently much greener. The dry season stretches over 7 to 8 months from Apr to Oct. During these months, the rolling landscape is dry and desolate; but during the rainy season the green grasslands of the W are not unlike those of Ireland. Rice can be cultivated only in the valleys where perennial rivers flow, and in the dry season these – like the Lewa Valley, mid-way between Waingapu and Waikabubak – are small oases of green in an otherwise parched landscape. In times past Sumba was known as the 'Sandalwood Isle' but destruction of these forests for commercial gain has left much of the island, especially in the E, fit only for extensive cattle grazing and horse raising. The island's population is about 425,000: 280,000 in the agriculturally richer W, the remainder in the E. These days Sumba's wealth is based on the export of horses and buffaloes; every year about 40,000 of each are exported to Java.

Historically, Sumba was known as a source of horses, slaves and sandalwood, but lying as it does to the S of the island arc of Nusa Tenggara, it managed to escape the successive streams of Hindu, Muslim and Christian interlopers who influenced the area. Although the island did come under the influence of the Majapahit Kingdom of Java from the 5th century, and rather later from the Sultanate of Bima in Flores, it was never directly ruled from the outside. The first Europeans to note the existence of the island were the crew of the Portuguese vessel *Victoria* in the 16th century, part of Magellan's expedition. Although marked on maps following this original sighting, it

The Sumbanese slave trade

Sumba's role as a source of slaves dates from as early as historical accounts exist. The Sultan of Bima on Sumbawa, and the sultans and kings of S Sulawesi, Flores, Lombok and Bali all obtained slaves from the island. At Ende, in Flores, it was said by the Dutch visitor Goronvius in 1855 that "there is hardly a man to be found, of moderate or even limited means, who is not the owner of some 20 slaves, all of them from Sumba". Dutch interest in Sumba as a source of slaves dates from the mid-18th century, and the island quickly became the major supplier to the colonial power.

Why Sumba should have filled this role is linked to the nature of society and the absence of a strong, central power. The structure of Sumbanese society was rigidly divided into an aristocratic (*maramba*) class, and a slave (*ata*) class. This social stratification was more prominent in the E and even today wealth and power lie in the hands of 4 or 5 men. The W is more diverse ethnically and culturally with 7 different languages spoken and more opportunity for advancement based on merit rather than heredity. The latter could be freely bought and sold, and even denied the right to marry, own property or to have a funeral – the essential qualities of human existence. When the first colonial administrator was dispatched to Sumba in 1866, he reported the island to be lawless and politically fragmented. By this time, the NW coast was effectively depopulated, such were the numbers of slaves plucked from the island by raiders. The trade was officially abolished in 1860, but continued until the early 20th century. The first Resident was even given a slave girl as a welcome gift when he first arrived on the island.

Sumba's megalithic tombs

👣 The construction of megalithic graves is characteristic of both E and W Sumba. However, in E Sumba the grave construction cannot begin until after the intended occupant is dead. This means that some families have to keep the corpse of their relative in a kind of limbo until enough funds and time have been found to build the monument. In W Sumba people help to build their own tombs. Here the socially ambitious seek enhanced prestige while they are still alive by having large gravestones hauled to their village; a feat which requires the expenditure of large sums of money for the many kinsmen needed to help, and for ceremonial feasting.

Limestone boulders weighing anywhere up to 30 tonnes are dragged on wooden rafts (*tena*) to the site of the grave. *Tena* means ship, and a textile sail is raised to help the stone on its journey. The graves are not spatially separated from the village houses, and many are used for more mundane purposes like drying corn or dyed textiles, or for lounging on during evening village events. There are four main types of megalithic tomb in Sumba: the first is a simple dolmen, with four stone pillars supporting a rectangular stone slab. The second, is similar to the first, but carved and ornamented. The third has stone walls enclosing the four pillars. And the fourth, the added feature of stone stairs leading up to the covering slab.

The purpose behind the many rituals and ceremonies, at which offerings of food and valuables are made, is to ensure good relations between the living and the ancestors to guarantee the former's well-being. (These days the government limits the number of buffalo which can be sacrificed to prevent families going into penury.) Even numbers, in particular four and eight, are considered auspicious.

was not until the Dutch arrived in the 17th century that western contact intensified. Even then, it was not until the early 20th century that a colonial administrator was installed.

Today, it is thought that over 50% of the population, predominantly in the W, still adhere to the traditional, animist, religion of ancestor worship *agama merapu*. The merapu are the original ancestors of each patrilineal clan. Another 35% are Protestant and the remainder, Catholic, Muslim, Hindu and Buddhist. The government has been trying – much as they have in the Toraja area of Sulawesi – to stamp out the slaughter of pigs, chickens and buffalo in 'wasteful' traditional ceremonies. Those who flout the ban and are caught are fined – even detained for a while. Success is patchy and many people have taken to clandestine slaughtering at night. Funerals and the ceremonies associated with blessing a new house 'demand' that guests be fed and animals killed – perhaps 25 pigs for a house ceremony, up to 100 buffalo for the funeral of an important personage.

Sumbanese villages and houses The layout of a *paraingu* – or village – in Sumba should conform to traditional rules. The village symbolizes a ship, with a bow (*tunda kambata*), deck (*kani padua*) and stern (*kiku kemudi*). The houses are arranged around the ancestors' burial place.

Important villages of clan chiefs are built on hills while less important villages surround them at lower elevations. Similarly, ancestral houses *uma merapu* have high peaked roofs whilst houses not associated with the ancestors have lower roofs and are called *uma kamudungu* 'bald houses'. Buffalo horns on the outside of houses are indicative of past sacrifices and denote wealth and prestige; they also protect the house and ward off evil spirits. Through their part in sacrifices buffaloes act as a link with the spirit world.

The ikat hinggi blankets of Sumba

Sumba produces perhaps the most distinctive warp ikat in Indonesia. Traditionally, the weaving of cloth was the preserve of aristocratic women who, free from agricultural and household chores, had the time to produce finely woven cloth. Ikat is still woven on backstrap looms, although natural indigo and red morinda dyes are being replaced by chemical substitutes. The most commonly produced cloth is the *hinggi*, a large blanket worn by men. Characteristic motifs include animals such as horses, dogs, snakes, monkeys, crocodiles, fish and lizards. Each has its own symbolism – dogs with warriors, snakes with rebirth and long life, crocodiles with the afterlife. Another common motif is the skull tree or *andung*, which draws upon the former practice of hanging the heads of vanquished enemies from a tree in the centre of a village to scare away evil spirits.

The quality of Sumba ikat is declining, and most lengths of cloth can only be described as 'tourist' material: large and simple motifs, often without the important border strip or *kabakil*, woven with machine spun yarn, coloured with chemical dyes, and showing 'bleeding' of dye across the borders between design elements. First-class cloth is almost exclusively reserved for burial, and no local, quite literally, would be seen dead in the blankets sold to visitors. Wrapping the body in fine ikat ensures that the spirit of the dead man or woman will reach *Parai Merapu* – Merapu heaven. The transition from the physical world to that of the spirits is critical, and the various elements of the death rite must be strictly adhered to.

Some people maintain that it is cheaper to buy cloth in Bali where shop owners purchase in bulk from villages with which they have special relations. Tour groups visiting villages like Rende have pushed prices up considerably. To buy a good piece of cloth expect to have to pay 300,000Rp or more.

In the open space in the centre of the more warlike villages can be found the 'skull tree' *andung*, a dead tree on which in earlier headhunting times the skulls of enemy taken in battle were hung. The life force believed to emanate from these heads was considered to be a source of fertility, and the tree acted as a symbol of strength and security for the village as well as the focal point for rites of war.

The striking, traditional, thatched houses – low-sided, yet high-peaked – are built around a fireplace which is positioned between the four main pillars. There are two doors: a front door for men, and a rear entrance for women. Due to poor ventilation, the smoke from the open fire tends to fill the houses, making them dirty and suffocating. Each consists of three 'floors': cattle are kept at ground level and most weaving takes place here.

The first floor is the main living area, with various rooms for sleeping (divided according to sex, age and rank), grain storage, cooking and eating. The upper section, known as the *uma deta* or *hindi merapu*, is for the spirits; here, sacred objects are stored. In W Sumba, some of the finest traditional houses can be seen at Anakalang, Tarung and Prai Goli; in E Sumba, at Prailiu and Pau. The dwellings in W Sumba tend to have higher roofs.

The right side of the house is symbolically male, the left side female. The four central posts supporting the house are also either male or female and must be placed following strict ritual customs. The front right corner post of the house is considered sacred; this is where the priest makes offerings, speaks to the ancestors in their language, and channels the power of the ancestors stored in the

Sumba Ikat motifs

IMS 306

A design based on the mamuli, a gold ear ornament and traditional marriage gift.

Cockatoos

Man with skull tree (andung), and cockatoos.

Roosters

Horses

heirlooms in the high peaked roof to the living. The right back corner post is the site of animal sacrifices. The left back corner post is the domain of women and is the place where domestic animals are fed. The left front corner post is where the sacred rice is cooked and served by the women who then pass it to the priest by the front right post.

The highest parts of the house are considered sacred and are connected with the ancestors; the house having become

Sumba death rites

🐾 A notable aspect of Sumbanese society is the very close association of the living with the dead. Graves are constructed on the doorstep of houses in the open space in the centre of each village. Death is viewed as the beginning of eternal life; life itself being merely a stage which is passed through en route to the attainment of eternal life. The transition from the physical world to the world of the spirits is critical to the Sumbanese and is ensured by strict adherence to the burial rite. Following a person's death, a close relative calls his or her name four times; should there be no answer, he or she is pronounced dead. No crying is allowed for 3 days following the death. The body is bathed, coated in coconut oil (in E Sumba the body is also coated with the blue dye used in ikat which protects the corpse) and dressed in ikat sarongs. The number, and quality, of the sarongs is indicative of status. The arms and legs of the body are broken, and the dead person placed in the foetal position, either in a wooden coffin, or wrapped in buffalo hide. The body is placed over a hole so that the blood can drain down a bamboo pole into the ground. The body, except if the dead person was of lowly status, is guarded by four men. During this period, the spirit of the deceased is still regarded as roaming the village.

The second stage of the burial ceremony involves the preparation of the tomb. A stone is dragged into the village by large numbers of people. Relatives bring cattle, horses or pigs to be sacrificed, the size of the sacrificial gift being dictated by the status and closeness of relationship with the deceased. The corpse is then taken to the tomb and buried with many valuable objects. In the past, if the person was of royal blood, a slave was buried alive along with the corpse.

The wealth consumed at funeral ceremonies was deemed necessary to ensure a safe passage to the world of the ancestors where the deceased could bring benefit to his clan. The greater the display of wealth at his funeral the higher the status he would merit in the spirit world. There is great wealth buried in the soil of Sumba and there have been cases of unscrupulous dealers, allegedly from Java, going out into likely areas of the countryside with metal detectors in search of buried treasure.

sacred as a result of the heirlooms being stored in its roof since the heirlooms represent the spirit of the founding ancestor residing in the house. The heirlooms are powerful objects used in rituals as a medium through which contact with the ancestors can be made; some heirlooms, particularly those that are very old and made of gold, silver or other metal are believed to be so powerful that disasters may result if they are mishandled; the most powerful are not even allowed to be looked at and are housed in sealed boxes or inside many different containers.

Some clan origin-houses in Sumba have accumulated so much sacred power leading to a wealth of taboos and prohibitions that living in them has become too dangerous for their owners who fear they might inadvertently break a taboo and incur the wrath and retribution of their ancestral spirits. They prefer to install more expendable family slaves as caretakers. This is the case with the ancestral house in Rende.

Visiting Sumbanese villages Part of the attraction of Sumba lies in the ease with which a traveller can witness traditional ceremonies and festivals which are genuine, entirely for the benefit of local clans and not part of a tourist charade. Having maintained its autonomy over the centuries, and lying off the main tourist routes, Sumba's age old traditions and beliefs remain largely intact, particularly in W Sumba. If you want to explore new territory there are countless traditional villages rarely, if ever, visited by travellers; ask at hotels as someone working there may come from just such a village worth visiting, this is particularly likely in W Sumba. Some travellers consider that the people in W Sumba are even friendlier than E Sumba's villagers as they are not so concerned with tourism and making money from selling ikat. Hotels are only full during high season (July/Aug) and at the time of the Pasola (Feb/Mar). At other times of the year surprisingly few visitors come to Sumba and you may well find yourself the only foreigner in town, even in Waikabubak.

Important When visiting local villages it is courteous and advisable to observe local etiquette and take a gift of betel nut to share with your hosts; it would be polite also to stop and chat or, bearing in mind any language restrictions, at least to partake of some betel nut with the headman. It can cause offence if visitors treat these villages as a zoo, you are after all invading their territory uninvited. If offered betel nut, it is impolite not to take some. It's fairly tasteless and even after half an hour of chewing you are unlikely to have swallowed any as it does not readily dissolve; without the lime it will not stain your mouth and you can remove it later. Alternatively, hide it to dispose of later. Betel is easily bought in the market where you will see stalls selling piles of 'betel' (in fact areca) nut (*pinang*) together with the catkin (*sirih*) for 500Rp or 1,000Rp for a double sized quantity, and in separate piles, lime (*kapur*) in the form of a white powder in little plastic packets for 100Rp. Alternatively, you could take coffee, sugar and cigarettes or simply make a donation of 1,000Rp at each village you visit. Don't expect to just wander in and look around. You will probably be asked for 1,000Rp for photographs.

Conduct and dress Women should avoid wearing short shorts and skimpy skirts, and men and women should avoid wearing singlets.

Transport New roads are being built and minibuses are also new, making travel to many places easy and painless. You are less likely to be hassled on Sumba than almost any other part of Indonesia. As Sumba prospers, more villages will become easily accessible by public minibus. Look out for the 'names' of individual minibuses and trucks brandished across their front windscreens, some unprintable!

The two luxury developments on Sumba's S coast, one 5 km from Baing in the SE and the *Sumba Reef Lodge* S of Waikabubak near Rua Beach, are currently closed. There is talk of re-opening the former, ask in Waingapu.

WAINGAPU

Waingapu is the capital of the regency of E Sumba, and the island's largest town with a population of 25,000. A hot dusty place spread out over a large area in two concentrations, one by the harbour, and the other about 1 km inland, convenient for the bus station and market and where many of the hotels are found. Waingapu suffers from having little attractive accommodation, and few restaurants serving appetising food. It is a base from which to explore the far more interesting surrounding countryside.

The **Old Docks** area (*Pelabuhan Lama*) can be entertaining: fishing boats, and the occasional inter-island mixed cargo boat, dock here. Watch Sumba's famous horses and buffaloes being loaded onto small inter-island boats and brand new Japanese minibuses being precariously unloaded. There is a pleasant walk along a street bordering the shore with views of the sea and harbour; follow one of the sidestreets off Jl Yos Sudarso to reach the sea. At night look out for the amazing neon lit decorations on minibuses. Overlooking the dock on Jl Kartini are some picturesque colonial-era buildings dating

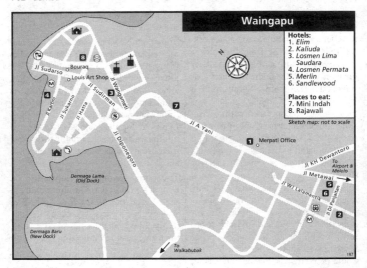

Waingapu

Hotels:
1. *Elim*
2. *Kaliuda*
3. *Losmen Lima Saudara*
4. *Losmen Permata*
5. *Merlin*
6. *Sandlewood*

Places to eat:
7. *Mini Indah*
8. *Rajawali*

Sketch map: not to scale

back to the first half of the century. Nearby, just off Jl Yos Sudarso, is a small **market**, with a larger market next to the bus station on the outskirts of town. Neither is particularly notable.

Excursions

Although Waingapu and E Sumba do not have the megaliths of W Sumba, it is the centre of fine ikat production (see page 758) and there are a number of weaving villages within easy reach of the town.

Prailiu is an ikat weaving village only 2 km SE of town. Stages in the ikat weaving process can usually be seen, or make arrangements in advance with the weavers. There is cloth for sale – it is even sometimes possible to buy good, finely-worked ikat here. The village has a small number of inferior 'megalithic' tombs, both modern and traditional in design. *Getting there*: walk or take one of the constant bemos that run from the bemo stop near the bus terminal (300Rp).

Kawangu is another weaving village, 11 km E of Waingapu. Like Prailiu, stages in the ikat process can often be witnessed and there is cloth for sale. *Getting there*: regular bemos run from the bemo stop

next to the bus station (300Rp). **Lamba-napu** is another ikat weaving village worth a visit, 7 km from Prailiu.

Melolo is a lovely, overgrown (with vegetation), little town 60 km SE of Waingapu and one of the most rewarding of excursions. It also makes a good base from which to visit the area SE of Waingapu. Melolo itself has few traditional houses but Rende and Pau (see below) are easily reached from here by bus or on foot. Market day is Fri. *Getting there*: buses run regularly until 1600 along a good and scenic road taking about 1½ hrs, 2,500Rp. From here there is local transport to the traditional village and weaving centre of **Rende**, 7 km on along the road S to Baing.

Rende not only produces good ikat, but also has some of the most impressive megalithic tombs in E Sumba, with carvings featuring animals, sea creatures and humans. There are traditional houses here, though many now have tin roofs. The largest of these is the recently rebuilt home of the Raja. It may be possible to stay with a family here. The inhabitants believe that the earth is built on five house posts like their own homes; earthquakes happen when a mouse chews the central post destabilizing the earth and causing it to shake. Wednesday is market day (see page 757). Unfortunately, because Rende is firmly on the tour group itinerary, prices of cloth are high and rising. Good pieces made with home-grown cotton and using natural dyes are around 1,000,000Rp. The best weaver in the village sells cloth from the house close to the *kepala desa's* (headman's) residence. From Melolo, there is a pleasant 4 km walk past rice paddys to another traditional village: **Pau**. There are more megalithic tombs, peaked traditional houses and ikat at the village of **Umabara**, about 5 km W of Melolo. Alternatively take a bemo from Melolo and ask to be dropped off at the turning for the village. Both Pau and Umabara are about a 30-min walk from the main road; follow the road until you reach a stone horse, take the right fork to reach Umabara and take the left for Pau. The Raja of Pau has a fine collection of ikat. At both these villages expect to sign the visitors book and pay 1,000Rp. **Lailuru** to the N of Melolo is another ikat weaving village. **Accommodation E** *Losmen Hermindo*, Melolo, owned by the local Chinese shop owner, clean, 5 rm with shared mandi, squat toilet and fan, 2 new rooms with attached bathroom and western toilet are being built and should be ready early 1996, price includes breakfast, meals available, or eat at the warungs which serve good cheap food. There is also a *homestay* in Rende (at the *kepala desa's*). *Getting to Melolo*: several direct buses from Waingapu starting from 0700 (2,500Rp, 2 hrs); from Melolo to Waingapu bemos run all day until about 1600.

Kaliuda is an ikat weaving village, 50 km past Melolo and 110 km from Waingapu, just off the road to Baing. The ikat produced here features, predominantly, chicken and horse motifs. Weavers from other villages make fun of the local artists saying – 'Oh, all they can do are chickens and horses'. Much of the ikat is unfinished (that is, without the border strip)

and clearly, therefore, for tourist rather than local consumption. **Accommodation** The *kepala desa* takes in visitors, but the rooms are very basic and rather dirty. *Getting there*: 2-3 buses each day from the bus terminal.

Kalala on the SE coast 5 km from Baing with a good beach and one of the best places to surf. The upmarket resort built here is currently closed; there are no plans to reopen it. *Getting there*: by bus from Waingapu, 4 hrs (4,000Rp), or from Melolo, 2 hrs (2,500Rp).

Northwest of Waingapu

Prailiang, reached down a rough road off the main road shortly before Mondu which has a Fri market. This is a good example of a traditional fortified hilltop village where ancient customs and rituals are still strong. The remnants of the encircling wall can be seen. The villagers work the land surrounding the hill. *Getting there*: by bus to Mondu; ask the driver to let you off at the turn off to Prailiang.

Maru, on the coast 60 km NW of Waingapu, is a traditional village with important rituals and ceremonies. Market day is Mon. *Getting there*: buses run daily 2,000Rp.

Kapundak This traditional area is difficult to reach though there are plans to upgrade the road. Local legend has it that this is the place where the ancestors landed when they first came to Sumba. In consequence it is an area of great significance to all Sumbanese; the village of **Wunga** is the religious focus where important ceremonies take place. *Getting there*: you can take the bus to Maru, but it is best to hire your own transport.

Tours

The *Elim*, *Merlin*, *Permata*, and *Sandle Wood Hotels* can arrange cars and guides to take tourists around the main sights. Ali Fa'daq at the *Permata* speaks excellent English and has the best background knowledge of Sumba. He has films of some traditional ceremonies. **Zaid Bachmid** (with some English) at the Tourist Office is also willing to guide tourists. Prices for the day, including car and guide, range from 75,000Rp to 125,000Rp.

Local information
● Accommodation
Most of Waingapu's hotels and losmen are found around the bus station, about 1½ km S of the town centre or in the harbour area.

C-D *Elim*, Jl Jend A Yani 73, T 21323, friendly owners are a good source of information, reasonable rooms, every type of room available from dorm beds to rooms with fan or a/c and private mandi, tours, guides and car/motorbike hire, restaurant (♦♦); **C-D** *Merlin Hotel*, Jl Dl Panjaitan 25, T 21300, F 21333, new with attractive decor, the best hotel in town and very reasonably priced, most rooms with modern private bathrooms, more expensive rooms have a/c, the stairs might pose a problem for old people and for the vertically challenged, as the treads are almost 1 ft in height, restaurant on 3rd floor (♦♦), excellent with commanding views, tours, guides and car/motorbike hire available, rec; **C-D** *Sandle Wood*, Jl Dl Panjaitan, T 21199, the second best place to stay but original rooms badly in need of redecoration, especially the bathrooms, rooms with shared and private mandis, kapok filled beds have compressed over the years and are now rock hard, the new wing with a/c rooms is better, breakfast incl but awful, restaurant (♦♦), not rec, unfortunately the Chinese owner always seems to be asleep and the staff have no authority (both a seemingly common occurrence on Sumba) so obviously complaints fail to filter back to him.

D *Lima Saudara*, Jl Wanggameti 2, T 21083, rooms rather dirty, attached bathrooms, average, price incl breakfast.

E *Kaliuda*, Jl Dl Panjaitan 3, T 21264, behind bus station, clean, well run, best of the budget places, some rooms with private mandi, all squat toilets; **E** *Losmen Permata* (aka *Ali's Place*), Jl Kartini 10, T 21516, overlooking the old docks nr the centre of town, basic rooms with private mandi, squat toilets, the owner Ali is very knowledgeable about local culture, nice position on grassed square.

● Places to eat
♦♦*RM Restu Ibu*, Jl IR Juanda, T 21218, rec.

♦*Mini Indah*, Jl A Yani (between the two halves of town), very variable, you might have an excellent meal or an inedible one; ♦*Rajawali*, Jl Sutomo 96, good Chinese, seafood, pleasant atmosphere, rec; *Sumbawa*, Jl Palapa (behind the bus station); ♦♦*Hotel Merlin* restaurant, rec.

● Airline offices
Bouraq, Jl Yos Sudarso 57, T 21363, 21906, Yanca is very helpful, speaks excellent English and will bring tickets to your hotel in the evening, a former tour guide in W Sumba he is very knowlegeable about the island; **Merpati**, Jl Jend A Yani 73 (at the *Elim Hotel*), T 323462, open Mon-Fri 0700-1700, Sat 0700-1400, Sun and holidays 0900-1300.

● Banks & money changers
Bank Rakyat Indonesia, Jl Jend A Yani 36, changes cash and TCs, open 0800-1200, except Fri when it closes at 1100.

● Hospitals & medical services
Hospitals: *General Hospital*, Jl Adam Malik, Hambala.

● Post & telecommunications
Area code: 0386.

General Post Office: Jl Sutomo 21, open 0800-1400, except Fri 0800-1100.

Perumtel: Jl Cut Nyak Din 19 (international telephone, telex & fax).

● Shopping
The best place to buy Sumba's ikat is on Bali where prices are more reasonable and dealers are prepared to negotiate. The ikat-producing villages tend to have only a limited selection of pieces as most, including the best pieces, is swiftly purchased by dealers, and the villagers rarely bargain. In town *LA 'Louis' Art Shop* has 2 branches: at Toko Kupang, Jl WJ Lalamentik 15 (just pass the *Sandle Wood Hotel*) and on Jl Yos Sudarso nr the port area, T 21536, 21132 (home); open 0800-2200 or by appointment, rec. The *Sandle Wood Hotel* has a large selection of mostly rather average ikat; they seem strangely reluctant to show any quality.

Sumba blankets vary a great deal in quality and a reasonable piece cannot be bought for less than 150,000Rp; good lengths are 400,000Rp or more.

● Tour companies & travel agents
Eben Haezer, Jl Jend A Yani 73, T 323, by the *Elim Hotel*.

● Tourist offices
Kantor Cabang Dinas Pariwisata, Jl Suharto T791, no useful maps or pamphlets, but helpful staff.

● **Transport**
173 km from Waikabubak, 178 km from Melolo, 185 km from Rende, 220 km from Baing.

Local Bemos: ply the main routes around town (300Rp); the central bemo stop is nr the bus terminal. **Car/minibus hire**: from the *Losmen Surabaya* (6,000Rp/hr); or the *Sandle Wood Hotel* (5,000Rp/hr); for longer journeys, charges are 50,000Rp return to Melolo, 60,000Rp to Paun and Rende, and 80,000-100,000Rp to Waikabubak and Baing. The *Merlin* and *Permata* will also hire out cars for the day (100,000Rp and 75,000Rp respectively). **Motorcycle hire**: available from most hotels, 15,000Rp/day.

Air Waingapu's Mau Hau Airport is 6 km SE of town. **Transport to town**: free transport provided by hotels. Drivers congregate in the arrivals hall. Taxi 3,000 Rp or catch one of the regular bemos that run along the road just outside the terminal to the bus station in town (200Rp). The Merpati minibus takes passengers from the Merpati Office (*Hotel Elim*) to the airport. Daily flights by Merpati and/or Bouraq to Kupang. By Merpati, 2½ hrs, 3 flights/week to Tambolaka (Waikabubak), 40 mins, on Mon, Thur and Sat, continuing on to Bima, 1 hr 40 mins, and 3 non-stop flights to Bima (also on Mon, Thur, Sat); 3 flights a week to Surabaya, 5 hrs, via Bima and Denpasar, 2¾ hrs, Mon, Thur, Sat. 4 flights a week to Denpasar by Bouraq non-stop, 2 hrs. DPS-Waingapu (185,000Rp), Kupang-Waingapu (128,000Rp), Waingapu-Waikabubak (Tambolaka) (50,000Rp).

Road Bus: the station is 1½ km S of town, nr most of the hotels, on Jl El Tari. Regular bemos link it with town. Several buses each day at approx 0700, 0800, 1200 to Waikabubak, 4 hrs (4,000Rp) (sometimes with over an hour cruising for fares). Also several departures each day to Melolo (for Rende), 1½-2 hrs (2,000Rp), Lewa, 2 hrs, and Baing, 4 hrs (4,000Rp). Buses will pick passengers up from hotels and losmen with advance warning. The best seats are up front next to the driver. These usually need to be reserved in advance either through your hotel or at the bus company headquarters. Buses to Waikabubak stop half way at Langa Leru for about 20 mins. There are stalls and warungs where you can get excellent strong coffee and something to eat. **Taxi**: for groups of 4 or more it can make sense to hire a car; public transport, though cheap, is slow (see Local transport).

Sea Boat: the Pelni ship *Binaiya* docks at the new harbour – Pelabuhan Baru; other vessels, including pioneer vessels *(Perintis)*, dock at the old harbour or Pelabuhan Lama. Though only 200m from the old harbour by water, the Pelabuhan Baru is a circuitous 7-km ride by bemo. The *Binaiya* docks twice a fortnight on its circuit through Nusa Tenggara (see route schedule, page 921). *Pelni* ships sail to Ende and Kupang via Sawu and Roti; ask at the Pelni office for details. There is also a weekly ferry linking Waingapu with Ende (Flores) and Savu (Sawu). At the time of writing, it docks on Wed am, leaves for Savu on Wed pm, returns to Waingapu on Fri am, and leaves for Ende on Fri night, 10-12 hrs (10-15,000Rp, both legs). There are also other, smaller boats heading out of Waingapu for other islands in Nusa Tenggara. Ask at the harbour. A Perintis ship currently sails from Waikelo Harbour to Larantuka on Eastern Flores, 8-12 hrs. The Pelni office is near the harbour (see map), T 21265, F 21027, staff are very helpful and some speak good English. Don't necessarily be put off if Pelni say there are no cabins available when you make a booking. Cabins frequently materialize on the day.

WAIKABUBAK

Waikabubak is the regency capital and the largest town in W Sumba. Even so, it is really little more than a village, with a population of only around 15,000. Situated at 800m above sea-level, the town is cooler than Waingapu and during the coldest months of Jun and Jul can be chilly at night.

Almost 70% of the population of this region are nominal Christians; unwilling converts, they still follow and attach much more importance to their animist religious practices. One of the unfortunate consequences of their conversion is that many of the old ancestral heirlooms have been sold and some of the important ceremonies are no longer performed.

Nonetheless, **Waikabubak** is a very pleasant town with trees, parks and four traditional hilltop 'kampungs' within its boundaries. It is a good base from which to see the fine megalithic tombs in this area of Sumba and at the appropriate time of year it is also possible to see the *Pasola*. This spectacular festival takes place in four different districts of W

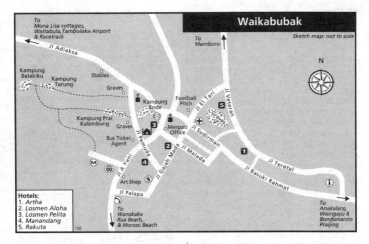

Waikabubak

Hotels:
1. Artha
2. Losmen Aloha
3. Losmen Pelita
4. Manandang
5. Rakuta

Sumba after the full moon; in Feb at Tossi Village in Kodi district (see Excursions, below) and Sodan village in Lamboya, and in Mar in Wanokaka and Gaura districts. Verify exact dates and location with your hotel or the tourist office. Alternatively, if when you are out walking you notice an endless stream of people converging on a village join them, they will probably be delighted to invite you along and will indicate appropriate behaviour which will include giving a gift or donation. Homestays are available in nearby villages (see Festivals, below).

The village of **Tarung** is only 500m W of town, set on a small hill. Being so close to Waikabubak, it has inevitably been influenced by the large number of tourists who walk up here. Nevertheless, it has several – rather plain – tombs and 33 traditional, thatched houses (see box, page 757). Tarung is the centre of the Marapu religion where many important rituals take place including the Wula Podhu New Year festival. Admission to village is by donation.

Another village that can be reached on foot from Waikabubak is **Bondomaroto**. This is an ikat-producing village with some rather inferior tombs and tradi-

tional high roofed dwellings. You may be lucky and witness a festival taking place – ask in town. On the last day of Tarungs' celebration of Wula Podhu the villagers have a day long celebration. Admission to the village is by donation. 2 km from Waikabubak, Bondomaroto is just off the main road to Waingapu. Follow the dirt track S and take the left hand path. To the right lies the beautiful village of **Praijing**. Weaving can be seen in both villages.

Excursions

Anakalang is a district 20 km E of Waikabubak and, conveniently, close to the main road to Waingapu. This district has the greatest concentration of megalithic tombs to be found in Sumba: a mass marriage ceremony is held here every 2 years in the summer to coincide with the full moon. At **Pasunga**, on the main road, there is one of the largest tombs in Sumba. It features a man and woman, and was carved over a period of 6 months in 1926. Over 150 buffalo were reportedly sacrificed as part of the funeral ceremonies. The tomb is for the clan elders. The nearby village of **Kabunduk** is the important 'origin village' of the local clan and also has some well-carved graves. It is the site of

Pasola: of worms and warriors

This fertility rite involves a battle between massed ranks of horsemen representing two villages. They use (these days blunted by Government order) spears, and the battle can last from morning until nightfall. It not unusually results in serious injury, even death. The pasola is also a ritual 'cleansing'. Anyone injured or killed is deemed to have transgressed against the gods; their injury is believed to be divine retribution, a price that must be paid by the individual to ensure the gods will not wreak revenge on the whole village or its harvest in the coming year. Human blood is the price of atonement. The battle is preceded by other traditional pursuits and ceremonies – traditional boxing (*pajura*), purification rituals, and the nyale ceremony (see below). The date of the pasola is determined by the appearance of the Nyale worms (see page 716) on the shores of the sea a few days after the full moon; their appearance is part of the worms' annual reproductive cycle in which their tails, filled with sperm or eggs, are deposited and are carried to the shore where they are much sought after as ritual food. Prior to the coming of the *Wua Nyale*, the combatants and supporting villagers go to the sacred beach. As the moon rises traditional boxing *pajura* commences; the blood that is spilled also acts as a blood offering to the gods. As dawn breaks, priests from the ancestral village inspect the nyale in order to foretell the coming harvest, the larger the number, the more abundant the crop. Following this the 'pasola' begins and continues for much of the day. The pasola is particularly popular in the districts of Wanokaka (18 km S of Waikabubak), Lamboya and Kodi. The combat itself symbolizes the contest between the upper and lower worlds – between Merapu, the gods of heaven, and Nyale, the goddess of the sea. The duality of male and female, the sky and the earth mirrors the duality so common in the rites and rituals of Nusa Tenggara. **NB** The timing of the festival is decided at the last moment; although the Jakarta-based national tourist office may decide the festival will occur on a certain day, if it does it is pure serendipity.

the largest tomb in Anakalang District, named 'Resi Mona', where the rajas of the district were buried. The layout of this village is typical: in the central space there are graves, a supplementary altar for crops, a village altar and a skull tree; some flat stones indicate the spot where a supplementary altar is placed to serve as the focus at rituals and ceremonies. **Accommodation**: it is possible to stay in one of the traditional houses by the altars which has been converted into a homestay. First see the kepala desa who has an interesting collection of old photographs taken by a Swiss anthropologist, and some ritual heirlooms. **Lai Tarung** – walking distance from Kabunduk – is regarded as an important ceremonial and spiritual centre. There are 10 carved stone pillars on which

sits a 'traditional' house. Reach this hilltop village of the ancestors by following the track uphill at the end of Kabunduk village and on past some houses and tombs. The *Purung Takadonga* ceremony is held here every 2 years to communicate with and honour the spirits of the ancestors of the Merapu religion and commemorate their arrival on Sumba. The priest speaks in the language of the ancestors for several hours; this is followed by dancing, some warlike, as clansmen wave their spears menacingly. From Kabunduk, it is a 20 mins walk to **Matakakeri**, where there is what is touted as being the heaviest megalith in Sumba – weighing 70 tonnes – and erected in 1939 following the death of the King of Anakalang. It is said (these figures are often quoted, but have not been substantiated) that 2,000 men were required to quarry the stone and then move it here, and that three people died in the process. 250 buffalo were slaughtered and 10 tonnes of rice consumed during the burial ritual. *Getting there*: take a bus heading for Lewa/Waingapu or for Anakalang.

Continue on the main road S of Kabunkuk for about 3 km to reach the village of **Galubakul**, site of Sumba's largest tomb (there seems to be considerable competition between the various claimants of the 'largest tomb in Sumba' title) where Umbu Sawola, one of the island's most important rajas, and his wife are buried.

1½ hrs' walk along this road S of Anakalang is the Mata Yangu waterfall with a pool at the base of the 60m drop.

There are many other traditional villages worthy of a visit. The *Artha Hotel* has details of some of these.

Some 40 km to the N of Waikabubak about 7 km inland from Mamboro is one of the oldest traditional hilltop villages, **Manuakalada**. **Mamboro** (market day Sat), on the coast 46 km N of Waikabubak, was a centre of the slave trade which made the local rajas some of the richest in Sumba.

Wanokaka lies 18 km S of Waikabubak and features several traditional villages. The main road S passes through a scenic, hilly landscape with brilliant green ricefields. This is one of the districts where the spectacular annual *Pasola festival* is held (see Festivals below). Nearby, the village of **Prai Goli** or **Paigoli** has one of the finest, best carved, tombs in Sumba. **Sodan**, 25 km SW of Waikabubak where an important New Year festival takes place at the time of the full moon in Oct, is a traditional hilltop village and another important centre of the Merapu religion. This is an area steeped in magic and taboos. Each evening at sunset the sacred drums are struck to call the spirits of the ancestors. One drum was made of human skin but 8 years ago a fire destroyed many of the traditional houses in the village and

the drum; this village is being rebuilt. **Waigalli**, **Pulli** and **Waiwuang** are other traditional villages in the area with carved tombs. *Getting there*: by hire car or motorcycle (see Local transport).

West of Waikabubak

Kodi District offers superb coastal scenery and many beautiful beaches as well as traditional villages and megaliths. En route to **Kodi** district look out for the rice paddies near **Waimangura** (market day Wed) about 28 km W of Waikabubak. Kodi is the main town and market day is also Wed.

Pero near Kodi on the W coast offers some basic accommodation on a spectacular stretch of coast, though the waves can be powerful and swimming is not always for the faint hearted. **Accommodation E** *Losmen Story* on the only street in this village, basic rooms with shared mandi and squat toilet, price incl 3 meals (there is nowhere else to eat in town), best to arrive on Wed, market day in Kodi, when there is an abundance of food; by the following Tues meals in the losmen offer little more than rice and noodles. *Getting there*: to catch the direct bus aim to be at the bus station by 0600, 2½ hrs (2,500Rp); alternatively you can catch a bus to Waitabula 1½ hrs (2,000Rp), then change to a connecting bemo.

There are good walks in the area around Kodi passing traditional villages and megalithic tombs. Follow the beach S to **Ratenggaro**, approximately 5 km, with superb sea views. From this raised village there are more grand views with the picturesque traditional village of **Wainyapu** just across the mouth of the river, easily reached at low tide. **Paronabaroro** is slightly inland enroute to Ratenggaro; here you will find the highest roofs in Sumba, as well as stone tombs and possibly even some women weaving. Going N from Pero follow the path along the coast for about 5 km to reach **Tossi**, the most traditional village in Kodi and one of the sites of the annual

Pasola festival (see Festivals, below). Other traditional villages include **Bondokawango** and **Bukarani**. *Getting there*: all these villages can be reached by road from Kodi if you have your own transport.

Pantai Rua, 26 km, and **Pantai Morossi**, 36 km further W still, are two beaches S of Waikabubak. Pantai Rua is good for surfing. The new *Sumba Reefs Hotel* is currently closed. The surfing at Pantai Morossi is reputed to be even better – the S coastline of Sumba is exposed to the onslaught of the Southern Seas – though both are considered safe for swimming. There are no losmen at Morossi, although it is possible to stay in surrounding villages. *Getting there*: it is easiest to hire a motorcycle, 1-2 hrs (see Local transport). You can go by public bus with a 20-min walk to the beach.

Festivals

Full moon (movable): *Wula Podhu*, a period of fasting, and a festival, held in the village of Tarung just outside Waikabubak. Traditional dances, musical celebrations and sacrifices, ending with an extravagant night of dance and song. The combat itself or *pasola* symbolizes the contest between the upper and lower worlds – between Merapu, the gods of heaven, and Nyale, the goddess of the sea. The duality of male and female, the sky and the earth mirrors the duality so common in the rites and rituals of Nusa Tenggara. For more background to the festival see the box on page 767. *Porung Takadonga* festival takes place every 2 years in Lai Tarung village (see village entry).

Apr/May (moveable): 'Pajura', traditional boxing, sometimes takes place during these months, where the hands are bound with straw and the winner is the first to draw blood, held to commemorate the harvest.

August (17th, public holiday): **Horse racing** takes place once a year to commemorate Independence and lasts a week. The spirited Sumba horses are broken in and ridden for the first time in a muddy 'field'. The mud serves as an anchor and prevents them from bucking wildly. Depending on size, a horse is worth 200,000Rp to 600,000Rp with stallions being worth more than mares. A large buffalo is worth 1-2 million Rp, the price being indicative of its symbolic and ceremonial role in the Merapu religion.

Tours

Hotels can provide guides and transport. Traditional dances can be arranged in Wanokaka (150,000Rp, performance lasts 45 mins), and at Kodi. An entire Pasola with 100 horses can be arranged for 3,400,000Rp, inclusive of the cost of police for security and health insurance for the Pasola team!

Local information
● Accommodation

B *Mona Lisa*, Jl Adyaksa 30, T 21364, roughly 3 km from the centre of town on the road to Waitabula, attractive bungalows with private bathrooms, shower, western toilet, hot water, restaurant (♦♦♦), the hotel provides a bus to the airport, prices highly negotiable off-season; **B-E** *Manandang*, Jl Pemuda 4, T 21197, 21292, 17 rm, the largest hotel in town, incl a new wing and there are plans to build a swimming pool, clean, rooms with private bathrooms, shower and western toilet, first class rooms have hot water, fan and satellite TV, economy rooms with shared mandi, price incl breakfast and tax, restaurant (♦♦) offers an extensive and reasonably priced menu, satellite TV in lobby, car hire available, rec.

C-D *Artha*, Jl Veteran No 11, T 21112, 21676, 16 rm, 10 mins' walk from town centre, this small, new hotel is well-run, clean with very friendly and helpful staff, set around an attractive garden, price incl breakfast and tea all day, restaurant (♦♦) serves good, simple food, the 3 cheapest rooms are the best value in town, all rooms with private bathroom, shower, western toilet, VIP rooms have fan and fridge, Jack the manager and Meno both speak English and are extremely helpful; they can arrange a visit to a local festival, advise on etiquette and explain what is happening, you might become the guest of the headman of the village of Tarung for one of that village's festivals, or you might be invited to a wedding, no fee will be asked but a gift would be in order, photographs of the more interesting villages, beaches and rituals are displayed at the reception desk, satellite TV in lobby, parking, car hire and guides available, highly rec.

D *Rakuta*, Jl Veteran, T 75, shared mandi, rather run down, all meals incl.

D-F *Pelita*, Jl A Yani 2, T 21104, 21392, communal areas and the cheaper rooms with shared mandi are basic and rather depressing, the new more expensive rooms with private mandi (shower and western toilet) are fine once you are inside, restaurant (♦), only stay here if everywhere else is full.

E *Aloha*, Jl Gajah Mada, T 21024, 8 rooms, very popular with budget travellers, clean, 4 cheaper rooms with shared mandi, 4 better rooms with private mandi, all squat toilets, restaurant (♦) good simple food, cars and motorbikes for hire, guide available, rec.

In addition to the above it is possible to stay in almost every village by making arrangements with the kepala desa, and thus gain a fascinating insight into local life and customs. Expect to pay about 10,000Rp/day.

● **Places to eat**
Most visitors eat in their hotels or losmen; the *Manandang* has the best food in town. Alternatively, there are a selection of cheap warungs on Jl Jend A Yani.

● **Airline offices**
Merpati, 1st floor of building, corner Jl Malada and Jl Jend A Yani.

● **Banks & money changers**
Bank Rakyat Indonesia, Jl Gajah Mada.

● **Post & telecommunications**
Post Office: corner Jl Jend A Yani and Jl Sudirman.

● **Shopping**
Art Shop, Jl A Yani 99, has photocopies of a 'book' by two Swedish anthropologists describing local customs, 5,000Rp. Many pieces and jewellery carved in W Sumba's villages from horn, bone, wood and stone, containers for betel nut, religious objects and stone statues.

Many of these objects show examples of local symbolism.

Textiles Ikat is best bought in E Sumba.

● **Transport**
137 km from Waingapu, 47 km from Waikelo.

Local Public transport is irregular but improving all the time. Hiring a car to visit out-of-town sights makes good sense for groups of 4 or more. Most losmen and hotels have vehicles for charter. Examples of return rates are: 15,000Rp to Waikelosawa; 35,000Rp to Wanokaka; 50,000Rp to Lamboya/Sodan and Waitabuta; 60,000Rp to Waikelo; 75,000Rp to Memboro; 85,000Rp to Kodi. A cheaper and equally flexible way to get around is by motorcycle taxi; alternatively, some losmen/hotels are willing to rent out motorbikes by the day (10,000-15,000Rp).

Air The airport is 42 km NW of town at Tambolaka. Merpati operate 3 flights/week to Kupang, $2\frac{1}{2}$ hrs, via Waingapu, and to Bima, 40 mins. There are share minibuses into town.

Road Bus: the terminal is on the SW edge of town, off Jl Jend A Yani. 3 morning departures daily for Waingapu, the first at about 0700, 0800, 1200, 4 hrs. Connections with regional market towns. From Waingapu, passengers are dropped-off at their losmen or hotel; those travelling to Waingapu will be picked-up at their hotel or losmen if given advance warning. There are several bus agents along Jl A Yani where you can buy tickets, arrange hotel pick up and reserve seats; Sumba Mas, Bumi, Indah and Tambora Indah all have newish buses.

Sea Boat: Perentis ships operate out of Waikelo harbour, bound for Larantuka on Flores. The trip takes 8-12 hrs. 60 km from Waikabubak on Sumba's N coast and nr the airport. It is also sometimes possible to hitch a ride on one of the inter-island mixed cargo boats that stop here

Timor

TIMOR is one of the driest islands in the Indonesian Archipelago. The terrain is beautiful but often bleak: rock strewn hills, isolated communities, and poor soils. In the West it is probably most often associated with the Indonesian invasion and annexation of the former Portuguese colony of East Timor in 1975 (see page 782).

Horizons

Administratively, Timor Island is slightly confusing. **West Timor** or **Timor Barat** consists of three districts which constitute part of the province of East Nusa Tenggara: Kupang (centred on the city of Kupang which is also the capital of East Nusa Tenggara), Timor Tengah Selatan and Timor Tengah Utara. The E section of Timor, and a small coastal enclave in West Timor known as Ambeno, is a province in its own right: **East Timor** or **Timor Timur**, formerly Portuguese East Timor.

The districts of West Timor cover a total of 16,500 sq km and have a population of 1.25 million. East Timor covers 14,500 sq km and has a population of about 750,000. The long dry season on both halves of the island stretches from Apr to Oct, with annual rainfall of 1,200 mm – 2,000 mm being concentrated in the months from Nov to Mar. Soils are generally thin and unproductive. Most of the population is concentrated in the slightly wetter interior where cattle raising is the principal occupation. Because

of the Portuguese and Dutch influences, the bulk of the population is Christian: 58% are classified as Protestant, 35% Roman Catholic.

HISTORY

Timor became a focus of European interest because of the valuable aromatic sandalwood that grows here. Formerly an important export of Sumba and Solor as well as Timor, the earliest reference to trade in perfumed sandalwood is contained in the chronicles of the Chanyu Kua Dynasty, written in 1225. The Chinese, sometimes using Javanese intermediaries, probably began buying the wood in the 10th century, perhaps even as early as the 3rd century. Their accounts describe Timor as being covered with sandalwood trees – something that is difficult to believe today.

European contact with the island dates from the early 16th century. The Portuguese may have sighted Timor in 1512 when an expedition was sent from Melaka to seek the famed and fabulously wealthy Spice Islands (see page 797). However, the earliest confirmed European reference to the island is contained in a letter from the Commander of Melaka, dated 6 January 1514. Physical contact with the island dates from 1561 when a Portuguese settlement was established on neighbouring Solor and Dominican friars began to evangelize on Timor. Though much of their time was spent on missionary activity, they also became involved in the sandalwood trade. Other important exports of the period were horses and slaves. It was at this time that the inter-marriage between Portuguese sailors, soldiers and traders from Melaka and Macao with local women laid the foundations for Timor's influential *mestizos* community – locally known as the *Topasses*, from the Dravidian word *tupassi*, meaning 'interpreter'.

The Portuguese began to lose influence to the Dutch at the beginning of the 17th century and the important harbour of Kupang was wrested from the Portuguese in 1637. However, the Dutch showed only a marginal interest in securing this distant colonial possession and the day-to-day administration of the island was left to 62 petty kingdoms, ruled by Catholic princes. Indeed, it was not until 1859 that a treaty was finally ratified determining the boundary between the Dutch and Portuguese territories. Even this agreement was unsatisfactory as it left the status of the Portuguese enclave of Ocussi (now Ambeno), ambiguous. This was not to be resolved until 1905. The friction between the Dutch and the Portuguese provided the basis for the later conflict between Indonesia and East Timor (see page 782).

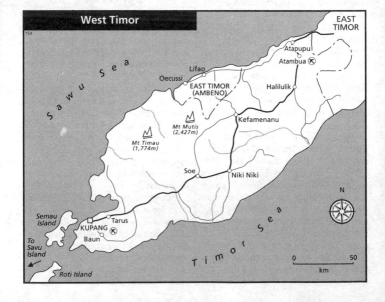

KUPANG

The origins of Kupang are not known, although the name is Timorese for 'Lord', probably referring to the ruler of the area. The Dutch first landed here in 1613, and received a warm welcome from the Kupang. He apparently even expressed an interest in being converted to Christianity. This was not pursued by the Dutch who left, not to return for another 40 years. In 1647 the Portuguese began construction of a fort, which was abandoned before it was completed. 6 years later, the headquarters of the Dutch in Solor were damaged by an earthquake, and they moved their operations to Kupang, building upon the fortifications left by the Portuguese. Kupang was to remain the centre of Dutch influence in the area until independence.

The town was initially focused on Jl Siliwangi, but quickly spread inland from the coast. Today, the city is the capital of the province of East Nusa Tenggara with a population of 120,000, most of them Protestants, and a university (the University of Nusa Cendana, 12 km outside town).

Places of interest

Kupang is not well-endowed with sights. Despite its history, there are virtually no pre-WW2 buildings. Jl Siliwangi, the seafront road (although the sea is usually out of sight), is the bustling heart of the city, as it has been since the Dutch settled here in 1637. Street salesmen and women market traditional herbal and spiritual cures, and there is a **market** at the E end of the street (where it becomes Jl Garuda). To the W of Jl Siliwangi, the coast road crosses **Air Mata**. This is the small river where Captain Bligh landed after his extraordinary 7,000 km, 41-day voyage in an open boat from the spot near Tonga in the Pacific where the mutineers on his ship *HMS Bounty* set him and his supporters adrift. Walking further W along the road, past the army barracks and church, are good views of the coast and the islands beyond. This was the site of the Dutch **Fort Concordia** built in 1653. Back in town and close to the Kota Kupang bemo terminal at Jl Soekarno 23, is a fine and well-maintained **Dutch church**, orginally constructed in 1873. It is simple and pure in conception, barring the ornate porchway.

About 4 km out of town, 300m from the long-distance bus terminal, is the **Museum of Nusa Tenggara Timur**. The exhibits are well displayed, but less well explained. The collection includes textiles, ceramics, traditional weapons and ethnographic pieces. Notable is the fine bronze Dongson (Vietnamese) drum (see page 377), collected on Alor, with its frogs symbolizing and promoting rain, along with the bronze *moko* dowry vessels, also from Alor (see box, page 753). The ikat process is illustrated with the use of a series of models and sets. Admission by donation. Open 0800-1400 Mon-Thur, 0800-1100 Fri, 0800-1230 Sat. *Getting there*: take a bemo from the city centre to Walikota (300Rp).

Excursions

Lasiana Beach lies 12 km E of Kupang, and is quiet during weekdays. At weekends it becomes popular as a picnic spot for locals. *Warungs* and drinks vendors operate on the beach and at the W end of the beach there is a small plateau where there are good views over Kupang Bay. Admission to beach: 400Rp. **Accommodation D** *Lasiana Beach Cottage*, not always open, attached bathrooms, rather grubby. *Getting there*: take a bemo heading for Tarus and ask to be let off at the entrance to the beach (300Rp).

Baun lies 30 km from Kupang and is a weaving town; the processes of ikat can be seen, although the quality of the work produced is variable. Visitors have recommended *Ibu Raja* as producing the best cloth. There is a **market** in Baun on Sat (from 0700). *Getting there*: take a bemo from the Kota Kupang terminal in town to Sikumana terminal (300Rp) and from

Kupang

Hotels:
1. Astiti
2. Backpackers
3. Cendana
4. Eden
5. Fatuleu Homestay
6. Flobamor II
7. Laguna Inn, Kelimutu & Adian
8. L'avalon Backpackers
9. Losmen Susi
10. Marina
11. Maya
12. New Orchid
13. Timor Beach

Places to eat:
14. Garnda Tomor
15. Happy Café
16. Karang Mas (Bar)
17. Palembang
18. Teddy's Bar

there another bemo to Baun (500Rp).

Semau Island is good for swimming and snorkelling but is best reached on a tour (see Tours) as there are no regular ferries. There is talk of running game-fishing boats (marlin) from the island, the season stretching from Mar-Sep. **Accommodation C** *Uiasa Beach Cottages*, attached mandi, price includes three meals; and *Flobamor II Cottages* (book through *Flobamor II Hotel* in Kupang, see below). *Getting there*: if not on a tour, catch a bemo bound for Bolok or Tenau (300Rp) from the Kota Kupang terminal and get off at Pantai (Beach) Namosain, SW of town. Boats can sometimes be hired from here for the trip to Semau (45 mins).

Sandalwood factory is open to visitors, lies 3 km N of town at Bakunase. *Getting there*: direct bemos to Bakunase from Terminal Kota (300Rp).

Tours

There are a number of well-organized tour and travel companies in Kupang. They offer city tours (US$17/person), tours to the weaving village of Baun (US$22/person), Lesiana Beach tours (US$15/person) and a number of other day trips (all these are prices for three people). They also arrange longer tours to destinations on Timor and the other islands of East Nusa Tenggara (Flores, Alor, Komodo, Sumba etc). *Teddy's Bar and Restaurant*, also run a less formal tour service, with day snorkelling tours to Semau Island (17,000Rp) departing 1000, Rote Island surfing safaris, city tours, fishing and camping expeditions.

Local information
● **Accommodation**

A *New Orchid*, Jl Fatuleu (facing the *Fatuleu Homestay*), T 33707, F 33669, a/c, restaurant, pool, central location, very clean, best in town; **A** *Sasando*, Jl Perintis Kemerdekaan 1,

T 22224, a/c, restaurant, pool, tennis, good views, but out of town nr bus terminal.

B *Flobamor II*, Jl Jend Sudirman 21, T 21346, a/c, hot water, comfortable but over-priced; **B-D** *Marina*, Jl Jend A Yani 79, T 22566, some a/c, small, friendly, central, price incl breakfast, cheaper rooms without attached bathrooms, rather gloomy.

C *Astiti*, Jl Jend Sudirman 96, T 21810, a/c, good mid-range hotel, well-run, expansion underway, rooms at front noisy, 3 km from town centre; **C** *Kelimutu*, Jl Gunung Kelimutu 38 (close to *Laguna Hotel*), T 31179, some a/c, clean and quiet, price incl breakfast and lunch or dinner; **C-D** *Cendana*, Jl Raya El Tari 23, T 21541, some a/c, some distance out of town nr the Kantor Gubernor, but regular bemos into city centre, nice garden atmosphere, popular, price incl breakfast, rec; **C-D** *Laguna*, Jl Gunung Kelimutu 36, T 21559, some a/c, painted entirely in a wonderful green, on a quiet side street but central, clean with good bathrooms, rec; **C-D** *Maliana*, Jl Sumatra 35, T 21879, clean, spacious rooms with fans, with mandi and western toilet en suite, friendly management, rec; **C-D** *Maya*, Jl Sumatra 31, T 32169, some a/c, good rooms and good value, garden, on sea front but still central, more expensive rooms with hot water, popular so often full, price incl breakfast, rec; **C-D** *Susi*, Jl Sumatra 37, T 22172, some a/c, on seafront but still central, undergoing expansion; **C-D** *Timor Beach*, Jl Sumatra (nr *Maya Hotel*), T 31651, some a/c, on seafront but still central, rooms are dirty and the hotel is poorly maintained, but position is some recompense.

D *Adian*, Jl; Kelimutu 40, T 21913, popular with Indonesians, good position; **D** *Fatuleu Homestay*, Jl Fatuleu 1, T 31374, quiet street in garden atmosphere, clean, and central, rec.

E *Losmen Safariah*, Jl Moh Hatta 34, T 21595, rooms only average, attached mandi, reasonable location.

F *Backpackers*, Jl Kancil 37B, Airnona (about 7 km from town centre but there are regular bemos), T 31291, clean, very popular, quiet and peaceful, good for information, price incl breakfast, rec; **F** *Eden*, Jl Kancil, Airnona, 7 km from town centre, regular bemos, T 21921, thatched bungalows in peaceful location, wonderful trees, but rooms shabby and poorly maintained, price incl breakfast; **F** *Losmen Isabella*, Jl Gunung Mutis 21, T 21407, central (just off Jl Siliwangi), but dirty; **F** *L'avalon Backpackers*, Jl Sumatra 1 No 8, T 32278, quiet, friendly place, with lots of travellers' information, but basic, price incl breakfast, tea and coffee.

● **Places to eat**

Local specialities incl *daging s'ei* (smoked beef).

Indonesian: ♦♦*Hemaliki*, Jl Soekarno, attractive garden and restaurant serving Indonesian, Chinese, seafood and Japanese; ♦*Bundo Kanduang*, Jl Jend Sudirman 49, Padang; ♦*Depot Makan Hattuba*, Jl Moh Hatta 54; ♦*Garuda Timor*, good food, clean restaurant, good value; ♦*Happy Café*, Jl Ikan Paus 3 (nr the bemo terminal), large portions of freshly cooked Indonesian and Chinese dishes, excellent value; ♦*Ibu Soekardjo*, Jl Moh Hatta 23, Indonesian; ♦*Tunggal Dara*, Jl Siliwangi (facing the market square), Indonesian dishes, hardly refined but one of the cheapest places to eat – 1,000Rp for *ikan bakar*, also serves *jeruk panas* (warm orange juice); ♦♦*Lumintu*, Jl Garuda 1 (by the market square), Indonesian, good and cheap *ikan bakar* (barbecue fish); ♦♦*Palembang*, Jl Mohammed Hatta 54 (nr the general hospital on bemo route 2), serves a wide range of excellent Chinese and Indonesian dishes, very popular and very good.

Chinese: ♦♦*Lima Jaya Raya*, Jl Soekarno 15, clean, reasonably priced, good range of dishes, Chinese, crab specialities; ♦♦*Mandarin*, Jl Jend Sudirman 148 (next to *Astiti Hotel* and intersection with Jl Harimau), good, simple, Chinese, rec; *Hemaliki*, Jl Soekarno good, cheap Chinese and seafood.

International: ♦♦*Teddy's Bar & Restaurant*, Jl Ikan Tongkol 1-3, western, seafood, lobsters, steak, live music.

Seafood: ♦♦*Timor Beach*, Jl Sumatra, seafood, overlooking beach.

● **Bars**

Teddy's Bar, Jl Ikan Tongkol 1-3, live music, popular with westerners, pricey. *Karang Mas*, Jl Siliwangi 84/88, one of the best places to watch the sunset clutching a cold beer, the bar has a terrace overlooking a small beach, small menu of mediocre food. *Pantai Bar*, *Timor Beach Hotel*, JL Sumatra, bar overlooking the sea, another place to watch the sunset over Kupang Bay.

● **Airline offices**

Bouraq, Jl Jend Sudirman 20A, T 21421; Garuda/Merpati, Jl Kosasih 13, T 21205.

● **Banks & money changers**

Bank Dagang Negara, Jl Soekarno 10, change most TCs and currencies; Bank Rakyat Indonesia, Jl Soekarno, Danamon, Jl Jend Sudirman 21, change most TCs in US$ and A$, plus major currencies cash;

● **Hospitals & medical services**
Hospitals: *General Hospital*, Jl Moh Hatta.

● **Post & telecommunications**
Area code: 0391.

General Post Office: Jl Palapa (out of centre).

Post Office: Jl Soekarno 29 (more convenient).

Perumtel: Jl Palapa. **Telephone Office**, Jl Urip Sumohardjoll.

● **Shopping**
Books: *Istana Beta Bookshop* on Jl Jend A Yani 58 (past the *Marina Hotel*) has town maps.

Crafts: *Loka Binkra Crafts Centre* is on the road to the airport, just before the 8 Km marker. Catch a bemo bound for Tarus or Penfui (200Rp).

Textiles: Kupang is a centre for the sale of Nusa Tenggara Timur ikat, but it is highly variable in quality. For *tenunan asli* (cloth woven from home-grown and spun cotton and coloured with natural dyes) expect to pay 150,000Rp upwards. Wrap-around sarong blankets or *selimut* worn by men are decorated with bright, bold geometric and stylized animal and bird motifs. Try: *Toko Dharma Bakti*, Jl Sumba, or the house (21D) on the side street off Jl Soekarno nr the 5 *Jaya Raya Restaurant*.

● **Tour companies & travel agents**
Natrabu, Jl Gunung Mutis 18, T 21095; *Pitoby Tours*, Jl Jend Sudirman 118, T 21443, F 31044, branch at Jl Siliwangi 75, T 21222; *Varanus*, Jl Perintis Kemerdekaan.

● **Tourist offices**
Kantor Pariwisata Parpostel, Jl Soekarno 29 (next to Post Office), central location but next to useless; **Provincial Tourist Office**, Jl Basuki Rakhmat 1, T 21540, 5 km from town off Jl Soeharto, catch a bemo travelling towards Baun and ask for Kantor Gubernor Lama, the turning is just past the Pentecostal Chapel, some useful handouts, open 0700-1400 Mon-Thur, 0700-1100 Fri, 0700-1230 Sat; **Tourist Information Desk**, Jl Soekarno 25 (next to church), helpful and convenient source of information, especially for independent travellers.

● **Useful addresses**
Immigration Office: Jl Soekarno 16, T 21077.

● **Transport**
110 km from Soe, 283 km from Atambua.

Local Bemos: there are a huge number of bemos, which must be among the noisiest and most ostentatious in Indonesia with names like James Bond and Givenchy (300Rp). Routes are marked over the roof, and most ply between the city bemo terminal (Terminal Kota Kupang) at the end of Jl Soekarno nr the intersection with Jl Siliwangi, and the out-of-town bus terminal, Walikota. A board at Terminal Kota Kupang gives all routes and fares.

Selected bus fares		
KUPANG to:		
Soe	2½ hrs	3,000Rp
Dili	13 hrs	15,000Rp
Atambua	6 hrs	8,000Rp
(Late 1995 fares)		

Air   Kupang's El Tari international airport is 14 km NE of town. **Transport to town**: taxis into the centre of town (7,500Rp). **NB** Taxi drivers encourage tourists to go to hotels of their choice, saying others are full – they receive a commission. Try to ask at reception without the taxi driver in company. Airport taxi service T 33824. Bemos running between Penfui/Baumata and town (300Rp) pass the airport turn off – it is a 1½-km walk from the airport buildings to this spot. Connections by Merpati and Bouraq with Jakarta, Dili and Bali, and other destination in Java, Sulawesi, Nusa Tenggara, Irian Jaya and Kalimantan. **International connections** with Darwin, Australia.

Road   Bus: the long-distance Oebobo bus terminal, better known as Walikota, is some way E of town. Regular bemos run between it, along different routes, and the central bemo terminal at the end of Jl Siliwangi. Buses from Oebobo to Baun, Bolok, Baumata, Tarus Kejamenanu 5 hrs, Soe 2½ hrs, Niki Niki 3 hrs, Atambua 7 hrs and Dili 13 hrs, with change of bus at Atambua. *Natrans*, who run buses to Dili via Atambua have a counter at the terminal; *Tunas Mekar*, who run night buses to Dili sell tickets at Jl Siliwangi 94 (nr the Terminal Kota bemo station).

Sea   Boat: Kupang's Tenau harbour is SW of town. Catch a bemo bound for Tenau or Bolok. The Pelni ships *Dobonsolo* and *Binaiya* visit Kupang on their 2 week circuits (see route schedule, page 921). The Pelni office is at Jl Pahlawan 3, T 21944 (5 mins walk W of Jl Siliwangi; a new building off, but visible from, the road). There are also a number of ferries serving surrounding ports and islands; these leave from the Bolok ferry terminal, a few kms further on from Tenau. Catch a bemo bound for Bolok (500Rp). The ferry office (Perum Angkutan Sungai, Danau dan Penyeberangan) is at Jl Cak Doko 20, T 21140. Ferry services are as follows: Kupang-Ba'a (Rote) 0900 (3,700Rp) Mon, Wed,

Fri and Sat (returning same day); Kupang-Ende (Flores) 1400 Mon and 1300 Tues (returning Wed), (about 18 hrs, ventilation in economy reportedly better than 1st class); Kupang-Larantuka (Flores) 1500 (11,450Rp) Sun and Thur (returning Tues and Sat); Kupang-Savu 1600 (11,900Rp) Wed (returning Thur); Kupang-Kalabahi (Alor) 1400 (14,900Rp) Mon (returning Tues).

International connections Air With Darwin, Australia on Merpati. No visa required for entering Timor as it is a 'gateway' port (this applies to nationals of those countries permitted visa-free entry), but you must have an onward ticket out of Indonesia or US$1,000. Flights from Darwin are usually not too booked up.

SOE

Soe is the cool, spread out capital of the regency of Timor Tengah Selatan, lying 800m above sea-level. During the coldest months of Jun and Jul it can be chilly and a sweater is needed during the day – it is always cool at night. The town is best-known for the large regional market held here every day of the week but on the whole the place cannot be said to ooze character.

Excursions The countryside around Soe represents the heartland of West Timorese culture. Typical villages can be found along the Soe-Kefamenanu road. There are also beautiful, traditional villages on the Soe-Kupang road, 20 km from Soe. *Getting there*: it is possible simply to hop on and off public buses. A better, though more expensive alternative, is to hire a car (40,000Rp/day) – see Local transport.

- **Accommodation C-D** *Bahagia*, Jl Diponegoro 72, good restaurant, some rooms have their own mandi; **D-E** *Mahkota Plaza*, Jl Suharto 11 (nr the bus station), T 21168, restaurant, new and reasonably comfortable, friendly and helpful staff, attached bathrooms, the hotel manager, Anton, speaks reasonable English and is a good source of information on Soe and the surrounding area; **E** *Sejati*, Jl Gajah Mada 18, T 101; **F** *Anda*, Jl Kartini 5, very friendly.

- **Transport** 111 km from Kupang, 86 km from Kefamenanu, 172 km from Atambua. **Local Car hire**: (40,000Rp/day). Ask Anton at the *Mahkota Hotel* to arrange it. **Road Bus**: regular connec-

tions with Kupang 2½ hrs, Kefamenanu 2 hrs, and Atambua 3½ hrs. For Dili it is necessary to go via either Kupang or Atambua.

KEFAMENANU

Kefamenanu is the capital of the regency of Timor Tengah Utara. Like Soe, this is a highland town, at an altitude of 500m, with chilly nights. During Jun and Jul, the coldest months, a sweater may be needed throughout the day. The town has simple accommodation and can be used as a base to explore the surrounding countryside.

Excursions The area around Kefamenanu is rarely visited by tourists. There are numerous **traditional villages** and towns including **Maslete** (4 km S) and **Nilulat** (at 1,300m).

Festivals Nov 30: *Culture and Art Festival*. Traditional dances, music, food and handicrafts on show and on sale.

- **Accommodation C-D** *Cendana*, Jl Sonbay, T 168, some a/c, breakfast incl, new losmen; **E** *Ariesta*, Jl Basuki Rakhmat 29, T 7, restaurant, large rooms; **E** *Sederhana*, Jl Pattimura; **E** *Sokowindu*, Jl Kartini, T 122, breakfast incl, friendly, rec; **E** *Victory*, Jl Kartini.

- **Transport** 197 km from Kupang, 86 km from Soe, 86 km from Atambua. **Road Bus**: regular connections with Soe 2 hrs, Kupang 4½ hrs, Atambua 1½ hrs, and Dili.

LIFAO AND THE AMBENO ENCLAVE

The Ambeno Enclave is administratively part of East Timor and Lifao is the largest town. In fact, it used to be the capital of Portuguese East Timor, until Lisbon, in 1769, decided Dili – largely for defensive reasons – would be more suitable. From that date Lifao languished in obscurity, which it still continues to do. The ruins of the former governor of East Timor's residence occupy the hill of Fatsuba. In fact the town is charming in its decrepitude, and the legacies of the Portuguese period are still in evidence.

- **Accommodation E** *Aneka Jaya*, Jl Soekarno (on the beach front), small, pleasant hotel with clean but basic rooms and friendly management.

● **Transport Road Bus**: connections with Atambua (and from there with Kupang or Dili) and with Kefamenanu.

ATAMBUA

The town of Atambua, the second largest in West Timor (after Kupang), is set at an altitude of 500m and is the last significant settlement before crossing from West Timor into the province of East Timor. The heart of the town is just 200m from the bus terminal. The market area is close to the terminal, and there is also a good range of restaurants, hotels, shops and supermarkets. Atambua's port of Atapupu is 24 km N of town. Travellers going by bus between Kupang and Dili have to change here.

Excursions Atapupu, Atambua's port 24 km N of town is little more than a fishing village and is worth visiting if there is time to kill. The coast here is protected by mangroves and local people extract salt from seawater using ancient brick ovens. *Getting there*: by bus from the terminal.

● **Accommodation C** *Intan*, Jl Merdeka 13, some a/c, new hotel in centre of town, clean rooms with attached bathrooms, rates incl breakfast – best available; **D** *Kalpataru*, Jl Jend Subroto 3, T 351; **D** *Nusantara*, Jl Sukarno 4, T 117, very friendly, reasonable rooms with attached bathrooms, breakfast incl in room rate, not far from bus terminal and market, also within reach of town centre; **E** *Klaben*, Jl Dubosinanaet 4, T 79; **E** *Liurai*, Jl Satsuitubun 12, T 84; **E** *Sahabat*, Jl Merdeka 7; **F** *Minang*, Jl Sukarno 12A, T 135, clean and central.

● **Transport** 283 km from Kupang, 173 km from Soe, 86 km from Kefamenanu. **Air** Merpati run 1 flight/week from Atambua to Kupang and Dili. **Road Bus**: regular connections with Atapopo 45 mins, Kupang 6 hrs, Soe 3½ hrs, Kefamenanu 1½ hrs, and Dili 4 hrs. **Sea Boat**: Pelni operate a ship which circuits between Kupang and Dili via Atapupu (Atambua's port), 24 km N of town.

ROTI

Roti Island, just off the SW tip of Timor, is administered as part of the regency of Kupang. It covers 1,214 sq km and has a population of nearly 100,000. The capital is the town of **Ba'a**, on the N coast.

Like Savu, the lontar palm is the traditional subsistence crop here (see page 779), although rice is increasingly cultivated. The tradition of making working clothes from the fibres of the lontar palm has now died out, but some people still continue to make shrouds for the dead from the fibres. At birth, each Rotinese baby is given, when it cries, a drop of Roti sugar – presumably indicating the former importance of the lontar palm to the islanders' collective livelihoods.

Namberala (or Dela) village, on the W coast, about 35 km from Ba'a, is close to the main surfing beach and there are a handful of homestays here for the really adventurous surfer. The best months for surfing are reputed to be from Apr to Sep. The villages both NE and SW from Ba'a are worth visiting for their markets and traditional architecture. *Getting there*: there is a direct bus from Pante Baru (the port) to Namberala on Tues and Fri, or hire a car or motorcycle for the day. **Oeseli Beach**, 58 km SW from Ba'a is good for swimming.

Island Information
● **Accommodation**
At Ba'a: **D** *Ricky's*, nr the mosque, some a/c. There are a number of other cheaper losmen.

At **Namberala**: **E-F** *Mr Thomas Homestay*, room rate incl all meals (and good ones) as well as tea, coffee and drinking water.

● **Shopping**
Textiles: the Rotinese produce a distinctive ikat, which is strongly influenced by *patola* cloth – Gujarati cloth from India which was imported in large quantities from the 16th century. Patola motifs – floral designs, diagonal crosses – were incorporated into the traditional textiles of the island, as they were through much of Nusa Tenggara. Cloth is often decorated with flower motifs using red, white, brown and black hues.

Unfortunately, there are few weavers left on Roti now – many of the local people have left the island, seeking work in Kupang – and it is becoming hard to find good cloth.

● **Transport**

Local Bemos and buses ply the main roads but not regularly. It is best, though, to hire a motorcycle, bemo or car for the day (ask at losmen).

Air Two flights/week on Merpati from Kupang; the service is unreliable.

Sea Boat: the ferry dock is at Pante Baru, about 30 km NE of Ba'a; bemos wait to take passengers to the capital. Pelni Perintis vessels leave Kupang every day at 0900, returning the same day at about 1400, 4 hrs (4,500Rp).

SAVU

Savu Island, over 250 km W of Kupang, is still part of the regency of Kupang. The island covers 460 sq km and supports a population of about 50,000 people, predominantly Protestants. The 'capital' of the island is the town of **Seba**, which has an airport and a dock. The dry season here extends over 7 months (Apr-Oct), sometimes longer, and the rains are intermittant. It is a dry, barren and unproductive island.

Traditionally, the slow-growing lontar palm (*Borassus sundaicus*) has met the subsistence needs of the population. The sap from this tree, known as *tuak*, is both drunk fresh and boiled into a sugary syrup (*gula air*). The fruit of the tree is eaten, and its wood and leaves are used for thatching and, in the past, for cloth and paper.

The women of Savu produce a distinct warp ikat cloth. It is said that about 300 years ago the people of Savu were divided into two distinct clans – the Greater Blossoms (*Hubi'Ae*) and the Lesser Blossoms (*Hubi'Ike*) – based on female blood lines. Within each clan there were several subgroups called Seeds (*Wini*). Each group wove distinctive motifs on their cloth and even today, local people can recognize cloth and its origin by its clan motif.

Island Information

● **Accommodation**

Basic accommodation in Seba.

E *Makarim Homestay*; **E** *Ongko Da'i Homestay*; **E** *Petykuswan Homestay*.

● **Shopping**

Textiles: a distinctive warp ikat cloth is handwoven on Savu, in bands of floral and geometric designs, set against a dark indigo and rust ground. The Savunese sarung is known as the *si hawu*, while the *higi huri* is a blanket. Men's clothing has tended to keep more faithfully to traditional designs, while women have been happy to incorporate western-inspired motifs such as vases of flowers, birds and rampant lions.

● **Transport**

Air 2 flights/week on Merpati from Kupang to Seba town; the service is unreliable.

Sea Boat: boats dock at Seba on the N coast. There is a weekly Pelni Perintis vessel from Kupang leaving on Wed at 1600 and returning to Kupang on Thur, 8 hrs (11,900Rp). Once a week, on Fri, a ferry docks from Waingapu (Sumba), returning to Waingapu and then continuing on to Ende (Flores) (10-15,000Rp). There are also other, irregular, departures from Kupang's Tenau harbour.

The lontar palm from G.E. Rumphius' *Het Amboinsche Kruydboek* (1741), labelled (A) a leafstalk; (B) a female inflorescence with young fruit; (C) the fruit; (D) three seeds; and (E) a male inflorescence with tiny flowers.

EAST TIMOR

The former Portuguese colony of East Timor was invaded by Indonesian forces in Dec 1975, and annexed in 1976 – to become the country's 27th province. It is this event for which East Timor is best remembered in the West and for the Indonesian government it seems to be an issue which simply won't go away. In Nov 1991, a British camera crew coincidentally captured a massacre of East Timorese demonstrators at the cemetery of Santa Cruz on film, rekindling the West's interest in this remote territory (see page 783). In 1994, a large group of foreign journalists were given a guided tour of the province. To the government's intense annoyance, rather than – as the *Economist* put it – being a trip with the theme of 'forget the killing, look at these nice new roads', there was a sequence of demonstrations by people willing to confront the authorities, and risk a heavy price. The commander of Indonesian forces in the province, General Adang Ruchiatna, was quoted as saying the East Timorese seemed 'ungrateful' for all the money lavished on the province by the authorities, and feared a renewed civil war should the army withdraw. As the *Economist* concluded, "Almost 20 years after Indonesian troops first entered East Timor, this is a sorry comment on their efforts at integration". During 1995 and 1996 East Timor continued to occupy column inches in newspapers in the West – the one thing the government has been so anxious to avoid.

East Timor is known locally as *Tim-Tim*, the shortened version of the Indonesian name for the province: Timor Timur. It covers a total of 14,500 sq km and has a population of about 800,000. By a quirk of colonial history, the province encompasses not only the E half of Timor Island but also a small coastal enclave in the W, known as Ambeno (formerly Oecussi, covered in this book in the West Timor section). The province is divided into 13 districts, two of which are in the W.

HISTORY

The Colonial Period (1701-1975)

East Timor became an official colony of Portugal in 1701 when a governor was appointed and placed under the control of the Viceroy of Goa, over 6,000 km away on the W coast of India. Before that date, Dominican friars were busy converting the East Timorese to Roman Catholicism, while making fortunes from the sandalwood trade. Most historians rate the moral rectitude of these priests as very low. Even after the appointment of a governor, control over East Timor was lax. In 1750 there were just eight white Portu-

East Timor

Savu Sea

Tutuala
Los Palos
Desa Rasa
Mt Matedia (2,315m)
Baucau
Viqueque
Manatuto
DILI
Aileu
Maubessi
Ermera
Maubara
Mt Tata Mai Lau (2,963m)
Ainaro
Same
Maliana
Suai
Batugede
Mt Toromon
Atambua
WEST TIMOR

Timor Sea

0   35
km

guese in the territory, and control really lay with the local chiefs, the Dominican friars, and the so-called 'Black Portuguese' – the descendants of Portuguese soldiers, merchants and sailors who had had children by local women.

During the early years of Portuguese 'rule', the capital of East Timor was the port of Lifao, in the enclave of Ambeno. It was only moved to Dili in 1769 when rebels took Lifao forcing the governor and his supporters to flee N. The boundaries between Dutch and Portuguese Timor were not finally demarcated until 1914. Foreign visitors who bothered to venture to East Timor during the early decades of this century invariably either derided Portuguese colonial rule or treated the administration with amused disdain. Officialdom was languid and ineffective, and the country was the most underdeveloped and primitive colony in all Southeast Asia. Incredibly, on the eve of WW2, East Timor's capital – Dili – had no electricity, no water supply, no paved roads, and no telephones.

In Feb 1942 the Japanese Imperial Army landed an army of 20,000 men in Dili and occupied the colony. A small force of 300 Australians of the 2/2nd and 2/4th Independent Companies fought a remarkably successful guerrilla campaign killing 1,500 Japanese and losing only 40 men themselves before withdrawing in Jan 1943. It is acknowledged as one of the finest episodes of the Allied war in Southeast Asia. But the battle for East Timor caused considerable suffering among the East Timorese. After the Australians were evacuated, the Japanese exacted a terrible revenge on the many locals who had provided support. The population of the territory declined from 472,000 in 1930 to 403,000 by 1946.

After the capitulation of the Japanese at Kupang in Sep 1945, East Timor returned to Portuguese control. The most that can be said of the Portuguese stewardship of East Timor is that they converted about half of the population to

Roman Catholicism (or nominal Roman Catholicism), and introduced some elements of Portuguese cuisine and culture. Otherwise, the authorities in Lisbon effectively ignored what was to them an insignificant colonial backwater.

Indonesia's independence leaders differed over East Timor's status. The radical politician Mohammad Yamin in May 1945 stated that like N Borneo, East Timor should "come within the control and complete unity of the State of Indonesia", noting that they were "not only physically part of us but have been inhabited by Indonesian people since history began, forming part of our motherland". In contrast, Mohammad Hatta, who was later to become Vice-President, was actively opposed to any incorporation. Overall, most Indonesian leaders did not support expansionism and the incorporation of East Timor.

The 1975 invasion and annexation

"50,000 people or perhaps 80,000 people might have been killed during the war in East Timor... It was war... Then what is the big fuss?" (Adam Malik, Foreign Minister of Indonesia, 30 March 1977).

In 1974 the rightist dictatorship in Lisbon was overthrown, paving the way for East Timor's decolonization. Three political groups emerged in the colony: the Social-Democratic Association of East Timor or ASDT, which was middle-of-the-road and supported a decolonization period of 5 years; the Timorese Democratic Union or UDT, a conservative party favouring continued Portuguese stewardship; and the Popular Democratic Association of Timorese or Apodeti which supported the incorporation of East Timor into Indonesia.

The third party was by far the weakest. In late 1974, Gough Whitlam, the Prime Minister of Australia, appeared to indicate that he would not oppose annexation – or at least this is the way the Indonesian military chose to interpret his comments. The US administration also seemed reconciled to Indonesian intervention. US Ambassador Newsom was reported as saying that his country hoped Indonesia should preferably do so "effectively, quickly and not use our [military] equipment". At the same time, the UDT changed its stance to one of independence from Portugal, while the ASDT changed its name to Fretilin, the Revolutionary Front for an Independent East Timor, and became more overtly revolutionary.

By late 1974, fears of an Indonesian invasion were growing while the authorities in Jakarta fermented stories of a 'reign of terror' in Dili. Independent journalists found no evidence to support such claims. On 11 August 1975 the UDT staged a coup in Dili. Fighting erupted between the UDT and Fretilin and thousands of East Timorese fled into West Timor. By Sep, Fretilin had emerged as victors in the civil war which had caused

The massacre at Santa Cruz, November 1991

Although the Indonesian government had some reason to believe that Fretilin was on the verge of defeat and the desire of the population of E Timor for independence almost extinguished, recent events have underscored the degree to which E Timorese still hanker for self-rule. In Nov 1991, during the funeral of a man allegedly killed by Indonesian forces, the army opened fire on mourners at Santa Cruz Cemetery in Dili. Not surprisingly, accounts are greatly at odds. Locals and Fretilin sympathizers, supported by eight foreign journalists who were also present at the cemetery, claim that the army opened fire without warning on a peaceful demonstration of 2,000-3,000 E Timorese, resulting in the death of between 50 and 100 mourners. One journalist, Amy Goodman of Pacific Radio Network, was reported as saying: "The Timorese didn't do anything to the troops. They just chanted *Viva Timor L'este*. These were truly defenceless people". The commander-in-chief of the Indonesian army General Try Sutrisno, by contrast, claimed that the army opened fire only after his men had been attacked, and that they seized many grenades, guns and knives. They also claim that only a handful of demonstrators were killed.

The film of the massacre was shown across the world and provoked international condemnation. The Indonesian government responded by setting-up an independent commission which published its findings in Dec 1991, confirming that 50 demonstrators had, indeed, been killed. The commission also placed blame on the army for excessive use of force. President Suharto sacked the two most senior commanders with operational control in the province, and ordered a military commission to investigate the matter. This commission published its results in Mar 1992, disciplining six officers and calling for the court martial of eight other soldiers. Although many observers believed that the two reports failed to uncover the whole truth, they were unprecedented in Indonesian political history. They also did just enough to deflect international criticism – for the time being at least. With the Cold War at an end, the western powers have been less restrained in their criticism of human rights abuses in pro-western countries. Significantly, however, in June 1992, it was reported by the human rights group Asia Watch that several of the demonstrators at Santa Cruz had been jailed for 10 years or more. In contrast Indonesian soldiers who fired on, and killed, the demonstrators have received sentences of 20 months, or less. At the end of 1992, General Syajei, who took over the East Timor command after the massacre, bragged that had he been in charge many more would have been killed. A strange way to win hearts and minds.

the death of 1,500-3,000 people. Their cause lost, the leaders of the UDT fled into Indonesian territory, whereupon the Indonesian government claimed they were pro-integrationist.

On the 7 December 1975, Indonesian forces invaded Dili, although the official Indonesian view is still that they were 'invited' in. The brutality of the invasion and its aftermath was verified by most journalists who witnessed it, and by independent scholars. Indonesian troops quickly gained control of the capital.

In Apr, the UN Security Council passed a resolution reaffirming East Timor's right to self-determination. The question is why did not the West do more to draw attention to the Indonesian annexation. Various explanations have been offered – although many would argue that they hardly amount to a justification. At the time, the West was preoccupied with the American withdrawal from Vietnam and the US, the countries of western Europe and Japan abstained in the vote. South Vietnam had just fallen to the N Vietnamese Communists, as too had Cambodia. America found its geo-political interests to be at odds with supporting a revolutionary party like Fretilin, especially as Indonesia was gradually becoming more pro-western. Even Portugal was in no state to offer support to its former colony, having just experienced political upheaval itself. In turn, the Indonesian government claimed that it could not live with a revolutionary state on its doorstep, noting that just a decade earlier they had had to contend with their own Communist-inspired coup. The fact that East Timor's population was 200 times smaller than Indonesia's seemed to make no difference.

East Timor: Indonesia's youngest province 1976-1990 From 1975 until 1990, East Timor was sealed to the outside world, while the Indonesian army quashed the secessionist threat. Despite East Timor's small population, Fretilin

has managed to sustain a long-term insurgency. Since the annexation, an estimated 100,000-200,000 East Timorese have died – either from violence or neglect – out of a population of only 750,000. At its worst, more than a quarter of the population may have been killed – a figure which puts East Timor on a par with Cambodia during the terrible Pol Pot years. The Indonesian government has always disputed the figures, Ali Alatas the foreign minister saying, for example, that they are without "a shred of evidence or factual underpinning". Unfortunately for the authorities, at the beginning of 1994 the governor of East Timor, Abilio Soares stated that he thought they were "probably true". Doubtless the numbers game will continue with few in the wider international community at least believing the Indonesian side of the story.

During the period of 'occupation' (the UN has still not recognized Indonesia's annexation of East Timor and marks it as a separate country on maps), an estimated 60,000 soldiers, policemen and informants have tried to keep the peace: one for every 10 East Timorese. But despite this (relatively) massive military presence, few foreign observers dispute that East Timor's pro-independence movement is far from dead. The reluctance of the Indonesian government to countenance any sort of plebiscite illustrates that they must have a good idea how most people would vote.

In Nov 1992 the government scored a considerable coup with the capture of Fretilin leader Xanana Gusmão. Gusmão was tried in Dili in May 1994, and on the 21st of the month the High Court judge presiding found the resistance leader guilty of a series of charges ranging from disrupting national stability to possession of fire arms and pronounced a sentence of life imprisonment – later reduced to 20 years. Amnesty International said the trial was a "travesty of justice", adding that "In view of the fact that Indonesia's sovereignty over East Timor has not been recognized by the UN, the competence of Indonesian courts to try Xanana Gusmão ... is open to question."

At the end of 1993, a US Congressional amendment linked arms sales to improvements in human rights – and specifically in East Timor. The Defence Minister Edi Sudrajat dismissed the move, explaining "we will [just] buy defence equipment from Britain, Germany, France and Russia". Attempts by countries like Britain to have assurances signed before arms – like the Hawk jet 'trainer' (also a very effective ground attack aircraft) – are sold to Indonesia are recognized not to be worth the paper they are written on.

The resistance movement in East Timor, after decades of fighting the massively larger and better armed Indonesian armed forces, appears to have dwindled to a handful of guerrillas – perhaps less than 100 armed rebels. But passive resistance, if anything, is becoming stronger as overt resistance crumbles. While the Indonesian government may reasonably have hoped that a generational change would dim the fires of resistance, there seems to be a younger generation of militants emerging, in some ways even more disenchanted that those that the years have led them to replace. During New Year celebrations at the end of 1994, riots broke out in Baucau and the security forces killed 3 demonstrators. In Feb 1995, 6 East Timorese were killed by soldiers in the moutainous Ermera district. Initially, the military claimed their were Fretilin guerrillas; later, that they might have been civilians. There have also been attacks on residents of the capital, Dili, by 'ninja' gangs – labelled by the government as East Timorese hooligans bent on destabilizing the province, and by most others as groups of thugs supported by the security forces to intimidate anti-Indonesian elements. Dili's residents responded by forming their own self-defence groups.

The latest events which have kept East Timor in the news have been a series of violent incidents by Catholic East Timorese against Muslim immigrants. At the end of 1995 mosques were razed in Dili and the disturbances spread to Maliana, Liquica and Viqueque. The riots seemed to be sparked by resentment that immigrants have captured so much business in the province, rather than religious animosities *per se*. It seems that some Indonesians are losing patience with East Timor. In late 1995 Amien Rais, the chairman of one of the country's largest Muslim organizations, Muhammadiyah, wrote in *Ummat*: "Its time for a sharp change in direction. Up until now, we have been so defensive, so cautious, so good-hearted, and very much spoiling our youngest province. Like a small child who has been spoiled too long with the utmost patience and tolerance, that child begins to disobey us."

Putting East Timor to rights

Over the years since the Santa Cruz débâcle of 1991 (see box), Indonesian leaders have been trying to find a way out of the diplomatic and PR quagmire that is East Timor. With remarkable understatement, towards the end of 1994 Foreign Minister Ali Alatas called East Timor "a stone in Indonesia's shoe". The *Financial Times*, in Jun 1995, quoted a foreign affairs specialist as saying "It's more like a bloody great rock", adding "They see the problem, but they don't know what to do about it." There can be little doubt that East Timor has hindered Indonesia's stuttering steps to become a leader among the countries of the developing world. With a population of nearly 200 million, a robust and fast-growing economy, and political stability, the country should be a leading light in the international community. Instead, whenever the media shines its lights on Indonesia, East Timor – to the intense irritation of foreign minister Ali Alatas – glows like a beacon to distract (and detract) attention from the Indonesian government's undoubted successes. Most recently, in 1994, the UN released the report of its special investigator Bacre Waly Ndiaye into the Santa Cruz killings of 1991. It was highly damming in its criticism of the government and military, and said that the conditions that created the massacre were still present in the province. "No solution to the problems of East Timor can be found before justice has been done", he concluded.

Perhaps with the gradual recognition – and acceptance – that East Timor is not just a military problem, but also a major and persistent diplomatic embarrassment and political challenge, the government and military appear to be beginning to take some faltering steps towards finding a solution. These steps include:

● Abri, the armed forces of Indonesia, have accepted that the policing of East Timor needs to be overhauled, with a fundamental reappraisal of the operation of its personnel in the province.

● Giving the province some sort of special status within the Republic of Indonesia. East Timor's governor, Abilio Jose Osorio, favours the view that East Timor become a *propinsi istimewa*, or special administrative area, like Aceh and Yogyakarta. The Catholic bishop of the province suggests 'autonomy'. These proposals, and others, indicate that Jakarta is looking for a political as well as, or perhaps instead of, a military solution to the problem. That said, Suharto has so far rejected all notions of a change in administrative status.

● There is greater contact and communication between Indonesian officials and resistance figures. In Oct 1994, Foreign Minister Ali Alatas and José Ramos Horta, representing the resistance movement, met for talks at the UN in New York. Though the parties agreed nothing, commentators were impressed that the meeting occurred at all.

● There appears to be a more co-ordinated attempt to deal with grievances and to court martial soldiers accused of violating accepted procedures. The killing of six East Timorese in Feb 1995 (see above) led to the establishment of a investigating team and a review board which has reported that the killings were illegal.

● In the middle of 1993 Suharto established an 'independent' human rights commission – only the Philippines has a similar body among the ASEAN nations. Early evidence is that the Commission is not just a puppet of the government, but is willing to tackle sensitive issues and go against the wishes of the government and military.

Taken together, these changes might herald a change in the way in which Jakarta is managing the East Timor problem, although as yet all is talk; there has been little substantive progress. In Aug 1995, on the occasion of Indonesia's 50th anniversary celebrations, Archbishop Belo of Dili declined to participate in the event – signalling his feeling that East Timor at least did not have much to celebrate.

ECONOMY

Since integration in 1976, Indonesia has allocated considerable investment to East Timor, on the theory – presumably – that it is possible to 'buy' allegiance. Since 1976, the population of East Timor has received more central government money – on a per capita basis – than any other province in the country. In 1995 it amounted to around US$100 pp – as against US$30 in East Java and just US$15 in West Java. (In 1995, Irian Jaya received more, although it also generated far more revenue for the government from its timber, copper and gold.) But the territory is still poor and undeveloped, and barely viable as an economic unit – which would pose problems for an independent East Timor. It is decades behind much of the country, with poorly developed schools, roads, hospitals and other physical and social infrastructure. Efforts to promote agricultural and industrial development have constantly been frustrated by security considerations, and much of the economic growth that has occurred has been linked to government activity. Manufacturing only accounts for 1% of the province's economy, and 90% of families depend on agriculture for their living. Despite this, the province has to import food. Among the cash crops cultivated, coffee is the most important.

There is also evidence that the fruits of the economic progress that has occurred have tended to accrue not to the 750,000 East Timorese but to immigrants from Java and Sulawesi – who have been arriving at the rate of about 25,000 a year. In a book published in 1994 and entitled *Ekonomi politik penbangunan Timor Timur* (The political economy of East Timor), Joao Mariano de Sousa Saldanha notes that the top-down approach to development has tended to create a class of dependents, and has also skewed development in favour of the few, not the majority. This has created frictions between the indigenous East Timorese and the 'foreign' immigrants who are perceived to be in league with the military and the provincial government, and denying local people jobs and income. On New Year's day in 1995, the riots that followed the death of three East Timorese (see above) in Baucau led to the burning down of most of the town's shops. It was not coincidental that the shops were owned and run by immigrants from Sulawesi.

ISLAND INFORMATION

● **Accommodation**

The province welcomes fewer tourists than any other in Indonesia and tourist facilities are limited. Dili is relatively well-provided with hotels – built to serve visiting officials – but in the countryside there is a dearth of accommodation. Note that some places may refuse to take foreigners because of fear of police/army harassment. Expect to be watched and scrutinized – probably by a government 'spy'.

● **Cost of living**

The cost of living in East Timor is probably higher than almost anywhere else in the country.

● **Travelling to, and in, East Timor**

East Timor was a closed province until 1990 when it was opened to visitors for the first time since 1975. Following the events at Santa Cruz at the end of 1991, the government became more suspicious of foreign visitors and the province was closed once more. It has since been opened again, but there is less freedom to travel here than elsewhere in the country. When travelling in the province, it is advisable to have the *Surat Tanda Melaporkan* form with you, dispensing with the need to fill in the form at every police station. In addition, it is advisable to have your passport with you at all times. **NB** Check entry regulations beforehand in Kupang. There are regular flights to Dili from Kupang and daily intercity buses, also from Kupang to Dili, via Kejamenamu and Atambua. The journey from Atambua to Dili is just 130 km, but it takes 4-5 hrs. Buses pass through 4 check points where the police check passports, and the road from the border to Dili is very poor (although currently being upgraded). The view of the coast, though, is stupendous. The Pelni ships *Kelimutu* and *Tatamalau* dock at Dili on their 2 week circuits (see page 921). So too do the smaller vessels *KM Dobonsolo* (which plys the route Dili-Kupang-Surabaya-Jakarta) and the *KM Tatamailau* (serving Dili, Larantuka and Labuanbajo).

● **Being sensitive to local concerns**

Note that local people often wish to keep their distance from foreign visitors. Association with foreigners attracts attention and can entice a reaction from the authorities. This means that the East Timorese are less open, and less welcoming, than other Indonesians – and for good reason.

● **Books on East Timor**

Budiardjo, Carmel and Liem Soei Liong (1984) *The war against East Timor*, Zed Books: London; Cox, Steve and Carey, Peter (1995) *Generations of resistance: East Timor*, London: Cassell, a 'coffee table' book, if there can be such a thing on East Timor, with almost 80 mostly black and white photographs and an excellent text by Peter Carey; Hiorth, F (1985) *Timor past and present*, James Cook University of Queensland: Townsville; Jolliffe, Jill (1978) *East Timor: nationalism and colonialism*, University of Queensland Press: St Lucia; Retboll, Torben (ed) (1984) *East Timor: the struggle continues*, IWGIA: Copenhagen; Kohen, ET and Taylor, John (1979) *An act of genocide: Indonesia's invasion of East Timor*, Tapol: London; Taylor, John G (1991) *Indonesia's forgotten war: the hidden history of*

East Timor, Zed Books: London.

ROUTES From the border to Dili The 'rapid' bus to Dili travels along the coast road via Batugede and Maubara. It is also possible to take a slightly longer, inland route via Maliana and Ermera.

MALIANA

Maliana is a large regional centre close to the border between East and West Timor.

Excursions The small local town of **Marobo** was known as a spa resort, and hot spring-fed pools are used by local people to cure various ills. As this area marked the border between Dutch and Portuguese Timor there are the remains of a number of fortresses in the area. The two largest are **Batugade** and **Balibo**.

● **Accommodation** There are two losmen in Maliana (**E**). The *Purwosari Indah* is said to be the better of the two, although they are both basic.

● **Transport Bus**: connections with Atambua and with Dili's Taci Tolu bus terminal.

ERMERA

Ermera is the coffee-growing capital of Timor, and the largest coffee plantation on the islands is said to be situated in the area. The town itself does not really do justice to its billing as a coffee 'capital' – a 300m-long high street, albeit dominated by a beautiful colonial-era church. Coffee is sold by vendors lining the main road and the aroma of the beans permeates the place.

Excursions Fatubesi is a small village a few kilometres outside Ermera dominated by a large coffee processing plant. It is owned by the government.

● **Accommodation** None available.

● **Transport** 62 km SW of Dili. **Road Bus**: accessible on a day trip from Dili, or en route to or from the city. Buses leave from the Taci Tolu terminal and travel via Gleno, where a change of vehicle is required. The road to Gleno is relatively good, 48 km, 1 hr 20 mins; from Gleno to Ermera it is very poor, 15 km, 45 mins.

DILI

Dili, the capital of East Timor, is situated in the heart of a bay, surrounded by dry, scrub-covered, hills. It is a shell of a city. There are few cars on the roads, shops seem more often to be shut than open, and there is little of the bustle and confusion so evident in other Indonesian towns. People appear generally glum and reserved – except for the children. It is difficult not to assume that this must be linked to the Indonesian invasion and annexation of this former Portuguese territory in 1975. With the enormous scale of human suffering over the intervening years, it is small wonder that people are not filled with zest for life.

Dili became the capital of the former Portuguese colony in 1769. Due to colonial mismanagement and the dislocations and ferment caused by the war since 1975, the city has failed to prosper. The population of the district of Dili – which also includes surrounding settlements and countryside – was only 81,000 in 1985. There are numerous examples of Indonesian investment in Dili – impressive municipal buildings for example – but these seem out of place in such a quiet town.

Places of interest

Dili has numerous architectural reminders of the Portuguese period, but few are noteworthy. On the seafront, just W of the port, is Dili's oldest church, **Motael Church**. It is rather too heavy to be elegant and is fronted by a hideous concrete statue of Joseph, Mary and the infant Jesus, perched on top of a globe and hand. In the evenings, the seafront on the W side of the bay is a pleasant area to walk. Food carts set up near the **lighthouse**, not far from the Motael Church, and there is usually a cooling on-shore breeze. Also in the W of the town is the new **Cathedral of the Immaculate Conception**, said to be the largest in Southeast Asia. It was inaugurated by President Suharto in 1988 and blessed by Pope Paul in Oct 1989. During the

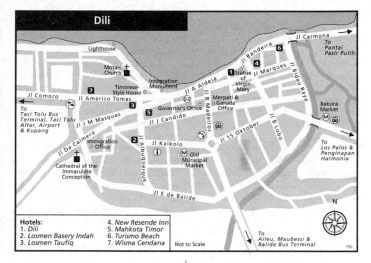

Hotels:
1. Dili
2. Losmen Basery Indah
3. Losmen Taufiq
4. New Resende Inn
5. Mahkota Timor
6. Turismo Beach
7. Wisma Cendana

Not to Scale

Pope's visit, over 250,000 people assembled to hear him preach. Not far away to the N is a reproduction traditional **Timorese house** (which used to have a craft centre associated, now closed). Across the road is the appalling **Integration Monument** showing a muscle-bound wild man breaking-off the shackles of colonialism. Locals must view it as a wry joke and certainly the weeds and generally unkempt feel seems to indicate that no one views it with any affection. The Christian statue outside the Motael Church is immaculately maintained by comparison.

In the centre of town, facing the seafront, is the **Kantor Gubernor** or Governor's Office, a long, arched and slightly Mediterranean-style building which was once surrounded by trees. The Indonesian assault is still starkly in evidence in the rusting **landing craft** that lie haphazardly on the beach in front of the *Dili Hotel*. It is peculiar that the authorities have not removed these obvious signs of the invasion. Perhaps they are designed to act as a reminder of Indonesia's military might to deter any erstwhile Fretilin supporters. Further E on the seafront, between the *Dili* and *Turismo* hotels, is a statue of the **Virgin**

Mary, said to be carved from marble shipped from Portugal. From the beach near the *Turismo Hotel* fishermen leave in the early evenings and return early the following morning with their catch. Fresh fish is sold by vendors a little further back along the beach, opposite the *Dili Hotel*.

Inland from the seafront, near the Perumtel Office at the intersection of Jl Kaikolo and Jl Bispo Medeiros, is the **Mercado Municipal Dili** – Dili's municipal market, which was closed for some years but is now operating once more. It is housed in a Portuguese-era building. But the best market is the **Bekora Market**, close to the Bekora Bridge and bus terminal. It is best, like most markets, in the early morning. It was here, in 1994, that a confrontation between local East Timorese and immigrants from Sulawesi led to the place being partially destroyed by fire. There is another market in Comoro, near the bus terminal to the W of town. The **Comoro Market**, though, was also destroyed by fire in late 1995, again by Catholic East Timorese registering their resentment that Muslim immigrants have taken control of so much trade in the capital.

Excursions

Pantai Pasir Putih or 'White Sand Beach', also known as *Areia Blanca*, lies 6 km E of town, on the far E side of Dili Bay. There is reasonable snorkelling here and it is becoming popular at weekends. The Indonesians claim that before 1975 it was a segregated 'whites only' beach, although foreign residents of the time maintain that in fact it provided ample evidence of the lack of colour consciousness within the Portuguese colonial administration: there would be blacks, Goans, *mestizos*, East Timorese and Portuguese whites all crowded onto the sand. *Getting there*: buses only run to the beach on Sun and public holidays (bus 'D'); on other days catch a taxi and arrange a pick-up time (or walk back).

Walking on from Pantai Pasir Putih to the **Fatumaka Promontory** there is a gigantic **Statue of Christ**. It was erected by the Indonesian government and is claimed to be the third largest such statue in the world – after those in Rio and Lisbon. There are also good views from the promontory towards Dili. *Getting there*: no public transport. Take a bus or taxi to Pantai Pasir Putih (see above) and then walk, taking the path.

The **Museum of Timorese Culture** on Jalan Comoro, about 1 km from the airport towards town (5 km from town), contains a poor display of East Timorese material and non-material art, even more poorly labelled. The museum is managed by the Department of Education and Culture but one wonders why it was built. It has no regular opening hours and is often closed. *Getting there*: by bus 'AB'.

The **Taci Tolu** altar is 7 km W of town near the bus terminal. The altar was built to commemorate the Pope's visit to Dili in 1989 when 250,000 people assembled here. The design is based on that of the traditional East Timorese house. *Getting there*: by bus 'AB'.

Manatuto is a pottery-making centre 64 km E of Dili and one of the driest places on an already arid island. There are beaches near the town and it is also possible to explore the Ilimanuk hills from here. *Getting there*: regular connections from the Bekora bus terminal, 1½ hrs (2,000Rp).

Ataturo Island can be seen in Dili Bay. There is no public transport to this large, 150 sq km island, but boats can be chartered, 1 hr (15,000Rp). There are no beaches but the underwater life is said to be plentiful. There is also no accommodation on the island.

Aileu is a largish town 47 km S of Dili. It is accessible as a day trip or *en route* to Maubessi (see page 793). *Getting there*: by bemo from the Balide terminal, 2 hrs (2,000Rp).

Ermera is the coffee producing capital of Timor, 62 km SW of the city (see page 788). *Getting there*: bus connections from the Taci Tolu terminal via Gleno, 2 hrs.

Tours

Day tours to Maubessi, Baucau and Los Palos. See Tour companies & travel agents for tour company addresses.

Festivals

End Feb-early Mar: 3-day carnival in Dili.
Apr (first week): Thanksgiving ceremony for the harvest.
May: *Annual Saint Mary Parade* (13th).
July: Anniversary of East Timor's integration into the Indonesian republic (17th).
Oct: Anniversary of Dili's founding (10th) on 10 October 1769. Festivities include musical performances and traditional dances.

Local information
● **Accommodation**

Few tourists make it to Dili; hotels are thin on the ground and expensive. There are no travellers' losmen.

B *Mahkota Timor*, Jl Gov Alves Aideia (opp the port), T 21664, F 21063, a/c, restaurant, a barn of a new hotel, totally lacking in character, though the rooms are comfortable; **B** *New Resende*, Jl Av Bispo Medeiros, T 22094, a/c, restaurant, the best equipped hotel in Dili, central with good service and clean rooms – popular with Indonesian officials, so often full, expect to be closely watched, as it is assumed that anyone visiting East Timor must have an ulterior motive and this place is government-owned, price incl breakfast.

A-C Turismo Beach, Jl Av Marechal Carmona, T 22029, F 22284, about 1 km from town centre, villa on seafront, some a/c, restaurant, rooms are clean and fan rooms are a good deal, best rooms with hot water and TV (but note that the rooms with an ocean view – which are more expensive – are noisy early in the morning as they front onto the main beach road), friendly staff, pleasant position, price incl breakfast.

D Dili, Jl Av Marechal Carmona, T 21871, some a/c, quaintly decrepit, rooms have sitting area, some character, with 1950s furnishings and bathroom fittings from Scotland, on seafront; **C Wisma Cendana**, Jl Americo Tomas (not far from the port), T 21141, a/c, looks nicer than it is, rooms have been allowed to deteriorate.

D Losmen Basery Indah, Jl Estrade de Balide, T 2731, dark rooms, shared mandi, rather grubby, grossly over-priced; **D Losmen Taufiq**, Jl A Thomas, T 21934, central location, basic rooms, clean enough.

E Penginapan Harmonia, 4 km E of town, T 22065, for a while the ownership of this place was taken over by a Javanese businessman – and it went rapidly downhill, fortunately the original, very friendly English and Portuguese manager, Pedro, should have taken over the membership once more; if so, it is rec!

● **Places to eat**

Timorese coffee is very good in Dili.

◆◆◆**Coto Cahaya Pangkep**, Komplek Bioskop Seroja 9 (facing the military port), popular among Dili's (mostly non-Timorese) middle class; ◆◆◆**Massau**, Jl Massau (nr the hospital), T 22599, good to excellent Portuguese food and wines, even a decent selection of Australian wines, rec; ◆◆**Beringin Jaya**, Jl Ameriko Tomas, Padang food, excellent; ◆◆**Djakarta**, Jl Kolmera 125, good, Chinese and steaks; ◆◆**Pantai Indah Kuring**, Jl Lobo (nr the square containing the statue of St Mary), excellent *Ikan bakar*, the owner (a Chinese) allows customers to choose their fish, cheap beer, the *ayam goreng* is also highly rec by the locals; ◆◆◆**Pantai Laut**, Airport Comoro, expensive but elegant restaurant serving good Chinese and Indonesian dishes; ◆◆**Turismo Beach Hotel**, Jl Av Marechal Carmona, Indonesian and Chinese, good selection of Portuguese dishes and wine; *Aru Bakery*, Jl M Alburqueque; *Golden Bakery*, Jl Jose Maria Marques 24.

● **Airline offices**

Merpati, Jl Bispo Medeiros 5, T 21880 (next to the *New Resende Hotel*).

● **Banks & money changers**

Bank Dagang Negara, Jl Bispo Medeiros, most major TCs; **Bank Summa**, Jl Bispo Medeiros, US$ cash and some TCs; **Danamon**, Jl Bispo Medeiros, US$ cash, no TCs.

● **Entertainment**

In the evenings Jl Bidau Raya becomes Dili's rather lack-lustre red light district. Warungs along this street double as brothels.

Cinemas: on the seafront, W past the Post Office.

● **Hospitals & medical services**

Hospitals: *General Hospital*, Jl Toko Baru Bidau.

● **Post & telecommunications**

Area code: 0390.

General Post Office: Jl Inf D Hendrique (next to *Kantor Gubernor*, on seafront).

Perumtel: Jl Bispo Medeiros (nr intersection with Jl Kaikolo). IDD available.

● **Shopping**

The main shopping street is Jl Jose Maria Marques. Shops shut in the afternoon for siesta.

Books: *Toko Dili Craft and Bookshop*, Jl Bispo Medeiros Il.

Crafts: the *Toko Dili*, Jl Bispo Medeiros 11. Crafts are generally poor quality. Street sellers hawk textiles (usually made from machine-spun cotton and chemically dyed) nr the larger hotels (eg *New Resende*).

● **Tour companies & travel agents**

Multi Perona Maya, Jl Jose Maria Marques 23, T 21274; *Dili Beach Tours and Travel*, Jl Kulu-Hun, T 21024, F 22284; *Timor Indah*, Jl Raya Komoro, T 22244.

● **Tourist offices**

Dinas Pariwisata, Jl Kaikolio Baru, T 21350, large new offices but, as yet, little information to offer. Seemingly none of the staff speaks any English; the maps and brochures seem too be almost intentionally inaccurate, and no one seems to be inured with any semblance of service or helpfulness.

● **Useful addresses**

Immigration Office: Jl Kolmera, T 21862.

● **Transport**

Local Town buses run fixed routes (200Rp). Bus 'A' runs from the main out-of-town bus termi-

Selected bus fares

	Ekonomi	Journey time
DILI (main bus terminal - Taci Tolu) to:		
Atambua	5,000Rp	3 hrs
Kupang	15,000Rp	15 hrs
Ermera	2,000Rp	2 hrs
Suai	4,000Rp	4 hrs
Liquica	1,500Rp	1 hr
Maliana	2,000Rp	3 hrs
DILI (Bekora bus terminal) to:		
Manatuto	2,000Rp	1½ hrs
Baucau	4,500Rp	3 hrs
Los Palos	7,000Rp	5-7 hrs
DILI (Balide bus terminal) to:		
Aileu	2,000Rp	2 hrs
Ainaro	4,000Rp	4 hrs
(Late 1995 fares quote)		

nal, 8 km W of Dili, to the Mercado Municipal. Bus 'B' runs from the bus terminal to the city centre passing many of the hotels en route. Bus 'D' runs from the bus terminal to the Bekora bus terminal, again passing most hotels. Bemo I runs from the Bekora terminal to the Mercado Municipal passing, en route, the Balide bus terminal (for bemos to Aileu), the university and the new Cathedral. Ancient, un-metered taxis can be easily hailed. The *New Resende Hotel* has a car for charter for day excursions out of town; the *Multi Perona Maya* tour company also has a car for charter.

Air Dili's Komoro Airport is on the coast 6 km W of town. Ancient taxis run into Dili, or walk 500m to the main road and catch a bus ('A' or 'B') (200Rp). Regular twice daily connections by Merpati with Kupang; daily connections with Denpasar (Bali); 1 flight/week to Atambua.

Road Bus: Dili's main bus terminal (Taci Tolu) is 8 km W of town. All buses from West Timor stop here, as do buses to/from western portions of East Timor such as Ermera, Suai, Liquica and Maliana, as well as Kupang and Atambua. *Tunas Mekar* run daily buses to Kupang; agents all over town sell tickets eg *Abundo Kanduang Padang Restaurant*, Jl 15 Oktober 29A; *Losmen Basery Indah*, Jl Estrade de Balide. City buses connect the terminal with the town centre. Buses to/from the eastern portion of East Timor (E of Dili) arrive or depart from the Bekora bus terminal, at the E edge of town, but within walking distance of Dili's hotels and guesthouses. Connections from here with Manatuto, Baucau and Los Palos.

There is a third, smaller, bus terminal: the Balide terminal, 1½ km S of town on Jl Bispo Medeiros. Buses leave here for Same and Aileu. Town bemo I stops at the Balide terminal on its cross-city circuit.

Sea Boat: Pelabuhan Dili is close to the town centre, to the E of the Motael Church. The Pelni ships *Dobonsolo* and *Binaiya* dock here on their 2 week circuits (see route schedule, page 921). The Pelni Office is at Avenido Aleixo Corte Real (next to the military airport), T 22478. Note that it is necessary to book Pelni tickets 48 hrs before embarking. Mixed cargo/passenger ships to other destinations also call at Pelabuhan Dili; check with the harbour master.

EAST FROM DILI TO LOS PALOS

The route E from Dili along the coast has only recently opened to tourists and facilities are few. The road, though, is very good – presumably to afford rapid movement of military traffic. The views are wonderful. After passing through the pottery-making town of Manatuto, the road continues to Baucau and Los Palos. Before Los Palos, the village of Rasa contains some of the few remaining examples of traditional Timorese architecture.

BAUCAU

Baucau is situated on the edge of a high plain and the surrounding area is an important agricultural zone. It is also the second largest town in East Timor. It was best known for its impressive Portuguese market – the **Mercado Municipal** – which was burnt out during a riot on New Year's Day 1995 and latest reports indicate is still abandoned. The riot followed the killing of three people by the military the day before, sparking the violent demonstration. The market, along with many shops – largely owned by immigrants from Sulawesi – were destroyed in the conflagration. Baucau is an important local centre with roads leading E to Los Palos and S to Viqueque. The town's public swimming pool is, by all accounts, usually empty.

Excursions Reflecting the (relative) wealth of the surrounding area in agricultural terms, the villages hereabouts show the remains of investments made during the Portuguese period. Perhaps the most beautiful village is **Veninale**, a tiny hamlet of just 10 houses with impressive, largely abandoned, colonial buildings and a Catholic mission. There is a rather squalid hot spring in Veninale and from here it is possible to venture further into the countryside – an area of rolling hills known as **Mundo Perdio**. On clear days it is possible to see both of Timor's coasts. *Getting there*: by bemo from Baucau to Veninale, 45 mins (1,000Rp).

● **Accommodation C-D** *Hotel Baucau/Hotel Famboyan* (formerly the *Flamboyant*, then the *Baucau* and now, apparently, the *Flamboyan*), elegant colonial structure, which has seen better days – it is run by the army, but is not a bad place, 26 basic rm, some with attached mandi; **E** *Wisma Goya Lida*.

● **Transport** 130 km from Dili. **Road Bus**: the station is nr the Mercado Municipal. Connections with Dili, 3 hrs (4,500Rp) and Los Palos, 2 hrs (2,500Rp), and S to Viqueque.

LOS PALOS

This is the most important town in the E, situated at an altitude of 500m and therefore considerably cooler than coastal towns. The Los Palos area is culturally distinct even within the context of East Timor. The people in the area speak Fateluco, apparently unintelligible to speakers of East Timor's most widely spoken language, Tetun. The area was closed to all bar residents until recently. It is a busy town but unattractive. The centre of town, such as it is, has a reconstruction of a traditional Timorese house. The Catholic church close by is surmounted with a steeple in Timorese-style.

Excursions **Tutuala Beach** is 15 km E of Los Palos, on Timor's East coast. **Accommodation** A small hotel has recently opened. *Getting there*: there are occasional bemos to Tutuala, but not every day and it may be necessary to charter a vehicle (10,000Rp). Ask when the last bemo leaves the beach for Los Palos, or arrange to be picked up.

Rasa Village is 10 km N of town and has some of the finest examples of traditional Timorese architecture – tall-roofed, elegant, wooden structures, raised off the ground on pillars (there is a poor imitation at the (now defunct) craft centre in Dili). The houses are still occupied and are probably in the best condition of any in the area. Ikat cloth is also woven here. *Getting there*: by bemo from Los Palos; the last bemo returns from Rasa to Los Palos at about 1600. **Lautem** is on the road to Baucau and Dili. The remains of (allegedly) the largest Portuguese fort in East Timor are to be found here. A little further along the road towards Baucau is a cave with prehistoric paintings. *Getting there*: by bemo towards Baucau.

● **Accommodation D** *Turismo* (branch hotel of the *Turismo* in Dili); **F** *Wisma Venissimo* (nr the hospital), small rooms but friendly management.

● **Transport Road Bus**: Los Palos' bus terminal is a few kilometres from the town centre; bemos link the terminal with town (200Rp). Bus connections with Dili, 5-7 hrs (7,000Rp) in the morning; it is best to book and reserve a seat – the bus will pick passengers up from their hotels. The *Lausari* bus company, which operates on the Dili-Los Palos route, has its offices next to the Catholic church. Note that buses from Dili leave from the Bekora terminal between 0600 and 0730 only; after that time it is necessary to travel to Baucau and catch a connection to Los Palos.

SOUTH FROM DILI TO MAUBESSI

The route S from Dili climbs into the rugged interior highlands. Aileu, 47 km from Dili, has a beautiful church, while the highland town of Maubessi, formerly a minor colonial resort, offers a bracing climate, mountain walks and good views. At Maubessi the road divides; S to Same and SW to Ainaro.

AILEU

Aileu is a major upland interior town 47 km S of Dili and 1,600m above sea level. The road to Aileu is enormously circuitous, but the views are worth the dizziness and nausea. On entering Aileu there is a small park with three examples of **East Timorese architecture**. Further on still is a **monument** commemorating those Australians and Portuguese who died fighting the Japanese during WW2. (The story of the Australian resistance is one of the finest examples from the war of bravery against overwhelming odds.) A daily **market** is also held in Aileu. **Accommodation** None available. *Getting there*: 47 km S of Dili, bemos to Aileu leave from the Balide terminal, S of town. Town bemo I runs to Balide on its cross-town circuit. Though it is only 47 km to Aileu, the journey takes 2 hrs (2,000Rp).

MAUBESSI

A beautiful highland town, 800m above sea-level, with fine views over the ocean. Maubessi is a centre of traditional arts, and good ikat cloth is still produced here. The hills that surround the town are good for walking. It gets cold at night, particularly during Jul and Aug, so take warm clothing.

Excursions Same is an attractive hill town to the S of Maubessi. There is some accommodation here. *Getting there*: by bus.

● **Accommodation F** *Wisma Udayana*, opp Martins' Kiosk, 8 clean rooms. Attractive, though basic, colonial guesthouse.

● **Transport Road Bus**: connections with Dili from the Balide terminal, via Aileu.

SUAI

Suai is on Timor's southern coast, not far from the border between East and West Timor. The area was earmarked for development linked to presumed oil reserves, but the investments intended by the Portuguese never really amounted to much and the remnants of the drilling efforts are still in evidence. The region is famed for its hand-woven textiles and handicrafts, and good quality ikat can be obtained from most villages in the area.

● **Accommodation** Two losmen in Suai.

● **Transport Road Bus**: accessible from either East or West Timor. From Dili's Balide terminal, buses travel via Aileu, Maubessi and Ainaro, 10 hrs. Alternatively, it is possible to catch a bus from Atambua in West Timor to Suai. In fact, buses leave from the main Taci Tolu terminal in Dili for Atambua where there are connections with Suai. In other words there is a loop possible, meaning that travellers do not have to retrace their steps.

AINARO

Ainaro lies close to Mount Tatamaliau, the highest peak in East Timor at 2,963m. There are several decrepidly attractive colonial buildings in town as well as the well maintained monument to Don Aleixo Corte Real in the centre of the town.

Excursions The countryside around Ainaro is lush and green compared with the rest of Timor. Villages hereabouts still have **traditional Timorese houses**, more like those in West Timor than East Timor. **Maubessi** is also accessible as a day trip. But more traditional and less visited is the village of **Hatubuilico**, right at the foot of Mount Tatamaliau. This is also a good point from which to start a climb of **Mount Tatamaliau**. It is said that on a clear day it is possible to see the North coast of Timor and the island or Alor from the summit.

● **Accommodation** None available in Ainaro, but there is a losmen in Hatubuilico (see Excursions) and also in Maubessi (see above). **F** *Tatamaliau*, Hatubuilico, very basic and grubby place but the only convenient place if intending to climb Mount Tatamaliau.

● **Transport Road Bus**: daily bemo from Dili's Balide terminal via Aileu, 4 hrs (4,000Rp).

Maluku

Horizons	795	Ternate and Tidore	825
Ambon	801	Halmahera	831
The Lease Islands	809	Morotai	832
Seram	813	South East Maluku	833
Banda Islands	815		

MALUKU, formerly known as the Moluccas, is not so much a province as an archipelago: it sprawls across 851,000 sq km, of which only one tenth is land, and consists of over 1,000 islands. Their total population is 1.9 million. The sea in this area is very deep – reaching 4,971m in the Bacan Basin, southeast of Halmahera. The highest mountain is Mt Binaiya on Seram, at 3,000m. The largest islands are Seram, Halmahera and Buru, although the most important economically are Ambon, tiny Ternate and the Bandas. Recent economic attention has focused upon the expansion of the fishing industry, especially tuna and shellfish, and on forestry. Other important crops include the sago palm (see page 798), coffee and coconut.

Horizons

Although the islands are very much at the edge of the Indonesian world, both geographically and economically, it was the spices of Maluku which initially attracted the European powers to Asia and to the E isles (see page 897 and below). They became known as the **Spice Islands**, or Spiceries. It was only here that cloves and nutmeg were cultivated and the early history of Southeast Asia was moulded and driven by the fabulous wealth that the Spice Islands had to offer the adventurous explorer.

Now that spices no longer generate the wealth that they once did, Maluku has been forced to find an alternative *raison d'être*. Not only are the islands more than 2,000 km from Jakarta, but they are very geographically dispersed: Morotai in the N is over 1,000 km from Tanimbar in the S.

CLIMATE

Maluku's climate is complex because it straddles the equator and covers such a vast area. In **N and central Maluku** there is rain throughout the year, but it is concentrated between May and Oct – the

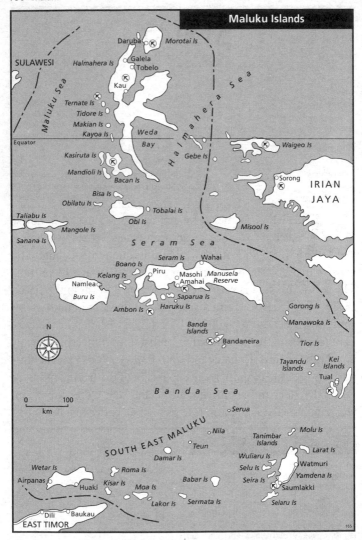

Maluku Islands

period of the E monsoon. In Ambon for example, the wettest month is Jul (590 mm), and the driest, Nov (104 mm). Total annual rainfall in Ambon is a very wet 3,450 mm. See the graph of monthly rainfall and temperature on page 801.

In **SE Maluku**, S of the equator, the climate is very different and more akin to that of Nusa Tenggara. The islands here experience a long dry season between Dec and Mar corresponding with the W monsoon and annual rainfall is 1,400 mm. As a result, while the islands to the N are clothed in forest, those in the S have savanna vegetation.

HISTORY

Maluku was important as a source of spices long before the first Europeans discovered the islands. Arab, Chinese, Malay and other seafarers traded here, and indeed the first Europeans had to employ the services of local pilots in Melaka to help them find the fabled Spiceries. The name *Maluku* is said to be derived from the words *Jaziratul Jabal Maluk* – meaning the 'Land of Many Kings', and the islands of *Miliku* are mentioned in 7th century T'ang Chinese documents.

The spices of Maluku

It was spices that initially enticed European mariners to Southeast Asia. The expedition of the Portuguese general Alfonso d'Albuquerque was the first to make landfall on the legendary Banda Islands in 1512. The General himself did not accompany the small fleet (he was resting in Melaka), but Ferdinand Magellan, then a lowly junior officer, probably did. The great attraction of the Spice Islands lay in the value of the spices that they seemed to produce in prodigious quantities, and the universal European belief that cloves (*Eugenia aromatica*), nutmeg (*Myristica fragrans*) and mace (another product of the nutmeg tree) could be grown nowhere else on earth.

Nutmegs are used for both medicinal and culinary purposes – they are said to be the secret ingredient in the flavouring of Coca Cola. In the Orient, nutmeg was – and is – used primarily for health purposes. It is an important ingredient in preparations to relieve illnesses from rheumatism and malaria to sciatica and indigestion. It is also considered to be an effective aphrodisiac. No wonder, then, that nutmegs were known as the golden fruit. Jan Huygen van Linschoten, a Dutchman who sailed with d'Albuquerque's expedition, wrote of the benefits of nutmeg: "The nutmeg comforts the brain, sharpens the memory, warms and strengthens the Maw, drives wind out of the body, makes a sweet breath, drives down Urine, stops the Laske, and to conclude, is good against all cold diseases in the head, in the brain, the Maw, the Lice and the Matrice". Cloves were similarly regarded; German naturalist George Rumphius viewed the clove tree as "the most beautiful, the most elegant, and the most precious of all known trees".

Having displaced the Portuguese from the Moluccas, the Dutch were intent on maintaining a monopoly of the spice trade and proceeded to extirpate every tree not under their control – they literally sent expeditions to neighbouring islands to uproot and destroy any potential competitor plants. They did this so successfully that it was 200 years before people began to question whether nutmeg and cloves could be grown beyond the Spice Islands.

Cloves and nutmeg proved to be very sensitive to transportation – a fact that helped perpetuate the myth. The clove is not a seed or fruit at all, but a dried flower and most trees were grown from so-called volunteer seedlings, not from seeds. A tree will produce about 2 kg of cloves a year, picked between Aug and Sep. Before the Dutch took control of the region, they were found on just five small islands of what is now N Maluku: Ternate, Tidore, Bacan, Makian and Motir. The nutmeg tree requires similar careful management. Sensitive to sunlight, it was grown under the protective shadow of huge *kenari* shade trees, which also provided an edible nut and hulls for dug-out canoes. The nutmeg itself is the seed of the nutmeg fruit (which looks in size and colour rather like an apricot), while the more valuable mace is the beautiful, scarlet filigree wrapped around the outside of the seed. The mace is removed prior to the nutmeg drying process, and left to dry in the sun.

The English and French spent much of the 18th century trying to break the Dutch spice monopoly but were not successful until 1770 when French missionary and naturalist Pierre Poivre (1719-1786) smuggled out nutmeg and clove seedlings and managed to propagate them in Mauritius. With the British soon following suit, the wealth of the Moluccas was effectively undermined. From this date, these distant eastern isles were relegated to obscurity and economic insignificance. But the importance of spices remains enshrined in

Multi-purpose tree par excellence: the sago palm

🌴 Sago, not rice, is the traditional staple of Maluku as well as parts of Nusa Tenggara. The sago palm (*Metroxylon sago*) grows to a height of 5-10m, and flowers once, after about 15 years. Shortly before the flowers open, the tree is cut down and the pith scooped out. This is then washed, removing the starchy flesh from the inedible fibrous material. After being sieved, this flesh, rich in carbohydrate – though of poor quality – is dried and becomes what is commercially known as 'pearl sugar'. Eaten with fish and fruit, it provides a balanced diet. The sago tree not only provides nutrition, but does so with virtually no toil whatsoever; it grows without cultivation, needs no maintenance and a man and a boy, leisurely working for half a day, can process a mature palm and produce sufficient pulp to feed a family of five for over a month. The palm also provides fibre for rope, matting and cloth, the leaves can be used for thatch, and the sap ferments into a liquor. It is the multi-purpose tree *par excellence*.

The first reference to sago appears in Antonio Pigafetta's account of his journey around the world with the Portuguese explorer Ferdinand Magellan at the beginning of the 16th century. Always an acute observer, he wrote: "They eat wooden bread made from a tree resembling the palm, which is made as follows. They take a piece of that soft wood from which they take certain long black thorns. Then they pound the wood, and so make the bread. They use that bread, which they call saghu, almost as their sole food at sea".

Many Europeans commented on the abundance of sago in island Southeast Asia, Arthur Russel Wallace and Stamford Raffles among them. Wallace thought the tree a curse because it induced extreme laziness. He explained in 1862 that the "habit of industry not being acquired by stern necessity, all labour is distasteful, and the sago-eaters have, as a general rule, the most miserable of huts and the scantiest of clothing".

The sago palm is not just an abundant source of food. It also has many other uses. Its leaves (*attap*) are used for roofing and to weave interior ceilings; its bark is laid clinker-style to form walls; and the trunk is used for walls and posts. An attap roof is made by drying green leaves and folding them over bamboo poles, holding the leaves in place with a stitching of bamboo fibres. These poles of attap are then placed on a sago wood frame and, when in place, the roofs can withstand hurricanes (usually) and heavy rainfall. An attap roof is said to last 7 years – longer than zinc-roofed houses which are said to have a lifespan of just 4-5 years.

There is almost no end to the uses of the sago tree. Long handled brooms are made from sago wood and, rather appropriately, witches in Maluku are said to fly on sago leaves – not on broomsticks. There is also a work dance, unique to Maluku, known as the sago dance. The dance re-enacts the process of harvesting and processing sago. Thus from tree, to food, to ritual, to art form, the sago tree threads together different aspects of Moluccan life.

the popular nursery rhyme 'I had a little nut-tree':

I had a little nut tree, nothing would it bear
But a silver nut-meg and a golden pear;
The King of Spain's daughter came to visit me,
And all for the sake of my little nut-tree.

CULTURE

One of the first things a visitor notices about this area are the **churches**. Even quite small villages will have several, often quite large churches; the size reflects the fact that they are competing for status with each other and also with the mosques in any adjacent Moslem villages. There is a Malukan proverb: "Keeping up with the Moslems." Try to peek inside these churches, as many have huge, flamboyant murals painted on their walls (an example is the one in Ambon on the opposite side of the road to the *Beta Hotel* going down in the direction of Jl Sangaji). The Ambonese in particular, are gifted singers and it is worth going to church, or hovering outside on a Sun just to hear them. The very lucky may even come across a choir and conch shell band (conch shells require some expertise to blow).

Adat

One unique aspect of *adat* in Maluku is *pela*, a pact of brotherhood between two or more villages to provide help, shelter and protection in times of need. (For a general background to *adat* see the box on page 55.) pela villages are frequently far apart, even on different islands. Those pela bonds which today exist between Moslem and Christian villages were probably formed before their conversion.

There are obligations and taboos associated with the bond; one of the latter states that people from villages united in a pela bond may not marry; it is considered incestuous. A Christian village will help a Moslem village build a mosque and vice versa. The traditional greeting between members of villages united by a pela pact is "wakeou" which used to mean – very approximately – "don't cut off my head" as well as "brother"; a reminder of the central role of headhunting in the adat customs of this region in times past.

The continuing survival of adat may appear peculiar when people have embraced Islam or Christianity. However, not only is adat and mainstream religion perceived to be complimentary rather than contradictory, but many adat practices also have a practical value. For example, the "cuci negeri", which besides being a symbolic purification is also a 'spring clean' of houses and villages in Dec each year. There is also a strong and continuing fear that perhaps the ancestors will punish someone who fails to follow adat practices.

It is in connection with marriage ceremonies that adat customs persist most visibly. There are three types of adat marriage: '*Kawin lari*' is the most common, a marriage of elopement, popular because it saves on the cost of formal feasts and ceremonies; '*Kawin Minta*' is the traditional marriage by request; and '*Kawin masuk*' is where the bridegroom enters the bride's family, possibly because her family has no son. It is no accident that there are three types of adat marriage for three (also seven) is a significant adat number. It is a number that can bring both good and bad luck. Three of anything is bad luck so people do not give gifts in threes; likewise, taking a picture of three people will bring bad luck to one of them.

ISLAND INFORMATION

GETTING THERE

AIR

When buying tickets for flights, only pay for one journey at a time – Merpati offices get a commission on each ticket they sell, and the 'down route' agents may refuse to accept a perfectly valid, paid-for ticket. In other words, if travelling Banda-Ambon-Ujung Pandang with a stop-over in Ambon and buying the ticket in Banda, only buy the Banda-Ambon ticket in Banda; buy the Ambon-UPG ticket in Ambon.

ON ARRIVAL

● **Conduct**
Most Malukuns are friendly and generous, and will go out of their way to be helpful. When travelling by boat, foreigners sometimes find themselves being treated as VIPs and offered the Captain's private cabin, or invited to join a family in their private cabin. However, be prepared for the fact that there is no concept of privacy in these parts; there are not that many travellers so expect to be an object of curiosity.

● **Sights**
Forts, museums etc usually have a sealed donation box and a visitors' book where tourists sign and note the amount of their donation. How much you give is optional; 1000Rp is average. The amount will probably have a few 0s added to it afterwards.

● **Sports**
Snorkelling and diving: when snorkelling wear shoes as there are several bottom-dwelling poisonous sea creatures including stone fish and scorpion fish as well as deadly sea snakes (although the latter's mouth is too small to actually bite a person except at a narrow point like an earlobe, so the threat they pose is small).

WHERE TO STAY

● **Accommodation**
Most toilets are Western style, sit-down. Many hotel prices are negotiable, particularly if Chinese owned (the Chinese control the food supply and are therefore in a better position to offer discounts). Indonesians prefer to be on the ground floor, so rooms on higher floors, which most Westerners prefer, are often cheaper.

GETTING AROUND

If making a trip by **bemo**, plan on returning by 1600 as bemos become scarce or non-existent by late afternoon. Always try and ascertain the correct fare on bemos and **prahus** (small public boats) prior to setting out as it is almost unheard of to be quoted the correct fare by the driver or captain. It is common for drivers to try to get foreign visitors to charter the whole vehicle or vessel.

AMBON

Ambon, or Amboina as it was known during the colonial period, is the capital of the province of Maluku and has a population of 250,000. The island goes by the same name and covers a total of 780 sq km. The origin of the name, which was in use before the arrival of the Dutch, is not certain; it could be derived from the word *Ambwan* meaning 'dew', or *Nusa Ombong*, 'dawn'.

For 200 years Ambon was the centre of the clove trade. At the height of the colonial period in the late 1600s Ambon was called "Queen of the East" and was more important than Jakarta. Despite this it was not a popular posting due to the very high death rate, and low pay.

Many Ambonese became Christians during colonial times; they looked up to the Dutch and tried to emulate their ways. Even as recently as the 1970s, Ambonese women, who could afford the expense, looked on a trip to Holland as an essential life pilgrimage, and still today some Malukan women aspire to marrying Dutch men in order to live in Holland.

Gradually, the Dutch colonial administration, having taken over control on the demise of the VOC in 1799, began to atone for past Dutch excesses. Schools and hospitals were opened and by the end of the 19th century the Ambonese were among the best educated people in Indonesia. For the Ambonese elite, this led to jobs working for the Dutch colonial administration in Ambon and beyond. Renowned as superb soldiers, many served in the Dutch colonial army in Indonesia. After WW2, Ambonese soldiers fought against the Nationalist forces on the side of the Dutch in the Royal Netherlands East Indies Army, or KNIL. Having identified so strongly with the Dutch, they felt they had little in common with the rest of Indonesia and as Independence loomed they attempted to create an Independent state incorporating Ambon, the Lease Islands and Seram – Republik Maluku Selatan (RMS), initially with Dutch backing. (Some notional RMS threat, however unlikely that seems, is the reason given for a request that travellers present their passport to the local police when staying overnight in some villages.)

The RMS were prepared to fight for their independence, but were eventually defeated by Indonesian forces in a guerilla war that carried on into the 1960s on the island of Seram. About 40,000 Ambonese, mainly ex-soldiers who had fought with the Dutch, escaped to Holland. Conditions were not good for these Malukan exiles and gradually they began to realize that their faith in the Dutch was misplaced. Today most Malukans living in Holland find themselves caught between two worlds and the Dutch and the Indonesian government are working on a repatriation package for at least some of the 12,500-odd KNIL members and their family members who still remain in Holland. The older Moluccans have never integrated into life in the Netherlands and many still speak only poor Dutch. Their children, by comparison, are more Dutch than Moluccan. The repatriation scheme, generously financed by the Dutch to the tune of 30,000 to 40,000 guilders per returnee, is targeting these

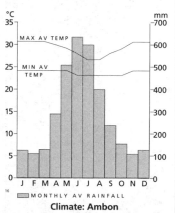

Climate: Ambon

°C / mm

MAX AV TEMP

MIN AV TEMP

⬜ MONTHLY AV RAINFALL

J F M A M J J A S O N D

16

older Moluccans who, so to speak, backed the wrong side in the nationalist struggle. Studies to date have revealed that 20% of returnees die within 6 months of arriving home, as if waiting to step back on the soil of their ancestors before succumbing to old age.

In the S of the island the people are mainly Christian, whereas along the N coast many villages, with their long history of contact with Arab traders, retain their Muslim beliefs. The Ambonese are renowned for their energy. They are also great singers and dancers; karaoke bars

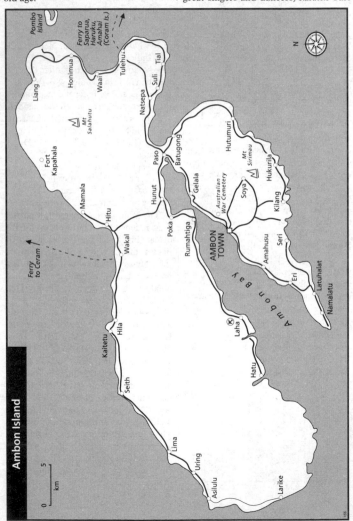

Ambon Island

are springing up everywhere – Fri night seems to be the big night, with singing going on till 0600. Ambon was traditionally a matrilinial society, as was Banda, so the equality of women is a deep-rooted concept. According to Shirley Deane, women were granted equal pay in 1900, 75 years before women in England.

Ambon Island is a modern, comparatively prosperous place compared with other parts of the archipelago, and in modernizing, it has lost much of its appeal. For example, the beautiful reddish-brown sago leaf roofs have given way to zinc corrugated roofs, even though the latter only last 4-5 years as against 7 years for sago. Ambon itself is a pleasant enough town although it was heavily bombed during WW2 so no old colonial buildings remain.

If you want to know more about the history of this fascinating region there is a fine collection of archive material and antiquarian books in the library belonging to the Bishop of the Catholic church on Jl Pattimura. Although not open to the public, if you are genuinely interested and the bishop is not too busy, he will take the time to show you his unique collection.

Places of interest

Ambon has more than its fair share of second-rate **heroic monuments**. The most interesting is that of **Saint Francis Xavier** outside the Catholic Cathedral of St Francis Xavier at Jl Raya Pattimura 1. The Spanish saint and co-founder of the Jesuit Order stands, bible in hand, on the shore while a crab offers him a crucifix. He visited the Moluccas between 1546 and 1547 and was struck by the volcanic violence of these islands, believing it to be the work of God. He wrote in his journal:

"It would seem that as these men have no one to warn them about the punishment of the wicked, God has been pleased as it were to open to them the abode of hell, and give them some pictures of the fires in which sinners are to be forever tormented, so that they may be admonished by that awful sight, and come to understand what punishments will await them unless they abandon their abominable vices and crimes".

Overlooking the stadium and running track is the **statue of Thomas Matulessy** – better known as the liberation hero **Kapitan Thomas Pattimura**. He looks rather like a cartoon pirate in cut-off jeans, wielding an enormous cutlass. He led a group of rebels who besieged and over-ran Fort Duurstede, on the island of Saparua in 1817, killing the Dutch Resident and his family, bar a baby boy. Pattimura was captured by the Dutch and hanged where his statue now stands.

Also facing onto the stadium is an army base, housed within the walls of **Fort Victoria**, the first of over 40 forts built on Ambon and constructed by the Portuguese in 1575 (when it was known as *Nossa Seinhora da Annonciada*). The guards will only allow visitors to see the gateway to the old fort (which originally stood on the sea front), with its faded crests and fine plaster ships over the apex, and may allow photographs to be taken on request (officially prohibited).

The lovely green-roofed and walled **Jame Mosque**, with its silver dome, is at the NW edge of town on Jl AJ Patty. Next door is the newer, bigger, and rather less attractive **Mesjid Raya**. Ordinarily, the old mosque would have been demolished on completion of its replacement, but in this case, locals were so fond of the old structure that it – thankfully – has been allowed to stand.

At the end of Jl AM Sangaji is the **Pelabuhan Ambon** – Ambon Port. This is where the Pelni liners and other large ships dock. Not far from the port, on both sides of Jl Yos Sudarso is the **Gotong Royong Market** – both a food (seaward side) and general (landward side) market, with delicious barbecued fresh tuna and fruit on sale. Walking along the seafront, is the new covered **Mardika Market**. It is most enjoyable in the morning, when

Gateway to Fort Victoria

fresh fish is on sale and fishing boats sell their night's catch along the promenade. This is also the central bus terminal.

The **Siwalima Museum** is 2½ km SW of town at Taman Makmur. Established in 1973, it is primarily an ethnographic collection with carved boats, ancestor figures, musical instruments and textiles. Open 0800-1400 Tues-Thur, 0800-1100 Fri, 0800-1300 Sat-Sun. *Getting there*: bus from the Mardika terminal for Amahusu (ask for 'musium').

About 2 km NE of the town centre, on **Karang Panjang Hill**, is the statue of 19-year-old **Marta Tiahahu**, a Christian Ambonese who gazes, spear in hand, over Ambon city and bay. When her father, who was leading a rebellion against the Dutch, was captured and imprisoned she took up the fight on Nusa Laut. Eventually captured herself, Marta was told of her father's execution while she was being taken to Java and starved herself to death. She was buried at sea on 2 January 1818. Get there by bus (150 Rp), or on foot. The **Doolan Memorial**, is on Jl Dr Kayadou in Kudamati (just past the Rehoboth Church) at the SW edge of town. This simple monument commemorates an Australian soldier who provided covering

fire for retreating comrades. He was only killed by the Japanese after tenacious resistance, and his body was spirited away by local Ambonese and buried beneath a gandaria tree on this spot.

Excursions

Soya, a village with strong traditions of adat (see page 799 and page 55) and magic, is a pleasant outing from Ambon town. Catch a bemo, marked 'Soya', at the bemo stand for the 20 mins ride up into the hills overlooking the town and bay. Alighting from the bemo the path to the top of Gunung Sirimau is signposted, a 20 mins walk. At 700m the path reaches the sacred site, a stone throne facing a panoramic view out over the bay. Behind the throne, follow a short path up the hill to the 'tempayan setan', a clay urn containing water which never dries up, even during the dry season. Local people come here in search of cures, good luck and a marriage partner. A concrete pillbox, a remnant from WW2, can be found about 15m further along the path going away from Soya, along with a trench dug by the Dutch. Visitors fortunate to be in Ambon on the second Fri in Dec, should try to visit Soya for the ceremony of 'Cuci Negeri' an annual ritual practiced in many villages to purify the village of evil spirits, an example of adat traditions which are still practiced. It also serves as an annual 'spring cleaning' when houses and village are given a thorough clean. The walk back down the hill into Ambon takes just over an hour past a church built by the Portuguese in 1817, a former baileo (meeting place, see page 810) surrounded by ceremonial stones, and through villages with attractive local houses. There are alternative scenic walks from Soya, continuing in the opposite direction to Ambon, through the villages of Hatalai and Naku to the coast at Hukarila. *Getting there*: by bemo (marked 'Soya') from the bemo stand in town (400Rp).

The Australian War Cemetery lies 5 km NE of town. Immaculately maintained, 2,000 Australian, British, Canadian, Dutch and US servicemen who fought and died during the Second World War are buried here. *Getting there*: bus to Tantui (150Rp).

Ambon's beaches are not the best. Most of the reefs have been destroyed or seriously degraded by dynamite fishing or killed by pollution, and the more accessible are busy at weekends. **Natsepa Beach** at Baguala Bay is 14 km NE of town, and one of the most popular. **Accommodation A+** *Maulana Hotel* at Waitatiri, Jl Raya Passo, Waitatiri, T 61466/61468, F 61497 (near Natsepa Beach, to get there take a bemo to Natsepa, and ask the driver to let you off at Waitatiri, 600Rp). This sister hotel to the *Maulana* on Banda Island has a/c rooms with satellite TV, a restaurant serving Indonesian, Chinese and European food, a fresh water swimming pool, which is open to non-guests for a fee of 5,000Rp. Boats are also available for diving and fishing. Losmen accommodation is also available. *Getting there*: bus from the Mardika terminal bound for Suli (450Rp). **Amahusu Beach** is 7 km SW of town. The reef here is depressingly degraded. This spot is the finish line for the annual Darwin-Ambon yacht race. Hotel accommodation available. *Getting*

there: bus from the Mardika terminal (250Rp). Finally, **Namalatu Beach** is 15 km from town, SW from Amahusu, at the tip of this arm of Ambon Island. Snorkelling is reasonable here and overall it is probably the best beach on Ambon Island. **Accommodation B** *Lelisa Beach*, a/c, and some losmen. The best of the cheaper places to stay are (**E**) *Ibu Eta's*, a house with use of the owner's own kitchen and (**D**) *Marthin Latuhihin's Place*, a very friendly place with great views over the ocean and just two clean rooms and attached mandi, breakfast included. *Getting there*: by bus bound for Latuhalat from the Mardika terminal.

Waai, 31 km NE of town, past Tulehu, possesses one of the strangest sights on Ambon: a pool of sacred eels. Waai has strong adat traditions and ancient myths surround its famed eels. The eels live in a pool, fed by clear spring water from a 50m-high waterfall. These days the eels are fed eggs to bring them into view, but in former times they rarely appeared and it was considered a sign of good fortune to see them – any wish would come true following a sight of them. The villagers believe that if the sacred eels and sacred fish disappear, disaster will strike. *Getting there*: by bemo from the Mardika terminal (1,100Rp).

Pombo Island is situated just off Ambon's NE coast (10 mins by boat). The surrounding waters are said by locals to offer the best snorkelling and swimming. The island is a national park and there are PHPA bungalows which visitors can use with prior booking (see Useful addresses for PHPA Office address). *Getting there*: boats to Pombo can be chartered from Tulehu, Waai, Honimua and Liang. Expect to pay 75,000 Rp for a day's charter. Buses to all four towns leave from the Mardika terminal.

Hila is a village on the N coast with a charming old Dutch church, the oldest still standing on Ambon, built in 1780, with an inscription in Dutch carved into the stone. Nearby are the ruins of Fort Amsterdam built on the site of a former

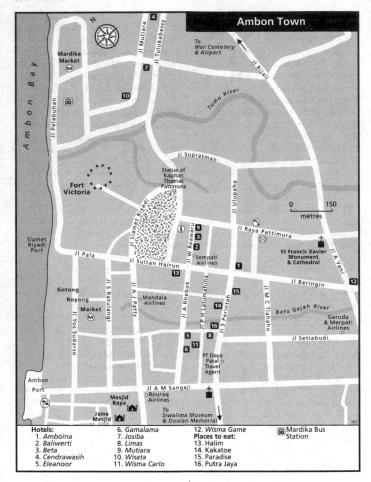

Ambon Town

Hotels:
1. *Amboina*
2. *Baliwerti*
3. *Beta*
4. *Cendrawasih*
5. *Eleanoor*
6. *Gamalama*
7. *Josiba*
8. *Limas*
9. *Mutiara*
10. *Wisata*
11. *Wisma Carlo*
12. *Wisma Game*

Places to eat:
13. Halim
14. Kakatoe
15. Paradise
16. Putra Jaya

Mardika Bus Station

Portuguese fort. *Getting there*: by bemo (1,300Rp).

Tours

Daya Patal Tours & Travel operate a range of tours around the island (US$50-60/day); *Natrabu* also run tours.

Festivals

Jul: *Darwin-Ambon yacht race*, first contested in 1976, the race is over a distance of more than 1,000 km.

Local information
● Accommodation

NB During the Darwin-Ambon yacht race (Jul) hotels are booked-up. Most rates quoted incl breakfast.

A *Manise*, Jl WR Supratman 1, T 42905, F 41054, a/c, standard rooms are windowless, superior rooms are OK.

A-B *Amboina*, Jl Kapt Ulupaha 5A, T 41725 / 41961 / 41641 / 41712 / Hunting 55515, F 53354/55723, Reservations T 55624, a/c, overpriced, even the most expensive rooms have slightly tatty cord carpets, long-term residents qualify for a substantial discount, standard double has a shower, the deluxe room has a bathtub, prices are very negotiable, a businessman's hotel, with Conference Room, shops, restaurant and bar, 24-hrs room service, laundry, etc, credit cards accepted.

B *Baliwerti Hotel*, Jl Wim Reawaru 9, T 55996, a/c, restaurant, new hotel with very attractive decor, rooms have colour TV, bathrooms with hot water, rec; **B** *Cendrawasih*, Jl Tulukabessy 39, T 52487, F 53373, a/c, hot water, on edge of town, comfortable; **B** *Mutiara*, Jl Raya Pattimura 90, T 97124, a/c, well-run, clean and modern rooms.

B-C *Josiba*, Jl Tulukabessy 27, T 41280, on the edge of town, rooms rather shabby and overpriced; **B-C** *Wisata*, Jl Mutiara SK 1/3-15 No 67, T 53293, F 53592, a/c, hot water, on edge of town in a quiet alley, friendly, rooms rather like ships' cabins with hotch-potch of furniture and fittings.

C *Eleanoor*, Jl Anthone Rhebok 30, T 52834, some a/c, not very good value, rooms seemed a bit dingy but positioned on quiet street; **C** *Limas Hotel*, Jl Kamboja 16, T 53269, some a/c, attractive international-style decor, full size bathtub in more expensive rooms, cheaper fan rooms are also modern and attractive with attached shower, breakfast and afternoon tea incl, rec; **C** *Penginapan Simponi*, Jl Tulukabessy 46, T 54305, some a/c, on edge of town, clean but no windows; **C** *Wisma Carlo*, Jl Philip Latumahina 24A, T 42220, some a/c, small hotel, modern rooms with attached mandi set around a courtyard but not as good value as other equivalent hotels, rates incl tax, breakfast and afternoon tea.

D *Beta Guesthouse*, Jl Wim Reawaru 114, T 53463, the *Beta* is an outstanding guest house and an invaluable source of travellers' information, owners are very friendly, the wife in particular speaks excellent English, rooms are simple but clean, with attached mandi, and fans, the hotel is on 3 flrs, with a pleasant verandah running outside all the rooms, at the entrance is a seating area with satellite TV (CNN news available for the homesick), a restaurant and bar with iced beer, price incl breakfast and an afternoon snack, highly rec; **D** *Gamalama*, Jl Anthone Rhebok 11, T 53724, bare rooms, attached mandi.

E *Wisma Game*, Jl Jend A Yani, T 53525, small rooms, we have received good reports about this hotel, all rooms with private mandi, clean, balconies, early morning aerobics class next door might be a problem.

● **Places to eat**

Black dog is a great delicacy for Ambonese Christians, it is said to taste much better than the meat of white dogs. Good Indonesian food served from small warungs along Jl Said Perintah. Try the *Putra Jaya* at No 38 with 2 white cockatoos on perches outside, good nasi goreng and mie goreng. Also rec on this road are *Roda Baru* (Padang food) at No 42, *Sonata* at No 92 and *Paradise* (good nasi campur). There are also restaurants selling cheap, tasty dishes nr the mosque on Jl Sultan Babullah. ♦♦♦*Halim*, Jl Sultan Hairun, seafood specialities but food generally rather bland and overall, disappointing; ♦♦*Asri*, Jl WR Supratman (next to *Manise Hotel*), Indonesian food in spotless restaurant; ♦♦*Kakatoe*, Jl Said Perintha 20, T 56142, Belgian chef, specializing in European food, good food incl breakfast, a meeting place for foreigners with a useful message board and book exchange, attractive garden setting, rec; *Amboina*, Jl AJ Patty 63, bakery and ice cream; *Utama*, Jl Setiabudi 58, good seafood, Chinese, dog sometimes served.

● **Airline offices**

Bouraq, Jl Sultan Babullah 19, T 52314, open 0800-1700 Mon-Sat; **Mandala**, Jl AJ Patty 19, T 42551, F 42377 (for Ujung Pandang, Jakarta and Surabaya) open 0800-1800 Mon-Sat, 0800-1400 Sun; **Merpati/Garuda**, Jl Jend A Yani, T 52481, open 0800-1700 Mon-Fri, 0800-1500 Sat, 1000-1500 Sun; **Sempati**, Jl Wim Reawaru (just down from *Beta* and *Baliwerti* hotels).

● **Banks & money changers**

Bank Central Asia, Jl Sultan Hairun 24; **Bank Dagang Negara**, Jl Raya Pattimura; **BNI**, Jl Said Perintah; **Danamon**, Jl Diponegoro; **Ekspor Impor**, Jl Raya Pattimura 14.

● **Entertainment**

Dance: there are a number of dances characteristic of Maluku; unfortunately it is rare to find them being performed in 'authentic' surroundings. The oddest is the *Bambu Gila* or Crazy Bamboo dance. The Maluku tourist office provides an enlightening description of the dance: '...it is a performance using a bamboo-pole, held by 7 young strong men. In using supernatural powers, the bamboo begin to move, while still held, and at a sudden moment, it throw down the men'. More interesting is the Cakalele

(Chakalaylee), a war dance which features dancers wearing headgear inspired by the helmets of Portuguese soldiers.

● **Post & telecommunications**
Area code: 0911.
General Post Office: Jl Raya Pattimura 20.
Perumtel: Jl Raya Pattimura 11. A new office has opened on Jl Dr JB Sitanala.

● **Shopping**
The main shopping street is Jl AJ Patty. There are a number of souvenir shops here selling pearls, silver, shell collages, shell lamps, jewellery and tortoise shell. Bargain hard.

Books: *Dian Pertiwi*, Jl Diponegoro 25 – for 2 books on the histories of Banda and Ternate/Tidore by Willard Hanna, shop closes at 1500, reopens 1700.

● **Sports**
Diving: not very well developed around Ambon (compared to, say, Manado) as most of the coral has been destroyed to make cement for buildings and roads. In Ambon Bay spots incl Eri, Silale and Tanjung Setan (Ghost Cape – good dropoffs here); around Saparua Island (E of Ambon) at Itawaka and Kulor, and at Tiga Island. But the best dive spot is off Amet on Nusa Laut Island (Mahu Diving Lodge offers dives here, 1 hr by boat from Mahu on Saparua Island). Rates are approx US$50 pp/day (2 tanks, ie 2 dives). Oct and Nov are the best months – the seas are calmest. *Daya Patal* on Jl Said Perintah 27A, T 3529, F 44709, can provide all diving equipment except regulators and BCDs; divers must bring their own, rates are approximately US$200 for 3 days, US$675 for 7 days.

● **Tour companies & travel agents**
One of the best is *Daya Patal*, Jl Said Perintah 27A, T 53344, F 54127, open 0800-1800 Mon-Sat, 0800-1400 Sun. The manager Karolis Anaktototy is very helpful and speaks excellent English. They offer a variety of tours and can also put together tailor made packages, eg 5 days Spice Island Tour featuring Ambon, Saparua and Seram for 2 people US$249 pp; Banda Tour (3 nights), US$302 pp in *Laguna Hotel*, US$160 in *Guest House*. They can also arrange diving holidays at the Mahu Diving Lodge on Saparua. High season for tourism is Aug, Sep and Oct. Other agents incl *Natrabu*, Jl Rijali 53, T 2593, F 3537; *Netral Jaya*, Jl Diponegoro 76.

● **Tourist offices**
Maluku Tourist Office, Jl Raya Pattimura 1 (in the large offices of the Gubernor Kepala Daerah Tingkat Maluku – ask for the Dinas Pariwisata), open 0830-1430 Mon-Thur, 0830-1130 Fri, 0830-1300 Sat, useful maps and other handouts.

● **Useful addresses**
Immigration Office: Jl Dr Kayadoe 48A, T 3066.
PHPA: Jl Tantui (nr the Australian War Cemetery outside town), T 41189.

● **Transport**
Local Bejaks: there are so many that different colours denote those which are allowed to operate on certain days; yellow (Wed, Sat), red (Tues, Fri), and white (Mon, Thur). A ride should cost about 700Rp. **Bemos & buses**: link most places on Ambon Island with the capital. The central Mardika terminal is next to the market of the same name, on the seafront, 1 km NE of town. In town, bemos take 1 of 5 routes or 'lines', all beginning and ending at the Mardika terminal (150Rp). **Taxis**: unmetered, can be hired for specific trips or by the hour (about 5,000Rp/hr, 25,000Rp half day). Taxi 'ranks' at the intersection of Jl Setiabudi and Jl Said Perintah, and nr the Gotong Royong market on Jl Pala/Slamet Riyadi (at the end of Jl Dr Sam Ratulangi). Taxis also wait outside the bigger hotels.

Air Ambon's Pattimura airport is only a few kms NW of town as the crow flies, but over 40 km by road. Regular connection with Merpati (CASA-designed planes made outside Bandung, Java) with Banda and on Sat via Seram (see Transport in Banda section for more details on the difficulties of getting to and back from Banda). **Transport to town**: Ancient taxis cost 20,000Rp. A much cheaper alternative is to catch a bus from just outside the airport to Poka, 14 km (350Rp); from here, there are ferries across Ambon Bay to Gelala (200Rp), where bemos wait to whisk passengers the final 5 km into town (250Rp). Going from town to the airport, catch a bemo to Gelala, take the ferry, and then board another bemo from Poka, bound for Laha. **NB** Sempati and Mandala both offer a free bus service to the airport – useful for early morning flights. *Airport facilities*: incl a useful tourist information desk (usually open when flights arrive). Ambon is Maluku's air transport hub with regular connections with Biak, Ternate, Banda, Ujung Pandang, Sorong, Langgur, Manado and Jayapura. Less frequent services to Amahai, Labuha, Langgur, Mangole, Namlea, Sanana, and Saumlaki.

Road Bus: see Local transport.

Sea Boat: larger ships dock at the Pelabuhan Ambon, nr the centre of town, at the intersection of Jl Yos Sudarso and Jl AM Sangaji. Pelni and other shipping companies have their offices in the port complex. The Pelni ships *Rinjani*, *Kerinci* and *Dobonsolo* leave for other destinations in Maluku, and for Sulawesi, Java and Irian Jaya (see route scedule, page 921). Smaller vessels use the Pelabuhan Slamet Riyadi at the end of Jl Pala near the Gotong Royong market, and leave for Banda (1 night), Seram Utara (Wahai – 18 hrs), Seram Timur, Irian Jaya and other ports. For Banda, the *Waisamar* leaves every 2 days, 19,000Rp (Ambon-Banda), 20,000Rp (Banda-Ambon). Cabins are available for 40,000Rp. For the Ambon-Banda leg buy the tickets from the ship's captain. Boats also leave daily for Seram, Saparua and Haruku from Hurnala Port, Tulehu, on Ambon's W coast. For Saparua, boats leave twice daily at 0900 and 1300, 2 hrs (a very pleasant journey); there are also speedboats to Saparua, which depart when full (4,500Rp). **NB** The speedboats leave from a different pier to the regular ferries. Boats for Seram from Tulehu leave daily at 1000 (5,000Rp). *Getting there*: bus from the Mardika terminal (30 mins, 800Rp).

THE LEASE ISLANDS

To the E of Ambon are a collection of other, less frequently visited, islands – Saparua, Haruku and Nusa Laut – collectively known as the Lease Islands.

SAPARUA

With a population of 50,000 and a fairly well developed infrastructure, Saparua offers good beaches, snorkelling and diving. This was the island where Kapitan Pattimura led his rebellion against the Dutch (see page 803).

Saparua town is the capital of Saparua and is a very relaxed place. Traditional houses made of coconut and sago palm, or entirely of sago palm, with their beautiful rust-red roofs are interspersed between old Dutch houses, cemeteries, and several rather grand churches. Many of the houses have gardens full of colourful shrubs and flowers. Walking through the streets at night provides the nosy (to be fair, though, privacy is not a concept much in evidence in these parts), with the opportunity to gaze into people's homes to see the interesting collections of ornaments and memorabilia, many of Dutch origin – a huge tapestry of windmills and tulips for example, carefully handed down from generation to generation. In

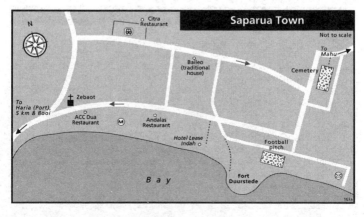

Nov the early arrival of the Christmas decorations provides yet more colour.

Even along the main street there are cloves drying on mats in the sun, scenting the air with a wonderful aroma. The green plump cloves are newly picked and by the end of the first day will have acquired a reddish tinge; at nightfall of the second day they will have turned brown but still be fairly plump; by the end of their final day (the process takes 3-7 days) they will be brown and shrivelled.

Places of interest

Fort Duurstede on the edge of town has been partially restored with commanding views over two bays. The latrine area and mandi are still standing (note the drainage system). Several of the sentry positions still have their cannon. Below are the remains of the 16th century pier, built by the Portuguese.

Saparua town holds a **colourful market** on Wed and Sat, selling excellent local smoked fish, huge cones of red palm sugar and sago pulp, and some curious, unrecognizable produce. People from the surrounding islands come here to sell their goods.

Climbing the hill outside town in the late afternoon offers the best views of the sunset. In 1817 the famous Malukan Independence leader, Pattimura, in an ultimately unsuccessful attempt to rid the area of the Dutch presence (inspired by his experience of the rather more honourable colonial conduct of the British during their brief period of occupation during the Napoleonic wars), took control of Fort Duurstede; he marched the captured Dutch soldiers to the top of this hill and slaughtered them at sunset; he then had them buried here. No wonder the hill is reputed to be haunted.

Excursions

Saparua has **beaches** which are far superior to those found on Ambon. **Waisisil** is one with white sand and good snorkelling. At present there is no accommodation but it is roughly midway between Saparua town and Siri Sore, both of which have good accommodation; many bemos go in this direction. **Kulor**, in the NW of the island has one of the best beaches. There is only one bemo a day at present from Saparua town, which leaves in the afternoon; otherwise you have to charter. At the end of 1995 some new accommodation is due to open at Kulor. Check in town for latest information. But perhaps the best place to stay on Saparua is on the beach S of **Ouw** at *Nukahoni* (see Accommodation for more details). The **village of Ouw** is also a worthwhile excursion from Saparua town. Ouw is locally renowned for its **pottery**. Attractive utilitarian pieces are made

The baileo

👣 The baileo is an open sided structure built on piles with a thatched roof, together with its sacred ancestral stone. The baileo was the traditional meeting place of the village elders, where all matters concerning the welfare of the village and of adat were discussed and decisions taken. This is where the ancestral spirits live, and in times past would have housed the clan heirlooms and sacred objects. To enter it one would have had to dress in adat costume and behave in an appropriate manner, having first asked the ancestors for permission to enter. This would have been achieved through an intermediary who would recite verses in bahasa tanah – earth language or language of the ancestors – and blow a conch shell. Traditionally, when a new baileo was built, adat custom required the work to be accompanied by headhunting rituals. The baileo would originally have been in the centre of the village. The welfare of the village was dependent on the baileo being well-maintained; should it have fallen into disrepair then the community would suffer and death would result. The land around the baileo was also considered sacred.

The Nuaula: warriors and house-builders

In times past the Nuaula were renowned as fierce warriors and headhunters. Adat ceremonies connected with the attainment of manhood, marriage or the building of a new house or baileo required, often, the offering of several severed heads to the ancestors. Fortunately, today, the heads of old have been replaced by red cloth, symbolizing blood, which most Nuaula wear.

There is a spatial separation in the village between men and women's places: the men's meeting house is in the centre of the village, the women's – including home gardens and menstruation huts – on the periphery. The process of house-building is one of the most important ceremonies, with an associated cycle of rituals. Like some societies in Africa, it is the act of building which is important, not the finished product, and houses may be torn down very soon after they have been completed. 'Building' is a performance infused with ritual meaning. As the anthropologist Roy Ellen has written, "The building of the house is...one of the eternal ceremonial cycles and a focus of ritual which regulates the Nuaula conception of time."

Numerous adat laws govern every step in the house-building process. Upright supports are 'planted' so that they remain true to the direction that the tree grew, maintaining continuity between the living tree and the 'living' house. Particularly important are the *numa mone*, traditional pile built houses that contain the sacred heirlooms of the clan or family. It is their role as a receptacle for these objects, rather than as places to live and sleep, which is important. The house becomes, in effect, the embodiment of the clan, a living object, that is referred to in anthropomorphic terms.

in great quantities, and used to store and carry water, make sago, and so on. The pots are used all over the island, and the production process can be seen at any one of numerous potteries. **Other sights** in Ouw include the cannon outside the Raja's new, and rather imposing, house; the mural on the wall in the Sunday School; and the old 'fort' which once had 99 windows but now is being hastened into ruin by the local people who use it as a source of building material. In her book *Ambon: island of spices*, Shirley Deane writes that "Ulath and Ouw – one town geographically, with only a narrow street dividing them – but considering themselves so very much two villages that every year one side attacks the other (for some reason now lost in the shadows of the past). That year (1972) five men had been killed in the fighting." This antagonism is itself, it seems, now a thing of the past too. *Getting there*: there are regular bemos from Saparua town that pass through Ouw.

Local information
● **Accommodation**

Saparua town: C-E *Lease Indah*, Jl Benteng Duurstede, T 21040, the hotel has recently expanded with 10 new a/c rm and 5 fan rm all clean and attractively decorated, the 4 older rm with shared mandi and much inferior, but considerably cheaper, many rooms have their own private verandah overlooking an attractive courtyard, separate dining area, price incl breakfast (with huge flask of boiling water plus tea and coffee) and afternoon tea which is often freshly cooked pisang goreng. The hotel is situated overlooking the bay next to Fort Duurstede and a remarkably quiet mosque. In a corner of the courtyard there is a small concrete tank with 5 baby crocodiles (being kept for their skins), highly rec.

Beyond the main town: A-B *Mahu Diving Lodge* (formerly *Mahu Village Resort*), the main reason to stay here is for the diving, which is good. The hotel has no beach, the rooms are overpriced (but spotless), and the site is marred by a large, empty swimming pool which gives a very slightly unkempt feel to the resort. Prices are negotiable especially in the low season, all meals incl in rates. *PT Daya Patal Travel Agent* in Ambon runs tours here (see Ambon section), though it is easy enough to travel independently; **D** *Sire Sore Losman* in Sire Sore village, well-run, caters to Dutch tour groups for whom they put on Malukan 'cultural evenings', rooms with fan and private mandi, excellent breakfast, very clean, dinner is 6,000Rp pp (there is nowhere else to eat in the village).

Nusa Laut and Haruku: no accommodation, but some homestays.

Ouw: D-E *Nukahoni*, 8 attractively furnished but simple rm with private mandi and shower. Rates incl 3 meals, tea, coffee and biscuits all day. Diving is available at 75,000Rp for 2 people, and the owners take residents to their 'secret' dive site, a submerged village. It is also possible to go fishing at night, and there is reasonable snorkelling in front of the bungalows. Arnold, the Dutch co-owner works here between Nov and Jan and is a mine of information. His wife's grandfather is the Raja of Ouw and her brother is co-owner of the bungalows. In front of the main house are 2 ancestor stones – this is ancestral land and the owners had to propitiate the ancestors before building, highly rec. To get to this place, take a bemo to Ouw, get off at the bus stop nr the start of the village opp the smaller of the 2 churches (Gereja Pantekosta Jemaat Ouw) – everyone knows him. You will then be taken by small boat, or dug out canoe, round the headland to a clearing in the jungle opp Nusa Laut Island (20 mins boat ride). There is good diving and snorkelling here, and a reasonable beach.

● **Places to eat**
Three are rec: ◆*Citra* in bus station, good beef rendang; *ACC Dua* and *RM Andalas* also both serve good food and are friendly places to eat.

● **Post & telecommunications**
There is a Post Office and Telecommunications centre (see map), but no banks.

● **Sports**
Diving: there is excellent diving off Saparua. The *Mahu Diving Lodge* at Mahu is the largest and most developed outfit, with the greatest range of amenities. However, perhaps the best ambience, accommodation and diving – if more basic conditions are being sought – is at *Nukahoni* nr Ouw. See Accommodation for details.
Boat hire: to go snorkelling etc 39,000Rp to Nusa Laut, ask at your accommodation for Francis. John who meets the boats at Haria, and the bemos at the bus station in Saparua town, and speaks good English, may also be able to help.

● **Transport**
Local Bemos: to all points on the island depart regularly throughout the day from the bus terminal in town. Check the fare in advance as drivers may try to get you to charter the whole vehicle. Most points on Saparua are within 10 km of town, so missing the last bemo is not a disaster – it is possible to walk back. *Fares*: Haria-Saparua 350Rp (5 km); Sire Sore 400Rp (6 km); Booi 300Rp (4 km); Mahu 500Rp (7 km); Ouw 500Rp (10 km).

Sea Boats/ferries: boats to Haria on Saparua (2 hrs) leave daily from Liang on Ambon's NE coast (get there by bus from the Mardika terminal). The dock at Haria is 5 km from Saparua town. Boats for Pelauw, on Haruku, also leave from Liang. There are boats from Haria to Nusa Laut. Two ferries daily from Haria to Tulehu on Ambon at 0900 and 1300, very pleasant 2 hrs crossing on uncrowded boat, 4,000Rp. Also speedboats which leave when full taking 1 hr, 4,500Rp (inconveniently, speedboats leave from a different pier so decide in advance which type of boat to take. Three ferries a week to Amahai on Seram, Mon, Wed, Fri, check times. Market days are a good time to visit the surrounding islands as boats run frequently from Haria.

SERAM

Seram is the largest island in Maluku with a land area of 18,400 sq km, and the most mysterious. It's densely wooded, mountainous (though non-volcanic) interior harbours animist tribal peoples whose traditional lifestyles remain remarkably intact; up to 75% of the population are animists. The Nuaula were renowned warriors and headhunters. The Bonfia, living in eastern Seram, are – by contrast – shy and peaceful. Few people visit the eastern interior due to the difficulty of access.

The island lies to the NE of Ambon and, in size at least, dominates its smaller neighbour. The capital, **Masohi** – Masohi's port is known as **Amahai** – is situated on the S coast, and the island's second town, **Wahai**, is on the N coast. Transportation between the two is not good although buses do make the journey. An alternative is to catch a bus from Masohi to Sawai and then a speedboat from there to Wahai.

A land of myth and superstition, Ambonese refer to Seram as the 'Nusa Ina' (Mother Island); they believe they came from here and it is here that Ambonese adat originated. Even today the island elicits both fear and respect from the worldly Ambonese. Seram is viewed as a land of mystery and magic, whose indigenous peoples had strange, often frightening powers. There are many legends connected with Seram, stories of witches and witchcraft, people who could fly or make themselves invisible at will. In the remote interior of this island, headhunting persisted into this century. During colonial times the Dutch found these interior tribes among the most troublesome and difficult to control.

Most of the population of 300,000 is found in the W and on the coasts. Since colonial times the government has found it expedient to enforce resettlement programmes. First by moving inland tribal peoples to the coast to make them easier to control, and more recently, people from the Lease Islands to relieve population pressure there.

Descriptions of the cuscus

The cuscus is a small furry animal, found only in Maluku (mainly Seram) and parts of New Guinea. Described by Alfred Russel Wallace in *The Malay Archipelago* he wrote that "They have small heads, large eyes and a dense covering of woolly fur....They live in trees....They move slowly....The natives everywhere eat their flesh, and as their motions are so slow, easily catch them by climbing; so it is wonderful that they have not been exterminated".

More recently Shirley Deane in *Ambon – Island of Spices* writes that:
"There are many legends in Seram about the cuscus, giving it human characteristics, assuming that groups of cuscus' have a 'kapitan' (a cuscus with the thickest tufts of white fur, like an elder's beard) and so on. Certain tribes are thought to be descended from cuscus, both in Seram and New Guinea. And the Nuaula tribe of South Seram believes that the ghost of a man killed while hunting cuscus is exceptionally evil.

The cuscus is an integral part of the adat of Nuaula – five roasted cuscus form a necessary part of their marriage wealth, and it is part of their birth ritual too. A new mother eats the meat and drinks the broth of a cuscus stewed inside a green bamboo to ensure a flow of milk. The ritual killing of the cuscus is an essential item of the male initiation ceremony, the cracking of its skull replacing the taking of a human head in earlier times. It is thought that the cuscus was chosen for the substitution because of its human characteristics – the large soulful eyes, its habit of sitting bolt upright and eating with its front paws, its wise white beard, and its tremendous courage in adversity."

Mount Binaiya – also known as Mt Manusela – is the highest peak in Maluku at 3,019m. There are several other mountains that exceed 2,000m on the island. Spectacular waterfalls, rivers big enough to raft down, and dense tropical forest are all features of the island. During the rainy season, trees across roads and landslides make travelling by road difficult. To get to Wahai from Masohi, travel by bemo to Saka, on the N coast (2-3 hrs) and from here take a speed boat to Wahai (2-3 hrs).

Superb snorkelling is to be found in a lagoon off an isolated small beach, 15 mins walk over rocks from the big beach at *Suamadaha*. There is a warm spring running into the bay and a wreck in the lagoon can easily be seen when snorkelling.

Manusela National Park, covering a 1,890 km^2 swathe of forest from Seram's N coast to S coast and including Mt Manusela, is Maluku's most important protected area. Many people who visit Seram do so to trek through the park. It supports a remarkably varied flora and fauna which is relatively well recorded as the park was selected as a research site for an Operation Raleigh expedition. The bird life is particularly rich, and it is also famous for its huge butterflies, including the spectacular *Papilio ulysses*. Visitors are recommended to take a guide, and to obtain a permit and/or advice from the PHPA office at Air Besar, 2 km E of Wahai, or from the PHPA office in Ambon. Visitors have gone missing in this wild area, and are presumed to have died. There is no accommodation in the park. Hikers need to be fit for this arduous trek, and to take all supplies. When trekking in Seram, it is essential to contact the village head, or *Bapak Raja*, to ensure your safety as you pass through each area. The trek through the Manusela reserve takes several days. Hiring porters presents its own problems. Due to local adat laws porters must be changed at each village; if they do not wish to continue trekkers have no choice but to wait with them. Days also tend to get shorter than

originally agreed. In short, be prepared and be patient.

Practical advice

There are few English speakers on Seram. John Lisapeli at the Kantor Pariwisata (tourist office) speaks good English and is knowledgeable about the Nuaulu people. He can take visitors to see the Nuaulu tribes. (Take a red scarf and tobacco as gifts; the red scarf has replaced the severed head in traditional adat ceremonies and rituals of these former head hunters, red being the colour of blood.) He can arrange tours to Bonara, Watane and Sepa, all Nuaulu villages. The cost is 20,000Rp for the guide and 30,000Rp for transport.

Festivals

Mar: once a year, usually in Mar, sea worms come ashore to breed, near Ouw. They are collected by local people and eaten, fried with chillies.

● **Accommodation** There are no good hotels on Seram, but a number of adequate losmen. Most are found in the capital, Masohi. Most are in our **C-E** range. **Masohi**: **C** *Lelemuku*, Jl Tiahahu 12, T 129; **C** *Nusantara*, Jl Abd Soulisa 15, T 21339; **D** *Nusa Ina*, Jl Banda 9, T 221; **D** *Sri Lestari*, Jl Abd Soulisa 5, T 178. **Wahai**: **D** *Sinar Indah*; **D** *Taman Baru*. **Tehoru**: **D** *Susi*.

● **Tourist offices** Dinas Pariwisata, Jl Banda 2, T 21462, helpful – see Practical advice, above.

● **Transport Air** One flight a week on Sat to Amahai (Masohi); this is the Ambon-Banda flight which transits Seram out and back. Return flights will have the usual problems associated with getting back from Banda (see Transport, Banda). **Sea Boat**: numerous boats leave for various destinations on Seram from various points on Ambon. For Amahai/Masohi there are daily boats from Hurnala Port in Tulehu, Ambon leaving between 1000 and 1200 and returning from Amahai at 0700, 3½ hrs (7,000Rp). There are less regular boats from Pelabuhan Slamet Riyadi in Ambon town to both Amahai and Wahai 18 hrs. A ferry makes a daily run from Liang (N coast of Ambon) to Kairatu 2 hrs, another from Hitu (also on Ambon's N coast) to Piru 4 hrs, and there are also said to be boat connections from Ambon's Honimua Beach to Seram.

BANDA ISLANDS

The nine tiny and beautiful islands that constitute the Banda archipelago lie SE of Ambon and cover a combined area of only 60 sq km. The capital Bandaneira is on the island of the same name (but spelt as two words, Banda Neira), separated from the active volcano Mt Api by a strait just a few 100m across. It has a superb setting, facing the lagoon formed by the crater of an extinct volcano and dominated by the imposing presence of Gunung Api with its near perfect cone and constant plume of smoke. The largest island in the group is Banda Besar (literally 'Big Banda') or Lontar, situated to the S of Banda Neira, while the smaller islands of Pulau Ai and Run to the W, and Pulau Rozengain to the E, make up this microscopic archipelago. The island of Ai was occupied by the British but was eventually handed back to the Dutch under the Anglo Dutch Treaty (1924) in exchange for Mahattan Island, New York.

The Bandas were 'discovered' by the Portuguese in 1512 in their search for spices, and as they were the only source of nutmeg and mace, brought vast profits to those able to control production and trade (see box). The nutmeg tree, *Myristica fragrans*, was for the Bandas the source of its wealth and the reason for its destruction (for background to the nutmeg and its role in the history of the Bandas see page 797). There are two harvests of nutmegs a year; the main harvest is in Jun and Jul, with a second, smaller harvest in Nov and Dec. Banda's nutmegs are still reputed to be the best in the world. In the Bandas, the outer fruit is also used to make delicious jams and drinks.

Thrust into obscurity with the fall in nutmeg prices in the early 19th century, the Bandas are now beginning to benefit from a new industry: tourism. With excellent game fishing, superb snorkelling and diving, and a rich history the islands have considerable potential. It is hoped that the development of tourism and fishing can arrest the slow depopulation of the islands – between 1971 and 1980 the population declined from 13,368 to 12,635.

Des Alwi, who owns the two most expensive hotels on Banda Neira and has a monopoly on diving, is the latterday king of the Bandas. It does not take long for a visitor to realize that little happens here without his involvement, or at least his consent. There are essentially two conflicting views as to his role in the development of the Bandas. One has it that the Bandas are Des Alwi's play thing; that

Banda Island

Sketch Map

Malole Beach

Malole

Lautaka

Mangku Batu

Boi Kherang

N

Tanah Rata

Mt Papenburg

see Town Map

Fort Belgika

Dr Cipto's House

Butchery in the Bandas: the curse of the spice trade

The Banda Islands' experience of colonialism is a case study in the excesses, inequities, inadequacies and inefficiencies of Dutch rule in Indonesia. The tiny size of the Bandas belies their former economic significance. These were the famous Spiceries of the E, on which Europeans depended for nutmeg and mace to flavour an otherwise monotonous diet. The first Europeans to arrive here were the Portuguese, under the captainship of Antonio de Abreu who landed on Banda in early 1512. The first Dutch vessel did not arrive until 1599, and the English landed in 1601.

The arrival of the Dutch coincided with increased activity from the volcano Mt Api, a portent – and taken as such by the Bandanese – of what was to follow. The Dutch established trading posts (known as *logies*) and proceeded to buy nutmeg and mace. Profits were vast: the spices were purchased at $1/320$ th of the price they realized in Amsterdam. From 1602, the Dutch presence in the Bandas was financed and administered by the VOC (Vereenigde Oost-indische Compagnie) or the United East India Company.

The appalling Dutch treatment of the local population can be traced back to 1609 when Admiral Verhoeven attempted to negotiate without a sufficiently large guard; he and 26 other Dutchmen were slaughtered by the Bandanese. This 'treachery' was not to be forgotten. In 1621 the new VOC governor-general Jan Pieterszoon Coen sailed for Banda with a large force to deal, once and for all, with the duplicitous locals. He forced a one-sided treaty upon the *Orang Kaya* (the rich men or chiefs) and when they failed to keep their side of the agreement proceeded to depopulate the islands. Many Bandanese were captured and shipped to Batavia to be sold into slavery, others committed suicide by throwing themselves from cliffs. Of a population of 15,000, only 1,000 remained – and most of these on the English controlled islands of Pulau Ai and Pulau Run. The 44 Orang Kaya faced a particularly vile fate, which even Dutchmen in Holland felt was beyond the realms of acceptable, civilized behaviour. The historian Willard Hanna quotes an eyewitness, Naval Lieutenant Nicolas van Waert:

The condemned victims being brought within the [Fort Nassau] enclosure, six Japanese [mercenary] soldiers were also ordered inside, and with their sharp swords they beheaded and quartered the eight chief orang kaya and then beheaded and quartered the 36 others. Their execution was awful to see. ... All of us, as professing Christians, were filled with dismay at the way the affair was brought to a conclusion, and we took no pleasure in such dealings.

his autocratic and domineering presence casts a shadow over the archipelago much as Gunung Api does. He is reputed to have closed down homestays that do not toe his line, and he controls diving hereabouts. The other view, turns this thread of logic on its head, and maintains that if it was not for Des Alwi then the Bandas would still be languishing in obscurity. That he has, personally, developed the islands' potential as a tourist destination, using his contacts and money, and doing so for the benefit of all islanders. Des Alwi is currently having talks with the Aman-resort group – which build possibly the most luxurious hotels in the world – to construct a 20-room hotel on Banda (although it will probably be a 'down market' version).

Flora and fauna

Unique to the Bandas are the Laweri fish,

Having disposed of the Bandanese, Coen had to find a way to maintain spice production. He chose to colonize the islands with *Perkeniers* – licensed planters who, for the most part, were 'free burghers' who had completed their contracts of service with the VOC. They leased the land from the VOC and had to sell all their production to the company at a fixed price. For their part, the VOC provided slaves, supplies and protection.

Life, even for the Perkeniers, was harsh and short. Mortality from disease was high, and earthquakes, eruptions, tidal waves and hurricanes periodically decimated the settlement of Banda Neira. Even company rule was unforgiving. A German resident between 1633 and 1638 recorded 25 executions: two buried alive, one broken on the wheel, nine hanged, nine decapitated, three garotted, and one arquebussed (shot with an early form of portable gun, supported on a tripod). Less fatal punishments were equally gruesome – one woman who had blasphemed had her tongue pierced by a red hot needle. Even the executioner was executed.

Despite the high mortality, the costs of maintaining a garrison, and the extensive smuggling and cheating on the part of the Perkeniers (for instance, substitution of inferior long nutmegs for Bandas' product), profits for the VOC remained high, and the Bandas were regarded as the jewel in the VOC crown. The Perkeniers, though usually in debt, lived in extravagant style.

The end of the Banda's monopoly position in nutmeg production is linked to the British period of control during the Napoleonic Wars. The British controlled the islands over two periods, between 1796 and 1803, and 1810 to 1817. During these years, nutmeg seedlings were taken to Bengkulu (Sumatra), Ceylon and Penang (Malaysia) for cultivation, while the French – a few years earlier in 1770 – had also obtained seedlings and planted them in Mauritius, Zanzibar and Madagascar (see page 798). Their monopoly in production lost, the VOC was never again in a position to set the price of nutmeg. As production elsewhere increased, so competition grew and prices fell, and the Banda Islands languished into obscurity. There was a brief period of excitement between 1936 and 1942 when two leaders of the fledgling Indonesian nationalist movement, Mohammad Hatta (to become Vice President) and Sutan Sjahrir (to become Prime Minister) were exiled here. But, other than this short period, the Bandas became just another group of breathtakingly beautiful islands in the eastern seas.

For an entertaining account of the Bandas see: Hanna, Willard A (1991) *Indonesian Banda: colonialism and its aftermath in the nutmeg islands*, Yayasan Warisan dan Budaya: Banda Neira. Available at the museum and the Hotel Laguna in Banda, or from the *Dian Pertiwi* bookshop in Ambon (see page 808).

Photoblepharon bandanensis, with eyes that light up and best seen on a moonless night. Their luminous eyes are the equivalent of a 5-watt light bulb and even after death they continue to glow for several days – the locals use them as bait when fishing at night. In times past these fish were also used as 'night lights' for children who were afraid of the dark.

Look out for the 'nutmeg pigeon', *Carpophaga concinna*, a fat pigeon which lives on the fruit of the nutmeg (similar in size and colour to an apricot). They are most common in nutmeg plantations, especially on Banda Besar. Other notable flora are the kapok tree, with its fluff that looks just like it does in the DIY cushion department, and the spectacular flame red flamboyan tree, which is quite a feature of Banda and adds greatly to the island's beauty (and after which many an Indonesian hotel is named).

Gunung Api erupting, reproduced from Valentijn, François (1724) *Oud en Nieuw Oost-Indiën*, Amsterdam

BANDA NEIRA

The core of the Banda archipelago, both geographically and economically, is the island of **Banda Neira**. It is here that most of the 15,000 strong population live and where the capital Bandaneira is to be found. The town is peaceful and attractive, and still contains a good array of Dutch mansions – gradually crumbling, due to lack of upkeep. A draw back of Banda Neira, and a surprising one, is that there are no good beaches. The nearest is a 50 mins' walk from town, and is nothing to speak of. Most visitors charter boats to go diving or snorkelling.

Places of interest

Fort Belgica, built in 1611 with stone shipped in from Holland, has been unsympathetically restored but enjoys a magnificent situation commanding views in three directions – go in the morning for photographs, late afternoon for atmosphere. Despite the cack-handed restoration efforts this is the most impressive and best preserved of the ruined forts in Central Maluku. Below it lies the mouldering ruins of **Fort Nassau**, built in 1609, somehow more authentic for not having been restored. Fort Belgica, was built in response to the growing threat posed by the British

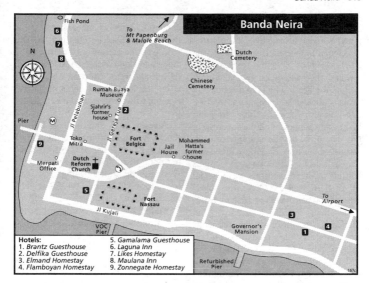

Banda Neira

Fish Pond

To
Mt Papenburg
& Malole Beach

Dutch
Cemetery

N

Chinese
Cemetery

Rumah Buaya
Museum

Jl Pelabuhan

Sjahrir's
former
house

Pier

Mohammed
Hatta's
former
house

Toko
Mitra

Fort
Belgica

Jail
House

Jl Gereja Tua

Dutch
Reform
Church

Merpati
Office

To
Airport

Fort
Nassau

Jl Kujali

VOC
Pier

Governor's
Mansion

Refurbished
Pier

Hotels:
1. Brantz Guesthouse
2. Delfika Guesthouse
3. Elmand Homestay
4. Flamboyan Homestay
5. Gamalama Guesthouse
6. Laguna Inn
7. Likes Homestay
8. Maulana Inn
9. Zonnegate Homestay

in this area and the site chosen because it commanded a far better military vantage point than Fort Nassau. Once the Dutch had established their monopoly of the spice trade, these forts' primary role was to protect the Dutch from any insurrection on the part of their badly treated slaves. Not far away, is the **Dutch Reform Church** (see map) with impressive coats of arms carved into the stone floor. This church is still in use.

The **former residences** of Banda's two most famous exiles, Mohammed Hatta and Sujan Sjahrir, have been turned into museums. These two were fervent anti-colonialists and members of the Nationalist party. Exiled by the Dutch to Banda, they eventually held high government office once Indonesia had won its independence. Hatta became Vice-President and Sjahrir went on to be Prime Minister.

On Jl Gereja are several fine, recently restored **Perkenier mansions**. A total of six of these impressive colonial houses have been restored on Banda; the original moulding, which symbolizes bread, has been recreated on the ceiling of the

verandah, while the columns are shaped to symbolize pineapples. The perkeniers (contract plantation owners), were a rum lot; many had been criminals and undesirables. They were brought in by the Dutch (who, under the ruthless leadership of the VOC Governor-General, Jan Pieterszoon Coen, had murdered most of Banda's population, see tinted box), and given tracts of land which they farmed using slave labour. The Perkeniers built magnificent mansions, some with marble floors, others with beautiful granite or ceramic tiles. They were often opulently decorated with crystal chandeliers and imported furnishings and European oil paintings. (It is said that the golden age of Dutch painting, represented by Rembrandt, was financed by fortunes made as a result of the spice trade.) These imports from Europe came out by ship from Holland as ballast, being replaced with spices for the return journey.

The **Rumah Buaya Museum** is housed in one of the restored colonial mansions. It houses an interesting collection of memorabilia and relics; maps, prints and drawings which bring to life Banda's past and give a fairly accurate portrait of what life was like for the Dutch in colonial Indonesia. Unfortunately the labelling is poor. Note the layers of clothing and the wigs, worn by the Dutch despite the heat. (The Dutch refused to adopt a 'tropical' lifestyle such as wearing non-European dress, taking frequent baths and changes of clothes, resting in the heat of the day, designing airy, well-ventilated houses.) They were renowned for their heavy drinking and copious feasting and it is easy to imagine the social life of these well fed Perkeniers, over-dressed in their layers of elegant European high fashion, dancing and consuming quantities of imported wine, gin, cigars, even preserved foods, and retiring to their gracious colonial mansions. (It is possible to do research in the museum archives; organize this through the tourist office.) Books by Willard Hanna on the history of the Bandas and Tidore & Ternate are on sale here.

But the **Governor's Mansion** is perhaps the grandest of the restored colonial buildings. Ask to see inside and look out for the poignant inscription scratched by a French prisoner on one of the walls:

"When will my happiness return? When will the bells toll the hour of my return, to the shores of my country, and the heart of my family, whom I love and bless."

There is a statue of King Willem III of Holland, in the garden behind.

Near the *Zonnegate Homestay* are some **old Dutch walls** and an arch made of coral. Watch the splendid sunsets from the refurbished pier in front of the Governor's Mansion.

There are **two cemeteries** on Banda; a Dutch and a Chinese one. Walk out of town past the *Delfika*, take the right fork going up the hill (past Des Alwi's new house and that of his daughter next door), and follow the road as it bends round. The Chinese cemetery is on the right: large, colourful, ornate tomb stones painted with symbolic dragons and plants, and depicting scenes of Chinese life. To get to the Dutch cemetery, continue on this road past the mosque also on the right, make a left turn along the road towards the telecom transmitter and the cemetery is on the left. Rather romantic in the evening with the scent of the Frangipane trees.

Papenburg is the highest hill on Banda, worth climbing for the superb views of Banda Neira. It is a steep climb but not difficult. Follow the path on the W side of the runway going away from town, fork left on the first minor path, which leads up the hill.

Malole Beach is a 50 mins walk to the far end of the island from town. It may be the best beach hereabouts but that is not saying much. To get there take the path running away from town at the W end of the runway; keep following this main path until reaching the beach.

There is an odd **fish pond** – a neglected concrete pool – on the edge of town which at low tide barely covers the imprisoned occupants. These poor creatures are interesting to see and in 1995 included a tiger shark and two medium sized turtles.

Excursions

Across the lagoon and overlooking Banda Neira is the volcano appropriately named **Gunung Api** – or Fire Mountain. A vulcanologist who climbed the peak in 1986, some 2 years before it last erupted, maintained that lava flows would always run down the side of the mountain away from the capital and the main centres of settlement. When Gunung Api did erupt in 1988 he was, fortunately, proved correct. A thin plume of smoke continually hangs over the island, a reminder to all residents and visitors of the volcano's continued activity. Hotels and guesthouses organize expeditions to climb the 600m-high cone, which takes about half a day; for the best views set off before 0600 (see tours). A guide is recommended.

Ay Island – also spelt Ai – is a highly recommended excursion, with beautiful beaches and good snorkelling.

A visit to **Banda Besar** with the **plantation home** of Wim Van den Broeke, **Fort Hollandia** and an **adat** house is highly recommended (see page 824).

Pisang Island is usually visited on a day boat tour. However there are also some very attractive bungalows on Pisang, with their own private beach and mandis. However, there is no fresh water on the island. *Getting there*: by chartered boat, 30,000Rp (see tours).

Tours

Most hotels and guesthouses run tours to various parts of the island, and to neighbouring islands. To climb Gunung Api, with a guide, should cost about 10,000Rp pp; for a large group, about 50,000Rp in total. To charter a boat costs between 45,000 and 150,000Rp, depending on the destination. Pisang, Ay, Hatta, Run and Nailaka islands are all easily accessible on a day boat tour.

Festivals

KoraKora races occur twice a year – the dates vary and can be postponed by a week or more at the very last minute – but roughly Apr and Oct/Nov. The competition is between boats from Banda, Selamon on Banda Besar and Ay Island, and the prize is a trophy and 2 million rupiah (the money comes from Jakarta). Ay Island always wins! The KoraKora canoes are quite impressive, the 37 men in each row in unison in a beautiful, stylized, almost balletic movement, accompanied by gongs and drums – quite a breathtaking spectacle. The race takes place in the lagoon between the town of Banda Neira and Gunung Api. The boats travel at enormous speed and the race is over in just 20 mins. The KoraKora are the boats which took part in the historic Hongi raids, commandeered by the Dutch to extirpate spice trees on islands that might fall into enemy hands, and to ensure their control of the spice trade. Accommodation may be a problem if you have no reservation; if coming

from Ambon, PT Daya Patal Travel Agent can find out the date and help with reservations, or ask other travellers coming back from Banda.

Local information
● Accommodation

Des Alwi, the self-crowned king of the Bandas is trying, apparently to corner the entire tourist industry in the islands. The *Maulana* and *Laguna* hotels are owned by him. To be able to dive it may be necessary to stay at one of his establishments or at the *Delfika* and *Flamboyan* guesthouses which also enjoy diving 'rights' (see Diving section). All the guesthouses meet planes and ships; those who take a ride into town are not obliged to stay at a particular place – passengers are shown the full range of accommodation. All the guesthouses listed below are rec; they each have their own plus points and all serve 3 meals incl in the price, and have fans.

A+-A *Maulana Inn*, Jl Pelabuhan, T 21022, F 21024, on the seafront, in the process of renovation and much needed redecoration, at present there are 52 rm but these are being redesigned to create 42 larger rm, with staff quarters over the road for any staff accompanying guests. Large bathrooms, but no hot water, conference facilities, and the restaurant serves good food – try the nutmeg juice. The building was originally the family home of the Baadilla family (Des Alwi's mother's maiden name); you can still see the original black granite flr. The rooms are overpriced and the hotel relies on its rather over-blown reputation.

A *Laguna Inn*, Jl Pelabuhan, a/c, like the *Maulana*, this hotel, though cheaper, is still overpriced. All rooms have private bathrooms but are rather drab and disappointing. Most people stay here for the diving, and a saving grace is the restaurant which serves good food. Like the *Maulana* this place is also owned by Des Alwi.

C *Likes Homestay*, Welky Riupassa, Jl Maulana, T 21089, enjoys possibly the best location of the homestays, on the waterfront, facing G Api, with a garden, one of the few homestays with a view. Welky, the owner, is very friendly and speaks some English, he makes his guests feel part of the family, but equally, respects their privacy. It is possible to watch how the local food is prepared and there is sometimes singing in the evenings. The best 3 rm with private mandi, 3 more rm with shared mandi, mosquito nets available. Welky is in the process of creating a private beach, and the house has been in his family for 90 years. It is said that Des Alwi would like to close this homestay down probably because he wants the land, and he resents his guests eating there in preference to his hotels; **C** *Delfika Guesthouse*, Jl Nusantara, T 21027, first guest house on Banda, opened in 1981, the best place to stay if you want to learn about Banda, Bahri the manager is very well-informed, speaks good English, and is very helpful and friendly, he is the nephew of Des Alwi and his uncle owns the *Zonnegate Homestay*. Lawrence and Lorne Blair stayed here when they were making their TV documentary 'Ring of Fire' which chronicled their epic 10-year journey through the Indonesian archipelago. The 8 new rm are very attractive and spotless with private mandi; the 4 older rm are distinctly inferior but have private mandi; plus 10% tax. Food here is excellent, Moslem owned so no liquor on premises, but they will recommend a bar, garden with lovely views of Gunung Api. The *Delfika* has an in town location, and is 1 of the 2 guest houses with rights for residents to go diving; **C** *Flamboyan Homestay*, Jl St Syahrir, T 21067, almost opp the *Brantz*, restaurant, fans, has 5 attractive, clean, new rooms in a modern house with a lovely garden, 1 rm has Indonesian style squat toilet, residents have the right to go diving; **C** *Gamalama Guesthouse*, T 21032, from 1995 6 rm will have a/c, 7 rm with fan, new attractive rooms with private mandi, attractive upstairs balcony for guests to sit on but very small garden, good food; **C** *Zonnegate Homestay*, T 21050, located on the waterfront but only has a balcony, no garden, next to market so no privacy (fishermen often try their luck from in front of the balcony), 3 new rm, very attractive, double with mandi.

C-D *Brantz Guesthouse*, Jl St Syahrir, T 21068, located 5 mins walk from town in a pretty area of tree lined streets and old Dutch Perkenier mansions, very popular, opened in 1991. The entrance is a handsome Dutch colonial plantation house, with 12 rm with private mandi set around a large garden filled with a variety of flowering trees and shrubs: nutmeg, tropical sweet olive, avocado. Cheapest rooms with shared mandi are in the old house; slightly dearer rooms with private mandi.

D *Elmand Homestay*, directly opp the *Brantz*, in an old colonial plantation house, only 2 rm – a genuine homestay, spotless, private mandi, owners don't speak English, this is the place to stay if you want to experience living in a Dutch plantation house.

Further accommodation is available on **Pisang Island**: **C** bungalows on a beautiful beach. **Pulau Ai** and **Banda Besar** have homestays.

● **Places to eat**

The best place to eat is in your accommodation; the restaurants are not up to much. ◆*Nusantara RM* (Rumah Makan), Muslim owned so no alcohol, mie goreng is awful, tiny portions, although the fish is said to be good. For a taste of the unusual, try the nutmeg jam if you are offered some. Available to buy from many homestays.

● **Airline offices**

Merpati open Mon, Wed and Sat 0900-1300, Sun 0800-1230, Tues and Thur 0800-1300, Fri 0800-1130. When you pay for your return ticket (which cannot be bought in Ambon) at their town office, a day or two before the flight, Merpati is oddly very reluctant to issue a ticket. They prefer to just write 'cash' on their list. Tickets are handed out at the airport before boarding. Ask for a receipt if concerned.

● **Banks & money changers**

There are no banks on the islands; bring sufficient Indonesian currency.

● **Post & telecommunications**

Area code: 0910.

● **Sports**

Diving: diving in the Bandas is run by a Dutch diving instructor. PADI course, 4 days, US$350, open water course up to Dive Master. Best visibility Oct-Dec when the seas are at their calmest. The diving is excellent, though expensive at US$80, the going rate in Maluku being US$50. Best dive site: off Hatta Island. Des Alwi has the monopoly on diving; in order to dive you either have to stay at his hotels or at the *Delfika* or *Flamboyan* guesthouses. In early 1995 guests at other places were not permitted to go diving. This might change though.

Fishing: excellent game fishing (tuna, swordfish); hotels hire out tackle. All hotels and guesthouses except the *Elmand* organize boat trips.

Snorkelling: there is no good snorkelling nr Banda itself and it is necessary to charter a boat. The sea surrounding Banda Neira (town) is full of rubbish, is polluted, and the plant life and coral are dying. Recommended is the boat trip to see the young coral which has grown since the 1988 eruption of Gunung Api (homestays can arrange this). Snorkelling off Hatta Island is also good.

Waterskiing & windsurfing: both available in Banda Bay.

● **Tourist information**
There is a desk at the airport which is manned for flight arrivals.

● **Transport**
Local The *Delfika* has its own bemo; the *Likes*, *Zonnegate*, *Brantz*, *Flamboyan* and *Gamalama* share a van.

Air The airport is a short distance from town; walkable with limited luggage. Regular connections on Merpati (CASA planes made outside Bandung, Java) with Ambon and on Sat via Seram. **NB** The baggage allowance is just 10 kg (see below). It is only possible to book the outward leg; the return journey has to be bought in Banda. This is partly because of the way that the Merpati system works (each local office receives a cut from fares bought there) and partly because while the planes take 18 passengers to Banda, they can only return with 12 – due to the short length of the runway on Banda. A further factor is that it seems that residents of Des Alwi's hotels – the *Maulana* and *Laguna* inns – take precedence over other passengers. Be prepared to be frustrated and arrange your stay with some element of inbuilt flexibility. Guesthouses meet the plane (see introduction to Accommodation) and Merpati will provide transport from town to the airfield – picking passengers up from their accommodation.

Sea Boat: the *Waisamar* leaves about every 2 days for Banda from Ambon, 19,000Rp (Ambon-Banda), 20,000Rp (Banda-Ambon). Cabins are available for 40,000Rp. For the Ambon-Banda leg, buy the tickets from the ship's captain. For Banda-Ambon, they are on sale at the Toko Mitra in Banda town. The Pelni ship *Rinjani* docks every 2 weeks at Banda on its circuit through the islands. The *Rinjani* is cheaper (fares 17,000Rp-54,000Rp for the Ambon-Banda leg) and more comfortable than the *Waisamar* but, of course, is far less frequent. Guesthouses send a van to meet ships.

AY ISLAND

Ay is a place rich in history. At the dawn of the colonial period it was controlled by the British, until 1667, where upon it came under Dutch administration. Next to Ay is Run Island, a tiny, almost deserted island, that the world has forgotten. Such was the importance of the Spice trade (spices were more valuable than gold at this time) that the British exchanged Run with the Dutch for New Amsterdam (present day Manhattan).

It is hard to imagine, when visiting this peaceful, remote island, that it was once the scene of heavy fighting between the British and the Dutch. In the early 17th century the British had established fortified trading centres on both Ay and Run. They paid higher prices for nutmeg and mace than the Dutch and therefore posed a threat to the Dutch. In 1615, the Dutch attacked the British on Ay with a force of almost 1,000 men. After a fierce battle they were ultimately repelled by the British, only to return the following year, killing the entire British force. In 1667, when the British traded Run for Manhattan the Dutch established themselves as effectively the sole European presence in the region, with a monopoly of the Spice trade.

Places of interest

There are **several beaches** on Ay. The nearest is down from the boat landing in the direction of Banda. The best way to find the second beach, which is at the end of Ay Island nearest Run Island (going away from Banda), is to ask your host to show you the way. Alternatively, follow the coast path which turns inland at the end of the village. After 2-300m, where the village peters out, turn right, follow the most well-trodden path which forks left after another 2-300m, and remain on the best trod path until reaching the beach; about a 30 mins walk. There is another beach round the tip nearest Banda which can be reached by canoe or by walking over the hill – although a guide may be needed.

Interesting **historical sights** include the crumbling remains of Fort Revenge, the Dutch plantation house of the Welfaren Estate, a Dutch church and cemetery (take the path in the centre of the village, by the monument, going inland, after 50m turn right and the church is on the left after another 50m). Everywhere are the crumbling remains of the colonial plantations – walls, foundations, massive arches and gate posts. When the Dutch divided up the land on the Bandas and leased it to the Perkeniers (see box), there were 31 Perken (tracts of land) on Ay, 34 on Banda Besar and three on Banda Neira.

There are many **pleasant walks** through the spice-scented forests following well-trodden paths past giant kanari trees with their fantastic, sculpted roots. The kanari trees provide much needed shelter for the delicate nutmeg trees, and produce a nut called the tropical almond (on sale in the market at Banda). Recently, there have been times when the oil from this nut has been worth more than nutmeg.

● **Accommodation** There are 4 homestays on Ay. Insist on seeing all of them before making a choice as personal preference and rapidly changing quality may well alter the comments below. At the time of writing, *Weltevreden* is outstanding and the only one with private mandis. All the homestays have generators; they are situated in the village, not on a beach. Room rates incl all meals. **C-D** *Weltevreden*, the first homestay opp the boat landing, spotless, with delicious food. Kacong and his wife take a real pride in making their guests feel at home, at the same time they respect privacy. Kacong takes visitors through the forests to the best beaches for snorkelling, and will identify the various spice trees – nutmeg, clove, cinnamon and the fantastically shaped, huge kanari trees. 2 rm with private mandi, western toilet, for 4 meals incl in room rate (huge home-baked teas, try the nutmeg jam and 'kue' biscuits made of spun sugar with spices and coconut), 2 cheaper rm with shared mandi; **D** *Ay Star Homestay*, this homestay doubles as a shop so can be noisy, and the owners are not friendly once you announce you are leaving, food is nothing special, shared mandi; **D** *Revenge Homestay*, 5 rm with shared mandi, the main feature is an upstairs balcony with a seaview; **E** *Welvaren*, 4 rm with shared mandi, the 'homestay' is in a separate house from the family.

● **Transport Sea Boat**: to reach Ay takes 1 hr by small boat (2,500Rp); the boat leaves at 1300 from Banda (from the left side of the port, as you face the sea, beside the market next to

the *Zonnegate Homestay*). To return to Banda the boat leaves Ay Island at 0800. There are 2 boats: the *Ay Indah* and the *Ay Star*, both leave at roughly the same time, when full. Returning on Sun to Banda can be a problem as the boats are often full.

BANDA BESAR

The highlight of Banda Besar is the **plantation home**, built in 1750 (with walls of coral), of Wim Van den Broeke. Mr Van den Broeke is a fascinating and informative gentleman, well-versed in the history of the Bandas, who welcomes all visitors with lychee juice and conversation. Although 75% Indonesian, he feels Dutch and speaks both English and Dutch.

Ask to see his 'nutmeg kitchen – *dapur pala*' – where he will explain the drying process, invented by the Dutch, which produces a superior product to the older method of drying nutmegs in the sun. 4,000 trees worth of nutmegs are dried at a time in Mr Van den Broeke's 'kitchen', which consists of two large rooms: on the ground floor is the small fire of kenari wood which produces a dry heat, while the nutmegs are laid out on the floor above to dry in the sauna-like atmosphere; the process takes 10 days. Visitors may be invited to hike in his nutmeg plantation, formerly 100 ha, now only 12½. Wim Van den Broeke makes, and sometimes has for sale, the rather beautiful and intricate device for picking nutmegs: a long pole at the end of which is a 'cage' with two prongs to pull the nutmegs off the tree. To reach his house either take the boat from Banda harbour that goes to Walang, the village nearest his plantation, or the boat to Lonthar village. From Lonthar village the walk is about 45 mins: alighting from the boat, turn left as you face inland and follow the path along the coast; to find his house just ask, everyone is very friendly and helpful. To reach Fort Concordia, continue past his house.

Fort Hollandia near the main village, Lonthar, is reached via a steep flight of steps that leads to the top of the central mountain spine that runs along this island, the largest of the Banda group and implicit in the name ('Big' Banda). The ruins of Fort Hollandia are off to the left, with superb views over the sea to Gunung Api and Banda Neira. To reach a fine **adat house**, go back to the steps and continue up through the village. At the top, the track levels off; a little further on turn right on the main track, and on the left the path comes to an imposing former **Perkenier mansion** which is now an adat house in the process of being renovated. Continuing down the far side of the hill, the path leads to a fine white sand beach.

● **Transport Boat**: from the harbour on Banda, public boats (*umum kapal*) run regularly from 0800 to 1600. Boats usually leave when full but the boatmen try very hard to encourage tourists to charter a boat (3,000Rp). Boats leave from left side of the market in town. The *Delfika* homestay also organizes trips to Banda Besar and Wim Van den Broeke.

TERNATE & TIDORE

The tiny, twin, circular islands of Ternate and Tidore, separated from one another by a narrow strait, lie just to the W of the far larger island of Halmahera. Neither Ternate nor Tidore measure much more than 10 km in diameter and both are dominated by volcanos: the former by the active Mt Gamalama (1,720m), and the latter by Mt Kiemtabu (1,740m). The largest town is Ternate, on the E coast of the island with a population of about 50,000. Tidore is more sparsely settled with 40,000 inhabitants. Taken together, the islands have a population of about 120,000.

Like the Bandas, these two pinpricks were once of enormous economic and hence strategic value. Many saw this as a curse rather than as a blessing, the Portuguese soldier and poet Luis Camões writing in the mid 16th century:

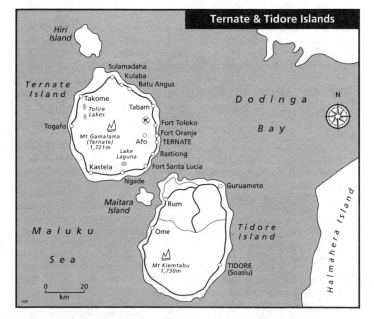

Ternate & Tidore Islands

Royal procession to the mosque in Ternate for weekly Friday prayer, 1599; a contemporary Dutch woodcut based on the description in "Rweede Boeck"

Tidore and Ternate, whence on high
From his hot crest and waves of fire are thrown.
There trees of burning cloves you may descry,
Portuguese blood has purchased for our own
(Camões, book 10, stanza 132)

History

Ternate, a sultanate rich in spices, was first visited by Europeans on 6 November 1521 when the expedition of Ferdinand Magellan dropped anchor off Tidore. Financed by King Charles of Spain, Magellan's devastated fleet arrived after 27 months at sea, having lost three ships as well as its illustrious leader in a skirmish in the Philippines. The remaining two vessels were worm-eaten, waterlogged and rotten. But the emaciated crew managed to fill the holds with spices and returned to Spain to sell their spoiled cargo for 5,100 pounds, 300 pounds more than it cost King Charles

to fit out the expedition. Only 17 of the original crew returned and a joyous procession through the city and a Mass in the cathedral marked their ragged arrival.

Though the crew did not return to Ternate, amazingly, Magellan's reconditioned flagship the *Victoria* did, in early 1527. The historian Willard Hanna writes:

It arrived...in even more woeful state than before, the rigging reduced to mere rudiments, the bottom barnacled and worm-eaten, the crew famished and exhausted. ...Don Garcias [the Portuguese captain of the island] exchanged grandiloquent messages of felicitation and abuse with the Spanish captain...engaged the ship in brief combat, discreetly retiring when its cannon proved still to be functional, and watched with gratification as it proceeded to sink of sheer decreptitude' (1990:39).

Like Banda to the S (see page 815), Ter-

A, the mosque; **B**, the procession; **C**, the palace of Ternate, built with Portuguese assistance.
Source: reproduced in Reid, Anthony (1988) *Southeast Asia in the age of commerce*, Yale University Press: New Haven.

nate and Tidore have had a remarkably colourful history. One uprising against the Portuguese in 1529 occurred after a pig escaped from their castle. The local Muslims, unsurprisingly, had it killed, whereupon the Portuguese Captain Menesez imprisoned the chief *ulama*. The locals rebelled and had their priest released, but not before his face had been daubed in pig fat. The apoplectic *ulama* called a holy war and the Portuguese garrison was effectively blockaded. Without supplies, Menesez captured three elders and demanded food before he would release them. These demands were ignored, and so two of the three captives had their ears sliced off, while the third was thrown to a mastiff who drove him into the sea. Seizing one of the dog's ears between his teeth, this third elder dragged both himself and the beast beneath the waves to their respective deaths.

A succession of Captains followed Menesez, all with instructions to increase trade and profits and mete out justice. In all areas they were generally unsuccessful. The only Governor to leave with any semblance of a good reputation was 'Good Governor Galvao' who arrived in 1536. As Hanna writes: "In the chronicles of the Moluccas during the 16th century, Galvao's is the only Portuguese name other than that of Francis Xavier to which, 4 centuries later, any very bright luster still adheres" (1990:68). The Portuguese left the island on 15 July 1575 after 60 years of ineptitude.

Other visitors to Ternate included the English explorer Francis Drake who moored here in the *Golden Hind* in 1579, after ravaging the Spanish on the Main. He appears to have got on famously with the rogue of a Sultan who ruled at the time, Sultan Baab (see page 42 for an account of Drake's voyage and his stay at

Ternate). The Dutch, who replaced the Portuguese as the dominant power (though harassed by the British), continued the tradition of blundering and provided their own cast of tragi-comedy characters to play next to a succession of colourful sultans. The terrible de Vlaming allowed his men to cut Prince Saidi up alive and throw morsels of his flesh over a cliff (1655), while Sultan Sibori had to cut the throat of the husband of a beautiful and seductive Chinese woman and then drown her mother-in-law in a bath before he was able to marry the cursed female.

For visitors interested in the history of Ternate and its sister island Tidore, Willard Hanna's history is highly recommended – *Turbulent times past in Ternate and Tidore*, Yayasan Warisan dan Budaya: Banda Neira 1990. It can be bought from the Tourist Office in Ternate at a rather inflated price or from the *Dian Pertiwi Bookshop* in Ambon (see page 808).

Places of interest

Ternate is a small, quiet town, where the bemos are driven at a refreshingly sedate pace and people stop to talk to visitors. Although the town is spread, ribbon-like, over 3 km or 4 km, and sandwiched between the lower slopes of Gamalama Volcano and the sea, it is manageable on foot. The main street is Jl Pahlawan Revolusi on which are found the major hotels, banks, shops and the **Gama Lama Market**. The **Pasar Sayur** ('Vegetable Market') is at the N edge of the town centre; the main bemo terminal is also here.

In Ternate town, **Fort Oranje** is on Jl Babullah, opposite the bemo station and Pasar Sayur. Built in 1607, it is the best preserved and largest fort on the island. Now the quarters for the local army garrison, it nevertheless has a rather abandoned, decayed and in some respects attractive, air about it. About 1 km N is the **Mesjid Sultan Ternate** dating from the 13th century. This mosque has a layered red-orange roof

above high yellow-wash walls. Inside, the absence of decoration and the bare soaring roof give it a satisfying purity. About 500m further N from the mosque, on a rise, is the **Kedaton Sultan Ternate**, the Sultan's Palace, but looking rather like a modest European hunting lodge. There was a palace on this site during the 13th century, although the present structure dates from the 19th century. It is now a small **museum**, displaying gifts presented to previous Sultans – armour, swords – along with basketry and some local costumes. The prize exhibit is, unfortunately, rarely on show. This is Sultan Awal's crown, still plastered with some of his hair (which is said to grow – see below, festivals), and kept locked away. Persistence and a modest payment (5,000-10,000Rp) may entice the officials to allow a peep. Good views from the verandah of the kedaton, back over the town. Admission by donation (ignore the vast sums stated in the visitor's book). Open 0800-1400 Mon-Thur, 0800-1100 Fri, 0800-1400 Sat.

Excursions

Circumnavigating Ternate is a good way to spend a day. It is easiest by chartered bemo, but is also possible by regular public bemo. Try walking on the W side of the island, where there are some interesting small settlements.

Sights travelling anti-clockwise from town: Benteng (Fort) Toloko is 2 km from town, and was built by Alfonso d'Alburqueque in 1512. Little remains, except the vegetation-covered walls. **Batu Angus** lies just before the village of Kulaba, and is the crumpled lava flow from Mt Gamalama's eruption of 1737. There is also a **Japanese war memorial** here. **Sulamadaha** is a village 16 km from town; close by are good black sand beaches. Finally, the **Tolire Lakes** lie almost diagonally opposite Ternate town about 25 km away, on the other side of the island and the mountain. There are two peaceful lakes here, Tolire Besar ('Big Tolire') and

The nutmeg plant

Tolire Kecil ('Little Tolire').

Sights travelling clockwise from town: **Fort Santa Lucia**, also known as Fort Kayu Merah (Red Wood) or Fort Kalamata, is just past Bastiong port and about 3 km from town. It was built by the English in 1518 right on the coast; only the walls of this small fortress remain. Good views over to Tidore. Admission by donation. **Lake Laguna** is inland from the village of Ngade, 7 km from town. Climb up above the lake for good views. Further on along the coast road, **Fort Kastella** has been almost weathered out of existence.

Mount Gamalama, which is in effect Ternate, rises to 1,721m. It erupted in 1737 and again in 1987 and 1990 and can be climbed (just) in a day. Ask at the tourist office for further information.

Afo clove tree is claimed to be the oldest clove tree in the world. It lies inland from Fort Oranje, 4 km from town. Known as Afo or 'Giant', it is 400 years old and still produces 600 kg of cloves each harvest. The path to the tree begins behind the town and branches off before the TVRI mast. Ask for 'Cekih Afo' along the way.

Tidore is Ternate's neighbouring and less developed twin island and can be visited in a day trip. There is a fort at Rum, where the ferry docks. Soasiu, the main town, is on the easternmost side of the island; good markets are held here on Tues and Fri. There is a basic losmen at Soasiu, *Losmen Jangi. Getting there*: take a ferry from Bastiong, 20 mins (500Rp). They run during daytime at fairly frequent intervals.

Festivals

Cutting the Hair of the Sultan's Crown, this is said to be performed once a year, although there is no fixed date for the ceremony. The crown is believed to hold supernatural powers, one manifestation of which is the alleged continued growth of the Sultan Awal's hair.

Local information

● **Accommodation**

B-C *Neraca*, Jl Pahlawan Revolusi 30, T 21668, a/c, hot water, new, clean, rather stark, in town centre; **B-D** *Elshinta*, Jl Pahlawan Revolusi 426, T 21059, some a/c, OK, with cars parked in lobby, all meals incl.

C *Chrysant*, Jl Jend A Yani 131, T 21580, a/c, friendly and quiet, rooms are reasonable but rather overpriced; **C-D** *Nirwana* (and fitness studio), Jl Pahlawan Revolusi 58, T 21787, F 21487, some a/c, hot water, in centre of town, noisy, good rooms, price incl breakfast.

D *Sejahtera*, Jl Salim Fabanyo 21, T 21139, dark, windowless rooms with shared mandi, all meals incl.

E *Penginapan Yamin*, Jl Pelabuhan Revolusi (by port), average rooms, verandah, shared mandi.

F *Penginapan Sentosa*, Jl Pahlawan Revolusi, T 21857, basic but friendly and popular, shared mandi.

● **Places to eat**

No excellent restaurants, but a number of mid-range establishments selling reasonable Indonesian and Chinese dishes. Most are found on Jl Pahlawan Revolusi – eg *Gama Lama* at No 248 (Chinese), *Garuda* (Indonesian), and *Roda Baru* (Padang food). The *Siola Restaurant* in Ternate town also comes rec. Stalls set up at night opp and N from the local government offices (Kantor Bupati Kapala Daerah). For local specialities, try the cakes and bread which use the kenari nut (from the huge shade tree that protects nutmeg groves) as an ingredient: *roti kenari* and *bagea kenari*.

● **Airline offices**

Bouraq, Jl Jend A Yani 131, T 21288, open 0800-1700 Mon-Sun; **Merpati/Garuda**, Jl Basoiri 2, T 21651, open 0800-1700 Mon-Sat, 1000-1230 Sun.

● **Banks & money changers**

Bank Rakyat Indonesia, Jl Pahlawan Revolusi 234; **BNI**, Jl Pahlawan Revolusi; **Ekspor Impor**, Jl Pahlawan Revolusi (nr corner with Jl Tenang).

● **Hospitals & medical services**

Hospitals: *General Hospital*, Jl Tanah Tinggi.

● **Post & telecommunications**

Area code: 0921.

General Post Office: Jl Pahlawan Revolusi 420.

Perumtel: Jl Pahlawan Revolusi (next to *Elshinta Hotel*), telephone and telegram.

● **Shopping**

Spices: nutmegs, cloves, etc are very cheap. Not always the best quality but this, after all, is where it all began, so they have a certain romantic appeal.

● **Tour companies & travel agents**

Indo Gama, Jl Pahlawan Revolusi 17, T 21681; *Noname*, Jl Jend A Yani 129 (next door to *Chrysant Hotel*).

● **Tourist offices**

North Maluku Tourist Office, Jl Pahlawan Revolusi (in the Kantor Bupati Kepala Daerah), open 0800-1400 Mon-Thur, 0800-1100 Fri, 0800-1200 Sat, limited information.

● **Transport**

Local Bemos: the main terminal is opp the Pasar Sayur at the N edge of the town centre. Give the destination, and the appropriate vehicle will be pointed out. Although there are routes, these are loosely adhered to – most passengers are dropped right outside their house, hotel or wherever. **NB** Although regular bemos travel both clockwise and anticlockwise, they rarely circle the island completely. Destinations at the far side of Ternate are more difficult to get to, and to get back from. Fares are 200-300Rp for short trips, up to 500Rp for longer journeys. For the more remote spots (or if in a group) it is best to charter a bemo; expect to pay 3,500Rp/hr. **Ferries**: regular ferries to Tidore leave from Bastiang, 20 mins (500Rp). Take a bemo the 3 km from town to the ferry dock.

Air Ternate's tiny airport is 5 km N of the town centre; planes brush the palm trees on landing. Regular connections by Merpati with Ambon and Manado; less regular flights to Galela and Kao on Halmahera, and to Gebe and Morotai. Bouraq also run 4 flights/week to Manado, Indoavia fly 3 times a week between Ternate and Ambon (146,000Rp). Taxis to town cost 3,000Rp. There is a tourist information counter at the airport, but it is usually unattended. To see the island on landing sit on the right-hand side of the aircraft.

Sea Boat: Ternate's main port is conveniently located just S of the town centre at the end of Jl Pahlawan Revolusi. Shipping companies, incl Pelni, have their offices in the port complex (T 21434). Arrivals and departures are posted on boards outside the offices. The Pelni ships *Kerinci* and *Ciremai* call here (see route schedule, page 921), as does the Kalla Lines vessel (page 683). Other vessels of various sizes and states of seaworthiness call at Morotai and Halmahera, Bitung, Laiwui, Madapolo, Babang, Mangoli, Sanana and Ambon, among other destinations.

HALMAHERA

The weirdly shaped island of Halmahera, something like a miniature version of Sulawesi, is the second largest in Maluku with a land area of 18,000 sq km. It is one of the least visited islands in the archipelago. Like the relationship between Ambon and Seram, Halmahera is overshadowed in historical and economic terms by its far smaller neighbour, Ternate.

Much of Halmahera remains forested and transport is distinctly limited. Tribal groups inhabit the interior and it is thought that there are some for whom life has only changed marginally over the last century. The establishment of transmigration settlements on the island for Javanese settlers (see page 377), and the financial attractions offered by Halmahera's primary forests may mean that this beautiful island will not remain isolated and beautiful for very much longer. Trekking in the forests and mountains of Halmahera may become an important alternative source of income, although even this will have its cultural costs. It was here, in Feb 1858, that Alfred Russel Wallace, the great Victorian naturalist, wrote his famous paper 'On the tendency of varieties to depart indefinitely, from the original type', which laid out his ideas on the principle on natural selection. Although the paper (published in the *Proceedings of the Linnean Society*) drew upon his observations in Borneo, South America and in other areas of Indonesia, perhaps it was the wonder of Halmahera which cemented his thoughts into this seminal paper.

At the N end of Halmahera, the largest settlement is the town of **Tobelo** with about 15,000 inhabitants. On the coast near the centre of the island, **Kao** is the biggest town with a population of less than 5,000. Kao was an important Japanese air base during WW2. There is a road linking Kao with Tobelo. There are flights to Kao and Galela (see below) and ferries link Ternate with Tobelo and Jailolo.

- **Accommodation Tobelo**: **C-D** *President*; **D** *Karunia*, Jl Kemakmuran, T 21202; **D** *Megaria*, Jl Bayankara; **D** *Pantai Indah*, Jl Lorong Pantai Indah, T 21068. **Kao**: **D** *Dirgahayu*, price incl 3 meals a day; **D** *Sejahtera*.

- **Airline offices** Merpati, Cabang PT Eterna Galela, Jl Kampung Soasiu, Galela.

- **Transport Local** Minibuses provide a reasonable service between Kao, Galela and Tobelo, and more limited links with other towns. **Air** There are connections between Kao and Ternate and Galela (2/week); and between Galela (60 km from Tobelo, take a shared taxi) and Ternate and Kao (2/week), and Morotai (1/week). **Sea Boat**: daily ferries from Ternate to Tobelo via Morotai (18-20 hrs); there is also an infrequent service from Ternate to Kao

MOROTAI

Morotai was an important airforce base for the allies as they advanced across the Pacific and there is a good deal of war scrap still lying about as evidence. Covering an area of over 1,800 sq km, the Japanese Private Nakamura holed-up here until 1973 when he emerged from the forest to surrender after nearly 30 years. **Daruba**, the capital, has a population of about 5,000 and the diving and snorkelling is reputed to be excellent. The population of the island is about 50,000.

- **Accommodation Daruba**: **E** *Tongga*, **E** *Angkasa*..

- **Sports Diving**: it is reported that some shopkeepers in Daruba are willing to hire out diving equipment; maintenance may be poor.

- **Transport Air** Merpati flies a once weekly loop between Ternate, Galela and Morotai. **Sea Boat**: daily ferry connections with Ternate 12½ hrs and Tobelo on Halmahera 3½ hrs.

SOUTH EAST MALUKU

The *Kabupaten*, or district, of SE Maluku is the remotest and least visited part of the province (or at least of that part which can be visited). The largest and most important islands are the Kei, Aru, Tanimbar, Babar, Wetar and Kisar Islands. The district covers almost 25,000 sq km and has a population of about 275,000. These islands were never important in the spice trade with Europe and they were largely insulated from the events that were so fundamentally altering life elsewhere in the archipelago. However, there were local trading links with the N Moluccas and S Sulawesi, and forest products were exchanged for metal implements.

Lying S of the equator, these islands are drier than those to the N and the people subsist primarily on yams, maize, millet, coconut and sago, rather than rice. Missionaries have converted most of the population to nominal Christianity, although traditional ancestor worship is still important.

Malaria in SE Maluku

It seems that the closer islands are to Irian Jaya, the worse the malaria problem is. The Aru Islands, Tanimbars and Kai Islands have swamps, so there is the potential for malaria. It seems to be less of a problem in the Tanimbars. Dobo, the largest city in the Aru Islands, has sea breezes which may mitigate the problem.

KAI

Places of interest

The **Kai Islands** consist of three islands with a total population of about 100,000. **Kai Kecil** and **Dullah** – on which is the capital Tual – are largely low lying and comparatively densely populated: much of the former swamp has been converted to crop land. **Kai Besar** is mountainous and only settled along the coastline. The forested interior of this magical place is home to no fewer than five species of bird, two species of lizard, one species of snake and a species of bat, all found nowhere else in the world. At Langgur town, on Kai Kecil (connected to Tual by the Watdek Bridge), the Catholics have a mission (reputedly, the oldest Catholic mission in Maluku), and have brought some prosperity to Langgur through various business enterprises, and excellent schools. (It may be possible to stay at the mission.) The local people are renowned for their boat building skills, and the **Laut Cave** on Kai Kecil contains enigmatic ideograms indicating a long period of human settlement.

Kai offers the intrepid visitor **fantastic beaches** with powdery white sand as fine as flour; some say the finest beaches in the world. A particularly stunning beach lies on the W coast of Kai Kecil – Pasir Panjang (or Pasir Sas Nadan). However, there have been reports that malaria is rampant on most beaches during the wet season. Cholera is also said to be a problem.

Dullah Island provides more attractive villages and beautiful beaches, especially to the N. The capital **Tual** is surprisingly busy for an area, seemingly, at the edge of the world. Kai Besar is very quiet in comparison with Kai Kecil and Dullah.

Festivals

Oct: boat races around Tual.

● **Accommodation Tual**: **D** *Linda Mas*, Jl Anthony Rhebok, outside of town, T 21271, coffee house, friendly, clean, some a/c, rooms with both private and shared mandis, price incl breakfast; **E** *Rosemgen I*, Jl K Sadsuitubun, T 21045, top of the range for Kai; **E** *Nini Gerhana*, Jl Pattimura, T 21343; **F** *Mira*, Jl Mayor Abdullah, T 21172, convenient for the harbour but nr to Mosque so noisy. **Langgur**: **D** *Ramah Indah*, Jl Baru Watdek, T 21232; **C** *Rosemgen II*, Jl Watdek, nr the bridge, T 21477, own mandi, some rooms with good views, good place for local information, restaurant. **Ohoililir Beach** (Kecil): **D** *Coaster Cottages* (book at *Mira Inn* in Tual), 6 km from town, rate incl breakfast, an extra 2,500Rp pp for all meals, food very, very basic, verging on the inedible (ie bring some provisions – biscuits, peanuts etc), a charter bemo to the village from Tual is 15-20,000Rp. It is possible, but complicated to get there by public bemo (in morning, can be a long wait) to Ngilgof village, then 20 mins walk along the beach to Ohoililir village.

● **Places to eat**   Restaurants in Tual not very good. The best restaurant on the Kai Islands is at Densiko nr Langgur.

● **Airline offices**   Merpati Rahmat Jaya, Jl Pattimura, T 21376, Langgur.

● **Banks & money changers**   It is possible to change US$ cash in some shops, but it is best to take enough for your stay.

● **Tourist offices**   On Tual side, close to bridge, T 21466, some useful information available.

● **Transport**   Local Bemos around Dullah leave from the terminal at Tual nr the mosque. For bemos around Kai Kecil, the terminal is nr the Ohijong Market in Langgur. Bemos are very crowded and rather infrequent. Chartering should cost about 8,000Rp/hr. The public transport system on Kai Besar has yet to be developed. **Air**   The airport lies 5 km from Langgur town. Beware rip-off bemo drivers. Daily connections on Merpati between Langgur and Ambon. **Sea Boat**: Ferries to Kai Besar leave from Langgur – the Pelabuhan Motor Watdek – nr the bridge, twice daily. Perintis ships leave Ambon every 2 weeks or so and call at the major ports of SE Maluku. There are 2 routes – one links Ambon with the Nr SE or Tenggara Dekat; the other linking Ambon with the Far SE or Tenggara Jauh (calling at harbours in the Babar and Kisar Islands). The Pelni ship the *Rinjani* sails from Banda to the Kai islands and on to Fakfak (Irian Jaya) every 2 weeks on its circuit through the islands. The *Tatamailau* also calls here. (Pelni office in Tual, nr the mosque, T 21181. They provide good clear information on all schedules.) From Kai there are boats roughly every 10 days (a 48 hrs journey) to Tanimbar (Saumlaki town), although expect delays and postponements. Check at the Pelni office or at the port for latest information.

TANIMBAR

The densely forested **Tanimbar Islands** (over 60 in all, population 75,000) are similarly endowed with beaches and sea gardens. The 'largest' towns are **Larat**, on the island of the same name, and **Saumlaki** at the southern end of Yamdena Island – the largest in this group of islands. Having said this, Saumlaki is little more than a ribbon of development along Jl Bhineka. The Christian inhabitants of Tanimbar have been influenced by Hinduism from India (evident in textile design), and by Polynesian and Micronesian cultures (for instance, the tradition of cooking food wrapped in banana leaves over hot stones). On the E coast of Yamdena, at the village of **Sangliat Dol** is a **megalithic** stone structure, approached up a stone staircase from the beach. To get there from Saumlaki, 2 buses a day, 1½-hr journey in uncomfortable bus.

● **Accommodation**   Saumlaki: **C-D** *Harapan Indah*, Jl Bhineka, T 21019, downstairs rooms are more expensive, with a/c, private mandi and TV, price incl good meals; **D** *Pantai Indah*, Jl Bhineka, T 2148, some rooms with own mandi, price incl food, clean, large rooms; **D** *Ratulei*, Jl Bhineka, T 21014.

● **Places to eat**   All three hotels provide food; there's not much else on offer, except a scattering of foodstalls.

● **Banks & money changers**   No bank will change money, but the *Toko Selatan* in Saumlaki may change cash for you, at a lower rate.

● **Airline offices**   Merpati in *Harapan Indah*, T 21017, Jl Bhineka, Saumlaki.

● **Transport**   **Air**   Flights to Ambon and Langgur on Thur and Sat. Confirm departure details by phoning Merpati here before arrival. **Boat** Pelni and Perintis boats link Tanimbar with the Kai Islands and East Timor, Ambon and Banda. The Pelni vessel *Tatamailau* is the most comfortable (see route schedule, page 921). For boats to Larat, there is a weekly ferry. The Pelni office is nr the port in Saumlaki.

Irian Jaya

Horizons	835	Jayapura	845
Island information	843	The Baliem Valley	848

IRIAN JAYA, known before 1973 as Irian Barat or W Irian, comprises the W half of the island of New Guinea – the world's second largest island after Greenland. It is Indonesia's largest, most remote, and least populated province. Large areas have yet to be explored, and this is one of the few parts of the world where maps can still legitimately be marked: 'Here be Dragons'.

HORIZONS

Irian Jaya has a population of only 1.7 million, scattered over an expanse nearly twice the size of Great Britain – about four people per sq km. The province is also one of the country's newest: Indonesian forces *de facto* occupied Irian Jaya in 1962, but *de jure* only annexed the province in 1969. The word *irian* is derived from a Biak word meaning 'pretty' or 'light'. *Jaya* is an Indonesian word meaning 'glorious'. The shape of the island of New Guinea is often likened to a bird. The inhabitants sometimes talk of Pulau Cassowary – or Cassowary Island – and the Dutch named the NW corner Vogelkop or 'Bird's Head' (now Kepala Burung, also meaning Bird's Head).

THE LAND

GEOGRAPHY

Irian Jaya was once part of a land bridge that linked Australia and Southeast Asia.

The main geological feature of the province is a central range of mountains that runs from NW to SE. Near the border with Papua New Guinea (PNG) is the Jayawijaya Range, separated from the W Sudirman Range by the fertile Grand Baliem Valley. The highest peak – and also the highest in Indonesia – is Mt Jaya at 5,030m. There are 10 other mountains which exceed 4,800m, making this the consistently highest part of Southeast Asia, and the only area with glaciers.

North of this impressive, central spine of mountains are a small range known as the Coastal Range or Van Rees Mountains. The highest peak here is 2,272m. To the S, the central mountains descend steeply to a vast, swampy, lowland plain.

As well as the W half of New Guinea, Irian Jaya also comprises a number of islands. The main ones are Japen, Biak-Supiori and Numfor to the N, and the Raja Amphat group – including Waigeo, Batanta, Salawat and Misool – to the NW.

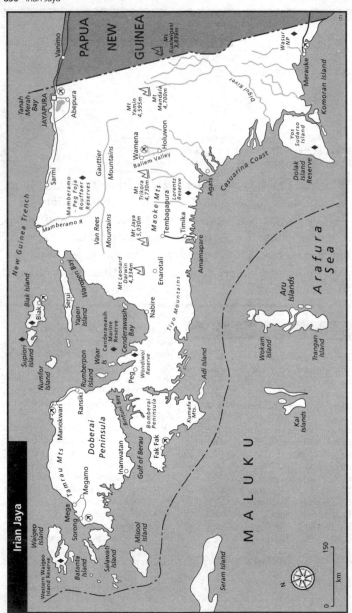

CLIMATE

Irian Jaya is hot, wet and humid. Rainfall tends to be heavy throughout the year, with only minor seasonal variations. On the N coast rainfall is about 2,500 mm/year; in the mountains it can exceed 8,000 mm/year, making this one of the wettest spots on earth. It is also one of the cloudiest (which poses a major problem for air transport). However, there are areas where rainfall is markedly less. Merauke in the SE, for example, receives less than 1,500 mm; also drier are sections of the NW and the N (eg Jayapura). Temperatures, except at altitude, average a fairly constant 29°C-32°C.

FAUNA AND FLORA

Irian Jaya's flora and fauna are complex and diverse. In total, 'Papuasia' – as the whole region is known – has over 20,000 species of plant, 200 mammal, 725 bird, 253 reptile and 80,000-100,000 species of insect. In the Arfak Nature Reserve alone, which covers only 70 km² outside

---

The bird of paradise: legless bird of God

When Ferdinand Magellan's ship the *Victoria* docked at Seville after her monumental circumnavigation of the globe, the hold contained, along with spices, five skins of the bird of paradise (*Paradisaeidae*) which had been given to the crew as a gift when they landed at Tidore in the Moluccas. Although the name was coined by a Dutchman, Jan van Linschoten in 1590, they had long been viewed as Birds of God or Golden Birds from 'a land of departed souls'.

'Paradise' referred not just to their spectacular plumage, but also to the fact that the birds were thought to be legless. The skins arrived in Europe with no legs, and sometimes no wings, and it was thought the birds were naturally this way and fed, bred and reared their young on the wing – only falling to earth when they died. Thomas Pennant, an 18th century British naturalist, went so far as to claim that "they lived on the dew of Heaven, and had no evacuation like other mortal birds". It was presumed that the female incubated her egg in a shallow depression on the male's back. Getting it there must have entailed some skilled aerobatics. Why they were transported legless is not certain. The British naval captain Thomas Forrest, who visited New Guinea between 1774 and 1776, maintained that it was for two reasons: because they could be more easily preserved that way, and because the Moors wanted to "put them in mock flight, on their helmets, as ornaments".

In all, there are 26 species of bird of paradise, of which the most valuable – because they have the most spectacular plumage – are those of the genus *Paradisae*, in particular the much sought-after Greater (*Paradisaeidae apoda*) and Lesser (*P minor*) bird of paradise. Naturalists point to these birds as an example of evolution run wild in the absence of predators. The wonderful plumage is necessary to attract a mate, so an ever larger, more magnificent, and less efficient plumage, tends to evolve, locking them into an evolutionary dead end.

Although it was demand for their feathers (in the West) which really threatened the bird, the magnificent plumage was in demand in the courts and among noblemen and women in Southeast Asia, China, India and Persia. The European fashion for hats decorated with feathers of the bird of paradise dates from the late 19th century, and between 1884 and 1889 50,000 skins were exported to Europe. Today, they are protected, but sadly it is still possible to buy birds of paradise skins, and their valuable plumage, in places like the market in Biak for only US$20. In the countryside around Biak, many of the churches – tragically and rather ironically – have been built on the back of the trade in the skins of these Birds of God.

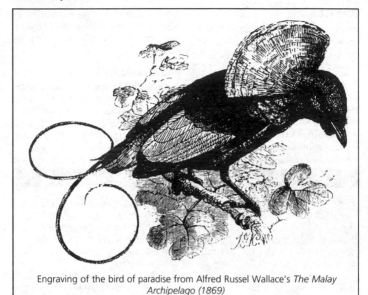

Engraving of the bird of paradise from Alfred Russel Wallace's *The Malay Archipelago (1869)*

Manokwari, 800 species of spider and 5,000 species of butterflies and moths have been recorded. Not only does the province cover a wide variety of ecological zones from coastal mangrove swamp, to lowland rainforest, montane forest, up to alpine grasslands; but it also lies at a biogeographical crossroads: the animals and plants are both Asian and Australasian in origin. In the mountains, for example, there are N latitude oaks from China such as *Quercus junghunii* growing alongside 'Antarctic' beeches (*Nothofagus*). Among the large number of fascinating plants are insectivorous pitcher plants (*Nepenthes*) and the weird and wonderful giant anthouse plant (*Myrmecodia brasii*), an epiphyte over 2 km in length with a bulbous, honeycombed stem inhabited by large numbers of ants.

Like Irian's flora, its fauna shows clear links with both Asia and Australasia. There are two species of primitive monotremes, the short-beaked (*Tachyglossus aculeatus*) and long-beaked (*Zaglossus bruijni*) echidna, marsupial mice (*Dasyuridae*), tree kangaroos (*Dendrolagus*), and the rare sea mammal, the dugong (*Dugong dugon*). Among its 725 species of bird, the best known are the 26 species of birds of paradise (see box). Other notable birds include nine species of bower bird (*Ptilonorhynchidae*), the large, flightless cassowary (*Casuarius*) and the orange and black pitohui. In 1992, the pitohui became the first bird to be proved poisonous. The feathers, skin and flesh of the pitohui contain homobatrachotoxin, powerful enough to kill a mouse in minutes. It explains why snakes and hawks – the birds' natural enemies – steer well clear of the three species of pitohui and why it is known locally as the 'rubbish bird'.

HISTORY

The first sighting of New Guinea by a European was by d'Abreu in 1512. Long before this date however, Chinese and Arab traders and seafarers from the Spice

Islands of Maluku were trading with the coastal communities of Irian Jaya, exchanging manufactured goods for forest products. In 1526, de Menses, the first governor of the Spice Islands, was forced to take shelter in a cove on Bird's Head (Kepala Burung) during a storm and named the land Ilhas dos Papuas or Islands of the Papuans. He took the word Papuas from the Malay *papuah* – for orang papuah, or 'frizzy-haired men'.

From the 16th century mariners continued to sail along and map the coasts, but there was no attempt at interior exploration or settlement. The first colony was established in 1793 by the English East India Company near Manokwari; it was abandoned after only 2 years. The Dutch did not establish a presence until 1828 when they built a fortress at Fort du Bus, in Triton Bay; it was abandoned less than 10 years later. They re-established a presence at the end of the 19th century, building forts at Manokwari, on the N coast of the Bird's Head, and at Fak-Fak, on the W peninsular, declaring all the land to the W of the 141st meridian as Dutch territory. In 1902 a settlement was established at Merauke in the SE and at Humboldt Bay (near present day Jayapura), on the N coast. However, the Dutch presence was restricted to the coastal regions, forays into the harsh, inpenetrable interior were intermittant and generally unsuccessful.

Coordinated exploration of the interior did not begin until the second decade of the 20th century. And it was only in 1938 that the American Richard Archbold, leader of the Archbold Expeditions, discovered the Grand Baliem Valley. The Japanese occupied New Guinea in 1942, and some of the bitterest fighting in the Pacific Theatre took place here. Legacies of the war include the large numbers of airfields built by the Allies and the Japanese, and topographic maps which are still in use today. The Japanese were defeated in 1945 and the territory was returned to the Dutch.

In 1962, the Dutch gave up control of W Papua to a United Nations Temporary Executive Authority (UNTEA). A year later, in May 1963, the territory was handed over to Indonesia to administer on the condition that within 6 years there would be an Act of Free Choice – a plebiscite – to ascertain whether the population wished to become a part of Indonesia. It is at this point that opinions – like those on East Timor (see page 784) – differ. According to the Indonesian government, in 1969 the people of Irian were given a choice of whether to become an independent country, or part of the Republic of Indonesia; they freely, chose the latter. Critics like the Anti-Slavery Society maintain that: "The Act was stage-managed by the Indonesians, who used a combination of bribery and brute force to persuade 1,025 local 'delegates' to approve the continued Indonesian occupation of W Papua" (1990:6). Despite a highly critical report by the UN observer Fernando Ortiz Sanz, the UN voted to endorse the Indonesian annexation of the territory in Nov 1969. Since that date, the Operasi Papua Merdeka (OPM) or Free Papua Movement have been fighting a largely ignored (but see the end of this introduction, page 843) guerrilla war of independence in Irian Jaya. In 1996 it was estimated that the OPM had a combined force of 300, but perhaps only 90 assorted firearms to share between them. In addition, with the death of their leader Thomas Wannggai in prison in Jakarta in early 1996 (the Red Cross confirmed he died of natural causes) it also lacks a charismatic leader or a coherent command structure.

CULTURE

PEOPLE

There are three ecological regions in Irian Jaya: the coast, the interior lowlands, and the highlands. Because travel is so difficult through the harsh terrain, the people of these different zones remained largely

Master craftsmen: the Asmat of Irian Jaya

The woodcarvings of the Asmat of SE Irian Jaya are regarded as some of the finest examples of 'primitive' art in the world. They now command high prices on the international art market. The Asmat are primarily hunter-gatherers who live on the banks of rivers and subsist on fish, sago and game. Their homeland is the area around the town of Agats. Formerly, the Asmat were headhunters and cannibals. The motivation was on the one hand revenge, and on the other the acquisition of prestige. Heads also became important objects in initiation ceremonies. Cannibalism was a product of headhunting: it gave the victor the strength of the vanquished.

The Asmat regard carving to be an almost religious experience and believe that their first ancestors were created out of wood by a mythical being. Traditionally, ancestral spirits or *ndet* could not be released from the world of the living until an enemy had been killed by a close relative. Until then, the spirit of the ancestor would persecute the living, and carving ritual objects named after particular ancestors was one way of placating the ancestors. Modern Asmat artists are just as likely to carve likenesses of living people as dead ancestors.

Although there is no word in Asmat for either art or artist – the latter is simply known as a *tsjestsju ipitsj* or 'clever man' – skilled artists were accorded the same prestige as successful warriors. Asmat art varies a great deal. Among more common works are:

● ancestor poles or *bis* made from mangrove wood, and sometimes as much as 5-6m high and carved with an ancestor figure and various motifs and symbols (one root of the mangrove tree is left attached to become the *tjemen* or penis).
● carved sago worm containers; carved drums with lizard skin drumheads; crocodile poles from the Casuarina coast area.

isolated from one another. Even today, the only feasible way to get around the province is by air. This inaccessibility is reflected in a huge diversity of languages; about 250 different dialects are thought to be spoken in Irian Jaya. About 30% of the population live in agricultural communities in the cool, temperate valleys of the Baliem Valley, Paniai Lakes and Anggi Lakes. In recent years however, there has been a dramatic increase in the urban population of such centres as Jayapura, Biak and Merauke. Most of this increase has been through an influx of immigrants from other regions of Indonesia, rather than a shift in population from rural areas in Irian Jaya. As the last great frontier zone in Indonesia, the province has also been targeted as a major destination for transmigrant settlers (see page 427).

The coasts The coastal people cultivate sago, taro and coconuts, raise pigs, and fish. Sago is their dietary staple (see page 798). Traditionally, they lived in large houses built on stilts, which could hold up to 100 people, with a central communal area for cooking and socializing and separate rooms for each family; this tradition has died out and most families now have their own homes. The people of the coasts grew rich on maritime trade; they were able to sell local products such as sea cucumber (trepang), rare woods, animal skins and exotic birds in exchange for foreign goods such as metals, textiles, glass beads and porcelain. In their turn, and despite the difficulties of communication, the coastal people would trade these imported goods to the inhabitants of the interior, where they became an important part of a bride's trousseau.

- carved paddles with handles over 2m long sometimes decorated with human heads or hornbills (symbols of head-hunting).
- 'soul' ships or *wuramon* (made only by the inland Asmat) in the form of dug-out canoes.
- incised war shields, carved from the trunks of mangrove trees and painted in red, black and white.

Pottery is unknown, and the area that the Asmat inhabit is almost devoid of stone, so wood and wood products are virtually the only materials used to produce 'art'.

The finest collection of Asmat art in the world is displayed at the **Asmat Museum of Culture and Progress** in Agats. The collection was assembled by the Crosier Mission under Bishop Alphonse Sowada and Father F Trenkenschug. They began buying Asmat art in the early 1960s, and when the Indonesian government ordered the destruction of carvings to stop headhunting and cannibalism in 1962, they frantically assembled as much as their limited funds allowed. The museum was opened in 1973.

Although evaluating the 'artistic', and hence commercial, value of Asmat art is difficult, fine pieces now command high prices on the international art market. It is said that there are only 40 master carvers still at work in Irian Jaya and well-produced ancestor poles sell for well over US$1,000; war shields for over US$500. **NB** Formerly, most Asmat art was carved from soft woods which deteriorate in the cold and dry climates of the N hemisphere. Now, with the introduction of metal tools, many carvings are made from far more durable ironwood (*belian*). Nevertheless, many cheaper pieces are still carved from softwood.

The lowland and highland interior Like the coastal people, the interior lowlanders also grow sago and taro, but hunting and gathering play a more important role in their livelihoods. They 'farm' the larvae of the capricorn beetle by cultivating fallen, rotting trees where the insects breed. The highlanders cultivate sweet potatoes and taro in a rotational field system, and also raise pigs for ceremonial and ritual events.

ARTS AND CRAFTS

The inhabitants of Irian Jaya produce fine woodcarvings – those of the Asmat are particularly highly regarded (see box). On the N coast, elaborately carved spatulas for serving food are the most distinctive art form. Food was traditionally served on carved plates, and large ceremonial platters were reserved for feasts and kept by the headman.

Betel nut holders – used to carry the lime powder that is a part of the betel nut preparation – are also common. These are made from gourds and are incised with patterns. Men's gourds are long and thin, whilst women's are short and fat. The incisions on a woman's gourd are also rubbed with lime. Spatulas with pointed ends were carved as stoppers for the gourds, sometimes with figures on the top.

There is no tradition of weaving in Irian Jaya. The inhabitants traditionally adorned their bodies with necklaces, armbands and head-dresses, and the women sometimes wore barkcloth skirts.

ECONOMIC AND POLITICAL CHANGE

The development of Irian Jaya by the Indonesian government has taken three main directions. On the one hand the government has allotted considerable sums to upgrading the province's infrastructure. This is partly for security reasons – the secessionist OPM (see above) is still active and there is continued political disaffection. Another important motivation however, is that the government sees Irian Jaya as a major source of primary resources (see the box on page 855). Already, oil and copper represent over 90% of the value of the province's exports and any expansion in exploitation is partly contingent upon improving the physical infrastructure. Finally, with a population density of only 4 people/sq km, Irian Jaya is seen as a vast un-tapped source of agricultural land to satisfy the land hunger of the poor in Java and Bali (see page 427). For a time during the 1980s a series of transmigration settlements were opened in the province and it seemed that Irian Jaya was gradually becoming the main focus of the programme. Then pressure from the World Bank which feared the environmental and cultural effects of the settlements in the province led to it being suspended in 1991. However it now seems that the Indonesian government is so intent on satisfying the needs of land hungry Javanese by opening the province to settlement that they are funding this part of the scheme themselves. The main focus of settlement appears to be on new sites around Merauke.

The need to develop the province has led to considerable investment by the government. It has also encouraged the immigration of large numbers of Indonesians from outside Irian Jaya – primarily Javanese, Makassarese and people from Maluku. This process is most obvious in the cities where nearly 90% of the population are non-Irian born. This has led to criticisms that the Irianese are failing to derive any benefit from the exploitation of the province and accusations that the central government is trying to 'Javanize' the area by swamping the locals with immigrants. Visitors may notice that almost all jobs of significance, almost all small businesses from bemo-operators, to losmen-managers, to warung-owners, are non-Irianese. Today, over 20% of the population are non-Irian born, and with only 1.7 million inhabitants in total, it may not be long before immigrants outnumber the indigenous inhabitants. Certainly, many of the Papuans of Irian Jaya feel little sense of common identity with the 'Asians' that dominate the rest of the country.

For the moment however, Irian Jaya remains one of the few true frontier areas left on earth. Vast expanses remain largely unexplored and traditional customs exert a dominant influence. On 19 March 1992, the Jakarta-based Indonesian daily newspaper *Kompas* reported that a tribesman had killed his wife when he hit her over the head with a bottle during an argument. He was fined 11 cows and ordered to part with his treasured collection of stones and seeds.

Recent years has seen a change in the Indonesian approach to the development of the tribal peoples of Irian Jaya. Until the 1980s, the view was that tribes like the Dani had to be 'civilized'. Measures were taken to promote such indicators of 'development' as the wearing of Western clothes. In the early 1970s, for example, the army's *Operasi Koteka* – or Operation Penis Gourd – tried to rather cack-handedly 'encourage' the Dani of the Baliem Valley to dispense with their 'primitive' penis gourds by airlifting jogging shorts and dresses into the province. The programme was spectacularly unsuccessful: the men found the shorts more usefully worn as hats, while the women adapted the dresses into holdalls. Now however, the Indonesian authorities have discovered that there is a tourist demand for people wearing penis gourds and other paraphenalia of 'primitive-ness'. Although many Indonesian officials still believe the Irianese to be backward, the prevailing argument seems to be that if there is money in it, then why change it.

In Wamena for example, a statue shows a Dani warrior resplendent in little more than a *koteka*, while new government-run handicraft co-operatives laud the artistic skills of the Dani.

Although the Organisasi Papua Medeka (OPM or Free Papua Movement) has languished with an almost non-existent international profile, the kidnapping of 13 environmentalists, including seven Europeans, on 8 January 1996 brought it more media attention than it had ever previously enjoyed. The fact that many of the kidnappers were armed with bows and arrows rather than uzis, M-16s and SAMs seemed to illustrate that this was an independence movement with at least one penis gourd in the past. General Prabowo Subianto, one of President Suharto's son-in-laws and an up-and-coming military commander, was put in charge of the operation to free the hostages. For a while it seemed that bows and arrows were getting the better of high-tech military equipment as the OPM managed to evade detection while they drew out the release of the hostages with a succession of demands. But, with the reputed aid of Israeli drones, a hand-picked squad of élite Red Berets were dropped into the jungle from helicopters wearing night vision goggles and freed the hostages after a brief firefight. Unfortunately, two of the Indonesian hostages were hacked to death by the escaping OPM rebels. Although it took over four months for the hostages to be freed, the operation was regarded as a success by most observers, leaving Prabowo's reputation enhanced. The Indonesian military showed a skill that many people thought it lacked, and instead it was the OPM and their murder of two of the hostages which received the opprobrium of the press. Nonetheless, the whole affair has once again highlighted that although Indonesia may be a unitary state it is not necessarily a united country.

ISLAND INFORMATION

PERMITS

A transit visa is required to visit Irian Jaya; and a *surat jalan* (literally 'travel letter') for all parts of the province outside the major towns of Jayapura, Sorong and Biak – for example, the Baliem Valley. *Surat jalan* can be obtained from the central police stations in Jayapura, Sorong and Biak and from the station outside Jayapura Airport (two passport photographs are required, along with your passport, or photocopies of the first page, the photo page, the date of issue and expiry page, the immigration entry stamp page, and immigration card). Officially, *surat jalan* should be returned to the issuing office when a visit is completed. Most hotels will organize *surat jalan* for a small fee (about 1,500Rp). There are some parts of the province which are off-limits to all visitors, even with a *surat jalan*. Check at the local police station.

MONEY

It is difficult to change money in Irian Jaya. Banks in Jayapura, Biak and Wamena (Baliem Valley) are the only places where TCs can be changed.

TOURS

The *Tropical Princess* cruises from Biak Island for 5-10 day scuba-diving trips. The boat can also be chartered. Contact: *Tropical Princess Cruises*, PT Prima Marindo Paradise, 3rd Flr., E Wing, Shop 36, *Borobudur Intercontinental Hotel*, Jl Lapangan Banteng Selatan 1, Jakarta, T 371108, F 370477.

GETTING AROUND

An ambitious road building programme is underway in Irian Jaya, but because of the size of the task, most of the country can still only be reached by air, sea, or on foot. For most visitors, the only feasible way to get around the country is by air. At last count, there were over 250 airstrips scattered over the province, most built by Christian missionary groups. Merpati operates services to the larger towns, and two missionary airlines – MAF (Missionary Aviation Fellowship) and AMA (Associated Missions Aviation) – to smaller settlements, as well as the main towns. **NB** The missionary airlines do take passengers but it should be stressed they are not commercial airlines and are under no compunction to carry fare-paying passengers.

BIAK

Biak is the capital of Biak Island, which covers less than 2,000 sq km off the mainland's N coast. The town has a population of about 25,000. It is a one road town – all the main hotels, restaurants and government offices are strung out along Jl Jend A Yani, with the harbour at the W end of town (where the road becomes Jl Sudirman) and the airport at the E (where the road becomes Jl Prof Moh Yamin).

There are no sights as such in the town, although the **markets** are colourful. The central **Pasar Panir** is on Jl Selat Makassar and sells, among other things, animal skins and live birds. At the W edge of town is the **Pasar Inpres**, next to the taxi terminal, which is mainly a food market. In the morning a **fish market** sets up just off the W end of Jl Sudirman near the harbour.

Excursions

There are a number of **idyllic beaches** within 2 hrs or so of Biak by public transport. To the E, in the vicinity of the market town of **Bosnik** (18 km from town), are white-sand beaches with good snorkelling. **Accommodation**: **A** *Biak Beach Hotel*, another Aerowisata monstrosity, 263 rooms in 6 ha of garden, little character and a real eyesore.

Korem is a market town about 50 km N of Biak on the island's N coast. A good market is staged here on Wed and Sats. *Getting there*: by bemo from town (1½ hrs).

Padaido Islands lie off Biak Island to the SE. These paradisical islands offer superb snorkelling and beaches. Equipment available for snorkelling from someone near the market in Bosnik. *Getting there*: charter a boat from town or from Bosnik, or go on a tour. Expect to pay about US$50-80 for the day, but bargain hard.

Supiori Island, right next to Biak Island, has little to offer, except mangrove swamps and upland forest.

Tours

Sentonsa Tosiga, organize tours around town and to such spots as the Padaido Islands.

Local information
● **Accommodation**

B *Irian*, Jl Prof Moh Yamin, T 21139 (2 km E of town nr the airport), some a/c, good restaurant, colonial feel (like something out of a Hemingway novel) and comfortable rooms, set in gardens and overlooking the sea; **B** *Arumbai*, Jl Selat Makassar 3, T 21835, a/c, hot water, pool, quiet and comfortable, rather expensive; **B-C** *Mapia*, Jl Jend A Yani, T 21383, some a/c, large, pleasant rooms with attached mandi, friendly but a bit grotty; **C** *Basana Inn*, Jl Imam Bonjol 46, T 22281, new and good value; **D** *Maju*, Jl Imam Bonjol 45, T 21841, small, but clean rooms with attached mandi; **D** *Solo*, Jl Monginsidi 4, T 21397, best of the 'budget' accommodation, nr the market.

● **Places to eat**

There are cheap warungs on Jl Monginsidi and stalls on Jl Jend A Yani nr the centre of town. ◆◆*Cleopatra*, Jl Jend A Yani, fish and chicken specialities and tables outside; ◆◆*Jakarta*, Jl Imam Bonjol, Indonesian and Chinese, good seafood; ◆several places along Jl Ahmad Yani.

Foodstalls: on Jl Sudirman and nr the markets.

● **Airline offices**

Garuda, Jl Sudirman 3, T 21416; Merpati, Jl Prof Moh Yamin 1, T 21386.

● **Banks & money changers**

Bank Rakyat Indonesia, Jl Sudirman, and Ekspor Impor, Jl Jend A Yani (nr intersection with Jl Imam Bonjol), will both change most major TCs and cash.

● **Hospitals & medical services**

Hospitals: *General Hospital*, Jl Sriwijaya Ridge 1.

● **Post & telecommunications**

Area code: 0961.

General Post Office: Jl Prof M Yamin (at the edge of town on the road to the airport).

Telkom office: Jl Yos Sudarso, out of town, towards airport.

● **Shopping**

Crafts: available from the markets and from shops like the *Pusaka Art Shop* at the Pasar Lama. **NB** Skins of the bird of paradise are available for US$20 – they are a protected species and their trade should not be encouraged.

● **Sports**
Diving: facilities opening up, as the potential is realized. No courses, and equipment not provided but *Tropical Princess* lays on tours (T Jakarta 5703500).

● **Tourist offices**
Opposite Post Office on Jl Prof M Yamin (airport road), T 21663.

● **Tour companies & travel agents**
Bawa Makmur, Jl Koti 72, T 22180; *Granda Irja*, Jl Imam Bonjol 16, T 21616; *Sentosa Tosiga*, Jl Jend A Yani 36, T 21398.

● **Useful addresses**
Central Police Station: Jl Selat Makassar (for *surat jalan*, see page 843).
Immigration Office: Jl Jend Sudirman 1, T 21109 (corner of Jl Sudirman and Jl Imam Bonjol).

● **Transport**
Local Minibuses/colts: run to most local destinations. The terminal is off Jl Airlangga at the W edge of town, nr the Inpres Market. **Taxis**: can be chartered for about 8,000Rp/hr.

Air The airport is on the outskirts of town, about 2 km E of the centre. Connections throughout Indonesia. **International connections** with Hawaii. International departure tax 11,000Rp. **Transport to town**: minibus or taxi (about 5,000Rp), or catch a public bemo, or it is possible to walk. Regular daily connections on Merpati with Jayapura, Ujung Pandang, Denpasar, Nabire and Serui; less regular connections with Ambon, Sorong and Timika. *International connections*: on Garuda with Los Angeles, via Honolulu and on to Denpasar.

Sea Boat: the harbour is at the W edge of town. The Pelni vessels *Ciremai* and *Dobonsolo* call here (see route schedule, page 921). The Pelni office is at Jl Sudirman 37, T 21065.

JAYAPURA

Formerly the Dutch city of Hollandia, Jayapura is the capital of Irian Jaya province and has a population of about 100,000. As most of the inhabitants – like those in other urban areas in Irian Jaya – are immigrants from other parts of Indonesia, it lacks any distinctive 'Papuan' atmosphere. The Irianese here are outnumbered by Javanese, Makassarese and others.

Jayapura is one of Indonesia's more featureless towns, and most visitors only use it as a base before venturing inland. It is a ribbon development stretching inland from the coast, with most commercial buildings on Jl Jend A Yani.

Excursions

Hamadi is a coastal suburb about 4 km NE of town. This was the spot where the Americans landed in Apr 1944 to wrest control of New Guinea from the Japanese. On the beach, a few rusting landing-craft and tanks half-buried in the sand bear testament to the event. After gaining control of the area, General Douglas McArthur made Jayapura – or Hollandia as it was then – into one of the major forward staging posts for the advance N. The beach is attractive; walk through the Indonesian military base to get there. The town also has an interesting central market and a number of shops and stalls selling souvenirs. **Accommodation** here includes: **C** *Asia*, T 22277, clean but expensive; **D** *Hamadi Jaya*, clean rooms, noisy, but probably the best of the 'budget' accommodation (both here and in Jayapura). *Getting there*: by colt from Jl Jend A Yani.

Base G is a beach 6 km W of town named after the US base established here at the end of the war. Swimming is moderate, but currents can be strong. Very popular at the weekend. *Getting there*: colts only run out to Base G on weekends; on weekdays, charter a colt for the journey.

Candrawasih University Museum is located at Abepura, about 25 km S of town. It displays a reasonable collection of ethnographic pieces and is worth a visit before venturing into the interior. Open 0800-1300 Mon-Fri. *Getting there*: by colt from the station or from Jl Jend A Yani.

Museum Negeri is situated just outside Adepura and has a collection of natural history exhibits as well as ethnographic pieces. Open 0800-1300 Mon-Fri. *Getting there*: by colt from the station or from Jl Jend A Yani to Adepura.

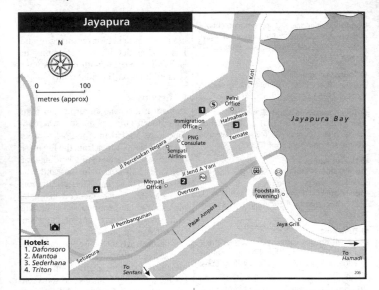

Jayapura

Hotels:
1. Dafonsoro
2. Mantoa
3. Sederhana
4. Triton

Sentani Lake This enormous lake lies SW of Jayapura and is worth a visit. Boats can be chartered to visit some of the islands in the lake from Sentani's harbour.

Tanah Merah Bay is about 55 km W of the city and offers some of the best swimming in the area, as well as reasonable snorkelling. *Getting there*: by colt to Depapre from the bus station.

Tours

There are a number of tour agents in town running tours outside the city and to more distant destinations in Irian Jaya.

Local information
● **Accommodation**

Accommodation in Jayapura is some of the most expensive in Indonesia. Sentani lies 37 km from town and only 3 km from the airport. It is recommended as a more attractive place to stay than Jayapura, where there is little to do. **B** *Mantoa*, Jl Jend A Yani 14, T 31633, a/c, hot water, best hotel in town, comfortable rooms with good facilities; **B** *Triton*, Jl Jend A Yani 2, T 21218, a/c, one notch down from the *Mantoa*, a bit grotty; **B-C** *Irian Plaza*, Jl Setiapura 11, T 34649, some rooms with a/c and hot water, very adequate, good information provided here;

C *Dafonsoro*, Jl Percetakan 20-24, T 31695, a/c; **C-D** *Ratna*, Jl Raya Sentani 7, T 91435, some a/c, own bathroom, good location 5 mins from airport, clean new rooms, rec; **C-D** *Sederhana*, Jl Halmahera 2, T 31561, some a/c, range of rooms some with attached mandi; **C-E** *Kartini*, Jl Perintis 2, T 22371, some attached mandi, central and clean.

Accommodation at Sentani, nr the airport: **C** *Mansapur Rani*, Jl Yabaso 113, 10-min walk from the airport (turn right on exiting the terminal), T 91219, price incl breakfast; **D** *Sentani Inn*, Jl Raya Sentani, T 91440, some a/c, price incl breakfast, basic accommodation with attached mandi, very helpful staff with good English; **C-D** *Semeru*, Jl Yabaso, T 91447, some a/c.

● **Places to eat**

The better restaurants are strung out along Jl Percetakan. Cheaper warungs can be found nr the mosque on Jl Jend A Yani. There is a night market by the Pelni office with good Indonesian stall food; for cheap seafood try the stalls on Jl Halmahera. ◆◆◆*Jaya Grill*, Jl Koti 5, seafood and steaks served on the waterfront, expensive; ◆◆*Nirwana*, Jl Jend A Yani 40, good Padang food.

● **Airline offices**
AMA, Sentani airport, T 91009; **MAF**, Sentani airport, T 91109; **Merpati/Garuda**, Jl Jend A Yani 15, T 33111; **Sempati**, Jl Percetakan 17, T 31612.

● **Banks & money changers**
Ekspor-Impor, Jl Jend A Yani, will change TCs and cash.

● **Embassies & consulates**
PNG, Jl Percetakan 23, T 31250.

● **Hospitals & medical services**
Hospitals: *General Hospital*, Jl Kesehatan 1.

● **Post & telecommunications**
Area code: 0967.
General Post Office: Jl Koti (on the waterfront).
Telkom office: Jl Koti, next door to Post Office.

● **Shopping**
Tribal art: is sold at Hamadi 4 km from town (see above, Excursions). It is mass produced, and usually ersatz, although good pieces do sometimes crop up. For better pieces, try the *Madinah Art Shop*, Jl Perikanan.

● **Tour companies & travel agents**
Bawa Makmur, Jl Koti 72, T 22180; *Dani Sangrila*, Jl Pembangunan 19, T 31060, F 31529; *Duta Baliem*, Jl Nindya Karya, T 21416; *Indonesia Safari*, Jl Kemiri, T 94; *Limbunan*, Jl Tugu 11, T 31633, F 31437; *Natrabu*, Jl Jend A Yani 72.

● **Tourist office**
Jl Soa Siu Dok II, T 23923.

● **Useful addresses**
Central Police Station: Jl Jend A Yani, T 22161 (for *surat jalan* permits for the interior, see page 843).
Immigration Office: Jl Percetakan 15, T 22147.

● **Transport**
Local Colts: the terminal is on Jl Percetakan, close to the waterfront.

Air Sentani airport is 35 km from town. There is some accommodation available nr the airport (see Accommodation). Minibuses take passengers into town, or walk out onto the main road and catch a public colt to town via Abepura. Taxi prices are very inflated. Regular connections on Merpati/Garuda with Biak, Wamena, and Ujung Pandang; less regular connections with Sorong, Nabire, Sarmi, Senggeh, Serui, Manokwari and Merauke. MAF and AMA fly to even less prominent destinations in Irian.

Sea Boat: the Pelni ships *Tatamailau*, *Ciremai* and *Dobonsolo* dock at Jayapura every fortnight on their various circuits (see route schedule, page 921). The Pelni office is at Jl Halmahera 1, T 33270, on the waterfront.

THE BALIEM VALLEY

The Grand Valley of the Baliem was one of the most remarkable finds of this century. In 1938, the American explorer Richard Archbold flew his seaplane over the Snow Mountain Range (now called the Sudirman Range), and peered out of the cockpit to see an extensive and lush, cultivated valley where he and everyone else expected to find only forest. The network of gardens and canals brought to mind the great civilizations of Asia and the Middle East – nothing like it was expected in New Guinea, let alone in this isolated spot. The expedition named the valley *Shrangrala*.

Today it is known as the **Baliem Valley**, a verdant and fertile upland valley set at an altitude of over 1,500m and encircled by mountain peaks. It is drained by the Baliem River and is about 55 km long and 15 km wide. The population of the area is 70,000, making this the most densely populated rural area in Irian Jaya. The inhabitants make up Irian Jaya's largest, and probably most famous, tribe: the **Dani**.

Despite conversion to Christianity and the intrusion of all the paraphernalia of Indonesian administration, the Dani continue to wear their traditional penis sheaths and to farm in the traditional manner. The economy is based upon a sophisticated system of gardens, allied with the raising of pigs. On the valley floors, canals help to control flooding in the wet season, and provide irrigation water during the dry. Fields located on the hillsides even have erosion control structures, giving lie to the notion that the inhabitants of New Guinea practised only an unsophisticated agriculture before the arrival of Europeans. Pigs, the other side of the Dani agricultural coin, are raised by the women and are only eaten in ritual or ceremonial situations. Among the tribes of Irian Jaya, the Dani have been among the most resistant to change. They do not seem to be attracted by the trappings of a 'western' lifestyle, and have clung to their traditions. Nathalie Seddon, a member of a scientific expedition to the area describes

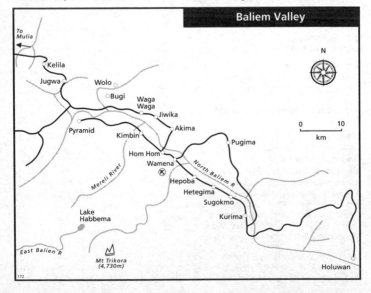

Baliem Valley

The Baliem Valley irrigation systems

When Richard Archbold and his expedition 'discovered' the Baliem Valley in 1938 they were astonished to find the Dani people maintaining a complex system of drainage and irrigation works. In an area where they expected to find only 'primitive' hunter gatherers and swidden farmers they found a people managing a system of agriculture capable of supporting a population density of over 200 people/km^2. As Brass, the expedition's botanist, explained in a paper published three years later: "...many of the slopes had a terraced appearance, and extensive flat lands were canalized in a manner which suggested drainage works to some of the observers and irrigation to others".

The Dani of the Baliem number approximately 50,000, making this the most densely settled agricultural area in New Guinea. The ability of the area to support such a relatively high density of population rests on a highly productive system of sweet potato cultivation. Pigs and sweet potatoes are the Dani's two most important food sources, together constituting about 90% of their diet. Most of the sweet potatoes are cultivated in an elaborate ditch system which dissects the valley floor into a curvilinear chequerboard of raised 'fields'. The sight of this regular field system from the air must have amazed Archbold and his fellow passengers. The ditches serve a three-fold purpose: during periods of heavy rain, they drain water from the land; during drought, they provide irrigation water; and throughout the year they are used for mulching – the rich mud which accumulates in the ditches being ladled onto the crops to promote growth and raise yields. Not only are population densities exceptionally high for the area, but the anthropologist Karl Heider maintains there is no evidence of over-population. Although it is the rice-based irrigation systems of Java and Bali which tend to attract the most attention, the Dani's intensive system of horticulture is no less sophisticated. It is perfectly in tune with environmental conditions in the area, and the antiquity of some of the terraces testifies to its sustainability over time.

her view of the Dani in the following way:-

"Never had I encountered such an uninhibited and affectionate people ... The Danis exude an overwhelming contentment and love of life, sharply putting into perspective the sad materialism, dissatisfaction and alienation that now characterize western society ... But irrevocable change dawns in Irian and our very being there has accelerated a westernisation that could obliterate an entire culture"

WAMENA

Wamena is the largest town in the Baliem Valley and most visitors use it as a base to explore the surrounding countryside. The settlement was established by the Dutch in 1958, at about the same time that missionaries began working in the valley. It is really just a small group of administrative buildings, hotels, tour companies and restaurants. Wamena is something of a boom town at the moment due to the imminent completion of the trans-Irian highway, linking Wamena with Jayapura. At present the town can only be reached by air. Small investors and large, no doubt assuming that the road will open up the Baliem area to tourists and other riches, are buying land and building shops, hotels and restaurants in anticipation. Others wonder whether the road really will herald a massive increase in business: are tourists likely to want to travel overland for hundreds of kilometres in uncomfortable buses when there are no other places worth stopping at? Time will tell.

Excursions

There are a number of Dani villages and other sights within easy reach of Wamena. Not surprisingly, these are relatively heavily touristed. Good maps of the surrounding area are available from most hotels. It is much more rewarding to go on an overnight(s) trek.

South-east and east of Wamena

Pugima is the closest Dani village to Wamena, about 1-hr walk E of town. Walk through **Wesaput** and then cross the Baliem River to reach the village. There are some traditional houses here, but being so close to Wamena it is changing fast. *Getting there*: on foot, 1 hr.

Kurima is a district capital about 30 km SE of Wamena. A market is held here on Tues and it can be used as a base for treks into the surrounding hills, particularly S through the **Baliem River Gorge**. **Accommodation** Basic accommodation available. *Getting there*: public bemos venture 15 km SE from Wamena to Hepoba; sometimes the drivers can be persuaded to continue to Hetegima or Sugokmo (another 5 km) for an additional charge. From these towns it is an easy hike to Kurima.

North and north-west of Wamena

Akima is famous for its blackened, **mummified warrior**. In former times, powerful or important men were not cremated but preserved through desiccation so that their influence could continue to benefit the village. The hunched figure is dressed in the regalia of a Dani warrior. To see the mummy, haggle with the keeper – expect to pay 5,000-10,000Rp depending on your bargaining skills. There is a market in Akima on Sun. *Getting there*: take the NW road out of town towards Hom Hom; at Hom Hom cross the Baliem River on the suspension bridge and then follow the track; the village is just off the road. In all, about 2 hrs walk. Bemos also run past Akima.

Jiwika is a district capital about 18 km NW of Wamena and the largest village in the area. Like Akima, there is a mummy here. Expect to pay about 5,000Rp to see the wizened figure. **Accommodation E** *Losmen Lauk*, very basic, shared mandi, fleas. *Getting there*: bemos run to Jiwika from Wamena, or walk.

Waga Waga is a small community on the track running N from Jiwika. The unexciting Kontilolo Cave attracts some visitors. Admission 2,000Rp. *Getting there*: by bemo, or walk.

Kimbin is a district capital NW of Wamena. **Accommodation** Homestay available. About 5 km further N still is the missionary centre of **Pyramid**, an oasis of civilization at the end of the road running N out of town. From Pyramid, follow the river to a world vision bridge. Cross over, and continue down river. There is a new road running parallel to the footpath, about 500m away. Bemos run along the road to **Manda**. The walk and bemo journey takes about 3 hrs. From Manda, another 3-hr hike through a gorge, leads up to **Wolo**. *Getting there*: public bemos run to Kimbin and sometimes on to Pyramid. To walk to Kimbin should take about 6 hrs, Pyramid 7 hrs. From Manda, there is a new road back to Wamena. Bemos available.

West of Wamena

A new road has reportedly just been completed (1994) from Wamena to the beautiful highland lake of **Habbema**. Previously reaching this idyllic spot, at an altitude of 3,000m took a strenuous 5-day hike; now the journey should take just a few hours in a vehicle. Environmental activists tried to lobby against the road: it penetrates an area of outstanding and fragile natural beauty, and they feared what effects further developments might have on the environment. Roads in themselves are not the problem; rather it is the increased accessibility that the roads afford. Locals in Wamena expect that lake-side hotels will soon open, in all likelihood with inadequate waste and sanitation facilities, leading to pollution of the lake and the rivers and streams that flow from it. *Getting there*: by chartered vehicle.

Tours

Organizing your own 'tour' It is essential for anyone intending to trek in the Baliem Valley – and who is not fluent in Dani – to hire a guide. Even Indonesian is not widely spoken. Given the necessity to have a guide, it is not surprising that there are always independent guides offering their services. Hotels will also have their own suggestions. These private guides will charge from 10,000-30,000Rp/day depending on their experience; you will be expected to meet all their costs. If staying in a village – usually in a teacher's or nurse/doctor's house – expect to pay 3,000-6,000Rp/night. There are likely to be additional costs incurred: photographing a person usually costs 100Rp or a cigarette; a Dani warrior might expect 1,000Rp for the privilege; while being present at a funeral might mean a charge of 25,000Rp or more. The Dani are well aware that their traditions have a market value. For a 5-day tour with a guide, porter and cook, inclusive of accommodation in villages and food, expect to pay about 250,000Rp for two people.

Organized tours Far less bother is to book a tour through one of the established tour companies who offer a variety of treks and expeditions from 3 nights to 2 weeks. It is best to have a day just to judge the competition and get an idea of prices. The prices of tours obviously vary depending on the itinerary, but expect to pay about US$60-120/day/person. At last count there were only three local companies: *Chandra Tours*, Jl Trikora; *Insatra*; and *Insos Moon*. However John Tabuni, (a Dani who speaks good English), c/o *Trendy Hotel*, Jl Trikora in Wamena has also come highly recommended by recent visitors.

When booking a tour, bear in mind the following:
- Does the guide speak good English, as he is your link with the Dani.
- How many people will be going on the trek?
- What is the mode of transport?
- What does the cost of the trek include?
- What is the route and destinations (more adventurous treks venture beyond the Baliem Valley)?

What to take
- good walking boots
- insect repellent
- sleeping bag
- toiletries
- medical kit
- candles/matches and a torch (there is no electricity and it is dark by 1800)
- light day clothes
- warm clothing for the night
- raincoat and/or collapsible umbrella
- food for trip; only vegetables and fruit are easily available outside Wamena. Taking high energy food is a good idea
- barter goods and gifts like cigarettes
- sun hat and sun cream
- ample small change

Local information
● **Accommodation**
Accommodation is some of the most expensive in Indonesia – understandably, as Baliem is only connected by air (or foot) with the outside world. **B** *Baliem Cottages*, Jl Thamrin, T 31370, 'traditional' thatched cottages, rather down-at-heel; **B** *Baliem Palace*, T 31043, hot water, large rooms, attractive garden; **C** *Anggrek*, Jl Ambon, T 31242, clean and well-run, some attached mandis; **C** *Jayawijaya*, 3 km out of town, inconvenient location, expensive; used only by tour groups; **C** *Nayak*, Jl Gatot Subroto 1, T 31067, good rooms, quiet, nr the airport, with attached bathrooms, Ricardo speaks some English, very accommodating; **C** *Sri Lestari*, Jl Trikora, Pasar Sentral, T 31221; **D** *Trendy*, T 31092, clean rooms and a seating area.

● **Places to eat**
NB Consumption of alcohol is not permitted in Wamena. Most visitors choose to eat in their hotels. There are a few warung in the market area but the quality is poor. *Sinta Prima*, Jl Trikora 17, best restaurant in Wamena with local crayfish and Chinese dishes.

● **Airline offices**
AMA, far end of airfield; MAF, Airport building, T 31263; Merpati, Jl Trikora 41, T 31488.

● **Banks & money changers**
Bank Rakyat Indonesia, will change most major TCs and cash.

● **Post & telecommunications**
Post Office: Jl Timor.
Telkom office: Jl Thamrin 22.

● **Shopping**
Tribal art: the Dani do not have a rich material culture, but hawkers sell what there is in town: penis gourds, well-made stone axes and adzes, spears, and bows and arrows. Try the souvenir shop nr the market first to get an idea of price.

● **Tour companies & travel agents**
Chandra Nusantara, Jl Trikora 17, T 31293. *Desa Tour and Travel*, T 31107.

● **Transport**
Local Public bemos run to local centres within about a 20 km radius of Wamena. Bemos can also be chartered to venture a little further off the beaten track – about 10,000Rp/hr. **Air** The airstrip is virtually in the town. Multiple daily connections on Merpati with Jayapura. **NB** Bad weather and over-booking are a perennial problem. MAF and AMA fly to numerous destinations in surrounding area, but only intermittantly.

MERAUKE

Merauke, near the SE border with Papua New Guinea, is as far from Jakarta as it is possible to get – and still stay a night in a hotel room. The area is an important transmigration settlement zone although the numbers targeted for settlement during Repelita IV (1985-89) – some 50,000 for the Merauke district – were not attained. Immigrants from S Sulawesi and from Java are also prominent in the town and in local trade, and many locals feel marginalized.

In 1990, only 50 foreign tourists made it to this distant outpost. However, the tourist office has big plans – almost all of them tied to the perceived potential of eco-tourism and the attractions of the Wasur National Park (see Excursions, below). The town itself is unremarkable; the old Dutch **Post Office** (built in 1920) and a few buildings near the **harbour** are quite interesting. The long sandy *beach* is popular with locals on a Sunday and the outlook provides good sunsets. The tidal **mud-flats** are not suitable for swimming but are excellent for **bird-watching**.

Nearby **kampungs** (villages) are worth a wander.

Local information
● **Accommodation**
All hotel prices include breakfast. *Megaria* and *Nirmala* hotels are the best in town; **B-C** *Flora*, Jl Raya Mandala 221, T 21879, a/c; **B** *Megaria*, Jl Raya Mandala 166, T 21932, a/c; **B** *Nirmala*, Jl Raya Mandala 6, T 21849, a/c, very good restaurant, but no atmosphere; **C-D** *Asmat*, Jl Trikora 3, T 21065, restaurant, some a/c, some rooms with own bathrooms, slightly more interesting accommodation than normal; **D** *Nikmat*, Jl Biak, T 21375, some a/c; **D-E** *Abadi*; **E** *Wisma Praja*.

● **Airline offices**
Garuda, Jl Raya Mandala, T 21084; Merpati, Jl Raya Mandala 163, T 21242.

● **Banks & money changers**
Close around 1300, earlier on Fri.

● **Hospitals & medical services**
Hospitals: *General Hospital*, Jl Sukarjowiryo-pranoto; *WWF*, Jl Biak 12, T 21397 for more information on visiting Wasur National Park.

● **Post & telecommunications**
Area code: 0971.

● **Shopping**
Good quality Asmat and Marind carvings. Shops close around 1300 (earlier on Fri) and open again from 1800-2100.

● **Tour companies & travel agents**
Sentosa Tosiga, Jl Raya Mandala, T 21821.

● **Transport**
Air Connections with Jayapura on Merpati on Sun, Tues, Thur and Fri. Flights to the Asmat area.

Sea Boat: The Pelni ship *Tatamailau* docks here on its fortnightly circuit (see page 921 for route schedule). Pelni office is at Jl Sabang 318, T 21591 (sporadic opening times).

WASUR NATIONAL PARK

This park is one of Indonesia's newest reserves and abuts Papua New Guinea's Tonda Reserve, creating a huge protected area. It occupies 400,000ha of wetlands, mangroves, lakes, areas of rivers and open savanna grasslands. The dominant forest formation is acacia, melaleuca and eucalyptus. It is richest in birdlife, with nearly 400 recorded species, including cranes, storks, pelican, ibis and spoonbills. Mammals include the agile wallaby (*Macropus agilis*), the spotted cuscus (*Spilocuscus maculatus*) and the short-beaked echidna (*Tachyglossus aculeatus*). About 2,500 people from the Marind and Kanum

tribal groups live in the park, and there has been no attempt (yet) to relocate them outside the park's boundaries. They are allowed to practise traditional hunting and gathering. Despite the fact that most visible elements of their culture have disappeared, these people retain a strong

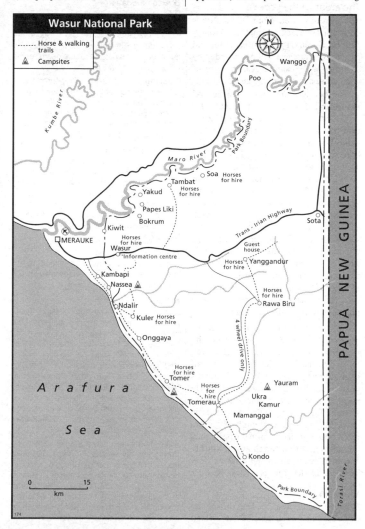

Wasur National Park

...... Horse & walking trails

△ Campsites

N

Wanggo

Poo

Kumbe River

Maro River

Park Boundary

Soa
Horses for hire

Tambat
Horses for hire

Yakud

Papes Liki

Bokrum

Kiwit

⊗ MERAUKE
Horses for hire
Wasur
Information centre

Kambapi

Nassea △

Ndalir

Kuler Horses for hire

Onggaya

Trans - Irian Highway

Sota

Guest house

Horses for hire Yanggandur

Horses for hire

Rawa Biru

4 wheel drive only

PAPUA NEW GUINEA

A r a f u r a

S e a

Horses for hire
Tomer

Horses for hire
Tomerau

△ Yauram

Ukra
Kamur

Mamanggal

Kondo

Park Boundary

Toraki River

0   15
km

family structure and moral code; western behaviour such as holding hands, kissing, and wearing scant clothing is certain to offend – so please refrain. In addition, please do not walk in their gardens uninvited.

The areas of the park

The **northern area**, from Wasur NE is dominated by acacia and melaleuca forest. Around **Tambat**, the forest is denser and patient birdwatchers will be rewarded by sightings of, for example, cassoway, birds of paradise and crowned pigeon.

The beach near **Ndalir** is wide and sandy, and the mudflats also make for good birdwatching (hundreds of pelicans collect here in the Southern Winter). The **central area** from **Onggaya** NE to the border is open savanna land. NE of **Tomer** is a good area for walking all year round. The **southern area** from **Tomerau** E and up to **Rawa Biru** is open savanna grasslands with some areas of permanent wetlands. This is the best area for viewing wildlife in the dry season; during this season, it is one of the last areas to contain water and tens of thousands of waterbirds such as pelican, ibis, egret, crane and stork congregate here. Near **Ukra**, there is a good lookout tree which provides wonderful views across the grassland plains, to watch wallabies and deer.

NB The park operates a 'zoning policy', which restricts access to some areas of the park for conservation reasons. However, the policy has been designed so that all habitat types are represented in the areas open to tourists. Trails are not yet clearly marked in the park, although it is fairly straight forward as far as Tomer. It is advisable to take a local guide if you are intending to go deeper into the park; they are worth it, as they can show you wildlife and introduce you to the local culture. The price of a local guide is 10,000Rp/day.

Viewing

Best time to visit: from Jul-Dec, during the dry season. Travel becomes restricted during the wet season, but if visitors don't mind the wet, it is possible to visit all year round. The tourist information centre provides information on which areas to visit at different times of year.

Park information

● *Accommodation*

D *Guesthouse* in Yanggandur, built in traditional style, sleeps 6, bring your own food (cooking facilities available) and mosquito net and bedding. The park is planning three new guesthouses. It is possible to stay in some of the villages, but there are no amenities.

Camping it is possible to camp almost anywhere in the park, there are several dedicated campsites. The best facilities are at Ukra, where there is a large permanent tent, which provides wildlife viewing by day and mosquito and snake protection by night.

● **Places to eat & bars**

It is advisable to buy provisions in Merauke (tinned and dried food is reasonably priced here). Local women may prepare your evening meal for you; it will consist of sago, cassava, sweet potatoes and maybe some fish or chicken. They can provide boiled water for drinking. If you are hiring a guide, remember to provide food for him too.

● **Tourist information**

There is a centre at Wasur, with cultural displays and general information sheets on where to go. There is a smaller post at Ndalir.

● **Transport**

It takes 30 mins by car from Merauke to the park. Large areas of the park are accessible because of the Trans Irian highway, which dissects the park, E to W. It is possible to hire a taxi, jeep or motorbike to get into the park. Motorized vehicles are allowed along the highway to Yanggandur, Rawa Biru and Sota. **Local** Within the park, it is possible to hire ponies (places where ponies are available for hire are marked on the map provided by the park information office). Hiring a pony costs about 10,000Rp/day. Cycling is allowed in the park.

Road Taxi: drivers may only agree to take you during the dry season. To Wasur, 30,000Rp return; to Rawa Biru, 80-90,000Rp one way; to Yanggandur 80,000Rp (drop and pick up same day or later); to Ndalir/Onggaya, 70,000Rp (drop and pick up same day or later). Taxis will agree to drop off at one point and pick up somewhere else. **Four wheel drive vehicles**: it is possible

Freeport Indonesia: the world's richest mine

Irian Jaya is one of the last, great, largely unsurveyed, sources of minerals on earth. And Freeport Indonesia, near Tembagapura in the southern highlands of the province, is arguably the richest mine in the world. The statistics are astounding. The Grasberg copper 'knob' has reserves of 1 billion tonnes of ore; a 118 km-long conveyer belt and pipeline transports the ore down over 3,000m to the port of Amamapare on the Arafura Sea; the copper and gold reserves of the mine are worth US$38bn at 1994 prices; over 70,000 tonnes of ore are moved each day; and a town – Kuala Kencana (River of Gold) – of 20,000 people has been built at a cost of US$500mn and was opened in December 1995 by President Suharto. To date there are two mines in the area. The Ertsberg is mined out, and in the process the effort has transformed a 180m-high mountain of copper into a 360m-deep hole in the ground. The Grasberg mine is still being expanded. Exploration for more deposits is being undertaken in areas where humans have probably never before set foot. All equipment and supplies are helicoptered into alpine meadows surrounded by precipitous cliffs.

Inevitably, environmentalists such as the Indonesian Forum for the Environment (Wahli) have highlighted the costs to people and nature at the scale of the Freeport operation and the further activities that might follow from the current wave of exploration. Already, the Grasberg is the second largest open-cast copper mine in the world, and James Moffatt ('Jim-Bob'), the colourful and outspoken Chairman of Freeport-McMoRan, the holding company based in the US, has been quoted as saying that they will "mine all the way to New Orleans" in their search for ore. The tailings or waste from the mine, though pobably non-toxic, are fed into the Agawagon River at a rate of 100,000 to 160,000 tonnes a day. The river has changed course as a result of the siltation. But it is arguable that the rewards of exploitation to Freeberg Indonesia and to the Indonesian government are simply too great for environmental – even human rights – worries to curtail work. Freeport is Indonesia's fourth largest taxpayer and their investments in the province are opening up the area for other developments. Infrastructure like roads for example is providing the means by which transmigrants from Java (see page 427) can settle in the area. This concerns environmental groups and some locals. It will open up this last untouched part of Indonesia in the way that the Trans-Amazon highway has done in Brazil. Pristine forest will make way for possibly unsustainable agriculture, displacing tribal peoples in the process. The inflow of transmigrants is also taking jobs away from local Irianese, creating social tensions in the process.

Until recently it seemed that Freeport-McMoRan and the Indonesian government had the situation under control. But the widely publicized death of several demonstrators at the hands – allegedly – of the military has changed the tempo and temperature of the debate. James Moffatt has been accused of 'killing for profit', while Moffatt has lambasted his opponents as 'radical groups cloaked as environmental organizations'. The fact that the area around the mine is also a centre of OPM (Organisasi Papua Merdeka, the Free Papua Movement) activity has raised the stakes for the government too.

The geologists at Freeport believe that there are yet more riches to be found along a 'trend line' that runs E-W through the middle of New Guinea. In a deal with the British mining company Rio Tinto Zinc, or RTZ, they are exploring two new sites at Etna Bay and Wabu – to be horror of environmentalists.

to hire these, with a driver, in order to visit some of the central grasslands, and villages such as Kondo and Tomerau in the dry season; the price remains high (200-250,000Rp/day) and numbers are controlled. Each additional day costs 50,000Rp. The park insists a local guide is employed to escort the vehicle.

TIMIKA, KUALA KENCANA AND TEMBAGAPURA

In December 1995 President Suharto presided at the official 'opening' of a new town – Kuala Kencana which, appropriately, means 'River of Gold'. The town, which will support a population of 20,000, exists to service the massive Freeport gold and copper mine to the N (see box). South of Kuala Kencana is the 'open' town and sub-district (*Kelurahan*) capital of Timika with a population of around 45,000. Most of these are immigrants from Java and Sulawesi as well as other parts of Irian Jaya. South of Timika is the port settlement of Amamapare. A road runs from Amamapare to Tembagapura (a settlement close to the mine) via Timika and Kuala Kencana, a distance of about 120 km. All four towns are effectively run by Freeport-McMoRan: they are by far the largest employer in the area and the government presence is minimal. (It has been said that Timika has just 40 civil servants ostensibly running the place.) The main

tribal groups living in this area are the Amungme, Kamoro and Dani.

During 1995 and into 1996 Timika has been the scene of demonstrations by Papuan tribespeople – orchestrated, some maintain, by the Organisasi Papua Merdeka (OPM), the Free Papua Movement – demonstrating against the Freeport mine and the alleged human rights abuses perpetrated by the Indonesian military and security personnel employed by Freeport-McMoRan. The allegations and counter-allegations are particularly sensitive because of the importance of the Freeport mine to the Indonesian economy and because of the political and security concerns that colour the Indonesian government's view.

● **Accommodation Timika**: *Sheraton Inn Timika*, PO Box 3, Timika, this 100-room hotel N of Timika opened towards the end of 1994 and the existence of a 4-star hotel in such a remote place is inextricably associated with the Freeport mine which attracts more than its fair share of visitors with company expense accounts.

● **Transport** 500 km E of Fakfak. **Air** The airport is a 5-min drive from Timika. **Sea** The Pelni vessel *Tatamailau* docks here on its fortnightly circuit (see route schedule page 795).

Notes

Information for travellers

Before travelling	859	Getting around	871
Getting there	861	Communications	877
On arrival	862	Entertainment	878
Where to stay	866	Holidays and festivals	878
Food and drink	868		

BEFORE TRAVELLING

ENTRY REQUIREMENTS

Passports

All visitors to Indonesia must possess passports valid for at least 6 months from their date of arrival in Indonesia and, in theory, they should have proof of onward travel. Many visitors find that immigration officials are happy with some indication that sufficient funds (eg TCs) are available to purchase a return flight.

Visas

Visas are not required for nationals of ASEAN countries, Australia, Austria, Belgium, Canada, Denmark, Finland, France, Germany, Greece, Iceland, Ireland, Italy, Japan, Liechtenstein, Luxembourg, Malta, the Netherlands, New Zealand, Norway, S Korea, Spain, Sweden, Switzerland, Turkey, the UK, and the USA. Tourists may stay for a maximum of 2 months (non-extendable). Entry or exit must be through one of the so-called 'Gateway' cities, namely Ambon, Bali, Balikpapan, Batam, Biak, Jakarta, Kupang, Manado, Medan, Pekanbaru, Pontianak and Surabaya airports, and the seaports of Ambon, Bali, Batam, Manado, Medan, Jakarta, Riau, Semarang and Surabaya. If entering the country through any other city, a visa is required. These can be obtained from any Indonesian Embassy or Consulate, are only valid for 1 month, but can be extended (apply at an immigration office).

For nationals of countries other than those listed above, visas can be obtained from any Indonesian Embassy or Consulate, but are valid for 1 month only (extension possible). Two passport photographs and a small fee are required, plus a confirmed onward flight.

Business visas People intending to work in Indonesia need to take their passport, two photos and a covering letter from their company to an Indonesian Embassy or Consulate. The application takes 24 hrs to process and costs between £10-22, maximum stay 5 weeks.

Visa extension Jl Teuku Umar I, Jakarta, T 349811.

Vaccinations

None required unless visitors have been in a cholera, yellow fever or smallpox infected area in the 6 days prior to arrival.

WHEN TO GO

Best time to visit

Indonesia spans several climatic zones and the 'best time to visit' varies across the country. The dry season for much of the archipelago, including Java and Bali, spans the months from May to Sep. For details on seasons elsewhere in Indonesia (see page 36) and the relevant regional introductions.

Clothing

Light clothing is suitable all the year round, except at night in the mountains. Shorts, miniskirts and singlets should be limited to beachwear only. Proper decorum should be observed when visiting places of worship; shorts are not permitted in mosques, shoulders and arms should be covered, and women must cover their heads. Formal dress for men normally consists of a batik shirt and trousers; suits are rarely worn. Local dress is *batik* for men and *kebaya* for women.

HEALTH

For general health information see page 899. Long-term residents of Indonesia, even doctors, often offer differing advice on how to stay healthy. In many hotels in Bali, none of the tips listed below will apply; in more remote areas it would be wise to observe them all. In general:

● Malaria tablets and mosquito repellent are essential. **Warning**: do not go diving if you are taking Larium (Mefloquine). Some local residents swear by *Minyak Gosok Tawan* (lemon balm oil) or *Minyak Kayu Putih* (camphor oil) to keep mosquitoes at bay. Tiger Balm is also good for itchy bites. **NB** There is no strong mosquito repellents available outside Jakarta. The locally produced *Autan* is not effective. See Jakarta shopping for details of repellent available. An American company has designed a tailored mosquito net which covers the wearer in fine mesh and offers protection as you move around;

contact *Ben's Bug Armor*, Long Rd, T 00 1 510 540 4763.

● Avoid drinking water unless you are sure that it has been boiled bottled (mineral water is widely available).

● Do not accept drinks with ice in them, except in more expensive hotels and restaurants.

● Fresh fruit and vegetables should be limited to those that you can peel yourself.

● Salads should be avoided, as many vegetables are fertilized with human excrement and the organisms remain even after washing.

● Avoid eating food (particularly meat) at sidestalls where it has been left standing in the open.

● Avoid ice-creams.

MONEY

Cost of living

Visitors staying in first class hotels and eating in hotel restaurants will probably spend about 150,000Rp/day (around US$75/day). Tourists staying in cheaper a/c accommodation, and eating in local restaurants will probably spend about 75,000-120,000Rp/day (around US$37-60). A backpacker, staying in fan-cooled guesthouses and eating cheaply, might expect to be able to live on 20,000Rp/day (US$10/day).

Credit Cards

Major credit cards are accepted in larger hotels, airline offices, department stores and some restaurants although this method of payment is often subject to a 3% surcharge. If you are visiting very remote areas for a long period, it can make sense to obtain Indonesian Post Office TCs in one of the big cities. These are then easily changed into rupiahs in any post office in the country. For lost American Express cards and TCs T (021) 5703310.

Currency

1Rp equals 100 sen. **NB** Denominations are 100Rp, 500Rp, 1,000Rp, 5,000Rp,

10,000Rp, 20,000Rp and 50,000Rp. Coins are minted in 25Rp, 50Rp, 100Rp and 500Rp denominations. The rupiah/US$ exchange rate in August 1996 was US$1=2,350Rp. But note that the rupiah had weakened considerably following the civil disturbances of July.

Travellers' cheques

Travellers' cheques can usually be changed in larger towns and tourist destinations. In smaller towns and more out of the way spots it may not be possible to change TCs. The US$ is the most readily acceptable currency, both for TCs and cash. If changing cash note that banks like bills in pristine condition, and a better rate is often given for larger denomination notes – eg US$50 or US$100. American Express US$ are easily changeable. Thomas Cook Cheques are not always accepted (Standard Chartered Bank will accept Thomas Cook Visa TCs and Hong Kong Shanghai Bank will accept Thomas Cook Mastercard TCs. Money changers often give better rates than banks. Hotels will sometimes change TCs (usually in popular tourist destinations), but rates vary a great deal from competitive to appalling, so it is worth checking.

GETTING THERE

AIR

The three main gateways into Indonesia are Jakarta, Bali and Medan (Sumatra). For information on connections with Bali see page 337, and for Medan see page 439. Batam is also becoming increasingly popular, although arrivals are mostly by sea, from Singapore (see page 501). Garuda, the national flag carrier, flies between Jakarta and Europe, the US, other Asian cities and Australia and New Zealand. Most of the major European carriers fly direct to Jakarta including British Airways, Lufthansa, Air France and KLM. The last 3 also have direct flights to Bali. Many visitors fly to Jakarta via Singapore. British Airways, Singapore Airlines, and Qantas all fly from London to Singapore. There are also flights via Bangkok, Kuala Lumpur and Hong Kong. Garuda and Singapore Airlines operate many flights a day from Singapore.

From Australasia

From Auckland twice a week with Garuda; from Sydney daily flights with Qantas, Garuda and Ansett; from Melbourne 6 times a week with Garuda; from Perth daily flights with Garuda, Qantas and Singapore Airlines.

From Europe

There are direct flights from London (BA and Garuda), Amsterdam (KLM and Garuda), Frankfurt (Lufthansa and Garuda), Zurich (Garuda), Paris (Air France and Garuda), Rome (Garuda), and Moscow (Aeroflot).

From the Far East

Japan Airlines and Garuda have daily flights from Tokyo; Garuda and Japan Asia Airlines fly 6 days a week from Osaka. From Hong Kong, Cathay Pacific, Garuda and China Airlines. From Seoul daily flights with Garuda and Korean Airlines. From Taipei daily flights with Garuda, Eva, China Airlines and Sempati. From Beijing Air China and Garuda each have 2 flights a week. From Ho Chi Minh City twice a week with Garuda.

From South Asia

Many direct flights from Singapore, Bangkok or Kuala Lumpur; also from Manila 5 days a week with Garuda and Philippine Airlines.

From the USA and Canada

From Los Angeles, Garuda fly direct 3 times a week.

BOAT

Visitors can enter Indonesia by sea without a visa at the gateway ports of Benoa (Bali), Balikpapan, Batam, Jakarta,

Medan, Pontianak, Semarang, Surabaya and Tanjung Pinang. There are regular ferries from Singapore to Batam (see page 502), and from Penang to Medan's Belawan Port (see page 439); there is also a ferry service from Melaka to the non-gateway city of Dumai (Sumatra). Otherwise visitors will have to take a freighter or some other form of irregular sea transport.

CUSTOMS

Duty free allowance

Two litres of alcohol, 200 cigarettes or 50 cigars or 100 grammes of tobacco along with a reasonable amount of perfume.

Currency regulations

A limit of 50,000Rp can be carried in or out of the country. There are no restrictions on the import or export of foreign currency, either cash or TCs.

Prohibited items

Narcotics, arms and ammunition, TV sets, radio/cassette recorders, pornographic objects or printed matter, printed matter in Chinese characters and Chinese medicines. In theory, approval should also be sought for carrying transceivers, movie film and video cassettes.

ON ARRIVAL

Airport information

Jakarta's **Soekarno-Hatta International Airport** lies 30 km NW of the city. It is Indonesia's main international gateway and has two separate terminal complexes 5 km apart: one for domestic connections (terminals A to D) and the other for international flights (E to H). The only exception is the national flag carrier, Garuda, which operates out of the international terminal (see route map, page 912).

Airport facilities Facilities at the airport include car rental (Avis, Blue Bird Limo and Hertz), currency exchange booths, left luggage facilities (outside the arrivals hall),

hotel booking counter (about which we have received complaints concerning the sending of visitors to sub-standard hotels for which the reservation office staff receive a commission), the *Transit Hotel* (see below), the *Transit Restaurant*, *Dunkin Donuts*, *McDonald's* a Post Office for 24 hrs long-distance calls, fax, telex and postal facilities. The faint aroma of Kretek (clove) cigarettes as one steps off the plane tells passengers they have clearly arrived in Indonesia.

Airport accommodation If in transit, it may not be worthwhile travelling into the city. **B** *Cengkareng Transit*, Jl Jurumudi, T 611964, 10 mins from the airport, neither very pleasant nor very good value, but may be necessary to stay here if in transit or catching an early flight. Free shuttle bus from and to the airport.

Transport to town Metered taxis to the city centre cost about 25-30,000Rp. The fare on the meter has a surcharge of 2,300Rp added on plus toll fees of 6,000Rp (for the airport and city toll roads). A/c Damri buses run every 30 mins (operating between 0500 and 2400) from the airport to five points in the city centre including Gambir train station (3,000Rp) and Blok M (see page 132 for more details on transport from the airport). It is a 10-min walk from Gambir to Jl Jaksa where most of the budget accommodation is to be found.

Other international airports Denpasar's (Bali) Ngurah Rai Airport has direct flights from Singapore, Kuala Lumpur, Hong Kong, Japan and Amsterdam (see page 337 for details). **Medan's Polonia Airport** has direct flights from Singapore, Penang and Kuala Lumpur on Garuda, Singapore Airlines and MAS (see page 439 for details). **Kupang's El Tari Airport** has flights from Darwin, Australia (see page 745), while there are flights from Los Angeles, via Honolulu, to **Biak**, Irian Jaya (see page 735). **Pontianak's**

Supadio Airport has connections with Kuching (E Malaysia) and Singapore (see page 735), as does **Balikpapan's Sepinggang Airport** (see page 377). From **Pekanbaru's Simpangtiga Airport**, there are flights to Melaka and Kuala Lumpur (Malaysia) and to Singapore (see page 782).

Airport tax
25,000Rp on international flights, 8,000Rp on domestic flights.

Conduct
As a rule, Indonesians are courteous and understanding. Visitors should be the same. As foreigners, visitors are often given the benefit of the doubt when norms are transgressed. However, it is best to have a grasp of at least the basics of accepted behaviour. In tourist areas and large cities, westerners and their habits are better understood; but in remote areas be more aware of local sensibilities. There are also some areas – such as Aceh in N Sumatra – that are more fervently Muslim than other parts of the country. With such a diverse array of cultures and religions, accepted conduct varies. Specific cultural notes are given in the appropriate introductory sections.

Calmness Like other countries of Southeast Asia, a calm attitude is highly admired, especially if things are going wrong. Keep calm and cool when bargaining, or waiting for a delayed bus or appointment.

Dress Indonesia is largely a Muslim country and women should be particularly careful not to offend. Dress modestly and avoid shorts, short skirts and sleeveless dresses or shirts (except at the beach). Public nudity and topless bathing are not acceptable.

Face People should not be forced to lose face in public; especially in front of colleagues. Putting someone in a position of *malu* or social shame, should be avoided.

Gifts If you are invited to somebody's home, it is customary to take a gift. This is not opened until after the visitor has left.

Heads, hands and feet The head is considered sacred and should never be touched (especially those of children). Handshaking is common among both men and women, but the use of the left hand to give or receive is taboo. When eating with fingers, use the right hand only. Pointing with your finger is considered impolite; use your thumb to point, beckon buses (or any person) with a flapping motion of your right hand down by your side. When sitting with others, do not cross your legs; it is considered disrespectful. In addition, do not point with your feet and keep them off tables. Shoes are often not worn in the house and should be removed on entering.

Jam karet or 'rubber time' is a peculiarly Indonesian phenomenon. Patience and a cool head are very important; appointments are rarely at the time arranged.

Open affection Public displays of affection between men and women is considered objectionable.

Religion Indonesia is the largest Muslim country in the world. In Java, Islam is a synthesis of Islam, Buddhism, Hinduism and animism – although the extent to which it is 'syncretic' is vigorously debated (see page 94). Orthodox Islam is strongest in northern Sumatra (Aceh), but is also present in parts of Sulawesi, Kalimantan and W Java. For a brief background to Islam see page 52.

Mosques are sacred houses of prayer; non-Muslims can enter a mosque, so long as they observe the appropriate customs: remove shoes before entering, dress appropriately (neatly and fully covered, avoiding singlets, shorts or short skirts), do not disturb the peace, and do not walk too close to or in front of somebody who is praying. During the fasting month of

Ramadan, do not eat, drink or smoke in the presence of Muslims.

Bali has remained a Hindu island (see page 324), and remnants of Hinduism are also evident in parts of central and E Java. To enter a temple or *pura* on Bali it is often necessary to wear a sash. Christianity is a growing religion in Sulawesi (see page 635) and in E Nusa Tenggara (page 729).

Although not a religion, **Pancasila** is the Indonesian state ideology and should not be slighted (see page 51).

For a more comprehensive background to do's and don'ts in Indonesia see: Draine, Cathy and Hall, Barbara (1986) *Culture shock! Indonesia*, Times Books: Singapore.

Hours of business

Hours of business are highly variable; there are not even standard opening hours for government offices. The listing below is a rule of thumb:

Banks: foreign banks 0800-1200 Mon-Fri and 0800-1100 Sat; local banks 0800-1300, 1330-1600 Mon-Sat. Banks in hotels may stay open longer.

Businesses: most businesses open 0800/0900-1200, 1300-1600/1700 Mon-Fri.

Government offices: 0800-1500 Mon-Thur, 0800-1130 Fri and 0800-1400 Sat.

Museums: 0830 or 0900-1400 Tues-Thur, 0900-1100 Fri, 0900-1300 Sat and 0900-1500 Sun, closed Mon.

Shops: 0900-2000 Mon-Fri, 0900-1300 Sat, sometimes on Sun. In smaller towns shops may close for a siesta between 1300 and 1700.

Official time

There are three time zones in Indonesia. *Western Indonesia* (Sumatra, Java, W and central Kalimantan) GMT + 7; *central Indonesia* (Bali, S and E Kalimantan, Sulawesi, Nusa Tenggara) GMT + 8; and *E Indonesia* (Irian Jaya and the Maluku islands) GMT + 9.

Safety

Indonesia is a safe country and violence is rare. However, single women should take care – it is unusual for women to travel alone and those who do will find Indonesians concerned for their safety. There is a notion held by too many Indonesians that western women, by definition, are loose, so pestering males may be a problem. Be firm, but be polite. Older women travelling alone will not be faced with such problems and will be treated with great respect.

Far more of a problem is theft and deception. It is advisable for travellers to carry all valuables in a moneybelt. Avoid carrying large amounts of cash; TCs can be changed in most major towns. Pickpockets frequent the public transport systems. Reports of robbery on the overnight trains through Java are common. Take great care of your belongings on these longer journeys on public transport. Do not leave valuables in hotel rooms; most of the more expensive hotels will have safety deposit boxes. Many guesthouses have 'open air' bathrooms, ie with only a

---

The Indonesian day

Indonesians divide the day into four periods:

pagi is from midnight to 1100.
siang is from 1100 to 1500.
sore is from 1500 to dusk.
malam is from dusk to midnight.
People greet one another accordingly – *selamat siang* (good afternoon), *selamat malam* (good evening).

partial roof. A favoured means of entering rooms is over the bathroom wall and through the bathroom door, therefore it is essential to lock bathroom doors in this type of accommodation. Petty theft is a growing problem in all places frequented by travellers. In Jakarta it is also recommended that passengers in taxis keep their doors locked: thefts while stuck in traffic jams are becoming more common.

Beware of the confidence tricksters who are widespread in tourist areas. Sudden reports of unbeatable bargains or closing down sales are usual ploys.

Shopping

Indonesia offers a wealth of distinctive handicrafts and other products. Best buys include textiles (batik and ikat), silverwork, woodcarving, puppets, paintings and ceramics. Bali has the greatest choice of handicrafts. It is not necessarily the case that you will find the best buys in the area where a particular product is made; the larger cities, especially Jakarta, sell a wide range of handicrafts and antiques from across the archipelago at competitive prices.

Tips on buying Early morning sales may well be cheaper, as salespeople often believe the first sale augurs well for the rest of the day. **Bargaining**: except in the larger fixed price stores, bargaining (with good humour) is expected; start bargaining at 50-60% lower than the asking price. Do not expect to achieve instant results; if you walk away from the shop, you will almost certainly be followed, with a lower offer. If the salesperson agrees to your price, you should really feel obliged to purchase – it is considered very ill mannered to agree on a price and then not buy the article.

Antiques There are some good antique shops in Jakarta and a handful of other regional centres, but bargains usually need to be 'rooted out' by visiting little out-of-the-way shops. Antiques include Dutch memorabilia and Chinese ceramics (Indonesia was on the trade route between China and India), as well as local products like Javanese carvings and Sulawesi metalwork. **NB** There are also a huge number of fakes on the market – you only have to walk down Jl Surabaya (Jakarta's most popular flea market) to see men openly 'distressing' work, then to be sold as 150-year-old heirlooms.

Batik Centres of batik-making are focused on Java. Yogyakarta and Solo (Surakarta) probably offer the widest choice, although Cirebon and Pekalongan (both on the N coast), offer their own distinctive styles. There is also a good range of batik on sale in Jakarta. The traditional hand-drawn batiks (*batik tulis*) are naturally more expensive than the modern printed batiks. For more information on batik see page 102.

Clothing Very reasonably priced western-style clothes can be found in most of the bigger cities. Large department stores and markets are the best places to browse. Children's clothes are also very good value (although dyes may run). Bali offers the best fashion clothing.

Ikat This dyed and woven cloth is found on the islands of Bali, Lombok and Nusa Tenggara (Sumba, Flores, Timor), although it is not cheap and is sometimes of rather dubious quality. For more information see page 408.

Jewellery Gems mined in Indonesia include diamonds and black opals from Kalimantan and pearls from Maluku. Contemporary-style jewellery is made in Bali (although some is of poor quality). There are several good jewellery shops in Jakarta, mostly found in 5-star hotels. West Sumatra and Aceh are both known for their silverwork.

Metalwork The traditional Malay sword, the *kris* is the most popular buy. Both antique and modern examples are available. For more information see page 118.

Painting Yogyakarta is a centre of painting, with several workshops of artists who have achieved world-wide acclaim. Work includes oil and batik painting. Ubud (Bali) has, since the 1930's, been a centre for local artists and is a good place to buy tropical-style paintings (see page 322).

Wayang puppets Wayang is a Javanese and Balinese art form and puppets are most widely available on these two islands, particularly in Yogyakarta and Jakarta. For more information see page 96.

Weaving Baskets of all shapes and sizes are made for practical, everyday use, out of rattan, bamboo, sisal and nipah and lontar palm. The intricate baskets of Lombok are particularly attractive.

Woodcarving This ranges from the clearly ersatz and tourist oriented (Bali), to fine classical pieces (Java), to 'primitive' (Irian Jaya). The greatest concentration of woodcarvers work in Bali producing skilful modern designs as well as more traditional pieces.

Tipping

Tipping is not usual in Indonesia. A 10% service charge is added to bills at more expensive hotels (in addition to tax of 11%). Porters expect to be tipped about 500Rp a bag. In more expensive restaurants where no service is charged, a tip of 5-10% is sometimes appropriate. Taxi drivers (in larger towns) appreciate a small tip (200-300Rp). *Parkirs* always expect payment for 'watching' your car – 200Rp, or 300Rp in Jakarta.

Voltage

220 volts, 50 cycles in the big cities; 110 volts in some areas. Plugs are usually rounded and two pronged although more expensive hotels often have 3-pin plugs. Power surges are not common and well protected electrical equipment such as lap-top computers can be used.

Weights and measures

Metric, although local units are still in use in some areas.

WHERE TO STAY

Tourist and business centres usually have a good range of accommodation for all budgets. Bali, for example, has some of the finest hotels in the world – at a corresponding price – along with excellent middle and lower-range accommodation. However, visitors venturing off the beaten track may find hotels restricted to dingy 'Chinese' establishments and over-priced places catering for local businessmen and officials. The best run and most competitively priced budget accommodation is found in popular tourist spots – like Bali and Yogya. It is almost always worth bargaining in Chinese hotels, and in middle and upper grade establishments. Cheaper places may not give discounts, although as a general rule it is worth negotiating. Note that Indonesians prefer to be on the ground floor, so rooms on higher floors are usually cheaper.

Terminology can be confusing: a *losmen* is a lower price range hotel; in parts of Sumatra and in some other areas, losmen are known as *penginapan*; a *wisma* is a guesthouse, but these can range in price from cheap to moderately expensive; finally, a *hotel* is a hotel, but can range from the cheap and squalid up to a Hilton. **NB** The government has recently introduced a ruling requiring all tourist accommodation to have Indonesian names rather than use Western words. Thus the *City Guesthouse* might be renamed *Wisma Kota*. It is not yet clear how far this edict will be taken, nor how assiduously it will be enforced. However, be prepared for hotel name changes.

Accommodation

Hotels are listed under seven categories, according to the *average* price of a double/twin room for 1 night. It should be noted that many hotels will have a range of rooms, some with a/c and attached bathroom facilities, others with just a fan and shared facilities. Prices can therefore vary a great deal. The best rooms in any hotel are usually termed 'vip'. If a hotel entry lists 'some a/c', then these rooms are likely to be in the upper part of the range, perhaps even in the next category. Hotels in the middle and lower price categories often provide breakfast in the room rate. In the more out-of-the-way places or in hotels geared to Indonesians this is usually fried rice or something similar. White bread, margarine and chocolate vermicelli is also strangely popular as a breakfast pick-me-up. In the more expensive hotels, service charge (10%) and government tax (11%) are added onto the bill; they are usually excluded from the quoted room rate. More expensive hotels tend to quote their prices in US$. **NB** During the off-season, hotels in tourist destinations may halve their room rates,

Hotel price guide

L: *US$200+ (400,000Rp+)* **Luxury**: hotels in this bracket number a handful and are to be found only in Jakarta and Bali. All facilities, combined with sumptuous rooms and excellent service.

A+: *US$100-200 (200,000-400,000Rp)* **International class**: only to be found in a few cities and tourist destinations. They should provide the entire range of business services (fax, translation, seminar rooms, etc), sports facilities (gym, swimming pool, etc), Asian and western restaurants, bars, and discotheques.

A: *US$50-100 (100,000-200,000Rp)* **First class**: will usually offer good business, sports and recreational facilities, with a range of restaurants and bars.

B: *50,000-100,000Rp* **Tourist class**: in tourist destinations, these will probably have a swimming pool and all rooms will have air-conditioning and an attached bathroom. Other services include one or more restaurants and 24-hrs coffee shop/room service. Most will have televisions in the rooms.

C: *30,000-50,000Rp* **Economy**: rooms should be air-conditioned and have attached bathrooms with hot water. A restaurant and room service will probably be available but little else.

D: *16,000-30,000Rp* **Budget**: rooms are unlikely to be air-conditioned although they should have an attached bathroom or mandi. Toilets may be either western-style or of the 'squat' Asian variety, depending on whether the town is on the tourist route. Toilet paper may not be provided. Many in this price range, out of tourist areas, are 'Chinese' hotels. Bed linen and towels are usually provided, and there may be a restaurant.

E: *8,000-16,000Rp* **Guesthouse**: fan-cooled rooms, often with shared mandi and Asian 'squat' toilet. Toilet paper and towels are unlikely to be provided, although bed linen will be. Guesthouses on the tourist route have better facilities and are sometimes excellent sources of information, offering cheap tours and services such as bicycle and motorcycle hire. Places in this category vary a great deal, and can change very rapidly. Other travellers are the best source of up-to-the-minute reviews.

F: *under 8,000Rp* **Guesthouse**: fan-cooled rooms, shared mandi and 'squat' toilet. Rooms can be tiny, dark and dingy, with wafer-thin walls. There are also some real bargains in this bracket. Standards change very fast and other travellers are the best source of information. **Homestays** are usually also in our **E-F** categories. The difference between a guesthouse (or losmen) and a homestay is that in the latter guests live within the family house, while in the former they sleep separately.

so it is always worthwhile bargaining or asking whether there is a 'special' price.

Peculiarities of Indonesian hotels include the tendency to build rooms without windows and, more appealingly, to design middle and lower range hotels around a courtyard. Baths and showers are not a feature of many cheaper losmen. Instead a *mandi* – a tub and ladel – is used to wash.

FOOD AND DRINK

Food

Although Indonesia is made-up of a bewildering array of ethnic groups dispersed over 5 million sq km of land and sea, the main staple across the archipelago is rice. Today, alternatives such as corn, sweet potatoes and sago, which are grown primarily in the dry islands of the E, are regarded as 'poor man's food', and rice is the preferred staple.

Indonesians will eat rice – or *nasi* (milled, cooked rice) – at least three times a day. Breakfast often consists of left-over rice, stir-fried and served up as *nasi goreng*. Mid-morning snacks are often sticky rice cakes or *pisang goreng* (fried bananas). Rice is the staple for lunch, served up with two or three meat and vegetable dishes and followed by fresh fruit. The main meal is supper, which is served quite early and again consists of rice, this time accompanied by as many as five or six other dishes. *Sate/satay* (grilled

Restaurant price guide

Prices

◆◆◆◆	30,000Rp+	Hotel restaurants and exclusive restaurants.
◆◆◆	10,000-30,000Rp	Restaurants in tourist class hotels and more expensive local restaurants.
◆◆	4,000-10,000Rp	Coffee shops and basic restaurants.
◆	under 4,000Rp	A warung or roadside stall.

skewers of meat), *soto* (a nourishing soup) or *bakmi* (noodles, a dish of Chinese origin) may be served first.

In many towns (particularly in Java), sate, soto or bakmi vendors roam the streets with carts containing charcoal braziers, ringing a bell or hitting a block (the noise will signify what he or she is selling), looking for customers in the early evenings. These carts are known as *kaki lima* – literally 'five legs'. There are two schools of thought as to the origins of the term. Most people maintain that they are named after the three 'legs' of the cart plus the two of the vendor. But *pedagang* (vendor) *kaki lima* (abbreviated to PK5 in newspaper reports) also refers to hawkers who peddle their wares from stalls and from baskets hung from shoulder poles. The second interpretation of the term maintains that *kaki lima* in fact refers to the pavement, which formerly used to have a width of 5 ft. This is a less obvious, and rather more attractive interpretation. Larger foodstalls where there is too much to cart around tend to set up in the same place every evening in a central position in town. These *warungs*, as they are known, may be temporary structures or more permanent buildings, with simple tables and benches. In the larger cities, there may be an area of warungs, all under one roof. Often a particular street will become known as the best place to find particular dishes like *martabak* (savoury meat pancakes) or *gado gado* (vegetable salad served with peanut sauce). It is common to see some warungs being labelled *wartegs*. These are stalls selling dishes from Tegal, a town on Java's north coast – *Warung Tegal = warteg*. More formalized restaurants are known simply as *rumah makan*, literally 'eating houses', often shortened to just 'RM'. Another term for cheaper restaurants is 'Depot', which is often rather appropriate. A good place to look for cheap stall food is in and around the market or *pasar* (from the

Arabic *bazaar*); night markets or *pasar malam* are usually better for eating than day markets.

Feast days, such as Lebaran marking the end of Ramadan, are a cause for great celebration and traditional dishes are served. *Lontong* or *ketupat* are made at this time (they are both versions of boiled rice – simmered in a small container or bag, so that as it cooks, the rice is compressed to make a solid block). This may be accompanied by *sambal goreng daging* (fried beef in a coconut sauce) in Java or *rendang* (curried beef) in Sumatra. *Nasi*

Popular Indonesian dishes

Bubur – rice porridge. *Bubur hitam* is black glutinous rice boiled with sugar, garnished with coconut milk and served warm.

Cap cai – mixed, stir-fried vegetables, with various additions – such as pork and squid – and served with rice (Chinese).

Gado-gado – steamed vegetable salad, hard-boiled egg, krupuk and tempe, served with a peanut sauce and sometimes rice.

Ketupat – compressed, boiled rice; usually served with satay.

Lumpia – spring rolls; fried egg pancake stuffed with chicken, shrimps and vegetables (Chinese).

Martabak – pancake, either sweet or savoury, the latter usually in Java when it is stuffed with mutton, eggs and onions; served crispy with a curry sauce.

Mie goreng – the same as nasi goreng, but the rice is replaced by noodles.

Nasi campur – a rice platter, similar to *nasi rames*; often cold, usually consisting of bean curd, chicken, beans and rice; campur means 'to mix'.

Nasi goreng – fried rice, served with shrimps, small pieces of meat, onion, garlic and cucumber.

Nasi gudeg – rice, chicken and jackfruit, cooked in coconut milk (Javanese).

Nasi kuning – yellow rice, usually a festival dish, cooked with turmeric and coconut milk; sometimes served with beef.

Nasi lemak – rice cooked with coconut milk and garnished with *ikan bilis* (fried anchovies), egg and cucumber.

Nasi liwet – rice and chicken cooked in coconut milk (Javanese).

Nasi rames – rice with meat and vegetables on top, accompanied by *serundeng* and *krupuk* (Padang).

Nasi uduk – rice cooked in coconut milk with spices.

Opor ayam – chicken cooked in a mild creamy coconut sauce.

Pisang goreng – banana fritters; coated in batter and deep fried.

Rendang – hot, dry beef curry (Padang) cooked in coriander, laos powder and tumeric; a W Sumatra speciality.

Rijstaffel – literally, 'rice table', rice served with as many as 16 other dishes (Dutch-Indonesian).

Sate – perhaps the Malay world's most famous dish: slivers of skewered meat, marinated, cooked over a charcoal fire and served with a peanut sauce and lontong (compressed rice).

Sayur lodeh – mixed vegetables in coconut milk (Javanese).

Serabi – scotch pancakes, made from rice flour, *santen* (coconut milk) and sugar (Javanese-Cirebon).

Soto – a soup of clear chicken stock, flavoured with lemon grass, to which is added glass noodles, hard-boiled eggs, chopped shallots, beansprouts, sambal and/or shredded chicken.

Tempe: soybean cake

Tempe has recently become a popular health food in the West, but its origins are Indonesian. It is believed to have originated in Java about 100 years ago, with the establishment of the soybean trade with China. In Indonesia, it is used as a meat-substitute by poorer communities, providing a cheap meal, rich in protein. During WW2, tempe became familiar to prisoners in Japanese prison camps. It is an easily digestible nutritious food, because it is fermented before being eaten. It contains no cholesterol or saturated fats, but does contain the vitamin B12. It is made by injecting cooked soybean with a fungal spore. The soybean is packed in banana leaves (now, more usually, plastic bags) and left to ferment. A solid white cake is formed, looking rather like a cheese, which is then cut into slices and may be deep fried (*tempe goreng*) or simmered in spicy coconut milk (*pechel tempe* – an E Javan speciality). Visitors to Indonesia are most likely to come across tempe in *gado-gado*, where it is served, along with a hard-boiled egg, on top of vegetables.

kuning (yellow rice) is traditionally served at a *selamatan* (a Javanese celebration marking a birth, the collection of the rice harvest or the completion of a new house).

In addition to rice, there are a number of other common ingredients used across the country. Coconut milk, ginger, chilli peppers and peanuts are used nationwide, while dried salted fish and soybeans are important sources of protein. In coastal areas, fish and seafood tend to be more important than meat. As Indonesia is over 80% Muslim, pork is not widely eaten, although Chinese restaurants usually serve it. For a **food glossary** see page 896.

Regional cuisines   Although Indonesia is becoming more homogeneous as Javanese culture spreads to the Outer Islands, there are still distinctive regional cuisines. The food of **Java** itself embraces a number of regional forms, of which the most distinctive is **Sundanese**. *Lalap*, a Sundanese dish, consists of raw vegetables and is said to be the only Indonesian dish where vegetables are eaten uncooked. Characteristic ingredients of Javanese dishes are soybeans, beef, chicken and vegetables; characteristic flavours are an interplay of sweetness and spicyness. Probably the most famous regional cuisine however is **Padang** or **Minang** food,

which has its origins in W Sumatra province. Padang food has 'colonized' the rest of the country and there are Padang restaurants in every town, no matter how small. Dishes tend to be hot and spicy (see page 487), using quantities of chilli and turmeric, and include *rendang* (dry beef curry), *kalo ayam* (creamy chicken curry) and *dendeng balado* fried seasoned sun-dried meat with a spicy coating). In **Eastern Indonesia**, seafood and fish are important elements in the diet, with fish grilled over an open brazier (*ikan pang-gang* or *ikan bakar*) and served with spices and rice being a delicious common dish. The **Toraja** of Sulawesi eat large amounts of pork and specialities include black rice (*nasi hitam*), and fish or chicken cooked in bamboo (*piong*). There are large numbers of Chinese people scattered across the archipelago and, like other countries of the region, **Chinese** restaurants are widespread.

Drink

Unboiled **water** may not be safe to drink. Hotels and most restaurants, as a matter of course, should boil the water they offer customers. Ask for *air minum*, literally 'drinking water', *air putih* or *air mendidih* (boiled water). You may have to try both *air putih* and *air mendidih* to get what you want; in some places if you ask for *air*

Jamu: herbal drink

Jamu is the generic word used for traditional herbal medicines, which have been used throughout the archipelago for hundreds of years. The Indonesian people put great faith in the healing powers of jamu (secret recipes of herbs, roots, flowers, bark and nuts), which are believed to be able to cure anything from flu to cancer. These herbs are usually taken in the form of muddy-brown elixirs, which usually claim to restore not only your health but also your youthfulness and sexual vigour. Jamu sellers wander the streets of every town, selling their own secret concoction. They are recognizable by the heavy baskets they carry slung over their backs, full of bottles of murky brown liquid.

mendidih you will get boiling hot water rather than the previously boiled water. On Bali *air putih* usually means cold but previously boiled water. Many restaurants provide a big jug of boiled water on each table. But in cheaper establishments it is probably best to play safe and ask for bottled water. Over the last few years 'mineral water' – of which the most famous is *Aqua* ('aqua' has become the generic word for mineral water) – has become increasingly popular. It is now available from Aceh to Irian Jaya in all but the smallest and most remote towns. There have been some reports of empty mineral water bottles being refilled with tap water: check the seal before accepting a bottle.

Western **bottled and canned drinks** like Sprite, Coca-cola, 7-Up and Fanta are widely available in Indonesia and are comparatively cheap. Alternatively most restaurants will serve *air jeruk* – citrus **fruit juices** – with or without ice (*es*). Ice in many places is fine, but in cheaper restaurants and away from tourist areas many people recommend taking drinks without ice. Javanese, Sumatran, Sulawesi or Timorese **coffee** (*kopi*), fresh and strong, is an excellent morning pick-you-up. It is usually served sweet (*kopi manis*) and black; if you want to have it without sugar ask for *kopi tidak ada gula*. **Milk** (*susu*) is available in tourist areas and large towns, but it may be sweetened condensed milk. **Tea** (*teh*) is obtainable almost everywhere.

Although Indonesia is a predominantly Muslim country, alcoholic drinks are widely available. The two most popular **beers** – light lagers – are the locally brewed Anker and Bintang brands. Imported **spirits** like whisky and gin are usually only sold in the more expensive restaurants and hotels. They are comparatively expensive. There are, however, a number of local brews including *brem* (rice wine), *arak* (rice whisky) and *tuak* (palm wine).

GETTING AROUND

AIR

This is the most convenient and comfortable way to travel around Indonesia. **Garuda** and **Merpati**, now sister-companies, service all the main provincial cities. Merpati tends to operate the short-hop services to smaller towns and cities, particularly in Eastern Indonesia (see route map). Garuda/Merpati offers a **Visit Indonesia Decade Pass**. The basic pass is for three 'stretches' (legs) and costs US$300. Each additional stretch costs a further US$110, up to a maximum of 8. The pass is valid for 90 days, with a minimum stay of 5 days, and can be used on all Garuda/Merpati routes except 'pioneer' services (perintis). These passes are obtainable by non-Indonesian citizens outside Indonesia in Japan, Hong Kong, Australia, New Zealand, Europe and US and are non-refundable. They are also available in Indonesia, if purchased within 14 days of arrival. **NB** There can be difficulties booking seats on some legs (particularly in Nusa Tenggara). But 'no shows' are many and it is always worth going to the airport even if the plane is said to be 'full'. The other main domestic airlines are **Bouraq**, **Mandala** and **Sempati** (see route map, page 753). Bouraq's network is concentrated in Kalimantan and Eastern Indonesia (Sulawesi and Nusa Tenggara); Sempati's in Kalimantan, Sumatra, Java and Sulawesi; while Mandala has the most restricted network, serving only a handful of cities in Java, Sumatra, Sulawesi and Maluku. Sempati has a growing international network, modern aircraft and allegedly the highest paid pilots in Indonesia. On some routes, Bouraq, Mandala and Sempati offer fares that are marginally cheaper than Garuda/Merpati but there is very little in it. There are also non-commercial air services such as the **Missionary Aviation Fellowship** (MAF) and **Associated Missions Aviation** (AMA) which offer non-scheduled flights in Irian Jaya, Kalimantan and Sulawesi to more out of the way spots. **NB** These are not commercial airlines and can refuse passage. See page 911 for a listing of air fares and page 911 for a map of major routes. See page 687 for an air route map of Nusa Tenggara.

TRAIN

Passenger train services are limited to Java and certain areas of Sumatra, including a route in Lampung and S Sumatra, and in N Sumatra. Trains are usually slow and often delayed. Single track connects many major cities. First class is a/c with a dining car. There are two main trunk routes on Java: Jakarta – Cirebon – Semarang – Surabaya and Jakarta – Bandung – Yogyakarta – Surakarta (Solo) – Surabaya. The principal services are identified by name, eg the **Bima** is the a/c night-express from Jakarta via Yogya and Solo, to Surabaya (16 hrs); the **Mutiara Utara** is the northern route train to Surabaya via Semarang; the **Senja Utama Solo** is the express train to Yogya and Solo; while the **Senja Utama Semarang** is the express train to Cirebon and Semarang. Reservations should be made well in advance; it is often easier through a travel agent in the town where you are staying. See page 917 for a train timetable and a basic fare listing.

BUS

Road transport in Indonesia has improved greatly in recent years, and main roads on most of the islands are generally in reasonably good condition. The single major exception is Irian Jaya, where air transport is the only sensible way to get around. It should be noted that in many areas in Indonesia during the rainy season and after severe storms, even main roads may be impassable. For details on road transport and conditions in a specific area, see the relevant regional introduction.

Most Indonesians, as well as many visitors, get around by bus. The network is vast – there are buses from Bali to Banda Aceh, a distance of almost 4,300 km – and although it is not always quick or comfortable, buses are the cheapest way to travel. Buses – and particularly non-a/c buses – are often overfilled and seats are designed for Indonesian, rather than western bodies. A/c buses are generally less cramped. The seats at the front are the most comfortable, but also the most dangerous (crash-wise). In May 1993, it was reported that the police had asked bus drivers to pray before setting off – presumably hoping that divine intervention might reduce the number of accidents. Some people recommend booking two seats for comfort, although on non a/c buses it is difficult to lounge over two seats free from guilt when the vehicle is packed. Roads are often windy and rough, and buses are badly sprung (or totally un-sprung). Despite harrowingly fast speeds at times, do not expect to average much more than 40 km/hr (particularly on Flores and Sulawesi) except on the best highways. Overnight buses (*bis malam*) are usually faster and recommended for longer journeys. However, a/c *bis malam* can be very cold and a sarong or blanket is useful. Their other disadvantages are that the scenery passes in the darkness and they invariably arrive at antisocial, inconvenient times of day (or night). **NB** Watch out for pickpockets.

The key word when travelling by bus is: patience. On non-a/c buses be prepared for a tedious 'trawl' around town (for up to an hour) collecting passengers, until the bus is full to overflowing. Buses stop regularly for refreshments at dubious looking roadside restaurants, hawkers cram the aisle, selling hot sate, fruit, sweets, sunglasses, magazines, even pornographic playing cards. Loud music and violent videos keep the passengers either in heaven or purgatory. As most Indonesians have still to be convinced that smoking is bad for your health ("that's only true with western cigarettes, *kreteks* [Indonesian clove cigarettes] are good for you") or that some people might find it distasteful, buses – and especially a/c buses – are also often fogged with cigarette smoke. The buses themselves are usually plastered with perplexing names such as 'No Problem – Banana on the Road', 'Sweet Memory', 'No Time for Love', 'Pash Boy's' and 'Khasoggi'. But, despite the drawbacks, buses are not only the cheapest and often the only way to get about, they are also one of the best ways to see the scenery and to meet Indonesians.

In many towns, bus companies have their offices at the bus terminal. However, this is not always true, and some long-distance buses may depart directly from a bus company's office located in another part of town to the terminal. Larger towns may also have several bus terminals,

serving different points of the compass. These are often out of town, with regular bemos linking the various terminals with one another and with the town centre. In smaller towns, buses will sometimes pick up passengers from outside their losmen or hotel (although occasionally passengers may be asked for a surcharge). They may also drop passengers outside a losmen at the other end of the journey.

Tickets can be obtained from bus company offices or through travel agents; shop around for the best fare, bargaining is possible. Estimated journey times are often wildly inaccurate. During Ramadan all forms of public transport are packed. For selected official bus prices see page 919. **NB** Bus fares vary a great deal depending on level of service (a/c, reclining seats, express etc), the size of the vehicle (coach or minibus), the number of seats, the time of departure, the age of the vehicle, and between bus companies (which is related to their reputation for safety and timeliness). The fares given in the table on page 919 should be viewed as only approximate rates.

In the main tourist areas on Java, Bali and Lombok look out for **shuttle buses**. These operate almost exclusively for the benefit of foreigners connecting the most popular destinations, with a fixed daily timetable. They will pick up and drop off passengers at their hotels and take a very great deal of the hassle out of ground travel, though you miss much of the local colour.

BICYCLING

We have had a number of letters from people who have bicycled through various parts of Indonesia. The advice below is collated from their comments, and is meant to provide a general guideline for those intending to travel by bicycle. There may be areas, however, where the advice does not hold true. (Some of the letters we have received even disagree on some points.)

Bike type: touring, hybrid or mountain bikes are fine for most roads and tracks in Indonesia – take an ordinary machine; nothing fancy.

Spares: are readily available for most machines, and even small towns have bicycle repair shops where it is often possible to borrow larger tools such as vices. Mountain bikes have made a big impact in the country, so accessories for these are also widely available – although their quality might not be up to much. What is less common are components made of unusual materials – titanium and composites, for example. It is best to use common accessories. It may also be worthwhile forging a good relationship with a bike shop back home just in case a spare is not available – and then it can be couriered out. It is better to have a 'free' rear wheel, as opposed to a free hub and cassette, as the latter are generally not available, while free rear wheels are widely sold.

Attitudes to bicyclists: the view seems to be, that it depends on the area. In Nusa Tenggara people are generally very welcoming and warm. In Bali bicyclists tend to be ignored. Officials, though, may view independent cyclists with some suspicion.

Road conditions: the maps in this guide are not sufficiently detailed for bicycling and a good, colour map is useful in determining contours and altitude, as well as showing minor roads.

Road users attitude to bicyclists: cars and buses often travel on the hard shoulder, and few expect to give way to a bicycle. Be very wary, especially on main roads.

Taking bikes on buses, ferries and taxis: expect to pay a surcharge of about one third to a half of the cost of the ticket for buses and ferries. They are used to taking bicycles (although the more expensive a/c tour buses may prove reluctant). Most taxi drivers are not so keen on carrying bicycles – be ready to throw it in the boot and have bungee cords close at hand to secure.

Bicycles on airlines: many international airlines take bicycles free-of-charge, provided they are not boxed. Take the peddles off and deflate the tyres. Domestic airlines sometimes charge, although there does not seem to be a hard-and-fast rule.

In general:
Avoid major roads.
Avoid major towns.
Avoid Java. (Most people report that such is the traffic on Java that even on small roads it can be worryingly lethal. The island is also very mountainous.)

Useful equipment
Pollution mask if travelling to large cities.
Basic toolkit – although there always seems to be help near at hand, and local workshops seem to be able to improvise a solution to just about any problem – including a puncture repair kit, spare tubes, spare tyre, pump.
Good map of the area.
Bungee cords.
First aid kit.
Water filter.

Unnecessary equipment: A tent is generally not needed. Every small town will have a guesthouse of some description. Nor is it worth taking a stove, cooking utensils, sleeping bag, food... it is almost always possible to get food and a place to sleep – and cheaply, too. The equipment is simply a burden. The exceptions to this are the really back-of-beyond areas of Indonesia. In addition, Kalimantan seems to be well provided with camping grounds, as are Sabah, Sarawak and Peninsular Malaysia.

A 'D' lock is not really necessary – they are hefty and a simple cable lock will suffice. Many bicyclists take their machines into their rooms at night.

Driving in Indonesia

Renting a self-drive car in Indonesia has several advantages: it is a flexible, relatively quick, convenient and comfortable means of travel, and is a good way of experiencing the countryside and getting to out-of-the-way spots. But there are several dangers worth highlighting. As in Thailand, 'might is right' – smaller vehicles give way to larger ones. A driver flashing his headlights normally means 'don't mess with me'. Although Indonesians are a very courteous people, this does not apply when in a car. Traffic does not always remain in the allotted lanes – it is best to adopt a strategy of follow-the-leader and go with the flow. Cutting in is an accepted way of changing lanes. After driving in Indonesia many people leave firmly beliving that the guiding principle adhered to by most road users is that 'Time is money and lives are cheap'.

If involved in an accident, it is best to go to the nearest police station to report the incident, rather than waiting at the scene. Signposting is generally poor, so be sure to get a good map. Many towns have complicated one-way systems, which take a bit of negotiating. Every town has its army of semi-official traffic wardens – often dressed in orange jumpsuits – waiting with whistle poised to usher motorists into a parking spot. All '*parkir*' must be paid for – 200-300 Rp in Jakarta. Petrol is cheap and Pertamina stations are found on all main highways.

CAR HIRE

Cars can be hired for self-drive (see box) or with a chauffeur. The latter are available by the hour or by the day, and cost about 10,000Rp/hr for use within a city, rather more if travelling out of town. A cheaper alternative is to simply charter a bemo for the day (about 50,000Rp). Generally, self-drive cars are only available at the more popular tourist destinations (eg Bali and Lombok) and in the bigger cities (eg Jakarta, Medan, Yogya and Surabaya); expect to pay about 50,000-100,000Rp/day depending on the company, and the condition and type of vehicle. In Bali and Lombok, there are numerous small operations that offer cars and jeeps for hire. For car rental offices, see appropriate town entry.

OTHER LOCAL TRANSPORT

Bajaj

Small 3-wheeled motor scooters similar to the Thai *tuk-tuk*. They are probably the cheapest form of 'taxi' after the becak, but are only available in big cities – in Jakarta, they are orange and usually rather scruffy.

Becaks

Becaks or bicycle rickshaws are one of the cheapest, and most important, forms of short-distance transport in Indonesia. Literally hundreds of thousands of poor people make a living driving becaks. However, they are now illegal in central Jakarta and often officially barred from main thoroughfares in other large cities. They are a good – and sedate – way to explore the backstreets and alleys of a city and can be chartered by the hour or for a particular journey. Bargain hard and agree a fare before boarding. Minimum fare 200Rp.

Bemos

These are small buses or adapted pick-ups which operate fixed routes. The name originates from 'motorized becak' (*becak motor*). They carry four-six passengers and are found in Jakarta, Bandung, Semarang, Surabaya and Surakarta (Solo). The bemo is gradually being replaced by the larger oplet. They can be chartered by the hour or day (bargain hard, about 50,000Rp/day).

Bis kayu

Trucks converted into buses with bench seats down each side. They are now only in use on minor roads on some islands in Nusa Tenggara, such as Flores. Slow and uncomfortable, they often ply unsealed roads.

Horsecarts

These come in various shapes and sizes. *Dokars* are 2-wheeled pony carts carrying two-three passengers found, for example, in Padang, W Sumatra. In Lombok dokars are known as *cidomos*, while in Bima-Raba (Sumbawa) they are proudly named *Ben Hurs*. *Andongs* are larger 4-wheeled horse-drawn wagons, carrying up to six people. These are found mainly in Yogya, Surakarta and a different version in Bogor. Horse-drawn transport is still very common in the countryside, and 'stands' of carts can be seen arrayed at most markets.

Inter-city taxis/share taxis

Share taxis make particular sense for a party of four or five. Inter-city 'share taxis' are more expensive than buses, but are usually a quicker and cheaper alternative to going by air or private taxi. They are not available in all towns and only tend to run the busier routes, like Jakarta to Bandung. They depart when all five seats are taken.

Motorbike hire

Available at many beach resorts. Rates per day vary according to size and condition of the machine, but range from 5,000-15,000Rp. It is illegal to ride without a helmet, although this can just be a construction worker's hard hat. Many machines are poorly maintained, so check brakes and lights before paying.

Ojeks

These are motorcycle taxis – a form of transport which is becoming increasingly popular. Ojek riders, often wearing coloured jackets, congregate at junctions, taking passengers pillion to their destination. Agree a price before boarding and bargain hard.

Oplets

Larger versions of bemos carrying 10-12 passengers. They have a bewildering number of other names – *Daihatsu* in Semarang, *Angkuta* in Solo, *Microlets* in Malang and Jakarta, while in rural areas they tend to be called *Colts*. In cities they operate on fixed routes at fixed fares (about 150-200Rp). In the countryside, routes can vary and so do fares; be prepared to bargain. Oplets can also be chartered by the hour or day (bargain hard).

Taxis

Taxis are metered in the major cities. Unmetered taxis can be shared for longer journeys. **NB** Drivers cannot usually change large bills. All registered taxis, minibuses and rental cars have yellow number plates; black number plates are for private vehicles, and red are for government-owned vehicles. Pirate taxis (with black number plates) tend to operate at airports, supermarkets and in city centres.

SEA

Boat

The national shipping company is **PELNI**, standing for Pelayaran Nasional Indonesia. Its head office is at Jl Angkasa 18, Jakarta, T 343307, F 3810341. For ticket offices, see relevant town entries. Note that many travel agents also sell Pelni tickets and although they levy a small surcharge may be far more convenient. Pelni operates an expanding fleet of modern passenger ships which ply fortnightly circuits throughout the archipelago (see timetables). The ships are well run and well maintained, have an excellent safety record, and are a comfortable and leisurely way to travel. Each accommodates 500-2,000 passengers in five classes, has central a/c, a bar, restaurant and cafeteria.

Between 1996 and 1998 an additional five ships are due to join the fleet. First Class cabins have attached bathrooms and TV sets. Classes I-IV are single sex – unless a group takes the whole cabin. Class II has 4 bunks per cabin, Class III, 6 bunks and Class IV, 8 bunks. Fares include all meals (no matter what class), and classes I-IV are cabin classes, while class V is 'deck' class (in fact, in a large a/c room where mattresses can be rented for 1,000Rp). Note that even First class cabins are 'inside', ie they have no portholes. It may be possible to leave bags at the ship's information desk. Booking ahead is advisable although in smaller ports of call it may only be possible to make reservations 4 days in advance.

In addition to these ships, Pelni also operates a so-called 'pioneer' service – *Pelayaran Perintis* – serving smaller, more out-of-the-way ports. Perintis vessels are important means of travel in Maluku for example. These ships have no cabins but take passengers 'deck' class. Like their more illustrious sister vessels, they are generally well-run and safe, if not always comfortable. Finally, there are the mixed cargo boats and ships which go just about everywhere. Passage can be secured just by visiting the port and asking around. **NB** Safety equipment may not be up to standard, and level of comfort is minimal. See page 896 for a timetable and fare listing.

COMMUNICATIONS

Language

The national language is *Bahasa Indonesia*, which is written in Roman script (see page 54). There are 250 regional languages and dialects, of which Sundanese (the language of W Java and Jakarta) is the most widespread. The Bataks of N Sumatra have a number of mutually intelligible languages which are, in essence, forms of primitive *Bahasa*. In Padang and elsewhere in W Sumatra, the population speak *Minang* – which is also similar to 'Bahasa'. Despite the bewildering array of regional languages, most of the younger generation will be able to speak Bahasa – about 70% of the population. English is the most common foreign language, although there are Dutch speakers amongst the older generation and some Portuguese is still spoken in E Timor.

Bahasa Indonesia is a relatively easy language to learn, and visitors may have a small but functional vocabulary after just a few weeks. Unlike Thai, it is not tonal and is grammatically very straight forward. However this does not mean it is an easy language to speak well. A small number of useful words and phrases are listed in the box below. For visitors interested in studying Bahasa Indonesia in more depth, the Cornell course, though expensive, is recommended. Cassettes are available from Southeast Asia Publications Office, East Hill Plaza, Ithaca, New York 14853, USA, T 607 2553827.

Language courses in Indonesia The best way to learn Indonesian is to study it intensively in Indonesia. In **Jakarta** courses are available through: *The Indonesian/American Cultural Centre*, Jl Pramuka Kav 30, T 8583241; *The Australian Cultural Centre* (the Indonesian Australia Language Foundation), Jl Rasuna Said (at the Embassy), T 5213350; *The French Cultural Centre*, T 3908585; *The Goethe Institute*, T 8581139. In **Yogyakarta**, another centre where overseas students study Indonesian, courses are run by: *The Realia Language School* which is recommended; it is cheaper if a group learns together.

Postal services

Post offices open from 0800-1600 Mon-Fri, 0800-1300 Sat. The postal service is not particularly reliable; important mail should be registered. Faxes and telexes can be sent from major hotels and

Perumtel and Wartel offices, found in most major towns. Post and telex/fax offices are listed under Post & telecommunications in each town entry.

Telephone services

Indonesia has a comprehensive telecommunications network which links the islands throughout the country and boasts its own satellite (Indosat). Every town has its communication centres (Warpostel) where you can make local, interlocal (between other areas within Indonesia) and international calls and faxes. Most Warpostels open early in the morning and operate until around midnight. Interlocal calls are cheaper after 2100, so centres tend to be very busy then. International calls have a cheap rate between midnight and 0800, and all Sat and Sun. Calls are expensive. A 1 page fax to England will cost 9,150Rp. There is a wide network of cardphones and coin phones throughout Jakarta and other main towns and cities in hotels, shopping centres, street corners. Telephone cards (*Kartu telepon*) are sold in Warpostel's, supermarkets and a wide range of shops. Sold according to number of units (100 unit 13,200Rp, 140 unit 18,400Rp, 200 unit 36,900Rp, 400 unit 52,800Rp, 600 unit 89,700Rp). International calls can be made from card phones. Indosat, is located at Jakarta Theatre, Jl Thamrin, Jakarta, just opposite McDonalds, 10 mins' walk from Jl Jaksa (open 24 hrs). Direct international dialling and collect calls can be made from here. **International enquiries**: 102. **Operator**: 101. **Local enquiries**: 106; in Jakarta: 108. All telephone numbers marked in the text with a prefix 'J' mean that they are Jakarta numbers.

ENTERTAINMENT

Newspapers

English language newspapers are the *Indonesia Times*, *Jakarta Post* (which carries international news from Reuters reports and English football league reports) and *Indonesia Observer/Sunday Observer*. Of the international newspapers available in Indonesia, the *Asian Wall Street Journal* and the *International Herald Tribune* can be purchased in Jakarta and some other major cities and tourist destinations; so too can the Singapore *Straits Times*. Among English language magazines, the most widely available are the *Economist*, *Time*, *Newsweek* and the Hong Kong-based *Far Eastern Economic Review*. The latter provides the most comprehensive regional coverage and is well-informed, but can be rather heavy going.

Radio

Radio Republik Indonesia (RRI) broadcasts throughout the country. News and commentary in English is broadcast for about an hour a day. Shortwave radios will pick up Voice of America, the BBC World Service and Australian Broadcasting. See page 890 for BBC and VoA frequencies.

Television

Many hotels now boast enormous 'parabola' – satellite dishes that receive TV signals from the Philippines, Singapore, Thailand and Malaysia. Large hotels may also offer CNN News.

HOLIDAYS AND FESTIVALS

NB All Islamic festivals and holidays are movable.

Jan: *Tahun Baru*, New Year's Day (1st: public holiday). New Year's Eve is celebrated with street carnivals, shows, fireworks and all-night festivities. In Christian areas, festivities are more exuberant, with people visiting each other on New Year's Day and attending church services.

Feb: *Imlek*, Chinese New Year (movable). It is not an official holiday, but many Chinese shops and businesses close for at least 2 days. Within the Chinese community, younger people visit their relatives, children are given *hong bao* (lucky money), new clothes are bought and any unfinished business is cleared up before the New Year. *Idul Fitri* or *Lebaran* (movable: public holiday). A 2-day celebration which marks the end of the month-long period of Ramadan, when Muslims observe *puasa* and fast from dawn to dusk. Mass prayers are held in mosques and squares. Muslims go to each others homes to ask forgiveness and there is a general air of celebration.

Mar/Apr: *Wafat Isa Al-Masih Good Friday* (movable: public holiday).

Apr: *Nyepi* (movable: public holiday). Balinese Saka New Year (1995 = 1917). *Kartini Day* (21st). A ceremony held by women to mark the birthday of Raden Ajeng Kartini, born in 1879 and proclaimed as a pioneer of women's emancipation (see page 257). The festival is rather like mothers' day, in that women are supposed to be pampered by their husbands and children, although it is women's organizations like the Dharma Wanita who get most excited. Women dress in national dress. *Idhul Adha* (movable: public holiday). This is the 'festival of the sacrifice' and is the time when burial graves are cleaned, and an animal is sacrificed to commemorate the willingness of Abraham to sacrifice his son.

May: *Waisak Day* (movable: public holiday). Marks the birth and death of the historic Buddha; at Candi Mendut outside Yogyakarta a procession of monks carrying flowers, candles, holy fire and images of the Buddha walk to Borobudur. *Kenaikan Isa Al-Masih or Ascension Day* (movable: public holiday). *Muharram*, Muslim New Year (movable: public holiday). It marks the Prophet Muhammad's journey from Mecca to Medina on the lunar equivalent of 16 July 622AD. Religious discussions and debates mark the day.

Jul: *Garebeg Maulad (birthday of the Prophet Mohammad)* (movable: public holiday). Celebrations begin a week before the actual day and last a month, with *selamatans* in homes, mosques and schools.

Aug: *Independence Day* (17th: public holiday). This is the most important national holiday, celebrated with processions, dancing and other merry-making.

Oct: *Hari Pancasila* (1st). This commemorates the Five Basic Principles of Pancasila (see page 51). *Armed Forces Day* (5th). The anniversary of the founding of the Indonesian Armed Forces, with military parades and demonstrations.

Nov: *Al Miraj* (movable: public holiday). The Prophet Mohammad is led through the seven heavens by the archangel. He speaks with God and returns to earth the same night, with instructions which include the five daily prayers.

Dec: *Christmas Day* (25th: public holiday). Celebrated by Christians – the Bataks of Sumatra, the Toraja and Minahasans of Sulawesi and in some of the islands of Nusa Tenggara, and Irian Jaya.

Rounding up

Acknowledgements	881	Travelling with children	907
Reading and listening	881	Fares and timetables	910
Internet	889	Glossary	927
Short wave radio	890	Temperature conversion and weights	
Useful addresses	891	and measures charts	932
Malaysian words and phrases	894	Tinted boxes	933
Food glossary	896	Illustrations	936
Distinctive fruits	897	Index	937
Health	899	Maps	955

ACKNOWLEDGEMENTS

Piero Scaruffi, USA; Meena Rugmini, Singapore; Peter Rendle, EK; Jürg Wüthrich, Switzerland; Eva Oberwiler, Switzerland; Stefano Magistretti, Italy; Andreas Kucher, Germany; Piergiorgio Pescali, Italy; Yasuko Higuchi, Italy; Dirk Zeiler, Germany; P Jacobson, USA; T Meijering, Netherlands; Jabar Lahadji, Friends of Morowali, Kolondale, Indonesia; Pius Elmiger, Switzerland; Pierre-Yves Saunier, France; Willy H Schoch, Switzerland; Thomas Enters, Indonesia; Catherine Lewis, UK: James Baxter, Indonesia; U Peter Degen, Canada; Ingo Korudörfu, Germany; Fred Braun and Astrid Jerjen, Bern, Switzerland; Peter Barrow, Florida, USA; Jayne Dyer and Nicholas Hird, UK; Tina Ottman, Cambridge, UK; Susan Fuhs, USA; Steve Scott, UK; Capt Harry Hilliard, Pelni, Jakarta; John Moxey, Garuda Indonesia, London; Martin Jones, UK; Robbie Payne, Australia.

READING AND LISTENING

MAGAZINES

Asiaweek (weekly). A lightweight *Far Eastern Economic Review*, rather like a regional *Time* magazine in style.

The Far Eastern Economic Review (weekly). Authoritative Hong Kong-based regional magazine; their correspondents based in each country provide knowledgeable, in-depth analysis particularly on economics and politics.

BOOKS ON SOUTHEAST ASIA

Cambridge History of Southeast Asia (1992). Two volume edited study, long and expensive with contributions from most of the leading historians of the region. A thematic and regional approach is taken, not a country one, although the history is fairly conventional. Published by Cambridge University Press: Cambridge.

Caufield, C (1985) *In the rainforest*, Heinemann: London. This readable and well-researched analysis of rainforest ecology and the pressures on tropical forests is part-based in the region.

Clad, James (1989) *Behind the myth: business, money and power in Southeast Asia*, Unwin Hyman: London. Clad, formerly a journalist with the *Far Eastern Economic Review*, distilled his experiences in this book; as it turned out, rather disappointingly – it is a hotch-potch of journalistic snippets.

Conrad, Joseph (1900) *Lord Jim*, Penguin: London. The tale of Jim, who abandons his ship and seeks refuge from his guilt in Malaya, earning the sobriquet Lord.

Conrad, Joseph (1915) *Victory: an island tale*, Penguin: London. Arguably Conrad's finest novel, based in the Malay Archipelago.

Conrad, Joseph (1920) *The rescue*, Penguin: London. Set in the Malay Archipelago in the 1860s; the hero, Captain Lingard, is forced to choose between his Southeast Asian friend and his countrymen.

Dingwall, Alastair (1994) *Traveller's literary companion to South-east Asia*, In Print: Brighton. Experts on Southeast Asian language and literature select extracts from novels and other books by western and regional writers. The extracts are annoyingly brief, but it gives a good overview of what is available.

Dumarçay, Jacques (1991) *The palaces of South-East Asia: architecture and customs*, OUP: Singapore. A broad summary of palace art and architecture in both mainland and island Southeast Asia.

Fraser-Lu, Sylvia (1988) *Handwoven textiles of South-East Asia*, OUP: Singapore. Well-illustrated, large-format book with informative text.

Higham, Charles (1989) *The archaeology of mainland Southeast Asia from 10,000 BC to the fall of Angkor*, Cambridge University Press: Cambridge. Best summary of changing views of the archaeology of the mainland.

King, Ben F and Dickinson, EC (1975) *A field guide to the birds of South-East Asia*, Collins: London. Best regional guide to the birds of the region.

Miettinen, Jukko O (1992) *Classical dance and theatre in South-East Asia*, OUP, Singapore. Expensive, but accessible survey of dance and theatre, mostly focusing on Indonesia, Thailand and Burma.

Osborne, Milton (1979) *Southeast Asia: an introductory history*, Allen & Unwin: Sydney. Good introductory history, clearly written, published in a portable paperback edition.

Rawson, Philip (1967) *The art of Southeast Asia*, Thames & Hudson: London. Portable general art history of Cambodia, Vietnam, Thailand, Laos, Burma, Java and Bali; by necessity, rather superficial.

Reid, Anthony (1988) *Southeast Asia in the age of commerce 1450-1680*, Yale University Press: New Haven. Perhaps the best history of everyday life in Southeast Asia, looking at such themes as physical well-being, material culture and social organization.

Reid, Anthony (1993) *Southeast Asia in the age of commerce 1450-1680: expansion and crisis*, Yale University Press: New Haven. Volume 2 in this excellent history of the region.

Rigg, Jonathan (1991) *Southeast Asia: a region in transition*, Unwin Hyman: London. A thematic geography of the ASEAN region, providing an insight into some of the major issues affecting the region today.

SarDesai, DR (1989) *Southeast Asia: past and present*, Macmillan: London. Skilful but at times frustratingly thin history of the region from the 1st century to the withdrawal of US forces from Vietnam.

Savage, Victor R (1984) *Western impressions of nature and landscape in Southeast Asia*, Singapore University Press: Singapore. Based on a geography PhD thesis, the book is a mine of quotations and observations from western travellers.

Sesser, Stan (1993) *The lands of charm and cruelty: travels in Southeast Asia*, Picador: Basingstoke. A series of collected narratives first published in the *New Yorker* including essays on Singapore, Laos, Cambodia, Burma and Borneo. Finely observed and thoughtful, the book is an excellent travel companion.

Steinberg, DJ *et al* (1987) *In search of Southeast Asia: a modern history*, University of Hawaii Press: Honolulu. The best standard history of the region; it skilfully examines and assesses general processes of change and their impacts from the arrival of the Europeans in the region.

Wallace, Alfred Russel (1869) *The Malay Archipelago: the land of the orang-utan and the bird of paradise; a narrative of travel with studies of man and nature*, MacMillan: London. A classic of natural history writing, recounting Wallace's 8 years in the archipelago and now reprinted.

Waterson, Roxana (1990) *The living house: an anthropology of architecture in South-East Asia*, OUP: Singapore. Illustrated, academic book on Southeast Asian architecture, fascinating material for those interested in such things.

Young, Gavin (1991) *In search of Conrad*, Hutchinson: London. This well-known travel writer retraces the steps of Conrad; part travel-book, part fantasy, it is worth reading but not up to the standard of his other books.

BOOKS ON INDONESIA

Other books relating to particular regions, towns and monuments are listed in the relevant sections of the text.

Western novels and biography

Conrad, Joseph: Perhaps the finest novelists of the Malay archipelago, books include *Lord Jim* and *Victory*, both widely available in paperback editions from most bookshops.

Couperus, Louis (1994) *The Hidden Force*, Quartet Books: London. A translation of this Dutch novel originally written in 1900, Couperus was a dandy, who liked to shock. His book deals with the culture clash of locals and colonials and the underlying corruption and decedence of the colonial way of life. All a little dated now but caused a stir at the time of writing.

Deane, S (1979) *Ambon: Isle of Spices*, Murray. An amusing and informative account of her 2 years spent teaching there in the 1970s. The second half is particularly interesting, with accounts of the customs and rituals of the islands and the continuing influence of Adat traditions and beliefs. Out of print, but found in public libraries.

Forster, Harold (1989) *Flowering lotus: a view of Java in the 1950s*, OUP: Singapore, Forster recounts his life as an English lecturer at Gajah Mada University in Yogya in the 1950s; closely observed and informative of the period just after independence.

Koch, CJ (1978) *The year of living dangerously*. Average novel transformed into a well-received film; romance based in Java during the 1965 attempted coup.

Van der Post, Laurens (1963) *The seed and the sower*, Penguin. The semi-autobiographical account of Laurens van der Post's internment in a Japanese prisoner of war camp outside Bandung. Was made into a film starring David Bowie, *Merry Christmas Mr Lawrence*.

Van der Post, Laurens (1970) *The night of the new moon*, Penguin. Like his better-known *The seed and the sower*, this is based on his internment in a Japanese prisoner of war camp; it is rather more introspective and philosophical though.

Indonesian literature available in English

Lubis, Mochtar (1957) *Twilight in Djakarta*. One of the finest works of modern Indonesian fiction; tells of the poverty and destitution in 1950s Jakarta; journalist Lubis was imprisoned for his writings.

Lubis, Mochtar (1968) *A road with no end*, Hutchinson. Originally published in Indonesian in 1952, regarded as one of the classic of Indonesian literature, draws heavily on French existentialist philosophy. The novel tells the story of Isa, a teacher in Java, and the turmoil of the early years of independence.

Lubis, Mochtar (1991) *Tiger!*, Select Books: Singapore. A novel based in Sumatra first published in Indonesian in 1975.

Toer, Pramoedya Ananta (1979) *This earth of mankind*, Penguin: Ringwood, Australia. Along with the other three books in this series – *Child of all nations*, *Footsteps*, and *Glass House* – this represents some of the finest of modern Indonesian writing. It tells the story of the writer Minke caught between the Dutch and modernity, and his own people and tradition. Toer was imprisoned on Buru Island between 1965-1979 and his books remain banned in Indonesia.

Travel

Barley, Nigel (1988) *Not a hazardous sport*, Penguin: London. Anthropologist Barley, in this humorous and entertaining book head off to Toraja and convinces a team of builders to travel to London to construct a traditional house for the Museum of Mankind.

Bickmore, Albert S. (1869) *Travels in the East Indian archipelago*, OUP: Singapore Published at the same time as Wallane's much more famous tome, this is not nearly as important a text but, written by an American, it does provide a very different gloss. Republished in 1991 by OUP, Singapore.

Bird, Isabella (1883 and reprinted 1983) *The Golden Chersonese*, Murray: London, reprinted by Century paperback. The account of a late 19th century female visitor to the region who shows her gumption facing everything from natives to crocs.

Bock, Carl (1985, first published 1881) *The headhunters of Borneo*, OUP: Singapore. Bock was a Norwegian naturalist and explorer and was commissioned by the Dutch to make a scientific survey of south-eastern Borneo. His account, though, makes much of the dangers and adventures that he faced, and is some of his 'scientific' observations are, in retrospect, clearly highly faulty. Nonetheless, this is an entertaining account.

King, Victor T. (edit.) (1992) *The best of Borneo travel*, Oxford University Press: Oxford. A compilation of travel accounts from the early 19th century through to the late 20th. An excellent companion to take while exploring the island. Published in portable paperback.

Lewis, Norman (1994) *An Empire of the East*, Jonathan Cape: London. Norman Lewis' latest travel book in which he explores three politically sensitive areas: E Timor, Irian Jaya and Aceh, N Sumatra. Given the regions to which he selected to travel, beneath the languid surface it is, inevitably, a highly critical book; well written and seemingly innocently provocative.

Mjoberg, Eric: *Forest life and adventures in the Malay archipelago*, OUP: Singapore.

Naipaul, V.S. (1981) *Among the believers*. A rather self-indulgent account of Naipaul's visit to Indonesia.

Wallace, Alfred Russel (1869) *The Malay Archipelago*. See the comments under Natural history, below.

Wilcox, Harry (1989) *Six moons over Sulawesi*, OUP: Singapore. First published in 1949 as *White stranger: six months in Celebes*, it recounts the 6 months sojourn of Harry Wilcox in Toraja who went to there to recover from the horrors of the war.

History

Abeyasekere, S (1989) *Jakarta: a history*, OUP: Jakarta. A skilful and comprehensive history of Jakarta; the best available.

Anderson, B (1972) *Java in a time of revolution: occupation and resistance 1944-1946*. The best study of the period by one of the world's leading political scientists.

Chapman, F. Spencer: *The jungle is neutral*. An account of a British guerrilla force fighting the Japanese in Borneo – not as enthralling as Tom Harrisson's book, but still worth reading.

Harrisson, Tom (1959) *World within*, Hutchinson: London. During the Second World War, explorer, naturalist and ethnologist Tom Harrisson was parachuted into Borneo to help organise Dayak resistance against the occupying Japanese forces. This is his extraordinary account.

Loeb, Edwin M (1972) *Sumatra: its history and people*, OUP: Kuala Lumpur (first published 1935). Despite being over 50 years old this book is still worthwhile reading, and the best of its type.

Marsden, William (1783, 1811) *The history of Sumatra*, OUP: Singapore. Like Raffles' study of Java, a book by a polymath who believed history was also geography, anthropology and natural history; now available as an expensive reprint.

Raffles, Thomas (1817) *The history of Java*, OUP: Singapore. The first history of Java, fascinating for Raffles' observations, sections have still yet to be bettered; available as a reprint, but large, cumbersome and expensive.

Ricklefs, MC (1981) *A history of modern Indonesia, c1300 to the present*, Macmillan: London. Dense but informative, and probably the best modern history of Indonesia. A new edition has recently been published.

Smithies, Michael (1986) *Yogyakarta, cultural heart of Indonesia*, OUP: Singapore. Good background to the city and its culture.

Times Travel Library (1987) *Jakarta*, Times Editions: Singapore. Photographic guide to Jakarta with reasonable background text.

Natural history

Cranbrook, Earl of (1987) *Riches of the wild: land mammals of South-East Asia*, OUP.

Holmes, Derek and Nash, Stephen (1989) *The birds of Java and Bali*, OUP: Singapore. Manageable, light weight book with good colour illustrations.

Payne, Junaidi *et al*: *Pocket guide to birds of Borneo*, World Wildlife Fund/Sabah Society

Payne, Junaidi *et al*: *A field guide to the mammals of Borneo*, World Wildlife Fund/Sabah Society. Good illustrations, reasonable text, but very dry.

Wallace, Alfred Russel (1869) *The Malay Archipelago: the land of the orangutan and the bird of paradise; a narrative of travel with studies of man and nature*. A classic of Victorian travel writing by one of the finest naturalists of the period. Wallace travelled through all of island Southeast Asia over a period of 8 years. The original is now re-printed.

Whitten, Tony and Whitten, Jane (1992) *Wild Indonesia*, New Holland: London. Illustrated large format coffee-table book but with good text written by a specialist on Indonesia's natural history. Provides background to the country's major national parks and characteristic species and forest formations. Wonderfully illustrated.

Whitten, Anthony *et al* (1984) *The ecology of Sumatra*, Gajah Mada University Press: Yogya. Like its sister book on Sulawesi, a dense but informative and authoritative account of the island's ecology.

Whitten, Anthony *et al* (1988) *The ecology of Sulawesi*, Gajah Mada University Press: Yogyakarta. Dense, comprehensive study of Sulawesi ecology.

Geography, anthropology, politics and development

Anti-Slavery Society (1990) *West Papua: plunder in paradise*, Anti-Slavery Society: London. Records the people of Irian Jaya's fight for independence – the title speaks for itself.

Budiardjo, Carmel (1996) *Surviving Indonesia's gulags*, London: Cassell. The author of this book is a Jewish Londoner who married an Indonesian, moved to Jakarta and worked as a civil servant and university lecturer during Sukarno's presidency. She was imprisoned in 1967 and the book recounts her horrific time in gaol. She now lives in London again and continues to campaign enthusiastically for human rights in Indonesia despite her age of over 70. She was awarded the Right Livelihood Award – a sort of alternative Nobel Peace Prize – in December 1995.

Belo, Jane (edit) (1970) *Traditional Balinese culture*, Columbia University Press: New York. Collection of academic papers mostly focusing upon dance, music and drama.

Carle, Rainer (edit) (1981) *Cultures and societies of North Sumatra*, Dietrich Rimmer Verlag: Berlin.

Covarrubias, Miguel (1937) *Island of Bali*, Cassell: London (reprinted, OUP: Singapore, 1987). The original, full treatment of Bali's culture; despite being over 50 years old it is still an excellent background to the island and is highly entertaining.

Donner, Wolf (1987) *Land use and environment in Indonesia*, Hurst: London. Rather laboured but detailed summary of Indonesia's environmental problems and prospects.

Geertz, Clifford (1963) *Agricultural involution: the process of ecological change in Indonesia*, University of California Press: Berkeley. Classic book by perhaps the foremost anthropologist of Indonesia; looks at rice and shifting cultivation and conditions in 19th and 20th century Java; some of his views have been vigorously attacked in recent years. Hard to get hold of.

Kis-Jovak, JI et al (1988) *Banua Toraja: changing patterns in architecture and symbolism among the Sa'dan Toraja*, Sulawesi, Royal Tropical Institute: Amsterdam. Wonderful black and white photo-essay with informative text.

Lansing, J Stephen (1991) *Priests and programmers: technologies of power in the engineered landscape of Bali*, Princeton University Press: Princeton. An anthropological account of Bali's irrigation system; interesting for rice fans.

Loeb, Edwin M (1972) *Sumatra: its history and people*, OUP: Kuala Lumpur (first published 1935). Despite being over 50 years old this book is still worthwhile reading, and the best of its type.

Nooy-Palm, Netty (1986) *The Sa'dan Toraja: a study of their social life and religion – rituals of the east and west*, Foris: Dordrecht. Dense but very informative anthropological work.

Petocz, Ronald G (1989) *Conservation and development in Irian Jaya*, EJ Brill: Leiden.

Stuart Fox, David (1982) *Once a century: Pura Besakih and the Eka Dasa Rudra Festival*, Penerbit Citra Indonesia: Jakarta.

Volkman, Toby A (1985) *Feasts of honour: ritual and change in the Toraja highlands*, University of Illinois Press: Urbana. Readable account – part academic, part personal – of an anthropologist's stay in Toraja.

Waterson, Roxana (1990) *The living house: an anthropology of architecture in South-East Asia*, Singapore: OUP. Although this is as academic anthropological work it is written in a style and presented in a format which makes it comparatively accessible. The colour and black and white illustrations combine with an excellent text to make it an invaluable companion (although it is rather heavy) for anyone interested in traditional houses.

Arts

Beek, Aart van (1990) *Life in the Javanese Kraton*, OUP: Singapore. Useful and interesting short history to the kraton or palace.

Djelantik, AAM (1990) *Balinese paintings*, OUP: Singapore. Concise history of Balinese painting also covering the major contemporary schools of art.

Dumarçay, Jacques (1978) *Borobudur*, OUP: Singapore. Concise account of Borobudur's construction and meaning. A good, light weight introduction to take along.

Dumarçay, Jacques (1986) *The Temples of Java*, OUP: Singapore. Short art history of Java's main temples; rather dry and, for the really interested, rather thin.

Eiseman, Fred and Eiseman, Margaret (1988) *Woodcarvings of Bali*, Periplus: Berkeley.

Heuken, Adolf (1982) *Historical sites of Jakarta*, Cipta Loka Caraka: Jakarta. Probably the best background text available.

Jessup, Helen I (1990) *Court arts of Indonesia*, Asia Society Galleries: New York. Lavishly illustrated book produced for the Festival of Indonesia exhibition; good background on the pieces displayed.

Miksic, John (1990) *Borobudur: golden tales of the Buddha*, Bamboo and Periplus: London and Singapore. Well illustrated book written by an academic in the history department at the National University of Singapore and therefore with a better text than most coffee table books.

Schneebaum, Tobias (1990) *Embodied spirits: ritual carvings of the Asmat*, Peabody Museum: Salem, Mass.

Smithies, Michael (1986) *Yogyakarta, cultural heart of Indonesia*, OUP: Singapore. Good background to the city and its culture.

Warming, Wanda and Gaworski, Michael (1981) *The world of Indonesian textiles*, Serindia Publications: London. Summarizes all the processes of production and provides an outline of the major regional styles; illustrated.

Other books

Draine, Cathie and Hall, Barbara (1986) *Culture shock! Indonesia*, Times Books: Singapore. A good summary of do's and don't's with some useful cultural background.

Horridge, Adrian (1986) *Sailing craft of Indonesia*, OUP: Singapore. Illustrated with concise, useful text.

Books on Indonesian Borneo (Kalimantan)

Note that some of the books below refer to events largely, even entirely, in Malaysian Borneo (ie Sarawak and Sabah) or Brunei. They are nonetheless recommended as highly descriptive of jungle and tribal life.

Bock, Carl (1985, first published 1881) *The headhunters of Borneo*, OUP: Singapore. Bock was a Norwegian naturalist and explorer and was commissioned by the Dutch to make a scientific survey of south-eastern Borneo. His account, though, makes much of the dangers and adventures that he faced, and is some of his 'scientific' observations are, in retrospect, clearly highly faulty. Nonetheless, this is an entertaining account.

Chapman, F. Spencer: *The jungle is neutral*. An account of a British guerrilla force fighting the Japanese in Borneo – not as enthralling as Tom Harrisson's book, but still worth reading.

Charles, Hose (1985, first published 1929) *The field book of a jungle wallah*, OUP: Singapore. Hose was an official in Sarawak and became an acknowledged expert on the material and non-material culture of the tribes of Sarawak. He was one of that band of highly informed, perceptive and generally benevolent colonial administrators.

Hanbury-Tenison, Robin (1980) *Mulu, the rain forest*, Arrow/Weidenfeld. This is the product of an Royal Geographical Society trip to Mulu in the late 1970s; semi-scholarly and useful.

Harrisson, Tom (1959) *World within*, Hutchinson: Lodon. During the Second World War, explorer, naturalist and ethnologist Tom Harrisson was parachuted into Borneo to help organise Dayak resistance against the occupying Japanese forces. This is his extraordinary account.

Keith, Agnes (1969) *Land below the wind*, Ulverscroft: Leicester. Perhaps the best-known English language book on Sabah.

King, Victor T. (edit.) (1992) *The best of Borneo travel*, Oxford University Press: Oxford. A compilation of travel accounts from the early 19th century through to the late 20th. An excellent companion to take while exploring the island. Published in portable paperback.

O'Hanlon, Redmond (1984) *Into the heart of Borneo*, Salamander Press: Edinburgh. One of the best recent travel books on Borneo. This highly amusing and perceptive romp through Borneo in the company of poet and foreign correspondent James Fenton, includes an ascent of the Rejang River and does much to counter the more romanticised images of Bornean life.

Payne, Robert: *The White Rajahs of Sarawak*. Readable account of the extraordinary history of this East Malaysian state.

Payne, Junaidi *et al*: *Pocket guide to birds of Borneo*, World Wildlife Fund/Sabah Society

Payne, Junaidi *et al*: *A field guide to the mammals of Borneo*, World Wildlife

Fund/Sabah Society. Good illustrations, reasonable text, but very dry.

Books on Bali

Belo, Jane (edit) (1970) *Traditional Balinese culture*, Columbia University Press: New York. Collection of academic papers mostly focusing upon dance, music and drama.

Covarrubias, Miguel (1937) *Island of Bali*, Cassell: London (reprinted, OUP: Singapore, 1987). The original, full treatment of Bali's culture; despite being over 50 years old it is still an excellent background to the island and is highly entertaining.

Djelantik, AAM (1990) *Balinese paintings*, OUP: Singapore. Concise history of Balinese painting also covering the major contemporary schools of art.

Eiseman, Fred and Eiseman, Margaret (1988) *Woodcarvings of Bali*, Periplus: Berkeley.

Lansing, J Stephen (1991) *Priests and programmers: technologies of power in the engineered landscape of Bali*, Princeton University Press: Princeton. An anthropological account of Bali's irrigation system; interesting for rice fans.

Stuart Fox, David (1982) *Once a century: Pura Besakih and the Eka Dasa Rudra Festival*, Penerbit Citra Indonesia: Jakarta.

Magazines on Indonesia

Far Eastern Economic Review, perhaps the most authoritative weekly magazine to the Southeast Asian region; they have correspondents based in Jakarta.

Inside Indonesia, published quarterly by the Indonesia Resources and Information Programme (IRIP) in Australia. Generally outspoken and radical (ie anti-government) in tone; excellent for background information on issues usually not covered in the press. For information on subscribing write to *Inside Indonesia*, PO Box 190, Northcote 3070, Australia.

Films about or based on Indonesia

Merry Christmas Mr Lawrence. A film starring David Bowie based on Laurens van der Post's novel *The Seed and the Sower*, an semi-autobiographical account of his internment in a Japanese prisoner of war camp outside Bandung.

The Year of Living Dangerously. Well-received film based on the romantic novel by CJ Koch based in Java during the 1965 attempted coup.

MAPS OF ISLAND SOUTHEAST ASIA

A decent map is an indispensable aid to travelling. Although maps are usually available locally, it is sometimes useful to buy a map prior to departure to plan routes and itineraries.

Nelles: publish a good series of maps of the major islands and island groups: Java, Bali, Sumatra, Kalimantan, Sulawesi, Maluku, Irian Jaya, and Nusa Tenggara.

Periplus Travel Maps: recent series of maps to the major islands including some to individual provinces – like Bali, East Java, and West Java. Good on tourist site information and often with good insert city maps.

Travel Treasure Maps (Knaus Publications): arty map series concentrating on the major tourist destinations – Bali, Lake Toba, Toraja etc. Sometimes with inset city plans and hiking trails.

Regional maps Bartholomew Southeast Asia (1:5,800,000); Nelles Southeast Asia (1:4,000,000).

Country maps Nelles Indonesia (1:4,000,000); Nelles Java and Bali (1:650,000); Nelles Java (1:1,500,000); Nelles Sulawesi (1:1,500,000); Nelles Sumatra (1:1,500,000); Nelles Irian Jaya and Maluku (1:1,500,000); Nelles Kalimantan (1:1,500,000); Nelles Java and Nusa Tenggara (1:1,500,000); Nelles Bali. Gescenter International Indonesia Malaysia (1:2,000,000); Periplus Bali; Periplus Lombok; Periplus Central Java and Yogyakarta; Periplus East Java and Surabaya; Periplus West Java and Bandung; Periplus North Sulawesi and Manado; Periplus South Sulawesi and Ujung Pandang; Periplus North Sumatra and

Medan; Periplus West Sumatra and Padang; Periplus Riau and Batam; Travel Treasure Map Sumatra: Lake Toba and the Minang Highlands.

City maps Nelles Jakarta.

Other maps Tactical Pilotage Charts (TPC, US Airforce) (1:500,000); Operational Navigational Charts (ONC, US Airforce) (1:500,000). Both of these are particularly good at showing relief features (useful for planning treks); less good on roads, towns and facilities.

Locally available maps Maps are not always available beyond Jakarta and a few larger cities, and often the quality of information is poor.

Map shops In London, the best selection is available from Stanfords, 12-14 Long Acre, London WC2E 9LP, T (0171) 836-1321; also recommended is McCarta, 15 Highbury Place, London N15 1QP, T (0171) 354-1616.

THE INTERNET

Listed below are Internet addresses which access information on Asia generally, the Southeast Asian region, or Indonesia. **Newsgroups** tend to be informal talking shops offering information from hotels and sights through to wide-ranging discussions on just about any topic. **Mailing Lists** have a more academic clientele, and probably are not worth plugging into unless you have a specific interest in the subject concerned. **Web sites** offer a whole range of information on a vast variety of topics. Below is only a selection.

Newsgroups on USENET with a Southeast Asian focus

Newsgroups are discussion fora on the USENET. Not every computer linked to the Internet has access to USENET – your computer needs Net News and a News reader. Newsgroups are informal fora for discussion; they are occasionally irreverent, usually interesting.

● *Asia general*
alt.asian.movies
alt.buddha.short.fat.guy
rec.travel.asia
soc.religion.eastern
talk.religion.buddhism

● *Southeast Asia*
soc.culture.asean

● *Indonesia*
alt.culture.indonesia
alt.sci.tech.indonesian
soc.culture.indonesia

Mailing lists

These are discussion groups with a more academic content; some may be moderate – ie the content of messages is checked by an editor. Mailing lists communicate using E-mail. The focus of the groups are in square brackets.

● *Asia general*
actmus-1@ubvm.bitnet
 [Asian Contemporary Music Discussion Group]
apex-1@uhccvm.bitnet
 [Asia-Pacific Exchange]
buddha-1@ulkyvm.bitnet
 [Buddhist Academic Discussion Forum]

● *Southeast Asia*
seanet-1@nusvm.bitnet
 [Southeast Asian Studies List]
seasia-1@msu.bitnet
 [Southeast Asia Discussion List]

● *Indonesia*
ids@suvm.bitnet
 [Indonesian Development Studies Network]
indonesi@dearn.bitnet
 [Indonesian student group in Europe]
permias@suvm.bitnet
 [Indonesian Student Association]
permon@mcgill1.bitnet
 [forum to discuss Indonesian issues]
gamelan@listserv.dartmouth.edu
 [Indonesian performing arts]
indonews@vm.gmd.de
 [news service]
indokul@cc1.kuleuren.ac.be
 [Indonesian forum]

indo-l@r3.uni-karlsruhe.de
[Indonesia mailing list]

Southeast Asia on the World Wide Web – Web sites

Web sites are on the World Wide Web. They can now be browsed using a graphical mouse-based hypertext system. The two in use are Mosaic and the newer, Netscape. They allow the user to browse through the WWW easily. Note, however, that images (especially) take time to download and if on the Web during the time of the day when the US is alive and kicking expect to spend a very long time twiddling your thumbs. The subject of the web site is in square brackets after the address.

● *Asia general*
http://none.coolware.com/infoasia/
[run by Infoasia which is a commercial firm that helps US and European firms get into Asia]
http://www.city.net/regions/asia
[pointer to information on Asian countries]
http://www.branch.com:80/silkroute/
[information on hotels, travel, news and business in Asia]
http://www.singapore.com/pata
[Pacific Asia Travel Association – stacks of info on travel in the Pacific Asian region including stats, markets, products etc]

● *Southeast Asia*
http://www.pactoc.net.au/index/resindex.htm
[Pacific talk homepage with lots of topics and links]
http://libweb.library.wise.edu/guides/SEAsia/library.htm
[the 'Gateway to Southeast Asia', lots of links]

● *Indonesia*
http://www.mawar.inn.bppt.go.id/
[Indonesia homepage based in Jakarta but good place to start a search of Web sites for Indonesia]
http://www.umanitoba.ca/indonesian/homepage.html
[another homepage with good links to other servers and broad range of information]

Terms

E-mail = Electronic mail
WWW = World Wide Web or, simply, the Web
HTML = Hypertext Markup Language

Source: the above was collated from *Internet news* published in the *IIAS Newsletter* [International Institute for Asian Studies Newsletter], Summer 1995; *IIAS Newsletter*, Spring 1996 and *Asian Studies Newsletter*, June/July 1996.

SHORT WAVE RADIO (KHz)

British Broadcasting Corporation (BBC, London) *Southeast Asian service* 3915, 6195, 9570, 9740, 11750, 11955, 15360; *Singapore service* 88.9MHz; *East Asian service* 5995, 6195, 7180, 9740, 11715, 11750, 11945, 11955, 15140, 15280, 15360, 17830, 21715.

Voice of America (VoA, Washington) *Southeast Asian service* 1143, 1575, 7120, 9760, 9770, 15185, 15425; *Indonesian service* 6110, 11760, 15425.

Radio Beijing *Southeast Asian service (English)* 11600, 11660.

Radio Japan (Tokyo) *Southeast Asian service (English)* 11815, 17810, 21610.

Useful Addresses

EMBASSIES AND CONSULATES

Australia
8 Darwin Ave, Yarralumla, Canberra, T 2733222. Consulates: Adelaide T 2236535, Darwin T 819352, Melbourne T 6907811, Perth T 2198212, Sydney T 3449933

Austria
Gustav Tschenmakgasse 5-7, 1180 Vienna, T 0222342533

Bangladesh
Gulshan Ave 75, Gulshan Model Town, Dhaka, T 600131

Belgium
Avenue de Turvueren 294, 1150 Brussels, T 7712014. Consulates: Antwerp T 32256136, Charleroi T 071 310050

Brunei
EDR 4303 Lot 4498 KG, Sungai Hanching Baru, Simpang 528, Jl Muara, PO Box 3013, Bandar Seri Begawan, T 330180

Canada
287 Maclaren St, Ottawa, Ontario K2P 0L9, T 613 2367403. Consulates: Toronto T 416 5916462, Vancouver T 604 682 8855

Denmark
Orehoj Alle 1, 2900 Hellerup, Copenhagen, T 01 624539

Finland
37 Berikinkatu, 00810 Helsinki 18, T 694 7744

France
47-49 Rue Contambert, 75116 Paris, T 45030760. Consulate
Marseilles, T 91713435

Germany
Bernkasteler Strasse 2, 5300 Bonn 2, T 0228 328990. Consulates: Berlin, T 4722002, Bremen T 0421 3322224, Dusseldorf T 0211 353081, Frankfurt/Main, T 06105 76003, Hamburg T 040 512071, Hannover T 511 103 2150, Kiel T 0431 603425, Munich T 089 294609, Stuttgart T 711 223729

Greece
Consulate: 11-13 Shyrou St, Athens 811, T 9914082

Hong Kong
Consulate: 127-129 Leighton Rd, Causeway Bay, Hong Kong, T 890 4421

India
50A Chanakyapuri, New Delhi 110021, T 602353. Consulates
Bombay T 368678, Calcutta T 460297

Italy
53 Via Campania, 00187 Rome, T 482 5951. Consulates
Genoa T 268322, Napoli T 400143, Trieste T 765601

Japan
2-9 Higashi Gotanda 5 Chome, Shinagawa-Ku, Tokyo, T 441 4201. Consulates: Fukuoka T 092 761 3031, Kobe T 078 321 1656, Sapporo T 011 251 6002

Laos
Route Phone Keng, Boita Postale 277, Vientiane, T 2372

Luxemburg
Consulate: Gote d'Eich 15, Luxemburg, T 0352 471591

Malaysia
Jl Tun Razak No 233, PO Box 10889, 50400

Kuala Lumpur, T 9842011. Consulates: Kota Kinabalu T 54100, Penang Island, T 25162

Myanmar (Burma)
100 Pyidaungsu Yeiktha Rd, PO Box 1401, Rangoon, T 81174

Netherlands
8 Tobias Asserlaan, 5517, s'-Gravenhage, T 070 3108100

New Zealand
70 Glen Rd, Kelburn, Wellington, T 758695

Norway
Gt 8 Inkognito, 0258 Oslo 2, T 441121

Pakistan
Diplomatic Enclave Ramna 5/4, PO Box 1019, Islamabad, T 811291. Consulate: Karachi T 531938

Philippines
185 Salcedo St, Lagaspi Village PO Box 372 MCC, Makati, Metro Manila, T 855061

Russia
12 Novokuznetskaya Ulitsa, Moscow, T 2319549

Singapore
7 Chatsworth Rd, Singapore 1024, T 737 7422

Spain
65 Calle de Agestia, Madrid 28043, T 413 0294. Consulate
Barcelona T 3171900

Sri Lanka
1 Police Park, Colombo 5, T 580113

Sweden
47/ V Strandvagen 11456, Stockholm, T 6635470

Switzerland
51 Elfenauweg, PO Box 270, 3006 Bern, T 440983

Thailand
600-602 Phetburi Rd, Bangkok, T 252 3135

UK
38 Grosvenor Square, London, T 0171 499 7661

USA
2020 Massachusetts Ave NW, Washington DC 20036, T 202 775 5200. Consulates: Chicago T 312 938 0101, Honolulu T 808 524 4300, Houston T 713 785 1691, Los Angeles T 213 383 5126, New York T 212 879 0600, San Francisco T 415 474 9571

Vietnam
50 Pho Ngo Quyen, Hanoi, T 256316.

TOURIST OFFICE INFORMATION

The Directorate General of Tourism is to be found in Jakarta. Administratively, it is under the Department of Tourism, Post and Telecommunications, which has offices throughout the country. These offices are known as *Kanwil Depparpostel*. Each of the 27 provinces also have their own tourist offices, known as *Deparda* or *Dinas Pariwisata*. The head office of the Directorate General of Tourism, with information on the whole country, is at Jl Kramat Raya 81, Jakarta. The Dinas Pariwisata Jakarta is at Jl Abdul Rohim 2, T 511073. For other offices, see relevant town entry. **Indonesian Tourist Promotion offices overseas** are

Asean and Hong Kong
10, Collyer Quay, 15-07 Ocean Bldg, Singapore 0104, T 5342837, F 5334287

Australia
Level 10, 5 Elizabeth St, Sydney NSW 2000, T 2333630, F 2333629

Europe
Wiessenhuttenplatz 17, Frankfurt am Main, Germany, T (069) 2336778

Japan
Asia Trans Co, 2nd Flr Sankaido Bldg, 1-9-13 Akasaka, Minato-ku, Tokyo, T 5853588, F 358 21397

UK
3-4 Hanover St, London W1R 9HH, T (0171) 4930030, F (0171) 4931747

USA
3457 Wilshire Blvd, Los Angeles, California 90010, T (213) 3872078, F (213) 3804876.

SPECIALIST TOUR OPERATORS

ASIA AND AUSTRALIA

Natrabu Tours & Travel
16 Westlane Carpark, Darwin NT-5794, Australia, T 813695 and at 6th Flr, Asabudai Bldg, 2-1, 2-Chome, Asabudai, Minato-ku, Tokyo, Japan, T (03) 5856209, F 5824479

Purawisata Cultural Workshops
Jl Brig Jend Katamso, Yogyakarta 55121, Indonesia, T (0274) 74089, F (0274) 78905 or in Jakarta at Jl Balai Pustaka Timur 1, Blok J-225, Rawamangun, Jakarta 13220, T (021) 4702983, F (021) 4702982, a 6 day package where the visitor immerses themselves in the local culture.

EUROPE

Arc Archipelago Journeys
39 Newnham Rd, Cambridge, CB3 9EY, UK, T (01223) 355976, F (01223) 460425, excellent cultural and natural tours of Indonesia led by people who understand and care for the country, its people and environment

Cross Country
Postbus 164, 2180 AD Hillegom, The Netherlands, T (02520) 77677, F 23670, trekking specialist dealing with Kalimantan

Mistral Tour Internazionale
24 Via Leonardo Da Vinci, 10126 Torino, Italy, T (011) 638444, F 633969

Natrabu Tours & Travel
129 Van Leyenberghlaan, 1028, Amsterdam, the Netherlands, T (020) 443429, F 423325

Nayak Travel and Expeditions
Steinengraben 42, CH-4001 Switzerland, T (061) 224343, F 224383, specialists in adventure tourism in Kalimantan

Noble Caledonia
11 Charles St, London W1X 7HB, T (0171) 491-4752, F (0171) 409-0834, specialist cruise company with cruises to more remote areas of Indonesia, well run with resident experts

P&O Spice Island Cruises
Jl S Parman 78, Jakarta, T (021) 5673401, F (021) 5673403, run excellent, luxurious cruises through the Spice Islands of Nusa Tenggara

Symbiosis Expedition Planning
113 Bolingbroke Grove, London SW11 1DA, UK, T 0171-924-5906, F 0171-924-5907, customized tours arranged by small company with an intimate knowledge of the region and an ethical stance

Windrose
D-1000 Berlin 15, Germany, T (030) 8813059, adventure and safari tour specialist.

USA

Forum International
91 Gregory Lane, 21 Pleasant Hill, Calif 94523, T (510) 671-2900, F (510) 946-1500, eco-tours to Indonesia, interesting and well-planned

Kingfisher Asian Tours (Friends in America Inc), PO Box 281, Hawthorne, New Jersey 07506, T (201) 4274551, F 4232775

Natrabu Tours & Travel
8th Flr 352, 27th Ave, New York, NY10001, T (212) 5641939/(800) 6287228 (toll-free) and at 433 California St, San Fransisco, CA 94104, T (800) 6546900 (toll-free)

Sobek Expeditions Inc
Angelo Camp, California 95222, T (209) 7364574, F 7362646, adventure tours to Kalimantan and elsewhere in Indonesia.

CANADA

ElderTreks
597 Markham St, Toronto, Ontario, T (416) 588-5000, F (416) 588-9839, specializes in adventurous tours for the elderly.

Useful Indonesian words and phrases

I N INDONESIAN, there are no tenses, genders or articles and sentence structure is relatively simple. Pronunciation is not difficult as there is a close relationship between the letter as it is written and the sound. Stress is usually placed on the second syllable of a word. For example, *restoran* (restaurant) is pronounced res-TO-ran.

VOWELS

a is pronounced as *ah* in an open syllable, or as in *but* for a closed syllable.
e is pronounced as in *open* or *bed*.
i is pronounced as in *feel*.
o is pronounced as in *all*.
u is pronounced as in *foot*.
The letter c is pronounced as *ch* as in *change* or *chat*.
The *r*'s are rolled.
Plural is indicated by repetition, *bapak-ba-pak*.

LEARNING INDONESIAN

The list of words and phrases below is very rudimentary. For anyone serious about learning Indonesian it is best to buy a dedicated Indonesian language textbook or to enrol on an Indonesian course. In Indonesia, there are courses on offer in Jakarta, Bali and Yogyakarta. A phrase book and/or some knowledge of the Indonesian language comes in very handy away from tourist sites.

Yes/no
Ya/tidak
Thank you [very much]
Terima kasih [banyak]
Good morning (until 1100)
Selamat pagi
Good day (until 1500)
Selamat siang
Good afternoon (until dusk)
Selamat sore
Good evening
Selamat malam
Welcome
Selamat datang
Goodbye (said by the person leaving)
Selamat tinggal
Goodbye (said by the person staying)
Selamat jalan
Excuse me, sorry!
ma'af
Where's the...?
...dimana?
How much is...?
...berapa harganya?
You're welcome, don't mention it
kembali

I [don't] understand
  Saya [tidak] mengerti

THE HOTEL

How much is a room?
  kamar berapa harga?
Does the room have air-conditioning?
  Ada kamar yang ada AC-nya?
I want to see the room first please
  Saya mau lihat kamar dulu
Does the room have hot water?
  Ada kamar yang ada air panas?
Does the room have a bathroom?
  Ada kamar yang ada kamar mandi?

TRAVEL

Where is the train station?
  Dimana stasiun kereta api?
Where is the bus station?
  Dimana stasiun bis?
How much to go to...?
  Berapa harga ke...?
I want to go to...
  Saya mau pergi ke...
I want to buy a ticket to...
  Saya mau beli karcis ke...
Is it far?
  ada jauh?
Turn left/turn right
  belok kiri/belok kanan
Go straight on
  terus saja

DAYS

Monday Hari Senin
Tuesday Hari Selasa
Wednesday Hari Rabu
Thursday Hari Kamis
Friday Hari Jumat
Saturday Hari Sabtu
Sunday Hari Minggu
today hari ini
tomorrow hari besok

NUMBERS

1 satu
2 dua
3 tiga
4 empat
5 lima
6 enam
7 tujuh
8 delapan
9 sembilan
10 sepuluh
11 se-belas
12– dua-belas...etc
20 dua puluh
21– dua puluh satu...etc
30– tiga puluh...etc
100 se-ratus
101 se-ratus satu...etc
150 se-ratus lima puluh
200– dua ratus...etc
1,000 se-ribu
2,000 dua ribu
100,000 se-ratus ribu
1,000,000 se-juta

BASIC VOCABULARY

all right/good baik
bank bank
bathroom kamar mandi/ kamar kecil
beach pantai
beautiful cantik
big besar
boat prahu
bus bis
bus station stasiun bis
buy beli
can boleh
chemist apotek
clean bersih
closed tutup
day hari
delicious enak
dentist doktor gigi
dirty kotor
doctor doktor
eat makan
excellent bagus
expensive mahal
food makan
fruit buah
hospital rumah sakit
hotel hotel/ losmen/ penginapan/
        wisma
hot (temperature) panas
hot (spicy) pedas
I/me saya

immigration office kantor imigrasi
island pulau
market pasa
medicine obat
open masuk
police polisi
police station stasiun polisi
post office kantor pos
restaurant rumah makan
room kamar
ship kapal
shop toko
sick sakit
small kecil
stop berhenti
taxi taksi
ticket karcis
that itu
they mereka
this ini
toilet WC ("way say")
town kota
train station stasiun kereta api
very sekali
water air
what apa

AN INDONESIAN FOOD GLOSSARY

asam tamarind; sold in a solid block, or still in the brown pod
atpokat avocado
ayam chicken
ayam goreng fried chicken
babek duck
babi pork
bakar roast
bakmi rice flour noodles
bakso meat balls
belimbing star fruit
bifstik beef steak
cabe chilli
cumi cumi squid
dadar omelette/pancake
daging beef/meat
durian durian
es ice
es krim ice cream
garam salt
goreng stir fry
gula sugar
gulai curry soup
ikan fish
istemiwa 'special' – nasi goreng istemiwa has a fried egg and other additions
jeruk
generic term in Java and Bali for citrus fruit
jeruk bali pomelo
jeruk manis orange
jeruk nipis lime
kacang generic term for bean or nut
kacang peanut sauce
kacang buncis french bean
kacang kedele soybean
kacang tanah peanut
kambing lamb/goat
kangkung 'greens' grown in water – some-times known as water spinach
kayu manis cinnamon
kecap asin salt-soy sauce
kelengkeng lychee
kemiri macadamia nut
kenari a shade tree which produces a nut similar to an almond
kepiting crab
ketimun cucumber

kodok frog

kopi coffee

kopi bubuk ground coffee (with grounds)

kopi saring filtered coffee

krupuk deep-fried tapioca crackers

kuah gravy

kue cake

kunyit turmeric

lombok chilli

lontong compressed rice, usually served with sate

madu honey

mangga mango

manggis mangosteen

manis sweet

merica black pepper

mie noodles

nangka jackfruit, eaten ripe as a fruit or unripe cooked as a vegetable

nasi rice

nasi putih plain white rice

nenas pineapple

pala nutmeg

panggang grill

papaya (kates) papaya

pisang banana

rambutan rambutan

rebus boil

roti bread

salak brown, pear shaped fruit, with a shiny, snake-like skin. The flesh is white, segmented and dry. Balinese salak are considered to be the sweetest

sambal chilli paste

santen coconut milk

sawi Chinese cabbage

sayur vegetables

semangka air watermelon

sereh lemon grass

serundeng grated coconut roasted with peanuts

sop soup

tahu soybean curd

telur egg

tempe fermented soybean cake (see box)

udang shrimp

udang karang lobster

DISTINCTIVE FRUITS

Custard apple (or sugar apple) Scaly green skin, squeeze the skin to open the fruit and scoop out the flesh with a spoon.

Durian (*Durio zibethinus*) A large prickly fruit, with yellow flesh, about the size of a football. Infamous for its pungent smell. While it is today regarded by many visitors as simply revolting, early Europeans (16th-18th centuries) raved about it, possibly because it was similar in taste to western delicacies of the period. Borri (1744) thought that "God himself, who had produc'd that fruit". But by 1880 Burbridge was writing: "Its odour – one scarcely feels justified in using the word 'perfume' – is so potent, so vague, but withal so insinuating, that it can scarcely be tolerated inside the house". Banned from public transport in Singapore and hotel rooms throughout the region, and beloved by most Southeast Asians (where prize specimens can cost a week's salary), it has an alluring taste if the odour can be overcome (it has been described as like eating blancmange on the toilet). Some maintain it is an addiction. Durian-flavoured chewing gum, ice cream and jams are all available.

Jackfruit Similar in appearance to durian but not so spiky. Yellow flesh, tasting slightly like custard.

Mango (*Mangifera indica*) A rainforest fruit which is now cultivated. Widely available in the West; in Southeast Asia there are hundreds of different varieties with subtle variations in flavour. Delicious eaten with sticky rice and a sweet sauce (in Thailand). The best mangoes in the region are considered to be those from S Thailand.

Mangosteen (*Garcinia mangostana*) An aubergine-coloured hard shell covers this small fruit which is about the size of a tennis ball. Cut or squeeze the purple shell to reach its sweet white flesh which is prized by many visitors above all others. In 1898, an American resident of Java wrote, erotically and in obvious ecstasy: "The five white segments separate easily, and they melt on the tongue with a touch of tart and a touch of sweet; one moment a memory of the juiciest, most fragrant apple, at another a remembrance of the smoothest cream ice, the most exquisite and delicately flavoured fruit-acid known – all of the delights of nature's laboratory condensed in that ball of *neige parfumée*". Southeast Asians believe it should be eaten as a chaser to durian.

Papaya (*Carica papaya*) A New World Fruit that was not introduced into Southeast Asia until the 16th century. Large, round or oval in shape, yellow or green-skinned, with bright orange flesh and a mass of round, black seeds in the middle. The flesh, in texture and taste, is somewhere between a mango and a melon. Some maintain that it tastes 'soapy'.

Pomelo A large round fruit the size of anything from an ostrich egg to a football, with thick, green skin, thick pith, and flesh not unlike that of the grapefruit, but less acidic.

Rambutan (*Nephelium lappaceum*) The bright red and hairy rambutan – *rambut* is the Malay word for 'hair' – with its slightly rubbery but sweet flesh is a close relative of the lychee of southern China and tastes similar. The Thai word for rambutan is *ngoh*, which is the nickname given by Thais to the fuzzy-haired Negrito aboriginals in the southern jungles.

Salak (*Salacca edulis*) A small pear-shaped fruit about the size of a large plum with a rough, brown, scaly skin (somewhat like a miniature pangolin) and yellow-white, crisp flesh. It is related to the sago and rattan trees.

Tamarind (*Tamarindus indicus*) Brown seedpods with dry brittle skins and a brown tart-sweet fruit which grow on a tree introduced into Southeast Asia from India. The name is Arabic for 'Indian date'. The flesh has a high tartaric acid content and is used to flavour curries, jams, jellies and chutneys as well as for cleaning brass and copper. Elephants have a predilection for tamarind balls.

Health

THE TRAVELLER to Southeast Asia is inevitably exposed to health risks not encountered in North America, Western Europe or Australasia. All of the countries have a tropical climate; nevertheless the acquisition of true tropical disease by the visitor is probably conditioned as much by the rural nature and standard of hygiene of the countries concerned than by the climate. There is an obvious difference in health risks between the business traveller who tends to stay in international class hotels in large cities and the backpacker trekking through rural areas. There are no hard and fast rules to follow; you will often have to make your own judgements on the healthiness or otherwise of your surroundings.

Medical care

Medical care is very variable; medical culture is quite different from the other neighbouring countries, although there are some good hospitals in Jakarta and other main cities. The likelihood of finding a doctor who speaks English and a good standard of care diminishes very rapidly as you move away from the big cities. In the rural areas – there are systems and traditions of medicine wholly different from the western model and you may be confronted with less orthodox forms of treatment such as herbal medicine and acupuncture. At least you can be sure that local practitioners have a lot of experience with the particular diseases of their region. If you are in a city it may be worthwhile calling on your embassy to provide a list of recommended doctors.

Medicines

If you are a long way away from medical help, a certain amount of self administered medication may be necessary and you will find many of the drugs available have familiar names. However, always check the date stamping (sell-by date) and buy from reputable pharmacists because the shelf life of some items, especially vaccines and antibiotics, is markedly reduced in hot conditions. Unfortunately, many locally produced drugs are not subjected to quality control procedures and so can be unreliable. There have, in addition, been cases of substitution of inert materials for active drugs. With the following precautions and advice you should keep as healthy as usual. Make local enquiries about health risks if you are apprehensive and take the general advice of European, Australian or North American families who have lived or are living in the area.

BEFORE YOU GO

Take out medical insurance. You should also have a dental check-up, obtain a spare glasses prescription and, if you suffer from a long-standing condition, such as diabetes, high blood pressure, heart/lung disease or a nervous disorder, arrange for a check-up with your doctor who can at the same time provide you with a letter explaining details of your medical disorder. Check the current practice for malaria prophylaxis (prevention) for the countries you intend to visit.

Vaccination and immunisation

Smallpox vaccination is no longer required. Neither is cholera vaccination, despite the fact that the disease occurs – but not at present in epidemic form – in some of these countries. Yellow fever vaccination is not required either, although you may be asked for a certificate if you have been in a country affected by yellow fever immediately before travelling to Southeast Asia.

The following vaccinations are recommended:

Typhoid (monovalent) One dose followed by a booster 1 month later. Immunity from this course lasts 2-3 years. An oral preparation is also available.

Poliomyelitis This is a live vaccine generally given orally but a full course consists of three doses with a booster in tropical regions every 3-5 years.

Tetanus One dose should be given, with a booster at 6 weeks and another at 6 months. 10 yearly boosters thereafter are recommended.

Meningitis and Japanese B encephalitis (JVE) There is an extremely small risk of these rather serious diseases; both are seasonal and vary according to region. Meningitis can occur in epidemic form; JVE is a viral disease transmitted from pigs to man by mosquitos. For details of the vaccinations, consult a travel clinic.

Children should, in addition to the above, be properly protected against diphtheria, whooping cough, mumps and measles. Teenage girls, if they have not had the disease, should be given a rubella (German measles) vaccination. Consult your doctor for advice on BCG inoculation against tuberculosis: the disease is still common in the region.

Infectious hepatitis (jaundice) This is common throughout Southeast Asia. It seems to be frequently caught by travellers. The main symptoms are stomach pains, lack of appetite, nausea, lassitude and yellowness of the eyes and skin. Medically speaking there are two types: the less serious but more common is *hepatitis A* for which the best protection is careful preparation of food, the avoidance of contaminated drinking water and scrupulous attention to toilet hygiene. Human normal immunoglobulin (gammaglobulin) confers considerable protection against the disease and is particularly useful in epidemics. It should be obtained from a reputable source and is certainly recommended for travellers who intend to travel and live rough. The injection should be given as close as possible to your departure and as the dose depends on the likely time you are to spend in potentially infected areas, the manufacturers' instructions should be followed. A vaccination against hepatitis A has recently become generally available and is safe and effective. Three shots are given over 6 months and confer excellent protection against the disease for up to 10 years. Eventually this vaccine is likely to supersede the use of gammaglobulin.

The other, more serious, version is *hepatitis B* which is acquired as a sexually transmitted disease, from a blood transfusion or an injection with an unclean needle, or possibly by insect bites. The symptoms are the same as hepatitis A but the incubation period is much longer.

You may have had jaundice before or you may have had hepatitis of either type before without becoming jaundiced, in which case it is possible that you could be immune to either hepatitis A or B (or C or a number of other letters). This immunity can be tested for before you travel. If you are not immune to hepatitis B already, a vaccine is available (three shots over 6 months) and if you are not immune to hepatitis A already, then you should consider having gammaglobulin or a vaccination.

AIDS

AIDS in Southeast Asia is increasingly prevalent. Thus, it is not wholly confined to the well known high risk sections of the population ie homosexual men, intravenous drug abusers, prostitutes and the children of infected mothers. Heterosexual transmission is probably now the dominant mode of infection and so the main risk to travellers is from casual sex. The same precautions should be taken as when encountering any sexually transmitted disease. In some Southeast Asian countries, Thailand is an example, almost the entire population of female prostitutes is HIV positive and in other parts intravenous drug abuse is common. Indonesia seems to be going the same way. The AIDS virus (HIV) can be passed via unsterile needles which have been previously used to inject an HIV positive patient, but the risk of this is very small indeed. It would, however, be sensible to check that needles have been properly sterilized or disposable needles used. The chance of picking up hepatitis B in this way is much more of a danger. Be wary of carrying disposable needles. Customs officials may find them suspicious. The risk of receiving a blood transfusion with blood infected with the HIV virus is greater than from dirty needles because of the amount of fluid exchanged. Supplies of blood for transfusion are supposed to

be screened for HIV in all reputable hospitals so the risk should be small. Catching the virus that causes AIDS does not necessarily produce an illness in itself; the only way to be sure if you feel you have been put at risk is to have a blood test for HIV antibodies on your return to a place where there are reliable laboratory facilities. However, the test does not become positive for many weeks.

MALARIA

Malaria is prevalent in Indonesia. Malaria remains a serious disease and you are advised to protect yourself against mosquito bites as above and to take prophylactic (preventative) drugs. Start taking the tablets a few days before exposure and continue to take them 6 weeks after leaving the malarial zone. Remember to give the drugs to babies and children, pregnant women also.

The subject of malaria prevention is becoming more complex as the malaria parasite becomes immune to some of the older drugs. In particular, there has been an increase in the proportion of cases of falciparum malaria which are resistant to the normally used drugs. It would not be an exaggeration to say that we are near to the situation where some cases of malaria will be untreatable with presently available drugs.

Before you travel you must check with a reputable agency the likelihood and type of malaria in the countries which you intend to visit. Take their advice on prophylaxis but be prepared to receive conflicting advice. Because of the rapidly changing situation in the Southeast Asian region, the names and dosage of the drugs have not been included. But Chloroquine and Proguanil may still be recommended for the areas where malaria is still fully sensitive. Doxycycline, Metloquine and Quinghaosu are presently being used in resistant areas. Halofantrine Quinine and tetracycline drugs remain the mainstays of treatment.

It is still possible to catch malaria even when taking prophylactic drugs, although this is unlikely. If you do develop symptoms (high fever, shivering, severe headache, and sometimes diarrhoea) seek medical advice immediately. The risk of the disease is obviously greater the further you move from the cities into rural areas, with primitive facilities and standing water.

OTHER COMMON PROBLEMS

HEAT AND COLD

Full acclimatization to tropical temperatures takes about 2 weeks and during this period it is normal to feel relatively apathetic, especially if the humidity is high. Drink plenty of water (up to 15 litres a day are required when working physically hard in the tropics). Use salt on your food and avoid extreme exertion. Tepid showers are more cooling than hot or cold ones. Large hats do not cool you down but do prevent sunburn. Remember that, especially in highland areas, there can be a large and sudden drop in temperature between sun and shade and between night and day so dress accordingly. Loose-fitting cotton clothes are best for hot weather. Warm jackets and woollens are often necessary after dark at high altitude.

INSECTS

These can be a great nuisance. Some, of course, are carriers of serious diseases such as malaria, dengue fever or filariasis and various worm infections. The best way of keeping mosquitos away at night is to sleep off the ground with a mosquito net and to burn mosquito coils containing Pyrethrum. Aerosol sprays or a 'flit gun' may be effective as are insecticidal tablets which are heated on a mat which is plugged into the wall socket (if taking your own, check the voltage of the area you are visiting so that you can take an appliance that will work; similarly, check that your electrical adaptor is suitable for the repellent plug; note that they are widely available in the region).

You can, in addition, use personal insect repellent of which the best contain a high concentration of diethyltoluamide (DET). Liquid is best for arms and face (take care around eyes and make sure you do not dissolve the plastic of your spectacles). Aerosol spray on clothes and ankles deter mites and ticks. Liquid DET suspended in water can be used to impregnate cotton clothes and mosquito nets. The latter are now available in wide mesh form which are lighter to carry and less claustrophobic to sleep under.

If you are bitten, itching may be relieved by cool baths and antihistamine tables (take care with alcohol or when driving), corticosteroid creams (great care – never use if any hint of septic poisoning) or by judicious scratching. Calamine lotion and cream have limited effectiveness and antihistamine creams have a tendency to cause skin allergies and are therefore not generally recommended. Bites which become infected (a common problem in the tropics) should be treated with a local antiseptic or antibiotic cream such as Cetrimide, as should infected scratches. Skin infestations with body lice, crabs and scabies are unfortunately easy to pick up. Use gamma benzene hexachloride for lice and benzyl benzoate for scabies. Crotamiton cream alleviates itching and also kills a number of skin parasites. Malathion lotion is good for lice but avoid the highly toxic full strength Malathion which is used as an agricultural insecticide.

INTESTINAL UPSETS

Practically nobody escapes intestinal infections, so be prepared for them. Most of the time they are due to the insanitary preparation of food. Do not eat uncooked fish, vegetables or meat (especially pork), fruit without the skin (always peel fruit yourself), or food that is exposed to flies (particularly salads). Tap water may be unsafe, especially in the monsoon seasons and the same goes for stream water or well water. Filtered or bottled water is usually available and safe but you cannot always rely on it. If your hotel has a central hot water supply, this is safe to drink after cooling. Ice should be made from boiled water but rarely is, so stand your glass on the ice cubes instead of putting them in the drink. Dirty water should first be strained through a filter bag (available from camping shops) and then boiled or treated. Bringing the water to a rolling boil at sea level is sufficient. In the highlands, you have to boil the water a bit longer to ensure that all the microbes are killed (because water boils at a lower temperature at altitude). Various sterilizing methods can be used and there are proprietary preparations containing chlorine or iodine compounds. Pasteurized or heat-treated milk is now fairly widely available as is ice cream and yoghurt produced by the same methods. Unpasteurized milk products, including cheese, are sources of tuberculosis, brucellosis, listeria and food poisoning germs. You can render fresh milk safe by heating it to 62°C for 30 mins followed by rapid cooling or by boiling. Matured or processed cheeses are safer than fresh varieties.

Fish and shellfish are popular foods throughout Indonesia but can be the source of health problems. Shellfish which are eaten raw will transmit food poisoning or hepatitis if they have been living in contaminated water. Certain fish accumulate toxins in their bodies at certain times of the year, which give rise to illness when they are eaten. The phenomenon known as 'red tide' can also affect fish and shellfish which eat large quantities of tiny sea creatures and thereby become poisonous. The only way to guard against this is to keep as well informed as possible about fish and shellfish quality in the area you are visiting. Most countries impose a ban on fishing in periods when red tide is prevalent, although this is often flouted.

Diarrhoea

Diarrhoea is usually the result of food poi-

soning, but can occasionally result from contaminated water. There are various causes – viruses, bacteria, protozoa (like amoeba), salmonella and cholera organisms. It may take one of several forms coming on suddenly or rather slowly. It may be accompanied by vomiting or severe abdominal pain, and the passage of blood or mucus (when it is called dysentery). The different types of diarrhoea and the best ways to treat them are listed in the box.

All kinds of diarrhoea, whether or not accompanied by vomiting, respond favourably to the replacement of water and salts taken as frequent small sips of some kind of rehydration solution. There are proprietary preparations consisting of sachets of oral rehydration electrolyte powder which are dissolved in water, or make up your own by adding half a teaspoonful of salt (3.5 grams) and 4 tablespoons of sugar (40 grams) to a litre of boiled water. If it is possible to time the onset of diarrhoea to the minute, then it is probably viral or bacterial and/or the onset of dysentery. The treatment in addition to rehydration is Ciprofloxacin (500 mgs every 12 hrs). The drug is now widely available as are various similar ones.

If the diarrhoea has come on slowly or intermittently, then it is more likely to be protozoal, ie caused by amoeba or giardia, and antibiotics will have no effect. These cases are best treated by a doctor as should any diarrhoea continuing for more than 3 days. If there are severe stomach cramps, the following drugs may help: Loperamide (*Imodium*, *Arret*) and Diphenoxylate with Atropine (*Lomotil*). The drug usually used for giardia or amoeba is Metronidazole (*Flagyl*) or Tinidazole (*Fasigyu*).

The lynchpins of treatment for diarrhoea are rest, fluid and salt replacement, antibiotics such as Ciprofloxacin for the bacterial types, and special diagnostic tests and medical treatment for amoeba and giardia infections. Salmonella infections and cholera can be devastating diseases and it would be wise to get to a hospital as soon as possible if these were suspected. Fasting, peculiar diets and the consumption of large quantities of yoghurt have not been found useful in calming travellers' diarrhoea or in rehabilitating inflamed bowels. Oral rehydration has, especially in children, been a lifesaving technique and as there is some evidence that alcohol and milk might prolong diarrhoea they should probably be avoided during, and immediately after, an attack. There are ways of preventing travellers' diarrhoea for short periods of time when visiting these countries by taking antibiotics but these are ineffective against viruses and, to some extent, against protozoa. This technique should not be used other than in exceptional circumstances. Some preventatives such as Enterovioform can have serious side effects if taken for long periods.

SUNBURN AND HEAT STROKE

The burning power of the tropical sun is phenomenal, especially in highland areas. Always wear a wide-brimmed hat, and use some form of sun cream or lotion on untanned skin. Normal temperate zone suntan lotions (protection factors up to 7) are not much good. You need to use the types designed specifically for the tropics or for mountaineers or skiers, with a protection factor between 7 and 15 or higher. Glare from the sun can cause conjunctivitis so wear sunglasses, particularly on beaches.

There are several varieties of heat stroke. The most common cause is severe dehydration. Avoid this by drinking lots of non-alcoholic fluid, and adding salt to your food.

Water purification

There are a number of methods for purifying water in order to make it safe to drink. Dirty water should first be strained through a filter bag, and then boiled or treated. Bringing water to a rolling **boil** at sea level is sufficient to make water safe for drinking, but at higher altitudes you have to boil the water for longer to ensure that all the microbes are killed.

Various sterilizing methods can be used, and there are propriety preparations containing **chlorine** (eg 'Puritabs') or **iodine** (eg 'Pota Aqua') compounds. Chlorine compounds generally do not kill protozoa (eg giardia).

There are a number of **water filters** now on the market, available both in personal and expedition size. There are broadly two types of water filter, **mechanical** and **chemical**. Mechanical filters are usually a combination of carbon, ceramic and paper, although they can be difficult to use. Ceramic filters tend to last longer in terms of volume of water purified. The best brand is possibly the Swiss-made Katadyn. Although cheaper, the disadvantage of mechanical filters is that they do not always kill viruses or protozoa. Thus, if you are in an area where the presence of these is suspected, the water will have to be treated with iodine before being passed through the filter. When new, the filter will remove the taste, although this may not continue for long. However, ceramic filters will remove bacteria, and their manufacturers claim that since most viruses live on bacteria, the chances are that the viruses will be removed as well. This claim should be treated with scepticism.

Chemical filters usually use a combination of an iodine resin filter and a mechanical filter. The advantage of this system is that, according to the manufacturers' claims, everything in the water will be killed. The disadvantage is that the filters need replacing, adding a third to the price. Probably the best chemical filter is manufactured by Pur.

SNAKE AND OTHER BITES AND STINGS

If you are unlucky enough to be bitten by a venomous snake, spider, scorpion, centipede or sea creature, try (within limits) to catch or kill the animal for identification. Reactions to be expected are shock, swelling, pain and bruising around the bite, soreness of the regional lymph glands, nausea, vomiting and fever. If in addition any of the following symptoms should follow closely, get the victim to a doctor without delay: numbness, tingling of the face, muscular spasms, convulsions, shortness of breath or haemorrhage. Commercial snake-bite or scorpion-sting kits may be available but these are only useful against the specific type of snake or scorpion for which they are designed. The serum has to be given intravenously so it not much good unless you have had some practice in making injections into veins. If the bite is on a limb, immobilize it and apply a tight bandage between the bite and the body, releasing it for 90 secs every 15 mins. Reassurance of the victim is very important because death from snake bite is very rare. Do not slash the bite area and try to suck out the poison because this sort of heroism does more harm than good. Hospitals usually hold stocks of snake-bite serum. The best precaution is not walk in long grass with bare feet, sandals or in shorts.

When swimming in an area where there are poisonous fish such as stone or scorpion fish (also called by a variety of local names) or sea urchins on rocky coasts, tread carefully or wear plimsolls/trainers. The sting of such fish is intensely painful. This can be relieved by immersing the injured part of the body in water as hot as you can bear for as long as it remains painful. This is not always very practical and you must take care not to scald yourself, but it does work. Avoid spiders and scorpions by keeping your bed away from the wall, look under lavatory seats and inside your shoes in the morning. In the rare event of being bitten, consult a doctor.

WATCH OUT FOR

Remember that **rabies** is endemic in many Southeast Asian countries. If you are bitten by a domestic or wild animal, do not leave things to chance. Scrub the wound with soap and water and/or disinfectant, try to have the animal captured (within limits) or at least determine its ownership where possible, and seek medical assistance at once. The course of treatment depends on whether you have already been satisfactorily vaccinated against rabies. If you have (and this is worthwhile if you are spending lengths of time in developing countries) then some further doses of vaccine are all that is required. Human diploid cell vaccine is the best, but expensive: other, older kinds of vaccine such as that derived from duck embryos may be the only types available. These are effective, much cheaper and interchangeable generally with the human derived types. If not already vaccinated then anti-rabies serum (immunoglobulin) may be required in addition. It is wise to finish the course of treatment whether the animal survives or not.

Dengue fever is present in Indonesia. It is a viral disease transmitted by mosquito and causes severe headaches and body pains. Complicated types of dengue known as haemorrhagic fevers occur throughout Asia but usually in persons who have caught the disease a second time. Thus, although it is a very serious type it is rarely caught by visitors. There is no treatment, you must just avoid mosquito bites.

Intestinal worms are common and the more serious ones, such as hook worm can be contracted by walking barefoot on infested earth or beaches.

Influenza and **respiratory diseases** are common, perhaps made worse by polluted cities and rapid temperature and climatic changes – accentuated by air-conditioning.

Prickly heat is a very common itchy rash,

best avoided by frequent washing and by wearing loose clothing. It can be helped by the use of talcum powder, allowing the skin to dry thoroughly after washing.

Athlete's foot and other **fungal infections** are best treated by sunshine and a proprietary preparation such as Tolnaftate.

WHEN YOU RETURN HOME

On returning home, remember to take anti-malarial tablets for 6 weeks. If you have had attacks of diarrhoea, it is worth having a stool specimen tested in case you have picked up amoebic dysentery. If you have been living rough, a blood test may also be worthwhile to detect worms and other parasites.

BASIC SUPPLIES

You may find the following items useful to take with you from home: suntan cream, insect repellent, flea powder, mosquito net, coils or tablets, tampons, condoms, contraceptives, water sterilizing tablets, anti-malaria tablets, anti-infective ointment, dusting powder for feet, travel sickness pills, antiacid tablets, anti-diarrhoea tablets, sachets of rehydration salts, a first aid kit and disposable needles (also see page 901).

FURTHER INFORMATION

Information regarding country-by-country malaria risk can be obtained from the World Health Organization (WHO) or in Britain from the Ross Institute, London School of Hygiene and Tropical Medicine, Keppel St, London WCIE 7HT which also publishes a highly recommended book: *The preservation of personal health in warm climates*. The Centres for Disease Control (CDC) in Atlanta, Georgia, USA will provide equivalent information. The organization MASTA (Medical Advisory Service for Travellers Abroad) also based at the London School of Hygiene and Tropical Medicine (T 0171 631-4408) will provide up-to-date country-by-country information on health risks. Further information on medical problems overseas can be obtained from the new edition of *Travellers health, how to stay healthy abroad*, edited by Richard Dawood (Oxford University Press, 1992). This revised and updated edition is highly recommended, especially to the intrepid traveller. A more general publication, with hints on health and much more besides, is John Hatt's new edition of *The tropical traveller* (Penguin, 1993).

The above information has been compiled by Dr David Snashall, Senior Lecturer in Occupational Health, United Medical Schools of Guy's and St Thomas' Hospitals and Chief Medical Adviser, Foreign and Commonwealth Office, London.

Travelling with children

MANY PEOPLE are daunted by the prospect of taking a child to Indonesia. Naturally, it is not something which is taken on lightly; travelling is slower and more expensive and there are additional health risks for the child or baby. But it can be a most rewarding experience, and with sufficient care and planning, it can also be safe. Children are excellent passports into a local culture. You will also receive the best service, and help from officials and members of the public when in difficulty.

Children in Indonesia are given 24-hrs attention by parents, grandparents and siblings. They are rarely left to cry and are carried for most of the first 8 months of their lives – crawling is considered animal-like. A non-Asian child is still something of a novelty and parents may find their child frequently taken off their hands, even mobbed in more remote areas. This can be a great relief (at mealtimes, for instance) or most alarming. Some children love the attention, others react against it; it is best simply to gauge your own child's reactions.

PRACTICALITIES

Accommodation
At the hottest time of year, air-conditioning may be essential for a baby or young child's comfort. This rules out many of the cheaper hotels, but air-conditioned accommodation is available in all but the most out-of-the-way spots. When the child is bathing, be aware that the water could carry parasites, so avoid letting him or her drink it.

Food and drink
The advice given in the health section on food and drink (see page 902) should be applied even more stringently where young children are concerned. Be aware that expensive hotels may have squalid cooking conditions; the cheapest street stall is often more hygienic. Where possible, try to watch food being prepared. Stir-fried vegetables and rice or noodles are the best bet; meat and fish may be pre-cooked and then left out before being re-heated. Fruit can be bought cheaply right across Indonesia: papaya, banana and avocado are all excellent sources of nutrition, and can be self-peeled ensuring cleanliness. Powdered milk is also available throughout the region, although most brands have added sugar. But if taking a baby, breast-feeding

is strongly recommended. Powdered food can be bought in most towns – the quality may not be the same as equivalent foods bought in the West, but it is perfectly adequate for short periods. Bottled water and fizzy drinks are also sold widely. If your child is at the 'grab everything and put it in mouth' stage, a damp cloth and some *dettol* (or equivalent) are useful. Frequent wiping of hands and tabletops can help to minimize the chance of infection.

Transport

Public transport may be a problem; trains are fine but long bus journeys are restrictive and uncomfortable. Hiring a car is undoubtedly the most convenient way to see a country with a small child. Back-seatbelts are rarely fitted but it is possible to buy child-seats in capital cities.

ESSENTIALS

Disposable nappies These can be bought in most large towns in Indonesia, but are often expensive. If you are staying any length of time in one place, it may be worth taking Terry's (cloth) nappies. All you need is a bucket and some double-strength nappy cleanse (simply soak and rinse). Cotton nappies dry quickly in the heat and are generally more comfortable for the baby or child. They also reduce rubbish – many countries are not geared to the disposal of nappies. Of course, the best way for a child to be is nappy-free – like the local children.

Baby products Many western baby products are now available in Indonesia: shampoo, talcum powder, soap and lotion. Baby wipes can be difficult to find.

HEALTH

Younger travellers seem to be more prone to illness abroad, but that should not put you off taking them. More preparation is necessary than for an adult and perhaps a little more care should be taken when travelling to remote areas where health services are primitive. This is because children can become more rapidly ill than adults (they often recover more quickly however). For more practical advice on travelling with children and babies see page 907.

Diarrhoea and vomiting are the most common problems so take the usual precautions, but more intensively. Make sure all basic childhood **vaccinations** are up to date as well as the more exotic ones. Children should be properly protected against diphtheria, whooping cough, mumps and measles. If they have not had the disease, teenage girls should be given rubella (german measles) vaccination. Consult your doctor for advice on BCG inoculation against tuberculosis: the disease is still common in the region. Protection against mosquitos and drug prophylaxis against malaria is essential. Many children take to "foreign" food quite happily. Milk in Indonesia may be unavailable outside big cities. Powdered milk may be the answer; breast feeding for babies even better.

Upper respiratory infections such as colds, catarrh and middle ear infections are common – antibiotics could be carried against the possibility. **Outer ear infections** after swimming are also common – antibiotic ear drops will help. The treatment of **diarrhoea** is the same as for adults except that it should start earlier and be continued with more persistence. Children get dehydrated very quickly in the tropics and can become drowsy and uncooperative unless cajoled to drink water or juice plus salts. Oral rehydration has been a lifesaving technique in children.

Emergencies

Babies and small children deteriorate very rapidly when ill. A travel insurance policy which has an air ambulance provision is strongly recommended. When planning a route, try to stay within 24 hrs' travel of a hospital with good care and facilities. Many expatriats fly to Singapore for medical care, which has the best doctors and facilities in the region.

Sunburn

NEVER allow your child to be exposed to the harsh tropical sun without protection. A child can burn in a matter of minutes. Loose cotton-clothing, with long sleeves and legs and a sun-hat are best. High-factor sun-protection cream is essential.

CHECKLIST

Baby wipes
Child paracetamol
Disinfectant
First aid kit
Flannel
Immersion element for boiling water
Kalvol and/or *Snuffle Babe* or equivalent for colds
Instant food for under-one-year-olds
Mug/bottle/bowl/spoons
Nappy cleanse, double-strength
ORS/ORT (Oral Rehydration Salts or Therapy) such as *Dioralyte*, widely available in the countries covered here, and the most effective way to alleviate diarrhoea (it is not a cure)
Portable baby chair, to hook onto tables; this is not essential but can be very useful
Sarung or backpack for carrying child (and/or lightweight collapsible buggy)
Sterilizing tablets (and an old baby-wipes container for sterilising bottles, teats, utensils)
Cream for nappy rash and other skin complaints such as *Sudocreme*
Sunblock, factor 15 or higher
Sunhat
Terry's (cloth) nappies, liners, pins and plastic pants
Thermometer
Zip-lock bags for carrying snacks, powdered food, wet flannel

FURTHER INFORMATION

Pentes, Tina and Truelove, Adrienne (1984) *Travelling with children to Indonesia and South-East Asia*, Hale & Iremonger: Sydney. Wheeler, Maureen *Travel with children*, Lonely Planet: Hawthorne, Australia.

Fares and timetables

To/From	Balikpapan	Banda Aceh	Banjarmasin	Batam	Biak	Denpasar	Jakarta	Jayapura	Manado	Medan	Padang	Palembang	Pekanbaru	Surabaya
Garuda domestic passenger tariff for economy class*														
Balikpapan			63	241		221	221			376				
Banda Aceh	447					419	315							
Banjarmasin		409					172							
Batam		194	230			278	163							
Biak		685		562		376	478	91						
Denpasar							156							
Jayapura		739		623		430	529							
Malang	168													
Manado		599		415		266	389							
Medan	376	81	349		638	326	240	752	504					
Padang	330		289		575	303	172	631	440					
Palembang	245		200		524	241	91	565	393					
Pekanbaru			315		619		174	767	459					
Pontianak							139							
Semarang		359		230			78			314	242	160	242	
Solo		372		228			89			295	241	156	252	
Surabaya		375		263	429	63	128	522	295	321	267	189	288	
Ujang P'dang		477		318	289	109	234	378	171	443	361	288	451	146
Yogyakarta		365		227	424	83	89	500		288	233	149	246	

*Economy class, one way, quoted in US$ for purchase outside Indonesia

Domestic passenger tariff – Merpati Nusantara – Pioneer (Perintis) flights

ROUTE	US$
Amahai to:	
Langgur	154
Ambon to:	
Labuha	97
Manggole	97
Ternate	123
Saumlaki	145
Bandaneira	61
Bula	76
Amahai	31
Taliabu	125
Sanana	81
Namlea	37
Langgur	138
Atambua to:	
Kalabahi/Alor	32
Bade to:	
Kepi	25
Kupang	91
Ende	31
Bajawa to:	
Ruteng	21
Balikpapan to:	
Kotabangun	39
Berau	111
Palu	88
Gorontalo	157
Tanjung Warukin	53
Tarakan	120
Samarinda	31
Banda Aceh to:	
Meulaboh	47
Tapaktuan	67
Lhokseumawe	53
Banda Neira to:	
Langgur	93
Bandar Lampung to:	
Tanjung Pandan	107
Jakarta	54
Bandung to:	
Jakarta	38
Batam	206
Banjarmasin to:	
Pangkalanbun	95
Palangkaraya	48
Gorontalo	220
Muaratewe	75
Tanjung Warukin	45
Sampit	61
Kotabaru	47
Trakan	181
Batam to:	
Dumai	70
Pangkal Pinang	123
Jambi	99
Rengat	72
Tanjung Pandan	140

	US$
Singkep	54
Berau to:	
Samarinda	79
Tarakan	39
Tanjung Selor	19
Biak to:	
Serui	24
Sarmi	83
Manokwari	64
Kokonau	136
Numfoor	35
Bintuni	85
Enarotali	102
Kaimana	109
Nabire	68
Ransiki	60
Bima to:	
Sumbawa	39
Ende	77
Tambulaka	35
Bajawa	72
Labuhanbajo	36
Kupang	157
Ruteng	64
Waingapu	58
Denpasar	106
Maumere	94
Bintuni to:	
Ransiki	30
Bokondini to:	
Jayapura	66
Buol to:	
Palu	100
Toli-Toli	22
Buton to:	
Kendari	43
Raha/Muna	26
Ujung Pandang	111
Dabo/Singkep to:	
Pangkal Pinang	70
Denpasar to:	
Sumbawa	68
Mataram	30
Ende	177
Ruteng	161
Tambulaka	134
Maumere	163
Waingapu	145
Solo	94
Malang	70
Dili to:	
Oecusi	41
Baucau	28
Maliana	26
Atambua	30
Suai	49
Dumai to:	
Sungai Pakning	24

	US$
Enarotali to:	
Kokonau	24
Ende to:	
Maumere	22
Kupang	72
Ruteng	42
Waingapu	55
Sawu	51
Fakfak to:	
Manokwari	70
Teminabuan	38
Sorong	68
Kaimana	53
Galela to:	
Manado	67
Kao	31
Morotai	21
Ternate	38
Gebe to:	
Ternate	71
Gorontalo to:	
Luwuk	47
Palu	83
Jakarta to:	
Cilacap	85
Cirebon	60
Rengat	177
Ketapang	170
Tarakan	340
Malang	144
Tanjung Pinang	177
Jambi to:	
Rengat	56
Sungai Penuh	70
Dabo/Singkep	40
Tanjung Pinang	96
Jayapura to:	
Sarmi	78
Wamena	59
Nabire	125
Kaimana to:	
Sorong	101
Ransiki	58
Wasior	34
Manokwari	83
Nabire	56
Kao to:	
Ternate	24
Manado	70
Kendari to:	
Luwuk	97
Namlea	147
Raha	38
Ketapang to:	
Pangkalanbun	58
Semarang	177
Kuala Pembuang to:	
Pangkalanbun	42

Kupang to:

Rote	24
Waingapu	102
Tambulaka	135
Alor	65
Ruteng	109
Lewoleba	64
Maumere	59
Sawu	56
Atambua	58
Oecusi	42

Labuha to:

Sanana	64

Labuhanbajo to:

Ruteng	29

Langgur to:

Dobo/Benjina	45
Saumlaki	86

Larantuka to:

Lewoleba	23
Maumere	31
Ruteng	81
Ende	45
Kupang	61

Luwuk to:

Manado	97
Palu	91
Soroako	63
Poso	81
Taliabu	57
Mangole	87

Manado to:

Taliabu	99
Tahuna/Naha	67
Gorontalo	70
Ternate	75
Poso	171
Melangguane	93

Mangole to:

Labuha	71
Sanana	21
Namlea	67
Taliabu	40
Manado	110

Manokwari to:

Numfoor	29
Sorong	97
Bintuni	38

Masamba to:

Soroako	34

Mataram to:

Malang	93
Bima	78
Sumbawa	40
Lunyuk	41

Maumere to:

Ujung Pandang	113
Ruteng	51

Medan to:

Lhokseumawe	73
Gunung Sitoli	76
Singkep	219

Sinabang	79
Tapaktuan	52
Tanjung Pinang	177
Rengat	144
Jambi	159
Meulaboh	77
Sabang	120
Dumai	93

Merauke to:

Tanah Merah	74
Kamur	86
Wamena	106
Bade	47
Aboge	87
Mindiptanah	79
Kepi	49

Meulaboh to:

Tapaktuan	40

Mindiptanah to:

Tanah Merah	18

Moanamani to:

Waghete	36

Nabire to:

Waghete	34
Serui	51
Moanamani	33
Enarotali	34
Kokonau	49

Naha/Tahuna to:

Melanggoane	40

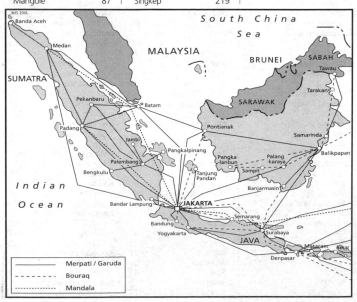

——————	Merpati / Garuda
- - - - - - -	Bouraq
··········	Mandala

Namlea to:
Luwuk 148
Taliabu 79
Padang to:
Sungai Penuh 56
Pekanbaru to:
Dumai 39
Tanjung Pinang 82
Singkep 131
Jambi 90
Sungai Pakning 39
Tanjung Balai 65
Rengat 33
Palangkaraya to:
Buntok 35
Tumbangsamba 38
Muara Tewe 48
Pangkalanbun 70
Sampit 35
Palembang to:
Rengat 92
Dabo/singkep 76
Dumai 120
Tanjung Pandan 82
Ranau 62
Tanjung Pinang 103
Lubuk Linggau 56
Palu to:
Toli-Toli 82
Poso 38

Pangkalanbun to:
Sampit 40
Tanjung Pinang 91
Tanjung Pandan 38
Pomala to:
Kendari 30
Pontianak to:
Tumbangsamba 38
Ketapang 53
Nangapino 93
Buntok 38
Sintang 63
Putusibau 113
Pangkalanbun 105
Singkawang 40
Semarang 163
Rote to:
Sawu 40
Waingapu 96
Samarinda to:
Tanjung Selor 93
Tarakan 113
Kotabangun 26
Sampit to:
Tumbangsamba 37
Kuala Pembuang 31
Sawu to:
Waingapu 47
Semarang to:
Tarakan 266
Pangkalanbun 129

Serui to:
Sarmi 77
Sibolga to:
Gunung Sitoli 40
Sinabang to:
Meulaboh 53
Singkep to:
Jakarta 188
Tanjung Pandan 104
Rengat 70
Tanjung Balai 58
Dumai 114
Sintang to:
Putusibau 54
Soroako to:
Tanatoraja 49
Poso 51
Sorong to:
Kambuaya 38
Teminabuan 33
Ternate 138
Sumbawa to:
Lunyuk 20
Surabaya to:
Waingapu 172
Maumere 209
Sampit 148
Tambolaka 163
Palangkaraya 145
Tarakan 205

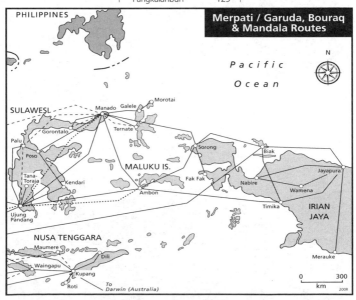

Merpati / Garuda, Bouraq & Mandala Routes

Taliabu to:

Ternate	128

Tana Toraja to:

Masamba	27
Mamuju	29

Tanjung Pinang to:

Tanjung Balai	38
Rengat	74
Batam	26
Singkep	61

Tanjung Santan to:

Samarinda	20
Tarakan	103

Tapak Tuan to:

Sinabang	38

Tarakan to:

Malinau	32

Tanjungselor	20
Longbawan	53
Toli-Toli	121
Nunukan	38

Ternate to:

Sanana	96
Labuha	45
Morotai	48
Mangole	97

Ujung Pandang to:

Gorontalo	103
Masamba	81
Mangole	206
Raha	91
Soroako	99
Luwuk	168
Tana Toraja	62

Pomala	86
Mamuju	65
Bima	99
Poso	122

Waingapu to:

Mataram	113
Tambulaka	38

Wamena to:

Ewer	53
Timika	70

Yogyakarta to:

Tarakan	305

US$ prices quoted for flights purchased outside Indonesia (one way). Note that although locally quoted rates have recently increased it is still significantly cheaper – about one third – to purchase tickets in rupiah within Indonesia.

To/From	Ambon	Balikpapan	Bandar L'pung	Bandung	Banjarmasin	Batam	Bengkulu	Biak	Denpasar	Dili
Ambon						447				
Balikpapan					63				153	
Banda Aceh										
Bandung									152	
Batam										
Bengkulu				114						
Biak	160									
Denpasar	232									
Dili									196	
Dumai										
Jambi				135						
Jayapura	244									
Kendari		173								
Kupang									159	52
Malang		168			109					
Manado					232					
Mataram						308				
Medan				230						
Merauke										
Padang				191		85				
Palangkaraya		67								
Pangkal Pinang				116						
Palembang			48	101			57			
Palu				122						
Pekanbaru										
Pontianak										
Semarang		166	128	59	112				104	
Solo				60						
Sorong	82							102	308	
Surabaya	289			102	95					260
Tanjung Pandan				109						
Timika								68	400	
Ujung Pandang	160									
Yogyakarta		188		53	134					

*one way, quoted in US$ for purchase outside Indonesia

Domestic passenger tariffs for economy class combination Garuda and Merpati flights

To/From	Jakarta	Jayapura	Manado	Mataram	Medan	Palembang	Pekanbaru	Pontianak	Surabaya	Ujung Pandang
Ambon	323									
Balikpapan			173	376	376		320	151	154	108
Banda Aceh				532						
Bandung							195			
Batam					126	83	59	115		
Bengkulu	108									
Biak			229							
Denpasar										
Dili	352									
Dumai	161									
Jambi	119									
Jayapura						38				
Kendari	298								200	65
Kupang	314								213	130
Malang										
Manado		291					335			
Mataram	178				455					
Medan										
Merauke	631	121		532						
Padang					97	101	38			
Palangkaraya	164									
Pangkal Pinang	91						37	100		
Palembang					180					
Palu	334		118						217	100
Pekanbaru				335	89					
Pontianak					241	241				230
Semarang									46	
Solo			306						38	181
Sorong	383	192	134						321	186
Surabaya		200	68	68						
Tanjung Pandan	37									
Timika	536	83							457	311
Ujung Pandang				92						
Yogyakarta			306						42	175

*One way, quoted in US$ for purchase outside Indonesia

Selected train timetables: Java

Trains to/from Jakarta
Daily night trains:

Bima:	*Jakarta (Kota) – Solo – Surabaya (Gubeng)*
Mutiara Utara:	*Jakarta (Kota) – Semarang (Tawang) –*
	Surabaya (Pasar Turi)
Gaya Baru Malam Utara:	*Jakarta (Pasar Senen) – Solo – Surabaya (Kota)*
Gaya Baru Malam Selatan:	*Jakarta (Gambir) – Solo – Surabaya (Kota)*
Bangun Karta:	*Jakarta (Gambir) – Semarang (Tawang) – Jombang*
Matamarja:	*Jakarta (Gambir) – Semarang (Tawang) – Malang*
Senja Utama/Semarang:	*Jakarta (Pasar Senen) – Semarang (Tawang)*

Daily day trains:

Cepat Siang:	*Jakarta (Pasar Senen) – Semarang (Tawang)*

Daily night trains:

Senja Utama/Solo:	*Jakarta (Gambir) – Cirebon – Yogya – Solo*

Daily day trains:

Fajar Utama:	*Jakarta (Gambir) – Purwokerto – Yogya*
Sawunggalih:	*Jakarta (Pasar Senen) – Purwokerto – Kutoarjo*
Cepat Solo:	*Jakarta (Senen/Tanjung Priok) – Yogya – Solo*
Cirebon Express:	*Jakarta (Kota) – Cirebon*
Gunung Jati:	*Jakarta (Kota) – Cirebon*
Tegal Arum:	*Jakarta (Kota) – Cirebon – Tegal*
Parahyangan (5 daily):	*Jakarta (Kota) – Bandung*
Parahyangan (3 daily):	*Jakarta (Gambir) – Bandung*

Trains to/from Surabaya
Day trains:

Argopuro:	*Surabaya (Kota) – Banyuwangi*
Mutiara Timur Daylight:	*Surabaya (Kota) – Banyuwangi*
Penataran:	*Surabaya (Kota) – Malang – Blitar*
Express Siang:	*Surabaya (Kota) – Solo – Bandung*
Tumapel:	*Surabaya (Kota) – Malang*
Dhoho:	*Surabaya (Kota) – Kertosono – Blitar*
Tumapel Utama:	*Surabaya (Kota) – Blitar*
Purboyo:	*Surabaya (Kota) – Purwokerto*

Night trains:

Mutiara Timur Night:	*Surabaya (Kota) – Banyuwangi*
Mutiara Selatan:	*Surabaya (Kota) – Solo – Bandung*

Selected train fares: Java

JAKARTA-CIREBON-SURABAYA

Train	Route	Arr	Dep	Fare in Rupiah			
				Spec.	Exc.A	Exc. B	Business
BIMA	Jakarta (Kota):		1555				
	Purwokerto	2126	1600	77,000	51,000	39,000	31,000
	Yogyakarta	0008		98,000	58,000	44,000	36,000
	Solo	0118		94,000	58,000	44,000	36,000
	Madiun (Gobeng)	0251		94,000	58,000	44,000	36,000
	Surabaya (Gobeng)	0515		94,000	58,000	44,000	36,000
MUTIARA UTARA	Jakarta (Kota):		1625				
	Cirebon	2012	2020	77,000	51,000	39,000	31,000
	Tegal			77,000	51,000	39,000	31,000
	Pekalongan			77,000	51,000	39,000	31,000
	Semarang	0014	0024	77,000	51,000	39,000	31,000
	Cepu	0332	0335	94,000	58,000	44,000	36,000
	Surabaya (Pasar Turi)	0520		94,000	58,000	44,000	36,000

JAKARTA-YOGYAKARTA-SOLO

Train	Route	Arr	Dep	Fare in Rupiah			
				Spec.	Exc.A	Exc. B	Business
SENJA UTAMA SOLO	Jakarta (Gambir):		1835				
	Purwokerto	0039	0050	-	40,000	28,000	18,000
	Yogyakarta	0405	0413	-	44,000	33,000	21,000
	Solo	0520		-	46,000	35,000	24,000
SENJA UTAMA SEMARANG	Jakarta (Pasar Senen):		1945				
	Cirebon	2256	2305	-	40,000	28,000	18,000
	Tegal	0025	0030	-	40,000	28,000	18,000
	Pekalongan	0124	0127	-	40,000	28,000	18,000
	Semarang (Tawang)	0311		-	40,000	28,000	18,000

Selected bus fares (Rp)*

Route		Distance (km)	Fares (RS = reclining seat)		
			Economy	A/c	A/c + RS + Toilet
SUMATRA					
Medan to	Banda Aceh	829	13,250	22,475	35,725
	Bukittinggi	736	11,675	19,800	31,475
	Bakauheni	1,917	30,650	52,000	82,650
	Jambi	1,701	27,200	46,150	73,350
	Padang	869	13,900	23,600	37,450
	Pekanbaru	783	12,550	21,250	33,750
	Palembang	1,614	25,800	43,775	69,600
	Takengon	492	7,850	13,350	21,200
Padang to	Bengkulu	820	13,100	22,250	35,350
	Jambi	775	12,400	21,050	33,400
	Pekanbaru	308	4,950	8,350	13,300
	Palembang	1,092	17,450	29,650	47,100
	Sungai Penuh	276	4,400	7,500	11,900
JAVA-SUMATRA					
Jakarta to	Bengkulu	897	14,350	24,350	38,700
	Bandar Lampung	214	3,400	5,800	9,250
	Bukittinggi	1,514	24,200	41,100	65,300
	Banda Aceh	2,851	45,600	77,350	122,950
	Jambi	1,054	16,850	28,600	45,450
	Medan	2,244	35,900	60,900	96,750
	Palembang	774	12,400	21,000	33,400
	Pekanbaru	1,441	23,050	40,000	62,150
	Padang	1,507	24,100	40,900	65,000
JAVA-BALI					
Jakarta to	Anyer	116	1,850	3,150	5,000
	Bogor (via Jalan Tol)	47	750	1,300	2,050
	Bandung (via Jalan Tol)	147	2,800	4,700	7,500
	Bandung (via Sukabumi)	191	3,050	5,200	8,250
	Cirebon	255	4,100	6,900	11,000
	Cilacap	468	7,500	12,700	20,200
	Denpasar	1,432	22,900	38,850	61,750
	Jepara	542	8,650	14,700	23,350

Route		Distance (km)	Fares (RS = reclining seat)		
			Economy	A/c	A/c + RS + Toilet
	Merak	116	1,850	3,150	5,000
	Surabaya	845	13,500	22,950	36,450
	Solo	554	8,850	15,050	23,900
	Tasikmalaya	273	4,350	7,400	11,750
	Yogyakarta (via Semarang)	660	10,550	17,900	28,450
	Yogyakarta	635	10,150	17,250	27,400
Bandung to	Cilacap	390	6,250	10,600	16,000
	Denpasar	1,268	20,300	34,400	54,700
	Semarang	395	6,300	10,700	17,050
	Solo	626	10,000	17,000	27,000
	Surabaya	691	11,050	18,750	29,800
	Tegal	204	3,250	5,550	8,750
	Yogyakarta	562	8,975	15,250	24,250
Yogyakarta to	Banyuwangi	779	12,450	21,150	33,600
	Denpasar	789	12,600	21,400	34,000
	Malang	388	6,200	10,550	16,750
	Mataram	876	14,200	23,950	38,000
	Solo	74	1,200	2,000	3,200
	Surabaya	341	5,450	9,250	14,700
	Tawangmangu	119	1,900	3,250	5,150
Surabaya to	Magelang	386	6,175	10,450	16,650
	Semarang	378	6,050	10,250	16,275
KALIMANTAN					
Banjarmasin to	Samarinda	620	13,950	20,850	30,750
SULAWESI					
Manado to	Palu	1,033	24,275	35,750	52,275
Ujung Pandang to	Kendari	355	8,350	12,300	17,950
	Palu	966	22,700	33,450	48,900

* 1995 prices quoted. **NB** Fares vary considerably according to age and type of bus, journey time, and facilities. See page 872 for more background information on bus travel.
 Note 1: bus fares vary a great deal depending on level of service (a/c, reclining seats, express etc), the size of the vehicle (coach or minibus), the number of seats, the time of departure, the age of the vehicle, and between bus companies (which is related to their reputation for safety and timeliness). The fares given in this table should be viewed as only approximate rates.

Pelni weekly sailing schedule

Day of arrival/ departure	Port	Time of arrival & departure	Day of arrival/ departure	Port	Time of arrival & departure
KERINCI			Sun	Ambon	1500-1900
Sun	Ambon	1000-1300	Mon	Bau Bau	1400-1700
Mon	Bitung	0800-1200	Tues	Ujung Pandang	0600-1000
Mon	Ternate	2100-2400	Wed	Surabaya	0800-1100
Tues	Ambon	1600-1900	Thur	Tanjung Priok	0800-1500
Wed	Bau Bau	1400-1700	Fri	Muntok	0600-0800
Thur	Ujung Pandang	0600-1000	Fri	Kijang	1900-2200
Fri	Surabaya	0800-1100	Sat	Dumai	1200-1600
Sat	Tanjung Priok	0800-1300	**UMSINI**		
Mon	Belawan	0900-1300	Sun	Kwandang	0400-0600
Wed	Tunjung Priok	0900-1700	Sun	Pantoloan	2200-2400
Thur	Surabaya	1400-1800	Mon	Balikpapan	1000-1300
Fri	Ujung Pandang	1800-2100	Tues	Ujung Pandang	0500-0900
Sat	Bau Bau	1000-1300	Wed	Surabaya	0700-1100
KAMBUNA			Thur	Tanjung Priok	0800-1500
Mon	Belawan	0900-1300	Fri	Muntok	0600-0800
Wed	Tanjung Priok	0900-1700	Fri	Kijang	1900-2200
Thur	Surabaya	1400-1800	Sat	Dumai	1200-1600
Fri	Ujung Pandang	1800-2200	Sun	Kijang	0600-0900
Sat	Balikpapan	1500-1900	Sun	Muntok	2000-2100
Sun	Pantoloan	0500-0800	Mon	Tanjung Priok	1300-1900
Sun	Toli Toli	1600-1800	Tues	Surabaya	1600-1900
Mon	Bitung	1200-1700	Wed	Ujung Pandang	1900-2200
Tues	Toli Toli	1000-1200	Thur	Balikpapan	1400-1800
Tues	Pantoloan	2000-2300	Fri	Pantoloan	0400-0700
Wed	Balikpapan	1000-1300	Fri	Kwandang	2300-0100
Thur	Ujung Pandang	0600-1000	Sat	Bitung	1100-1800
Fri	Surabaya	0800-1100	**TIDAR**		
Sat	Tanjung Priok	0800-1300	Sun	Balikpapan	1000-1300
RINJANI			Mon	Surabaya	1300-1700
Sun	Kijang	0600-0900	Tues	Pare Pare	1900-2200
Sun	Muntok	2000-2100	Wed	Pantoloan	1200-1500
Mon	Tanjung Priok	1300-1900	Thur	Nunukan	0900-1200
Tues	Surabaya	1600-1900	Thur	Tarakan	1700-2000
Wed	Ujung Pandang	1900-2100	Fri	Balikpapan	1600-1900
Thur	Bau Bau	1100-1300	Sat	Pare Pare	0800-1100
Fri	Ambon	1000-1200	Sun	Surabaya	1100-1600
Fri	Banda	1900-2100	Mon	Ujung Pandang	1600-2000
Sat	Tual	0700-0900	Tues	Balikpapan	1200-1500
Sat	Fak Fak	1800-2100	Wed	Tarakan	1200-1600
Sun	Banda	0600-0800	Thur	Pantoloan	0700-1000

Day of arrival/departure	Port	Time of arrival & departure
Fri	Ujung Pandang	0300-0700
Sat	Surabaya	0500-0800
CIREMAI		
Sun	Ujung Pandang	1300-1700
Mon	at sea	
Tues	Tanjung Priok	0600-1500
Wed	at sea	
Thur	Ujung Pandang	0800-1500
Fri	Bau Bau	0400-0700
Fri	Banggai	1900-2100
Sat	Bitung	0800-1200
Sat	Ternate	2100-2300
Sun	Sorong	1500-1900
Mon	Manokwari	0700-0900
Mon	Biak	1600-1800
Tues	Jayapura	1000-1600
Wed	Biak	0700-1000
Wed	Manokwari	1700-1900
Thur	Sorong	0600-1000
Fri	Ternate	0200-0700

Day of arrival/departure	Port	Time of arrival & departure
Fri	Bitung	1400-1800
Sat	Banggai	0500-0700
Sat	Bau Bau	2200-2400
DOBONSOLO		
Sun	Sorong	1500-1900
Mon	Manokwari	0700-0900
Mon	Biak	1600-1800
Tues	Jayapura	1000-1600
Wed	Biak	0700-1000
Wed	Manokwari	1700-1900
Thur	Sorong	0600-1100
Fri	Ambon	0400-0900
Sat	Dili	0200-0500
Sat	Kupang	1400-1600
Sun	Benoa (Bali)	1700-1900
Mon	Surabaya	1000-1300
Tues	Tunjung Priok	0900-1500
Wed	Surabaya	1100-1500
Thur	Benoa (Bali)	0700-0900
Fri	Kupang	1100-1300

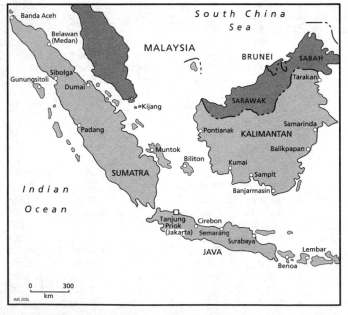

Day of arrival/ departure	Port	Time of arrival & departure
Fri	Dili	2200-2400
Sat	Ambon	1800-2200
BINAIYA		
Sun	Lembar	1300-1400
Mon	Surabaya	0900-1400
Tues	Benoa	0900-1100
Tues	Lembar	1500-1600
Wed	Bima	0700-0900
Wed	Labuanbajo	1500-1700
Wed	Waingapu	2300-2400
Thur	Ende	0700-0900
Thur	Kupang	1900-2100
Fri	Kalabahi	0600-0700
Fri	Dili	1400-1500
Sat	Maumere	0900-1100
Sat	Bone Rate	1800-1900
Sun	Ujung Pandang	1000-1300
Mon	Balikpapan	1000-1300
Tues	Ujung Pandang	1000-1300
Wed	Bone Rate	0400-0500

Day of arrival/ departure	Port	Time of arrival & departure
Wed	Maumere	1300-1500
Thur	Dili	0800-1000
Thur	Kalabahi	1700-1800
Fri	Kupang	0500-0800
Fri	Ende	1800-2000
Sat	Waingapu	0300-0500
Sat	Labuanbajo	1200-1400
Sat	Bima	2000-2200
LAWIT		
Sun	Semarang	0500-0900
Mon	Pontianak	1800-2000
Tues	Tanjung Pandan	1200-1400
Wed	Tanjung Priok	0600-1100
Thur	Enggano	(FAC)
Fri	Padang	0800-1300
Sat	Gunung Sitoli	0400-0900
Sat	Sibolga	1500-1700
Sun	Padang	0800-1100
Mon	Enggano	(FAC)
Tues	Tanjung Priok	0700-1300

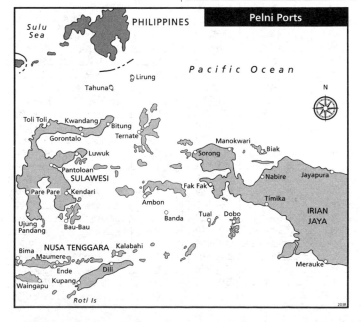

Day of arrival/ departure	Port	Time of arrival & departure
Wed	Tanjung Pandan	0500-0700
Wed	Pontianak	2200-2400
Thur	at sea	
Fri	Semarang	0800-1100
Sat	Kumai	0800-1100
	SIRIMAU	
Sun	Tanjung Pandan	1400-1600
Mon	Pontianak	0900-1100
Tues	Cirebon	1800-2300
Wed	at sea	
Thur	Banjarmasin	0900-1300
Fri	Ujung Pandang	1400-1700
Sat	Lembar	1400-1700
Sun	Ujung Pandang	1300-1600
Mon	Banjarmasin	1800-2200
Tues	at sea	
Wed	Cirebon	0400-0900
Thur	Pontianak	1700-1900
Fri	Tanjung Pandan	1100-1300
Sat	Panjang	0600-0800
Sat	Tanjung Priok	1700-2200
	TATAMAILAU (circuit 'A')	
Sun	Tual	(0300-)
Mon	Timika	(FAC)
Tues	Merauke	*
Wed	Timika	*
Thur	Dobo	*
Thur	Tual	-2000
Fri	Saumlaki	0700-0800
Sat	Kisar	0000-0100
Sat	Dili	1000-1300
Sun	Larantuka	0000-0300
Sun	Labuanbajo	1900-2100
Mon	Badas	0900-1100
Tues	Banyuwangi	0400-1300
Tues	Banoa (Bali)	2000-2200
Wed	Badas	0900-1100
Wed	Labuanpajo	2200-2400
Thur	Larantuka	1500-1700
Fri	Dili	0500-0800
Fri	Kisar	1500-1600
Sat	Saumlaki	1000-1200

Day of arrival/ departure	Port	Time of arrival & departure
	TATAMAILAU (circuit 'B')	
Sun	Tual	0400-
Sun	Dobo	*
Mon	Timika	*
Tues	Agats	(FAC)
Wed	Merauke	*
Thur	Timika	(FAC)
Fri	Tual	-1000
Fri	Kaimana	2000-2200
Sat	Fak Fak	0900-1100
Sat	Sorong	2200-2400
Sun	Manokwari	1700-1900
Mon	Nabire	0700-0900
Mon	Serui	1600-1800
Tues	Jayapura	1500-2300
Wed	Serui	1800-2000
Thur	Nabire	0500-0700
Thur	Manokwari	1800-2000
Fri	Sorong	1000-1600
Sat	Fak Fak	0400-0700
Sat	Kaimana	1600-1800
	TILONGKABILA	
Sun	Ujung Pandang	1400-1600
Mon	Labuanbajo	0800-1000
Mon	Bima	1600-1700
Tues	Benoa	0800-1000
Tues	Banyuwangi	1600-
Wed	Benoa	0800-1300
Thur	Bima	0400-0700
Thur	Labuanbajo	1300-1500
Fri	Ujung Pandang	0600-0900
Sat	Bau Bau	0400-0600
Sat	Raha	0900-1000
Sat	Kendari	1600-1800
Sun	Kolonedale	0600-0800
Sun	Luwuk	1700-1900
Mon	Gorontalo	0600-0800
Mon	Bitung	2100-2300
Tues	Siau	0600-0700
Tues	Tahuna	1200-1300
Tues	Lirung	2100-2300
Wed	Tahuna	0700-0900
Wed	Siau	1400-1500

Day of arrival/departure	Port	Time of arrival & departure
Wed	Bitung	2100-0700
Thur	Gorontalo	2000-2200
Fri	Luwuk	0700-0800
Fri	Kolonedale	1700-1800
Sat	Kendari	0900-1100
Sat	Raha	1600-1700
Sat	Bau Bau	2000-2200
LEUSER		
Sun	Samarinda	1200-1500
Mon	Pare Pare	1100-1400
Tues	Batulicin	0800-1000
Wed	Surabaya	0700-1000
Thur	Sampit	0800-1000
Fri	Semarang	0600-1300
Sat	Sampit	1000-1300
Sun	Surabaya	1100-1400
Mon	Batulicin	1300-1500
Tues	Pare Pare	0900-1200
Wed	Samarinda	0900-1100
Thur	Toli Toli	0800-1200
Fri	Tarakan	0600-0900
Fri	Nunukan	1600-1900
Sat	Toli Toli	1300-1600
KELIMUTU		
Sun	Surabaya	1200-1500
Sun	Bawean	2100-2200
Mon	Banjarmasin	1200-1400
Tues	Surabaya	0800-1300
Wed	Banjarmasin	0900-1100
Thur	Semarang	1000-1300
Fri	Banjarmasin	1300-1500
Sat	Surabaya	0900-1300
Sun	Banjarmasin	0900-1300
Mon	Surabaya	0700-1100
Tues	Banjarmasin	0700-1000
Wed	Semarang	0900-1300
Thur	Banjarmasin	1300-1500
Fri	Bawean	0500-0600
Fri	Surabaya	1300-1500
Sat	Sampit	1300-1500
BUKIT RAYA		
Sun	Surabaya	0700-1100
Mon	Kumai	1100-1300

Day of arrival/departure	Port	Time of arrival & departure
Tues	Karimun	0100-0200
Tues	Semarang	0800-1100
Wed	Pontianak	2000-2300
Thur	at sea	
Fri	Tanjung Priok	0600-1200
Sat	Pontianak	2000-2200
Sun	at sea	
Mon	Semarang	0500-0900
Mon	Karimun	1400-1500
Tues	Kumai	0600-0800
Wed	Surabaya	0800-1100
Wed	M Lembo	2100-2200
Thur	Batulicin	1200-1600
Fri	Samarinda	0900-1300
Sat	Batulicin	0600-0800
Sat	M Lembo	2100-2200
ARU		
Sun	Kuala Enok	0400-0700
Mon	Tanjung Priok	1200-1600
Tues	Kuala Enok	2100-2300
Wed	Batam	0800-1000
Wed	Kijang	1500-1800
Thur	Tarempa	0700-1000
Thur	Natuna	1800-2000
Fri	Pontianak	1400-1600
Sat	Bawean	2100-2300
Sun	Surabaya	0500-1000
Mon	Lembar	0500-0700
Mon	Banoa	(FAC)
Tues	Surabaya	0600-1100
Tues	Bawean	1700-2000
Wed	at sea	
Thur	Pontianak	0600-1000
Fri	Natuna	0500-0700
Fri	Tarempa	1600-1800
Sat	Kijang	0700-1000
Sat	Batam	1400-1800

NB Pelni ships operate on fortnightly circuits which can change from year to year. The above tables give the day of arrival/departure for 1996. Please confirm all

Selected Pelni fares (US$)*

	I	II	III	IV	Economy
Jakarta to:					
Ambon	348	261	192	161	122
Balikpapan	245	184	135	114	86
Banda	355	267	196	164	124
Banjarmasin	280	211	155	130	98
Batam	152	115	85	71	54
Bau-Bau	232	175	129	108	81
Belawan	189	142	105	88	67
Biak	521	392	288	241	182
Bitung	380	285	210	176	133
Cirebon	201	152	112	93	71
Denpasar	441	332	244	204	154
Dili	285	214	157	132	100
Dumai	161	121	89	75	57
Fak-Fak	398	299	220	184	139
Gn Sitoli	176	133	98	82	62
Jayapura	579	435	319	267	202
Kupang	253	190	140	117	89
Kwandang	336	253	186	156	119
Lembar	405	304	223	187	141
Manokwari	485	372	273	229	173
Muntok	73	55	41	35	27
Padang	132	99	73	62	47
Pantoloan	279	210	154	129	98
Pontianak	275	207	152	127	96
Samarinda	400	301	221	185	140
Semarang	203	152	112	94	71
Sibolga	196	147	108	91	69
Sorong	454	341	251	210	159
Surabaya	381	286	210	176	133
Ternate	428	321	236	198	149
Toli Toli	308	231	170	143	108
Tual	367	276	203	170	128
Ujung Pandang	350	263	193	162	123

* 1996 prices quoted. I-IV = 1st-4th class; Economy = deck class. Children travel at 75% of full fare; infants 1-2 years old travel at 25% of full fare; less than 1 year olds at 1-10%. Note that the less plush and comfortable vessels may charge a lower tariff. Thus, travelling first class between Tanjung Priok and Surabaya on the *Bukit Raya* costs US$297, on the *Awu* US$381, and on the *Kerinci* and *Rinjani*, just US$95. Note also that rupiah prices are considerably less than these quoted US$ prices.

Glossary

A

Abdi dalem
court servants of Java

Adat
custom or tradition

Alang
Torajan rice barn

Amitabha
the Buddha of the Past
(see Avalokitsvara)

Andesite
volcanic building stone

Andong
horse-drawn carriage

Angklung
traditional Javanese bamboo musical instrument
(see page 175)

Arhat
statues of former Buddhist monks

Atavaka
flesh-eating ogre

Avadana
Buddhist narrative, telling of the deeds of saintly souls

Avalokitsvara
also known as Amitabha and Lokeshvara, the name literally means "World Lord"; he is the compassionate male Bodhisattva, the saviour of Mahayana Buddhism and represents the central force of creation in the universe; usually portrayed with a lotus and water flask

B

Bahasa
language, as in Bahasa Malaysia and Bahasa Indonesia

Bajaj
three-wheeled motorized taxi

Banaspati
East Javan term for kala makara (see kala)

Banjar
Balinese village organization (see page 324)

Banua
Torajan house (see page 636)

Batik
a form of resist dyeing common in Malay areas (see page 101)

Becak
three-wheeled bicycle rickshaw

Bendi
2-wheeled, horse-drawn cart

Bhaga
cult altar of Flores (see page 736)

Bodhi
the tree under which the Buddha achieved enlightenment (*Ficus religiosa*)

Bodhisattva
a future Buddha. In Mahayana Buddhism, someone who has attained enlightenment, but who postpones nirvana in order to help others reach the same state

Brahma
the Creator, one of the gods of the Hindu trinity, usually represented with four faces, and often mounted on a hamsa

Brahmin
a Hindu priest

Budaya
cultural (as in Muzium Budaya)

Bupati
regent

C

Candi
sepulchral monument (see page 90)

Candi bentar
split gate, characteristic of Balinese pura (see page 795)

Cap
batik stamp (see page 103)

Chedi
from the Sanskrit *cetiya* (Pali, *caitya*) meaning memorial. Usually a religious monument (often bell-shaped) containing relics of the Buddha or other

holy remains. Used interchangeably with stupa

Cidomo
Lombok's two-wheeled, pony carts (see page 695)

Cukong
Chinese-owned corporations

Cultuurstelsel
the Dutch 'culture system' introduced in Java in the 19th century (see page 88)

Cunda
see Tara

Cutch
see Gambier

D

Dalang
wayang puppet master

Dayak/Dyak
collective term for the tribal peoples of Borneo

Delman
horse-drawn carriage

Dharma
the Buddhist law

Dipterocarp
family of trees (Dipterocarpaceae) characteristic of Southeast Asia's forests

Dokar
horse-drawn carriage

Durga
the female goddess who slays the demon Mahisa, from an Indian epic story

Dvarapala
temple door guardian (see page 272)

E

Epiphyte
plant which grows on another plant (but usually not parasitic)

F

Fahombe
stone-jumping of Nias Island (see page 477)

Feng shui
the Chinese art of geomancy

G

Gambier
also known as cutch, a dye derived from the bark of the bakau mangrove and used in leather tanning

Gamelan
Javanese and Balinese orchestra of percussion instruments (see page 101)

Ganesh
elephant-headed son of Siva

Garuda
mythical divine bird, with predatory beak and claws, and human body; the king of birds, enemy of naga and mount of Vishnu

Gautama
the historic Buddha

Golkar
ruling party in Indonesia (see page 58)

Gopura
crowned or covered gate; entrance to a religious area

Gunung
mountain

H

Hamsa
sacred goose, Brahma's mount; in Buddhism it represents the flight of the doctrine

Hariti
child-eating demon who is converted to Buddhism

Hinayana
'Lesser Vehicle', major Buddhist sect in Southeast Asia, usually termed Theravada Buddhism

I

Ikat
tie-dyeing method of patterning cloth (see page 408)

Indra
the Vedic god of the heavens, weather and war; usually mounted on a 3 headed elephant

Islam Waktu Telu
Islam of Lombok (see page 692)

J

Jaba
front court of Balinese temple (see page 319)

Jaba tengah
central court of Balinese temple (see page 320)

Janur
Balinese bamboo 'pennants' (see page 325)

Jataka(s)
birth stories of the Buddha, of which there are 547; the last ten are the most important

Jeroan
back court of Balinese temple (see page 320)

K

Kabupaten
regency, Indonesian unit of administration (see page 30)

Kala (makara)
literally, 'death' or 'black'; a demon ordered to consume itself; often sculpted over entranceways to act

as a door guardian, also known as kirtamukha

Kalanaga
same as the kalamakara but incorporating the mythical naga (serpent)

Kepala desa
village headman

Kerangas
from an Iban word meaning 'land on which rice will not grow'

Kerapan sapi
bull races of East Java and Madura (see page 291)

Keraton
see kraton

Kinaree
half-human, half-bird, usually depicted as a heavenly musician

Kirtamukha
see kala

Klotok
motorized gondolas of Banjarmasin

Kraton
Javanese royal palace (see page 92)

Kris
traditional Malay sword (see page 118)

Krishna
an incarnation of Vishnu

Kulkul
Balinese drum

Kuti
living quarters of Buddhist monks

L

Lapar biasa
'normal hunger' (see page 692)

Laterite
bright red tropical soil/stone sometimes used as a building material

Linga
phallic symbol and one of the forms of Siva. Embedded in a pedestal shaped to allow drainage of lustral water poured over it, the linga typically has a succession of cross sections: from square at the base through octagonal to round. These symbolize, in order, the trinity of Brahma, Vishnu and Siva

Lintel
a load-bearing stone spanning a doorway; often heavily carved

Lokeshvara
see Avalokitsvara

Lontar
multi-purpose palm tree (see page 779); the fronds were used for manuscript sheets (see page 416)

Losmen
guesthouse

M

Mahabharata
a Hindu epic text written about 2,000 years ago (see page 56)

Mahayana
'Greater Vehicle', major Buddhist sect

Mandi
Indonesian/Malay bathroom with water tub and dipper

Maitreya
the future Buddha

Makara
a mythological aquatic reptile, somewhat like a crocodile and sometimes with an elephant's trunk; often found, along with the kala, framing doorways

Mandala
a focus for meditation; a representation of the cosmos

Meru
name given to the tapered shrines of Bali (see page 412)

Meru
the mountain residence of the gods; the centre of the universe, the cosmic mountain

Moko
bronze dowry 'drums' of Nusa Tenggara (see page 753)

Mudra
symbolic gesture of the hands of the Buddha (see page 208)

N

Naga
benevolent mythical water serpent, enemy of Garuda

Naga makara
fusion of naga and makara

Nalagiri
the elephant let loose to attack the Buddha, who calmed him

Nandi/Nandin
bull, mount of Siva

Negara
kingdom and capital, from the Sanskrit

Negeri
also negri, state

Ngadhu
cult altar of Flores (see page 736)

Nirvana
'enlightenment', the Buddhist ideal

Nyi Loro Kidul

Goddess of the South Seas (see page 151)

O

Odalan
festival celebrating a Balinese temple's anniversary (see page 317)

Ojek
motorcycle 'taxi'

Ondel-ondel
paired human figures given to newly-weds in Java

P

Paddy/padi
unhulled rice

Padmasana
stone throne

Padu-raksa
ceremonial gate

Paliwijaya/Palawija
a second crop, planted after rice

Pamedal Agung
main gate

Pancasila
Sukarno's five guiding principles (see page 51)

Pantai
beach

Pasar
market, from the Arabic 'bazaar'

Pasisir
Javanese coastal trading states

Pelni
Indonesian state shipping line

Pemuda
literally 'youth', but historically refers to the Pemuda Movement against the Dutch (see page 48)

Pendopo
open-sided pavilion of Java

Perahu/prau
boat

Peranakan
'half caste', usually applied to part Chinese and part Malay people

Perintis
'pioneer' ships which ply minor routes between Indonesia's islands

PKI
Perserikatan Komunis di Indonesia, the Indonesian Communist Party

Pradaksina
pilgrims' clockwise circumambulation of a holy structure

Prajnaparamita
the goddess of transcendental wisdom

Prang
form of stupa built in the Khmer style, shaped rather like a corncob

Prasada
see prasat

Prasat
residence of a king or of the gods (sanctuary tower), from the Indian prasada

Pribumi
indigenous (as opposed to Chinese) businessmen

Priyayi
Javanese aristocracy

Pulau
island

Puputan
'fight to the death' (see page 317)

Pura
Balinese temple (see page 319)

Pusaka
heirloom

R

Raja/rajah
ruler

Raksasa
temple guardian statues

Ramayana
the Indian epic tale (see page 56)

Rumah adat
customary or traditional house

S

Sago
multi-purpose palm (see page 798)

Sal
the Indian sal tree (*Shorea robusta*), under which the historic Buddha was born

Saka
Hindu calendar used in Bali (see page 326)

Sakyamuni
the historic Buddha

Sawah
wet rice (see page 80)

Silat
or bersilat, traditional Malay martial art

Singha
mythical guardian lion

Siti Inggil
literally 'High Place' in a kraton; used for enthronements

Siva
one of the Hindu triumvirate, the god of destruction and rebirth

Songket
Malay textile interwoven with supplementary gold and silver yarn (see page 529)

Sravasti
the miracle at Sravasti when the Buddha subdues the heretics in front

of a mango tree
Sri Laksmi
the goddess of good fortune and Vishnu's wife
Stele
inscribed stone panel or slab
Stucco
plaster, often heavily moulded
Stupa
see chedi
Subak
Balinese irrigation society (see page 314)

Susuhunan
Hindu king or sultan

T

tamu
market
Tara
also known as Cunda; the four-armed consort of the Bodhisattva Avalokitsvara
Tau tau
Torajan effigies of the deceased (see page 639)
Tavatimsa
heaven of the 33 gods at the summit of Mount Meru
Theravada
'Way of the Elders'; major Buddhism sect also known as Hinayana Bud-

dhism ('Lesser Vehicle')
Tirta
holy water
Tongkonan
Torajan ancestral house (see page 636)
Totok
'full blooded'; usually applied to Chinese of pure blood
Transmigration
the Indonesian government sponsored resettlement of people from the Inner Islands to the Outer Islands (see page 427)

U

Ulama
Muslim priest
Ulu
jungle
Urna
the dot or curl on the Buddha's forehead, one of the distinctive physical marks of the Enlightened One
Usnisa
the Buddha's top knot or 'wisdom bump', one of the physical marks of the Enlightened One

V

Vishnu
the Protector, one of the

gods of the Hindu trinity, generally with four arms holding the disc, the conch shell, the ball and the club
VOC
the Dutch East India Company or Vereenigde Oost-Indische Compagnie

W

Wali
the nine Muslim saints of Java (see page 95)
Wallace's Line
division between the Asian and Australasian zoological realms (see page 690)
Waringin
banyan tree
Warung
foodstall or small restaurant
Wayang
traditional Malay shadow plays (see page 96)
Wayang Topeng
masked dance of Java (see page 99)
Wuku
Hindu-Javanese calendar, now primarily in use only in Bali (see page 326)

TEMPERATURE CONVERSION TABLE

°C	°F	°C	°F
1	34	26	79
2	36	27	81
3	38	28	82
4	39	29	84
5	41	30	86
6	43	31	88
7	45	32	90
8	46	33	92
9	48	34	93
10	50	35	95
11	52	36	97
12	54	37	99
13	56	38	100
14	57	39	102
15	59	40	104
16	61	41	106
17	63	42	108
18	64	43	109
19	66	44	111
20	68	45	113
21	70	46	115
22	72	47	117
23	74	48	118
24	75	49	120
25	77	50	122

The formula for converting °C to °F is:
$$°C \times 9 \div 5 + 32 = °F$$

WEIGHTS AND MEASURES

Metric

Weight
1 Kilogram (Kg) = 2.205 pounds
1 metric ton = 1.102 short tons

Length
1 millimetre (mm) = 0.03937 inch
1 metre = 3.281 feet
1 kilometre (km) = 0.621 mile

Area
1 heactare = 2.471 acres
1 square km = 0.386 sq mile

Capacity
1 litre = 0.220 imperial gallon
= 0.264 US gallon

Volume
1 cubic metre (m³) = 35.31 cubic feet
= 1.31 cubic yards

British and US

Weight
1 pound (lb) = 454 grams
1 short ton (2,000lbs) = 0.907 m ton
1 long ton (2,240lbs) = 1.016 m tons

Length
1 inch = 25.417 millimetres
1 foot (ft) = 0.305 metre
1 mile = 1.609 kilometres

Area
1 acre = 0.405 hectare
1 sq mile = 2.590 sq kilometre

Capacity
1 imperial gallon = 4.546 litres
1 US gallon = 3.785 litres

Volume
1 cubic foot (cu ft) = 0.028 m³
1 cubic yard (cu yd) = 0.765 m³

NB 5 imperial gallons are approximately equal to 6 US gallons

Tinted boxes

INTRODUCTION AND HINTS

Exchange rates (August 1996)	18
Tourism development guidelines	23
A tourism checklist	25

HORIZONS

The regions of Indonesia	30
Volcanoes	31
Indonesia's climate	36
Heat and lust: colonial impressions	37
Durian: king of fruits	38
Major pre-colonial powers	41
Sir Francis Drake in Indonesia	42
The expansion of Dutch influence and control	45
A stroll along Jalan history	49
Pancasila: Sukarno's five principles	51
The practice of Islam: living by the Prophet	52
Much ado about *adat*	55
The Ramayana and Mahabharata	56
Art forms	57
Rising hopes	60
In the nick of time	63
The politics of envy: the Chinese in Indonesia	67
Asian values	70
The Asian miracle: why it happened: the story according to the world bank	72
Total and percentage of the population defined as poor, 1979-1990, using the BPS poverty line	75
Indonesia fact file	77

JAVA

Sawah: wet rice cultivation in Java	80
The curse of the kris-maker	83
A summary of Javanese history 400-1870	85
The building sequence in Java (late 6th-late 15th century)	89
The Javanese candi	90
The Javanese kraton	92
The nine walis of Java	95
Making a wayang kulit puppet	96
A Batik primer	102
Jakarta highlights	107
The Chinese of Java and Jakarta	108
Jakarta's heroic monuments	115
The kris: martial and mystic masterpiece of the Malay world	118
The Javan Rhinoceros (*Rhinoceros Sondaicus*): the rarest mammal on Earth	143
The legend of Nyi Loro Kidul, the Queen of the South Seas	151
Bandung's Art Deco heritage	157
Bandung – factory visits	159
The angklung	162
Cirebon rock and cloud designs	175
The Hamengkubuwono Sultans of Yogyakarta (1749 -1996)	186
Diponegoro: prince and early freedom fighter	192
Courtship Javanese-style – the *lamaran*	196
Barobudur: what's in a name?	205
Mudras and the Buddha image	208
Prambanan as a holy water sanctuary	217
A short history of the Susuhunan of Surakarta	227
Out of Java: Homo erectus	229
The traditional Kudus house	254

The life-blood of the Indonesian male: the clove or 'kretek cigarette' 256
Raden Kartini 257
The Madiun affair 263
The magic saus of Gudang Garam 265
Dvarapala or temple guardians 272
The battle for Surabaya, 1945 280
Tambak fisheries and the perils of over-production 287
Kerapan Sapi (bull racing) 291
Traditional boats of Madura 292

BALI

Bali highlights 313
The gift of water: rice and water in Bali 314
The sign of the swastika 317
The banjar 324
Penjor and janur 325
The Balinese calendars: saka and wuku 326
Self-immolation and human sacrifice in a Dutch account of 1633 328
Dance performances on Bali 330
Tourism and culture in Bali 335
Getting around Bali by bemo 341
Bronze kettledrums of Vietnam 377
The 1979 festival of Eka Dasa Rudra at Pura Besakih 391
The Bali Aga: the original Balinese 406
Cloth as art: Ikat in Southeast Asia 408
The Balinese pagoda: the meru 412

SUMATRA

Transmigration 'a matter of life and death' 427
Sumatra: good buys 430
The Aceh War (1873-1878) 444
Buses down the west coast 450
Karo Batak architecture 452
Trekking in Gunung Leuser National Park: check list 457
The Bataks of North Sumatra 462
Hiking across the central highlands 468
Toba Batak architecture 470
The main temples at Padang Lawas 474
The earthquake-proof houses of Nias 477
Pencak silat: martial art of West Sumatra 483

Islam versus tradition: the Padri Wars (1803-1838) 486
Rafflesia arnoldi: the largest flower in the world 490
Places of interest around Batusangkar: the Minang Darek 492
Batam – Singapore's industrial zone and holiday playground 501
Business milestones 507
Black gold: Indonesia's oil industry 509
Small and hairy: the Sumatran rhinoceros 522
The Kubu: remnant hunter-gatherers of Sumatra 524
Cloths of gold and silver: kain songket 529
Bangka's tin mines 532
Caripaksa: sanctioned kidnapping 537
Ship cloths and tapis: textiles of Lampung 541

KALIMANTAN

River roads 544
20/20 vision: Kalimantan bushfires 545
The Iban hornbill festival 552
Piracy: the resurgence of an ancient scourge 553
Konfrontasi 554
The Palang – the stimulant that makes a vas diferens 555
Main Dayak groups in Kalimantan 556
Traditional Banjarese architecture – high ridged roofs 558
Skulls in the Longhouse: Heads you win 561
The tree of life 563
Tribal tattoos 565
The Hill Dayaks of Kalsel - a fragile culture 571
Sasirangan tie-dyes – from the shaman to the shop shelves 577
Balikpapan's streetnames – selamat jalan-jalan 583
Deforestation in Kalimantan – the chainsaw massacre 587
The tough life of a turtle 588
A ceramic inheritance 593
The longhouse – prime-site apartments with river view 596
The massacre at Long Nawang 597

Pontianak's red-light district –
forlorn hopes   602
Visiting longhouses: house rules   606
Entikong's fiscal advantages   608

SULAWESI

A Noah's ark: endemic animals of
Sulawesi   613
Billiards Indonesian style   614
The original bogeymen – the Bugis
of South Sulawesi   617
Bogeymen and antimacassars   619
The Pinisi schooner of Sulawesi   620
Buginese textiles of Sengkang   631
The buffalo: symbol of wealth
and power   634
Torajan mortuary effigies (tau tau)   639
Trekking around Rantepao   644
Torajan Ikat blankets   645
Lake Poso   659
Tangkoko Batu Angus National Park   678
The extraordinary maleo bird   684

WEST NUSA TENGGARA: LOMBOK AND SUMBAWA

Island hopping in Nusa Tenggara   687
Lombok highlights   688
Wallace's line   690
Islam Waktu Telu   692
Lombok's crafts   693
Mount Tambora and the year without
summer   722

EAST NUSA TENGGARA AND EAST TIMOR

Indonesia's living dinosaur:
the Komodo dragon   731
The textiles of Flores   735
To build in pairs: the Ngadhu
and Bhaga of Flores   736
The old Catholics of Larantuka   751
Lamalera's whaling   752
The Moko drum currency debâcle   753
The Sumbanese slave trade   756
Sumba's megalithic tombs   757
The ikat hinggi blankets of Sumba   758
Sumba death rites   760
Pasola: of worms and warriors   767

The massacre at Santa Cruz,
November 1991   783

MALUKU

Multi-purpose tree par excellence:
the sago palm   798
The baileo   810
The Nuaula: warriors and
house-builders   811
Descriptions of the cuscus   813
Butchery in the Bandas: the curse
of the spice trade   816

IRIAN JAYA

The bird of paradise: legless
bird of gold   837
Master craftsmen: the Asmat
of Irian Jaya   840
The Baliem Valley irrigation systems   849
Freeport Indonesia: the world's
richest mine   855

INFORMATION FOR TRAVELLERS

The Indonesian day   864
Hotel price guide   867
Restaurant price guide   868
Popular Indonesian dishes   869
Tempe: soybean cake   870
Jamu: herbal drink   871
Driving in Indonesia   875

ROUNDING UP

Water purification   904
Garuda domestic passenger tariff
for economy class   910
Domestic passenger tariff – Merpati
Nusantara – Pioneer (Perintis) flights   911
Domestic passenger tariffs for economy
class combination Garuda and Merpati
flights   915
Selected train timetables: Java   917
Selected train fares: Java   918
Selected bus fares (Rp)   919
Pelni weekly sailing schedule   921
Selected Pelni fares (Rp)   926

Illustrations

Bali distance chart	340
Bali pura	320
Bird of Paradise	838
Borobudur – 9th century ship	212
Borobudur plan	211
Borobudur reliefs	207
Buddha Image, The	210
Candi Jabung	297
Candi Sukuh	226
Candis on the Dieng Plateau	237
Chief's house and rice barn	487
Chinese bird motif	177
Cockerel motif	101
Dongson drum	376
Dvarapala from Candi Sewu	272
Early map of Bali	316
Fahome or 'stone-jumping' in Nias illustrated on a Bank of Indonesia 1,000Rp note	479
Garuda, Indonesia's national symbol	51
Gateway to Fort Victoria	801
Gedung Songo	240
Gudang Garam kretek cigarette logo	265
Gunung Api erupting	818
Iban hornbill	552
Javanese Candi	91
Karang sae	90
Karo Batak House end	452
Kidnapping	327
Lake Toba illustrated on a Bank of Indonesia 1,000Rp note	461
Legong costume	329
Locals bringing nutmeg to sell to Dutch factors	44
Lontar palm	780
Madura boats	292
Megalithic sarcophagi or *waruga* at Sawangan	677
Megalithic stone figures from the Bala, Besoa and Napu Valleys	666
Meru	412
Mudras	210
Nias ancestor figure	476
Nutmeg plant	829
Orang utan	549
Orang utan illustrated on a Bank of Indonesia 500Rp note	442
Pejeng moon	378
Prahu jaring – stern decoration	293
Pinisi schooner	620
Prambanan – Siva temple plan	218
Rangda	332
Royal procession, Ternate	826-827
Ship of the dead	559
Skull	561
Sumba blankets	759
Tau tau with articulated arms	639
Toba Batak cross section	471
Toraja House	637
The Budha Image	210
The famous *pinisi* schooner illustrated on a Bank of Indonesia 500Rp note	620
Traditional Boats of Madura	292
Traditional East Kalimantan house illustrated on a Bank of Indonesia 500Rp note	592
Warrior with dongson drum	526
Wayang gunungan	98
Wayang kresna	97
Wayang semar	97
Weekly tournament, Tuban	289
Yogya Kraton	189

Index

A

Abian Soan   410
accommodation   20
    Bali   339
    East Timor   787
    Flores   735
    See also individual town's local information
    Lombok   695
    Maluku   800
    Sumatra   430
Aceh Museum   444
acknowledgements   881
Adam Malik Museum, Jakarta   120
adat   55, 799
Adityavarman Museum   512
Afo clove tree   829
Agung Demak Mosque   249
Agung Gianyar Palace   385
Agung, Mount   390
AIDS   901
Aileu   790, 793
Ainaro   794
Air
    Bali   337
    discounts   19
    getting there   18, 861
    internal transport   20
    Lombok   694
    Maluku   800
    pass   19, 871
    Sumatra   429, 430
    within Indonesia   871
Air Manis   512
Air Sanih   420
Air Terjun Gigit   418
Air Terjun Gitgit   414
Airmadidi   676
Airport facilities
    Bali   338

Jakarta   862
Airport tax   338
Akima   850
Al Miraj   879
Al-Aqsa Mosque, Kudus   254
Al-Manar Mosque, Kudus   254
Alamada Hotsprings   496
Alas   719
Alas River   454
ALOR   753-755
aluk rambe matampu', the   638
Alun-alun   171
Alun-alun Lor   188
Amahai   813
Amahusu Beach   805
Ambarawa   249
Ambarawa Railway Museum   242
Ambarita   470
Ambeno Enclave   777
Ambon   801
Ambon's beaches   805
Ambulance
    See individual town's local information
Amed   410
Amlapura   405
Ampel Mosque   280
Ampenan   696
Ampera Bridge   526
Anakalang   766
Ancient Inscription Museum   116
Anda   450
angklung   101, 162
antiques   865
Anyer   140
Api, Gunung   820
Apo Kayan   596
archaeological museum, Blitar   267

Architecture
    Bali   318
    Dutch provincial   671
    East Java   261
    East Timor   794
    Indonesia   52
    Java   88
    Minangkabau   486
    Sasak   715
    Toraja   636
    tropical Art Deco   158
Area code
    See telephones
Armed Forces Day   879
army   64
Army Museum   490
Arosbaya   293
Arsip Nasional   113
Art
    Bali   318, 321
    Indonesia   52
    Irian Jaya   841
    Lombok   693
    Java   88
Art festivals
    See festivals
Asak   394
Asam Kumbang Crocodile Farm   435
Asia-Pacific Economic Cooperation   65
Asmat Art   840
Asta Tinggi   294
Atambua   778
Ataturo Island   790
Atavaka   212
Australian War Cemetery, The   805
Ay Island   821, 823
Ayer, Pulau   136

B

Ba'a 778
Bada Valley 666
Badmington 58
Badut, Candi, Malang 270
Bahari Museum, Jakarta 112
Bajaj 131, 875
Bajawa 740
Bajoe 630
Bakauheni 541
Bakungan 450
Balai Kota 177, 433, 535
Balai Kota Malang 269
Balai Seni Rupa 113
Bale Kembang 393
Balekambang 274
Balekambang swimming pool 233
BALI 310-423
  airport facilities 338
  banks 338
  before travelling 337
  best time to visit 337
  Botanical Gardens 414
  craft villages 371
  East 393
  emergency numbers 338
  ferries 337
  festivals 343
  getting there 337
  North coast 416
  road 337
  sea 337
  shopping 338
  shuttle bus 341
  South 349
  sports 342
  tipping 339
  tourism 335
  tours 342
  train 337
  West 422
Bali Barat National Park 422
Balibo 788
Baliem River Gorge 850
Baliem Valley 848
Balikpapan 581
Balimbiang 493
Balina Beach 398
Balinese
  dancing course 417
  names 323
  painting 322

pura 319
Ballakalua 654
Ballapeu 654
Baluran National Park 298
Baluran Reserve 305
Ban Hing Kiong Chinese temple 674
Bancea Orchid Reserve 662
Banda Aceh 443, 450
Banda Besar 824
Banda Islands 815
Banda Neira 818
Bandar Baru 435
Bandar Lampung 537
Bandengan Beach 258
Bandung 121, 155
Bandung Institute of Technology 159
Bandung Plain 155
Bandungan 240, 251
Bangka Island 530
Bangkalan 293
Bangko-Bangko 697
Bangli 387
Bangsal 703
Bangsal Kencono 190
Bangsal Manis 190
Bangsal Proboyekso 190
Bangsal Witana 224
banjar 324
Banjarmasin 569
Banjarsari market 245
Bank of Indonesia 158, 433
Banks
  See also individual town's local information
Banten 121, 138
Banten Lama 138
banteng 551
Bantimurung Falls 622
Banyumulek 715
Banyuwang 298
Banyuwangi 305
bargaining 865
Barito River Dayaks 557
Barrang Lompo Island 621
Barung 654
Barusjahe 453
Base G 845
Bataks 462
  Architecture 470
  houses 470
Batam Island 499
Batang Palupuh 491

Batavia 109
batik 101, 865
  lessons 200
  Museum 244
Batu 274
Batu Angus 828
Batu Bangga Beach 671
Batu Koq 711
Batuan 371
Batubolong Temple 701
Batubulan 341, 371
Batugade 788
Batur, Lake 387
Batur, Mount 387
Batur, Pura, Bali 388
Batusangkar 492
Batutumonga 648
Baubau 657
Baucau 792
Baun 773
Bawamataluo 479
Bayan 709
Beaches
  Amahusu 805
  Balina 398
  Bandengan 258
  Batu Bangga 671
  Berewa 358
  Bungus 512
  Carita 140
  Cimaja 151
  Florida 139
  Karang Bolong 195
  Karanghawu 151
  Kencana 719
  Labuan 140
  Lasiana 773
  Lawata 725
  Lerahinga 752
  Lovers 448
  Lovina 417
  Malole 820
  Matako 663
  Medewi 423
  Namalatu 805
  Nangalala 742
  Natsepa 805
  Nirwana 657
  Oeseli 778
  Padang 512
  Pandan 473
  Panjang 505
  Paradise 448
  Pasir Panjang 605

Seger 716
Siri 709
Telur Sei Pisang 512
Trikora 504
Tutuala 793
Waicicu 737
*See also highlights and individual
towns*
bearded pig 551
Bebandem 394, 407
becaks 875
Bedugul 414
Bekora Market 789
Belitung Island 531
bemos 340, 875
Bena 740
Bengkulu 533
Benoa 367
Benteng (Fort)
Anna Victoria 522
Pendem 182
Toloko 828
Ujung Pandang 617
Berewa Beach 358
Beringharjo Market 191
Besakih 390
Besakih, Pura, Bali 390
Best time to visit 17
Bali 337
Indonesia 860
Kalsel 569
Sumatra 429
surfing 343
Biak 844
Bicycle hire
Bali 341
Lombok 695
Indonesia 873
*See also individual town's local
information*
Bidadari, Pulau 136
Bima-Raba 724
Binjei 435
Bintan Beach International
Resort 505
Bintan Besar, Mount 505
Bintan Island 502
Bird of Paradise 837
Bird watching
Bali 378
Birds
Kalimantan 551
Kutacane and the Gunung
Leuser National Park 457

Bis kayu 876
bites 904
Blanco, Antonio 373
Blanjong Inscription 359
Blankejeren 459
Blikan Blewut Museum 748
Blitar 267
blowpipes 567
Boat 21, 876
*See also individual town's local
information*
Bodhisattva Avalokitesvara
212
Bogor 121, 146
Bogor Army Museum 148
Bohorok River 441
Bonang 260
Bondokawango 769
Bondomaroto 766
Bondowoso 303
Bone Bone
Watampone 630
Bontang 586
Books
East Timor 787
Indonesia 883
SE Asia 881
textiles 104
Bori 646
Borobudur 82, 204, 213
Bosnik 844
Bosscha Observatory 160
Botanical gardens
Bali 414
Bogor 146
Cibodas 154
Brastagi 451
Bratan, Lake 414
Brawijaya Museum 269
British Council 433
British Residency 534
Bromo, Mt 298, 306
Bromo-Tengger-Semeru National
Park 298
Bronjonolo Gate 189
Bugbug 394
Bugis 617
Bukarani 769
Bukit Barisan Museum 435
Bukit Barisan Selatan National
Park 540
Bukit Lawang 440
Bukit Peninsula 365
Bukittinggi 488, 514

Bukittinggi zoo 488
Bula 654
bull fights, Tapen 303
bullock races, Bali 423
Bunaken National Marine Park
683
Bunaken sea garden 678
Bunaken Sea Garden, Manado
674
Bungaya 394
Bungus Beach 512
Buntu Kalando Museum 646
Buntu Kesisi 654
Buntuballa 654
burial chamber
Torajan 640
buses 21
Bali 341
Indonesia 872
lombok 694, 695
Sumatra 430
*See also individual town's local
information*
Butak, Mt 306
Buton Island 657
Buyan, Lake 414

C

Cakranegara 696
Calang 450
Camp Leakey 580
camping
See accommodation
Camplong 294
Candi 90
Candi Arjuna 239
Candi Bajang Ratu 286
Candi Banon 212
Candi Banyunibo 220
Candi Bima 239
Candi Brahma 218
Candi Brahu 286
Candi Bubrah 219
Candi Cangkuang 163
Candi Ceto 225
Candi Dasa 399
Candi Dasa temple 400
Candi Dvaravati 238
Candi Gatukaca 239
Candi Gumpung 523
Candi Hindu 434
Candi Jabung 296
Candi Lumbung 218
Candi Prambanan 225

Candi Puntadewa 239
Candi Semar 239
Candi Sembadra 239
Candi Sojiwan 220
Candi Songgoriti 274
Candi Srikandi 239
Candi Sukuh 225
Candi Tikus 286
Candi Vishnu 218
Candi Wringin Lawang 287
Candrawasih University Museum 845
Canggu 357
Cangkuang, Candi 169
Canti 538
Car hire 21
  Bali 341
  Indonesia 875
  Lombok 695
  See also individual town's local information
Carita Beach, Java 140
casuarina forest 548
catamaran 694
Cathedral of Larantuka 751
Cathedral of the Immaculate Conception 788
Catholic Cathedral, Jakarta 117
Caves at Taman Purbakala Leang Leang 622
Cekik 422
Celuk 371
Cemora Sewu 235
Cemoro Lawang 300
Cempaka 573
Central Highlands 134
Central Javanese Period 89
central mosque 512
Ceto, Candi 227
Chapel of Christ 751
Chapel of the Virgin Mary 751
Checklist
  See what to take
Chinatown 113, 248, 526
Chinese Pagoda 254, 433
Chinese temple 182, 214, 530, 617
Chinese, Indonesia 67
Christmas Day 879
Church
  See gereja and individual town's local information
Ciater Hot Springs 162

Cibodas 154
Cidomos 695
Cilacap 182
Cimaja beach 151
Cipanas 154
Cipanas hot springs 170
Circumnavigating Ternate 828
Cirebon 174
Cisarua 152
Cisolok Hot Springs 152
Ciwidey 163
Clara Bundt 619
Climate
  Bali 314
  Indonesia 33
  Irian Jaya 837
  Java 81
  Kalimantan 546
  Lombok 691
  Maluku 795
  Sulawesi 612
  Sumatra 425
Climbing
  See Trekking
Clothing **860, 865**
Communist puputan 318
Comoro Market 789
conduct
  Bali 338
  Flores 735
  Indonesia 863
  Maluku 800
  Sumatra 429
Confidence tricksters **19**
Conservatory of Dance and Music 617
corruption 69
Cost of living
  East Timor 787
  Indonesia 860
courses
  language 877
Court dances 100
Craft villages
  Bali 374
crafts
  Bali 322
  Irian Jaya 841
  Kalimantan 564
  Lombok 693
credit cards **338, 860**
Cremation
  Bali 327
Cruises 339

cuisines, regional 870
Culture
  Bali 323
  Flores 734
  Indonesia 52
  Irian Jaya 839
  Java 93
  Kalimantan 554
  Lombok 693
  Maluku 799
  Toraja 635
Culture System 88
Currency **860**
Curup 535
custard apple 897
Cut Nyak Dhien Museum 446
cycling **21**

D

Daerah Museum 294
Dago Teahouse 160
Dakota DC3 446
Dance
  Bali 329
  Barong 329
  Indonesia 56
  Java 96
  Jegog 333
  Kalimantan 564
  Kecak 329
  Kris 329
  Legong 332
  Sanghyang dedari 330
  Topeng 333
Dani, Irian Jaya 848
Daruba 832
Dayak groups, Kalimantan 555
Demak 84, 249, 255
Dendam Tak Sudah Lake and Botanical Gardens 535
dengue fever 905
Denpasar 345
Deri 648
Desa Sunga 492
Diarrhoea 903
Dieng Plateau 214, 237
Dili 788
Diponegoro 192
Diponegoro Museum 192
distinctive fruits 897
Diving
  Ambon 808
  Amed 342, 410

Bali   342
Bandas   822
Benoa   367
Gilis   708
Lembongan   342
Manado   672
Maumere   749
Menjangan, Pulau   422
Nusa Lembongan   363
Nusa Penida Islands   342
Nusantara Diving Centre   680
Padangbai   342
Sangiang, Pulau   140
Saparua   809
Tepekong Island   342
Tulamben   342
Weh   447
See also highlights and individual
town's local information
Djarum kretek factory   254
dolphins, Lovina Beach   417
Dompu   723
Donapratopo Gate   190
Donggala   668
Doolan Memorial   804
Drake Francis Sir   42
Drama
Bali   329
Gambuh   333
Indonesia   56
Java   96
Kalimantan   564
Dress   863
drugs   19
Dua, Pulau   139
Dullah   833
Durian   38, 897
Dutch arrival   315
Dutch fort   719
Dutch Reform Church   819
Dutch, The   691
Dutch-era drawbridges   112
Duty free allowance   862
Dwi Dharma Bhakti Chinese
Temple   602

E

East Javanese Period   91
**EAST NUSA TENGGARA
727-794**
EAST TIMOR   781-794
accommodation   787
cost of living   787
getting around   787

Economy
Bali   334
East Timor   786
Indonesia   68
Irian Jaya   841
Mentawi Islands   517
Torajan   641
Egon, Mount   750
Eka Dasa Rudra   325
Ekas   716
Electricity   866
Elephant   550
Embassies   891
Jakarta   127
See also useful addresses
Emergency numbers
See individual town's local
information
encephalitis   900
Ende   741
Eng An Kiong Chinese Pagoda
269
Enggano Island   537
English East India Company
87
Ermera   788, 790
Ethnological Museum   471
exchange rates   18

F

Face   863
fact file
Indonesia   77
Factory Visits, Bandung   159
Fares
buses   919
Garuda   910
Merpati   911
Pelni   926
trains   918
Fatahillah Museum   112
Fatahillah Square, Jakarta   112
Fatumaka Promontory   790
Fauna and flora
Indonesia   37
Irian Jaya   837
Kalimantan   546
Kutacane and the Gunung
Leuser National Park   457
Mentawi Islands   517
Sulawesi   612
Feet   863
Ferries
Bali   337

Lombok   695
Sumatra   429
Festivals   878
Bali   325, 343
Jakarta   122
fish   903
FLORES   733-753
accommodation   735
conduct   735
Florida Beach   139
Food   20
glossary   896
Sumatra   430
See also restaurants
Forts
Belgica   818
Concordia   773
de Kock   488
Duurstede   810
Hollandia   824
Kastella   829
Marlborough   534
Nassau   818
Oranje   828
Santa Lucia   829
Victoria   803
fossils   40
Freeport Indonesia   855
Friends of Morowali   661
funeral and ritual slaughter
Torajan   639

G

Galubakul   768
Gama Lama Market   828
Gamalama, Mount   829
Gamelan orchestra   101
Garebeg Maulad   879
Garut   169
Gede-Pangrango National Park
154
Gedong Kirtya   416
Gedong Agung   191
Gedung Keputrian   190
Gedung Kopo   190
Gedung Merdeka   158
Gedung Pancasila   117
Gedung Sate   158
Gedung Songo   240
Gembira Loka Zoo and
Amusement Park   192
General Sudirman   278
Geography
Bali   312

Flores 733
Indonesia 31
Irian Jaya 835
Java 81
Kalimantan 544
Lombok 689
Sulawesi 612
Sumatra 425
Geological Museum 158
Gereja Blenduk 247
Gereja Immanuel 117
Gereja Kristen Protestan 535
Gereja Sion 113
geringsing 401
Getting around
air 20
Bali 339
boat 21, 876
cycling 21
East Timor 787
Flores 735
hitchhiking 21
Irian Jaya 843
Lombok 695
Maluku 800
road 21, 340
Sumatra 430
train 21
Getting there 18
Bali 337
boat 861
Lombok 694
Maluku 800
overland 19
sea 19
Sumatra 429
Gianyar 385
Gifts 863
Gili Air 705
Gili Gede 697
Gili Ketapang 296
Gili Meno 705
Gili Nanggu 697
Gili Poh 697
Gili Trawangan 704
Gilimanuk 422
Gilis, The 704
Glodok, Jakarta 113
Glombang 450
Goa Gajah, Bali 374
Goa Lawah 394
Goa Susu 711
Godang 460
Golkar 58

Gorontalo 671
Gotong Royong Market 803
Grahadi 278
Grajagan Bay 307
Grand Mosque 188, 222, 433, 526
Graves
  Pangeran Samudera 571
  Sunan Bonang 288
  tree 641
Gresik 281
Grobogan 249
Grojogan Sewu Waterfall 233
Grupuk (Desert) Point 716
Gua Selomangleng 264
Gudang Garam 264
Gunung Leuser National Park 455, 457
Gunung Leuser Nature Reserve 454
Gunungan, Banda Aceh 445
Gunungsitoli 479
Gurah 458

H

Habbema lake 850
Halmahera 831
Hamadi 845
Handicrafts
  See crafts
Hands 863
Haranggaol 472
Harau Canyon 493
Hari Pancasila 879
Hariti 212
Harvest Festival 560
Hatubuilico 794
Head-hunting 561
Heads 863
Health 17, 899
  kit 906
  Lombok 694
  Sumatra 429
Heath forest 548
hepatitis 900
Herman Daendels 87
Highlights 12
  beaches 14
  culture 15
  diving 14
  entertainment parks 16
  fairs 16
  handicrafts 16
  historical sites 15

museums 16
national parks 12
natural features 13
palaces 15
rafting 14
shopping 16
surfing 14
temples 15
towns 15
trekking 13
wildlife 12
Hiking
  See Trekking
Hila 805
Hilisimaetano 480
Hill stations 12
  Batu 274
  Bogor 121
  Cibodas 154
  Cipanas 154
  Cisarua 152
  Malino 621
  Sangiran 228
  Selekta 274
  Tawangmangu 228, 233
  Tretes 276
  Ubud 372
Hindu and Buddhist monuments 193
Historical and Archaeological Institute 617
History
  Bali 315
  East Timor 781
  Flores 734
  Indonesia 40
  Irian Jaya 838
  Jakarta 107
  Java 81
  Kalimantan 552
  Lombok 691
  Maluku 797
  Mentawi Islands 517
  Riau Archipelago 497
  Sulawesi 613
  Sumatra 426
  Ternate 826
  Timor 771
  Toraja 634
hitchhiking 21
Hok An Kiong 280
Homo erectus 229
Homo erectus erectus 40
Hornbill 551

Hornbill Festival   552
Horsecarts   876
Hospitals
   Jakarta   128
   See also individual town's local information
hot springs, Penatahan   413
Hotels
   See accommodation
Hours of business   864
Hu'u   723
Hutan Wisata Puntikayu   527

I

Ia, Mount   742
Ibans, Sarawak   561
Iboih Recreational Forest   448
Ibu Tien   63
Idhul Adha   879
Idul Fitri   879
Ijen Crater   303, 304
ikat   865
   double   401
   geringsing   401
Imlek   878
Immanuel Protestant Church   434
immunisation   900
Imogiri   193
Independence Day   879
Indonesia
   airport information   862
   architecture   52
   art   52
   before travelling   859
   bicycling   873
   boat   876
   bus   872
   car hire   875
   clothing   860
   communications   877
   credit cards   860
   culture   52
   customs   862
   departure tax   863
   entertainment   878
   entry requirements   859
   food and drink   868
   fossils   40
   getting around   871
   getting there   861
   health   860
   holidays and festivals   878
   literature   55
   money   860
   oil   69
   on arrival   862
   postal services   877
   press   66
   regions   30
   religion   863
   safety   864
   shopping   865
   sport   58
   telephones   878
   tipping   866
   tourism   72
   train   872
   when to go   860
   where to stay   866
Indonesia Decade Pass   871
Inpres market   740
insects   902
Integration Monument   789
Internet, Southeast Asia   889
IRIAN JAYA   835-856
   money   843
   permits   843
   tours   843
Irian Jaya Liberation Monument   117
Isak   460
Ise Ise   460
ISIC   18
Islam   52, 94
Island information
   Bali   337
   East Timor   787
   Flores   735
   Irian Jaya   843
   Lombok   694
   Maluku   800
   Sulawesi   616
   Sumatra   429
   See also information for travellers
Island of Weh   446
Istana
   Ballampoa   621
   Bogor   146
   Cipanas   154
   Kaibon   139
   Maimun   433
   Merdeka   116
   Sultan Deli   433
   Tua   719
Istiqlal Mosque, Jakarta   117

J

jackfruit   897
Jagaraga   418
Jago, Candi, Malang   273
JAKARTA   105-133
   accommodation   122
   Central   113
   embassies   127
   entertainment   128
   excursions   120
   festivals   122
   hospitals   128
   kampungs   117
   Kota   110
   places of interest   110
   places to eat   125
   shopping   129
   South   120
   Sunda Kelapa   111
   tour companies   130
   tours   121
   West   119
Jakarta Lloyd   433
Jalan Braga   158
Jalan Otista   148
Jalan Pasar Selatan   160
Jalan Pasar Utara   160
Jalan Pemuda   278
Jalan Sultan Patah   249
Jambi   523
Jame Mosque   803
Janggala   83
Janur   325
Japanese occupation   47
Japanese war memorial   828
Jasi   394
Jatijajar caves   182, 194
JAVA   79-309
   Central   180
   East   261
   Far East   295
   Far West   136
   North Coast   174
   West   134
Java cuisine   870
java man   40
Java War   87
Javanese dance course   284
Jawi, Candi, Malang   271
Jayapura   845
Jembatan Merah   280
Jember   306, 308
Jembrana   423

Jempang 595
Jepara 256
jewellery **865**
Jimbaran 366
Jiwika 850
Joko Dolog 278
Jopu 745
Jungle treks
  See Trekking

K

Kabanjahe 453
Kabunduk 766
Kadazans, Sabah 560
Kadriyah Palace 601
Kaget, Pulau 572
Kai 833
Kai Besar 833
Kai Kecil 833
Kakas 676
Kakas Kasen 674
Kakek Bodo Waterfall 277
Kalabahi 753
Kalabat, Mount 676
Kalala 763
Kalasan, Candi, Prambanan 220
Kalbar 546, 599
Kali Besar 112
Kali Mas 278
Kaliklatak 305
KALIMANTAN 542-608
Kaliuda 763
Kaliurang 193, 204
Kalsel 544, 568
Kalteng 544, 579
Kaltim 545, 581
Kamanga Cave 492
Kamarora Forest 669
Kampung Arab 280
Kanoman, Kraton, Cirebon 175
Kantor Gubernor 789
Kantuq 562
Kao 831
Kapal 411
Kapitan Thomas Pattimura 803
Kapuas Indah 602
Kapuas River 599, 606
Kapundak 763
Karang Bolong Beach 195
Karang Panjang Hill 804
Karangasem 405

Karanghawu 'cliff' beach 151
Kariango 654
Karimunjawa Islands 258
Karo Batak 451
Karo Batak villages 453
Kartasura 225
Kartini Day 879
Kartini Museum 257
Kasepuhan, Kraton, Cirebon 174
Kasunanan Palace, Solo 222
Katangka Mosque 621
Kawah Sikidang 239
Kawangu 762
Kawi, Gunung 384
Kayangan Island 622
Kayu Poli 660
Kayun Flower Market 281
Ke'te Kesu' 644
Keben 189
Kebun Binatang 159, 281
Kedah 459
Kedaton Sultan Ternate 828
Kediri 83, 264
Kedisan 388
Kedungwuni 245
Kefamenanu 777
Kehen, Pura 387
Kelabit, Sarawak 559
Kelenteng Sam Poo Kong Temple 247
Kelimutu 745
Kelimutu, Mount 742, 745
Kemakanan 190
Kemandungan Gates 224
Kemangdungan 189
Kembang, Pulau 572
Kemenuh 371
Kemiri, Gunung 458
Kenaikan Isa Al-Masih 879
kenari nut 676
Kencana Beach 719
Kendari 656
Kenjeran 281
Kenyah and Kayan, Sarawak 557
Keong Mas Theatre 120
Keramik Museum 113
Kerapan Sapi 291, 293
Kerek 288
Kereneng 341
Kerinci, Lake 520
Kerinci, Mount 520
Kerinci-Seblat Nature Reserve

514, 520
Kersik Tuo 520
Kesatrian 190
Ketambe 458
Ketapang 306
Kher Khoff 445
Kherta Ghosa 393
Kidal, Candi, Malang 273
Kimbin 850
King's Coffin 468
Kinilow 674
Kintamani 388
Klenteng 138
Klenteng Kwa Sam Yo 526
Klenteng Kwan Sing Bio 287
Klungkung 393
Kodi District 768
Kolaka 656
Kolam Segaran 286
Kole 654
Kolo 725
Kolonodale 659
KOMODO 730-738
Konfrontasi 554
Koningsplein Paleis 116
Kopian 654
KoraKora races 821
Korem 844
Kota 110
Kota Baru 491
Kota Gadang 489
Kota Gede, Yogya 193
Kota Raja 713
Krakal 203
Krakatau 144, 538
Krakatau Steelworks 139
Kraton 92
Kraton Kacirebonan 176
Kraton of Yogyakarta 188
Kraton Ratu Boko, Prambanan 219
Kraton Surakarta Hadiningrat 222
kretek museum 254
Kruengluck 450
Kudus 249, 254
Kudus Menara 254
Kukup 203
Kulor 810
Kupang 773
Kurima 850
Kuta 349
Kuta Beach, Lombok 715
Kutacane 455

Kutai National Park   586
Kwandang   671

L

La Bangenge Museum   628
Labuan Beach, Java   140
Labuan Lalang   422
Labuanbajo   737
Labuhan Lombok   714
Labuhan Sape   726
Labunan Poh   697
Ladalero   748
Lae Lae Island   621
Laguna, Lake   829
Lagundi Bay   480
Lai Tarung   767
Laki, Pulau   136
Lambaleda   739
Lambung Mangkurat State
  Museum   573
Lamno   450
Lampung Textiles   541
Lampuuk   446
Land
  Bali   312
  Flores   733
  Indonesia   29
  Irian Jaya   835
  Java   81
  Kalimantan   543
  Lombok   689
  Sulawesi   612
  Sumatra   425
Langa   740
Langoan   676
Langse Cave   203
Language   21, 877, 894
  Bali   323
  courses Yogya   200
  courses   877
  East Nusa Tenggara   729
  Indonesia   54
Lapangan Banteng   117
Larantuka   750
Larat   834
Lasem   259
Lasiana Beach   773
Laut Cave   833
Lautem   793
Lawang Sewu   248
Lawang Top   496
Lawata Beach   725
Tri Dharma Poo An Kiong temp
  267

Le Mayeur Museum   358
Lease Islands   809
Legian   354
Lembang   160
Lembata   752
Lembongan, Nusa   363
Lemo   645
Lempo   648
Lendang Nangka   713
Lerahinga Beach   752
Les waterfall   420
Leuser National Park   455
Leuser, Gunung Reserve   440
Lewoleba   752
Lho'seuda   446
Lhoknga   446
Lhokseumawe   442
Liang Pia   645
Lifao   777
Linau, Lake   675
Lingga   453
Lingga Island   505
Lingsar, Lombok   713
Literature   55
Loko   654
LOMBOK   688-717
  accommodation   695
  bicycles   695
  bus   695
  car hire   695
  Cidomos   695
  getting around   695
  health   694
  Motor bikes   695
  road   694
  sea   694
  sports   696
  tours   696
Londa   644
Long Iram   595
Long Lunuk   595
Lookout Tower   112
Lore Lindu National Park   662, 665
Loro Jonggrang, Candi,
  Prambanan   215
Los Palos   793
Lovers Beach   448
Lovina Beach   417
Loyok   713
Lubang Buaya   121
Luhur, Pura   413
Lumajang   306, 309
Lumut, Indonesia   460

Lutungan Island   671
Luwu, Palopo   654

M

Ma'anyan   557
Mada, Gajah   84
Madiun   263
Madura   281
Madura Island   290
magazines   881
Magelang   213
Mahabharata   56
Mahakam River   586, 591
main market   512
Majapahit   84
Makale   642
Malabo   654
Malang   269, 306
Malaria   901
Malaria in SE Maluku   833
Maleo bird   684
Maliana   788
Malino   621
Malole Beach   820
Maluk   719
MALUKU   795-834
  accommodation   800
  air   800
  conduct   800
  getting around   800
  getting there   800
  sports   800
Mamasa Town   652
Mamasa Valley   650
Mamboro   768
Mambulilin   654
Mampu caves   630
Manado   672
Manatuto   790
Mancong longhouse   595
Manda   850
Mandala Bhakti Museum   248
mango   897
mangosteen   897
Mangrove   548
Maninjau, Lake   490, 496
Manuakalada   768
Manusela National Park   814
maps   888
Maranda   663
Marante   646
March 1st Monument   191
Mardika Market   803

Margo Mulyo Church   191
Maria   725
Marobo   788
Maros   622
Marriage, Bali   326
Marta Tiahahu   804
Martapura   573
Maru   763
Mas   371
Mas, Gunung Tea Factory and Estate   153
Masbaggik   713, 715
Maslete   777
Masohi   813
Matakakeri   767
Matako beach   663
Mataram   84, 696
Maubessi   794
Maumere   746
Maumere Cathedral   746
Mayang Mengurai Park   523
Mayura Water Palace and Gardens, Cakranegara   697
Mbongawani market   742
Medan   432
Medan Merdeka, Jakarta   113
Medewi Beach   423
megalithic culture   476
Megaliths   533, 646
Megaliths in Lahat District   528
megaliths of Pagaralam   535
Melak   595
Melayu   428
Melintang   595
Melolo   762
Mendut, Candi, Borobudur   211
Mengwi, Bali   413
meningitis   900
Menjangan, Pulau   422
Mentawai Islands   517
Merak   139
Merak Belantung   538
Merapi, Mount   193, 203, 304, 448, 492
Merauke   852
Mercado Municipal   792
Mercado Municipal Dili   789
meru   412
Meru Betiri National Park   306, 307
Mesa Kada   654
Mesjid
    Agung   138, 171, 175, 520,

526
Agung Tegal   244
Agung Tuban   288
An Nur   508
Baitul Ma'mur   258
Baiturahan   247
Baiturrachman   305
Jami   602
Jamik Mosque   294
Nurul Huda   719
Raya   433,803
Raya Baiturrahman, Banda Aceh   444
Raya Sultan Riau   502
Sultan Ternate   828
metalwork   865
Meulaboh   450
Middle Mahakam   595
Minang cuisine   487
Minanga   654
Minangkabau   483
Minangkabau matrilineal society   483
Mining museum   530
Miri   228
Modern Bali   334
Modern Jakarta   110
Modern Riau   498
Moko Drum   753
Monas, Jakarta   115
Monasteries
    Tri Dharma Buddhist Dharma   264
Money   *18*
Irian Jaya   843
Sumatra   429
    See also information for travellers
Moni   745
monsoon   36
Montane forest   548
Monumen Perjuangan Rakyat Sumatera Bagian Selatan   526
Monumen Rakyat Pejuang   628
Moon of Pejeng, Bali   378
Moramo Waterfall   656
Morotai   832
Morowali Nature Reserve   660
Mosque
    Agung Demak   249
    Ampel   280
    Grand   433
    Istiqlal   117

Jame   803
Katangka   621
Mesjid Agung Tegal   244
Mesjid Agung Tuban   288
Mesjid Agung   138, 171, 175
Mesjid Agung   520, 526
Mesjid Baitul Ma'mur   258
Mesjid Baiturahan   247
Mesjid Baiturrachman   305
Mesjid Jami   602
Mesjid Jamik   294
Mesjid Nurul Huda   719
Mesjid Raya Baiturrahman   444
Mesjid Raya   433
Mesjid Raya   803
Mesjid Sultan Ternate   828
Sabila Muhtadin   570
Syech Yusuf   619
Motael Church   788
Motorbike hire   *876*
Bali   341
Lombok   695
Mountains
    Gunung Leuser National Park   455
Moyo Island   719
Mt Baru   711
Mt Belirang hot springs   472
Mt Lokon   674
Mt Mahawu   675
Mt Meja   742
Mualang   562
Muara Jambi   523
Muara Muntai   595
Muara Takus   508
Mudras   208
Muharram   879
Muko Muko   496, 522
Mulawarman Museum   593
mummified warrior   850
Muna Island   657
Mundo Perdio   793
Museum
    Aceh   444
    Adityavaran   512
    Ambarawa Railway   242
    Ancient Inscription   116
    Bali, Denpasar   345
    Batik   244
    Blikan Blewut   748
    Bogor Army   148
    Brawijaya   269
    Budaya Sultan Mahmud

Bandaruddin 526
Bukit Barisan 435
Buntu Kalando 646
Candrawasih University 845
Central Sulawesi 668
Cut Nyak Dhien 446
Daerah 294
Diponegoro 192
Ethnological 471
Fatahillah 112
Indonesia 120
Kartini 257
Keramik 113
Kereta Karaton 190
King Soribunto Sidabutar 468
Komodo 120
kretek 254
Lambung Mangkurat State 573
Lapawawoi 630
Le Mayeur 358
Mandala Bhakti 248
mining 530
Mulawarman 593
Negeri Jambi 523
Negeri Propensi Sumatera Selatan 526
Negeri 845
Neka 373
Nusa Tenggara Timur 773
Perjuangan 191
Post and Philately 158
Prabu Geusan Ulun 168
Prince Diponegoro 214
Provincial 538
Purbakala Archaeological 378
Puri Lukisan 373
Radya Pustaka 225
Railway 249
Riau Kandil 503
Rumah Buaya 819
Satriamandala 120
Simalungun 455
Situs Kerpurbakalaan 138
Sonobudoyo 188
Sumatera Utara 434
Taman Prasasti 116
Tantular 281
Timorese Culture 790
West Java 160
West Nusa Tenggara Provincial 696
Zoological 147
Museum of the History

Jakarta 112
Musi River 528
Music
Bali 329, 333
Java 96
Kalimantan 564
Indonesia 56
Musium Negeri 600
Mussa 654

N

Nagoya 499
Namalatu Beach 805
Namberala 778
Nangalala Beach 742
Nanggala 646
Narmada 712
National Archives 113, 617
National Museum, Jakarta 116
National Park
Bali Barat 422
Baluran 298
Bromo-Tengger-Semeru 298
Bukit Barisan Selatan 540
Gede-Pangrango 154
Indonesia 39
Komodo 730
Kutacane 455
Kutai 586
Leuser 455, 457
Lore Lindu 665
Manusela 814
Meru Betiri 306
Meru Betiri 307
Penanjung 172
Seventeen Island 741
Tangkoko Batu Angus 678
Tanjung Puting 579
Ujung Kulon 141
Wasur 852
Way Kambas National Park Elephant Reserve 538
Natsepa Beach 805
Ndalir 854
Negara 423
Negeri Museum 845
newspapers **878**
Ngadas 274, 300
Ngaju 557
Ngalupolo 743
Ngarai Canyon 489
Nggela 743, 745
Ngis 394

Ngliyep 274
Nias Island 475
Niha settlements 476
Nilulat 777
Nirwana Beach 657
Nita 748
North Sulawesi Provincial Museum 674
Northern Coastal Plain 134
Nuabosi 743
Nusa Ceningan 363
Nusa Dua 343, 368
Nusa Kambangan 182
Nusa Lembongan 363, 394
Nusa Penida 363, 394
Nusa Tenggara, Island-hopping 687
Nyepi 879
Nyi Loro Kidul 150

O

Odalan 326, 333
Oeseli Beach 778
Official time **864**
oil 69
Oil Industry 509
Ojeks 876
Old Gowa 619
Onggaya 854
Onrust, Pulau 136
Oplets 876
Orang utan 548
Orang Utan Rehabilitation Centre 435, 440
Orobua 654
Osango 654
Ot Danum 557
Ouw 810

P

Paceren 451
Paciran 281
Pacitan 228, 234
Padaido Islands 844
Padang 511
Padang beach 512
Padang cuisine 870
Padang Lawas 474
Padang Port 512
Padangbai 396
Padangsidempuan 473
Padri Wars 486
Pagai Selatan 517

Pagai Utara 517
Pagaralam 532
Pagaruyung 492
Pagelaran 222
Pageleren 188
Pah Auman 607
Paigoli 768
painting 866
Pajak Ikan Lama 435
Pajak Petisar 435
Paku Alam's Palace 192
Palang 555
Palangkaraya 579
Palawa 646
Palembang 525
Pallu 654
Palopo 654
Palu 667
Palung, Mount Wildlife Reserve 608
Pamekasan 294
Pamona Cave 662
Pana 648
Panataran, Candi, Blitar 267
Panca Walikrama 326
Pancasila 51, 864
Pandaan 273
Pandai Sikat 491
Pandalarang 155
Pandan Beach 473
Pangandaran 171
Panggung Songgobuwono 224
Pangkal Pinang 530
Pangkalanbun 580
Pangli 646
Panguuran 472
Panjang Beach 505
Panjang, Pulau 136
Panorama Park 490
Pantai Cecil 396
Pantai Citepus 151
Pantai Morossi 769
Pantai Panjang 535
Pantai Pasir Putih 790
Pantai Rua 769
Panua Reserve 671
Paotere Harbour 619
Papandayan, Mount 163, 170
papaya 898
Papenburg 820
Paradise Beach 448
Parang Wedang hot springs 203

Parangtritis 194, 203
Pare Pare 628
Pariangan 493
Parigi Bay 172
Paringgitan 225
Paronabaroro 768
Parr, Thomas 534
Pasar 16 Ilir 526
Pasar Bambaru 668
Pasar Barde 296
Pasar Baru 160
Pasar Barukoto 534
Pasar Besar 269
Pasar Bunga 269
Pasar Cikini 120
Pasar Ikan 111, 151, 182, 446, 602
Pasar Inpres 844
Pasar Jatayu 160
Pasar Johar 249
Pasar Kanoman 175
Pasar Klewer 225
Pasar Kota Kembang 160
Pasar Malam 502
Pasar Masomba 668
Pasar Ngasem 190
Pasar Niaga 573
Pasar Panir 844
Pasar Potulando 742
Pasar Satya Pradja 671
Pasar Sayur 828
Pasar Senggol 269
Pasar Sentral 619, 671
Pasar Terapung, Banjarmasin 570
Pasar Triwindu 225
Pasir Kencana 245
Pasir Panjang beach 605
Pasir Putih 302, 538
Pasongsongan 294
Passports 859
Pasunga 766
Pasuruan 295
Patai Sumur Tiga 448
Pati 259
Pau 763
Pawon, Candi, Borobudur 211
PDI 59
peat swamp 548
Pekajangan 245
Pekalongan 244
Pekalongan Port 245
Pekan Tigaraja 463
Pekanbaru 507

Pelabuhan (Port) Pasuruan 295
Pelabuhan Ambon 803
Pelabuhan Cilacap 182
Pelabuhan Kota 671
Pelabuhan Lama 571
Pelabuhan Manado 674
Pelabuhan Tegal 244
Pelabuhanratu 150
Pelangi, Pulau 136
Pelni 876
Pelni sailings 921
Pemangtangsiantar 455
Pemuteran 422
Penan, Sarawak 560
Penanjakan, Mt 300
Penanjung National Park 172
Penatahan 413
Pencak silat 483
Pendem Fort 182
Pendolo 659
Pendopo Agung 224
Penelokan 388
Pengsong, Gunung 697
Penida, Nusa 363
Penuba Island 505
Penujak 715
Penyenget Island 502
People
  Bali 323
  Flores 734
  Irian Jaya 839
  Kalimantan 554
  Java 93
  Lombok 693
  Riau Archipelago 497
People's Amusement Park 281
Perasi 394
Perintis fares 911
Perkenier mansion 819, 825
permits, Irian Jaya 843
Pero 768
perumtel 877
Piracy 553
Pisang Island 821
Plaosan, Candi, Prambanan 219
Police 19, 338
Politics, Indonesia 58
Pombo Island 805
Pongkor 739
Pontianak 600
poor 75
population 30

Portuguese church 748
Portuguese fort 258
Poso 663
Poso, Lake 659
Postal services 877
Prabu Geusan Ulun Museums 168
Prai Goli 768
Praijing 766
Prailiang 763
Prailiu 762
Prambanan 82, 215
Prambanan, Candi 215
Pramuka Hill 737
Prapat 462
Pre-Colonial kingdoms: Srivijaya, Melayu and Aceh 426
pre-colonial powers 41
Presidential Palace 146
prickly heat 905
Prince Diponegoro 87, 617
Prince Diponegoro Museum 214
Pringgasela 713, 714
Prisoners abroad 19
Probolinggo 296, 298
Proboscis monkey 549
Prohibited items 862
Proklamasi Monument 535
Provincial Museum 538
Pua kumbu 565
Pugima 850
Pugung Raharja Archaelogical Park 538
Pulau Kotok 136
Pulli 768
Puncak Lawang 490
Puncak Pass 152
Puputan 318
Puputan Square 345
Pura
  Agung Girinatha Temple 719
  Balinese 319
  Beji 417
  Besakih 390
  Blanjong 359
  Bukit Sari 374, 413
  Dalem Agung Padangtegal 374
  Dalem 418
  Gelap 392
  Jaganatha 345
  Kebo Edan 378
  Maduwe Karang 418

Mangkunegaran, Solo 224
Masopahit 345
Mayura 697
Panataran Sasih 378
Penataran Agung 390
Pengubengan 392
Pusering Jagat 378
Sada 411
Saraswati 374
Suranadi 713
Tirta 392
Ulun Danau Bratan 414
Uluwatu 367
Yeh Gangga 413
Purajati 388
Purbakala Archaeological Museum 378
Puri Agung 406
Puri Saren 374
Puri Smarapura 393
Purwaretna 190
Purwodadi Botanical Gardens, Malang 271
Putri, Pulau 136
Putung 410
Putussibau 607
Pyramid 850

R

rabies 905
Raden Kartini 257
radio 878
Rafflesia flower 490, 535
Rafting
  Alas River 458
  Ayung River 343
  Banjarmasin 574
  Mamasa 648
  Maulu River 649
  Pinoh River 602
  Sa'dan River 649
  Telaga Waja River 348
Ragunan Zoo 121
Raha 657
Railway Museum 249
Rajabasa, Mount 538
Ramayana 56
Ramayana ballet 100, 333
Rambusaratu 654
rambutan 898
Rambut Siwi Temple 423
Randayan, Pulau 606
Rante Balla 654
Rante Katoan 654

Rante Sopang 654
Rantepao 643
Ranu Lake 660
Rao Rao 492
Rasa Village 793
Ratenggaro 768
Raung, Mt 306
Rawa Biru 854
Regency of Karangasem 394
Regional Houses of Parliament 503
Rejo Agung sugar mill 263
Religion
  Bali 324
  Indonesia 52, 863
  Java 94
  Kalimantan 562
Rembang 255, 259
Rembang market 259
Remboken 677
Rende 762
Reo 739
rhinoceros 551
  Javan 143
  Sumatran 522
Riau Archipelago 497
Riau Kandil Museum 503
rice, cultivation 32
Rigaih 450
Rikit Gaib 460
Rinca Island 731, 738
Rinjani, Mount 709, 714
Riung (Nangamese) 741
Roman Catholic Cathedral of the Immaculate Conception 434
ROTI 778
rubber processing plants 441
Rubiah Sea Garden 448
rumah adat 486
Rumah Buaya Museum 819
rumah gadang 486
rumah panjang 520
Rungkang 715
Ruteng 739

S

Sa Seng Keng 602
Sa'dan 646
Sabang 446, 447
Sabanga Elephant Training Camp 509
Sabila Muhtadin Mosque 570
Sade 715
Safety 864

confidence tricksters 19
drugs 19
police 19
theft 19
sago palm 798
Saguling Dam 155
Sailendra 81
Saint Francis Xavier 803
Saka Year Festivals 344
Sakenan, Pura 359
salak 898
Salatiga 242
Salotangah 632
Saluopa waterfall 662
Samalona Island 621
Samarinda 586
Sambirenteng 420
Sambisari, Candi, Prambanan 221
Same 794
Samosir Island 464, 466, 472
Samudera Pasai 443
Sandalwood factory 774
Sangeh 374, 413
Sangiang, Pulau 140
Sangihe 684
Sangiran 228
Sangliat Dol 834
Sangsit 417
Sanjaya 82
Santa Cruz 783
Sanur 343, 358
Sao Wisata 746
Saparua 809
Sape 726
Sapit 711, 714
Sarangan 233, 235, 263
Sarapang 645
Sari, Candi, Prambanan 220
Sasana Sewaka 224
Sasirangan 577
Sasono Wirotomo 192
Satriamandala Museum 120
Saumlaki 834
Savu Island 779
Sawah 80
Sawangan 676
Sawentar, Candi, Blitar 268
SE Maluku 833
Sea transport 19
  Bali 337
  Lombok 694
  Sumatra 429
Seba 779

Seberuang 562
Sebesi 538
Sebuku 538
Segara Anak 711
Seger Beach 716
Seketeng Market 719
Selekta 274
Selo 203, 228
Selong Blanak 716
Semar Cave 239
Semarang 247
Semau Island 774
Semayang 595
Sembalun Bumbung 711
Sembalun Lawang 711
Semeru, Mt 300
Sempang 632
Senaru 711
Sendang Duwur 281
sendratari 100
Senggigi 700
Sengkang 631
Sengkidu Village 398
Sentani Lake 846
Seram 813
Serang 138
Serangan Island 359
Seribu, Pulau 121, 136
Sesajen 325
Seulawah 446
Seventeen Island National Park 741
Sewu, Candi, Prambanan 219
shellfish 903
shifting cultivation 33
Shopping
  Bali 338
  bargaining 865
  Jakarta 129
  Sumatra 430
  tips 865
Short Wave Radio Guide 890
Si Jagur 113
Si Piso Piso 453
Siak Sri Indrapura 508
Siallagan village 470
Siantar 455
Siantar Zoo 455
Sibayak, Mount 453
Siberut 517
Sibolga 473
Sideman 410
Sidikalang 450, 455

Sikka 748
Simanindo 471
Simarmata 472
Simpang Lima 247
Singapore, ferries from 429
Singaraja 416
Singasari 83
Singasari, Candi, Malang 271
Singgalang, Mount 492
Singkarak, Lake 493
Singkawang 605
Singkep Island 505
Sintang 607
Sipora 517
Sirandah 512
Siri Beach 709
Siti Inggil 189, 222
Situbondo 303
Siva, Candi, Prambanan 215
Siwalima Museum 804
snake bite 904
Sodan 768
Soe 777
Soekarno-Hatta International Airport 862
Solo 221
Sonder 676
Songket 529
Sonobudoyo Museum 188
Sore Island 505
Southeast Sulawesi 656
Soya 83
Spellwijck Fortress 138
Spice Islands 44, 795
spices of Maluku 797
Sport 58
  Bali 342
  Lombok 696
  Maluku 800
  See also individual town's local information
Srimanganti 190
Srivijaya 426
Sriwedari 225
State Palace 116
Suai 794
Suaya 645
Suci 341
Suggested reading
  Bali 336
  Borneo 567
Suharto, President 62
Sukamade 307
Sukarara 715

Sukarno's house   535
Sukarno's house and museum   742
Sukarno's mausoleum   267
Sukarnoputrii, Megawati   59
Sukuh, Candi   225
Sulamadaha   828
SULAWESI   609-685
   boat   616
   getting around   616
sulphur lake   239
Sultan's Palace   724
Sumatera Utara Museum   434
SUMATRA   424-541
   accommodation   430
   best time   429
   bus   430
   conduct   429
   ferry   429
   food   430
   getting there   429
   health   429
   money   429
   northern   432
   sea   429
   shopping   430
   southern   482
   taxi   430
   tours   429
   train   430
   west coast   449
SUMBA   755-771
Sumbanese villages and houses   757
SUMBAWA   717-726
Sumbawa Besar   719
Sumedang   168
Sumenep   294
Sunburn   904
Sunda Kelapa, Jakarta   111
Sungai Penuh   520
Sungaipua   492
Sungei Ular   502
Sungguminasa   621
Sunyaragi   176
Supiori Island   844
Surabaya   277
Surakarta   221
Suranadi   713
Surfing
   Bali   343
   best time   343
   Bingin   343
   Bukit Peninsula   365

Canggu   343, 357
Carita Beach   140
Cimaja Beach   151
Grajagan Bay   307
Hu'u   723
Labuan Beach   140
Lagundi Bay   480
Lhoknga   446
Kalala   763
Maluk   719
Medewi   343
Medewi Beach   423
Namberala   778
Nusa Lembongan   363
Nyang Nyang   343
Padang Padang   343
Pantai Rua   769
Parigi Bay   172
Suluban   343
Ujung Kulon NP   141
Uluwatu   343
Surosowan Palace   138
Surowono temple   264
Sutera Alam Silk Factory   619
Syech Yusuf Mosque   619

T

Taci Tolu   790
Tahun Baru   878
Tahuna   684
Taibassi   654
Takengon   460
Talaud Islands   684
Taliwang   719
Tallunglipu   646
Tamalate   621
Taman Anggrek   676
Taman Ayun, Pura   413
Taman Bundokandung   488
Taman Burung Bali Bird Park   371
Taman Chandra Wilwatika   273
Taman Fatahillah   112
Taman Gili   394
Taman Hutan Raya Bung Hatta   514
Taman Impian Jaya Ancol, Jakarta   121
Taman Kyai Langgeng   214
Taman Margasatwa Zoo   435
Taman Mini-Indonesia, Jakarta   120
Taman Narmada   712

Taman Nasional Bali Barat   423
Taman Prasasti Museum   116
Taman Purbakala Waruga   676
Taman Safari   148, 153
Taman Sari   191, 294
Taman Wisata   677
tamarind   898
Tambat   854
Tambora, Mount   720
Tampangallo   645
Tanah Lot   411
Tanah Merah Bay   846
Tanate   654
Tangkoko Batu Angus National Park   677, 678
Tangkuban Prahu Crater   161
Tanimbar Islands   834
Tanjung Aan   716
Tanjung Api Reserve   665
Tanjung Berakit   504
Tanjung Harapan   580
Tanjung Isuy   595
Tanjung Pinang   502
Tanjung Puteh Orang Utan Sanctuary   574
Tanjung Puting National Park and Orang Utan Rehabilitation Centre   579
Tanjungkarang   537
Tantular Museum   281
Tao   471
Tapaktuan   450
Tapan   522
Tapen   303
Tarakan   598
Taru Martani   193
Tarum River   155
Tarung   766
Tasik Malaya   171
Tatale   654
Tatamaliau, Mount   794
Tattoos   565
Taun   697
Taupe   654
Tawangmangu   228, 233
taxis   *876*
Tegal   244, 341
Tegen Koripan, Pura   388
Tegurwangi   264
Telaga Warna   239
Telephones   *878*
   Bali   342
   Lombok   696
television   *878*

Teluk Bayur   512
Teluk Penyu   182
Telukbetung   537
Telukdalam   479
Telur Sei Pisang Beach   512
Temajo, Pulau   606
Tempe   632
Tempe, Lake   631
temple etiquette   338
Temples
  Ban Hing Kiong Chinese   674
  Batubolong   701
  Candi Dasa   400
  Dwi Dharma Bhakti Chinese   602
  Kelenteng Sam Poo Kong   247
  Pura Agung Girinatha   719
  Rambut Siwi   423
  Surowono   264
  Tri Dharma Poo An Kiong   267
  Uluwatu   366
  Waktu Telu   713
Tenganan   400
Tenggarong   593
Tentena   662
Terkulai Island   505
Ternate & Tidore   825
Terunyan   388
Tetebatu   713
Textile Museum, Jakarta   119
textiles   101
Thay Kak Sie Pagoda   249
The Baliem Valley   849
The Kubu   524
theft   19
Tidore   829
Tikala   648
Tilanga   644
Timbrah   394
time zones   864
timetables
  Pelni   921
  train   917
Timetabling a visit   12
Timika, Kuala Kencana and Tembagapura   856
TIMOR   771-794
Timorese house   789
Tipping
  Bali   339
  Indonesia   866
Tirta Empul   385
Tirtagangga   407
To'karau   646

Toba, Lake   461
Tobelo   831
Togian Islands   667
Toko Merah   113
Toli-Toli   671
Tolire Lakes   828
Tomalanti   654
Tomb
  Arief Mohammad   170
  Imam Bonjol   674
  Laga Siallagan   470
  Matarm Sultans   193
  Prince Diponegoro   617
  Sri Aji Joyoboyo   265
  Sultan Iskandar Muda   445
  Sunan Gunung Jati   177
  Sunan Kudus   254
  Torajan   640
Tombiano   663
Tomer   854
Tomerau   854
Tomini Bay   667
Tomohon   675
Tomok   468
Tomori Bay   660
Tondano   677
Tondano, Lake   676, 677
Tooth-filing
  Bali   328
Toraja   634
  Village and house   636
Torajan death ritual   638
Toranggo Buya   648
Tossi   768
Tour companies
  Jakarta   130
  specialists   893
Tourism   22
  and art   24
  and culture   22
  and environment   24
  and the traveller   25
  Bali   334
  guidebooks   26
  Lombok   694
  pressure groups   27
  reading list   27
Tourist offices
  Jakarta   131
  overseas   892
Tours
  Bali   342
  Indonesia   72
  Irian Jaya   843

  Jakarta   121
  Lombok   696
  Mentawai Islands   519
Toya Bungkah   388
Traditional society and religion
  Toraja   635
Train   872
  Bali   337
  Sumatra   430
Transmigration   427
Transport
  Jakarta   131
Transport and travelling   9
travellers' cheques   861
Travelling
  Bali   9
  East Nusa Tenggara   11
  East Timor   11
  See also information for travellers
  Irian Jaya   12
  Java   9
  Kalimantan   10
  Lombok   11
  Maluku   11
  Sulawesi   11
  Sumatra   10
Travelling independently
  Mentawai Islands   519
Travelling with Children and Babies   907
tree graves   641
Trekking   13
  Apo Kayan   596
  Baliem Valley   851
  Balikpapan   582
  Banjarmasin   574
  Bawamataluo   480
  Blankejeren   459
  Bromo-Tengger-Semeru NP   300
  Bukit Lawang   440
  Gede-Pangrango NP   154
  Gunung Leuser   458
  Ijen crater   304
  Kaliurang   204
  Komodo   730
  Lake Batur   388
  Lake Tempe   632
  Lore Lindu NP   662
  Mamasa   648
  Mamasa Valley   653
  Mamasa-Rantepao   654
  Manusela NP   814
  Mentawai Islands   518

Mount Egon 750
Mount Kelimutu 745
Mount Kerinci 520
Mount Merapi 203, 304
Mount Rinjani 709
Mount Tambora 720
Ngadas 274
Rantepao 644
Samosir Island 468
trans-Borneo 546
Trans-Sumatra 478
Wamena 849
Tretes 276
Tri Dharma Buddhist monastery 264
Tribal art
   See art and culture
Trikora Beach 504
tropical forest 32
Trowulan 277, 281, 285
Trusmi 177
Tua Peh Kong Bio 449
Tual 833
Tuban 287, 355
Tugu Khatulistiwa 602
Tugu Muda 248
Tugu Pahlawan 280
Tuju, Gunung 520
Tuk Tuk 469
Tulamben 421
Turtle Bay 182
Tutuala Beach 793
typhoid 900

U

Ubud 372
Ubung 341
Ujung 406
Ujung Blang 443
Ujung Kulon National Park 141
Ujung Pandang 616
Ujung Pandang State Museum 617
Ukra 854
Ulun Siwi Temple 366
Uluwatu Temple 366, 367
Umabara 763
Upper Mahakam 595
Useful addresses 891
Uwak 460

V

vaccinations 859
Van den Bosch 88
Veninale 793
Vereenigte Ooste-Indische Compagnie 86
Vihara Gunung Timur 434
Villa Isola 160
Virgin Mary 789
Visas 859
visiting a funeral ceremony 640
VOC 86
volcanoes 31
Voltage 866
Vredeburg Fort 191

W

Waai 805
Wafat Isa Al-Masih 879
Waga Waga 850
Wahai 813
Waiara 746
Waicicu Beach 737
Waigalli 768
Waikabubak 765
Waingapu 761
Wainyapu 768
Waisak Day 879
Waisisil 810
Waiwuang 768
Waktu Telu Temple 713
Walis 94
Walking
   See also Trekking
Wamena 849
Wanokaka 768
warpostel 878
wartel 877
Wasur National Park 852
Watampone 630
Water 20, 870
   See also health
Watu Pinabetengan 676
Watu Ulo 308
Watublapi 748
Way Kambas National Park Elephant Reserve 538
wayang 96
   kulit 333
   Museum, Jakarta 112

orang 100
puppets 866
topeng 99
weaving 866
weaving factories 696
Weh 447
Werdi Budaya Art Centre 345
Wesaput 850
West Coast 511
West Nusa Tenggara 686, 726
West Nusa Tenggara Provincial Museum 696
WEST TIMOR 780
whaling village of Lamalera 752
What to take 17
Where to stay 20
   See also accommodation
White-river rafting
   See highlights and rafting
Wildlife
   highlights 12
   See also fauna and flora
Wodong 748, 750
Wogo 740
Wolio Kraton 657
Wolo 850
Wolotopo 743
Wolowaru 745
Women travelling alone 20
Wonosobo 235
woodcarving 477, 866
words and phrases 894
worms 905
wrapping and lamentation Torajan 638
Wuku Year Festival 343
Wunga 763
Wuruk, Hayam 84

Y

Yeh Pulu 375
Yogya Kembali Monument 193
Yogyakarta 184
Youth hostels
   See accommodation

Z

Zaid Bachmid 763
Zoological Museum 147

Maps

Ambon Island 802
Ambon Town 806
Around Banjarmasin 574
Around Mount Rinjani 710
Bali 311
  North & East 386
  South 349
Baliem Valley 848
Balikpapan 582
Banda Aceh 445
Banda Islands 815
Banda Neira 819
Bandar Lampung 539
Bandung 156
  centre 164
  environs 161
Bangka Island 531
Banjarmasin 572
Banjarmasin, around 574
Banten Lama 139
Batam Island 500
Bemo stops for onward
  connections from Amlapura
  407
Bengkulu 534
Bima 724
Bintan, Pulau 503
Bogor 147
Bone Bone 630
Borobudur 206
Brastagi 451
Bromo – Crater and Trails 299
Bukit Lawang 441
Bukittinggi 489
  environs 491
Bunaken marine park 683
Candi Dasa – Padangbai and
  environs 399
  west 400
  East 401
Candi Siva 218
Cilacap 183

Cirebon 176
Denpasar 346
Dieng Plateau 238
Dili 789
East Timor 781
Ende 742
  environs 741
Flores Island 734
Gedung Songo 241
Gili Islands 706
Goa Gajah 375
Gunung Kawi 384
Gunung Leuser National Park
  456
Indonesia 10-11
  climate 34-35
  compared with Europe 48
  national parks 38-39
  Merpati/Garuda, Bouraq
    & Mandala Routes 912-913
  Pelni Shipping Routes
  922-923
Irian Jaya 836
Jakarta
  Blok M and Pasar Raya 130
  Centre 114
  General 106
  Jalan Jaksa 123
  Kota & Sunda Kelapa 111
Java
  East 262
  Central 181
  West 135
Jayapura 846
Jimbaran Bay 366
Kalimantan Selatan 570
Kalimantan 543
Karangasem 395
Kediri 266
Kerinci-Seblat Reserve 521
Komodo National Park 730
Krakatau 144

Kraton Ratu Boko 219
Kudus 255
Kupang 774
Kuta 350
Lake Poso 658
Legian 355
Lombok Island 689
Lovina Beach 418
Madura Island 290
Magelang 214
Mahakam River 594
Malang Surroundings 271
Malang 270
Maluku 796
Mamasa 652
  surroundings 651
Manado 679
  centre 673
  environs 675
Mataram 698-699
Maumare 747
Medan 434
  centre 436
Morowali National Park 660
Mount Bromo Surroundings
  300
Nias Island 475
Nusa Dua 364
Nusa Lembongan 364
Nusa Tenggara 728
  Route map of flights within
  687
Padang 513
Padangbai 396
Palembang 527
Palopo 655
Palu 630
Panataran Complex 268
Pangandaran 172
Pare Pare 629
Pekalongan 245
Pekanbaru 508

Pontianak centre 603
Pontianak 601
Poso 664
Prambanan Group 216
Prambanan sanctuary complex 217
Prapat 464
Pulau Seribu 137
Pura Basikh, Bali 390
Rantepao 647
Riau Archipelago 498
Sabang Island 448
Samarinda 620
Samosir Island 467
Sanur 359
Saparua 809
Semarang 248
  centre 250
Senggigi Beach 701
Sengkang 632
Siberut Island (Mentawi) 518
Singaraja 417

Solo 223
Sulawesi 610-611
  Central 632
  South 627
Sumatra
  Northern 431
  Southern 484-485
Sumba Island 755
Sumbawa Besar 720
Sumbawa Island 718
Surabaya 279
  detail 283
Surakarta – see Solo 223
Tana Toraja 642
Tanjung Pinang 504
Tegal 244
Tentena 662
Ternate & Tidore Islands 825
Toraja 642
Tribes of Borneo 557
Trowulan 286
Tuban 288

Ubud 374
  centre 380
  environs 372
Ujung Kulon National Park 142
Ujung Pandang centre 623
Ujung Pandang 618
Uluwatu 368
Waikabubak 766
Waingapu 762
Wasur National Park 853
Watampone See Bone Bone
Weh Island 448
West Timor 772
Wonosobo 236
Yogya environs 194
Yogya Kraton 189
Yogyakarta Jalan Prawirotaman 198
Yogyakarta 185

Map Symbols

Administration

International Border	
State / Province Border	
Cease Fire Line	
Neighbouring country	
Neighbouring state	
State Capitals	□
Other Towns	○

Roads and travel

Main Roads (National Highways)	
Other Roads	
Jeepable Roads, Tracks	
Railways with station	

Water features

River	*Mahakam River*
Lakes, Reservoirs, Tanks	
Seasonal Marshlands	
Sand Banks, Beaches	
Ocean	
Waterfall	
Canals	
Ferry	

Topographical features

Contours (approx), Rock Outcrops	
Mountains	
Mountain Pass	
Glaciers	
Gorge	
Escarpment	
Palm trees	

Cities and towns

Built Up Areas	
Main through routes	
Main streets	
Minor Streets	
Pedestrianized Streets	
One Way Street	→
National Parks, Gardens, Stadiums	
Fortified Walls	▲ ▲ ▲
Airport	⊗
Banks	Ⓢ
Bus Stations (named in key)	
Hospitals	⊕
Market	Ⓜ
Police station	Ⓟₒₗ
Post Office	⊜
Telegraphic Office	◔
Tourist Office	ⓘ
Key Numbers	1 2 3 4 5
Bridges	
Stupa	
Mosque	
Cathedral, church	†
Meru	
Guided routes	

National parks, trekking areas

National Parks and Bird Sanctuaries	♦
Hide	
Camp site	▲
Refuge	
Motorable track	
Walking track	

Other symbols

Archaeological Sites	
Places of Interest	○
Viewing point	
Golf course	
Pelni shipping office	

Writing to the editor

Many people write to us - with corrections, new information, or simply comments. If you want to let us know something, we would be delighted to hear from you. Please give us as precise information as possible, quoting the edition and page number of the Handbook you are using and send as early in the year as you can. Your help will be greatly appreciated, especially by other travellers. In return we will send you details about our special guidebook offer.

For hotels and restaurants, please let us know:

- each establishment's name, address, phone and fax number
- number of rooms, whether a/c or air-cooled, attached (clean?) bathroom
- location - how far from the station or bus stand, or distance (walking time) from a prominent landmark
- if it's not already on one of our maps, can you place it?
- your comments - either good or bad - as to why it is distinctive
- tariff cards
- local transport used

For places of interest:

- location
- entry, camera charge
- access - by whatever means of transport is most apropriate, eg time of main buses or trains to and from the site, journey time, fare
- facilities - nearby drinks stalls, restaurants, for the disabled
- any problems, eg steep climb, wildlife, unofficial guides
- opening hours
- site guides

Footprint Handbooks

All of us at Footprint Handbooks hope you have enjoyed reading and travelling with this Handbook, one of the first published in the new Footprint series. Many of you will be familiar with us as Trade & Travel, a name that has served us well for years. For you and for those who have only just discovered the Handbooks, we thought it would be interesting to chronicle the story of our development from the early 1920's.

It all started 75 years ago in 1921, with the publication of the Anglo-South American Handbook. In 1924 the South American Handbook was created. This has been published each year for the last 73 years and is the longest running guidebook in the English language, immortalised by Graham Greene as "the best travel guide in existence".

One of the key strengths of the South American Handbook over the years, has been the extraordinary contact we have had with our readers through their hundreds of letters to us in Bath. From these letters we learnt that you wanted more Handbooks of the same quality to other parts of the world.

In 1989 my brother Patrick and I set about developing a series modelled on the South American Handbook. Our aim was to create the ultimate practical guidebook series for all travellers, providing expert knowledge of far flung places, explaining culture, places and people in a balanced, lively and clear way. The whole idea hinged, of course, on finding writers who were in tune with our thinking. Serendipity stepped in at exactly the right moment: we were able to bring together a talented group of people who know the countries we cover inside out and whose enthusiasm for travelling in them needed to be communicated.

The series started to grow. We felt that the time was right to look again at the identity that had brought us all this way. After much searching we commissioned London designers Newell & Sorrell to look at all the issues. Their solution was a new identity for the Handbooks representing the books in all their aspects, looking after all the good things already achieved and taking us into the new millennium.

The result is Footprint Handbooks: a new name and mark, simple yet assertive, bold, stylish and instantly recognisable. The images we use conjure up the essence of real travel and communicate the qualities of the Handbooks in a straightforward and evocative way.

And for us here in Bath, it has been an extraordinary exercise working through this dramatic change. Already the 'new us' fits like our favourite travelling clothes and we cannot wait to get more and more Footprint Handbooks onto the book shelves and out onto the road.

James Dawson

The Footprint list

Caribbean Islands Handbook
East Africa Handbook
Egypt Handbook
India Handbook
Indonesia Handbook
Malaysia & Singapore Handbook
Mexico & Central America
  Handbook
Pakistan Handbook
South Africa Handbook
South American Handbook
Sri Lanka Handbook
Tibet Handbook

New in Spring 1997
Andalucía Handbook
Brazil Handbook
Cambodia Handbook
Chile Handbook
Ecuador and Galápagos Handbook
Laos Handbook
Morocco Handbook
  with Mauritania
Myanmar (Burma) Handbook
Namibia Handbook
Peru Handbook
Thailand Handbook
Tunisia Handbook with Libya
Vietnam Handbook
Zimbabwe & Malawi Handbook
  with Botswana, Moçambique &
  Zambia

Mail Order

Footprint Handbooks are available worldwide in good bookstores. They can also be ordered directly from us in Bath (see below for address). Please contact us if you have difficulty finding a title.

Footprint T-shirt

The Footprint T-shirt is available in 100% cotton in various colours.

There are always more titles in the pipeline. For the most up-to-date information and to join our mailing list please contact us at:

Footprint Handbooks

6 Riverside Court
Lower Bristol Road
Bath BA2 3DZ, England
T +44(0)1225 469141
F +44(0)1225 469461
E Mail handbooks@footprint.compulink.co.uk